Economics

Third Edition

Robert B. Ekelund, Jr.
Auburn University

Robert D. Tollison
George Mason University

HarperCollins*Publishers*

For my mother and for faithful friends, who are the medicine of life
RBE

For Anna, April, Mark, and my parents
RDT

Sponsoring Editor: Bruce Kaplan
Development Editor: Kathy Richmond
Project Coordination, Four-Color Text Design, and Cover Design: Proof Positive/
    Farrowlyne Associates, Inc.
Text Design: Russell Schneck Design
Photo Research: Kelly Mountain
Production: Michael Weinstein
Compositor: Omegatype Typography, Inc.
Printer and Binder: R. R. Donnelley & Sons Company
Cover Printer: New England Book Components

Economics, Third Edition
Copyright © 1991 by HarperCollins Publishers Inc.

Library of Congress Cataloging-in-Publication Data

Ekelund, Robert B. (Robert Burton), 1940–
    Economics / Robert B. Ekelund, Jr., Robert D. Tollison.—
3rd. ed.
        p.   cm.
    Includes index.
    1. Economics.   I. Tollison, Robert D.   II. Title.
HB171.5.E47   1990   90-21324
330—dc20   CIP

ISBN 0-673-52096-X (student edition)
ISBN 0-673-49950-2 (teacher edition)

 91 92 93 9 8 7 6 5 4 3 2

CONTENTS

PART TWO   THE MICROECONOMIC BEHAVIOR OF CONSUMERS, FIRMS, AND MARKETS   **145**

supplementary

PREFACE

Ask students what first comes to mind when they think of the term *economics,* and the majority will answer "money." Some students may think of economics as a set of dry, analytical concepts or tools used in financial matters. But economics is much more than this. The third edition of *Economics* was written to stress that economics is a way of thinking. It is not concerned primarily with money. It is not dry and boring. It is a vibrant, exciting way of weighing the costs and benefits of actions and policies in every facet of life. It is true that the economic way of thinking can be used to analyze the function of money and prices. But it can also be used to understand how roommates are selected or what factors affect a job search. The versatility and depth of an economic way of thinking is shown in a broad array of examples drawn from daily life and history, as well as contemporary policy issues that one finds in the newspapers and that one traditionally classifies as economics.

Economics is packed with applications. These are not opportunities for the authors to display how much they know of the technical apparatus of the discipline or to overwhelm students with impenetrable terminology. Rather, we think that only by appealing to student intuition and common sense in these applications can we show the usefulness and power of an economic way of thinking. This is why we include important elements of college life such as roommate selection and tuition costs, as well as more traditional market and global applications. This helps shun the more arcane applications often found in other principles of economics texts.

This third edition of *Economics* is thoroughly modern in its scope. We firmly believe that the economic way of thinking comes alive in the immediacy of current issues, events, and policies. Sprinkled throughout are such current global concerns as the 1992 integration of the European Community, the opening of Eastern Europe to a different kind of economic structure, debt repayment, environmental regulation, and the participation of women and minorities in the labor force. But "modern" means more than this. We discuss the direction that modern economic research is taking. In this way, we hope to give students a sense of the excitement that is generated when the economic way of thinking is used at the frontiers of knowledge, revising or discarding old concepts and approaches and creating new ones. Time costs, transaction costs, game theory, and an entire chapter on the new views of industrial organization are thoroughly modern topics that facilitate student understanding of the power and ramifications of an economic way of thinking.

NEW TO THE THIRD EDITION

The third edition of *Economics* expands its presentations of the economic way of thinking into new examples, applications, and topics. Changes and additions can be grouped into five main categories:

1. *Modern topics.* Three new chapters provide some sense of the ferment in portions of microeconomic theory. Oligopoly is now given increased importance in its own chapter (Chapter 12), with simple game theory and cartel problems as the vehicles for delineating welfare and efficiency implications of oligopolistic markets. Chapter 13 is the capstone of the market structures developed in the previous four chapters. This focuses on traditional views of industrial organization and the modern challenges to such things as concentration ratios as indicators of competition. This new chapter brings in recent work on contestable markets, price discrimination, vertical restraints, and advertising. Chapter 19, a new policy chapter, gives the immediacy of the issue of regulation and deregulation by concentrating on areas such as health and safety, the environment, and government franchising.

   In the macroeconomic portion of the text, Chapter 30 has been reworked to bring in recent views on the effects of government debt and deficits on saving rates and the ability of the economy to grow. Chapter 35 brings up "the activist versus non-activist" policy debate in terms of the new classical and new Keynesian positions. Finally, Chapter 39 relates trade deficits and budget deficits to the overall competitiveness of the U.S. economy.

2. *Globalization.* To show the international dimensions of the economic way of thinking, we have tried to globalize the coverage throughout—from beginning to end. In Chapter 2, contemporary problems of trade and protection immediately follow a traditional discussion of specialization and trade; Chapter 3 brings up the importance of economic institutions by discussing the "two Koreas"; and Chapter 4 employs the world cashmere market to demonstrate the forces affecting supply and demand. Other international examples follow: Chapter 12 brings up cartels, Chapter 13 emphasizes the impact of international competition on domestic market structure, Chapter 14 explores the effects of immigration on domestic labor supply. Japanese unemployment problems are considered in Chapter 23. The possibilities for European inflation under a common currency agreement in 1992 are developed in Chapter 34. Also in Chapter 34, a boxed feature outlines the worldwide economic effects of Iraq's invasion of Kuwait. Chapter 40 provides some sense of the turmoil faced by Eastern European nations and the Soviet Union as they attempt to modify their political and economic systems in an attempt to become more economically efficient.

3. *Streamlined coverage.* We have reorganized much of the material appearing in previous editions. These structural improvements are most apparent in Parts Five, Six, and Seven—the portion of the text given over to macroeconomic theory and policy. An entire chapter, Chapter 25, is now devoted to classical macroeconomics. This chapter provides the contrasting coun-

terpoint to two reorganized chapters on Keynesian economics (Chapters 26 and 27). Taken together, these three chapters provide the basis for a complete and solid understanding of aggregate demand and aggregate supply analysis (covered in Chapter 28), fiscal and supply-side policies (Chapter 29), and the macroeconomic issues of taxation and debt (Chapter 30). We have made an effort in this edition to more fully integrate monetary control and inflation into the discussion. Chapters 31, 32, and 33 cover money, the role of banking, and the social regulation of money in the United States. This prepares the way for the thorough discussion of monetary policy and inflation in a newly organized Chapter 34. Our treatment of unemployment and its attendant problems is now combined with the principles and problems related to business cycles in Chapter 36. The organizational changes made throughout the third edition represent much more than a shuffling of preexisting elements; our aim was a more logical presentation of the principles of economics. To that end we have also endeavored to eliminate unnecessary, potentially confusing details throughout the text.

4. *Applications*. We have added an abundance of applications. Chapter 7 features leveraged buyouts and the merger mania of the 1980s, Chapter 10 examines the viability of the postal monopoly in the face of new technology, Chapter 20 discusses global pollution caused by acid rain and economic aspects of the greenhouse effect, Chapter 32 considers the economic fallout from the "war on drugs," and Chapter 40 explores *perestroika,* or the restructuring of the Soviet economy—to name just a few of the many new applications.

5. *Pedagogical innovations*. New to this edition are full-color sections that both summarize key economic ideas and show important trends. In this way, students have an effective way of reviewing key material and enriching their understanding of movements in the economy.

With these additions, *Economics* has tried to freshen its use of the economic way of thinking to shed new light on many seemingly unrelated aspects of daily life.

ORGANIZATION

Economics is divided into eight parts: "The Power of Economic Thinking," "Microeconomic Behavior of Consumers, Firms, and Markets," "Microeconomic Principles of Input Demand and Supply," "Microeconomics and Public Policy," "Private-Sector and Public-Sector Macroeconomics," "Money: Its Creation and Management," "Monetary and Macroeconomic Problems and Policy," and "International Trade and Economic Development."

The Power of Economic Thinking

Part One introduces the basic tools of economic analysis, including opportunity cost, marginal analysis, specialization, trade, comparative advantage, supply and demand, market equilibrium, and elasticity. We have packed these chapters with lively, interesting issues and applications. In Chapter 2, for example, the concept of specialization and trade via comparative advantage is illustrated with an example of marriage and roommate selection. Chapter 4 discusses how rent controls affect the allocation of apartments in a college town, then gives an example of international price controls. The importance of time and other transaction costs, mentioned initially in Chapter 1, is stressed in the discussion of full price in Chapter 4. With more than a dozen applications, Chapter 5 brings home to students the important concept of elasticity; students come to understand how the prices of products as diverse as jogging shoes and salt are affected by elasticity of demand and supply.

Microeconomic Behavior of Consumers, Firms, and Markets

Part Two covers consumer choice, the firm, the firm's costs of production, and output market structures from pure competition through monopoly. The general description of production principles and costs to firms in Chapter 8 leads to an examination of the differences among firms, beginning in Chapter 9 with the competitive firm. We treat monopolistic competition separately in this edition (Chapter 11) and in Chapter 12 use game theory to facilitate understanding of oligopoly and cartels. Having delineated firms by type, we turn in Chapter 13 to the logical policy implications of market structures in which competition is impaired through some form of monopoly. However, much of Chapter 13 is given over to new views on monopoly power, to the question, Is *big* necessarily *bad?*; to this end, ample attention is paid to contestable markets theory and to the efficiency-inducing effects of advertising.

Microeconomic Principles of Input Demand and Supply

Part Three covers demand and supply in factor markets for labor, land, and capital. Chapter 14's discussion of the supply of and demand for labor provides a basis for understanding how labor is organized, the topic of Chapter 15. After a look at capital and interest (Chapter 16) and at the modern theory of rent-seeking behavior and the economic role of entrepreneurs, issues of income distribution—including poverty, economic discrimination against women and minorities, and welfare reform legislation—round out Part Three.

Microeconomics and Public Policy

Part Four formally integrates microeconomic theory with four areas of modern economic policy. Chapter 19 deals with the principles and policy of regulation and deregulation in our economy, highlighting both the impact of deregulation and the increasing importance of health, safety, and environmental regulation. Chapter 20, "Market Failure and Public Policy," applies the modern theory of externalities to such diverse problems as endangered species, shrinking oil reserves, and environmental pollution. Chapter 21 shows how principles of microeconomic theory apply to taxation and the effects on individual and business behavior. Chapter 22 shows how economic analysis gives insights into political decision making. Readers will discover, for example, why lobbyists are such a major part of the political machinery in this country, the role of ideology in explaining the voting behavior of legislators, and political reasons for the growth of government.

Private-Sector and Public-Sector Macroeconomics

Part Five opens with two chapters on the basic tools of macroeconomics—concepts such as real and nominal GNP, two-flow models of national income, and price indexes. A simple, intuitive explanation of aggregate demand and aggregate supply is given. Chapter 25 analyzes the classical view of the long-run, self-regulating economy and discusses how classical theory and policy are related. Formal Keynesian models as reactions to classical thought are fully developed in Chapters 26 and 27. Chapters 28 and 29 build upon classical and Keynesian theories to develop a modern approach to macroeconomics—the theory of aggregate demand and aggregate supply. Chapter 29 makes the theory more concrete by discussing fiscal and supply-side policies and the influence of politics within the aggregate demand–aggregate supply framework. Chapter 30 completes our integration of theory and policy with a discussion of taxation, deficits, and debt, including an analysis of crowding out.

Money: Its Creation and Management

Part Six is a complete introduction to money, monetary institutions, monetary policy, and monetary theory—with particular attention paid to the enormous changes in money use and financial institutions. For example, a "Focus" in Chapter 32 contemplates the future of cash in society, and the "Economics in Action" for Chapter 33 discusses Federal Reserve policy and the savings and loan crisis. In addition to a full discussion of inflation in Chapter 34, the role of money is analyzed according to classical, Keynesian, and modern views.

Monetary and Macroeconomic Problems and Policy

Part Seven extends macroeconomic theory into current policy debates. Chapter 35 shows how new Keynesians and new classical writers—those leaning toward monetarist or rational expectationist theories—view fiscal and monetary policy. Chapter 36 links the problem of unemployment to business cycles and shows how macroeconomic policy varies with business conditions and politics. Finally, Chapter 37 deals with some key features of U.S. economic growth, past and present.

International Trade and Economic Development

The three chapters of Part Eight cover international trade and finance, comparative economic systems, and economic development. Chapter 38 extends the theory of comparative advantage—first covered in Chapter 2—into the area of international specialization and trade, touching on such things as tariffs and quotas. Chapter 39 details many pressing international financial problems, including debt repayment by developing countries. Finally, Chapter 40 reviews changing economic systems worldwide, focusing on Eastern Europe and the Soviet Union; we emphasize the potential for substantial economic gains following such restructuring, of course, but we do not neglect the potential costs.

SPECIAL FEATURES

Each chapter opens with an overview of the topics covered and a bulleted list of chapter objectives. Many other pedagogical elements appear in the text.

1. Key concepts and key trends in microeconomics and macroeconomics are shown in special full-color sections. These sections summarize important economic principles and demonstrate current data trends to enhance text discussion.
2. Key terms are **boldfaced** at the first text mention, and definitions appear in the margin.
3. Graphs are drawn simply, some with background grids to help students understand the relationships portrayed. Standard notation is used in graphs and equations. Many graphs are color-coded: demand curves in black, supply curves in color. Shifts in both types of curves move from darker to lighter shades.
4. "Focus" boxes in each chapter give interesting perspectives on theory and institutions. Titles include "Would You Sell a Used Car to This Franchisee?", "Unions and Sympathy Strikes: The Eastern Airlines Case," "Entrepreneurs from Edison to Milken," "1992: Dawn of the European Community," and "Economic Repercussions of Iraq's Invasion of Kuwait."
5. "Economics in Action" sections, which end most chapters, provide applications of chapter topics. Topics in "Economics in Action" sections range from things students likely have always wondered about—How do retailers mark up merchandise? How can state lottery commissions pay out jackpots running to tens of millions of dollars?—to things most students have never thought to consider—Does the postal monopoly make sense? Is it rational to vote?
6. Chapters conclude with a summary, a list of key terms, questions for review and discussion, and, where appropriate, problems to work.
7. Each part of *Economics* concludes with a historical Point-Counterpoint. This feature gives short biographies of two important economic thinkers and compares or contrasts their theories. For example, Part Eight, "International Trade and Economic Development," ends with a Point-Counterpoint on P. T. Bauer and Gunnar Myrdal—economists with very different views on development in the Third World.
8. Special appendixes to selected chapters (for instance, "Working with Graphs," "Indifference Curve Analysis," and "General Equilibrium in Competitive Markets") give instructors the option of more extensive coverage.
9. A glossary of terms with text page references and a thorough index at the back of the book provide useful tools for study.

THE COMPLETE *ECONOMICS* PACKAGE

Printed Supplements

- The *Study Guide* to accompany this third edition of *Economics,* by John Keith Watson, University of Southwestern Louisiana, helps students learn and review key concepts. Each chapter includes a summary, learning objectives, study tips, and fill-in reviews. Students can use the true-false, multiple-choice, and short essay questions to test mastery of concepts; then they can check their answers to discover where more study is needed. Timely articles from newspapers and magazines like the *Wall Street Journal* and *Business Week* guide students in using an economic way of thinking about real-world situations. Every question in the study guide is answered, and answers to the questions in the "Economics in Action" sections in the text are provided.
- The *Instructor's Manual* to accompany *Economics,* also by John Keith Watson, contains chapter outlines, lecture suggestions, and answers to all text questions and problems. Additional readings and problems are included for many chapters.
- The *Test Bank* to accompany *Economics,* prepared by Neal Davis, has doubled in size from the previous edition. It now includes more than six thousand multiple-choice items—for an average of 150 questions per chapter. Questions closely follow topic coverage; each is keyed to the corresponding text page. Test items are coded to indicate different forms of the same question, and they are divided into four categories: recall, inference, calculation, and graph/table interpretation. Instructors can use the categories and codes to tailor each exam. All test items are available on microcomputer software.
- Over 100 two-color overhead *Transparencies* of important figures and tables from the text are provided.

Software Supplements for Students

An economics software package is available. EconSim, by Robert Brooks, University of Alabama, and David Swanger and Chuck Warlick, Auburn University, contains simulations that stimulate student interest in major economic concepts. Students can explore what happens to specific micro and macro models when variables are changed. It is available on floppy disk for the IBM PC.

Software Supplements for Instructors

TestMaster operates on IBM PC and compatible microcomputers to provide the printed *Test Bank* questions in a computerized format. In addition to allowing you to develop, maintain, and revise the *Test Bank,* TestMaster enables you to add your own questions or even create your own test bank. This test generator has been designed for easy use.

ACKNOWLEDGMENTS

The extensive scope of this revision would have been impossible without the help and advice of scores of friends and critics. We gratefully acknowledge the following colleagues, friends, and students who selflessly gave their advice and time: John Allen, Andy Barnett, Raymond Battalio, Randy Beard, Don Boudreax, Katherine Boudreaux, Bill Breit, Butch Browning, Steve Caudill, Roy Cordato, Pat Culbertson, Elynor Davis, Charles DeLorme, David Gay, Kathy Gilbert, Dan Gropper, Bob Hebert, Randy Holcombe, John Jackson, Ethel Jones, Dave Kaserman, Roger Koppel, Dwight Lee, Jim Long, Charles Maurice, François Melese, Margaret O'Donnell, Karen Palasek, Chris Paul, Phil Porter, Ed Price, Jennie Raymond, Richard Saba, David Saurman, Tom Saving, Henry Thompson, and David Whitten. For special help and assistance we thank Gary Anderson, Richard Beil, Bill Shughart, and, especially, Mark Thornton. We are also grateful to Debra Beil for her expert proofreading and advice and to Rand Ressler for able help in data gathering and checking. Neal Davis has done yeoman's work on our *Test Bank*. To our good friend Keith Watson, who wrote the *Study Guide* and *Instructor's Manual* and who provided expert assistance throughout the entire project, we owe a special thanks.

No one other than the authors is more responsible for the direction and quality of *Economics* than Richard Ault, Auburn University. His firm and intuitive control of traditional and modern principles of economics helped us immeasurably.

We thank graduate assistants Manisha Perrera, Bharat Vijayan, Brian Goff, Ladd Jones, Dan Berry, Doug Bunn, Yvan Kelly, Paul Gentle, Kendall Somppi, Jim Tillery, Deborah Walker, and Biff Woodruff for help with all three editions of *Economics*. Secretaries Cathy Kruse and Kim Johns were of very able help.

We also wish to thank our developmental editor Kathy Richmond, who went beyond all job expectations, and Bruce Kaplan, our economics editor, for solid support of this third edition. Will Sanford of Proof Positive/Farrowlyne Associates, Inc., saved us from many errors.

Official reviewers and contributors for the third edition are Douglas K. Agbetsiafa, Indiana University at South Bend; Ralph E. Ancil, Southwestern Missouri State University; Robert A. Baade, Lake Forest College; Dean Baim, Pepperdine University; J. Lloyd Blackwell, IV, University of North Dakota; Robert Carbaugh, Central Washington University; John Dennis Chasse, State University of New York–Brockport; George Shih-Fan Chu, University of Nevada at Reno; Paul A. Cleveland, University of Central Florida; Cheryl Cohen, Millikin University; Barbara Craig, Oberlin College; Robert D. Crofts, Salem State College; Steve Cunningham, University of Connecticut; William W. Davis, Western Kentucky University; David Denslow, University of Florida; Carl E. Enomoto, New Mexico State University; Donald H. Farness, Oregon State University; Andrew W. Foshee, McNeese State University; Jack Goddard, Northeastern State University; Anthony Greco, University of Southwestern Louisiana; William B. Green, Sam Houston State University; Anthony O. Gyapong, Wayne State University; Jan M. Hansen, University of Wisconsin–Eau Claire; Steven C. Hine, State University of New York–Binghamton; James H. Holcomb, Jr., The University of Texas at El Paso; Arthur E. Kartman, San Diego State University; Philip King, San Francisco State University; Gary F. Langer, Roosevelt University; Stephen E. Lile, Western Kentucky University; Marvin S. Margolis, Millersville University; Lawrence W. Martin, Michigan State University; Mary Ann Meiners, Middle Tennessee State University; Khan Mohabbat, Northern Illinois University; Emmanuel Nnadozie, Northeast Missouri State University; Edd Noell, Westmont College; Don Owen, Ottawa University; Ken Patterson, Oregon State University; Gerald Pelovsky, College of the Sequoias; Steven C. Pitts, Houston Community College; J. M. Pogodzinski, San Jose State University; Munir Quddus, University of Southern Indiana; Doralia Reynolds, Seward County Community College; Peter Rupert, West Virginia University; Carlos E. Santiago, State University of New York–Albany; Abraham Usumang, Bowling Green State University; John Wakeman-Linn, Williams College; Harold Warren, East Tennessee State University; Walter J. Wessells, North Carolina State University; and Mahmood Yousefi, University of Northern Iowa.

Thanks also go to the reviewers of the second edition.

RBE and RDT

PART ONE

The

Power of

Economic

Thinking

1

Economics in Perspective

Does economics matter? More to the point, why should you spend precious time and money learning economics when there are so many other activities, products, and services—not to mention other college courses—competing for your attention? The answer: Economics touches all facets of our lives from the trivial to the fundamental as consumers of gasoline and home computers, as voters for political candidates, and as workers and employers. Economics analyzes why we are poor or rich as individuals and extends its scope to government policies about inflation, unemployment, economic growth, and international trade. Economics not only deals with large issues, but with personal decisions as well—how much time to spend cleaning the apartment or studying, how to decide whether more education is called for, how to select a mate. Close study of economics gives us a new perspective on a wide variety of human activities and institutions. When you finish Chapter 1 you should understand

- how individuals, societies, and nations solve the basic economic problem caused by scarce resources and unlimited wants.
- the functions of prices and how they act as signals to producers, consumers, and governments in any economy.
- the basis on which all individuals actually make economic decisions.
- how economics gives insight into human behavior and social problems.

WHAT ECONOMICS
IS (AND WHAT IT ISN'T)

Goods:
All tangible things that satisfy people's wants and desires.

Services:
All forms of intangible but useful activities that are valued by people.

Most people would say that economics deals with the stock market or with how to make money by buying and selling gold, land, or some other commodity. This common view contains a grain of truth but does not touch on the richness, depth, and breadth of the matter. Economics is a social science—the oldest and best developed of the social sciences. As such, it studies human behavior in relation to three basic questions about an economy: What **goods** and **services** are produced? How are goods and services produced? For whom are goods and services produced?

All societies and all individuals have faced these three questions. Since goods and the means to produce them have never existed in limitless amounts, the insistent questions—How? What? and For whom?—must be asked; for at least two hundred years, economists have tried to analyze how individuals and societies answer them. Consider some famous economists' definitions of economics:

Adam Smith (1776): Economics or political economy is "an inquiry into the nature and causes of the wealth of nations."[1]

Nassau William Senior (1836): Political economy is the "science that treats the nature, the production, and the distribution of wealth."[2]

Alfred Marshall (1890): "Political Economy or Economics is a study of mankind in the ordinary business of life . . . it is on the one side a study of wealth; and on the other, and more important side, a part of the study of man."[3]

Lionel Robbins (1935): "Economics is the science which studies human behavior as a relationship between ends and scarce means which have alternative uses."[4]

Milton Friedman (1962): "Economics is the science of how a particular society solves its economic problems."[5]

Paul Samuelson (1980): "Economics is the study of how people and society end up *choosing,* with or without the use of money, to employ *scarce* productive resources that could have alternative uses—to *produce* various commodities and *distribute* them for consumption, now or in the future, among various persons and groups in society. Economics analyzes the costs and the benefits of improving patterns of resource use."[6]

Economics: A Working Definition

There is merit in each of the preceding definitions. Economics *is* the study of how nations produce and increase wealth. Economics also studies the activities of people in producing, distributing, and consuming wealth. It analyzes how people and societies choose among competing goals or alternatives.

A common thread runs through all definitions of economics. Each definition emphasizes the inescapable fact that **resources**—the wherewithal to produce goods and services—are not available in limitless quantities and that people and societies, with unlimited desires for goods and services, must make some hard choices about what to do with the resources that are available. Our working definition of economics may be expressed as follows:

Resources:
Those things used to produce goods and services. These include land, machines, energy, and human labor and ingenuity. Resources are also called factors of production.

---

[1]Adam Smith, *An Inquiry into the Nature and Causes of the Wealth of Nations,* ed. Edwin Cannan (1776; reprint, New York: Modern Library, 1937).

[2]N. W. Senior, *An Outline of the Science of Political Economy* (1836; reprint, New York: A. M. Kelley, 1938).

[3]Alfred Marshall, *Principles of Economics* (London: Macmillan, 1920), p. 1.

[4]Lionel Robbins, *The Nature and Significance of Economic Science,* 2nd ed. (London: Macmillan, 1935), p. 16.

[5]Milton Friedman, *Price Theory* (Chicago: Aldine, 1962), p. 1.

[6]Paul A. Samuelson, *Economics* (New York: McGraw-Hill, Inc., 1980), p. 2.

Economics is the study of how individuals and societies, experiencing virtually limitless wants, choose to allocate scarce resources to satisfy their wants.

Unlimited wants, scarcity, and the choices they force on us are thus the key elements in understanding economics and the economic problem. Consider the nature of scarcity.

The Economic Condition: Scarcity

Scarcity:
The condition whereby the resources, goods, and services available to individuals and society are limited relative to the wants and desires for them.

What, exactly, is **scarcity**? More to the point, what are scarce resources? Dorothy Parker, an American humorist, once said, "If you can't get what you want, you'd better damn well settle for what you can get." The entire study of economics amplifies and expands on Parker's proposition. As individuals and as a society, we cannot get all of what we want because the amount of available resources is limited. The role of the economist and of economics in general is to explain how we can make the most of this problem of scarcity—in Parker's terms, how to get as much as we can of what we want.

The most important problem in economics is that while the wants of individuals and societies must be satisfied by limited resources, the wants themselves are not limited; rather, they are endless. We are never satisfied with what we have. Individuals are forever lured by more tempting foods, more cleverly engineered computers, more up-to-date fashions. Societies continually desire safer highways, more national security, greater Social Security benefits, or more cancer research. Problems of scarcity and unlimited wants—economics itself—apply to all nations regardless of political, social, and religious orientation. Moslems, Jews, and Christians all face the eternal problem of satisfying limitless wants with limited means. Methods of dealing with scarcity will, of course, differ from society to society depending on cultural differences and on particular endowments of resources within political boundaries, but the fundamental problem is the same everywhere.

Scarcity is relative to time and fortune. Our generation has many more services and goods to choose from than our parents and grandparents did. The quantity and quality of goods and services may have grown from primitive to modern times, but the supply of resources needed to produce them is limited, and human wants are not.

Economic goods and services:
Goods and services that are scarce.

Costs:
An implication of scarcity; the necessary sacrifices associated with making any choice.

All scarce goods—from television to chlorinated water—are called **economic goods.** Their scarcity leads to **costs.** While it is customary to associate cost with the money price of goods, economists define *cost* as the value of the good or activity given up in place of the good or activity actually chosen. Since all unlimited wants cannot be met with scarce resources, individuals have to make choices—between, for instance, more steaks and more computer games. Societies may have to choose between safer highways and more accurate missiles. Cost is, therefore, the direct result of the scarcity of resources. Scarcity of resources means that both individuals and societies must endure the costs of acquiring more of any good or service. That cost is the value of the good or activity given up in place of the good chosen. Think for a moment about that scarce resource, time. Being absolutely limited in supply for each of us, time—or, rather, the use of time—bears a definite cost. No college student, certainly, has escaped being confronted with economic decisions arising from the need to allocate this costly resource. (See Focus, "Scarcity, Economizing, and the College Student's Time.")

FOCUS   Scarcity, Economizing, and the College Student's Time

College students know the principle of scarcity all too well. Indeed, a successful student needs an ability to make sound and efficient economic decisions, not only in the more obvious case of scarce monetary resources but in the allocation of scarce time resources as well. Time is a valuable resource to all human beings, but it exists in finite quantities of 24 hours a day, 168 hours a week, and (approximately) 720 hours a month.

Every student knows that he or she cannot have and do everything and that *economic* decisions, whether they are recognized as such or not, must be made every day. Most familiar is the weekly or monthly monetary budget derived from savings, family support, or private or government loans. Too grand a splurge on meals, clothes, or entertainment in the first weeks of the month demands a Spartan existence (peanut butter and TV) in that last week. (Poverty is a hard taskmaster!) Likewise, summer school attendance will produce a degree sooner, but at the expense of income from a summer job or other alternatives.

A student's time often must be allocated over a day or a week. A weekend trip to an out-of-town football game must be "paid for" not only in monetary terms but also in less time to work on the English paper due on Wednesday. The end of a term always necessitates economizing: Given the limited time available, should an additional two hours be directed to chemistry or art history? Actual choices will depend on perceived net gain or potential net gain from the array of alternatives. Ordinarily, most activities or goods and services selected, if they are divisible, will be combined by the choice-maker to maximize satisfaction (for example, one hour spent on chemistry and one hour spent on art history).

College students are not alone, of course. For anyone, the choice may be between listening to a rock band or attending a Bach organ recital. We may have chosen a career in acting or dance instead of law or computer programming. A retiree may choose to return to the classroom rather than to spend time fishing or playing bridge. Economizing—maximizing the value of monetary or time resources under conditions of scarcity—forms the foundation of human behavior. Students, workers, politicians, philanthropists, business executives—all must make choices, and an analysis of these choices forms the basis of the social science of economics.

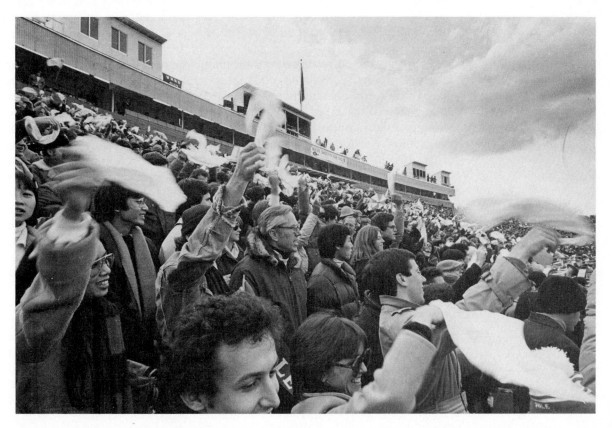

Free goods and services: Things that are available in sufficient amounts and provide all that people want at zero cost.

You may feel that some things are not scarce and that some things—such as love, sunshine, and water—are free. In economic terms, **free goods** are goods that are available in sufficient amounts to satisfy all possible demands. But are many things truly free? Surface water is usually unfit for drinking except in areas far from human habitation. Water suitable for drinking must be raised to the surface from deep wells or piped from reservoirs and treatment plants, operations involving resources that are scarce even when water itself is not. Scarcity of winter sun in the North results in costly winter vacations in the snowbird states. And if you think love is free. . . .

Scarce Resources and Economic Problems

There are basically two categories of scarce resources: human resources and nonhuman resources (see Table 1). **Human resources** encompass all types of labor, including specialized forms of labor such as management or entrepreneurship. **Nonhuman resources** include the rest of the bounty: land, natural resources such as minerals and water, and capital.

Human resources: All forms of labor and skill used to produce goods and services.

Nonhuman resources: All resources other than human resources, such as machines and land.

Examples of human resources abound. By definition, all human resources apply talent and energy to produce goods and services. The cook at the Chicken Shack, the hairstylist at the Mad Hacker, the chief executive of a computer firm, and the assembly-line worker at a General Motors plant all represent human resources. Obviously, labor includes a huge variety of skills, both general and precise. Knowledge, or know-how, is also part of human resources. Economists are interested not only in the scarcity of labor but in its quality. The quality of human resources can be enhanced through investments in education and training.

Economists view *entrepreneurship* as a special form of labor. An entrepreneur is a person who perceives profitable opportunities and who combines resources to produce salable goods or services. Entrepreneurs attempt to move resources from lower- to higher-valued uses in the economy and take the risk that they can make profits by doing so. Lemonade-stand entrepreneurs, for example, see an opportunity to make a profit by combining lemons, ice, and cups and by selling the resulting beverage product. *Management,* a second special form of labor, guides and oversees the process by which separate resources are turned into goods or services. The successful lemonade entrepreneur could hire a manager to oversee the opening of new stands around the neighborhood.

Human resources utilize nonhuman resources such as land, minerals, and natural resources to produce goods and services. A plot in Manhattan, an

TABLE 1	**Economic Resources**
	Economic resources include all human and nonhuman resources that are scarce in supply.

Human Resources	Nonhuman and Other Resources
Labor, including entrepreneurship and management	Land
	Natural resources, including minerals and water
	Capital

acre in Iowa, a coal deposit in Pennsylvania, a uranium mine in South Dakota, and a timber stand in Oregon are all scarce nonhuman resources. New deposits of minerals can be discovered, forests can be replanted, and agricultural land can be reclaimed from swamps. But at any one time, the available supply of nonhuman resources is limited.

Capital, another category of nonhuman resources, comprises all machines, implements, and buildings used to produce goods and services either directly or indirectly. A surgeon's scalpel, a factory, an electric generator, and an artist's brush are all used to produce goods and services and, thus, are considered capital.

Many different forms of capital may be needed to produce a single economic good. With a wheat harvesting machine, a South Dakota farmer can reap a huge crop. But the wheat must also be milled into flour and transported from South Dakota to bakeries in California. Once the wheat has arrived, bakeries must utilize brick or convection ovens to produce bread. The harvesting and milling machines, the railroad, and the baker's ovens are all capital goods, created to increase the amount of final production.

Capital—and the resources used to produce it—is scarce. To create capital, we must sacrifice consumer goods and services because the production of capital takes time away from the production of goods that can be consumed in the present. Societies and individuals must therefore choose between immediate consumption and future consumption. That choice is crucial to growth and ultimate economic well-being. We return to this important issue in Chapter 2.

Other Factors Affecting Resources and Growth

Quantities of human and nonhuman resources are only one prerequisite for economic growth and well-being in an economy. The institutional framework of an economy, such as the nature of its legal system and its form of government, is also critical for economic growth and development, as are other factors such as technology and information. Consider, first, the nature of technology and information.

Technology:
Knowledge of production methods associated with producing a particular good.

Technology and information assist resource utilization in a modern, functioning economy. **Technology,** in general, is composed of know-how, inventions, and innovations that help us get more from scarce resources. An improvement in technology implies that we can produce more. Existing technology is the outcome of many inventions, some of which were the invention of new resources—such as aluminum and hybrid plants. All inventions that increase the productivity of labor and capital can be considered improvements in technology. Innovation is the application of technology to the production of goods and services. Technology, then, helps make other resources less scarce.

Information:
A scarce and important element in the process of economic exchange and growth.

Information is a scarce and costly ingredient in the economic process. The acquisition of information for economic decision making has never been free. In the nineteenth and early twentieth centuries, businesses hired armies of bookkeepers to provide sufficient information for managers to make decisions. The development of the digital computer in the mid-twentieth century made the storage and retrieval of information less costly (while having little effect on the scarcity of the information itself). Technology has progressed so rapidly that the quantity of information that could be stored in a warehouse-sized computer in 1950 can now be placed on a chip the size of a fingernail! Advertising is a form of information that can help us economize on the use of scarce time. With price, quality, and other information provided through advertising, we can spend less time searching for goods and services. Information, then, helps us economize on the use of scarce resources.

Resources, both human and nonhuman, never operate in a vacuum; they always exist in some real-world setting that includes government, a legal system, and a structure of property rights. **Property rights** are those rules that establish and govern the ownership and control of resources. Property rights are established by laws developed within a society's traditions and social relations. **Institutions** are the sum total of the traditions, mores, laws, and governmental structures of an economy. Institutions in the United States include the Constitution and the laws of the fifty states. Some of these institutions restrict and define the rights to own and use resources. Others enhance the flow of resources between individuals and states. The U.S. Constitution, for example, guarantees the free movement of resources from state to state.

We live in a world filled with many governments representing many different institutional structures. Some countries are blessed with huge quantities of land and natural resources but still do not manage to achieve economic growth and development beyond the barest minimum. Prior to the 1980s, China's communist government directed almost all human and nonhuman resources from the highest levels of bureaucracy. Despite China's huge resource base, these institutions reduced the country's ability to produce economic development. More recently, and in spite of periodic political repression, the Chinese government has tentatively embraced a Western-style free market system in which some areas of the economy, such as agriculture, are given over to self-interested production, distribution, and exchange. However slowly, Western institutions and technology *are* being adopted in China because they have encouraged a more efficient use of human and nonhuman resources in producing goods and services.

When property rights are not assigned to scarce resources, the resources tend to be wasted. The old adage "What is owned by all, is cared for by none" means the failure to legally assign property rights to specific resources will ensure that the resources will not be utilized in the most efficient fashion. Most Western economists believe that private rights over property—combined with free and unregulated private markets for human and nonhuman resources—are essential to growth in any nation. The success stories of relatively free and unrestricted economies such as Hong Kong, Taiwan, and Singapore—each endowed with very modest quantities of resources—are often presented as proof that noninterventionist institutions contribute greatly to economic development. The shift in New Zealand's economy from more to less regulation of resources has produced heightened growth there, while the coexistence of private property and extensive controls on resource use in the Indian economy has produced stagnation. The lesson to be learned from these cases is that institutions—especially the form of government and the nature of controls over resources and resource utilization—are keys to productivity and economic growth in any society.

Scarcity of resources *and* scarcity of imagination in designing institutions to facilitate resource use are at the heart of all economic problems. Resources can be augmented over time; indeed, we are much better off materially than our grandparents, and our grandparents were better off than their

Property rights:
Any legal and/or enforceable rights to the use of resources of any kind.

Institutions:
The sum total of the traditions, mores, laws, and governmental structures of an economy.

grandparents. At any one time, however, individuals and societies cannot get all of what they want. Given scarcity, individuals and societies must make choices, and a primary role of economists is to analyze scarcity and the process of choosing. With their analyses they make predictions and recommendations regarding productivity and economic growth.

THE POWER OF ECONOMIC THINKING

All economists of all political stripes have common fundamental ways of thinking. These perspectives, at the core of the science of economics, appear many times throughout this book. When properly and consistently used, they brand a person as adept in the economic way of thinking. A look at these economic perspectives in simple, commonsense language should convince you that economics and economic reasoning are closely related to decisions you make every day. Indeed, economics may be usefully characterized as a way of thinking about both familiar and unfamiliar events.

Resources Cost More Than You Think

Accounting costs:
Actual money expenditures associated with any activity; out-of-pocket costs.

Explicit costs:
Accounting costs.

Implicit costs:
Nonpecuniary costs associated with the consumption of a good or service.

Opportunity costs:
The highest-valued alternative forgone in making any choice.

What does it cost you to take a skiing weekend in the mountains or to make a trip to the beach during spring break? Your instant reply might include the costs of gasoline, auto depreciation, airfare, lift tickets, food, drink, entertainment, and a motel room. These money expenditures are called **accounting costs,** or explicit money costs.

Economists define *costs* more broadly than accountants do. In addition to the **explicit** (money) **costs** considered by accountants, economists consider additional **implicit costs** associated with an action. In the case of a ski trip, an economist would recognize that an additional implicit cost of a ski weekend is the forgone opportunity of using the time in its next most valuable use when all viable alternatives are considered. For example, if the student who goes skiing would otherwise have spent the weekend watching TV or working at a part-time job, an implicit cost of skiing is the income that would otherwise have been earned, if working is the highest-valued alternative. Therefore, the full economic cost of the ski weekend—the **opportunity cost**—equals the explicit money costs (that money does have an alternative use) plus the implicit costs of the forgone income. (See Focus, "Opportunity Cost: The Case of Professional Line-Standers.") Opportunity costs always include all accounting costs.

Greg is a self-employed lawyer who charges $125 per hour for his services. A next-door neighbor owns four large cats who howl at night, disturbing Greg's sleep. Unable to convince his neighbor to quiet the cats, Greg spends 10 work hours preparing a lawsuit to demand satisfaction. Greg bears an opportunity cost, although he paid no lawyer to handle his case. If Greg's next best alternative was to work for a client (and we assume that it is), he could have earned $1250. An economist would say that his opportunity cost of the lawsuit against his neighbor was $1250, for that is what his choice to prepare the lawsuit cost him in terms of forgone legal billings. Therefore, bringing the suit is costly to the lawyer even though no explicit costs (accounting costs) are incurred.

Such opportunity costs also exist for society. Use of government lands in Wyoming and Montana as recreation areas or national forests entails a cost. Through lease or purchase, these lands could be used as a source of oil, minerals, and timber. Such use would contribute to society's well-being, but park land serves the recreational needs of society as well. Whatever choice society makes for the use of the land will imply a cost in economic terms. An opportunity must be forgone when the land is used in either manner.

A favorite saying of economists is "There is no such thing as a free lunch." The first fundamental principle of economics is that most things in life come at the opportunity cost of something forgone. They are never free. For many activities, accounting, or out-of-pocket, costs understate opportunity cost. In economics, opportunity cost is the true, total measure of the costs of anything.

Economic Behavior Is Rational

Rational self-interest:
The view of human behavior espoused by economists. Given circumstances and preferences, people weigh the costs and benefits of choices in order to do the best they can for themselves.

The second fundamental principle of economics is that people behave according to **rational self-interest.** Economists selected from a number of alternative views of human behavior and settled on a very simple one—that of *Homo economicus* (economic man or woman). Rather than viewing humans as inconsistent, incompetent, selfish, or altruistic, economists argue that human behavior is predictably based on a person's weighing the costs and benefits of decisions. This choice making is influenced by constraints such as the availability of options, personal tastes, values, and social philosophy. A student will choose to eat lunch at the local health food restaurant rather than the fast-food cafeteria on campus if the personal benefits of doing so, say eating nutritious food in a pleasant atmosphere, outweigh the costs, such as longer lines and greater distance to be walked.

When costs or benefits change, behavior will change. Consider Jack, a poor but honest man. When he finds $100 cash in a phone booth, he turns it in to authorities. Had Jack found $1000, he might have acted similarly, but discovery of $100,000 might have caused Jack to pause. It may be more costly to be honest under some circumstances.

The view of the individual espoused by economists has always been subject to misinterpretation. When economists say that humans are self-interested, they do not mean that other views of human behavior and motivation are unimportant or irrelevant. Altruistic or charitable behavior, for example, is perfectly compatible with *Homo economicus*. If a person values altruism, then an act that benefits others will carry emotional benefits and will therefore be in that person's rational self-interest. Economists simply maintain that people calculate the costs and benefits of their decisions in acting in their own self-interest.

If the IRS were to quadruple the income tax deduction for charitable contributions, economists would predict an increase in charity. No economist would deny that love, charity, and justice are important aspects of human behavior. Indeed, an economist has argued that "that scarce resource Love" is in fact "the most precious thing in the world" and that humans are therefore compelled to conserve it in ordering the affairs of the world.[7] Economists

---

[7]D. M. Robertson, "What Does the Economist Economize?" in *Economic Commentaries* (London: Staples, 1956), p. 154.

FOCUS   Opportunity Cost: The Case of Professional Line-Standers

Matters of opportunity cost fill our lives, although we seldom stop to think of the mechanics of this central principle of economics. Our time, for example, may be thought of as a resource of 24 hours a day. Consider the plight of a Washington, D.C. doctor who was faced with the opportunity cost of an unpleasant task. According to the *Washington Post,* " . . . last month, Dr. Howard Hoffman took a morning off from work to try to register his son's 1983 Honda Prelude. He got to the District's Department of Motor Vehicles [DMV] at 'what I thought was the crack of dawn, and it seemed like there were 300 people in there,' Hoffman said. 'I was overwhelmed by this sense of futility when I saw this line of people armed with newspapers and sandwiches. I would have had to spend my whole morning in there.' "[a] The opportunity cost of standing in line was high to Dr. Hoffman. His opportunity cost of standing in line was the highest-valued alternative, for example, working, sleeping later, or playing tennis. (Note that the highest-valued alternative does not have to be lost income from missed work time.)

Dr. Hoffman, however, did not stand in line. Robert Long came to his rescue. Long is a professional line-stander—he stands in line for pay. Hoffman filled out the automobile registration forms, gave them to Long, who, for $25, handled the DMV transaction on the same day. Hoffman concludes: "I was really very tickled by the whole thing. It was well worth whatever I paid."

Robert Long is not alone. Two brothers in the Washington, D.C. area have started a business handling DMV trans-

actions for customers. They drop by professional offices, pick up the completed forms, take them to the DMV office, and return with car registrations for their customers. As one of the brothers, Nicholas Montgomery, observes: "These are really people who don't have time to do these things. . . . Some of them are a bit wary about handing over their cars, but then, the people who use the service tend to have pretty expensive cars."

The economics of the professional line-stander illustrates that individuals have different opportunity costs of time. The brisk business in expensive car registration reflects the fact that high-earning, high-income individuals, whose opportunity costs are high, are using the service. When opportunity costs of any given activity (e.g., waiting in line) become large compared to the benefit derived from the activity, individuals will seek alternatives to their advantage. In all such cases, it can be profitable for people to part with their money instead of their time.

The emergence of professional line-standers also illustrates the concept of entrepreneurship. The entrepreneur is someone alert to new opportunities to provide valuable goods and services. The professional line-stander is an entrepreneur who makes himself or herself and those who are willing to pay to avoid standing in line better off economically.

[a]*Washington Post,* July 28, 1986, p. A5.

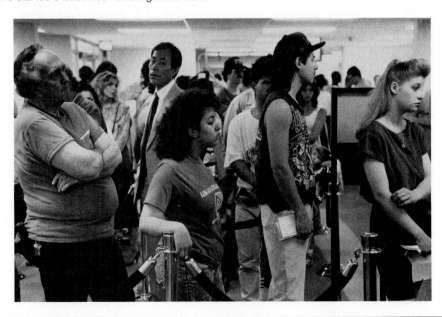

have merely advanced the simple but powerful proposition that, given personal tastes, values, and social philosophy, rational self-interest is a better guide to predicting behavior than any other assumption about why people act as they do.

The economists' view of the rational self-interested individual applies not only to economic behavior but also to other realms of behavior. Animals other than humans, such as birds or rats, can be shown to be self-interested in that they act to maximize their own well-being given their constraints. Politicians maximize their self-interest by wooing voters to elect and reelect them. Since politicians face periodic elections, political behavior such as garnering support from particular voters can be predicted using the economic self-interest assumption. Even activities such as dating, marriage, and divorce have been analyzed using the self-interest assumption! After more than two hundred years of economic theorizing, rational self-interest remains a most powerful predictor of behavior.

Choices Are Made at the Margin

Margin:
The difference between costs or benefits in an existing situation and after a proposed change.

Economists do not ordinarily analyze all-or-nothing decisions but are concerned with decisions made at the **margin**—the additional costs or benefits of a specific change in the current situation. An individual consumer, for example, does not decide to spend his or her entire budget solely on food, cassette tapes, or weekends at the beach. Consumers purchase hundreds of goods and services. Their choice to purchase or not purchase additional units of any one good is based on the additional (or *marginal*) satisfaction that that single unit would bring to them.

Marginal analysis:
Looking at changes in the costs and benefits of a change from the status quo to a proposed new situation. These marginal changes in the costs and benefits are the basis for rational economic choice.

Marginal analysis is a method of finding the optimal, or most desirable, level of any activity—how much coffee to drink, how much bread to produce, how many store detectives to hire, and so on. In an economic sense, every activity we undertake involves *both* benefits and costs, so an optimal level of an activity is the point at which the activity's benefits outweigh its costs by the greatest amount. For example, the optimal level of coffee drinking is reached when coffee's total benefits (its taste and stimulating effects, perhaps) exceed its costs (the expense, the health risks, the acid indigestion) by the greatest degree.

Students make marginal decisions all the time, whether studying for exams, purchasing a new sweater, or maintaining a car. Clearly, additional study for a mathematics examination will improve the grade you receive. But doing your best will not mean devoting *all* available time to the project. The total gain in terms of grade achieved will rise, but the total costs due to the opportunity cost of time will rise also. Additional hours spent studying math may require forgone activities such as work, sleep, studying history, or even recreation. The rational student will stop studying for an examination when the *marginal* benefits from another hour of study equal the *marginal* costs of study. Beyond this point, additional study hours would likely raise the exam grade by a few more points, but the additional study would not be worth the additional cost in terms of other activities given up. The *net* benefits of studying math (net benefits = total benefits − total costs) are always maximized where the marginal benefits equal the marginal costs.

The marginal principle carries over into all we do. Regular automobile maintenance (for example, getting an oil change or having the tires rotated) costs money and time, but there are benefits in terms of the quality of the car's performance. What is the optimal amount of miles to drive between oil changes? As usual, marginal analysis helps us decide on an answer. Obviously a change every 1000 miles would produce some benefits in terms of the maintenance of the car's engine, whereas an oil change only every 20,000 or 25,000 miles would likely produce positive harm. Given the marginal costs (time and money) and the marginal benefits from periodic servicing, the car owner will probably choose a length of time between changes that is less than 25,000 miles but greater than 1000 miles. More frequent changes would increase total benefits but at higher total costs. The individual will maximize the *net* benefits of the service where the additional or marginal benefits of getting the oil changed just equal the marginal costs incurred.

The marginal principle in economics adds new meaning to the familiar statement "Whatever is worth doing, is worth doing well." We never want to maximize the total benefit or return from an activity—studying for an examination, purchasing and eating hamburgers, or getting an oil change—without weighing the cost. We "do well" by maximizing the *net* benefits from purchases or activities, which means that we follow the marginal principle. Rational self-interest requires isolating and considering the specific effects of specific changes—of choices at the margin, in the area of change. (Economics in Action at the end of this chapter provides further illustrations of marginal analysis.)

Prices Are Signals to Producers and Consumers

What products and services are produced in our economic system and how are they produced? Consumers decide what is to be produced—TVs, automobiles, beets—with the scarce resources in our society. Economists say that consumers transmit their desires through **markets,** which are simply arrangements where buyers and sellers exchange goods or services for money or some other medium. Buyers and sellers can be physically together in a market, as in a livestock market, or they can be separated by geographic distance or by wholesalers and other intermediaries, as when the buying and selling of a company's stock is carried out through stockbrokers. A market may even be an abstraction, as is the labor market, in which the supply of and demand for jobs and workers are juggled on a broad scale. The prices established in these markets (through mechanics to be explored in Chapter 4) are the key to understanding what gets produced and how much is produced in our economic system. Economists, therefore, give a great deal of attention to the role and function of prices and markets in explaining how things get done.

Market:
A collection of buyers and sellers exchanging resources, goods, or services.

In a market economy **prices** are the essential signals that tell producers and resource suppliers what and how to produce. Take, for example, a fairly new product, the compact disc (CD) player. Scarce resources—integrated circuits, electronic components, lasers, and fabricated metals—are used in producing CD players, and someone finds it profitable to do so.

Prices:
The market-established opportunity costs of goods and services obtained through exchange.

What happens if consumers suddenly want CD players instead of cassette decks or turntables in their homes and automobiles? Consumers express this desire by buying many more CD players and leaving cassette decks and turntables to gather dust on store shelves. Meanwhile, the relative unavailability of CD players causes their price to rise, because, temporarily, there are insufficient resources and production to meet the new demand. Manufacturers observe the increased sales and rising prices and realize that producing more CD players will be profitable. They react by producing more players, which means ordering more electronics and circuitry and plastics, and hiring more labor and machinery. Higher prices for integrated circuits, fabricated metals, and wiring give producers in Silicon Valley and other resource suppliers a signal to supply more of their inputs and services. Why do they do it? Because higher prices mean greater profitability to resource suppliers as well. Resources are diverted to CD players as both demand for and production of cassette decks and turntables decline.

Consumers also view prices as signals that help them decide what, and how much, to buy. Prices are both a mechanism that signals the degree of scarcity of goods and services to consumers and an allocator of the available quantities of goods and services among consumers.

Suppose, for example, that one-half of Brazil's coffee crop is destroyed by frost. Less coffee would be available, and coffee would become scarcer on supermarket shelves in the United States. The economic system informs consumers of the scarcity by a rise in the price of coffee. The economic system also allocates the smaller amount of coffee among consumers through a price increase. Consumers will purchase a smaller amount when coffee becomes more expensive. Prices ration the available quantity among consumers by influencing the amount consumers will want to buy. Prices perform this rationing function no matter how much coffee is actually available. Likewise, a decrease in price signals consumers that a good has become less scarce. Price reductions allocate or ration increased amounts of goods by making them less expensive and by encouraging larger purchases.

Prices serve two basic functions in an economy. They serve to determine how much and what goods and services are produced by producers. They also serve to ration available commodities among different consumers and competing end uses.

Economists Do Not Decide Who Gets What

Economists study poverty and wealth; but as economists they have no unique knowledge to comment on how rich people should be or how much poverty is tolerable. Economists do not decide whether a college football coach deserves $16 million on a five-year contract or whether a Nobel Prize–winning physicist deserves more. Economists basically explain that the economic value of all individuals—expressed as their income—is determined by the relative desires for their services and by the relative scarcity of their talents and abilities. Perhaps good football coaches are relatively more scarce and more highly desired than good physicists.

Most products and services—such as food, vacations, and domestic help—are allocated to those with the greatest desire and ability to pay for them. Our ability to pay is determined by the economic value of our own particular services or resources in the marketplace. This value depends on our education, on-the-job training, health, luck, inheritance, and a host of other factors.

The distribution of "public" goods and services—such as highways and bridges, space weapons, and "free" movies on campus—is conducted by national, local, and student governments through the filter of politics and voting. A decision whether to add seating capacity to the football stadium or to double the size of the English department at a public university may be made by a university committee appointed by the president and board of trustees, who may be appointed by the governor, who is elected by the citizens of the state. Ultimately, therefore, decisions on how resources are to be distributed are made by voter choices. If voters do not like the decisions made in the political process, they have a right to change the decision-makers. Chosen by voters, politicians make economic decisions based on their perceptions of costs and benefits to the public—as well as to their own chances of reelection. In government, as in the workings of the market, the chief role of economists is not to say who should get what, but to describe and analyze the process—the costs, benefits, and incentives—through which the distribution of all products and services takes place.

We All Need Money, But Not Too Much

Barter:
Direct exchange of one good or service for another without the use of money.

Economists also place a special significance on the role of money in our lives. The trade of goods for goods, called **barter,** will not work in any economy that completes billions of transactions every day. Barter may have been sufficient in primitive societies where few things were produced and traded, but as individuals became specialized, using more and more of their talents and skills, the number and kind of traded commodities and services grew. As the number of commodities grew, the cost of transacting by barter grew enormously. A common denominator, acceptable to all, developed within economic societies to reduce the costs and inconveniences of barter. That common denominator is **money,** which serves as a medium of exchange.

Money:
A generally accepted medium of exchange.

Money is not limited to coins and paper dollars. Throughout history many things—shells, feathers, paper, gold, and cattle, for instance—have served as money. The important point to economists is that money, whatever it is, reduces the costs associated with barter and increases specialization and trade. At the same time, economists are concerned that money should not be available in such quantities as to become unacceptable and valueless to people who produce, buy, and sell. For society, at least, huge increases in the money supply may be too much of a good thing. For example, in post–World War I Germany the government attempted to solve the nation's economic problems by printing more money. Eventually, money was worth more as paper than as a medium of exchange; buying a loaf of bread required a wheelbarrow full of money.

Inflation:
A sustained increase in the general level of prices; inflation reduces the purchasing power of money.

When the quantity of money increases beyond its use as a means of making transactions, confidence in the medium of exchange and its value (in terms of the quantity of goods and services a unit of it can purchase) deteriorates. Economists call this phenomenon **inflation.** Inflation was an especially sad fact of American life during the 1970s, and it is a persistent element in nations around the world. Inflation, if left untamed, can result in the collapse of entire economies with reversion to primitive barter conditions. Economists therefore are very concerned with the relation between the production and trade of goods and the quantity of money available to facilitate these crucial activities. Breakdowns must be prevented, and economists have valuable insights on preventive measures.

Voters Choose the Role of Government—The Economist Analyzes

In a functioning democratic system, society chooses an economic role for government by electing politicians. In general, that role has included such activities as taxation for and provision of collective goods such as national defense, highways, and education; the regulation of monopoly; pollution control; control of the money supply; and alleviation of poverty through welfare programs. In its economic role of taxing and spending, government can affect economic factors such as inflation, the degree of unemployment, economic growth, and international trade.

Economists have always been concerned with the effects of government activity in these areas. In the United States, economists are in the thick of government. Since 1946 an official Council of Economic Advisers has been appointed by the president to aid in the formulation and implementation of economic policy. Almost every agency of government employs economists to give advice in their areas of expertise.

In their role as advisers, economists primarily evaluate, from the perspective of economic theory or analysis, the effects of proposals or, more correctly, of marginal changes in economic policies. Economists do not argue, for example, that additional funds should be allocated to Social Security and taken away from water reclamation projects. They simply evaluate and communicate the costs and benefits of such proposals.

Economists are not confined to giving advice on specific issues such as the Social Security program or the effects of advertising regulation by the Federal Trade Commission. Larger issues are within economists' purview as well. Predicting the effects of government taxing and spending policies on employment, interest rates, and inflation is a very large part of economists' role. Economists might predict, for example, the impact of a tax cut on private spending, interest rates, the private production of goods and services, and inflation. As such, economists are concerned with *economic stabilization*.

Despite economists' influence, however, the economic role of government is ultimately decided by voters in periodic elections. Specific economic functions are not decided in elections, but politicians run on platforms pledging to "increase social welfare spending," "increase defense spending," "reduce the debt," "balance the budget," and "increase environmental regulation." In a loose sense, then, voters decide economic policies. Economists evaluate the implications of government's economic policies. Economists advise. They do not make ultimate decisions about what the government should do.

THE ROLE OF THEORY IN ECONOMICS

Economists must be able to discern fundamental regularities about human behavior. Only if behavior is regular and consistent, on average, among individuals or from generation to generation will economists be able to predict the results of behavior. Economists organize their thoughts about human behavior and its results through **models.** Economists, like all scientists, construct models to isolate specific phenomena for study. Constructing models requires assumptions and abstractions from the real world.

Model:
A simplified abstraction of the real world that approximates reality and makes problems easier to analyze; also called a theory.

The Need for Abstraction

The economist, the biochemist, or the physicist could never handle all the details surrounding any event. Thousands of details are involved in even the simple act of buying a loaf of bread. The friendliness of the clerk, the way the buyer is dressed, and the freshness of the bread are all details surrounding the purchase, and these details may be different each time a buyer makes a purchase. Likewise many details surround a particular chemical reaction or an astronomical event like the appearance of a comet. Economists, like chemists or astronomers, are interested in particular details about an event, such as how much the bread cost or how many loaves the buyer purchased.

Economists must *abstract* from extraneous factors to isolate and understand some other factor because, as one economist put it, people's minds are limited and nature's riddles are complex. Economists must assume that the extraneous factors are constant—that "other things are equal"[8]—or that, if altered, they would have a predictable effect on the relations or model under consideration. Humanity has never progressed very far in understanding anything—be it chemistry, astronomy, or economics—without abstracting from many factors that are not central to a given problem. *Thus, all economic models are of necessity abstractions. Good models, those that perform and predict well, use relevant factors; poor models do not.*

An economic model (or, essentially the same thing, a theory) can be expressed in verbal, graphical, or mathematical form. Sometimes verbal explanation is sufficient, but graphs or algebra often serve as convenient shorthand means of expressing models. Economics is like other sciences in this regard. A complicated chemical or physical process can be described in words, but it is much more convenient to use mathematics. All methods of expressing models will be used in this book, but we rely primarily on words and graphs. The appendix to this chapter explains how to read and interpret graphs.

The Usefulness and Limitations of Theory

In recognizing the regularities of human behavior and in committing them to a model, economists or scientists do not have to rethink every event as it occurs. Theory saves time and permits extremely useful predictions about future events based upon regularities of human behavior.

Economic theory has its limits, though. Since a complex world is the economist's workshop, economic theory cannot be tested in the way chemical or physical theories can. Economists can seldom find naturally existing conditions that provide a good test of a model, let alone a sequence of such conditions, and it is difficult to conduct controlled laboratory experiments on

---

[8]The Latin phrase *ceteris paribus,* meaning "other things being equal," is common economic shorthand for this assumption about human behavior.

human beings to determine their economic behavior. Because of the difficulties of testing, economists are less certain than, say, geneticists or biologists. The accuracy of economics is somewhat more like that of meteorology. Total accuracy is not within the meteorologist's abilities. At least, total accuracy is not worth what it would cost to obtain in either weather forecasting or economics. The unusual weather conditions of 1988, including a severe drought in the far western and southwestern parts of the United States, were caused by a complicated host of factors related to air currents, stalled high-pressure fronts, and other weather phenomena. It took meteorologists a good deal of time to sort out the relevant causes by testing and applying their models.

In economics, the problem of imperfect conditions for testing is a limitation to theory, but theory is essential nonetheless. Nothing can substitute for the usefulness of theory in organizing our thoughts about the real world and in describing the regularities of economic behavior.

In constructing models, moreover, economists and all other scientists must be careful to follow the rules of logic and to avoid common fallacies. Two of these are the **fallacy of composition** and the *post hoc* **fallacy.** The fallacy of composition involves generalizing based on a particular experience. Suppose that you had never seen a fox, and then the first one you saw was white. Should you conclude that all foxes are white? If you did, you would commit the fallacy of composition. The conclusion that if everyone stands up at a crowded football game, each will get a better view founders on the same fallacy.

The *post hoc* fallacy (from *post hoc, ergo propter hoc,* "after this, therefore because of this") is the faulty reasoning of cause-and-effect relations between events. The ancient Aztec Indians of Mexico believed that the spring ritual of sacrificing children and virgins appeased the gods of agriculture, bringing a bountiful harvest. When crops appeared in the fall, high priests insisted that the good crop was caused by the sacrifice. If the crop was insufficient, more children and virgins had to be wary the following spring. In economic analysis, the *post hoc* fallacy may be involved in statements such as "high interest rates cause inflation" or "after hoarding sugar, the price of sugar rises" or "the government subsidy to Chrysler Motor Company saved the business." Economists and all who are interested in sound thinking must constantly guard against such fallacies.

Positive and Normative Economics

Economics is usually a positive rather than a normative science. Positive statements describe what is or predict what will be under certain circumstances, whereas normative prescriptions entail value judgments about what should be. For the most part, economists confine themselves to positive statements. Individual values, concepts of justice, or tastes are normative matters and generally do not enter economists' analyses of issues. These matters are not testable in any accepted scientific sense and are therefore excluded from economics.

Consider U.S. welfare programs. To say that additional tax dollars should be spent on welfare would involve a normative judgment on the part of economists. Once society has decided to spend more on welfare, however, economists can make positive statements about the effects of such spending. Or economists may observe the welfare system and analyze how the system could

Fallacy of composition: Incorrectly generalizing that what is true for a part is also true for the whole.

Post hoc fallacy: The incorrect linking of unrelated events as a cause-and-effect relationship simply because one event happens after the other.

Positive economics: Observations, explanations, or predictions about economic life; scientific economics.

Normative economics: Value judgments based on moral principles or preferences about how economic life should be.

work more efficiently in achieving its goals. In other words, economists must show, once society has decided on a welfare system and on some dollar amount to be devoted to welfare, how alternative systems of welfare distribution would alter the effectiveness of the program. Economists make positive statements in presenting alternatives and their effects so that society might get the most for the dollars spent.

On the smaller scale, imagine a student facing an afternoon choice between watching soap operas and studying for an economics quiz. In positive terms, economists can only describe the alternatives open to the student. An observer would be on normative grounds if he or she insisted that the student should avoid TV all afternoon and spend the time preparing for the quiz. Free choice is, in this as in all cases, the prerogative of the economic actor. Economists can only array the alternatives. On occasion, normative statements slip into economic discussion, as they undoubtedly do in this book. Beware of them and learn to distinguish them from positive economics.

Microeconomics and Macroeconomics

The first half of this book concerns what economists call microeconomics, and the second half deals with macroeconomics. **Microeconomics,** like microbiology, concerns the components of a system. Just as a frog is made up of individual cells of various kinds, individual sales and purchases of commodities from potatoes to health care are the stuff of which the whole economy is composed. Microeconomists are thus concerned with individual markets and with the determination of relative prices within those markets—the price of potatoes versus the price of hot dogs. Supply and demand for all goods, services, and factors of production are the subject matter of microeconomics. Microeconomists address questions such as the following: Will the use of larger quantities of solar energy reduce the total energy bill of Americans? Will an increased tax on cigarettes increase or decrease federal revenues from the tax? Will the quality and quantity of nursing services in the state of Wyoming be changed by the licensing of nursing in that state?

Macroeconomics is the study of the economy as a whole. The overall price level, inflation rate, international exchange rate, unemployment rate, economic growth rate, and interest rate are some issues of concern to macroeconomists. Macroeconomists analyze how these crucial quantities are determined and how and why they change.

Some issues contain elements of both microeconomics and macroeconomics—for instance, a proposed U.S. tariff on Japanese auto imports. Microeconomists would be interested in the effects of the tariff on auto prices, on the American auto industry, and on the quantity of cars bought by U.S. consumers. Macroeconomists would be primarily interested in the effects of the tariff on international trade, the balance of payments, and total spending. They might address such questions as: Would the tariff increase or decrease economic growth in the United States and in Japan? Would total employment in the United States or Japan change because of the tariff?

Daily television reports and newspapers are filled with discussions of both macroeconomic and microeconomic issues: Do tax cuts to business spur investment and economic growth? Will an OPEC price decrease or an alteration in supply affect oil and gas prices in America? Is the economy headed for more inflation, greater unemployment, or both? Will a tightening of the

Microeconomics:
Analysis of the behavior of individual decision-making units, including individuals, households, and business firms.

Macroeconomics:
Analysis of the behavior of an economy as a whole.

money supply cause an increase or decrease in interest rates? Does foreign competition mean fewer jobs for domestic autoworkers? Will price competition cause some airlines or trucking firms to shut down? Should the federal government balance the budget or not? A mastery of the fundamental and general principles of economics will give you a good foundation for formulating intelligent and reasoned answers to important questions such as these.

Why Do Economists Disagree?

Government or academic economists are forever predicting economic doom or economic prosperity for the same future time period. If economics contains fundamental principles agreed on by all, why do economists always seem to be arguing over predictions or over causes and effects? Why do economists disagree? One of the limitations of economic science is its inability to test theory. This imperfection means that alternative theories may be offered to explain the same events, such as the effects of government budget deficits or of the Great Depression of the 1930s. Alternative theories mean divergent policy prescriptions and different perspectives on the effects of policy prescriptions.

Even when economists agree on theoretical apparatus, they may differ on the magnitude of the effects suggested by the theory. And secondary effects—effects not considered in a theory—can occur after the initial impact of a policy change has taken place. Economists often disagree on the nature and importance of these secondary effects. Would new monetary incentives for an all-volunteer army increase or decrease our military effectiveness? Economists of good faith and common fundamentals might disagree. We do not

© Sam C. Rawls 1984.

wish to overemphasize economists' disagreements or the ambiguous nature of economics. Meteorologists of equal training and ability might well disagree over whether it will rain tomorrow.

Economics, like meteorology, is an inexact science, and it is likely to remain so. But economic theory and prediction are accurate and testable enough to provide extremely important insights into numerous issues that touch our lives. And the science of choice and scarcity is (like meteorology) constantly being improved from both theoretical and empirical perspectives. The well-established power of economic thinking is the result of two hundred years of such continuing improvements. Sound understanding of the principles of economic thinking will improve your understanding of the world.

SUMMARY

1. Economics is basically concerned with three questions: What goods and services are produced? How are goods and services produced? For whom are goods and services produced?
2. Economics is the study of how individuals and societies choose to allocate scarce resources given unlimited wants.
3. Scarce resources include human and nonhuman resources as well as time and technology. Human resources consist of labor, including entrepreneurship, and management. Nonhuman resources include land and all natural resources such as minerals, technology, information, and capital.
4. All scarce resources bear an opportunity cost. This means that individuals or societies forgo other opportunities whenever scarce resources are used to produce specific goods and services.
5. Economic behavior is rational: Human beings are assumed to behave predictably by weighing the costs and benefits of their decisions and their potential actions.
6. Economic choices are made at the margin—that is, the additional costs or benefits of a change in the current situation. Prices are the signal that indicates individual and collective choices for goods and services as well as the relative scarcity of the resources necessary to produce the goods and services.
7. The study of prices of individual products and inputs is called *microeconomics,* and the study of inflation, unemployment, and related problems is called *macroeconomics.*
8. Economics is a more inexact and imprecise science than chemistry or physics. It is accurate enough to predict much economic behavior, however, and to provide insight into a large number of important problems.

KEY TERMS

goods	information	marginal analysis	*post hoc* fallacy
services	property rights	markets	positive economics
resources	institutions	prices	normative economics
scarcity	accounting costs	barter	microeconomics
economic goods	explicit costs	money	macroeconomics
free goods	implicit costs	inflation	
human resources	opportunity costs	models	
nonhuman resources	rational self-interest	fallacy of	
technology	margin	composition	

QUESTIONS FOR REVIEW AND DISCUSSION

1. What problem creates the foundation of economic analysis? Is this problem restricted to the poor? Why or why is it not relevant to the animal kingdom?

2. Can wants be satisfied with existing resources?

3. What are resources? How is the resource capital different from the resources land and labor?

4. What is the difference between behaving in one's self-interest and behaving selfishly?

5. What functions do prices have in the economy? Why were things rationed during World War II?

6. You have already paid your tuition. What does it cost you, at the margin, to attend your afternoon economics class on Friday? On Tuesday? (*Remember:* The margin refers to the additional cost of attending one additional class.)

7. Is air a free good? Is clean air a free good? Is cleaner air a free good?

8. Why do economists abstract from reality when formulating theories? Does this imply that their theories have no relevance in the real world?

9. "The stock market crash of 1929 preceded the Great Depression. Therefore, the fall in stock prices caused the Great Depression." "Periods of inflation are frequently followed by increases in the stock of money. Therefore, inflation causes increases in the money supply." "*A* occurs after *B*. Therefore, *B* causes *A*." These statements violate which fallacy? How?

10. "The distribution of income in the United States is not fair." What type of statement is this? Can "fair" be used to describe something without being normative?

ECONOMICS IN ACTION
Marginal Analysis in Business and Politics

Far from being an abstract, theoretical exercise, marginal analysis—making decisions at the margin—is central to the everyday life of individuals, businesses, governments, and politicians. Suppose you manage a large department store and want to reduce the amount of shoplifting that takes place. By hiring additional store detectives, you will benefit from fewer thefts. But the detectives must be paid, so the net benefit is the amount you save minus the costs of the detectives. You might perform an experiment to determine whether you have enough detectives. Hire an additional detective and see whether losses from shoplifting fall by more than the $300 per week you pay each detective. If losses decrease by more than $300, hire additional detectives; if not, let detectives go. Stop hiring when the reduction in losses per week (the marginal benefit) is exactly equal to the weekly wage of detectives (the marginal cost to the store). (Note that the optimal level of shoplifting you will permit is not zero! Something worth doing is not necessarily worth doing well if "doing well" means eliminating *all* shoplifting.)

Suppose you are the manager of a large grocery store close to campus. On what basis would you decide to stay open all night rather than close at midnight and open at 6 A.M.? The costs would include the additional electricity required to stay open later plus the additional labor cost of cashiers and stock persons. The additional benefit is the sales revenue the store would make from staying open six more hours each day. In other words, the decision would not be based on the costs of building the grocery store, installing shelves, and so on. The decision, like all decisions, will be based on marginal, forward-looking considerations.

Government, through the political process, also makes decisions at the margin. The completion of the Strategic Defense Initiative ("Star Wars") program or the decision to finish a nuclear power plant are pertinent examples. These decisions will not be made on the basis of how much has already been spent on the projects but on the additional costs and benefits attached to completion. Political opposi-

tion, for example, will increase the marginal costs to those who vote to complete the "Star Wars" project, whereas political (voter) support will increase their marginal benefits. If the benefits of completing a nuclear power plant no longer outweigh the costs of ample electric power, then the plant will probably sit half-finished.

Politicians also gauge costs and benefits in running for election. In a presidential election, a candidate cannot campaign continuously all over the country. He or she must make marginal decisions about where to spend scarce campaign time and funds based upon factors such as the strength of support in various states and regions, the likelihood that undecided voters will commit in any particular area, and the number of electoral votes obtainable in any "noncommitted" state or region. Each political party conducts polls to determine this sort of information. Some states or areas may be "given up as lost," which means, in economic terms, that the marginal costs far outweigh the marginal benefits of campaigning there. As election day approaches and time becomes more scarce, candidates usually visit states and regions where the marginal benefits (in terms of the probability of obtaining electoral votes) to campaigning exceed the marginal costs. The marginal principle holds true for state and local politicians.

Every one of these decisions, and millions more like them, employ marginal analysis. It is one of the foundations of economics.

Questions

1. In the store detective example, why wouldn't it be considered optimal to permit no shoplifting at all?
2. On what will you base your decision whether to eat another piece of pizza at a pizza parlor that advertises "all you can eat" for $5?
3. Would a rational person in a hurry ever give away money to a beggar on the street? Use both the concepts of opportunity cost and marginal analysis to explain your answer.

Working with Graphs

Economists frequently use graphs to demonstrate economic theories or models. This appendix explains how graphs are constructed and how they can illustrate economic relations in simplified form. By understanding the mechanics and usefulness of graphs, you will find it much easier to grasp the economic concepts presented in this book.

THE PURPOSE OF GRAPHS

Most graphs in this book are simply pictures showing the relation between economic variables, such as the price of a good and the quantity of the good that people are willing to purchase. There are many such pairs of variables in economics: the costs of production and the level of output, the rate of inflation and the level of unemployment, the interest rate and the supply of capital goods, for example. Graphs are the most concise means of expressing the variety of relations that exist between such variables.

Figure 1 illustrates these ideas. It is a bar graph that shows the relation between the U.S. gross national product (GNP), a measure of the value of all goods and services produced annually, and time, in this case, the period between 1960 and 1990. The GNP variable is plotted along the vertical line on the left side of the graph. The time variable is plotted along the horizontal line at the bottom of the graph. From this graph you can roughly estimate the level of GNP for each year between 1960 and 1990. For instance, GNP in 1967 was somewhere around $800 billion. You can also see that GNP tended to increase over the years 1960–1990. By working with the graph, you could estimate the rate of increase of GNP from year to year or the percentage increase over a particular period, such as 1965–1970.

This one concise picture—the graph—contains a great deal of information. Aside from economy of expression, graphs have a great deal of cognitive appeal: People can more easily grasp concepts demonstrated through pictures than concepts demonstrated through words.

Some of the graphs in this book are bar graphs; many others use the Cartesian coordinate system, which consists of points plotted on a grid formed by the intersection of two perpendicular lines. See Figure 2. The horizontal line is the **x-axis,** and the vertical line is the **y-axis.** The intersection of the two lines is the point 0, called the *origin*. Above the origin on the vertical axis, all values are positive. Below the origin on the vertical axis, all values are negative. Values to the right of the origin are positive; values to the left are negative. The economic variables we use in this book are usually positive; that is, to plot economic relations we will usually use the upper-right portion, or quadrant, of a graph such as the one in Figure 3.

FIGURE 1

This graph shows the levels of U.S. GNP between the years 1960 and 1990 at five-year intervals. (1990 figure is an estimate.)

Source: Council of Economic Advisers, *Economic Report of the President* (Washington, D.C.: U.S. Government Printing Office, 1990) p. 294.

A Bar Graph

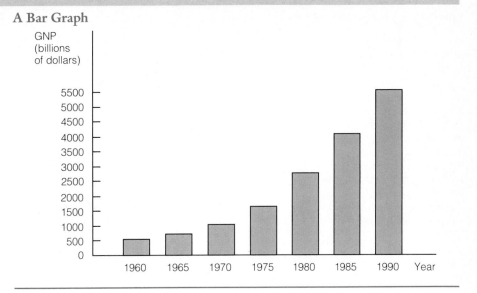

FIGURE 2

Any pair of numerical values can be plotted on this grid. The upper-right quadrant, shaded here, is the portion of the graph most often used in economics.

A Grid for Plotting Graphs

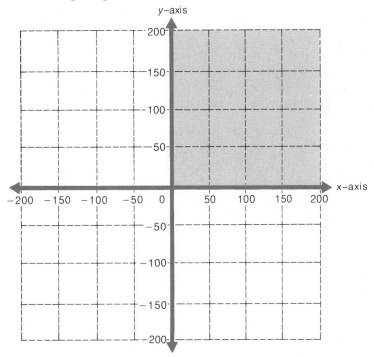

FIGURE 3

A Simple Line (or Linear) Graph

Curve *AE* shows the essential relation between two sets of variables: the number of words memorized and the number of minutes spent memorizing. The relation is positive; as the variable on the *x*-axis increases or decreases, the variable on the *y*-axis increases or decreases, respectively. A positive relation is shown by an upward-sloping line tracing the intersection of each pair of variables.

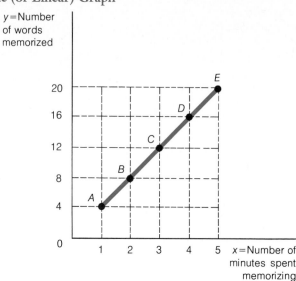

HOW TO DRAW A GRAPH

Suppose you wish to graph the relation between two variables. Variable *y* is the number of words memorized, and variable *x* is the number of minutes spent memorizing words. Table 2 presents a set, or schedule, of hypothetical data for these two variables.

We can plot the data from Table 2 on a graph using points in the upper-right quadrant formed by the *x*-axis and the *y*-axis. See Figure 3. The variable, number of words memorized, is measured along the *y*-axis and is considered the *y* value. The variable, number of minutes spent memorizing, is measured along the *x*-axis and is the *x* value. From the data in Table 2 we see that each increase of 1 minute of memorizing resulted in 4 more memorized words. The graph in Figure 3 illustrates this relation.

The points marked as large dots in Figure 3 represent pairs of variables. Point *A* represents the pair on the first line of Table 2: 4 words and 1 minute. Point *B* represents 8 words and 2 minutes, and so on. When we connect the points, we have a straight line running upward and to the right of the origin. Lines showing the intersection of *x*- and *y*-values

on a graph are referred to as **curves** in this book, whether they are straight or curved lines.

Curves show two types of relations between variables: positive and negative. The relation between the *x* and *y* values in Figure 3 is positive: as the *x* value increases, so does the *y* value. (Or, as the *x* value decreases, the *y* value decreases. Either way, the relation is positive.) On a graph, a **positive,** or **direct, relation** is shown by a curve that slopes upward and to the right of the origin. In a **negative,** or **inverse, relation,** the two variables change in op-

TABLE 2
Schedule of Hypothetical Data

Number of Words Memorized (*y*)	Number of Minutes Spent Memorizing (*x*)
4	1
8	2
12	3
16	4
20	5

posite directions. An increase in *y* is paired with a decrease in *x*. Or a decrease in *x* is paired with an increase in *y*. Figure 4 shows a negative, or inverse, relation on a graph. The curve for a negative relation slopes downward from left to right—the opposite of a positive relation.

General Relations

Throughout this book, some graphs display general relations rather than specific relations. A general relation does not depend on particular numerical values of variables, as was the case in Figure 3. For example, the relation between the number of calories a person consumes per week and that person's weight (other things being equal) is positive. This suggests an upward-sloping line, as shown in Figure 5a, with calories on the *x*-axis and weight on the *y*-axis. Figure 5 represents a general relation, so it does not need numerical values on either axis. It does not specify the particular number of calories required to maintain a particular body weight; it simply shows that an increase in the number of calories consumed increases body weight. Figure 5b shows an inverse relation between body weight and the amount of exercise per week, again a general relation. Sometimes two variables are not related. Figure 5c shows that a per-

son's weight is independent of a neighbor's caloric intake. Thankfully, no matter how much your neighbor eats, it has no effect on your weight.

At this point you should be able to construct a graph showing simple relations. For example, graph the relation between the weight of a car and the miles per gallon it achieves or between the length of the line at the school cafeteria and the time of day. If the relationship between any two variables you select is a straight line, it is said to be **linear.** A linear relationship means that for every unit change (increase or decrease) in one of the variables (the weight of a car), the other variable (miles per gallon of gasoline) changes (increases or decreases) by some fixed amount.

Nonlinear Relations

Often, relations between two variables are not the simple linear relationships depicted in Figures 3, 4, and 5. For example, unlike in Figure 3 where each additional minute spent studying enables one to memorize 4 additional words, it may be that the number of additional words memorized changes as the number of minutes changes. Such a **nonlinear** relationship is depicted in Figure 6. There, 1 minute of studying enables a student to memorize 6 words, but 2 minutes of studying enables a student

---

FIGURE 4   A Negative Relation Between Two Variables

As the price of a cup of coffee increases, the number of cups drunk each day decreases. When variables move in opposite directions, their relation is negative, or inverse. Negative relations are shown by a curve that slopes downward and to the right of the origin.

FIGURE 5   General Graphical Relations

General relations are (a) positive, (b) inverse, or (c) independent. General relations are not measured numerically on the *y*- or *x*-axis.

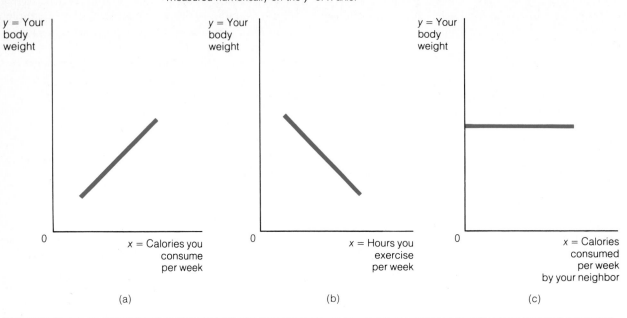

(a)   (b)   (c)

to memorize only 11 words—the second minute adds only 5 additional words to the total. Additional minutes of studying beyond 2 lead to even smaller increases in the total number of words memorized. Therefore, there is a positive relationship between the two variables, but the relationship is *nonlinear.*

Occasionally nonlinear relations are more complex than the one depicted in Figure 6 and do not fall into the simple category of positive or negative. Figure 7 shows that for some relatively low *x* values, the variables on the graph are positively related, but as the *x* value increases, a point is reached where the two variables become inversely related. In Figure 7 from the origin to x^* the curve slopes positively. But for values greater than x^*, the curve slopes negatively. To illustrate, we let the *x*-axis show the number of pieces of pizza that a friend consumes in an evening and the *y*-axis show the total amount of pleasure she receives from each additional slice. At first, the more she eats, the happier she becomes, but eventually a critical point is reached, after which the more she eats, the less pleasure she receives from each additional slice.

FIGURE 6
A Nonlinear Graph

Curve *AE* shows the nonlinear relation between the number of minutes spent studying and the number of words memorized.

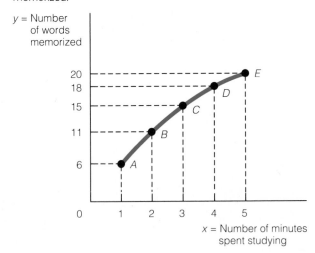

FIGURE 7

For lower values of *x*—in this example, the number of pizza slices eaten—the *y* value—the amount of satisfaction—increases. After some point, say 3 slices, the *y* value decreases with increasing values of *x*.

Variables Both Positively and Negatively Related

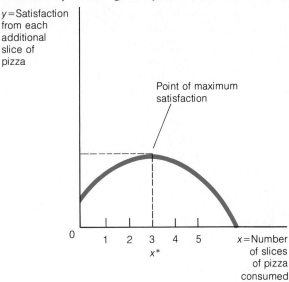

FIGURE 8

Some relations yield a U shape. Variables along the *x*- and *y*-axes are inversely related at first, but after some critical value, here shown as *x**, they become positively related.

A U-shaped Curve

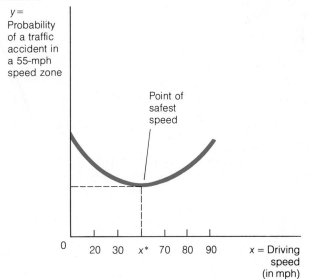

Many other relations can exist. A U-shaped curve, as graphed in Figure 8, shows that the x value is at first inversely related to the y value and then positively related. After some critical value, x^*, the y value begins to rise as the x value increases. The y-axis in this example might represent the probability of having an accident on an interstate highway and the x-axis might show the miles per hour at which a car travels. To avoid accidents, x^* is the optimal, or "best," speed. Driving at speeds lower than x^* increases the probability of an accident, but rates faster than x^* mph also increase the chances of an accident.

SLOPE OF THE CURVE

In graphical analysis the amount by which the y value increases or decreases as the result of an increase or decrease in the x value is the **slope** of the curve. The slope of the curve is an important concept in economics. Much economic analysis studies the margin of change in a variable or in a relation between variables, and the slope of a curve mea-

sures the marginal rate of change. In Figure 3, for example, every change in the x value—every increase of 1 minute—is associated with an increase of 4 words memorized. The slope of the curve in Figure 3 is the rate of change. Economists express the concept "change in" with the symbol Δ. So in Figure 3 the slope of the line AE is $\Delta y/\Delta x$, or $4/1 = 4$.

For the straight-line curves in Figures 3 and 4, the slope is constant. Along most curves, however, the slope is not constant. In Figure 8, an increase in driving speed from 55 to 60 mph may increase the probability of an accident only slightly, but an increase from 60 to 65 mph may increase the probability by a greater amount. Not only does the probability increase for each mile-per-hour increase in driving speed, but it increases by a greater amount. This indicates that the slope not only is positive but also is increasing.

The slope of a curved line is different at every point along the line. To find the slope of a curved line at a particular point, draw a straight line tangent to the curve. (A tangent touches the curve at one point without crossing the curve.) Consider point A in Figure 9. The slope at A on the curved

---

FIGURE 9   Slope Along a Curve

The slope of a curve at a particular point is the slope of a straight line tangent to the curve at that point.

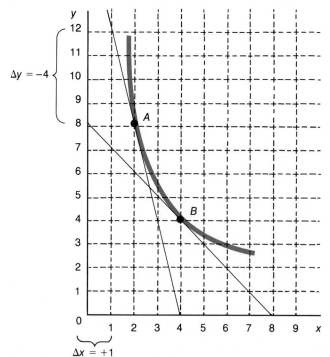

FIGURE 10   A Curve with an Increasing Slope

As the *x* variable increases, the
change in the *y* variable
increases.

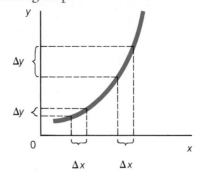

line is equal to the slope of the straight line tangent to the curved line. Dividing the change in the *y* variable (Δy) by the change in the *x* variable (Δx) yields the slope at *A*. In Figure 9, every change in *x* from 0 to 1 and 1 to 2, and so on, results in a change in *y* along the curve. At point *A*, the change in $y = -4$. So $\Delta y / \Delta x = -4/1 = -4$. At lower points along the curve, such as *B*, the curve is flatter—that is, less steep. The line tangent at *B* has a slope of -1. As we move from point *A* to point *B*, equal increases in *x* result in smaller and smaller decreases in *y*. In other words, the *rate* at which *y* falls decreases as *x* increases along this particular curve.

Other relations lead to different slopes and different changes in the slope along the curve. Along the curve in Figure 10, not only does the *y* value increase as the *x* value increases but the slope increases as the *x* value increases. For equal increases in the *x* value, the incremental changes in the *y* value become larger.

Interpreting the essential concepts illustrated in graphs is a necessary part of learning economic principles. Should you encounter difficulty in interpreting any of the graphs in later chapters, a brief review of this Appendix will prove helpful.

SUMMARY

1. Graphs are a concise expression of economic models, or theories. Graphs usually show the relation between two variables, such as price and quantity.
2. Linear graphs are drawn with two perpendicular lines, called axes. The *x*-axis is a horizontal line. Variables measured along the *x*-axis are called *x* values. The *y*-axis is a vertical line. Variables along it are called *y* values.
3. Lines showing the correlation between *x* and *y* values are called curves. An upward-sloping curve indicates a positive, or direct, relation between variables: As the *x* value increases or decreases, the *y* value does likewise. A downward-sloping curve indicates a negative, or inverse, relation between variables: As the *x* value increases, the *y* value decreases and vice versa.

4. Relations between variables may be specific or general. Specific relations are based on numerical quantities measured on either the *x*- or *y*-axis or both. General relations are not based on specific numerical quantities.
5. Relations between two variables can be either linear or nonlinear.
6. Variables can be both positively and negatively related. In such complex relations, the curve is either bow-shaped or U-shaped.
7. The slope of a curve measures the ratio of change in the *x* value to changes in the *y* value, expressed as $\Delta y / \Delta x$. Along a straight-line curve, the slope is constant. Along a curved line, the slope is different at every point.

KEY TERMS

x-axis, *y*-axis

curve

positive, or direct, relation

negative, or inverse, relation

linear relation

nonlinear relation

slope

QUESTIONS FOR REVIEW AND DISCUSSION

1. Explain how the slope of a line tells you whether the relation between the two variables illustrated is direct or inverse. If you drew a line illustrating your score on a history test as you study more hours, which would its slope be?

2. Plot the following points on a graph with X on the horizontal axis and Y on the vertical axis. Connect the dots to show the relation between X and Y.

	X	Y
A	0	2
B	2	4
C	4	8
D	6	14
E	8	22

What is the slope of the line between the points A and B? What is the slope between C and D? Is this a straight line?

3. Curves can be represented in algebraic form by an equation. For example, the points along a certain line can be demonstrated by the equation

$$Y = 10 - 2X.$$

The value of Y can be found by inserting different values of X and solving the equation for Y. Some of the values of Y for different values of X are shown in the following table. Fill in the blanks by solving the equation for the values of Y for each value of X given.

X	Y
0	10
2	6
4	—
6	—
8	—
10	—
12	—

Draw this set of points on a graph. Does this show a direct or inverse relation between X and Y? What is the slope of this line between the first and second points? Between the second and third? Is this a straight line?

4. If you measured body weight on the horizontal axis and the probability of dying of heart disease on the vertical axis, what would be the slope of a curve that showed the relation between these two variables?

2

Economic Principles

The essence of the economic problem is how to get as much value as we can from limited and costly resources. To do so, we constantly make choices. One college student may choose to spend a weekend at the beach rather than buy a new sweater and skirt. Another may choose to sleep late rather than attend an eight o'clock chemistry class. Every choice must be made at some cost.

Economists emphasize that decisions to use scarce resources bear an opportunity cost. The **opportunity cost** of a decision is the next most preferred or next-best alternative to a good or activity (the new clothes or the class instruction) that one must forgo in order to obtain some other good (a beach weekend or extra sleep). Economists have developed tools for expressing the choice and opportunity cost that are central to all decisions. After reading Chapter 2 you should understand

- how individuals and societies actually make decisions given that they are always costly.
- how individuals make practical decisions, since all-or-nothing choices are rare.
- how specialization and trade increase quantities of output for parties who exchange goods and services.
- how exchange, transaction costs, and other barriers reduce the benefits from specializing and trade.

Opportunity cost:
The highest-valued alternative forgone in making any choice.

OPPORTUNITY COST: THE INDIVIDUAL MUST CHOOSE

Suppose that a student is trying to decide what to do with 4 hours of time on a Sunday evening. One alternative is to work at the library, where the student earns $4 per. The other choice is studying for an economics quiz to be given Monday morning. The student views these two activities as the highest-valued uses of the 4 hours of time on Sunday evening. Table 1 depicts five different ways the student can allocate the 4 hours of time. Also depicted are

TABLE 1

The Individual Chooses: Working or Studying

Individuals must make choices from many alternatives available. In this example, the individual has choice options involving various combinations of studying and working in the library. These options range from no studying and all work to no work and all studying, with various other options in between these two. The trade-off involved in these choices is clear—more work (and more income) comes at the expense of less study time and a lower grade, and vice versa.

Choice of Time Allocation	Income Earned (in dollars)	Grade Earned (in percent)
(1) 0 hours working, 4 hours studying	0	100
(2) 1 hour working, 3 hours studying	4	90
(3) 2 hours working, 2 hours studying	8	75
(4) 3 hours working, 1 hour studying	12	55
(5) 4 hours working, 0 hours studying	16	0

five different combinations of income earned and percentage quiz scores the student could "produce" with the five different allocations of time. Choice (1), no work and 4 hours of study, yields the student a perfect quiz score but no income. Choice (2), allocating 1 hour to library work and 3 hours to study, produces an income of $4 and a score of 90 percent. The third, fourth, and fifth alternative choices mean still more income but lower quiz scores. Choice (5) involves no study time at all—and a score of 0 percent—but the student earns the highest income possible for the evening's work, $16.

Table 1 sets forth an important point. The student must spend time working and studying to obtain some income and a positive quiz score. The student's scarce resource, time, is used to produce two economic goods, grades and income.

Consider the two right-hand columns in Table 1. These two columns show the five different combinations of income and grades that the student can obtain from allocating the evening's available 4 hours of time five different ways. In Figure 1 these combinations are plotted as black dots and connected with a smooth curve. Choice (3) from Table 1, $8 of income and a score of 75 percent, is shown as point (3) in Figure 1. This particular combination of goods produced implies 2 hours of time allocated to library work and 2 hours to study.

Several aspects of Figure 1 are important. *All possible combinations* of income and quiz scores that the student could conceivably earn are represented by the curved line. This means that the choices between working and studying are *continuous*. Continuous choice implies that the five combinations in Table 1 are not the only ones available with 4 hours of time. The student could choose any combination of income and quiz score that together required 4 hours of time to produce—say, $2 of income for ½ hour worked and a score of 95 percent with 3½ hours of study. If choices were *discrete*, the student would be limited to only the five choices labeled (1) through (5). (Discrete

FIGURE 1

As the hours spent working increase, the score on the economics quiz falls.

The Individual Chooses: Income or Grades

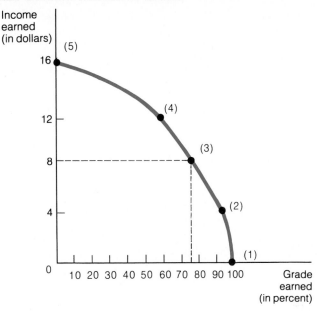

choices are fixed in number.) For convenience, economists ordinarily assume that economic relations are continuous.

A second crucial point is that Figure 1 and Table 1 constitute what economists call a *model*. Economists construct models to isolate specific phenomena for study. The model summarized in Figure 1 and Table 1 assumes a number of things about the student in the example. First, as just explained, the choices are continuous rather than discrete. Second, we assume as given that the total amount of time that the student has available for both activities combined is fixed—in this case, 4 hours. The general relationship governing the amount of time put into an activity and the resultant amount of the activity produced is also assumed given. Each hour worked yields $4 and only $4 of income. The first hour of study always yields a score of 55 percent, never 60 or 50 percent. Two hours of study produce a grade of 75 percent, not 74 or 76 percent. Other factors, such as the total amount of time the student has already put into the course before Sunday evening and the student's IQ, are assumed given. Does the student have the flu, a factor that would detract from performance on the quiz? Is the income more important to the student than the economics quiz? Are there other alternatives such as washing a car or spending time in language lab? Is the fact that one alternative has a future payoff, such as a job, relevant to the choice? Certainly matters such as these are significant, but we assume them as given with respect to the choice at hand.

Economists also emphasize that the decision to study or to work is made at the margin. Practically, making decisions at the margin means that we are faced not only with all-or-nothing choices but also with degrees of balancing units of one choice against another. Each choice would be made in terms of the costs of an additional hour of study or work forgone. Satisfactions from both activities are thus balanced **at the margin.** For example, suppose the

Choices at the margin: Decisions based on the additional benefits and costs of small changes in a particular activity.

student had originally planned on working 2 hours and studying 2 hours. This division of the evening's time would produce $8 of income and a grade of 75 percent on the economics quiz. Suppose the student considers choosing to earn $4 more income. This would entail working 1 additional hour, which means studying 1 less hour. A reallocation of the time resource means that a quiz grade of 55 percent will be earned rather than 75 percent. The student must make a decision at the margin. Does the additional satisfaction of the extra $4 of income outweigh the quiz score falling by 20 percentage points? The drop of 20 points is the opportunity cost of choosing to earn an additional $4 (whether or not the extra $4 is "worth it" to the student is a question to be addressed in Chapter 6).

In making decisions at the margin we assume that all other factors are equal, or fixed. Each time we make a decision some fixed or given factors resulting from previous decisions come into play. In our example, the student would weigh, for instance, the amount of previous study, a fixed factor in choosing work or study on the evening in question.

Previous decisions cannot be changed and are gone forever, but that does not mean that they have no impact on current choices. It simply means that we make choices in the present with unchangeable past choices as given and unalterable. This is another aspect of making choices at the margin.

OPPORTUNITY COST AND PRODUCTION POSSIBILITIES: SOCIETY MUST CHOOSE

So far we have focused on individual choices, but the same principles apply to society's choices. Just as an individual is limited by the scarcity of time in choosing among options, society is constrained by scarce resources in producing and consuming alternative goods. Let us examine an abstract example. Suppose a society produces only two goods—oranges and peanut butter—and that all its resources and technology are fixed and constant in amount and level.

Given the state of technology and assuming that the society uses all its resources, the society could produce either 100 million jars of peanut butter or 16 million tons of oranges (see Table 2). Or the society may choose to

---

TABLE 2	Society Decides: Oranges or Peanut Butter

Society must choose among many alternative combinations of goods to produce. The cost of one good is the lost production of other goods.

Choice	Peanut Butter (millions of jars)	Oranges (millions of tons)
A	100	0
B	90	4
C	75	8
D	50	12
E	0	16

devote some of its resources to producing peanut butter and some to producing oranges. These choices, called society's *production possibilities,* are listed *A–E* in Table 2. From this information a production possibilities curve can be constructed (see Figure 2). A production possibilities curve depicts the alternatives open to society for the production of two goods, given full utilization of all existing resources, human and nonhuman, and an existing state of technology. When resources are fully employed, moreover, society is said to be producing on its **production possibilities frontier.**

At choice *A* in Figure 2, society produces 100 million jars of peanut butter and no oranges, while at choice *E* society uses all its resources in orange production. Choices in between, with some of both commodities produced, are shown at points *B*, *C*, and *D*. Continuous choices of all other possible combinations are shown along the curve; resources are assumed to be fully employed at all points on the curve. The curve therefore shows all of the possibilities for the production of oranges and peanut butter, assuming resources are fully employed. Points such as *G* lie beyond the production possibilities frontier. The country's resources and technology do not permit it to produce at points such as *G* that lie outside the frontier.

Production possibilities frontier:
The curve that graphs all the possible combinations of two goods that an economic entity can produce given the available technology, the amount of productive resources available, and the fact that these resources are fully utilized.

The Law of Increasing Costs

Just as there was an opportunity cost to the student in choosing to study for the quiz or to work in the library, there is an opportunity cost for society in any choice between producing oranges and peanut butter.

Consider a society that produces nothing but peanut butter, choice *A* in Figure 2. The opportunity cost of that choice is that no oranges can be produced. A move to choice *B*, representing a shift of some resources from

FIGURE 2

As more and more oranges are produced, the opportunity cost per orange increases. The opportunity cost of producing the first 4 million tons of oranges is 10 million jars of peanut butter. The opportunity cost of producing the next 4 million tons of oranges is an additional 15 million jars of peanut butter, and so on.

Production Possibilities Curve

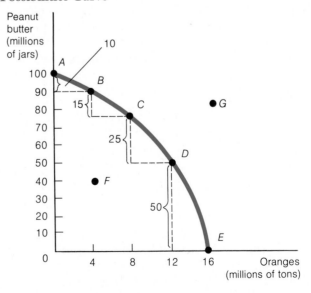

peanut butter production to orange production, means a sacrifice of 10 million jars of peanut butter, but society gains 4 million tons of oranges. Thus the opportunity cost of producing the first 4 million tons of oranges is 10 million jars of peanut butter. To get the second 4 million tons of oranges, however, a larger quantity of peanut butter must be given up—15 million jars. Thus as society becomes more specialized in production of either oranges or peanut butter, the opportunity cost per unit of the good rises. This effect is called the **law of increasing costs.**

Why does the law of increasing costs hold? Resources, training, and talents are not all alike and are not perfectly adaptable to alternative uses. Land suited to orange growing is not equally suited to peanut farming and vice versa. Orange pickers are not equally adept at the manufacture of metal lids for peanut butter jars or even peanut farming without additional training. The most-suited human and nonhuman resources are moved into production first, but as production of a good increases and becomes more specialized, less-adaptable resources must be used to produce it. The costs of producing additional units of the good rise because it requires larger amounts of these increasingly less-adaptable resources to produce each successive unit. This means that greater quantities of another good do not get produced and must therefore be sacrificed in the process. A society of peanut butter lovers might be growing peanuts in greenhouses in North Dakota, and concert pianists and nuclear technicians might be operating machinery in peanut butter processing plants.

Law of increasing costs:
As more scarce resources are used to produce additional units of one good, production of the other good falls by larger and larger amounts.

Unemployment of Resources

The law of increasing costs always applies when resources are fully employed. When there is a degree of **unemployment of resources,** however—such as a certain amount of land lying idle—society finds itself producing at a point *within* the production possibilities curve. Point *F* in Figure 2 represents such a situation. From point *F* to the curve, additional oranges or peanut butter can be produced without any increase in opportunity costs until resources become fully employed. The production possibilities curve is thus referred to as a *frontier* because it represents full employment of resources. Full employment means that society is realizing its maximum output potential. Many economic problems are the result of unemployment.

Unemployment of resources:
A situation in which some human and/or nonhuman resources that can be used in production are not used.

Choices Are Made at the Margin

As with individuals, society's choices are made at the margin. Suppose, for example, that a society has for years been one of peanut butter lovers and orange haters. Suppose further that long-time devotion of society's resources to peanut butter production "warped" resources—made them more adaptable over time—to peanut butter production. Past decisions to warp the resources would make current additional orange production more costly. A sudden decision by society to produce more oranges would have to be made at the present—not some past—margin. Thus past decisions obviously affect current costs, but past decisions cannot be changed.

WHY THE PRODUCTION POSSIBILITIES FRONTIER SHIFTS

If we keep in mind the meaning of the production possibilities frontier, we will also understand that an increase or decrease in society's human or non-human resources can shift society's output potential. An understanding of such changes is central to the understanding of economic growth—or the lack of it.

The Shifting Frontier

The production possibilities frontier can only shift leftward or rightward in response to any change in the quantity of human resources, any change in the quantity of nonhuman resources, or any change in technology. Changes in these factors shift the production possibilities frontier because we previously assumed they were constant.

Suppose a technological improvement occurs in peanut butter production that increases the productivity of peanut harvesters—perhaps a fertilizer or new crop techniques. In such a case, society's production possibilities relating to peanut butter are increased without a similar decrease in orange production. The result is a shift rightward on the peanut butter end of the production possibilities curve. Such a change is shown in Figure 3a as a shift from the PP_1 curve to the PP_2 curve.

In Figure 3b, a productivity change brought about by technological improvement occurs in orange production. Here the production possibilities curve shifts rightward on the orange end; if society prefers, additional oranges can be produced without any sacrifice of peanut butter.

In Figure 3c, a general change in productivity, technology, or resource supply is assumed. An increase in the quantity of labor (through a simple growth in population), for example, shifts the entire production possibilities frontier rightward from PP_1 to PP_2. Suppose society now chooses the peanut butter/orange combination A_1. More of both goods are produced and consumed as a result of the technological improvement. But society faces new trade-offs once it is producing on its new frontier. Opportunity costs arise again in resource utilization, just as they did at combination A on production possibility curve PP_1. Society cannot escape scarcity, yet it can improve its production possibilities through growth in technology, quantity of human or nonhuman resources, or resource productivity.

Economic Growth: How Economies Progress

We can understand the nature of economic growth with the aid of the production possibilities curve model. The key to economic growth in society is related to the growth or change in capital stock and other crucial resources.

The creation of **capital stock** (a supply of items used to produce other items) takes time and bears an opportunity cost in present consumption. The benefits of creating capital, however, are in increased amounts of future consumption. In other words, forming new capital stock requires that people save—that is, abstain from consuming in the present. When investment in

Capital stock:
The amount of nonhuman resources available in the economy. These include tools, land, machinery, equipment, and so on.

FIGURE 3   Shifting the Production Possibilities Frontier

(a) A technological improvement in peanut butter production shifts the production possibilities curve outward at the peanut butter end. (b) A technological improvement in orange production shifts the production possibilities curve outward at the orange end. (c) A general increase in technology or resource supply shifts the entire production possibilities curve outward.

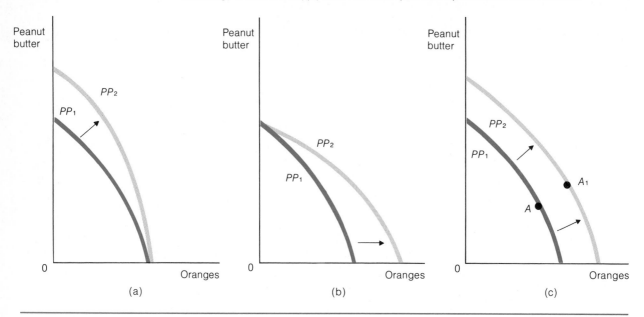

(a)   (b)   (c)

capital stock results from this saving, capital formation and growth occur. The formation of capital goods—tools, tractors, computers and so on—requires a redirection of resources from consumption of goods to production of capital goods. The opportunity cost of acquiring capital is thus consumption goods forgone, but the reward for society is an increase in future productive capacity in consumption goods, capital goods, or both.

We can illustrate this phenomenon with the production possibilities curve. Figure 4 shows two production possibilities frontiers that contrast capital goods production (the vertical axis) with consumption goods production (the horizontal axis) for two hypothetical societies with initially similar production possibilities curves. Consider society A's choice of consumption and capital goods in 1990, represented by point E_A in Figure 4a. Clearly, society A devotes a larger proportion of its resources to capital goods production than to consumption goods production. Saving (abstaining from current consumption), investing, and capital formation are all high in that society. The payoff for society A will come later, say in 2000, with vastly enlarged productive capacity, designated by the shift of the production possibilities curve to PP_{2000} in Figure 4a.

Society B chooses to use almost all of its resources in 1990 for consumption goods, with only a small quantity of resources devoted to capital goods, a combination represented by point F_B in Figure 4b. The consequence of this choice is low economic growth over the following decade. By 2000, the production possibilities of that society have grown by only a small amount, as curve PP_{2000} in Figure 4b indicates. Thus **economic growth** in the future is

Economic growth:
A permanent increase in the productive capacity of the economy.

FIGURE 4   Growth Choices on the Production Possibilities Curve

(a) By producing more capital goods, E_A, in 1990, society A can produce more consumption goods in the future than (b) society B, which produces only F_B capital goods in 1990.

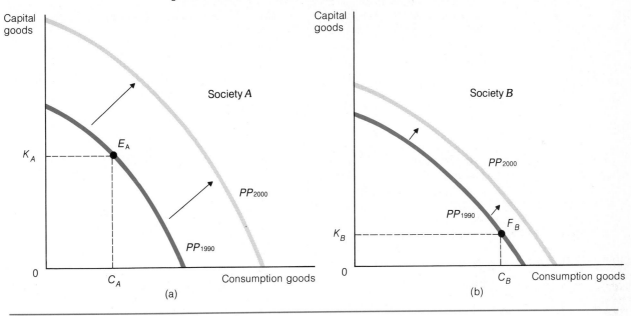

(a)

(b)

largely determined by current decisions about production. Technological changes are important factors in the progress of society, but to take advantage of technology, society must sacrifice some present consumption. (See Focus, "How Societies Can Regress and Progress: Black Death in the Middle Ages.")

In addition to choosing to put some resources into the creation of capital stock, societies can increase their output by specializing in and trading, or exchanging, goods and services. **Specialization** simply means that the tasks associated with the production of a product or service are divided—and sometimes subdivided—and performed by many different individuals to increase the total production of the good or service. The principles of specialization are therefore related to how all societies and economic organizations try to overcome the basic problem of scarcity.

Specialization:
An economic entity producing only one good or service or the performance of a single task in a production process by an individual.

SPECIALIZATION AND TRADE: A FEATURE OF ALL SOCIETIES

Virtually all known peoples have engaged in specialization and trade, and theories and principles related to specialization and trade have been part of economists' tool kits for more than two hundred years. Adam Smith (1723–1790), the Scottish philosopher and recognized founder of economics, published his great work *An Inquiry into the Nature and Causes of the Wealth of Nations* in 1776 (a year of declarations). It formally established the science of what we now call economics. (For more on Adam Smith, see Point-Counterpoint, pp. 142–144.)

FOCUS How Societies Can Regress and Progress:
Black Death in the Middle Ages

As we know from the ancient Greek and Roman experiences, civilization and its production possibilities can decline or be lost. Perhaps the greatest calamity ever visited on the Western world was the bubonic plague—the so-called Black Death. Between 1347 and 1350, rats infested with plague-ridden fleas spread death throughout Europe; between 33 percent and 65 percent of the population perished.

In 1300, before the Black Death, Europe's production possibilities (even given feudal institutions and technology) were considerably larger than after the catastrophe. The Black Death, by decimating a large percentage of the working population, reduced the production possibilities frontier of European society. It did not, however, eliminate the trade-off between consumer goods (goods in the present) and capital goods (goods for producing more goods in the future). (See Figure 5.)

Since labor had been cheap and plentiful relative to other resources before the plague, agricultural methods had been oriented to the large, untrained labor supply. The scarceness of labor following the plague—even given the smaller number of mouths to feed—meant society had to devote a large proportion of its resources to consumption goods (such as food) to survive. In 1350, European society was forced to a point such as *B* on the innermost production possibilities curve in Figure 5.

Relatively expensive labor, brought about by the general population reduction, meant that businesses "economized" or "rationed" labor by trying to substitute capital and other resources for it. In this process, many "labor-saving" inventions were discovered (new uses for water power, new agricultural implements, and so on). Later, steam power supplemented or replaced water power. The Black Death of the fourteenth century may have ultimately made the production possibilities curve PP_{1700} possible for Europeans.[a] At points such as *C* on the furthermost production possibilities curve in Figure 5, the choices available to society between

FIGURE 5
Production Possibilities and the Black Death

The loss of labor resources caused by the bubonic plague shifts the production possibilities curve toward the origin for 1350. Technological advances in and inventions of labor-saving capital, in part created by the shortage of labor, created a huge rightward shift in the production possibilities curve by 1700—the beginning of the Industrial Revolution.

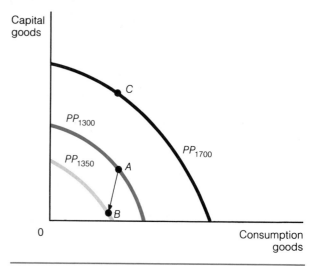

consumer and capital goods were greatly enhanced. It is an ill wind that does not blow some good ultimately (somewhere).

[a]This position is developed in Charles Maurice and Charles W. Smithson, *The Doomsday Myth: 10,000 Years of Economic Crises* (Stanford: Hoover Institution Press, 1984), pp. 86–91.

At the very core of economics, according to Smith, is the ability of individuals and societies to deal with the facts of scarcity through specialization and trade. In the *Wealth of Nations,* Smith used the example of a pin factory, a seemingly trivial manufacturing activity he had observed directly, to evaluate specialization. Smith observed that pin making was no longer a trade peculiar to a single individual but instead was "divided into a number of branches, of which the greater part are likewise peculiar trades."[1] Straighten-

[1]Adam Smith, *An Inquiry into the Nature and Causes of the Wealth of Nations,* ed. Edwin Cannan (1776; reprint, New York: Modern Library, 1937), pp. 4–5.

ing wire, cutting it, putting a point on it, constructing a head to the pin, and inserting the pins into paper for ease in handling were all separate "trades" performed by individuals. (Smith, in fact, counted up eighteen distinct operations in some pin factories.)

How does Smith's description of a pin factory promote an understanding of output growth? Smith's point is that when tasks are divided, permitting each individual to concentrate on a single element in the production of a good, output increases over what it would be if each individual produced the entire good. Specialization and the **division of labor** led to increased output. As a result, people became more dependent on one another for all goods. We may work in an automobile plant, for example, but we still want eggs for breakfast. Smith recognized that mutual dependence could be a problem but thought that the potential for increased output with given resources was well worth the cost.

Division of labor:
Individual specialization in separate tasks involved with a production process; the result of specialization.

If an analysis of a pin factory does not stir your imagination, think of any organization and try to list the number of distinct divisions of labor in it. Think of a larger factory, a steel mill, a football team, a fraternity, a church. Specialization exists in almost everything we do. (See Focus, "Economic Specialization in Everyday Life: Marriage and Roommate Selection," for illustrations.)

All modern nations, states, firms, and individuals specialize in the production of economic goods and services, in varying degrees. The individual, the most basic economic entity, specializes to the greatest extent. Your teacher for this course specializes in economic research and teaching. Other people specialize in mechanical engineering services or in breeding thoroughbred racehorses. Some businesses produce only one product, whereas others offer a multitude. One very critical point must be made about all specialization and trade—it is as significant as having more and better resources or improved production techniques. As Smith noted, specialization and division of labor leads to increased output and it does so without any additional resources. The gains from specializing in and exchanging goods and services are, in effect, *equivalent* to acquiring or developing additional natural resources or capital.

The notion of specialization can also be applied to entire nations. Table 3 shows that large percentages of many of the goods consumed by Americans are obtained from other countries. For commodities like crude rubber and diamonds, there is no domestic production; the entire supply is imported. While nations specialize in the production of a multitude of goods, patterns of specialization across countries may be observed nonetheless. Exotic spices are not commercially grown in Canada, for example, although they *could* be grown there with greenhouses, sufficient heating expenditures, and so on. Canada does produce a fair proportion of the world's wheat. Likewise, no fine silk is produced on the tiny Caribbean island of Grenada, but nutmeg and other spices are. The explanation for such general production patterns across countries and more complete patterns of specialization among individuals resides in concepts that are at the very core of economics—comparative advantage, specialization, and trade.

Comparative Advantage

While Adam Smith developed the fundamentals underlying specialization and trade, it was left to his English followers David Ricardo (1772–1823) and Robert Torrens (1780–1864) to develop the critically important principle of

TABLE 3

Selected Imports and Exports as a Percentage of the U.S. Market

A look at leading U.S. exports and imports provides an indication of how specialization and trade apply to every country of the world. The nature of these tradables changes over time with shifting comparative advantage. (Data are for 1976.)

Industry	Exports as a Percentage of Output	Industry	Imports as a Percentage of New Supply
Wheat	66%	Crude rubber	100%
Oilfield machinery	63	Diamonds	100
Missiles, space vehicles	62	Bauxite	94
Milled rice	58	Crude petroleum	53
Medicinals, botanicals	47	Motorcycles, bicycles, and parts	51
Construction machinery	43	Finfish, shellfish	47
Aircraft	41	Potash	47
Corn	39	Raincoats	47
Soybeans	38	Zinc	47
Tobacco	37	Radios and TVs	43
Pulpmill products*	35	Iron ore	39
Solid-state semiconductor devices	34	Pulpmill products*	33
Turbines	32	Watches and clocks	32
Cotton farm products	29	Textile machinery*	30
Textile machinery*	28	Sugar	29
Electronic computing machinery	26	Women's shoes	27
Industrial trucks, tractors	20	Passenger cars	20

Source: U.S. Department of Commerce, Bureau of the Census, *U.S. Commodity Exports and Imports as Related to Output, 1976 and 1975* (Washington, D.C.: Government Printing Office, 1980), pp. 1–4.

*Note that textile machinery and pulpmill products are significant on both sides of the international market.

specialization—the theory of comparative advantage. Comparative advantage (and its relation to specialization and trade) is best understood with a simple, hypothetical example. Table 4 describes three production combinations of silver and lumber for two different locales, Canada and Mexico. The production possibilities information in Table 4 is reproduced graphically in Figure 6. The production possibilities curves of Figure 6 do not look exactly like the production possibilities curves we have discussed so far. For simplicity, we have temporarily assumed that the law of increasing costs does not hold in the two locales—at least not where lumber and silver production are concerned. Instead, we assume that in each locale both silver and lumber production are subject to constant opportunity costs of production.

Table 4 indicates that production of the first 30,000 ounces of silver in Canada means 300,000 board-feet of lumber do not get produced. Moving from point *A* to point *B* on Canada's production possibilities curve reduces the production of lumber from 1 million to 700,000 board-feet. In such a move, each additional ounce of silver produced has an opportunity cost of 10

FOCUS Economic Specialization in Everyday Life:
Marriage and Roommate Selection

Specialization and trade has increased economic welfare and human progress from the very beginning of time. These gains have depended on the diverse talents of individuals as well as the different resources of great nations. Consider two examples that do not often come to mind when considering the economic principles of specialization—the selection of a marriage partner and selection of a roommate.

Although relationships like marriage have many bases—love, security, etc.—one of them is surely economic. The greatest gains from trade occur when individuals (or countries) with widely differing skills or resources trade. In a society in which males and females acquire widely different skills, the incentive to marry is quite strong. If, as in primitive society, women do not know how to hunt or fish and men cannot prepare food or make clothing, the gains to both partners in a marriage relationship are immense. In fact, survival outside of a marriage-type relationship may be impossible. In such societies, nearly everyone would marry, and individuals would abandon a marriage relationship only to enter another one.[a] In societies where men and women acquire similar skills, the gains from exchange between marriage partners are much smaller. Individuals, therefore, have a weaker incentive to marry or to remain married. The slowing marriage rate and the growing divorce rate in Western societies in recent decades may partly be attributed to greater occupational equality. As the incomes of women rise (the opportunity cost of child rearing) a lower birth rate may be expected. Specialization may even be reversed, with men taking more active roles in raising children. "Mr. Mom" may become more common due to economic specialization and trade.

Roommate selection, an activity perhaps closer to your experience, also takes place, in part, on the basis of economic specialization and trade. Students room together to save money, but they also do so, in part, because of the gains from specialization and trade. Communal arrangements ranging from fraternities and sororities to clubs and study groups work best when the participants have tradable skills. Ideally, then, one roommate would be an excellent cook, say, while another roommate would be an expert carpenter, and yet another would be adept at yard work. Even if individuals' skill levels are pretty much the same, trade is still profitable when roommates' tastes and preferences for specific jobs differ and trade is possible. Problems and disputes arise most often between roommates when trade agreements or "contracts" are not enforceable. You may do the cooking, but can you "force" your roommate to clean up the kitchen—assuming you both agreed she would?

The benefits of specialization and trade are not just of academic interest, nor do they pertain only to trade in goods and services between nations such as Japan and the United States. As workers, club members, marriage partners, roommates, or friends, these principles affect us every day.

[a]For some fascinating details of the emergence of modern humans and the family, see Richard E. Leakey, *The Making of Mankind* (London: Abacus, 1982).

Marginal opportunity production cost:
The number of units of one good that do not get produced when one additional unit of another good is produced.

Comparative advantage:
An economic entity's ability to produce a good at a lower marginal opportunity production cost than some other entity.

board-feet of lumber. If Canada is producing 30,000 ounces of silver and shifts productive resources from the lumber industry to produce 70,000 more ounces of silver (for a total of 100,000 ounces), lumber production drops by 700,000 board-feet. Each additional ounce of silver produced has a constant opportunity cost of 10 board-feet of unproduced lumber, regardless of how many ounces of silver are already being produced.

The situation may be viewed from another angle, and the same information may be expressed in a different manner. In Canada, the additional, or **marginal opportunity production cost** of 1 board-foot of lumber is constant and equal to $\frac{1}{10}$ of an ounce of silver. Silver and lumber production in Mexico are also subject to constant (marginal opportunity) production costs. For each additional ounce of silver produced, only 1 board-foot of lumber goes unproduced. The marginal opportunity cost of producing 1 ounce of silver in Mexico, 1 board-foot of lumber, is *less* than it is in Canada, where it is equal to 10 board-feet of lumber. Mexico is said to possess a **comparative advantage** over Canada in producing silver. A comparative advantage exists because the marginal opportunity cost of producing an ounce of silver in Mexico (1 board-

TABLE 4

Production Possibilities in Canada and Mexico

Canada has a comparative advantage in lumber. If Canada were to move to producing combination *A* instead of *B*, 300,000 board-feet of lumber could be had at an opportunity cost of 30,000 ounces of silver. Each board-foot of lumber has a marginal opportunity cost of $\frac{1}{10}$ of an ounce of silver going unproduced. If Mexico were to move from *B* to *A*, 40,000 more ounces of silver could be had at an opportunity cost of 40,000 board-feet of lumber. Each ounce of silver costs Mexico 1 board-foot of lumber. Likewise, Mexico has a comparative advantage in producing silver. In Canada an extra ounce of silver costs 10 board-feet of lumber.

	Canada's Production Possibilities			Mexico's Production Possibilities		
	A	*B*	*C*	*A*	*B*	*C*
Silver (ounces)	0	30,000	100,000	0	40,000	80,000
Lumber (board-feet)	1,000,000	700,000	0	80,000	40,000	0

foot of lumber) is less than it is in Canada (10 board-feet). So, any locale with a lower marginal opportunity cost of producing a good possesses a comparative advantage over some other locale in producing that good.

Canada has a comparative advantage over Mexico in lumber production, as indicated in Table 4. Canada can produce lumber at a lower marginal opportunity cost ($\frac{1}{10}$ of an ounce of silver) than can Mexico (1 ounce of silver). If Canada has a comparative advantage in lumber production, this necessarily means that Mexico has a comparative advantage in silver production. One ounce of silver costs Mexico only 1 board-foot of lumber, whereas in Canada the cost is 10 board-feet. Each country has a comparative production advantage over the other, but in a different good.

Suppose that both Mexico and Canada are initially self-sufficient in silver and lumber. That is, each locale produces and consumes some of both goods and does not trade with the other nation. Specifically, suppose that both countries produce and consume the combination of silver and lumber labeled *B* in Table 4 and Figure 6. We assume that combination *B* represents the most desirable consumption combination for both Canada and Mexico that is attainable from self-production.

How might Mexicans and Canadians be made better off economically? The residents could consume more of both goods or more of one good and the same quantity of the other good. Economic growth, either from technological improvement or from increased quantities of productive resources in each country, would shift the production possibilities curve rightward, enabling greater quantities of silver and lumber than those represented by *B* in Figure 6 to be produced and consumed. Economic growth would, therefore, make residents of either country better off in economic terms.

Excluding economic growth, residents of each locale could improve their economic situation through specialization and trade. Each could specialize in producing the good for which that locale has a comparative advantage and then *trade* some of its output for the other good.

FIGURE 6

Canada's and Mexico's Production Possibilities Curves

Both locales agree that each 1000 ounces of silver trades for 5000 board-feet of lumber, or a board-foot of lumber for ⅕ of an ounce of silver. Each agrees to trade on these terms because obtaining a good through trade is less costly than obtaining the good by producing it at home. After specialization and trade, each locale will consume combination *D*, a combination that lies beyond each country's production possibilities curve.

(a)

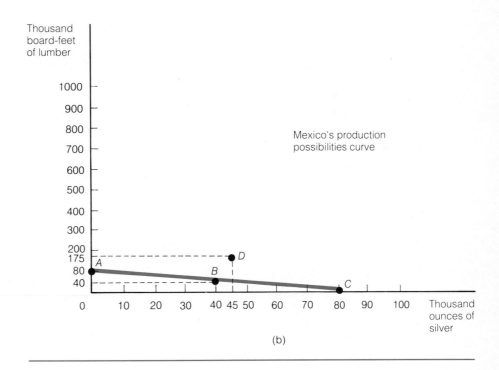

(b)

Specialization

Suppose that Mexico and Canada happen to hire the same economic consultant to help them improve their respective economic fortunes. After a study of each economy, the consultant brings representatives of both locales together and suggests a plan that will leave each economically better off: Specialize according to comparative advantage and trade with each other.

The benefits of specialization and trade are shown in the four parts of Table 5. Table 5a shows the situation in each locale before specialization and trade occur. Specifically, it reproduces combination *B* from each locale's production possibilities curves shown in Figure 6a and b. Combination *B,* recall, is assumed to be the most desirable consumption combination for each locale. Also shown in Table 5a is the sum total of both locales' production and consumption of each good. It is assumed that Canada and Mexico constitute the "world."

Table 5b depicts the production situation in each locale, and, therefore, the world, after Canada and Mexico have specialized in production according to comparative advantage. After specialization, total world output of silver is 10,000 ounces *greater* than it was at combination *B* on the production possibilities curves in Figure 6. World production of lumber has also increased. It is 260,000 board-feet more than before specialization. The world is economically better off (more of both goods), but we have yet to show that each individual locale is made better off as a result of specialization according to comparative advantage.

There is one more step to the process, that of trade.

TABLE 5a

Canada and Mexico Before Specialization and Trade

The amounts actually produced and thus consumed in Canada and Mexico are the combinations labeled *B* in Table 4. Amounts of each good for the "world" are the sums of the two countries' production.

	Canada Produces and Consumes	+	Mexico Produces and Consumes	=	World Produces and Consumes
Silver (ounces)	30,000		40,000		70,000
Lumber (board-feet)	700,000		40,000		740,000

TABLE 5b

Canada and Mexico After Specialization but Before Trade

Specialization in production according to comparative advantage yields a world gain in the output of both goods.

	Canada Produces	+	Mexico Produces	=	World Produces	World Gains
Silver (ounces)	0		80,000		80,000	+10,000
Lumber (board-feet)	1,000,000		0		1,000,000	+260,000

Trade: The Fruits of Specialization

Our consultant realizes that neither Canada nor Mexico would voluntarily agree to an exchange that would leave them worse off (than before trade). For voluntary exchange to take place, each nation must end up economically better off. With this in mind, the consultant proposes that Canada trade 175,000 board-feet of lumber to Mexico in exchange for 35,000 ounces of silver, or 5 board-feet of lumber for each ounce of silver. The Canadians would agree to this trade since domestic production of the 35,000 ounces of silver would cost them 10 board-feet of lumber each, for a total of 350,000 board-feet. This exchange allows the Canadians to obtain silver from the Mexicans cheaper than to produce it themselves.

The Mexicans would also agree to the proposed trade. Each board-foot of lumber costs them 1 ounce of silver to produce, but the proposed trade allows them to obtain each board-foot for $\frac{1}{5}$ of an ounce of silver. The trade with Canada enables Mexico to obtain 175,000 board-feet of lumber for 35,000 ounces of silver. The opportunity cost to Mexico of producing 175,000 board-feet of lumber would be 175,000 ounces of silver. It is less costly for Mexico to obtain lumber through trade than through self-production. This trade is depicted in Table 5c.

The number of board-feet of lumber that trade for an ounce of silver is called the **terms of trade.** The terms of trade is really a price that is not measured in terms of either country's money. In this example, Canada pays Mexico 5 board-feet of lumber for each ounce of silver. Mexico pays $\frac{1}{5}$ ounce of silver for each board-foot of lumber. The terms of trade is a price that defines the number of units of one good that exchange for one unit of some other good. The terms of trade will always fall somewhere between the mar-

Terms of trade:
The number of units of one good that exchange in the market for one unit of some other good. Although not expressed in terms of money, it is a price nonetheless.

TABLE 5c   **The Trade Between Canada and Mexico**

Canada and Mexico agree that each ounce of silver trades for 5 board-feet of lumber, or a board-foot of lumber trades for $\frac{1}{5}$ of an ounce of silver. Each agrees to trade on these terms because obtaining a good through trade is less costly than obtaining it by producing it at home.

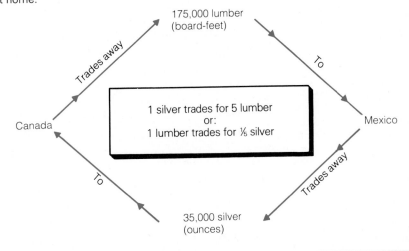

ginal opportunity production costs of a given good in each of the two countries. In this case an ounce of silver has an opportunity cost of 10 board-feet of lumber in Canada and 1 board-foot of lumber in Mexico, so the terms of trade will be at least one board-foot of lumber for an ounce of silver, but at most 10 board-feet of lumber for 1 ounce of silver. Terms of trade outside these limits would cause trade to be counter to the interests of citizens in one of the countries—for instance, Canadians would be better off producing their own silver than paying more than 10 board-feet per ounce for Mexican silver.

Table 5d summarizes the economic positions of Canada and Mexico after specializing in production and trading. Most important, both countries end up with more of both the goods to consume than before trade. Canada consumes 125,000 more board-feet of lumber than it did initially and Mexico an additional 135,000 board-feet. Both enjoy 5000 more ounces of silver than in the prespecialization and trade period. In Figure 6a and b, both locales are consuming combination D—combinations of goods that lie beyond the respective production possibilities curves. Without specialization and trade, these combinations could only be attained through economic growth. It is as if additional resource quantities of silver and lumber were actually created through specialized production and division of labor. Residents at *each* locale are economically better off. Specialization according to comparative advantage and trade has led to increased living standards in both parts of the world.

Factors Explaining Comparative Advantage

There are basically two reasons why a locale would have a comparative advantage over some other locale in producing any given good relative to other goods—differences in technology or differences in the quantities of productive inputs in the two locales. Relative differences in production technologies of the goods in the two locales can lead to a comparative advantage for each locale. With a given level of productive resources, Mexico might be able to produce an ounce of silver relatively more cheaply than Canada owing to technological differences in each good's production process in the two locales.

TABLE 5d   **Canada and Mexico After Specialization and Trade**

Specialization in production according to comparative advantage and trading yields a world gain and a gain for each locale.

	Canada					Mexico				
	Produces	Trades For (+) Away(−)	Consumes After Trade	Consumed Before Trade	Gains From Trade	Gains From Trade	Consumed Before Trade	Consumes After Trade	Trades For (+) Away (−)	Produces
Silver (ounces)	0	+35,000	35,000	30,000	+5,000	+5,000	40,000	45,000	−35,000	80,000
Lumber (board-feet)	1,000,000	−175,000	825,000	700,000	+125,000	+135,000	40,000	175,000	+175,000	0

Lumber production technology may be identical in each locale, but the technical know-how of making silver may be more advanced in Mexico.

Alternatively, if production technologies are identical in both locales, an abundance of the productive resources used in producing lumber in Canada compared to Mexico's amounts of these resources could exist. This would give Canada a comparative advantage in lumber. But a relative abundance of lumber-producing trees in Canada implies a relative abundance of silver inputs in Mexico. These relative, or comparative, differences in the amounts of productive resources in the two locales can produce the pattern of comparative advantage shown above. Patterns of comparative advantage may, of course, shift over time with either natural or artificially induced changes in resource prices and supplies or with changes in technology. (See Economics in Action, "When Is a Rose Not a Rose? Shifting Comparative Advantage in the Flower Industry," at the end of this chapter.)

Consider another aspect of the situation in Mexico and Canada. Table 5 indicates that Canada has the ability to produce more lumber in absolute numbers than Mexico if each country produces only lumber (1 million board-feet versus 80,000 board-feet). Canada also has the capacity to produce absolutely more silver (100,000 ounces versus 80,000 ounces) than Mexico. Canada has what economists call an **absolute advantage** in production of both goods. That is, Canada can specialize in silver production and simply produce more silver than Mexico. The same holds for lumber production. Any time a country can specialize in producing a good and produce absolutely more of it than some other country, the first country has an absolute advantage over the second. An absolute advantage can arise because of technological factors or from one country being larger in terms of the quantity of productive resources it possesses. Although Canada has an absolute advantage in producing both goods, it has a comparative advantage only in lumber. Mexico has an absolute disadvantage in both goods, but it still can produce silver at a lower marginal opportunity cost than Canada. Both countries still benefit from specialization and trade according to comparative advantage.

Finally, we must clearly understand the simplifications attached to the discussion. Differences in marginal opportunity costs explain comparative advantages, but the economic system does not actually require an "economic consultant" to tell locales (or businesses or individuals) about the potential gains from specialization and trade. Relative scarcities based on differences in marginal opportunity costs are transmitted to producers and consumers through the price system. Prices "inform" producers and consumers about what, how much, and when to supply and consume millions of goods and services. The details of how prices are formed through the interaction of supply and demand are reserved for Chapter 4. Nonetheless, it is useful to remember that prices, not hypothetical economic consultants, "discover," signal, and reflect the comparative advantages that exist between nations, states, locales, businesses, and individuals.

Absolute advantage:
The ability of an economic entity to specialize and produce a greater amount of some good than another entity can.

Exchange Costs

The model of comparative advantage and trade—along with all other economic models—is a simplification of reality. A number of important assumptions hide behind our simple discussions. But there are also costs to the

Exchange costs:
The opportunity costs of the resources used in making trades; includes transaction costs, transportation costs, and artificial barriers to trade.

Transaction costs:
The opportunity costs of the resources directly associated with trade; includes time costs, brokers' fees, and so on.

process of the exchange that must be accounted for when calculating the benefits of specialization and trade. We classify these **exchange costs** as transaction costs, transportation costs, and artificial barriers to trade.

Transaction Costs. Transaction costs are all the resource costs (including time-associated costs) incurred because of exchange. Transaction costs occur every time goods and services are traded, whether exchanges are simple (purchase of a pack of gum) or complex (a long-term negotiated contract with many contingencies).

Here's a simple example: Gwen goes to the supermarket to purchase a pound of coffee. What are the costs of the transaction? Gasoline and auto depreciation must of course be considered as resource costs, but the principal cost is the opportunity cost of Gwen's time. Gwen might have spent this time working or playing tennis instead of grocery shopping. Gwen's wage rate might then serve as her opportunity cost. If the shopping trip takes 30 minutes and if Gwen's wage rate is $15 an hour, the time part of her transaction costs is $7.50.

In this simple case the contracting and negotiating are instantaneous—Gwen simply gives the money to the checkout person, takes her coffee, and the transaction is complete. In other, more complex exchanges—such as the purchase of a house, a car, or a major appliance or the negotiation of a long-term labor contract—contracting and negotiating costs can be substantial. Think of the time and other resource costs associated with long-term supply contracts such as U.S. arms deals with allies or negotiations for ammonia plants in China. Every detail must be studied, formulated, and then spelled out.

The important point is that transaction costs include resources used by each party to the exchange. The higher the resource costs, the lower the benefit that comes from specialization and trade. Institutions—new legal arrangements, new marketing techniques, new methods of selling—have emerged, and are continually emerging, to reduce all forms of transaction costs. Gwen could have purchased coffee at a convenience store nearer to her house. The price of the coffee might have been somewhat higher, but Gwen's time costs, and therefore her total transaction costs, would have been lower. In a broader sense, laws about contracts, and law itself, are means by which transaction costs are reduced. The invention of money and the development of various forms of money and financial instruments are responses to transaction costs associated with barter and more primitive means of exchange.

In addition to money, intermediaries such as wholesalers and advertisers developed over the ages to facilitate exchange. The creative marketing of goods and services from bazaars to discount stores to media advertising has increased consumer information and thus reduced the costs of making transactions. Middlemen have lowered transaction costs by decreasing the risk of exchange. The production of some goods entails some risk and uncertainty on the part of buyers and sellers. Planting wheat in the spring for sale in the fall obviously entails some uncertainty about what prices will be at harvest. Middlemen-speculators who deal in futures provide sellers and buyers assurance of prices in the future. This type of middleman makes profit on the miscalculations of buyers and sellers but reduces uncertainty and thereby increases trade and specialization.

Transportation costs:
The value of resources used in the transportation of goods that finalize any trade.

Transportation Costs. A second impediment to trade is transportation costs, resource costs associated with the physical transport of products from place to place. The higher these resource costs, the lower the benefits from specialization and trade.

We did not include transportation costs in our initial examples of comparative advantage with Canada and Mexico. Let's do so now. Suppose that transportation costs associated with the trade amounted to 10,000 board-feet of lumber to each country. Even after paying these transportation costs, Canada and Mexico still enjoy more lumber than they did before specializing and trading (see Table 5d). Even if the "consultant," or the intermediary who organized trade, also charged a fee of 5000 board-feet of lumber to each country, both would still gain from specialization and trade. If transportation costs were high enough, possible advantages to specialization and trade could be wiped out completely. Cheaper transportation costs permit more trade and open up opportunities for new forms of and increases in specialization. The invention of the railroad in the nineteenth century, the spread of the automobile and the truck, and the dawning of air freight transport in the twentieth century were all boons to specialization and increased output.

Artificial barriers to trade:
Restrictions created by the government that inhibit or prevent trade; includes import quotas and tariffs.

Artificial Barriers to Trade. The final impediments to specialization and trade are government-imposed restrictions such as tariffs, quotas, and outright prohibitions on the import or export of goods. More localized restrictions include minimum-wage laws and specific restrictions on an industry or in an area. Such impositions, known as artificial barriers, either reduce or eliminate the benefits of specialization and trade.

Governments always have reasons for these restrictions, but the reasons must be closely scrutinized because the benefits from international and domestic specialization and trade are potentially huge for all consumers. Artificial barriers have the power to reduce economic welfare by reducing or eliminating the benefits of specialization according to the law of comparative advantage.

The possible effects of restrictions on trade can be seen in the growing volume of trade between Japan and the United States in commodities such as TVs, automobiles, stereo equipment, and musical instruments. Special-interest groups—such as American autoworkers and manufacturers—have lobbied for import tariffs and other trade restrictions to protect their own interests, which include increased demand for American-made products and therefore increased domestic production. Government-enforced tariffs make Japanese goods more expensive, however, causing a reduction in the general well-being of Americans. Artificial restrictions on trade, whatever their purpose, reduce the advantages of specialization and trade. As a matter of economic principle, therefore, most economists generally advocate free trade over any type of trade restriction. Further, any institution or mechanism that reduces the costs of exchange usually gets the support of economists because greater specialization permits better utilization of scarce resources. Specialization, in other words, helps us get more of what we want, given a limited amount of resources.

Real-World Patterns of Trade. The previous sections suggest that trade occurs between two countries when the countries have differences in opportunity costs of producing various goods (when comparative advantages exist), when transaction costs and transportation costs are small, and when the countries promote free trade. Real-world evidence reported in Table 6 and Figure 7 supports these arguments. For example, Canada is the leading trade partner of the United States. Transportation costs between the two countries are very low, and the two countries have one of the freest trade relationships in the world. In contrast, the United States trades substantially less with the United Kingdom because its trade policies are more restrictive and transportation costs are much greater than those with Canada.

The same factors explain the relative importance of foreign sales in the economies of different nations. Foreign trade is more important to the Dutch economy than to the New Zealand economy largely for geographic reasons that affect transportation costs. In addition, the Netherlands has historically pursued less restrictive trade policies.

The tremendous volume of trade between Japan and the United States is best explained by the strong comparative advantages between the two countries. Because the types of productive resources found in the two countries differ greatly, certain goods that have high opportunity costs in Japan have low costs in the United States, and vice versa. A huge trade volume, therefore, exists between the two countries, even though they both pursue policies to restrict foreign trade, and despite the large transportation costs of moving goods between the two countries.

TABLE 6	Leading Trading Partners of the United States, 1987

In terms of exports, Canada is the biggest customer of the United States. However, Americans import more goods and services from Japan than from any other country.

Country	Value of U.S. Imports (in billions)	Value of U.S. Exports (in billions)
All countries, total	$405.9	$252.9
Canada	71.1	59.8
Japan	84.6	28.2
West Germany	27.1	11.7
United Kingdom	17.3	14.1
Mexico	20.3	14.6
France	10.7	7.9
Netherlands	3.9	8.2
South Korea	17.0	8.1
Hong Kong	9.9	4.0
Singapore	6.2	4.1

Source: U.S. Bureau of the Census, *Statistical Abstract of the United States* (Washington, D.C.: U.S. Government Printing Office, 1989), pp. 788–791.

FIGURE 7

Foreign Trade as a Percentage of Gross Domestic Product (1987) in Various Countries

International trade is clearly more important in percentage terms to some countries—Korea or Belgium—than to others, such as the United States and Japan.

Source: International Monetary Fund, *International Financial Statistics Yearbook* (Washington, D.C., 1988).

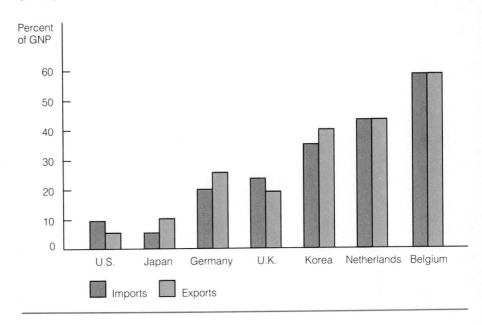

SUMMARY

This chapter described several principles that provide a foundation to economic thinking.

1. Economic choices, both for the individual and for society, always involve an opportunity cost.
2. Opportunity cost is the highest-valued alternative forgone in the decision to engage in a particular activity.
3. The law of increasing costs means that as more of one good is produced by a society, the opportunity costs of obtaining additional units of that commodity rise. The increase in cost is the result of resources becoming less adaptable as production becomes more specialized.
4. Choices are ordinarily made not in all-or-nothing fashion but at the margin. Both individuals and societies, therefore, calculate the cost of consuming additional units of some good or service.

5. The production possibilities curve shows the possible quantities of two goods that could be produced given the state of technology and society's scarce resources.
6. Changes in technology or increases (or decreases) in the amount of resources cause rightward (or leftward) movements in the production possibilities frontier.
7. Greater quantities of output can be obtained with society's scarce resources when people specialize and trade. Trade takes place according to the principle of comparative advantage.
8. Trade can take place between two individuals or economic entities even if one of the entities is more efficient at producing all goods. All that is required is that each entity be relatively more efficient than the other in some production.
9. Transaction costs, transportation costs, and artificial trade barriers such as tariffs and quotas reduce the benefits obtainable from specialization and trade.

KEY TERMS

opportunity cost
choices at the margin
production possibilities frontier
law of increasing costs
unemployment of resources
capital stock

economic growth
specialization
division of labor
marginal opportunity production cost
comparative advantage
terms of trade

absolute advantage
exchange costs
transaction costs
transportation costs
artificial barriers to trade

QUESTIONS FOR REVIEW AND DISCUSSION

1. What did reading this chapter cost you? Did you include the price of the book? What will reading the next chapter cost? Does that include the price of the book?

2. Do government-sponsored financial aid programs for college students influence the amount of education produced? Do these programs shift the production possibilities curve?

3. What does a movement along the production possibilities frontier suggest? What does a point inside the curve suggest?

4. A subsidy to farmers who purchase tractors and combines increases the production of this farm machinery. Does this cause an increase in the production possibilities curve or just a movement along the curve? Can subsidies cause economic growth?

5. Why would a country with an absolute advantage in the production of all goods be willing to trade with other countries?

6. Alpha can produce 60 bottles of wine or 40 pounds of cheese. Beta can produce 90 bottles of wine or 30 pounds of cheese. Both have constant costs of production. Draw their production possibilities curves. What is Alpha's cost of 1 bottle of wine? What is Beta's cost of 1 pound of cheese? If they trade, who should specialize in cheese?

7. What are the costs of going to college? Does the marginal benefit outweigh the marginal cost?

8. Is the lost present consumption associated with the production of capital goods worth the benefit of the new capital?

9. Does Japan have an absolute advantage over the United States in the production of televisions and stereo equipment, or is it just a comparative advantage?

10. Who is hurt by and who benefits from an import quota on foreign beef?

11. How does the cost of purchasing a loaf of bread at a supermarket compare with the cost of purchasing a loaf of bread at a convenience store?

PROBLEMS

Countries A and B both produce golf balls and golf clubs. The table shows what each country can produce at full employment.

1. Graph the production possibilities curve of each country.
2. Do both production functions exhibit constant costs?
3. Who has the absolute advantage in both golf ball and golf club production?
4. Who has the comparative advantage in the production of golf balls?
5. Who has the comparative advantage in the production of golf clubs?

A		B	
Golf balls	Golf clubs	Golf balls	Golf clubs
1200	0	900	0
1000	50	750	25
800	100	600	50
600	150	450	75
400	200	300	100
200	250	150	125
0	300	0	150

ECONOMICS IN ACTION
When Is a Rose Not a Rose? Shifting Comparative Advantage in the Flower Industry

Changes in technology, in capital investment, and in resource prices will often alter comparative advantage and trade in surprising ways. Consider conditions in the American flower industry, particularly among flower and plant growers.

Imported plants and cut flowers were a mere trickle in 1973 compared to recent years. Colombia, Mexico, the Netherlands, and Israel have made huge incursions into U.S. wholesale and retail markets for fresh cut flowers (especially roses, carnations, and chrysanthemums), and Belgium, Canada, Denmark, the Netherlands, Israel, and Costa Rica have done the same in the plant market. Colombia, America's largest foreign source of cut flowers, exported almost 73 million roses to the United States in 1982 and half a billion carnations. In fact, cut flowers were second only to coffee as Colombia's leading legal export item in recent years. Israel also has come on strong as a rose supplier to the United States with the aid of Israeli government subsidies. A survey taken by Professor Kenneth Sanderson of Auburn University in 1986 revealed that 82 percent of the roses, 79 percent of the carnations, and 41 percent of the chrysanthemums used by Alabama retail florists were imports.[a]

A number of reasons related to shifting comparative advantage can be offered for the lower prices and increased supplies of cut flowers and plants from foreign sources. The energy crisis of the 1970s raised the price of heating greenhouses, putting a cost squeeze on many domestic growers, especially those in the colder climates of North America. In 1986, according to U.S. Department of Agriculture (USDA) estimates, the states of Florida and California combined accounted for approximately half of the entire U.S. greenhouse and permanent-cover growing area. Under the high energy price conditions of the 1970s and early 1980s, nations such as Colombia had a new source of comparative advantage in flower growing—no heating of greenhouses is necessary.

A second reason for the new strength of imports is the technical possibility of avoiding historical restrictions on the importation of plants potted in soil. Modern techniques permit plant cultivation in such media as sphagnum moss, unused peat, plastic particles, glass wool, and inorganic fibers. Dutch growers have become especially adept at these new techniques for commercial propagation. Such plants (with some limitations) are allowed into the United States under a USDA regulation called Quarantine 37. Under Quarantine 37, plants grown under very rigid specifications in foreign countries may be preinspected by USDA teams in the foreign country and admitted into U.S. markets.

While higher energy prices might help explain the initial shift in comparative advantage from the United States to Colombia and other nations in flower and plant growing, it does not explain why comparative advantage has not been regained by the United States since the collapse of OPEC and lower energy prices in recent years. Other factors related to comparative advantage are clearly relevant. An important factor is that foreign growers are able to use insecticides and chemicals that are not allowed in the United States. Environmental Protection Agency (EPA) and Occupational Safety and Health Administration (OSHA) regulations on plant and flower growers may, in part, explain why the United States is not recapturing comparative advantage. Flower growers also may be hurt relatively more than greenhouse plant and food growers if blanket restrictions apply to all greenhouse propagation.

More important, perhaps, is the fact that significant technological advances occurred in flower growing and transportation during the 1970s and 1980s. Growers in such nations as Colombia started up with state-of-the-art capital and growing techniques. In the case of Canada, the low price and high quality of flower and plant products were "the outcome of general improvements pushed by former European growers who had emigrated to Canada" in the 1960s and 1970s.[b] Modernization of greenhouses and equipment together with a willingness to risk capital will be required before the United States can recapture its comparative advantage.

Predictably, efforts to institute artificial barriers to trade, such as tariffs and quotas, have been made by lobby groups and trade organizations of the various segments of the American flower industry in the late 1980s. Protectionists, especially those representing flower growers, drew battle lines, declaring "cheap foreign labor," "inferior-quality products," "unemployment in the flower industry," "foreign government subsidies," and "health hazards through damaging

---

[a]Market Letter, News Edition, *Florist's Review* (September 29, 1986), p. 1.

[b]Rick Davis, "Canadian Imports Up as Relations Strain," Market Letter, Market Edition, *Florist's Review* (August 25, 1986), p. 2.

insect pests." Leading the fight in 1986 and 1987 was the Washington-based lobby group of the industry called the Society of American Florists (SAF). Roses, Inc., a floral trade association, called for legislation against countries who supposedly sell ("dump") flowers in the United States below their costs of production.

These groups have had a measure of success. In March 1987 a thinly disguised protectionist "Anti-Dumping Duty" was imposed on U.S. importers of carnations and pompon chrysanthemums from several Latin American countries and in January 1989 duties were imposed on flower containers and silk flowers imported from South Korea, Taiwan, Hong Kong, and Singapore (all formerly duty-free nations). Industry experts estimated an increase of flower costs to American consumers of $4 million dollars in 1987, with equal or higher losses calculated for 1988 and 1989.[c] The price of flower arrangements to consumers rose by approximately 33 percent in 1989, with further increases predicted.

None of the reasons given by the flower industry, except the possible problem of the importation of damaging insects, holds a drop of water when compared to the benefits of comparative advantage, specialization, and free trade. If Colombian or Israeli roses are of inferior quality, as U.S. growers allege, the market soon adjusts prices and quanti-

[c]"Duty Debate Continues," *Florist's Review* (January 1988), p. 46; Spencer, Elaine, "Christmas Costs Climb Higher and Higher," *Florist's Review* (July 1988), p. 16.

ties accordingly. (In fact, Colombia's initial stock of the Visa rose, the hearty mainstay of its export trade, had to be imported from France because American rose propagators refused to trade.) If other nations wish to subsidize exports of flowers to the United States, American consumers gain.

It is as yet unclear how much more protection will be supplied in the flower industry. Not all interests in the U.S. flower business are the same. Flower growers and other groups such as container manufacturers favor protection, while flower importers are, in general, fighting it. Politicians and government agencies have demonstrated that they will respond to protectionist pleas from the industry. The economic principles of comparative advantage, specialization, and trade suggest that gains to one small group of producers would be more than offset by higher prices and welfare losses to other industry segments and to flower consumers as a whole.

Question

Suppose that Japan has a comparative advantage in certain types of automobiles and that the elimination of all quotas and tariffs on U.S. imports of Japanese automobiles would reduce employment in the American automobile industry by 200,000 jobs. Would you support the immediate elimination of all artificial barriers to trade? Would you support a gradual elimination? No elimination? Would you support the implementation of retraining programs and subsidies to auto workers? Answer the questions on the basis of comparative advantage. Are there other problems to consider?

3

Economic Institutions and the Role of Government

The vehicles for economic growth, as we have seen, are technology and resource development, specialization, and trade. But what makes these vehicles possible? Why are they more apparent in some societies than in others? To better understand the answers to these questions and the workings of the American market economy, we give an overview of the American economic system and contrast it to other contemporary economic systems and societies. When you finish Chapter 3 you should know

- the major institutions of market, socialist, and mixed economies that channel the problems of scarcity and unlimited wants.
- the roles governments play in the major economic societies and nations of the world.
- the specific role government plays in the U.S. economy with respect to free markets, property rights, law, and public goods and services.
- whether expanding government's role in mixed economies enhances or detracts from production and economic well-being.

THE U.S. MARKET SYSTEM IN PERSPECTIVE

Economic system:
The part of the social system determining what, how, and for whom goods and services are produced.

Rice paddies in China, nut-and-fruit-gathering societies in Africa, government enterprise in Russia, free-trade zones in Hong Kong, computer hardware development in California's Silicon Valley—all these arrangements represent different answers to the "what," "how," and "for whom" questions under different economic systems. An **economic system** is the particular form of social arrangements through which the three fundamental questions are answered. In this chapter we focus on the capitalist system as it exists in the United States.

Comparative Systems

Two basic types of economic systems have emerged in response to scarcity of resources: capitalism and communism. All societies, including the United States, actually contain some elements of each type. It is very difficult to identify a pure type of economic system in contemporary societies.

Capitalist, Communist, and Mixed Economies.   The comparison of economic systems in different countries is made easier by the classification of systems along a spectrum that ranges from pure capitalism to pure communism. A **pure capitalist** economy is one in which most property is owned and most economic decisions are made by private individuals and in which government economic control is minimal. An economic system characterized by common ownership of productive resources, both human and nonhuman, is called **pure communism.** A **pure socialist** economy is one in which most of the nonhuman resources are owned by the state, which in turn makes most production and some consumption decisions.

The real world is complex, however; there simply are no examples of pure capitalist, pure socialist, or pure communist systems (although there are examples that come fairly close to each). Moreover, it would be a mistake to draw a single line between pure capitalism and pure communism and attempt to place various countries on either side of it. Some countries have economic systems in which most property is privately owned but in which government regulation and control is extensive; in other countries the opposite is true. For example, Sweden permits free ownership of resources, but a very high share of the economy's total output goes to taxes. In Poland there are still extensive controls of property, but people are relatively free to spend incomes as they choose. Ranking economic systems with respect to degrees of economic freedom is problematic. Distinctions may be made about the degree of capitalism and communism or socialism in *many* dimensions. What's more, many economic and political systems are now in a state of flux; a distinction that holds today may not hold tomorrow. Figure 1 illustrates the differences between existing economic systems in just two dimensions—degree of economic freedom and per capita GNP. The per capita GNP is shown on the horizontal axis and the degree of government control is shown on the vertical axis.

Mixed Capitalism.   To varying degrees, the economies of France, Canada, and England display the characteristics of **mixed capitalism.** In such systems, the state is an important participant in the economy, but by and large the bulk of productive activity is undertaken by private firms and individuals. (One economy in Figure 1—that of Hong Kong—does come close to the pure capitalism model.)

In a large number of countries the dominant economic institutions are fundamentally different from those in capitalist societies. These are the socialist economies, such as in China and the Soviet Union. Socialism is basically a system of economic organization in which resource allocation is determined by central planning rather than by market forces. Many socialist economies are undergoing rapid change, however—mainly in the direction of capitalism. (See Focus, "Capitalism: Wave of the Future?")

Pure capitalism:
An economic system in which most resources are owned, and most relevant decisions are made, by private individuals.

Pure communism:
An economic system in which most productive resources, both human and nonhuman, are publicly owned.

Pure socialism:
An economic system in which most nonhuman productive resources are owned by the state.

Mixed capitalism:
An economic system in which most economic decisions are made by the private sector but in which government also plays a substantial economic and regulatory role.

FIGURE 1

Economic Systems and Per Capita Income

Figure 1 links the per capita income produced in various economies, shown on the horizontal axis, to the degree of government control in them, shown on the vertical axis. No economies exactly fit the extremes of pure capitalism and pure communism, but China and Hong Kong come close. Furthermore, there is no exact relation between per capita income and the type of economic system in countries.

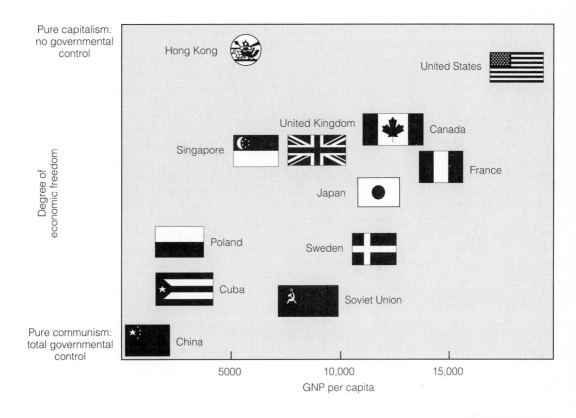

Market society:
An economic system in which individuals acting in their own self-interest determine what, how, and for whom goods and services are produced, with little government intervention.

Market Societies. In a **market society,** personal and impersonal forces lead consumers and producers to answer the three fundamental questions of production. Consumers answer the "what" question through their participation in the marketplace. Production of goods and services such as personal computers and auto repair is determined by "dollar votes." Just as political votes elect a president, dollar votes—or money spent on products and services—express consumers' demands. Suppliers of products and services, interested in making profits, respond to these votes by providing the products and services in just the right quantities. (Chapter 4 explains exactly how this occurs, through the laws of supply and demand.)

The "how" question in the market society is, at any one time, answered by available technology and by suppliers' profit-motivated desire to produce goods most cheaply given the price of resources. Most goods can be produced by a variety of methods. Avocadoes, for example, can be picked by hand or by harvesting machines. The avocado grower will choose whatever method min-

FOCUS Capitalism: Wave of the Future?

Historically, the economic experience of most societies has been one of government controls, economic stagnation, and abysmal living conditions. In ancient Egypt, in Rome, and in France under Louis XIV the privileged few reached economic and cultural highs, but the dreadful conditions of the average citizen were the shameful downside of such opulence. In contrast, eighteenth-century capitalism emphasized free, unregulated markets in a new industrial setting and a government that was small relative to the private economy. This new system of Adam Smith replaced a system of controls in Great Britain and eventually in the United States and parts of Western Europe. To this day, most economic systems are based on government controls in the form of regulation of the private sector, plus outright government ownership and direction in some sectors of the economy.

Ideas and policies, however, come and go. Following a period of increased government controls in most Western nations after World War II, the United States, Great Britain, and France have recently taken steps to deregulate their economies. For example, the shift away from regulation and control has dramatically affected the transportation and banking industries in the United States, and the full effects are not as yet completely known. However, the most startling experiments with capitalism are taking place in societies that previously had very tight economic and political controls. The Soviet Union, China, Poland, Hungary, and many Third World nations are trying a system of freer markets along with alternative, or freer, political systems.

In a number of cases, the changes represent dramatic reversals of long-standing policy. The Soviet Union is attempting, through *perestroika* and *glasnost* (openness), to increase free farm production (which was tightly controlled in the past) and to pursue freer trade with Western nations. In some cases, the "new openness" in the Russian economy is merely the legalization of activities that were taking place in the "second economy," where markets previously functioned in an illegal or quasi-legal environment. China, too, has moved toward capitalistic production and trade. Specifically, the Chinese government has established clearer property rights in land and embraced Western technology and business practices in an attempt to foster economic growth. The Beijing Kentucky Fried Chicken restaurant—at 500 seats, the world's largest—opened in 1987. It is a symbol of new directions for the Chinese economy, although political repression continues.

Countries from the Third World and Soviet bloc have also taken steps to deregulate their economies. In 1988 the government in Poland passed laws that, for the first time, enabled business firms to be established with relative freedom. The communist government in power has since opted to relinquish control to popularly elected leaders. In Latin America, Chile relaxed many restrictions on domestic businesses and experienced a period of rapid economic growth. Countries as diverse as Pakistan and New Zealand have similarly removed many long-standing economic controls and adopted free-market policies.[a]

The motives for adopting new policies differ from country to country. Much of the change in Poland has been forced on the government by popular uprisings and open dissent. In the Soviet Union, change seems to have been imposed from the very top of the Soviet government with little evidence of popular support. In nearly every case, supporters of free enterprise have convincingly argued that their policies are essential to the economic well-being of average citizens. Although there are exceptions, evidence generally supports that argument. Factors such as climate, natural resources, and history undoubtedly play important roles in determining a country's production level, but Figure 1 indicates a strong connection between a country's degree of economic freedom and its economic success as measured by GNP per capita. People throughout the world will be paying close attention to the economic successes or failures that occur in countries where freer markets have been permitted. Depending upon the economic experiences of these countries, capitalism may again be the wave of the future.

[a]These and other matters are discussed by Nobel laureate Milton Friedman in "Why Liberalism Is Now Obsolete," *Forbes* (December 12, 1988), pp. 161–68.

---

imizes the cost of production. In a market economy prices are the signals not only for what to produce and how to produce now but also for how new technologies and new resources can be brought into production over time.

When one highly demanded resource becomes scarce and therefore high-priced, producers will attempt to substitute other resources for it. If possible substitutions are limited, alternative technologies and new types of resources may be developed. In mid-nineteenth-century America, for example, whale oil—used primarily for lighting—became scarce and high-priced as the supply of whales depleted. Price provided the incentive to develop alternative lighting fuel such as fossil fuels. Some historians believe that the depletion of the whales encouraged both the discovery of petroleum and the widespread use of oil derived from petroleum.

Prices also answer the "for whom" question in a market society. Just as the prices and quantities of all goods and services available in a market system are determined by the demands of buyers and sellers, so are the "prices" (such as wage rates, rental rates, and interest rates) of resources used to produce them. The value of particular resources in general depends on the demand for the product that the resource helps produce. For example, the owner of property bordering Central Park in New York City may expect to receive a higher rental than one who owns desert property in Nevada. Luciano Pavarotti, a world-renowned operatic tenor, may be expected to receive a higher wage than a college president. The money rewards to these resources are determined not only by the demand for them but also by their relative scarcity. First-class tenors are scarcer than college presidents.

Most Western economists see the market system as the greatest force for economic growth within the context of political and economic freedom. The U.S. market economy—its functioning and its problems—therefore receives the lion's share of attention in this book. The American economy is one of a kind, but it shares some important features with other, similar market systems. One shared feature is the use of money and a circular flow between money, goods, and resources.

Money in Modern Economies

Barter:
The trading of goods for other goods without using a medium of exchange such as money.

Despite their differences, a feature of all economic systems is the use of money. **Barter**—the exchange of goods for goods—is cumbersome and costly. For a system to take advantage of specialization, output must grow steadily. For output to expand, trade must take place at a low cost. But the costs of bartering goods are numerous, for the value of each good must be recorded in terms of the other goods traded. As the number of goods traded increases, calculations become overwhelming. Money was invented as a medium of exchange and as a unit of accounting. It is a good in terms of which the value of all other goods can be calculated. Money lowers the cost of transacting and is therefore essential to any modern society.

We can think of money as a substitute for real things traded. Wages, for example, represent a trade of the output of a worker for the goods and services consumed by the worker. We may earn wages as a bricklayer and purchase fried chicken at a fast-food establishment. In a real sense, we are bartering bricklayer labor for fried chicken. Money simply substitutes for real trades.

The Circular Flow in a Market Economy

Circular flow of income:
The movement of real goods and services, payments, and receipts between households and business firms.

The exchange of money for goods and services takes place throughout the United States and other developed economies. One can conceptualize this exchange as a **circular flow of income** (Figure 2), a cyclical pattern of money payments and goods and services produced.

In Figure 2 the arrows on the outer circle represent the flow of real goods and services between business firms and households, while the arrows on the inner circle represent the reciprocal flow of money payments. In the circular flow of products, business firms produce products and services with resources

FIGURE 2   The Circular Flow of Income

Economic activity between business firms (producers) and households (consumers) takes place in a cyclical pattern. The arrows on the outer circle represent the flow of real goods and services (consumer products and factors of production such as labor); the arrows on the inner circle represent the reciprocal flow of money payments for real goods and services.

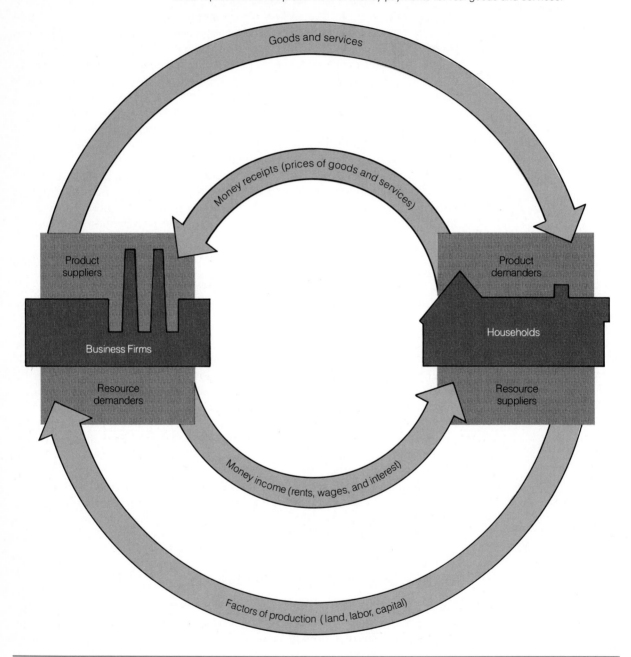

(land, labor, and capital) from resource suppliers. To complete the circle, households that purchase products and services are virtually all resource suppliers—of labor, land, or capital. The flow of products has a corresponding and counterbalancing money flow in the opposite direction. For goods and services, firms receive money payments (business receipts) from households, and for resources (labor, land, and capital), resource owners receive money income in the form of rents, wages, and interest from firms. The quantities and the mix of resources used and products produced are determined by price signals. These signals, as we will show more clearly in Chapter 4, are the result of the impersonal forces of supply and demand.

Figure 2 is not meant to depict a functioning economy in detail but to serve as a model for product and money flows. Missing are the complexities of flows by which producers supply goods to other producers and of the tax and expenditure flows by which government provides public goods and services.

INSTITUTIONS OF AMERICAN CAPITALISM

While money and real goods circulate through all modern economic systems like blood through the veins and arteries of the body, societies vary in the institutions they create for ownership and use of goods and money. A *capitalist economy* relies primarily on market forces and the profit motive for production, distribution, and consumption of goods and services. Capitalism is characterized by individual ownership of property, free enterprise, open competition, and a minimal role for government.

Property and the Law

In the American economy the individual's right to own and dispose of property is regarded as basic. Property includes both physical property (such as houses and automobiles) and intellectual or intangible property. For example, the ownership of poems, songs, and books by their authors is protected by copyright laws; inventions are protected by patents. The legal apparatus set up to protect such rights may even make a distinction between property and property rights. Rental of a carpet cleaner from U-Rent-Um gives the renter certain property rights over the cleaner but not ownership of the property itself. In all societies, rights to use property are limited. For example, the Environmental Protection Agency has used its legislatively derived power to limit the rights of businesses to pollute air and water and has established worker protection standards (such as those limiting the use of asbestos) that restrict businesspeople's free use of property.

In a capitalist society, the law protects property rights; the proper assignment of property rights is thought to be a key to economic efficiency. (See Focus, "Property Rights, Incentives, and Economic Development.") Without some guarantee that property rights will be protected, there would be little incentive to accumulate capital stock and, therefore, to grow economically. Without state guarantees of rights to property, individuals would have to protect their own property at high personal cost.

FOCUS   Property Rights, Incentives, and Economic Development

Why does rental property, jointly owned property, leased equipment, or public parkland tend to be abused or used inefficiently compared to the property of an individual owner? Economists argue that resources attain economic efficiency when governments or legal systems assign few or no limits to property use. Consider what this means in terms of practical examples of property rights assignment.

In past centuries, property rights to land were limited or restricted by tradition or by law. One institution that emerged in Western Europe and the American South—sharecropping—illustrates the economic point about rights and efficiency. Under sharecropping, tenants do not *own* the land but are given rights by the owner to farm it, with certain terms and conditions attached. In return for these temporary rights, owners receive a portion (typically, one-half or one-third) of the product or its value. Unfortunately, tenants have no incentive to conserve property (land, capital, and other resource inputs) to maximize production under this system. When users do not own the capital or land they employ, there are few incentives to conserve resources, which may lead to overutilization (overfarming) of land, little conservation, or lack of capital improvements (deterioration of plows, fences, or other farm implements). Although own-

ers and tenants might create contracts to try to avoid problems, maximum output and full economic efficiency in resource use is not expected without complete ownership.

These problems apply to many current land reforms undertaken by developing nations. Concentrations of land ownership are, in some cases, dissolved by governments only to be replaced with systems that do not produce economic efficiency. Farmers and peasants are often given limited terms of ownership or limited rights to farm or develop land and other resources. If the property, for example, is leased for a specified number of years or over the farmer's lifetime (restricting or eliminating rights of survivors), there will be no incentive to farm efficiently and to maximize output over the life of the lease. (If restrictions on the *use* of the property limit land use to agricultural production or to a certain type of agricultural output, even less efficiency may be expected.) The point is that the incentive to conserve property and to use it efficiently is directly related to the user's ability to own the property. Economic theory teaches us that, in general, a full assignment of property rights—with full costs and benefits assigned to the owner—is necessary for maximum economic efficiency.

Legal protection of property rights often emerges as a response to market activities. Consider an example from the American frontier West. In the early days of silver and gold prospecting, individuals were forced to protect their own mining claims. As their claims grew, individual protection entailed higher opportunity costs—that is, higher costs in time spent away from mining or prospecting and in potential loss of equipment or mined ore. Thus, the collective benefits of enforcement through police, courts, and prisons outweighed the costs of such enforcement to individual prospectors—paying taxes, serving on posses, and the like. Property rights and the laws that protect them emerge when benefits to the parties involved begin to exceed the costs of acquiring and enforcing the rights. Such rights to private property, established by law, have been a part of American capitalism since the founding of the nation.

Free Enterprise

Free enterprise:
Economic freedom to produce and sell or purchase and consume goods without government intervention.

Free enterprise, the freedom to pursue one's economic self-interest, is an intrinsic part of the capitalist system. Men and women are free to choose their line of work with few or no governmental restraints or subsidies, and businesspeople are free to combine any resources at their command to produce products and services for profit. Laborer-consumers are free to produce, purchase, and exchange any good or service so long as their activity does not infringe on other's rights. (Bear in mind that participants are also *not* free of the constraints of limited resources and unlimited wants.) Free enterprise, in sum, means that

1. Laborers are free to work at any job for which they are qualified;
2. Business firms and entrepreneurs can freely combine resources, at competitive market prices, to take advantage of profit opportunities;
3. Consumers can decide what products and services will be produced; and
4. There is freedom within constraints (for example, within a rule of law).

Competitive Economic Markets

Competition:
A market situation satisfying two conditions—a large number of buyers and sellers and freedom to enter and exit the market—and resulting in prices equal to the costs of production plus a normal profit for sellers.

The American economic system is characterized by free competitive markets. **Competition** entails two important conditions: a large number of buyers and sellers and free entry and exit in the market. When these two conditions are met, the self-interested actions of buyers and sellers tend to keep prices of goods and services at a reasonable level, usually the costs of production plus a normal profit for the sellers.

When the number of buyers and sellers is large, no individual buyer or seller can affect the market price of a product or service. Many millions of individuals purchase canned soup, for example, but no one buyer purchases enough to affect the market price of the soup. Likewise, the existence of competing suppliers means that no individual seller can acquire enough power to alter the market for his or her gain. Sellers of canned soup are numerous enough that no one seller can affect the price of soup by increasing or decreasing output.

Crucial to the effects of large numbers is the condition that firms be free to enter and leave markets in response to profit opportunities or actual losses. New firms entering particular lines of business, bankruptcies, and business failures are expected consequences of a competitive system. New fast-food restaurants open every day in anticipation of profits. Airlines declare bankruptcy and leave the industry—a sure sign of losses. Competition requires that entry and exit into business be free and unregulated. The Focus, "Adam Smith's 'Invisible Hand,'" discusses the competitive system.

Coordinating the billions of individual decisions involved in competition is an interconnected system of prices for inputs and outputs that is so complex that no individual or computer can fully comprehend it. We begin to study the intricacies of the price system in Chapter 4.

The Limited Role of Government

Laissez-faire economy:
A market economy that is allowed to operate according to competitive forces with minimal government intervention.

American capitalism as an economic system requires an attitude of laissez-faire (from the French, meaning roughly "to let do"). Laissez-faire has come to mean minimum government interference and regulation in private and economic lives. In a pure **laissez-faire economy,** government has a role limited to setting the rules—a system of law establishing and defining contract and property rights, ensuring national defense, and providing certain goods that the private sector cannot or would not provide. The last category includes roads, canals, and national defense.

THE MIXED SYSTEM OF AMERICAN MARKET CAPITALISM

In truth, no society ever conforms totally to the laissez-faire ideal. The ideal is modified in two ways: in an altered notion of the competitive process and in an expanded role for government. Such a modification is called *mixed capitalism*.

An Evolving Competitive Process

Was any country ever composed of so many competing buyers and sellers to become, in Adam Smith's phrase, a "nation of shopkeepers"? Although historical data are less than perfect, we are fairly certain that purely competitive market structures did not exist even in Adam Smith's time. With the Industrial Revolution, capital requirements of firms were such that the most efficient firms—those producing goods at lowest cost—became larger. Certain industries and markets no longer had large numbers of competing sellers. Economists call such markets imperfectly competitive. They are also called *oligopolies* (characterized by a few competitors) or *monopolies* (having a single producer).

Some economists have argued that the decline in the number of competitors in some markets has led to concentrations of economic power in the hands of a few and to the demise of the laissez-faire competitive system. Modern economic research into the competitive process disputes this position, however. In the new view, competition is not to be described by a given number of sellers and buyers but rather by a rivalry for profits—that is, a process. Such rivalry—or even the potential for it, as long as individuals and businesses are free to enter and exit the market—produces results similar to competition among many buyers and sellers. One or two sellers in an industry can be competitive as long as entry and exit in the market is possible.[1]

The Expanded Role of Government

The most important modification in the traditional conception of laissez-faire capitalism is an expanded social and economic role of government. Since the turn of the century, and especially since the 1930s, the relative size of government in the United States has grown dramatically in both social and economic spheres. In the 1960s and 1970s we saw large increases in government payments to individuals through Social Security, Aid to Families with Dependent Children, Medicare and Medicaid, unemployment compensation, and other welfare programs. The direct economic activity of government has grown apace.

Public Goods and Externalities. Theoretically, underlying the government's role in economic life is the failure of a free-market society to satisfy all of its

---

[1]See Israel M. Kirzner, *Competition and Entrepreneurship* (Chicago: University of Chicago Press, 1973), for more details on rivalrous competition.

FOCUS   Adam Smith's "Invisible Hand"

Economists tend to praise a free and unfettered competitive market system because the rational and self-interested forces that characterize economic behavior lead not to a permanent state of chaos but to a harmony of interests. Adam Smith had great insight into the matter more than two hundred years ago in his "invisible hand" message in the *Wealth of Nations:*

> Every individual necessarily labours to render the annual revenue of the society as great as he can. He generally, indeed, neither intends to promote the public interest, nor knows how much he is promoting it. By preferring the support of domestic to that of foreign industry, he intends only his own security; and by directing that industry in such a manner as its produce may be of the greatest value, he intends only his own gain, and he is in this, as in many other cases, led by an invisible hand to promote an end which was not part of his intention. Nor is it always the worse for

the society that it was no part of it. By pursuing his own interest he frequently promotes that of the society more effectively than when he really intends to promote it. I have never known much good done by those who affected to trade for the public good.[a]

Smith felt that individuals' tendency to act in their own self-interest is a natural law and a natural right that precedes the existence of government. The exertion of these individual rights in a competitive market setting, furthermore, creates the greatest good for the greatest number in society. Smith's view, although a mainstream perspective in American capitalism, has been amended to accommodate government provisions of goods when the market fails to provide them in sufficient quantities.

[a]Adam Smith, *An Inquiry into the Nature and Causes of the Wealth of Nations,* ed. Edwin Cannan (1776; reprint New York: Modern Library, 1937), p. 423.

Public goods:
Goods that no one individual can be excluded from consuming once they have been provided to another, such as national defense.

members' needs. The market society can fail in its ability to provide **public goods** such as national defense. Since national defense protects all citizens regardless of whether they pay for it, no one is likely to contribute to defense voluntarily. The private market fails in the sense that public goods such as defense would not be provided (or provided in sufficient quantity) unless government assumed responsibility.

Another cause for government intervention in a free-market economy is what economists call an *externality*. An externality is an unintended by-product of some activity, and it often involves environmental protection. A beautiful garden creates a **positive externality** in that it confers benefits to neighbors for which they do not pay. A **negative externality** might arise from a factory belching smoke or a firm dumping chemical wastes into a stream. In such a case, costs are imposed on members or segments of society, for which they are not compensated, rather than limited to the perpetrators of the externality. Both positive and negative externalities involve inefficient allocations of resources. Externalities have led to various government interventions to correct the inefficient resource allocations of the market. Taxes, subsidies, quotas, prohibitions, and assignment of legal liability are examples of government intervention (see Chapter 20).

Many problems that justify government intervention involve negative externalities. Regulations prohibiting overfishing in the open seas attempt to limit the externalities imposed by self-interested commercial or sport fishermen. Elimination of garbage and industrial waste at sea, highlighted in the summer of 1988 by the medical waste that washed ashore on the east coast of the United States, is another example of an externality. Climatologists warn of a very difficult and complex negative externality—a worldwide "greenhouse effect." The greenhouse effect is a persistent rise in global temperature caused

Positive externality:
A benefit of producing or consuming a good that does not accrue to the sellers or buyers but can be realized by a larger segment of society, such as vaccinations.

Negative externality:
A cost of producing or consuming a good that is not paid entirely by the sellers or buyers but is imposed on a larger segment of society, such as pollution.

by the human use and production of products that emit carbon dioxide, fluorocarbons, and other gases. Overuse of these gases lets sunlight in but does not let heat out of the earth's atmosphere. Self-interested actions contribute to the possibility that the earth may eventually warm up between three and nine degrees Fahrenheit. Some scientists fear that this warming could shift weather patterns, causing devastation in the form of droughts in once fertile regions and excess rainfall in deserts. Melting glaciers could raise the sea level as much as six feet, disrupting agriculture, coastal economic activity, and water resources. All of the consequences of continued global warming are not known at present. These kinds of negative externalities, like the problem of acid rain in the northeastern United States and Canada, require multinational political solutions.

Income Distribution. The price system, where goods and services are produced and distributed within markets, does not necessarily produce what society might regard as a "just" distribution of income. In the market system, individuals earn income according to their abilities, education, and drive. Inheritance augments the incomes of some individuals. Some individuals, as a result of economic discrimination, poor education, or lack of abilities or incentives, earn less income or no income at all. Other people are poor because they are physically or mentally handicapped, indigent, old, or unable to work. We are, sadly, all familiar with poor and homeless people. Our society, like most others in history, is unwilling to endure a high degree of such income disparity.

At times, and in different degrees, the market system fails to provide the amount of income equality desired by society. When this happens, provisions for the poor, indigent, and needy are made through the political process, primarily through tax redistributions. These provisions take a number of forms. Until the Tax Reform Act of 1986 income tax rates were sharply graduated upward. In this progressive system of income taxation, the rich (higher-income individuals and families) were taxed at higher marginal tax rates than the poor (lower-income individuals and families). One of the stated objectives of the Tax Reform Act of 1986 was to simplify the tax system (basically to two income tax rates) and, at the same time, to remove approximately six million of the poorest families from the tax rolls altogether. Public goods and other government expenditures will still be paid for by wealthier, higher-income individuals and families, which is, in effect, an income redistribution through the governmental process.

The government administers other more direct forms of income redistribution in society. **Public assistance,** or welfare, **programs** are designed to aid the needy, the indigent, the handicapped, and the unemployed with income assistance derived from government taxation. Programs such as Aid to Families with Dependent Children, the food stamp program, and Medicaid bring relief to those who have little or no income. The Medicare and Social Security programs are designed to supplement the fortunes of the old, the retired, and the ailing members of society. Other kinds of assistance and subsidies are available to specific groups in society. Direct farm subsidies were oriented as a price support system for certain agricultural commodities when prices fell below that deemed "fair" in the political process. (The recent reduction or elimination of these subsidies has caused disruptions in the farm sector.) Finally, artificial barriers to trade, including quotas and tariffs on imported

Public assistance programs: Efforts by government to provide a more equitable distribution of income.

goods, form a "subsidy" to domestic producers. In many cases, such as in the plant and flower industry (see Economics in Action, Chapter 2), in textiles, and in the automobile industry, the government redistributes income from domestic consumers of products to businesses and laborers in the protected industries.

Government has always functioned as a redistributor of income in the United States, but that role has expanded greatly in the past twenty-five years. As always in economics, the question is not essentially *whether* income should be redistributed to the poor, sick, and needy, but *how much* should be transferred within the political process. President George Bush called for a new initiative of private charity to care for those in need (a "thousand points of light"), but critics charge that an entirely private redress of the problems of the poor will always be insufficient. Economists do not ordinarily comment on the normative aspects of such policies. The economist, however, has a role to play in assessing the problems of income distribution. As we will see in Chapter 18, the economist analyzes income distribution and the costs and benefits of initiating, expanding, or contracting specific welfare programs.

Antitrust and Monopoly Regulation. Another broad area of increased government participation in the U.S. free-market economy is **industry regulation.** Early in this century, antitrust laws prohibiting price discrimination, collusion among producers, and deceptive advertising practices were passed in an attempt to restore competition where it no longer existed. Such laws continue to be enforced today.

Industry regulation: Government rules to control the behavior of firms, particularly regarding prices and production techniques.

Even earlier, however, economists and politicians believed that government had a role whenever competition could not exist, perhaps because of economies of large-scale production, or what economists call *natural monopolies.* Such monopolies are created when each seller can produce more and more output at lower and lower costs. Eventually it becomes profitable for only one seller to supply the *total* quantity demanded of a good, thereby creating a monopoly. Federal, state, and local governments undertook the regulation—not the ownership or operation—of transportation, communications, energy, and many other industries that were regarded as natural monopolies. Government regulation was considered a substitute for competition where viable competition could not exist because of industry production and cost conditions.

Some economists have strongly disputed this view (see Chapter 19) and question the existence of large-scale economies (natural monopoly) in many of these regulated industries. Some contemporary economists believe that regulation of prices and profits must fail, either because regulation has been ineffective or because these industries are more competitive than previously thought. Questions have been raised about the self-interested supply of regulation by politicians combined with the self-interested demand for regulation by firms and industries. Do industries and other interest groups use the government regulatory apparatus for their own benefit? Should broad areas of regulation of industry, such as regulation of transportation and communications be eliminated? Has the deregulation of airlines fostered competition and benefited consumers, as many economists allege? These and many other issues concerning the expanded role of government are in hot debate. A firm foundation in economic theory is required to answer these important questions.

Economic stabilization:
The goal of governments' attempts to prevent adverse swings of inflation rates, interest rates, unemployment rates, and economic growth rates over time in the economy.

Economic Stabilization. A final, but crucially important, part of the expanded role of government is in macroeconomic **stabilization** of the economy—that is, the government's efforts to promote full employment of resources without creating increases in the price level (or inflation). Taxation, expenditure policies, and the money supply can be intentionally changed by the federal government to help maintain full employment and promote economic growth at noninflationary levels.

Whether the government is capable of achieving macroeconomic goals of full employment without inflation is a subject of debate among economists. The mission to stabilize business cycles of inflation and unemployment has been a generally accepted role of government since the 1930s—the years of massive unemployment of resources known as the Great Depression. Much of the impetus to assign this new function to government came from the writings of the British economist John Maynard Keynes (1883–1946). Keynes believed that government could actually influence employment and inflation through spending and taxing policies and could thereby prevent depressions or severe reductions in economic activity.

The role of government in American economic life is much larger than it was fifty years ago. The American market system is modified laissez-faire. Government has provided a large number of social and economic goods, regulated markets and externalities such as pollution, and attempted to establish a high rate of economic growth through full employment without inflation. These microeconomic and macroeconomic functions of government receive a great deal of attention later in this book. A brief look now at the relative size of government's role in the private economy will provide some perspective on the modified system of laissez-faire that constitutes the American market system.

GROWTH OF GOVERNMENT

Private sector:
All parts of the economy and activities that are not part of government.

How big is government in our mixed American economy? Should the economic role of government be larger or smaller in relation to that of the **private sector**—all nongovernment activities? This is the subject of an ongoing debate among political candidates, members of Congress, journalists, intellectuals, academics, and private citizens. Rather than developing value judgments about how big government should be, economists analyze the probable effects of political decisions on the past and present role of government. To provide background information for such an economic analysis, we examine the size of the U.S. government's economic role by looking at its expenditures and the taxes it levies to support them, contrast the level of U.S. government taxation and spending with that of some other developed nations, and then relate this information to patterns of economic growth.

The Size of the Federal Budget

We can get an overview of the role of the federal government in the U.S. economy by looking at a gross measure of government expenditures and receipts over the past four decades. Figure 3 depicts the federal budget (expenditures and tax receipts) for the years 1950–1991 (estimated). After a slow

FIGURE 3   ## Growth of the Federal Budget, 1950–1991

Since 1950 the federal budget (the total of expenditures and receipts) has grown both absolutely, in total dollars, and as a percentage of the gross national product. Federal deficits grew dramatically in the first half of the 1980s but have begun to decline since then. The deficits for 1990 and 1991 are estimates.

Sources: Board of Governors of the Federal Reserve System, *Historical Chart Book* (Washington, D.C.: U.S. Government Printing Office, 1986); Council of Economic Advisers, *Economic Report of the President* (Washington, D.C.: U.S. Government Printing Office, 1990), p. 383.

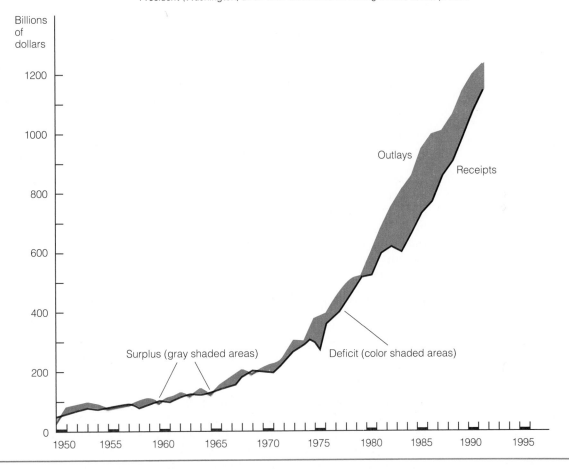

rate of growth through the mid-1960s, expenditures and tax receipts began to increase at a faster pace.

The Great Society welfare programs begun by President Lyndon B. Johnson in the mid-1960s and the defense expenditures of the Vietnam War were partly responsible for the absolute increases in government spending and taxation. Especially during the 1970s, deficits appeared when expenditures exceeded tax revenues. The government's growth is not only of recent origin, however. The Franklin D. Roosevelt administration's social and economic programs in the 1930s—a response to the largest worldwide depression in modern history—were an initial and important force for the expansion of government into a mixed economy. The participation of government at all levels—federal, state, and local—has increased dramatically since 1930.

Since prices of goods and services have risen considerably during the twentieth century, the absolute dollar increase in government expenditures

Gross national product (GNP):
The dollar value measured at market prices of all final goods and services produced in an economy in one year.

does not necessarily indicate whether government has grown bigger relative to the private sector. For this information, economists often look at government expenditures as a percentage of the **gross national product,** or GNP. The GNP is the aggregate value of all goods and services produced in the country over some period, usually a year. Using this measure, economists have found that while the government accounted for less than 10 percent of all purchases of goods and services as a percent of gross national product in 1929, by 1989 government purchases of goods and services were responsible for more than 20 percent of GNP. Since 1960, government's percentage of purchases of goods and services has remained fairly constant at 20 percent, but this constancy understates the growth of the government's role in the economy. The government's tax receipts at all levels in 1989 accounted for more than 32 percent of GNP. We can understand the discrepancy between expenditures and receipts and the expanding role of government by examining the kinds or distributions of expenditures at the various levels of government and then looking at the ways the government collects revenues.

Government Expenditures

Direct government purchases:
Real goods and services, such as equipment, buildings, and consulting services, purchased by all levels of government.

Government transfer payments:
Money transferred by government through taxes from one group to another, either directly or indirectly; also called income security transfers.

There are two kinds of government expenditures: direct purchases of goods and services and transfer payments. **Direct purchases** of newly produced goods and services include such items as missiles, highway construction, police and fire stations, consulting services, and the like. In other words, the government purchases real goods and services. **Transfer payments** are the transfers of income from some citizens (via taxation) to other citizens; these are sometimes called *income security transfers* or payments. Examples of transfer payments are Social Security contributions and payments, Aid to Families with Dependent Children, food stamp programs, and other welfare payments. These transfers do not represent direct purchases by the government of new goods and services, but they influence purchases of goods and services in the private sector. They are a growing part of government's role in the mixed economy.

The Distribution of Federal Expenditures. Out of the thousands of items in the federal budget, we can use six major categories to compare expenditures as a percentage of the total federal budget in 1960 and 1989 (see Figure 4). Since providing national defense is one of the major functions of the federal government, we would expect defense to account for a large proportion of federal outlays, and it does. National defense expenditures represented about one-quarter of all federal outlays in 1989. The largest single item in the 1989 federal budget, however, was not defense expenditures but income security transfers, which made up 33 percent of total outlays. Expenditures on interest service of the federal debt, education, and natural resources ranged from almost 15 percent to about 1 percent, respectively. The remainder, accounting for only 10 percent of the federal budget, went to such activities and projects as the administration of justice, science and technology, transportation, agriculture, international affairs, energy, the environment, revenue sharing, and the running of general government.

A mere recital of the proportions of outlays in the 1989 budget is not as interesting as a more dynamic picture of how these outlays changed over the preceding three decades. Using Figure 4, compare the distribution of expenditures in 1960 and 1989. In 1960, fully 50 percent of federal expenditures

FIGURE 4

These two illustrations show percentage shares of federal spending. Expenditures at the federal level between 1960 and 1989 underwent dramatic changes. The percentage spent on defense was cut in half and the percentage of the budget spent for income security transfers increased by 14 percent. Education and health also received increased shares of expenditures.

Source: Council of Economic Advisers, *Economic Report of the President* (Washington, D.C.: U.S. Government Printing Office, 1990), p. 385.

Federal Expenditures, 1960 and 1989

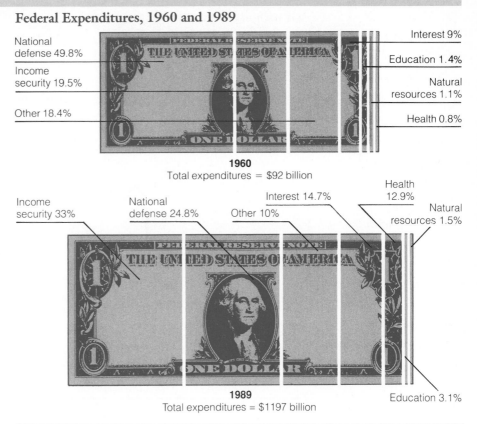

National defense 49.8%
Income security 19.5%
Other 18.4%
Interest 9%
Education 1.4%
Natural resources 1.1%
Health 0.8%

1960
Total expenditures = $92 billion

Income security 33%
National defense 24.8%
Other 10%
Interest 14.7%
Health 12.9%
Natural resources 1.5%
Education 3.1%

1989
Total expenditures = $1197 billion

went to national defense, while only 19 percent went to income security. Health-related expenditures have grown from less than 1 percent in 1960 to more than 12 percent in 1989.

Changes in defense spending and in transfer payments between 1960 and 1989 are part of a clear trend over the period, shown in Figure 5. Over most of the 1960s, transfer payments grew at a faster rate than defense purchases, reflecting the decisions of President Johnson and Congress to attack poverty and social imbalance. In spite of the fiscal pressures of the Vietnam conflict, transfer payments overtook defense purchases in absolute amounts—that is, in actual billions of dollars spent—in about 1970 and have exceeded them every year since.

Will this trend continue? Ronald Reagan campaigned for and won the presidency in 1980 and 1984 partly on this issue, promising to slow the growth rate in income security expenditures and to raise it on defense expenditures. To an extent he succeeded, but President George Bush, promising to work toward budget balance, has had to moderate all spending. The final outcome is still unclear.

State and Local Expenditures. Figure 6 shows that the primary public goods provided by state and local government are education, highways, public welfare, health and hospitals, police and fire protection, and other goods and services. Economists, voters, and other observers view the federal government as the principal economic agent in the mixed economy. The truth is, however,

FIGURE 5

The dramatic growth rate in transfer payments over the 1960s and 1970s is shown in the figure. Absolute amounts spent on transfer payments overtook defense expenditures in about 1970.

Sources: Board of Governors of the Federal Reserve System, *Historical Chart Book* (Washington, D.C.: U.S. Government Printing Office, 1984), p. 53; Council of Economic Advisers, *Economic Report of the President* (Washington, D.C.: U.S. Government Printing Office, 1990), p. 389.

Growth in Government Expenditures, 1950–1989

FIGURE 6

Principal expenditures at the state and local levels of government are on education, highways, public welfare, and health and hospitals.

Source: Facts and Figures on Government Finance (Washington, D.C.: The Tax Foundation, 1988), p. 168.

State and Local Expenditures by Category

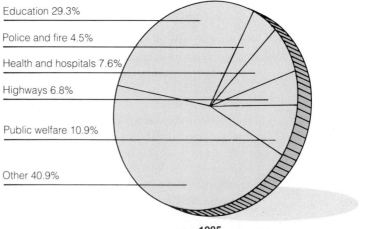

Education 29.3%

Police and fire 4.5%

Health and hospitals 7.6%

Highways 6.8%

Public welfare 10.9%

Other 40.9%

1985
Total state and local outlays = $658 billion

that state and local governments combined approximate the level of goods and services provided by the federal government. The big difference between the economic impact of the federal government and state and local governments is the huge federal redistribution of funds through the tax system from some citizens to others. When income security transfers are included, the economic impact of the federal budget is larger than that of state and local governments.

Government Receipts: The U.S. Tax System in Brief

Goods and social transfers provided at all levels of government are paid for out of taxation. The type of taxes levied at federal, state, and local levels varies a great deal.

Federal Taxation. The principal source of federal revenues, as shown in Figure 7, is the individual income tax. In 1990, the individual income tax is expected to account for 45.6 percent of total federal receipts.

Second in order of importance at the federal level, representing 35.9 percent of receipts in 1990, are receipts from social insurance taxes and other contributions. These taxes are, principally, the payroll taxes paid jointly by employees and employers that finance Social Security, disability compensation, and other payments. Receipts from these taxes have grown, dramatically, from less than $10 billion in 1950 to more than $600 billion in 1990.

Taxes on corporate income accounted for about 10 percent of revenues in 1990 and have generally declined since 1970 as a percentage of federal revenue. Other sources of federal revenues include federal excise taxes on goods such as liquor, tobacco, and gasoline, customs deposits paid on imports and exports, and estate and gift taxes.

FIGURE 7

Social insurance tax receipts have more than doubled as a percentage of total receipts between 1959 and 1990, while the relative contribution of the individual income tax has remained almost constant. (Data for 1990 are estimated.)

Source: Council of Economic Advisers, *Economic Report of the President* (Washington, D.C.: U.S. Government Printing Office, 1990), p. 385.

Distribution of Federal Tax Receipts, 1959 and 1990

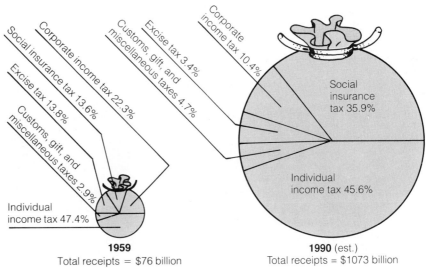

Social insurance tax 13.6%
Corporate income tax 22.3%
Excise tax 13.8%
Customs, gift, and miscellaneous taxes 2.9%
Individual income tax 47.4%

1959
Total receipts = $76 billion

Customs, gift, and miscellaneous taxes 4.7%
Excise tax 3.4%
Corporate income tax 10.4%
Social insurance tax 35.9%
Individual income tax 45.6%

1990 (est.)
Total receipts = $1073 billion

State and Local Receipts. State and local governments rely primarily on property taxes and sales taxes for revenue. Additional revenue sources, of varying importance from state to state, are the state income tax and state lottery. Only about 10 percent of state receipts were from state income taxes in 1990. Transfers of revenue from the federal to state and local governments, called *grants-in-aid,* have assumed increasing importance over the past twenty years. In 1990, for example, federal grants accounted for the highest single percentage of revenue for states and municipalities.

The United States and Other Mixed Economies

The preceding discussions indicate the kinds of activities pursued by government in a mixed economy as well as the kinds of taxes the government relies on for revenue. The relative size of government is only hinted at by the breakdowns of outlays and receipts, however. To understand how mixed the American economy is, we can consider some international comparisons.

Figure 8 shows the growth of the government's public expenditures as a percentage of gross domestic product for five Western industrialized nations

---

FIGURE 8   **Relative Growth Rates of Government Public Expenditures in Five Western Democracies, 1965–1988**

The bars represent government expenditures as a percentage of gross domestic product (GDP). By this measure, the U.S. economy is the least mixed of five Western democracies.

Sources: Organization for Economic Cooperation and Development, *Main Economic Indicators,* various issues; *Government Finance Statistics Yearbook* (Washington, D.C.: International Monetary Fund, 1989).

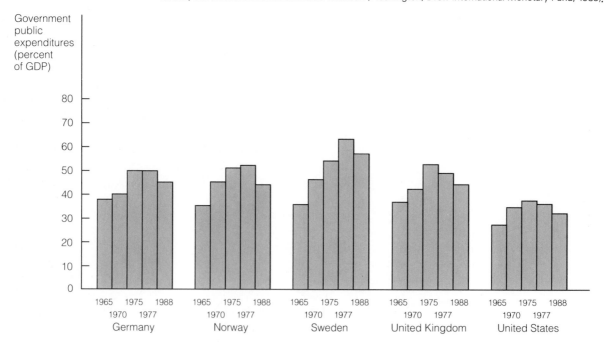

**Gross domestic product
(GDP):**
A measure of the final goods
and services produced by a
country with resources
located within that country.

between 1965 and 1988. **Gross domestic product** (GDP), like GNP, is a measure of a country's production of goods and services, but GDP measures final goods and services produced using domestic resources. (GDP is determined by subtracting income earned by foreign investments from the GNP.)

Public expenditures as a percentage of GDP grew between 1965 and 1977 in all of the countries shown in Figure 8, although the percentage has declined since 1985. The percentage of government expenditures in Sweden almost doubled between 1965 and 1977. By 1977, more than 60 percent of spending in Sweden was directed by the government. Germany, Norway, and the United Kingdom were about evenly divided in their mix between public and private participation in the economy by 1977. The trend over the past fifty years, until the 1980s, at least, has been toward more government participation in Western democracies. The bottom line: Of the leading Western industrialized nations, the U.S. economy is the least mixed in that the government directs only one-third of the country's spending.

The Economic Effects of Increased Government

Do economists care about how mixed economies are? Most economists believe that rational self-interested forces and private enterprise are the key factors leading to maximum output, growth, and efficiency. In their view, government-directed enterprises—of self-perpetuating bureaucracies—do not normally provide maximum incentives for work, creativity, technology, and economic progress.

An ever growing federal debt, the result of previous deficits, is also a major feature of the increased size of government in the United States. The sheer size of the debt is staggering—over three *trillion* (3319 billion) dollars in 1990. Growing deficits (the difference between government expenditures and tax collections) create this debt, which must be financed through borrowing from individuals or from banks. Government borrowing competes with businesses who borrow and use the private savings of individuals for investment. Some economists argue that the pressure of government debt finance reduces private investment and the future production possibilities of society. Further, there is the important question of whether and in what manner future generations will be burdened by the debt. There are alternative views on these complicated issues. At this point it is important to remember that an enormous federal debt has accompanied the recent progress of American capitalism; that debt, and the growth in deficits that created it, may alter that progress.

Government, as we have seen, has important and legitimate functions. Few economists, moreover, would question some redistribution of income based on a concept of justice since a market system does not automatically produce a just distribution of income or wealth. The question plaguing economists is a marginal one: Will added government control over a given amount of private resources increase or decrease satisfaction and economic incentives to work, produce, and invest? Is the relative size of government a tonic to economic society or a sedative? These are extraordinarily difficult questions to answer. Much of this book is devoted to both microeconomic and macroeconomic analyses of these critical questions since American capitalism is a blend of larger government combined with free-market forces.

SUMMARY

This chapter discussed alternative economic systems and their characteristics, with particular emphasis on the American economy.

1. Specialization and trade, which are responses to the problem of scarcity, take place within economic systems. The two main types of economic systems are socialist and capitalist.
2. Market societies allocate resources and consumer goods and services through the interplay between consumers' dollar votes and the free and unregulated decisions of producers and resource suppliers.
3. All real-world systems are combinations of socialist and capitalist characteristics. Further, modern economic systems are mixed economies because they contain elements of both free-market forces and government provision of goods, services, and income security transfers.
4. Some of the important features of American capitalism include the individual's right to own and dispose of property, a legal system protecting property and contracts, free enterprise, competitive economic markets, and a traditionally limited economic role for government.
5. An expanded economic role for government characterizes contemporary American capitalism. The basis for this role is the provision of goods such as national defense that would not be produced in sufficient quantity by the private sector. Government also intervenes in the market to block the effects of negative externalities, to regulate industry competition, and to help achieve economic stabilization.
6. Local, state, and federal governments directed about one-third of America's resources in 1990 through purchases of goods and services and through the redistribution of income. Income security transfers are, in absolute terms and as a percentage of total spending, the largest item in the federal budget, whereas expenditures on defense are half the percentage today that they were in 1960.
7. Economists study mixed economies and the role of government to determine whether an enlarged public sector increases economic well-being or reduces incentives to work and to invest capital.

KEY TERMS

economic system
pure capitalism
pure socialism
pure communism
mixed capitalism
market society
barter
circular flow of income

free enterprise
competition
laissez-faire economy
public goods
positive externality
negative externality
public assistance programs
industry regulation

economic stabilization
private sector
gross national product
direct government
  purchases
government transfer
  payments
gross domestic product

QUESTIONS FOR REVIEW AND DISCUSSION

1. How are the "what," "how," and "for whom" questions determined in a market society and in a command society?
2. "They don't build cars like they used to. These days cars wear out before they are paid for." This type of statement is heard frequently. Who determines the quality and durability of products?
3. What is capitalism and what does it have to do with property rights and economic freedom?
4. What are some of the roles of government in the U.S. economy? Has the role of government increased in size and scope? Does this hinder or help the rate of economic growth?

5. What are the primary activities of state and local governments?
6. Can free enterprise exist in a country where a dictator or king has absolute power?
7. "The local cable TV company provides slower services, and it doesn't have many channels." If this cable company has a monopoly granted by the government, is Adam Smith's invisible hand at work?

8. The Baltimore city government was disappointed when the Colts, a professional football team, moved to Indianapolis. Is a professional football team a public good? Explain.
9. Does individual self-interest hinder economic growth and well-being if there is competition?
10. What can government do to improve the general economic welfare? Has it done such things?

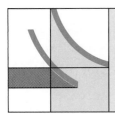

ECONOMICS IN ACTION
Contrasts in Economic Institutions: The Two Koreas

Can differences in social, political, and economic institutions be pinpointed as a major cause of differences in economic development? The experiences of North Korea and South Korea—neighboring countries with vastly different institutions—suggest the answer to this question is yes.

The two Koreas were one nation for hundreds of years. When the two separated in 1950, they adopted diametrically opposed paths to economic development. The People's Democratic Republic of (North) Korea has adhered strictly to the central planning model. It has one of the world's most highly socialized and centrally planned economies. All industrial enterprises are either directly owned by the state or are cooperatives owned indirectly by the state. Agriculture is carried out on either collective or state farms. Following the Soviet model (that is, the Soviet model *before* Gorbachev's economic reforms), the central planning system has allocated priority to investment in heavy industry at the expense of consumer and agricultural sectors. Despite this emphasis, the performance of the industrial sector has been disappointing. Productivity is low, and virtually all plants and equipment are obsolete, although North Korea has recently begun to purchase Western equipment and technology, including complete plants. Nominal per capita income in 1988 was approximately $1200 per year. There is little variety in consumer goods, and quality is uniformly low. Shortages are common, and standing in long lines to purchase basic necessities is a way of life. Consumer durables like appliances are usually unavailable.

Although the land, climate, and people of South Korea are similar to those of North Korea, there are dramatic dif-

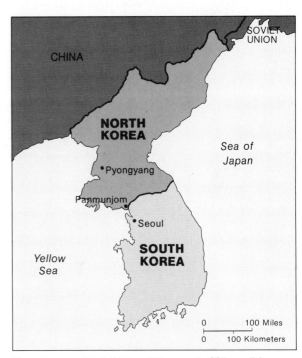

The arbitrary political division of Korea at the 38th parallel following World War II produced two very different nations.

ferences between the two countries. The Republic of (South) Korea has an economy based on private enterprise and a market economy. In a little over twenty years South Korea transformed itself from an economy dominated by subsistence agriculture (which is characteristic of most poor nations) to a modern economy with an emphasis on light industry. A thriving export market has led to South Korea's surge of development, and exports increased annually between 1974 and 1989. This growth reflects, in part, the improving quality of its exports, which include many finished goods, such as Hyundai automobiles and trucks and Reebok shoes. The standard of living is among the highest in modern Asia; per capita income for South Koreans in 1988 was over $2000, with a diverse array of high-quality consumer goods available. Interestingly, South Korea has only 10 to 20 percent of the Korean peninsula's deposits of mineral resources.

Similar contrasts may be made between the ethnically and culturally identical mainland Chinese and their freer neighbors in Hong Kong and on Taiwan. Estimates of GNP per capita in 1985 put China at $253, Taiwan (1986) at $3784, and Hong Kong at $6258. The standard of living in the latter two countries is high and visibly improving with relatively low levels of government regulation and thriving entrepreneurship. Despite some continued political repression, communist China is currently experimenting with capitalist elements in its own economy (as you discovered in Focus, "Capitalism: Wave of the Future?").

Such real-world examples suggest that different systems of property rights and incentive structures play a vital role in relative economic development. In other words, economists believe that many differences in economic development between North and South Korea can be explained on the grounds of different institutions. These institutional differences, especially those relating to political controls or to regulation of markets and economic processes, are often more important than the endowment of resources in determining economic progress.

Question

Why do you think countries with centrally planned economies typically have lower output and standards of living than countries with a free-market economic system, even when the countries have similar natural resources?

4

Markets and Prices: The Laws of Demand and Supply

Simple specialization began to take place in primitive cultures as individuals recognized unique abilities in themselves and in others. As we have seen, increasing specialization led to organized markets where people bought and sold goods, to the use of money, and to increasingly large groups of buyers and sellers. Economists define these organized markets—such as bazaars, the stock exchange, or Saks Fifth Avenue—as places or circumstances that bring together demanders (buyers) and suppliers (sellers) of any goods or services.

   After reading Chapter 4 you should understand

- the motivations of demanders and suppliers in the exchange of goods and services in markets.
- how and why some goods and services get produced and sold at certain prices while other items are not produced or sold at all.
- what happens to demand and supply when governments or other agencies institute price or rent controls.
- that the full price we pay for goods and services includes the money price and such things as time and the other costs involved in a transaction.

AN OVERVIEW OF THE PRICE SYSTEM

Every day the news media provide dramatic evidence of the workings of the market system. The price of silver rises by 45 percent in one day as massive investments in silver futures by two of the world's richest oil magnates trigger a bandwagon effect. Leak of a technological breakthrough in a certain computer firm creates a frenzy of stock buying, driving up the price of the firm's stock overnight. Crude oil prices fall sharply when the OPEC cartel has trouble policing its members.

   In the familiar economic transactions of everyday life, we too enter markets where buyers and sellers congregate to buy and sell a great variety of products and services. The typical American supermarket sells thousands of products, and as we wander through the store we can view a price system in action. In the produce section, for instance, quantities and prices of fruits and vegetables depend on the quantities consumers want and on the season. Early crops usually bring in the highest prices. Watermelon may sell for more than two dollars a pound in March but only fifteen cents a pound by the Fourth of July.

What determines who will get the early melons or how they will be rationed among those who want them? Why are prices and quantities constantly rising and falling for millions of goods and services in our economy? How do new products find their way to places where buyers and sellers congregate? The answers are simple. In a market society, the self-interest of consumers and producers, of households and businesses, determines who gets what and how much. To paraphrase Adam Smith, it is not to the benevolence of the butcher and the baker that we owe our dinner but to their self-interest. The primary way that consumers and producers express their self-interest is through the economic laws of supply and demand. Sticking a price tag on a product does not imply price-setting power, as anyone who has run a garage sale knows. In a market system, demand and supply determine prices, and prices are the essential pieces of information on which consumers, households, businesses, and resource suppliers make decisions. High melon prices in March will encourage suppliers and discourage demanders, whereas low prices in July will encourage demanders and discourage suppliers. Before investigating the mechanics of these laws of supply and demand, we consider a simple overview of the price system.

As market participants, households and businesses play dual roles. Businesses supply final output of products and services—rock concerts, bananas, hair stylings—but also must hire or demand resources to produce the outputs. Households demand rock concerts, bananas, and hair stylings for final consumption. But they also supply labor and entrepreneurial ability as well as quantities of land and capital to earn income for the purchase of products and services.

Product market:
The forces created by buyers and sellers that establish the prices and quantities exchanged of goods and services.

Resource market:
The forces created by buyers and sellers that establish the prices and quantities exchanged of resources such as land, labor services, and capital.

As Figure 1 shows, businesses and households are interconnected by the **products** (outputs) **market** and by the **resources** (inputs) **market.** Each market depends on the other; they are linked by the prices of outputs and inputs. The particular mix of goods and services exchanged in the products market depends on consumer demands in that market plus the cost and availability of necessary resources. For example, which groups are featured at a rock concert will depend on what the targeted audience wants to hear plus the ability of that audience to pay the price asked by the groups and the groups' availability on the chosen date. Similarly, the particular mix of resources available at any one time or through time is determined by what households are demanding—subject also to the availability of the resources. If land suitable for banana growing is available, it is most likely to be sold for banana plantations if households are demanding a lot of bananas, thereby making it possible for banana growers to pay landowners handsomely for their land.

Prices are the impulses of information that make the entire system of input and output markets operate. Take the prices of fad goods: At times, certain goods or services—such as hula hoops and Nintendo video games—have quickly appeared and then disappeared. When a fad begins to catch on, prices tend to be high because there is a high and rapidly growing demand and because resources necessary to produce the good may be scarce and command a high price. It takes time to adapt resources to the production of

FIGURE 1   The Product and Resource Markets: A Circular Flow

Businesses play a dual role in the market economy: They are the suppliers of goods and services as well as the demanders of resources. Households also have a dual role: They are both demanders of goods and services and suppliers of resources.

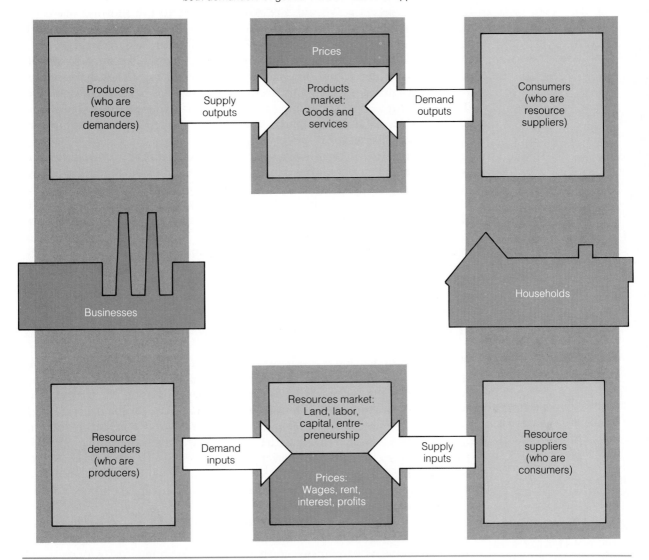

the fad good. Labor must be drawn from other uses and trained in the new production techniques. Marketing channels must be established so that sellers and buyers can converge at convenient points of trade. Demand for the fad good is transmitted through businesses to the factors of production through a system of prices. Initially high prices signal the scarcity of goods and resources. As more entrepreneurs and businesses perceive the profit opportunities associated with the fad and as more resources are discovered or developed to produce it, prices of both the inputs and the outputs change accordingly.

The price system reacts similarly with goods that remain in the market for a longer time. Consider the development of computers and computer technology in the 1960s. Initial investments by producers were substantial as businesses rushed to introduce computer systems. In particular, the wages of computer programmers and technicians were high because there was a relative scarcity of workers possessing the skills necessary to use and produce computers. High demand and relative scarcity mean high wages. However, high wages are also an excellent piece of information that may encourage changes that ultimately lower wages. From the 1960s to the present, many schools teaching computer technology have emerged, reducing the scarcity of this resource. Demand for computer technology, however, has grown over time. The wages for people supplying services essential to production depend on consumers' demand for computers and on price(wage)-signaled supply conditions in the market for these services.

The informative signals of a price system work whether goods have short or long lives. The prices formed in both product and resource markets reflect the relative desires of consumer-demanders for particular goods and services as well as the relative scarcity of the resources required to produce them. The very fact that a product or service bears a price means that scarcity exists. Supply and demand in all markets is at the core of scarcity and, therefore, of economics. These critical notions must be understood with the greatest possible clarity. We begin with demand.

THE LAW OF DEMAND

The concept of demand is intuitive. The notion that the amount of goods sold depends on the prices charged seems to "just make sense." The amount of any one good bought during a sale, for example, depends upon the **relative price** of the good on sale—the price in relation to the price of some other good or of goods as a whole. The actual money price of the good in isolation does not determine what we purchase. If the relative price of shoes declines—that is, the item is put "on sale"—the price has fallen relative to other shoes, shirts, or camcorders. Intuitively, we understand that more shoes will be purchased. By formally expressing this easily understood relationship, economists merely make intuition more rigorous.

What determines how much of any good or service—camcorders, compact discs, or hair styling—consumers will purchase during some period of time? Economists have answered that question for hundreds of years in the same manner—by formulating a general rule, or law, of demand. The **law of demand** states that, other things being equal or constant, the quantity demanded of any good or service increases as the price of the good or service declines. In other words, **quantity demanded** is inversely related to the price of the good or service in question.

The relation between price and quantity demanded is a fact of everyday experience. The reaction of individuals and groups to two-for-the-price-of-one sales, cut-rate airline tickets, and other bargains is common proof that quantities demanded increase as prices decrease. Likewise, gas price hikes will lower the quantity of gasoline demanded. The formalization of the inverse relation between price and quantity demanded is called a law because econo-

Relative price:
The price ratio or "trade-off" in consumption between one product (or service) and another product (or service) or between one good and other goods taken as a whole.

Law of demand:
The price of a product or service and the amount purchased are inversely related. If price rises, then quantity demanded falls; if price falls, quantity demanded increases, all other things held constant.

Quantity demanded:
The amount of any good or service consumers are willing and able to purchase at various prices.

Demand curve:
A graphic representation of the quantities of a product that people are willing and able to purchase at all possible prices.

mists believe it is a general rule for all consumers in all markets. Imagine a graphic representation of the law of demand—called a **demand curve**—for two hypothetical consumers.

The Individual's Demand Schedule and Demand Curve

Suppose that we observe the behavior of Dave and Marcia over one month. These two music lovers own compact disc players and are willing and able to purchase, or demand, CDs. To determine Dave's and Marcia's demand for CDs, we need only to vary the price of discs over the month, assuming that all other factors affecting their decisions remain constant, and observe the quantities of CDs they would demand at various prices. This information is summarized in Table 1.

Table 1 shows a range of CD prices available to Marcia and Dave over the one-month period and the quantities (numbers) of discs that each would purchase, all other things being equal. (For simplicity we have kept CD prices low.) Given factors such as their income and the availability of other forms of entertainment, neither person would choose to purchase even a single CD at $10 per disc. Dave, however, would buy one CD per month at $9 and two at $8. Marcia would not buy her first CD until the price was $7. Each would purchase more discs as the price falls. Thus, Dave's and Marcia's CD-buying habits conform to the law of demand.

We obtain the individuals' demand curves by simply plotting or transferring the information from Table 1 to the graphs in Figure 2a and b. The prices of CDs are given on the vertical axis of each graph, and the quantities of CDs demanded per month are given on the horizontal axis. The various combinations of price and quantity from Table 1 are plotted on the graphs. Each demand curve is then drawn as the line connecting those combinations of price and quantity. For both Dave and Marcia, the demand curve slopes

TABLE 1

Two Consumers' Demand Schedules

While individuals' demand schedules may differ, they do not violate the law of demand. For both people, the quantity demanded increases as the price falls.

Price of Compact Discs (dollars)	Quantity Demanded (per month)	
	Dave	Marcia
10	0	0
9	1	0
8	2	0
7	3	1
6	4	2
5	5	3
4	6	4
3	7	5
2	8	6
1	9	7
0	10	8

FIGURE 2

A consumer's demand for a product is the quantity that he or she is willing to purchase at each price. The demand curve is downward-sloping for both Dave (a) and Marcia (b): As the price falls the quantity demanded increases, and as the price rises the quantity demanded decreases.

Demand Curves for Two Consumers

(a)

(b)

downward and to the right (a negative slope), indicating an increase in quantity demanded as the price declines and a decrease in quantity demanded as the price rises.

Factors Affecting the Individual's Demand Curve

In addition to the price of a good or service, there are dozens, perhaps hundreds, of other factors and circumstances affecting a person's decision to buy or not to buy. These **factors affecting demand** include income, the price of related goods, price expectations, income expectations, tastes, the number of consumers, and time. Even when the list of other factors is limited, as here, it is not possible to handle simultaneous variations among all factors in expressing a demand curve or schedule.

Factors affecting demand: Anything other than price, such as consumer income and preferences, that determines the amount of a product or service that consumers are willing and able to purchase.

Ceteris paribus: The Latin phrase for "all other things held constant."

Holding Factors Other Than Price Constant. To isolate the effect of price on quantity demanded, the nonessential factors must be stripped away. We want to know what quantity of CDs Dave and Marcia would choose to purchase in a month at various possible prices, given that other factors affecting their decision do not change. This condition is called *ceteris paribus* ("other things being equal") by economists. It is essential to the development of any economic theory or model dealing with real-world events since all events cannot be controlled. Economists hold factors such as income and the price of related goods constant when constructing a demand schedule or curve.

This does not mean that these factors cannot change, but if they do change, the demand schedule or curve must be adjusted to account for them. Laboratory scientists are in a better position than economists to hold conditions constant. Chemists can perform controlled experiments, but economists, like weather forecasters, deal with a subject matter that can rarely be controlled. Economics, after all, is a social science; it deals with human nature and with people in society. The very subject matter of economics makes most factors affecting demand difficult to control. But like their scientific counterparts, economists must use scientific methods to organize real-world events into theories of how things work. The economist can use these theories to predict some of the effects on the demand schedule of changes in factors other than price.

Shift

Changes in Demand Versus Changes in Quantity Demanded. A simple but crucial distinction exists between a change in Dave's or Marcia's *demand* for CDs and a **change in** their **quantity demanded** of CDs. Other things being equal, a change in the price of CDs will change the quantity demanded of CDs, as we have seen. Figures 3 and 4 illustrate an increase and a decrease in quantity demanded, respectively. The graphs illustrate a movement along a single demand curve, indicating that factors like buyers' incomes and preferences are held constant. Figure 3 shows that a decrease in the price of discs leads to an increase in the quantity demanded. Figure 4 shows that an increase in the price of discs reduces the quantity demanded. A change in any factor other than the price will shift the entire demand curve to the right or left. Economists call this a **change in demand.** An increase in demand is shown as the rightward shift of the entire demand curve in Figure 5. A decrease in demand, shown in Figure 6, is a leftward shift in the entire demand curve.

Change in quantity demanded:
A change in the amount of a good a consumer is willing and able to purchase that is caused by a change in the price of the good or service.

Shift

Change in demand:
A shift of the entire demand curve to the right or left.

FIGURE 3
Increase in Quantity Demanded

Holding Marcia's demand constant, a decrease in the price of CDs from $4 to $3 will lead to an increase in the quantity of CDs demanded from 4 to 5 per month.

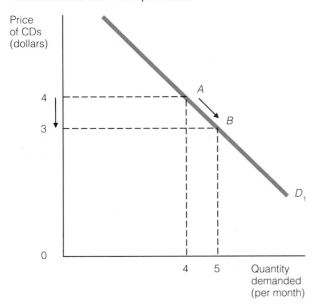

FIGURE 4
Decrease in Quantity Demanded

Holding Marcia's demand constant, an increase in the price of the CDs from $4 to $6 will cause Marcia to decrease the quantity of CDs demanded from 4 to 2 per month.

FIGURE 5
Increase in Demand

A change in any factors affecting demand causes a shift to the right or left in the demand curve. In this case, Marcia's income increases, causing an increase in her quantities demanded for CDs at every price. The demand curve shifts to the right. At a price of $4 per disc, Marcia previously would purchase 4 CDs, but given her increased income, she would now purchase 8 CDs. In this representation, D = demand.

FIGURE 6
Decrease in Demand

A leftward shift of the demand curve indicates a decrease in demand. In this case, the price of a substitute good decreased, causing Dave to demand fewer discs at every price. The demand curve shifts to the left. Before the price change in the substitute good, Dave would purchase 5 CDs at $5 each, but given the change in the substitute good's price, he would purchase only 2 CDs at $5 each.

Normal good:
A good that a consumer chooses to purchase in smaller (larger) amounts as income falls (rises).

Inferior good:
A good that a consumer chooses to purchase in smaller quantities as income rises or in larger amounts as income falls.

Change in Income. Marcia's or Dave's income may change, and such a change would necessitate a redrawing of the entire demand curve for CDs. For most goods, a rise in income means an increase in demand. For instance, if Marcia's income increases from $1500 to $2000 a month, she will demand more CDs at every price because she can afford more. Figure 5 shows that, given a new, higher income, Marcia's demand curve shifts to the right for every price of CDs. When demand increases, quantity demanded is increased at every price.

Although the theory that rising income means greater demand for goods holds true for most goods, it does not apply to all goods. Economists distinguish between normal goods and inferior goods. **Normal goods** are those products and services for which demand increases (decreases) with increases (decreases) in income; the demand for **inferior goods** actually decreases (increases) with increases (decreases) in consumers' income. Joe's demand for Honda automobiles may decrease as his income increases; a Honda automobile is an inferior good to him. Beth purchases less Häagen-Dazs vanilla ice cream as her income falls, indicating that Häagen-Dazs ice cream is a normal good for her.

The terms *normal* and *inferior* contain no implications about intrinsic quality or about absolute standards of goodness or badness. Indeed, a good or service that is normal for one consumer in a given income range may be inferior for another consumer in the same income range. It is even possible for a good to be normal for an individual consumer at certain levels of income and inferior at other levels. As one's income rises, for example, hamburgers or compact cars may change from normal to inferior. We will discuss this distinction in more detail later, but it is important to note that a change in income will produce a shift in the demand curve.

Prices of Related Goods. Suppose that the price of a good closely related to CDs—such as cassette tapes or CD players—changes during the month for which Dave's and Marcia's demand curves are drawn. What happens? Clearly, one of the assumptions about other things being equal has changed, and the demand curve will shift right or left depending on the direction of the price change and on whether the closely related good is a **substitute** for or a **complement** to the product under consideration.

Suppose that other forms of entertainment can substitute for CDs in Dave's or Marcia's budgets. If ticket prices for movies or tape prices decline during the month, the demand curve for CDs for both consumers would shift to the left; that is, the demand for CDs would decline. For every price of CDs, the quantity demanded would be lower. This shift is represented in Figure 6. If the price of a substitute good increased during the month, the demand for CDs would increase.

If the price of a good or service complementary to CDs rises or falls, the demand curve for CDs would shift. Such a complementary good or service might be compact disc players for home or auto. If the price of the complement increases, the demand for CDs would decrease (shift left). If the price of the complement decreases, demand for CDs would increase (shift right).

Other Factors Shifting the Demand Curve. A number of factors other than income and the price of related goods can cause a shift in the demand curve. Among these are consumers' price and income expectations and consumers' tastes. If the price of CDs or the income of consumers is expected to change in the near future, the demand for CDs during the month will be altered. Marcia may discover during the month that she will receive an inheritance. The basis under which her original demand curve was derived changes because she anticipates a change in income. Or back-to-school CD sales might be announced for August during the middle of July, causing a decrease in demand during July. Likewise, any alteration in the time period under examination—changing from a month to a day, week, or year—will alter the construction of the demand curve. A purchase of four pizzas per month at a price of $6.95 each would be represented differently than a weekly consumption of one pizza. A change in the time period requires a redrawing of the demand curve. Also held constant is the quality of the good or service. Changing the amount of ice in a 10-ounce soft drink, for example, will alter the quality of the drink. The change in quality will alter quantity demanded at any price.

Reviewing the Law of Demand

The demand curve expresses an inverse relation between the price of a good and the quantity of the good demanded, assuming a number of constant factors affecting demand. As price rises, quantity demanded falls; as price falls, quantity demanded rises. When any of the other factors affecting demand change, we must reevaluate the demand schedule and curve. In general, we

Substitutes:
Products that are related such that an increase in the price of one will increase the demand for the other or a decrease in the price of one will decrease the demand for the other.

Complements:
Products that are related such that an increase in the price of one will decrease the demand for the other or a decrease in the price of one will increase the demand for the other.

identify only the most important factors affecting demand curves. If we have missed some important factor affecting demand—Dave's carburetor unexpectedly burns out in the middle of the month, for example—that factor must be accounted for in analyzing demand.

Economists predict that individuals (and collections of individuals), all things being equal, will purchase more of any commodity or service as its price falls. To verify this prediction, the individuals in question do not even have to be fully aware of their behavior; they need only act in the predicted manner. Individuals' response to sales of any kind—they buy more when price declines—is evidence that a general and predictable law of demand exists. That law is a fundamental tool of economists' analyses of real-world events.

From Individual to Market Demand

Market demand:
The total amount consumers are willing and able to purchase of a product at all possible prices, obtained by summing the quantities demanded at each price over all buyers.

While an individual's demand curve is sometimes of interest, economists most often focus on the **market demand** for some product, service, or input such as automobiles, intercontinental transport, or farm labor. Market demand schedules are simply the summation of all individual demand schedules at alternative prices for any good or service. An increase in the number of consumers increases the market demand curve and a reduction decreases market demand. The key is to add up the quantities demanded by all consumers at alternative prices for the good or service in question.

We can use the CD demand example to understand market demand. We constructed individual demand schedules for Dave and Marcia by varying the price and observing the quantities of discs that they would buy at those prices, other things being equal. To determine the market demand schedule we simply observe the behavior of all other consumers in the same market situation.

Table 2 begins with the data on Dave's and Marcia's demand from Table 1. The table also contains a summary of quantity demanded for all other

---

TABLE 2   Market Demand Schedule

The total market demand for a product is found by summing the quantities demanded by all consumers at every price.

Price of CDs (dollars)	Quantity Demanded (per month)			
	Dave	Marcia	All Other Consumers	Total Market Quantity Demanded
10	0	0	0	0
9	1	0	39	40
8	2	0	78	80
7	3	1	116	120
6	4	2	154	160
5	5	3	192	200
4	6	4	230	240
3	7	5	268	280
2	8	6	306	320
1	9	7	344	360
0	10	8	382	400

consumers at every price and, finally, the total quantity demanded for all consumers, or the total market demand. At a price of $10 no one, including Dave and Marcia, wants to buy CDs. At a slightly lower price, $9 per disc, Marcia does not choose to buy, but Dave and 39 other consumers buy 1 disc. The total market demand is, therefore, 40 discs at a price of $9. (Note that actual numbers of discs sold to all consumers would be much higher. We use low numbers for simplicity. The important point is that the market demand schedule for CDs or any other privately produced product or service is constructed in precisely this manner.)

The market demand schedules can be represented graphically as market demand curves (see Figure 7). Dave's and Marcia's demand curves are repeated from Figure 2. The demand of all other consumers, taken from Table 2, is plotted in Figure 7c. The total market demand, shown in Figure 7d, is simply the horizontal addition of the demand curves of Figure 7a, b, and c.

As in the case of individual demand curves, the market demand curve is downward-sloping (negatively sloped) and drawn under the assumption that all factors other than the price of CDs remain constant. If the incomes of consumers change, or the price of goods or services closely related to CDs is altered, the market demand would shift right or left, as in the individuals' demand curves. Economists must focus closely on these related factors in any real-world application. Changes in the demand for any product—compact cars, energy, crude oil—will be closely related to factors such as income changes and the price of substitutes and complements.

The important concept of market demand summarizes only half of the factors determining and affecting prices. Like the cutting blades of a pair of scissors, two sets of factors—demand and supply—*simultaneously* determine price.

FIGURE 7   Market Demand Curve

The total market demand curve for a product is obtained by summing the points on all the individual demand curves horizontally. This is accomplished by selecting prices and summing the quantities demanded by all individuals to obtain the total quantity demanded at each price.

SUPPLY AND OPPORTUNITY COST

Indirectly, we have already encountered a supply concept—that of opportunity cost along a production possibilities frontier, which we discussed in Chapter 2. We will briefly review those concepts before shifting attention from the behavior of the consumer to that of the producer.

An opportunity cost—the highest-valued alternative product forgone—is incurred whenever any good or service is produced. Consider the trade-off between producing automobiles and wheat in a two-good world. See Figure 8a. A given stock of resources is available for the production of these two goods. Society, of course, will choose some combination of the two, and there is an opportunity cost in terms of automobiles forgone making a choice of more wheat.

Consider what the real **marginal** (or additional) **opportunity cost** of producing more automobiles is in terms of wheat forgone. The marginal cost (short for marginal opportunity cost) of more automobiles is simply the amount of wheat sacrificed to produce the additional automobiles. This is plotted in Figure 8b. From Figure 8a we see that society's choice of the first million automobiles is made at a cost of 10 million tons of wheat (point G in Figure 8b). An additional, or marginal, million automobiles can be produced

Marginal opportunity cost:
The extra cost associated with the production of an additional unit of a product; this cost consists of the unproduced amounts of some alternative product.

FIGURE 8

The marginal opportunity cost of a product rises as more and more of that product is produced. This is shown in the production possibilities curve as well as in the marginal opportunity cost curve.

Production Possibilities and Marginal Opportunity Cost

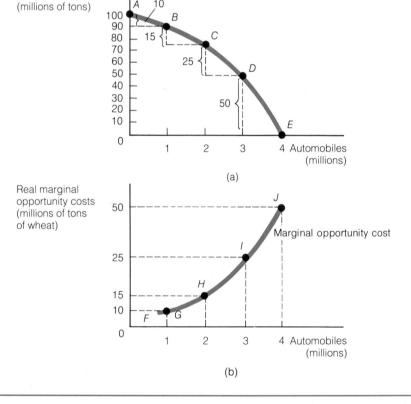

at an additional cost of 15 million tons of wheat (point *H*). Additional automobiles will be produced at higher and higher opportunity costs of wheat. Figure 8b gives the marginal cost curve in terms of real opportunity cost. Note that marginal cost increases as more automobiles are produced. Why? Common sense suggests that there are increasing costs of transforming resources from wheat production to automobile production. At first the resources drawn from wheat are easily adapted to producing automobiles (that is, there is a low opportunity cost); as more and more automobiles are produced, less-adaptable and less-talented resources must be used. The concept of the law of supply is totally analogous to this real opportunity cost except that prices (or opportunity cost in money terms) serve as the proxy for the real output of some good given up (wheat) to produce another good (automobiles).

Thus, any production involves a real opportunity cost to society. The increasing money costs of producing additional CDs, for example, is merely a reflection of the higher real opportunity costs of drawing resources from other productions. Money prices, which represent real opportunity costs, are merely representations of the real factors underlying the economy. Scarcity and opportunity cost do not vanish, in other words, in a highly developed economy. Relative resource prices and, consequently, costs of production are but relative signals of scarcity.

THE LAW OF SUPPLY AND FIRM SUPPLY

Law of supply:
The price of a product or service and the amount that producers are willing and able to offer for sale are positively related. If price rises, then quantity supplied rises; if price decreases, then quantity supplied decreases.

Quantity supplied:
The amount of any good or service that producers are willing and able to produce and sell at some specific price.

Supply curve:
A graphic representation of the quantities of a product or service that producers are willing and able to sell at all possible prices.

The **law of supply** states that, other things being equal, firms and industries will produce and offer to sell greater quantities of a product or service as the price of that product or service rises. There is a direct relationship between price and quantity supplied: As price rises, **quantity supplied** increases; as price falls, quantity supplied decreases. The assumption of other things being equal is invoked, as in the case of demand, so that the important relation between price and quantity supplied may be specified exactly. This relation, called a **supply curve,** shows the quantities of any good that firms would be willing and able to supply at alternative prices over a specified time period.

The method for constructing an individual firm's (and the market's) supply schedule is identical to the method we used for individual and market demand. All factors affecting supply except the price of the good or service are held constant. The price of the good or service is varied and the quantities that the firm or the industry will supply are specified.

To see how the supply curve is drawn, we turn to the supply side of CDs. Suppose that there are a number of firms supplying CDs in a given geographic area and that the output per month of two typical firms (Oranges Inc. and Joe's Audio) and all other firms combined is as shown in Table 3. The supply schedules of Oranges Inc. and Joe's Audio are given in the table by the combination of price and quantity supplied. That is, given alternative prices of CDs and the assumption that all other things are equal, Oranges Inc. and Joe's Audio specify the quantity of CDs that they would be willing to supply during a one-month period. (Again, numbers are kept arbitrarily low for simplicity.)

TABLE 3

Individual Firm and Market Supply Schedules

Individual firms' supply schedules follow the law of supply: As the price of the product increases, the quantity supplied increases. The total market supply is obtained by summing the quantities supplied by all firms at every price.

Price of CDs (dollars)	Quantity Supplied (per month)			
	Oranges Inc.	Joe's Audio	All Other Firms	Total Market Quantity Supplied
10	24	16	410	450
9	21	14	365	400
8	18	12	320	350
7	15	10	275	300
6	12	8	230	250
5	9	6	185	200
4	6	4	140	150
3	3	2	95	100
2	0	0	50	50
1	0	0	0	0
0	0	0	0	0

At a price of $10 per disc, Oranges Inc. would be willing and able to supply 24 discs, but if the price falls to $3 per CD, Oranges Inc. will supply only 3 discs.

As in the case of demand schedules, the information from supply schedules can be graphically expressed as supply curves (see Figure 9). The individual supply curves for Oranges Inc. and Joe's Audio conform to the law of supply—other things being equal, as price rises, the quantity supplied increases and as price falls, quantity supplied decreases. Note that the supply curve for the individual firm is sloped upward and to the right. This is because the marginal opportunity cost of resources used for increased CD production rises as more discs are produced. As more CDs are produced, less-adaptable resources are drawn into disc production, just as in the case of wheat and automobile production. To increase the quantity of CDs supplied, a firm may have to enlarge its quarters by buying and converting buildings formerly used for other purposes, incur the costs of hiring and training workers who have never made CDs before, and perhaps redesign its product to use alternative materials as original materials become more scarce. These increases in marginal costs may make it unprofitable for the firm to supply more CDs unless the price of CDs rises.

Change in quantity supplied:
A change in the amount of a good a producer is willing and able to produce and sell that is caused by a change in the price of the good or service.

Change in supply:
A shift of the entire supply curve to the right or left.

Changes in Quantity Supplied and Shifts in the Supply Curve

As in the case of demand, a change in price will alter the quantity that producers are willing to supply, indicated by a movement along a given supply curve, and a change in any other factor will cause a **change in supply,** indicated by a shift in the supply curve either right or left. An increase in price will increase the quantity supplied, but a decrease in price will reduce the quantity

FIGURE 9   Market Supply Curves

The market supply curve of a product is obtained by summing the quantities that will be supplied by the two individual firms and by all other firms at every price. For example, at a price of $7 the total quantity supplied is 300 (15 + 10 + 275).

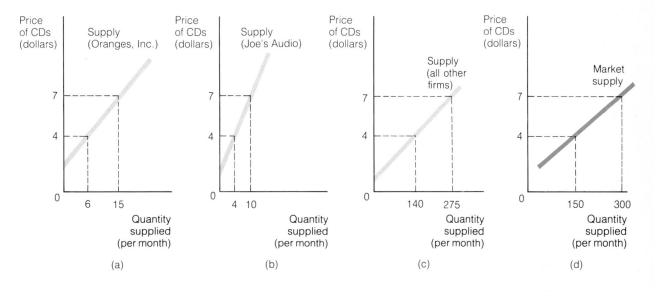

(a)   (b)   (c)   (d)

supplied. The supply curve is positively sloped—upward and to the right—and, as we saw, the demand curve is negatively sloped—downward and to the right. When **factors affecting supply**—that is, factors other than the price of the good—change, the whole curve shifts.

Changes in Cost of Production.   The most important influence on the position of the supply curve is the cost of producing a good or service. The price of resources—labor, land, capital, managerial skills—may change, as may technology or production or marketing techniques peculiar to the product. Any improvement in technology or any reduction in input prices would increase supply; that is, it would shift the supply curve to the right.

Suppose that the price of plastic materials used in compact disc construction falls or that the wages of salespeople available to CD stores decline. As the production or sales costs to firms producing and selling CDs decline, the quantity supplied increases and the supply curve shifts to the right for every price of CDs. An increase in supply is shown in Figure 10a. At price P_0, the firm was willing to supply quantity Q_0 of discs when the supply curve was S_0. After the firm (and all other firms) experiences a reduction in costs, the supply curve shifts rightward to S_1, indicating a willingness to supply a quantity Q_1 at price P_0. An improvement in production or sales techniques or a reduction in the price of some resource shifts the supply curve to the right. A decline in production or sales or an increase in any input cost shifts the supply curve to the left, as shown in Figure 10b.

Other Determinants of Supply.   Factors other than cost of production changes can affect the location of the supply curve. One such factor is changes in

FIGURE 10

As factors other than price change, the supply curve shifts. When input costs fall, the quantity supplied increases from Q_0 to Q_1 at the price P_0, shifting the supply curve to the right from S_0 to S_1. An increase in input costs causes a decrease in quantity supplied from Q_0 to Q_2, and the supply curve shifts to the left, from S_0 to S_2.

A Shift in the Supply Curve

(a)   (b)

producer-seller price expectations. The supply curve, like the demand curve, is drawn for a certain time period. If expectations of future prices change drastically in a market—for example, prices of the good or service are expected to rise suddenly—suppliers would withhold current production from the market in anticipation of higher prices. The current supply would be reduced, causing the supply curve to shift to the left, as in Figure 10b.

One other factor deserves mention. The supply curve is drawn for a given time period. A change in the time period (from one month to one week or one year) will alter the dimensions of the supply curve; it must be redrawn if the time period changes.

Market Supply

Market supply:
The total amount producers are willing and able to offer for sale of a product at all possible prices, obtained by summing the quantities supplied at each price over all producers.

Market supply is simply the addition of all firms' quantities supplied for every price. If the number of firms in a given market increases or decreases, the supply curve would increase or decrease accordingly because the market supply curve is constructed by adding all the supply curves of individual firms. The market supply of CDs represented by the price-quantity combinations of the first and last columns of Table 3 is plotted in Figure 9d. The market supply curve is obtained by plotting the total quantities of CDs that would be produced and sold at every price during the time period.

The market supply curve is positively sloped—that is, total quantity supplied increases with increases in price—because the real marginal opportunity cost of CD production rises as more discs are produced. Resources become more costly as more and more inputs are diverted from other activities into CD production. Remember that money cost is simply a proxy for real marginal opportunity cost.

MARKET EQUILIBRIUM PRICE AND OUTPUT

Market:
The interaction of buyers and sellers producing and buying goods and services. Prices tend towards equality through the continuous exchange between suppliers and demanders.

Perfect market:
A market in which there are enough buyers and sellers that no single buyer or seller can influence price.

Law of one price:
In perfect markets, the market forces of supply and demand produce a single, equilibrium price for a good or service.

Surplus:
The amount by which quantity supplied exceeds quantity demanded at a price above the equilibrium price.

We now put the concepts of supply and demand together to understand how market forces work to establish a particular price and output. A **market** is any area in which prices of products or services tend toward equality through the continuous interactions of buyers and sellers. Competitive (self-interested) forces of both buyers and sellers guarantee this result. All other things being equal, a buyer of dog food will always choose the seller with the lowest price, whereas a seller will choose if possible to sell at higher prices. Buyers will not pay more than price plus transportation costs, and sellers will not take less. Only one price is possible.

In a **perfect market,** both buyers and sellers are numerous enough that no single buyer or seller can influence price. In addition, buyers and sellers are free to enter or exit the market at any time. In this case of perfect competition, no single seller sells enough of the commodity and no buyer buys enough of the product or service to influence price or quantity. In a perfect market the **law of one price** holds: After the market forces of supply and demand, of buyers and sellers, are at rest or in equilibrium, a single price for a commodity (accounting for transportation and other costs) will prevail. If a single price did not prevail, someone could get rich by buying low and selling at a higher price, thereby driving prices to equality. The self-interested, competitive forces of buyers and sellers acting through supply and demand guarantee this important result.

The Mechanics of Price Determination

Price and output are determined in a market by the simple combination of the concepts of supply and demand already developed in this chapter.

Tabular Analysis of Supply and Demand. Table 4 combines the data on the market supply and demand for compact discs and contrasts the quantities supplied and quantities demanded at various prices. The numbers used in Table 4 come from Tables 2 (market demand for CDs) and 3 (market supply of CDs). The principles discussed here apply to supply and demand functions in any market.

Consider a price of $10 for CDs in Table 4. At the relatively high price of $10, the quantity of discs supplied would be 450 while quantity demanded would be zero. That is, suppliers would be encouraged to supply a large number of CDs at $10, but consumers would be discouraged from buying CDs at that high price. If a price of $10 prevailed in this market, even momentarily, a **surplus** of 450 CDs would exist and would remain unsold on the sellers' shelves.

These unsold inventories of CDs would create a competition among sellers to rid themselves of the unsold discs. In this competition sellers would progressively lower the price. Consider Table 4 and assume that the price is lowered to $7. At $7 the quantity supplied of discs is 300, while the quantity demanded is 120—a surplus of 180. Only when price falls to $5 per CD is there no surplus in the market.

TABLE 4   Market Supply and Demand

The equilibrium price is established when quantity supplied and quantity demanded are equal. Prices above equilibrium result in surpluses; prices below equilibrium result in shortages.

Price (dollars)	Quantity of CDs Supplied (per month)	Quantity of CDs Demanded (per month)	Surplus (+) or Shortage (−)
10	450	0	450 (+)
9	400	40	360 (+)
8	350	80	270 (+)
7	300	120	180 (+)
6	250	160	90 (+)
5	200	200	0
4	150	240	90 (−)
3	100	280	180 (−)
2	50	320	270 (−)
1	0	360	360 (−)
0	0	400	400 (−)

Shortage:
The amount by which quantity demanded exceeds quantity supplied at a price below the equilibrium price.

Now consider a relatively low price: $3 per CD. As the hypothetical data of Table 4 tells us, the quantity demanded of CDs at $3 would far exceed the quantity that sellers would willingly sell or produce. There would be a **shortage** of 180 CDs—that is, 280 minus 100. Clearly some potential buyers would be unable to buy CDs if CD prices remain at $3. In fact, some buyers would be willing to pay more than $3 per CD rather than go without music. These buyers would bid CD prices up—offer to pay higher prices—in an attempt to obtain the product.

As the price bid by buyers rises toward $5, sellers will be encouraged to offer more CDs for sale; simultaneously, some buyers will be discouraged (will buy fewer CDs) or drop out of the market. For instance, at a price of $4 per disc, sellers would sell 150 CDs while buyers would demand 240, creating a shortage of 90 CDs. The shortage would not be eliminated until the price reached $5.

Equilibrium price:
The price at which quantity demanded is equal to quantity supplied; other things being equal, there is no tendency for this price to change.

Equilibrium price in this market is $5; equilibrium quantity is 200 compact discs supplied and demanded. At this price there is no shortage or surplus. A price of $5 and a quantity of 200 is the only price-output combination that can prevail when this market is in equilibrium—that is, where quantity demanded equals quantity supplied. The very existence of shortages or surpluses in markets means prices have not adjusted to the self-interest of buyers and sellers. *Equilibrium* means "at rest." In economic terms, equilibrium is that price-output combination in a market from which there is no tendency on the part of buyers and sellers to change. It is the price-output combination that clears the market. The free competition of buyers and sellers leads to this result.

Graphic Representation of Supply and Demand. The most common and useful method of analyzing the interaction of supply and demand is with graphs.

Figure 11 displays the information of Table 4 on a graph that combines the market demand curve of Figure 7d with the market supply curve of Figure 9d.

The interpretation of Figure 11 is identical to the interpretation of Table 4, but the point of equilibrium is pictured graphically. Equilibrium price and quantity for CDs is established at the intersection of the market supply and demand curves. The point where they cross is labeled *E,* for equilibrium. At equilibrium, both demanders and suppliers of CDs are mutually satisfied. Any price higher than $5 causes a surplus of CDs; that is, a higher price eliminates some demanders and includes more suppliers. Any price below $5 eliminates some suppliers and includes more demanders so that a shortage of CDs results.

The theory of supply and demand is one of the most useful abstractions from the world of events that is available to economists. Here we will discuss a few of the implications of supply and demand for society and for public policy.

Price Rationing

Rationing:
The allocation of goods among consumers with the use of prices. The equilibrium price rations the limited amount of a good produced by the most willing and able suppliers, or sellers, to the most willing and able demanders, or buyers.

Prices, which are formed through the interaction of supply and demand, are **rationing** devices. Scarce resources are channeled to those who can produce a desired product in the least costly fashion for demanders who most desire the product. Another way of saying this is that resources flow to their most highly valued uses. Consider our hypothetical market for compact discs again. Suppliers who are able and willing to produce or sell CDs at a cost below $5

FIGURE 11

The equilibrium price is established at the point where the demand and supply curves intersect. At this price, quantity demanded equals quantity supplied. At prices below equilibrium, the quantity demanded exceeds the quantity supplied and the price is bid upward. At prices above equilibrium, the quantity supplied exceeds the quantity demanded and the price is bid downward.

Equilibrium Price and Quantity

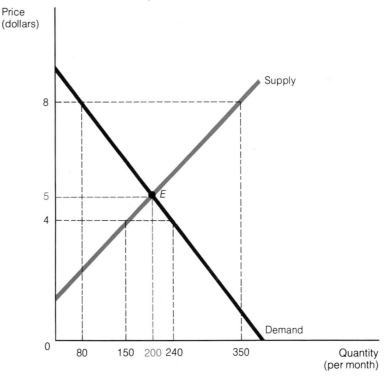

(including a profit) are "successful" in that their discs will be purchased. Demanders who are willing and able to purchase CDs at a price at or above $5 are the successful buyers of CDs. Only the most able sellers and buyers of CDs are successful in this market. High-cost producers (above $5) and buyers with a low preference for CDs (below $5) are eliminated from the market. CDs and all other goods are rationed by a price system—by the free interplay of supply and demand. In such a system no conscious attempt is made by any organization (such as government) to allocate scarce resources on the basis of factors such as presumed need, eye color, morals, skin color, or ideas of justice. As such, the market system plays no favorites. A price rationing system ensures that only the most able suppliers and demanders participate in markets.

Effects on Price and Quantity of Shifts in Supply or Demand

Both individual and market supply and demand functions are constructed by assuming that other things are equal. What happens if other things do not remain equal? We can summarize these other factors and indicate their influence on equilibrium price and quantity in any market obeying the law of one price.

Demand Shifts. Any change in a factor other than the price of a good will alter the basis on which a demand curve is drawn; that is, it will shift the curve left or right. (Remember the difference between a change in demand, which is caused by a change in other factors, and a change in quantity demanded, which is caused by a change in price.) A number of shifting factors are summarized in Table 5, which indicates the nature of the change, the direction in

---

TABLE 5   Factors Shifting the Demand Curve

Changes in factors other than the price of a good or service will shift the demand curve either to the right or to the left, changing equilibrium price and quantity.

Factors Changing Demand	Effect on Demand	Direction of Shift in Demand Curve	Effect on Equilibrium Price	Effect on Equilibrium Quantity
Increase in income (normal good)	Increase	Rightward	Increase	Increase
Decrease in income (normal good)	Decrease	Leftward	Decrease	Decrease
Increase in income (inferior good)	Decrease	Leftward	Decrease	Decrease
Decrease in income (inferior good)	Increase	Rightward	Increase	Increase
Increase in price of substitute	Increase	Rightward	Increase	Increase
Decrease in price of substitute	Decrease	Leftward	Decrease	Decrease
Increase in price of complement	Decrease	Leftward	Decrease	Decrease
Decrease in price of complement	Increase	Rightward	Increase	Increase
Increase in tastes and preferences for good	Increase	Rightward	Increase	Increase
Decrease in tastes and preferences for good	Decrease	Leftward	Decrease	Decrease
Increase in number of consumers of good	Increase	Rightward	Increase	Increase
Decrease in number of consumers of good	Decrease	Leftward	Decrease	Decrease

which demand will shift, and the effects on equilibrium price and quantity. Note that when demand changes, equilibrium price and quantity move in the same direction.

These facts can be seen graphically in Figure 12. Factors causing an increase in demand from Table 5 will have the effects on price and quantity shown in Figure 12a. An increase in demand shifts the whole demand curve rightward from D_0 to D_1. A shortage appears at price P_0. All the self-interested market forces that we discussed earlier now come into play. Demanders bid price up to P_1, where additional quantities are supplied by firms and where a new equilibrium, E_1, is established. Thus, an increase in demand has the effect of increasing the equilibrium price and the quantity of the product demanded and supplied. A decrease in demand causes the demand curve to shift leftward (shown in Figure 12b). This has the effect of reducing equilibrium price and quantity demanded.

Supply Shifts. The effect of supply changes are summarized in Table 6. Any increase or decrease in a factor such as resource prices or price expectations will cause increases or decreases in the whole supply schedule. Effects of such changes are shown graphically in Figure 13.

Figure 13a shows the effects on price and quantity of an increase (rightward shift) in the supply schedule. At price P_0 a surplus is created and self-interested competitive firms and buyers bid price down to P_1. Note, however, that while equilibrium price decreases, equilibrium quantity *increases* from Q_0 to Q_1. A price decline from P_0 to P_1 means that an additional quantity of the product or service will be demanded by consumers. Figure 13b shows the effects on price and quantity of a factor that decreases the supply curve (shifts it leftward). A decrease in supply has quantity-decreasing (from Q_0 to Q_1) but

---

FIGURE 12

(a) An increase in demand from D_0 to D_1 will increase equilibrium price and equilibrium quantity. (b) A decrease in demand from D_0 to D_1 will decrease both equilibrium price and quantity.

Shifts in the Demand Curve

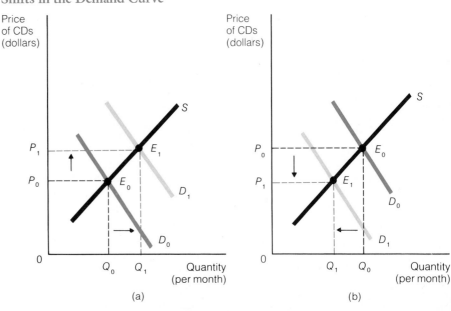

(a)

(b)

TABLE 6   Factors Shifting the Supply Curve

Factors changing the supply schedule will change equilibrium price and quantity in opposite directions.

Factors Changing Supply	Effect on Supply	Direction of Shift in Supply Curve	Effect on Equilibrium Price	Effect on Equilibrium Quantity
Increase in resource price	Decrease	Leftward	Increase	Decrease
Decrease in resource price	Increase	Rightward	Decrease	Increase
Improvement in technology	Increase	Rightward	Decrease	Increase
Decline in technology	Decrease	Leftward	Increase	Decrease
Expect a price increase	Decrease	Leftward	Increase	Decrease
Expect a price decrease	Increase	Rightward	Decrease	Increase
Increase in number of suppliers	Increase	Rightward	Decrease	Increase
Decrease in number of suppliers	Decrease	Leftward	Increase	Decrease

price-increasing (P_0 to P_1) effects, as Figure 13b shows. With supply shifts, unlike demand shifts, equilibrium price and quantity change in opposite directions.

Shifts in Both Supply and Demand. In the previous two sections, shifts in either the demand curve or the supply curve were considered; however, simultaneous shifts in both curves are also possible. If both curves shift simultaneously, changes in both equilibrium price and quantity are possible, but it will only be possible to predict the direction of change for one of the two—not both. In Figure 14 initial positions of demand for wheat (D_0) and supply of wheat (S_0) are shown with the equilibrium price of $6 per bushel and the equilibrium quantity of 240 tons per year. Suppose there is an increase in the number of farmers who grow wheat, causing the supply curve to shift from S_0 to S_1 in Figures 14a and 14b. If demand remained unchanged, the increase in supply would unambiguously lead to a decline in the equilibrium price to some level below $6 and an increase in the equilibrium quantity above 240 tons per year. Suppose, though, that during the same time period that supply increases, Russian buyers arrange to purchase wheat, which leads to an increase in the demand for U.S. wheat. Figure 14a depicts this as a shift in demand to D_1. The new equilibrium point is where D_1 intersects S_1. If we compare the new equilibrium with the old one, we can see that the equilibrium quantity has increased. Since both increases in demand and increases in supply lead to higher equilibrium quantities, simultaneous increases in both also lead to a higher equilibrium quantity. However, it is impossible to say what happens to equilibrium price when both supply and demand increase. The increase in demand raises equilibrium price, but the increase in supply lowers it. Depending on which shift is greater, equilibrium price can increase, decrease, or remain unchanged. In Figure 14a, equilibrium price appears to remain unchanged. If the increase in demand were greater, the equilibrium price would

FIGURE 13

(a) An increase in supply from S_0 to S_1 will lower the equilibrium price and increase the equilibrium quantity. (b) A decrease in supply from S_0 to S_1 will increase the equilibrium price and lower the equilibrium quantity.

Shifts in the Supply Curve

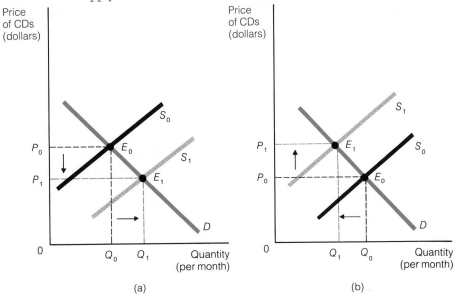

(a)   (b)

FIGURE 14

Simultaneous Demand Shifts and Supply Increases

(a) When the supply curve shifts to the right and demand increases, quantity will always increase, but the price change will depend on the size of the two shifts. (b) When demand decreases and supply increases, price will always decline, but the new equilibrium quantity will depend on the size of the two shifts.

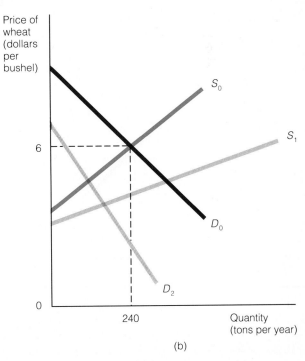

(a)   (b)

rise; it would fall if the increase in demand were smaller than that depicted in the diagram.

It is also possible that when the supply of wheat increased, demand for wheat decreased—perhaps because of a change in taste by wheat buyers who, for example, now prefer corn. In Figure 14b these changes are depicted by a shift in supply from S_0 to S_1 and a shift in demand from D_0 to D_2. Since each of the shifts occurs independently of the other and each causes the equilibrium quantity to fall, the price will fall below $6 per bushel. In this case, it is impossible to say what will happen to the equilibrium quantity—the decrease in demand causes it to fall, but the increase in supply causes it to rise. Depending on the magnitude of the two shifts, the equilibrium quantity can increase, decrease, or remain unchanged.

The same complexities arise if a decrease in supply is accompanied by changes in demand. Figure 15 depicts initial positions of demand and supply of wheat. Instead of considering an increase in supply of wheat, imagine that the price of inputs used in wheat production rises. This will cause the supply of wheat to fall from S_0 to S_1 in the diagrams. If demand for wheat simultaneously increases (see Figure 15a), the equilibrium price of wheat will rise, but the equilibrium quantity can rise, fall, or remain unchanged. Figure 15b shows that a simultaneous decrease in demand and supply will cause the equilibrium quantity to fall since both changes have this effect. However, price

FIGURE 15   Simultaneous Demand Shifts and Supply Decreases

(a) A simultaneous supply decrease and demand increase will have the effect of raising prices, but the change in quantity will depend on the size of the shifts. (b) A decrease in both supply and demand will always reduce quantity, but the effects on price will depend on the size of the shift.

(a)

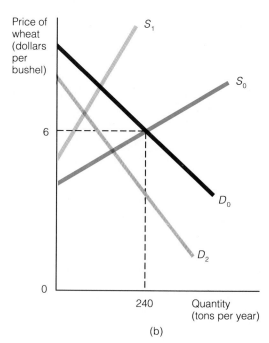

(b)

can rise, fall, or remain unchanged depending on the size of the two shifts. If the decrease in supply is large relative to the decrease in demand, the equilibrium price will rise. The price will fall if there is a small reduction in supply and a large reduction in demand.

SIMPLE SUPPLY AND DEMAND ANALYSIS: SOME FINAL CONSIDERATIONS

Many real-world events—new entrants into markets, oil price increases, new computer technology—can be analyzed using the simple laws of supply and demand. Some seemingly unrelated events also affect supply and demand. (See Economics in Action, "Global Problems in the Cashmere Market.") The theory of supply and demand is one of the most powerful tools the economist has to analyze the real world. It is important to understand some limitations and some possible applications and extensions of the simple mechanics described in this chapter.

Price Controls

Price control:
The setting, by government, of a price in a market different from the equilibrium price.

As we have seen, a major effect of the free interplay of supply and demand is the rationing of scarce goods by a system of prices. One of the best ways to understand price rationing and its usefulness is to examine what happens when government intervenes with regulation in freely functioning markets. One such intervention into the natural functioning of supply and demand is called a **price control.** Rent controls, price controls, agricultural price supports, usury laws (controls on interest rates), and numerous other policies are examples of such tinkering in free markets. We deal with many of these matters elsewhere in the book, but simple supply and demand analysis provides the basis for an initial discussion of the rationing of goods and services by nonprice means.

Price ceiling:
A form of regulation in which a maximum legal price is established by government above which exchange between buyers and sellers is illegal.

Price Ceilings and Price Floors. Imagine a hypothetical market for wheat. The market demand and supply curves are depicted in Figure 16. Without government interference, the equilibrium price of $7 per bushel would be reached with 12 million bushels of wheat being bought and sold each month. Government officials could become concerned about the high price of food and impose a **price ceiling** of, say, $5 per bushel. The government is declaring that wheat can be sold only at prices of $5 per bushel or less. While the intent of the legislation is to enable buyers to obtain all the wheat they want at a lower price, Figure 16 shows that at the ceiling price of $5 per bushel, the number of bushels that buyers would like to buy (14 million bushels) exceeds the quantity that sellers are willing to sell (9 million bushels) by 5 million bushels. In other words, at the $5 price, there will be a shortage of wheat equal to 5 million bushels. Clearly, the desires of buyers and sellers are not synchronized at that price. Wheat buyers who cannot obtain desired quantities of wheat will offer to pay more than $5 per bushel (in some cases even more than $7 per bushel) rather than go without.

To prevent the price from rising above legal levels, the government must engage in potentially costly enforcement activities. If the government succeeds in preventing illegal price increases, some other means will be used to determine which buyers get wheat. Any number of allocation plans could be used. Sellers could make the wheat available on a first-come, first-served basis, in which case long lines would form. Consumers could buy wheat at a reduced dollar price, but they would also pay with their time. Alternatively, the government could impose rationing so that each consumer is restricted to buying a fraction (nine-fourteenths) of their desired quantity of wheat. Other possibilities would be for government to establish priority schemes, with some consumers being permitted to buy and others being denied that opportunity. At any price below the equilibrium level there is an insufficient amount of wheat to meet demand, and some nonprice rationing scheme must be used to determine who does and does not obtain wheat.

Alternatively, given the same circumstances, government officials might decide that the equilibrium price of $7 per bushel is too low to assure prosperity to wheat growers. They might decide to keep the price of wheat up by imposing a **price floor**—a minimum legal price of perhaps $9 per bushel—on the sale of wheat. Figure 17 shows that at $9 per bushel, the quantity supplied of wheat (16 million bushels) exceeds the quantity demanded (10 million bushels) by 6 million bushels. In this case, a *surplus* of wheat of 6 million bushels exists. Wheat producers would find it difficult to locate buyers at the legal price, and they would have an incentive to reduce the price (in the absence of government enforcement). With effective enforcement, only 10 million bushels will be purchased at $9 per bushel; the government would be forced to use taxpayers' money to buy the surplus.

Price floor:
A form of regulation in which a minimum legal price is established by government below which exchange between buyers and sellers is illegal.

FIGURE 16
A Shortage Caused by a Price Ceiling

When the price of wheat is not allowed to rise above $5 per bushel, quantity demanded exceeds quantity supplied, creating a shortage of wheat.

FIGURE 17
A Surplus Caused by a Price Floor

When a price floor above equilibrium price is placed on any commodity, quantity supplied exceeds quantity demanded.

The U.S. government has supported prices of products such as milk, cheese, and peanuts, and these purchase and storage programs can be costly. This experience also shows why world trade of agricultural products has caused serious disputes among countries. For a variety of reasons, governments in Great Britain, Japan, the United States, and several Western European countries have imposed price floors on various agricultural products. As a consequence, the cost of storing surpluses has grown dramatically. Each of the governments, therefore, is eager to get rid of domestic surpluses by selling in world markets. Simultaneously, each government wants to prevent the inflow of foreign agricultural products. An inflow will force the government to purchase larger quantities of its own product to keep its price from falling below the price floor. For example, the Japanese government has a strong incentive to prevent American rice from entering the Japanese market; the U.S. government has an equally strong motive for providing American growers access to Japanese markets.

Price Controls and Quality Changes. One additional implication of price controls is interesting and relevant to understanding the competitive market process. We have assumed in the foregoing that the quality of goods and services produced remains the same when price controls are established. This is not generally the case.

Consider the recent deregulation of the airline industry. Prior to deregulation in the late 1970s, airline fares were controlled (regulated) by the Civil Aeronautics Board, a government agency, at levels above equilibrium. This price floor created a surplus of passenger seats and unfilled airplanes. The reaction of the airlines, since they were by law forbidden to lower airfares, was to alter the quality of passenger air service in an effort to compete. Higher quality is more costly to suppliers, in effect shifting the supply curve to the left. Higher quality is, at the same time, more valuable to consumers, shifting the demand curve to the right. Both effects tend to eliminate the surplus. In the case of airlines, gourmet meals, more frequent flights, and other extras were offered a pampered flying public. These activities increased the quality of air travel at the controlled fares. Quality competition, which eventually became too costly for airlines and contributed to their deregulation, sidestepped the money price control imposed by the government and effectively lowered the price of air services to customers through increased quality.

Price ceilings also may be avoided through quality changes. New York, Washington, D.C., Los Angeles, and a host of other U.S. cities impose rent controls on apartments and other rental housing. This means that the rental price of these apartments is fixed by law. While such price controls are often enacted to "protect" low-income families, quality changes may often mean lower quality to these groups over time. When landlord-owners cannot by law raise rents as the demand for housing increases or as the cost of supplying housing rises, equilibrium rents rise above the controlled ones. If these rates are adequately enforced, the available housing will be rationed to housing demanders as a result of the shortage. Since some of the demanders will be willing to pay higher prices than the controlled rate for the lower available quantity of housing, *black markets* (extralegal markets) may develop. Illegal side payments to landlords, known as "key money," are common in rent-controlled cities.

FOCUS   Palace Ruins, Key Money, and "Togetherness": Price Controls in Lisbon

Rent controls were instituted in Lisbon in 1948 and were applied in all of Portugal in 1974. The freezes brought about a dreadful housing situation and serious decay of large numbers of once-glorious old buildings because landlords' maintenance costs exceeded rental income received. Prior to 1986, rents ranged from 40 to 1000 escudos per month (200 escudos is currently approximately equivalent to $1.35).

The effects of rent control on Lisbon's rental housing were predictable. Buildings decayed over time as a result of the controls, which left landlords with not only insufficient income but also insufficient incentives for repairs. Once-elegant palaces and apartment buildings have been left crumbling and in ruins despite persistent tenant complaints.

The reactions to quality decline also were predictable. Those lucky enough to find an apartment "sublet" to other tenants. Although the practice was (and is) strictly illegal, as many as 20 lodgers were crowded into cheap flats, each paying thousands of escudos per month. Little new housing was built, since both new and old housing were subject to

rent controls. Those seeking new housing could obtain it only after paying millions of escudos to landlords in key money. Such paid-in-advance key money compensated owner-landlords for future rent depreciations from inflation. Many new buildings remained empty and thus decayed because tenants preferred not to pay.[a]

In 1986, new rental laws went into effect as worsening conditions were partially recognized. New levels were established, with as high as 300 percent rent increases and yearly adjustments for inflation. Many observers do not believe that Lisbon's (and Portugal's) rental problems are over or that progress has been made. A 1000-escudo apartment before rent control cost $6.75 per month. Assuming the worst, a 300 percent increase would be to 3000 escudos, a rent of $20.75 per month. This amount would likely not cause landlords to order mortar and hire stonemasons. It is not clear that, over the long run, most Portuguese consumers will benefit from rent controls.

[a]"Rent a Ruin," *The Economist* (July 12, 1986).

Another possibility exists, however. If controls are effectively enforced and black markets are prohibited, landlords have little incentive to maintain rental property. Excess demand for apartments at the controlled price makes it possible to obtain tenants even if the unit deteriorates. For example, imagine a landlord in a college town who is compelled by law to lower the rent on a unit from $550 per month to $300 per month. Unless the unit is allowed to deteriorate to the point that it is no longer worth $300 to any potential tenant, the owner will receive $300 per month in rent. It will be in the landlord's interest to save money on maintenance and to allow the unit to deteriorate until it is worth no more than $300. Regulations that prevent prices from adjusting to equilibrium levels cause predictable changes in quality. Experience with rent controls in cities as diverse as New York City and Lisbon (see Focus, "Palace Ruins, Key Money, and 'Togetherness': Price Controls in Lisbon") shows that such programs produce low prices and substandard housing. Markets can clear at very low prices if quality can be reduced to a sufficiently low level. This type of nonprice competition has thwarted the best intentions of many regulators.

Static Versus Dynamic Analysis

The analysis discussed in this chapter is called *static equilibrium analysis*. This means that (1) time does not enter into the discussion—it is not dynamic; and (2) price-quantity combinations move from one equilibrium to another (E_0 to E_1, for instance, in Figure 13) with no indication of the process by which firms and consumers actually move. The *dynamic analysis* of market supply and demand considers the time and process involved in moving from one equilibrium situation to another. How long, for example, does it take for a world oil price increase to influence prices in the various markets that use oil as an input? A static analysis cannot tell us. It can indicate only the probable direction of change in price and quantities. What is the role of the entrepreneur in seeking profit opportunities when demand or supply schedules shift and markets are in disequilibrium—that is, in markets that experience shortages or surpluses? Again, static analysis provides no method for answering questions about disequilibrium. A number of these issues will be discussed and supply and demand will be analyzed more thoroughly in a real-world context in the following chapters.

Full Versus Money Prices

Money price:
The dollar price that sellers receive from buyers; a price expressed in terms of money, not in terms of an amount of another good.

Full price:
The total opportunity cost to an individual of obtaining a good; includes money price and all other costs such as transportation costs or waiting time costs.

Another distinction must be made about prices resulting from the forces of supply and demand: There is a difference between the **money price** of a product or service and the **full price.** Consider the money price of a haircut for which the customer pays $12.50 in cash. Is this the full price of a haircut?

Money price is often not the only cost to consumers. In the case of a haircut, we must account for the time spent traveling to and from the salon, the time spent waiting, and the time spent with the hairdresser. The economist accepts the truth of the adage "time is money." Time, like diamonds, is a scarce resource, and it bears an opportunity cost. Time costs are often estimated in terms of the wage rate forgone, the leisure time forgone, or, generally, as the opportunity cost of the consumer's next-best alternative. Thus the full price of a haircut or any other good or service includes the price in money terms plus any other resource costs required in the purchase of the commodity. (See Focus, "Full Price and a New Orleans Restaurant.") Prices as interpreted in the simple model of demand and supply of this chapter are to be regarded as full prices. Consumers react to full prices, not money prices. No one, for example, should take an advertisement for "free puppies" or "free kittens" literally. There is no such thing! Do consumers react to the money price of products and services or to what economists call the full price? The theory of supply and demand discussed in this chapter has not explicitly stressed the distinction between money prices and full prices. But it is important to interpret even basic supply and demand theory as a theory of full, not money, prices. With this distinction taken into account, the theory of supply and demand forms the foundation for understanding how markets function and, therefore, for the whole science of economics.

FOCUS   Full Price and a New Orleans Restaurant

New Orleans is considered a restaurant town by gourmets. Restaurants such as Le Ruth's, Antoine's, Brennan's, and Commander's Palace consistently offer some of the best cuisine to be found anywhere. One of our favorite French Quarter restaurants, however, is Galatoire's. Galatoire's has earned a reputation for producing some of the highest-quality meals in the city. Menu prices, however, have remained low relative to other famous establishments over the past several decades.

Have both menu prices and full prices remained low at Galatoire's? If not, why not? Finally, what evidence might be offered for a real price increase? How would an economist view the matter?

The economist would focus on elements in the full price of a meal at Galatoire's. The restaurant has not enlarged its classic physical plant over the years but, over time, longer and longer lines form outside the door during the day and evening. Galatoire's, unlike most of its competition, does not take reservations or accept credit cards—only cash will do. Moreover, Galatoire's enforces a dress code—tie or coat for men (evenings and all day on Sundays) and, until a few years ago, dresses (no pants) for women.

All these factors would tend to increase the full price of dining at Galatoire's. There are opportunity costs to waiting for a table (time is a scarce resource); the time and resources spent dressing for dinner are also applicable to the full price. The length of the line at the restaurant can also make the real price higher or lower than anticipated, although diners can form hunches about when the line is apt to be shortest or nonexistent.

These additional costs mean that the full price exceeds the money price printed on the menu. However, the economist must calculate all benefits as well as all costs associated with purchasing products or services. Consider the possibility that some customers get positive benefits from dressing for dinner and from being surrounded by those similarly attired. Others may value the prestige or satisfaction of dining at the legendary restaurant. Such factors would tend to increase the benefits to these consumers. The full price paid for a meal at Galatoire's varies among consumers, depending on opportunity cost. However, consumers will marginally balance the perceived costs of buying products and services with the perceived benefits associated with consumption. When price or price formation is discussed in this book, it is therefore the full price, not the nominal or money price, that is being considered.

SUMMARY

1. The extension of specialization from earlier societies is the modern market society, where individuals and collections of individuals buy and sell—demand and supply—millions of products and services.

2. Demand can be expressed as a schedule or curve showing the quantities of goods or services that individuals are willing and able to purchase at various prices over some period of time, all other factors remaining constant.

3. Supply can be expressed as a schedule or curve of the quantities that individuals or businesses are willing and able to sell at different prices over a period of time, other factors remaining constant.

4. Equilibrium prices and quantities are established for any good or service when quantity supplied equals quantity demanded.

5. A change in the price of a good or service changes the quantity demanded or quantity supplied along a given demand or supply curve. A change in demand or supply occurs when some factor other than price is altered. When these factors change, the demand or the supply curve shifts to the right or left, either raising or lowering equilibrium price and quantity.

6. The market system, through supply and demand, rations scarce resources and limited quantities of goods and services among those most willing and able to pay for them. Products and services, moreover, appear and disappear in response to the market system of supply and demand.

7. Price controls instituted by governments tend to create shortages or surpluses of products. Market forces usually result in some form of rationing other than price rationing under such circumstances.

KEY TERMS

product market
resource market
relative price
law of demand
quantity demanded
demand curve
factors affecting demand
ceteris paribus
change in quantity
    demanded
change in demand
normal good
inferior good

substitutes
complements
market demand
marginal opportunity cost
law of supply
quantity supplied
supply curve
change in quantity
    supplied
change in supply
factors affecting supply
market supply
market

perfect market
law of one price
surplus
shortage
equilibrium price
rationing
price control
price ceiling
price floor
money price
full price

QUESTIONS FOR REVIEW AND DISCUSSION

1. What happens to demand for a product if the price of that product falls? What happens to the quantity demanded?

2. What happens to the supply of coal if the wages of coal miners increase?

3. If income falls, what happens to the demand for potatoes? Are potatoes inferior goods?

4. If price is above equilibrium, what forces it down? If it is below equilibrium, what forces it up?

5. What is a shortage? What causes a shortage? How is a shortage eliminated?

6. If the demand for compact disc players increases, explain the process by which the market increases the production of CD players. What are the costs of CD players?

7. A price ceiling on crude oil has an effect on the amount of crude oil produced. With this in mind,

explain what happens to the supply of gasoline if there is a price ceiling on crude oil.

8. What happens to the supply of hamburgers at fast-food restaurants if the minimum wage is increased?

9. What is the full price of seeing a movie? Is it the same for everyone?

10. "Lately the price of gold keeps going up and up, and people keep buying more and more. The demand for gold must be upward-sloping." Does this statement contain an analytical error?

PROBLEMS

Examine the data in the table below.

1. Graph the supply and demand curves.
2. What is the equilibrium price?
3. What is the equilibrium quantity?
4. At what price does a shortage of 280 exist?
5. At a price of $19, how much of a surplus exists?

Price	Quantity Demanded (per month)	Quantity Supplied (per month)
$0	400	0
3	340	60
5	300	100
8	240	160
10	200	200
13	140	260
16	80	320
19	20	380

ECONOMICS IN ACTION
Global Problems in the Cashmere Market

A formal discussion of the factors that affect demand and supply rarely includes real events that affect market prices and quantities traded. Yet the factors that affect supply and demand, such as changes in income or in the price of related goods, always occur in some framework of social, political, and economic institutions. As an example, let's consider how international events affect the market for a popular gift item—the cashmere sweater.

Cashmere is a wool fiber derived from the down (found under the coarse outer hair) of goats raised in mountainous or arid regions. It has long been the material of choice for fine garments, especially sweaters, jackets, and coats. The world supply of cashmere comes almost exclusively from three countries: Iran, Afghanistan, and China, which alone has produced 75 to 80 percent of the world's supply of raw cashmere. The material is precious, indeed; the down output of approximately four goats is required to make one pullover sweater. Fibers are woven into fabric, and one yard of 100 percent cashmere can cost as much as $140 from an American mill. Products such as sweaters or coats are then constructed from the fabric by clothing manufacturers.

Worldwide demand for cashmere products rose by 25 to 40 percent in early 1989.[a] Increased affluence in Japan and Western Europe played a role in the increase, as did supply

[a]Lena H. Sun, "A Crisis Is Shaping Up for Cashmere," *Washington Post* (December 21, 1988), pp. G1, G4.

restrictions. Figure 18 shows how demand increase shifts the demand curve rightward from D_0 to D_1. If supply had remained constant, price would have risen and the world quantity traded of cashmere would have increased. But supply did not remain constant. The supply of cashmere has diminished, shifting the supply curve to the left, from S_0 to S_1. If demand had remained constant, the equilibrium price would have increased and equilibrium quantities of cashmere would have declined. With the two influences—a simultaneous demand increase and supply decrease—price will definitely rise, but the resulting equilibrium quantities traded are unpredictable. The effects of these changes on quantity are unpredictable because they depend upon the size of the relative shifts in demand and supply. If the demand change is greater, quantity will rise; if the supply shift is greater, as we assume to be the case in Figure 18, quantity will fall. Price will rise in either event.

Why has the supply of cashmere shifted leftward? The curve shifts when any nonprice factor affecting supply, such as costs of production, changes. Costs of production are determined by many factors, including the availability of raw material resources. When raw materials, such as cashmere fibers, become scarce, costs of production rise. Higher-priced fibers mean higher-priced fabric, which inevitably means higher-priced cashmere sweaters. But this does not explain why cashmere fibers are less available. For that, we

must consider the real-world institutional framework in which the fibers are produced.

Political disruptions in Iran and Afghanistan occurred throughout the 1980s. The Russian occupation of Afghanistan and Iran's war with Iraq brought chaos to those countries and dislocated local producers of goats. Such dislocations decreased the availability of cashmere fiber from these countries. An entirely different institutional change reduced the supply of fiber from China. The "capitalist revolution" in China—the partial conversion of some controlled markets to free production and exchange—reduced the supply of cashmere. Goat and fiber producers in many Chinese localities were no longer forced to sell to government "marketing collectives." Instead, they chose to follow market instincts and establish their own factories to process fiber, manufacture fabric, and produce final goods. Traditional channels for marketing fiber to producers in the developed nations have been disrupted. The overall effect has been a reduction in the supply of cashmere garments, including sweaters.

Along with a demand increase, these political and economic factors explain the worldwide price increase of cashmere products. That price increase may be modified with changes in the circumstances affecting supply. For instance, the price increase has encouraged other countries such as Australia, New Zealand, and even the United States to at-

---

FIGURE 18 **Demand and Supply in the Market for Cashmere Products**

In 1989, demand increases for cashmere and cashmere fibers along with decreased supplies created an increase in the price of cashmere sweaters and other products. Supply decreases were caused by political and market disruptions in Afghanistan, Iran, and China.

tempt to breed cashmere-producing goats. Success would have price-reducing effects on world markets; however, agricultural experts believe that the climates and terrain in these countries may not be suitable. Though goats may be raised successfully under lush agricultural conditions, fat goats produce little down. Also, when marketing channels develop for sale of finished products from China, price will tend to fall.

Some important lessons may be learned from the example of cashmere. Although a solid knowledge of demand and supply is essential to understand real-world market functioning, a keen knowledge of complex economic, social, and political factors is important as well. The theory of demand and supply is an invaluable tool in helping us to organize our thoughts about how prices and quantities behave in any actual market. As critical in analyzing any particular market is an understanding of the factual institutional framework through which demand and supply function.

Question

If a synthetic fabric were developed that was relatively inexpensive to produce and possessed similar characteristics to cashmere, what changes would occur in the cashmere market? Include supply, demand, price, and quantity in your answer.

5

Elasticity

Studying the laws of supply and demand helps economists organize their thoughts about real-world problems. But it is not enough to understand that an inverse relation exists between price and quantity demanded or that a decrease in supply causes price to rise in a market. For supply and demand theory to explain and predict economic events, economists must be able to say how much the quantity demanded or supplied of a product will change after a price change. The laws of supply and demand tell us nothing about how responsive quantity demanded or quantity supplied is to a price change. But if, for example, you owned a fast-food restaurant, you would be very interested to know how responsive your customers would be to a hamburger price discount. The law of demand tells you that you would sell more hamburgers, but it does not tell you how many more.

Economics does provide a means of determining how many more (or less) goods and services will be bought when prices or other factors change: the application of the concept of **elasticity.** When you finish Chapter 5 you should understand

Elasticity:
A measure of the relative responsiveness of one variable to a change in another variable; the percentage change in a dependent variable divided by the percentage change in the independent variable.

- the general nature of elasticity and how it is measured.
- how elasticity relates to the impact of a percentage change in prices on the percentage change in quantity demanded.
- how elasticity relates to many quantifiable economic events and relations.
- what factors determine elasticity of demand and supply.
- how time affects consumers' responses to changes in prices.

THE CONCEPT OF ELASTICITY

The following examples—one relating to drugs and the other to the business world—demonstrate the practical nature of the questions that the concept of elasticity allows us to answer.

The Drug Enforcement Administration initiates a crackdown on the import of illegal drugs such as crack cocaine. With stepped-up enforcement, a smaller quantity of higher-potency drugs is smuggled into the country by organized crime. As a result, the money price of these drugs goes up steeply. Will the revenues of organized crime increase or decrease? There will be some reduction in quantity demanded; that is, fewer drugs will be sold at higher prices. The important question is, how much of a reduction? The answer will depend on the responsiveness of drug users to the increase in price.

You are contemplating two business alternatives: buying a gourmet delicatessen or opening a new travel agency. Best estimates tell you that consumers' incomes are expected to rise by 5 percent per year over the next eight years. On these grounds, which business should you enter? By what percent will an increase in consumers' incomes increase the amounts of gourmet foods purchased compared to the amounts of travel and leisure services consumed?

To answer these questions we must gauge the relative responsiveness of decision-makers—consumers—to changes in price or income, or the elasticity. Elasticity is calculated as the ratio of the percentage change in some effect (quantity demanded of illegal drugs; quantity demanded of gourmet food or travel services) to the percentage change in the cause (price change, income change, or any other change). You should keep in mind that while elasticity most often relates changes in demand to changes in price or income, the calculation may be applied to *any* cause-and-effect relationship. Elasticity is *always* a percentage change divided by a percentage change, resulting in a number that is independent of any *absolute* change in a cause or an effect.

Consider the relation between egg production and the weather. Assume that egg production falls with increasing henhouse temperatures. The elasticity of egg production with respect to changes in temperature is calculated by dividing the percentage change in production by the percentage change in temperature. If, according to a farmer's records, a 10 percent increase in henhouse temperature resulted in a 30 percent reduction in egg production, we say that the chickens are very responsive to temperature changes; that is, egg production dropped by a larger percentage than temperature rose. If a 10 percent increase in temperature reduced egg production by only 2 percent, we say that the chickens are not very responsive to temperature changes.

All kinds of elasticities are measured in the same way. More drug enforcement reduces supply and increases prices by some percentage. Drug purchases are reduced by some percentage depending on buyers' responsiveness to the price change, but, given the effects of addiction on drug users, the decrease in purchases will probably be small. Percentage increases in income will, similarly, cause percentage increases in gourmet food and travel consumption. The percentages of these changes can be estimated from similar past experiences, and businesses can use the information to make decisions.

PRICE ELASTICITY OF DEMAND

Elasticity, as these examples suggest, is a general and wide-ranging concept with many applications. The most common and important applications relate to demand.

Formulation of Price Elasticity of Demand

Price elasticity of demand:
A measure of buyers' relative responsiveness to a price change; the percentage change in quantity demanded divided by the percentage change in price.

The formal measurement of demand elasticity, like the generalized concept itself, is simple and straightforward. **Price elasticity of demand** is the percent change in quantity demanded divided by the percent change in price.

$$\epsilon_d = \frac{\text{price elasticity of}}{\text{demand coefficient}} = \frac{\text{\% change in quantity demanded}}{\text{\% change in price}}$$

Price elasticity of demand is expressed as a number. If, for example, a 10 percent reduction in the price of jogging shoes causes a 15 percent increase in the quantity of jogging shoes demanded, then the ratio, called the **demand elasticity coefficient, ϵ_d,** is

Demand elasticity coefficient:
The numerical representation of the price elasticity of demand: $\epsilon_d = (\Delta Q / Q) \div (\Delta P / P)$.

$$\frac{15\%}{10\%} = 1.5.$$

This elasticity coefficient or ratio, 1.5, and the percent changes in price and quantity demanded from which it was calculated are independent of the absolute prices and quantities of jogging shoes. If a 10 percent rise in the price of jogging shoes causes a 2 percent decline in sales, the price elasticity coefficient is calculated in the same way:

$$\frac{2\%}{10\%} = 0.2.$$

The price elasticity of demand coefficient (or, more simply put, the demand elasticity coefficient) always measures consumers' responsiveness, in terms of purchases, to a percent change in price.[1] To determine the effect of price changes alone, all other changes—such as differences in the quality of goods—must be held constant.

Elastic, Inelastic, and Unit Elastic Demand

The size of the elasticity coefficient is important because it measures the relative consumer responsiveness to price changes. If the number obtained from the elasticity calculation is greater then 1.00, we say that demand is **elastic** over the given price and quantity range; the percent change in quantity

Elastic demand:
A situation in which buyers are relatively responsive to price changes; the percentage change in quantity demanded is greater than the percentage change in price: $\epsilon_d > 1$.

---

[1]Notice that in actual calculation, the demand elasticity coefficient will always be negative owing to the inverse relation between price and quantity demanded (the law of demand). If price goes up, quantity demanded for a good or service goes down, and vice versa. Unless otherwise noted, this point is irrelevant to the interpretation of elasticity. We will accordingly eliminate use of a negative sign before the demand elasticity coefficient.

demanded is greater than the percent change in price. Above a coefficient of 1.00, degrees of elasticity vary. A demand elasticity coefficient of 1.5 for jogging shoes means that consumers are somewhat responsive to a price change. A coefficient of 6.0 for pizza means that buyers of pizza are much more responsive to a change in pizza price than they are to a change in the price of jogging shoes (four times more responsive, in fact). The larger the demand elasticity coefficient is above 1.0, the more elastic demand is said to be. (*Remember:* Price elasticity of demand measures the *relative* response of quantity demanded to a price change, the percentage change in quantity demanded caused by some percentage change in price.)

Unit elasticity of demand:
A condition where the percentage change in quantity demanded is equal to the percentage change in price: $\epsilon_d = 1$.

Inelastic demand:
A situation in which buyers are relatively unresponsive to price changes; the percentage change in quantity demanded is less than the percentage change in price: $\epsilon_d < 1$.

Unit elasticity of demand means that the elasticity coefficient equals 1. In this case, a given percent change in price is exactly matched by the percent change in quantity demanded. If, for example, a 2 percent increase in the price of candy bars causes a 2 percent reduction in purchases, demand would be of unit elasticity. The same would be said if an 8 percent decrease in the price of Volkswagens caused an 8 percent increase in quantity demanded.

An **inelastic demand** coefficient is a number less than 1, meaning that a percent change in quantity demanded is less than the percent change in price that caused the change in quantity. If the price of salt increases by 5 percent and the quantity demanded decreases by 2.5 percent, the demand elasticity coefficient would be 0.5, placing it in the inelastic category. An elasticity number lower than 0.5 for salt would mean that demand is relatively more inelastic.

The various categories of price elasticity of demand can be shown with demand curves. Figure 1 depicts three responses to a 20 percent increase in pizza prices over a given time period in a small college town. In Figure 1a, a 20 percent increase in price causes a 5 percent reduction in quantity demanded. This means that pizza consumers are not very responsive to a change in price: ϵ_d is inelastic—it equals 0.25, which is less than 1. In Figure 1b, a 20 percent increase in pizza price reduces pizza consumption by exactly 20 percent, meaning that demand is of unit elasticity: $\epsilon_d = 1$. Figure 1c shows an elastic demand—a 20 percent price increase causes a 50 percent reduction in the quantity of pizzas demanded: ϵ_d is 2.5 (greater than 1).

The elasticity of two special forms of the demand curve is also of interest in analyzing economic problems. Figure 2 shows a completely inelastic and a completely elastic demand curve. Total or complete price inelasticity means that consumers are not responsive at all to price changes, a condition that is seldom met in the real world. Increases or decreases in price leave quantity demanded unchanged—the demand curve is vertical, as in Figure 2a. One might think of the demand for addictive drugs—at least for certain price ranges and certain levels of use—as being completely inelastic. The price elasticity of demand coefficient is zero along such a curve: $\epsilon_d = 0$.

A completely elastic demand curve—along which an infinitely large or small quantity is demanded at a given price—is shown in Figure 2b. Individual businesses in competitive markets view the demand for their products as totally elastic. In a competitive market, producers are so numerous that they are unable to affect prices. The huge number of wheat farmers, for example, means that a single small producer cannot affect the market price by altering production. If the wheat farmer raises his or her price by even a small amount, buyers will not purchase any of the farmer's production. Buyers can get all the wheat they want at the (lower) prevailing market price. In these competitive circumstances, a single wheat farmer faces an infinitely elastic demand curve

FIGURE 1   Price Elasticity of Demand

(a) The percent reduction in quantity demanded (from Q_0 to Q_1, 5%) is less than the percent increase in price (from P_0 to P_1, 20%). Demand is inelastic, $\epsilon_d < 1$. (b) The percent reduction in quantity demanded equals the percent increase in price. Demand is unit elastic, $\epsilon_d = 1$. (c) The percent reduction in quantity demanded is larger than the percent increase in price. Demand is elastic, $\epsilon_d > 1$. The same relations hold for reductions in price or increases in quantity demanded.

FIGURE 2   Demand Curves May Be Totally Inelastic or Totally Elastic

(a) Quantity demanded is unresponsive to price changes (totally inelastic). (b) Quantity demanded is completely responsive to price changes (totally elastic); a small increase in price will cause quantity demanded to disappear. Perfectly competitive suppliers view the demand for their output as totally elastic.

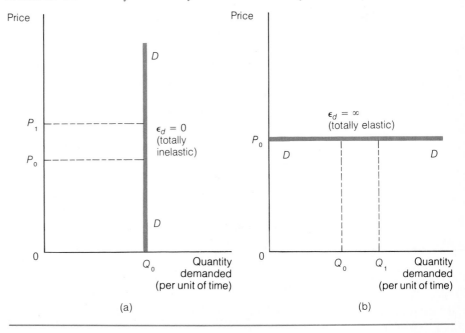

($\epsilon_d = \infty$). Quantity demanded is supersensitive to price increases. The farmer can sell as much or as little as he or she desires at the market price.

To summarize, an elasticity coefficient less than 1.0 means that demand is inelastic, and a coefficient greater than 1.0 means that demand is elastic. A coefficient equal to 1.0 indicates unit elasticity of demand. In all cases, elasticity values apply over a given range of prices. The demand curve can, under certain circumstances, be completely elastic or completely inelastic.

Elasticity Along the Demand Curve

Our discussion of demand elasticity has contained a crucial qualification: that the coefficient (whether elastic, inelastic, or unitary) has meaning only over certain (or relevant) price ranges. We now investigate exactly what this means. To do so requires that we be even more specific about the basic elasticity concept and its algebraic formulation.

Table 1 and Figure 3 show the market demand function—or price quantity pairs—that constitute the demand schedule for cassette tapes. (Table 1 and Figure 3 are similar to Table 2 and Figure 5d of Chapter 4, which relate to the market demand curve for compact discs.)

Is it ever correct or meaningful to ask, "What is the elasticity of this or any other demand curve?" Some simple calculations from the market demand function of Table 1 or Figure 3 will tell us that the answer is no. Remember that demand curves are downward-sloping because quantity demanded drops as price rises. Every negatively sloped demand curve will, in general, contain portions that are elastic, unit elastic, and inelastic. The elasticity coefficient will vary along any straight (linear) or curving (nonlinear) demand curve in

TABLE 1
Market Demand Schedule for Tapes

Price of Tapes (dollars)	Quantity Demanded (per month)
10	0
9	40
8	80
7	120
6	160
5	200
4	240
3	280
2	320
1	360

(handwritten annotations: "elastic ↓" next to prices 7–6; "inelast ↓" next to prices 4–3)

FIGURE 3

The elasticity of demand is different between various points along a downward-sloping demand curve. If prices fall by $1 between *A* and *B*, demand is elastic. If prices fall by $1 between *C* and *D*, demand is inelastic. The calculated elasticity is different depending on whether it is measured from *A* to *B* and *C* to *D* or from *B* to *A* and *D* to *C*.

Differing Elasticities Along a Market Demand Curve

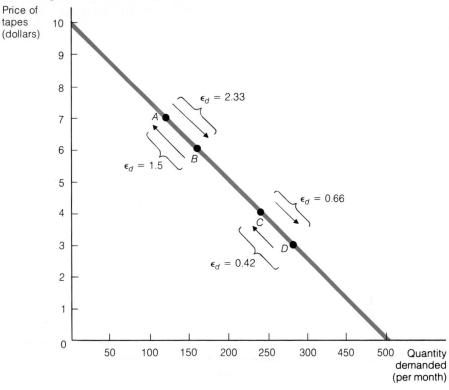

all but a few special cases. To verify this fact, consider the simple elasticity expression and its algebraic counterpart once more.

$$\epsilon_d = \frac{\%\ \text{change in quantity demanded}}{\%\ \text{change in price}} = \frac{\Delta Q/Q}{\Delta P/P}$$

In the algebraic expression, Q means quantity, Δ means "a change in," and P means price. In the numerator, percent change in quantity demanded is determined by dividing the change in quantity demanded by the initial quantity demanded ($\Delta Q \div Q$). The same is done in the denominator for initial price and change in price to determine the percent change in price. Then elasticity can be expressed as the percent change in quantity demanded ($\Delta Q/Q$) divided by the percent change in price ($\Delta P/P$). This formulation can be rearranged thus:

$$\frac{\Delta Q/Q}{\Delta P/P} = \frac{\Delta Q}{Q} \times \frac{P}{\Delta P}.$$

We will use this expression to make some calculations.

Suppose from Table 1 and Figure 3 that the price of tapes declines from $7 to $6. Quantity demanded would increase from 120 to 160 tapes. How would elasticity be calculated? Returning to our simple formula, we can calculate the elasticity across this price range as follows:

$$\epsilon_d = \frac{\Delta Q/Q}{\Delta P/P} = \frac{\Delta Q}{Q} \times \frac{P}{\Delta P} = \frac{40}{120} \times \frac{7.00}{1.00} = 2.33.$$

The number of tapes sold increased by 40 over the original quantity of tapes, those purchased at $7 (120). Thus, 40/120 is multiplied by the ratio of the original price, $7, to the change in price, $1. The elasticity coefficient is 2.33, which means that demand is elastic over this range of prices. Consumers are responsive to a price reduction from $7 to $6.

Now assume that tapes are selling at $4 and that the price is reduced to $3. Using the same method, we see that

$$\epsilon_d = \frac{\Delta Q/Q}{\Delta P/P} = \frac{\Delta Q}{Q} \times \frac{P}{\Delta P} = \frac{40}{240} \times \frac{4.00}{1.00} = 0.66.$$

compare w/ 0.42 →

The coefficient indicates that for a decline in price over the price range from $4 to $3 demand is inelastic. Consumers are far more responsive to a one-dollar price reduction from $7 to $6 than they are to a one-dollar price reduction from $4 to $3.

The formula for elasticity used above may be simplified even further. It can be reorganized

$$\epsilon_d = \frac{\Delta Q}{\Delta P} \times \frac{P}{Q}.$$

This equation tells us that elasticity and slope are different concepts.[2] The slope of the demand curve is $\Delta P/\Delta Q$; slope shows how price changes with unit or other changes in quantity. Elasticity is the inverse of the slope ($\Delta Q/\Delta P$)—that is, the slope "turned upside down"—multiplied by the ratio of some specific price and quantity (P/Q) that varies along the demand curve. So elasticity may be expressed

$$\epsilon_d = \frac{1}{slope} \times \frac{P}{Q}.$$

If a demand curve is a straight line (linear), its slope is negative and constant; therefore, the value of the slope divided into 1 is also constant. However, the *ratio* of price to quantity changes along the demand curve, meaning that elasticity also changes up and down the demand curve.

---

[2]You might want to reread portions of the Appendix to Chapter 1 on the value of slopes in linear and nonlinear situations. Along nonlinear demand curves, the slope changes along with the ratio of price to quantity, which (ordinarily) gives different values to the elasticity coefficient.

Again, suppose that \$7 tapes are reduced in price to \$6 and that \$4 tapes are reduced to \$3. As determined from the data in Table 1, the slope of the demand curve for tapes is 1/40, so the reciprocal of the slope (1/slope) is 40—a number that does not change as we calculate different elasticities along the demand curve. The *ratio* of price to quantity, the other part of the elasticity calculation, does change—from 7/120 in the first calculation to 4/240 in the second. The first calculation produces a number greater than 1 (40 × 7/120 = 2.33), or an elastic demand; the second yields a number less than 1 (40 × 4/240 = 0.66). The demand for any item—salt, cigarettes, tapes—cannot be called elastic or inelastic without first identifying some specific price range for that item.

The knowledge that elasticity changes along demand curves suggests another difficulty in accurately calculating elasticity. Since elasticity varies at all points along the demand curve, it also varies along the arc, or length, A to B or C to D. In other words, there will be different elasticity coefficients for price changes *between* \$4 and \$3, such as a price increase from \$3.25 to \$3.75. We will even get a different elasticity coefficient for a price *increase* from \$3 to \$4, as we verify in the following calculation (also see Figure 3):

$$\epsilon_d = \frac{\Delta Q/Q}{\Delta P/P} = \frac{\Delta Q}{Q} \times \frac{P}{\Delta P} = \frac{40}{280} \times \frac{3.00}{1.00} = 0.42.$$

Whereas a price decrease from \$4 to \$3 yielded an elasticity of 0.66, a price increase from \$3 to \$4 yields an elasticity of 0.42, a more inelastic consumer response. The difference reflects the fact that *initial* prices and quantities are plugged into the formula.

Arc elasticity:
A measure of the average elasticity between two points on the demand curve.

One compromise solution to the problem of determining the exact elasticity of demand over such a price range is to find the **arc elasticity,** or the average elasticity within the arc between the two price-quantity combinations.[3] There are other methods of calculation as well. Naturally, the smaller the price change, the more precise the simple formula $\epsilon_d = (\Delta Q/Q) \div (\Delta P/P)$ is at estimating the true elasticity between two points.

There are several means of calculating elasticity. While all these calculations (as with many other representations of actual economic data) are approximations, elasticity is often useful in assessing real-world problems and policies. We will continue to use the simple formula as our approximation.

---

[3] To calculate the arc elasticity in the \$3 to \$4 price range for tapes, the prices \$3 and \$4 and the quantities 240 and 280 are given equal weight. To express the formula algebraically, we can call one quantity Q_1 and the other Q_0. The price at Q_1 is P_1; the price at Q_0 is P_0. The average elasticity of their relation can then be calculated as:

$$\epsilon_d = \frac{\dfrac{Q_1 - Q_0}{(Q_1 + Q_0)/2}}{\dfrac{P_1 - P_0}{(P_1 + P_0)/2}} = \frac{Q_1 - Q_0}{Q_1 + Q_0} \times \frac{P_1 + P_0}{P_1 - P_0} = \frac{280 - 240}{280 + 240} \times \frac{3 + 4}{3 - 4} = 0.53.$$

The average elasticity coefficient is thus between those calculated for a price increase and for a price decrease. This is one method of handling the difference in elasticity between two points.

Relation of Demand Elasticity to Expenditures and Receipts

It is often necessary to estimate the effect of a proposed increase or decrease in price on total revenue—how much for instance, a fast-food chain will make (or lose) by offering a half-price sale on hamburgers. Estimates of elasticity from previous experience can make such projections possible. Or, if the price change and consumer response have already occurred, we can look at what happened to determine the elasticity of demand by examining either what customers have spent for a good or what businesses have received for it.

Common sense tells us that an industry's revenues are the same as consumer's expenditures for the industry's product. The number of items bought by all consumers multiplied by the price paid for each item is the same as the number of items sold by all producers multiplied by the average price charged for the items. Elasticity, therefore, is related both to **total expenditures** of customers and to **total revenues** or receipts of businesses.

To understand how elasticity is related to consumer expenditures, we return to the example from Chapter 4 of a single consumer purchasing compact discs. Table 2 reproduces Dave's demand and total expenditures (quantity times price) for CDs, and Figure 4 reproduces his demand curve with the associated elasticities. Dave's total expenditures on CDs begin to rise as the price of CDs falls below $10. As the price falls to $9, $7, and $5, Dave's quantity demanded *and* his total expenditures on CDs rise. For decreases in price, if elasticity is greater than 1, total expenditures will increase. Why?

Total expenditure:
The total amount spent by consumers on a good or service; calculated as equilibrium price times equilibrium quantity.

Total revenue:
Total receipts of businesses; always equal to total expenditures by consumers.

TABLE 2

Elasticity and Consumer Expenditures

The average elasticity of demand is greater at higher prices and falls as price falls. At the midpoint (near $5), the elasticity is equal to 1 and total expenditures are at a maximum.

Price of CDs (dollars)	Quantity Demanded (per month)	Total Expenditure	Average Elasticity of Demand
10	0	0	
			−19
9	1	9	
			5.66
8	2	16	
			3
7	3	21	
			1.85
6	4	24	
			1.22
5	5	25	
			0.81
4	6	24	
			0.53
3	7	21	
			0.33
2	8	16	
			0.17
1	9	9	
			0.05
0	10	0	

FIGURE 4

The elasticity of demand varies along a downward-sloping demand curve. As price falls, the elasticity falls.

An Individual's Elasticity of Demand

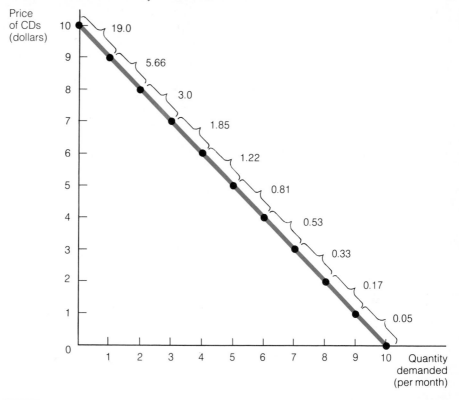

When demand is elastic, there is an inverse relation between price and total expenditures because the percent change in quantity demanded dominates (is larger than) the percent change in price. But as price is reduced below $5, Dave's total expenditures begin to decline, even though his consumption of CDs continues to increase. In the price range in which demand is inelastic (a coefficient of less than 1) total expenditures decrease as price falls. Here the percent decline in price dominates the percent increase in quantity, and total expenditures fall. In other words, prices and total expenditures change in the same direction if demand is inelastic.

The same relation between price and total expenditures is found when prices increase. If demand is inelastic, expenditures rise as prices increase from some low level, say $2, to a new level or over a range. If demand is elastic for that price range, total expenditures actually fall as prices increase. At some price-quantity combination, demand is unit elastic, $\epsilon_d = 1$. For Dave in Figure 4, unit elasticity of demand occurs around $5, when Dave's total expenditures for CDs will remain constant whether price is increasing or decreasing by some minuscule amount. At this point Dave's expenditures are at a maximum.

Being able to estimate the ways that price elasticity of demand affects the total expenditures of consumers is of obvious value to businesses seeking to maximize revenues.

If total expenditures are known, the relations between the direction of the price changes and total expenditures can be used as an informal method for determining elasticity, though not of calculating elasticity coefficients. The relations between the direction of the price change, the elasticity, and total expenditures (or revenues) are summarized in Figure 5. As the price falls from P_1, where consumption of the good is zero, to P_2, the midpoint on the demand curve, demand is elastic; total expenditures (TE) and therefore total receipts (TR) are rising. At P_2, price elasticity of demand is unitary, and total receipts and expenditures remain constant as the price rises or falls around this price. As the price falls below price P_2 (where quantity Q_2 is demanded), the demand elasticity coefficient falls below 1. Below P_2, total expenditures and receipts fall, and demand is inelastic, becoming more inelastic as the price approaches zero.

The major point to remember is that elasticity varies along any ordinary demand curve. It makes no sense to say, for instance, that salt is an inelastically demanded commodity without reference to some price range. The demand for salt may be elastic over some price range and inelastic over another. In the next section we consider what makes the demand elasticity coefficient greater than, equal to, or less than 1 and what factors determine consumer responses to price changes. (See Focus, "How to Tell Who Your Friends Are," for a broad application of elasticity.)

FIGURE 5

As the price falls ($P \downarrow$) along the demand curve, both total receipts (TR) and total expenditures (TE) rise, indicating that elasticity is greater than 1. At the point of unit elasticity, TE and TR remain constant. As the price falls from the midpoint, TE and TR decline owing to inelasticity of demand. Rising price ($P \uparrow$) has the opposite effects on expenditures and receipts.

Total Expenditures and Total Receipts Along a Demand Curve

FOCUS   How to Tell Who Your Friends Are

Elasticity is a general measure of the responsiveness of one thing relative to another. In economics we speak of price elasticity of demand, income elasticity of demand, elasticity of supply, and so on. The concept of elasticity is more than an intellectual device to examine strictly economic data. It can be useful to you in a practical manner. It can help you classify the quality of your friends.

Friendship elasticity can be interpreted from an economic perspective. A "good friend" is someone who has a low price elasticity of demand for your companionship. In other words, the person in question desires your company pretty much independently of what it costs him or her. You can raise the "price" of your friendship to a friend by behaving badly—being late for dates, being loud and obnoxious, grinding your teeth, not keeping your word, lying, and so on. But your friend will not desert you at the higher "price." The demand for your friendship is inelastic; consumption of your friendship does not change much at all when its price rises.

Other people will not pass the friendship test. Their demand for your companionship will be very elastic. If things get even slightly more difficult, they will desert you. Perhaps there are larger numbers of substitutes for your friendship available.

Figure 6 illustrates this phenomenon. The "price of friendship" on the vertical axis is what it costs an individual to be your friend—Are you easy to get along with? Are you fun? Are you a good conversationalist? Are you trustworthy? and so on. Higher or rising prices mean that being your friend becomes more costly in terms of your behavior. The quantity of friendship on the horizontal axis may be thought of as the amount of time you spend with a friend. The two demand curves in Figure 6 illustrate two types of behavior. The steeper demand curve D_F is relatively less elastic than D_{NF} (NF = no friend). Demand curve D_F represents the behavior of someone who is a "true friend." At high prices or low that person has a fairly constant desire to be around you. Demand curve D_{NF} proxies a "fickle friend." At a slightly higher

FIGURE 6
Demand Curves for Friendship

Good friends express demand curves of relatively lesser elasticity for your friendship. Poorer friends show more elasticity of demand.

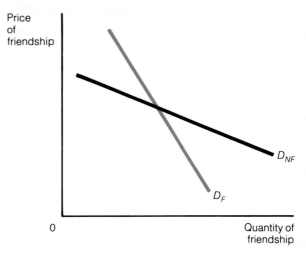

price (suppose you get sick), the demand for your company is radically reduced. Friendship is an inelastic demand curve for you; a relatively higher elasticity of demand implies a weaker concern.

Think of your own personal relationships. Do you know of people who have a high elasticity of demand for you? How do they behave—missed phone calls, only call when they need something, always insisting on doing what they want to do? And what about your good friends? Need we say more? Elasticity can be applied to the interpretation of friendships. Indeed, is not "love" a relatively inelastic demand curve?

DETERMINANTS OF PRICE ELASTICITY OF DEMAND

There are three major determinants of price elasticity: (1) the number and availability of substitutes, (2) the size and importance of the item in the consumer's budget, and (3) the time period involved. Since all three factors interact, the condition of other things being equal must be invoked to determine the specific effect of any one factor.

Number and Availability of Substitutes

By far the most important predictor of demand elasticity is the ability of consumers to find good substitute products. If the price of one brand of toothpaste rises, many consumers may respond by switching to a different brand. This substitution will happen only when alternatives are available.

Food is a vital commodity. Everyone must eat; elasticity of demand for nutrients in general is probably very low over relevant price ranges. For most of us, there is no substitute for food. But it is possible to substitute between kinds of food. While the demand for food as a whole tends to be inelastic, the consumer may substitute between broad food groups such as meat and seafood and also between foods within the broad groups. Consumers of meat, for instance, have a wide choice of substitutes, such as chicken, beef, pork, duck, possum, or alligator. Consumers are far more sensitive to changes in the price of beef when other substitutes are available. Elasticity of demand for meat itself is lower than that for kinds of meat over the same price ranges.

What about the elasticity of demand for beef versus beef products such as hamburger, sirloin steak, oxtails, and so on? The consumer can substitute among beef products. When the price of sirloin rises relative to hamburger, the consumer can substitute hamburger for sirloin. The elasticity of demand for hamburger is therefore higher than the elasticity of demand for meat. By now, the general rule must be apparent: The broader the product or service group, the lower the elasticity because there are fewer possibilities for substitution. We expect the elasticity of demand for Budweiser beer to be more elastic than the demand for beer, just as the demand for a Ford or Mercedes-Benz is more elastic than the demand for automobiles. Ordinarily, the wider the selection and substitutability of similar products and services, the larger the elasticity of demand for those products.

In Chapter 9 we will see that elasticity is a crucial factor in determining how competitive markets are structured. One view of competition is that it exists when products are perfectly substitutable—one seller's wheat is identical to another seller's, for example. A number of closely substitutable products—such as hair stylists in a large city—would also indicate a very competitive market. When goods are demanded and produced with few or no close substitutes, the market changes from competition to monopoly.

The Importance of Being Unimportant

The size of the total expenditure within the consumer's budget is another determinant of elasticity. Ordinarily, the smaller the item in the consumer's budget, the less elastic the consumer's demand for the item will be over some price ranges. A salt user may be insensitive to price increases in salt simply because expenses for salt are a small part of his or her budget. If the price of salt were to rise too high, the user might substitute alternatives, such as artificial salt or lemon juice. Thus, in calculating elasticity it is important to analyze both substitutability and the size of the item in the consumer's budget.

On the other hand, the effects of size in one's budget and substitutability may offset each other in determining elasticity of demand. Take, for instance, the demand for electricity by the poor and the aged living on Social Security or other transfer payments. Inflation and rising energy costs caused electricity rates to soar during the 1970s. How would such consumers respond to rising electricity prices, which take up a large portion of their total budget? We might be tempted to say that their demand for electricity is highly elastic. But economic theory and common sense tell us that electricity consumers will not be very responsive to price increases because there are few viable substitutes for electricity (except perhaps for intolerable house temperatures or highly expensive conversion to oil heat, when electricity is used for heating and cooling). Thus, substitutability—the second determinant of elasticity—outweighs the importance of being unimportant.

The condition of other things being equal clears up our understanding of the elasticity determinants. Given some constant degree of substitutability, the more unimportant the commodity is to a consumer—that is, the smaller the item in the consumer's budget—the lower demand elasticity will be. This indicates that tastes, substitutability, and importance of the commodity in the consumer's budget must all be examined in gauging the demand elasticity of products over given price ranges.

Time and Elasticity of Demand

Time is the final factor affecting the elasticity of demand. We alluded to this at the beginning of the chapter, but now we expand on the effects of time.

Let's assume a local market for tennis rackets is represented in Figure 7. (For simplicity, we may neglect the supply function.) Assume that the initial price is P_0 and the initial quantity demanded is Q_0. What happens to elasticity of demand over time if tennis rackets go on sale—that is, if that price falls to P_1 per unit, a 15-percent decline?

FIGURE 7

As time goes by, a given price change (ΔP) may be associated with larger and larger changes in quantity demanded (ΔQ). Since the percent change in quantity demanded grows over time, the elasticity of demand grows as well.

Elasticity of Demand over Time

The answer depends on how long it takes for consumers and potential consumers to adjust to the new price. If the sale is totally unpublicized, there may be no immediate reaction to the new price. As consumers gain information, however, demand increases. Thus, we may think of the demand curve as rotating around a point (*A* in Figure 7) as news of the sale becomes more widespread. Greater quantities (Q_1, Q_2, and so on) will be sold *through time* at the new lower price. For the given price change, the elasticity of demand will be different at different times—that is, it will depend on whether it is calculated on the first day of the sale ($\epsilon_d = 0.33$) or one week ($\epsilon_d = 0.66$) or one month later ($\epsilon_d = 1.33$). Percent changes in quantity demanded are greater as time passes, meaning that the demand elasticity coefficient is larger and larger (up to some limit). The general rule holds: Given quality and consumer preferences, elasticity of demand increases the longer any given price change is in effect.

The time period of adjustment is a crucial factor in calculating or estimating all types of actual elasticities. Not only do tastes, substitutability, and size within the consumer's budget affect elasticity, but the ability of consumers to recognize and adjust to changes also plays a part.

OTHER APPLICATIONS OF ELASTICITY OF DEMAND

The concept of elasticity is not restricted to price elasticity of demand. In general, we can calculate an elasticity of any dependent variable (effect) to a change in any independent variable (cause). We will consider two other important applications of this versatile and useful economic concept: income elasticity of demand and cross elasticity of demand.

Income Elasticity of Demand

Income elasticity of demand:
A measure of consumers' relative responsiveness to income changes; the percentage change in quantity demanded divided by the percentage change in income, holding price constant.

As you will recall from Chapter 4, a consumer's income is an important determinant (independent variable) of the demand for goods and services. It is often very informative to inquire about consumers' **income elasticity of demand.** Producers of all kinds are interested in the magnitude of consumption changes as incomes rise or in consumption habits within various income groups. Budget data compiled by the government and other sources can be used to calculate recent and historical trends in changing consumption patterns as incomes change.

The mechanics of income elasticity of demand are identical to those involved in the calculation of price elasticity; only the independent variable changes. With price held constant, income elasticity is the percent change in quantity demanded resulting from (divided by) a given percent change in income. It is expressed as ϵ_y, with Y representing income.

$$\epsilon_y = \frac{\% \text{ change in consumption of a good}}{\% \text{ change in income}} = \frac{\Delta Q}{Q} \div \frac{\Delta Y}{Y}$$

The income elasticity coefficient, ϵ_y, may be positive or negative depending on whether the good is normal or inferior. (Recall from Chapter 4 that a good is normal if an increase in income results in greater consumption and inferior if an increase in income results in a reduction in product consumption.) When applying the income elasticity formula, if ϵ_y is greater than zero, the good is normal; if ϵ_y is less than zero, the good is inferior. For the moment we discuss only normal goods.

If the elasticity coefficient ϵ_y is greater than 1, demand (or consumption) is said to be income elastic; if ϵ_y is less than 1, the product is income inelastic; and if ϵ_y equals 1, income is unit elastic. Suppose that income in the United States rises by 10 percent in 1990 and that the quantity of new automobiles consumed over the year increases by 8 percent. New automobiles are a normal good since their consumption increases along with the increase in income. But what is the income elasticity? The simple computation is

$$\epsilon_y = \frac{8\%}{10\%} = 0.8.$$

The income elasticity of demand for automobiles in this hypothetical calculation is less than 1 but greater than zero. What does this mean for the auto industry? Other things being equal (such as price and tastes), the demand for automobiles will rise, but at a slower pace than income. This fact is important to groups such as auto manufacturers, investors, boat dealers, and airlines.

Income elasticity for a particular good may be determined for any individual consumer or for consumers as a group. The practical importance of this calculation is undeniable. An individual deciding between opening a gourmet food shop and a travel agency during a period of rapidly rising income would be very interested to know, for example, that income elasticity for gourmet foods is perhaps 0.2, while the same coefficient for Mediterranean vacations is 6.2. However, to achieve accuracy in actual use, all other factors, such as substitutability and the price of the product, must be kept constant. If these factors vary, as they often do in the real world, their impact on consumption must be determined and integrated into the analysis.

Cross Elasticity of Demand

Cross elasticity of demand:
Measures buyers' relative responsiveness to a change in the price of one good in terms of the change in the quantity demanded of another good. The percentage change in the quantity demanded of one good divided by the percentage change in the price of another good.

Substitutes:
Two goods whose cross elasticity of demand is positive: $\epsilon_c > 0$.

Cross elasticity of demand reveals the responsiveness of the quantity demanded of one good to a change in the price of another good. As such, a cross elasticity coefficient can define either substitute or complementary products or services. In more general terms, cross elasticity is an extremely useful economic tool for identifying groups of products whose demand functions are related. Cross elasticity is calculated as the ratio of the percentage change in the quantity demanded of one good, A, to the percentage change in the price of another good, B, or

$$\epsilon_c = \frac{\Delta Q_A}{Q_A} \div \frac{\Delta P_B}{P_B}.$$

If the price of one good rises and, other things being equal, the quantity demanded of another good increases, those products are **substitutes.** If Dorothy's demand for Bayer aspirin rises 85 percent following a 10 percent rise in the price of Bufferin, her cross elasticity of demand for aspirin is $+8.5$. The coefficient of cross elasticity of demand is calculated thus:

$$\epsilon_c = \frac{\% \text{ change in quantity demanded of Bayer}}{\% \text{ change in price of Bufferin}} = \frac{85}{10} = +8.5.$$

For substitute commodities, the cross elasticity coefficient is positive because an increase in the price of one good causes an increase in the quantity demanded of the other. The larger the elasticity coefficient (in absolute terms), the more substitutable the products or services are.

Some items that are complements in consumption—bacon and eggs; gasoline and automobiles; light bulbs, lamps, and electricity. Goods are **complements** when an increase in the price of one good results in a decrease in the quantity demanded of the other. Gin and vermouth are the two essential ingredients (besides olives) in a martini. If there is a 4 percent increase in the price of vermouth and a 16 percent reduction in the quantity consumed of gin, other things being equal, we can call gin and vermouth complementary products. Note that the cross elasticity coefficient is negative.

$$\epsilon_c = \frac{\% \text{ decrease in quantity demanded of gin}}{\% \text{ increase in price of vermouth}} = \frac{-16}{4} = -4.0$$

A negative number is obtained for the cross elasticity coefficient for complementary goods, since the increase in the price of one is always associated with a decrease in the demand for the other.

In calculating cross elasticity, therefore, a positive sign indicates that goods are substitutes and a negative sign indicates that they are complements. The absolute size of the coefficient, moreover, tells us the degree of substitutability or complementarity. A coefficient of -28.0 indicates a greater degree of complementarity than one of -4.0, for example.

ELASTICITY OF SUPPLY

The versatile concept of elasticity, applied thus far only to demand, can also be applied to problems related to supply. **Elasticity of supply** is the degree of responsiveness of a supplier of goods or services to changes in the price the supplier receives for those goods or services.

A price elasticity of supply coefficient can be mechanically calculated in the same manner as all other elasticities. To determine the relation between a change in quantity supplied and a change in price, this simple formula can be applied:

$$\epsilon_s = \frac{\% \text{ change in quantity supplied}}{\% \text{ change in price}} = \frac{\Delta Q_s}{Q_s} \div \frac{\Delta P}{P} = \frac{\Delta Q_s}{Q_s} \times \frac{P}{\Delta P}.$$

Such a simple coefficient or some more elaborate "average elasticity" can be calculated for any supply curve at any instant in time just as it can be for the elasticity of demand. Elasticity of supply can also be applied to any kind of supply curve, from beets to ball bearings. We turn to an input supply curve—a labor supply curve.

Complements:
Two goods whose cross elasticity of demand is negative; $\epsilon_c < 0$.

Elasticity of supply:
A measure of producers' or workers' relative responsiveness to price or wage changes; the percentage change in quantity supplied divided by the percentage change in the price or wage rate.

The Elasticity of Labor Supply

A labor supply curve, such as the one shown in Figure 8, simply shows the amount of work (measured in number of hours) that a laborer, whom we will call Sam, would be willing to supply at alternative wage rates. Factors such as the worker's wealth, tastes, preferences, and other factors affecting work decisions are held constant. Each person's labor supply function differs because of these factors.

Ordinarily the labor supply curve is positively sloped, like the supply curve for any commodity or service. An increase in the wage rate from W_0 to W_1 in Figure 8 causes Sam to increase the number of hours he is willing to work from L_0 to L_1; likewise, a wage increase from W_2 to W_3 increases Sam's quantity of work supplied from L_2 to L_3. What is the elasticity of the labor supply schedule and what does it tell us?

The elasticity of labor supply shows the responsiveness of labor supply to a percentage change in the wage rate. It is calculated

$$\epsilon_{L_s} = \frac{\% \text{ change in quantity of labor supplied}}{\% \text{ change in the wage rate}} = \frac{\Delta L}{L} \div \frac{\Delta W}{W} = \frac{\Delta L}{L} \times \frac{W}{\Delta W}.$$

We can make an elasticity calculation for two different segments of Sam's supply curve. Starting from a relatively low wage rate, W_0, an increase in wages of 10 percent will produce a 25 percent increase in the number of hours worked. The coefficient ϵ_{L_s} is 2.5, which indicates an elastic supply of work effort (because it is greater than 1).

But notice what happens to an identical wage rate increase (10 percent) starting from a higher wage, W_2. Sam increases the number of hours worked

FIGURE 8

Starting from a relatively low wage rate (W_0), a 10 percent increase in Sam's wage leads him to supply 25 percent more work, an elastic response. A 10 percent rise at a higher wage (W_2) increases Sam's hours worked by only 3 percent, an inelastic response.

Elasticity of Labor Supply

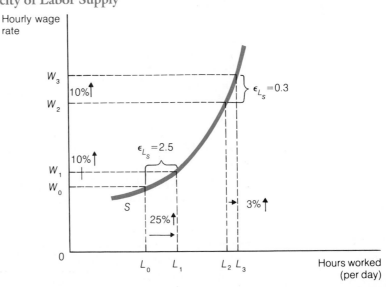

by 3 percent, producing an elasticity coefficient, ϵ_{L_s}, of 0.3—clearly an inelastic response. Why the drastic change in Sam's response to wage increases?

Some personal reflection will give us clues to Sam's work behavior. Work and leisure are two ways of using the scarce resource of time. The more hours we work, the less time we have for leisure. As we work more hours per day in response to wage rate increases, the relative opportunity cost of working (leisure forgone) begins to increase. At some point, laborers start to substitute leisure for work and income. Elasticity of labor supply is one method of calculating this trade-off (although other factors such as income level also shape labor supply). Other things being equal, an inelastic labor supply co-efficient for a given wage rate change means that the laborer demonstrates a preference for leisure over work (nonmarket time over market time).

Time and Elasticity of Supply: Maryland Crab Fishing

An extremely important issue concerns the time dimension over which the economist calculates supply elasticities. A time dimension exists in all facets of life and human activity, and it is important in the economic activities of suppliers and producers.

A supply elasticity coefficient would not ordinarily capture the full response of suppliers over time to a given price change. To illustrate, consider a crab fisherman from Chesapeake Bay who daily brings in a catch and offers it for sale. The supply curve for crabs on any given day would be totally inelastic. On any given day, the quantity supplied of crabs would be completely unresponsive to price changes.

How then does the market establish a price? Price is determined by the interaction of supply and demand. If the demand for crabs on some particular day happens to be D_0 in Figure 9, price will settle at P_e and the entire quantity of crabs (a commodity that we assume, unrealistically, is not storable) will be sold.

Now suppose there is a change in consumers' taste. Maryland crabs become more desirable, and the demand curve shifts permanently to D_1. The fisherman's good fortune is revealed when his usual catch of Q_0 crabs brings a higher price P_0. How will the fisherman respond? If the price P_0 is higher than his average production costs, meaning a higher-than-normal profit, the fisherman will adjust by shifting available resources into crab fishing as soon as possible. If he has idle boats or nets and if there is plenty of labor available, all will be put to use. The act of producing more crabs takes time because resources are not instantly adaptable to crab fishing.

During ensuing days, weeks, or months, more crabs will be offered for sale per day, resulting in a more elastic supply curve for crabs. Such a supply curve over the initial adjustment period may look like S_1 in Figure 9. The price may temporarily fall to P_1 given that the demand for crabs remains stationary at D_1. Comparing the quantity Q_1 sold at price P_1 with the previous quantity of crabs sold, Q_0, shows us that over some adjustment period the supply curve for crabs is not completely inelastic but that quantity supplied is responsive to the initial price change. The response of the fisherman to price changes on any given day will still be nil; but over time, he will adjust resources to increase the amount of crabs he offers for sale.

FIGURE 9

If the demand for crabs shifts from D_0 to D_1, then price rises quickly to P_0. As time goes by and crab fishermen are able to adjust inputs, the price begins to fall to P_1. After a long period of time and all adjustments are made to the increased demand, price falls to P_2. Over time, elasticity of supply increases.

Time and Elasticity of Supply

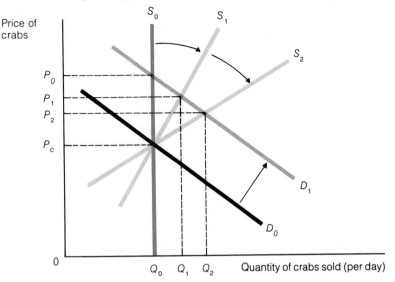

If price P_1 is still abnormally profitable, the fisherman will continue to shift resources into crab production by purchasing new boats and equipment and by training new workers. Again, such activity takes time, but the effect will be to increase crab supply (perhaps to S_2). The end result in the crab market will depend on the adaptability and availability of resources for crab fishing and on the cost of producing new inputs. But the general rule is that elasticity of supply will tend to increase over time. The longer the time period of adjustment to an initial change in price—whether price is rising or falling— the more elastic supply schedules will be. This principle applies to all supply curves, including market or industry supply curves. In the case of market supply curves, the adjustment to a change in demand and price will depend on how long it takes to draw on unused or idle capacity or on resources from other industries; in the case of a permanent price drop, the adjustment will depend on the time it takes to decrease the use of resources. The full impact of economic policy changes—levying taxes on industries, for example—often hinges on the elasticity of supply over time.

Real-world events are seldom so isolated and data so accurate as to provide the economist with means to calculate elasticities precisely. It is nonetheless important to a great number of economic and practical problems that elasticities can be estimated. To estimate elasticities, the economist must apply precise analytical tools to often complicated policy situations. In Economics in Action, "Cigarettes, Gasoline, and Elasticity: The Effects of an Excise Tax," we provide an example of two such situations.

SUMMARY

1. Elasticity is the ratio of the percent change in effect to the percent change in some cause. If changes in quantity demanded (the effect) are caused by changes in price, elasticity of demand is the percent change in quantity divided by the percent change in price. This ratio is called the demand elasticity coefficient (ϵ_d).

2. A demand elasticity coefficient greater than 1 means that consumers are responsive to price changes; demand is elastic. When $\epsilon_d = 1$, demand is unit elastic. When ϵ_d is less than 1, consumers are not very responsive to price changes; demand is said to be inelastic.

3. Elasticity can also be derived (in a general, short-hand manner) by examining total expenditures (or total revenues) as price rises or falls. If total expenditures rise (fall) as price rises (falls), ϵ_d is less than 1. If total expenditures remain constant as price rises or falls, $\epsilon_d = 1$. If total expenditures fall (rise) as price rises (falls), the demand elasticity coefficient is greater than 1—that is, it is elastic.

4. There are three major determinants of demand elasticity: (1) the number and availability of substitutes; (2) the size and importance of the item in the consumer's budget; and (3) the time period over which the coefficient is calculated.

5. Other applications of the elasticity concept related to demand are the relation between income changes and changes in quantity demanded (income elasticity of demand) and between price changes for one good and changes in quantity demanded for another complementary or substitute good (cross elasticity of demand between two goods).

6. An elasticity coefficient can be calculated for all kinds of supply curves. A supply elasticity coefficient is simply the percent change in quantity supplied divided by the percent change in price. The concept can be applied to all input and output supply curves, including labor supply.

7. Time is at the center of most important economic calculations, including elasticity. A general rule regarding time and elasticity is that the elasticity of demand and supply increases with the time that a change (in price, for instance) is in effect.

KEY TERMS

elasticity
price elasticity of demand
demand elasticity coefficient
elastic demand
unit elasticity of demand

inelastic demand
arc elasticity
total expenditure
total revenue
income elasticity of demand

cross elasticity of demand
substitutes
complements
elasticity of supply

QUESTIONS FOR REVIEW AND DISCUSSION

1. The formula for elasticity is

$$\frac{\%\Delta Q_d}{\%\Delta P} = \frac{\Delta Q_d/Q}{\Delta P/P} = \frac{\Delta Q_d}{Q} \times \frac{P}{\Delta P}.$$

Using this formula, derive the elasticity of demand for a product when the price changes from $1 to $1.50, $2 to $2.50, $3 to $3.75, and the change in quantity demanded is 15 to 10, 25 to 5, 50 to 30, respectively.

2. What are the three determinants of consumers' sensitivity to a change in price? Do these always work in the same direction?

3. Is it feasible to talk about *an* elasticity all along a single demand or supply curve? Why or why not?

4. Given that a price change remains in effect over a period of time, will elasticity increase or decrease? Why?

5. What is meant by cross elasticity? How is it algebraically different from elasticity of supply and elasticity of demand, which we calculated earlier?

6. What do cross elasticities indicate about relations between two goods?

7. What might reports about the link between aspirin consumption and heart attacks do to the elasticity of demand for aspirin?
8. Is the demand elasticity coefficient for large industrial consumers of electricity larger or smaller than that for residential users? If electric companies lower the price to both groups, would total revenues from each group change in the same direction?
9. Suppose a friend has an allowance of $25 per week. She spends all of her weekly income on banana splits. What is her income elasticity of demand for banana splits?
10. A college town pizza parlor decides to offer a back-to-school two-for-one special, in effect cutting the price of pizza in half. More pizzas will be sold according to the law of demand. Will the total receipts of the parlor increase, decrease, or remain the same if pizza consumption increases by 30 percent? By 80 percent?

PROBLEMS

1. Compute the price elasticity of demand for a change in price from $5 to $3.
2. Is the resulting value elastic, inelastic, or unit elastic?
3. Will the firm's total revenue rise or fall from such a price change?

ECONOMICS IN ACTION
Cigarettes, Gasoline, and Elasticity: The Effects of an Excise Tax

An excise tax is a simple per unit tax on the sale of a particular item. Tax collectors determine the amount of the taxable good sold by a retail or wholesale firm and require that the firm pay the amount of the tax times the quantity sold.

The equilibrium effects of an excise tax on cigarettes are shown in Figure 10. The hypothetical supply and demand curves for cigarettes before the excise tax are S_1 and D. The equilibrium price, E_1, is $1.75 per pack and the quantity is 50 million packs per day. The effect of a 30-cent-per-pack excise tax can be shown by shifting the supply curve vertically upward by 30 cents to S_2. For each quantity along S_2 the price at which producers were willing to offer that quantity has now increased by 30 cents. Producers were previously willing to offer 50 million packs for $1.75 each, but now they must receive $2.05 per pack to offer 50 million packs.

The new equilibrium quantity, E_2, is lower, at 40 million. This change occurs because buyers respond to price changes; their elasticity of demand for cigarettes is greater than zero. As the excise tax puts upward pressure on the price, a smaller quantity is demanded. Producers were willing to offer 40 million packs at a price of $1.60 before the tax. The posttax equilibrium price to consumers, P_c, is $1.90. From this price, producers must pay the 30-cent excise tax and receive the net price, P_p, of $1.60 per pack.

The total revenues received by the government from the tax may not be as great as some politicians expected. Before the tax was instituted, the quantity bought was 50 million. A simple multiplication of 30 cents times 50 million would yield an overestimate of tax revenues. The actual tax revenues are 30 cents times 40 million, the new equilibrium quantity. For any excise tax the elasticity of supply and demand must be taken into account before a projection is made for tax revenues.

The elasticities of supply and demand also determine the relative burden of the excise tax. Who actually pays the tax—producers or consumers—is shown by the change in price to the buyers and sellers. In this example, the price to consumers increased 15 cents and the net price to producers fell 15 cents. Here the burden is shared equally by consumers and producers, but this is not necessarily the case.

If demand had been relatively less elastic, then price would have increased more to consumers than it fell to producers. Figure 11a shows that with less elastic demand, more of the burden is shifted to consumers. Also, Figure

FIGURE 10
Effect of an Excise Tax on Cigarettes

When a 30-cent excise tax is added to the price of a pack of cigarettes, the entire supply curve for cigarettes shifts from S_1 to S_2. At the new equilibrium price, $1.90, the elasticity of demand is greater than zero; specifically, consumers will reduce their consumption of cigarettes by 10 million packs and total tax revenues will equal 40 million times the tax. The shaded area represents government tax revenues, the 30-cent excise tax per pack multiplied by the number of packs of cigarettes sold after the tax is imposed.

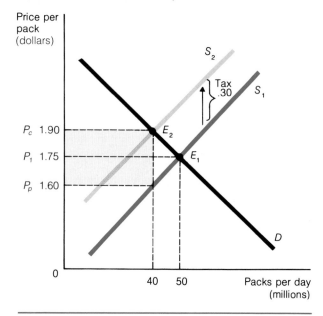

11b shows that if supply had been less elastic, more of the burden would have shifted back to the producers. Figure 11c shows that a more elastic demand also shifts more of the burden to producers.

Similarly, the effect of proposed changes in excise taxes on gasoline depends on demand and supply elasticity. In view of the large federal deficit and the stated opposition of the Bush administration to increased taxes, considerable attention is being given to raising federal excise taxes on gasoline by 15 to 20 cents per gallon, calling the tax a "user

FIGURE 11   Elasticity and the Relative Burden of a Tax

(a) With less elastic demand, more of the burden of an excise tax is shifted to consumers: At Q_1 consumers pay the equilibrium price P_1, but at Q_2 following a tax, consumers must pay P_c. (b) With less elastic supply, more of the burden of a tax is shifted to producers. (c) More elastic demand also shifts more of the burden to the producers.

(a)   (b)   (c)

fee." Given the nature of elasticities, such an increase would likely generate increased federal revenue. This is less certain to be the case, however, for states considering increases in gasoline excise taxes. If federal taxes are increased, gasoline prices will tend to rise uniformly in all states. This will induce consumers everywhere to conserve gasoline, but it will provide no incentive for consumers to switch gasoline purchases between states. In contrast, if a single state increased its excise taxes, gasoline prices there would rise. Consumers in that state would have an incentive both to conserve gasoline and to purchase gas in neighboring states. For certain regions, many buyers either reside in other states or can conveniently travel to adjacent states. Delaware officials, for example, should expect significant interstate substitution if they were to raise gasoline taxes. Demand for gasoline in Delaware (where substitutes are readily available in New Jersey or Maryland) is more elastic than demand in Montana, where most buyers must travel great distances to escape state taxes. Therefore, gasoline tax increases in states like Montana would likely prove more successful in generating tax revenue than they would in states like Delaware.

What would be the effects of a new and higher federal excise tax on gasoline? The price would rise, but not by the full amount of the increase. Producers and consumers would share the burden of the tax. However, the burden might not be shared equally. The tax revenues would equal the amount of the tax times the quantity sold *after* the tax was instituted. The change in price, the burden of the tax, and the level of tax revenues all would be determined by the elasticity of supply and demand.

To summarize the effects of an excise tax: The lower the elasticity of demand, the greater the price increase or tax burden to consumers. The lower the elasticity of supply, the greater the net price decrease or burden to the producers. And the greater the elasticity of supply or demand, the lower the total tax revenues.

Question

Why are federal and state taxes on alcoholic beverages so prevalent? If "moral objections" to such beverages are the reason for raising excise taxes, do you believe that the taxes have had the desired effects? Why or why not?

Adam Smith

Karl Marx

Adam Smith and Karl Marx: Markets and Society

ADAM SMITH, one of the most important figures in the history of economics, actually began his career as a lecturer in moral philosophy at Scotland's Glasgow College in 1751. Moral philosophy in Smith's time encompassed a wide range of topics, including natural theology, ethics, jurisprudence, and economics. In 1776, coincident with the Declaration of Independence, Smith published his second book (his first was a treatise on moral behavior), *An Inquiry into the Nature and Causes of the Wealth of Nations,* known usually by the shorter title *Wealth of Nations.* The book won much attention from scholars of the day, and it brought together most of what was then known about the workings of the market system. Smith was one of the most eloquent defenders of free markets and the promise of capitalism. More than two hundred years later, his insights are still being taught.

Smith was born in Kirkcaldy on the east coast of Scotland in 1723 and lived most of his life in his native country. Although known for his brilliant lectures (and for his many eccentricities), Smith did not devote his entire career to teaching. In 1778, he accepted a well-paying job as commissioner of Scottish customs, a post in which he remained until his death in 1790.

KARL MARX "*looked* like a revolutionary," writes Robert Heilbroner in *The Worldly Philosophers.* "He was stocky and powerfully built and rather glowering in expression with a formidable beard. He was not an orderly man; his home was a dusty mass of papers piled in careless disarray in the midst of which Marx himself, slovenly dressed, padded about in an eye-stinging haze of tobacco smoke."[a]

Marx wrote in response to the miseries of the European working class during the Industrial Revolution of the late eighteenth and nineteenth centuries. Coauthor with Friedrich Engels of the *Communist Manifesto,* which predicted the inevitable downfall of capitalism and the triumph of communism, Marx spent most of his life in difficult circumstances. His activities as a radical in the communist movement caused his exile from his native Germany as well as from Belgium and France. In 1849, a year after the publication of the *Manifesto,* he settled in London, where he and his family survived through the benevolence of Engels and where Marx researched and wrote *Das Kapital,* a theory and history of capitalism and its ills. Marx died in 1883 in London at the age of sixty-five.

---

[a]Robert L. Heilbroner, *The Worldly Philosophers* (New York: Simon and Schuster, 1953), p. 131.

THE "INVISIBLE HAND"

Smith's views of the free-market system are summarized in a passage from the *Wealth of Nations* in which he writes that individuals pursuing their own self-interest are "led by an invisible hand to promote an end which was no part of [their] intention."[b] Smith believed that by freely exchanging goods and services across markets, individuals contribute to the public good—the aggregate wealth of society—even though they act from purely self-interested motives. In other words, markets cause individuals to benefit others even though they intend only to benefit themselves.

To Smith, voluntary market exchange coordinated the decisions of consumers and producers and generated economic progress. Producers compete with one another to satisfy consumers with the most appropriate and cheapest goods and services, not out of the goodness of their hearts, not because government planners instruct them to do so, but simply because they maximize the profits of their enterprises by doing so. Markets coordinate supply and demand by way of the price system. Consumers express their preferences in their decisions about what to buy; producers attract customers by producing goods at the least cost. In this system of coordination without command, individuals pursuing their own interests are led "as if by an invisible hand" to mesh their interests with those of other individuals trading across markets.

Smith was not opposed to government, but argued that its proper role in society was to provide a legal framework—police and courts—within which the market could operate, as well as to provide certain other services (including national defense, highways, and education) that the market itself would either not supply or would tend to supply in inadequate amounts. Smith also felt that government should provide welfare services for the poor. But he strongly believed that government could best assist the market economy achieve growth by stepping out of the way—that is, by not regulating and by not granting monopoly privileges to favored groups and individuals.

In Smith's view, income was distributed in a market economy by the production of wealth. An individual's income was a strict function of the value of his or her output. Smith did not feel that income inequality by itself was unfair because the invisible hand ensured that individuals' wealth (or lack of it) was a measure of how much their efforts benefited society as a whole. Anyone can increase his or her income in a free market by serving the consumers in a new, better, or faster way.

THE "ANARCHY OF PRODUCTION"

Karl Marx rejected Smith's view of the market process. In *Das Kapital* he argued that Smith's writing represented merely the interests of the ruling capitalist class. To Marx, the market process was a system of exploitation by which owners of capital robbed their employees by paying them wages less than the worth of their labor (a situation he termed the *alienation of labor*).

The alternative social system that Marx thought would eliminate this exploitation and at the same time greatly increase the efficiency of production was a "general organization of the labor of society . . . [that] would turn all society into one immense factory."[c] He viewed the market economy as one of general disorganization. Its main feature was "the anarchy of production" where producers overproduced and consumers were forced to accept goods they neither wanted nor needed. He claimed that the market process, left to itself, could not coordinate diverse individual plans.

In Marx's view, Smith's "invisible hand" was a euphemism for describing the economic system in which "chance and caprice have full play in distributing the producers and their means of production among the various branches of industry. . . . [T]he division of labour within the society [the theme of much of Smith's *Wealth of Nations*] brings into contact independent commodity-producers, who acknowledge no other authority but that of competition, of the coercion exerted by the pressure of their mutual interests. . . . [T]he same bourgeois mind which praises division of labour in the workshop [as a conscious organization that increases productivity] denounces with equal vigour every conscious attempt to socially control and regulate the process of production."[d] Smith's "invisible hand" was not only invisible but also unbelievable to Marx. Only the central planning of economic activity by society (government), which owned all means of production, could coordinate the needs of consumers and producers and eliminate the wastefulness of capitalism. To Marx it was nonsense to describe the market as organized economic activity because there was no organizer. Coordination of economic activity requires the conscious, centralized control of the economy.

While Adam Smith described the emerging market economy of his day and offered reforms (mostly summarized by the phrase *less government*), Marx offered a vision of economic organization that did not exist at the time he wrote but that he maintained was the inevitable wave of the future. In a sense he was proven correct. Followers of the teachings of Marx and his admirer Lenin (who filled in many details of

[b]Adam Smith, *An Inquiry into the Nature and Causes of the Wealth of Nations,* ed. Edwin Cannan (1776; reprint, New York: Modern Library, 1937), p. 423.

[c]Karl Marx, *Das Kapital,* ed. Max Eastman (1867; reprint, New York: Modern Library, 1932), p. 83.

[d]Marx, *Das Kapital,* p. 83.

what a central planning system would look like in practice) imposed avowedly Marxist-socialist, centrally planned economies on Russia (1917), China (1949), most of the countries of Eastern Europe, and some African and Latin American nations.

In another sense Marx's teachings appear to have failed, as recent developments in the Eastern bloc have demonstrated. The centrally planned economies seem to function poorly—providing low per capita income and poor rates of economic growth—relative to the modern versions of the capitalist economies whose central principle of market organization was so clearly seen by Smith.

Microeconomics: Key Concepts

We have culled some of the most important principles of microeconomics from the pages of this book for presentation in this section. Separating these important concepts out from the text and presenting them as a group serves two purposes. First, it gives beginning students an idea of the scope of microeconomics and sets them on the road toward an economic way of thinking. Second, it provides students familiar with the basics of microeconomics an opportunity for review and—through the generous use of color, especially—an opportunity to see new relationships.

Simple Circular Flow

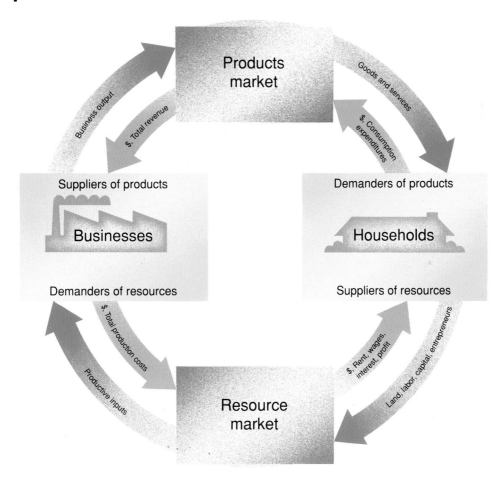

The simple circular flow diagram is an abstract view of the market economy in operation. Money flows from households—consumers, or demanders of products—through the products market to businesses and from businesses through the resource market back to households (in the form of rents, wages, interest, and profit). Resources—land, labor, capital, entrepreneurship—flow from households through the resource market to businesses, which use the resources to produce products that flow through the products market to households.

Production Possibilities Curve

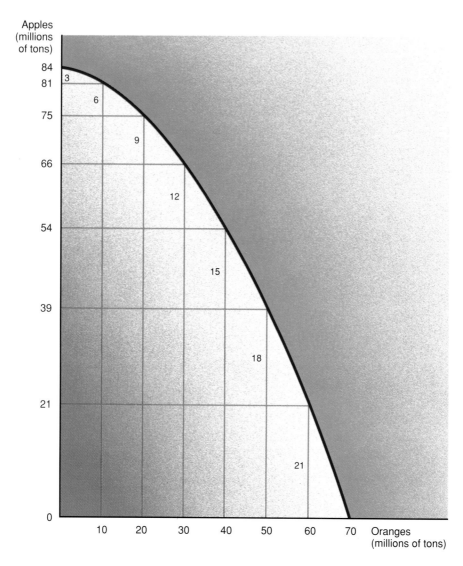

Apples (millions of tons) vs. Oranges (millions of tons)

A production possibilities curve shows all of the combinations of two goods that can be produced with a given amount of resources and with a given level of technology. The curve itself may be viewed as a boundary or frontier that separates the combinations of goods that can be produced—represented by points beneath and along the curve—from the combinations that cannot be produced—points lying beyond the curve.

The production of goods has an opportunity cost: As the production of one good increases, the amount produced of the other good must decrease. Here, the first 10 million tons of oranges produced costs society 3 million tons of apples. Further production increases of 10 million tons will decrease apple production by more than 3 million tons each time, however. This is the law of increasing opportunity costs, and it accounts for the bowed shape of the curve.

Supply, Demand, and Equilibrium Price

(a)

(b)

The prices of goods and the quantities produced are determined in markets by demand and supply. (a) The quantities of a given product that buyers are willing and able to purchase at various prices are shown by the demand curve; for example, buyers will purchase 24 units at a price of $55. (b) The quantities that sellers are willing and able to offer at all of the various prices are shown by the supply curve; at $55, sellers will offer 57 units. (c) Together, the demand and supply curves determine the equilibrium price—the price at which quantity demanded equals quantity supplied. The intersection of the demand and supply curves indicates the price at which there is no shortage and no surplus.

Here, equilibrium price is $37 and the equilibrium quantity is 38 units. The market will adjust—upward or downward—to this point under conditions of free competition among buyers and

(c)

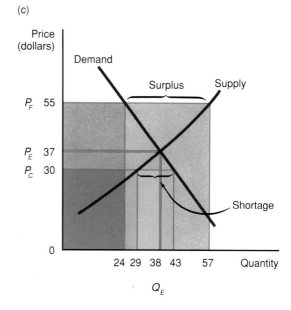

sellers. Sometimes, however, governments interfere with this process by mandating, or controlling, the prices for certain goods—price floors (minimum prices) or price ceilings (maximum prices). In this example, a price floor of $55 means that sellers will produce 33 more units than buyers will demand. Supply and demand are also out of sync with a price ceiling of $30; in this case, buyers' desires for 43 units of the product will outpace sellers' willingness to supply the product by 14 units.

Total and Marginal Utility

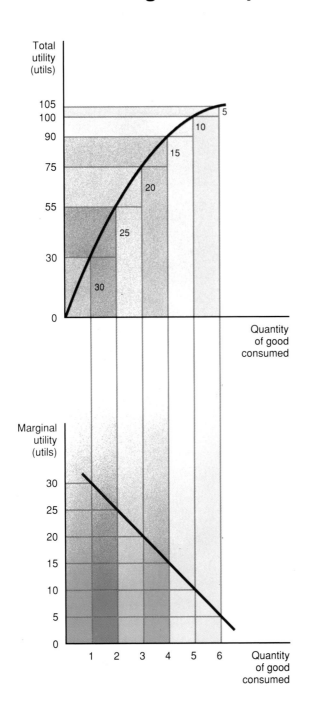

Total utility, or the total amount of satisfaction received from consuming a good, rises as more of the good is consumed. According to the principle of diminishing marginal utility, however, this satisfaction rises at a decreasing rate; the first unit adds more to total satisfaction than the second unit, and the second adds more than the third. Another way of stating this is to say that as more is consumed, the additional satisfaction, or marginal utility, falls. Marginal utility is the change in total utility that results from consumption of one more unit of the good. Marginal utility accounts for the decreasing slope of the total utility curve with each additional unit consumed.

PART TWO

The

Microeconomic

Behavior of

Consumers, Firms,

and Markets

6

The Logic of Consumer Choice and Demand

We have seen in Chapters 4 and 5 that the law of demand is an accurate and useful generalization about human behavior. Other things being equal, individuals will consume more of a good when its price is lower. Knowing that the law of demand works, however, does not tell us why it works. In this chapter we examine why individuals increase their purchases of a good or service when its price falls. The heart of the analysis involves how consumers deal with the problem of scarcity. In other words, given that a consumer has a fixed budget or income, how does he or she allocate the budget among goods and services to obtain the most satisfaction from consumption? When you finish Chapter 6 you should understand

- how consumers affix value to goods and services in the marketplace.
- how scarcity affects individual behavior.
- how the economic theory of consumer behavior explains the law of demand.
- how marginal utility explains consumer behavior.

This chapter analyzes consumer choice in two alternative but largely equivalent forms. In the body of the chapter, individual choice is analyzed in terms of marginal utility; in an appendix at the end of the chapter, the same analysis is cast in terms of indifference curves. Both approaches to the analysis of individual choice-making behavior are useful and introduce new tools and insights with which to study economic behavior.

UTILITY AND MARGINAL UTILITY

Utility:
A measure of the satisfaction that the consumption of goods or services yields an individual.

Why do we demand anything at all? The obvious answer is that we get satisfaction or pleasure from consuming goods and services. A vacation at the beach, a ticket to the big game, dinner at a fine restaurant all give us pleasure. Economists call this pleasure or satisfaction **utility.** Economics, unlike psychology, does not provide any fundamental answers to questions such as why some people prefer red shirts to blue shirts or why so many people like chocolate. Economics analyzes the results of people's preferences—the observations that people will demand or pay for those things that give them utility.

Although economics cannot offer an answer to questions such as why people like chocolate, economics is interested in the intensity of consumer desires for goods. Why will individuals pay $2.50 for a magazine and $1000 for a vacation at the beach? In other words, why is the intensity of demand, as reflected in the prices people are willing to pay, greater for some goods than for others? Economists address questions like these with the aid of the **principle of diminishing marginal utility.** This principle is a simple proposition: As people consume a good in greater and greater quantities, eventually they get less and less extra utility from that good.

Although the utility derived by a consumer from some good—shoes, books, raspberries—depends on many factors, such as past experience, education, and psychological traits that we may not be able to explain, the principle of diminishing marginal utility allows us to predict certain bounds for consumption behavior. Other things being equal, an individual will not be willing to pay more for an additional unit of good than what was paid for the last unit. Sooner or later, as the amount consumed increases, the consumer will be willing to pay even less for an additional unit because of diminishing marginal utility.

The principle of diminishing marginal utility is based on common sense. At lunch you might be ravenously hungry from skipping breakfast. The satisfaction, or utility, you get from eating the first hamburger in the cafeteria would likely be great. But after one giant burger, or certainly after two or three, the additional satisfaction you experience from one additional hamburger must decline. The amount of money that you would be willing to pay for additional burgers—amounts that reflect their **marginal utility** for you—would also decline.

Some given time period of consumption also must be specified in order for the principle of diminishing marginal utility to be relevant to behavior. Why, for example, do vending machine sellers of soft drinks and foods use costly and elaborate procedures to prevent buyers from stealing, while newspaper sellers usually permit the purchaser to take as many papers as he or she wants after the first is purchased?[1] It is because the marginal utility of the second or third candy bar, sandwich, or soft drink does not diminish much or at all after the first is consumed if the consumer paces his or her consumption of them through time. The additional utility you get from the fifth soft drink or prepackaged sandwich is clearly less if all are consumed over the period of an hour. However, packages of peanuts and diet drinks can be saved for later consumption. The utility of a daily newspaper, once read, is ordinarily used up immediately. The *marginal* utility of a second daily paper is low or zero, and vendors do not ordinarily use up costly resources in order to prevent you from taking three or four papers after paying for one. More "honesty" is therefore expected among paper buyers than would be expected from consum-

---

[1]The example is suggested by the delightful mystery novel by Marshall Jevons, *The Fatal Equilibrium* (Cambridge, Mass.: MIT Press, 1985), pp. 113–14. We highly recommend this book, which employs marginal utility and other basic economic concepts to solve a series of murders.

ers of other products from vending machines, and the theory of diminishing marginal utility explains why.

The principle of diminishing marginal utility can be numerically and graphically illustrated. Most people use umbrellas as shields from rain and sun. Unfortunately, umbrellas are items that are easily misplaced or lost; in addition, they are sometimes not available when we need them. Many of us, therefore, own more than one umbrella, although the first umbrella we own obviously yields us the most satisfaction, since, without it, we would go unprotected from the elements. Consider the data in Table 1 and Figure 1. Table 1 indicates the relation between the number of umbrellas a consumer owns, the **total utility** the consumer derives from umbrellas, and the marginal utility of each additional umbrella to the consumer. For convenience, economists construct imaginary units called *utils* with which to measure quantities of utility derived by the umbrella consumer. Note that as the number of umbrellas owned increases, total utility—a measure of the total satisfaction gained from the entire amount consumed—increases, but at a decreasing rate. Marginal utility—the satisfaction gained by the consumer from each additional umbrella—declines as the consumer acquires additional umbrellas.

In Figure 1a, the dotted step lines measure the total utility generated by the consumption of umbrellas. A smooth curve has been drawn through the steps to show the positive relation between units of consumption and total utility. Notice that as consumption increases, total utility increases, but at a decreasing rate. The downward-sloping curve in Figure 1b shows the corresponding marginal utility associated with each umbrella acquired. As more umbrellas are consumed, the marginal utility of each additional umbrella declines.

Total utility:
The total amount of satisfaction derived from consuming any given quantity of a good or service.

TABLE 1   **Total Utility and Marginal Utility**

The umbrella consumer buys and uses between 1 and 5 umbrellas. The satisfaction the consumer gains from the umbrellas is measured in imaginary units called *utils*. Total utility increases as the consumer adds more umbrellas to his or her stock, but marginal utility—the satisfaction associated with each additional umbrella—decreases.

Umbrellas Acquired	Total Utility (utils)	Marginal Utility (extra utils per umbrella)
1	6	6
2	11	5
3	15	4
4	18	3
5	20	2

FIGURE 1

(a) Total utility increases, but at a decreasing rate, as more and more umbrellas are added to the consumer's stock. (b) Marginal utility declines with each additional umbrella.

Total Utility and Marginal Utility

(a)

(b)

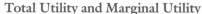

CONSUMER EQUILIBRIUM: DIMINISHING MARGINAL UTILITY PUT TO WORK

If the principle of diminishing marginal utility applies only to a consumer's choices regarding umbrellas, then it is not very useful. To be useful, the concept of diminishing marginal utility must help us explain behavior in a world in which many different goods are consumed.

Basic Assumptions

To use diminishing marginal utility to understand consumer behavior, four postulates of consumer behavior need to hold.

many goods substitutable

1. Each consumer desires a multitude of goods, and no one good is so precious that it will be consumed to the exclusion of other goods. Moreover, goods can be substituted for one another as alternative means of yielding satisfaction. For example, the consumer good of exercise can be satisfied by jogging, playing basketball, hiking, swimming, or a number of other activities. Dinner offers a variety of choices—steak, chicken, pizza, and so on.

fixed, const. prices

budget constraint

Consrs max satisfaction or utility

2. Consumers must pay prices for the things they want. This seems obvious, but for the purposes of the following analysis it is convenient to assume that consumers pay fixed, constant prices for the things they choose to buy. We will ignore such things as consumers searching out bargains, different prices at different stores, and quantity discounts. Each good carries a given price no matter how much is bought or where it is bought.

3. Consumers cannot afford everything they want. They have a budget or income constraint that forces them to limit their consumption and to make choices about what they will consume.

4. Consumers seek the most satisfaction they can get from spending their limited funds for consumption. Consumers are not irrational. They make conscious, purposeful choices designed to increase their well-being. This does not mean that consumers do not make mistakes or sometimes make impulsive purchases that they later regret. By gaining experience over time as they deal in goods and services, consumers try to get the most possible satisfaction from their limited budgets given their past experience.

Balancing Choices Among Goods

Armed with these postulates, we can better understand the behavior of consumers in the real world. To see how diminishing marginal utility works in a practical setting, assume that you—a consumer—are deciding how much of two goods to choose: movies and rock concerts. For each additional dollar you spend on movies, you experience an increase in utility. Simultaneously, you forgo the utility you could have experienced by spending the dollar on concerts. Because you seek to maximize the satisfaction you get from your consumption expenditures (postulate number 4), you will spend your additional dollar on the good that yields you the largest increase in utility—that is, the good with the greatest marginal utility for you.

According to the principle of diminishing marginal utility, whether the utility of one good is greater than the other depends on the amount of each good consumed. If, during a month, you have already attended a large number of concerts but have seen relatively few movies, the marginal utility of concerts will tend to be low and that of movies high for you. You are therefore more likely to spend an additional dollar on movies than on concerts.

In this simple world of two goods, you will continue to spend additional dollars on movies until the marginal utility you receive from an additional dollar spent on movies is equal to the marginal utility of an additional dollar spent on concerts. This process of reaching equality in the two marginal utilities per dollar occurs naturally because the marginal utility of movies declines relative to the marginal utility of concerts as you pay to attend more movies. When the marginal utility per dollar of consuming the two goods is equal, you have maximized the total utility of your purchases, subject to the resources you have to spend. In other words, at the point of equality of marginal utility per last dollar spent, you will have no incentive to alter the pattern of your choices between rock concerts and movies. This condition of balance in consumer purchases, from which there is no tendency to change, is called **consumer equilibrium.**

How do economists take the differing goods—as well as their differing marginal utilities—into account? Note that consumer equilibrium occurs

Consumer equilibrium: A situation in which a consumer chooses quantities of goods that maximize total utility given a budget constraint; equilibrium implies that the per-dollar marginal utility obtained from the last unit of each good consumed is equal for all goods.

where the marginal utility of a dollar's worth of concerts is equal to the marginal utility of a dollar's worth of movies. To accommodate the differing goods, the following equation is used to describe the condition of consumer equilibrium:

$$\frac{\text{Marginal utility of concerts}}{\text{Price of concerts}} = \frac{\text{Marginal utility of movies}}{\text{Price of movies}}.$$

Equilibrium is reached when the marginal utility of the last concert attended divided by the price of a concert is equal to the marginal utility of the last movie seen divided by the price of a movie.

This equation is just a representation of consumer equilibrium. To see what it means, assume that concerts cost $12 and movies cost $6, and that you, the consumer, are initially not in equilibrium. This means that the above equation does not hold for you—that is,

$$\frac{\text{Marginal utility of concerts}}{\$12} \neq \frac{\text{Marginal utility of movies}}{\$6}.$$

Suppose that you begin by buying a movie ticket because its marginal utility to you is initially higher than that of concerts.

$$\frac{\text{Marginal utility of movies}}{\$6} > \frac{\text{Marginal utility of concerts}}{\$12}$$

As you attend more movies the marginal utility of an additional movie seen declines relative to the marginal utility of an additional concert attended. At each point you are trying to get the most possible satisfaction from your expenditures on the two goods—you are balancing the marginal utility of spending a dollar toward an additional movie against the marginal utility of spending a dollar on another concert.

At the end of the process, as the ratio of the marginal utility of movies to the price of movies declines relative to the ratio of the marginal utility of concerts to the price of concerts, equality between the two ratios is reached. Consumer equilibrium is restored at the point where additional movies seen add 2 times as much utility as a concert. Put another way, you will adjust your consumption of the two goods until the marginal utility of a dollar's worth of movies is equal to the marginal utility of a dollar's worth of concerts. This is what the equation of consumer equilibrium means and how it is reached by a consumer. (See Focus, "Marginal Utility and the Allocation of Students' Time," for an example of how marginal utilities are balanced in everyday situations.)

The Budget Constraint and Consumer Equilibrium

Consider a more specific and highly stylized example of how a consumer maximizes utility in the everyday world. Assume that a student consumer, Keith, is trying to allocate his (hypothetical) food budget on two goods—macaroni and cheese and pizza—over some given time period. (As everyone recognizes, the real world offers thousands of goods and opportunities to increase one's budget over time through hard work or borrowing.) Call macaroni and cheese product X, pizza product Y and Keith's relative preferences

FOCUS   Marginal Utility and the Allocation of Students' Time

It is a typical Sunday evening, and you have to decide whether to watch television or prepare for a history exam scheduled for Tuesday. This is not an "either/or" proposition since you can spend a portion of your time on each of the two activities. This kind of time management, which college students confront daily, is a straightforward application of basic economic theory. Assuming that each of the television programs you like to watch is an hour long and that each history chapter assigned takes two hours to read, the price to you of each chapter of history is twice the price of each television program. The price you must pay for each chapter you read is two hours of your time—twice the price of each hour-long program. Therefore, to equate the ratios of marginal utility per unit of cost (measured in terms of time), you should work on history as long as an additional chapter gives you at least two times the marginal utility you receive from watching one more television show. In other words, you should "solve" the problem in the following way:

$$\frac{MU_H}{P_H} = \frac{MU_T}{P_T},$$

where MU_H is the marginal utility to you of mastering an additional history chapter, MU_T is your marginal utility of watching an additional television program, P_H is the time cost of reading a history chapter, and P_T is the time cost of watching a television program.

Usually students do not consciously think in terms of ratios of marginal utilities and prices in making such decisions. When you find yourself closing your history book and saying, "I'm tired of studying history," you are really saying that you have reached the point where the return per hour of studying has fallen below the return per hour of watching

television. Under these circumstances, your decision will not maximize your history grade, but it will maximize your utility.

The same framework of analysis applies if the cost of competing activities includes both time and money. If, for example, preparing for the history exam requires you to do outside reading at the library and you must pay for parking there, the price of history will have risen. Therefore, your initial allocation of time would no longer equate marginal utility per unit of cost for the two activities. To maximize your utility, you should increase the time spent watching television and decrease the time on history, with the full price of history being higher, $MU_H/P_H \leq MU_T/P_T$.

This framework can also explain why choices of this type differ systematically between types of students. Other things equal, one would predict that premed students will devote proportionately more time to studying than other students. To them, the marginal utility from improved grades is high compared to other students. It also explains why students with great interest in either sports or old movies generally make lower grades; for them, the marginal utility from time spent watching television is high, so they allocate more time to television. Similarly, speed-readers are generally better prepared for exams, because the price to them in terms of time studying history is lower. Although the behavior of individual students differs widely, each behaves in a utility-maximizing way.

All students have received such advice as "Study at least three hours per night," or "Never watch television until you have completed all your assignments." This advice may boost your grades, but it will not necessarily maximize your happiness. To do that, you must equate the ratios of marginal utility to price for all your activities.

for macaroni and cheese versus pizza MU_X and MU_Y, respectively. It is clear from Table 2 that Keith prefers pizza to macaroni and cheese. The marginal utility of the first unit of pizza consumed brings Keith 80 utils, whereas the first box of macaroni and cheese yields only 50. Likewise, for every successive unit from the first to the seventh of the two meals consumed, Keith's utility preference is for pizza over macaroni and cheese. How, then, do we explain why individuals always buy combinations of goods in order to maximize their utility? What rule do we apply to Keith's consumer behavior to explain how choices are actually made? The rule is simple: *Consumers will always balance the consumption of all of the various goods purchased so as to maximize utility given their respective budget constraints.*

Knowing that Keith prefers pizza to macaroni and cheese is not enough to explain the decisions he makes. Many of us would say that we would prefer (have a higher preference for) a Maserati or a Porsche to a Ford or a Yugo.

TABLE 2

A Consumer's Utility Maximization

Keith, a consumer with preferences for two goods, chooses a utility-maximizing combination of macaroni and cheese and pizzas by equating the "adjusted" marginal utilities of the two goods under an income constraint. When his income is $34, he buys 2 boxes of macaroni and cheese and 3 pizzas.

Units of Product	Product X: Macaroni and Cheese (boxes) Price: $2 per box		Product Y: Pizzas (12-inch) Price: $10 per pizza	
	(1) Marginal Utility (utils)	(2) Marginal Utility (per dollar's worth)	(3) Marginal Utility (utils)	(4) Marginal Utility (per dollar's worth)
First	50	25	80	8
Second	8	4	50	5
Third	4	2	40	4
Fourth	2	1	20	2
Fifth	0	0	10	1
Sixth	−2	−1	0	0
Seventh	−10	−5	−40	−4

Most of us do not buy high-priced sports cars, however, when our utilities are adjusted for the relative prices of these two categories of automobile and when, for most of us, our incomes are considered. Thus, the marginal utilities of *all* goods consumed must be adjusted by the prices of those goods before we can explain the choices consumers make.

Price adjustments are made to the marginal utilities of macaroni and cheese and pizza in columns (2) and (4) of Table 2. If we assume that the price of macaroni and cheese is $2 per box and pizzas are $10 each, the marginal utilities *per dollar's worth* of the two goods may be readily calculated. For the first unit of macaroni and cheese, for example, the marginal utility per dollar's worth, or MU_X/P_X, is equal to 25 (50/$2). For the first unit of pizza, the marginal utility per dollar's worth, or MU_Y/P_Y, is equal to 8, or 80 divided by $10. Just as in the case of movies and rock concerts, consumers will attempt to balance these "adjusted" marginal utilities to maximize satisfaction given their income or budget constraint. Consider Keith's choices. As soon as he has an income of $2 per time period he will buy a box of macaroni and cheese. Why? Because the marginal utility per dollar's worth of this item is greater than that of the first unit of pizza.

As Keith's budget or income constraint becomes less stringent, his consumption pattern changes, as Table 2 shows. Suppose that his budget rises to $12 over the time period. Table 2 tells us that he will buy the first unit of pizza in preference to more macaroni and cheese. The first unit of pizza would add 50 utils to his total utility, whereas 5 more boxes of macaroni and cheese would add only 12 utils to his satisfaction. (With consumption of 5 more units of macaroni and cheese, he would gain 8 + 4 + 2 + 0 + (−2) = 12, as verified in column (1) of Table 2.) Indeed, Keith would never want to buy a unit of any commodity that yielded a negative marginal utility as the sixth unit of macaroni and cheese would. To maximize satisfaction, Keith will buy the first pizza with the additional $10 in income.

When his budget rises to $34 for these two products, Keith is in equilibrium when he buys 2 units of product X (macaroni and cheese) and 3 units of product Y (pizza). To see why this level of consumption is an equilibrium level, simply calculate the *total* utility that Keith receives. His total satisfaction on good X will be 58 utils (50 + 8), and the total utility obtained from good Y will be 170 (80 + 50 + 40), for a total of 228 utils of satisfaction. With $34 Keith could buy other possible combinations of products such as 7 boxes of macaroni and cheese and 2 pizzas, but this purchase would yield a lower total satisfaction (52 utils on X and 130 on Y, for a total of 182 utils). Keith is looking for the *utility-maximizing combination*, and that is always found where the marginal utilities per dollar's worth of the two (or more) goods or services are equal. In terms of the simple problems considered in Table 2, equilibrium occurs when the dollar-adjusted marginal utilities of the items purchased are equal,

Eqm cond^n →

$$\frac{MU_{\text{macaroni and cheese}}}{P_{\text{macaroni and cheese}}} = \frac{MU_{\text{pizza}}}{P_{\text{pizza}}}$$

or where

$$\frac{8}{\$2} = \frac{40}{\$10}.$$

All of us, moreover, are subject to a budget constraint. In Keith's case, the income constraint is assumed to be $34 dollars; the sum of the total expenditures for both items must equal that amount.

Budget constraint →

$$P_{\text{mac}} \times Q_{\text{mac}} + P_{\text{pizza}} \times Q_{\text{pizza}} = \$34$$

$$\$2 \times 2 + \$10 \times 3 = \$34$$

Here we assume that Keith, the consumer, expends all of his income on macaroni and cheese and pizza. This assumption is a simplification, since any consumer typically purchases hundreds or even thousands of goods and saves and borrows, as well. Some of these complications are treated below, but the same principles of utility maximization in equilibrium always apply. Symbolically, the equilibrium conditions for maximum consumer satisfaction may be stated

$$\frac{MU_X}{P_X} = \frac{MU_Y}{P_Y}.$$

This equilibrium condition for maximum consumer satisfaction is always subject to a budget constraint, or

$$P_X X + P_Y Y = \text{Income.}$$

Let's consider some other aspects of utility-maximizing behavior. Suppose that Keith receives an additional $8 in income to add to his $34, enlarging his constraint to $42. What would he do? Keith would be in temporary disequilibrium, since he cannot purchase a fourth pizza and gain an additional 20 utils. Four more boxes of macaroni and cheese (the third through the sixth) would net him only 4 units of utility. Keith is in this quandary due to a problem of indivisibility. If boxes of macaroni and cheese and pizza were divisible, Keith would purchase a bit more of each of these consumables so that he would be in equilibrium. He would make the adjusted marginal utilities equal, and he would meet the budget constraint. In many cases, commodities are divisible. The lesson, however, is this: In the real world indivisibilities may exist, meaning that consumers may find themselves in temporary disequilibrium.

Another interesting aspect of the consumer equilibrium described above is that Keith or any consumer will never knowingly consume a unit of any good or service that brings him or her *negative* marginal utility. Even if Keith's budget constraint permitted him to purchase 7 boxes of macaroni and cheese and 7 pizzas over the time period, he would never do so. Even if both of the commodities were *free*, Keith would never consume more than 5 boxes of macaroni and cheese and 6 pizzas. The purchase of units of goods giving negative marginal utilities will reduce the total utility produced in these consumptions. The two last boxes of macaroni and cheese would reduce total utility by 12 utils and the last pizza would cause it to decline by 40 utils. No rational consumer would spend scarce resources to reduce utility.

Consumers Maximize Satisfaction Among Thousands of Goods

The two-good examples for entertainment and for food consumption are simplifications of consumers' actual choices among thousands of goods and services. We not only consume food and entertainment but such items as electricity, medical services, music lessons, and cable television. To express the general condition of consumer equilibrium, the two-good equation may be expanded, with N denoting the total number of goods and services consumed. If $X, Y, Z, \ldots N$ are goods in the consumer's budget; $MU_X, MU_Y, MU_Z, \ldots MU_N$ are the marginal utilities of these goods and services; and $P_X, P_Y, P_Z, \ldots P_N$ represent the corresponding prices of these goods and services, then

$$\frac{MU_X}{P_X} = \frac{MU_Y}{P_Y} = \frac{MU_Z}{P_Z} = \ldots \frac{MU_N}{P_N}.$$

The only numbers we have to put in the consumer equilibrium equation are the prices of the goods. We do not know—or need to know—what the subjective marginal utilities of the consumer are. The important point about the equation is that it is a proposition about individual behavior. It outlines how consumers will achieve balance or equilibrium in allocating their incomes among goods and services. In a sense, consumers assign their own utility numbers and arrange their patterns of consumption to achieve equilibrium; that is, they buy less of one good in order to buy more of another. Consumers solve the equation for themselves as an expression of their rational choices.

Consumers will equate the "adjusted" marginal utilities in the consumer equilibrium equation subject to an income constraint; in other words, the sum of all expenditures made on each item in the budget equals total income.

$$P_X X + P_Y Y + P_Z Z + \ldots P_N N = \text{Income}.$$

In the budget constraint equation, prices of all the various goods and services as well as the consumer's income must be supplied, reminding us that utility is maximized only under an individual's budget limitations. As noted in the case of Keith's choices, the individual can only maximize satisfaction subject to given prices (of macaroni and cheese and pizzas in Keith's case) and to income. The explanation given here of the rational consumer's behavior only states that the individual *always* acts to maximize his or her satisfaction or utility—whatever that may be to any individual—given the economic environment. That environment always includes the prices of individual goods and services and the consumer's income, as the equations for consumer equilibrium indicate.

Is consumer choice always rational? In describing the famous diamond-water paradox (see Focus, "The Diamond-Water Paradox"), Adam Smith pondered what seemed to be an irrational willingness of consumers to spend vast sums of money on "useless" goods like diamonds. The principle of diminishing marginal utility, developed many years after Smith's writings, helps us understand the rationality behind such choices.

FROM DIMINISHING MARGINAL UTILITY TO THE LAW OF DEMAND

The marginal utility equation helps us understand the relation between diminishing marginal utility and the law of demand. Assume that you, the consumer, are in equilibrium with movies priced at $6 and concerts priced at $12. The equation of consumer equilibrium then looks like this:

$$\frac{MU_{\text{movies}}}{\$6} = \frac{MU_{\text{concerts}}}{\$12}.$$

If the price of concerts falls to $6, this equality will be upset. The resulting disequilibrium will be temporary, however, for you will act to restore equality by attending more concerts. As you attend more concerts, the principle of diminishing marginal utility tells us that the marginal utility of concerts for you will fall in proportion to their lower price. When the marginal utility of concerts has fallen by the same proportion that their price has fallen, consumer equilibrium will be restored.

Note the relation of this behavior to the law of demand. Because the price has been reduced, you will attend more concerts until a dollar's worth of concerts generates no more utility for you than a dollar's worth of movies— or anything else. The law of demand says that consumers will respond to a fall in the relative price of a good by purchasing more of that good. Diminishing marginal utility thus provides a behavioral basis for the law of demand. When price falls, consumption increases until consumer equilibrium is again established.

The Substitution Effect and Income Effect

Substitution effect:
The change in the quantity demanded of a good that results only from a change in the relative price of the good.

Consumers' tendency to buy more of a good when its price drops in relation to the price of other goods is called the **substitution effect.** The relatively cheaper good is substituted for other now relatively more expensive goods. Concerts are substituted for movies when the price of concerts drops. Technically, the substitution effect refers to that portion of the increase or decrease in quantity demanded of a good that is the direct result of its change in price relative to the price of other goods.

FOCUS   The Diamond-Water Paradox

Adam Smith formulated the diamond-water paradox when he observed:

Things which have the greatest value in use frequently have little or no value in exchange; and on the contrary, those which have the greatest value in exchange have frequently little or no value in use. Nothing is more useful than water; but it will scarce purchase anything, scarce anything can be had in exchange for it. A diamond, on the contrary, has scarce any value in use; but a very great quantity of other goods may frequently be had in exchange for it.[a]

Water is useful but cheap; diamonds are not useful but expensive. This seems paradoxical. But using the principle of diminishing marginal utility, what errors can we find in Smith's reasoning about the paradox?

First, Smith failed to grasp the importance of the relative scarcity of a commodity in determining its value in use, or marginal utility. He compared a single diamond with the total

[a]Adam Smith, *An Inquiry into the Nature and Causes of the Wealth of Nations,* ed. Edwin Cannan (1776; reprint, New York: Modern Library, 1937), p. 28.

supply of water. Had he compared the marginal utility of a single diamond with a single gallon of water, no other water being available, the paradox would have disappeared, for the scarce water would be considered quite valuable. As economic theorists later discovered, water commands little in exchange because its supply is so abundant relative to the intensity of consumer desire for it. Diamonds are scarce relative to consumer desires and therefore command much in exchange. There is no diamond-water paradox when one focuses on the value of the marginal unit of supply to the consumer. Water is plentiful and cheap; diamonds are scarce and expensive.

Second, Smith makes a personal judgment of utility when he suggests that diamonds have no value in use. Many wearers and investors in diamonds would disagree on this point. Modern utility theory does not allow judgments to be made that some preferences are good and others bad.

Of course, Adam Smith did not have modern utility theory available to him when he wrote his statement. Indeed, it was in trying to resolve this simple paradox that modern utility theory was developed by economists in the nineteenth century in Europe and England.

Price, however, is not the only relevant factor affecting the quantity demanded of a good. Changes in wealth or income will also tend to shift the demand curve for goods, as we saw in Chapter 4. The larger an individual's income, the more he or she will demand of most goods.[2] Other things being equal (primarily the prices of other goods remaining the same), the fall in price of a particular good will raise the **real income,** or buying power, of the individual consumer. This change in real income means that the consumer can buy more goods under the same budget constraint as before. This **income effect** can be stated more technically: It is that portion of the change in the quantity demanded of a good that is the direct result of the change in the individual's real income that resulted from a price change.

Real income:
The buying power of a consumer's budget; determined by the consumer's money income and the prices of goods and services.

Income effect:
The change in the quantity demanded of a good that results from a change in real income.

Marginal Utility and the Law of Demand

The principle of diminishing marginal utility and the law of demand are thus closely related. A price change leads to a change in quantity demanded, which is composed of a substitution effect and an income effect. When the price of a good falls relative to the prices of other goods, the principle of diminishing

---

[2]Increases or decreases in quantity demanded as a result of an increase in income will depend upon whether the good in question is normal or inferior. Goods for which consumption increases as the consumer's income rises, such as medical care, are called *normal goods*. When the consumption of a good falls with increases in income, we say that such goods are *inferior goods*. Used cars may be an example of an inferior good. See Chapter 4 for a discussion of these terms.

marginal utility, acting by means of the substitution effect, tends to increase the quantity of the good that the consumer demands. The income effect is a separate and distinct influence that generally reinforces the substitution effect; that is, the income effect tends to increase the quantity demanded of the good whose price has fallen. Though there are cases where the income effect can pull in the opposite direction from the substitution effect, as in the case of an inferior good, economists generally predict that the strength of the substitution effect will outweigh the strength of the income effect, leading to an increase in the quantity demanded of a good whose relative price has fallen.

Sometimes people claim that they have found exceptions to the law of demand, but the exceptions turn out, on close examination, to be based on simple mistakes in reasoning. For example, sometimes a fall in price of a good seems to result in a decline in the quantity demanded of that good. A department store may actually sell less furniture after it lowers furniture prices. If we look closer at such cases, we may find that, in the calculations of consumers, the relative price of furniture has not fallen. Consumers may judge that the store is phasing out its furniture department and, as a result, expect that furniture prices will soon be even lower. What is crucial to consumers is that, relative to the expected future price, the present "sale" price of furniture has actually risen. This is the law of demand in action—relative and not absolute prices matter to consumers.

One more of the many possible examples of an apparent, but not real, exception of the law of demand is the case of a "prestige" good. The demand for caviar, for example, is sometimes said to be much higher as an expensive item than it would be if its price per pound were comparable to, say, tuna fish. The high price of caviar is said to actually increase the quantity demanded of caviar, contrary to the law of demand. But this notion is confused. Would the quantity demanded of caviar continue to increase as the price rose to $1000, $10,000, or $1 million per pound? It would not. Although prestige goods are usually expensive goods, they do not defy the law of demand. If they did, we would see their prices rise without limit, which does not happen.

Although there may be exceptions to the law of demand, they are extremely hard to find. You might at first think of exceptions that are probably not really exceptions after all. The law of demand seems to describe the way people behave in virtually all cases.

SOME PITFALLS TO AVOID

The principles of diminishing marginal utility and marginal utility analysis are useful constructs for analyzing individual behavior. As we have seen, they help explain individual choice behavior and they offer a richer understanding of the law of demand. In using this analysis, however, some fairly common misunderstandings must be avoided.

1. The individual wishing to maximize utility is motivated by personal self-interests, but the principle says nothing about what those interests may be. They may be based on purely selfish, greedy goals or on humanitarian concern for others. Marginal utility analysis does not specify the goals or desires of individuals; it is useful only in understanding and analyzing individual behavior once those goals have been specified.

2. Only individuals make economic decisions. When we refer to a government agency, a corporation, or a snorkeling club as making a decision, we are only using a figure of speech. Take away the individual members who compose these organizations, and nothing is left to make a decision. This reminder is a principle of positive economics, necessary to avoid confusion.

3. Economics is concerned with the effects of scarcity on the lives of people. It does not address the issue of human needs. A need is not an object that can be measured in a way that everyone can agree on (like the size of a desk or the height of a building). Needs are subjective, just like love, justice, and honor. Economics is neutral with respect to subjective judgments. Marginal utility analysis and the law of demand allow us to discuss resource allocation without having to argue about what "real needs" are.

4. Marginal utility analysis is an explanation, not a description, of individual choice behavior. Economists do not claim that individual consumers actually calculate marginal utility trade-offs before they go shopping. Indeed, most consumers, if asked, would probably deny that they behave in the way that marginal utility analysis suggests they do. The proof is obviously in the pudding. Individuals behave so as to generate the same outcomes they would generate if they actually did calculate and equate marginal utilities. Marginal utility analysis explains the outcomes we observe rather than describing the mental process involved.

SUMMARY

1. As individuals, we demand goods and services because the consumption of material things gives us utility, or satisfaction.

2. The principle of diminishing marginal utility says that the more we consume of a good, the less utility we get from consuming additional amounts of that good.

3. Consumer equilibrium occurs when individuals obtain the most possible utility from their limited budgets. Their respective consumption patterns are in balance, and they cannot increase total utility by altering the way they allocate their given budgets among goods.

4. In equation form, consumer equilibrium for N goods (the total number of goods and services that a consumer chooses from) is

$$\frac{MU_X}{P_X} = \frac{MU_Y}{P_Y} = \frac{MU_Z}{P_Z} = \ldots \frac{MU_N}{P_N}.$$

In other words, the ratio of marginal utility to price is equal among all the goods a consumer purchases. The consumer's purchases, however, are always limited by a budget constraint.

$$P_X X + P_Y Y + P_Z Z + \ldots P_N N = \text{Income}$$

5. The principle of diminishing marginal utility underlies the law of demand. In the first equation above, if the price of X falls, the equality of the marginal utility ratios is upset. To restore equality, the consumer will consume more of the good that has fallen in price, driving its marginal utility down proportionate to its fall in price. This is equivalent to the type of behavior predicted by the law of demand. Other things being equal, more of a good is consumed when its price falls.

6. The increase in consumption of a good when its price falls is caused by two effects. More is consumed because the price of the good has fallen relative to the prices of other goods. This is called the substitution effect. In addition, more is consumed because the consumer has more real income owing to the fall in price. This is called the income effect.

7. Generally, the substitution and income effects taken together lead to increased consumption of a good when its price falls.

8. The law of demand is a widespread empirical regularity. We observe its action everywhere. Supposed exceptions to the law are usually just misapplications or misunderstandings of basic economic principles.

9. Marginal utility analysis does not specify or judge goals, address issues of social needs, refer to group behavior, or describe the mental process by which consumers make choices; it merely explains the observed patterns of consumers in making those choices.

KEY TERMS

utility	marginal utility	substitution effect
principle of diminishing marginal utility	total utility	real income
	consumer equilibrium	income effect

QUESTIONS FOR REVIEW AND DISCUSSION

1. What is meant by *utility*? Is it calculable? Why do economists not speak of *economic needs*?
2. Define *marginal utility*.
3. What are the four postulates of consumer preference?
4. Express consumer equilibrium algebraically in terms of marginal utility. Explain what your expression means in words.
5. "I love seafood so much that I could never get enough of it." Why would an economist disagree with this statement? Could there ever be a time when the person making this statement might actually receive negative utility from consuming more seafood? Give your answer in a graph and in words.

6. Explain the difference between substitution effects and income effects. Which would we expect to dominate during a period of changing demand? During economic downturn and deflation? During economic prosperity and inflation?
7. Oil is essential to the economic life of the nation. Our machines and homes cannot run without it. Yet a quart of oil is cheaper than a ticket to the Super Bowl. How can oil be so precious and yet so cheap? Resolve this oil–Super Bowl paradox.
8. Two economists are walking past a Porsche dealer's showroom. One says, "I really want one of those Porsche 928s." The other says, "Obviously not." Who is right, and why?

PROBLEMS

1. Let the following table represent the total utility you receive from consuming chocolate chip cookies and glasses of milk. Calculate the marginal utilities.

Number of Cookies	Total Utility	Marginal Utility	Number of Glasses of Milk	Total Utility	Marginal Utility
1	14	——	1	10	——
2	26	——	2	18	——
3	36	——	3	24	——
4	44	——	4	28	——
5	48	——	5	28	——
6	48	——	6	27	——
7	44	——	7	24	——

2. Suppose you visit a friend's house whose family's policy is "all-you-can-eat-and-drink." According to the table how many cookies and how many glasses of milk will you consume?

3. Suppose the price of cookies at a cookie shop in the mall is 25 cents each and the price of milk is 50 cents per glass. Calculate the marginal utility per dollar to you at these prices.

Cookies	MU/$	Glasses	MU/$
1	——	1	——
2	——	2	——
3	——	3	——
4	——	4	——
5	——	5	——
6	——	6	——
7	——	7	——

4. If you only had $2.25 to spend, would you buy 4 cookies and 2 glasses of milk at the prices charged? Why or why not?
5. If you had $4, how many cookies and glasses of milk would you buy? If you had $7.25, how many of each would you buy?

ECONOMICS IN ACTION
Is It Rational to Vote?

You decide to vote in a presidential election. Typically, more than 60 million people cast their votes for their favorite candidate—Democratic, Republican, Socialist, Libertarian, or other. Your vote therefore has only 1/60,000,000 worth of influence on the outcome of the election, and it is, of course, filtered through the Electoral College process in the United States.

We also know that voting is not costless. To make a trip to the polling place, voters must pay for transportation, take time off from work or leisure, and so forth. Moreover, prior registration often means another trip to the voter registration office. Thus, voting is not free—it clearly places opportunity costs on the voter.

Suppose, in a radical simplification, that all these opportunity costs equal $1; that is, it costs you $1 to vote. Given that you are 1 out of 60 million voters who vote and that it costs you $1 to vote, what must your vote be worth to you to make it rational for you to go to the polls on election day? Since you have only a tiny effect on the election, the outcome would have to have an enormous impact on you to make it worth your while to vote. This concept can be represented algebraically by the formula

$$\frac{1}{60,000,000} \times benefits = \$1,$$

which gives the large value of $60 million necessary in benefits to you to justify the cost of voting. In terms of this analysis, it is hardly reasonable to expect the outcome of any given election to be worth $60 million to the average voter. Therefore, no one should vote, and democracy should fall on its face.

Yet herein lies a paradox. A great number of people do vote, and the question is, why? Economics provides a simple explanation for the conditions under which it is rational to vote. Obviously, voters are smarter than to view themselves as only 1 vote out of 60 million. They have identified—before the election and during the campaign—with parties and individual candidates, and they will make their own estimates of the prospects of the candidates in the election.

Economics says that voters will behave in terms of the marginal utility and marginal cost of voting. Notice that the above example was stated in terms of the *average* influence of a voter on the election. The fact that the average influence of any one voter is low does not tell us anything about his

or her marginal influence on the election. (As we stress repeatedly, the distinction between average and marginal is a crucial one in economics.) While we cannot directly measure the marginal influence of a voter in an election, we can indirectly gauge the marginal benefit from voting. The marginal influence of a vote will be greater the closer the election is predicted to be. Your vote counts for more in a close election than in a lopsided election. Therefore, economic theory leads to the following prediction: Voting turnout will be positively related to expected closeness of the election. In other words, voter turnout will be heavier the closer the election is expected to be.

This is precisely what Barzel and Silberberg found in studying gubernatorial elections in the United States. The closer an election was predicted to be, the larger the voter turnout was.[a] So the simple economic proposition that individuals behave according to marginal cost and marginal benefit provides an explanation for the conditions under which voting is rational. This is not to argue that the only reason people vote is to obtain narrow personal benefits. Benefits can be construed in a wide variety of ways, such as patriotic

[a]Yoram Barzel and Eugene Silberberg, "Is the Act of Voting Rational?" *Public Choice* (Fall 1973), pp. 51–58.

duty, citizenship, support for an ideological cause, voting for a friend, and so forth. The point is not what the benefits are but that, depending on the closeness of the election, these benefits are likely to be higher or lower relative to costs. Thus, if your friend is running for Congress, you are more likely to vote if he or she is in a tight contest than if your friend is a shoo-in.

Question

Logically, how should each of the following situations affect voter turnout on election day?

    a. Rain
    b. An international crisis
    c. A close race
    d. Television coverage

APPENDIX

Indifference Curve Analysis[3]

Suppose that we want to determine how a consumer feels about consuming various combinations of two goods, such as mystery and science fiction ("sf") novels. One approach would be to ask the person how much utility she gets from consuming 4 mystery novels and 9 sf novels per year. She would perhaps answer, "50 utils." This would not be a very helpful answer because we do not know how much 50 utils represents to this person.

A second approach would be to observe how the individual chooses among various combinations of mysteries and sf books over a specified period of time, such as a year. We could then see, through her **revealed preferences,** how she ranks the various combinations. For example, does she prefer a combination of 4 mysteries and 9 sf's to a combination of 9 mysteries and 4 sf's? That is, when offered a choice of the two combinations, does she choose one over the other? Proceeding in this way, we are more likely to derive useful information about preferences. This type of approach yields the concept of an indifference curve.

INDIFFERENCE CURVES

Indifference curves are based on the concept of **indifference sets.** Indifference sets can be easily illustrated. Suppose that four possible combinations of two goods confront an individual—say, four possible combinations of quantities per year of mystery and science fiction novels. Four combinations are given in Table 3. Assume that the consumer, through her revealed behavior, obtains the same total utility from consuming 10 mysteries and 3 sf's as she would from consuming 7 mystery novels and 5 science fiction novels, and so on through the table. Each combination is equivalent to the others in terms of the total utility yielded to the consumer. For example, if we compare combinations C and D, an additional mystery in combination C exactly makes up for the utility lost by consuming 2 fewer science fiction novels. The consumer reveals herself to be indifferent among these various combinations of the two goods; each combination yields the same level of total utility to her. An indifference set, then, is all combinations of the two goods among which the consumer is indifferent.

With this information about the individual's evaluation of the combinations, we can draw an indifference curve, as in Figure 2. Each point on the graph represents a combination of mystery and science fiction novels per year. The points representing combinations A through D are shown on the

---

[3]We present indifference curve analysis in an appendix because it is not necessary to know the technique to understand any of the basic points about economics presented in this book. Indifference curve analysis is, however, an integral part of more advanced courses in economics, and many students who plan to do more work in economics will want to learn the technique.

TABLE 3
Combinations of Novels Yielding Equal Total Utility

The data represent the consumer's observed behavior. The consumer derives as much satisfaction from consuming combination A, 10 mystery novels and 3 sf novels per year, as she does from consuming combination D, 4 mystery novels and 9 sf novels. The total utility of each combination, A, B, C, and D, is the same.

Combination	Novels per Year	
	Mystery	Science Fiction
A	10	3
B	7	5
C	5	7
D	4	9

graph. These points and points in between them are joined by a smooth curve because they are members of an indifference set. The curve is the **indifference curve,** a curve made up of points that are all members of a particular indifference set. Any point on the indifference curve is equally preferred to any other by the consumer; all yield the same level of total utility.

Characteristics of Indifference Curves

Indifference curves have certain characteristics designed to show established regularities in the patterns of consumer preferences. Five of these characteristics are of interest to us.

1. Indifference curves slope downward from left to right. This negative slope is the only one possible if the principles of consumer choice are not to be violated. An upward-sloping curve would imply that the consumer was indifferent over the choice between a combination with less of both goods and another with more of both goods. The assumption that consumers always prefer more of a good to less requires that indifference curves slope downward from left to right.

2. The absolute value of the slope of the indifference curve at any point is equal to the ratio of the marginal utility of the good on the horizontal axis to the marginal utility of the good on the vertical axis. In Figure 2, the slope of the indifference curve between A and B is about −1.5, or simply 1.5 in absolute value. This absolute value tells us that in the area of combinations A and B, the marginal utility of sf novels is approximately one and one-half times that of mysteries. In this region, about 3 mysteries can

FIGURE 2   An Indifference Curve

This indifference curve is based on the data in Table 3. The curve shows the various combinations of mystery and science fiction novels among which the consumer is indifferent. The marginal rate of substitution of one good for the other is given by the slope of the indifference curve. The indifference curve is usually convex, which means that its slope decreases from left to right along the curve. The decreasing marginal rate of substitution is due to the principle of diminishing marginal utility.

be substituted for 2 sf's without lowering the consumer's total utility. For this reason, the slope of the indifference curve is called the **marginal rate of substitution**—in this case, substitution of science fiction for mystery novels. The marginal rate of substitution tells us the rate at which one good can be substituted for another without gain or loss in utility.

3. Indifference curves are drawn to be convex: The slope of an indifference curve decreases as one moves downward to the right along the curve. This convexity reflects diminishing marginal utility. As the quantity consumed of one of the goods increases, the marginal utility of that good declines. Hence, the ratio of the marginal utilities—the slope of the indifference curve—cannot be the same all along the curve. The slope must decrease as we move farther down and to the right because the quantity of science fiction novels consumed is increasing and their marginal utility is therefore decreasing, whereas the quantity of mystery novels is decreasing and the marginal utility of mysteries is therefore increasing.

In Figure 2, the marginal rate of substitution of sf's for mysteries falls from 1.5 between points A and B to 0.5 between points C and D. As more science fiction novels are consumed, their marginal utility (measured by how many mystery novels the consumer is willing to give up per year in order to get an additional science fiction novel while remaining on the same indifference curve) falls. Fewer mysteries are consumed, and their marginal utility rises. Between A and B, the consumer is indifferent between 3 more mysteries and 2 less science fiction novels per year. Between C and D, fortified with more sf's, the consumer is indifferent between 1 additional mystery and 2 fewer sf's. The marginal utility of mystery novels has risen, and the marginal utility of science fiction novels has declined.

4. A point representing any assortment of consumption alternatives will always be on some indifference curve. Figure 3 presents a graph of combinations of bacon and eggs. We can select a point on the graph—such as A, representing 10 eggs and 1 bacon strip, or D, representing 9 bacon strips and 1 egg—and that point will have a corresponding indifference curve through it showing other bacon and egg combinations that

FIGURE 3
An Indifference Map

This consumer indifference map illustrates combinations of bacon and eggs. Any point on the graph will be associated with an indifference curve. Since a large number of indifference curves can be placed on the graph, it is called an indifference map. Indifference curves that are farther from the origin, such as I_1, represent higher levels of utility for the consumer because greater quantities of both goods are consumed.

generate the same level of total utility for the consumer. We can see from the graph that this particular consumer is indifferent among 10 eggs and 1 bacon strip (A), 5 eggs and 4 bacon strips (B), and 3 eggs and 8 bacon strips (C) per week.

Moreover, we know that the consumer will prefer any point on the *ABC* indifference curve, I_1, to any point on the *FED* indifference curve, I_2, because points on I_1 contain more of both goods than do points on I_2. The farther from the origin the indifference curve lies, the higher the level of utility the individual will experience.

We can draw as many indifference curves on the graph as there are indifference sets confronting the consumer. However many we draw—two or two hundred—the resulting graph is termed an **indifference map.**

5. Indifference curves never cross. The reason for this is **transitivity of preferences,** which simply means that if an individual prefers carrots to

squash and squash to artichokes, he or she will also prefer carrots to artichokes. Indifference curves that cross would violate this assumption. Figure 4 illustrates this point.

In this graph two indifference curves *do* cross. The point where they cross (point *A*) lies on both indifference curves, I_1 and I_2. Since, by definition, all points along one indifference curve are equally preferred by the individual, the consumer will be indifferent among choices *A*, *B*, and *C* on I_1 and *A*, *D*, and *E* on I_2. This implies that the consumer is indifferent among all these points. But we see that this is impossible—if the consumer were indifferent between point *B* on I_1 and point *D* on I_2, this would mean that having more of both bacon and eggs (point *B*) made him or her no better off than having less of both (point *D*). Other things being equal, consumers always prefer more to less, so indifference curves cannot intersect without implying a type of irrationality that we do not observe in the real world.

FIGURE 4
Indifference Curves Cannot Cross

Because preferences are transitive, point *A* cannot lie on two different indifference curves. If it did, the consumer would be indifferent among the combinations of bacon and eggs at point *B* with higher quantities of both, and point *D* with lower quantities of both.

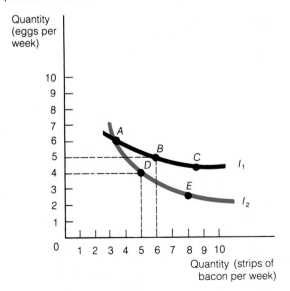

The Budget Constraint

Although we know that an individual consumer prefers a point on an indifference curve that is farther from the origin to a point closer to the origin, this knowledge does not enable us to establish which indifference curve represents the best an individual can achieve with a limited budget. We can solve this problem by introducing a **budget constraint,** represented on the graph by a budget line.

In Figure 5a, we have assumed that the prices of two goods—apples and oranges—are the same: $1 per pound. If the consumer has a weekly budget of $10, the budget line will be a straight line running from the $10 level of apples (on the vertical axis) to the $10 level of oranges (on the horizontal axis). This line simply reflects the fact that the consumer can allocate his budget between apples and oranges in any way he sees fit—$10 on apples and zero on oranges, $10 on oranges and zero on apples, or any other combination that adds up to $10, such as point *A*: $5 for each.

How does a change in price affect the budget line? Figure 5b shows that the individual's budget remains the same ($10) but that the relative prices of the two goods have changed. While the price of apples remains at $1 a pound, the price of oranges has risen to $2 a pound. Although the consumer can still allocate his entire income to the purchase of either apples or oranges, $10 spent on apples would purchase 10 pounds of apples, while the same amount spent on oranges would yield only 5 pounds of oranges.

The budget line is thus drawn to reflect any combination of prices for the two goods. The budget line is also called the consumption opportunity line because it shows the various combinations of goods that can be purchased at given prices with a given budget. The absolute value of the slope of the budget line is equal to the ratio of the price of the good on the horizontal axis to the price of the good on the vertical axis. As illustrated in Figure 5b, where the price of oranges is $2 a pound and the price of apples $1 a pound, the absolute value of the slope is 2.

Consumer Equilibrium with Indifference Curves

The combination of an individual's indifference curves and budget line allows us to represent consumer equilibrium in a way that is equivalent to the

FIGURE 5   **Budget Constraint**

The budget line, or consumption opportunity line, depends on the relative prices of the two goods. The absolute value of the slope of the budget line is the ratio of the price of the good on the horizontal axis to the price of the good on the vertical axis. (a) The budget line represents all possible combinations of apples and oranges at $1 per pound each within a budget constraint of $10 per week. The absolute value of the slope of the line is 1. (b) The budget line, still with the budget constraint of $10 per week, has changed to reflect an increase in the price of oranges to $2 per pound. The absolute value of the slope of the line is 2.

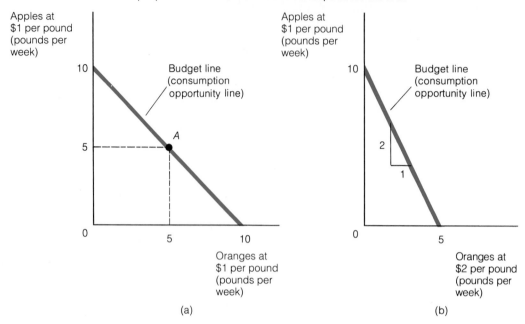

method of marginal utility analysis. This alternative method is illustrated in Figure 6, which combines the budget line from Figure 5b with a set of indifference curves.

We can see that the consumer represented here will prefer point C to point F because C lies on a higher indifference curve. She will also prefer point A to point C. All three of these points are actual opportunities confronting the consumer; she can afford them, given her budget constraint. Other things being equal, she would prefer point G to point A. However, point G is beyond the limit of her budget line. The best point she can achieve—the point on the highest indifference curve that can be reached within her budget constraint—is point A. This point represents consumer equilibrium—the combination yielding maximum utility from a given budget.

At A, the relevant indifference curve is exactly tangent to the budget line. This means that the slope of the budget line is equal to the slope of the indifference curve. We therefore know that in equilibrium the ratio of the marginal utility of the good on the horizontal axis (oranges) to the marginal utility of the good on the vertical axis (apples), indicated by the slope of the indifference curve, is equal to the ratio of the price of oranges to the price of apples, indicated by the slope of the budget line. Or, expressed somewhat differently,

$$\frac{\text{Marginal utility of oranges}}{\text{Marginal utility of apples}} = \frac{\text{Price of oranges}}{\text{Price of apples}}.$$

With terms rearranged, this formula is exactly the same result we arrived at earlier in the chapter when we discussed consumer equilibrium in marginal utility terms without the aid of indifference

FIGURE 6

Determining Consumer Equilibrium with Indifference Curves

The consumer attains maximum satisfaction at point A, where the budget, or consumption opportunity, line is tangent to the highest possible indifference curve. At A the slope of the indifference curve, or the ratio of the marginal utilities of the two goods, is equal to the slope of the budget line, or the ratio of the prices of the two goods. This relation reflects the same condition for consumer equilibrium as that suggested by marginal utility analysis.

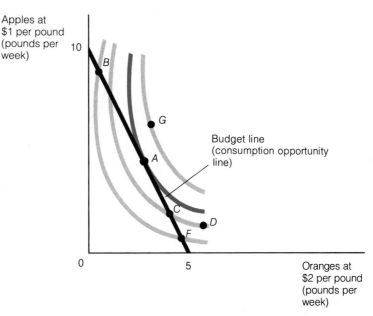

curves; that is, the preceding expression is equivalent to

$$\frac{\text{Marginal utility of oranges}}{\text{Price of oranges}} = \frac{\text{Marginal utility of apples}}{\text{Price of apples}}.$$

The two approaches thus yield similar predictions about consumer behavior.

INDIFFERENCE CURVES AND THE LAW OF DEMAND

Indifference curve analysis also can be used to demonstrate the law of demand. A demand curve can be derived by first allowing the price of a good to change, then finding the new equilibrium quantity of the good, and finally graphing the new and old price/equilibrium quantity combinations. Figures 7 and 8 together show how this is accomplished. Budget line B_1 is drawn by assuming that the price of oranges is $2 per pound and the price of apples is $1 per pound. Given these prices, and the consumer's income, the equilibrium quantity of oranges and apples for this consumer is shown as E_1

in Figure 7. Point E_1 is where indifference curve I_1 is tangent to budget line B_1. The consumer buys quantity O_1 of oranges per week when the price of oranges is $2 per pound.

If we allow the price of oranges to fall from $2 per pound to $1 per pound, the budget line rotates outward to line B_2. Indifference curve I_2, which is tangent to the new budget line at point E_2, lies farther from the origin than indifference curve I_1. This indicates that the lower price of one good leads to an increase in total utility. As Figure 7 shows, the lower price of oranges results in a larger quantity of oranges purchased, O_2.

By taking some of the information from Figure 7 and transferring it to Figure 8, the consumer's demand curve for oranges can be plotted. Figure 8 shows that at a price of oranges equal to $2 per pound, the consumer will purchase quantity O_1 of oranges per week. This information has come from the beginning situation in Figure 7, where the initial price of oranges was $2 per pound, the budget line was B_1, and the equilibrium quantity of apples and oranges consumed was E_1.

Figure 8 also shows that when oranges are priced at $1 per pound, the consumer will buy quantity O_2 of oranges per week. This information came

FIGURE 7

Indifference Curves and the Law of Demand

As the price of oranges falls from $2 a pound to $1 a pound, the budget line rotates to the right from B_1 to B_2. The consumer reaches a higher level of utility and maximizes satisfaction by attaining the highest indifference curve, I_2 rather than I_1, possible. As the price of oranges falls, the consumer purchases a larger quantity; O_2 is larger than O_1. This is precisely what the law of demand predicts—that, other things being equal, quantity demanded varies inversely with price.

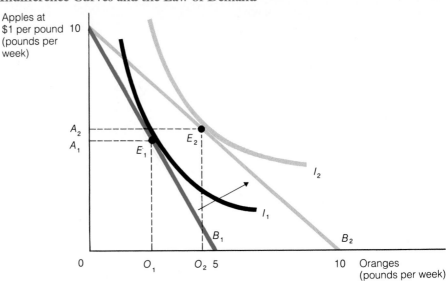

from budget line B_2, where the price of oranges is $1 per pound and equilibrium quantity is E_2. The smooth line connecting the two points in Figure 8, labeled D_{oranges}, is the consumer's demand curve for oranges. It is downward-sloping, indicating that the lower the price of oranges, other things being equal, the larger will be the amount of oranges purchased per week. The consumer equilibrium obtained through indifference curve analysis thus yields the type of demand curve predicted by the law of demand.

Substitution and Income Effects

This chapter discussed the two reasons why consumers buy more of a good when its price falls, or why demand curves are downward-sloping. When a good's price falls, the good becomes relatively less expensive in comparison to other goods. Other goods become relatively more expensive when this happens. As a result, consumers tend to substitute relatively less expensive goods for relatively more expensive goods in their purchases. This is what we referred to as the substitution effect.

However, when the price of only one good falls, the total buying power of the consumer's budget increases. This rise in what economists call real income induces the consumer to buy more of any given good. The increase in consumption of a good due to the consumer's increased buying power

(which, in turn, is due to a drop in some good's price) was called the income effect.

The substitution and income effects of a change in the price of oranges can be depicted graphically by using a graph similar to Figure 7. Parts of Figure 7 have been reproduced in Figure 9. Combination E_1 on indifference curve I_1 is the initial combination of apples and oranges consumed when apples are $1 per pound and oranges are $2 per pound. Combination E_2 and budget line B_2 are also the same in both figures. Figure 9 ignores the effects on apple consumption in order to concentrate on the two effects on orange consumption.

Both Figures 7 and 9 show that when the price of oranges falls from $2 to $1 per pound, the equilibrium quantity of oranges consumed rises from O_1 to O_2. However, Figure 9 shows how much of this increased orange consumption is due to the substitution effect (the amount O_s minus O_1) and how much to the income effect (O_2 minus O_s). To see why these amounts are the substitution and income effects, we need to apply the formula for consumer equilibrium.

Consider point E_1 in both Figures 7 and 9. Combination E_1 is the initial amounts of the goods consumed. For this to be a point of consumer equilibrium, we know that

$$\frac{\text{Marginal utility of oranges}}{\text{Marginal utility of apples}} = \frac{\$2}{\$1} = \frac{\text{Price of oranges}}{\text{Price of apples}}.$$

FIGURE 8

The consumer's equilibrium quantity of oranges consumed increases from O_1 to O_2 if the price of oranges falls from $2 to $1 per pound. The demand curve for oranges is downward-sloping.

The Demand Curve for Oranges

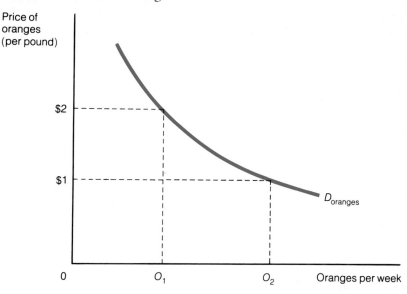

FIGURE 9

When the price of oranges is $2 per pound, O_1 pounds of oranges are consumed per week. When the price of oranges falls to $1 per pound, two things happen. The consumer substitutes oranges for apples because oranges have become relatively cheaper. Orange consumption changes from O_1 to O_s due to the substitution effect. The buying power of the fixed budget also rises. Orange consumption rises from O_s to O_2 due to the income effect.

Substitution and Income Effects

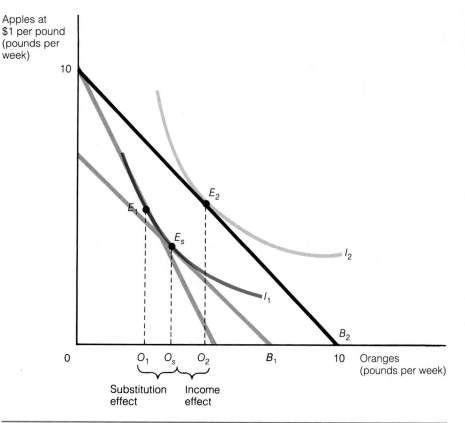

At point E_1 in each figure, the ratio of the marginal utilities, given by the slope of I_1 at point E_1, equals the ratio of prices, given by the slope of the budget line. The substitution effect conceptually measures by how much consumption of a good would change if the consumer's real income remained unchanged when a price changes. This is accomplished by finding a combination of goods *on the original indifference curve I_1* that would be chosen by the consumer if the ratio of the prices were \$1/\$1 instead of \$2/\$1. This combination of goods, E_s in Figure 9, yields the consumer the same level of total utility as does combination E_1. Keeping total utility constant is the economist's way of hypothetically preventing a change in real income when a price changes. At combination E_s in Figure 9, the ratio of the marginal utilities (the slope of the indifference curve) is equal to the new price ratio, \$1/\$1. Conceptually holding real income, or total utility, constant, this consumer would buy amount O_s pounds of oranges if the price of oranges were to fall to \$1 per pound. The substitution effect of a drop in the price of oranges is then measured as O_s minus O_1 pounds of oranges.

We know, however, that when one price decreases, the buying power of the consumer's budget increases. Figures 7 and 9 both show the consumer buying combination E_2 (O_2 pounds of oranges) after all is said and done. Both figures also indicate that the consumer's total utility has increased as a result of the price decrease. This increased total utility results from the increased buying power of the budget, which in turn is caused by the price decrease. The change in orange consumption per week due to the budget's larger buying power is measured as O_2 minus O_s pounds of oranges in Figure 9. This is the income effect of the decrease in the price of oranges. It is that part of the increased consumption of oranges that is not explained by the substitution effect.

The sum of the substitution effect (O_s minus O_1) plus the income effect (O_2 minus O_s) equals the total effect (O_2 minus O_1) on orange consumption of a fall in the price of oranges. This is so because the single price change affects the consumer's environment in two ways. It alters the relative price of one good compared to another. This induces the consumer to substitute one good for another in consumption—the substitution effect. It also changes the budget's purchasing power, allowing the consumer to buy more (in the case of a price decrease) of the good and thus increasing the consumer's total utility. While we could never actually see these two effects separately (we can only observe the total effect in the real world), they nonetheless exist and are important in explaining consumer behavior. These effects are analogous to the concept of gravity in physics. We cannot "see" gravity, but we can conceptually understand its effect and observe the results it produces.

SUMMARY

1. The method of indifference curves is an alternative way to study the process of individual choice and consumer equilibrium. It is based on the idea of observing how an individual chooses among consumption alternatives.
2. An indifference set is a group of consumption alternatives that yield the same total utility to the consumer.
3. An indifference curve is a graphical representation of an indifference set. Each point on the curve represents the same total utility to the consumer.
4. Indifference curves have negative slopes, are convex, and do not intersect.
5. The slope of an indifference curve is called the marginal rate of substitution of one good for another.
6. An indifference curve is associated with any combination of goods selected by the consumer. An indifference map consists of a set of possible indifference curves of the consumer.

7. The budget line shows the relative prices of the goods an individual consumes and the amounts of the goods that he or she can consume without spending beyond the budget constraint.
8. In the indifference curve approach, consumer equilibrium occurs at the point where the consumer's budget line is tangent to the highest possible indifference curve. This condition is the same as that derived for consumer equilibrium using marginal utility analysis—namely, $MU_X/P_X = MU_Y/P_Y$.
9. The indifference curve technique can be used to show that the quantity consumed of a good is inversely related to its price—in other words, the law of demand.
10. In terms of indifference curves, the substitution effect shows how a change in a good's relative price affects consumption of the good. The income effect shows the impact on consumption of a change in the consumer's real purchasing power.

KEY TERMS

revealed preference
indifference set
indifference curve
marginal rate of substitution

indifference map
transitivity of preferences
budget constraint

QUESTIONS FOR REVIEW AND DISCUSSION

1. Explain why indifference curves cannot intersect.
2. What is the relation between the principle of diminishing marginal utility and the marginal rate of substitution?
3. Suppose that the consumer feels that each combination of x and y in the table at right yields the same total utility. What comment would you make about the individual's choice process?
4. What are the characteristics of indifference curves? What is the rationale for each characteristic? What would be the consequences of violating each of these characteristics?
5. How does the indifference curve approach show that consumer demand curves are negatively sloped? Explain.
6. Suppose that the price of oranges increases rather than decreases in Figure 9. Using indifference curve analysis, show the income and substitution effects of this price increase.

Combinations	Goods	
	x	y
A	10	7
B	15	8
C	20	9
D	25	10
E	30	11

7

The Firm

We are now at the point in our study of microeconomics where the concept of the business firm comes into play. If you look back briefly at the circular flow of income diagram in Chapter 3, you will see that firms occupy a critical role in a market economy. In fact, there are over 17 million business firms in the United States, ranging in size from the small corner grocery store owned by one individual to the immense multinational corporations owned by millions of stockholders.

In broad terms, the economic function of a business **firm** is to combine scarce resources (factors of production) to produce goods and services demanded by consumers. Firms that perform this function well make profits and survive; firms that perform this function poorly experience losses and fail. This brief definition of a firm, however, touches only the surface of the matter. To understand the role of firms in a market economy, we need to explore how a firm organizes resources. Specifically, we need to explore certain key questions about firms and their characteristics so that, after reading Chapter 7, you will understand

- the characteristics that all firms have in common.
- some problems of organization that firms face in their attempts to purchase, organize, and assemble resources to produce goods and services.
- why firms are organized in different ways.
- who controls modern firms and to what end.

Firm:
An economic institution that purchases, organizes, and assembles resources to produce goods and services.

MARKET AND FIRM COORDINATION

Production in a market economy is based on the principle of the **division of labor:** Individuals specialize in different productive activities, all of which are coordinated by the price system. The division of labor in a market economy is a vast network of activities based on such factors as the different levels of skill possessed by members of the labor force. Some individuals find their calling in farming, others in medicine. But what coordinates the division of

Division of labor:
An economic principle whereby individuals specialize in the production of a single good, service, or task, thereby increasing overall productivity and economic efficiency.

172

labor so that we can be assured of a supply of food and a supply of medical services? What is the mechanism by which the production of goods and services by millions of individuals is coordinated so that we can get what we want when we want it?

Basically, there are two methods of economic coordination in a market economy: market coordination and firm coordination.

Distinguishing Market and Firm Coordination

Market coordination:
The process that directs the flow of resources into the production of goods and services through the price signaling mechanism.

Market coordination is what we have studied so far in this book. It is the use of the price system to provide incentives to suppliers and demanders to produce and consume goods and services in the appropriate amounts. Market coordination refers to the myriad daily economic activities that are guided by the "invisible hand" of the market. Our study of demand and supply is the study of how the market coordinates activities.

Not all activities in a modern economy are coordinated by the market, however. Part of the division of labor is carried out within firms. Automobile assembly-line workers do not sell their output directly in a market. Rather, they supply labor to the auto company, which employs managers to direct and coordinate the uses of their labor within the firm. **Firm coordination** is a productive process that depends on managerial rather than market direction.

Firm coordination:
The process that directs the flow of resources into the production of a particular good or service through the forces of management organization within the firm.

In some respects a business firm is like a socialist economy within a market economy. Decision making in the firm is centralized and performed by **managers.** Managers decide what and how to produce, just as central planners do in a socialist economy. Within the firm, resources are not bought and sold but are transferred at the command of a manager. The firm, in short, seems to be a contradiction in the marketplace; it appears to conduct its production activities outside the price system.

Manager:
An individual or group of individuals that organizes and monitors resources within a firm to produce a good or service.

The analogy between capitalist firm and socialist economy is somewhat misleading, however. One critical difference relates to incentives and property rights. State-owned and -operated enterprises in socialist countries typically divorce reward (wages, salaries) from productivity; managers and workers cannot gain from efficient activities and do not suffer for losses based on poor performance. This situation creates weak incentives for individual managers and workers to excel. A capitalist firm, on the other hand, is a voluntary institution in which individuals cooperate through free contractual relationships and through the establishment of strong incentives to produce. The manager acts as a specialist in overseeing production and makes decisions that can only figuratively be called commands. Employees agree to follow the manager's directions when they agree to join the firm.

The distinction between market and firm coordination is not absolute. Resource allocation within the firm is not really outside the price system, although it might superficially look that way. Managers transfer and allocate resources within the firm in ways that are efficient given the prices for equivalent resources on the market. The manager's decision to transfer a quantity of a particular resource within the firm is based on prices, even though resources are not actually bought and sold within the firm.

To understand this point, consider the example of a hypothetical gourmet restaurant, the Greenhouse. It has a luncheon and dinner trade five days a week, it serves brunch on Sundays, and it runs a catering business. After two years of operation, luncheons and Sunday brunch are very crowded, while there are few customers in the evening. In response, the manager of the restaurant will probably transfer resources such as labor, linens, and food from nighttime to daytime use. The transfer is within the firm, but the manager will make the decision by judging the marginal cost of transferring resources—linens, buspersons, waiters, and so on—as if each were being hired or purchased afresh outside the firm. Transfer of resources within the firm is therefore subject to the laws of supply and demand just as if the resources were newly contracted from outside the firm.

If market and firm coordination are so similar, what accounts for the existence of firms? In actuality, much production is undertaken by independent individuals, and it is common for individual demanders to contract with individual suppliers for particular goods and services. For example, Saks Fifth Avenue, Tiffany's, and Neiman-Marcus contract with individual artists and artisans for their wares. Many publishers hire work out to freelance editors and art directors rather than having all editorial services performed by in-house staff. It is often cheaper or more efficient to do so. Economic coordination between contracting individuals in such cases is achieved directly through the operation of the price system. So an interesting question arises: Why is all production not undertaken by freelance individual operators? In other words, why will an owner of capital goods hire employees for long periods of time instead of contracting out for the performance of specific tasks as they arise?

Least Cost and Most Efficient Size

Ronald H. Coase was the first economist to pose and answer this important question.[1] His answer was simple and profound: Firms exist when they are the least costly form of economic coordination; their size is determined by what is most efficient (least costly) for production. We do not use the market to organize all production because it is not costless to use markets. Using the market necessitates finding out what prices are, negotiating and enforcing contractual agreements with suppliers, going to court when promises are not kept, paying transaction costs, and engaging in various other costly and resource-using activities. For these reasons, not all production in a market economy is coordinated through market exchange. It costs less in many cases to organize production in a firm where resource allocation is directed and coordinated by managers.

Recall the Greenhouse restaurant and some of the reasons that it organized as a firm. The production of food services—luncheons and dinners—requires labor and many other inputs such as refrigeration, stoves, and silverware. It would be too costly to hire cooks or waiters sporadically for specific tasks—catering a wedding or simply serving the regular dinner hours. Using the market to contract for every single input or task required would be costly and inefficient. Instead, a firm is organized to manage and coordinate a variety of inputs. Waiters and cooks are hired on a long-run basis, and some (but possibly not all) capital is leased or purchased through similar long-run arrangements.

mkt costs

---

[1] Ronald H. Coase, "The Nature of the Firm," *Economica* (November 1937), pp. 386–405.

In firm production, the inside of the firm will be run by managerial coordination; the firm will deal with the outside world through market coordination. Which activities the firm chooses to organize internally will be related to the cost of organizing the same activities through market exchange. Automobile manufacturers can buy tires in a contractual arrangement with tire companies, or they can make their own tires. The relative costs of these alternatives will determine how the auto company gets its tires. The restaurant may go into the direct market to obtain bookkeeping services or lease, in the short term, specialized capital such as silver serving trays for special catering jobs. It may be too costly to purchase silver trays for one or two occasions a year or to hire a permanent bookkeeper or accountant.

Firms exist in a market economy because they represent a least-cost means of organizing production. However, firms will not grow without limit because at some point the marginal cost of organizing a task within the firm will exceed the marginal cost of organizing the same task through market contracting. This limit on firm size will evolve naturally because the managerial cost of organizing and keeping track of inside production rises along with the number of tasks the firm undertakes. There will be a natural division of production in an economy between firms and markets, determined by the relative costs of producing goods and services in each way.

Suppose an automobile company in its early years produces many of its car parts, such as the seat covers and the spark plugs, because buying these inputs from independent suppliers entails too many risks. This future supply may be uncertain, perhaps because the courts do not strongly enforce supplier contracts for failure to supply these inputs. If, over time, the courts become more concerned about this type of problem and supply contracts come to be more strongly enforced in the event of a failure to supply inputs, the automobile firm can begin buying the auto parts it needs from independent suppliers rather than making them in-house. In the new legal environment, the future supply of seat covers is more certain. In principle, this is how Coase's theory works over time.

TEAM PRODUCTION

It will further our understanding of why firms exist and how they are organized if we look at the internal operations of a firm in more detail. A fundamental principle involved in the operations of many firms is **team production,** by which several people work together to accomplish a task. None of the individual team members produces a separate product. The classic example is the method of assembly-line production invented by Henry Ford.

Production by means of a team is sometimes more efficient than production by individuals working separately. For example, two workers making jogging shoes—one stamping out the material and the other stitching it together—may be able to produce more pairs of shoes than the two could produce if each were independently assembling whole shoes. Or it may be possible to repair more automobile engines per day if two or three mechanics work on one engine together than if each mechanic concentrates on repairing a separate engine. Assembly-line production, carried to extreme, may create

Team production:
An economic activity in which workers cooperate as team members in order to accomplish an objective.

boredom or "burn-out," but the technique is undeniably efficient because it permits specialization and focused refinement of individual talents.

Management of the firm can be seen as a device that organizes and **monitors** team production. Management, as such, functions as a substitute for the discipline of market competition. Management is the firm's solution to a problem that would otherwise limit productive efficiency in group efforts: shirking.

The Problem of Shirking

In individual production, a person's output can easily be measured, but in team production, only the total output of the team as a whole is observable. The contribution of each team member to the total output is harder to detect. Since only the total output of a team is observable, each team member has an incentive to shift the burden of work onto the rest of the team. Such behavior is called **shirking.** This term is not used in a negative sense. We are not saying that workers are naturally lazy; we are simply saying that shirking can be a rational form of behavior when the worker is part of a team production process. Shirking reduces the total output and productivity of the team, but the individual worker who shirks does not bear the full consequences of his or her reduced effort; part of the consequences are shifted to the other team members. Anyone who has ever played basketball, worked in an office or a fast-food restaurant, or participated in any team production process is aware of this problem.

Where team production does not exist, individual producers are disciplined by competition from other producers and other products. The individual producer can dawdle or take frequent work breaks if he or she chooses, but the individual bears the cost of reduced production directly in lower income.

In a team setting, it is costly to monitor the performance of each team member. When the increased productive efficiency of team production exceeds this cost of monitoring, team production will replace independent production by individuals. In other words, when teams can produce products at a lower cost than individuals can, firms will exist.

Enter the Manager

The manager is that individual (or group) assigned by the firm to monitor team members and direct them to perform their tasks in a manner that enhances team productivity. The manager is more than just a specialist relieving individual team members of the responsibility for monitoring each other's performance. He or she coordinates the production process in an effort to minimize the costs of production. Managers have the power to hire or fire team members and to renegotiate wage contracts and redirect work assignments. As a result, they are able to discipline shirking and to reward superior productive contributions by team members more effectively than would be possible in a system in which every member monitors every other.

Return momentarily to the Greenhouse restaurant example and suppose that an elaborate banquet is planned for one hundred people. The chef, kitchen crew, waiters, and buspeople are alerted. Without management, all members

Monitor:
An individual in management who coordinates team production, measures the performance of team members, and discourages shirking.

Shirking:
A sometimes rational type of behavior of team members in which the individual exerts a less than expected or normal productive effort.

of the team would be responsible for monitoring each other's performance; all would have an incentive to shirk work, placing responsibility on other members of the team. If the food does not appear on time or if it is cold and unpalatable, the chef may blame the kitchen help, the kitchen personnel may blame the waiters, and the waiters may blame the buspeople. It might be more efficient for a manager to organize team activity and to monitor the effort of each member of the food-producing and food-serving team. The manager-monitor would discipline shirking and reward outstanding performance by individual members of the team. The manager, in other words, would attempt to minimize the costs of producing the banquet. Moreover, the manager's performance rating usually depends on his or her group's individual performance, which is a further incentive for effective monitoring.

Monitoring the Manager

Within any firm there remains another monitoring problem: Who will monitor the monitor? That is, what is to prevent the manager from shirking? Here competition serves to discipline shirking. More specifically, the threat of losing his or her job to a competing manager will force a manager to avoid shirking. Inefficient managers can and will be fired when more efficient managers are available.

Residual claimant:
The individual or group of individuals that shares in the profit of the firm.

Another incentive to avoid shirking is positive rather than negative: making the managers **residual claimants** who share in the profits of team production. Extra profits that result from more efficient management can be used to reward managers. Managers are commonly given a share of the profits so that they will manage the company effectively, thereby increasing their own wealth. For example, in 1988 Michael D. Eisner, the chief executive officer of Walt Disney Company, made over $7 million in wages and salary, plus an additional $32 million in stock gains (*Forbes,* May 29, 1989). This reward resulted from Walt Disney stock performing well under his stewardship. In contrast, the chief executive officer of First Florida Banks received a salary and bonus of only $9000 and nothing in stock gains. Most CEOs receive no stock gains—either because of the design of their respective compensation packages or because their respective firms are performing poorly. (See Focus, "The Wages of Success: Big Pay in Large Corporations," for additional statistics on managerial pay.)

Voluntary Acceptance of Managers' Commands

What incentive is there for team members to accept the manager's dictates? The manager's power is entirely contractual; team members have voluntarily agreed to accept the manager's commands within the firm. Team members will enter into such contracts because they are better off with a monitor than they would be without one. At first, this appears paradoxical. How can employees be better off if they are made to work harder or more efficiently? Why would they voluntarily contract to be disciplined? Even though each team member might be better off if he or she alone could shirk, if every team member shirks, each will bear the full burden of lowered production in reduced income. Hence, every team member will prefer that the entire team be monitored, even if this reduces his or her own opportunities for shirking.

FOCUS The Wages of Success: Big Pay in Large Corporations

Major corporations reward successful managers handsomely. A *Business Week* survey of 356 of the 500 largest corporations in the United States found that the average compensation of CEOs in this country was almost $1.9 million in 1989. Unfortunately for the CEOs, that figure represents a decline of 9 percent from 1988! Table 1 shows a wide range of salary and bonuses in 1989—from a little under $300,000 to over $14 million. The highest salary was earned by Paul Fireman of Reebok International.

In terms of total compensation, the highest-paid executive was Craig O. McCaw of McCaw Cellular Communications. Interestingly, all of the CEOs surveyed except one earned more than McCaw in salary and bonuses. McCaw, however, racked up nearly $54 million in stock options. Under stock-option programs, executives have the option of buying some limited quantity of their company's stock over a specified future time period at a fixed price. For example, a company may allow its chief executive to buy up to 200,000 shares of stock over the next five years at a price of, say, $40 per share. Should the price of the company's stock rise above $40 in that time period, the executive can acquire stock at less than its market price. In this example, if the price of the stock rose to $46 per share, the option would be worth, on paper, $1.2 million ($6 × 200,000).

As Table 1 shows, all of the top executives do not achieve stock gains in any given year, and few profit from stock-option programs the way McCaw has. Still, executives stand to gain millions if their respective companies' stock prices rise, giving them a strong incentive to make managerial decisions that maximize the value of company stock.

TABLE 1 Earnings of the Top Twenty CEOs in 1989

Long-term compensation in the form of stock options is becoming an increasingly important part of CEO payment packages. The salaries of all but two of the twenty highest-paid chief executives were supplemented by stock options.

Company	Chief Executive	Salary + Bonus (000)	Stock Gains (000)	Total (000)
McCaw Cellular	Craig O. McCaw	$ 289	$53,655	$53,944
Time Warner	Steven J. Ross	4,800	29,400	34,200
Lin Broadcasting	Donald A. Pels	1,363	21,428	22,791
Lotus Development	Jim P. Manzi	991	15,372	16,363
Reebok International	Paul Fireman	14,606	—	14,606
Torchmark	Ronald K. Richey	1,078	11,588	12,666
Paramount	Martin S. Davis	4,095	7,540	11,635
Coca-Cola	Roberto C. Goizueta	2,542	8,173	10,715
Walt Disney	Michael D. Eisner	9,589	—	9,589
Anheuser-Busch	August A. Busch III	1,464	7,397	8,861
MCI	William G. McGowan	1,325	7,341	8,666
Freeport McMoRan	James R. Moffett	1,350	5,950	7,300
Ford Motor	Donald E. Petersen	3,050	4,097	7,147
Merck	P. Roy Vagelos	2,340	4,423	6,764
Unisys	W. Michael Blumenthal	725	5,786	6,511
Morgan Stanley	S. Parker Gilbert	5,475	35	5,510
Louisiana-Pacific	Harry A. Merlo	575	4,739	5,314
Colgate-Palmolive	Reuben Mark	1,407	3,597	5,004
Alexander & Baldwin	Robert J. Pfeiffer	1,467	3,476	4,943
Ralston Purina	William P. Stiritz	1,064	3,790	4,854

Source: Reprinted from May 7, 1990 issue of *Business Week* by special permission, copyright © 1990 by McGraw-Hill, Inc.

SIZE AND TYPES OF BUSINESS ORGANIZATIONS

Firms evolve when team effort can produce goods and services at a lower cost than individual effort. This occurs because of the increased efficiency that may be gained when labor and capital are coordinated through managerial talents. In the following sections, we consider the varying size of firms and the advantages and disadvantages of various ways that firms can be organized.

Scale of Production

Scale of production:
The relative size of a physical plant, which can be measured by the amount or value of the firm's capital.

The most efficient size for firms (the size that performs at the lowest cost of production) varies greatly. The most efficient **scale of production** can be as small as a hot dog stand on a street corner or as large as a General Motors assembly plant.

A firm's scale of production affects the amount of capital equipment it needs. Owners of firms that require large-scale production are forced to make large expenditures on buildings, inventories, machines, and other tools of production. These purchases can amount to millions of dollars. On the other hand, owners of firms with a small scale of production may spend only a few thousand dollars on capital equipment.

When an individual decides to start a business, the amount of money required is determined by the desired scale of production. The larger the scale of production, the larger the amount of funds needed to purchase capital equipment. Often an individual is not able or willing to provide all of the necessary capital. Fortunately, there is more than one way to finance a new firm. An individual may seek other people with complementary talents, ambitions, and funds to start a new business enterprise, sharing the responsibilities, risks, and profits. The way in which a firm's ownership is organized depends on many things—the scale of production, the required capital funds, and the individual talents of owners.

Categories of Ownership

Generally, a firm is organized to fit one of three legal categories: a proprietorship, a partnership, or a corporation. The nature of ownership is different in each category.

Proprietorship:
A firm with a single owner–residual claimant who has unlimited liability for the firm's debts.

Unlimited liability:
A legal principle implying that the owner(s) of or partners in a firm are personally responsible for the debts of the firm up to the total value of their wealth.

Proprietorships. A **proprietorship** is a firm that has a single owner who is liable—or legally responsible—for all the debts of the firm, a condition termed **unlimited liability.** The sole proprietor has unlimited liability in the legal sense that if the firm goes bankrupt, the proprietor's personal as well as business property can be used to settle the firm's outstanding debts.

More often than not, the sole proprietor also works in the firm as a manager and a laborer. Thus, most single-owner firms are small. Many small retail establishments are organized as proprietorships.

The primary advantage of the proprietorship is that it allows the small businessperson direct control of the firm and its activities. The owner, who is the residual claimant of profits over and above all wage payments and other expenses, monitors his or her own performance. The sole proprietor faces a market price directly. It is up to the sole proprietor to decide how much effort to expend in producing output. In other words, the sole proprietor can be his or her own boss.

The primary disadvantage of the proprietorship is that the welfare of the firm and the liability for its activities largely rest on one person. The typical sole proprietor is the chief stockholder, chief executive officer, and chief bottle washer for the firm. Since there are only twenty-four hours in a day, the sole proprietor faces problems in attending to the various aspects of the business.

Nevertheless, as Table 2 shows, proprietorships are the dominant form of business organization in the American economy. In 1985, they constituted 71 percent of all firms. Though plentiful, they generated only 6 percent of total business revenue. The small business sector is composed of many small firms.

Partnership:
A firm with two or more owner–residual claimants with unlimited liability.

Partnerships. A **partnership** is an extended form of the proprietorship. Rather than one owner, a partnership has two or more co-owners. These partners—who are team members—share financing of capital investments and, in return, the firm's residual claims to profits. Jointly they perform the managerial function within the firm, organizing team production and monitoring one another's behavior to control shirking. A partnership is a form well suited to lines of team production that involve creative or intellectual skills, areas in which monitoring is difficult. Imagine trying to direct a commercial artist's work in detail or monitoring a lawyer's preparation for a case. If the lawyer is looking out the window, is he or she mentally analyzing a case or daydreaming? By making lawyers residual claimants in their joint efforts, the partnership ensures self-monitoring.

The partnership also has certain limitations. Individual partners cannot sell their share of the partnership without the approval of the other partners. The partnership is terminated each time a partner dies or sells out, resulting in costly reorganization. And each partner is considered legally liable for all the debts incurred by the partnership up to the full extent of the individual partner's wealth, a condition called **joint unlimited liability.** Because of these limitations, partnerships are usually small and are found in businesses where monitoring of production by a manager is difficult.

Joint unlimited liability:
The unlimited liability of a partnership, which is shared by all partners.

As Table 2 shows, partnerships constitute a small percentage of firms and business revenues in the U.S. economy. One should not underestimate the

TABLE 2

Types of Firms and Total Receipts, 1985

While the absolute number of sole proprietorships is greater than the number of corporations, their volume of business (total receipts) is much lower.

	Number of Firms (thousands)	Percent of Total Firms	Total Receipts (billions)	Percent of Total Receipts
Proprietorships	11,929	71	$ 540	6
Partnerships	1,714	10	368	4
Corporations	3,277	19	8,398	90
Total	16,920	100	9,306	100

Source: Statistical Abstract of the United States, 1989, Table 846, p. 516.

significance of partnership firms, however, since many important services, such as law, accounting, medicine, and architecture, are organized as partnerships.

Corporations. While **corporations** are not the most numerous form of business organization in the United States, they conduct most of the business. In 1985, corporations accounted for just 19 percent of the total number of firms in the economy but 90 percent of total business revenues. This means that many large firms are corporations and that this form of business organization must possess certain advantages over the proprietorship and the partnership in conducting large-scale production and marketing.

In a corporation, ownership is divided into equal parts called **shares** of stock. If any stockholder dies or sells out to a new owner, the existence of the business organization is not terminated or endangered as it is in a proprietorship or partnership. For this reason the corporation is said to possess the feature of continuity.

Share Transferability. Another feature that makes the corporation radically different from other forms of business organization is **share transferability**—the right of owners to transfer their shares by sale or gift without having to obtain the permission of other shareholders. For many large organizations, shares of stock are traded on a stock market such as the New York Stock Exchange. Other corporations, however, are smaller, and their shares are traded so seldom that they are not even listed on formal stock exchanges. The shares of these firms are traded by independent stockbrokers on the over-the-counter market.

Share transferability is the most economically important feature of the corporation; in fact, share transferability is one reason for the origin of the corporation. (See Focus, "The Birth of the Corporation: All in the Family?") It allows owners and managers to specialize, increasing efficiency and profitability in the firm. Owners of stock in a corporation do not need to be concerned with the day-to-day operations of the firm. All that owners need to do is observe the changing price of the firm's shares on the stock market to decide whether the company is being competently managed. If they are dissatisfied with the performance of the company, they can sell their stock. Managers, on the other hand, specialize in reviewing the day-to-day operations of the corporation.

Accumulation of Capital. Specialization in ownership means that relatively large amounts of capital can be accumulated because ready transferability of shares renders investment by individuals feasible. Because stock can be traded at the individual owners' discretion, the risk of owning it is reduced. If the firm's performance sags, dissatisfied investors can sell their shares with a minimum of loss.

Many people who have neither the time nor the inclination to bear the burden of management in a firm nevertheless want to invest in firms operated by skilled specialists and to share in the firms' profits. The resources provided by this investment enable the firms to operate on a larger scale. The stockholders primarily bear the changes in value for those resources—both increases and decreases—and thereby partially free the managers from bearing those risks.

Corporation:
A firm owned by one or more individuals who own shares of stock that define ownership and rights to profits. Liability is limited to the value of corporation assets.

Shares:
The equal portions into which ownership of a corporation is divided.

Share transferability:
The ability of an economic entity to sell ownership shares in a corporation without the approval of other shareholders.

FOCUS   The Birth of the Corporation: All in the Family?

The most significant developments leading to the modern corporation occurred during the mercantile period (roughly, 1500–1750) in England. Mercantilism, a system of internal and external governmental controls on production and trade, was the system assailed by Adam Smith in *Wealth of Nations*. Among other things, the mercantilist system was characterized by grants of monopoly economic power by monarchs to regulated firms such as the English Merchant Averturers, the Levant Company, and the Muscovy Company—all closely-held family partnerships.

The modern corporation evolved from these regulated companies, through joint-stock companies—although both company types coexisted for a time. You know that one of the most attractive features of the corporation is limited liability. This means that shareholders are liable for corporate debts only up to the value of the stock they hold. Limited liability permits firms to attract and accumulate capital for large-scale investments.

As noted in the text, ownership of easily tradable stock with limited liability allows individuals to participate in investments without the obligation of managing the firm. In the family-held regulated companies, shares were either not tradable or sold only with difficulty. The viability of the firm over time depended upon the passing of shares within families through inheritance. Participation of some family member or members in the management of the firm was required for the firm to survive.[a] Since there was no market where ownership rights could be traded, a problem still associated with partnerships arose: A partner's exit from the firm was restricted by the requirement that a new partner be satisfactory to those partners remaining in the firm.

Successfully continuing a regulated company, a family of partners, through time was fraught with difficulties. What would guarantee that sons, grandsons, or nephews would constitute the most effective and efficient owner-managers? A profligate, spendthrift son could go through a fortune with abandon, paying no attention to the management of the firm he inherited. Even today, less than one-third of all family businesses survive to the second generation, and, of these, less than one-half make it to the third—only in part due to adverse tax laws.[b]

It became clear that profitability and viability of firms would be enhanced over time if shares could be traded more readily. Share transferability would allow managers to specialize in the day-to-day operations of the company. Owner-shareholders of joint-stock companies, like their modern counterparts trading on the New York Stock Exchange, could express confidence in or disgust with managerial behavior by buying or selling stock at any time. When the shareholder gained this right, family ties would no longer protect inefficient managers from the possibility of being replaced—and the corporation as we know it was born.

[a]For details, see Robert B. Ekelund, Jr. and Robert D. Tollison, ''Mercantilist Origins of the Corporation,'' *The Bell Journal of Economics* (Autumn 1980), pp. 715–20.

[b]See Rita Koselka, Fleming Meeks, and Laura Saunders, ''Family Affairs,'' *Forbes* (December 11, 1989), pp. 212–18.

Limited liability:
A legal principle implying that the owner(s) of a corporation are not personally responsible for the firm's debts, except up to the value of the shares.

4) ***Limited Liability.*** Another feature of the corporation that distinguishes it from other forms of business organization is **limited liability.** Corporate shareholders are responsible for the debts or liabilities of the corporation only to the extent that they have invested in it. For example, if an investor is a millionaire and has invested $10 in one share of XYZ corporation, under no circumstances will he or she risk the loss of more than the invested $10, even if XYZ declares bankruptcy, leaving large unpaid debts. (By contrast, sole proprietorships and partnerships are characterized by unlimited liability; sole owners or partners are legally responsible for the firm's debts up to the amount of their entire personal wealth.) Many investors prefer investments in which their risk of personal loss is strictly limited; the amount of direct investment in corporations is therefore increased as a result of the limited liability involved.

 2) ***The Separation of Ownership and Control.*** Not all observers see the corporation as the goose that lays the golden egg. Critics of the modern corporation often claim that it is inefficient because ownership and control

are separated: Shareholders are the owners of the firm, but the control of the firm is vested in professional managers. Except for the cases in which managers are also large stockholders in the firm, the problem of separating ownership and control is that management and shareholders have different objectives for the firm. Shareholders are interested in increasing profits and raising the value of their shares. Incumbent managers often have other objectives. They may want to be captains of industry and heads of large firms; they may seek job security or plush corporate headquarters; or they may want to work with friendly rather than competent colleagues. To the extent that managers can pursue such goals at the expense of firm profitability, the separation of ownership and control is a real problem, and shareholder wealth is reduced as a consequence.

This problem may be more apparent than real, however. The corporate shareholder is not held in bondage by the corporation's management—he or she can sell shares at any time. Because the shareholder has this salable right in the capital value of the firm, changes in the behavior of managers that produce losses will provide the inducement to replace inefficient managers with more efficient ones. Such a change may come through a corporate takeover (in which another firm or group of investors buys controlling interest in the firm), a stockholder rebellion (where inefficient management is thrown out of office), or some other means. The point is simply that mechanisms exist to pull errant managers back into line. A subsequent rise in stock price would provide shareholders a gain from the managerial replacement. This potential gain provides a powerful incentive for stockholders to ride herd on management by monitoring the value of their shares (but not by monitoring managerial activities in detail).

Takeovers: The Corporation in the 1980s. The potential value of a corporation's assets is sometimes not accurately represented by the price of its stock shares. This can happen when managers are incompetent—that is, when they fail to maximize the wealth of the shareholders by failing to maximize the value of the company's assets. When stock prices do not reflect the value of the corporation's assets, the corporation and its present management are vulnerable to *corporate raiders.* These investor-entrepreneurs may engage in what is called a **takeover bid strategy.** First, the entrepreneur finds a corporation whose stock prices are undervalued. He or she then offers to buy stock in the corporation, driving the value of shares upward. (The entrepreneur is usually joined by other investors in these purchases.) Individual shareholders are then faced with a choice: They can either sell their stock at the higher prices or stick with existing management. However, if sufficient shares are acquired to gain voting control of the corporation, the entrepreneur may attempt to take over the corporation entirely. The takeover entrepreneur in effect gives the management of the corporation a choice: It can buy back the stock at the new (higher) price or it can submit to new corporate control and face possible firing. Management may try to prevent stockholders from selling their shares by employing various legal maneuvers, or it may attempt to stave off the raider by selling assets to buy stock.

Corporate takeovers became popular "sport" in the 1980s, with battles and tactics taking on the characteristics of medieval warfare. (See Focus, "To the Jousts: A Short Guide to Corporate Takeover Terminology.") In 1984 and 1985, for example, T. Boone Pickens twice attempted to take over the Phillips

Takeover bid strategy:
The attempt by one or more entrepreneurs to gain voting control over a corporation by buying vast quantities of that corporation's stock.

Grandma's PIES

UNDER NEW MANAGEMENT

Drawing by Frascino; © 1990 The New Yorker Magazine, Inc.

Greenmail:
Stock purchase made by incumbent management of a corporation to prevent corporate takeover by a hostile stockholder or group of stockholders.

Petroleum Company of Bartlesville, Oklahoma. Rather than relinquish control of the company, Phillips management paid $89 million for the Phillips stock held by Pickens; his takeover bid failed, but Pickens made millions on the deal! Such "blackmail" of the corporation is called **greenmail.** In 1988 and 1989, entrepreneur William Farley, who controls the Fruit of the Loom Company, courted stockholders and took over the Westpoint-Pepperell textile company. Despite a deeply hostile counterattack by Westpoint-Pepperell management, Farley's bid proved successful.

What are the economic implications of takeover bids? While such entrepreneurial activities may carry a "robber baron" flavor, they reflect the free market at work. If individual returns are to be maximized—to say nothing of economic productivity and growth in general—investors must be able to make rational choices among investments, including stocks, works of art, and rare stamps. Due to poor or improper management, stock prices may not reflect the underlying value of the assets of a company. Not only will investors receive less than maximum returns from their investments in such a case, but their abilities to make informed choices among investment alternatives will be impaired as well. The takeover entrepreneur brings the value of the tradable stock assets to its highest potential level. If the entrepreneur makes a mistake and acquires a corporation whose value is below the price he or she paid for it, the entrepreneur will suffer the consequences. Although takeovers have become controversial (see Economics in Action, "Leveraged Buyouts of Firms and the Takeover of RJR/Nabisco"), they may be viewed as indicators of economic efficiency.

FOCUS   To the Jousts: A Short Guide to Corporate Takeover Terminology

Like the warfare of medieval knights, modern corporate takeovers are filled with strategy, tactics, and intrigue. Wall Street brokerage firms, banks, and traders have developed their own slang to describe the happenings.[a] The action begins with the *raider* who is attempting to gain control of a company's stock in an "unfriendly" manner—that is, against the wishes of current management. The company's management has a number of defense options when rumors of takeover or unfriendly raiders appear. When management suspects that a takeover attempt may take place, it can employ a *scorched earth tactic* by selling off the company's most attractive assets or by committing it to long-term contracts, which may make the company less desirable as a takeover target. Or it might use the *lollipop*

defense, which permits current shareholders to sell their shares at premium prices *only* if the raider acquires a predetermined quantity of the outstanding shares. In the *pac-man defense,* the targeted company tries to purchase control over the raider before the raider is successful in the takeover.

The company can also attempt to get a *showstopper*—a legal maneuver designed to stop the takeover attempt. In *feemail,* attorney's fees might have to be paid by self-interested stockholders to prevent existing management from ransoming shares held by raiders attempting to get *greenmail.* Existing management may also court *white knights*—people or corporations who are encouraged to purchase sufficient shares to save the business from the unfriendly takeover. To protect themselves against the possibility that their defenses may fail, managers may vote themselves a *golden parachute*—termination or other retirement benefits that will make them financially secure no matter what happens to the company.

[a]For more fascinating details of the slang of the corporate and financial world, see Allan H. Pessin and Joseph A. Ross, *More Words of Wall Street: 2000 Investment Terms Defined* (Homewood, Illinois: Dow-Jones-Irwin, 1986).

Other Types of Enterprises

The proprietorship, the partnership, and the corporation are not the only possible types of firms in the economy. Other types of firms are not generally numerous, nor do they account for a large portion of economic activity in the United States, but we mention some briefly.

Labor-managed firm:
A firm that is owned and managed by the employees of the firm, who are also the residual claimants to firm profits.

Labor-Managed Firms. Most firms in Yugoslavia are owned and managed by the employees. The employees share in the profits of the enterprise in addition to earning their normal wages. This form of profit-sharing enterprise is gaining popularity in West Germany and exists to a limited degree in the United States. Profit-sharing programs in U.S. firms allow employees to share in their respective firms' performance. While this is not strictly labor management of the firm, since the workers do not make managerial decisions, it is perhaps a step in the direction of labor management. Other examples include the phenomena of workers buying a plant when management decides to shut it down, as happened at a Bethlehem Steel plant in Johnstown, Pennsylvania, and the addition of union leaders to the boards of directors of corporations. The most notable example of this is in the automobile industry, where the president of the United Auto Workers sits on the board of Chrysler Corporation. Also in this vein are numerous cooperatives around the country in which individuals band together to produce simple clothing or craft goods such as quilts, furniture, and Christmas tree ornaments.

Labor-managed firms are very attractive to employees. Any increase in profits resulting from increased productivity accrues to the workers, which adds an incentive to be efficient and avoid shirking. Increases in wages and strikes only serve to decrease profits and thus occur less often. Also, since the workers manage the firm, they can determine their own working conditions, safety standards, and fringe benefits.

This type of firm faces one important constraint, as do all other kinds of firms. For a firm to survive in the long run, it must be efficient with respect to its costs of production. To compete with other firms, the labor-managed firm must keep its costs as low as possible. Excessive wages, fringe benefits, or costly programs such as office beautification could force firms out of business. Any management decisions by labor must be as efficient as decisions made by traditional managers of other firms. For this reason the working conditions and incomes of employees of successful labor-managed firms do not and cannot differ significantly from those in other firms in a market economy.

In addition, management by labor does not completely eliminate incentives to shirk. When an individual worker's extra effort or lack of it are shared equally with a large number of other employees, then the rewards or costs of these activities to the individual are diminished.

In the long run the survival of firms is in the hands of owners and managers whose incomes depend on their special talents and efficiency. Labor-owned and -managed firms must provide this talent and efficiency as well as the labor.

Nonprofit firm:
A firm with no residual claimant(s) or shareholders. Such a firm may have a charitable or research objective for which it raises and expends funds.

Nonprofit Firms. Nonprofit firms—such as churches, country clubs, colleges, cooperatives, and mutual insurance companies—do not have a group of owners to whom a residual return accrues. No one owns a college in the sense of making a profit from its operation. Generally, funds raised by such organizations must be spent to further the purposes of the organization. Since the reward for good performance is spread among members of the organization, the individual incentive to do a good job is much reduced. Theoretically, workers in nonprofit institutions may have greater incentives to shirk and to pursue their own interests on the job than workers in profit-making institutions.

Publicly owned firm:
A firm owned and operated by government.

Publicly Owned Firms. Governments sometimes own and operate basic public services, such as railroad, airline, and water companies. One issue in these cases is whether government is a more efficient provider of these services than privately owned enterprises. The answer seems to be no. Note the distinction between publicly owned firms and private firms that are subject to public regulation. (Publicly regulated firms are treated in detail in Chapter 19.) Government water tends to cost more than private water; government garbage collection often costs more than private garbage collection; with few exceptions, government airlines are less efficient than private airlines. Why? The answer appears to be that operators of government enterprises do not face the test of profit or loss as directly as do their private counterparts. Losses in a publicly owned firm can be made up from general tax revenues, for example. Without the discipline of profit and loss, costs can be higher in public than in private enterprises. (We will take up the issues of profits and losses in succeeding chapters.)

THE BALANCE SHEET OF A FIRM

Balance sheet:
An accounting representation of the assets, liabilities, and net worth of a firm.

Asset:
Anything of value owned by a firm that adds to the firm's net worth.

Ownership claims:
The legal titles that identify ownership of the assets of a firm.

Liability:
Anything owed as a debt by a firm, reducing net worth.

Net worth:
The owners' net value of a firm, determined by subtracting liabilities from assets; also called equity.

The financial status of a business enterprise is represented by a **balance sheet,** a statement in which the dollar value of all the firm's **assets** corresponds to an equal total value of **ownership claims.** This correspondence is necessary and exact. An asset is a resource owned by the firm; an ownership claim identifies each party who has a property right or a claim to the firm's assets or wealth. A **liability** is simply a debt of the company—what the company owes to various creditors.

Underlying the balance sheet is a fundamental identity:

Value of assets − value of total claims to ownership = value of liabilities (the amount owed) + value of owned property in the firm.

Another familiar way of expressing this identity is

$$\text{Assets} = \text{liabilities} + \text{net worth.}$$

Net worth, also called equity, is the amount of a firm's wealth left over for the owner(s) after all liabilities are met from the firm's assets. If liabilities exceed assets, the firm's net worth is negative. Net worth is

$$\text{Net worth} = \text{assets} - \text{liabilities.}$$

A simplified hypothetical balance sheet of a sole proprietorship is presented in Table 3. In the sole proprietorship, all the firm's assets are owned by a single individual who is personally liable for all of the firm's debts. The proprietor's own stake in the business is his or her net worth, or equity; this is the difference between the firm's assets and the firm's debts. In this case, Joan Robinson's net worth is $110,000.

Table 4 reproduces a simplified balance sheet for a hypothetical partnership. Note that it is identical to the sole proprietorship's balance sheet except that the net worth of the firm is divided equally between partner Smith and partner Ricardo. Equity in partnerships need not always be divided equally between the two (or more) partners. However they divide the equity, each of the partners is individually liable for the firm's entire debt.

In Table 5 we present a simplified balance sheet for a hypothetical corporation. The corporation is legally defined as an individual separate and distinct from its shareholders. Hence, all of its assets are held in the name of the firm. The firm's assets minus its liabilities equals its net worth, termed the *capital stock.* Shareholders hold claims to this capital stock, which represents their equity in the firm. This equity may be paid out to shareholders in the form of dividends or plowed back into investments in the firm in the form of retained earnings. Shareholders are legally liable for the firm's debts up to, but not exceeding, the extent to which they have invested in the firm.

Income statement:
A summary of a firm's revenues and expenses over a month, a quarter, a year or some other time period; facilitates assessments of a firm's well-being.

Another important accounting document is the **income statement,** which reveals the financial condition of the firm over some *specific* time period. The income statement summarizes a firm's revenues and expenses over certain accounting periods—months, quarters, or years—so that comparisons of the firm's financial well-being can be made. Table 6 is such a statement for a

TABLE 3

Balance Sheet of Joan Robinson, a Sole Proprietor

The net worth or equity of the firm to Joan Robinson is equal to total assets minus total debts. In a sole proprietorship the single owner has complete claim to all of the equity.

Assets		Debts	
Cash holdings	$ 4,000	Accounts payable	$ 8,000
Equipment	20,000	Mortgage payable	20,000
Warehouse inventory	14,000	Total debts	28,000
Land and building	100,000	Joan Robinson's equity	110,000
Total assets	$138,000	Total debts plus equity	$138,000

TABLE 4

Balance Sheet of Smith and Ricardo, a Partnership

The balance sheet of a firm that is a partnership is very much like that of a sole proprietorship. In this case, the firm's equity is divided equally between the partners.

Assets		Debts	
Cash holdings	$ 60,000	Accounts payable	$ 11,000
Equipment	10,000	Mortgage payable	40,000
Warehouse inventory	52,000	Total debts	51,000
Land and building	120,000	Adam Smith's equity	95,500
		David Ricardo's equity	95,500
Total assets	$242,000	Total debts plus equity	$242,000

TABLE 5

Balance Sheet of Robert Malthus, Inc., a Corporation

The capital stock of a corporation is the firm's net worth. This equity is divided among the shareholders, the owners of the firm.

Assets		Debts	
Cash holdings	$ 60,000	Accounts payable	$ 13,000
Equipment	10,000	Mortgage payable	40,000
Warehouse inventory	52,000	Total debts	53,000
Land and buildings	120,000	Capital stock	189,000
Total assets	$242,000	Total debts and capital stock	$242,000

hypothetical corporation—J.S. Mill, Inc.—for the years 1989 and 1990. Basically, the income statement shows expenses subtracted from revenues over comparable periods. Net sales—representing revenues—top the statement, after which all of the various costs are deducted. Notice the two intermediate values for net income in Table 6. Net operating income is calculated by subtracting from net sales all of the corporation's expenses except corporate income taxes and interest. Earnings before taxes are found by calculating the difference between net operating income and interest expense. When taxes are deducted (calculated at 40 percent) from earnings before taxes, the income statement yields the net income after taxes, or the amount available to common stockholders in the firm. (Some net income may be reinvested in the firm as retained earnings rather than devoted to the payment of stockholders.) Again, an advantage of the income statement is that it allows an analysis of the firm's condition over time.

The firm is a fascinating and complex institution. It continues because of its efficiencies relative to simple exchange within markets. Some people see the modern corporation as an unchained beast that seeks to rule the world. The analysis in this chapter leads to a benign view of the corporation as a powerful instrument for economic good—which is not to say that corporations should be completely unfettered from public control. We explore such matters in Chapter 19 on economic regulation. We turn our attention in the next chapter to the conditions of real production and costs in the business firm.

TABLE 6

Income Statement of J.S. Mill, Inc., a Corporation

The income statement of the firm is a "still picture" of the revenues and expenses of the firm over some specific time period—in this case, the years 1989 and 1990, ending December 31. As such, it represents the financial condition of the firm over some period of time.

	1990 (thousands of dollars)	1989 (thousands of dollars)
Net sales	3000	2850
Costs and expenses		
Labor and materials	2544	2413
Depreciation	100	90
Advertising and selling	22	20
Other expenses	68	63
Total costs	2734	2586
Net operating income, or earnings before interest and taxes	266	264
Less interest expense	66	47
Earnings before taxes	200	217
Taxes (at 40%)	80	87
Net income after taxes available to stockholders	120	130

Summary

1. The basic function of a business firm is to combine inputs to produce outputs.

2. Economic coordination in a market economy can take place through prices and markets or within firms. Market coordination relies on price incentives; firm coordination relies on managerial directives.

3. Firm coordination of economic activities exists because there are costs to market exchange and efficiencies in large-scale production.

4. Team production takes place in firms. In team production, group output can be observed but individual output cannot.

5. Team production makes it natural for individual team members to shirk—that is, to reduce individual effort in achieving the team goal. It is the function of managers in the firm to control shirking.

6. A proprietorship is a single-owner firm whose owner faces unlimited liability for the contractual obligations of the firm. With unlimited liability, the personal wealth of the owner, above and beyond what

he or she has invested in the firm, can be drawn on to settle the firm's obligations in the event of bankruptcy.

7. A partnership is owned by two or more individuals who face shared unlimited liability for the contractual obligations of the firm.

8. A corporation is owned by shareholders who have limited liability. Shareholders are liable only for the amount they have invested in the corporation.

9. Corporations are owned by shareholders and typically controlled by professional managers. This potential division of interests has been a source of criticism of the modern corporation.

10. A balance sheet is a financial statement of the economic well-being of a firm. Net worth, which can be positive or negative, is a measure of the wealth of a firm's owner(s). It can be derived from a balance sheet and is defined as assets minus liabilities. An income statement summarizes the revenues and expenses of a firm over some specific period of time.

Key terms

firm	residual claimant	share transferability	asset
division of labor	scale of production	limited liability	ownership claims
market coordination	proprietorship	takeover bid strategy	liability
firm coordination	unlimited liability	greenmail	net worth
manager	partnership	labor-managed firm	income statement
team production	joint unlimited liability	nonprofit firm	
monitor	corporation	publicly owned firm	
shirking	shares	balance sheet	

Questions for review and discussion

1. Describe the workings of a balance sheet as presented in this chapter; be sure to include definitions for assets, liabilities, and net worth.

2. Compare and contrast limited liability and unlimited liability. Which of them characterizes (a) a sole proprietorship, (b) a partnership, (c) a corporation?

3. What are the major advantages and disadvantages of the corporation as a form of business organization?

4. What is the concept of team production? Does shirking mean that workers are naturally lazy? Give some examples of team production.

5. What type of firm is your college or university? How would you expect it to operate compared to a private corporation?

6. Is it inefficient for the control and ownership functions of large corporations to be separated?

7. What is the single most efficient way to extract effective performance from managers?

8. Since it would be easy for members of a team to shirk on their work, why does team production exist, from the firm owners' point of view?

9. What types of business activity should be organized as partnerships? Why?

10. A football team is by definition a team production process. Determine three ways that the coaches at your school work to monitor and control individual players' performances on the football team. Do they, for example, film practices and games or do they give differential rewards for superior performance?

ECONOMICS IN ACTION
Leveraged Buyouts of Firms and the Takeover of RJR/Nabisco

Takeovers are everyday news in the ever-changing United States business environment. In the early 1970s, takeover mania surrounded the oil and petroleum industries during the price rise created by OPEC (Organization of Petroleum Exporting Countries), an international cartel. In the late 1980s, what could best be described as a "food fight" developed on Wall Street when firms such as Kraft, Pillsbury, Holly Farms, Gerber Products, Church's Fried Chicken, and other food-related businesses became the objects of takeover attempts. The granddaddy of all takeovers, however, was the successful acquisition of the RJR/Nabisco company, a huge corporation composed of the combined R. J. Reynolds tobacco company (which makes Winston and Salem cigarettes) and Nabisco, one of the largest food sellers in the United States (owning such brands as Del Monte, Oreo cookies, Ritz crackers, and Life Savers). In October of 1988, a group of RJR/Nabisco managers tried to purchase the corporation from stockholders, offering $17 billion for their shares. In early December, the bidding stopped with a successful and record-setting offer of $24.7 billion ($109 per share). The winner: the investment firm of Kohlberg Kravis Roberts & Co. (KKR).

All financial observers were shocked by the sheer size of the KKR bid, for it entailed the largest *leveraged buyout* in history. A leveraged buyout (or LBO) occurs when a company's shareholders are bought out with cash raised largely through loans borrowed against the acquired firm's assets. The raiders (new management) then attempt to streamline the firm by lowering costs or by selling off pieces of the firm (often well-known brand names) to reduce the size of its debt. (This device is also sometimes called a *bootstrap acquisition.*)

In the case of KKR, $18 billion in cash had to be raised by setting up an LBO fund and by offering investors high returns for their participation. In such funds, low-rated high-interest bonds (*junk bonds* in industry slang) are often issued. Investors in KKR's LBO funds have done extremely well, as KKR sold off pieces of its companies at prices far above their stock market values. KKR itself takes a percentage of these profits plus transaction fees and management fees for putting the deals together. The possibility for such profits indicates that the assets of the individual companies (or brand names) were not being efficiently managed before the takeover.

There are both critics and defenders of leveraged buyouts in the business community and in government. Critics charge that recessions (downturns in business activity) or reductions in demand could put investors and even the banking system in *greater* jeopardy due to highly leveraged deals such as KKR's acquisition of RJR/Nabisco. If lower prices materialized during a recession, for example, KKR might have to sell pieces of its companies at unprofitable rates. Some unions and other labor organizations also charge that workers are sometimes displaced when large firms are bought and sold. When the Safeway supermarket chain was sold in a takeover, hundreds of employees lost their jobs. Politicians have complained that the government loses tax revenue on such deals since much of the cash flow of acquired businesses must go for nontaxable interest payments on debt. Huge debt, moreover, means that little may be left over from company earnings for research and for new investment.

Defenders of corporate takeovers, mergers, and leveraged buyouts point out that all business activity involves risk. In the event of recession, all kinds of investors stand to lose, including those who invested in high-risk (but high-yield) securities. The term *junk bonds* is simply an unflattering name for a risk that only some of us wish to take. Risk is inherent in business activity; yearly, 90 percent of all new businesses fail. In any market economy, businesses and workers are *continuously* being displaced as the demand for goods and services shifts and as technology changes. Change and adaptation in firms and in the worker population are part of the process of a market society. Moreover, U.S. firms that do not change and streamline to meet international competition in the 1990s will not revitalize America's competitive edge. Firms that do not engage in research and development for the future will either fail or become the object of takeovers. Ultimately, according to their defenders, takeovers would not be profitable if firms were being managed efficiently.

Question
Do you think corporate takeovers via leveraged buyouts should be prohibited by law? What might result from such legal action?

8

Production Principles and Costs to the Firm

All profit-oriented business firms are alike in one basic sense: Firms purchase inputs in resource markets and use these inputs to produce a product or service, which is then sold to consumers. The fact that inputs to a production process are not free—that they carry an opportunity cost—leads to the concept of production costs.

In this chapter we develop the concept of production cost from the perspective of the economist. When you complete Chapter 8 you should understand

- how production costs are actually a form of opportunity costs.
- how an accountant's out-of-pocket costs may sometimes differ from an economist's measure of opportunity cost.
- how costs of production influence a firm's behavior.
- how the various types of costs relate to both business decision making and to market functioning.

TYPES OF COSTS

Consumers have virtually unlimited wants, but resources to satisfy their wants are limited. Costs of production arise from the fact that resources have alternative uses. The same resources that are used to produce a good to satisfy consumers' demands can also be used to produce other goods. For resources to be drawn into the production of a particular good, they must be bid away from their present uses. Production of a newspaper might require, among other things, that wood pulp be turned into newsprint rather than notebook paper, that photographers be enticed to work as photo journalists rather than as portrait photographers, and that youngsters be hired to distribute newspapers rather than earn money by baby-sitting or mowing lawns. The expenditures representing the opportunity costs necessary to do all of these things are called **opportunity costs of production.** Costs of production are therefore the value of resources in their next-best uses. The Focus, "The Opportunity Cost of Military Service," illustrates this point.

Opportunity cost of production:
The opportunity cost of resources used to produce goods and services.

192

FOCUS   The Opportunity Cost of Military Service

Recent attempts to establish an all-volunteer army have been based on the concept of opportunity costs. That is, to induce people to volunteer for military service, the U.S. government offers them benefits comparable to those they would receive in civilian careers.

Assume that potential recruits have civilian jobs and that economics is the only consideration in deciding to join the army. If government can offer recruits a package including salary, room and board, clothing, education, health care, and travel opportunities that is equal to or greater than their opportunity cost—that is, what they would earn as civilians—then people will sign up in numbers considered sufficient for national defense.

If the opportunity cost to new recruits is not balanced by the army's offer, people will not volunteer in sufficient num-

bers. In this case, the government may return to the draft to meet its quota for national defense. When this happens, forced conscription can be seen as a tax—"the draft tax." The draft tax is equal to what an individual could have earned as a civilian minus any compensation he or she gets from serving in the military. If a recruit was earning $10,000 as a civilian but receives only $5000 in the military (including the value of benefits such as food and shelter), the draft tax is $5000.

This example assumes that only money wages matter to the individual. If the individual is concerned about the choice between civilian and military work—if he or she strongly prefers to work as a civilian no matter what the pay for military service is—the financial cost of $5000 understates the real opportunity cost of the draft to the individual.

Explicit and Implicit Costs

The opportunity costs of production include both explicit and implicit costs. Take, for example, a small, owner-operated dry cleaning firm organized as a sole proprietorship. The dry cleaner has to purchase labor, cleaning fluids, hat blocks, bagging machines, insurance, accounting and legal services, advertising, and so on, to produce dry cleaning services. The costs of these resources, entered onto the firm's balance sheet, are called **accounting**, or explicit, **costs.** They are so named because they are quite visible; they are the wages and bills the sole proprietor must pay to conduct business.

Accounting costs:
Payments a firm actually makes to resource suppliers; out-of-pocket costs or explicit costs.

The firm does not make explicit payments for all the resources it uses to produce dry cleaning services. The owner of the firm may not enter a wage for his own services on the balance sheet. Omitting his salary from the balance sheet, however, does not mean that the owner's services are free. They carry an **implicit cost,** valued by what the owner could have done with his time instead of working in the firm. Implicit costs are the opportunity costs of resources owned by the firm. They are called *implicit costs* because they do not involve contractual payments that are entered on the firm's balance sheet.

Implicit costs:
The opportunity cost of resources used in production, for which no explicit payments are made.

Opportunity cost of capital:
The return that could be received from the next-best alternative investment.

The main implicit cost is the **opportunity cost of capital.** Individuals who invest in firms expect to earn a normal rate of return on their investment. For instance, they could have placed their capital in money market certificates and earned at least a 6 percent rate of return. In this case, the 6 percent rate of return represents the opportunity cost of capital invested in business ventures. Unless investors earn at least the opportunity cost of capital, they will not continue to invest in a business. (Here we neglect the fact that individuals may also receive implicit returns—for example, satisfaction from investing in environmentally conscious businesses—that would have to be included in their calculations.)

Total cost of production:
The total opportunity cost of all resources used in production; the sum of all explicit and implicit production costs.

The **total cost of production** is the sum of explicit and implicit costs. Total cost is the value of all the alternative opportunities forgone as a result of production of a particular good or service.

The Nature of Economic Costs

Opportunity cost is a forward-looking concept. Opportunity costs are incurred when the decision-maker decides about the future use of resources; they are the expected costs of possible alternatives available to an owner.

An owner must choose, for example, among potential plants of different sizes. The plants do not yet exist—they are only in the planning or blueprint stage of development. The owner will base his or her estimate of what the costs look like on past experience in the industry or in other industries, so the past is of some help in estimating what will happen in the future. The choice of plant size, however, involves looking into the future and making a decision under uncertainty. To select a plant size means forgoing certain future alternative plant sizes.

Historical costs:
Costs measured by the cost of a resource at the time the resource was purchased.

Sunk costs:
Previously incurred, irretrievable costs of a currently owned resource.

In contrast, accounting costs are **historical costs,** or costs that have been incurred in the past. While historical costs can be useful in estimating economic costs, historical costs look backward; opportunity costs look forward. Historical costs are often poor guides to opportunity costs. Consider the case of **sunk costs,** which are closely related to historical costs. The essential characteristic of sunk costs is that some productive activities require specialized forms of capital that are not easily converted into other productive uses. More precisely, current sunk costs are the difference between the initial cost—which exists prior to a commitment to a given investment or project—and the value that can be recovered after commitment to the given investment or project. Sunk costs are the irretrievable part of any fixed or historical investment.

For better or worse, certain portions of earlier decisions cannot be reversed. Economists consider certain of the costs of previous decisions—the sunk costs—to be irrelevant to current decisions. Suppose that you buy a farm in Vermont for $300,000 and spend an additional $200,000 refurbishing the old farmhouse, which you plan to operate as a bed and breakfast. After a year you realize that your location prevents you from profitably remaining in business. If you decide to sell, should your asking price be dictated by your having spent $500,000 on the property?

The answer is no. A portion of the $500,000 in costs you have already incurred is a sunk cost. Some of the alterations you made may have no value if the property is to be put to a use other than serving as a bed and breakfast—in fact, some changes may actually reduce the property's value for other uses. You must realize that some of your costs cannot be recaptured. Some of the money you invested is gone forever. It may be that we have to learn this the hard way—from experience. However, viewed rationally, current decisions *should* be based on current or expected costs and benefits, not on sunk costs and past benefits.

Economic Profits Versus Accounting Profits

Economic profit:
The amount by which total revenues exceed total opportunity cost.

$$E\pi = TR - TC(expl + impl)$$

Businesspeople must compare their total costs with their total revenues (all the money they take in) to determine whether they are making a profit. **Economic profit** is the difference between total revenue and total opportunity cost. It exists when the revenue of the firm more than covers all of its costs, explicit and implicit. Economic loss results when revenue does not cover the total opportunity cost. A firm's economic profit is said to be zero when its total revenue equals its total cost. Zero economic profit does not mean that the firm is not viable or about to cease operating. It means that the firm is covering all the costs of its operations and that the owners and investors are making a normal rate of return on their investment.

Since accounting costs do not usually include implicit costs—such as the value of the sole proprietor's time or the opportunity cost of capital invested in the firm—accounting costs are an understatement of the opportunity costs of production. **Accounting profits** will generally be higher than economic profits because economic profits are calculated after taking both explicit and implicit costs into account.

Private Costs and Social Costs

We have so far discussed a world of **private costs,** in which the firm pays a market price for the resources it uses in production. The dry cleaner's costs of production were private costs, equal to the sum of explicit and implicit costs. The key aspect of the concept of private costs is that someone is responsible for them; that is, someone pays for the use of the resources. The owner of the dry cleaning firm incurred both explicit and implicit costs in business, and he paid these costs to engage in business.

But what if the dry cleaner dumps used cleaning fluid into the town lake adjacent to the plant? In this case he is using the lake as a resource in his dry cleaning business—as a place to dispose of a by-product of his production process—but he pays no charge for the use of the lake as a dumping site. No one owns the lake for purposes of dumping, and it is therefore unpriced for this use. The private costs of the dry cleaner thus do not reflect the full costs of his operation. The cost of the use of the lake is not reflected in the dry cleaner's costs of production. Such a cost is called an **external cost** because the cost is borne by someone other than the owner of the firm.

When external costs arise from a firm's activities—such as polluting the air or water—the firm imposes **social costs.** These are the total of both private and external costs; the total cost to society of the firm's production includes the costs of using environmental assets such as the town lake, as well as its input costs.

In Chapter 20 we further analyze external costs, including ways in which society can correct problems arising from external costs. The important point here is that private costs of production do not always reflect the full opportunity costs of production; the use of unpriced resources, such as the environment, may also carry a hidden price to society.

ECONOMIC TIME   SR, LR

The passage of time is fundamental to the theory of costs. Economic time is not the same thing as calendar time. To the economist analyzing costs, the firm's time constraints are defined by its ability to adjust its operations in light of a changing marketplace. If the demand for the firm's product decreases, for example, the firm must adjust production to the lower level of demand. Perhaps some of its resources can be immediately and easily varied to adapt to the changed circumstances. In the face of declining or increasing sales, an automobile firm can reduce or increase its orders of steel and fabric. Inputs whose purchase and use can be altered quickly are called **variable inputs.** The auto firm with declining sales cannot immediately sell its excess plants and equip-

---

$A.\pi = TR - Texp.C.$

Accounting profit:
The amount by which total revenues exceed total accounting, or explicit, costs.

Private costs:
The opportunity costs of production that are borne, or paid, by producers.

External costs:
The opportunity costs of production that are not borne, or paid, by producers.

Social costs:
The opportunity cost of all resources used in the production of goods and services; the sum of private plus external costs.

Variable input:
A factor of production whose level of usage may be changed in the short run.

Fixed input:
A factor of production whose level of usage cannot be changed in the short run.

Short run:
An amount of time insufficient to allow the usage of all inputs to vary.

Long run:
An amount of time sufficiently long that all input usage levels can be varied.

ment or its inventory. Such resources are called **fixed inputs;** a reduction or increase in their use takes considerably more time to arrange.

There are two primary categories of economic time: the short run and the long run. The **short run** is a period in which some inputs remain fixed. In the **long run** all inputs can be varied. In the long run, the auto firm can make fewer cars not only by buying less steel but also by reducing the number of plants and the amount of equipment and labor it uses for car production. The time it takes to vary all inputs is different for different industries. In some cases, it may take only a month, in others a year, and in still others ten years. In August 1983, for example, the Chrysler Corporation announced that it planned to be able to respond to an increase in sales by boosting its output by 50 percent within twelve months. The relative brevity of this period needed to increase output was made possible by its purchase of a former Volkswagen assembly plant, an increase in work shifts, the return to production of resources left idle during earlier cutbacks, and a sharp increase in purchases of new capital stock. Increased demand for home entertainment in the latter half of the 1980s encouraged Turner Broadcasting System (TBS) and Home Box Office (HBO) to make new investments in cable television programming. Some of these—the purchase of old film libraries, for example—were accomplished relatively quickly, but others, such as the production of new motion pictures for broadcast, required a far longer time horizon.

SHORT-RUN COSTS

In the short run, some of the firm's inputs are fixed and others are variable. Building on this distinction, the short-run theory of costs emphasizes two categories of costs—fixed and variable.

Fixed Costs and Variable Costs

Fixed costs:
The costs of inputs that cannot be varied in the short run.

A **fixed cost** is the cost of a fixed input. In the short run, the fixed cost does not change as the firm's output level changes. Whether the firm produces more or less, it will pay the same for such things as fire insurance, local property taxes, and other costs that are independent of its output level. Fixed costs exist even at a zero rate of output. Perhaps the most important fixed cost is the opportunity cost of the firm's capital equipment and plant—that is, the next-best alternative use of these resources. This cost exists even when the plant is idle. The only way to avoid fixed costs is to shut down and go out of business, an event that can occur only in the long run. Total fixed costs (TFC) equal the price of fixed inputs multiplied by the quantity of fixed inputs employed.

Variable costs:
The costs of inputs whose usage levels can be changed in the short run. Variable costs change as output changes.

Variable costs are costs that change as the output level of a firm changes. When the firm reduces its level of production, it will use fewer raw materials and perhaps will lay off workers. Consequently, its variable costs of production will decline. Variable costs are expenditures on inputs that can be varied in short-run use. Total variable costs (TVC) equal the price of variable inputs multiplied by the quantity of variable inputs employed. **Total cost** (TC) is the sum of total fixed and total variable costs.

Total costs:
All the costs of a firm's operations; total variable costs plus total fixed costs.

It is useful to determine how the cost of producing output changes in the short run as the level of output is increased or decreased. The fixed cost

Average fixed cost:
Total fixed costs divided by the level of output.

per unit is called **average fixed cost** (AFC) and is found by dividing the total fixed cost (TFC) by the firm's total output of the good (referred to as q throughout this chapter). Since total fixed costs are the same at all levels of output, AFC will decline continuously as output increases. This relation is defined in Table 1 and shown graphically in Figure 1a. Symbolically, average fixed cost is expressed

$$AFC = \frac{TFC}{q}.$$

Average variable cost:
Total variable costs divided by the level of output.

Average variable cost (AVC) is found by dividing total variable cost (TVC) by the firm's output. It is also drawn in Figure 1a and defined in Table 1. Average variable cost ordinarily has a U shape and may be expressed in the formula

$$AVC = \frac{TVC}{q}.$$

Average total cost:
Total costs divided by the level of output.

Average total cost (ATC) is total cost divided by total output. Average total cost also can be found by adding average fixed costs and average variable costs. Thus, in Figure 1a, the ATC curve is shown as the vertical sum of the AFC and AVC curves. Average total cost is sometimes referred to as *unit cost,* and it is total cost (fixed plus variable) divided by the firm's output, or

$$ATC = \frac{TC}{q}.$$

Although the average total cost curve provides useful information, economic decisions are made at the margin. In considering a change in the level of production, firms must determine the marginal cost of the change.

Marginal cost:
The additional cost of producing one more unit of output; the change in total costs divided by the change in output.

Marginal cost (MC) is the cost of producing each additional unit of output; it is found by dividing the change in total costs by the change in output. Symbolically, marginal cost may be expressed

$$MC = \frac{\Delta TC}{\Delta q}.$$

TABLE 1   Short-Run Cost Relations

Terms	Symbols	Definition
Average fixed cost = Total fixed cost ÷ Output	$AFC = TFC/q$	A fixed cost does not vary with output. Average fixed cost per unit declines as output rises.
Average variable cost = Total variable cost ÷ Output	$AVC = TVC/q$	Average variable cost exhibits a U-shaped pattern as output increases.
Average total cost = Total cost ÷ Output = Average fixed cost + Average variable cost	$ATC = TC/q$ $ATC = AFC + AVC$	Total cost is the sum of fixed and variable costs. Average total cost also forms a U-shaped curve when graphed from very low to very high output levels.
Marginal cost = Change in total cost ÷ Change in output	$MC = \Delta TC/\Delta q$	Marginal cost first falls and then rises as the short-run capacity of a firm's fixed plant is approached.

FIGURE 1 Short-Run Cost Curves of the Firm

(a) The behavior of average fixed cost (AFC), average variable cost (AVC), and average total cost (ATC) as output changes. ATC is the sum of AVC and AFC. (b) The behavior of the firm's marginal costs (MC) as output increases. MC ultimately rises as the short-run capacity limit of the firm is approached at $\bar{q}$. (c) All the short-run cost curves. Notice in particular the U shape of the ATC curve. ATC is high where the firm's plant is underutilized at low rates of output or overutilized at high rates of output. The rate of output is measured per unit of time.

(a) (b) (c)

Fixed plant:
A given amount of equipment and size of production facilities with which the firm can use variable inputs in the short run.

The result of such calculations is a marginal cost curve, shown in Figure 1b. As output rises, marginal cost declines, reaches a minimum, then rises—because it becomes increasingly hard to produce additional output in a **fixed plant.** Extra workers needed to produce additional output begin to get in each other's way; inefficiencies proliferate as workers must take turns using machines; storage room for inputs and outputs becomes filled. At some point the firm's maximum output from its fixed plant will be reached (shown at $\bar{q}$).

Figure 1c brings all the short-run cost curves together. Notice that the ATC curve is U-shaped. At low levels of output a firm does not utilize its fixed plant and equipment very effectively. The firm does not produce enough relative to the fixed costs for its plant, causing the average total cost to be high. At high levels of output the firm approaches its capacity limit ($\bar{q}$). The inefficiencies of overloading the existing operation cause marginal costs to rise, raising the average total cost. These two effects combine to yield a U-shaped average total cost curve. Either low or high utilization of a fixed plant leads to high average total cost. The minimum point on the ATC curve, q, represents the lowest average total cost—the lowest cost per unit for producing the good. Table 1 provides a shorthand reference to all these concepts.

Diminishing Returns

Law of diminishing marginal returns:
A situation in which adding more and more of a variable input to a fixed plant results in smaller and smaller amounts of additional output produced.

The behavior and shape of the short-run marginal cost and average total cost curves can be understood more completely with the **law of diminishing marginal returns.** The law of diminishing marginal returns states that as additional units of a variable input are combined with a fixed amount of other resources, the amount of additional output produced will start to decline beyond some point. The returns—additional output—that result from using more and more of the variable input will ultimately diminish.

Though the language sounds formidable, the law of diminishing marginal returns is little more than formalized common sense. Suppose that the dry cleaner in our previous example has a plant of a given size that we will view as his fixed input. He begins operations by adding workers one at a time and observes what happens to the resulting output of dry cleaning. The first few additional workers are very useful. One specializes in cleaning, another in pressing, another in bagging, and so on. The output of dry cleaning increases as the laborers are added. But the process cannot go on forever. At some point the output provided by one additional laborer will begin to diminish because capacity of the existing physical plant will be reached.

The law of diminishing marginal returns is a fact of nature. Imagine how the world would work if it were not true: All the world's dry cleaning could be done in a single plant. And if diminishing returns did not exist in agriculture, all of the world's food could be grown on a fixed plot of land, say an acre.

The law of diminishing marginal returns can be illustrated numerically and graphically. A standard example comes from agriculture; we experiment by adding laborers to a fixed plot of land and observe what happens to output. To isolate the effect of adding additional workers (the variable input), we keep all inputs except labor fixed and assume that agricultural technology does not change.

Table 2 is a numerical analysis of the results of such an experiment. The first column shows the amount of the variable input—labor—that is used in combination with the fixed input—land. The simplified numbers for **total product** and **marginal product** represent real measures of output such as tons of soybeans grown per year.

Marginal product is the change in total product caused by the addition of each additional worker, or

$$MP = \frac{\text{change in output}}{\text{change in quantity of variable input}}.$$

At first, as workers (the variable input) are added, total product, or output, expands rapidly. The first three workers show increasing marginal products (10, 12, and 14 extra tons of soybeans with the addition of each worker). Diminishing marginal returns set in, however, with the addition of the fourth worker. That is, the marginal product of the fourth worker is 13 tons, down from the 14-ton marginal product gained by adding the third worker. Marginal product continues to decline as additional workers are added to the plot of land. This agrees with our earlier definition of the law of diminishing marginal returns: As additional units of a variable input are added to a fixed amount of other resources, beyond some point the amount of additional output produced will start to decline. In fact, the addition of the ninth and tenth workers leads to reductions in total product. Marginal product in these cases is negative, meaning that the addition of these workers actually reduces output. It becomes more and more difficult to obtain increases in output from the fixed plot of land by adding workers. At some point the workers simply get in each other's way.

Total product:
The total amount of output produced.

Marginal product:
The additional output produced by employing one additional unit of a variable input.

TABLE 2

Law of Diminishing Marginal Returns

If units of a variable input (labor) are added one at a time to a production process with a fixed plant (growing soybeans with no change in technology on a fixed plot of land), the total product, marginal product, and average product all increase at first. But eventually, as more workers are added, they begin to get in each other's way. Total output gained by adding more workers begins to decline, as predicted by the law of diminishing marginal returns.

Variable Input (units of labor)	Total Product (tons per year)	Marginal Product (tons per year)	Average Product (tons per year)
0	0		0
		10	
1	10		10.00
		12	
2	22		11.00
		14	
3	36		12.00
		13	
4	49		12.25
		11	
5	60		12.00
		10	
6	70		11.67
		5	
7	75		10.71
		3	
8	78		9.75
		-2	
9	76		8.44
		-6	
10	70		7.00

Average product:
Total output divided by the number of units of the variable input used to produce the total output; output produced per unit of variable input used.

The last column in the table introduces the concept of **average product,** which is total product divided by the number of units of the variable input, or

$$AP = \frac{q}{\text{quantity of variable input}}.$$

It is the average output per worker. Average product increases as long as marginal product is greater than average product. Thus, average product increases through the addition of the fourth worker. The marginal product of the fifth worker is 11, which is less than the average product for five workers, and beyond this point the average product falls.

Figure 2 graphically illustrates the law of diminishing marginal returns with the data from Table 2. Figure 2a illustrates the total product curve. Total product increases rapidly at first, as the marginal product of the first three workers increases. Diminishing returns set in with the fourth worker, and thereafter the total product increases less rapidly. Beyond eight workers, the total product curve turns down and starts to decline. The maximum total product is reached with eight workers. The marginal product and average product curves are shown in Figure 2b. The marginal product curve is simply the slope of the total product curve. It rises to a maximum at three workers and then declines as diminishing returns set in. Eventually, it becomes negative past eight workers, indicating that total product is decreasing. The average

FIGURE 2

(a) Total product curve, plotting the data from Table 2. (b) Average product and marginal product curves. Marginal product is the rate of change of the total product curve. The area of diminishing marginal returns begins when marginal product starts to decline. Average product rises when marginal product is greater than average product, and it falls when marginal product is less than average product.

Total, Average, and Marginal Product Curves

(a)

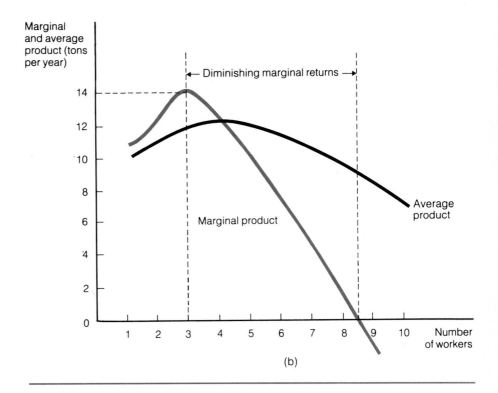

(b)

product curve rises when marginal product is greater than average product, and it declines when marginal product is less than average product.

How can the law of diminishing marginal returns be applied to economic decision making? Consider the thinking of the farmer who owns the plot of land in this experiment. How many workers will he or she choose to hire? Before the area of diminishing marginal returns is reached, additional workers have an increasing marginal product. The farmer will add these workers and will go no further in hiring than the point where the marginal product falls to zero. Even if labor were free, the farmer would not go beyond this point because there would be so many workers on the land that the marginal product of an additional worker would be negative and the total product would decline. This implies that it is rational for the farmer to operate somewhere in the area of diminishing marginal returns.

Precisely how many workers will maximize profits? The answer depends on the cost of the workers. Assume that each worker is paid a wage rate equivalent to 4 units of output. The farmer will compare the marginal product of each worker with the wage rate. The fourth worker adds 13 units of output and costs the farmer the equivalent of only 4 units. In fact, the marginal product of the first seven workers exceeds their wage rate. However, the marginal product of the eighth worker is 3 units of output, which is less than the wage rate. The rational farmer will therefore hire seven workers. This is the law of diminishing marginal returns in action. It points the farmer toward the rational utilization of factors of production.

Diminishing Marginal Returns and Short-Run Costs

What does the law of diminishing marginal returns imply about the behavior of the firm's short-run cost curves? Once diminishing marginal returns set in, more and more of the variable input—in our example, labor—is needed to expand output by an additional unit. If the price of the variable input is fixed, the firm's marginal costs will rise as a reflection of diminishing returns. Adding more workers to the plot of land at a fixed wage rate eventually leads to both diminishing returns and rising marginal costs. These are two ways of looking at the same thing.

To see this point more clearly, let's work through the formulas. Recall the definition of marginal cost from Table 1:

$$MC = \frac{\text{change in total cost}}{\text{change in output}}.$$

Since a change in total cost is equal to a change in the number of units of the variable input times the price of the variable input (which we assume is constant), the expression can be rewritten

$$MC = \frac{\text{change in quantity of variable input}}{\text{change in output}} \times \text{price of variable input}.$$

We know that marginal product is defined as the change in output divided by a change in the quantity of the variable input. Thus, the first term in the MC expression is the reciprocal of marginal product. MC can further be rewritten

$$MC = \frac{1}{\text{marginal product of variable input}} \times \text{price of variable input}$$

$$= \frac{\text{price of variable input}}{\text{marginal product of variable input}}.$$

This means that marginal cost is inversely related to marginal product. That is, if the price of the variable input is constant, then increases in marginal cost are associated with decreases in marginal product. If, for example, the marginal product of the input is 20 units of output and the input price is $5 per unit, the marginal cost is $0.25 per unit. If the price of the variable input is $5 and its marginal product is 10 units of output, the marginal cost of each of those units is $0.50 per unit. To argue that marginal returns are diminishing is to argue that marginal costs are rising: As the quantity of variable inputs increases, marginal product (and output) rises and then falls. This means that as output rises marginal cost, too, rises and then falls.

Similarly, average variable cost is the inverse of the average product curve. Average variable cost is equivalent to the firm's total expenditure on variable inputs divided by the output of the firm, or TVC/q. The expenditure on variable inputs is also their price multiplied by the quantity used. The average expense on variable inputs is thus found by dividing their cost by the output of the firm, or

$$AVC = \frac{\text{quantity of variable inputs}}{\text{output of the firm}} \times \text{price of variable input}.$$

We know, however, that the average product of any input is its total product divided by the quantity of variable inputs employed. Thus, the first term in the expression for AVC is the reciprocal of average product, so that AVC may be rewritten

$$AVC = \frac{1}{\text{average product of variable input}} \times \text{price of variable input}$$

$$= \frac{\text{price of variable input}}{\text{average product of variable input}}.$$

Average variable cost, then, is inversely related to average product. Since the price of the variable input is assumed constant, reductions in AVC are associated with increases in average product and increases in AVC are associated with decreases in average product. If, for example, the price of a variable input is $5 per unit and the average product of the input is 5 units of the firm's output, the AVC at 5 units of output is $1 per unit of input. If the average product of the input is 10 units of output, the AVC is $0.50 per unit, and so on.

Table 3 presents a numerical illustration of how the law of diminishing marginal returns affects a firm's short-run costs. Columns (2), (3), and (4) show how total costs behave as output increases in the short run, and columns (5), (6), and (7) show the behavior of the corresponding average cost concepts.

In this example, we keep the numbers low for simplicity. Total fixed cost is constant at $10 per day; average fixed cost per unit is the total fixed cost divided by output. Fixed costs must be paid in the short run regardless of whether the firm operates. The level of average fixed cost falls continuously as output is increased. For the first unit produced, for example, both total fixed cost and average fixed cost are $10. Total fixed cost remains at $10 for the second unit, but average fixed cost falls to $5 per unit. As business grows, average fixed cost falls.

Remember, total variable cost is the sum of the firm's expenditures on variable inputs. As Table 3 shows, in order to produce more output, more must be spent on variable inputs. It takes an additional expenditure of $1.60

TABLE 3   Short-Run Cost Data for a Firm

The various concepts of short-run costs are expressed in both total and average terms. Columns (1) through (4) present the firm's total cost data; columns (5) through (8) present the cost data in marginal and average terms. Notice especially that short-run marginal cost ultimately rises because of the law of diminishing marginal returns.

	Total Cost Data (per day)			Marginal and Average Cost Data (per day)			
(1)	(2)	(3)	(4)	(5)	(6)	(7)	(8)
Output (units)	Total Fixed Cost	Total Variable Cost	Total Cost (2) + (3)	Average Fixed Cost (2) ÷ (1)	Average Variable Cost (3) ÷ (1)	Average Total Cost (4) ÷ (1)	Marginal Cost Δ(4) ÷ Δ(1)[a]
0	$10.00	$ 0.00	$10.00	$ —	$ —	$ —	$ —
1	10.00	1.60	11.60	10.00	1.60	11.60	11.60
2	10.00	3.05	13.05	5.00	1.53	6.53	1.45
3	10.00	4.40	14.40	3.33	1.47	4.80	1.35
4	10.00	5.70	15.70	2.50	1.43	3.93	1.30
5	10.00	6.90	16.90	2.00	1.38	3.38	1.20
6	10.00	8.00	18.00	1.67	1.33	3.00	1.10
7	10.00	9.00	19.00	1.43	1.29	2.71	1.00
8	10.00	9.90	19.90	1.25	1.24	2.49	0.90
9	10.00	10.20	20.20	1.11	1.13	2.24	0.30
10	10.00	10.85	20.85	1.00	1.09	2.09	0.65
11	10.00	12.15	22.15	0.91	1.10	2.01	1.30
12	10.00	13.65	23.65	0.83	1.14	1.97	1.50
13	10.00	15.40	25.40	0.77	1.18	1.95	1.75
14	10.00	17.80	27.80	0.71	1.27	1.99	2.40
15	10.00	21.05	31.05	0.67	1.40	2.07	3.25
16	10.00	25.30	35.30	0.63	1.58	2.21	4.25
17	10.00	30.65	40.65	0.59	1.80	2.39	5.35
18	10.00	37.20	47.20	0.56	2.07	2.62	6.55
19	10.00	45.00	55.00	0.53	2.37	2.89	7.80
20	10.00	54.30	64.30	0.50	2.72	3.22	9.30

[a]Δ means "the change in."

on variable inputs to expand output from 0 to 1 unit, but an additional expenditure of only $1.55 to expand output from 1 to 2 units. The increases in total variable cost get progressively smaller as output is expanded to 9 units; after 9 units the increases grow progressively larger. Since average variable cost is the total variable cost divided by output, it first declines and then rises at the tenth unit of output. Further, as we have shown above, average variable cost mirrors average product.

Total cost is the sum of total fixed and total variable costs. Average total cost is the sum of average variable and average fixed costs, or total cost divided by output. Average total cost, like average variable cost, is U-shaped. Since the influence of declining average fixed cost is less and less as output rises, the average total cost curve takes on the U shape of the average variable cost curve, which reflects rising average product.

Marginal cost, shown in column (8), is the change in total cost that results from producing one additional unit of output. The behavior of marginal cost reflects the law of diminishing marginal returns. In this example, marginal cost falls through the production of the ninth unit of output and rises thereafter. The rising portion of the marginal cost schedule reflects diminishing marginal returns for additions of the variable input.

The data in Table 3 are plotted in Figure 3, which graphically demonstrates the behavior of short-run cost curves. Figure 3a illustrates the concepts of total cost, and Figure 3b presents the corresponding average and marginal cost concepts. In Figure 3b, MC intersects AVC and ATC at their minimum points. This is because marginal cost bears a definite relation to average variable cost and average total cost. In the case of average total cost, marginal cost lies below average total cost when average total cost is falling and above average total cost when average total cost is rising. Marginal cost is equal to average total cost when average total cost is at a minimum. In Table 3, this occurs between the thirteenth and fourteenth units of output. At lower levels of output, the MC values in column (8) are less than the ATC values in column (7). ATC therefore declines. At higher levels of output—in this case 14 and over—the MC values are greater than the ATC values, and ATC rises. The same analysis holds for the relationship between MC and AVC. Here, MC becomes greater than AVC at 11 units of output.

FIGURE 3

Short-Run Cost Curves

(a) Total cost data plotted from Table 3. (b) Average cost and marginal cost data. Notice the U-shaped average total cost curve. At low levels of output, ATC is high because AFC is high, and the firm does not utilize its fixed plant efficiently. At high levels of output, ATC is high because MC is high as the firm approaches the capacity limit of its plant.

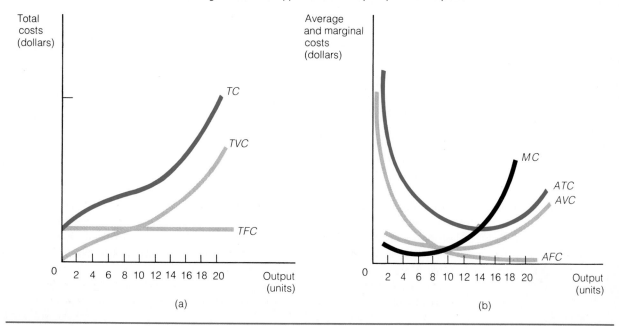

This type of relation holds for marginal-average series in general. If a baseball player is batting .400 and goes 3 for 4 today (.750), his batting average rises because the marginal figure (.750) lies above the average (.400). If he goes 1 for 4 today (.250), his average falls because the marginal figure (.250) lies below the average (.400). An example can be found closer to home. Suppose that your average grade in economics to date is 85. If you score 90 on your next exam, your average will rise. If you score 80, it will fall. When the marginal figure is above the average, it pulls the average figure up and vice versa. This same relation holds for average total cost and marginal cost, which both Table 3 and Figure 3 verify.

In sum, the firm's short-run cost curves show the influence of the law of diminishing marginal returns. First, the firm has certain fixed costs independent of the level of output. These costs correspond to what the firm must pay for fixed inputs, and they must be paid whether or not the firm operates. Second, assuming the price of variable inputs is constant, marginal costs reflect the behavior of the marginal product of the variable input. As output rises, marginal costs first decline because marginal product is increasing and it requires less and less of the variable input to produce additional units of output. At some point, however, diminishing marginal returns set in, and it takes more and more of the variable input to produce additional units of output. When this happens, marginal costs start to rise. Third, marginal cost will eventually rise above average variable cost and average total cost, causing these costs to rise as well, which results in a U-shaped average total cost curve.

LONG-RUN COSTS

In the short run, some inputs are fixed and cannot be varied. These fixed inputs generally are characterized as a physical plant that cannot be altered in size in the short run. Short-run costs therefore show the relation of costs to output for a given plant. In the long run, however, all inputs are variable, including plant size. As economic time lengthens and the contracts that define fixed inputs can be renegotiated, a firm owner can adjust all parts of his or her operation. In fact, the scale of a firm's operations can be adjusted to best fit the economic circumstances that prevail in the long run; an owner can choose to arrange the organization in the best possible way to do business. Stated in terms of plant size, the owner will seek the plant size that minimizes long-run costs of producing the profit-maximizing output.

Adjusting Plant Size

The choice of plant size affects production costs. An owner might have the choice of four plants, such as those depicted in Figure 4. The ATC curves are short-run average total cost curves that correspond to four plant sizes. Which plant is best from the owner's point of view? The answer depends on the profit-maximizing level of output. If the firm wants to produce less than q_1, the plant represented by ATC_1 is the lowest-cost plant for those levels of output. For outputs between q_1 and q_2, ATC_2 is the lowest-cost plant. For outputs between q_2 and q_3, ATC_3 is the lowest-cost plant. For even larger outputs—beyond q_3—the plant represented by ATC_4 is the lowest-cost plant.

FIGURE 4

The figure shows short-run average total cost curves for four plant sizes. If these are the only alternative plant sizes available, the long-run average total cost (or planning) curve will be given by *PLAN*. That is, starting with plant size *P,* the rational owner expands plant size to *L, A,* and then *N* in the long run. Each point represents movement to a larger and lower-cost plant size.

Adjusting Plant Size to Minimize Cost

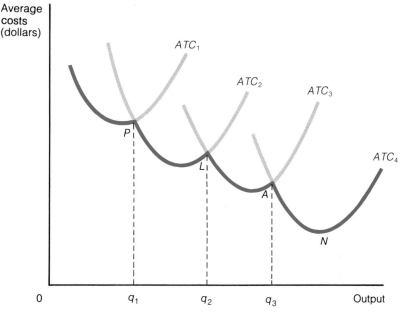

Long-run average total cost:

The lowest per-unit cost of producing any level of output when the usage of all inputs can be varied.

In effect, the owner's best course of action is depicted by *PLAN* in Figure 4. Given that inputs can be varied to build any of these plants, the owner will move along a path such as *PLAN,* gradually expanding output by expanding plant size, seeking the lowest-cost way to produce the profit-maximizing output in the long run.

To determine the optimum long-run plant size, we introduce a new concept: **long-run average total cost** (*LRATC*). This measure shows the lowest-cost plant for producing each level of output when the firm can choose among all possible plant sizes. In Figure 4, *PLAN* is the long-run average total cost curve when only four plants are possible. Indeed, the number of possible plant sizes is unlimited. In effect, the owner sees the world of possibilities in terms of a long-run average total cost (or planning) curve such as that drawn in Figure 5. The long-run average total cost curve is smoothly continuous and allows us to see the full sweep of a firm owner's imagination. On its downward course, the long-run average total cost curve is tangent to each short-run average total cost curve *before* the point of minimum cost for each given plant size. On its upward course it touches each short-term average total cost curve *past* the point of minimum cost. Only at the bottom of the long-run U shape do the minimum points of the long-run and short-run average total cost curves coincide. In effect, the long-run average total cost curve is an envelope for short-run average total cost curves.

Long-run marginal cost:

The additional cost of producing an additional unit of output when all inputs, including plant size, can be varied.

Figure 5 also contains the firm's **long-run marginal cost** curve, *LRMC*. It is similar to the short-run marginal cost curve in that it shows the additional cost arising from producing an additional unit of output. However, the long-run marginal cost curve depicts the change in total cost associated with a one-unit expansion in output when all inputs can be varied. Expansions in output in the long run are accomplished not only by increases in labor (variable)

FIGURE 5

LRATC is the planning curve of the firm owner. It shows how plant size can be adjusted in the long run when all inputs are variable. The plant size shown at *q* represents the lowest possible unit cost of production in the long run. Economies of scale prevail before *q* on the curve, and diseconomies of scale prevail past *q*. *LRMC* is the long-run marginal cost curve. It shows the additional cost of producing output under the condition that all inputs can be varied or that plant size can change.

Long-Run Average Total Cost and Marginal Cost Curves

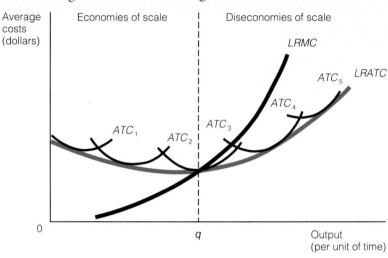

inputs, but also by changing the scale of operations or the plant size. Thus long-run marginal cost measures *all* additional costs of changing output. Notice that the *LRMC* curve intersects the *LRATC* curve where the *LRATC* curve reaches a minimum. At output levels greater than *q* in Figure 5, *LRMC* is greater than *LRATC,* which implies that *LRATC* must be rising. Just the opposite is true at output levels less than *q* in Figure 5.

Economies and Diseconomies of Scale

Why does long-run average total cost have a U shape, falling to *q* and rising thereafter? The answer involves two new concepts: economies and diseconomies of scale.

Economies of scale:
A situation in which long-run unit costs (*LRATC*) decline as plant output increases.

The initial falling portion of the *LRATC* curve is due to **economies of scale.** To a certain point, long-run unit costs of production fall as output increases and the firm gets larger. There are a number of reasons why a larger firm might have lower unit costs: (1) A larger operation means that more specialized processes are possible in the firm. Individual workers can concentrate and become more proficient at more narrowly defined tasks, and machines can be specially tailored to individual processes. (2) As the firm grows larger and produces more, workers and managers gain valuable experience in production processes, learning by doing. Since workers and managers of a larger firm produce more output, they acquire more experience. Such experience can lead to lower unit costs. (3) Large firms can take advantage of mass production techniques, which require large setup costs. Setup costs are most economical when they are spread over a large amount of output. Production techniques such as the assembly line used by large automobile manufacturers would result in very high unit costs if used by a small producer of specialized cars.

Diseconomies of scale:
A situation in which, beyond a point, the long-run average total cost of producing output increases as plant size increases.

The fact that the *LRATC* curve rises after q is due to **diseconomies of scale.** In this range of outputs, the firm has become too large for its owner to control effectively. Managers do not have the monitoring technology to hold costs down in a very large firm, and bureaucratic inefficiencies creep in. If such bureaucratic problems did not exist, firms would be much larger. However, diseconomies may be hard to observe in the real world because it is in the firm's self-interest to correct its operations to keep costs down. Large firms will reorganize, spin off component parts, hire new managers, and seek ways to avoid diseconomies of scale. The Focus, "Survivorship and Long-Run Average Total Costs," shows that the survival of a business firm depends on success in adjusting its output.

Other Shapes of the Long-Run Average Total Cost Curve

The *LRATC* curve in Figure 5 shows a unique ideal plant size at q. There is only one minimum point on this U-shaped curve. This means that there is a small range of plant sizes that are efficient in a particular industry, and plant sizes in the industry will tend to cluster at the level of q. The fact that most discount department stores are approximately the same size illustrates this point.

Constant returns to scale:
As plant size either increases or decreases, long-run average total cost does not change.

Figure 6 shows two other possible shapes the *LRATC* curve can take. Figure 6a illustrates **constant returns to scale.** In certain industries an initial range of economies of scale prevails up to a minimum efficient size of q_1. Beyond q_1, a wide variation in firm size is possible without a discernible difference in unit cost. Small firms and large firms can operate with the same unit costs over this range of outputs. This flat portion of the *LRATC* curve shows constant returns, or the same unit costs, for a range of output levels

FIGURE 6

Not all *LRATC* curves are U-shaped. (a) Constant returns to scale. The lowest possible production costs per unit exist within a large range between output levels q_1 and q_2. Both small and large firms can have the same long-run unit costs between q_1 and q_2. (b) Increasing returns to scale. The more output the firm produces, the lower its long-run average total cost.

Alternative *LRATC* Curves

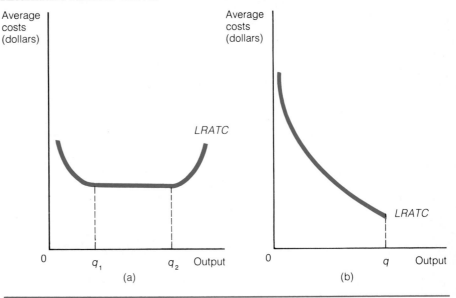

from q_1 to q_2. Beyond q_2, diseconomies of scale begin. This is apparently a very common *LRATC* curve in the real world because we observe both small and large firms surviving—even prospering—side by side in such industries as publishing and textiles.

Figure 6b shows an *LRATC* curve that exhibits economies of scale over its whole range; this is called **increasing returns to scale.** In such cases, the larger the firm, the lower its costs. This type of *LRATC* curve is representative of such industries as utilities and telephone service. Large firms are more efficient in the provision of these services. Where one large firm prevails in a marketplace, some form of regulatory control over the pricing power of the firm may be required.

Increasing returns to scale:
As plant size increases, long-run average total cost decreases.

SHIFTS IN COST CURVES

Our analysis of cost curves has been based on the familiar *ceteris paribus,* or other things constant, assumption. In other words, we held certain factors constant in the discussion of short-run and long-run costs. What factors did we hold constant, and how do they affect cost curves?

Resource prices have been held constant. If resource prices rise or fall, the firm's cost curves will rise or fall by a corresponding amount. If the price of gasoline falls, the cost curves of a trucking firm fall; this is illustrated by the fall from ATC_1 and MC_1 to ATC_2 and MC_2 in Figure 7.

Taxes and government regulation have been held constant. If government increases the excise tax on gasoline, the trucking firm's cost curves will rise. In fact, the average and marginal costs of the trucking firm will rise by the

---

FIGURE 7

The Effect of a Decrease in Resource Prices on Costs

As resource prices decrease, the cost curves of the firm fall from ATC_1 and MC_1 to ATC_2 and MC_2. If resource prices increased, the cost curves of the firm would rise.

FOCUS   Survivorship and Long-Run Average Total Costs

The theory of long-run costs concerns the productive efficiency of firms over a period of time (the long run) during which any size of firm can be chosen. Under competitive conditions, firm sizes will be chosen for reasons of economic efficiency; they are employed to produce some quantity of output at least cost. When the long-run average total costs are U-shaped, as in Figure 5, a single size of firm is best. (In Figure 5 this size is designated as q.) Where long-run average total costs are flat, or constant over a range of outputs, as in Figure 6a, a range of sizes is efficient (lowest-cost) in producing outputs.

The long-run cost conditions in an industry can be studied in a number of ways. One could talk to engineers who build plants in an industry and get estimates of the costs of new construction, or one could gather data on costs and output in an industry and use statistical techniques to estimate long-run cost functions. The *survivorship technique* is a shorthand and useful way to conceptualize long-run costs and optimal firm size in an industry, given that technology and the legal environment of business remains unchanged over the term of the study.[a] The use of this technique is fairly simple, as a hypothetical example from the steel industry in Table 4 shows.

The first column represents the range of firm sizes in the industry from smallest to largest. The second and third columns show the percentage of total industry output accounted for in 1980 and 1990 by the various size categories of firms in the industry. Company size and industry output can be measured in terms of sales, assets, or real production, such as metric tons of steel. Finally, the last column indicates whether a particular size category of firms gained ($+$) or lost ($-$) ground as a percentage of industry sales or output over the period. (Remember that the long run is a period long enough that all inputs can be varied in the industry.)

In the case described in Table 4, small firms (less than 2½ percent of industry output) lost ground over the ten-year period, as did very large firms (more than 25 percent). Gainers were midsize firms producing from 2½ to 25 percent of industry output. Thus, for example, the category of 1 to 2½ percent lost 4.9 percent of industry output from 1980–1990, whereas the category of 2½ to 5 percent gained 6 percentage points of industry output over the period.

These results demonstrate the essence of the survivorship technique. Survivorship measures adjustments in opti-

TABLE 4
Firm Size Change and Survivorship in the Steel Industry

Using hypothetical data on firm size in the steel industry, the table shows that both small and large firms lost ground in the period 1980–1990. The most efficient *scales* of plant appear to be midsize firms in the industry.

Company Size as a Percent of Industry Output	Percentage of Industry Output		Change
	1980	1990	
Less than ½ percent	7.2	6.1	–
½ to 1 percent	5.9	5.1	–
1 to 2½ percent	13.2	8.3	–
2½ to 5 percent	10.6	16.6	+
5 to 10 percent	11.2	14.0	+
10 to 25 percent	13.2	14.0	+
Greater than 25 percent	38.7	35.9	–

mal firm size in the long run in the broadest possible sense. If a particular firm size category is gaining share over time, firms in the category must be doing something better than their rivals in other size categories. Gains could result from simple technical efficiencies such as better plants, from better labor-negotiating skills, or from any of the thousands of things that differentiate one firm from another. Survivorship means doing well in the face of *all* circumstances. Firms that can adapt and expand do well and grow in importance in an industry. Less able firms lose share and decline.

The survivorship method offers us information about optimal firm size in an industry and about the probable shape of the long-run average total cost curve. In the case shown in Table 4, the data show a range of optimal firm sizes from 2½ to 25 percent. This means that the *LRATC* looks like that given in Figure 6a, where $q_1 = 2½$ percent and $q_2 = 25$ percent. The fact that there is more than one optimal firm size in most industries in the long run proves that there is "more than one way to skin a cat."

[a]See George J. Stigler, "The Economies of Scale," *Journal of Law and Economics* (October 1958), pp. 54–71.

amount of the tax. Similarly, if government imposes more stringent highway weight limits for trucks, the costs of trucking firms will increase.

Technological change has been held constant. Advances in technology make it possible to produce goods and services at lower costs. The invention of the diesel engine, which is more durable and less expensive to operate than the conventional gasoline engine, shifted the cost curves of trucking firms downward. Trucking services can now be produced with fewer resources because of this technological improvement. As the Economics in Action, "Technological Change and the Future of Small Farms," shows, changes in technology can also alter the shape of the long-run average total cost curve.

COSTS AND SUPPLY DECISIONS

Costs help explain the supply or output decisions of firms. Firms compare their expected costs and expected revenues in deciding how much output to produce. In the short run, the relevant comparison is between marginal cost and expected revenue. If the latter exceeds the former, the firm will supply additional units of output. In the long run the owner of a firm decides whether to enter an industry or to expand output within an industry by comparing long-run marginal cost with additional expected revenue. Again, if additional expected revenue exceeds long-run marginal cost, the firm enters or increases production, and industry output is expanded. There is a critical link between firm costs and the industry supply curve; we examine this link in the next chapter.

SUMMARY

1. Costs result from the fact that resources have alternative uses. An opportunity cost is the value of resources in their next-best use.

2. Explicit costs are like accounting costs; they are the bills that the firm must pay for the use of inputs. Implicit costs are the opportunity costs of resources owned by the firm. The total cost of production is the sum of explicit and implicit costs.

3. Economic or opportunity costs are the expected future costs of forgoing alternative uses of resources. Accounting or historical costs are costs that have been incurred in the past. Sunk costs are irretrievable historical costs and are not relevant to present decisions.

4. Private costs are payments by the firm for the use of inputs. External costs arise when the firm uses an input without paying for its services. The sum of private and external costs is social cost.

5. The short run is a period of economic time when some of the firm's inputs are fixed. The long run is a period over which all inputs, including the size of the firm's plant, can be varied.

6. The law of diminishing marginal returns states that when adding units of a variable input to a fixed amount of other resources, beyond some point the resulting additions to output will start to decline.

7. The law of diminishing marginal returns implies that the marginal cost curve of the firm will ultimately rise. As the firm adds more variable inputs to its fixed plant, diminishing marginal returns set in at some point, and marginal cost will start to rise as the firm approaches its short-run capacity.

8. Short-run costs are (a) fixed costs—costs that do not vary with the firm's output; (b) variable costs—the costs of purchasing variable inputs; (c) total costs—the sum of fixed and variable costs; and (d) marginal

costs—the change in total cost with respect to a change in output. These costs can be expressed in total or average (unit) terms. The short-run average total cost curve is U-shaped. When marginal cost is below average total cost, the latter falls. When it is above average total cost, the latter rises.

9. Long-run average total cost shows the lowest-cost plant for producing output when the firm can choose among all possible plant sizes. It is the planning curve of the firm; it helps the firm pick the right plant size for long-run production.

10. Long-run marginal cost is the additional cost associated with producing an additional unit of output when all inputs can be varied. It measures additional costs arising from producing more output not only with more labor, but also by altering plant size.

11. A U-shaped long-run average total cost curve results from economies and diseconomies of scale. Economies of scale cause long-run unit costs to fall, and diseconomies of scale cause long-run unit costs to rise as output is expanded.

12. Other shapes of the long-run average total cost curve are possible. Most important, the long-run average total cost curve can have a flat range with constant returns to scale, or it can be downward-sloping over its entire range, reflecting a condition called increasing returns to scale.

KEY TERMS

opportunity costs of production	private costs	total costs	marginal product
accounting costs	external costs	average fixed cost	average product
implicit costs	social costs	average variable cost	long-run average total cost
opportunity cost of capital	variable input	average total cost	long-run marginal cost
total cost of production	fixed input	marginal cost	economies of scale
historical costs	short run	fixed plant	diseconomies of scale
sunk costs	long run	law of diminishing marginal	constant returns to scale
economic profit	fixed costs	returns	increasing returns to scale
accounting profit	variable costs	total product	

QUESTIONS FOR REVIEW AND DISCUSSION

1. Explain the difference between explicit and implicit costs.
2. State and explain the law of diminishing marginal returns.
3. What is the definition of marginal cost? How is it linked to the law of diminishing marginal returns?
4. Define economies and diseconomies of scale and give an example of each.
5. How long is the long run? How does it compare to the short run?
6. When is the marginal cost curve below the average total cost curve? When is it above the average total cost curve?
7. An engineering student invests in obtaining an engineering degree. Let us say that the degree cost $50,000 in opportunity costs. Five years later, the engineer decides to become an artist. Is the $50,000 investment in the engineering degree relevant to the decision to become an artist?
8. Derive the long-run cost model using the short-run model. Be sure to include short-run average total cost (ATC), marginal cost (MC), and long-run average total cost (LRATC). Where is the single most preferred operating position in the long-run model?
9. Suppose that the long-run average total cost curve in an industry exhibits increasing returns to scale. How will firms compete in such an industry? Will there be many suppliers in the industry in the long run?

PROBLEMS

Use the table to answer the questions.

1. What is the average total cost of producing 4 units of output?
2. What is the total cost of producing 3 units of output?
3. What is the marginal cost of producing the third unit?

Units of Output	Total Fixed Cost	Total Variable Cost
1	$1000	$300
2	1000	550
3	1000	900
4	1000	1400
5	1000	2050

ECONOMICS IN ACTION
Technological Change and the Future of Small Farms

For years most of the milk consumed in the United States was obtained either from a family cow or a neighboring dairy farmer who had a few dairy cows. In the last forty or fifty years, however, most small family dairy farms have disappeared, replaced by large producers. To understand this fundamental change in the dairy industry, consider the effect of technological change on the cost curves of milk producers.

In the past, dairy cows were milked by hand; very little machinery was used. Thus, any economies of scale could be fully exploited at relatively low levels of production. Because milk was perishable and costly to transport, there were diseconomies of scale as farms grew larger. Large producers had to transport milk to more distant consumers, putting themselves at a cost disadvantage relative to local milk producers. Consequently, a huge number of small producers emerged in the market. The long-run cost curve apparently reached its minimum point at low output levels and rose for higher output levels. This put large producers at a cost disadvantage.

Several technological changes that occurred after World War II altered the shape of the long-run average total cost curve. One was the development of mechanical milkers, which provided larger-scale producers with a cost-effective alternative to hand-milking. Also, the public came to accept pasteurized milk, which meant a greatly increased shelf life compared to raw milk. In addition, refrigerated trucking was perfected and the highway system was greatly improved, making it economical to transport milk over greater distances than was possible previously. By the early 1960s these changes provided a substantial cost advantage to large-scale producers. Economist Leonard Weiss[a] has used Department of Agriculture statistics to estimate average cost curves of producing milk on dairy farms of various sizes. Figure 8 shows his estimates. Class I farms have sales in excess of $40,000 per year; Class II farms, $20,000–$40,000; Class III farms, $10,000–$20,000; Class IV farms, $5000–$10,000; Class V farms, $2500–$5000; and Class VI farms, 0–$2500. The curves labeled I through VI show average costs for farms in the corresponding classes. Figure 8 shows that the average cost of producing milk is more than twice as high for the small Class V and VI dairy farms than for the large Class I and II farms.

Economic theory suggests that over time firms tend to adjust to the size at which average costs are lowest. Table 5 provides evidence of such adjustment in the dairy industry.

TABLE 5
Percentage of Dairy Farms of Various Sizes

The data in the table reveal an increasing number of larger farms in the dairy industry between 1959 and 1982.

| Year | Number of Acres | | | |
	Less than 50	50–99	100–219	220 or more
1959	19.5%	18.8%	32.4%	29.6%
1982	6.1%	8.5%	32.6%	52.7%

Sources: United States Bureau of the Census, *Census of Agriculture* (Washington, D.C.: U.S. Government Printing Office, 1959) vol. 2, pp. 384–85; United States Bureau of the Census, *Census of Agriculture* (Washington, D.C.: U.S. Government Printing Office, 1982) vol. 1, p. 82.

[a]This feature is adapted from Leonard Weiss, *Case Studies in American Industry,* 2nd ed., p. 76. Copyright © 1971 John Wiley & Sons, Inc. Reprinted by permission.

FIGURE 8

Approximate Average Costs of U.S. Dairy Farms by Size, 1964

The curves labeled I through VI show average costs for dairy farms in different size classes. Note the substantial cost advantages to larger firms.

Source: Leonard Weiss, *Case Studies in American Industry,* 2nd. ed., p. 76. Copyright © 1971 John Wiley & Sons, Inc. Reprinted by permission.

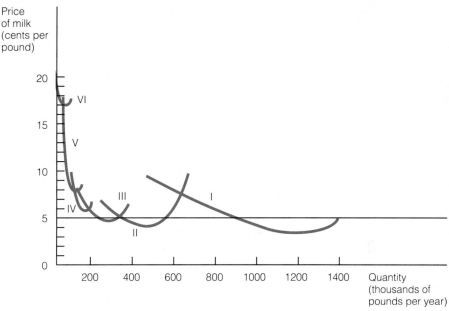

Farms in Classes V and VI generally had herds of milk cows of less than 20 and used less than 50 acres. As Table 5 shows, 19.5 percent of all the dairy farms were of that size in 1959. By 1982, the corresponding figure was 6.1 percent. Over the same time period the percentage of large, efficient dairy farms grew rapidly. In 1959, less than one-third of the dairy farms contained more than 220 acres. More than half of the dairy farms were larger than 220 acres in 1982.

While changes in technology have led to the demise of small dairy farms, technological change does not always have this effect. For example, recent technological changes in the typesetting sector of the publishing industry have altered the shape of the long-run cost curve in a way that enhances the competitiveness of small firms. Historically, typesetting was done by hand and represented a huge fixed cost for any printing run. Companies that typeset many publications had a substantial cost advantage over smaller companies. Recent technological changes have made desktop publishing and electronic typesetting economical. These changes have eliminated many of the cost advantages of the large typesetting firms and have enhanced the competitiveness of small firms. As a consequence, publication of specialty books and periodicals for limited audiences has become economically feasible; also, many new small firms have entered the market successfully.

Question

Over the past few decades, the trend in many school districts has been toward consolidation—merging several smaller schools to form one large school. Is there any evidence that the larger schools provide education at a lower cost? Do you think that this change was in response to an underlying change in the technology used to operate public schools?

9

The Competitive Firm and Industry

Competition exists in virtually every aspect of life. Students compete for grades, animals compete for habitat, sports teams compete for championships, government agencies compete for budget appropriations, firms compete for customers. In each case, scarcity causes the competition. Funds available to support government agencies are limited; defense and social agencies therefore compete for scarce budget dollars. Likewise, there can be only one World Series champion. Major league baseball teams therefore compete for this scarce distinction. If resources were freely available, there would be no competition. Everyone could have all they wanted of whatever they wanted.

This chapter introduces the economist's model of firm and industry behavior under pure competition (a market with many buyers and sellers, with sellers producing nearly identical products). It is the first of five chapters that analyze the impact of industry structure on price and output. Four chapters look at models of industry behavior: pure competition, monopoly, monopolistic competition, oligopoly, and cartels. The fifth relates industry structure to government policies. In this chapter we discuss the usefulness of the abstract model of pure competition and its relevance for real-world problems. After reading Chapter 9 you should understand

- the difference between competition as a dynamic rivalrous process and the economist's static model of a competitive market.
- the principles underlying the behavior of competitive firms in both the short run and the long run.
- the nature of the supply curve of a perfectly competitive firm.
- how economic profits (or losses) motivate competitive firms to expand, contract, or go out of business.

THE PROCESS OF COMPETITION

Naturally, most people think of competition as the process of competition or the conduct of competitors. Seen in this way, the important question in determining whether firms are competing with one another is whether they are exhibiting rivalrous, competitive behavior. Do they compete hard for customers? Do they try to outperform one another? Do they use a variety of methods—persuasive advertising, a carefully chosen location, and attractive price—to win and keep customers? Do they seek the best managerial talent available? Are they forward-looking and innovative? Do they seek to eliminate waste and inefficiency? The list could go on, but the point is clear: Competition is normally thought of as a process of rivalry among firms.

This process of rivalry leads to better and less expensive products for consumers. Business firms compete to make profits, but the competitive process actually forces firms to meet consumer demands at the lowest possible level of profit. As Adam Smith observed more than two hundred years ago, firms' self-interest is harnessed by the competitive process to promote the general well-being of society:

> It is not from the benevolence of the butcher, the brewer, or the baker, that we expect our dinner, but from their regard for their own interest. We address ourselves, not to their humanity but to their self-love, and never talk to them of our own necessities but of their advantages.[1]

The process of competition channels the pursuit of individual self-interest to socially beneficial outcomes, and for this reason economists put the study of the competitive process at the heart of their science.

The process of competition takes place in an uncertain world. Individuals have to make conjectures as they make resource commitments for the future. Some conjectures will turn out to be correct, and individuals who forecast correctly will survive and prosper. Individuals whose conjectures turn out not to be correct will not fare so well in the future. The concept of competition as a process of rivalry under uncertain conditions is especially important for understanding entrepreneurial behavior in the economy.

Although competition generally benefits consumers by harnessing the self-interest of producers, producers have incentives to subvert the competitive process to increase their profits. Adam Smith also recognized this tendency:

> People of the same trade seldom meet together, even for merriment and diversion, but the conversation ends in a conspiracy against the publick, or in some contrivance to raise prices.[2]

Independent action among competitors is by no means guaranteed. Indeed, firms may have incentives to avoid competition and independent action in favor of collusion and higher profits. This tendency leads to monopolies of one sort or another, which we discuss in more detail in Chapters 11 and 12. Yet society can influence the rules under which firms compete. Price fixing may or may not be allowed; property rights may or may not be defended; business taxes may be high or low. The process of competition is affected by government regulations, which may be more or less restrictive. Indeed, this is a two-way street: government affects business, and business affects government. Chapter 19 is devoted to an analysis of government regulation of business.

---

[1] Adam Smith, *An Inquiry into the Nature and Causes of the Wealth of Nations*, ed. Edwin Cannan (1776; reprint, New York: Modern Library, 1937), p. 14.

[2] Smith, *Wealth of Nations*, p. 128.

A PURELY COMPETITIVE MARKET

In contrast to the concept of the competitive process just described, pure competition is an abstract model of competitive behavior that emphasizes the importance of industry structure. In particular, it stresses the number of independent producers in an industry. The difference between the competitive process model and the pure competition model can be compared with the behavior of runners in a race. To determine how close a race will be, the competitive process approach would ask how intensely the runners are competing. Are they striving hard to win? The pure competition approach would ask how many equally qualified runners are in the race. The process view is a richer, more natural interpretation of competition. Nonetheless, the model of pure competition is a useful abstraction that, interpreted carefully, can help us understand the competitive behavior of producers in real-world industries.

Market:
The interaction of buyers and sellers for the purpose of making transactions.

The model of pure competition is based on the concept of a **market.** As you recall, market prices are subject to the laws of demand and supply, and within a market the price of a good or service will tend toward a single value. Market forces even transcend geographical boundaries, given free flow of information. Buyers at point x will not pay more for a commodity than the price at point y plus transportation costs. Buyers at point y will not pay more for a commodity than the price at point x plus transportation costs. Price deviations will quickly be spotted by buyers, restoring the market's tendency to one price. Suppose that the price at point y fell below the price at point x plus transportation costs. What would happen? Buyers would shift their purchases from point x to point y, decreasing demand and lowering price at point x and increasing demand and raising price at point y. This shift of buyers would restore the tendency to a single price.

The behavior of sellers in a market is equally predictable. In fact, one way to determine if two commodities are in the same market is to check whether price reductions or increases for the commodity in one area are matched by price reductions or increases in other areas, accounting also for transportation costs. If the price of gasoline goes down in Atlanta, does it also go down in Charlotte? In Chicago? In Seattle? In other words, do sellers in other areas of the country respond with competitive price reductions? To the extent that they do, we can delineate the market for gasoline from the tendency of all sellers to adjust prices in the same direction. Perhaps there is an Atlanta-Charlotte gasoline market, but probably not an Atlanta-Seattle market.

Purely competitive market:
The interaction of a large number of buyers and sellers under the condition that entry and exit are not restricted.

Building on this concept of a market, we can define four conditions that characterize a **purely competitive market.**

Homogeneous product:
A good or service for which the consumer is indifferent as to which firm produces it; each firm's product is a perfect substitute for other firms' products in the eyes of the consumer.

1. Firms in a purely competitive market sell a **homogeneous product;** that is, they sell identical or nearly identical products that are perfectly substitutable for one another. This means that advertising does not exist in a purely competitive market. Why would one firm want to advertise the advantages of its product if it cannot be distinguished by consumers from the products produced by a large number of competing firms? *milk*

2. A large number of independent buyers and sellers exists in a purely competitive market. This assumption rules out the possibility of collusion among buyers or sellers to affect price and output in the industry. More-

over, the large number of buyers and sellers ensures that the purchases or sales of any one buyer or seller will not affect the market price. Each buyer and seller is small relative to the total market for the commodity and exerts no perceptible influence on the market.

3. There are no barriers to entry or exit in a purely competitive market. Features of economic life such as control of an essential raw material by one or a few firms or government regulation of firms' behavior in the market do not exist under pure competition.

4. A perfectly competitive market also offers **perfect information** to buyers and sellers. Everybody in the market has equal, free access to information about the location and price of a product. This assumption provides the basis for a single price to prevail in a perfectly competitive market. Buyers and sellers are constantly informed about price differences and act in turn to drive industry price to a single value.

Perfect information:
A situation that arises when information about prices and products is costless to obtain; complete knowledge about the market.

These four conditions are the assumptions on which the theory of pure or perfect competition is based. This theory is designed to explain the behavior of many independent buyers and sellers, none of whom has any perceptible influence on the market. The assumptions may seem unrealistic. Products, for example, are rarely homogeneous. But in economics, the realism of the assumptions is not the point of this or any other model. The point is the empirical relevance of the model. Does it explain behavior in real-world markets? As we will see, the purely competitive model helps us analyze important actual markets and industries such as the stock market and agriculture. (See Focus, "The Stock Market: An Example of Pure Competition," for one application of the concept of pure competition.) Moreover, the purely competitive model gives us an analytical framework for what might be loosely described as the ideal working of an economy. In this sense the model provides a benchmark against which other industry models, such as pure monopoly, can be measured.

THE PURELY COMPETITIVE FIRM AND INDUSTRY IN THE SHORT RUN

How then do firms behave within a purely competitive industry? We focus first on the purely competitive firm's decisions about how much output to supply in the short run—that is, over a period of time when it cannot adjust its plant size.

The Purely Competitive Firm as a Price Taker

In a purely competitive market an individual firm cannot influence the market price for its good or service by increasing or decreasing its output. Because each seller is only a small part of the total market, its actions have no perceptible influence on the market. The competitive firm is called a **price taker:** It must accept the going market price for its product.

Price taker:
An individual seller who faces a single market price and is able to sell as much as desired at that price.

As an example of price-taking behavior, consider the world cotton market. World cotton output was estimated to be 65,337,000 bales in 1989. Of this total, assume that Virginia produced a minuscule amount—100 bales in

FOCUS   The Stock Market: An Example of Pure Competition

The stock market—the market in which shares of ownership of firms are traded—might at first seem like an implausible example of a competitive market. The popular press typically portrays the stock market either as little more than a gambling casino or as a kind of free-for-all of combat among a few elite investment tycoons.

Closer observation dispels these misconceptions. The stock market is a highly competitive market. Many thousands of firms engaged in hundreds of distinct lines of business offer their shares to many thousands of potential buyers every day. Entry into the market on both sides of potential transactions is practically unrestricted. Shares are highly substitutable as potential investments to buyers, making them essentially homogeneous goods.

The highly competitive nature of the stock market is obscured by the fact that only a few hundred of the largest corporations are traded in the organized stock exchanges. (In the United States, these exchanges are collectively referred to as Wall Street.) Since the shares of large corporations are traded frequently, it is efficient for trade to occur among exchanges organized for this purpose. The organized exchanges radically reduce transaction costs, benefiting both buyers and sellers. It is misleading to confuse the overall stock market with the organized stock exchanges. Many thousands of other, smaller firms offer stock shares for sale in the over-the-counter market, outside of the larger organized exchanges. All these firms—those participating in the organized exchanges and those trading over-the-counter—are competing for the funds of potential investors. Entry into the market is open even to the tiniest firm that wants to offer its shares to the public.

On the buyers' side, although large institutional investors—for instance, well-known mutual funds like the Dreyfus Fund—receive much publicity, there are many small investors; the costs of entry into the market—the transaction costs—are very low, both in the organized exchanges and in the market generally. In 1989, for example, General Motors had more than 1 million common stockholders, General Electric more than 500,000 shareholders, and Eastman Kodak more than 200,000. In each case, the overwhelming majority of these shareholders were individuals with relatively small investments.

The price of the firm's shares reflects, at any given moment, the sum of all economically relevant information that the market possesses with respect to that firm's past, present, and expected future performance. That price is the result of bidding in the market, which in turn reflects the judgment and relevant knowledge of all interested parties. Hence, stock prices are extremely sensitive to information about any change that affects the firm and its future prospects. An accidental oil field explosion in Sumatra will be reflected in the price of oil company stock in seconds, as will be the influence of a flash flood in Alaska on the price of shares in a civil engineering firm. The stock market's first and foremost function is as a communications mechanism: However imperfectly, it facilitates the flow of information among buyers, sellers, and firms.

In short, the stock market, rather than representing a floating financial dice game, is one of the most efficient and competitive markets imaginable.

1989 and 200 in 1990. Further assume that, over a given price range, the price elasticity of demand for cotton worldwide (e_m) is 0.25, which means that the market demand curve for cotton is inelastic.

First consider what happened to the world price of cotton as a result of the 100-bale increase in Virginia's cotton production between 1989 and 1990. Other things being equal, the percent change, in this case a decline, in world price is given by

$$\frac{\text{percent change in world output}}{e_m} = \frac{100 \text{ bales}/65,337,000 \text{ bales}}{0.25}$$
$$= 0.0000061 = 0.00061\%.$$

(Remember that e_m equals percent change in world output divided by percent change in world price, so percent change in world output divided by e_m equals percent change in world price.)

Now we can derive the elasticity of demand facing Virginia producers of cotton (e_v). Since we know the 1989–1990 percent change in Virginia output (100 to 200 bales, or 100%), and since we have just computed the percent change in world price caused by the increase in Virginia production, we have all the information we need to calculate the price elasticity of demand facing Virginia producers.

$$e_v = \frac{\text{percent change in Virginia output}}{\text{percent change in world price}}$$
$$= \frac{100\%}{0.00061\%}$$
$$= 163,934$$

The Virginia producers face an extremely elastic demand curve for their output of cotton. If we took only one Virginia producer of cotton as a representative purely competitive firm, the elasticity result would be dramatically larger. For all intents and purposes, then, the demand curve the perfectly competitive firm faces can be characterized as perfectly elastic.

The Demand Curve of the Competitive Firm

From this example it is easy to see why the competitive firm is called a price taker. Expansions or contractions in an individual firm's output within a competitive market have virtually no effect on the market price. To capture this condition analytically, we draw the firm's demand curve as a straight line at the level of market price in Figure 1.

Figure 1a shows the demand curve (d) facing a Virginia cotton producer, and Figure 1b shows the world market demand (D) and supply (S) curves for cotton. The demand curve of the Virginia producer is perfectly elastic with respect to the price of cotton; it is drawn as a flat line at the level of market price (P). A perfectly elastic demand curve means that the firm can sell all it wants to sell at the prevailing market price. If it tried to sell its output at a slightly higher price, demand for its product would vanish because buyers can purchase cotton at the lower price in whatever quantities they choose. If the firm is trying to maximize its profits, it has no reason to sell its product for less than the market price.

perf. elastic dd curve

FIGURE 1　　　　　**Firm and Industry Demand in a Purely Competitive Market**

In a purely competitive industry, demand for an individual firm's product is perfectly elastic. The perfectly elastic demand curve facing one individual Virginia cotton producer is shown in (a) at the level of *P*, which is also the equilibrium price for the world market in (b) at an output of 65.3 million bales per year. Note that the scale for price is the same for both the individual producer and the world market but that the scale for quantity is much different for the two.

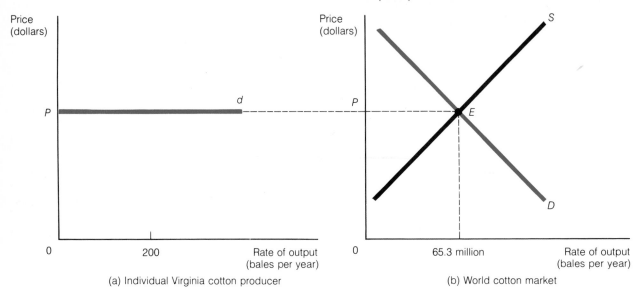

(a) Individual Virginia cotton producer　　　　　(b) World cotton market

The scale for price is the same in both parts of Figure 1. They obviously are not the same for quantity because of the Virginia producer's minuscule proportion of world output. Keep this in mind as you interpret the diagrams in this chapter. Always check to see if the horizontal axis represents *firm* or *industry* quantity. Capital Q will be used to represent industry output; small q will represent individual firm output.

To summarize: Every firm in a purely competitive industry is a price taker and faces a demand curve such as that of the Virginia cotton producer in Figure 1a. And every purely competitive firm produces a tiny proportion of industry output.

Short-Run Profit Maximization by the Purely Competitive Firm

The purely competitive firm is a price taker and faces a given price represented by a perfectly elastic demand curve. Under these circumstances how does the firm decide how much to produce? The simple answer is that the firm compares the costs and benefits of producing additional units of output. As long as the added revenues from producing another unit of output exceed the added costs, the firm will expand its output. By following this rule, the firm is led to maximize its **profits** in the short run.

The added cost of producing an additional unit of output is the marginal cost. We know from our analysis in Chapter 8 that the short-run marginal cost

Profits:
The amount by which total revenue exceeds total opportunity cost of production.

curve of a firm will eventually rise. This is due to the law of diminishing marginal returns, which comes into play as the firm uses its fixed plant more intensively in the short run.

Marginal revenue:
The change in total revenue resulting from the sale of one additional unit of output; the change in total revenue divided by the change in output.

The extra revenue from producing an additional unit of output is **marginal revenue** (*MR*). Simply, marginal revenue is the addition to total revenue from the production of one more unit of output, or

$$MR = \frac{\text{change in total revenue}}{\text{change in output}} \cdot \quad \frac{\Delta TR}{\Delta q}$$

In a purely competitive market, the denominator is 1—a one-unit increase in output—and the numerator is always the market price (*P*) because the demand curve facing the competitive firm is perfectly elastic. Therefore, marginal revenue equals market price, *MR* = *P*, for the purely competitive firm.

The purely competitive firm will decide how much to produce in the short run by comparing marginal cost with marginal revenue. To maximize its profits, the firm will produce additional units of output until marginal cost and marginal revenue are equal. Figure 2 illustrates this process.

MR = MC

The firm's perfectly elastic demand curve (*d*) in Figure 2a is drawn at the level of market price (*P*) from Figure 2b. As we have just seen, *d* is also the marginal revenue curve for the firm. Revenue will increase by the market price each time output increases by one unit. In other words, *MR* = *P*. We have also drawn the marginal cost (*MC*) and average total cost (*ATC*) curves of the firm.

FIGURE 2   **Short-Run Output Choice and Profit Maximization**

(a) The short-run choice of output confronting the individual firm. At rates of output less than *q*, additional production adds more to revenue than to cost. Beyond *q*, additional production adds more to cost than to revenue. Therefore, the purely competitive firm will produce at *q*. At this rate of output the firm earns an economic profit equal to the difference between total revenues and total costs: *PAq0 − BCq0 = PACB*. (b) Prevailing market conditions in the industry.

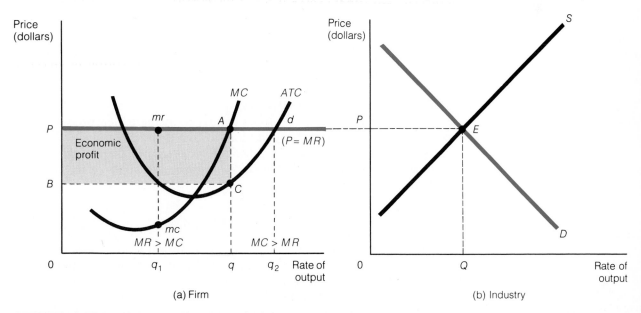

(a) Firm   (b) Industry

The owners of the firm want to make as much money as possible, so their problem is to find the level of production or output that yields the largest profit. Suppose that the firm is producing 5-gallon jars of hot pepper sauce, the kind one is apt to find in restaurants and school cafeterias. (We will neglect the fact that hot pepper sauce of various qualities is sold by brand name in grocery stores—and will focus instead on the generic, competitively produced variety.) The firm presently produces a certain quantity q_1. Should the owners expand their level of production? The answer is yes because additional units of pepper sauce add more to revenue than to costs. In other words, marginal revenue exceeds marginal cost at q_1, as you can see by comparing points mr and mc at quantity q_1. Since the owners want to maximize their profits, they will expand output beyond q_1 as far as q.

Suppose instead that the owners are operating at an output q_2. What will their profit-maximizing reaction be in this case? At this level of production, an additional unit of output adds more to cost than it adds to revenue. That is, marginal cost exceeds marginal revenue. The rational profit-maximizing response of the owners will be to lower production. Through a process of trial and error, they find that their best level of output is q. At a market price of P, they can do no better for profits than to produce q jars of hot pepper sauce. The short-run equilibrium level of production for the purely competitive firm is therefore defined by the condition $P = MC$. Since we know that price and marginal revenue are the same for the purely competitive firm, we can also write $P = MR = MC$.

Using the average total cost curve in Figure 2, we can see exactly how well the hot pepper sauce firm fares by producing at level q. The total revenue of the firm equals its sales, which are the level of output q times the price P for the output. **Total revenue** at q therefore equals P_q, represented by the rectangular area $PAq0$ in Figure 2a. Total cost is the level of average total cost (C) times the level of output q. Total cost at output q thus equals C_q, represented by $BCq0$. Total revenue exceeds total cost in this case: $PAq0 - BCq0 = PACB$. This firm's short-run economic profit is shown by area $PACB$, the return in excess of the total opportunity cost production.

In the real world, businesspeople do not spend a lot of time trying to draw marginal cost and marginal revenue curves for their firms. Moreover, they operate in an uncertain environment where future costs and prices cannot be known with certainty. Despite these considerations, however, the $P = MR = MC$ rule for profit maximization has predictive power. It is a rule based on common sense. If additional production promises to add more to revenue than to cost, most businesses will try to increase their production. If additional units will probably add more to cost than to revenue, most businesses will cut back production. Such behavior leads to the $P = MR = MC$ result even when businesspeople know nothing about the economic rule involved.

A Numerical Illustration of Profit Maximization

Another way to understand how the choice of output levels allows a competitive firm to maximize profits is to examine the specific costs and revenues at each level of production. Table 1 presents a numerical schedule for the hot pepper sauce firm. The firm's output level is given in column (1). Column (2) shows that the firm confronts an unvarying market price of $2.40 per jar for

Total revenue:
The total money receipts of a firm from selling its product; calculated as market price multiplied by the amount of output sold; the dollar value of sales.

TABLE 1

Profit Maximization for a Purely Competitive Firm

This numerical schedule of the costs and revenues the hot pepper sauce firm faces at each level of output provides data for determining the profit-maximizing rate of output. Marginal revenue equals marginal cost when the firm produces 14 jars per day, and profit is maximized at $5.80 per day.

(1) Rate of Output (jars/day)	(2) Price = Marginal Revenue	(3) Marginal Cost	(4) Total Revenue (1) × (2)	(5) Total Cost	(6) Profit (4) − (5)
0	2.40	—	0.00	110.00	−10.00
1	2.40	1.60	2.40	11.60	−9.20
2	2.40	1.45	4.80	13.05	−8.25
3	2.40	1.35	7.20	14.40	−7.20
4	2.40	1.30	9.60	15.70	−6.10
5	2.40	1.20	12.00	16.90	−4.90
6	2.40	1.10	14.40	18.00	−3.60
7	2.40	1.00	16.80	19.00	−2.20
8	2.40	0.90	19.20	19.90	−0.70
9	2.40	0.30	21.60	20.20	1.40
10	2.40	0.65	24.00	20.85	3.15
11	2.40	1.30	26.40	22.15	4.25
12	2.40	1.50	28.80	23.65	5.15
13	2.40	1.75	31.20	25.40	5.80
14	2.40	2.40	33.60	27.80	5.80
15	2.40	3.25	36.00	31.05	4.95
16	2.40	4.25	38.40	35.30	3.10
17	2.40	5.35	40.80	40.65	0.15
18	2.40	6.55	43.20	47.20	−4.00
19	2.40	7.80	45.60	55.00	−9.40
20	2.40	9.30	48.00	64.30	−16.30

its output. Price equals marginal revenue ($P = MR$) since this is a purely competitive firm. The marginal cost and total cost data in columns (3) and (5) are taken from Table 3 in Chapter 8, where these cost concepts were introduced and discussed. Total revenue in column (4) is the sales of the firm, or price times output, column (1) × column (2). Profit, in column (6), is the difference between total revenue and total cost, or (4) − (5).

There are two methods by which the firm will choose a rate of output to maximize profits. Suppose, with reference to Table 1, that managers do not actually draw the cost curves of the firm, as most real businesses do not. Instead, they operate the firm under a simple rule: Produce and sell output until profits begin to decrease. Examine column (6) in Table 1, which measures the firm's profits (total revenue minus total cost) from producing and selling various amounts of output. At a low rate of output, 1 to 8 units per day, profits are negative; that is, the firm is making losses. But as the firm expands output in the 1 to 8 unit range, losses decline from $9.20 per day to $0.70. This is the same thing as saying that profits are rising in this range.

When the firm produces the ninth unit of output, profits rise further and become positive ($1.40 per day). Profits continue to rise as the firm expands output up to the 13 unit per day level, at which profits are $5.80 per day. When the firm produces the fourteenth unit of output, profits level off at $5.80. With the firm's production rule of producing and selling output as long as profits do not fall, we know that at least 14 units of output will be produced.

If the firm were to continue to expand output, profits would decrease. The production of 15 jars instead of 14 would yield the firm a profit of $4.95 rather than $5.80. If the firm produced 18 jars, it would again suffer a loss, this time equal to $4. As output expands in the 15 to 20 unit range, profits decline and eventually turn to losses.

The simple decision to stop production when profits begin to decrease leads the firm to produce a rate of output, 14 units per day in Table 1, that maximizes profits for the firm. By comparing the total revenue and the total cost of producing and selling additional amounts of output, the firm will choose to produce that rate of output that maximizes profits.[3]

Figure 3a illustrates the total revenue–total cost approach to maximizing profits. The figure graphs columns (4) and (5) with respect to the output of the firm. The maximum profits possible in the short run occur where the total revenue line (TR) exceeds the total cost curve (TC) by the largest vertical difference. As Table 1 indicates, this takes place at 14 jars of sauce.

The second way to find the profit-maximizing rate of output using the numerical schedule in Table 1 is to compare marginal revenue and marginal cost, columns (2) and (3). As long as marginal revenue is greater than marginal cost, it pays to produce additional units of output. Clearly, marginal revenue ($2.40) is greater than marginal cost up to and including an output of 14 jars of sauce. This means that the point of maximum profit occurs at 14 jars per day. If the firm can turn out jars only one at a time, the firm will cease producing additional sauce after 14 jars, since the marginal cost of producing the next jar is $3.25 and the marginal revenue is only $2.40. Units of output beyond 14 add more to costs than to revenue; that is, they cause profits to decline. Both the total revenue–total cost and the marginal revenue–marginal cost approaches yield the same answer for the profit-maximizing rate of output.

Figure 3b illustrates the marginal revenue–marginal cost approach. Again, note the equivalence of the two approaches by comparing the optimal rate of output, at 14 jars per day in both graphs.

Economic Losses and Shutdowns

What will the firm do if the short-run situation changes for the worse? What if, for example, demand for hot pepper sauce declines because the government publishes an adverse report on the health consequences of eating too much hot pepper sauce? In this case, the market demand curve for pepper sauce will decrease, as shown in Figure 4b, shifting to the left from D_0 to D_1. This results in a price reduction in the hot pepper sauce market, causing the market price confronting the firm to fall from P_0 to P_1. The firm's situation is shown in

---

[3]Even though profits are maximum ($5.80) at both 13 and 14 units of output, the marginal condition for maximum profit $MC = MR$ is true only at 14 units of production.

FIGURE 3

Profit-Maximizing Output for a Purely Competitive Firm

(a) Total revenue–total cost approach to profit maximization. The profit-maximizing rate of output occurs when the vertical distance between total revenue and total cost is greatest.
(b) Marginal revenue–marginal cost approach. Profit maximization occurs where price, or marginal revenue (which are identical for the purely competitive firm), equals marginal cost ($P = MR = MC$). Both approaches result in the same profit-maximizing rate of output.

Figure 4a. Note that the average variable cost curve (AVC) has been added because it is now an important consideration.

We see in Figure 4a that the firm incurs an economic loss because the new market price, P_1, is below its average total cost curve. The firm's revenues are not sufficient to cover its total costs, and it therefore loses money on its operations. What will the firm do in the face of an economic loss? The firm has two options in the short run.

If it expects the adverse effect on sales to be short-lived, the firm can continue to operate in the face of short-run losses. While the price remains depressed at P_1, the firm can minimize losses by following the same rule it followed to maximize profits: It determines the output level at which price is equal to marginal cost and lowers production to that level, q_1 in the figure. Total cost at an output of q_1 is ABq_10, and total revenue is P_1Cq_10. The firm therefore incurs an economic loss equal to the difference between the two: $ABCP_1$. Why might the firm continue to operate in this case while making a loss? It covers all of its variable costs and some of its fixed costs at a price of P_1. If the firm stopped operating, it would still have to pay its fixed costs. These payments must be made whether or not the firm operates. By continuing to operate at price P_1, the firm earns *something* toward the payment of its fixed costs and pays all of its variable costs. Another way to understand this point is to compare the average fixed and average variable costs of producing q_1 rate of output. At q_1, the vertical distance between the average total cost curve and the average variable cost curve is average fixed cost. Figure 4a shows that the

FIGURE 4

Short-Run Loss Minimization

(a) Firm's behavior in the face of economic losses caused by (b) decreased industry demands from D_0 to D_1 and a price drop from P_0 to P_1. At P_1, the firm will minimize losses by continuing to operate in the short run because it covers all of its variable costs and some of its fixed costs by operating. At P_2, the firm may either operate, covering its variable costs, or shut down, eliminating its variable costs. At P_3, the firm will shut down in the short run because the price is too low to cover even its variable costs. It minimizes losses by shutting down and paying only its fixed costs, which must be paid whether the firm operates or not.

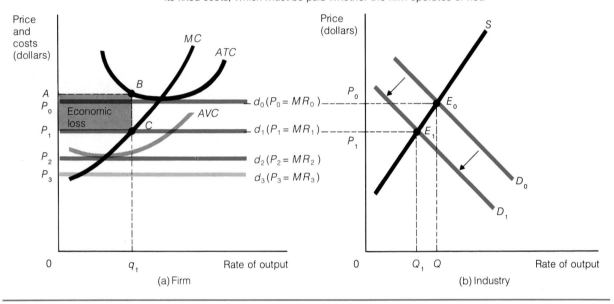

(a) Firm

(b) Industry

losses per unit of output incurred by producing q_1, the vertical distance BC, are less than average fixed cost. If the firm shuts down, its losses would equal fixed costs. It "pays" the firm to stay in business in that its losses are lower than if the firm were to shut down.

Suppose, however, that the market price for hot pepper sauce continues to fall in the industry, say to P_3. At P_3, the firm does not take in enough revenue to cover even its variable costs of production. The loss-minimizing policy for the firm at this point is to cease operations. By shutting down, the firm is ensured of having to pay only its fixed costs. If it tried to operate at a price below its average variable cost, such as P_3, it would not only have to pay its fixed costs but also would incur a deficit in its average variable cost account. The loss-minimizing policy for the firm is to **shut down** when the price falls below its AVC curve.

Suppose that the market price falls to point P_2, where it is just equal to the minimum AVC. What can the firm do in this case? Either operating or shutting down is a reasonable option. If it operates, it can cover its variable costs but none of its fixed costs. If it shuts down, it still may pay its fixed costs. Other things being equal, the firm should be indifferent about whether it operates in the short run under these conditions.

Keep in mind that we are discussing *short-run* policies for the firm. The short run is a period of time in which fixed inputs cannot be varied. Given that fixed costs must be paid, the firm's objective in the short run, when price

Shutdown:
A loss-minimizing procedure in which the firm stops production to eliminate all variable costs, although it must still pay fixed costs.

falls below *ATC* and losses begin, is to minimize its losses. The firm's long-run adjustment will depend on what it expects to happen to prices and costs in the industry. If it expects prices to rise, the firm may shut down temporarily, keep its plant intact, and plan to reopen at some time in the future. Indeed, the firm may use the shutdown period to reorganize in an effort to have lower costs when production begins again. If the firm expects price to remain so depressed in the industry that losses are likely to continue into the future, it may act to sell off its plant and equipment and go out of business.

Supply Curve of a Purely Competitive Firm

The previous considerations help us understand a competitive firm's willingness to supply products as the market price changes, even when it declines. We saw in Chapter 4 that a supply curve shows the relation between the quantity supplied of a good and its price, other things being equal. What is the supply curve of a purely competitive firm in the short run? We answer the question in Figure 5.

We have drawn the firm's marginal cost curve and average variable cost curve and a series of different price levels that the firm faces from a competitive market. We know that the general profit-maximizing rule for the competitive firm is to operate at the level of output at which $P = MR = MC$. We also know that the loss-minimizing rule for the firm is to shut down when price falls below the minimum average variable cost. With these two facts, we can derive a supply curve for the competitive firm.

We know that the firm will not produce at a price such as P_0 in Figure 5. Since P_0 is below the minimum *AVC*, the firm will shut down and produce no output at that price. (Notice that no output corresponding to P_0 is given along the horizontal axis.) This decision of the firm applies at any price below P_1, which is the point of minimum *AVC*. At P_1, the firm will just cover its

---

FIGURE 5

The short-run supply curve of the purely competitive firm is its marginal cost curve (*MC*) above the point of minimum average variable cost. The firm will not operate below P_1 because it cannot cover its variable costs of production. Above P_1, the firm produces where $P = MR = MC$.

Short-Run Supply Curve of the Purely Competitive Firm

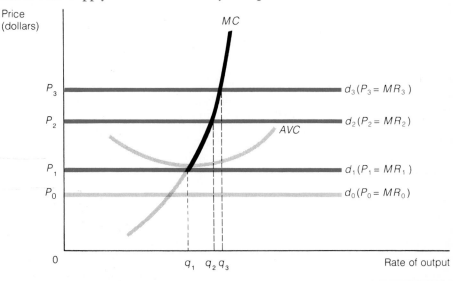

variable costs and will be economically indifferent about whether it operates. We show the firm producing q_1 units of output at the price P_1. At prices above P_1, the firm will operate in the short run and produce at the output level at which $P = MR = MC$. We show two such cases, at P_2 and P_3. In other words, the firm responds to changes in price above P_1 by producing output along its marginal cost curve. The marginal cost curve of the purely competitive firm above the point of minimum average variable cost is the **short-run firm supply curve**; it shows the relation between price and quantity supplied in a period of time when the firm's plant size is fixed.

Short-run firm supply curve:
That portion of a firm's marginal cost curve above the minimum point on the average variable cost curve.

Short-run industry supply curve:
The horizontal sum of all existing firms' short-run supply curves.

From Firm to Industry Supply

It is a simple step from the competitive firm's short-run supply curve to the short-run industry supply curve. The **short-run industry supply curve** is the horizontal sum of the individual firms' marginal cost schedules above their points of minimum average variable cost. This process, which is analogous to the way in which we derived market demand curves from individual demand curves in Chapter 4, is illustrated in Figure 6.

For simplicity, assume that the industry consists of two firms producing hot pepper sauce. At a price of P_0, firm A produces 3 jars per day and firm B produces 2 jars; at these outputs, $P = MR = MC$ for each firm. In each case P_0 is above the firm's minimum AVC. This point on the industry supply curve

FIGURE 6   **From Firm to Industry Supply Curves**

The short-run supply curve of a competitive industry is the horizontal sum of individual firms' marginal cost curves above their respective points of minimum average variable cost. At price P_0, firm A supplies 3 units of output, and firm B supplies 2 units. Market supply is 5 units at P_0. Other points on the industry supply curve, such as $5 + 4 = 9$ units at P_1, are derived in the same way.

is 5 jars per day at a price of P_0. That is, 5 jars is the horizontal sum of 3 and 2 jars produced by the two firms. If price rises to P_1, the firms expand production, to 5 and 4 jars, respectively, along their MC curves. The corresponding point for the industry is at 9 jars of pepper sauce. Other points on the short-run industry supply curve (S_{SR}) are obtained in the same manner. The short-run supply curve of a competitive industry is the horizontal sum of all the individual firms' marginal cost curves above their respective points of minimum average variable cost.

Three points should be kept in mind about this discussion. First, a purely competitive industry encompasses many independent producers; the two-firm model used to illustrate the derivation of the industry supply schedule is an abstraction. In a real case of pure competition, thousands of marginal cost curves would have to be summed horizontally. Second, our analysis is conducted in the economic time frame of the short run, in which firms adjust to price changes within the limits imposed by their fixed plant sizes. Third, the intersection of the industry demand curve and the short-run market supply curve determines the market price for the industry. Both firm and industry are in short-run equilibrium. The firm produces at a level where $P = MR = MC$ for its fixed plant, and industry demand equals industry supply. These two conditions define a short-run equilibrium for the purely competitive model.

THE PURELY COMPETITIVE FIRM AND INDUSTRY IN THE LONG RUN

The long run is a period of economic time during which firms can select the lowest-cost plant to produce their output and firms can enter and exit the industry. The result of these adjustments by firms in the face of economic profits and losses is to move the industry toward long-run equilibrium.

Equilibrium in the Long Run

Long-run competitive equilibrium:
A market situation in which economic profits are zero for all firms; each firm produces output at minimum average total cost.

Zero economic profits:
A condition in which total revenue equals total opportunity cost of production. Firms earn a normal rate of return and $P = MR = LRMC = LRATC$.

Long-run competitive equilibrium occurs when two conditions are met: (1) quantity demanded equals quantity supplied in the market and (2) firms in the industry are making a normal rate of return on their investments, a situation called **zero economic profits.**

Economic profits are returns above and beyond the total (explicit plus implicit) costs to the owner of or investor in a firm. They are returns above the opportunity cost of the owner's capital investment in the firm; that is, they are above the normal return that an owner could expect to make on an investment of some other form such as a money market certificate. Economic profits therefore attract the notice of other investors. They are a signal that prods others to try to capture above-normal returns by entering the industry. Economic profits also lead firms already in the industry to seek to expand their scale of operations. Both cases will result in an increase in output in the industry. This causes the short-run industry supply curve to increase and the market price to fall, erasing economic profits and returning the rate of return in the industry to a normal level. This level is referred to as zero economic profits; investors do make a profit, but no more than what their money would have earned through the prevailing rate of return on any other investment.

If firms in the industry are making economic losses, the opposite situation holds. Firms will cut back operations, and some firms will leave the industry. The short-run industry supply curve decreases, causing the market price to rise and restoring a normal rate of return to surviving firms.

A long-run equilibrium state for a purely competitive industry is depicted in Figure 7. The two conditions for this equilibrium are illustrated in the diagram: (1) quantity demanded equals quantity supplied at the industry level of output, and (2) price just equals the minimum average total cost of the firm. In other words, each firm earns a normal rate of return on its investment in the industry. Notice also that in a long-run equilibrium situation, the market price of output equals long-run marginal cost. Thus the price consumers pay for the good or service just equals the additional cost of producing the good or service.

The Adjustment Process Establishing Equilibrium

Establishment of equilibrium is a continual process in the purely competitive industry. (The Appendix to this chapter discusses how this process of adjustment takes place in agriculture.) To see how the position of long-run equilibrium is reached, consider a condition of long-run equilibrium in the hot pepper sauce industry, which is depicted in Figure 8.

Rightward Shift in Demand. Now imagine that hot pepper sauce not only is given a clean bill of health by government researchers but also is praised as a

---

FIGURE 7   **The Purely Competitive Industry in Long-Run Equilibrium**

In a long-run equilibrium, two conditions are met: (a) the competitive firm earns a zero economic profit, or a normal rate of return, and (b) at the equilibrium market price, industry quantity demanded equals industry quantity supplied. Market price is exactly equal to minimum long-run average total cost. The market price of the good also equals the long-run marginal cost of producing the good.

FIGURE 8

Industry Adjustments to Long-Run Equilibrium: An Increase in Market Demand

Demand increases from D_0 to D_1 in the industry, and price rises from P_0 to P_1 (b). As demand and price rise, firms now earn profits in excess of their average total costs (a). The opportunity for higher-than-normal profits induces entry by new firms. As this expansion of output takes place, the industry supply curve shifts to the right until a normal rate of return and the original price P_0 are restored in the industry.

(a) Firm   (b) Industry

cure for the common cold by a prominent scientist. The industry demand curve for hot pepper sauce suddenly shifts to the right, as shown in Figure 8b, raising the market price to P_1 from the previous equilibrium price P_0.

At first, individual firms in the industry (Figure 8a) adjust to the higher price P_1 by expanding output from q_0 to q_1 within their fixed plant sizes—that is, along their *SRMC* curves. This increase in firms' output is reflected at the industry level (Figure 8b) by the movement along S_0 as price rises from P_0 to P_1. Industry output thus initially rises from Q_0 to Q_1. However, P_1 is above the firm's *SRATC*, so firms in the industry are earning economic profits. Other firms will therefore be attracted to the industry. The effect of this adjustment will be to shift the market supply curve to the right, from S_0 to S_1. Eventually, long-run equilibrium is restored at the original price P_0, where firms again earn a normal rate of return. In the process, industry output has further expanded, from Q_1 to Q_2. The economy now produces and consumes more hot pepper sauce. In this case, larger industry production is accomplished with simply a larger number of firms, each operating at the plant size depicted by *SRATC* in Figure 8a.

Two points should be noted about this process. First, the long-run adjustment process in this example returned price to the original level of minimum average total cost—that is, to the previously prevailing price P_0. This is a special case of long-run adjustment in an industry in which the prices of resources do not change when industry output is expanded.

Second, entry can take place from both without and within the industry. Entry from without is the entry of new firms. Entry from within is the expansion of old firms. Entry from within can take place only if there is a range of long-run firm sizes consistent with minimum-cost production. If the long-run average total cost curve of firms in the industry were U-shaped, only one firm size would offer lowest cost in the long run. When this is the case, entry takes place entirely by new firms. The existing firms will not expand their scale of operations because they are already operating with the lowest-cost plant size. An existing firm can expand its scale of operations only if its *LRATC* curve exhibits a range of constant returns to scale (see Figure 6a in Chapter 8 and its accompanying discussion).

Leftward Shift in Demand. Whereas economic profits lead to the expansion of output in an industry, economic losses lead to a contraction of industry output. Figure 9b illustrates a reduction in industry demand from D_0 to D_1. At the resulting lower price of P_1, firms incur economic losses because P_1 is less than firms' average total cost (Figure 9a). In the short run, firms' output is reduced, depicted by movement down the *SRMC* curve, or firms shut down if P_1 is less than their minimum average variable cost. The short-run drop in production by individual firms causes quantity supplied in the industry to fall to Q_1 along S_0. In the long run some firms will leave the industry by going out of business. The decrease in the number of firms in the industry causes the industry supply curve to shift to the left, from S_0 to S_1. This causes a decrease in total market output from Q_1 to Q_2 and puts pressure on the industry price to rise. Ultimately, price will rise enough to restore the original price P_0 and a normal rate of return to firms in the industry. Here again, the size of each firm producing output is the same initially and after the long-run industry adjustments to the decrease in demand have taken place. Lower industry output is produced by a smaller number of firms, each operating a plant size represented by *SRATC* in Figure 9a.

What are some of the uses of these analyses? First, they depict the desirable effects of competition on the use and allocation of resources. Signals to producers about what consumers want are sent through the market system, and producers respond by adjusting and supplying what consumers want in a way that minimizes the cost of production. Second, the model generates testable propositions, such as the assertion that excess returns should promote entry in a competitive market, from both without and within. An indirect way to test for the presence of a competitive market is to see if excess returns or the presence of economic profits leads to an expansion of output in the industry, or if a decline in output follows economic losses. Such an application of this model could be useful to antitrust analysts, for example, whose job is to detect the presence of monopolistic behavior in the economy.

The Long-Run Industry Supply Curve

Long-run industry supply: The quantities of a product that all firms in an industry are willing and able to offer for sale at various prices when the number of firms and the scale of operations of each firm are allowed to adjust.

The **long-run industry supply** curve represents the quantities of a product that all firms in the industry will be willing to supply at alternative prices in the long run—that is, during a period long enough for entry into and exit out of the industry to occur and for firms to adjust their plant sizes to the lowest-cost level. The long-run supply curve reflects what happens to the prices of inputs as the output of an industry is increased or decreased. In our example of long-run equilibrium, depicted in Figures 8 and 9, price returned to its original level after first rising or falling with rise or fall in demand. As we

FIGURE 9

Industry Adjustment to Long-Run Equilibrium: A Decrease in Market Demand

Industry demand declines from D_0 to D_1, and market price falls from P_0 to P_1 (b). At P_1 firms incur economic losses and cut back production to q_1 (a). Industry output falls to Q_1. Losses cause some firms to leave the industry. The overall decline in production shifts the industry supply curve to the left, from S_0 to S_1, thus restoring the original price P_0 and a normal rate of return to firms that remain in the industry.

(a) Firm

(b) Industry

noted, this is a special case that does not always apply because the costs of inputs may change as industry output changes. There are three possibilities related to input costs: They may remain constant, increase, or decrease, depending on the nature of the industry.

Constant Cost. In Figures 8 and 9, long-run adjustments led to the restoration of the original price in the industry (P_0). In the first case the size of the industry expanded, and in the second case the size of the industry contracted. In both cases, price returned to the level of P_0 as entry and exit and adjustments by firms in the industry took place.

Figures 8 and 9 are examples of a **constant-cost industry**, an industry in which expansions or contractions of industry output have no impact on input prices or costs of production. The long-run industry supply (LRS) curve in this case is perfectly elastic—a flat, straight line at the level of the long-run equilibrium price in the industry, as shown in Figure 10. Notice that the curve is derived by connecting points E_0 and E_1, the points where long-run industry demand intersects supply—that is, points of long-run equilibrium.

Constant cost is most likely to occur in industries where the resources used in industry production are a small proportion of the total demand for the resources in the economy. Take, for example, the toothpick industry. A major expansion, say a tripling, of the output of toothpicks would probably not have much impact on the price of wood used in the industry because far more wood is consumed in other uses, such as building materials, paper, and

Constant-cost industry:
An industry in which the minimum $LRATC$ of production does not change as the number of firms in the industry changes; expansion (contraction) of the number of firms does not bid up (down) input prices; long-run industry supply is horizontal.

FIGURE 10

The long-run industry supply curve (*LRS*) for a constant-cost industry is horizontal at the level of the market price. Expansions in industry output do not change resource costs to individual firms.

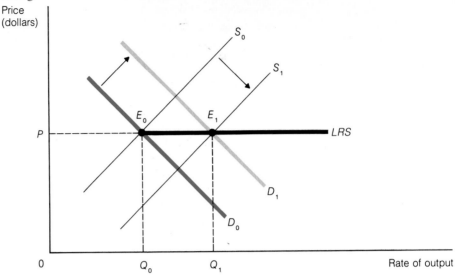

Long-Run Price in a Constant-Cost Industry

firewood. The cost of wood to toothpick producers would therefore remain the same as the industry expanded.

Increasing-cost industry: An industry in which the expansion (contraction) of the number of firms bids up (down) input prices; minimum *LRATC* of production changes as the number of firms in the industry changes; long-run industry supply is upward-sloping to the right.

Increasing Cost. In an **increasing-cost industry,** expansions of industry output lead to higher input prices and therefore higher costs of production for individual firms. This type of industry exhibits the common slope of the long-run industry supply curve because the expansion of most industries puts upward pressure on costs in the industry. An increase in the demand for chicken meat will cause the prices of chicken feed, farmland, and chicken coops to rise. An increase in the demand for newspapers will lead to higher prices for paper, printers, reporters, and so on. These increases in cost lead to a higher long-run price for the goods produced. To obtain more of these goods, consumers must pay higher prices in the long run in order to attract additional resources into their production.

The effects of industry expansion on price and supply in an increasing-cost industry are shown in Figure 11. Initially, the firm and industry are in equilibrium at E_0, with a market price of P_0. Demand increases, the market demand curve shifts to the right from D_0 to D_1, and price rises initially to P_1. Entry into the industry and increased production are encouraged by the higher price, with the additional entry represented by a shift in the supply curve from S_0 to S_1. As production expands, however, resource costs to producers in the industry rise, causing the individual firms' cost curves to shift upward. Thus, as entry takes place, price falls from its height at P_1, and costs to producers rise until a new equilibrium is reached at E_1. This new equilibrium price is higher than the initial equilibrium price of P_0. Connecting the two equilibrium points at E_0 and E_1 yields the long-run industry supply curve. The long-run industry supply curve in an increasing-cost industry slopes upward to the right because additional resources needed to produce additional output in such an industry come at higher costs.

FIGURE 11

Expansions of industry output in response to higher demand D_1 and resulting higher price P_1 lead to higher resource costs facing individual producers in the industry. Equilibrium is reached at P_2 as costs to producers rise and price falls from P_1 to P_2. The long-run industry supply curve (*LRS*) for an increasing-cost industry, determined by connecting equilibrium points E_0 and E_1, slopes upward to the right.

Long-Run Price Changes in an Increasing-Cost Industry

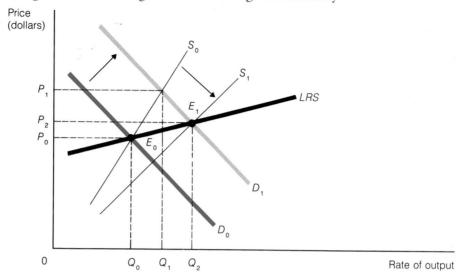

Decreasing-cost industry: An industry in which the long-run industry supply is downward-sloping; expansion (contraction) of the number of firms bids down (up) input prices; minimum *LRATC* of production falls as the number of firms in the industry increases.

Decreasing Cost. A less typical type of long-run industry supply is demonstrated by a **decreasing-cost industry.** In this industry, expansion of industry output leads to lower input prices and lower costs for individual firms and hence to a lower long-run market price for the product. This case is depicted graphically in Figure 12. When industry demand increases and the market demand curve shifts from D_0 to D_1, price first rises from P_0 to P_1. In response, the industry supply curve shifts from S_0 to S_1, and price to consumers falls to P_2. Connecting the two points of industry equilibrium, E_0 and E_1, yields a downward-sloping long-run industry supply curve.

This is an unusual type of long-run industry supply, but a decreasing-cost industry is logically possible. As the clothing industry expands, for example, the costs of certain inputs may fall. Producers of cutting and sewing machines may experience economies of scale, leading to lower prices for their machines. Hence, it is possible for the long-run supply curve of clothing producers to exhibit the decreasing-cost phenomenon.

PURE COMPETITION AND ECONOMIC EFFICIENCY

The model of a purely competitive market is often used by economists as a benchmark or ideal against which other models of market structure are compared. This point will be more obvious in Chapter 10, where we discuss the market structure of pure monopoly. But we first need to understand in what sense the operation of the purely competitive market represents an ideal outcome in the economy and in what sense the model is only an ideal.

FIGURE 12

Though an unusual case, it is logically possible that industry expansion can lead to lower input costs. As demand increases from D_0 to D_1 and the supply curve shifts from S_0 to S_1, prices ultimately settle at P_2, lower than both the initial market price P_0 and the short-run price P_1.

Long-Run Price Changes in a Decreasing-Cost Industry

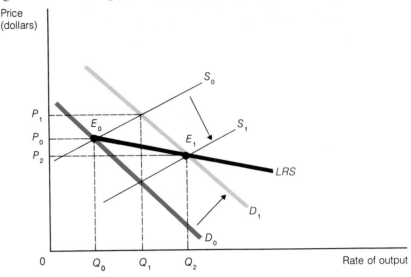

The Competitive Market and Resource Allocation

Pure competition produces what most economists would agree is an ideal or optimal resource allocation. Purely competitive allocation of resources is optimal or best in two fundamental senses.

Productive efficiency:
A condition in which total industry output is produced at the lowest possible opportunity cost of resources.

First, a competitive industry minimizes the resource costs of producing output. In effect, competition forces firms to produce their output at the minimum long-run average total cost and at a price just sufficient to cover that cost. This **productive efficiency** can be seen in long-run equilibrium in competitive firms, which produce at the point where $P = LRATC = LRMC$. It is the minimum possible opportunity cost of producing the good or service. Consumers benefit because they get the goods they desire at the lowest possible cost. This is so because market equilibrium price equals minimum long-run average cost of production. Inefficient, high-cost firms will incur economic losses and will be driven from competitive markets. Surviving will be firms who can provide industry output at the lowest cost. The 1978 lifting of government regulations on the airline industry created a highly competitive situation in which a number of airlines with excess costs suffered severe losses. Some were forced out of business. By contrast, Northwest Airlines thrived because of the leanness of its operations. By avoiding frills such as lavish company headquarters and by promoting values such as employee productivity, Northwest has kept its cost per passenger seat mile below the industry average. Such productive efficiency characterizes firms that survive in highly competitive markets.

Allocative efficiency:
A situation in which the socially optimal amount of a good or service is produced in an industry; the socially optimal amount depends on the tastes and preferences of society and on the opportunity cost of the resources used to produce the good or service.

Second, a competitive market also results in **allocative efficiency.** Allocative efficiency exists when the price paid by consumers for one more, or the last, unit of a good or service just equals the cost of the resources that produce the additional, or last, unit of the good or service. It is the socially optimal output of the good or service. In a competitive market, consumer demands are met as long as consumers are willing to pay a price for the production of an additional unit of output equal to the cost of the additional resources required to produce the additional output. In competitive markets, resources flow to their most highly valued uses, resulting in allocative efficiency.

This situation is expressed in the now familiar condition $P = LRMC$. Price reflects the desire of consumers for additional units of a good. Long-run marginal cost represents the opportunity cost of the resources necessary to produce an additional unit of the good. If P is greater than $LRMC$, consumers will pay more for additional units of production than the cost to produce them. When this is the case, resources in the economy will be reallocated from other uses considered less valuable by consumers. If a chicken farmer, for instance, finds that consumers will now pay more for the relatively scarce rooster hackle feathers prized for fly-fishing than they will pay for relatively abundant chicken meat, the farmer will shift the use of some chicken coops, chicken feed, and farmhands from production of meat birds to production of roosters bred for hackle feathers. Chicken lovers might find fewer chickens for sale.

If P is less than $LRMC$, consumers will pay less for additional units of production than the cost to produce them. Resources will be reallocated out of such production. If the price for hackle feathers is less than the cost, then fewer hackle feathers will be available for fly-fishing. If P equals $LRMC$, resource allocation is ideal in the sense that the things consumers want are produced by competitive firms in the exact quantities and combination (of feathers and food, for instance) that consumers desire and at the lowest cost.

The competitive model is really Adam Smith's concept of the "invisible hand" at work. Acting in their self-interest, consumers and producers create a mutually beneficial outcome. Looking out for their own interests, producers seek to maximize profits, and yet in a competitive market the result is that consumers' desires are met in the most efficient way possible. Consumers selfishly demand the goods and services they want, but competitive producers balance those demands against other demands for other goods and services. An incredibly complex process of consumer demand and producer response is put in motion by the behavior of each individual in heeding his or her own interest. No central planner is required, and yet a result emerges that is ideal.

Perfect competition is not perfect in every sense, however. While a purely competitive world leads to an ideal resource allocation, it might not lead to an ideal distribution of income among people. Equity will conflict sometimes with the achievement of economic efficiency. In other words, competitive solutions will not always result in equitable solutions (or what is considered equitable in law or by society). Equity might require a reduction in pure economic efficiency in order to achieve some greater good—for example, government subsidies to the homeless. Also, while pure competition accommodates consumers' preferences, these preferences themselves may not conform to anyone's image of the ideal state of human existence. Individuals are free to buy and sell as they see fit. If consumers want gadgets rather than great books, they are free to make this choice.

Competition in the Real World

Many critics of free-market policies admit to the virtues of perfectly competitive markets but argue that in the real world it is nearly impossible to find examples of perfectly competitive markets. To these critics, evidence that products sold by rival firms are not homogeneous, that prices charged by these firms are not identical, or that buyers are not perfectly informed proves that the competitive model is not applicable.

Defenders of free markets, in turn, argue that the competitive model can explain real-world behavior in a variety of markets. To them, the assumption of homogeneous products is not essential. Further, differences in money prices among rival firms are not important so long as the full prices charged by these firms are, for the most part, equal.

The market for student apartments is one in which we can readily contrast the two conflicting points of view. As any student who has shopped for an apartment knows, the units are not homogeneous, and prices are not uniform. Should one infer from these real-world facts that the market for apartments is not perfectly competitive?

Advocates of free markets would argue that use of the competitive model in this case is quite appropriate. Instead of viewing apartment units as goods being bought and sold, imagine a market for some intangible good called *housing services*. Although a unit of housing services cannot be defined exactly, each apartment can be viewed as giving some quantity of services to its tenant. Luxury units in prime locations have a large number of units of housing services; substandard units in undesirable locations have a small quantity of housing services. In the rental housing market there are many students who are buyers of housing services and many landlords who sell housing services.

From this perspective, the disparity in rental prices among apartment units is entirely consistent with the theory of perfect competition. If a particular apartment is perceived to be twice as good as another unit (yielding twice the quantity of housing services), we would expect the first apartment to rent for twice as much. The two units are physically quite different and have different locations, but the apartment owners still compete with each other. Although student tenants have imperfect information about apartment prices, students do have an incentive to acquire such information. The real-world alternative to perfect information is *some* information—not complete ignorance. The assumption of complete information is not totally unrealistic. (See Focus, "The Economics of Information: Searching for the Best Deal," for details about how consumers obtain information in competitive and other markets.)

Price differences among auto dealers or among gasoline stations also can be reconciled with the competitive model. In each case, sellers are competing for the sale of services to buyers, so price differences may only reflect differences in the units of service provided to customers.

From these examples, one should feel comfortable using the competitive model to analyze markets even if all the underlying assumptions are not met. Economies of scale have created industries comprised of only a few large firms. Economists have developed alternatives to the competitive model to analyze the behavior of firms in such industries. They have also developed useful models for examining forms of nonprice competition in markets that are not easily explained by the competitive model. The following three chapters develop several of the alternative models.

FOCUS   The Economics of Information: Searching for the Best Deal

The model of perfect competition is based on several key assumptions. One of these assumptions is that information about the price of products and services is free. Consumers, therefore, are immediately aware at zero cost of any price differences in a given market for a given product. By acting to buy low and sell high, they will drive price in the market to a single value. One price for a product will prevail when a perfectly competitive market is in equilibrium.

We live, of course, in a more complex world. Information—about prices, quality, or anything else—is rarely free. It is an economic good that is costly to produce and to obtain. For example, when gas stations post price signs, an act of producing information, they must pay for materials, pay for the labor to make and place the signs, pay for any changes that might be made, and so on. Consumers must spend valuable time and other resources looking for posted prices. Because information about prices is costly to produce and obtain in most markets, there will be a dispersion of transaction prices (more than one price) for the same commodity when the market is in equilibrium.

Figure 13 illustrates the economics of information. The MC curve represents the marginal cost to the consumer of searching for a lower price for some particular product or service. Additional search is typically more and more costly, so MC rises to the right. If you are in the market for a used car, for example, the marginal cost of search can be considered as the costs of visiting and negotiating with one or more used car dealers. Moreover, the level of the MC curve will vary across goods. It will be low, for example, when shopping for clothes by mail-order catalogue. It will be high, for example, when searching for a wedding dress.

The MB curve represents the marginal benefit to the consumer of searching for a lower price. As you check the prices of more and more sellers, the prospect of finding a lower price from the next seller declines, and so MB declines to the right. The marginal benefits of additional search also will vary across markets. When the value of the product is large (for example, consumer durables—houses, refrigerators, cars), it will pay the consumer to search more for a lower price. However, it will not pay the consumer to search widely for a lower price of toothpicks. Ordinarily, the larger proportion that the item is in the consumer's budget, the greater is the benefit of longer search—that is, the further to the northeast the MB curve would be in Figure 13.

The consumer will search until the MC of search equals the MB of search. This is the point of optimal or efficient

FIGURE 13
Marginal Costs and Marginal Benefits from Search

Consumers, without free information about the prices or qualities of products or services, will spend resources to discover these attributes until the marginal benefit just equals the marginal cost of search.

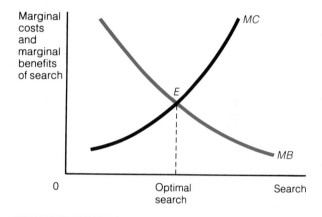

search, depicted by point E in Figure 13. At levels of marginal cost and benefit before point E, the extra benefits of more search exceed the extra costs. After point E, marginal costs of search exceed the marginal benefits. Point E represents the correct or equilibrium amount of search for a given consumer (for a particular good). Consumers will employ such optimal search procedures in their shopping behavior, not exactly as in the diagram, but in an intuitive, instinctive manner. Since point E will not be the same for all consumers (for all products), the fact that information about prices is costly to produce and to obtain means that in most markets there will be a dispersion of final transaction prices and not a single price for a product at all locations.

Common sense and experience reinforce this idea. In your own college community, for example, you can conduct the following experiment. Collect the prices for a single product, such as a particular brand of toothpaste, at five different stores. What you will observe will be an array of prices across locations, a result consistent with our analysis of costly information.

SUMMARY

1. Economists study competition in two basic senses: as a rivalrous, natural process among competitors and as an abstract concept described by the model of a purely competitive market.

2. A purely competitive market is characterized by many buyers and many sellers, a homogeneous product, no barriers to entry or exit by firms, and free information. Examples include the stock market and agricultural markets.

3. The purely competitive firm is a price taker: The firm is so small in relation to the total market for its product that its output has no influence on the prevailing market price. The demand curve facing the purely competitive firm is perfectly elastic at the level of the prevailing market price.

4. Marginal revenue is the change in total revenue caused by an increase in output. Since the purely competitive firm faces a perfectly elastic demand curve, each unit is sold at the prevailing market price. Thus, marginal revenue is equal to market price for the pure competitor.

5. In the short run, the pure competitor decides how much output to produce by setting marginal cost equal to market price. If price is above the average total cost, the firm earns an economic profit in the short run. If price is below the minimum average variable cost, the firm will shut down in the short run to minimize its losses.

6. The supply curve of a purely competitive firm is its marginal cost curve above the point of minimum average variable cost. The supply curve of a purely competitive industry in the short run is the horizontal sum of individual firms' marginal cost curves above their respective points of minimum average variable cost.

7. Short-run equilibrium for the purely competitive firm and industry occurs when the quantity supplied and quantity demanded are equal in the market and each firm is producing at the level where $P = MR = SRMC$.

8. In the long run, firms in a purely competitive industry can enter and exit the industry and seek the optimal plant size in which to produce their output. The presence of economic profits leads to entry and expansion in the industry, and economic losses lead to the opposite.

9. Long-run equilibrium in a purely competitive industry results when firms in the industry earn zero economic profits and industry demand and supply are equal. In the long run, the purely competitive firm's position is such that price equals marginal cost equals long-run average total cost: $P = LRMC = LRATC$.

10. The long-run industry supply curve in a purely competitive industry reflects what happens to firm costs as industry output expands or contracts. In a constant-cost industry, resource prices and firm costs are unchanged by industry expansion, and the long-run industry supply curve is perfectly elastic. An increasing-cost industry experiences rising costs as industry output expands; the long-run industry supply curve slopes upward to the right. In a decreasing-cost industry, resource prices fall as industry output expands, and the long-run industry supply curve slopes downward to the right.

11. The working of the purely competitive model represents a benchmark against which the working of the economy can be measured. In this model, resources flow to their most highly valued uses, and output is produced at the lowest cost in terms of resources used. The model of pure competition is also useful in some applications such as agricultural markets.

KEY TERMS

market
purely competitive market
homogeneous product
perfect information
price taker
profits
marginal revenue

total revenue
shutdown
short-run firm supply curve
short-run industry supply curve
long-run competitive equilibrium
zero economic profits

long-run industry supply
constant-cost industry
increasing-cost industry
decreasing-cost industry
productive efficiency
allocative efficiency

QUESTIONS FOR REVIEW AND DISCUSSION

1. What is a market? What is a purely competitive market?

2. Why are price and marginal revenue the same thing for a purely competitive firm?

3. What is the supply curve of a purely competitive firm? Of a purely competitive industry?
4. Describe the adjustment process between points of long-run equilibrium in an increasing-cost industry.
5. Suppose that the media reports the contamination of oyster fisheries in the coastal waters off the United States. The news creates a decrease in demand for oysters. If oyster production is a constant-cost industry, describe the adjustment to the new equilibrium using graphical analysis.
6. Suppose that a competitive firm is earning economic profits because its owner figured out a way to lower the costs of production. Since the source of the reduced costs is known only to the owner, how can

entry take place? Should such information be proprietary (belong to the owner), or should the owner be required to tell potential competitors the reason for the lower costs?
7. Which of the following markets could be analyzed with the competitive model: (a) automobiles; (b) Swiss cheese; (c) blue jeans; (d) cheeseburgers; (e) trash collection; (f) television news; (g) janitorial services?
8. How long will a firm in a competitive industry endure economic losses before it leaves the industry? In your answer, assume that price is above minimum $SRAVC$ but below $SRATC$.

PROBLEMS

The following data and graph pertain to a competitive firm.

1. How much output should this competitive firm produce?
2. What will be the firm's profit at its profit-maximizing rate of output?
3. Why can't the firm charge a long-run price of $10?

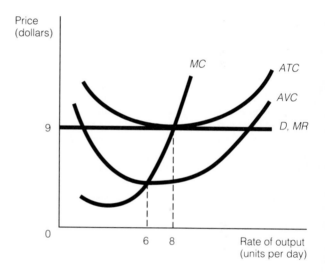

Output	MC	MR	TR	TC	Profit
1	5.00	9.00	9.00	10.00	−1.00
2	4.10	9.00	18.00	14.10	3.90
3	4.25	9.00	27.00	18.35	8.65
4	4.67	9.00	36.00	23.02	12.98
5	5.50	9.00	45.00	28.52	16.48
6	6.60	9.00	54.00	35.12	18.88
7	7.66	9.00	63.00	42.78	20.22
8	9.00	9.00	72.00	51.78	20.22
9	10.75	9.00	81.00	62.53	18.47
10	12.50	9.00	90.00	75.03	14.97

ECONOMICS IN ACTION
The Role of Speculators in Competitive Markets

After a harvest, the supply of wheat is fixed until the next harvest. An important economic problem consists of how the fixed supply of wheat can be made to last until the next harvest. What keeps the economy from running out of wheat between harvests? Why can wheat still be purchased to be processed into flour and made into bread in August, just a month before the new harvest?

Someone must have an incentive to buy wheat after the harvest and to hold and store the wheat over the year between harvests, gradually selling off the wheat over the course of the year and helping to ensure that the wheat lasts. Farmers generally do not want to store wheat; they want their money at harvest time. Users of wheat such as flour millers also do not want to store wheat—nor do consumers. Both producers and consumers of wheat shy away from the job of storing wheat because the job is risky—the price of wheat can change day-to-day, which means one can make or lose money by holding wheat.

Enter the speculator. The speculator is an individual who is willing to bear the risk of changes in the price of a commodity—such as wheat—over time and who tries to make money by bearing this risk. How does this process work?

Suppose this year's wheat harvest has been purchased by speculators. The speculators contract with owners of storage facilities to have their wheat stored. The speculators make deals buying and selling wheat for future delivery at specified prices. These deals are called *futures contracts* and are made on a futures market. Suppose, for example, that the current market price (the spot price) of wheat is $2 per bushel. This is just after harvest in September. Over the course of the year, this year's crop of wheat will be sold off and used. Next summer, just before the next harvest, the amount of wheat in storage will be low, and its price will be relatively higher. Thus, this September a wheat speculator might agree to sell wheat for delivery next July for $2.25 per bushel. The $2.25 price is a futures price of wheat. It reflects the speculator's prediction of what wheat will be worth in July. If the actual price in July is greater than $2.25 per bushel, the speculator loses money because he or she has to sell at the price agreed on today, $2.25 per bushel. If the price is less than $2.25, the speculator makes money. This process of buying and selling wheat in the future serves the important economic function of allocating the fixed supply of wheat over the course of a year. Speculators bear the risk of a change in the price of wheat, and their speculation on the future price of wheat helps to make the available wheat last until next year. For example, as this year's crop runs out, its price will rise to cut back consumption of the relatively scarcer wheat in July.

Suppose, in an alternative scenario, that after this year's harvest but before next year's, a severe drought hits the nation's wheat belt. This means that next year's wheat crop will be less than expected. What happens to the current spot price of wheat? Even though the same amount of wheat is still available in the storage bins, the future supply of wheat has been reduced. This means that the present price of wheat will rise, and owners (speculators) of this wheat will make a profit by withholding it from the market in expectation of even higher wheat prices in the future. Are the gains of the speculator ill-gotten? No, anyone can buy and sell wheat. The speculator's reward comes from a willingness to bear risks. Since the drought has reduced the future supply of wheat, the price of wheat must rise to allocate the available supply over an even longer time period, until the harvest after next. The higher prices deter consumption (remember the law of demand!), making the available wheat last longer, which it now has to do before new supplies become available. Speculators assist in this process by adjusting the price of wheat both today and in the future for changing conditions in the wheat market.

Thus speculators and speculation play an important economic function in a competitive economy. Keep in mind also that speculators made money when the price of wheat suddenly went up. They then owned a more valuable commodity. Suppose the harvest had been much larger than expected. In this case, the current and future price of wheat would have fallen, leaving speculators with a loss. Speculators do not always make a profit—that is the risk.

There are futures markets in many commodities, including cotton, pork bellies, common stocks, soybeans, and gold. The prices of these commodities at various future points in time are listed on the financial pages of most daily newspapers. Speculators buy and sell these commodities for future delivery and in so doing participate in a process that helps the economy allocate stocks of these commodities to consumption and production over time. In other words, speculators help to allocate the use of goods over time, confronting users of commodities with prices that reflect the relevant scarcity at a given point in time. Speculators keep us from consuming the supplies of commodities too fast, before more supplies can be produced.

Question

Word hits Wall Street that a severe freeze in Brazil has damaged the next coffee bean crop. What will happen to the price of coffee in the grocery store? Who wins and who loses from the change in coffee prices? Why did the price of coffee change, since the same amount of coffee existed before and after the freeze?

Agricultural Problems in the United States

When economists are asked to provide real-world examples of perfectly competitive markets, agricultural examples are among the first mentioned. There is a good reason for this. First, the total number of farms in the United States is huge—currently about 2.2 million. In addition, the number of competing producers within each segment is also quite large; for example, there are about 30,000 poultry producers and about 165,000 dairy farmers in this country. Therefore, the competitive model, which assumes a large number of competing producers of homogeneous products, is entirely appropriate for analyzing agricultural markets. Although economists consider competitive markets models of efficiency, agricultural markets continue to experience many economic difficulties. Year-to-year income instability plagues the nation's farmers. Poverty on the farm continues, with many farmers forced out of business each year despite numerous government assistance programs. By applying some of the economic principles we've covered in the text to this point we can gain insight into these problems.

ELASTICITY AND SHORT-RUN INCOME INSTABILITY

Evidence suggests that both the demand for and the supply of specific types of food are relatively inelastic over short time periods. Estimates of the price elasticity of demand (which is defined as the percentage change in quantity demanded divided

by the percentage change in price) for various food products are presented in Table 2. Although there are fewer estimates of supply elasticities, agricultural experts say that for specific food products " . . . over a period of one or two years, the supply elasticity is generally in the range of 0.1 to 0.3."[a] This means that relatively small changes in the sup-

---

[a]R. D. Knutson, J. B. Penn, and W. T. Boehm, *Agricultural and Food Policy,* (Englewood Cliffs, N.J.: Prentice-Hall, 1983), p. 103.

TABLE 2

Estimates of Demand Elasticities for Various Agricultural Products

The demand elasticity for specific food products varies, but demand elasticity for food is clearly inelastic.

Commodity	Elasticity
Cotton	0.1
Wheat	0.02–0.2
Corn	0.03–0.5
Citrus Fruit	0.8
All Fruit	0.6–1.1
Beef	0.8–1.1
Pork	0.7–1.0
All Meat Products	0.4–0.6
Eggs	0.3–0.4
All Food	0.2–0.5

Source: Adapted from Leonard Weiss, *Case Studies in American Industry,* 2nd ed., p. 38. Copyright © 1971 John Wiley & Sons, Inc. Reprinted by permission.

ply of food will cause large changes in the price. If, for example, weather conditions are particularly favorable to the production of corn, good weather may lead to a 10 percent increase in the supply of corn. However, with inelastic demand, the price will fall by more than 10 percent, causing the income (the total revenue) of corn growers to fall. With inelastic demand, reductions in price cause reductions in total revenue. Furthermore, the less elastic the demand for corn, the greater the decrease in income to corn growers.

On the other hand, drought or some other natural disaster would lead to a decrease in the supply of corn and to an increase in price larger in percentage terms than the decrease in supply. In turn, the incomes of corn growers increase; the size of the increase depends on how inelastic the demand for corn is. The less elastic the demand, the greater will be the increase in revenue. These situations are depicted graphically in Figure 14.

Relatively small changes in demand for food will similarly lead to large swings in the income of food producers if supply is inelastic. A relatively small increase in demand for a particular type of food will lead to a large increase in both the price and the income of producers. Small decreases in demand will lead to large decreases in price and large decreases in the income of producers. The low elasticities of demand and supply of food products explain why for farmers it is often either boom or bust. Figure 15 details the erratic nature of farm income.

LONG-RUN AGRICULTURAL PROBLEMS

A greater problem than short-term income instability among farm families is the long-term problem of poverty and bankruptcy. Except for the years 1973 and 1974, when agricultural prices were unusually high, average income for American farm families has been substantially less than the average income for nonfarm families. The extent of these differences is only hinted at in Table 3; about 50 percent of farm families receive less than $10,000 per year from the sale of agricultural products and must supplement their farm incomes with income from nonfarm sources.

Numerous factors have contributed to the joint problems of poverty and bankruptcy among farm families, but the most important is the rapid increase in farm technology. Expenditures on research and development by the U.S. Department of Agriculture and by land grant universities have resulted in a tremendous increase in farm productivity. The supply of agricultural products has increased more rapidly than demand, causing the *relative* price to fall, as shown in Figure 16. Since the rate of productivity growth has exceeded the rate of growth in demand, an increasing amount of agricultural output is being produced with *fewer* productive resources. According to Department of Commerce statistics, between 1947 and 1987, American farmers increased their total output by about 90 percent while using, on average, 18 percent *fewer* inputs. However, the quantity of all inputs used in agriculture did not fall by a uniform 18 percent. In 1947, there were about 10.3 million workers employed on farms. By 1987, the number had fallen by almost 75 percent, to 2.7 million. Over the same time period, the total number of acres used in farming decreased by 13 percent, the quantity of farm equipment increased by 33 percent, and the quantity of chemicals used increased

FIGURE 14
Short-Run Fluctuations of Food Prices

The demand for agricultural goods is relatively inelastic, and short-run supply fluctuations (shifts to S_0, S_1, or S_2) affect price and revenues dramatically. If farmers' output rises from Q_1 to Q_2, then price falls substantially along with total revenue. If output falls from Q_1 to Q_0, price and total revenue rise substantially.

FIGURE 15

Net Farm Income 1950–1989 (in 1982 dollars)

On balance, farm income declined dramatically during the period 1950–1989.

Source: Council of Economic Advisers, *Economic Report of the President* (Washington, D.C.: U.S. Government Printing Office, 1990), p. 403.

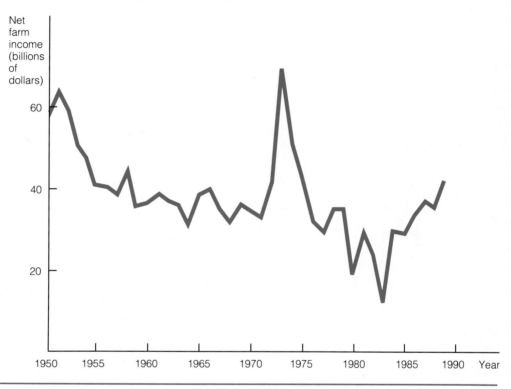

by about 700 percent. Between 1947 and 1987, the number of farms declined by about 4 million, and the percent of the U.S. population living on farms

TABLE 3
Median Family Income for Farm and Nonfarm Families

There is a persistent differential in farm and nonfarm median family income, with farm families earning only about 80% as much as nonfarm families.

Family Type	Median Family Income (1983 dollars)		
	1975	1980	1983
Farm	$20,076	$19,049	$18,925
Nonfarm	25,599	25,573	24,751

Source: United States Department of Agriculture, *Agricultural Statistics* (Washington, D.C.: U.S. Government Printing Office, 1986), p. 620.

fell from 21 percent to less than 3 percent. A comparison of the profiles of the typical farm in 1947 and the typical farm in 1987 is telling: The typical farm in 1987 was much larger (over 450 acres, on average, compared to about 200 acres), produced more output, and employed fewer workers.

These trends suggest that changing technology in agriculture has led not only to a downward shift in agriculture cost curves but also to a change in their shape. As shown in Figure 17, farms initially had to produce at least Q_0 units of output to reach a minimum efficient size. Changing technology has shifted the long run average cost curve from $LRAC_0$ to $LRAC_1$; farms today must be much larger (produce at least Q_1 units) in order to remain competitive. This shift helps explain the tremendous decrease in the number of farms and the increasing difficulty of smaller farms to remain competitive. Farms that were once competitive have adjusted to changing technology by growing larger or have been faced with economic ruin.

FIGURE 16
Long-Run Changes in Food Prices

In recent years the relative price of agricultural products has been falling. Supply has been shifting to the right owing to tremendous strides in food production technology (S_1 to S_2 to S_3). These supply shifts have outstripped increases in the demand for agricultural goods (D_1 to D_2 to D_3) caused by growth in population.

FIGURE 17
The Effect of Changes in Technology on Long-Run Average Costs

Changing technology in agriculture has caused the long-run average cost curve to shift downward and to decline over larger levels of output. As a consequence, farms have had to grow larger to remain competitive.

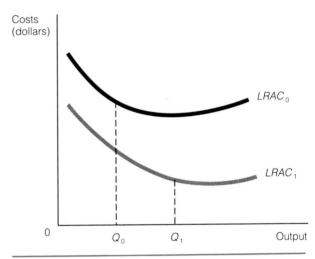

GOVERNMENT ATTEMPTS TO SOLVE BASIC AGRICULTURAL PROBLEMS

Since the 1930s, the federal government has implemented thousands of assistance programs aimed at reducing price instability or subsidizing the incomes of American farmers. Among them were programs to directly support agricultural prices, restrict production, promote consumption, and subsidize exports and restrict imports. All the programs fall into one of two categories. In the first category are programs that attempt to alter the demand or supply curves of farm products while allowing markets to clear at equilibrium prices. In the second type of program, the government regulates farm prices with direct price supports but does not attempt to manipulate demand or supply.

Agricultural Programs That Manipulate Demand and Supply

Since both demand and supply of agricultural products tend to be inelastic with respect to price,

relatively small shifts in either curve can affect incomes. Therefore, government policies that increase demand for farm products lead to large price increases and to huge increases in farmers' incomes. In Figure 18a, an increase in demand from D_0 to D_1 for apples causes the equilibrium price to rise from 10 cents per pound to 15 cents per pound and the equilibrium quantity to rise from 6 to 8 billion pounds per year. Such a shift would cause the receipts of apple producers to double from $600 million to $1.2 billion. Over the years, the federal government has implemented a number of policies that have affected demand in this way, including the school lunch and breakfast programs, food stamp programs, and export subsidy programs.

Programs that restrict the supply of agricultural products have similar effects on farmers' incomes. Figure 18b shows that a decrease in supply from S_0 to S_1 will cause the price to rise from 10 cents per pound to 16 cents per pound and increase the receipts of apple growers from $600 million to $880 million per year ($5,500,000,000 \times \$0.16 = \$880,000,000$). Over the years, the federal government has implemented acreage restriction programs that limit the number of acres farmers can use for production of certain crops; land retire-

FIGURE 18   **The Economic Consequences of Government Programs That Shift Demand or Supply**

(a) Government subsidy programs that increase demand cause price and quantity to rise.
(b) Government programs that restrict supply cause price to rise but quantity to fall. If demand is inelastic, farmers' incomes will rise.

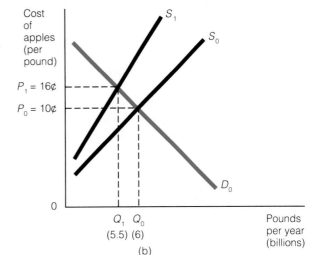

ment programs that pay farmers to withdraw land from production; and conservation programs that subsidize farmers to plant cover crops in place of cash crops to improve soil fertility. The federal government has also, at times, restricted imports of agricultural products. Assuming that supply curve S_0 in Figure 18b includes apples produced by foreign growers, programs that restrict apple imports will also increase incomes of domestic apple growers.

Each of these programs has increased incomes of domestic farmers; however, the programs have done little to stabilize farm incomes. In fact, when programs are changed from year to year, the effect can be a destabilization of farm prices. For example, when the Carter administration banned the sale of wheat to Russia, demand fell and there was great uncertainty in the market. The resulting volatility in wheat prices, then, resulted largely from government intervention.

Agricultural Programs That Regulate Prices

In addition to the various government programs designed to affect demand and supply of certain

agricultural products, the government has also implemented two general types of programs that directly control prices. The first is a standard price support program. Under this program, the government establishes some minimum price for a particular commodity and agrees to buy the commodity at that price.

Figure 19 shows the effect of setting a minimum price on wheat at $7.50 per bushel. When the government offers to buy wheat at $7.50 per bushel, growers will be unwilling to sell in private markets at any price below $7.50. As a consequence, growers will harvest 3.25 billion bushels but will sell only 2.25 billion bushels at $7.50 per bushel. The federal government must then buy the surplus 1 billion bushels of wheat at a price of $7.50 per bushel for a total cost of $7.5 billion. Farmers' incomes will go up, but consumers will pay higher food prices and higher taxes to provide the required subsidy. Having purchased the surplus wheat, the government must also determine what to do with it. It would do no good to sell the wheat—this would decrease the amount of wheat that could be sold privately at $7.50 per bushel and increase the surplus the government had to purchase. Instead, the alternatives are storing the wheat (and paying to do so), destroying it, or giving it away (to buyers who do not under any circumstances purchase American wheat).

Figure 19 illustrates how a direct price support program can become costly to finance. Increased supply due to improved technology leads to larger surpluses and greater government costs. Therefore, price support programs have usually been accompanied by programs to limit supply. In this way, the price can be kept at the support level without causing large surpluses.

The Department of Agriculture has phased out the simple price support system. Under the new system, the government sets a target price for affected commodities and agrees to make up the difference between the farmer's selling price and the target price. Figure 20 illustrates the operation of target prices, using demand and supply curves identical to those in Figure 19. If the government sets the target price at $7.50 per bushel, producers will supply 3.25 billion bushels. They are willing to supply this quantity because with the government subsidy included, the price they will receive is $7.50 per bushel. As the graph shows, producers will be able to sell that quantity at a price of $5.50 per bushel. Therefore, the government must pay a subsidy of $2 per bushel (the difference between $7.50 and $5.50) for each of the 3.25 billion bushels. The total subsidy cost of this program will be $6.5 billion.

The government has replaced traditional price supports with target prices for several reasons. One reason is that a given level of income can be generated with lower government subsidies. The subsidies in Figures 19 and 20 produce equal incomes to farmers, but the target price subsidy saves taxpayers $1 billion. In addition, the target price program keeps prices down for consumers and makes it easier for agricultural output to be sold abroad. And target prices do not require expensive storage or wasteful destruction of surpluses.

Government's Impact on Agriculture: An Assessment

Table 4 shows the extent of subsidy spending on various types of farms, but the data are deceptive:

FIGURE 19
The Economic Effects of a Price Support Program

A government support price of $7.50 per bushel will lead to a wheat surplus of 1 billion bushels, which the government is forced to purchase.

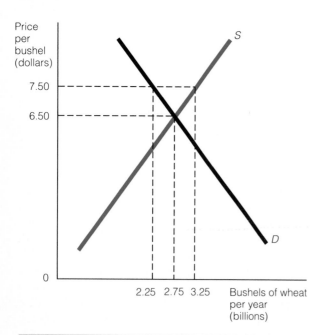

FIGURE 20
The Economic Effects of a Target Price Program

A target price of $7.50 per bushel causes wheat farmers to harvest 3.25 billion bushels, which they sell for $5.50 per bushel. The government pays $2.00 per bushel to farmers to raise the price to the target level.

TABLE 4

Size of Government Payments to Farms of Various Sizes

The amount of farm sales is a measurement of farm size. According to the statistics in the table, payments to smaller farms declined from 1975 to 1985, while payments to farms with sales over $100,000 rose dramatically.

Amount of Farm Sales	Average Payments per Farm				
	1975	1980	1982	1984	1985
Less than $2,500	$46	$37	$94	$59	$17
$2,500–$4,999	123	79	201	123	80
$5,000–$9,999	174	165	420	364	233
$10,000–$19,999	260	206	527	921	678
$20,000–$39,999	445	521	1330	2341	2040
$40,000–$99,999	729	1169	2986	5650	5193
$100,000–$249,999	1091	1700	4341	13,837	12,885
$250,000–$499,999	1665	2412	6160	21,877	21,783
$500,000 and over	5193	3849	9829	35,559	37,499

Source: United States Department of Agriculture, *Agricultural Statistics* (Washington, D.C.; U.S. Government Printing Office, 1986), p. 632.

Many government programs (particularly those that manipulate supply and demand) make no direct government payments to farmers. Despite massive government expenditures, the woes of American farmers continue. Land debt has increased from $30 billion in 1970 to more than $100 billion today, and farm foreclosures and auctions have become weekly events in many regions.

Critics of U.S. farm policy argue that government subsidies are in fact responsible for many of these problems. With unrestricted competition, gains in productivity would create only short-run problems for farmers. As fewer farmers were needed, competitive forces would drive some out of business. In the long run, surviving farms would earn a normal profit. Government subsidy programs, however, encourage farmers to continue despite economic losses. While these programs alleviate the risks of farming and ensure an overabundance of agricultural products for consumers, they also contribute to long-run problems. For example, when drought conditions struck much of the United States in 1986 and again in 1988, the government provided emergency assistance even to farmers who had not purchased government-sub-

sidized crop insurance. Rather than encouraging farmers to remain in an unprofitable industry, government reeducation and retraining programs could be instituted to encourage farmers to leave the industry. Such a policy would eliminate losses and the need for government income support programs.

In summary, the low income of farmers is the legacy of improved productivity, low short-run elasticities of supply and demand, and, indirectly, government subsidy programs. Government support of farmers is very much a product of the social problems—hunger and malnourishment, in particular—of the 1930s. Whether farm support programs should continue in the 1990s is debatable. Proponents argue that the loss of the small farmer would eliminate an American tradition and would create other social and economic problems, such as urban overcrowding and higher unemployment. Opponents believe that we have too many farmers and that this oversupply is an unnecessary burden on taxpayers. The fate of government subsidy programs, like other considerations of equity, will be left to the political process.

10

Monopoly: The Firm as Industry

In a purely competitive market, each firm's production is such a small proportion of industry output that a single firm has no influence on the market price. As we have seen, the competitive firm is a price taker. The opposite extreme to a purely competitive firm is a pure monopoly: a single seller in an industry. The pure monopoly, in fact, *is* an industry. It alone faces the industry demand curve for its output, and it can affect market price by changing the amount of output that it produces. For this reason, we refer to the pure monopoly firm as a **price searcher:** It must seek the price that maximizes its profits. The ability of the pure monopoly firm to affect market price is not absolute, however. Even a single seller in an industry is subject to competitive pressures from the makers of substitute products. When you finish Chapter 10 you should know

Price searcher:
A firm that is able to choose a profit-maximizing price from a range of prices rather than have price imposed by market conditions and competition; such a firm faces a downward-sloping demand curve.

- how barriers to market entry can create and sometimes maintain monopoly power.
- the principles underlying the economist's (static) model of monopoly behavior, including how the monopolist makes profits or sustains losses.
- how, under specific circumstances, monopolists can charge different prices to different consumer groups for the same product or service.
- the costs of monopoly in redistributing income from consumers to monopoly producers of goods and services.

WHAT IS A MONOPOLY?

Pure monopoly:
An industry in which a single firm produces a product that has no close substitutes and in which entry of new firms cannot occur.

A **pure monopoly** is an industry composed of a single seller of a product with no close substitutes and with high barriers to entry. This definition seems clear, but we must use some care in applying it.

Examples of pure monopoly in the sense of a single seller in an industry are rare. In sixteenth- through eighteenth-century Europe, monarchs granted monopoly rights to individuals for a variety of productive undertakings. These were pure monopolies because each was given the exclusive right to run an entire industry. For example, the king of England created only one English East India Company, which was empowered with a monopoly over the trade with India. This monopoly power was manifested in the high prices the East India Company charged for the goods it brought back from India and sold in England. (See Focus, "Mercantilism and the Sale of Monopoly Rights," for a more detailed discussion of such historical monopolies.)

Even in these historical cases of monopoly, the monopoly was usually granted to a group of merchants. These monopolies were therefore not technically a single seller; rather, they were a group of sellers acting as a single seller. This is a broader meaning of monopoly. In fact, we typically observe monopoly in the real world in groups of sellers acting together. Such associations of sellers are called *cartels*. The analysis of pure monopoly presented in this chapter is relevant to cartels, but pure monopolies and cartels are not the same. A group of sellers must somehow organize to form a cartel agreement; the single pure monopolist faces no such organizational problem. In this chapter, we discuss pure monopoly in the sense of a single seller facing the industry demand curve. In Chapter 12, we return to the cartel problem and see what extra elements have to be added to monopoly theory to account for cartel behavior.

A second problem in applying the definition of monopoly concerns the criterion that there be no close substitutes. All products exhibit some degree of substitutability. The monopolist's isolation from competition from substitute products is therefore a matter of degree. Consider electricity, usually sold by firms holding local monopolies on its distribution. Are there good substitutes for electricity? The answer depends on what the electricity is used for. If it is used for lighting services in residential homes, the few possible alternatives—such as candles and oil lamps—are not very good substitutes for the convenience of electric lighting. If it is used for heating, however, the range of substitute products is greater. The wood stove, oil, and gas industries are competitors with the electric utility company in the market for home heating. The degree of substitutability for the monopolist's product is an important determinant of monopoly behavior. Where there are close substitutes, the monopolist cannot substantially raise prices without losing sales. Where there are no close substitutes, the monopolist has more power to raise prices.

A third consideration in defining monopolies is high barriers to new entry by potential competitors, the basic source of a pure monopoly. There are several types of barriers to new competition: legal barriers, economies of scale, and control of an essential resource.

Legal Barriers to Entry

Sometimes the power of government is used to determine which industry or firm is to produce certain goods and services. Such **legal barriers to entry** take several forms.

First, it may be necessary to obtain a **public franchise** to operate in an industry. As noted previously, the English monarch granted a franchise determining who could sell Asian goods in England in the seventeenth and eighteenth centuries. In modern times, franchises are granted by government for a variety of undertakings. The U.S. Postal Service, for example, has an exclusive franchise to deliver first-class mail. (See Economics in Action, "Technology, Economics, and the Postal Monopoly.") Similar arrangements for food and

Legal barriers to entry:
Government actions that prohibit other firms or individuals from producing particular products or entering particular occupations or industries; such barriers take the form of legal franchises, licenses, and patents.

Public franchise:
A firm or industry's exclusive, government-granted right to produce and sell a good or service.

FOCUS   Mercantilism and the Sale of Monopoly Rights

Mercantilism refers to the form of economic organization that dominated Western Europe from, roughly, 1500 to 1776. The English and French economies of the time were typical mercantile economies. Both were characterized by monarchies in which a king or queen represented the central government. As practiced by these monarchs, mercantilism involved widespread and detailed regulation of the economy. Often, this regulation created monopoly rights for favored individuals. The mercantile economies therefore came to be characterized by the existence of pure monopolies in such diverse areas as brewing, mining, trading, playing cards, and so on.

The creation and protection of these monopoly rights had a clear purpose—to raise revenue for the needs of the sovereign. Such needs included the expenses of the king's court and the resources to fight foreign wars. In other words, the monarchies sold monopoly rights to raise revenue.

Why did sovereigns use monopolies rather than taxes for revenue? Fundamentally, tax collection was a relatively inefficient means to raise revenue for the central state be-

cause the costs of monitoring and controlling tax evasion were high. Barter and nonmarket production were widespread in the agricultural economy; moreover, there was little commercial record keeping. Tax collection was a difficult and unattractive alternative source of revenue.

The granting of monopoly rights as a means to raise revenue did not have the same deficiencies as taxation. Most important, competition among potential monopolists revealed to the state authorities the worth of such privileges. There were no problems of evasion or guessing at taxable values. Those who wanted the monopoly right would make an offer for the right to the king or queen. The potential monopolists were buying the agreement of the ruler to protect and enforce the monopoly privileges granted.

Thus, pure monopoly has a prominent place in economic history because of its effectiveness at raising revenue for the state. However, as the state's power to tax has increased in modern times, the revenue-raising role of monopolies has diminished.

Government license:
A legal right granted by state, local, or federal governments to enter an occupation or industry.

gas service are made along toll roads such as the New Jersey Turnpike. The essence of an exclusive public franchise is that a monopoly is created; competitors are legally prohibited from entering franchised markets.

Second, in many industries and occupations a **government license** is required to operate. In most states a license is required to practice architecture, dentistry, embalming, law, nursing, medicine, or veterinary medicine; to dispense drugs; and to teach. At the federal level, an operating license is required from the Federal Communications Commission to open a radio or television station. If you want to operate a trucking firm that carries goods across state lines, you must obtain a license from the Interstate Commerce Commission. Licensing therefore creates a type of monopoly right by restricting the ability of firms to enter certain industries and occupations.

Patent:
A monopoly right granted by government to an inventor for a product or process; valid for seventeen years in the United States.

Third, a **patent** grants an inventor a monopoly over a product or process for seventeen years in the United States. The patent prohibits others from producing the patented product and thereby confers a limited-term monopoly on the inventor. The purpose of a patent is to encourage innovation by allowing inventors to reap the exclusive fruits of their inventions for a period of time. Yet a patent also establishes a legal monopoly right. In effect, the social benefit of innovation is traded off against the possible social costs of monopoly.

Economies of Scale and Natural Monopoly

In some industries, low unit costs may be achieved only through large-scale production. Such economies of scale put potential entrants at a disadvantage. To be able to compete effectively in the industry, a new firm has to enter on a large scale, which can be costly and risky. The effect is to deter entry. Only rarely have new domestic firms attempted to enter the automobile manufacturing industry, for example, because it uses highly automated production techniques on a large scale to keep costs down.

Natural monopoly:
A monopoly in which the relation between industry demand and cost structure makes it possible for only one firm to exist in the industry.

In a **natural monopoly,** economies of scale are so pronounced that only a single firm can survive in the industry. In such a case, competition will not work, and government enacts some sort of regulatory scheme to control the natural monopoly. Public utilities such as natural gas, water, and electricity distribution are examples of natural monopolies that are regulated. The regulation of natural monopoly is discussed in more detail in Chapter 19.

A firm may own all of an essential resource in an industry. In this case new entry is barred because potential entrants cannot gain access to the essential resource. The De Beers Company of South Africa, for example, controls 80 percent of the world's known diamond mines. This makes the company a virtual monopolist in the diamond market.

MONOPOLY PRICE AND OUTPUT IN THE SHORT RUN

Even though pure monopoly is rare, the theory of monopoly can be applied to a large number of situations in the economy. These range from the behavior of government-created monopolies to natural monopolies, patent rights, and diamond companies. Moreover, virtually every firm has some control over the prices it charges. The degree of control varies with the type of market in which the firm sells, but the fact that the firm can choose its prices makes the concept of the monopoly firm as price searcher relevant to understanding firm behavior in general. In other words, the analysis of pure monopoly is useful in helping us understand the pricing behavior of all firms, from the corner grocer to IBM.

The monopoly firm, like the competitive firm, faces both long- and short-run production and pricing decisions. In this section we define more carefully what the concept of price searching means, and we examine how the monopoly firm decides how much output to produce and what price to charge in the short run.

The Monopolist's Demand Curve

The demand curve of the pure monopolist is fundamentally different from that of the pure competitor. The purely competitive firm is a price taker; it accepts market price as given but can sell as much as it wants at the prevailing market price because demand for its product is perfectly elastic. The monopoly firm faces a downward-sloping market demand curve and must find the price that maximizes its profits. This means that to sell more, the monopolist must lower price. The monopoly firm therefore confronts the problem of finding the best price-output combination. For this reason, we say that the monopolist is a price searcher. The process of price searching occurs in any firm that faces a downward-sloping demand curve, however slight the downward slope may be. A local dry cleaning firm, for example, has some control over its price and must therefore search for the best price for its service.

Figure 1 illustrates the difference in the demand curves facing price takers and price searchers: The former is perfectly elastic, while the latter slopes downward. How elastic is the price searcher's demand curve? Economic theory does not give us a single answer to this question. Recall from Chapter 5 that the degree of elasticity along a demand curve depends on a number of variables, including the price and the number of close substitutes for the monopolist's product. Even though monopolists are synonymous with the industries they occupy, they are not immune to competition from producers of substitute products. The cheaper and more numerous these substitutes are, the more elastic the monopolist's demand curve will be. The more elastic a monopolist's demand curve, the less valuable is its monopoly position in setting prices. Figure 1b represents the demand curves for two monopoly industries. The demand curves for these two industries, D_1 and D_2, both slope downward, but D_1 is more inelastic than D_2 at price P_m because the latter monopoly faces stiffer competition from substitutes.

For this reason a monopoly in tuna fishing, for example, would not be a tremendously valuable monopoly right. While tuna is a unique product, significant price increases for tuna would cause consumers to switch to other protein sources, such as chicken or beef. A monopoly over crude oil production, however, where consumers have few viable consumption alternatives in the short run, has proved to be tremendously valuable, as the price-raising success of OPEC in the 1970s testifies.

FIGURE 1   **Demand Curves for Competitive and Monopoly Firms**

(a) A perfectly elastic demand curve *d* facing a purely competitive firm. This firm is a price taker: It can sell all of its product that it wants at the prevailing market price. (b) Two market demand curves facing different monopolists. The firm facing demand curve D_1 has more leeway then the firm facing curve D_2 in choosing price-output combinations because consumers cannot easily find substitutes for the former's product. But both monopolies are price searchers. They face a downward-sloping demand curve; to sell more, they must lower their price.

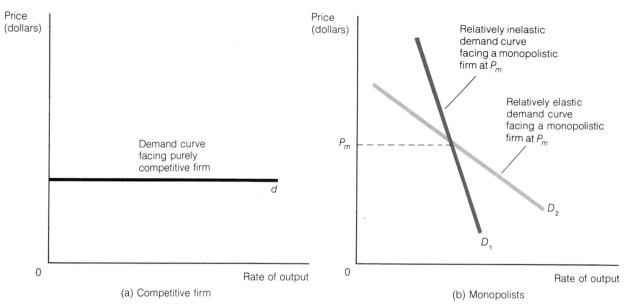

The basic point to remember about the demand curve facing the monopolist is that it is <u>downward-sloping</u>. This means that the monopoly firm must lower price to sell more and must search for the best, or profit-maximizing, level of output. In other words, the monopolist must be able to answer the question: Does the revenue <u>gained from lowering price</u> exceed the revenue lost from lowering price? To answer this question, the monopolist must employ the concept of marginal revenue.

The Monopolist's Revenues

To understand the usefulness of marginal revenue figures in price searching, consider yourself the owner of a monopoly. You have discovered a special kind of rock on your land that, when split, reveals a natural hologram. The mysterious beauty of these rocks is highly appealing to rock collectors and gift purchasers. If your aim is to earn the maximum profit from the production and sale of the rocks, how do you decide what price to charge for them?

By trial and error—for you have no previous experience on which to base your pricing decision—you find that the revenues, costs, and profits you encounter at different prices vary considerably, as illustrated in Table 1. Columns (1) and (2) show the decreasing prices you must charge to sell increasing

TABLE 1   Revenues, Costs, and Profits for the Pure Monopolist

These data are for the hologram rock monopolist. Columns (1) and (2) show the components of the demand curve facing the firm. Column (3) gives total revenue, or sales. Column (4) is the important concept of marginal revenue, which is the change in total revenue divided by the change in output. Columns (5) and (6) are the cost data. Maximum profits in column (7) occur where marginal cost equals marginal revenue, at 6 units of output per day.

(1) Rate of Output (units per day)	(2) Price (per unit)	(3) Total Revenue (per day) (1) × (2)	(4) Marginal Revenue $\Delta TR \div \Delta Q$	(5) Total Cost (per day)	(6) Marginal Cost	(7) Profit (per day) (3) − (5)
0	—	—		$40.00		−$40.00
			$24.00		$10.00	
1	$24.00	$24.00		50.00		−26.00
			22.00		8.00	
2	23.00	46.00		58.00		−12.00
			20.00		7.00	
3	22.00	66.00		65.00		1.00
			18.00		10.00	
4	21.00	84.00		75.00		9.00
			16.00		12.00	
5	20.00	100.00		87.00		13.00
			14.00		13.00	
6	19.00	114.00		100.00		14.00
			12.00		15.00	
7	18.00	126.00		115.00		11.00
			10.00		20.00	
8	17.00	136.00		135.00		1.00
			3.50		25.00	
9	15.50	139.50		160.00		20.50
			.50		30.00	
10	14.00	140.00		190.00		−50.00

numbers of rocks. Together, columns (1) and (2) represent the market demand curve for hologram rocks, of which you are the sole seller. Your total revenue per day (also known as *sales*) is column (1) × column (2), or price × quantity.

Marginal revenue:
The change in total revenue arising from a one-unit change in output; the change in total revenue divided by the change in output.

Marginal revenue (*MR*) is the change in total revenue brought about by a change in output, or $\Delta TR/\Delta Q$. In Table 1, column (4) reflects the change in column (3) each time you lower price and produce an additional rock. In Chapter 9, we saw that for the purely competitive firm, *MR* was equal to price because the firm did not have to lower its price to sell additional units of output (see Table 1 in Chapter 9, p. 225). However, as Table 1 here shows, *MR* is not equal to price for you as a monopoly firm, except for the very first unit you sell, because you face a downward-sloping demand curve. When you cut your price, as for example from $22 to $21, two conflicting influences affect your total revenues. You gain additional revenue from the additional units you sell at the lower price. In this case, you sell one more rock for $21. But since the price reduction also applies to output that you were previously able to sell at a higher price, in effect you *lose* revenue on these units. In other words, the three rocks per day you could previously sell at $22 are now priced at $21, a reduction of $3 from your total revenues. Your marginal revenue is therefore $21 − $3 = $18 in this case.

When demand is downward-sloping, *MR* ($18) is less than price ($21) by the amount of the revenue lost on units that would have sold at the higher price. For price searchers, marginal revenue is less than price ($P > MR$) because of the need to lower price to sell additional units of output.

Figure 2 provides another way of looking at the fact that marginal revenue is always lower than price for the monopoly firm. At a price of P_1, total revenue is $P_1 \times Q_1$. At a price of P_2, total revenue is $P_2 \times Q_2$. Marginal revenue is the difference between these two total revenue rectangles. To see its components more clearly, consider what happens when price is cut from P_1 to P_2. First, additional revenue is generated by the sale of extra units at the lower

$$TR = P \times q$$

FIGURE 2

When the monopoly firm lowers price, it gains revenue from the additional output sold, Q_1 to Q_2, and loses revenue on the output previously sold at price P_1 and now sold at a lower price, P_2. The net effect is a marginal revenue curve that lies below and inside the demand curve.

The Dual Effects of a Price Reduction on Total Revenues

price. This additional revenue is indicated in the shaded rectangular area CBQ_2Q_1 above increased sales. Second, there is a loss of revenue on units previously sold for P_1 but now sold for P_2. This loss is represented by the shaded area P_1ACP_2. Thus, the marginal revenue derived from a price reduction by the monopolist is less than the new price charged. Except for the first unit of output, the *MR* curve of the monopolist therefore lies below or inside the demand curve.

Even though the monopoly firm faces no direct competition, it still must search for its best price. This search for the most profitable price-output combination explains why the monopoly firm lowers price even though it has no direct competitors.

Total Revenue, Marginal Revenue, and Elasticity of Demand

The demand curve facing the monopoly firm shows the amount of output that can be sold at different prices. It also shows how the firm's revenues vary as price and output are changed. By observing this, we can learn something about the elasticity of the monopolist's demand curve over various ranges. Figure 3 illustrates the relation between total revenue, marginal revenue, and the elasticity of the monopolist's demand curve at various points. Suppose that we are joint owners of a firm with a monopoly on Gas-Saver, a unique additive that doubles gas mileage if one can is added to each tankful of gas. If we conduct a pricing experiment along our demand curve, we can observe its effects on our revenues. We start with a high price of $12 per can and lower it gradually to $6. At $12, we will not sell any of the stuff, for consumers know that a can will cost them more than the gas they save. As we lower the price toward $6, we sell more and more.

Figure 3b shows what happens to our total revenue as the price falls. Over the range of sales up to 30 cans per day, our total revenue rises. In Figure 3a, this rise is reflected by the positive marginal revenue. A demand curve is elastic when price reductions cause total revenue to rise. Thus, our demand curve is elastic up to the level of 30 units of output and a price of $6. Beyond 30 units of output, however, we observe that as we further lower our price, our total revenue falls, and our marginal revenue is negative. This drop means that we have reached the inelastic portion of our monopoly demand curve. Here, price reductions cause our sales to decline.

The regions of our Gas-Saver demand curve that are elastic and inelastic are labeled $\epsilon_d > 1$ and $\epsilon_d < 1$, respectively, in Figure 3. (ϵ_d is the symbol for price elasticity of demand.) The point labeled $\epsilon_d = 1$ is where the demand curve is unit elastic. This point occurs where marginal revenue equals zero and where total revenue is at a maximum. It is the dividing line between the elastic and inelastic portions of the monopolist's demand curve. The link between *MR* and elasticity of demand can be stated thus: *MR* goes from positive to negative as demand goes from elastic to inelastic.

With this simple model, we can begin to discuss the rational pricing strategy of the monopolist. Suppose that our Gas-Saver monopoly firm has no costs of production so that profits are equal to total revenue. What price should we set to maximize our revenue? Figure 3b clearly illustrates that we can do no better than to be at the top of the total revenue curve. At this point, we reach our total maximum revenue: $180 per day. Reading vertically up to Figure 3a, you can see that to earn this maximum total revenue, we should

FIGURE 3

Changes in Elasticity of Demand and Total Revenue as Price Changes

The elasticity of the monopolist's demand curve is linked to the behavior of total revenue as price changes. In the elastic ($\epsilon_d > 1$) portion of the demand curve, price reductions cause total revenue to rise. When demand is unit elastic ($\epsilon_d = 1$), price reductions leave total revenue unchanged. When demand is inelastic ($\epsilon_d < 1$), price reductions lead to a fall in total revenue. The point of unit elasticity in Figure 3a, beyond which marginal revenue becomes negative—30 cans per day—is also the point in Figure 3b at which total revenue stops rising and starts declining.

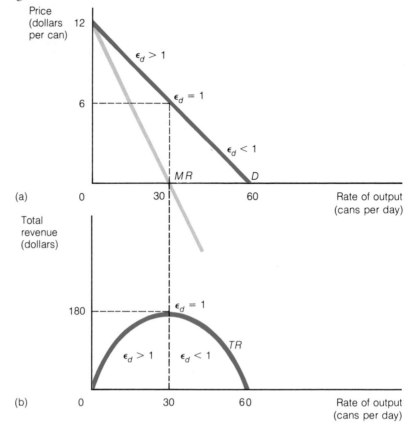

produce 30 cans of Gas-Saver per day and sell them for $6 each. The profit-maximizing monopolist with no costs of production will set price along the demand curve where demand is unit elastic, or equal to 1. A monopoly firm will never operate along the inelastic portion of its demand curve because marginal revenue is negative along this portion. Increases in output and reductions in price actually cause total revenue to fall.

This simple analysis helps us understand the pricing behavior of any firm facing a downward-sloping demand curve. Such firms will not set price in the inelastic part of their demand curve because they can earn more revenue by raising price. This result and the discussion of this section are based on the properties of a straight-line, or linear, demand curve.[1]

---

[1]With a linear demand curve, the marginal revenue curve will bisect the horizontal axis and any line parallel to the horizontal axis. In Figure 3, for example, *MR* bisects the horizontal axis at 30 units of output.

Short-Run Price and Output of the Monopolist

Although for simplicity we did not consider input costs in the previous discussion, we introduce them now, because all firms incur costs of production. The fact that the monopolist possesses a monopoly in the output market says nothing about its position in input markets. In this respect the monopoly firm is like the competitive firm; it is one of many buyers of inputs. The cost curves of the monopolist therefore resemble those of the competitive firm.

By combining the cost and revenue concepts of monopoly, we can analyze the choice of the best, or profit-maximizing, rate of output and price for the monopoly firm in the short run. To maximize profits, the monopolist follows the same rule that the competitive firm follows—it sets marginal cost equal to marginal revenue. The logic is identical in both cases. If MR is greater than MC, it pays to produce additional units of output because they add more to revenues than to costs. If MR is less than MC, it pays to reduce production because extra output adds more to costs than to revenues. The monopolist will therefore do best by producing at the output level where MC equals MR.

Look back at the cost and profit data in Table 1 for the hologram rock monopoly to check the viability of this rule for profit maximization. Comparing marginal revenue in column (4) with marginal cost in column (6), we see that the first 6 rocks produced per day add more to revenue than to costs; that is, $MR > MC$ over this range of outputs. The sixth unit of output adds $14 to revenues and $13 to costs. It pays to produce that sixth unit. Producing the seventh rock, however, has a marginal cost of $15 and a marginal revenue of $12. The firm would be losing money if it increased operations to 7 rocks a day. The maximum profit occurs at a rate of output of 6 rocks per day and a price of $19 for each. The profitability of this decision is recorded in column (7), which is the difference in total revenue from column (3) and total cost from column (5). The maximum daily profit of $14 occurs when 6 rocks are produced, the point at which MR equals MC.

The same point is illustrated graphically in Figure 4, where a monopoly's marginal cost curve is combined with its demand and marginal revenue curves. To determine the profit-maximizing rate of output, the monopolist would find the point along the horizontal axis where $MR = MC$—in this case Q_m. For outputs less than Q_m, $MR > MC$, and it pays the monopolist to expand production. In this area, extra units of output add more to revenue than to cost. For outputs greater than Q_m, it pays the firm to reduce output. At Q_m, $MR = MC$, and the firm can do no better than produce this output. Profits are maximized at Q_m.

The monopolist sets a price for Q_m units of output by reading the market value of this output off the demand curve at a point directly above the point where $MR = MC$. In other words, the price for this output is read off the demand curve by drawing a straight line from the intersection of MR and MC to the demand curve and over to the price axis, as shown by the dashed lines in the figure. Price is not set where $MR = MC$ on the marginal revenue curve; it is set by reference to the demand curve. In Figure 4, P_m is the **profit-maximizing price.**

Figure 4 illustrates a principle based on economic behavior, but in real-world firms, executives do not calculate MR and MC and set them equal to one another to determine their best price. Business decisions are more com-

Profit-maximizing price:
The price associated with the quantity sold at which the difference between total revenue and total cost is greatest; the price associated with the quantity sold at which marginal revenue equals marginal cost.

FIGURE 4

The monopoly firm maximizes profits where $MR = MC$. This means that Q_m is the profit-maximizing output and P_m, read off the demand curve, is the profit-maximizing price for the monopoly firm.

Profit-Maximizing Price for a Monopoly

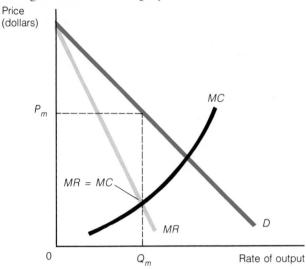

plicated; more often than not, businesspeople will be observed using rough-and-ready approaches to pricing and production decisions. However, through a process of trial and error, price-searching firms will grope toward the $MR = MC$ solution. It may not seem as if they are applying the $MR = MC$ rule, but the practical effect of their decision making ultimately works itself out in these terms.

Although both the purely competitive firm and the pure monopolist follow the $MR = MC$ rule, the result is fundamentally different in the two cases. For the competitive firm, marginal revenue is the same as price. The competitive firm therefore maximizes profits by producing where $P = MC$. Marginal revenue is not the same as price for the monopolist; as we have seen, the monopolist produces where $P > MC$. We will elaborate further on this important difference between competition and monopoly later in the chapter.

Monopoly Profits

Figure 4 shows how the monopolist applies the $MR = MC$ rule, but it does not tell us anything about the level of profits the monopoly earns. To discuss this concept we add the monopolist's average total cost to the analysis in Figure 5.

Nothing is changed from Figure 4. The monopolist continues to set $MR = MC$, selling Q_m units at a price of P_m. Just as in the case of the purely competitive firm, the monopolist's profits are determined with respect to the average total cost curve. At point B, the monopolist would just cover its average total cost. But its monopoly position and the demand for its product allow it to set price at P_m on its demand curve, creating economic profits in excess of its costs. In Figure 5, these profits are given by the shaded area $P_m ABC$, or the amount by which total revenue, the area $P_m A Q_m 0$, exceeds the total cost of

FIGURE 5

At point *B*, the monopoly firm would just cover its average total cost. But since it holds a monopoly, it can charge price P_m, creating economic profits equal to $AB \times Q_m$, represented by the area P_mABC. In other words, P_mABC is equal to total revenue, P_mAQ_m0, minus total costs, CBQ_m0.

Monopoly Profits

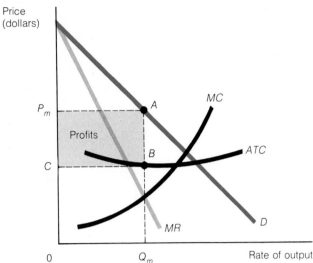

producing Q_m, the area CBQ_m0. Another way to look at monopoly profits in such a graph is to say that the monopolist makes *AB* profits per unit of output, where $AB \times Q_m = P_mABC$.

This is a profitable monopoly. These returns are in excess of the total costs of the firm, which means that they are above the opportunity cost of the monopolist's capital investment. Were this a purely competitive firm, these excess returns would stimulate new entry and expansion in the industry. Remember, however, that this is a pure monopoly. Entry cannot occur here, by definition. So, unlike the profits of the competitive firm, which ultimately are restored to a normal rate of return, the profits of the monopolist can persist in the long run.

Not all monopolies make monopoly profits. Some lose money. Such a case is graphed in Figure 6. In this case, demand is not sufficient to cover the average total cost of the monopolist at the level of output where $MR = MC$. Total revenue at Q_m is represented by P_mCQ_m0; total cost is represented by the larger area ABQ_m0. Total cost exceeds total revenue by the amount of the shaded area, $ABCP_m$. This monopolist makes an economic loss in the short

Shut-down point.

run. As long as P_m is high enough to cover the monopolist's variable costs, the monopoly will continue to operate in the short run if it expects market conditions for its product to improve. Over time, however, if the losses depicted in Figure 6 persist, the monopolist will cease operations and go out of business. The investment in the monopoly firm is not earning a normal rate of return, and by closing down, the firm is free to move its investment where it can earn higher rates of return.

It may seem curious that monopolists should make losses, but this is a very real phenomenon. Many holders of patents, for example, never market their products because there is no demand for them. The fact that one has a monopoly does not automatically make it a valuable monopoly.

FIGURE 6

Not all monopolies make profits. This monopoly makes *BC* losses per unit of output because demand for its product is not sufficient to cover its average total costs. Its total revenue at Q_m is represented by P_mCQ_m0, and its total cost by ABQ_m0. Therefore, its total losses are represented by the shaded area, $ABCP_m$. If the situation does not improve in the long run, this monopoly will go out of business.

An Unprofitable Monopoly

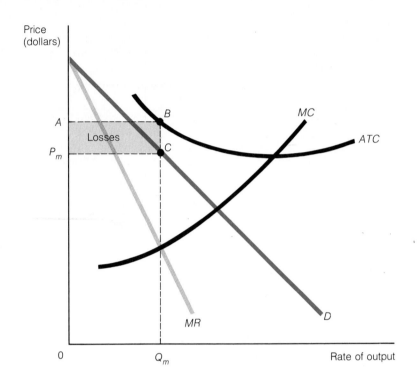

Differences from the Purely Competitive Model

Before we move on to long-run considerations for the monopolist, we note two important differences between the monopoly firm and the purely competitive firm. First, in a pure monopoly no distinction is made between the firm and industry. The pure monopoly *is* the industry, so there is no room for a separate theory of industry versus firm behavior, such as the one we presented for pure competition.

Second, recall that the marginal cost curve of a competitive firm (above the point of minimum average variable cost) is its supply curve because the firm sets marginal cost equal to price to maximize profits. Its pricing behavior traces out a relation between quantity supplied and price. No such relation exists for pure monopoly. The monopolist controls the quantity of output produced and sets $MR = MC$, but MR does not equal price for the monopolist. Because the monopolist does not set MC equal to price, no unique relation exists between MC and price in the case of pure monopoly. To know what the monopolist will produce at a given price, we need to know more than the firm's MC; we need to know the shape and position of its demand and marginal revenue curves as well. The lesson is simply that the monopolist does not have a supply curve—that is, a unique relation between the amount it produces and the price.

PURE MONOPOLY IN THE LONG RUN

Like all firms, the pure monopolist must face the long run, the period of economic time over which the firm can vary all of its inputs and enter or exit the industry. The long run for the pure monopolist is not analogous to the long run for a purely competitive firm and industry. Certain adjustments take place, such as the capitalization of monopoly profits, but entry and other efficiency-enhancing adjustments do not take place. Monopoly and its effects persist in long-run equilibrium.

Entry and Exit

A pure monopoly may not be profitable and, hence, may leave the industry. Exit is a distinct possibility. Entry is not. By definition, high and prohibitive barriers to entry exist with monopoly; entry by new firms is barred. Long-run adjustments in the form of competitive entry do not take place in the case of the monopoly.

Adjustments to Scale

The monopoly firm can adjust its scale of operations in the long run. Given that it makes a profit, the monopolist can seek to produce the profit-maximizing rate of output in the most efficient plant. Figure 7 illustrates one possible plant size result of a long-run adjustment for the monopolist.

The monopoly firm produces a rate of output Q_m where $MR = MC$ and operates to the left of the point of minimum long-run average total cost. In contrast, the purely competitive firm was forced by competition to produce at the level where long-run average total cost was at a minimum, at Q_c. The monopolist produces Q_m in the most efficient plant that it can, given by short-run average total cost ($SRATC$) for the lowest-cost plant in which to produce Q_m. But compared with the purely competitive firm, it is operating inefficiently—that is, in a plant size with unit costs greater than minimum long-run average total cost. This result is by no means unique. It depends on the specific demand and marginal revenue curves drawn in Figure 7. Different demand and marginal revenue curves would result in the monopolist's choosing a different scale of plant ($SRATC$ curve) to produce output in the long run. The important point is that the monopoly produces output in the long run with a higher-cost plant size than will a competitive industry.

Capitalization of Monopoly Profits

The final long-run adjustment by the monopoly firm concerns what happens to its profits in the long run. We have said that entry is not possible with pure monopoly. But there is no reason that the monopoly cannot be sold to aspiring investors. In this respect, monopoly rights are like any other resource: Where competition is free, resources will flow to their most highly valued uses. Figure 8 shows the outcome of this process.

The monopoly is earning profits represented by $P_m ABC$ in long-run equilibrium. Suppose that its owners decide to retire and sell the firm. What

FIGURE 7

The monopoly firm can adjust its plant size in the long run along its *LRATC* curve. Typically, this adjustment results in the selection of an efficient plant size to the left of minimum long-run average total cost, at Q_c, the point at which competitive firms must operate.

Monopoly Plant Size in the Long Run

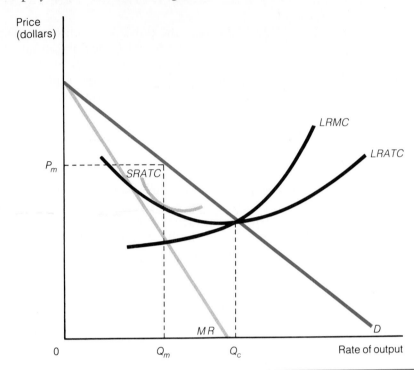

would they ask for the firm? Rationally, they would include in their asking price the value of the monopoly profits. They would not give these profits away to a buyer. As a result, the average total cost to the buyer would rise to reflect the value of the monopoly profits, from $LRATC_1$ to $LRATC_2$ in Figure 8. The selling price of the monopoly firm will be determined by the sum of all future years' economic profits that the monopoly could be expected to earn. Not only this time period's profits P_mABC in Figure 8, but all profits over the expected life of the monopoly would figure into what the owners could sell the firm for today (see the discussion in Chapter 16 on present values for a more precise way of determining the current value of a monopoly firm). The value today of all future monopoly profits is called the **capitalized monopoly profits.**

Capitalized monopoly profits:

What the sum of all future monopoly profits is worth today.

A useful principle has emerged. When monopoly profits are capitalized in this manner, the new owners of the monopoly firm may not earn any monopoly profits; they will most likely earn a normal rate of return on their investment in the monopoly right. Remember that a normal rate of return is embodied in the long-run average total cost curve. The *LRATC* curve faced by the new owners of the monopoly is $LRATC_2$, which is just tangent to the demand curve at P_m. At P_m, the new owners just cover their total costs, including a normal rate of return on their investment. The monopoly profits are taken by the original owners, who captured the value of P_mABC when they sold the firm. This does not mean that the monopoly must cease to exist because it is not profitable. P_m and Q_m continue to prevail in the marketplace, but the current owners make only a normal rate of return on their investment.

FIGURE 8

If the monopoly is sold, the asking price will include the value of the monopoly profits, represented by P_mABC. The average total cost to the buyers is depicted by a shift in the $LRATC$ curve from $LRATC_1$ to $LRATC_2$. The new owners therefore face an $LRATC$ curve of $LRATC_2$; they will not make monopoly profits but will make only a normal rate of return on their investment.

Capitalization of Monopoly Profits

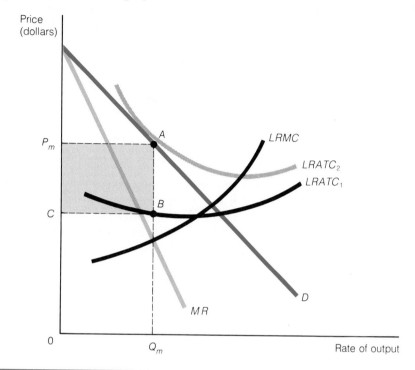

Why, then, did the new owners buy the firm? They might think they can run the firm at a lower cost than the old owner and make profits through more efficient management of the monopoly. Or they might believe, counter to existing owners, that demand will increase in the near future.

PRICE DISCRIMINATION

In our discussion of monopoly theory so far, the profit-maximizing monopoly has charged a single price for its product. Each customer who buys the product pays the same price. Under certain conditions, however, a monopoly can make more money by charging different customers different prices for its product. For example, movie theaters and airlines often charge lower prices to children and senior citizens than to others, and utilities charge different rates for electricity to businesses and residences. This method of pricing is called **price discrimination.**

Price discrimination:
The practice of charging one buyer or group of buyers a different price than that charged to others. The price difference is not due to differences in the cost of supplying the two groups.

Two points should be kept in mind as we discuss price discrimination. First, price differences that reflect cost differences do *not* constitute price discrimination. For example, large buyers (those purchasing more goods) are often charged less per unit for some goods than are small buyers. The general reason for this difference is that selling costs per unit are lower when dealing with the large buyer. Each sale may require the same paperwork, but the paperwork cost is lower per unit of sales for the large buyer. The lower price charged to the large buyer is not the result of price discrimination; it reflects the seller's different costs of serving the two customers. Second, equality of prices across buyers does not necessarily imply the absence of price discrimination because the costs of supplying the buyers may be different. For these reasons, price discrimination is a tricky concept, and care must be used in asserting its presence in the economy. Some forms of price discrimination are illegal under the Robinson-Patman Act (1936), which is enforced by the Federal Trade Commission. For example, different prices charged to different buyers *not* based on differences in costs to sellers are often held to be illegal under the act.

When Can Price Discrimination Exist?

Price discrimination can occur only under certain conditions. First, the firm must have monopoly power and face a downward-sloping demand curve for its output. In other words, the firm must be a price searcher, not a price taker. A price taker cannot charge different prices to different customers because the price it charges is determined by the prevailing market price, over which it has no influence. Second, the monopolist's buyers must fall into at least two clearly and easily identifiable groups of customers who have different elasticities of demand for the product. Third, the separation of buyers is crucial. Without the ability to separate buyers, the seller will not be able to keep buyers who are charged a low price from reselling the product to buyers who are charged a high price. Such behavior (normally called *arbitrage*) would undermine a price discrimination scheme and lead to a single price for the monopolist's product. The identification and separation of groups of consumers must be possible at low cost to make price discrimination worthwhile for the firm.

A Model of Price Discrimination

Figure 9 shows how a monopolist can gain from price discrimination. There are two groups of customers for the monopolist's product. The demand of buyers in market *A* is relatively more elastic than the demand of buyers in market *B* at a given price.

Two points are crucial in understanding the analysis in Figure 9. First, the marginal cost to the monopolist of supplying both markets is the same. The best way to think about this condition is to assume that the output sold to each market is produced in the same plant. *MC* is thus at the same level in both market *A* and market *B*. Second, to maximize profits, the monopolist sets marginal cost equal to marginal revenue in each market.

Following the $MC = MR$ rule in this case, the monopoly firm sets $MC = MR$ in both markets. In market *A* this leads to a price of P_1; in market *B* it leads to a price of P_2. The buyers in market *B* with the less elastic demand are charged a higher price than the buyers in market *A* $(P_2 > P_1)$. These are the profit-maximizing prices in the two markets. The monopolist benefits from price discrimination to the degree that its profits go up relative to what they would be if it sold its output at a single price to all buyers.

The monopolist must be able to keep the two markets separate to sustain a price discrimination scheme. If it does not, buyers in market *A* could profitably resell the product to buyers in market *B* and break down the price discrimination system. In 1984 Apple Computer Inc. offered to sell all stu-

FIGURE 9

Price Discrimination

The figures demonstrate a case of price discrimination for the same product in two markets. Consumers in market A have a relatively more elastic demand than those in market B. The profit-maximizing monopolist confronts market A consumers with a lower price. That is, $P_1 < P_2$. For a price discrimination scheme to be viable, the monopolist must prevent buyers in market A from reselling its product to buyers in market B.

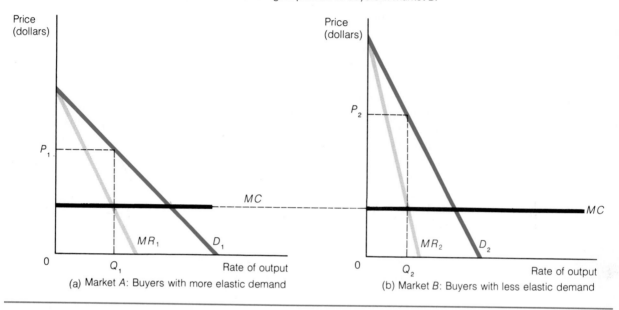

(a) Market A: Buyers with more elastic demand   (b) Market B: Buyers with less elastic demand

dents at twenty-four universities its then-new Macintosh computer for less than half of the full price being charged to other customers. Students and profiteers immediately saw the potential for profit in reselling the computers to nonstudents at marked-up but still below retail prices. Communication between students with the cut-rate Macintoshes and nonstudents desiring Macintoshes quickly sprang up through newspaper ads.

The seller who wants to practice price discrimination must therefore be able to distinguish and separate customers on the basis of their elasticity of demand. Moreover, the seller must be able to perform this feat without a large expenditure of resources. Thus, most real-world price discrimination schemes are based on general characteristics of customers, such as age, education, income, and sex. For example, children and older people are often charged lower prices for certain products because their age is thought to mean that they have more elastic demand for these products.

A subtle factor that provides a basis for price discrimination is differences in the opportunity cost of time among customers. The practice of giving discount coupons for grocery purchases, for example, allows sellers to separate buyers into elastic and inelastic demand categories. Buyers in the inelastic demand category will not take the time and trouble to collect coupons and redeem them. These are customers who place a relatively high value on their time. They value other uses of their time and do not want to clip coupons. Buyers in the elastic demand group place a lower value on their time and will take the time to clip coupons and convert them into lower prices at the store.

Sellers use coupons to separate buyers into classes and charge them different prices based on their different elasticities of demand.

X Price Discrimination on Campus

Many examples of price discrimination can be found on college and university campuses. Most government-funded institutions charge different tuition rates to in-state and out-of-state students, even though the marginal cost of educating each type of student is the same. In Figure 10, the marginal cost of educating each type of student is equal, given by MC. The price-discriminating university sets marginal revenue in each submarket equal to marginal cost. $P_{\text{in-state}}$ is the tuition charged to in-state students, with the higher price $P_{\text{out-of-state}}$ charged to out-of-state students. The students separate themselves into two groups when they complete the institution's application form and give their addresses. An in-state student cannot transfer registration in a class to an out-of-state student. Other things equal, this pricing behavior will reap the institution larger tuition revenues than would the practice of charging one price to all students.

The following representative 1986 data in Table 2 show how widespread and varied the practice of price discrimination is among state-supported col-

---

FIGURE 10　　　　Price Discrimination at the University

The graphs show how a college or university separates the markets for in-state and out-of-state students. MC is the marginal cost to the institution of educating either type of student. Out-of-state students have a relatively more inelastic demand for the institution's services and pay a higher price equal to $P_{\text{out-of-state}}$. In-state students, the relatively more elastic group, pay a lower price of $P_{\text{in-state}}$.

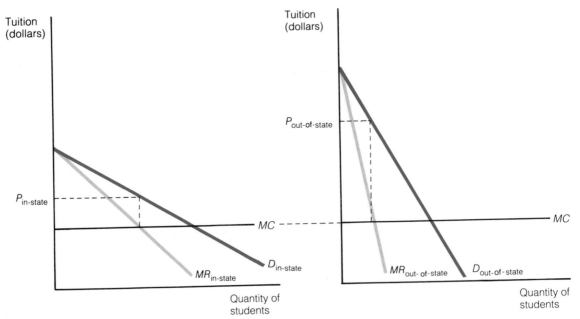

TABLE 2   In-State and Out-of-State Tuition for Selected Universities, 1986

Wide differences exist for tuitions paid by in-state and out-of-state students at universities across the United States. The principle of monopoly price discrimination may be used to explain some of these variations, expressed in terms of ratios in the table.

Institution	(1) In-State Tuition	(2) Out-of-State Tuition	(3) Difference (2) − (1)	(4) Ratio (2) ÷ (1)
Arizona State	$1172	$4260	$3088	3.63
University of Arkansas	1030	2542	1512	2.47
UCLA	1296	5382	4086	4.15
University of Colorado	1779	6559	4780	3.69
University of South Florida	1124	3738	2614	3.33
University of Georgia	1662	4422	2760	2.66
University of Illinois	2082	5141	3059	2.47
Louisiana State University	1727	4127	2400	2.39
Central Michigan University	1569	3925	2356	2.50
University of Minnesota	1970	4495	2525	2.28
University of Mississippi	1727	2909	1182	1.68
State University of New York	1495	3345	1850	2.24
Miami University-Ohio	2584	5458	2874	2.11
Oklahoma State University	889	2680	1791	3.01
Texas A&M University	870	3990	3120	4.59
North Texas State University	896	4016	3120	4.48
San Francisco State	679	4909	4230	7.23
University of Virginia	2238	5468	3230	2.44
University of Wisconsin-Madison	1570	4914	3344	3.13
University of Washington	1605	4461	2856	2.78

Source: Excerpted from *USA Today* (November 10, 1986), p. 11A. Copyright © 1986, *USA Today.* Excerpted with permission.

leges and universities. Tuition and fees from twenty colleges and universities for both kinds of students are listed, along with the differences in costs and the ratio of out-of-state to in-state charges. San Francisco State University charges out-of-state students more than seven times the fees that are charged to California residents. The University of Mississippi charges out-of-state students only about one and a half times more.

State colleges and universities often argue that the reason for this pricing behavior is that out-of-state students' parents do not pay taxes in the institution's state. However, economics tells us that tuition revenues will be higher if such pricing behavior exists than if all students are charged the same tuition. Out-of-state students have an incentive to become residents of the state in which they matriculate so that they can pay the lower tuition price. Some state legislatures have passed laws that prevent out-of-state students from becoming legal residents, preserving their educational institutions' ability to separate the two markets. The out-of-state student is the relatively more inelastic demander of any given college or university. Fewer substitutes exist (in the student's mind) for certain out-of-state schools. A student eliminates some substitutes based on parental ties, willingness to travel, or excellence in some particular area of study.

Colleges and universities also practice tuition discrimination by way of academic scholarships. Students with better academic credentials (high school GPA, SAT or ACT scores, and so on) generally find themselves with a larger number of schools to which they are accepted. The number of close substitutes they have for any particular institution is larger. This implies that their price elasticity of demand for a particular institution is relatively greater and that they will be charged a lower tuition than less adept students. The college or university lowers price to them through the granting of a scholarship. Again, the institution of higher education is seen to be a practiced price discriminator.

THE CASE AGAINST MONOPOLY

Monopoly is generally viewed as bad for the economy in comparison to the good expected from a competitive organization of markets. Critics base their indictment of monopoly on arguments that monopolies are lacking in both efficiency and equity, or fairness. After considering arguments against monopoly, we will examine the theory that monopolies provide certain social benefits that may offset their social costs.

Consumers' Surplus

Consumers' surplus:
The difference between the amount of money that consumers would be willing to pay for a certain quantity of a good and what they actually pay; the area above the price line and below the demand curve.

To understand the case against monopoly, you must first understand the concept of consumers' surplus. **Consumers' surplus** is the difference between the amount of money that consumers would be willing to pay for a quantity of a good and the amount they actually pay.

Figure 11 shows a demand curve. If the price of the good is P_c, a quantity of Q_c would be purchased, and consumers would spend a total of P_c times Q_c, or the area P_cEQ_c0, on the good. But consumers would be willing to spend a lot more than that for Q_c units. For some lower quantity of output, Q_m, consumers would be willing to pay a price of P_m, which is higher than P_c. For even lower quantities, some consumers would be willing to pay even more than P_m.

The highest price any buyer is willing to pay for a unit of the good is the distance up to the demand curve at a quantity of one unit—a distance of approximately $0C$ dollars. The consumer who values this good at about $0C$ dollars receives a surplus of approximately $0C - P_c$ if he or she can buy the good at a price of P_c. Another buyer is willing to pay slightly less for the second unit, so that consumer surplus (at a price of P_c) is lower than the surplus for the first unit. Each successive unit yields a lower surplus; the last unit sold at price P_c (Q_c) yields a surplus of zero. Thus, the whole area below the demand curve but above the price line can be identified as the dollar value of consumers' surplus. If the price is P_c, consumers' surplus is equal to area CEP_c. At a price of P_m, the consumers' surplus is equal to area CAP_m. Therefore, an increase in the price from P_c to P_m makes consumers worse off, and the size of this loss can be represented in terms of consumers' surplus. Instead of getting a surplus of CEP_c, consumers' surplus is only CAP_m. Consumers are worse off by an amount P_mAEP_c, the difference between the two surpluses.

FIGURE 11

Welfare Loss Due to Monopoly Power

This graph illustrates the hypothetical case of converting a competitive industry into a monopoly. Consumer surplus at price P_c and output Q_c in a constant-cost industry is represented by CEP_c. When the industry becomes a monopoly, it cuts back output to Q_m, resulting in a decreased consumer surplus of CAP_m and monopoly profits of P_mABP_c. The welfare loss to the economy—that is, the amount of real income that does not reappear for anyone after the monopoly is formed—is represented by AEB. The area of monopoly profits can be considered a transfer from consumers to the monopoly or an additional social cost of the monopoly.

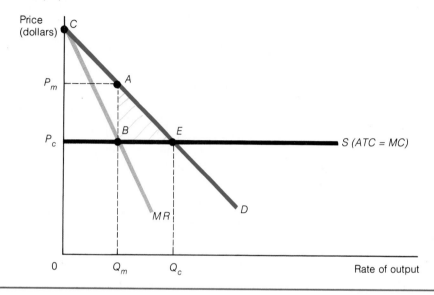

The Welfare Loss Resulting from Monopoly Power

Contrived scarcity:
A situation in which a monopoly produces an output below what a competitive industry would produce; the contrived scarcity results in price and profits above competitive levels.

The main efficiency argument against monopoly is that this market structure leads to **contrived scarcity**—that is, that a monopoly withholds output from the market to maximize its profits. The monopolist not only sets price where $MC = MR$ but where $P > MR$. At the profit-maximizing output for the monopolist, price therefore exceeds marginal cost. In the case of pure competition, price reflects the marginal benefit that consumers place on additional production, and marginal cost reflects the economic cost of the resources necessary for additional production. When price is greater than marginal cost, this is a signal to producers to increase output. The monopoly firm will not do so because this approach is not consistent with maximizing its profits. Given market demand and the cost curves, the monopolist will produce a smaller quantity of output than would a competitive industry. So we say that the monopolist causes a contrived scarcity, a condition in which the monopoly's product is short in supply and high in price. For example, the gas crisis of the 1970s was a contrived scarcity put into effect by the OPEC cartel. The price of gasoline rose as the supply of oil was reduced.

A contrived scarcity is a social cost to the economy. Its nature and magnitude can be estimated with an economic model that contrasts the effects of monopoly and competition in a given market, as shown in Figure 11.

Figure 11 shows the industry demand and supply functions, D and S, for some commodity, say cranberry juice. There are no economies of scale in this industry. The average total cost of producing cranberry juice is the same at all levels of output. This is a constant-cost industry with a flat long-run supply curve, along which $MC = ATC$.

Suppose that the industry is organized competitively, with many producers of cranberry juice. Long-run industry equilibrium is established at E, where industry demand and supply are equal. The juice output of the various firms is priced according to the marginal cost of producers along the industry supply curve and according to the wishes of the consumers along the demand curve. In other words, price is equal to the long-run marginal cost of production.

At the competitive price-output combination P_c and Q_c, how much surplus do consumers receive? They are willing to pay the amounts given by the demand curve, but they pay only P_c. They thus receive a surplus of real income, in this case represented by the large area above the industry supply curve and below the industry demand curve, or CEP_c. This triangle represents the concept of consumer surplus: the amount that consumers would be willing to pay over what they actually pay for a commodity.

Now suppose that the cranberry juice industry is turned over to a single seller, a monopolist. As a result, the monopolist restricts juice output to Q_m (contrived scarcity) and raises price to P_m to maximize its monopoly profits. What has happened to the level of consumer surplus in this market? The consumer surplus before monopoly is given by CEP_c, but consumer surplus after monopoly is only CAP_m. The difference in these two areas is the trapezoid P_mAEP_c.

The area P_mAEP_c is made up of two components. First we consider the rectangle P_mABP_c, depicting monopoly profits, to represent a transfer from consumers to the monopolist. In other words, these dollars do not leave the economy: They are taken out of the pockets of consumers and put into the pocket of the monopolist. The triangle AEB is left over. Who gets the real income represented by this triangle? No one—it simply vanishes when the monopoly is formed. This triangle is therefore called the **welfare loss due to monopoly**, or the *deadweight cost*. It is a cost to the economy because it does not reappear as income to anyone.

Arnold Harberger was the first scholar to attempt to state the total amount of this welfare loss in the manufacturing sector of the U.S. economy.[2] Using some complicated economic formulas, he found that the losses in the U.S. manufacturing sector for 1929 were on the order of 0.1 percent of GNP. In other words, the simple welfare loss to monopoly did not loom large in the economy. Subsequent scholars have used variations of Harberger's technique and have generally found the welfare losses due to monopoly to be low. Thus, even though the welfare loss due to a single monopoly looks large in Figure 11, it does not appear to be large in the context of the whole economy.

Welfare loss due to monopoly:
The consumers' surplus lost by consumers and not gained by the monopolist that results from a monopoly producing a less-than-competitive amount of output and charging a greater-than-competitive price; also called *deadweight cost*.

---

[2]Arnold Harberger, "Monopoly and Resource Allocation," *American Economic Review* 44 (May 1954), pp. 77–87.

(2) ## Rent Seeking: A Second Social Cost of Monopoly Power

The results of Harberger and other scholars suggest that in terms of the welfare loss it imposes, monopoly is not a big problem in our economy. This finding seems paradoxical in an economy dominated by very large and powerful firms. How could the social cost of these giant, powerful concerns be so small?

Gordon Tullock has suggested a solution to this apparent paradox.[3] He considered the area P_mABP_c in Figure 11—previously defined as monopoly profits, a simple transfer from consumers to the monopolist—and asked the question: What happens if people compete for these transfers? That is, suppose the monopoly procures its price by hiring lawyers to lobby the government for a monopoly right. The expenditure of resources on lawyers to win the transfer is socially wasteful because these expenditures add nothing to the social product. The opportunity cost of hiring lawyers consists of the productive activities they would otherwise perform. To pay lawyers to take a dollar out of the pockets of consumers and put it into the pocket of the monopolist reduces GNP by the amount the lawyers would have produced if engaged in productive pursuits. Not only lawyers but also lobbyists, economists, accountants, executives, and secretaries may be involved in the effort to secure a monopoly transfer. If the competition to capture these transfers is sufficiently strong, resources will be wasted up to the amount of the transfer. This amount, when added to the welfare loss, is the amount represented by P_mAEP_c. When the loss is equal to the trapezoid P_mAEP_c and not the triangle AEB, the social cost of monopolies may no longer be small.

This process of competing for transfers is called **rent seeking,** and it is normally associated with the process of seeking monopoly privileges from government. The "rents" that are sought are the monopoly profits created by government regulation or other restrictions resulting from the political process. The central proposition of rent-seeking theory is that the expenditure of resources to gain a pure monopoly transfer is a social cost.

Rent seeking:
The behavior associated with the use of scarce resources in the pursuit of monopoly profits created by government action.

(3) ## Production Costs of a Monopoly

Recall from our discussion of Figure 7 that the typical monopoly firm, after long-run adjustment, does not produce at the point of minimum long-run average total cost. In other words, the monopoly firm does not produce its output in the most efficient plant size in the long run. We learned in Chapter 9 that the competitive firm was compelled by competition to produce at the point of minimum long-run average total cost. By comparison, the monopoly produces its output inefficiently, resulting in another social cost of the monopoly relative to the competitive outcome.

This result assumes that the monopoly and the competitive firm operate along the same long-run average total cost curve. If they do not, a further social cost of monopoly power is possible. This cost was proposed by Harvey

---

[3]Gordon Tullock, "The Welfare Costs of Tariffs, Monopolies, and Theft," *Western Economic Journal* 5 (June 1967), pp. 224–32.

X-inefficiency:
The increase in costs of a monopoly resulting from the lack of competitive pressure to reduce costs to the minimum possible level.

Leibenstein, who called it **X-inefficiency.**[4] Purely competitive firms must minimize costs of production to survive in the long run. Are monopolists similarly constrained? Leibenstein's answer is no. He argues that the monopolist can afford to live a quiet life; although the monopoly firm gains from reducing costs, there is no competitive pressure to force it to do so. The monopoly firm will not be driven out of business if it fails to minimize costs of production. So the monopolist can take part of its income in terms of a looser, less efficient organization. The higher production costs caused by this X-inefficiency are also a social cost of monopoly power.

Estimates of the costs of X-inefficiency are hard to derive, so its possible magnitude in the economy is subject to speculation. Moreover, there are forces working to mitigate X-inefficiency costs. As we saw in our discussion of monopoly in the long run, the right to operate a monopoly can be bought and sold like any other asset in the economy. If the monopoly firm is operated inefficiently, investors can take it over, operate it more efficiently, and make a profit. The competitive pressure of such takeovers may or may not be sufficient to erase X-inefficiency costs, but takeovers surely play a role in keeping such costs to a minimum.

(4) Monopoly and the Distribution of Income

In addition to the potential efficiency cost arguments against monopoly—welfare loss, rent seeking, and inefficient levels of production—there is an equity argument. The creation of a monopoly transfers wealth from consumers to the monopolist. In Figure 11, this transfer is represented by the area of monopoly profits, P_mABP_c. The average consumer gets poorer; the monopolist gets richer. Most people would regard this transfer to the monopolist as unfair, but what is fair? The economist is no better than anyone else at answering such a question.

We can make some economic points about the transfer of monopoly profits, however. As we saw in the discussion of the capitalization of monopoly profits, the original monopolist receives the transfer. The current owners of a monopoly may be making only a normal rate of return on their investment in the monopoly right. Thus, if the government sets out to break up monopolies in the economy on the grounds that they undesirably affect the distribution of income, government would have to take care to distinguish between current and original owners of monopolies. Also, the concept of rent seeking states that monopoly profits are competed away in wasteful competition to obtain the monopoly right from government. In this sense, the monopoly profits are not transferred to the monopolist but to the inputs used in rent seeking, such as economists and lawyers.

THE CASE FOR MONOPOLY

We have seen that monopoly leads to economic inefficiency compared with a purely competitive organization of the economy. The monopolist essentially produces too little output at too high a price ($P > MC$). This type of ineffi-

---

[4]Harvey Leibenstein, "Allocative Efficiency vs. X-Inefficiency," *American Economic Review* 56 (June 1966), pp. 392–415.

Static inefficiency:
A condition associated with the welfare loss due to the presence of a monopoly. The loss can be summarized as the production of too little output sold at too high a price.

Dynamic efficiency:
A condition summarized in the idea that monopolies may, over time, be more innovative and efficient than competitive firms at developing new products and new production techniques.

ciency, called **static inefficiency,** can be seen as a social cost of monopoly given that other things are equal.

What if other things are not equal? Specifically, what if the monopoly produces more new ideas and products than the competitive firm? If this is the case, there may be an offsetting **dynamic efficiency** that makes monopoly a desirable form of market organization. One way to look at these counterforces is that the static inefficiency caused by monopoly pushes the economy inside its production possibilities frontier. This loss of production is the cost of monopoly power. But the dynamic efficiency of monopoly pushes the production possibilities curve outward over time, potentially swamping the short-run costs of monopoly power. In other words, monopoly has costs and benefits for the economy, and the benefits (dynamic efficiency) may outweigh the costs (static inefficiency).

This view of the potential efficiency of large-scale, monopolistic enterprise was put forth by Joseph Schumpeter.[5] He stressed the advantages of the ability of large firms to finance large research laboratories and hire thousands of scientists. While these firms with well-known, productive research labs—such as Du Pont, AT&T, and IBM—are not typically pure monopolies, they usually are large firms with dominant positions within their industries.

To Schumpeter, the traditional theory that competition spurred innovation seemed wrong. Small competitive firms were at a disadvantage in the innovation process because they could not afford large-scale research. Large firms were the key to innovation and success in the industrial order.

In Schumpeter's theory, the innovative monopolist did not possess a perennial advantage in the marketplace. He believed that innovation would proceed apace, and no one large firm would have more than a transitory monopoly in the face of a constant supply of new ideas and innovations by other large firms. The monopoly that any one large firm achieved by being creative was short-lived.

Other famous economists have advanced Schumpeter's vision of the industrial economy. John Kenneth Galbraith, for example, has argued forcibly that large firms are the source of innovation and economic advance.[6] Is the Schumpeter-Galbraith vision of the economy correct? That is, what are the sources of major innovations in the modern economy? Large firms? Small firms? Independent entrepreneurs and inventors?

Some studies have examined the relation between patents as a measure of innovation and firm size and have concluded that, in most industries, midsize firms have an advantage over both very large and very small firms in the innovation process.[7] Although the reasons for this finding are not entirely clear, more patents are issued to midsize firms in most industries. (For more on patents, see Focus, "Patents: The Inventor's Monopoly.")

Studies of the source of major inventions indicate that a surprisingly large number of innovations have come from the backyard shops of independent inventors. John Jewkes, David Sawers, and Richard Stillerman found, for example, that more than half of sixty-nine important inventions were produced

---

[5]Joseph A. Schumpeter, *Capitalism, Socialism, and Democracy* (New York: Harper, 1942).

[6]See, for example, John K. Galbraith, *American Capitalism* (Boston: Houghton Mifflin, 1956) and *The New Industrial State* (Boston: Houghton Mifflin, 1967).

[7]See Fredric M. Scherer, *Industrial Market Structure and Economic Performance* (Chicago: Rand McNally, 1970), chap. 18, for a survey of such studies.

FOCUS   Patents: The Inventor's Monopoly

A patent is an exclusive right given to an inventor for his or her invention. Alternatively, a patent is a monopoly right given to the inventor for the invention. A patent confers on the inventor the right to price and to sell the invention in any way he or she desires. In the United States, seventeen-year patents are granted by the Patent Office. Although economists generally condemn monopoly as a form of market organization since monopoly imposes costs on the economy, patents present a more subtle case for monopoly theory. Specifically, can patent monopolies be justified?

In general, economists complain about the costs of monopoly because they believe that the same industry could be organized competitively. A patent monopoly grant for seventeen years presents a different problem. That is, the purpose of the patent system is to encourage invention. The issue is not monopoly versus competition but, more fundamentally, invention versus no (or little) invention. Is the world better off with the invention, even though it is monopolized for seventeen years? In other words, what are the costs and benefits of a patent?

Consider the simple case, depicted in Figure 12, of a new consumer product with a positive demand, such as a camera utilizing a new exposure process. The costs of the patent monopoly are simply the deadweight costs of monopoly as discussed in this chapter. These are measured by the area BCD in Figure 12. Area BCD is the lost consumers' surplus from the seventeen-year patent monopoly. This cost must be assessed carefully in the context of an invention, however. *Remember:* The issue is for consumers to pay BCD for seventeen years or not have the new camera at all.

Obviously, the incentive to the inventor to reveal his or her new product and to market it resides in the monopoly profits that he or she hopes to capture as a result. These are given by the area P_mBDP_c. These profits are a transfer from consumers to the inventor, and as such, they represent neither a cost nor a benefit of the patent systems. Even here, however, we must be careful because the profits are the ultimate source of the inventor's incentive to invest.

What are the benefits of the patent system? First, there is the increase in consumer well-being brought about immediately by a desirable invention. This is measured by the area ABP_m. This area of consumers' surplus would not have existed without the new product. In seventeen years, the patent monopoly ends, and a second source of benefits arises: The price of cameras will fall to a competitive level,

---

FIGURE 12   A Camera Patent Monopoly

An inventor's patent confers a temporary monopoly on the holder. Price of the patented good is P_m in contrast to the competitive price P_c. Consumers' surplus of BCD is the temporary loss due to the patent.

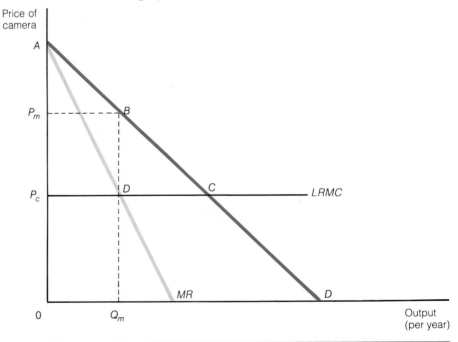

such as P_c, and consumers will reap the benefits of the camera at a lower price. Thus the patent system generates benefits in the amount ABP_m now and in the amount of an additional BCD seventeen years later. Consumers also receive a transfer from the monopolist in seventeen years in the amount of P_mBDP_c.

In sum, the theory of monopoly helps us to assess the costs and benefits of the patent system. The costs are BCD for seventeen years. The benefits are ABP_m forever plus BCD forever after seventeen years. P_mBDP_c is a transfer to the inventor from consumers of his or her product, which he or she gives back to consumers in seventeen years.

One can quibble about patent monopolies, arguing, for example, that they are granted for too long a time. In the end, the patent system creates goods and services and technologies that did not previously exist. In this respect it is a valuable system for the economy. The patent system also underscores the importance of property rights to ideas as a source of economic growth and progress.

---

by individual academics or by individuals unaffiliated with any research organization.[8] Among these inventions were air conditioning, the Polaroid Land camera, the helicopter, and xerography. Much invention is individually inspired and created in small-scale, personal labs and workshops. Industrial creativity thus seems to stem from something other than size alone.

Evidence suggests that the Schumpeter-Galbraith vision of the economy is not exactly accurate. But, then, neither is the vision that pure competition is best for the economy. Innovation springs from many sources, from the backyard or basement lab of the inventor to the lab of the large industrial company. Diversity produces innovation, or better yet, *individuals* produce innovation, whether they work in their own workshops or a large firm. Perhaps the most typical scenario is that an individual or small firm comes up with a new idea, and a large firm provides the vehicle by which the idea is realized.

Finally, what kind of balance is struck between the costs and benefits of monopoly? It is hard to generalize on this issue. In filling out a report card on firms, the best approach is to be pragmatic. Does the firm possess monopoly power? If so, can we judge how large this power is and how much it costs the economy? Does monopoly power carry with it some redeeming merit such as increased innovation? These are not easy questions to answer or to weigh in the balance, but they are the type of issues that must by confronted if the costs and benefits of monopoly are to be understood and its model applied intelligently.

SUMMARY

1. A pure monopoly is a single seller of a product for which there are no close substitutes in a market characterized by high barriers to new entry.
2. The monopoly firm faces the industry demand curve. When it lowers price, it must accept a lower price for all units previously sold for a higher price. The total revenue at the lower price minus the total revenue at the higher price is equal to the marginal revenue of the monopoly firm. For the monopoly, marginal revenue is less than price.
3. The monopoly selects an output to produce by setting marginal cost equal to marginal revenue. Since marginal revenue is less than price, the monopoly firm sets prices where price is greater than marginal cost.
4. Not all monopolies make profits. In the short run it is possible for the monopoly to incur a loss. If the loss persists in the long run, the monopoly will go out of business.
5. In the long run the monopoly firm can adjust its plant size. Normally, however, the monopoly does not operate at the point of minimum long-run average total cost.

---

[8]John Jewkes, David Sawers, and Richard Stillerman, *The Sources of Invention* (New York: St. Martin's, 1959).

6. Price discrimination requires that a seller be a monopoly firm, be able to separate buyers on the basis of their elasticities of demand, and be able to prevent buyers in the low-price market from reselling to buyers in the high-price market.

7. Where buyers can be separated into two classes, the monopoly firm will set marginal cost, which is the same in both markets, equal to marginal revenue in each market. This is the definition of price discrimination—price differences that do not reflect cost differences.

8. There are three potential efficiency costs of monopoly: the welfare loss due to monopoly power—the deadweight cost—which is the lost consumer surplus caused by monopoly; the rent-seeking cost of monopoly, which is the value of the resources used to capture monopoly profits; and the degree to which the monopoly firm has higher costs of production than a competitive firm.

9. Monopoly affects the distribution of income. Monopoly transfers wealth from consumers to the monopolist.

10. A potential advantage of monopoly is that large firms may be more effective developers of new products. The monopoly or large firm might thus possess a dynamic advantage over a small, competitive firm. The evidence on this issue is mixed; it appears that midsize firms are the most progressive in most industries.

KEY TERMS

pure monopoly
legal barriers to entry
public franchise
government license
patent
natural monopoly

price searcher
marginal revenue
profit-maximizing price
capitalized monopoly profits
price discrimination
consumers' surplus

contrived scarcity
welfare loss due to monopoly
rent seeking
X-inefficiency
static inefficiency
dynamic efficiency

QUESTIONS FOR REVIEW AND DISCUSSION

1. What is a barrier to entry? Why is it important in the definition of monopoly?

2. Depict the short-run equilibrium of a pure monopolist. Can the monopoly firm make a loss? If so, diagram what the loss situation for the monopoly might look like.

3. What conditions need to be met before a monopolist can price-discriminate?

4. What are three efficiency costs of monopoly? What is a potential advantage of a monopoly firm?

5. Insurance companies offer lower rates for life insurance to individuals who do not smoke and who jog. Is this an example of price discrimination? Why or why not?

6. Why is lobbying for an income transfer such as monopoly profits a social cost?

7. Entry is not possible with pure monopoly, but the monopoly can sell its monopoly right. What is the difference?

8. Monopolies and large firms are sometimes seen as the culprits in causing prices to rise. Does the theory of monopoly presented in this chapter imply that prices under monopoly will rise quickly or will be high? Explain.

PROBLEMS

1. At what price and quantity will the monopolist operate?
2. Do monopolists produce more or less than competitive firms?
3. If the demand curve crosses the x-axis when $Q = 500$, what does Q equal when the marginal revenue curve crosses the x-axis?

ECONOMICS IN ACTION
Technology, Economics, and the Postal Monopoly

The postal monopoly has been criticized since it began operating under federal protection in 1775; but the criticism has intensified over the past two decades.[a] The cost of mailing a one-ounce first-class letter has risen by 750 percent since 1958—twice as fast as the increase in the general price level (see Table 3). While the Constitution gives Congress the power to "establish post offices and post roads," it does not require postal service to be a monopoly or to be a government monopoly. Congress placed piecemeal restrictions on private carriage of mail throughout the nineteenth century. Since 1872, with the elimination of the Pony Express, only government employees can legally deliver a letter. The monopoly applies to first-class mail but not to second-class mail (newspapers and magazines), third-class mail (direct-mail advertising), or to parcels (fourth-class mail). The U.S. Post Office became the independent Postal Service in 1970 and retained the right to define a letter, which includes bills, receipts, IBM cards, magnetic cards, magnetic tapes, and other business documents.

In this chapter's terms, the Postal Service is a nonprofit monopoly with the power to price-discriminate among customers. Since it is not permitted to retain profits, the Postal

Service has little incentive to hold costs down or to improve the quality of service. Recall that price discrimination often accompanies monopoly and takes place when rates are not based upon differences in costs of providing service. *Equal rates are discriminatory when the costs of provision differ.* This is the kind of price discrimination practiced when the

TABLE 3
Postal Rates, 1919–1991

Between 1958 and 1991, the cost of mailing a one-ounce first-class letter has risen by 750 percent. Given technological changes, such as electronic banking and inexpensive facsimile transmitting (fax) machines, critics are questioning the necessity of a government monopoly on the delivery of first-class mail.

1919–2 cents	1978–15 cents
1958–4 cents	1981–18 cents
1963–5 cents	1981–20 cents
1968–6 cents	1985–22 cents
1971–8 cents	1988–25 cents
1975–10 cents	1991–30 cents*
1975–13 cents	

*Increase to go into effect February 1991.

[a]For more details see James C. Miller III, "End the Postal Monopoly," *Cato Journal* (Spring/Summer 1985), pp. 149–55; also, James Bovard, "The Slow Death of the U.S. Postal Service," *Policy Analysis,* Cato Institute (April 3, 1988).

Postal Service charges the *same* price to deliver a first-class letter from New York to Hawaii as it does to deliver the same letter across town, since costs are lower in the latter case. In effect, the price of a first-class stamp enables the Postal Service to internally subsidize distant customers and customers in small towns and isolated locales at the expense of urban, local, and business consumers.

The Postal Service also engages in price discrimination in pricing first-class mail compared to other classes. The Postal Service exploits its monopoly on first-class mail by pricing well above its marginal and average costs. It is then able to price lower classes of mail below cost by using profits from first-class mail to cover these losses. In this way it succeeds in extending its first-class monopoly to other classes of mail.

Criticism of the Postal Service is not limited to its rate structure. Despite rapid increases in postal rates since 1970, service has continued to deteriorate. Twice-a-day delivery has been halted, and most door-to-door delivery for businesses and multifamily dwellings has been abandoned. Many post offices have been closed, and many remaining offices no longer provide Saturday window service. Despite the adoption of ZIP codes, mail delivery is slower than it has been in decades.

Some postal authorities deny that service quality has declined and ask for larger subsidies to pay for improved service. There is little evidence, however, that poor quality is the result of underfunding. During the Reagan administration, the number of Postal Service employees increased by over 14 percent. The average Postal Service employee receives over $32,000 in wages and perks, although relatively few Postal Service jobs require much skill. Postal Service employees receive much higher pay than their counterparts at private firms like United Parcel Service. Critics charge that inefficiency may be inherent in any enterprise that is given a monopoly position and operated on a not-for-profit basis. In this view, managers of such enterprises may neglect innovations that permit cost containment and quality service.

According to critics, privatization or repeal of the laws giving the Postal Service a monopoly is the only way to obtain rational, cost-based, and efficient service. Technological change poses threats to any monopoly, and the Postal Service is no exception. In 1974, the Postal Service's failure to develop an innovative way to transport parcels created the United Parcel Service (UPS). By introducing mechanization and containerization, UPS reduced both breakage and costs. Despite the Postal Service's attempts to learn from UPS's success, UPS remains a viable competitor in the area of parcel service. Other private commercial carriers developed in the 1960s and 1970s—these specializing in the rapid and reliable carriage of commercial documents. Despite past threats of legal action by the Postal Service, firms such as Federal Express and Emery Air Freight now openly and freely compete for overnight service. The Postal Service's "Express Mail" overnight service, despite a lower and subsidized price, has not been successful in eliminating private services. Lower-quality service—specifically, fewer cities covered and fewer services offered—is one reason for the lack of success.

Rapidly developing electronic and computer technology promises to offer serious competition for both the Postal

Service and private overnight services. Banks, increasingly, are offering electronic bill paying services. In 1989, 32 percent of U.S. households utilized such services, paying 469 million bills. (In that same year, however, 20 billion checks were written.) Offered at a price below that for stamps, envelopes, and checks, electronic bill paying services provide stiff competition, especially for first-class mail.[b] Yet more troubling to the Postal Service and overnight carriers is the remarkable increase in the use of facsimile transmitting (fax) machines. Virtually unheard of when they sold for almost $4500 in the early 1980s, fax machines now cost, on average, less than $2000 and are considered standard pieces of office equipment.

The Postal Service's reaction to these and other developments—namely, the criticism of the 1988 bipartisan Presidential Commission on Privatization that agencies such as the Postal Service have become "muscle-bound to the point of paralysis"—has been to defend the monopoly. Morris Biller, president of the American Postal Workers Union, for example, denounces privatization as "profitization" and argues that rates would rise if the monopoly were subjected

[b]"Banks Hope to Stamp Out Paying by Check," USA Today (April 27, 1990).

to open competition. Such Postal Service defenders claim that "skimming" would take place under open competition. The argument is that private carriers would rush to provide service in high-density, low-cost areas, leaving the Postal Service stuck with unprofitable rural deliveries. But, critics retort, this defense is an admission that the current rate structure is discriminatory. While it is true that private firms would be willing to deliver letters to rural areas only at a price higher than that charged for urban deliveries, this does not mean that rural customers would necessarily be worse off. Their rates would be higher than urban rates, but with improved efficiency, the rates could be lower than those presently charged. Critics of the monopoly estimate that open competition for postal customers in all classes of mail could save $10 billion annually. While it is difficult to predict the exact form of the market with no postal monopoly, many economists, politicians, and observers argue that competition should be given a try.

Question

In what way does the Postal Service currently engage in price discrimination? How does the absence of competition facilitate slow mail delivery and high postal rates?

II

Monopolistic Competition

Until the 1930s, microeconomic theory analyzed only two basic market structures: pure competition and pure monopoly. These structures are, of course, opposite extremes. In a purely competitive market, prices tend to equal costs in the long run and consumers' economic welfare is theoretically maximized, whereas in a monopoly market the single monopolist may restrict output, raise prices, and capture economic profits. In the 1930s, two economists, E. H. Chamberlin of Harvard University and Joan Robinson of Cambridge University, wrote books developing models of market structures that did not fit the mold of either pure competition or pure monopoly. Both Robinson and Chamberlin emphasized that the real world was characterized by market structures that did not easily fit into existing economic theory.

All models of firms and markets other than the extremes of pure competition and pure monopoly are called theories of **imperfect competition.** The word *imperfect* means that not all the conditions for pure competition are met.

Some imperfectly competitive markets contain large numbers of sellers (as in pure competition) selling slightly different products (unlike in pure competition). These are monopolistically competitive markets.

Other structures are composed of small numbers of competing sellers who recognize that their actions affect one another's sales, prices, and profits. Under these circumstances, firms may engage or try to engage in various forms of combination or collusion. Such associations are called oligopoly or cartel market structures. They are closer in economic results to pure monopoly than to pure competition. The spectrum of market structures, therefore, runs from pure competition to monopolistic competition to oligopoly and cartels to pure monopoly.

This chapter focuses on monopolistic competition. Oligopolies and cartels are examined in the next chapter. In assessing market structures, we pay particular attention to the contrasts between each of these models and the purely competitive model. Governmental attempts to steer certain industries toward market structures considered more socially beneficial are covered in Chapter 19.

Imperfect competition: Market models, such as oligopoly, cartels, monopoly, and monopolistic competition, in which individual sellers' actions influence price.

284

Because real-world markets seldom fit into the neat categories of competition or monopoly, it is very important to develop more realistic models. The economist, moreover, must assess the effects of these real-world market structures on consumers' and producers' welfare and on economic efficiency in general. We begin with monopolistic competition, the economic model closest to pure competition. After reading Chapter 11 you should understand

- the formal characteristics of monopolistic competition as a model of how firms behave when many sellers are selling different products or services.
- advertising's role in differentiating products.
- how economically efficient monopolistically competitive markets are when compared to pure competition and pure monopoly.
- how monopolistic competition can be useful as an economic model of a firm's behavior.

MONOPOLISTIC COMPETITION

In his search for more realistic models of firms and markets, E. H. Chamberlin developed a model close but not equivalent to pure competition. Since the model contained some monopolistic elements, Chamberlin labeled this theory "monopolistic competition."

Characteristics of Monopolistic Competition

Monopolistic competition:
A market model with freedom of entry and exit and firms producing similar but differentiated products.

Monopolistic competition is a market structure in which a large number of sellers sell similar but slightly different products and in which no barriers to entry or exit exist. Advertising is a principal tool for differentiating products within monopolistic competition.

Large Number of Sellers. Monopolistic competition, like pure competition, is characterized by a large number of competing sellers. The effect of large numbers is the same in both cases: Collusion to fix prices or other kinds of cooperation is costly—so costly that it ordinarily does not occur. The presence of many sellers is a competitive element in monopolistic competition. Unlike pure competitors, however, monopolistic competitors are not always price takers because of another characteristic—product differentiation.

Differentiated product:
A product with features that make it distinct, in consumers' eyes, from close substitutes.

Nonprice competition:
Any means other than pricing decisions that firms use to sell output.

Product Differentiation. Competitive sellers sell a homogeneous or identical product, such as corn. Monopolistic competitors sell products that are highly similar but not identical. Products may be distinguished by brand names, location, services, even differences merely perceived by the consumer. Because the monopolistic competitor is selling a slightly **differentiated product,** the firm will have a degree of control over price, unlike the competitive firm. Product differentiation is an example of **nonprice competition,** a term commonly used to refer to any action other than price cuts taken by a competitor to increase demand for its product.

(1) There are many varieties of nonprice competition. One is differences created in the products themselves. Consumers shopping for personal computers can choose among many firms' products, each differing slightly in hardware, software, styling, sturdiness, and user-friendly or state-of-the-art appeal. (2) Sometimes distinctions between brands are more illusory than real. Although aspirin is essentially a homogeneous product, monopolistically competitive firms produce it under many different brand names—Bayer, Excedrin, Bufferin, and so on—often at very different prices. The reason for the different prices for aspirin is that each brand is differentiated in consumers' minds, often through advertising or some other form of sales effort. Consumers who are convinced that brands actually differ will have some allegiance to a particular brand. This brand allegiance permits the seller to set price, within limits.

(3) Location may also differentiate a seller's products. There may be ten Exxon gas stations within a city, alike in every respect, including the gasoline they sell. The gas stations each occupy a different location, however, and thus are free to set different prices. The Exxon station near the interstate might charge a higher price than the station downtown because travelers in a hurry are willing to pay more. In fact, many businesses have failed because of poor location.

(4) Service is another form of nonprice competition. Physically identical products may be offered for sale in supermarkets at identical money prices. However, one store may be untidy, another may employ rude cashiers, and still another may suffer chronically slow-moving checkout lines. Markets with well-swept aisles, neat shelves, automated checkout, and friendly clerks will have differentiated their products by the services they offer.

Subtle product differentiation, whether by packaging, service, location, or any other variable, is a common fact of life, but the degree of substitutability among such products is high. While demand is highly elastic under monopolistic competition, it is not infinitely elastic, as in perfect competition. A sudden tenfold increase in the price of one brand of aspirin would send buyers scurrying for substitutes. The monopolistically competitive firm, in other words, like the firm in pure competition, is primarily a price taker. It has a small and limited degree of control over price, however, stemming from its ability to differentiate its individual product from those of its many competitors. This limited control over price is the monopoly element in these markets. Chamberlin's ideas are verified by common observation: *Practically no market exists that is not characterized by monopoly elements through some form of differentiation.*

3. **No Barriers to Entry.** Just as with competitive markets, entry into and exit from the monopolistically competitive market is free. This fact follows from the high cost of collusion in a market occupied by a large number of sellers. Although monopolistic competition shares the free-entry conditions of perfectly competitive markets, entry is not costless in either market structure. *Free entry* means that there is no government regulation over entry and that essential raw materials are not controlled by one or a few firms. There are resource costs and commitments in opening any business: hiring labor, investing capital in fixed items such as buildings, managing or hiring managers, and so forth.

In addition to the start-up costs of entering any new business, entry into monopolistically competitive markets entails the cost of introducing a new product. New product development and market entry through advertising and other sales efforts constitute a cost that the competitive firm does not face. A farmer's entry into the winter wheat market, for example, will not involve a sales or advertising campaign, whereas entry into the deodorant, paper towel, or restaurant market will. Product differentiation is simply part of the cost of entry under monopolistic competition. Entry is nonetheless assumed to be free, and in this characteristic, monopolistic competition is very much like perfect competition.

Advertising and Monopolistic Competition

The keystone of monopolistic competition is product differentiation and advertising. Advertising, in fact, helps create product differentiation, giving individual firms some control over the product price. How does advertising affect the demand for products, and what is the economic assessment of such activity?

The Importance of Advertising. With the general characteristics of the monopolistically competitive structure in mind, we examine a typical firm's demand curve and assess the impact of **advertising** on it. The existence of nonprice competition coupled with a high degree of substitutability means that the firm's demand curve, while highly elastic, is downward-sloping. Such a demand curve is drawn in Figure 1 for a hypothetical antacid product, Relief. The demand curve for Relief approximates that of a competitive firm, but it is downward-sloping because Relief is not the same product as competitors Tums, Rolaids, Mylanta, and Maalox.

Advertising:
Any communication or information that firms offer consumers to increase demand for a product.

FIGURE 1

The demand curve for the monopolistic competitor slopes downward because the firm sells a product differentiated from its competitors. The marginal revenue curve lies below the demand curve because additional units can be sold only at a lower price.

Demand Curve Facing Monopolistically Competitive Firm

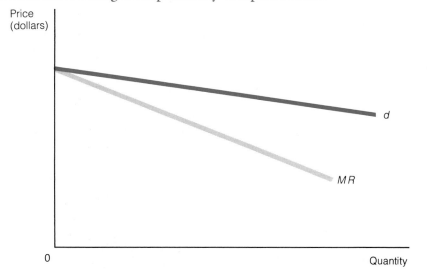

As with the pure monopoly firm, the monopolistically competitive firm's marginal revenue curve lies below its demand curve, and for the same reason: Additional units can be sold only at a lower price. The main difference between a monopoly firm and a monopolistic competitor is that the monopoly firm sells a unique product—one with no close substitutes—while substitutes abound for the monopolistic competitor's product.

How elastic or inelastic will the demand curve be for Relief? The answer will depend on the size and intensity of consumer preferences for Relief, given the range and price of substitutes. Naturally, the firm will be interested in increasing the size of its market and in intensifying consumers' preferences for its product. The firm accomplishes these goals through product advertising. Advertising is essential to the introduction of new products in monopolistic competition. It is also a crucial tool in the manipulation or management of demand for existing products.

Advertising is a variable under the monopolistically competitive firm's control, within the limits imposed by its advertising budget. The firm in monopolistic competition will seek, along with all firms who advertise, to equate the addition to revenue from the final dollar spent on advertising to the marginal addition to cost from the advertising. Firms seeking to enter markets will often spend large amounts of money to introduce their products. But whether the firm is an established competitor or a new entrant, the purpose of advertising is the same: to increase demand for the firm's product.

In Figure 2, demand curve $d_0 d_0$ depicts a monopolistically competitive firm's demand curve. The hoped-for effect of increased advertising is a shift rightward in the position of the demand schedule $d_1 d_1$ *and* a reduction in the elasticity of the curve at a given price. Thus advertising is intended not only to increase demand but to intensify demand by differentiating the good or service in consumers' minds so that the firm can raise the product's price. If

FIGURE 2

The firm advertising its product hopes to shift its demand curve to the right and to reduce its elasticity at a given price. In doing so, the firm tries to intensify demand for the product by distinguishing it in the minds of buyers.

The Effects of Advertising on the Firm's Demand Curve

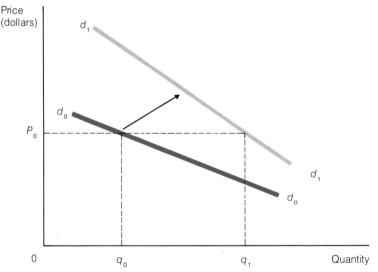

the advertising of Relief is able to convince consumers that the product is "easier to swallow," "has no unwanted side effects," and the like, demand becomes more inelastic (less substitutable), and consumers are willing to pay for it.

The Pros and Cons of Advertising. Few subjects in economics have been debated as vigorously as advertising. Critics argue that ads are tasteless and wasteful assaults on consumers' senses. Since the products of monopolistically competitive firms are close substitutes, actual differences between the products of competing producers, if any, may be difficult to discern. Advertising creates perceived differences among similar goods and allocates demand among firms that produce products that are fundamentally alike. Some economists, then, view advertising as the squandering of society's resources on a costly exercise by which rival firms divide total sales.

Another criticism of advertising is that advertising expenditures raise both the costs of producing goods and services and the prices consumers pay. The resources used in advertising have opportunity costs, which means that the firm that advertises will bear higher costs and charge higher prices than the firm that does not advertise.

John Kenneth Galbraith argued that advertising **private goods** results in an oversupply of such goods. With limited resources, any society has to choose between producing private goods such as cars, running shoes, and cat food and public goods such as highways, parks, and libraries. Galbraith argued that the public, continually assaulted by advertisements for private goods, develops an unnatural preference for these goods. So conditioned, society resists higher taxes for public goods, in order to buy more private goods.

Defenders of advertising deny that advertising is wasteful. They argue that advertising provides consumers with valuable information concerning the existence, characteristics, and location of goods and services. Such information reduces consumers' search costs and thereby reduces the full price that consumers pay.

Defenders of advertising also deny that advertising systematically leads to higher prices. While advertising is costly, it has two price-reducing effects. Since advertising can increase sales, advertising enables some firms to take advantage of economies of scale and produce output at a lower average total cost. Advertising also provides firms with a means of entry into markets and product lines. Without the ability to advertise, the process of new firms entering a market and competing away profits is short-circuited. The Focus, "Advertising and the Price of Eyeglasses," examines the impact of advertising on prices in a specific market.

One counterpoint to Galbraith's argument is that the social-balance issue should not be settled by subjective opinion concerning needs or tastes but by the behavior of the consumer-voter-taxpayer instead. Just as social wants filter through the political process in a democracy, private wants register through the dollar votes of consumers. The balance between the private and social goods that society produces is determined by these two kinds of votes. Furthermore, it would be a mistake to consider advertising the exclusive tool of producers of private goods. Elected officials and government agencies have extensive public relations budgets, which they routinely use to promote the virtues of increased spending on public goods.

Private good:
A good over which a consumer can establish property rights.

FOCUS Advertising and the Price of Eyeglasses

The issue of advertising's effect on prices is an empirical (or statistical) issue. Economic theory suggests that two different effects on prices can exist. Since advertising requires scarce resources, it adds to the cost of producing output. In this sense, advertising would tend to cause prices to be higher than otherwise. But advertising also can be viewed as a tool of competition and as one vehicle businesses use to enter markets and product lines. From this perspective, advertising would exert price-lowering effects. Whether advertising raises or lowers price cannot be resolved through economic theory alone. The answer must be found by looking at actual markets and data.

In trying to gauge the effect of advertising on prices, economist Lee Benham considered the effect that a prohibition or ban on advertising has on prices.[a] In the 1960s (and today still) a number of states had severe legal restrictions and outright prohibitions on the advertising of eyeglasses and eye examinations by physicians and optometrists. Other states had few or no restrictions on such advertising. Benham argued that the different states provided a good laboratory for the economic study of the relationship between advertising and prices. After adjusting for such factors as family income, sex, and customer age, any difference in prices paid in the two different types of states could be reasonably attributed to advertising (or the lack of it).

Some of Benham's findings are presented in Table 1. (Benham used prices during 1963. We have converted his results to 1989 dollars for easy comparison.) Table 1a contains average price differences for both glasses and glasses plus an eye exam between states with wide-ranging advertising restrictions and states with essentially no advertising prohibitions. Table 1b compares average prices in the most restrictive and least restrictive areas of the country in terms of legal limitations on advertising. North Carolina had the most severe advertising restrictions, whereas in Texas and Washington, D.C., suppliers enjoyed the widest latitude in their legal ability to advertise. Both parts of the table suggest that the price-lowering effects of advertising dominate in the eyewear market.

[a]Lee Benham, "The Effect of Advertising on the Price of Eyeglasses," *Journal of Law and Economics* 15 (October 1972), pp. 337–52.

TABLE 1
Advertising Restrictions and the Price of Eyeglasses

Part (a) compares average prices in states with severe advertising restrictions to prices in states with few, if any, legal advertising restraints. Part (b) compares prices in the most and least restrictive areas. These prices, originally measured in 1963, have been converted to their 1989 equivalents.

(a)	States with Restrictions	States without Restrictions	Average Price Difference	Average Price Difference
Eyeglasses	$134.72	$102.41	$27.31	26%
Eyeglasses plus exam	$167.02	$151.28	$15.74	10%

(b)	North Carolina	Texas and Washington, D.C.	Average Price Difference	Average Price Difference
Eyeglasses	$152.83	$73.31	$79.52	109%
Eyeglasses plus exam	$206.85	$122.21	$84.64	69%

Source: Lee Benham, "The Effect of Advertising on the Price of Eyeglasses," *Journal of Law and Economics* 15 (October 1972), p. 342.

Although Benham's study made no attempt to adjust for quality, it suggests empirical support for the proposition that advertising is a part of the competitive process. The prevention of advertising appears to have made prices higher than they would have been had advertising been allowed in the market.

This study and others like it seem to indicate that the added cost effects of advertising are swamped by the competitive, price-lowering properties of advertising, at least in some markets. The issue has not been settled however; some economists have uncovered evidence that in the cigarette market the overall effect of advertising is to raise prices. The safest approach, then, is to reserve judgment on such matters until specific data have been collected and properly analyzed on a case-by-case basis.

One's stand on these issues depends on, among other things, an awareness of the facts and one's preconceptions. However, some familiarity with the arguments regarding advertising, pro and con, is useful when studying monopolistic competition or any market structure where advertising is observed.

Short-Run and Long-Run Equilibrium Under Monopolistic Competition

Now that we have defined the overall conditions for monopolistic competition, we can discuss how firms set prices. The firm in monopolistic competition has some control over price, but its control differs in the short run and the long run.

Short-Run Equilibrium. Monopolistically competitive firms, like firms in all other market structures, always equate marginal cost to marginal revenue to maximize profits or minimize losses. In the short run, the firm may enjoy economic profits or endure losses.

Figure 3a gives a firm's short-run cost curves, demand curve, and marginal revenue curve. MC intersects, or is equal to, MR at quantity q_0. The firm produces that quantity and sets price P_0 for q_0 units of output. At this price and quantity, the firm will earn economic profits. These profits are calculated by multiplying price times quantity sold ($P_0 \times q_0$) to get the firm's total receipts, and then subtracting the total cost of q_0 units, $ATC_0 \times q_0$. Profits to the firm are shown in the shaded area of the figure. The firm's demand curve is highly elastic because of the large number of substitutes but it is still negatively sloped because, under monopolistic competition, products are differentiated through advertising and other forms of nonprice competition.

FIGURE 3	**Short-Run Profits and Losses for the Monopolistically Competitive Firm**

(a) The firm earns short-run profits. It sets price P_0 for q_0 units of output. Its profits are the difference between its revenue ($P_0 \times q_0$) and its costs ($ATC_0 \times q_0$). (b) The firm suffers short-run losses. Costs are greater than revenue. The firm will continue operating, however, because its total revenue ($P_0 \times q_0$) exceeds its total variable costs ($AVC_0 \times q_0$).

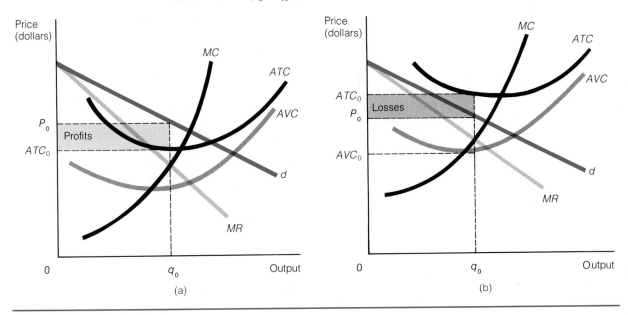

Like firms in all other market structures, monopolistically competitive firms do not always make profits. Figure 3b depicts a loss-minimizing short-run equilibrium for a monopolistically competitive firm. In the case illustrated, the firm will sell q_0 units at price P_0—the price-quantity combination selected for loss minimization (where MC equals MR). This time, however, total receipts, $P_0 \times q_0$, are exceeded by total costs, $ATC_0 \times q_0$. Losses (the shaded rectangle) are incurred. The firm, however, will remain in business in the short run because its total variable costs $AVC_0 \times q_0$ are covered by its total receipts, so there is some contribution to fixed costs. If these conditions prevailed in the long run, the firm (like the competitive or pure monopoly firm) would go out of business. In the long run, expenditures that are fixed in the short run become variable expenses and must be covered.

The monopolistic competitor does have one advantage over the pure competitor in the short run: the ability to manipulate demand through advertising and intensified product differentiation. The loss-minimizing firm in Figure 3b may increase short-term outlays on advertising or sales effort, thereby shifting the demand and marginal revenue curves rightward. Such an increase may permit the firm to break even or to earn profits. Optimum advertising outlay for the firm occurs when one dollar of additional selling costs adds exactly one dollar to the firm's receipts. In this sense, the cost of advertising is treated like the cost of any other input, such as capital or labor.

Long-Run Equilibrium: The Tangency Solution. Long-run equilibrium for the firm in monopolistically competitive markets may take a number of forms. One of them, described by E. H. Chamberlin, is the **tangency solution,** wherein the firm ends up making zero economic profits; that is, it simply breaks even. We now summarize the assumptions of this model of the firm's economic behavior.

Tangency solution:
A long-run equilibrium situation in which the firm's downward-sloping demand curve is tangent to its *LRATC* curve; zero economic profits are earned.

1. The firm operates in an industry composed of many sellers selling substitutable products, with the number of sellers constant throughout the period of adjustment.
2. Each seller assumes that its price actions will not provoke a response from rivals.
3. The degree of product differentiation (and thus advertising budgets) is constant and is determined by all competing firms; firms, therefore, manipulate prices to increase profits.
4. The firm represents all competitors in that their cost curves and demand curves (as well as their reactions) are identical.

A model conforming to these assumptions is shown in Figure 4b. Two demand curves, d_0d_0 and d_1d_1, are reproduced along with a long-run average cost curve for the firm. Suppose that the representative firm (out of perhaps a hundred firms producing similar products) initially finds itself at point A, charging price P_0 and selling quantity q_0. (The marginal revenue curves associated with d_0d_0 and d_1d_1 are omitted in Figure 4b for simplicity.) From the perspective of profitability, the firm, along with all other competitors, is earning economic profits in the amount represented by P_0ABC, B being the long-run average cost of producing quantity q_0. Collusion to maintain profits at this level is impossible because of the large number of producers, so these economic profits cannot be sustained. The initial price and quantity combination selected, P_0 and q_0, will not be permanent in the face of Chamberlin's assumptions about firms' behavior.

FIGURE 4   The Tangency Solution

Figure 4a shows the monopolistically competitive firm's perceived and actual reactions to a price cut. The firm believes that, due to its price cut, output will expand along the more elastic curve from q_0 to q_1. The actual increase is smaller (to q_2) because rivals respond to the price decrease by imitating the price-cutting firm. When all firms lower price from P_0 to P_1, the perceived demand curve shifts leftward for each firm as in Figure 4b. In final equilibrium E, the point of tangency with the *LRATC* curve, all firms break even.

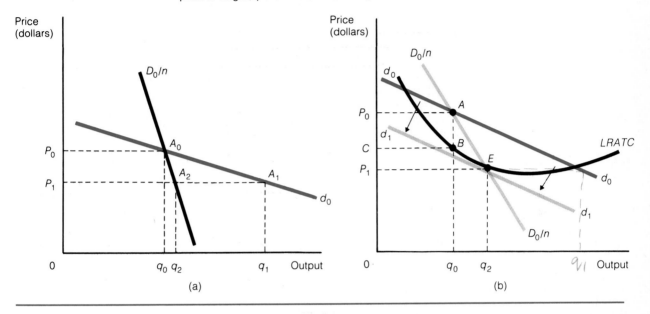

ad v. elastic ←

ie ↓p ⇒ people buying firm's product

Why? Because each firm believes that it can increase profits by lowering its price, which would, if correct, increase the firm's sales from q_0 in Figure 4a to q_1. That is, sales would increase substantially for the firm. The firm, however, will be mistaken because all rival sellers will lower their prices, causing the actual share of total sales to the initial price cutter to expand from q_0 to q_2 in Figure 4a. Demand curve d_0 is the demand curve *perceived* by the price-cutting firm, whereas demand curve D_0/n is the *actual* pro rata industry demand curve faced by the price-cutting firm. In other words, each firm believes that its demand curve is more elastic than it really is because it believes, erroneously, that rivals will not reduce prices when it does. In fact, rivals usually react to one another's price drops by lowering their own prices. This widespread lowering of price causes the demand curve for each seller to shift leftward until economic profits are zero—that is, until each firm breaks even. Finally, demand curve d_1d_1 becomes tangent to the long-run average total cost function, *LRATC* (thus the term *tangency solution* to describe this case).

At point E in Figure 4b, all firms will produce q_2 units of output and charge price P_1 per unit. Quantities above this amount and prices below P_1 would force firms out of business. Quantities less than q_2 and prices higher than P_1 would provoke the price adjustment responses described above. Under these circumstances, a stable equilibrium characterized by zero economic profits for all firms is generated.

A word of warning: While the tangency solution is perhaps the best-known analytical approach to monopolistic competition in the long run, it is only one of a large number of possibilities. A little reflection on the realism of the four assumptions in Chamberlin's model will tell us why.

1. The initial existence of economic profits will encourage the entry of new firms into the market, altering the effects of price responses.
2. We cannot assume that firms will continue to think that price reductions will not provoke similar responses from their competitors. Managers will probably become aware of other firms' repeated and identical responses to their respective firms' price reductions.
3. Monopolistic competitors can use product differentiation and advertising as well as price manipulation to maintain demand and profits. The degree of differentiation is artificially held constant in the model in Figures 4a and 4b.
4. All firms are not alike with respect to demand and costs.

Thus the model described in Figure 4b reflects but one set of behavioral assumptions among many possibilities. Its value is considerable, however, because it describes a tendency to tangency. Real-world tangency solutions will likely not exist, but as long as the assumptions of Chamberlin's famous model *approximate* reality, an approach to a tangency solution may be observed and predicted in markets displaying the features of monopolistic competition. Additionally, the tangency model of monopolistic competition provides a convenient benchmark for a comparison of the attributes and economic effects of pure competition and those of monopolistic competition.

Does Monopolistic Competition Cause Resource Waste?

A charge commonly leveled at monopolistic competition—unrelated to the alleged wastes of advertising—is that the tangency solution requires (1) underallocation of resources in production or (2) generation of excess capacity and prices higher than minimum long-run unit costs of production. This unflattering portrayal of monopolistic competition is possible when it is compared with the long-run competitive model.

Monopolistic Competition Versus Pure Competition. Long-run equilibrium in the perfectly competitive model, discussed in Chapter 9, results in the following three conditions:

1. Price = long-run marginal costs;
2. Price = minimum long-run average total costs; and
3. Total revenue = total costs.

The first condition means that the consumer's marginal sacrifice (price) just equals the marginal opportunity cost of producing the last unit of a product or service consumed. The second condition means that consumers are getting the product at the lowest price at which the product can be produced. The third conclusion means that no competitive firm earns more than a normal profit in the long run. Firms are price takers under competition. Freedom of entry guarantees normal profits in the long run.

Consider, with the aid of Figure 5, how monopolistic competition compares to pure competition in these respects. Figure 5a shows the demand

FIGURE 5

A Comparison of Pure Competition and Monopolistic Competition

In a technical sense, the monopolistically competitive firm (b) charges a higher price, P_m, than the purely competitive firm (a), P_c. The monopolistically competitive firm sets output at q_m to maximize profits, but the most efficient use of its plant would be an output of q_{m_1}. The firm therefore produces with excess capacity, or underutilization of its scale of plant.

(a) Pure competition

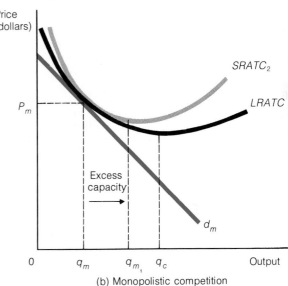

(b) Monopolistic competition

curve $P_c d_c$ and the short-run and long-run average cost curves for the typical firm in pure competition. Both long-run and short-run costs are tangent to the perfectly elastic demand curve for the firms in competition. Quantity q_c is produced at price P_c, which equals long-run (and short-run) marginal cost. Figure 5b shows the downward-sloping demand curve d_m of a monopolistically competitive firm in a tangency solution with the firm's long-run average cost curve. Given that the firms' cost curves are identical under both market structures, how do they compare in economic efficiency?

As Figure 5 shows, the following features result from monopolistic competition:

1. Price > long-run marginal costs;
2. Price > minimum long-run average costs; and
3. Total revenue = total costs.

The first conclusion means that the additional sacrifice (price) that consumers are willing to make for an additional unit of the good is greater than the marginal opportunity cost of producing that additional unit. In other words, resources are underallocated in the production of goods by monopolistically competitive firms, just as they usually are in production by pure monopolies.

The second conclusion is that consumers pay more for goods produced under conditions of monopolistic competition than they do when goods are supplied by perfect competitors. The fact that P_m in Figure 5b is greater than P_c in Figure 5a means that price is higher and output lower under monopolistic competition than under pure competition. Consumers are not paying the lowest possible unit cost. However, like perfect competitors, monopolistic competitors do not earn economic profits because a tangency solution means that total revenues equal total costs to the firm (or, alternatively, that the firm's average cost equals its average revenue).

Excess capacity:
A situation in which industry output is not produced at minimum average total cost. The output actually produced is less than the output that would minimize average total cost.

Critics of monopolistic competition raise still another issue: **Excess capacity** is generated under the monopolistically competitive market structure. This criticism ordinarily holds for any less-than-perfectly competitive market. To understand what excess capacity means, consider Figure 5 again. The *LRATC* function is called an envelope curve because it is composed of a series of tangencies of points on the short-run average total cost curves (see Figure 5, Chapter 8, on page 208). The short-run curves $SRATC_1$ and $SRATC_2$ drawn in Figure 5 are two such curves. To utilize fully any scale of plant or to produce at an optimum rate of output in the short run, the existing scale of plant or existing resources invested must be used at the lowest average cost of production. For the monopolistically competitive firm depicted in Figure 5b, the output corresponding to that lowest short-run average total cost of production is q_{m_1}, not q_m, the profit-maximizing quantity the firm has chosen. From society's point of view, the firm producing at q_m is wasting, or underutilizing, resources. Excess capacity is the unused capacity of the scale of plant that the firm has built. From the firm's perspective, however, the scale of plant represented by $SRATC_2$ is perfect or optimal in that it produces the quantity q_m more cheaply than any other scale of plant could. Thus, critics argue that monopolistic competition creates excess capacity as well as the long-run resource inefficiencies outlined above.

Economic efficiency:
The correct allocation of resources, from the firm's perspective, so that maximum benefit is achieved at minimum cost.

Economic welfare:
The value society places on goods and services consumed.

A Defense of Monopolistic Competition. Is monopolistic competition as inefficient as the critics say? In assessing this issue we must be careful to distinguish between pure **economic efficiency** and **economic welfare.** Economic efficiency means that resources are properly allocated (at minimum cost for a given output) from the firm's perspective. Pure economic welfare is the value that society places on goods and services consumed. Chamberlin argued that the monopolistically competitive market structure is not wasteful in either sense because product differentiation creates variety and extends the array of consumers' choices.

If price is established close to minimum long-run average total cost, some pure inefficiency might exist with monopolistic competition, but consider what consumers get in return: varied products and a vastly expanded number of products and services from which to choose. If this variety is socially valued, advertising and product differentiation are not necessarily wasteful. Such differentiation, summed across all consumers, means that monopolistic competition may increase social welfare. A society that produces only white shirts may be efficient in a technical sense, but the repeated purchase of other colors of shirts at higher prices means that consumers are willing to pay for differentiation.

Depending on a given consumer's preferences, excess capacity may be either a cost or a benefit. Resource costs other than money are involved in the purchase of goods. Time, for example, is an important cost for some consumers. Since excess capacity reduces the time cost of making purchases, it reduces consumption costs. For consumers who place a high value on time, excess capacity is likely to be beneficial. For example, in cities where cab fares are relatively high, cabs typically line up in front of hotels and airports. Business executives who place a high value on their time are willing to pay a high dollar price rather than wait for a less expensive means of transportation. For them, excess capacity is clearly beneficial. In contrast, consumers who place a low value on their time will choose to pay lower money prices but higher time prices by taking public transportation or the hotel van. The Economics in Action, "The Economics of Markup Pricing," shows other potential benefits to consumers from monopolistic competition.

How Useful Is the Theory of Monopolistic Competition?

When models of monopolistic competition and pure competition are subjected to real-world observation, is there a dime's worth of difference between them? How useful, in other words, is the model of monopolistic competition?

If the demand curve is very elastic when products are differentiated, the model of monopolistic competition is a close approximation of pure competition. The perfectly competitive model is primarily an idealized benchmark with which real-world markets can be compared. Most actual markets conform to the set of characteristics we have defined as monopolistically competitive.

Thus, a study of markets with differentiated products and rapid and free entry of substitutes is a study of what is usually called *competition*. With the ready emergence of substitutes, the adjective in *monopolistic competition* may be downplayed. Firms' ability to set prices is critically restricted by such entry and even by potential entry. Viewed in this light, the model of monopolistic competition, with its emphasis on product differentiation and other forms of nonprice competition, is of great value in helping us understand how dynamic real-world markets function, change, or thrive.

SUMMARY

1. Monopolistic competition is a market structure that contains a large number of firms. Each firm sells a product that is similar to but slightly differentiated from the products of other firms in the industry. Freedom of entry and exit exists in this model.

2. Advertising is a means by which firms distinguish their products and attempt to increase demand for them. Advertising and other forms of nonprice competition characterize monopolistic competition.

3. In the long run, a tangency between the firm's demand curve and its average long-run cost exists under monopolistic competition. If this tangency occurs, then the firm produces a rate of output less than the rate associated with minimum average total cost—that is, excess capacity exists.

4. The excess capacity that exists in a monopolistically competitive market may have value. A large variety of differentiated products offers consumers a wider variety of choice than they have in a purely competitive market where firms sell a homogeneous product.

5. The long-run equilibrium of the monopolistically competitive firm is similar to a competitive firm in that its price is equal to its average cost. It is similar to a monopolist in that its price is greater than its marginal cost.

KEY TERMS

imperfect competition
monopolistic competition
differentiated product
nonprice competition

advertising
private good
tangency solution
excess capacity

economic efficiency
economic welfare

QUESTIONS FOR REVIEW AND DISCUSSION

1. Select two products or services that you regularly consume. Are these goods produced under monopolistically competitive conditions? What information must you have before giving a definite answer to this question?

2. What, exactly, is the role of product differentiation and advertising in monopolistic competition?

3. How many forms of competition can you name and analyze in addition to price competition? How is location a factor in competition?

4. Suppose that Pepsi is the best-selling soft drink in the market. Is it wasteful for the firm to continue to advertise on a large scale? Give reasons for your answer.

5. Suppose you are moving to a new town and must find an apartment. What benefits do you receive from apartment advertisements? What costs do you incur?

6. What is the tangency solution to the market model of monopolistic competition? Are half-empty airplanes on the New York–San Francisco route definite evidence of excess capacity and economic waste? Give reasons for your answer.

7. Compare the results of long-run equilibrium in pure competition and monopolistic competition from the standpoint of both efficiency and welfare.

ECONOMICS IN ACTION
The Economics of Markup Pricing

Retail businesses buy goods at wholesale prices and mark up the prices by some percentage. Goods sold in grocery stores are marked up, on average, by about 15 percent, while goods sold in clothing stores are marked up by about 50 percent. The fact that retailers mark up prices does not imply that retail firms make economic profits, however. Any firm incurs costs other than the cost of purchased goods, so the break-even price must include some markup. In explaining why markup percentage is different for different types of retail stores, economists emphasize the cost of services provided by sellers. For this reason, restaurants, which provide much more expensive services for customers than do grocery stores, must mark their food prices up by a percentage far greater than 15 percent. Similarly, full-service department stores charge higher markups than discount stores.

A recent study by economist Peter Pashigian, however, reveals fashion to be a second factor in determining standard department store markups. Pashigian focuses on the problem of pricing merchandise when the seller is uncertain which brands, colors, or fabrics will be in fashion after the orders arrive. Although merchandisers try to anticipate fashion trends, they can never predict with certainty which goods consumers will want. In fact, the breadth of most fashion trends can be detected only after merchandise is made available and consumers start buying. For this reason, retailers generally price similar merchandise (say all colors of men's dress shirts) at a standard markup; retailers expect that some colors will sell at full price and that other colors will move only at clearance prices. The Pashigian model implies that where fashion plays a minor role, as in the case of men's dress shirts, retailers can match orders to sales fairly successfully, selling most merchandise at full price.

Pashigian's analysis also implies that as fashion becomes more important, both the percent by which prices are marked up and the percent of goods sold at discount will rise. Therefore, arguments about which groups of consumers are more style-conscious can be resolved by observing average markups and the frequency of clearance sales. The data in Figure 6 document attitudes toward fashion in the clothing industry since World War II. Especially since the mid 1960s, both average markups and the percentage of merchandise sold at discounted prices have risen rapidly. When buyers are classified into different types (see Table 2), the

FIGURE 6

Average Markups and Percent of Goods Discounted, 1945–1985

(a) Since World War II, department store markups have risen sharply. (b) During the same time the percentage of sales at discounted prices has also risen. This suggests that fashion has grown in importance over this period.

(a)

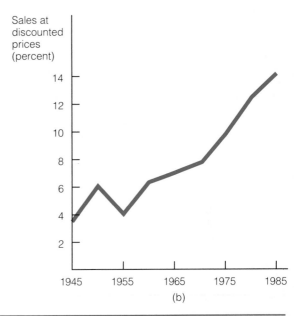

(b)

evidence—that is, the percent of goods sold at clearance prices—suggests that fashion is now equally important for

TABLE 2
Average Department Store Markups and Percent of Goods Sold at Discount

The table shows increases in markups (a) and in the percent of goods sold at discount (b) for all types of clothing for selected years since 1965. The data suggest that fashion plays as large a role in the purchase of men's apparel as it does for women's apparel.

Year	All Groups	Women's Apparel	Men's Apparel	Teens and Junior Apparel	Infant Apparel
(a)	Average Markups in Department Stores (%)				
1965	39.6	42.2	40.6	39.2	38.0
1977	46.0	48.9	48.6	49.1	42.3
1984	48.0	51.9	50.6	52.1	44.0
(b)	Percent of Goods Sold at Clearance				
1965	7.0	10.2	6.6	10.8	7.0
1977	10.2	11.8	10.8	18.2	10.3
1984	16.8	19.8	19.3	27.0	18.4

men and women, and that buyers in the teens and junior market are the most fashion-conscious of all.

Finally, Pashigian's model implies a somewhat ironic connection between consumers who are fashion-conscious and those who are not. Critics of product differentiation often argue that consumers would be better served if product differentiation were eliminated. Then producers would make homogeneous products and sell them under conditions of perfect competition. In terms of Figure 5, these critics argue that such a change would benefit consumers because products would be purchased at a price of P_c, which is less than P_m. Without fashion there would be lower standard prices (lower markups), but there would also be no need to discount out-of-fashion items. In markets where fashion is important, some items end up so heavily discounted that the final sale price is far below the cost of the item. Since consumers with no interest in fashion are likely to purchase goods on sale, the price paid will be far below the price paid in the absence of product differentiation.

Question
In general, how widespread is the practice among retailers of marking up goods that are in style and discounting goods that are not? Be sure to provide some examples.

Source: B. Peter Pashigian, "Demand Uncertainty and Sales: A Study of Fashion and Markdown Pricing," *American Economic Review* 78 (December 1988), pp. 936–53.

12

When Competitors Are Few: Game Theory, Oligopoly, and Cartels

In Chapter 11 we examined one type of imperfectly competitive market—the market consisting of large numbers of competing firms that sell similar products, or the monopolistically competitive market. Where sellers of a particular product or service are few or where a few large market leaders coexist with a large number of "fringe" competitors selling an insignificant amount of total output, the market is called an **oligopoly.** Beer, automobiles, cigarettes, steel, and aluminum are just some of the products of oligopoly markets.

The key element in these markets composed of small numbers of competing sellers is that they recognize that their actions have an impact on one another's sales, prices, and profits. The fate of any one competitor is linked to the actions of each of the other competitors in the market; further, each competitor *recognizes* that this is the case. Economists call this condition **mutual interdependence.** Under such oligopoly conditions firms may, for survival or profit, try to engage in various forms of combination or collusion, such as cartels. A **cartel** is a formal or informal alliance among producers to restrict competition and to achieve some or all of the gains of monopoly. Such a structure may be closer in economic results to pure monopoly than to pure competition, but this does not occur in all oligopolies. We may not think of hamburger, canned soup, or pizza sellers as oligopolists or cartels, but they certainly behave (compete) in ways that reveal that they are mutually interdependent. National purveyors of hamburgers or pizzas, especially in local markets, will never know exactly what the demand will be at any given price for a burger or a 12-inch pizza. What they will sell at some price will depend on a number of factors—including the quality and price competitors are offering and the competitors' advertising and promotion efforts.

This chapter focuses on those market structures in which mutual interdependence is a factor in the functioning of the market and is recognized as such. When you finish reading Chapter 12 you should understand

- the implications of game theory for explaining mutual dependence and for the behavior of oligopoly firms and cartels.
- the conditions under which collusion or cheating may be expected when large competitors are few.

Oligopoly:
Market models characterized by a few firms producing either homogeneous or differentiated products, with entry of new firms very difficult or prevented.

Mutual interdependence:
A relation among firms in which the decisions and actions of one firm have a significant impact on the decisions, actions, and profits of other firms.

Cartel:
An alliance of firms that act collusively to reduce output and increase price in an industry in order to increase profits.

- how strategic behaviors are important in understanding oligopoly market structures.
- the nature of legal and illegal cartels in U.S. and world markets.

GAME THEORY AND MUTUAL INTERDEPENDENCE

Game theory:
A theory involving decision making in an atmosphere of mutual interdependence and imperfect information.

Game theory is a tool that is often used in the analysis of strategic behavior between political entities such as the United States and the Soviet Union.[1] In economics, game theory permits us to focus on the central feature of oligopoly—mutual interdependence—and the principles behind the strategies of firms in markets where the number of firms is small. First, we consider the matter of mutual interdependence more closely.

Mutual Interdependence in the Economic World

The key to the existence of oligopoly is that mutual interdependence develops among a small number of sellers. Mutual interdependence is a relation among firms such that what one firm does with its price, product, or advertising budget directly affects other firms in the market, and vice versa. For example, if Chrysler Corporation introduces two new types of automobiles or if the company increases its overall advertising budget by a significant percentage, sales of General Motors, Ford, and foreign automobile manufacturers will be directly affected. These oligopolistic competitors know that their sales and profits are affected by Chrysler's actions and are likely to react accordingly. Firms therefore devote resources to keeping track of their competitors' actions.

When competitors recognize mutual interdependence, each firm will base its market decisions (on price, product innovation, and advertising) on what it thinks its rivals will do. Due to the uncertainty facing sellers in oligopoly markets, mutual interdependence can lead to a variety of outcomes. The outcome of any action an oligopoly firm takes depends on the responses—both actual and assumed—of rival firms.

Game Theory: A Basis for Small Numbers Behavior

The basic problem facing oligopolies should be familiar to everyone; we all find ourselves in situations of mutual interdependence every day. Anyone who has ever played games of any sort—tennis, blackjack, bridge—will immediately recognize the problem. Our actions are interdependent when playing games because our actions affect other players' behavior, and *our own* behavior is

---

[1]See John von Neumann and Oskar Morgenstern, *Theory of Games and Economic Behavior* (Princeton: Princeton University Press, 1944), the classic work applying game theory—of which the prisoner's dilemma is an example—to economic analysis. Data for and discussion of several of the games considered in this chapter are taken, with permission, from Richard O. Beil, Jr., *Collusion in Experimental Oligopoly Markets* (Unpublished doctoral dissertation, Texas A&M University, 1988).

conditioned by what we *expect* other players' reactions to our own behavior to be. Suppose that you and Joan have a weekly tennis match. Respectful of your powerful serve, Joan has learned to stand well behind the baseline when receiving. This position allows her to return an increasingly high percentage of your serves. Noticing this, you decide to surprise her with a shallow slicing serve. If you serve this way consistently, Joan will likely *change* her behavior. Joan's actions and yours are clearly interdependent—and recognized to be so. Game theory is the formalization of the effects of mutual interdependence on strategy.

The Prisoner's Dilemma as a Basis for Game Theory. An intriguing basis for game theory as applied to economic rivalry is called the **prisoner's dilemma.** The prisoner's dilemma originated in a story told by mathematician A. W. Tucker. It involves two criminals (here, Butch Cassidy and the Sundance Kid) and their likely behavior after capture. Suppose that the police have captured Butch and Sundance. Further, suppose that the police have sufficient evidence to convict both of lesser crimes but suspect that Butch and Sundance have committed more serious offenses that are punishable by lengthier stays in jail. The police separate the prisoners and attempt to obtain confessions. Butch and Sundance are each informed that (1) if one confesses, the confessor will receive a light sentence and the other a more severe sentence; (2) if neither confesses, both will receive the modest penalty that goes with the lesser crime; (3) if both confess, both will receive a sentence that, while severe, is short of the sentence that would be given to each individual if he did *not* confess and the other did.

The decisions facing Butch and Sundance are organized in Figure 1. Figure 1 represents the prisoner's dilemma by arranging the "payoffs" (in this case, punishments in years in jail) faced by the two decision-makers. (Figure 1 is the *payoff table* for this situation.) The potential number of years of

Prisoner's dilemma:
A scenario that illustrates the mutual interdependence of decision making; the basis for game theory.

FIGURE 1

Butch Cassidy and the Sundance Kid Face the Prisoner's Dilemma

If Butch and Sundance want to minimize their time in jail, the prisoner's dilemma leads both of them to confess. Each receives a seven-year sentence.

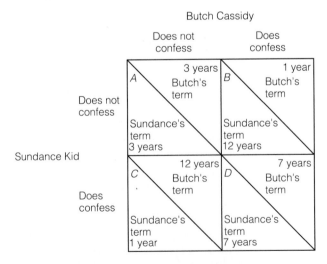

incarceration for Sundance is shown on the left side of each individual block, or quadrant, and the potential time served for Butch is shown on the right side. The police will try to get Butch and Sundance to testify against each other. If Butch confesses, but Sundance does not confess, Sundance gets twelve years in prison to Butch's one. Similarly, if Sundance confesses to the greater crime and Butch holds out, Sundance serves only one year in jail and Butch serves twelve. If both refuse to confess, each receives three years, but if both confess, they each serve seven years.

What is the most likely outcome of this "game" of strategy between Butch and Sundance? The outcome depends upon the assumptions that each makes about the other's behavior. We may reasonably assume (1) that both Butch Cassidy and the Sundance Kid want to minimize their time in jail and (2) that neither is concerned about the cost his decision imposes on the other. Given these two assumptions, the solution to the game is for *both* Butch and Sundance to confess. Look at Figure 1 and consider the potential years served. What is Sundance's best strategy? If Butch confesses, Sundance gets seven years if he confesses, too, *but twelve years if he doesn't*. If Butch does not confess, Sundance gets one year if he confesses and three years if he does not confess. Sundance is better off confessing. Given that Sundance cannot know Butch's decision, and can in no way influence that decision, a confession is the only way for Sundance to ensure a lesser jail term for himself. A look at Figure 1 will verify that the same is true for Butch; the best choice for each criminal is to confess and serve seven years. (If the two could communicate, however, and if each could hold the other to his word, the best choice for both Butch and Sundance would be to not confess.) In the terminology of game theory, the choices offered to Butch and Sundance have a **dominant solution:** each player has the same best choice, no matter what strategy the other player chooses. In the game represented by Figure 1, the dominant solution is to confess.

Dominant solution:
A situation in game theory in which each player has the same best choice no matter what course of action other players may choose.

The Prisoner's Dilemma as Economic Game. The prisoner's dilemma can be directly related to economic behavior. Contests offered by fast-food chains can be viewed within the context of simple game theory. A contest increases the restaurants' production costs (prizes, promotion fees, and so on) and at the same time tends to reduce profits. Yet contests are often offered by firms acting in their own self-interest. Their reasoning is illustrated in Figure 2, in which profits to the restaurant chains replace the time in prison spent by Butch Cassidy and the Sundance Kid. Here, the two fast-food chains are trying to maximize their profits, represented by the dollar figures in the boxes.

From the industry's standpoint, the best decision for both firms is represented in Box *A* of Figure 2. Industry profits total $120 million in Box *A* ($65 million for Wendy's and $55 million for Burger King), as opposed to $100 million in Boxes *B* and *C* and $90 million in Box *D*. Yet Box *A* does not represent the individual profit-maximizing choice for either firm separately. If Burger King offers a contest and Wendy's does not (Box *B*), Burger King's profits are $70 million, up $15 million. If it offers a contest and Wendy's does likewise, Burger King's profits will be only $40 million (Box *D*). But if Burger King does not offer a contest and Wendy's does, Burger King's profits will drop to $30 million (Box *C*). Wendy's management considers its own set of options and reaches a similar conclusion: namely, that acting independently, Wendy's will always be better off giving customers a contest to play. If each

FIGURE 2

Various possible combinations exist when Wendy's and Burger King try to maximize profits by deciding whether to offer contests. Profits for the firms' decisions are given in millions of dollars. The best choice for the industry as a whole is Box *A*, where neither firm offers a contest. The best profit-maximizing option for each individually is to offer a contest.

The Prisoner's Dilemma and Fast-Food Contests

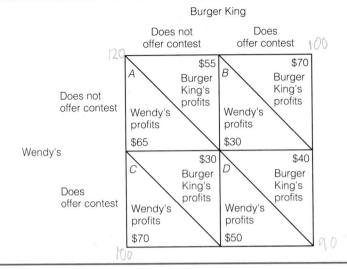

chain makes a decision that tends to maximize its individual profits, both will introduce contests and together earn smaller profits ($90 million) than they would have earned in the absence of contest offerings by both ($120 million).

The dilemma for Burger King and Wendy's is this: Both parties would be better off if they could communicate and stay in Box *A*; but firms cannot legally communicate because of the fear that they might talk about more than contests—that is, would collude or cooperate to raise prices. Therefore, the best option for each firm acting alone is Box *D*. In economic and game theory jargon, the solution to this, the prisoner's dilemma, is known as the **Cournot-Nash solution.** (See Economics in Action, "The Cournot-Nash Model of Game Theory: Cheating, Punishment, and Repentance.") The Cournot-Nash solution in oligopoly behavior produces profits, prices, and outputs halfway between pure competition and pure monopoly. Unfortunately, consumers may be left with even worse solutions in the real world.

Cournot-Nash solution:
The likely outcome of a one-shot game or a game with a known end point; in this case, both firms cheat, thus bringing profits below the joint profit-maximizing level.

Tacit collusive solution:
A possible outcome in game theory when, given an indefinite time horizon and no formal communication, rivals recognize that it is in their best interest to act so that joint profits are maximized.

One-Shot Versus Infinite Series Games. Two keys to the actual outcome of such "games" in real-world situations are (1) the conjecture made about rivals' responses and (2) the time frame over which combatants work out their responses and strategies. The two games presented in Figures 1 and 2 are one-shot games; in each case, each party has just one chance to make the best decision. If these games were played repeatedly, perhaps both parties in each game—both Sundance and Butch *and* Wendy's and Burger King—would eventually decide to do what's best for both. Butch and Sundance might eventually get to Box *A* in Figure 1, with each serving three years; Burger King and Wendy's might eventually get to Box *A* in Figure 2, with neither offering contests. Such **tacit collusive solutions**—or outcomes without specific, formal agreement—exist when, over an indefinite period of time, firms recognize that their own interests will best be served when joint or combined profits are maximized.

Backward induction:
The incentive each player has to cheat in the last period of the game; exists because there are no future periods left to play in which possible consequences from cheating could occur.

Cheating:
The act of violating a collusive agreement; may result in an increase in short-run economic profits to the firm that cheats, followed by zero economic profits in the long run.

When the time horizon facing two rivals is finite—that is, when the game has a known end point—the outcome is shaped by the principle of backward induction. **Backward induction** results from an incentive to cheat in the last period of the game.

Suppose Wendy's and Burger King's contest "game" will last three "periods." If the two firms have been in Box *A* of Figure 2 for two periods, it would be in either Burger King's or Wendy's best interest to **cheat** in the third and final period. Why? To do so would mean bigger profits for the cheater—*but only if the other does not cheat*. If you think your rival will cheat in the third period, then you have an incentive to get there first—to cheat in the second period. If you think your rival will cheat in the second period, then you will cheat in the first period. The collusive, or joint profit-maximizing, solution tends to break down when the end period of the game is known. Each player has an incentive to cheat *before* the joint profit-maximizing solution has a chance to get off the ground; the outcome in such a case is identical to the outcome of a one-shot game.

OLIGOPOLY MODELS

As noted previously, industries with a few sellers or with a few large sellers and a large number of fringe competitors are characteristic of the modern marketplace. Oligopolies may sell homogeneous products such as steel or differentiated products such as automobiles or soft drinks. Outwardly, oligopolies may resemble either pure competitors or monopolistically competitive firms.

Characteristics of Oligopoly

The simple principles of game theory tell us that pricing decisions by oligopolistic firms are much more complex than for firms in monopolistic or monopolistically competitive markets. Unlike other types of firms, oligopolistic firms find it extremely difficult to estimate their demand curves. If Ford is considering a 5 percent increase in prices, there is no reliable way of estimating sales at that higher price without knowing the price response of other firms like General Motors or Toyota.

Game Theory and Oligopoly Behavior. While game theory becomes extremely complex in models using more than two competitors or when complicated strategies are involved, simple models provide many insights into the problems of small numbers competition. Indeed, many of the conclusions of game theory models discussed previously have been verified experimentally.[2] Unlike monopoly, where a firm's fortunes are largely dependent on that firm's behavior, game theory reveals an oligopoly firm's profits, prices, and output

---

[2]For nontechnical explanations of some of these interesting experiments, see A. Roth, "Laboratory Experimentation in Economics," *Economics and Philosophy* 2 (1986), pp. 245–73; Vernon Smith, "Experimental Methods in the Political Economy of Exchange," *Science* 234 (October 10, 1986), pp. 167–73; or Charles Plott, "Laboratory Experiments in Economics: The Implications of Posted-Price Institutions," *Science* 232 (May 9, 1986).

to be the result of mutually interdependent behavior. Further, game theory shows how mutual interdependence creates incentives to collude, as well as contradictory incentives to cheat on collusive agreements. Before turning to some specific models of oligopoly, let's consider another characteristic of all oligopolies: barriers to entry.

Barriers to Entry. Oligopoly firms are normally thought to possess a large degree of **market power.** Subject to the reactions of competitors and to the ability of new competitors to enter the market, oligopoly firms are able to set prices and make economic profits, much like pure monopolists. But how does a firm achieve market power in the oligopoly market structure?

Market power:
A situation in which an established firm has influence over price and profit levels due to barriers impeding the entry of rival firms.

The source of the market power of oligopolists, as in any market structure, is barriers to entry. The pure monopolist is the sole supplier of a product because of barriers to entry into its industry. In any locality, for instance, there is ordinarily no close substitute for cable TV or residential power service, and there are legal barriers to firms wishing to enter these markets. If entry were free in these markets, new competitors would be attracted by higher-than-competitive prices, and excess profits would be eroded. Entry barriers are likewise essential to the maintenance of market power by oligopolists.

For an oligopoly, an entry barrier is essentially a cost that confronts a potential entrant into the industry but does not affect the incumbent firms. There are both natural and artificial entry barriers in an oligopoly market.

Natural Barriers. Economies of scale are an example of a natural barrier to entry. The economies of large-scale production and distribution mean that long-run average costs decline as output grows. Minimum average cost is not reached until the firm is producing a huge proportion of the total industry output. Economies of scale in the U.S. automobile industry, for example, have promoted the presence of a few firms in the long run—far fewer than the hundreds of automobile manufacturers at the beginning of this century. Other natural entry barriers include high fixed costs, high risk, scarce managerial talent, personal technological knowledge, and high capital costs.

Great care must be used in interpreting natural entry barriers, since most of these barriers reflect the different efficiencies of firms in producing output. Society benefits when firms achieve economies of scale, produce with the best technology, and allocate scarce managerial talent carefully. If a natural force like economies of scale leads to the possibility of market power, then the firm may be subject to antitrust prosecution. This means that the firm may be subject to laws enforced by the Federal Trade Commission and the Justice Department, which limit or eliminate anticompetitive practices.

Artificial Barriers. Government restrictions—patents, government regulations, licensing, tariffs, quotas, and other government actions—constitute artificial barriers to entry for oligopolists. Such restrictions are fairly self-evident, but consider some examples. Patent protection is the exclusive right to market an invention for a given number of years. Patent protection is said to promote inventions, but the patent law also creates and protects oligopolies or temporary monopolies. Patents on new drugs and such products as the Polaroid camera create temporary monopolies within oligopoly industries.

Government-sponsored import tariffs on foreign automobiles or steel are an example of government restrictions that encourage and protect oligopolies. Cartels or legal agreements to collude—in such industries as railroads, ocean transportation, communications, TV, and radio—are sponsored and enforced by government. Cartel arrangements legalized through regulation are probably the most important artificial barriers to entry established by government. The basic point is that oligopoly theory rests on the concept of barriers to entry, both natural and artificial. Without barriers to entry, oligopoly could not exist.

Models of Oligopoly Pricing

Like other firms, oligopolies seek to maximize their profits. To do so, however, the oligopolist can pursue many different strategies because firms can compete on a number of bases—product development, prices, advertising budgets, and so on—and can form a whole spectrum of opinions about how rivals will react. Many theories of oligopoly based on price or nonprice competition have been developed. We present some of the standard models, representing how economists have analyzed oligopolistic markets.

Kinked demand:
A demand curve in which the marginal revenue curve has a discontinuous segment; the result of qualitatively different price reactions by competitors to increases and decreases in the firm's price.

The Kinked Demand Model. The Great Depression of the 1930s provided a setting for the development of a famous model of oligopolistic competition. The **kinked demand** theory of oligopolistic pricing was developed by Paul M. Sweezy in the 1930s to explain why prices in oligopolistic industries with few sellers did not seem to change very much in the face of large-scale reductions in demand during the Depression. Prices were "sticky"—that is, they refused to fall or they fell slowly—over this period.

Figure 3 illustrates Sweezy's kinked demand model of oligopolistic pricing. The graph looks complicated, but it is not if we keep in mind Sweezy's

FIGURE 3

Sweezy's basic assumption is that rivals will not follow price increases by a firm but will follow price decreases. This causes MR to be discontinuous over the range BC. If MC cuts MR in this segment, there will be no tendency for price or output to change when the level of marginal costs rises or falls between B and C. Prices will be "sticky."

Sweezy's Kinked Demand Curve Model

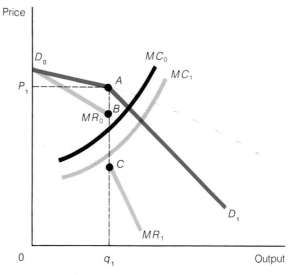

main assumption about oligopoly firm behavior: Rival firms will follow price decreases but will not follow price increases. In Figure 3, the price being charged is P_1, and output is q_1. As you can see, the market demand curve facing the firm has a "kink" in it. The slope of the upper portion, D_0A, reflects the assumption that if the firm raises its price, no rival will follow the price increase. D_0A is an elastic portion of the kinked demand curve. The slope of the portion AD_1 is based on the assumption that rivals will match price decreases by the firm. Thus, the firm loses sales if it raises price above P_1 and does not gain sales if it lowers price below P_1. This market situation results in a kink in the demand curve at point A.

very much

The two segments of the kinked demand curve are associated with two marginal revenue curves. MR_0 is the marginal revenue curve corresponding to D_0A, and MR_1 is the marginal revenue curve corresponding to AD_1. Connection of the two differently sloped MR curves results in a discontinuous marginal revenue curve. MR hits the dashed line in Figure 3 at B and "jumps" to C, where it begins again as MR_1. The marginal revenue curve has a gap (or discontinuity) over the distance BC. It is useful to think of marginal revenue as consisting of MR_0, BC, and MR_1 in this case.

Now we can easily see why prices are "sticky" in this model. Applying the $MC = MR$ rule, we see in Figure 3 that the MC curve cuts MR in the gap BC. Within this gap, MC can rise as high as B or fall as low as C, but applying the $MC = MR$ rule will yield the same optimal price for the firm. Thus, changes in marginal costs do not automatically lead to lower prices or higher quantities. In Figure 3 for example, when the firm's MC falls to MC_1, there is no change in its price.

Sweezy's assumption may or may not hold. Careful empirical studies tend to show a reasonable amount of upward and downward price flexibility in concentrated markets. Moreover, the kinked demand model is strictly a short-run theory of oligopoly pricing. It does not tell us how price comes to be set at P_1 or how firms adapt to situations where MC shifts outside the gap of MR.

2. **Dominant Firms.** Many industries consist of one or a few large firms and many smaller rivals. Examples are the airlines, steel manufacturers, and personal computer industry. Pricing in such a market is often characterized by **price leadership,** which means that there is an unwritten agreement that the largest firm sets pricing policy for the industry. When the largest firm announces that it is raising its price by 5 percent, the other firms in the industry follow suit (and usually on the same day!). This unwritten code of industry conduct is one way to solve problems of interdependent pricing.

It is not always the largest firm that is the price leader; sometimes it is the most respected firm in the industry or the firm, called a "barometric" firm, that best reflects average cost, demand, and other conditions in the industry. And sometimes the role of price leader shifts among firms. Jones-Laughlin, though not the largest firm in the market, was for years the steel industry's price leader, whereas General Motors, clearly the dominant firm, provided a similar role for the automobile industry.

Figure 4 illustrates the dominant-firm model. The diagram looks more complicated than it is. D is the industry demand curve; ΣMC_f is the horizontal sum of the MC curves of the "fringe suppliers" in the industry. These are competitive firms that behave like price takers; they set MC equal to price. D_d

Price leadership:
A market where a single firm sets industry price, with the remaining firms charging what the price leader charges. Industry price changes are initiated by the leader.

FIGURE 4

A Dominant-Firm Model

MC_d is the marginal cost curve of the dominant firm, and ΣMC_f is the marginal cost curve of fringe suppliers. At price P_1, the competitive fringe supplies the whole market. At prices below P_1, a residual demand faces the dominant firm $(D_d = D - \Sigma MC_f)$. The dominant firm, which has lower MC than the fringe suppliers, sets a monopoly price, P_d, over this portion of the market. The dominant firm produces q_d. The fringe firms accept P_d as given and set $MC = P_d$, producing q_f; $q_d + q_f = Q_T$. The dominant firm is therefore the price leader in the industry, and the fringe suppliers are price takers.

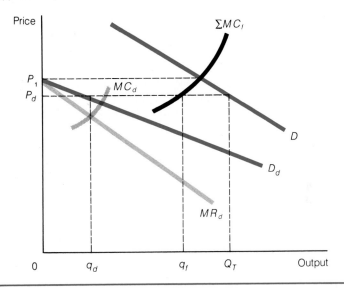

is the demand curve facing the dominant firm (or groups of firms), and MR_d is the associated marginal revenue curve. The marginal cost curve of the dominant firm, MC_d, is lower than the marginal cost curves of the fringe suppliers. Its lower costs derive from economies of scale.

How does the model work? The dominant firm takes the existence of the fringe suppliers as a given, and it prices accordingly. At any given price, the dominant firm derives its demand curve by considering what the fringe firms will do. At price P_1, the fringe suppliers will supply the whole market— $\Sigma MC_f = D$. There is nothing left for the dominant firm to exercise its monopoly power over. At prices below P_1, fringe suppliers cannot supply the whole market; something is left over for the dominant firm to supply. This portion of the market is given by the horizontal difference between ΣMC_f and D at points below $\Sigma MC_f = D$. In other words, at prices below P_1, the demand curve of the dominant firm is equal to the difference between ΣMC_f and D.

Over this residual portion of the market, the dominant firm is a price setter. According to its own MC_d and MR_d, it sets price at P_d and produces q_d units of output. The fringe firms accept P_d as given and produce by equating ΣMC_f to P_d. Fringe suppliers supply q_f. Since $q_d + q_f = Q_T$, market demand equals market supply at a price of P_d.

The dominant-firm model mixes elements of monopoly and oligopoly theory. The dominant firm sets price for the industry, and other firms follow this pricing policy, but it sets price by acting like a conventional monopolist over the residual portion of the market not supplied by the fringe firms.

Oligopolists with Differentiated Products. Just as there are many cases of pure oligopoly, there are many cases in which few sellers supply differentiated products. Under such conditions, oligopolists may compete with each other and perhaps try to bar new entrants through advertising, quality variations, or pricing strategies.

Advertising. In oligopoly, as in monopolistic competition, advertising is used by rival firms to increase demand for their products (shift demand curves rightward) through the creation of brand loyalty and product identity. Heavy advertising by a few large firms is often held to be an entry barrier to new competition. The argument is that new firms cannot enter because they cannot afford the heavy advertising expenses necessary to establish a presence in the market. But what is at stake in advertising? Basically, what advertising does is establish a firm's brand name, which represents the quality of the firm's products and services. A brand name reflecting reliable performance is quite valuable and reflects what might be called the advertising capital of the firm. However, if firms lie or produce shoddy products, their brand name capital value will fall.

If advertising creates a barrier to entry, we would expect to see firms earning excess profits (greater than a competitive rate of return) on their advertising capital investments in brand names. If they are earning only competitive returns on their advertising capital, advertising is not a barrier to entry. Incumbent firms and potential entrants would face an essentially competitive market in establishing brand names.

Quality Variations. Quality variation and product development are other familiar methods of nonprice competition by oligopolists. Oligopolists, like monopolistic competitors, will alter products to increase their demand curves and to make demand more "intense" and inelastic in consumers' minds. Adding new colors to toothpaste, more or less chrome to automobiles, and more service to airline travel are familiar attempts to differentiate products and services.

Not all this nonprice competition by oligopolists promotes efficiency in the economy. Our discussion of fast-food contests with regard to game theory illustrates how this sort of competition can lead to wasteful results.

Limit Pricing. In oligopoly industries with a differentiated product, incumbent firms may seek to deter potential competition by limit pricing. **Limit pricing** is the incumbent's practice of reducing price as much as necessary to limit entry.

Limit pricing:
A pricing policy consisting of temporarily setting a price lower than the short-run profit-maximizing price in order to deter entry and maximize profits in the long run.

Imagine a situation in which a new firm wants to enter an industry. Since other firms' products have already been differentiated, the new firm will have to incur heavy advertising expenses to become competitive with incumbent firms assumed to be earning economic profits. If a new entrant is successful in its bid for a share of the market, its sales will come at the expense of the incumbent firms. To block this challenge, an incumbent firm may lower price and increase output in response to the threat of entry, voluntarily (if temporarily) reducing its profits. In general, the incumbent firm could set a price at which entry would not be worthwhile for any potential rival.

We are talking about oligopolistic behavior. The potential entrant must make an estimate of what the incumbent firm will do in the face of entry. If the incumbent firm practices or even threatens limit pricing, entry may not be feasible. Indeed, the most rational thing for the incumbent firm to do is to keep price at profitable levels and at the same time make it clear to potential entrants that it will lower price and increase output if they enter.

CARTEL MODELS

To this point in our discussion of oligopolies, we have assumed that competitor firms will not cooperate to set prices. But what if firms do cooperate? This question brings us to the topic of cartels.

Cartels and oligopolies are close cousins. The distinguishing feature of a cartel is an agreement among firms to restrict output in order to raise price and to achieve monopoly power over a market.

Characteristics of Cartels

Normally cartels are supported by agreements that limit entry and restrict and segment output among markets. Mutual interdependence exists prior to cartel agreements; the purpose of a cartel agreement is to limit or constrain rivals' actions that affect the prices and profits of the group of suppliers.

Cartel agreements may be legal or illegal. In countries like the United States with antitrust laws, cartels are illegal, but they sometimes operate covertly. An illegal cartel rests on private, collusive agreements that are out of sight of the antitrust authorities. In the 1960s certain firms made a secret agreement to fix the prices of electrical generators sold to municipalities; this illegal collusion was discovered and prosecuted under antitrust laws, with the guilty firms paying damages. Beyond the threat and reality of antitrust prosecution, such secret arrangements may tend to fall apart on their own. Reasons for the fragile nature of cartels will be discussed later in the chapter, but most are related to the incentives for some members to cheat on the agreement.

A legal cartel is supported by a law limiting entry and restricting competition among members. Such cartels may be made legitimate by the legal and political organization of an industry—communications, electrical distribution, and railroads, for example—under the umbrella of government regulation restricting competition and allowing price fixing. Or cartels may be made legitimate by legislation granting exceptions to antitrust statutes. Such is the case for some exporters, labor unions, and farm organizations.

Legal status does not protect such cartels from breaking down in the long run. Technology and competition have all but destroyed the railroad cartel in the United States enforced by the Interstate Commerce Commission since the late nineteenth century. OPEC (the Organization of Petroleum Exporting Countries) was unable to maintain its full cartel status, not because it was illegal within the participating countries, but because of the lack of adequate enforcement and the unwillingness of certain nations, notably Saudi Arabia, to meet the terms demanded by other members. The Colombian coffee cartel of the 1960s broke down for similar reasons, and the De Beers diamond cartel (see Focus, "All That Glitters: The De Beers Diamond Cartel"), though legal, had some shaky times in the early 1980s. Both legal and illegal cartels tend to be fragile, therefore, though agreements enforced by law and the government are less so.

FOCUS   All That Glitters: The De Beers Diamond Cartel

Recession and falling demand have been the ruination of many cartels. There is great temptation to cheat during periods of declining demand. However, the De Beers diamond cartel successfully warded off a threat of dissolution in the recession of the 1970s and 1980s.[a] De Beers' maneuvering provides interesting insights into the enforcement powers of a cartel.

De Beers Consolidated Mines markets more than 80 percent of the uncut diamonds of both gem and industrial quality sold yearly in the world. De Beers owns South African mines and acts as the marketing agent for virtually all other diamond-producing and -supplying nations, including the Soviet Union. De Beers pays royalties out of its retail sales to these nations for exclusive rights to market their stones. Retailers have no choice but to purchase wholesale boxes of diamonds from De Beers; if they refuse, they are not necessarily invited to purchase diamonds again. Thus De Beers may be thought of as a marketing or middleman type of cartel.

The De Beers cartel system worked well until 1979, when the Arggle diamond mine was discovered in Australia. Even worse for the cartel, a worldwide recession created massive reductions in demand for diamonds. De Beers' earnings fell from $673 million in 1979 to $183 million in 1982. Rather than reduce price in the face of declining demand, De Beers removed massive supplies of diamonds from the market by cutting production at its own mines to shore up the cartel price. De Beers also reduced purchases

[a]John R. Emshwiller and Neil Behrmann, "Restored Luster: How De Beers Revived World Diamond Cartel After Zaire's Pullout," *Wall Street Journal* (August 7, 1983).

from participating nations in return for lump-sum payments. In all, De Beers added more than $1 billion worth of diamonds to its inventory between 1979 and 1982.

In May 1981, Zaire, the world's largest producer of diamonds, pulled out of the cartel and entered into a five-year contract with three independent producers of low-priced industrial-quality diamonds (called *boart*) from Zaire's Miba mine. De Beers' reaction was decisive. Though stockpiling diamonds in general, the company poured boart onto the market and encouraged illegal diamond smuggling by Zairian citizens. The result: Zaire's revenues and profits fell precipitously. The country was even refused loans from international agencies to upgrade its mines. In March 1983, Zaire returned to the fold, dropping the three independent marketers in mid-contract.

The biggest coup for De Beers to date was the securing of Australia as a member of the cartel. The two majority stockholders of Australia's huge Arggle mine had indirect ties to De Beers through a chain of stock ownership. Though there was opposition, De Beers' Australian friends helped bring Arggle within the cartel, but with some concessions: Australia is now free to market 25 percent of its industrial stones and 5 percent of its gemstones outside the cartel.

Some observers believe that De Beers' concession sets a precedent that could weaken the cartel. Others believe this outcome unlikely. The Soviet Union, for example, could produce and sell enough diamonds to create chaos in world markets but chooses instead to play the cartel game. The Soviet Union apparently thinks that long-run price stability is preferable to possible short-run gains. Zaire, through costly misadventure, learned this lesson all too well.

Cartel Formation

Assume for the sake of simplicity that cartels do not violate any law and that we are analyzing a case in which the cartel is to be privately enforced by the cartel members and not by government. The first problem facing any potential cartel or association of sellers is how to get organized. In this respect the cartel is no different from any other group. The usual problem in getting any group to do anything can be roughly summarized as "passing the buck." If somebody else forms the cartel or takes the lead in restricting output, other members can generally enjoy the benefits of the cartel without bearing any of the costs of organization. This behavior is called *free riding*.

Of course, if everybody in the cartel were a free rider, the cartel would never be formed. All potential members would hold back and expect to benefit from the organizational efforts of others. Suffice it to say that a cartel has to get organized. Someone has to get the individual suppliers in the industry together and hammer out an agreement to restrict output in order to raise price. The details of this feat are not simple. Which firms will reduce output and by how much? How will the resulting cartel profits be shared? How will deviations from cartel policies be monitored and enforced? And so on.

None of these are easy questions for the cartel manager to answer or to reach agreement on. The problem becomes more pronounced the more firms there are in the industry. As a rule, smaller groups are easier to deal with than larger groups.

The Cartel in Action

Figure 5 illustrates how a cartel operates. Imagine that orange juice producers try to form a cartel. Initially, the orange juice industry is competitively organized. Orange juice industry demand and supply intersect to yield price P. Industry output is Q.

A cartel manager emerges and strikes an agreement among the competitive producers to cut back production from the industry's Q to Q_c and to raise price from P to P_c. Cartel output Q_c will ordinarily not be equivalent to the output a pure monopolist would select. Why? In an industry such as orange juice production, with a relatively large number of suppliers, the costs of eliminating all competitive behavior—the costs of enforcing the cartel agreement against free riders—would be too high. Some competitive behavior will remain. Cartel price will therefore tend to be lower than the profit-maximizing price of a pure monopolist.

The incentive to form cartels is nevertheless clear. Cartel members who were previously earning a competitive rate of return in a competitive industry now earn an agreed-upon portion of P_cABP—an equal share of cartel profits.

FIGURE 5

Price rises from P to P_c as the cartel is formed and output is cut back from Q to Q_c. In the extreme case, the cartel price, P_c, is equivalent to the monopoly price.

Organizing a Competitive Industry into a Cartel

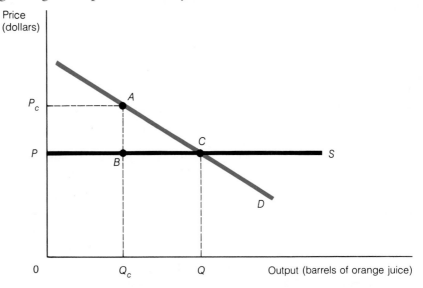

Cartel Enforcement

Holding the cartel together is not easy. Once the cartel has been organized, has restricted output, and has raised price to P_c, what is the position of the individual orange juice firm in the cartel? If an individual firm in the cartel lowers its price slightly below P_c, it will face a very elastic demand curve for its output. Buyers will prefer the lower price and will switch their purchases to the lower-priced firm. The fact that individual firms in a cartel can significantly increase their sales and profits by secretly lowering their price puts tremendous pressure on the cartel to fall apart. Given that individual firms have a large incentive to cheat on the agreement, cartels must give careful

Cartel enforcement:
Attempts by members of the cartel to prevent other members from cheating and thus destroying economic profit potential.

consideration to the matter of **cartel enforcement** from the outset.

Of course, to expect the price cutter's profits to hold up in the long run is unrealistic. Other firms would easily discover what was going on because they would suffer a drastic loss of sales. If they responded in kind with price reductions, the result would be that the second price cutter would not experience an increase in sales and profits for long. Further spates of secret price cuts and price competition would lead to a return to competitive equilibrium.

Recognizing these possibilities, the individual firm in the cartel must form an estimate of what it can reasonably expect to gain from secret price reductions and compare this estimate to its share of cartel profits. A cartel will not be stable if the former magnitude is larger than the latter.

The general case in which a firm might expect to gain by secret price cutting is illustrated in Figure 6. Cartel equilibrium is at price P_c and output q_c, represented by E_c. D/n represents the prorated firm demand curve, where n is the number of firms in the industry, and d_i represents the gains to an individual cartel member from secretly cutting price; d_i is more elastic than D/n. With the more elastic d_i curve, price increases would cause a sharp drop in sales, but price reductions cause a sharp gain sales and profits at the expense

FIGURE 6

P_c is the agreed-upon cartel price at cartel output q_c. E_c is therefore the cartel equilibrium. If secret price cuts cannot be detected, the cheating firm will face the more elastic demand curve, d_i, and can gain from cheating on the agreement. If such behavior can be detected, movements will be along D/n, the prorated firm demand curve. The degree to which d_i diverges from D/n reflects the efficiency of the cartel enforcement system.

Cheating in a Cartel

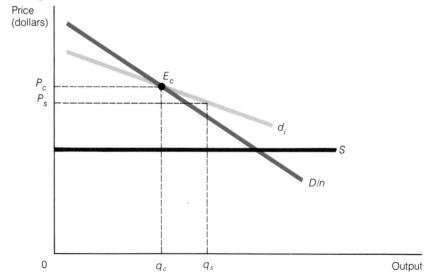

of other cartel members. The gains of a secret price cut to P_s are traced out by d_i below P_c.

The key to cartel enforcement is now apparent. Means must be found to make d_i approximate D/n. Perfect cartel enforcement exists when each cartel member knows that secret price cuts are not possible and will be matched by other members. In this case, the prorated demand curve, D/n, is the relevant demand curve. If a firm cuts price, it will immediately be matched by other cartel members. There is thus no gain to cutting price. Movements will be along the prorated firm demand curve, D/n. Where it is costly to detect secret price cuts, a demand curve like d_i will confront each cartel member. Each firm must decide whether to cheat, depending on the expected profits from cheating relative to the expected profits from staying in the cartel. In general, we can gauge the effectiveness of cartel enforcement by the degree to which the cartel is able to make the cheating demand curve d_i coincide with the prorated firm demand curve D/n. That is, how good is the cartel at detecting cheating?

Cartels will spend resources to control the incentive to cheat. Historically, many devices have been used. Perhaps the most effective device is a common sales agency for the cartel. All production is sold through the agency, and individual producers do not negotiate sales for themselves. Cheating is not a viable strategy under such a condition. Producers produce their allotted quotas, and the sales agency markets the agreed-upon cartel output (q_c). Exclusive sales territories and customer lists are other ways to control incentives to cheat on the cartel price. For example, exclusive territories are a way to divide markets, and intrusions by other cartel members are easy to spot.

Why Cartels May or May Not Succeed

Collusive cartel agreements are more likely to occur under some circumstances than others. We offer now a menu of factors thought to be conducive to cartel-like behavior. Our list is not meant to be exhaustive—just illustrative of the types of economic conditions associated with a great likelihood of cartel activity.

1. A cartel is easier to form among a smaller number of sellers than a larger number. The costs of any group decision-making process rise with the number in the group.
2. It is easier to reach a cartel agreement when members produce a homogeneous product; nonprice competition is less problematic. Sellers do not have to worry that their competitors will secure bigger market shares through advertising.
3. Collusion is easier to effect in growing and technologically progressive industries than in stagnant or decaying industries. In the latter case, excess capacity created by declining demand puts great pressure on individual firms to compete for customers and to cheat on the cartel agreement.
4. The costs of collusion are reduced when there are many small buyers. Large buyers have a clear incentive and the power to seek to undermine collusion among sellers. In effect, large buyers make cheating on the cartel price very worthwhile to individual sellers.
5. Low turnover among buyers makes collusion easier. If sellers cheat on the cartel agreement, frequent turnover of buyers makes it difficult to detect who is cheating.

Other factors could be added to this list of conditions favorable to the formation of private collusive cartels. Indeed, an easy way to find out what makes collusion attractive is to look at the areas of the economy in which the antitrust authorities typically find such behavior (discussed in Chapter 19).

At this point, one fact should be clear: Private collusive agreements are hard to sustain. The incentive to cheat on such agreements is very strong, as game theory suggests, and cartels therefore tend to be unstable. Moreover, where antitrust law prevails, cartels must operate on the sly to avoid law enforcement; this secrecy further reduces their ability to control cheating. Exclusive sales territories, for example, would likely be spotted by antitrust authorities, for customers would complain about high prices and the lack of competitive sales or service alternatives. It is little wonder, then, that cartels rarely last long unless they are supported by law.

Groups that have difficulty sustaining a private cartel agreement can petition government to pass a law making their cartel legal. More than this, the government can enforce the cartel by outlawing entry and price competition among members. So to say that private cartels are not stable and are unlikely to sidestep the social benefits of competition in the long run is inaccurate if government steps in to reinforce such agreements.

FROM COMPETITION TO MONOPOLY: THE SPECTRUM REVISITED

We are at last in a position to take an overview of the economic characteristics and welfare effects of market structures from pure competition (Chapter 9) to pure monopoly (Chapter 10) to those in between (Chapters 11 and 12). Table 1 organizes the long-run economic tendencies and conclusions of the various structures we have examined.

TABLE 1 **Characteristics and Consequences of Market Structures**

When static market structures are considered, only pure competition yields an efficient and welfare-maximizing allocation of resources. Resources are underallocated to the production of goods and services under all other structures from consumers' perspective.

Type of Market Structure	Number of Sellers	Barriers to Entry	Type of Product	Long-Run Market Tendencies
Pure competition	Many	No	Homogeneous	$P = MC$ $P = ATC$
Monopolistic competition	Many	No	Differentiated	$P > MC$ (tangency soln) $P = ATC$
Oligopoly	Few	Yes	Homogeneous or differentiated	$P > MC$ $P > ATC$
Cartels	Relatively few, acting as one	Yes	Homogeneous or differentiated	$P > MC$ $P > ATC$
Pure monopoly	One	Yes	Unique	$P > MC$ $P > ATC$

The table distinguishes the five market structures by number of sellers, barriers to entry, product characteristics, and long-run market tendencies. The number of sellers ranges from many under competition and monopolistic competition to one in the case of pure monopoly. Significant entry barriers characterize oligopolies, cartels, and monopolies. Oligopolies and cartels are characterized by the sale of *either* homogeneous or differentiated products, unlike the purely or monopolistically competitive structures. Pure monopolies sell unique products.

Most important, Table 1 provides a category—long-run market tendencies—that gives us some insight into the consumer and economic welfare created under these alternative structures. As the table reveals, price tends to equal long-run average total cost in only two of the structures—pure and monopolistic competition. Price, moreover, tends to equal long-run marginal cost only in the purely competitive market structure. What does this mean in terms of consumers' economic welfare?

An important concept introduced in Chapter 10 aids us in interpreting the effects of market structure on social welfare. In Chapter 10, we introduced the concept of consumers' surplus, defined as the difference between the amount of money that consumers would be willing to pay for a quantity of a good and the amount that they actually pay for the good.

Figure 7 contrasts what happens to consumers' surplus for a given hypothetical market—personal computer software—if the market is organized along monopolistic rather than competitive lines. The industry demand curve for this market has the usual negative slope, but the industry has a flat supply curve in this simplified conception. In other words, this is a constant-cost industry, in which additional output may be produced at a constant average cost that is also equal to marginal cost. The supply curve is simply a flat line.

To verify what happens to consumers' surplus under the different market structures represented in Figure 7, look again at the long-run market tenden-

FIGURE 7

In contrasting the higher price and lower quantity (P_m and q_m) produced under a monopolistic market structure with the lower price and higher quantity (P_c and q_c) theoretically possible in a purely competitive situation, ACP_c represents the area of consumer surplus. This is real income available to anyone who can capture it. Under competition, it goes to consumers. Under monopoly, cartels, and oligopolies, part of it (P_mBFP_c) typically goes to producers and part (BCF) is lost to society.

The Effects of Competitive Versus Monopolistic Markets

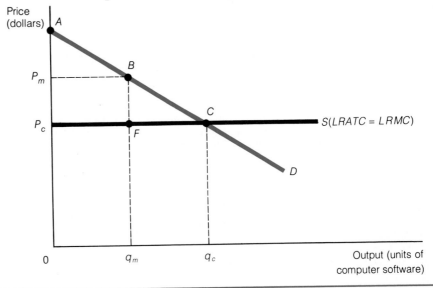

cies of the various models in Table 1. If the computer software industry is purely competitive, it will theoretically be producing an output of q_c at price P_c, which is the lowest possible price because it is equal to both the average cost and the marginal cost of production. In this situation, consumers enjoy a surplus represented by ACP_c. In contrast, price exceeds both average cost and marginal cost in the market models of oligopoly, cartels, and pure monopoly. Economic profits are therefore captured at the expense of consumers in these markets. In Figure 7, P_m and q_m represent the effects of a market structure on the monopoly end of the spectrum; the area P_mBFP_c is redirected from consumers' surplus to producers' profits. In addition, society must also pay a deadweight loss (the area BCF in Figure 7) because price exceeds cost. This deadweight or social loss due to monopoly power or the power of cartels and oligopolies causes some economists to condemn such structures as reducers of consumer and social welfare.

As we have seen, monopolistic competition is something of a special case. Under monopolistic competition, there is a long-run tendency for price to equal average total cost, although not marginal cost when economies of scale are considered. The benefits of differentiated products—a greater range of choices—also exist in this structure. But the only unambiguously welfare-maximizing structure is that of pure competition. As Table 1 and Figure 7 indicate, only competition provides the product in this example, computer software, at the lowest possible price (equal to both $LRATC$ and $LRMC$) and in the greatest quantities possible, q_c. Only pure competition maximizes society's welfare by maximizing consumers' surplus. Important deviations from this norm are prime subjects for society's economic policy concerns. The following two parts of this book, especially Part Four, discuss a number of important economic issues related to market structure.

SUMMARY

1. Oligopoly is a market structure characterized by a few firms that recognize that their actions have an impact on one another's sales, prices, and profits. They may sell either homogeneous or differentiated products. Entry into the industry is difficult because of natural or artificial barriers.

2. When oligopolists recognize their mutual interdependence, they will engage in a variety of strategic behaviors, often trying to tacitly combine or collude. When these behaviors are successful, the market structure more closely resembles pure monopoly than pure competition, but tacit collusion does not result in all cases.

3. Game theory is an important tool for understanding oligopoly behavior because it focuses upon the variety of possible outcomes when mutual interdependence is recognized by a small number of firms selling competing products in the market.

4. The Cournot-Nash solution to the prisoner's dilemma in game theory is an important potential outcome in oligopoly markets. When the Cournot-Nash solution results from oligopoly behavior it produces profits, outputs, and prices at levels midway between those produced under pure competition and pure monopoly.

5. The kinked demand curve theory of oligopoly encompasses two distinct reactions of firms to price changes. It suggests that if one firm increases its price, no other firms will follow the price increase. On the other hand, if one firm lowers its price, all other firms will lower their prices as well. The resulting demand curve can result in an unchanging price structure.

6. Cartels are formal or informal agreements among firms within an industry to restrict output or to segment the market in an effort to increase profits. The result may be similar to monopoly price and output in the industry.

7. There are potential profits for firms that cheat individually on a cartel. Cartels are therefore difficult to establish and maintain. The costs of enforcing the cartel agreement frequently prevent the cartel's survival.

8. Cartels can be legal or illegal. Those created and enforced by the government or those allowed to exist by government sanctions are legal. Otherwise, cartels in the United States are breaches of antitrust laws.

KEY TERMS

oligopoly
mutual
   interdependence
cartel
game theory
prisoner's dilemma

dominant solution
Cournot-Nash
   solution
tacit collusive solution
backward induction
cheating

market power
kinked demand
price leadership
limit pricing
cartel enforcement

QUESTIONS FOR REVIEW AND DISCUSSION

1. What are the general characteristics of the oligopolistic market model? Compare and contrast these to the characteristics of the monopolistic competition model discussed in Chapter 11.

2. Imagine a student cartel. If your professor promised to assign a fixed number of each letter grade, regardless of class performance, is there any type of agreement that you could make with classmates to exploit this grading system? Under what circumstances (for instance, class size) would your student cartel be most likely to succeed?

3. Although it is easy to draw a hypothetical demand curve, it is difficult to determine the position of real-world demand curves. In order to maximize profits, however, managers must accurately estimate the demand for their products. In which case is this estimation more difficult—when the good in question is sold in a monopolistic market or when it is sold in an oligopolistic market? Explain.

4. Sweezy presents an oligopoly model that assumes that rivals match price cuts but ignore price increases. Suppose, instead, that a manager makes optimistic assumptions—namely, that rivals will always react in a manner most beneficial to him or her. What will the manager's demand curve look like? What would a pessimistic manager's demand curve look like?

5. What does the free-rider effect mean? Cite three personal experiences in which you have observed free-riding behavior.

6. Suppose that firms forming a cartel have different marginal costs. Describe, both in words and in a graph, how this situation complicates the various problems that a cartel must solve to be effective in raising prices.

7. Which of the following factors make collusion more or less likely: (a) the purchase of an input in the same market (such as pigs at the stockyard); (b) long-term contracts with buyers; (c) selling to governments; (d) salespeople staying in the same motel on the road; (e) an industry trade association and price list?

PROBLEM

Suppose that you are one of two people hired to sell ads for a local newspaper during the summer. Your employer agrees to pay $350 per week plus a $2000 bonus to be divided by the two of you in proportion to the number of ads you sell. For example, if you sell three-fourths of the total, you get three-fourths of the bonus. Construct a simple payoff table, like the ones in Figures 1 and 2 of this chapter, in which the options for both you and your co-worker are spending little time trying to sell ads, spending some time trying to sell ads, or spending a lot of time trying to sell ads. Are there incentives for you to form a cartel? To cheat on it?

ECONOMICS IN ACTION
The Cournot-Nash Model of Game Theory: Cheating, Punishment, and Repentance

The discussion of game theory in the text of this chapter suggests that models of game-playing can become very complex. This complexity is due to the large number of possible assumptions or conjectures that can be made about someone else's behavior and about one's own reactions to that behavior. A slightly more complex model than those presented in Figures 1 and 2 of this chapter can add to our understanding of strategic behavior in oligopolistic markets. The principles underlying our discussion were first put forth in 1838 by the French economist Augustin Cournot (1801–1877), and they were extended by mathematician John Nash in the 1950s. These principles are called the Cournot-Nash solution in game theory.

Our discussion of the prisoner's dilemma may be expanded in order to understand an important model described by Cournot and Nash. Specifically, imagine a model of two competitors—for example, Sony and Motorola—considering three marketing or advertising strategies for the sale of high-resolution television sets. As shown in the payoff table in Figure 8, these three marketing strategies are labeled X, Y, and Z, giving Sony and Motorola nine possible combinations of choices, with the profits given in the nine individual boxes. If, for example, Sony chooses strategy Z and Motorola chooses X, profits to Sony are $544 million and Motorola's profits are $220 million.

The same basic solutions apply to the three-choice game as to the two-choice games discussed in this chapter. The addition of an intermediate solution, however, helps us understand some other possible features of small numbers behavior. As in simpler games, a one-shot or single play of the strategies open to Sony and Motorola will produce the prisoner's dilemma and result in the Cournot-Nash solution (Z, Z), where each earns profits of $256 million. When the time frame becomes infinite we expect the tacit collusive arrangement (X, X) to emerge, where the rivals each earn $400 million in profits. The same is generally true when the competitive game is finite, provided that neither competitor knows the end point. Even when these competitive games are considered infinite or of unknown duration, there is still room for strategic behavior, due to the mutually interdependent nature of the competition.

Cheating appears as strategic behavior in most games. A close look at Figure 8 reveals that even if Sony and Motorola reach their joint profit-maximizing strategies (X, X), there is room for short-term profits from cheating by either party. Suppose Sony continues "playing" the joint profit-maximizing marketing strategy, X, but that Motorola begins to employ strategy Y or Z. Sony's profits decline to $310 million or $220 million, while Motorola raises its returns from $400 million to $481 million or $544 million. Examination of Figure 8 tells us that Sony has a similar incentive to cheat on the tacit agreement with Motorola. In the real world, some cheating may be difficult to detect, but in this simple two-firm game any cheating is detected immediately by the victim's reduced profits.

One safeguard against cheating on the tacit collusive solution is to punish the offender. If Motorola moved to "cheating" strategy Y, Sony could immediately move to strategy Z, thereby restoring its returns to $400 million and reducing those of Motorola from $481 million to $247 million. Should Sony continue with strategy Z, Motorola could do no better than to also shift to strategy Z. We can easily verify that the Cournot-Nash solution (Z, Z) is the likely result once cheating begins.

Signals between game players are common in many games. As the dynamics of this game reveal, Motorola will be punished for cheating, but Sony's profits also fall with the movement to the Cournot-Nash solution. If the length of the game is infinite, or even just sufficiently long, cooperation and re-establishment of the collusive solution is the most likely result. Either party, Sony or Motorola, may signal the other that they would like to return to collusion from the (Z, Z) level of profits. Either may do so by moving to another strategy for a few periods, taking temporary losses, and giving their rivals gains for those periods. Having been the first to cheat, if Motorola initiated this behavior, the move would be considered repentance. Such temporary losses may be a relatively small sacrifice if the joint profit-maximization, or collusive, solution can be maintained (or restored) over the long run.

These simple principles of games are more than just theory. They help explain a good deal of the maneuvering that actually occurs among firms. Clearly, it would be in the interests of businesses selling similar products to collude and to reach the joint profit-maximizing level of returns. But as the complexities of game theory tell us, such collusion is far less likely as the number of sellers increases. Successful collusion with little or no cheating is also less expected when firms compete in a large number of areas—for example, service, product qualities, and advertising. As games grow

FIGURE 8

In an "infinite" or many-period game, we expect Sony and Motorola to arrive at the joint profit-maximizing, or tacit collusive, solution (X, X). In a one-shot game or in one with a known end point, the Cournot-Nash solution (Z, Z) is most likely. (Payoffs are expressed in millions of dollars.)

Sony and Motorola Caught in the Prisoner's Dilemma

more complex—that is, accommodate a larger number of participants and items upon which competition is based—the possibilities for collusive behavior are drastically reduced. Simple game theory, including the prisoner's dilemma or Cournot-Nash game, is nevertheless of great value in helping economists understand the dynamics of competition and market processes.

Questions

1. As information becomes more readily available, would you expect the degree of collusiveness between firms to increase or decrease?
2. Why does the entrance of new firms into a market inhibit the effectiveness of collusive agreements?

13

Industrial Organization

Monopoly is often in the news. Mergers and their effects on economic performance, for example, are hot topics, compelling microeconomic issues. Monopoly power in any form may be costly to the economy; it can result in lost output, higher prices, and lessened economic efficiency. Industrial organization theory uses the lens of microeconomics to study firms and industries in the economy. Industrial organization theory helps us study monopoly power by focusing on how to measure and how to detect monopoly power and monopolistic behavior in the structure, conduct, and performance of businesses.

Until recently, many economists considered number of firms to be the critical determinant of the conduct and performance of firms and industries: Unequivocally, in this view, more firms lead to more competitive conduct and performance. A new approach to the theory of industrial organization cautions against making automatic assumptions about conduct and performance in an industry based on number of firms; this view allows for the possibility that fewer firms can be conducive to competitive conduct and performance. This chapter covers both approaches to the theory of industrial organization. When you finish Chapter 13 you should understand

- how big business might be good or bad for the economy.

- some of the principles economists use to evaluate industries and merger activity in the economy.

- industrial organization and, more specifically, how a broader view of competitive processes might alter traditional views of merger restrictions and advertising.

MEASURING INDUSTRIAL CONCENTRATION

In the days when monopolies were almost universally vilified, a need for systematic methods of recognizing monopoly power arose. Economists devised several methods of detecting the existence of monopolies—all of which assumed that the number of firms in an industry indicates the degree of competition present. We examine two rough estimates of the degree of concentration of market power within an industry—aggregate concentration and industry concentration ratios. We also question why some industries exhibit high concentration ratios while others don't, noting that changing demands or costs will change the number of firms in an industry and thus the potential for monopoly concentration.

Aggregate Concentration

Aggregate concentration: A measure of the percentage of the total productive assets in an economy owned by the largest one hundred or two hundred firms in the economy.

One method of gauging the extent to which productive assets are dispersed among different firms is to examine the **aggregate concentration** of firms in the economy as a whole. These statistics measure the percentage of all business assets that are owned by the largest one hundred or two hundred firms in the economy. This approach ignores the percentage of individual industries' assets that firms own and instead focuses on the percentage of the nation's total assets held by the largest enterprises. Instead of determining the degree to which General Motors controls the assets of the automobile industry, aggregate concentration is a measure of the degree to which General Motors, IBM, Allied Chemical, and other manufacturing giants control assets among all manufacturing firms.

Table 1 shows trends in aggregate concentration for firms in the manufacturing sector between 1925 and 1984. The share of total manufacturing assets held by the top one hundred companies increased by about ten percentage points over the past sixty years, but the aggregate concentration has remained remarkably stable since 1958. Table 1 suggests that there is little cause for concern that the productive assets of this country are becoming increasingly concentrated in the hands of fewer and fewer firms.

Industry Concentration Ratios

Industry concentration ratios: A measure of the degree to which the largest firms in an industry account for total industry assets, sales, or some other factor.

An alternative method of looking at business structure is to calculate **concentration ratios** (*CR*) for various industries. Concentration ratios are determined by ranking firms within an industry from largest to smallest and then calculating the share of some aggregate factor such as sales, employment, or assets held by the largest four or eight firms. Sales is the most common factor used in these calculations.

Figured by this method, the concentration ratio will lie between zero and one hundred. If an industry is totally monopolized, one firm will have 100 percent of industry sales, or $CR = 100$. If an industry has several firms but the four largest have 50 percent of the market sales, then $CR = 50$. If a very large number of companies each have a very small market share, then CR will be close to zero, suggesting the existence of competition.

TABLE 1   **Trends in Aggregate Concentration in the Manufacturing Sector, 1925–1984**

To determine aggregate concentration, we measure the percentage of assets owned by the largest firms in the country. Since 1958, the percentage of assets held by the top one hundred and top two hundred firms in the U.S. manufacturing sector has remained fairly stable. (Data series altered after 1984.)

Year	Percentage of Assets Held by the Largest Firms	
	100 Largest	200 Largest
1925	34.5%	—
1929	38.2	45.8%
1935	40.8	47.7
1939	41.9	48.7
1948	38.6	46.3
1950	38.4	46.1
1958	46.0	55.2
1963	45.7	55.5
1967	47.6	58.7
1972	45.3	56.5
1974	46.1	57.6
1975	46.0	57.3
1976	46.1	57.3
1977	45.6	56.6
1978	45.5	58.3
1979	46.1	59.0
1980	46.7	59.7
1981	46.8	60.0
1982	47.7	60.8
1983	48.3	60.8
1984	48.9	60.7

Sources: Richard Duke, "Trends in Aggregate Concentration," *FTC Working Paper No. 61* (June 1982), p. 18; *Statistical Abstract of the United States* (Washington, D.C.: U.S. Government Printing Office, 1986), p. 524.

Table 2 displays four-firm and eight-firm concentration ratios for a small sample of manufacturing industries. A brief look at the concentration ratio data indicates that quite a bit of variation in business structure was hidden within the aggregate concentration percentages shown in Table 1. Some industries are very highly concentrated. In 1982, for example, the top eight producers of flat glass accounted for 97 percent of industry shipments, indicating that the remaining flat-glass manufacturers were very small businesses indeed. In contrast, the eight largest firms supplying ready-mix concrete had only a 9 percent share of total sales in 1982, suggesting that this industry is made up of a large number of relatively small companies.

Table 2 also reveals trends in concentration. Concentration ratios that have risen over the years indicate that the leading firms have grown relative to other industry members, either by internal expansion, merger, or decreases in the number of other firms. Declining concentration ratios imply that more and more competitors have made successful inroads into the industry and thereby reduced the dominance by leading firms. While examples of each pattern appear in the table, concentration ratios remain fairly stable in general.

TABLE 2 — Selected Concentration Ratios in Manufacturing

Concentration ratios measure the share of sales held by the largest four or eight firms in an industry. The data shown here represent a selected group of manufacturing industries for the years 1963, 1977, and 1982. In some industries—such as men's and boys' suits—the concentration ratio increased through the years, suggesting that the largest firms obtained a larger share of total industry output. In some cases—such as petroleum refining—the ratio fell, suggesting a more competitive situation.

| | Concentration Ratios | | | | | |
| | 1963 | | 1977 | | 1982 | |
	Four-Firm	Eight-Firm	Four-Firm	Eight-Firm	Four-Firm	Eight-Firm
Meat packing	31	42	19	37	29	43
Fluid milk	23	30	18	28	16	27
Cereal breakfast foods	86	96	89	98	86	97
Distilled liquor	58	74	52	71	46	68
Roasted coffee	52	68	61	73	65	76
Cigarettes	80	100	–	–	–	–
Men's and boys' suits and coats	14	23	21	32	25	37
Women's and misses' dresses	6	9	8	12	6	10
Logging camps and contractors	11	19	29	36	30	37
Mobile homes	–	–	24	37	24	39
Pulp mills	48	72	48	76	45	70
Book publishing	20	33	17	30	17	30
Pharmaceutical preparations	22	38	24	43	26	42
Petroleum refining	34	56	30	53	28	48
Flat glass	94	99+	90	99	85	97
Ready-mix concrete	4	7	5	8	6	9
Blast furnaces and steel mills	48	67	45	65	42	64
Metal cans	74	85	59	74	50	68
Electric lamps	92	96	90	95	91	96
Radio and TV receiving sets	41	62	51	65	49	70
Motor vehicles, car bodies	–	–	93	99	92	97
Jewelry, precious metal	26	33	18	26	16	22
Pens and mechanical pencils	48	60	50	64	41	62

Sources: U.S. Department of Commerce, Bureau of the Census, *Census of Manufactures* (Washington, D.C.: U.S. Government Printing Office, 1977); U.S. Department of Commerce, Bureau of the Census, *Concentration Ratios in Manufacturing* (Washington, D.C.: U.S. Government Printing Office, 1982).

One problem with using concentration ratios to determine the degree of competition in an industry is that the data can obscure quite vigorous competition. Since the ratios do not identify individual firms, the concentration ratio can remain stable over time even though the leading firms rapidly turn over. For example, if the first and fourth companies in meat packing change places, the four-firm concentration ratio would remain unchanged. Additionally, concentration ratios usually ignore the impact of foreign firms that sell goods and services in a country on that country's industry structure. Concentration ratios calculated solely from the assets or sales of domestic firms will understate the degree of competition in an industry when domestic firms in the industry face stiff foreign competition. This understatement is clearest for such product categories as motor vehicles or radios and TVs (see Table 2).

A further difficulty with the concentration ratios in Table 2 is that they are based on the Commerce Department's Standard Industrial Classification (SIC) groups. The SIC codes group firms that produce similar products, but

FOCUS Merger Guidelines

The merger guidelines issued by the Department of Justice in 1982 list conditions under which the department's Antitrust Division will "more often than not" challenge a proposed merger or acquisition. The conditions, which focus on the pre- and post-merger concentration levels, are expressed in terms of the Herfindahl index.

In brief, the Herfindahl index seeks to summarize in one number the extent to which a market is "concentrated" or dominated by a few firms. The index is calculated by squaring and then summing the individual market shares of all firms in the market. That is,

$$H = s_1^2 + s_2^2 + \ldots + s_n^2,$$

where, for example, s_1 is firm 1's percentage market share (usually its percentage of industry sales) and there are n firms in the market.

H will always be between zero and 10,000. If the industry is monopolized, one firm will have 100 percent of the market, so $H = 100^2 = 10,000$. In contrast, if each of a very large number of firms has a very small market share, H will be close to zero.

The advantage of the Herfindahl index over the more traditional four- and eight-firm concentration ratios is that it gives information about the dispersion of firm size within a market. The Herfindahl index does this by giving greater weight to large market shares than to small rather than treating all market shares equally. A disadvantage of the Herfindahl index is that its calculation requires the gathering of information on the market shares of every firm in the industry.

The 1982 Justice Department merger guidelines label a market as concentrated if H is equal to 1800 or more. (This situation would occur, for instance, if four firms in an industry accounted for approximately 50 percent of sales.) In such cases a merger that causes H to increase by 100 will gen-

erally be challenged by the Antitrust Division. In unconcentrated markets (where H is 1000 or less), mergers leading to a change in H of 200 or more will usually trigger antitrust action.

Suppose that an industry is made up of three firms of equal size. The Herfindahl index would work out to

$$H = 33^2 + 33^2 + 33^2 = 3267.$$

A merger between any two of the firms would raise H by 1178.

$$H = 66^2 + 33^2 = 5445$$

Since the industry was already concentrated by Justice Department standards, this merger would undoubtedly draw legal action.

In contrast, suppose that one firm accounts for 25 percent of sales in an industry and that one hundred other sellers each have a 0.75 percent market share.

$$H = 25^2 + 0.75^2 + 0.75^2 + \ldots + 0.75^2$$
$$= 683.25$$

If the large firm merges with one of the smaller firms, H rises accordingly.

$$H = 25.75^2 + 0.75^2 + 0.75^2 + 0.75^2 + \ldots + 0.75^2$$
$$= 719.56$$

This merger would generally go unchallenged.

Note that both the Herfindahl index and the merger guidelines are based on the assumption that firm size is an indication of market power. That is, concentration is considered bad because markets dominated by one or a few firms are thought to exhibit prices and profits exceeding the competitive level. Of course, firms can be large because they are efficient and serve consumers well. Thus, one should look beyond simple concentration levels before concluding that antitrust action is warranted.

these codes do not account for substitutability by buyers. For example, plastic panes may frequently be substituted for flat glass, but the SIC codes compare glass manufacturers only with other glass manufacturers. Thus, the concentration ratios do not show the competition among groups that results from actual market structures. Moreover, the SIC categories include sales data for the entire nation and therefore do not give information about concentration levels in different geographic regions. The four- and eight-firm concentration ratios were replaced after 1982 by the Herfindahl index, described in Focus, "Merger Guidelines," but the Herfindahl index is subject to similar problems.

Determinants of the Number of Firms

Why are there so few firms, sometimes only one, in some industries, while other industries have several hundred? The answer lies in the relation between the industry demand and firms' average cost of production.

For simplicity's sake, consider a hypothetical industry in which all firms have identical products and costs of production. Let the curve $LRAC_1$ in Figure 1 represent any one firm's average costs. The output that minimizes average long-run costs, q_1, is the equilibrium output for each firm. In other words, the optimal size for the individual firm in the long run is the output level that allows the lowest possible per unit cost of production. On an industry-wide level, D represents the entire demand in the industry. The amount demanded in the industry at price P_1 is Q_1. The equilibrium number of firms in the industry is therefore Q_1 divided by q_1. If the optimal output for each firm is 100 units and the amount demanded in the market is 10,000 units, then the optimal number of firms for efficient use of resources is 100.

The greater the industry demand relative to the firm's output at minimum average cost, the greater the number of firms will be. Highly concentrated industries result from industry demand that is insufficient to support a large number of firms of optimal size. In fact, a **natural monopoly** exists when industry demand is just great enough relative to a firm's average cost to support one firm.

Figure 2 shows two types of natural monopolies. In Figure 2a, a natural monopoly develops because demand is insufficient to support more than one firm; the monopolies held by small-town newspapers provide a familiar example. Demand for local news in small towns often is not great enough to support more than one newspaper. In such a case, D_A represents the industry

Natural monopoly:
A combination of market demand and cost conditions that results in only one firm being able to produce output in an industry profitably; occurs when decreasing long-run average costs exist up to the level of total industry demand.

FIGURE 1

The equilibrium number of firms is determined by the magnitude of industry demand relative to the firm's average cost of production. The long-run average cost curve for one representative firm is given as $LRAC_1$. The minimum average cost determines the optimal rate of output and plant size for each firm. The total number of firms is equal to the output per firm, q_1, divided into the amount demanded in the industry, Q_1, at the price that is equal to minimum average cost. If $q_1 = 100$ and $Q_1 = 10,000$, then the equilibrium number of firms in this industry would be 100.

Determination of the Number of Firms in an Industry

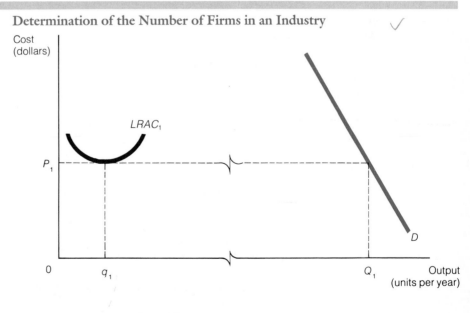

FIGURE 2   Demand-Cost Relations of Natural Monopolies

When industry demand is not great enough to support more than one firm of optimal size, then a natural monopoly results. (a) Only one firm can survive because half of industry demand, MR_A, the demand that each firm faces when there are two firms in the industry, does not rise above the firms' average cost. (b) A single firm survives because one large firm, through economies of scale, can achieve lower average cost than two smaller firms.

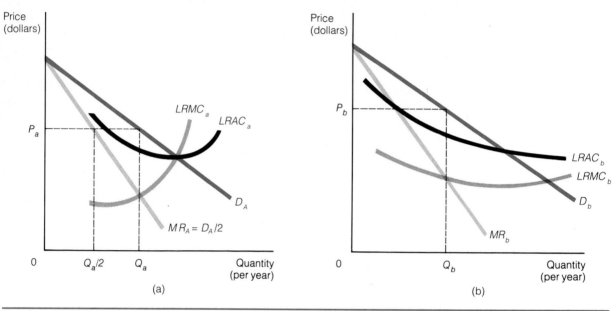

(a)

(b)

demand—the demand for local news in the small town; Q_a represents the quantity of newspapers demanded at price P_a—a quantity that can be produced profitably by only one firm. $LRAC_a$ and $LRMC_a$ represent this newspaper firm's long-run average and marginal costs. In this industry, only one firm can survive because industry demand is not great enough to support two firms. If another firm enters the market, industry sales will be divided by two. For example, at P_a the total industry output demanded is still Q_a, and thus each firm's sales are $Q_a/2$. Indeed, the marginal revenue curve represents each firm's demand curve when the industry demand is shared by the two firms. Since the individual firm's demand curve lies below $LRAC_a$ at all levels of output, two local newspapers cannot profit and survive; only one firm can exist under these market conditions.

Figure 2b demonstrates a natural monopoly created by economies of scale. A single cable television company might dominate the market in a given area because it can supply the entire existing demand among customers at lower cost than two or more smaller firms. One large cable TV company serving many customers can therefore offer lower commercial prices than several firms serving fewer customers. The key feature of the model shown in Figure 2b is that the industry demand intersects the average cost curve at a point where average costs are still declining owing to economies of scale. Even though two firms could survive in this industry because their demand curves lie above $LRAC_b$ at some points, we expect that price competition would eliminate one firm. The reason is that a single firm with a larger output can produce the entire industry output at a lower cost than two smaller firms. The existence of economies of scale yields a cost advantage for a single large firm.

Comparing the industry demand to the firm's average cost is a useful approximation of the number of firms that can exist in an industry. This method does have some limitations, however, for its assumptions may be unrealistic. For one thing, not all firms have identical costs. Firms in different parts of the country are confronted with different input prices and different economic environments. Consequently, the optimal size of the firm varies from one location to another, and the number of firms becomes difficult to predict. The assumption of identical products may also be false. If firms in an industry produce products that are not perfect substitutes for one another, then industry demand and product price will be difficult to determine.

Changes in the Number of Firms

Since the number of firms in an industry is determined by the magnitude of industry demand relative to each firm's long-run average cost, any change in demand or cost can lead to a change in the equilibrium number of firms. If the demand in a particular industry increases, then we expect to see more firms enter the industry. As demand for computers has soared, IBM's previous dominance of the computer market has decreased. On the other hand, if the price of inputs changes such that the long-run average cost curve shifts to the right, then the optimal plant size increases. Such a shift will lead to a decrease in the number of firms. Changes in technology can also affect the optimal plant size and thus the number of firms. Such changes have led to a decrease in the number of automobile manufacturers in the United States.

Since the economy is dynamic, we expect fairly frequent changes in production cost and industry demand. The number of firms in various industries will therefore change through time. New firms enter and old ones go out of business. The concentration ratio of an industry may thus change because of events external to the firms.

Figure 3 gives an indication of the turnover rate in U.S. markets between 1929 and 1987. The turnover rate is the rate at which new businesses open and older ones that are failing close their doors. The first point to note in Figure 3 is that many new enterprises are formed and quite a few fail in any given year. In 1987, for example, more than 685,000 new firms were incorporated, and over 60,000 businesses went bankrupt. (It should be noted that the business failure data in Figure 3 does not include failures of firms in the service industries, such as banks, real estate and insurance firms, travel agencies, and so on, until 1985. Thus, the 1985 and 1987 data are not strictly comparable with data from previous years.) The business failure rate during the Great Depression was very high. There were only one-half the number of business failures in 1980 that there were in 1929, and the rate of business failure in 1980 was about one-third of what it was in 1929. Though the failure rate has declined since 1929, the business failure rate is still significant. Starting a new business continues to be a risky proposition. However, the increase in new business formations indicates that there seems to be no shortage of entrepreneurs willing to take those risks in the hopes of succeeding.

FIGURE 3

During the Great Depression, the business failure rate was quite high. The chances for survival have generally improved since that time, yet business formation remains risky. The number of new incorporations has increased steadily since 1950, indicating that an increasing number of individuals are willing to take the risk.

Source: Council of Economic Advisers, *Economic Report of the President* (Washington, D.C.: U.S. Government Printing Office, 1989), p. 417.

Note: Prior to 1985, data for number of business failures exclude failures of banks, railroads, real estate, insurance, financial, and other service-oriented firms. Failure rate in Figure 3b is per 10,000 listed enterprises.

Business Formation and Business Failures, 1929–1987

(a) Number of business failures

(b) Business failure rate

(c) New business incorporations

MONOPOLY PROFIT SEEKING

Entrepreneurs organize and operate businesses in an effort to obtain profits. The profit motivation is socially desirable, for businesses earn profits by producing products that are most highly valued by society while simultaneously using the fewest and least expensive resources. However, the level of profits is limited in purely competitive industries. When new firms are able to enter profitable industries and act independently in seeking profits, economic profits are forced to zero. On the other hand, firms that are natural monopolies may enjoy positive economic profits—a greater than normal return on their investments. More important, from the perspective of resource allocation, the existence of monopoly means that society's resources are misallocated. Too little of the good is produced, as evidenced by price being greater than the marginal cost of producing the good.

Even though profits in competitive industries are no greater than normal, there is a potential for obtaining greater profits by decreasing the amount of competition. If all the firms in a competitive industry could agree not to compete and simultaneously could prevent new firms from entering the market, monopoly-level profits could be obtained.

As explained in Chapter 10, converting a constant-cost competitive industry into a monopoly results in loss of part of the consumer surplus. Consumer surplus is the amount that consumers would be willing to pay for a good above the price actually charged for it. This difference translates into real income to consumers. In Figure 4, a competitive market reaches equilibrium price and quantity for a certain good—perhaps lime juice—at price P_c and quantity Q_c, with D and S indicating industry-wide demand and supply conditions. At the competitive price and quantity, consumers enjoy a surplus equal to FCP_c, the area beneath the demand curve but above the supply curve.

If competition is eliminated in the lime juice industry, firms with monopoly power can create contrived scarcity by restricting output to Q_m and raising the price of lime juice to P_m. At this level, consumer surplus shrinks to the area FAP_m, shifting the profits represented by P_mABP_c to the lime juice monopolist. The monopoly profits of the lime juice producer, gained at the expense of consumers, do not constitute a welfare loss to society because the profits are merely a transfer of equal value from consumers to the lime juice producer. The area ACB, however, is lost to everyone. It is neither transferred to the monopolist in the form of profits nor retained by consumers as consumer surplus. This area is treated by economists as a **welfare loss due to monopoly** to society—the cost to society of having a monopolist produce a product rather than having the good supplied by a competitive industry.

To capture monopoly profits, firms may engage in a variety of activities designed to decrease competition. As described below, anticompetitive activities include the formation of cartels, mergers, trusts, collusive agreements, and government franchises.

Welfare loss due to monopoly:
The consumers' surplus lost but not transferred to the monopolist when a competitive industry is monopolized.

Cartels

Cartels represent an alliance among producers of a good. The firms agree not to engage in price competition and agree to restrict output in order to extract monopoly profits. To be successful, a cartel must prevent member firms from

FIGURE 4

With pure competition, the demand *D* and supply *S* intersect at *C* and the price and quantity at P_c and Q_c. The consumer surplus is FCP_c. If this industry is monopolized, then the profit-maximizing price and quantity are P_m and Q_m. Monopoly profits are the area P_mABP_c, and consumer surplus is decreased to area FAP_m. The welfare loss is the lost consumer surplus (*ACB*) that is not transferred to the monopoly in the form of profits; it is simply lost to the economy as a whole.

Welfare Loss Resulting from Monopoly

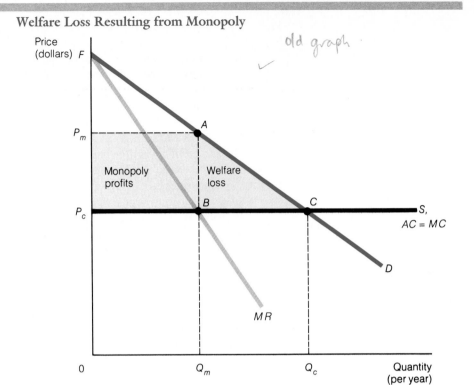

charging a price below the monopoly price. The cartel must also be able to prevent entry of new firms—otherwise, cartel profits are dissipated by the entry of competitive firms.

OPEC (Organization of Petroleum Exporting Countries) was a fairly successful cartel throughout most of the 1970s. OPEC firms are prevented from cheating on the cartel by the governments of the countries in the organization. New firms are prevented from entering by the endowments of nature—new firms cannot produce oil unless they acquire an oil deposit. These features explain the longevity of OPEC. Most cartels that are not able to police cheating and limit entry are short-lived.

The endowments of nature are unknown until exploration becomes profitable. Indeed, OPEC's initial success made exploration and development profitable to firms that formerly would not have entered the oil business. Consider the new production from the North Sea, Mexico, China, and the North Slope of Alaska. OPEC is now much weaker, in part as a result of the entry of these new "firms."

Trusts

Trust:
An institution that organizes firms in the same industry in an effort to increase profits by decreasing competition.

In the late 1800s, during the Industrial Revolution, the optimal size of firms—the size allowing the lowest possible per unit cost of production—began to increase. This trend lowered the number of firms in some industries and increased concentration ratios. Firms in some industries joined holding companies called **trusts** that monitored the activities of members. For example,

John D. Rockefeller capped his concentration of power in the oil-refining industry by forming the Standard Oil Trust, an organization to which stockholders of almost all oil-refining companies turned over controlling amounts of their stock in return for dividend-paying trust certificates. Such unifying organizations allowed firms to act as a cartel. Antitrust legislation has since been enacted to prevent most such organizations.

Collusion

Collusion:
An explicit or implicit agreement among firms in an industry not to engage in competitive behavior.

When there are very few firms in an industry but antitrust laws prevent formal organization, businesses sometimes engage in informal agreements to restrict output or raise prices, a form of **collusion.** Price competition can be diminished through explicit or implicit agreements. Firms may simply agree to charge a monopoly price and restrict output. The success of simple collusion is particularly rare since price cheaters and new entrants cannot be controlled informally.

Mergers

Merger:
The combining of the ownership of two firms' assets, which results in a single firm.

One way that concentration ratios may rise is through **mergers.** If there are only a few firms in an industry, the combination of two or more firms into one may decrease the degree of competition. However, the types of mergers vary and thus their effect in the market varies. There are three basic types of mergers: horizontal, vertical, and conglomerate. Each type is distinguished by the relation between the products produced by the merging firms.

A horizontal merger occurs when the merger partners produce the same product. Examples include mergers between two beer producers, two manufacturers of glass containers, two retail grocery stores, and so forth. Horizontal mergers usually decrease competition because they have the direct effect of raising industry concentration ratios and moving the affected market closer to monopoly.

AT&T → McCaw

Mergers are characterized as vertical if the product of one firm serves as an input for the other firm—that is, if the merging companies are at different stages of a production process. A vertical merger would occur if a company producing crude oil acquired a petroleum refinery, if a steel producer purchased iron ore deposits, or if an automobile manufacturer acquired a string of retail car dealerships. Vertical mergers do not raise industry concentration levels and are usually motivated by the prospect of lower costs. Accordingly, vertical mergers do not normally decrease competition.

Conglomerate mergers occur when the products of the firms are unrelated—when an insurance company buys a firm that produces bread or when a cigarette producer merges with a soft drink company. The usual explanation for such mergers is that they are motivated by a desire to spread the risks associated with economic ups and downs across products. However, spreading risks can be accomplished much more simply by, for example, purchasing shares of a variety of businesses. Rather, conglomerate mergers can better be explained by the desire to diffuse managerial expertise across firms. That is, if an efficient corporate management team believes that its executive talents can be profitably applied to some other firm, it will have an incentive to acquire another company regardless of the product produced by the other firm. Since conglomerate mergers do not raise industry concentration levels, they do not generally decrease competition.

Government-Managed Cartels

Given the problems associated with organizing and policing a cartel in an industry with a large number of firms, it is not surprising that firms turn to the power of government when seeking profits. Sometimes firms are able to entice the government to enforce a higher-than-competitive price or a lower-than-competitive output or to prevent new firms from entering their otherwise competitive industry. Long before OPEC, for example, the Texas Railroad Commission limited the rate at which oil could be pumped from wells in Texas. This action, ostensibly undertaken to conserve oil, bolstered price above the competitive level.

NEW VIEWS OF INDUSTRIAL ORGANIZATION

Traditionally, private cartels, trusts, mergers and collusive behavior, and government-managed cartels have been linked to monopoly power. The number and size of firms were the critical elements in determining the extent of that power over markets and consumers. In the last two decades major developments have boldly challenged these ideas. Widely accepted propositions about the nature and function of firms and business operations have been reconsidered and, in some cases, significantly revised.

Structure-conduct-performance:
A theory of industrial organization that emphasizes the importance of structural elements such as the number of firms in determining the competitive conduct and performance of the industry.

The organizing principle of industrial organization theory from World War II to about 1970 was **structure-conduct-performance.** Among other things, *structure* referred to characteristics of an industry's products, number of consumers of those products, and number of firms in the industry. An industry's structural elements were determined by such easily observable "measures" of competition as concentration ratios. Backed by statistics, economists could turn to two sets of assumptions to predict the conduct and performance of firms within an industry. First, it was assumed that under less-than-perfect competition firms would tend to restrict entry in order to keep the number of competitors small; entry barriers were thought to include, but were not believed to be limited to, advertising, brand proliferation, and capital requirements. After barring entry, firms could engage in monopolistic pricing. This brings us to the second assumption: Efforts to ensure monopolistic pricing were believed certain to result in less-than-competitive prices and outputs.

Bigness Is Not Necessarily Badness

An alternative to the structure-conduct-performance approach to industrial organization theory has emerged recently. A number of prominent lawyers and economists have advanced the notion that a high degree of concentration within an industry may result from the relative efficiency of the largest firms. Firms often become large simply because they produce better goods at lower cost than do their competitors. Legal scholar and antitrust expert Robert Bork maintains, for example, that a single large firm can be efficient when it faces competition from only *one* other firm. Industries with only two firms tend to perform in ways similar to industries with *many* firms. In order to obtain this result, however, firms must not collude but must act as real competitors.

> If the leading firms in a concentrated industry are restricting their output in order to obtain prices above the competitive level, their efficiencies must be sufficiently superior to that of all actual and potential rivals to offset that behavior. Where this is not so, rivals would be enabled to expand their market shares because of the abnormally high prices and would thus deconcentrate the industry. Market rivalry thus automatically weighs the respective influences of efficiency and output restriction and arrives at the firm sizes and industry structures that serve consumers best.[1]

The new view of industrial organization also challenges the implication, usually drawn from the structure-conduct-performance theory, that monopoly itself is always and necessarily inefficient from the standpoint of society. The principal insight of the new view is that firms can achieve substantial market power—that is, relatively large size—because larger firms are sometimes able to enjoy significant efficiencies compared to smaller firms. Monopoly (that is, only one firm in a particular market) may conceivably result from one big firm facing lower costs than multiple smaller firms. Other things being equal, lower costs represent gains in efficiency.

Figure 5 illustrates the efficiency theory of monopoly. This view does not claim that efficiency losses due to monopoly do not occur, but rather that

FIGURE 5

AEB represents the welfare loss of monopoly. P_cBCMC_m represents the cost savings of the larger monopoly firm. Sometimes the increased efficiency of a large firm can offset any monopoly power that it possesses—that is, $AEB < P_cBCMC_m$.

Possible Efficiencies Under Monopoly

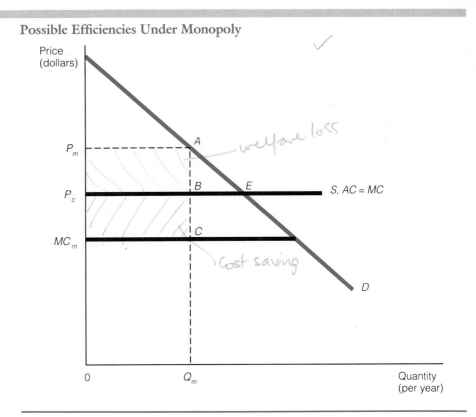

[1]Robert H. Bork, *The Antitrust Paradox: A Policy at War with Itself* (New York: Basic Books, 1978), p. 178.

social welfare does not necessarily go down simply because of monopoly waste. A countervailing "monopoly gain" may result from lower costs. In other words, the outcome of monopoly may be a *net* gain to society despite the usual monopoly welfare loss triangle. In effect, there is a welfare trade-off under monopoly, and the potential losses of welfare due to monopoly must be compared with the potential gains in welfare (the efficiency gains from large size). P_c represents both price and long-run marginal cost (MC) under competition. Transition to monopoly raises price to P_m. Simultaneously, the industry achieves real efficiency gains (for example, from greater economies of scale) along with the reduction in the number of firms in the industry. This new situation is shown by a new and lower long-run marginal cost curve, MC_m. If we assume that no resources are engaged in wasteful rent seeking, and treat P_mABP_c as a pure wealth transfer from consumers to the monopolist, the net efficiency result becomes ambiguous. (Equity is another matter altogether.) The triangle AEB (monopoly welfare loss) must be compared with the area of social gain from increased efficiency, P_cBCMC_m. The latter area represents the value of resources that have been freed up for other social uses. In other words, these resources are no longer required to produce the output of this industry and can be used elsewhere. The area of efficiency gain may be either larger than the triangle of monopoly welfare loss or just large enough to reduce substantially the net effect of the latter.[2] Again, however, treating the transfer of income from consumers to the monopolist, P_mABP_c, as ethically neutral is an assumption that many people would question.

2 Contestable Markets

Some contemporary economists argue that even where there is only *one* firm in a given industry, the firm may not behave as a monopolist. Under some conditions, single-firm industries will operate as if there were actually many firms in the industry. This is called the **contestable markets theory.** William J. Baumol, John C. Panzar, and Robert D. Willig have shown that firms in less-than-perfectly competitive markets may behave like perfectly competitive firms; that is, they will only earn normal rates of return on capital, and price will tend to equal marginal cost.[3] The only requirement is that entry and exit be "unimpeded," or "frictionless" and "costless." A market that meets these conditions is considered "perfectly contestable."

Figure 6 illustrates the basic idea. Here, the industry demand curve (D) intersects the long-run average cost curve ($LRAC$) at the minimum long-run average cost. According to the theory of contestable markets, this does not necessarily mean entry into this market is barred by economies of scale. Assuming low-cost entry and exit, the monopolist—that is, the firm currently operating in the one-firm industry—will not be able to raise price to P_1, because other firms could easily enter. These firms could set a price such as

Contestable markets theory:
A theory of industrial organization that suggests that where entry and exit are costless, a single supplier in an industry will produce the same price and output result as a competitive firm.

---

[2]Economist Howard P. Marvel shows that given reasonable assumptions about the elasticity of demand, relatively small percentage reductions in cost due to scale economies can offset the reductions in social welfare due to monopoly. See "Competition and Price Levels in the Retail Gasoline Market," *Review of Economics and Statistics* (May 1978), pp. 252–58.

[3]William J. Baumol, John C. Panzar, and Robert D. Willig, *Contestable Markets and the Theory of Industry Structure* (New York: Harcourt Brace Jovanovich, 1982).

FIGURE 6

In a contestable market, the incumbent supplier cannot raise price to P_1 without provoking the entry of a new supplier at a lower price. This threat disciplines price to remain at the competitive level of P_2.

Market Contestability

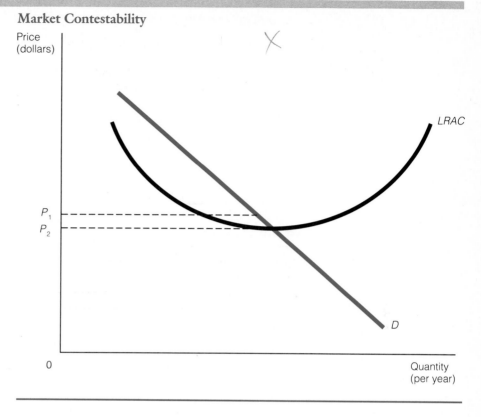

↑p ⇒ entry of new firms.

P_2, or slightly above P_2, and force the former monopolist to reduce price. Since exit from the industry is costless, the "entrant" can become an "exitor" by closing down operations and moving on as soon as the former monopolist lowers price to match the new entrant's price. This is called *hit-and-run* entry.

Thus, if a market is perfectly contestable—if entry and exit are free and costless, if the incumbent and potential entrants face identical cost functions, and so on—a perfectly competitive price might result even though the market is only occupied by a single firm. This is sometimes referred to as competition for the field: One firm serves the whole market and is disciplined to serve this market competitively by potential entrants. If entry is costless, even a hint of monopoly profit will induce entry and restore competitive conditions in the industry.

Nevertheless, defenders of contestable markets theory are willing to admit that, in general, "perfect contestability" is unrealistic. Note that this is not the same as saying that the model is irrelevant to real-world cases of apparent monopoly.

Perfect contestability is not likely to be satisfied exactly by any real market. Yet it does provide a standard against which actual markets can be compared, no matter if the relevant production techniques and market demands dictate production by a single giant firm or by a multitude of independent enterprises. . . . [T]here are objective structural conditions that can be examined to determine the relevance of contestability in practice. And where these conditions do not hold even approximately, actual industry configurations can, nevertheless, be usefully compared to those that would result if the markets were structurally contestable.[4]

Airline service between pairs of cities closely resembles the model of a perfectly contestable market. The markets for airline service between city pairs are "characterized both by easy entry and exit and significant economies of scale. Even if a route is flown by a single carrier, other carriers who have stations at both end-point cities can readily enter if monopoly profits become evident".[5] In the Economics in Action at the end of this chapter, we consider airline routes as contestable markets.

3 Vertical Restraints

Vertical restraints:
Agreements between manufacturers and retailers that restrict the marketing options of one or both parties.

Vertical restraints represent a particularly troublesome problem for industrial organization theorists attempting to analyze business behavior. **Vertical restraints** encompass a variety of agreements between manufacturers and wholesalers, manufacturers and retailers, or franchisers and franchisees that restrict the marketing options of one or both parties. Most often, the manufacturer—who markets nationally or internationally—will ask local retailers to agree to restrictive conditions in return for other advantages.

These restrictive conditions, or vertical restraints, exist in a number of ways in the real world. Are these practices designed to establish or extend monopoly power, or are they part of the competitive process? The courts have ruled both ways. Let's consider two examples—the use of exclusive territories and the imposition of resale price maintenance by manufacturers.

Exclusive territories:
Given geographic areas in which one retailer or wholesaler has the exclusive, manufacturer-granted right to sell or distribute the manufacturer's product.

At first glance, exclusive territories might seem to represent an obvious form of monopoly practice. **Exclusive territory** refers to a manufacturer's granting the exclusive right to sell its product to one particular wholesaler or retailer in a given area, thus eliminating competition among dealers for the product. The Miller Brewing Company grants wholesalers exclusive rights to distribute Miller products within given geographic regions; General Motors gives similar rights to retailers of Chevrolets and Cadillacs. Over the years, various court decisions—both those upholding and those overturning the use of exclusive territories—have been based on the premise that such arrangements automatically tend to reduce competition.

Resale price maintenance:
A stipulated minimum price for a product imposed on a retailer by a manufacturer.

Another hotly debated form of vertical restraint is **resale price maintenance** (RPM). In resale price maintenance, the manufacturer requires that retailers not sell the manufacturer's products below a stipulated minimum price. (After a retailer buys goods from the manufacturer, he or she resells them to consumers, hence the reference to "resale.") Traditionally, resale price maintenance was considered a form of price-fixing by the manufacturer, which restricted competition among dealers and harmed consumers.

Recent studies suggest that both exclusive territories and RPM may foster economic efficiency. Specifically, exclusive territory arrangements relieve manufacturers of the dual burden of having to produce advertising for multiple local markets and having to place advertising in local media. This responsibility shifts to local dealers, who can accomplish both jobs at lower cost.

---

[4]Baumol, Panzar, and Willig, *Contestable Markets,* pp. 35, 45.

[5]Elizabeth E. Bailey, Foreword to Baumol, Panzar, and Willig, *Contestable Markets,* p. xxi.

A local dealer is more likely to promote a national brand if the dealer has been granted an exclusive territory. Without exclusivity, each dealer would have an incentive to free ride on advertising investments made by other local dealers for the same product. This would result in a level of advertising less than that needed to maximize profits for the national manufacturer—possibly, in no advertising at all. Economic efficiency would suffer. Consumers would be harmed by too little advertising. Advertising is the primary means for providing consumers with information concerning both price and nonprice attributes of goods and services.

Industrial organization economists also emphasize the role of RPM in protecting manufacturers, retailers, and consumers from the effects of free riding.[6] In addition to advertising, other promotional investments can be made at less cost by local wholesalers or retailers than by the manufacturers who market nationally or internationally. Attractive showrooms, knowledge-able salespersons, delivery and repair services, and adequate stock of the product and spare parts are examples of such investments. However, customers are always free to visit full-service dealers, confer with their informed salespeople, inspect and try out their attractively displayed floor models—and then proceed somewhere else to make the purchase. By providing only minimal promotional services, hence reducing the cost of providing the manufactured good to buyers, the second store may be able to sell the product at a significantly lower price. Discount stores and mail-order outlets represent such low-overhead, low-service kinds of retail outlets. Salesclerks at low-overhead retailers may even advise customers to examine the product at a full-service outlet and return to the discount store to purchase it at a lower price. Such behavior is perfectly legal and represents the exercise of free choice on the part of customers.

This behavior presents a free-rider problem. If promotional services are not somehow "bundled" with the product itself, retailers will have an incentive to free ride on the promotional investments of their competitors. Eventually, in such a case, dealers' services will be eliminated. Dealers who continue to provide such services will be driven out of business, incurring higher costs and suffering losses while their nonservice competitors attract customers with lower prices. In requiring all dealers to sell the product at an identical price, resale price maintenance eliminates this form of free riding. Along the way, RPM may provide an increased incentive for dealers to provide high-quality service—as a form of nonprice competition for customers. Dealers will have an incentive to provide high-quality services because RPM makes *price* competition impossible. Nonprice competition brought about by RPM benefits consumers, retailers, and even the manufacturer—who is able to ensure the provision of a profit-maximizing level of promotional activity for his or her products.

Do vertical restraints such as exclusive territories and RPM contribute to overall economic efficiency and consumer welfare, or do they constitute means to monopoly power? The answer likely will depend upon the kind of

---

[6]For additional information on these views, see Lester G. Telser, "Why Should Manufac-turers Want Fair Trade?" *Journal of Law and Economics* (October 1960), pp. 86–105; Lawrence J. White, "Vertical Restraints in Antitrust Law: A Coherent Model," *Antitrust Bulletin* (Summer 1981), pp. 327–45; and, especially, Roger D. Blair and David L. Kaserman, *The Law and Economics of Vertical Integration and Control* (New York: Academic Press, 1983).

product or service that is restrained. The new industrial organization theory simply raises the possibility that consumers might actually benefit from business practices that in the past have been widely regarded as monopolistic and damaging to economic welfare.

Franchising

Franchising:
A form of vertical relationship in which, for a fee, a franchisee is granted the right to sell a good or service in a format designed and controlled by the franchiser.

Franchising is an increasingly popular form of vertical restraint, in some respects similar to the granting of exclusive territories. Traditional industrial organization theory holds that franchising creates local monopolies and reductions in consumer welfare. In the newer view, franchising is seen as a means of maintaining desirable levels of service and quality that are in the interests of both sellers and consumers.

What, exactly, is franchising? For a fee, a franchisee is granted the right to engage in selling or distributing goods or services under a market format designated by a franchiser (McDonald's, say, or Holiday Inn). This permits the franchisee to use the franchiser's trademark, name, and advertising. Basically, the franchisee obtains the opportunity to utilize proven methods of operation and the benefits of the franchiser's familiar, trusted advertising campaigns, brand names, or trademarks.

The franchisee enters business with the benefit of an established product or service name (Wendy's, Kentucky Fried Chicken). In addition to the existing reputation, the franchiser usually agrees to invest substantial resources in an ongoing effort to keep the public aware of the product. Technical and managerial assistance are often provided to the franchisee, including management training, selection of store layout and location, advice on the composition of stock, and so on. Quality-control standards are typically imposed and maintained by the franchiser. A consistent image is important for the franchisee to succeed; and a few poorly run stores can significantly harm the reputation of the franchiser and its product line.

Several advantages accrue to the franchiser from the arrangement. Perhaps the single biggest advantage is that franchising allows the entrepreneur's business to expand with a limited amount of capital. The franchisee bears much of the risk associated with starting a marketing operation in a location that the original entrepreneur is unfamiliar with. When a company expands without the use of franchising, the capacity of central management to control the growing business activity may be limited, resulting in higher costs. In contrast, expansion by means of a franchising network eliminates the need for central management of the expanded operations' activities. Finally, the franchisee is a residual claimant, who directly benefits from efficient business decisions by keeping the resulting profits. Granted, a company could expand and make the managers of its new branches residual claimants using profit-sharing schemes, but, in general, franchising secures these advantages at a lower cost.

Typically, the franchisee pays the franchiser fees or royalties. These are usually combined, and the exact combination is a compromise that helps to ensure compliance by both parties.[7] If successful marketing of a good or

---

[7]The principles by which the exact combination of fixed fee or royalty payment may be determined is discussed in Roger D. Blair and David L. Kaserman, "Optimal Franchising," *Southern Economic Journal* (October 1982), pp. 494–505.

service tends to depend heavily on the franchisee's personal initiative or effort, the franchiser will prefer to utilize a fixed fee. Under these conditions, a fixed fee gives the franchisee the most incentive to do a good job—the franchisee keeps all of the residual his or her effort generates, over and above the fee. Franchise arrangements in which the franchisee purchases technical assistance rather than a brand name or reputation from the franchiser usually utilize fixed fees. The more influence the brand name has on sales, the more likely it is that the franchiser will rely on a royalty payment instead of a fixed fee. As the royalty payment increases and the fixed fee decreases, the franchisee receives a smaller return from each additional sale and has less incentive to work towards additional sales. If the brand name is the main factor influencing sales, there is less danger of reducing total sales by lowering the percentage of revenues received by the franchisee. (The Focus, "Would You Sell a Used Car to This Franchisee?" illustrates the evolution of franchising in the automobile business.)

Overall, franchising allows for an efficient distribution of products and services on a larger scale than would be possible without this form of vertical integration. Contracts between franchiser and franchisee are negotiated and designed to the advantage of each party and, indirectly, to consumers. Franchising is a means of assuring consistent quality and service.

Advertising and the New Industrial Organization Theory

The economic analysis of advertising underwent enormous change throughout the 1960s and 1970s. Prior to this time a mostly critical view of advertising by economists found little of economic value in the practice, as you learned in Chapter 11. In general, the critics stressed the incompatibility of advertising with competition and, indeed, maintained that advertising contributes directly to monopoly power. The thinking was that high advertising expenditures might form entry barriers into markets. A number of challenges to this view of advertising have emerged within the context of advertising's effects on consumers and on the structure of industry.

Advertising and Consumer Information: A Modern Approach. The foundation of the modern defense of advertising is the analysis of the individual consumer. Some contemporary economists ask this question: By and large, do consumers make choices in their own self-interest? The assumption by contemporary economists that consumers do act rationally accounts for the differences between contemporary and traditional views on advertising and economic activity. According to modern theorists, advertising facilitates the consumer's search for lowest-cost goods and services. There are real costs consumers face in obtaining price and other relevant information, just as there are real costs consumers face in obtaining any other type of scarce economic resource. But because goods differ in price and quality, consumers can expect to benefit from the search for the best quality at the lowest price. These benefits of searching are real and measurable.

In deciding how much of a product to consume, the consumer will equate the marginal benefits to the marginal cost accrued from additional units of the search for a product in order to maximize the net benefit of the

FOCUS   Would You Sell a Used Car to This Franchisee?

Currently, there are about 21,000 automobile dealerships in the United States. Each of these is an independently franchised dealer. The manufacturer agrees to allow the dealer to sell its cars in some specific area in exchange for the performance, by the dealer, of various sales and service obligations. Among other things, the dealer agrees to provide certain repair services to customers and to advertise the manufacturer's cars in local markets. Today, car manufacturers nearly always sell their products through franchised dealers who are *not* employees of the manufacturers.

Between 1900 and 1920, the auto industry tried many different ways to distribute cars to consumers. Some manufacturers sold cars directly through factory stores; others tried mail order; some used consignment arrangements; some sold cars in retail stores like Sears; still others employed traveling sales representatives. By the 1950s, however, almost all cars were sold through franchised independent dealerships. Such a widespread voluntary change in the market for auto distribution implies that franchising was more efficient than other forms of distribution, but why was it more efficient?

Early cars were technologically simple, and the products of different manufacturers tended to be similar. Thus, consumers did not demand continuing service and support—the provision of spare parts, for example—from the automaker. When a person bought a car, it was not bundled with any future services of the manufacturer. Consumers sacrificed little or nothing by buying a car from a dealer who was entirely independent of the automaker. Eventually, vehicles became more sophisticated. Repairs and regular maintenance now required specialized skills, equipment, and facilities. The manufacturer could provide such services to the consumer at less cost if the consumer purchased a car from a dealer who represented the automaker.

The service problems associated with the increasing complexity of cars might have resulted in a distribution system in which manufacturers sold their own cars in "company stores." However, automobiles are highly durable goods. Because cars wear out slowly, buyers normally seek to replace them before they quit running. As the automobile market expanded, the number of used cars increased, and trade-ins for new cars became common. The acceptance of trade-in cars made each sales transaction unique; no two used cars of the same make and model would likely ever be in exactly the same condition. On-the-spot flexibility was necessary so that the best offer could be made in each customer negotiation.[a]

There may have been other reasons for the rise of franchising. For example, yearly model changes complicated inventory decisions, and increasing production lead times made forecasting future consumer demand more difficult. But the growth of the used car market, especially, pushed the industry toward decentralized decision making by dealers who were contractually bound to the manufacturer, but who were full residual claimants in their operations.

[a]See Thomas G. Marx, "The Development of the Franchise Distribution System in the U.S. Automobile Industry," *Business History Review* 59 (Autumn 1985), pp. 465–74.

---

activity. Consider Figure 7, in which the marginal cost of searching for lower prices is represented by the line labeled MC_s. (You might reread Focus, "The Economics of Information: Searching for the Best Deal," in Chapter 9.) Assume that the marginal cost of search is constant for any amount of search, with search time measured on the horizontal axis. (The additional cost of the tenth search, for example, is the same as the additional cost of the ninth search or the eleventh search.) Further, assume that an additional search takes 1 hour and that the marginal cost of the search equals the consumer's wage rate (the income given up in order to engage in the search).

The additional benefits obtained through more search decrease as the amount of search increases. Benefit to the consumer from search consists of finding a price lower than the lowest one currently known. Generally, there will be some "lowest" price in the market, reflecting the cost of producing the good. As the consumer searches more and more, the prices uncovered become closer to this minimum price, and the *reduction* in price (MB_s) the consumer can expect from one more search gets smaller and smaller. In other words, the marginal benefits decrease as the amount of search increases. In Figure 7, the

FIGURE 7

The rational consumer will
search for a lower price until
the marginal cost of search
equals the marginal benefit, or
$MC_s = MB_s$.

The Cost and Benefits of Product Search

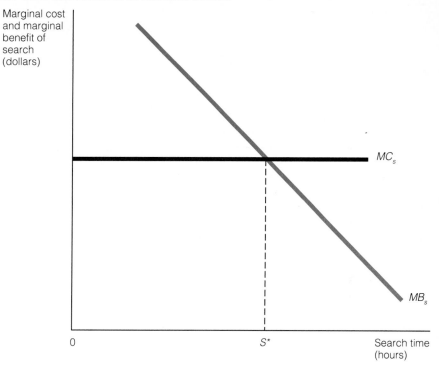

"optimal" amount of search for this consumer is shown as S^*. Search time
greater than S^* involves additional costs—with resultant welfare losses to the
consumer. Additional search simply would not be "worth it." For search time
less than S^*, additional benefits of more search are greater than the additional
costs, which would "pay" the consumer to search more. Thus, an S^* search
would maximize the consumer's economic welfare.

Where does advertising fit into all of this? The consumer has two methods of acquiring information about prices—through search and through advertising. Figure 8 helps explain how price advertising affects consumer
search. Suppose MC_s for this consumer is $5: An additional search (1 hour)
involves giving up $5 of income. Let MB_s represent the marginal benefit to
search assuming that the consumer knows nothing about existing prices. The
optimal amount of search time for this consumer, then, is $MC_s = MB_s$.

Alternatively, suppose that through newspaper advertising the consumer
already knows some of the prices charged by some sellers. Knowing some
prices, the consumer cannot expect to find price differentials as large through
search as in the first case. Therefore, the additional benefit to any given amount
of search (in terms of finding price reductions) is less when the consumer has
some price information. Marginal benefits to search in this case are depicted
in Figure 8 as MB_s'. The shift in the marginal benefits to search curve reflects
the fact that for any given amount of search time, additional benefits to search
are less if consumers have some information ahead of time. Advertising *reduces*
the amount of time consumers spend searching for lower prices. If consumers
spend less time searching for lower prices, they necessarily have more time left
over to devote to activities such as earning income or enjoying leisure.

FIGURE 8

Advertising affects the rational consumer's search process. It provides low-cost information about comparative prices so that less search time is required ($S < S^*$).

Advertising and Search Time

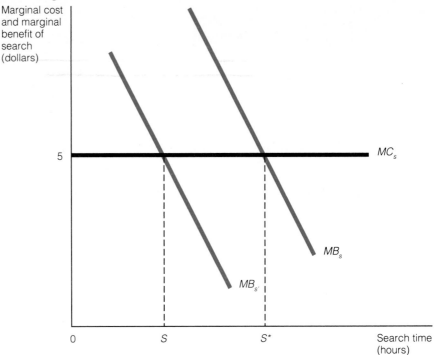

The number of dollars that consumers are willing to pay for a good after searching for the optimal price, or the money price, constitutes one part of the consumer's sacrifice in obtaining the good. For most purchases, however, there is a second sacrifice. In the example depicted in Figure 8, a consumer with a $5 per hour time cost searches 7 hours to find an optimal money price of a good, say, $200. The $200 money price *plus* the $35 ($5 per hour times 7 hours of searching) in search costs, or $235, represents the *full price* of the good purchased. Full price is the total value of resources sacrificed by a consumer—money price plus time costs—associated with the purchase of one unit of a good or service.

Full price—at least the full price consumers expect to pay—is the relevant variable upon which consumers base purchase decisions. Money price may be relatively more important than time costs in some cases, but this does not mean that full price is not the correct economic measure of resources sacrificed for a good or service.

Advertising has the general effect of lowering prices in the marketplace. Certain kinds of advertising might lower both money price and time costs, while other kinds might reduce only one measure of cost. Either way, the full price faced by consumers falls.

Advertising and Competition. Advertising has no place in the model of perfect competition introduced in Chapter 9. This traditional view does not prove, however, that advertising indicates or supports monopolistic forms of market structure, as some critics have suggested. When market functioning is viewed as a process, advertising is seen to promote competition, to be an essential aspect of the competitive process. Viewed as part of a process, advertising may be more logically consistent with competition than with monopoly or oligopoly.

Traditional criticism of advertising begins and ends with this straightforward proposition: Advertising is a barrier to entry into industries and, as such, contributes to monopoly power. This notion views the consumer as being manipulated by advertising in a manner that may not be beneficial. The assertion that a firm can use advertising to attach customers more firmly to itself evolved into the notion that advertising produces a type of "consumer inertia." This notion raises the prospect of a group of consumers unresponsive enough to advertisements for other firms that new firms are effectively prevented from entering a given market. In the view of contemporary industrial organization economists, traditional analysis begs an essential question: Why would consumers become attached to one firm's product or service through advertising but be impervious to advertising of new firms in an industry? The notions of consumer inertia and attachment are logically inconsistent.

Certain advantages are likely to accrue to the first firm in any market—with or without advertising. However, consider a market in which the pioneering firm has advertised to provide consumers with information about its product. Initially, consumers are induced to purchase the product by the informational content of the firm's advertising. This provides the first firm with a large market share, sales, and perhaps profits. Through the informative advertising and their purchases, consumers become knowledgeable about the good. The advertising of firms trying to enter this market would have to induce consumers to switch from the established product to one they know little about. Potential entrants would almost certainly find their costs of entering and staying in the market to be higher than the pioneer's.

Whether advertising produces an entry barrier or a higher cost of entry to potential entrants seems to depend largely on how one views consumers' responses to advertising. Traditional industrial organization theory treats the consumer as something of a helpless victim with regard to advertising. Newer views allow for the possibility that consumers may *choose* to ignore some advertising, including the initial advertising efforts of potential entrants. It may take time for a new firm to discover profit opportunities, to build the best size of plant, to organize efficiently, and to bear all the start-up costs of a business, including advertising. Modern views of industrial organization stress that it is misleading to blindly label these problems as "entry barriers"—they do not necessarily bar entry of capable, efficient firms from an industry. At base, advertising may provide a means *for* efficient entry into industries, although economists continue to debate the matter.

The Role of International Competition

An essential aspect of competition in the modern American economy is the presence of sellers from abroad competing for U.S. sales. Global competition is stiff, and it assumes various forms. Japanese and Canadian imports compete with American industries in such markets as computer components and agricultural products. Many foreign firms even institute production facilities in the United States. All of the major Japanese automobile manufacturers have built extensive production facilities in the United States; Honda is one of the leading automobile producers in the country. Other foreign auto firms ship their products into the United States and compete for sales with local auto dealer- and distributorships. There are various points of view concerning the challenge to the American economy that foreign competition offers. In the context of industrial organization in U.S. markets, however, foreign competitors play a vital role. Free international trade can be seen as a powerful substitute for domestic antitrust policies. Foreign entry, actual or potential, disciplines domestic firms, who would otherwise monopolize industries and raise prices. This discipline is a basic function of foreign competition; it produces a higher degree of competition at home. Remember: Competition serves the general interest of consumers and society at large.

Conclusion

Sometimes, size and concentration among sellers leads to poor performance and conduct in an industry. Modern industrial organization theory suggests that size and high concentration might also promote efficiencies and business practices such as vertical restraints and advertising that may benefit society. We do not completely understand the actual operation of firms and industries. In the past, economists tended to label business practices that they did not completely understand "monopolistic." As the discussion of vertical restraints illustrates, business practices that appear monopolistic in design often can justifiably be called competitive in the complex setting of an actual market. If nothing else, our examination of modern industrial organization theory should caution you against leaping to conclusions about monopoly power. Careful study is required to assess the degree of competitiveness of any given industry.

SUMMARY

1. Aggregate concentration ratios have not increased significantly in the past several decades. This suggests that big businesses have not been gaining greater control over the nation's productive assets. Industry concentration ratios change through time because the optimal number of firms changes as demand and cost conditions change.
2. The number of firms in an industry is determined by the number of firms of optimal size that industry demand is able to support. A natural monopoly exists when industry demand is sufficient to support only one firm of optimal size in an industry.
3. Monopoly is costly to society. This cost is called the welfare loss due to monopoly power. According to new industrial organization theory, this loss may be tempered by cost-saving efficiencies possible with monopoly.
4. Firms seek to increase profits by increasing their respective shares of industry demand, by decreasing production costs, and by decreasing the number of competitors. They may decrease competition by creating cartels, trusts, or mergers; by collusion; and by government grants of monopoly power.
5. Industrial organization theory uses microeconomics to study actual firms and industries. Traditional industrial organization theory follows a structure-conduct-performance approach that stresses the importance of industry structure, such as the concentration of sellers, in determining industry conduct and performance.
6. In recent years, the theory of industrial organization has shifted away from the structure-conduct-performance approach. Some economists now argue that large firms bring to the economy efficiency gains that offset other negative effects of large firms.
7. Other economists have developed a theory of contestable markets. This theory emphasizes that if entry and exit in an industry are costless, competitive

results can be obtained with a single supplier of industry output. Such a theory has been applied to the competition for airline routes.

8. Recent industrial organization theory has focused on the role of vertical restraints in promoting efficient sales by manufacturers and retailers. Two of the most commonly analyzed vertical restraints are exclusive territories and resale price maintenance.

9. Franchising is another form of vertical restraint. Franchising is a way to achieve efficient distribution of certain products on a larger scale. The contract between franchiser and franchisee can be structured to emphasize effective sales by local franchisees.

10. The modern economic theory of advertising emphasizes the competitive impact of advertising. Rather than erecting a barrier to entry, advertising is seen as lowering the full price (search costs plus list price) of advertised goods for rational consumers.

KEY TERMS

aggregate concentration
industry concentration ratios
natural monopoly
welfare loss due to monopoly
trust

collusion
merger
structure-conduct-performance
contestable markets theory
vertical restraints

exclusive territories
resale price maintenance
franchising

QUESTIONS FOR REVIEW AND DISCUSSION

1. Suppose that the output of an entire industry is produced by one firm and that there are no barriers to entry or exit. Should the antitrust authorities be concerned about this industry?

2. What is the Herfindahl index of concentration? How is it used by government to screen mergers?

3. Do a few large firms control all the wealth in the economy? Does the composition of the nation's largest firms change or does it remain constant over time?

4. What is a conglomerate merger? What is the rationale for it?

5. Suppose that a merger reduces the costs and increases the market power of two firms. Can you show this shift graphically? How should antitrust officials decide such a case?

6. Can public policy change an industry characterized as a natural monopoly into a competitive industry that results in competitive equilibrium?

7. Is there a competitive justification for exclusive territories for automobile distributorships?

8. How would you predict whether a franchisee would pay a lump-sum fee for franchise rights or be charged a royalty rate over time?

9. Is advertising a barrier to entry or a means of entry? Discuss.

ECONOMICS IN ACTION
Airline Routes as Contestable Markets

How has the theory of contestable markets stood up to tests using evidence from the real world? For about a decade, researchers have been attempting to arrive at a definitive answer to this question. Consider the implications of contestable markets theory for government policy. If economists conclude that contestable markets theory is valid, government regulation to increase competition by preserving a larger number of firms in an industry may be superfluous: In some cases, an industry with only one firm may already *be* competitive.

Most of the studies thus far have focused on the airline industry. In their 1982 book that presented the contestable markets theory, Baumol, Panzar, and Willig maintain that air travel provides real examples of contestable markets.[a] Later studies make the same point.[b] The portion of the airline market that represents the most likely example of contestable markets is airline service between city pairs—for example, between Chicago and Denver or between Las Vegas and San Francisco. These markets are typically characterized by easy entry and exit by airlines, and economies of scale are likely to be significant. Although the route may only be flown by a single carrier, carriers with gates in terminals at both city end points might easily enter the market if they detected that economic profits were being earned by the sole supplier of service. For example, Fly-by-Nite airlines may be the only air carrier that flies between Provo, Utah, and Salt Lake City; if Wing-and-a-Prayer airlines also operates out of both cities it could easily begin flying between the two, even though it does not do so now. Hence, the *possibility* of competition represented by Wing-and-a-Prayer might effectively force Fly-by-Nite to behave competitively—that is, set price equal to marginal cost.

The consensus of the literature that tests this theory is that the existence of potential entrants has some effect on the behavior of sole suppliers. Also, an emerging view is that the degree of contestability is not a perfect substitute for actual competitors—that is, more than one firm—in a particular market. Some studies of the airline industry have shown that various measures of competitive behavior (for example, price-cost ratios) are affected by the number of actual competitors.[c] Because this exercise of market power is inconsistent with the (perfect) contestability hypothesis, each of these studies concluded that airline markets are not contestable. Using similar procedures, other researchers found that in some cases the number of actual competitors does not influence efficiency.[d] They attribute this lack of influence on actual competitors to the presence of potential competitors and conclude that airline markets are "basically contestable."

While interesting, these studies have significant limitations. For example, market concentration apparently has some influence on market efficiency; to evaluate the hypothesis that contestability provides a kind of competitive pressure independent of the actual industry concentration, it is necessary to employ some measure of the degree of contestability *per se.*

Recent research by Morrison and Winston[e] provides such a direct test. They collected data on airline fares for 769 pairs of cities that were connected by only one airline and located at least 100 miles apart; at least one other airline served one or both of the cities without providing direct service between the two cities. This definition recognizes that immediate, or hit-and-run, entry into an airline market requires that a carrier already be present in the market by serving at least one of the relevant airports.

Morrison's and Winston's findings suggest that potential competitors *do* serve a significant disciplining function in these markets. Each additional *potential* competitor reduced the fare by about $0.0015 per mile. Three potential competitors thus have approximately the same effect on price as one actual competitor.

These results support the view that airline markets are *imperfectly* contestable; that is, the existence of firms *outside* the market that might easily compete with a sole service provider induces the monopolist to *behave* more like a competitive firm. Theoretical and empirical measures of contestability continue to appear in the literature; some recent studies have called into question the competitive effects of airline deregulation, particularly at "hub" airports.[f] However, contestability—as an important part of the new industrial organization theory—appears to offer much promise as a method for analyzing the effects of real-world market structures.

Question

What other types of businesses involving route structures could be analyzed according to the theory of contestable markets?

[a]William J. Baumol, John C. Panzar, and Robert D. Willig, *Contestable Markets and the Theory of Industry Structure* (New York: Harcourt Brace Jovanovich, 1982).

[b]Elizabeth E. Bailey and William J. Baumol, "Deregulation and the Theory of Contestable Markets," *Yale Journal of Regulation* 1 (1984), pp. 111–28.

[c]Thomas Gale Moore, "U.S. Airline Deregulation: Its Effects on Passengers, Capital, and Labor," *Journal of Law and Economics* 29 (1986), p. 1; Gregory D. Call and Theodore E. Keeler, "Airline Deregulation, Fares and Market Behavior: Some Empirical Evidence," in *Analytical Studies in Transport Economics,* ed. Andrew Daugherty, 1985; David R. Graham, Daniel P. Kaplan, and David S. Sibley, "Efficiency and Competition in the Airline Industry," *Bell Journal of Economics* 14 (1983), p. 118.

[d]Elizabeth E. Bailey and John C. Panzar, "The Contestability of Airline Markets During the Transition to Deregulation," *Law and Contemporary Problems* 44 (1981), p. 125.

[e]Steven A. Morrison and Clifford Winston, "Empirical Implications and Tests of the Contestability Hypothesis," *Journal of Law and Economics* 30 (1987), pp. 53–66.

[f]See Severin J. Borenstein, "Hubs and High Fares: Airport Dominance and Market Power in the U.S. Airline Industry," *Rand Journal of Economics* 20 (1989), pp. 344–65. Borenstein argues that certain marketing practices, such as frequent-flyer programs and computerized reservations systems, have led to airline dominance and some monopoly power at "hub" airports such as Atlanta's or Miami's. Borenstein acknowledges, however, that deregulation has provided important benefits to consumers.

Alfred Marshall

Joan Robinson

Alfred Marshall and Joan Robinson: Perfect Versus Imperfect Markets

ALFRED MARSHALL (1842–1924), an English economist, was the strong-willed son of a harsh father, who early on tried to coerce young Alfred into the ministry. Much to his parent's dismay, Marshall rejected a theological scholarship to Oxford University and entered Cambridge, where he showed early brilliance as a mathematician and received his M.S. in mathematics in 1865. From mathematics, Marshall veered into metaphysics, joined a philosophy discussion group at Cambridge, and lectured for almost ten years in moral science at Cambridge. During this period Marshall became convinced of the overriding importance of economics to individual and social action. In 1877, Marshall married Mary Paley, a former student, and moved to Bristol, where they both lectured on political economy at University College. In 1885, they returned to Cambridge, where Marshall continued his long and illustrious career as a lecturer in political economy.

The most important of Marshall's books was the modern bible of microeconomics *Principles of Economics* (1890),[a] which he revised through nine editions. Many of the concepts presented in today's introductory economics courses including the principles of perfect competition among firms, were first set down systematically by Marshall. His mathematical precision and fondness for lucid examples made the text and economics generally accessible and popular. In 1903, while his work on *Principles* continued, Marshall succeeded in establishing economics as a discipline separate from moral science. He is also credited with founding the neoclassical tradition in economics—the modern version of economic principles established by Adam Smith.

JOAN ROBINSON (1903–1983), like Alfred Marshall, spent most of her academic career at the University of Cambridge. She completed her B.A. in economics at Cambridge in 1925, the year after Marshall's death. She began a forty-year teaching career at Cambridge in 1931, at a time when Marshall's influence over the principles and methods of economics study was still great. Robinson is perhaps best known for her book *The Economics of Imperfect Competition* (1933),[b] which expands and enlarges many of Marshall's conclusions about business organization and his theory of perfect competition among firms.

Robinson's contributions to economics reach well beyond her theory of imperfect competition. In the mid-1930s she and a small group of Cambridge economists helped John Maynard Keynes write his monumental *General Theory of Employment, Interest, and Money,* which ushered in a new era of macroeconomic theory. She also wrote in the areas of economic development, international trade, capital theory, and Marxian economics.

Although Robinson later questioned her own analysis of imperfect competition, her critique of Marshall's assumptions of the way the economy operates presents an interesting chapter in the development of economic thought.

[a]Alfred Marshall, *Principles of Economics,* 8th ed. (London: Macmillan, 1920).

[b]Joan Robinson, *The Economics of Imperfect Competition* (London: Macmillan, 1933).

THE WORLD OF PERFECT COMPETITION

To Marshall, the microeconomic behavior of firms and individuals was kept in constant check by the competitive nature of markets. The dynamics of free enterprise, of limitless entry to and exit from markets, enforced the norm of perfect competition among buyers and sellers. By his terms, each market is made up of sufficiently large numbers of competing firms buying and selling virtually identical products and services. No single demander or supplier of goods can affect the market price because no single firm has a large enough stake in the market. Given these conditions, the market price for goods would always gravitate to a level equal to the firm's costs of production. As a result, economic profits could not persist. Under the rigors of perfect competition, no firm would be able to rise above its equals.

To demonstrate his model of perfect competition, Marshall chose a number of illustrations, including the market for fresh fish. Marshall noted that the ordinary daily price of fish varies according to factors such as the daily intensity of demand along with weather and luck, which affect the size of the catch. He then introduced into this illustration a cattle plague that permanently increased the demand for fresh fish over beef. How would the competitively organized fish market react? (Remember that no freezing or cold storage facilities were readily available in Marshall's day.)

Under competitive conditions, the price per pound of fish would immediately rise. Recognizing that the price rise was not a temporary phenomenon, fishermen would respond to the increased profits (since price would now be greater than costs of production) by using their boats, fishing crews, and nets more intensively. Supply would be increased by these activities, as it would by the entry into the market of new fishing firms attracted by profits. Supply increases would ultimately bring price down to the average cost of catching fish.

Marshall's vision of perfect competition comports well with Adam Smith's theory of "the invisible hand." In fact, Marshall's theory of perfect competition describes the invisible hand at work. In his illustration, new fishing firms enter the market and old firms expand not for the benefit of customers but in the hopes of earning more profits. They act only in their own self-interest but in doing so promote the interest of society. The price of fish falls to the costs of production in the long run, and more fish are provided in the market.

Although Marshall did acknowledge the existence of monopolies and oligopolies, he believed that these market structures were a special case. Natural monopolies—those with large economies of scale in production (the phone company, the gas company, and so on)—could exist, as could monopolies due to artificial barriers to entry (government regulation, control of vital resources, and so on), but these were rare exceptions to competitive organization.

PERFECT COMPETITION TURNED ON ITS HEAD

"It is customary," Joan Robinson wrote in *The Economics of Imperfect Competition*, " . . . to open with the analysis of a perfectly competitive world, and to treat monopoly as a special case. . . . It is more proper to set out the analysis of monopoly, treating perfect competition as a special case." Beginning with these words, Robinson set out to turn Marshall's theory of perfect competition upside down.

Modern industrialized societies, she contended, were dominated by monopolies (a single firm in a market) or oligopolies (a few large firms in a market). To a greater or lesser degree, most markets were influenced by the power of monopoly control. In other words, individual firms in these markets were large enough to affect market prices on their own. Given these assumptions, Robinson pointed out, the prices of goods and services would not gravitate to a level equal to the firm's costs of production. Economic profits could persist, enabling the dominant firms to maintain or even increase their dominance.

Modern examples of imperfect competition include the automobile industry, dominated by industrial giants such as General Motors, or the fast-food industry, dominated by firms such as McDonald's. A single seller or a few sellers of running shoes and athletic equipment in a small college town is an example of monopoly on a smaller scale.

To further illustrate her point that imperfect, rather than perfect, competition was the norm, Robinson pointed to the pervasive evidence of price discrimination in markets. Whereas Marshall contended that only one market price could prevail under perfect competition, Robinson saw many instances in which a single good or service could command several different prices in the same market. Multiple prices for the same product could be possible, Robinson emphasized, only in a world of imperfect competition.

Robinson's theory of imperfect competition was not the only challenge made against Marshall's system of perfect competition. A similar theory was offered by American economist E. H. Chamberlin in his *Theory of Monopolistic Competition*,[c] also published in 1933.

Other important additions have been made to Marshall's theory of competition. Modern economists stress the manner in which information affects suppliers and demanders, the consequences of potential competition and rivalry on markets, and the impact on Marshall's model of interpreting price as "full price." The new theory of competitive markets has again come to dominate microeconomic analysis as the simple theory of competition did in Marshall's time.

---

[c]Edward H. Chamberlin, *The Theory of Monopolistic Competition: A Re-orientation of the Theory of Value*, 8th ed. (Cambridge: Harvard University Press, 1962), originally published in 1933.

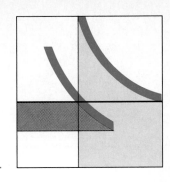

PART THREE

Microeconomic

Principles

of Input Demand

and Supply

14

Marginal Productivity Theory and Wages

In Chapter 4 we presented an overview of resource and product markets (see the circular flow model in Chapter 4, Figure 1). We showed business firms as both suppliers of goods and services and demanders of inputs such as land, labor, capital, and entrepreneurship. Households were depicted both as demanders of goods and services and as suppliers of inputs. Up to this point in our study of microeconomics, we have focused on the upper part of the circular flow model and studied how the prices of final products such as psychiatric services, personal computers, or diapers are determined. We now turn to the lower part of the model to view ourselves as demanders or suppliers of inputs such as labor services, land, or capital. Specifically, we now inquire how input prices—wages of day laborers or engineers, lumber or machine prices—are determined. Once we know the economic process by which input values are determined, we will be able to understand better how and why people earn the incomes they do as owners of their own labor and other resources. When you have mastered the ideas in Chapter 14, you should understand

- how the demand for labor or any other input is related to its productivity and the demand for the product that the resource produces.
- the principles under which competitive firms demand labor and how income is generated by such demands.
- how human capital and its acquisition is related to individuals' wage rates and income-earning capacity.
- how comparable worth proposals are related to the market for labor inputs.

Factor market:
A market in which the prices of productive resources (factors of production, or inputs) are determined by the interaction of firms acting as buyers with households and firms acting as suppliers of resources.

FACTOR MARKETS: AN OVERVIEW

The markets in which input prices are determined are called **factor, or resource, markets.** The prices of factors such as wages, rent, and interest are determined through the interplay of supply and demand. Indeed, the theory of factor prices is just the familiar theory of demand and supply applied to factors of production.

We begin this chapter by presenting the marginal productivity theory of demand for one factor of production, labor. Although our example is labor, the marginal productivity theory is equally applicable to other factors of production, as we will see in Chapters 16 and 17, where we apply the theory to land and capital inputs. In the second part of this chapter, we present the theory of labor supply. Since wages are intimately linked to the level of income earned by labor, we devote the final section of the chapter to discussing the relevance of marginal productivity theory to income distribution. The price and quantity of inputs such as labor and land are determined by the same laws of supply and demand that we have discussed for outputs. To understand why this is so, consider the general characteristics of factor markets.

Derived Demand

Derived demand:
The demand for factors of production that exists because of the demand for the products that the factors produce.

The demand for labor or any other factor of production is a **derived demand.** This term means that the demand for labor is directly related to the demand for the goods and services that the labor is used to produce. If the demand for computers increases, the derived demand for computer scientists and engineers will increase. If the demand for physical fitness increases, the derived demand for health foods and aerobics instructors will increase. If the demand for law and order increases, the derived demand for police officers will increase.

Derived demand also obeys the law of demand. All things being equal, if the price of health foods falls, more will be consumed; if the price of paper rises, fewer or shorter books will be published; if the rental prices on office space fall, more offices will be rented. So even though we call the demand for factors of production a derived demand, the law of demand applies to it in the same way that it applies to demand for final output.

Firms as Resource Price Takers

Just as there are different types of output market structures—such as competition, oligopoly, and monopoly—similar differences can occur in resource markets. There can be perfectly competitive sellers and buyers of labor, for example. In such cases, there are large numbers of both buyers (employing firms) and sellers (workers) of a homogeneous type of labor. There can also be various types of imperfect competition in buying and selling labor, as we will learn in the next chapter. We limit this chapter to a competitive labor market. The following discussion of labor demand examines labor markets in which a large number of firms hire a single type of labor and a large number of people are willing to supply the labor. There are, of necessity, simplifications in our discussion. For example, we all know that labor comes in many alternative "qualities" depending on training, education, and other matters. To keep matters simple, however, we assume that labor is homogeneous. Another important simplification relates to the nature of the "wage rate." In reality, the wage that workers receive includes many factors other than the money wage. A full wage includes all nonmoney wage benefits, such as retirement plans, health insurance, vacation policy, and so on, in addition to the money wage payment. Although we mention only a wage rate in this chapter—without any elaboration of the nonwage benefits—we are referring to the full wage paid to workers.

Competitive labor market: A labor market in which the wage rate is determined by the interactions of a large number of sellers (suppliers) of labor and a large number of demanders (buyers) of labor. Neither group acts in a collusive manner.

Market demand for labor: The total quantity of labor demanded at various wage rates, other things constant. The sum of all individual firms' demands for a type of labor. The firms may or may not all be in the same industry.

Market supply of labor: The sum of all individuals' supplies of a type of labor. The total quantity of labor people will offer to the market at various wage rates, other things being equal.

In a **competitive labor market,** the wage rate is determined by the familiar forces of supply and demand. The horizontal **market demand for labor** is the sum of all firms' demand for the type of labor in question. All the firms may not be in the same industry—that is, they may not all produce the same product—but they all employ the same type of labor. For example, the demand curve in Figure 1a could represent the market demand for electricians. This overall demand would be found by summing the demand for electricians by all buyers of their labor, from AT&T and General Motors to construction companies, cable television companies, and even homeowners.

The **market supply of labor** is obtained by horizontally summing the supply of individual workers. As indicated by the supply curve S_m in Figure 1a, as the wage rate rises, a larger quantity of labor is supplied. The supply of labor to any particular occupation thus follows the familiar law of supply.

The interaction of supply and demand for labor results in an equilibrium wage W_0. Once this wage is established, the individual buyers of labor are price takers. That is, the firms must accept W_0 as the prevailing wage and may hire as many workers as they are willing and able to hire at that wage. Being perfectly competitive buyers of labor, employing firms face an infinitely elastic labor supply curve, as shown in Figure 1b. All buyers of any good or service who are price takers face an infinitely elastic supply curve.

FIGURE 1

The Firm as a Wage Price Taker

(a) The equilibrium wage, W_0, is determined in the competitive market by the market supply, S_m, and demand, D_m, for a particular type of labor. (b) The firm must pay wage rate W_0 for workers but is able to hire all it wants at that wage. The supply of labor to the competitive firm, S_f, is totally elastic at the prevailing wage.

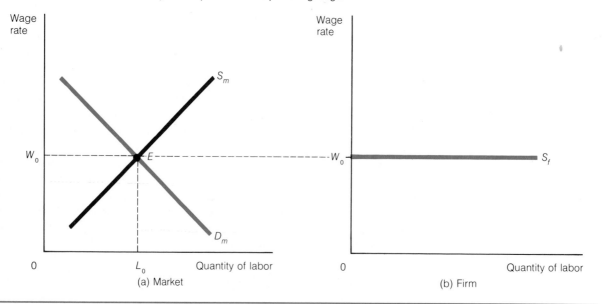

MARGINAL PRODUCTIVITY THEORY

We cannot say exactly how many electricians or computer programmers will be demanded within a given time period, but we can present some general rules about how the numbers of people demanded in these occupations might rise or fall. In this analysis, we reencounter many principles from earlier chapters. All apply equally to the demand for resource inputs, including labor.

The Profit-Maximizing Level of Employment

The firm hiring labor in a competitive market faces a market-determined wage. Since the equilibrium wage is established, the point of interest becomes the quantity of labor that an individual firm chooses to hire. If a firm is selling its product in a perfectly competitive product market, then how much labor will it hire at a particular wage rate?

To answer this question, let us say that the firm has many inputs, one of which is labor. Also, let the quantities of all inputs except labor be fixed. Labor, in other words, is the only variable input. (These circumstances, as you may recognize, describe a short-run situation for the firm.) To produce more output, the firm must hire more labor. The firm wishes to maximize profits and must therefore hire the profit-maximizing amount of labor.

Suppose the firm in this instance is a corn farmer who must decide whether to hire a worker to help pick and husk corn. How does the farmer make this decision? Hiring the worker will increase output, and the increase in production will be sold to obtain revenue. At the same time, hiring the worker will increase the cost of production because the farm worker must be paid. The farmer makes a profit-maximizing decision *at the margin*. If hiring the worker increases total revenue more than it increases total cost, then hiring the worker will increase profits. The farmer will always hire a worker if doing so increases profits.

Suppose the farmer is thinking about hiring a second worker. The same decision process is repeated. If the second worker adds more to revenue than to cost, then he or she will be hired. This process continues with every prospective worker. An important principle is in action: the *law of diminishing marginal returns.* As more and more of a variable input is added to a production process in which there is a fixed input, the marginal product of the variable input eventually declines. As more workers are hired, the extra output of each worker eventually falls. Since each additional worker adds less and less to total output, the additional revenues that each worker produces eventually fall below the additional cost of hiring. At some point, the farmer will stop hiring altogether. In short, the profit-maximizing farmer should hire all workers that add more to revenue than to cost but stop hiring at the point where the addition of revenue is just equal to the addition to cost.

The example of a corn farmer can also be expressed in economic terms. The extra output that each additional unit of labor adds to total output is called the **marginal product of labor (MP_L):**

$$MP_L = \frac{\Delta TP}{\Delta L},$$

Marginal product of labor (MP_L):
The additional output produced that results from hiring an additional unit of labor; change in total output divided by change in quantity of labor input used.

where MP_L is the marginal product of labor and ΔTP is the change in total product brought about by adding one unit of labor, ΔL. Adding units of the variable input to other fixed inputs will eventually lead to a decrease in the marginal product of the variable input in the short run.

Table 1 summarizes the hypothetical choices available to the corn farmer. The first column shows the units of labor, in number of worker-hours. The second column shows the marginal product of the workers—the amount by which total output increases as one more unit of labor is added to the production process. MP_L decreases as the amount of labor increases, according to the law of diminishing marginal returns. The first unit of labor adds 14 units of output (bushels of corn), the second adds 12 units of output, and so forth.

When the extra corn produced by each additional unit of labor is sold, the resulting increase in total revenue is called the **marginal revenue product of labor (MRP_L):**

Marginal revenue product of labor (MRP_L): The additional revenue that results from selling the additional output produced by hiring an additional unit of labor; marginal revenue times marginal product of labor.

$$\times\ MRP_L = \frac{\Delta TR}{\Delta L},$$

where MRP_L is the marginal revenue product of labor, ΔTR is the change in total revenue, and ΔL is the change in the amount of labor hired.

Another method of expressing MRP_L is

$$MRP_L = MR_C \times MP_L,$$

where MR_c is the marginal revenue under competitive conditions (the increase in total revenue resulting from selling one more unit of output) and MP_L is the marginal product of labor.

For the firm that sells its product in a perfectly competitive market, marginal revenue is equal to the price of the product. Thus, the marginal revenue product (MRP) is simply the price (P) of the product times the

---

TABLE 1

A Marginal Revenue Product Schedule for Labor

The marginal revenue product of labor in column (4) falls as more units of labor are employed because the marginal product of labor in column (2) falls. The firm will hire additional units of labor up to the point where the extra revenue these units generate just equals the extra cost of paying for them. At this point, 6 units of labor, $MRP_L = MFC_L$.

(1) Units of Labor (worker-hours)	(2) Marginal Product of Labor MP_L (bushels of corn)	(3) Marginal Revenue $MR_C = P_C$ (dollars per bushel)	(4) Marginal Revenue Product $MRP_L = MR_C \times MP_L$	(5) Marginal Factor Cost (dollars per hour) MFC_L = Wage
1	14	$2	$28	$8
2	12	2	24	8
3	10	2	20	8
4	8	2	16	8
5	6	2	12	8
6	4	2	8	8
7	2	2	4	8
8	0	2	0	8

marginal product (*MP*) of each unit. As shown in Table 1, the marginal revenue product of the first unit of labor is found by multiplying its marginal product, 14, by the price of the product, $2, to obtain $28. The MRP_L declines as more workers are hired because MP_L declines.

Regardless of which economic shorthand is used, the profit-maximizing firm will continue adding units of labor as long as the additional revenues the labor produces are greater than the additional costs of the labor. The firm will stop hiring when the additional reserves are less than the additional costs of hiring. The extra cost of hiring one more unit of labor is called the **marginal factor cost of labor (*MFC_L*)**:

Marginal factor cost of labor (*MFC_L*):
The change in total costs associated with employing one additional unit of labor.

$$MFC_L = \frac{\Delta TC}{\Delta L},$$

where MFC_L is the marginal factor cost of labor and ΔTC is the change in total cost. Under competitive conditions, the firm may purchase all of the labor it wants at the prevailing wage rate. Each additional unit of labor has in Table 1 a marginal factor cost equal to the wage rate (shown as $8 on the schedule).

The profit-maximizing firm will hire labor up to the point where $MRP_L = MFC_L$. With the numbers in Table 1, this equation indicates that it will be most profitable for the farmer to hire 6 units of labor. Each unit from the first to the sixth adds more to revenue than to cost. By hiring 6 units, the farmer adds as much as possible to profit. However, the seventh unit adds more to cost than to revenue and therefore will not be hired.

This process should sound familiar: It is the mirror image of how the competitive firm determines its profit-maximizing output. The firm follows the same process to equate its marginal cost to marginal revenue in hiring inputs as it does in selling its output. In fact, when the firm hires the profit-maximizing quantity of labor, that amount of labor will produce the profit-maximizing level of output.

The numbers used in Table 1 are presented in graph form in Figure 2. The MP_L curve is drawn in Figure 2a by plotting the points from columns (1) and (2). The demand curve for the farmer's corn is shown in Figure 2b, where $P = \$2$. The MRP_L is found by multiplying marginal revenue by marginal product; the result is the marginal revenue product curve in Figure 2c.

The prevailing wage is $8, stated as MFC_L. The profit-maximizing quantity of labor is the point where the MFC_L curve crosses the MRP_L curve. At this point, the marginal revenue product equals the marginal factor cost of labor.

Profit-Maximizing Rules for All Inputs

Firms employ many inputs other than labor. The profit-maximizing rule for the level of employment is the same for each resource. The corn farmer may be planning to use fertilizer, for example. If he applies 1 unit of fertilizer—a 100-pound bag—the amount of corn produced will increase. The extra corn is treated as the marginal product of the first bag of fertilizer. The extra revenue that results is the marginal revenue product, and the extra cost of the bag is the marginal factor cost. If the *MRP* of the fertilizer is greater than or equal to the *MFC,* then the farmer will purchase and use the fertilizer. The profit-maximizing amount of fertilizer is found at the point where the *MRP* of fertilizer is just equal to the *MFC*.

FIGURE 2   **The Firm's Marginal Revenue Product Curve**

(a) The farmer's marginal product of labor (MP_L) curve is plotted from columns (1) and (2) in Table 1. (b) The demand curve for the farmer's product is determined by the product price ($P_c = MR_c$ in this perfectly competitive market). (c) The marginal revenue product of labor (MRP_L) curve is found by multiplying MP_L by MR_c. The profit-maximizing firm hires labor up to the point where marginal revenue product of labor equals marginal factor cost of labor (MFC_L). With a wage of $8 and a product price of $2, the firm will hire up to 6 units of labor.

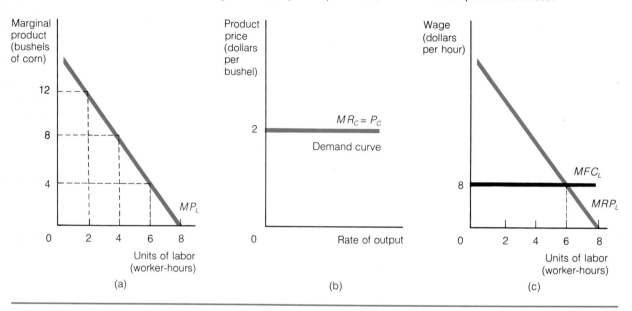

This rule applies to all inputs, such as tractors, seed, land, tractor drivers, and water. The profit-maximizing quantity of all inputs is the amount that makes the *MRP* of each input equal to the *MFC* of each input, or

$$\frac{MRP_1}{MFC_1} = \frac{MRP_2}{MFC_2} = \frac{MRP_3}{MFC_3} = \cdots = \frac{MRP_N}{MFC_N} = 1,$$

where the subscripts 1, 2, and 3 indicate the *MRP* and *MFC* of the first, second, and third inputs, and N indicates the total number of inputs used. Each ratio of *MRP* to *MFC* is equal to 1 because the *MRP* of each is equal to the *MFC* of each. Under this condition, all inputs are employed in the profit-maximizing amounts.

THE DEMAND FOR LABOR

Marginal productivity theory gives insight into the purchasing behavior of firms. In the short run, when labor is the only variable input, the firm is willing to purchase or hire additional units up to the point at which *MRP* = *MFC*. The firm's marginal revenue product curve (Figure 2c) thus traces the relation between the price of labor (the wage rate) and the amount of labor a firm is willing to purchase. In other words, the marginal revenue product curve is also the firm's short-run demand curve for labor. Figure 3 illustrates this. At

FIGURE 3

The firm hires labor up to the point where the wage is equal to the marginal revenue product of labor (MRP_L). The marginal revenue product curve shows the various quantities of labor the firm is willing to hire at all the different wage rates when labor is the only variable input.

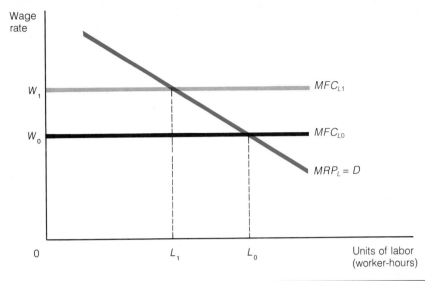

The Firm's Short-Run Demand for Labor

wage W_0 the firm chooses L_0 units of labor. A higher wage such as W_1 results in less labor hired. For each wage, the firm adjusts the level of employment to maintain the equation $MRP_L = MFC_L$.

In the following sections we examine the demand for labor from several perspectives.

The Short-Run Market Demand for Labor

A single firm's demand for labor in the short run is equivalent to its marginal revenue product of labor. To obtain the overall market demand for labor in the short run, we must make some additional calculations.

Each firm will demand labor up to the point where $MRP_L = MFC_L$. Thus, at a particular wage, the market demand for labor may be shown as the sum of all the firms' MRP_L curves. Figure 4 shows such a curve, MRP_{L0}. This curve represents the sum of all the firms' short-run demand curves for a particular type of labor. The curve labeled MRP_{L0}, however, is not the short-run market demand curve for this type of labor, although it does establish one point on the short-run market demand curve, D.

To establish the whole demand curve, we must examine what happens when the wage rate changes. Imagine the overall demand for corn huskers. Many farmers employ huskers at wage W_0; the total number of corn huskers employed at W_0 is L_0. Recall that the MRP_L curve is obtained by multiplying the price of corn by the marginal product of labor. If the wage rate rises to W_1, then each firm's costs of production will rise. The increased costs of production will decrease the supply of corn and increase the equilibrium price. To obtain the new MRP_L curve (MRP_{L1}), we multiply the marginal product of labor by the new, higher price of corn, and we sum this quantity over all the firms. The new wage, W_1, and level of employment, L_1, establish a second point on the short-run market demand curve. The short-run market demand curve, D, differs from the sum of the MRP_L curves because it allows for increases in the price of the product that result from wage increases. Note,

FIGURE 4

MRP_{Lo} represents the sum of all the firms' marginal revenue product curves for a particular occupation. When the wage for this occupation is W_0, the firms hire L_0 units of labor. If the wage rises to W_1, the firms initially hire the lower L_{0_1} units of labor. However, the increase in wages causes an increase in the price of the product. The higher product price shifts the sum of the firms' MRP_{Lo} to MRP_{L_1}. At W_1, when labor is the only variable input, the firms hire L_1 units of labor. D represents the short-run market demand curve for labor because it allows for changes in the wage rate.

The Short-Run Market Demand for Labor

however, that the demand curve, D, obeys the law of demand. When the wage rate rises, given other factors, less labor is ultimately employed.

Firm's long-run demand for labor:
The relationship between all possible wage rates and quantities demanded of labor at those wage rates, given that the firm has enough time to vary the usage of all inputs.

The Firm's Long-Run Demand for Labor

We have so far concentrated on the short-run demand for labor, in which labor is the only variable input. In the long run, many adjustments occur when wages change. Allowed enough time, firms may vary all inputs. Also, at the industry level, not only does the price of products change directly with wages, but the number of firms changes as well.

Suppose that the market wage rate for corn huskers increases. What happens in the long run? First, farmers will adjust to the higher price of labor by hiring fewer corn huskers; given enough time, they may turn to substitute inputs for this type of labor, perhaps by buying combines rather than hiring human huskers. Second, the increase in the price of labor increases the farmers' costs of production. With the increase in costs, the supply of the product decreases, and its price rises. Finally, the number of firms will adjust, establishing a new equilibrium. The number of firms, in the end, is likely to decrease. When wages rise, a larger number of workers lose their jobs in the long run than in the short run; or, if wages fall, a larger number of workers are hired. The long-run market demand is more elastic than the short-run market demand.

Change in the demand for labor:
A shift of the entire labor demand curve; caused by a change in the marginal product of labor, by a change in the demand for the product produced by the type of labor in question, or by a change in the price of some other factor of production.

Changes in the Demand for Labor

In applying the law of demand to labor, we have seen some adjustments at the firm level and at the industry level in response to wage rate changes. An increase in the wage rate changed the price of the product, the employment of other inputs, and the number of firms. However, in establishing the demand curve for labor, many other things were held constant, such as the demand for the product, the prices of other inputs, and the level of technology. If these things were not held constant, then we would not have been able to establish the relation of the wage rate to the amount of labor demanded.

What causes an increase or decrease in the demand for a particular type of labor? Why would the demand for chemical engineers suddenly increase? Or why would a restaurant suddenly hire more waiters and cooks? Such questions may be answered by examining the origins of the demand for labor and the behavior of profit-maximizing firms.

The demand for labor is derived from the demand for the product the labor produces and the marginal product of the labor itself. If either of these increases or decreases, then the demand for labor will increase or decrease in the same direction. Understanding this relation simplifies things; however, further details are of value.

1. *If the demand for the product that labor produces changes, then the demand for labor will change in the same direction.* Remember that for a competitive firm, the marginal revenue product is equal to marginal revenue (the output price) times marginal product. If the demand for the good increases, then its price increases and the demand for labor (*MRP*) and all other inputs also increases. The demands for electronics technicians and computer components have therefore increased since the demand for personal computers has increased.

The opposite situation occurs when the demand for a product decreases. If the price of a product falls, then the demand for inputs used to produce that product falls. When the demand for American-made cars decreases, the demand for domestic autoworkers decreases (along with the demand for tires and steel).

2. *If the marginal product of labor changes, then the demand for that labor will change in the same direction.* The productivity of a particular type of labor depends to a very large extent on the firm's employment of other inputs in the production process. Additional expenditures on other inputs often increase the productivity of labor. For example, the marginal product of farm workers is influenced by the amounts of other inputs that the farmer buys, such as land, equipment, seed, fertilizer, and water. If such inputs increase the workers' productivity, their use will also increase demand for the workers' labor.

These effects on the firm's demand for labor can be shown graphically. Suppose that the price of the firm's product rises and/or that, through worker training, the marginal product of labor increases. Either or both of these effects will increase the firm's demand for labor, as shown in Figure 5. Under competition, the supply of labor facing the firm is horizontal at the market-determined wage rate, W_c. When demand increases from D_0 to D_1 in Figure 5, the firm hires a greater quantity of labor, L_1 rather than L_0. Reductions in the firm's product price and/or reductions in labor's marginal productivity will have opposite effects.

The relation between the quantity of nonlabor inputs and the productivity of labor can be direct or inverse. In other words, increasing the amount of one input may either increase or decrease the productivity of labor. If increased usage of one input due to a decrease in that input's price increases the marginal product of labor and thus increases the amount of labor hired at any given wage, then this input and labor are **complementary inputs.** For example, if the farmer uses more fertilizer, then corn huskers can produce

Complementary inputs: Inputs with a relation such that increased usage of one input due to a fall in its price results in increased employment of the other(s).

FIGURE 5

The supply of labor to the firm is totally elastic at the market-determined wage rate, W_c. The firm can purchase as much labor as it desires at W_c without affecting the market wage rate. When the firm's demand for labor increases from D_0 to D_1, a larger quantity of labor, L_1 instead of L_0, is purchased at the given wage rate than previously.

A Change in the Firm's Demand for Labor

Substitute inputs:
Inputs with a relation such that increased employment of one input due to a fall in its price results in decreased usage of the other(s).

more output; their marginal product increases. Increases in inputs that complement labor will increase the demand for labor.

If increased usage of one input due to a decrease in that input's price decreases the marginal product of labor and thus decreases the amount of labor hired at any given wage, then that input is called a **substitute input** for labor. For corn pickers and huskers, a combine that picks and husks is a substitute input. If the farmer uses more combines, then the marginal product of human huskers and pickers will decrease, and so will the demand for them.

Why would a farmer suddenly choose to purchase more fertilizer or combines? A firm makes decisions on the basis of expected profits. For example, if the price of fertilizer falls, then it is in the farmer's interest to purchase more fertilizer. If the price of combines falls, then the farmer will purchase more combines. Thus, if the price of a complementary input falls, the demand for labor rises. If the price of a substitute input falls, the demand for labor decreases.

In addition to changes in the quantity of inputs, technological advances may shift the demand for labor. New production techniques may increase or decrease the demand for labor in a particular occupation. In fact, technological change generally increases the marginal product of some workers and decreases that of others. Technological change can, for example, result in robots being more adept than factory workers at performing certain tasks. As a consequence, the marginal product of factory workers falls and the demand for their labor decreases. At the same time, the marginal revenue product of workers who make robots rises as the demand for and the price of robots increases. This produces an increase in the demand for workers who make robots.

The Elasticity of Demand for Labor

We have shown how to find the firm's demand for labor, how to find the market demand for labor, and how the demand curve for labor can shift. We still need to say something about the **elasticity of demand for labor.** Remember that elasticity measures the relative responsiveness of buyers to changes in price. Specifically, the elasticity of demand for labor is equal to the percent change in the quantity of labor demanded divided by the percent change in the wage rate.

Keep in mind that we are not talking about labor in general. We are talking about the derived demand for a specific type of labor. For example, we want to understand why the level of employment of corn huskers decreases by 30 percent when the wage rate increases by 10 percent; or why the level of employment of nuclear physicists falls by only 10 percent when their wages increase by 30 percent. There are three useful rules to apply when analyzing the elasticity of demand for labor.

1. *The elasticity of demand for labor is directly related to the elasticity of demand for the product that labor produces.* If the demand for a product is highly elastic, then a small percent increase in price will decrease the quantity demanded by a large proportion. If the increase in price is caused by an increase in wages, the resulting large decrease in production will cause a large decrease in the quantity of labor demanded. Suppose that the demand for houses is very elastic, and the wage of carpenters increases. The increase in the price of houses that results from the higher wages will decrease the quantity of houses purchased by a relatively large amount. The decreased production of houses will then decrease the quantity of carpenters demanded by a relatively large amount.

The greater the elasticity of demand for corn, the greater the elasticity of demand for corn huskers. The less elastic the demand for nuclear reactors, the less elastic the demand for nuclear physicists. The elasticity of demand for labor is in part derived from the elasticity of demand for the product that labor produces.

2. *The elasticity of demand for labor is directly related to the proportion of total production costs accounted for by labor.* The total amount of money that a firm pays for labor is a percentage of its total costs. The larger the percentage of total costs accounted for by labor, the greater the elasticity of demand for labor. This relation occurs because of the effect of wage increases on the price of the product. If wages rise by $2 an hour and labor represents a large percentage of total costs, then total costs and thus product price will increase by a large amount. The large price increase will decrease the amount of the product purchased and will decrease greatly the quantity of labor demanded. On the other hand, if labor accounts for a very small percentage of total costs, the same $2-an-hour wage increase will have little effect on overall cost and price. The decrease in the amount of the product demanded will be very small, making the decrease in labor demanded also small.

If the percentage of corn huskers' wages in the farmer's total costs is very large, then an increase in the huskers' wages will result in a relatively large decrease in the number of workers that the farmer hires. Conversely, if the percentage of huskers' wages in the farmer's total costs is very small, then the same wage increase will result in a relatively small decrease in the number of huskers hired.

Elasticity of demand for labor:
Measures the relative responsiveness of employment of a type of labor to changes in the wage rate; percent change in amount of labor hired divided by percent change in wage rate.

3. *The elasticity of the demand for labor is directly related to the number and availability of substitute inputs.* The demand for labor is highly elastic if there are good, relatively low-priced substitutes for labor. If the wage rate rises and there is another comparably priced input that can do the job of labor, then the relative amount of labor hired will decrease significantly. If there are no close substitutes for labor, or the substitutes are of a much higher price, then a wage increase will reduce employment by a lesser amount.

Once again, we see that the behavior of firms is similar to the behavior of consumers. The determinants of the elasticity of demand for labor and other inputs parallel the determinants of the elasticity of demand for goods by consumers. A larger percentage of total expenditures for purchases of some item—labor by firms or a good by consumers—creates greater elasticity of demand. A large number of substitutes for an item creates a highly elastic demand.

Monopoly and the Demand for Labor

We have spoken so far of demand for labor only under conditions of competition. What if the firm demanding labor enjoyed a monopoly in its output market but was still a purely competitive buyer of labor? For example, what would the farmer's demand for labor be if he were the only producer of corn? Recall from Chapter 9 that the demand curve for the monopolist's product is downward-sloping. This suggests that as the firm hires more workers and increases output, the price of the product must fall for the firm to sell the extra output. As the firm hires more labor, not only is the marginal product of labor falling but the product price is falling as well.

Even though the price of the product is falling as more output is produced, marginal revenue product, *MRP,* still describes the change in total revenue that results from hiring one more unit of labor. As before, *MRP* is equal to marginal revenue times marginal product. The difference is that the marginal revenue of the competitive seller is equal to the market price, whereas the monopolist's marginal revenue is a downward-sloping curve, derived from its demand curve.

Table 2 is a numerical example showing the difference between the marginal revenue product of labor under competition (MRP_c) and under monopoly conditions (MRP_m). The MRP_c is calculated as shown in Table 1: marginal product of labor (MPL) multiplied by the *constant* marginal revenue of the competitive firm (MR_c). *Remember:* Under competition, marginal revenue equals the price charged, since—being a price taker—the competitive firm can sell all of its units of output at the same competitive price. This means that $MR_c = P_c$.

The marginal revenue product of labor under monopoly is found by multiplying the marginal product of labor (MP_L) by monopoly marginal revenue (MR_m). The marginal product of labor (MP_L) is the same under competition or monopoly conditions. What changes is the marginal revenue that the monopoly firm can obtain from selling more units of its product or service. The marginal revenue obtainable from selling additional units of output declines with each additional unit sold. As the monopolist sells more, he or she must reduce prices for the previous number of units sold, which means that the marginal revenue from additional sales declines more rapidly than price.

TABLE 2

Calculation of Marginal Revenue Product Under Competition and Monopoly

Since the marginal product of labor declines, the marginal revenue product falls with increases in labor input under both competition and monopoly in product markets. Under monopoly, MRP_m also declines because marginal revenue falls as the monopolist expands output.

(1) Units of Labor (worker-hours)	(2) Marginal Product of Labor MP_L (bushels of corn)	(3) Marginal Revenue (Competition) $MR_c = P_c$ (dollars per bushel)	(4) Marginal Revenue (Monopoly) $MR_m > P_m$	(5) Marginal Revenue Product (Competition) $MRP_c = MR_c \times MP_L$	(6) Marginal Revenue Product (Monopoly) $MRP_m = MR_m \times MP_L$
1	14	$2	$8	$28	$112
2	12	2	7	24	84
3	10	2	6	20	60
4	8	2	5	16	40
5	6	2	4	12	24
6	4	2	3	8	12
7	2	2	2	4	4
8	0	2	1	0	0

In Table 2 this declining marginal revenue is shown in column (4). Since MR declines as more units of labor are hired (and more units of output are produced), the MRP falls more rapidly under monopoly conditions, shown in column (6), than in competitive conditions, shown in column (5).

A graphical comparison of the purely competitive firm's demand for labor and the monopolists' demand for labor is shown in Figure 6. The competitive firm's demand for labor is MRP_c in Figure 6c, obtained, as before, by multiplying MR_c from Figure 6a by MP_L, the marginal product of workers in Figure 6b. The monopolist's demand for labor, MRP_m, is obtained by multiplying MR_m in Figure 6a by MP_L in Figure 6b. The marginal product of workers, MP_L, falls at the same rate whether they are working for monopolists or for purely competitive firms. But the monopolist's MRP diminishes more quickly than the pure competitor's because not only is the marginal product of labor falling, but the monopolist's marginal revenue is falling as well.

A firm that enjoys a monopoly in its output market does not necessarily have any advantage in resource markets. For example, your local electric company may have exclusive rights as the only seller of electricity in your area. But this monopoly position does not imply that the electric company is the only employer of electricians, computer programmers, or bookkeepers. For these occupations, the monopoly is a purely competitive buyer of labor and must pay a competitive market wage for its labor. The marginal factor cost of labor is equal to the wage rate because the supply of labor to the firm is infinitely elastic.

In the end, the monopolist's decisions in hiring labor require the same marginal analysis as for any other firm. The firm will hire any unit of labor when its marginal revenue product is greater than its marginal factor cost and will continue to hire labor up to the point where the MRP_L is equal to MRC_L. The only difference for a monopoly firm is that its marginal revenue falls along

FIGURE 6

The Monopolist's *MRP* Versus the Competitive Firm's *MRP*

(a) The marginal revenue curves for a monopoly (MR_m) and for a competitive firm (MR_c). (b) The marginal product of labor curve is the same for both the monopolist and competitor because it depends only on production relationships (assumed the same here) that are independent of the type of product demand curve facing the firm. (c) The marginal revenue product for each firm, obtained by multiplying marginal revenue by marginal product. The monopolist's marginal revenue curve is downward-sloping, and the competitive firm's is equal to a given and constant product price; therefore, the monopolist's demand for labor, MRP_m, diminishes more rapidly than the competitive firm's, MRP_c.

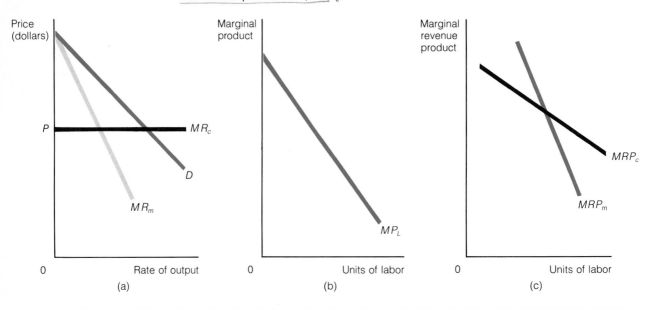

with the labor's marginal product. The Focus, "The Marginal Revenue Product of Professional Baseball Players," discusses these ideas as they relate to a special labor market.

THE SUPPLY OF LABOR

Now that we have some insight into the demand for labor, the next logical category is labor supply. We know that labor supply in competitive markets is highly elastic. But this fact does not answer two important questions: What determines the overall, or aggregate, supply of labor and how are wage rates and labor supply interrelated?

Individual Labor Supply

Nonmarket activities: Anything an individual does that directly or indirectly yields utility while not working.

Individuals in free markets are able to choose whether to offer their labor services in the market, and individuals' labor market decisions are based on the principle of utility maximization. The individual must choose between time spent in the market earning the wage that he or she may command and time spent in **nonmarket activities,** such as going to school, keeping house, tending a garden, or watching television.

FOCUS   The Marginal Revenue Product of Professional Baseball Players

The extra revenue that a firm obtains from hiring a worker is the marginal revenue product; if this is higher than the extra cost of the worker's wages, then the firm adds to its profits by employing the worker. Baseball players' salaries have increased sharply in the last few years, especially for superstars. Are they worth it? Are their *MRP*s greater than their wages?

To answer this question, economist Gerald Scully calculated the extra revenues that team owners received from hitters and pitchers. He first found that a player's contribution to his team's win-loss record was best measured for pitchers by the percent each added to the team's strikeout-to-walk ratios and for batters by the contribution of each to the team's batting average. Using this information, Scully then estimated the total team revenue, where revenue is simply the number of tickets sold per season times the average ticket price. After adjusting for the size of the city in which the team played its home games, the age of the stadium, the team's league, and other factors affecting revenue, he calculated that every point added to the team batting average by a batter increased the team's revenue by $9504. Similarly, every .01 point added to the pitching staff's strikeout-to-walk ratio increased revenue $9297.

Once he estimated player *MRP*s, it was a straightforward calculation for Scully to determine whether the salary paid to a particular player was commensurate with the amount the player added to team revenue (see Figure 7). For example, star hitters added from $250,000 to $383,700 to team revenues. Star pitchers contributed even more, from $321,700 to $479,000. However, during the 1968 and 1969 seasons, no player in Scully's sample was paid more than $125,000. He concluded, therefore, that players' salaries were well below their *MRP*s, with the greatest deficiency being the superstars' salaries. Scully's results explain in part free agency and the huge increases in players' salaries in the 1970s and 1980s.

Source: Gerald W. Scully, "Pay and Performance in Major League Baseball," *American Economic Review* 64 (December 1974), pp. 915–30.

FIGURE 7

Average Salary of Major League Baseball Players, 1970–1988

From less than $30,000 in 1970, the average salary for major league baseball players skyrocketed to $438,779 in 1988.

Source: Major League Baseball Players Association.

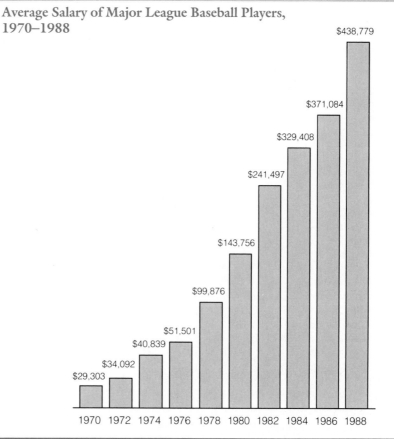

Fortunately, the individual does not have to make an all-or-nothing choice. No one chooses to work twenty-four hours a day, seven days a week. People can divide their time between market and nonmarket activities. How many hours would one choose to work during an average week? This question cannot be easily answered, but we can speculate about the effect that the wage rate may have on an individual's labor supply choices.

A supply curve relates the quantity supplied of a commodity to its price. Applied to labor supply, it is a schedule that relates the quantity of work offered and different wage rates. The labor supply curve of an individual is given in Figure 8. The first thing to observe about this person's labor supply curve, S_i, is that below w_1 she would prefer not to work at all; she chooses all nonmarket activity. This cutoff occurs because wages below w_1 do not meet her opportunity cost; she receives more utility from nonmarket activities than she would from the income received from working. Wage w_1 may not be high enough to encourage her to forgo fishing, painting the house, or attending school, for example. At wages immediately above w_1, the hours of labor she supplies respond positively to increases in pay. As her wage rate rises from w_1 to w_2, the hours she is willing to supply increase accordingly, to q_2.

The value of one hour of market time (one hour spent working) is equal to the wage rate. This means that for each hour an individual chooses to enjoy nonmarket activities, he or she is forgoing an hour of pay. In other words, the opportunity cost or the price an individual must pay for an hour of leisure time is the wage rate. As the wage rate rises, the price of nonmarket time also rises. An individual's demand for nonmarket time is downward-sloping, just as it is for any other good. If the wage rate rises, the individual is encouraged to opt for less nonmarket activity; that is, he or she is encouraged to substitute hours of work for hours of leisure.

The substitution effect, however, may be offset by an income effect. As the wage rate rises, the individual's income rises. If nonmarket time is a normal

leisure

FIGURE 8

The individual labor supply curve, the number of hours offered at various wages, may be positively or negatively sloped. If the substitution effect is greater than the income effect, the curve is upward-sloping, as shown from w_1 to w_3. The individual substitutes hours of work for hours of nonmarket activities. As the individual's wage rises beyond w_3, his or her demand for nonmarket time increases. The income effect is greater than the substitution effect, and the curve is negatively sloped above wage rate w_3.

Individual Labor Supply

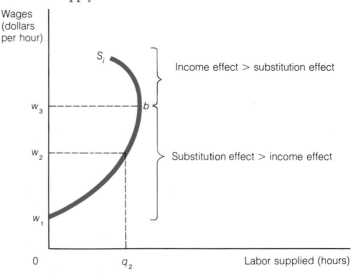

good, as we might expect, then the demand for nonmarket time will increase as income rises. This type of income effect will encourage the individual to enjoy more nonmarket time and less work.

As the wage rate rises, the two effects pull the worker in opposite directions. The effect that dominates will determine whether higher wages encourage more or fewer hours of work and determine whether the labor supply curve is positively or negatively sloped. If the substitution effect is greater than the income effect, higher wages will bring more hours of labor. In Figure 8, the substitution effect is greater than the income effect from w_1 to w_3, so the slope is positive. However, the income effect is greater than the substitution effect at wages above w_3. In this range, higher wages bring fewer hours of labor, so the curve is negatively sloped. At point b, where the income and substitution effects are equal, the supply curve begins to bend backward.

The labor supply curves of different individuals would, in all likelihood, be shaped differently. Within a given range of wage rates, one person's labor supply curve may be positively sloped, while another person's may be negatively sloped. This could be due to differences in tastes and preferences for leisure time. The wage level that initially entices people to enter the labor market may vary across individuals for the same reason. Additionally, it would be theoretically difficult to say at which particular wage rate any one person's labor supply curve becomes backward-bending—that is, the wage rate at which the income effect becomes greater than the substitution effect.

Since the shapes of individual labor supply curves are difficult to determine, the slope of the total or aggregate labor supply curve is difficult to predict with accuracy. The aggregate labor supply curve is theoretically obtained by summing individuals' labor supply curves horizontally. The aggregate curve shows the total amount of labor supplied at all the different wages. Even though some individuals have backward-bending labor supply curves, we expect the aggregate labor supply curve to be positively sloped, as in Figure 9, for two reasons. First, as wages rise, many workers will work more hours.

FIGURE 9

The aggregate labor supply curve, S_A, representing the numbers of hours of labor supplied by all individuals, is likely to be upward-sloping. As wages rise, more people join the labor force, and many people work more hours.

The Aggregate Supply of Labor

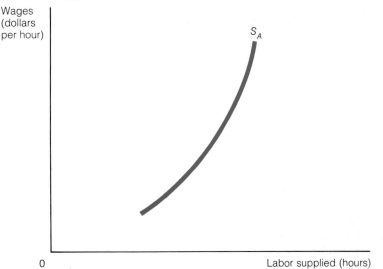

Second, as wages rise, more people will enter the labor force. Naturally, aggregate labor supply is influenced by other factors, such as immigration. (For a discussion of the impact of immigration, legal and illegal, on the U.S. labor supply, see Economics in Action, "Immigration and Labor Supply in the Southwestern United States," at the end of this chapter.)

Although the wage rate has an influence on the number of hours people may choose to work, individuals may also choose their wage rate, within limits. They do so by choosing an occupation. Some occupations must pay higher wages than others to induce people to join.

Human Capital

Some occupations, such as medicine, law, and nuclear physics, require many years of training. The fact that the wages in these skilled professions are higher than the wages of unskilled labor is not coincidental. Before people are willing to endure the years of training to become highly skilled professionals, they must be reasonably sure that their investment of time and other resources will pay off in the long run. People frequently choose to invest in some form of training to make themselves more productive and to enhance their income-earning potential. While a person is going to college, attending trade school, or gaining on-the-job training, he or she is building **human capital.**

Human capital:
Any quality, characteristic, or skill an individual has that enhances the individual's productivity, such as education and job experience.

Gaining human capital requires an investment period, such as four years in college. This investment involves a large opportunity cost. A college student loses the next-best alternative when attending college. For many students, the lost opportunity is the income they would have earned if working. Figure 10 portrays a simplified version of two alternative lifetime income streams for an individual.

After graduating from high school at age eighteen, individuals have a choice. They may enter the labor market immediately and earn income stream

FIGURE 10

An individual may choose to earn income Y_N from age eighteen to retirement at age sixty-five. Or an individual may attend college, lose income from age eighteen to age twenty-two, pay the direct costs of college, and then earn income Y_c from age twenty-two to retirement. The total costs of college are represented by the shaded area C, the lost income and direct costs; the benefits of college are shaded area B, the extra income earned with a college degree. In monetary terms it pays to go to college if B is greater than C.

The Economic Costs and Benefits of College

Y_N from that time until retirement at age sixty-five. This income stream could rise through the years as the individuals acquire job-related skills, but for simplicity we let it remain constant.

Some individuals may go to college. From age eighteen to twenty-two, they do not earn steady, full-time income. The opportunity cost of going to college—that is, the income the individuals forgo by choosing not to work—is represented by the shaded area above the x-axis between ages eighteen and twenty-two. In addition, they must pay the direct costs of college—tuition, books, and so on. The shaded area below the x-axis between ages eighteen and twenty-two represents the direct costs of college, a negative income. The total cost of going to college is the sum of both the opportunity cost and the direct costs of college, the entire shaded area C. After graduation, these individuals enter the labor market and begin earning positive income. Figure 10 indicates that their starting pay at age twenty-two after attending college is higher than it would have been had they not gone to college. They earn negative income for four years and then Y_C as a lifetime average from age twenty-two until retirement.

Which is the best choice? If the deciding factor is money, then one determines the relative values of the two income streams and chooses the higher. One method of doing so is to compare the area C (the investment period) with area B. Area C represents the total cost of going to college: the direct costs plus the lost income. Area B represents the benefits of going to college; it is the extra income earned with a college degree. If area B is greater than area C, then it pays to go to college.[1]

Some investments in human capital require more time and some require less time than others. Regardless of the length of the investment period (the number of years spent in school), if there is pure competition in the labor market and enough individuals choose the higher-income streams, then in the long run the sum total of the various income streams will be equal. That is, high school graduates will work at lower wage rates but for a greater total number of years than will college graduates. With a given retirement age for both groups, the lifetime earnings of high school graduates working more years but at a lower wage should just equal the lifetime earnings of college graduates working fewer years but at a higher wage. (This equilibrium requires that the wage rates for occupations with long investment periods be greater than the wage rates for occupations with short investment periods. The difference in wages is what equalizes the lifetime income streams.) The Focus, "Does It Pay to Go to College?" elaborates on the economic decision-making process of whether to go to college.

Other Equalizing Differences in Wages

A long investment period is not all that discourages individuals from entering a particular occupation. Other characteristics make it necessary for some occupations to offer higher wages to induce workers to enter. People will evaluate their alternative work possibilities in both monetary and nonmonetary terms. Pay will be important, but so too will be working conditions, location, coworkers, risk, length of contract, personality of the boss, and myriad other

---

[1]The values of C and B must be discounted for time, as is the case for any investment; this point is discussed in Chapter 16.

FOCUS Does It Pay to Go to College?

The decision to go to college is a decision to invest in human capital with alternative payoffs for different levels of investment (see Table 3). As with all investments, there are costs and benefits. The monetary costs are the forgone income one could earn by working and the direct costs such as tuition and books. The monetary benefits are the years of extra income that one may earn with a degree. Is college a good investment? Is the rate of return on an investment in education higher than that of other investments?

Richard Freeman calculated the rate of return on a college degree over an individual's life cycle.

Year	Rate of Return
1959	11.0%
1969	11.5%
1972	10.5%
1974	8.5%

These rates of return represent the interest rates that individuals receive on their investments in education. From 1969 to 1974 there was clearly a downward trend.

Freeman investigated whether the trend has continued into the 1980s. He found that through the 1970s the rate of return to college education fell considerably, suggesting that Americans were becoming "overeducated." That is, additional years of education did not seem to generate the additional income they once did. However, the trend seems to have bottomed out. Freeman predicted that during the 1980s the market for college graduates would improve and increase the rate of return on investment in a college education. The available evidence suggests that Freeman's prediction was on the mark.

Sources: Richard Freeman, "Overinvestment in College Training," *Journal of Human Resources* 10 (Summer 1975); and "The Overeducated American in the 1980s: A Report to the National Commission on Student Financial Assistance," *Higher Education Marketing Journal* 11:9 (Summer 1983).

TABLE 3

Estimated Lifetime Earnings of 24-Year-Old Men and Women by Education Level (1988 dollars)

The figures show the total earnings of various individuals, assuming that work life begins at age twenty-four and continues until age sixty-five. Expected earnings from additional education rise for both men and women. However, the figures probably underestimate true lifetime earnings because they do not account for future earnings growth due to human productivity changes over work life. Also note the disparity in estimated future earnings between men and women, a difference partially due to sex discrimination, which we discuss in Chapter 18.

Education Level	Male Lifetime Earnings	Female Lifetime Earnings
1 to 3 years of high school	$ 647,082	$ 289,570
4 years of high school	974,556	448,408
1 to 3 years of college	1,168,262	614,882
4 years of college	1,487,088	847,090
More than 4 years of college	1,842,162	1,079,942

Source: U.S. Department of Commerce, Bureau of the Census, Current Population Reports—Consumer Income, *Money Income of Households, Families, and Persons in the United States: 1988* (Washington, D.C.: U.S. Government Printing Office, 1988), pp. 42–43.

factors. Although some of these factors are nonmonetary or psychological, this does not mean that they are not income. They are a part of workers' pay. The total compensation of a worker in a given occupation consists of the wage plus any nonmonetary aspects of the job.

The principle of equalizing differences in wages works in the following way. In a competitive labor market, laborers choose the occupation with the highest total compensation, other things equal. This brings the wage down until the total compensation for the occupation is on a par with that of other

$\uparrow SS_L \Rightarrow \downarrow w$

occupations. If total compensation is too low in some occupation, then people leave that occupation until the wage rises enough to equalize the total compensation. When total compensation is equalized across occupations, the competitive equilibrium is achieved. If this condition is not met, workers will move around and change jobs until it is met.

One student who spends the summer in an air-conditioned office may make a lower wage but more nonwage pay per hour than another student who spends the summer on a construction crew. As students compete for summer jobs, total pay between jobs will be equalized. This is the principle of equalizing differences at work in a competitive labor market.

The basic point is that observed wage differences across occupations may reflect differences in nonmonetary aspects of employment. Of course, labor markets may not always be competitive as we have assumed here. Some jobs may pay more and have more attractive working conditions if there are barriers to entry into the occupation. However, under competition, wage differences can exist. The following are just a few of the many reasons for wage differences other than those caused by human capital differences.

Wages will vary directly with the disagreeableness of a job. The more uncomfortable the job, the higher the pay will be. To induce workers to accept jobs that create discomfort—such as tarring roofs in the heat of summer—a higher monetary reward must be offered. Workers will not offer their labor below a certain wage, given that they have alternatives.

The more seasonal or irregular a job, the higher the pay will be. To induce individuals to supply labor to irregular employments, the wage must compensate them for the likelihood of being laid off frequently. For example, construction workers often experience periods of unemployment between jobs. To have readily available workers, construction employers must pay a higher wage.

Jobs that require trustworthiness carry a higher wage. Armored truck drivers, blackjack dealers, and some bank employees receive relatively high wages. One reason that such occupations pay more is that being trustworthy is both an extra burden and a form of human capital; employers must compensate such workers for their extra efforts. Since workers have a choice between stealing and thereby losing future wage income and not stealing but keeping the job, the wage must be high enough to induce continued honesty in supplying labor.

Jobs with greater risk to health will have higher pay. Occupations with higher than average probabilities of death or disability must compensate employees for taking a risk. People are not willing to risk lost future income because of injuries unless they can receive higher income in the present. Steelworkers who construct frames for one-hundred-story skyscrapers must be paid more than those who work on the ground.

Jobs that carry the possibility of tremendous success will have a lower wage. Acting is a good example of such a profession. Many young people aspire to be actors and are arguably attracted into acting by the sumptuous lifestyle of movie stars. Most never make it that big; the average salary of all actors is quite low. Yet some people are willing to take the plunge, feeling that they are good enough to be big winners. Attitudes toward risk are therefore important in determining relative wages. The wages for most actors will be lower because some successful actors make startlingly high pay, a possibility that induces many young people to enroll in acting school.

Wages will vary by region. Wages in any region are determined by supply and demand. However, if wages in market *A* exceed the wages in market *B*, then we expect to see labor flow from B to A. (There may be a time lag if additional training is necessary for the job shift from B to A.) The shifting short-run supply brings wages into equilibrium. Wages fall in A and rise in B.

The equality of wages is the result of individuals' actions. Furthermore, an individual's decision to move is based on the costs and benefits of doing so. Relocation requires resource expenditures that must be offset by extra income. Indeed, the decision to move to a higher-paying location within the same occupation represents an investment in human capital.

Suppose a worker could stay in location B and earn wage W_B or could move to location A and earn a higher wage W_A. The direct costs of moving are the expenses incurred in transporting the worker, her family members, and their personal belongings. There are also additional opportunity costs. The act of moving requires time, and so might finding a job in A. This is time that could have been spent earning income in B. The lost income is a cost of relocation, as shown in Figure 11.

At time 0 the individual must choose between earning wage W_B from T to retirement and spending time moving so as to earn wage W_A. The time $0T$ is the amount of time spent moving from B to A plus the amount of time spent seeking employment in A. The total cost of moving is the shaded area between 0 and T above and below the x-axis, which represents the income forgone plus direct moving expenses. The benefit of moving—represented by the shaded area between T and retirement—is the extra income that may be earned after the move. It pays to move if the area of extra benefits is greater than the area of costs.[2]

FIGURE 11

An individual must choose whether to remain in location B and earn wage W_B from time 0 to retirement or move to location A and earn wage W_A from time T to retirement. The decision to move to A necessitates costs in terms of the time $0T$ spent moving and income forgone while making the move, represented by the shaded area from 0 to T above the x-axis. After the move, the individual earns extra income represented by the shaded area from T to retirement. If this area of extra income is greater than the area of total costs of moving, the individual will choose to move.

Wage Differences Across Regions

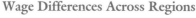

---

[2]As in the earlier example of the economic costs and benefits of a college education, these values must be discounted for time, as explained in Chapter 16.

If benefits outweigh costs, then many people will choose to move to A—the move is a good investment in human capital. However, the shifting labor supplies will increase wages in B, where workers are now scarcer, and decrease them in A. The maximum amount by which W_A can exceed W_B in the long run is the amount that forces the area of benefits to equal the area of costs. Therefore, the lower the costs of moving, the smaller the difference in wages needs to be.

In fact, there are many reasons why we expect little variation in wages across the country within the same occupation in today's markets. First, the duration of lost income for most movers is very small. Indeed, it is quite possible to work until 5:00 P.M. on Friday in New York City and start work at 9:00 A.M. on Monday in Los Angeles. Many people will not move unless they have already found employment in the new location. If the amount of time it takes to travel across the country today were as great as it was two hundred years ago, then wage differences could be very large.

Another reason that regional differences in wages are small is that young workers have small costs and large benefits in moving. Young workers typically have small families or no families and few material possessions to move. Also, the years of receiving extra benefits are longer for young people. Thus, the difference in wages can be smaller to induce them to move.

Another important aspect of regional wage differences involves the demand side of the labor market. Firms will be encouraged to expand operations in areas where there are low costs of production and decrease operations where costs are high. Firms will invest more capital in low-wage area B and decrease investment in high-wage area A. Capital moves around the country just as labor does, and this movement tends to equalize wages. In fact, all resources that are mobile move to the locations that yield the resource owners the highest income.

In spite of this equalizing tendency, we observe that wages in the North are about 10 percent higher than in the South in the same occupations. Economist Don Bellante suggests that the difference occurs only in money wages and not in real wages.[3] The cost of living in the South is about 10 percent lower than in the North. This difference in costs equalizes the real wage, just as we expect in the long run.

Comparable Worth: Government Regulation of Wages

Traditionally, in a market economy the pay of various types of workers is assumed to be determined solely by the interaction of supply and demand. As a consequence, wages differ greatly between occupations, with carpenters earning more than secretaries and physicians earning more than teachers. However, the resulting pay differences are viewed by many as failing to meet some standards of equity. It is not hard to find workers (ourselves, perhaps) who will argue that the demands on them are great and that they are underpaid compared with workers in other occupations. Often these complaints include charges that the inequities are, in part, the consequence of discrimination by employers against female or minority workers.

---

[3]D. Bellante, "The North-South Differential and the Migration of Heterogeneous Labor," *American Economic Review* 69 (March 1979), pp. 166–75.

Comparable worth:
A proposal that advocates government regulations requiring employers to pay employees in different but comparable occupations equally. Comparability between occupations is based on the amount of training and education required for each job and on working conditions.

In recent years a movement has started that advocates an increased role for the government in assuring greater equity in pay. The aim of this movement is to assure that the pay for different occupations reflects the **comparable worth** of the services provided by workers in various occupations. Advocates of comparable worth argue that the value of each type of worker can be objectively determined in terms of the job qualifications and work conditions. Under their proposed system, impartial experts would rate each occupation and assign a number that reflects the worth of each particular job. In one specific case involving a discrimination lawsuit against the state of Washington, consultants working for state employees ranked delivery truck drivers, auto mechanics, secretaries, civil engineers, registered nurses, and senior computer analysts.[4] Each occupation was evaluated on the categories of knowledge and skills, mental demands, accountability, and work conditions. Points were assigned in all categories of the rated occupations, and higher numbers reflected greater demands or more difficult working conditions. For example, in the category of mental demands, the evaluators assigned truck drivers 10 points, civil engineers 53 points, and nurses 70 points. In the category of knowledge and skills, auto mechanics were given 106 points, secretaries received 122, and registered nurses got 184.

When point totals were compiled for each occupation, secretaries outscored truck drivers by more than two-to-one, 197 to 97. At the time of the study, secretaries employed by the state were paid $306 per week and truck drivers were paid $382. Similarly, nurses received nearly twice the points of auto mechanics (341 compared to 175), but they were paid about 10 percent less. The implementation of comparable worth would require massive pay increases for secretaries and nurses, large pay cuts for mechanics and truck drivers, or some combination of the two.

To date, the comparable worth issue has been confined largely to the government sector. However, advocates are working for its implementation across the economy. Many would like to see the U.S. Secretary of Labor issue pay guidelines based on comparable worth to ensure that businesses that receive government contracts comply with comparable worth standards.

Critics of comparable worth argue that it is impossible to assign points objectively to different occupations. The working conditions of a forest ranger are different from those of a registered nurse, but it is impossible to say which conditions are more demanding—it depends on the preferences of particular workers. In addition, it is impossible to determine objectively how much importance should be placed on the physical requirements of a job compared with the mental ones. A baggage handler does more heavy lifting than an air traffic controller, but air traffic controllers have greater mental demands. It is impossible to say who has better working conditions. Even if the difficulties of objectively assigning points to different occupations could be resolved, a wage system based on comparable worth would still be subject to serious practical problems. A crucial role played by labor markets is to attract new workers into growing occupations. For example, as the number of older Americans increases, there is a need for additional nurses and other health care personnel. As a nursing shortage starts to develop, the wages of nurses will

---

[4]For a more complete discussion of this case, see Barbara A. Bergmann, "Does the Market for Women's Labor Need Fixing?" *The Journal of Economic Perspectives* (Winter 1989), pp. 43–60.

rise *if* market forces are allowed to operate. This increase will lead to increases in the number of nurses. If, however, wages are regulated by comparable worth considerations (or by artificial entry barriers), the nursing shortage could persist indefinitely. Under that pay system, the increase in demand for nurses will not cause nursing wages to rise.

MARGINAL PRODUCTIVITY THEORY AND INCOME DISTRIBUTION

The profit-maximizing tendency of competitive firms to set marginal revenue product (*MRP*) equal to marginal factor cost (*MFC*) leads to a wage that equals the value of a worker's marginal product. This result applies to the prices of all factors of production in competitive markets. Each resource—be it labor, land, or capital—is paid the value of its marginal product.

The marginal productivity theory of factor prices is a positive, not a normative, theory. It explains *how* factor prices are determined in markets, not how factor prices *should be* determined. It is not meant to be an ethical theory of income distribution, though it is sometimes attacked as such. It is meant as a demand and supply theory that explains the behavior of input prices and the allocation of factors of production to different employments.

However, the marginal productivity theory has been criticized even as a positive theory. Labor markets are not perfect, and resources do not seem to flow around the economy in a smooth, frictionless way to equalize rates of return in factor markets. Labor and physical capital are particularly difficult to characterize as easily movable. People and machines and buildings generally like to stay put. In this sense the marginal productivity theory may not always offer a realistic explanation of short-run factor prices. At any time we might observe different wage rates in a market for equally skilled workers, which marginal productivity theory may have difficulty in rationalizing. Wages also differ across regions, although some of the differences may be explained by differences in the cost of living.

Over a longer period of time, marginal productivity theory does offer a good explanation of factor prices. In the long run, resources will relocate to take advantage of higher rates of return. For this reason, marginal productivity theory is alive and well as a scientific explanation of factor prices. Given proper time, it is the best explanation we have of factor prices.

Another criticism of marginal productivity analysis is that business managers could not possibly estimate the marginal revenue products of their inputs. How hard it is to estimate *MRP* is an interesting question, but the fact is that, on an ongoing basis, business managers are forced to make some sort of estimate of what their inputs are capable of doing. For example, firms must decide whether to promote from within or hire managers from other firms. Why do firms typically promote from within? One answer is that it is less costly to form an estimate of the *MRP* of inside candidates. The firm has observed the performance of the inside candidate but must take letters of recommendation and other types of indirect evidence about the outside candidate.

It should now be clear that the theory of marginal productivity implies many things about income distribution. Where there is competitive voluntary contracting for labor services, labor's share of national income will be directly related to its marginal product. "To each according to the demand and supply for what he or she produces" perhaps best describes what happens in marginal productivity theory. Of course, factor markets are not perfect, and various other forces affect income distribution in a society. These issues will be carefully addressed over the next several chapters. Our argument in this chapter is not that the marginal productivity theory is necessarily a good normative theory of how income should be distributed (although you might believe it so), but rather that it provides an objective basis for understanding the economic behavior of demanders and suppliers of inputs.

SUMMARY

1. The demand for labor is a derived demand; it is derived from the demand for the product that labor produces.

2. The demand curve for labor is a function of its marginal product and the demand for the product it produces. In the short run, demand is equivalent to marginal revenue product: $MRP_L = MP_L \times MR$.

3. The competitive firm hires the profit-maximizing amount of labor at the point where MRP equals the wage rate. The short-run market demand curve for labor shows the amount of labor that firms hire when labor is the only variable input and the number of firms is constant, but it allows for changes in product price as wages change.

4. The long-run market demand curve for labor shows the amount of labor hired at different wages when all inputs are allowed to vary and firms are in long-run competitive equilibrium.

5. The demand for labor changes when the demand for the product changes or when the marginal product of labor changes. The elasticity of demand for labor is directly related to the elasticity of demand for the product it produces, the percentage of total cost accounted for by labor, and the number and availability of substitute inputs for labor.

6. The relation between the wage rate and the number of hours of labor an individual supplies depends on the substitution and income effects. If the substitution effect is greater than the income effect, then the individual's labor supply curve is positively sloped; the curve is negatively sloped if the income effect is greater than the substitution effect. The aggregate labor supply curve is the sum of individual labor supply curves and is usually positively sloped.

7. Human capital is anything an individual acquires that increases his or her productivity. In an occupation that requires human capital, the longer and more costly the investment period, the higher the wages.

8. The total compensation in all occupations in competitive markets is equalized by differences in wages. The long-run supply of labor to each occupation ensures the equilibrium difference in wages.

9. Because of changes in either supply or demand, wage levels may vary across the United States. However, migration of workers will tend to eliminate regional wage differences.

10. The government may elect to eliminate inequities in pay by requiring that workers be paid on the basis of comparable worth. However, such regulation might seriously impede the ability of labor markets to attract new workers into occupations where they are needed.

11. In competitive markets, resources are paid a price that is equal to their marginal product. Labor's share of the overall income distribution is related to its marginal product.

KEY TERMS

factor market
derived demand
competitive labor market
market demand for labor
market supply of labor
marginal product of labor (MP_L)

marginal revenue product of labor (MRP_L)
marginal factor cost of labor (MFC_L)
firm's long-run demand for labor
change in the demand for labor
complementary inputs
substitute inputs

elasticity of demand for labor
nonmarket activities
human capital
comparable worth

QUESTIONS FOR REVIEW AND DISCUSSION

1. Suppose that the demand for each of the following goods and services increases. What derived demands will increase as a result? (a) Automobiles, (b) candy, (c) government regulation, (d) physical fitness, (e) education.
2. Explain why an individual's supply of labor curve may bend backward at some sufficiently high wage level.
3. What does the law of diminishing marginal productivity have to do with the demand curve for labor?
4. What is the difference between the demand curve for labor of a monopolist and of a perfectly competitive firm in the output market?
5. Apply the principle of equalizing differences to explain why the relative wage of the following occupations is high or low: (a) politicians, (b) schoolteachers, (c) morticians, (d) actors, (e) brain surgeons.
6. In what sense is the marginal productivity theory of wages a positive theory? In what sense is it a normative theory?

7. What activities will frustrate the equalization of total wages across jobs in the labor market? Does this mean that there is such a thing as nonequalizing wage differences?
8. On the basis of comparable worth, a new professor of English may have the same value to a university as a new engineering professor. However, the market salary for engineering professors is currently about twice as high. If your college or university were to base faculty pay on comparable worth, what would the consequences be? Should your college or university make this change?
9. Are tractor drivers substitutes for human cotton pickers? What happens to the demand for tractor drivers if cotton pickers' wages fall?
10. Is the demand for toothpicks elastic or inelastic? What about elasticity of demand for a machine that makes toothpicks?

PROBLEMS

The data in the table apply to a competitive firm.

1. What is the marginal factor cost of labor for this firm?
2. If you are the personnel manager of this firm, how many units of labor will you hire?

Units of Labor	Marginal Product	Marginal Revenue	Marginal Revenue Product	Hourly Wage Rate
1	21	$1.50	$31.50	$9.00
2	18	1.50	27.00	9.00
3	15	1.50	22.50	9.00
4	12	1.50	18.00	9.00
5	9	1.50	13.50	9.00
6	6	1.50	9.00	9.00
7	3	1.50	4.50	9.00
8	0	1.50	0.00	9.00

ECONOMICS IN ACTION
Immigration and Labor Supply in the Southwestern United States

The U.S. labor supply not only depends on U.S. population growth, but on both legal and illegal immigration. The current level of legal immigration is about 750,000 persons per year, the majority from Asia and Latin America (primarily Mexico). Figure 12 describes immigration trends in the United States from 1820 to 1989. Although Europeans dominated immigration over most of American history, an "open door," antidiscriminatory policy was instituted in the 1960s that changed the face of American immigration and encouraged resettlement by other groups. Since then, the proportion of Asians and Latin Americans has been greater than that from all other places combined.

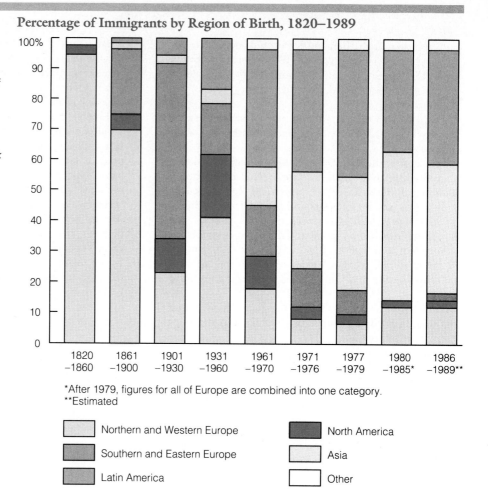

FIGURE 12

Percentage of Immigrants by Region of Birth, 1820–1989

For approximately 140 years, most immigrants to America were of European extraction. Since 1960, the percentages of Asians and Latin Americans have increased dramatically.

Source: Robert Reinhold, "Flow of Third World Immigrants Alters Weave of U.S. Society," *New York Times* (June 30, 1986), p. 11. Copyright © 1986 by The New York Times Company. Reprinted by permission.

*After 1979, figures for all of Europe are combined into one category.
**Estimated

Northern and Western Europe · North America · Southern and Eastern Europe · Asia · Latin America · Other

Legal immigration at present levels is viewed by most economists as a healthy and necessary trend to counterbalance slowed indigenous U.S. population growth and to create a base for U.S. economic development into the twenty-first century. Between 1980 and 1988, legal immigration averaged 580,000 persons per year—about one-quarter of 1 percent of the U.S. population. Illegal immigration bothers some politicians and interest groups in our society, although the economic effects of legal and illegal immigration are virtually the same. In particular, a flood of illegal immigrants—primarily, but not only, from Mexico—swells the ranks of unskilled workers, especially in the states that border Mexico. It is estimated that illegal immigrants total more than 10 million people. Some charge that such "illegals" put pressure on the U.S. welfare and educational systems and take jobs away from unskilled American workers. While these charges may have some merit, low-skilled illegal workers take many jobs that would go unfilled by domestic workers—at least at the wages the illegal immigrants are willing to accept. Another important issue is whether both legal and illegal immigrants add more (or less) to the present and future product of the United States than they add to costs.

In October 1986, Congress passed the Simpson-Mazzoli Bill (the Immigration Reform and Control Act of 1986), which revised immigration laws and, in the process, altered the markets for both skilled and unskilled labor—particularly in the southwestern United States. The legislation took a carrot-and-stick approach to enforcing immigration restrictions. The "carrot" was amnesty and provisional citizenship granted to all illegals who could prove that they were working (albeit illegally) in the United States prior to 1981. Under the law, 1.8 million illegals obtained amnesty. California accounts for 54.8 percent of the total, Texas for 17.8 percent, and New York for 6.9 percent. Other states that have large numbers of illegals who were granted amnesty include Illinois (6.7 percent), Florida (2.7 percent), Arizona (1.6 percent), New Jersey (1.6 percent), and New Mexico (1.0 percent). The law's "stick" required that employers police the papers of all workers hired to ensure that the workers are in the United States legally. A branch of the Justice Department

Thousands of new American citizens take part in a naturalization ceremony.

enforces the law. Infractions (or mistakes) make employers liable for fines up to $10,000 per illegal hired and/or jail terms. (The illegals are deported.)

A provisional analysis of the economic effects of Simpson-Mazzoli on unskilled labor in both the short run and the long run is now possible. One effect has been a decrease in demand for illegal labor due to the potential legal costs facing employers. The law has turned employers into police officers, particularly in Texas and California, although limited resources make it impossible for federal authorities to check on the compliance of all employers. Some employers have not been efficient in policing the law, and resource costs have risen for those who continue to hire Mexican-American laborers. More bureaucracy and paperwork for employers has meant reduced demand for certain types of labor. Discrimination against Americans of Hispanic descent has occurred, as employers have tried to cut costs by hiring "clearly" legal—that is, non-Mexican-American—workers. It can be argued, then, that an "undemocratic" incentive has been built into the law—making it difficult for the Justice Department to determine whether discrimination is being practiced or if employers are simply trying to follow the law.

Simpson-Mazzoli was oriented to demand conditions in low-skilled labor markets; it did not address the supply problem. There are few signs that the supply of illegal workers from Mexico and Central American countries has been sig-

nificantly affected. The nominal penalty for an illegal is exactly the same as before 1986—deportation by the Immigration and Naturalization Service (INS). But some illegals *reenter* the United States as often as five or ten times per year. Increased government expenditures on hiring and training additional border guards is no match for the determination of many of the people fleeing poverty or oppression in their own countries. Short of even stricter and much more costly enforcement—in other words, converting border cities into police states—the problem of illegal immigrants will continue.

The economic effects of Simpson-Mazzoli in the illegal and legal labor markets have been dramatic. Some American citizens of Hispanic or Asian descent are experiencing discrimination. In the face of reduced demand for *both* legals and illegals, lower wages are being paid in real and/or nominal terms, as the labor supply facing employers has changed. (Some increase in the employment of Anglo-Americans would be the expected result of the 1986 law.) Because the Justice Department cannot rigidly enforce the law—not at its current level of funding anyway—some employers cheat by knowingly hiring illegals at lower nominal pay than the market wage of legal unskilled laborers. Low unemployment rates in the late 1980s made hiring illegals more tempting; and unscrupulous employers now have even less incentive to treat illegal workers well. Counterfeiters have profited from devising and selling improved documents to prove legality, further taxing the meager resources of illegals.[a] One observer has noted that up to two-thirds of amnesty applications to the INS were tainted by forgery and fraud.[b]

More, not less, real poverty may have been the result of the 1986 law, although Simpson-Mazzoli did have at least one more clear-cut benefit—the amnesty granted millions of workers. Far from eliminating the entrenched two-tiered wage system for legal and illegal workers, however, Simpson-Mazzoli—specifically, the way the bill structures incentives—may encourage inequality. Stricter enforcement of the law would tend to raise the relative price of service and farming outputs, reducing the demand for *all* unskilled labor. This potential effect would be due to a reduced input requirement in these businesses and a significant economic effect on large parts of the Southwest.

The Simpson-Mazzoli bill of 1986 has not addressed the fundamental problems of illegal immigration; widespread unemployment, poverty, and slow economic growth in Mexico and Central America are well beyond the scope of a single piece of domestic legislation. With brighter conditions existing a stone's throw away, the tired, poor, and hungry will continue to cross the Rio Grande. The same motivations of our immigrant grandparents and great-grandparents—economic gain and political and religious freedom—are motivating modern-day Latin Americans and Asians. Historical studies tend to confirm that the pre-1900 open immigration provided the stimulus for economic growth in the United States.[c] A recent study cited by the President's Council of Economic Advisers noted that between 1970 and 1980, high immigration in 120 U.S. cities had a negligible effect on the employment status of less-skilled native workers. (Real wages of these workers were estimated to have fallen by only 1 percent over the ten-year period.)[d] Despite some short-run problems, open immigration may well produce long-run benefits: economic growth, innovation, and creativity. In 1847, the last Mexican governor of California allegedly stated the following: "We find ourselves suddenly threatened by hordes of Yankee emigrants whose progress we cannot arrest."[e] That threat proved an economic boon—something it may behoove us to keep in mind.

Questions

1. Would you support or oppose open immigration to the United States on economic grounds? Present a case, pro or con, considering the possible impact on U.S. workers, pressure on government programs and expenditures, and social effects.

2. If no border restrictions between the U.S. and Mexico existed, what do you think would happen to the average cost (and therefore the price) of labor-intensive goods produced in the United States? Include an analysis of the labor market in your answer.

[a]Jim Pfiffer, "Illegal Workers Snap Up Fake IDs," *USA Today* (March 22, 1990), p. 3A.

[b]Jeff Riggenbach, "The Law Won't Work: Open Our Borders," *USA Today* (November 30, 1988), p. 10A.

[c]Harry Jerome, *Migration and Business Cycles* (New York: National Bureau of Economic Research, 1929).

[d]Council of Economic Advisers, *Economic Report of the President,* 1990 (Washington, D.C.: U.S. Government Printing Office, 1990), p. 165.

[e]Robert Reinhold, "Flow of Third World Immigrants Alters Weave of U.S. Society," *New York Times* (June 30, 1986), p. 11.

15

Labor Unions and Imperfect Competition

The previous chapter discussed demand and supply conditions in a competitive labor market, where the wage rates tend toward equality. Although we see a great deal of wage discrepancies in competitive markets, many of these can be attributed to circumstances such as the amount of risk a particular job involves or the amount of training it requires. We naturally expect brain surgeons to make more than dishwashers in a competitive environment because of the human capital investment brain surgeons must make to perform their services. The mobility of a work force also affects its wage. The wages of workers will often vary because many of us are simply unable to move to fill available jobs.

All labor markets, of course, are not strictly competitive. In general, factor markets can assume the same kinds of imperfect market structures that we studied in Chapters 11 and 12. The imperfection in labor markets can occur on the supply side, the demand side, or both. On the supply side, labor unions account for the largest source of imperfect competition.

In this chapter we will look at how imperfectly competitive labor markets work. Specifically, we will look at the effects of labor unions. When you finish Chapter 15 you should understand

- the goals of labor unions and the changes unions have undergone in the United States.
- how unions achieve goals such as higher wages and better working conditions for their members.
- the impact of labor unions on consumers and nonunion labor.
- some of the effects on labor when a single employer exists in an individual market.

TYPES OF LABOR UNIONS

Labor union:
A group of individual workers organized to act collectively in an attempt to affect labor market conditions.

A **labor union** is a group of workers who organize collectively in an effort to increase their market power. By acting as a collective unit, they are able to exert a greater influence over working conditions or wages. In this sense, a labor union is similar to a cartel (discussed in Chapter 12). In a union, the sellers of labor agree not to compete among themselves but to act as a single seller of labor.

The first labor unions in the United States started as workers' guilds in the late 1700s and early 1800s. These organizations of workers within the same trade—carpenters, cordwainers (shoemakers), hatters—began meeting to set standards and prices for their output. These loosely organized trade unions were typically short-lived but were the beginnings of the American labor movement.

The Industrial Revolution brought about new opportunities for labor unions. Large manufacturing plants employed many workers with similar skills and interests who could organize at relatively low costs to pursue their common goals. The early stages of the new industrial growth also brought the buyer of labor—the factory owner—considerable market power, the effects of which further encouraged workers to unify to enhance their own power. Today there are three major types of labor unions: craft unions, industrial unions, and public employees' unions.

Craft Unions

Craft union:
Workers with a common skill who organize to restrict the supply of labor in their trade and obtain some market power; also called a trade union.

In 1886, the American Federation of Labor (AFL) was started in an effort to organize craftspeople into local unions. **Craft unions,** which flourished in the Middle Ages, organize workers according to particular skills—such as electricians, carpenters, or plumbers—regardless of the industry in which they work. The main function of the guilds is to advance their members' economic well-being. When workers act as a unit, their power in the market can limit competition and raise total compensation above the competitive level. In this sense, the American Medical Association (AMA) or the American Bar Association (ABA) may be viewed as effective unions because they restrict membership in the medical and legal professions, raising professional fees above competitive levels.

Trade or craft unions increase members' total compensation by decreasing the supply of skilled workers. They do so by excluding potential workers from membership. Frequently, trade unions require high initiation fees, monthly dues, and long apprenticeship programs in an effort to discourage potential entrants. Existing members enjoy the higher wage brought about by the limited supply of workers in their trade. Figure 1 shows the impact of this decreased supply on wages: Wages rise from the competitive level, W_c, to the unionized level, W_u.

Trade unions are very much like cartels in the sense that supply is artificially restricted so as to command a higher price. As such, craft unions face the same problems as cartels. Just as cartel members have an incentive to cheat on the cartel price, workers outside the union who offer their labor at a wage lower than the union wage can obtain jobs at the expense of union members.

Industrial Unions

Large manufacturing plants first appeared during the late 1800s and early 1900s. A large firm in the textile, automobile, steel, or coal industry would frequently be the only employer in a small, isolated town. As a single buyer of labor, such a firm would be able to keep wages below the competitive level.

FIGURE 1

Craft unions decrease the supply of workers in a particular craft by limiting the number of people who may join the union. When a union organizes, the supply of labor decreases to S_u from the competitive supply, S_c. Wages rise from the competitive level W_c to the unionized level W_u. Employment falls from L_c to L_u.

A Craft Union's Effect in the Labor Market

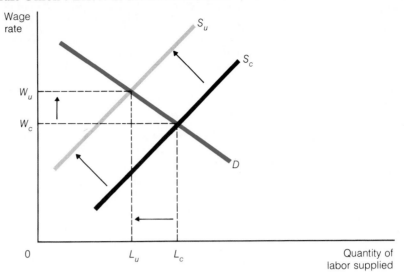

Industrial union:
Workers in a given industry organized independently of their skills in an effort to obtain market power.

Public employees' union:
Workers employed by federal, state, or local governments who organize in an effort to obtain market power.

Under these circumstances, workers often found it in their interest to organize. Rather than organize individual craft unions according to different skills, all workers within the same industry would organize a single industry-wide union. In 1938, John L. Lewis formally organized the Congress of Industrial Organizations (CIO), which unified workers first at the firm level and then at the level of the industry as a whole. Contemporary examples of these **industrial unions** include autoworkers' unions and steelworkers' unions.

For an industrial union to be effective, it must unionize all firms in an industry. Otherwise, the lower-cost, nonunionized firms would prosper while the higher-cost, unionized firms would dwindle. Thus, industrial unions often encourage membership rather than restrict it.

Public Employees' Unions

Public employees' unions are organizations of government workers. Such unions cover a wide variety of jobs—such as fire fighting, police work, teaching, and clerical work—and include both blue-collar and white-collar workers. This sector of the union movement has been one of the fastest growing in recent years. The American Federation of State, County, and Municipal Employees (AFSCME) is now among the ten largest unions in the country. Indeed, membership in AFSCME tripled between 1968 and 1988.

The problems of public employees' unions have received a great deal of attention in recent years. Each fall finds teachers on strike for higher wages and benefits in cities across the country. The decertification of the Professional Air Traffic Controllers Union (PATCO) in the early 1980s resulted from a technically illegal strike by a public employees' union. Despite these much publicized problems, public employees' unions continue to grow in membership relative to private-sector unions.

Changes in Union Membership

Membership in labor unions as a percentage of the U.S. labor market grew steadily throughout the first half of this century; by 1953, about 26 percent of the workers in the U.S. were members of labor unions. That percentage remained nearly constant until 1975, when a precipitous drop-off in union membership began. Today, less than 16 percent of American workers belong to labor unions. The composition of union membership has changed dramatically, as well. In 1953, less than 5 percent of union members were government employees. Today, about 35 percent of all union members are employed by the government. Such traditionally heavily unionized sectors of the economy as mining, construction, and manufacturing currently have a smaller percentage of workers represented by labor unions than does the government sector. Trends in unionization for various industries are shown in Table 1.

Several economic factors have contributed to the decline in union membership. Structural changes in the U.S. economy—brought about in part by the pressure of foreign competition—have resulted in a decline in the number of manufacturing and mining jobs relative to service sector jobs. Workers in the service sector have always been more difficult to organize because they tend to be dispersed over a large number of relatively small business firms. Another factor that has contributed to the decline in union membership is the increased participation of women in the labor force. While women have traditionally expressed stronger support for the labor union movement than have men, they have always participated in labor unions in smaller proportions than men; this reflects the concentration of women in the service sector.

UNION ACTIVITIES

Regardless of the means of organization, when workers successfully unite to act as a single seller of labor, the union gains monopoly power in its labor market. The union and its members are therefore no longer wage rate takers.

TABLE 1   **Percent of Union Members in Various Industries**

Except for government employees, the percentage of workers in every major industry who are members of labor unions declined sharply between 1953 and 1988.

Year	Industry					
	Manufacturing	Mining	Construction	Transportation	Services	Government
1988	21.1%	18.7%	21.7%	33.1%	5.9%	36.6%
1984	26.0	20.7	27.5	42.4	7.7	34.3
1980	32.3	32.1	31.6	48.0	11.6	35.0
1975	36.0	32.0	35.4	46.6	13.9	39.5
1966	37.4	35.7	41.4	50.3	9.3	26.0
1953	42.4	64.7	83.8	79.9	9.5	11.6

Sources: Percentages for 1984 and 1988 are calculated from data in *Employment and Earnings,* U.S. Department of Labor, Bureau of Labor Statistics. Data for prior years are from *U.S. Union Source Book,* 1st ed., Industrial Relations Data Information Services, Bureau of National Affairs, 1985.

There is a downward-sloping demand curve for the members' labor, and the union may seek any wage along this curve. However, the level of employment for union members is inversely related to the wage rate. Higher wages are gained at the expense of fewer jobs. In the face of this fact, a union's activities will depend on its choices among conflicting objectives, the elasticity of demand for its workers' product, and the union's effect on demand for its workers' labor.

Union Goals

The ultimate goals of the union may depend on many competing objectives. Understandably, the union's elected, policy-making officials suggest that members want improved economic well-being: higher wages, more jobs, greater job security, safer jobs, more retirement pay, more fringe benefits, and so on. But relating union policy to a particular objective is difficult. For example, the union objective may be to maximize any number of options, some of which may be inconsistent—such as the utility of the union officials, the utility of members, the wage rate, the level of employment, the level of membership, the total wage income of members, the total wage income of senior members, and so on. The ramifications of three of these objectives are discussed below.

Employment for All Members. One objective of a union may be to achieve full employment for all members. To do so would require a wage rate that ensures that the quantity of labor demanded by firms is equal to the quantity of labor supplied by existing members. Suppose that the demand for the union's labor can be represented by curve D_L in Figure 2. If the amount of labor offered by the union is L_1, then wage W_1 will ensure full employment of union members.

Maximizing the Wage Bill. Although wage W_1 means that everyone in the union is working, full employment may not be the union's goal. Unions frequently have members sitting on the unemployment bench. Any wage higher than W_1 will leave some members unemployed, but there may also be some benefits to a higher wage. For example, it may increase the total wage bill. The **total wage bill** to firms hiring union workers is the wage rate times the total amount (in person-hours) of labor hired. This total wage bill is not only the total cost of labor to the firms; it is also the collective wage income of all the union members. Since workers prefer more income to less, all things being equal, the union may choose to maximize the wage bill. If the full employment wage occurs where the elasticity of demand is less than 1 (inelastic demand), then an increase in the wage will increase total union income $(W \times L)$.

To understand this possibility, recall from Chapter 5 how price, total revenue, and elasticity are related. Total revenue is maximized at the price where the elasticity of demand is equal to 1. If elasticity is less than 1, then an increase in price increases total revenue; if elasticity is greater than 1, it takes a price decrease to increase total revenue. In analyzing labor demand, the total wage bill, the wage rate, and the elasticity of demand have the same relation. If the union's objective is to maximize the total union income, then the wage is set where the elasticity of demand is equal to 1.

Total wage bill:
The total cost of labor to firms; equal to wage rate times total quantity of labor employed.

In Figure 2, wage W_2 maximizes the wage bill. However, with L_1 amount of labor in the union, unemployment in the amount $L_1 - L_2$ results. This may not be a problem because the total union income ($W_2 \times L_2$) is now higher than at W_1. All members can still be better off at a higher wage if the working members provide unemployment compensation to unemployed members. On the other hand, a trade union may choose to limit union membership to L_2.

In considering attempts by unions to maximize the wage bill, it is important to interpret the wage rate as a full wage. This includes both the hourly pay and the value of fringe benefits such as hospitalization insurance, retirement benefits, and paid vacation. For many union contracts, a large portion of the full pay takes the form of fringe benefits.

Maximizing Income for Limited Members. While wage W_2 would maximize income for the union as a whole, a higher wage such as W_3 in Figure 2 would increase income only for those who remain fully employed. L_3 workers would be hired, and their incomes would be higher so long as they are working the same number of hours. The workers on the unemployment bench would receive no income. For example, senior members usually retain employment under a seniority system. Thus, wages above W_2 would probably increase senior members' incomes at the expense of younger members. These unemployed members could be phased out of the union so that remaining members could retain higher incomes.

FIGURE 2

The Union's Wage Goals

In setting its wage rate, a union must choose among many goals. If there is L_1 amount of laborers in a union, then wage W_1 must be chosen to achieve full employment of all members. If the elasticity of demand at W_1 is less than 1, then an increase in wages up to W_2 will increase the total wage bill while bringing about union unemployment in the amount $L_1 - L_2$. Still-higher wages such as W_3 will decrease total union income, although those union members who are working enjoy greater incomes. In trying to maximize total wages, the union will face some degree of unemployment, according to this model.

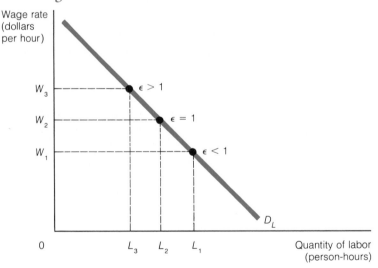

Union Objectives and the Elasticity of Demand

A union's ability to accomplish its goals is limited by the elasticity of demand for its members' labor. Increases in wages decrease the level of employment, but the percent decrease in employment is determined by the elasticity of demand. Unions would like to see large increases in wages with minor effects on employment; in other words, they would like the demand for their members' labor to be as inelastic as possible. The elasticity of demand for union labor is determined by many factors. Unions themselves often engage in activities that decrease the elasticity of demand for union members. Such a change in elasticity of demand is shown in Figure 3 as a rotation of the demand curve from D_1 to D_2. Wages are increased without causing so much unemployment. The following are some familiar examples of this process.

Elasticity of Demand for the Product. The more inelastic the demand for the good or service that the union produces, the more inelastic the demand for the union's labor. While a union would like the demand for the good or service its workers produce to be inelastic, it cannot do much to decrease this elasticity. Union workers are mostly at the mercy of the market, although in some circumstances they can and do affect elasticity of demand. For example, an item's elasticity of demand is determined in part by the number and availability of substitutes. If a union can limit the amount of substitutes for the product they produce, then the elasticity of demand for the union workers' labor decreases. We see this happening in the automobile industry. Through the political process, U.S. autoworkers encourage import quotas, which have the effect of limiting the supply of foreign autos and decreasing the elasticity of demand for U.S.-made cars. With import quotas, increases in autoworkers' wages have less effect on employment than the same increases in wages if quotas are not imposed.

FIGURE 3

Unions attempt to decrease the elasticity of demand for their members' labor. For example, unions support immigration laws that retard or block the flow of competitive foreign labor into this country. The effect of such activities is represented by a rotation of the demand curve from D_1 to D_2. This rotation of the demand curve indicates that future wage increases result in smaller employment decreases. If wages rise from W_1 to W_2, employment falls only to L_2 rather than L'_2.

Decreasing the Elasticity of Demand for Union Labor

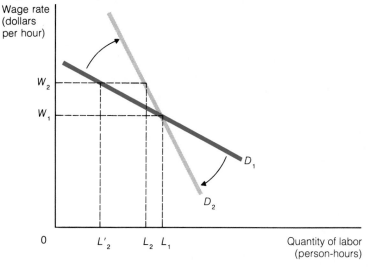

Availability of Substitute Inputs. The fewer substitute inputs for union labor, the lower the elasticity of demand for union labor. Unions would prefer that there be no substitute inputs for their members' labor. If this were true, then wage increases would have minimal effects on union employment. However, there are almost always some inputs that may be substituted for union labor. Typically, nonunion labor is a good substitute. For this reason, labor unions try to form contracts with firms that maximize the use of union labor. (Closed shops—which legally bind firms to hire *only* union labor—are now illegal in the United States.) Unions also take direct actions to limit the amount of nonunion labor available. For example, unions support laws that restrict immigration to the United States because such laws decrease the availability of immigrant workers who could substitute for union members in the work force.

Union Labor as a Proportion of Total Costs. The smaller the percentage of firms' total costs accounted for by unions, the more inelastic the demand for union labor. If labor represents a very small percentage of total costs and if wages increase substantially, then the increase in total cost and thus product price will be very small. For this reason, the level of employment will fall by only a very small percent. In such a situation, union goals conflict. If unions attempt to maximize the total wage bill and increase the number of unionized occupations, then their ability to affect wages might decrease.

Increasing the Demand for Union Labor

Regardless of the goals of unions, the members are always in favor of an increase in the demand for their labor. With increased demand, wages, employment, or both are increased. The curve representing demand for labor shifts to the right, as shown in Figure 4, when one of two basic things happens: an increase in the demand for the product or an increase in the marginal product of workers.

FIGURE 4

Labor unions encourage increases in the demand for their members' labor. Increasing the demand from D_1 to D_2 allows an increase in wages from W_1 to W_2 with a constant level of employment at L_1. Alternatively, employment can increase from L_1 to L_2 with wages constant at W_1. Or there can be an increase in both wages and employment to W_3 and L_3.

Increases in Demand for Union Labor

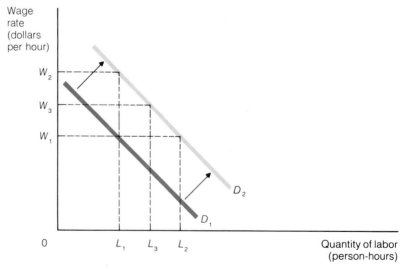

Unions can and do engage in activities that affect the demand for their members. Some of this activity is unproductive—for example, the practice of featherbedding. *Featherbedding* is the attempt to increase demand for union labor through contractual obligations to hire what some would regard as unnecessary labor. When diesel locomotives replaced steam locomotives, firemen were no longer needed to shovel coal. Railway workers nevertheless required firemen to be hired. The union contracts of journeyman carpenters or electricians stipulate that each union member must be provided with an apprentice—regardless of need. Contracts negotiated by musicians' unions routinely require that a minimum number of players be hired—again, without regard to any reasonable expectation of need. Some of these demand-increasing activities also decrease elasticity of demand for labor.

Increasing Product Demand. Unions frequently attempt to increase the demand for the products they produce. Garment workers advertise the union label and encourage consumers, as well as union members, to buy union-made clothes. Autoworkers strongly encourage union members to buy domestically produced cars. As we have seen, unions sometimes try to influence lawmakers to decrease the supply of foreign products that are substitutes for union-made goods. Import tariffs or quotas increase the demand for U.S.-made products.

Increasing Substitute Input Prices. If unions can increase the relative price of inputs that are substitutes for union labor, then the demand for union labor will increase. Unskilled nonunion workers using machines can substitute for skilled union labor, for example. Unions have therefore supported increases in the minimum wage. As the relative price of unskilled nonunion labor rises, the demand for union labor increases.

Increasing Productivity of Members. Unions prefer that their members be very productive. If the marginal product of new members joining the union is relatively high, then the demand for all members increases. Apprenticeship programs offered by unions train new entrants in an effort to increase overall productivity.

MONOPSONY: A SINGLE EMPLOYER OF LABOR

Having examined unions' attempts to build the economic power of laborers, we now turn to the nature of the firms they face as employers. Before the Industrial Revolution, large manufacturing plants were not common. In most towns or regions there were several potential employers for most workers. As a matter of fact, most skilled craftspeople were self-employed. However, as technology changed, the benefits of mass production increased. Large manufacturing plants such as steel mills, textile mills, and coal mines became the principal employers of labor in some regions. In some areas only one firm employed workers.

Monopsony:
A single buyer of a resource or product; sometimes found in labor markets as the single buyer of labor.

A single buyer of a resource in a market is known as a **monopsony.** The monopsonist buyer has market power because rather than purchase all that it is willing and able to purchase at a market-determined price, the monopsony faces an upward-sloping supply curve. From along this curve it seeks the price that yields the profit-maximizing quantity of resource employment.

Consider Figure 5. The firm sells its product in a competitive market; its marginal revenue product curve for labor is MRP_L. Since it is the only buyer of labor in the market, it faces an upward-sloping market supply curve of labor, S_L. To hire more labor, the firm must offer higher wages. Under these circumstances, the marginal factor cost of labor is no longer equal to the wage rate. The increase in total cost that results from hiring one more unit of labor is greater than the price paid for one more unit. And to attract one more unit of labor, the firm must offer a higher wage to all units of labor. For this reason, the MFC_L curve has the same relation to the upward-sloping supply curve as the marginal cost curve has to the average cost curve (discussed in Chapter 8). Indeed, the supply curve of labor represents the average factor cost curve.

The firm will hire all units of labor that add more to revenue than to cost. Thus the monopsonist firm will maximize profit by hiring labor up to the point where MFC_L equals MRP_L. (The monopsonist makes the same marginal analysis as the competitive buyer of labor.) The monopsonist hires L_m amount of labor and must pay wage W_m to attract that amount of labor.

The monopsonist wage and level of employment may be compared to those of pure competition under the same circumstances. If MRP_L in Figure 5 had been the summation of many firms' demand curves for labor, then competitive forces would have forced wages to W_c and employment to L_c. Under the same supply and MRP_L conditions, the presence of monopsony results in lower wages and lower employment.

Exploitation of labor:
A situation in which the wage rate paid to an input is less than the input's marginal revenue product.

The fact that the monopsonist pays a wage rate less than the MRP_L is known as **exploitation of labor.** If individuals are not being paid the value of their marginal product, then the monopsonist is extracting value from them. In the small regional markets of early days, monopsonists were actually exploiting the immobility of labor. As single employers, firms were able to pay

---

FIGURE 5

A monopsonist faces an upward-sloping supply curve of labor, S_L. It maximizes profit by hiring the amount of labor that equates its marginal factor cost (MFC) to its marginal revenue product for labor (MRP_L). The monopsonist's levels of employment and wage, L_m and W_m, fall below the competitive levels, L_c and W_c.

Monopsony in the Labor Market

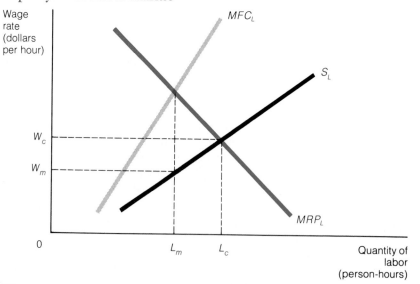

lower-than-competitive wages in isolated areas because the cost of transportation was very high. It was very difficult for individuals to move around the country to work for other employers.

The more mobile an employee, the greater the number of potential employers and the more elastic the labor supply. Today, the costs of transportation are relatively low. The opportunity cost of moving from one side of the country to another or commuting to all firms within a sixty-mile radius is lower today than it was a hundred years ago, although the costs of moving may be rising along with the increase in dual-career households. It is extremely rare to find an individual who has only one potential employer. (However, see Economics in Action, "Monopsony in College Athletics," at the end of this chapter.)

Bilateral Monopoly and the Need for Bargaining

Bilateral monopoly:
A market in which there is only one buyer and only one seller of a resource or product.

If there is a monopoly in a market, then the single seller has the power to determine price. If there is monopsony in a market, then the single buyer has the power to determine price. But in some markets, **bilateral monopoly**—a single seller and a single buyer—could exist. In such a case, what determines the price?[1]

Theoretically, the price in a bilateral monopoly market cannot be determined. No competitive forces determine a single price, and the seller has a preferred price that is higher than the buyer's preferred price. However, if the maximum price the buyer is willing to pay is greater than the minimum price the seller is willing to accept, then a bargain can be reached. Bargaining between two parties is the process by which price is determined.

Consider a labor market with bilateral monopoly. Suppose a monopsony exists in an isolated mining town with only one employer, a mining firm. The firm must rely on the town's supply of labor. As Figure 6 illustrates, the mining firm maximizes profit by hiring L_m workers and by paying wage W_m. The workers, though, are unhappy with wage W_m and decide to form a union. They manage to sign up workers of all skill levels throughout the community to the union, maximizing its bargaining strength.

The wage most preferred by the union is not clear. If the union's goal is to maximize employment, then W_c, which coincides with the competitive wage, would be most preferred. However, a higher wage such as W_u may result in the maximum total wage bill.

There is a maximum wage that the union can obtain. Any wage above the maximum would result in no union employment at all because of the high production costs that would be imposed. If wages are too high, then the monopsony may actually go out of business, turn entirely to substitutes for the union labor, or relocate in a lower-cost area. The union's ability to extract value from the firm is limited by the mobility of the firm, just as the firm's ability to extract value from the workers is limited by the mobility of the workers.

---

[1]The complexities of input price determination under bilateral monopoly are explored in Roger D. Blair, David L. Kaserman, and Richard E. Romano, "A Pedagogical Treatment of Bilateral Monopoly," *Southern Economic Journal* 55 (April 1989), pp. 831–41.

FIGURE 6

When a monopsonist chooses lower-than-competitive wage W_m and a monopoly union chooses higher-than-competitive wage W_u, the wage theoretically cannot be determined. But it can be determined by bargaining, and it will be between W_u and W_m. Although the wage is indeterminate, there is an incentive for the two parties to agree on employment level L_m because joint profits are maximized at that employment level.

Bilateral Monopoly

Collective Bargaining

When labor bargains collectively with a monopsonist, the final wage will be somewhere between the wage chosen by the monopsonist (W_m in Figure 6), and the wage most preferred by the union (W_u in the figure). The party that comes closest to establishing its goal is the one with the best bargaining strength. In **collective bargaining,** all buyers and all sellers of labor act as a unit to enhance their bargaining power.

Bilateral monopoly brings forth the need to negotiate. The absence of competition on both sides of the market creates a situation in which neither employers nor workers are able to dictate a wage rate. Indeed, there may be no need for bargaining unless a bilateral monopoly exists. Yet each year collective bargaining contracts are negotiated that cover the pay and working conditions for six to nine million American workers. Unions definitely limit wage competition among their members in many markets, but are there that many monopsonies?

In some industrial unions, such as the autoworkers' union, the union representatives bargain with a single firm. Under these circumstances, a firm that employs a very large percentage of a union's members does have some monopsony power. Wages cannot be dictated by the union. On the other hand, craft unions' members are employed by many firms. Hundreds of firms in different sectors of the United States employ carpenters, for example. It might seem that a union would not have to negotiate with an employer that has no monopsony power. However, the potential employers of craft union members may form a coalition, a buyer's cartel, to negotiate with unions as a single buyer of labor. Thus, when labor bargains as a unit to gain market power, previously competitive employers would do the same. When wage contracts are determined by bargaining negotiations there is, in effect, a bilateral monopoly in the market.

Collective bargaining:
The process of buyers and sellers negotiating, rather than competing individually, in order to determine a wage rate.

Strikes

The ability of a union to achieve higher wages depends on its bargaining strength, and its strongest weapon is the strike. When firms fail to meet labor's demands for a higher wage or any other demand, the union can withhold the labor services of its members. Such a **strike,** or refusal to work, can severely limit or even eliminate the firm's ability to continue production. By striking, a union withholds not only its members' labor but also that of other unions who respect the picket line. Under some circumstances, members of non-negotiating unions also withhold their labor from the negotiating firm. A firm's failure to concede to labor's demands can therefore be very costly. Of course, conceding to higher wages is costly as well.

Strike:
A collective refusal to work at the current wage or under current working conditions.

Yet the strike is a double-edged sword. Not only does it cost firms income, but union members lose income as well. A strike is not attractive to either party, but it is the best weapon labor has to force firms to accept the union wage. The union must decide if the lost income is worth its members' increased future income.

Similarly, firms have the power to reject employment at the union's desired wage. By doing so, a firm in effect refuses to hire labor at a particular wage or any higher wage. In a sense, the firm strikes against employing labor at too high a wage rate.

The potential costliness of a strike leads to serious bargaining by both management and labor because both sides have significant incentives to arrive at a new labor contract without a strike. In fact, negotiation is the general pattern of collective bargaining in the United States. Each year, some 120,000 labor contracts are renegotiated in collective bargaining processes. In more than 96 percent of these cases, labor and management arrive at a new agreement without recourse to a strike.

Table 2 provides some data about strikes since 1950. Perhaps the most relevant statistic in the table is the percentage of working time lost to strikes. As the data make clear, this figure has fallen over time and generally constitutes less than 0.5 percent of total working time, a figure far less than the time lost to worker absenteeism each year. The fact that little working time is lost to strikes means that strikes are a powerful union weapon. The threat of a strike may be sufficient to make collective bargaining work smoothly.

Sometimes, if negotiations are not successful, both parties can agree to **binding arbitration.** Such an agreement brings in a third party acceptable to labor and management to make a decision that both sides must abide by. Binding arbitration is often used for public sector union disputes because public employees usually are forbidden by law to strike. Public sector strikes in basic service activities—such as commuter transportation, garbage collection, teaching, and fire and police protection—have the potential to bring the economy to a halt. If essential services provided by government cease to be performed because of a strike, much private economic activity will cease as well.

Binding arbitration:
An agreement between the buyers and sellers of labor to allow a third party to determine the conditions of a work contract.

In private sector strikes, lost output can be made up to some extent if workers work overtime after the strike is settled. Moreover, substitute products and services are available to consumers during a private sector strike. Purchasers of new cars can buy used cars or drive their present cars until an autoworkers' strike is over, for example.

TABLE 2   Work Stoppages Involving 1000 Workers or More, 1950–1988

As these data for selected years since 1950 show, strikes have played a steadily declining role in the lives of American workers and the U.S. economy over the last four decades.

Year	Number	Workers Involved	Number of Idle Days	Percentage of Work Time Lost
1950	424	1698	30,390	0.26
1955	363	2055	21,180	0.16
1960	222	896	13,260	0.09
1965	268	999	15,140	0.10
1969	412	1576	29,397	0.16
1973	317	1400	16,260	0.08
1975	235	965	17,563	0.09
1977	298	1212	21,258	0.10
1979	235	1021	20,409	0.09
1980	187	795	20,844	0.09
1981	145	729	16,908	0.07
1982	96	656	9,061	0.04
1983	81	909	17,461	0.08
1984	62	376	8,499	0.04
1985	54	324	7,079	0.03
1986	69	533	11,861	0.05
1987	46	174	4,481	0.02
1988	40	118	4,381	0.02

Source: U.S. Bureau of Labor Statistics, *Handbook of Labor Statistics,* 1989, p. 543.

Political Influence in Bargaining

The bargaining power of unions and management is affected by legislation, which in turn is affected by the political environment. Legislation can favor either management or labor in the negotiating process. Until the 1930s, the struggle between management and labor in the United States was tilted toward management. The strike was not a strong labor weapon because employers could obtain a court order against a strike. Employees suspected of having union sympathies could be fired or roughed up by company thugs. New employees could be required to sign a "yellow-dog" contract, which forbade the employees from joining the union.

The New Deal response to the Great Depression changed all of this. The Norris–La Guardia Act (1932) and Wagner Act (1935) denied management the use of anti-union tactics and granted labor the right to organize and engage in collective bargaining in a legal framework regulated by the National Labor Relations Board (NLRB). The NLRB has five members appointed by the president for five-year terms. Its functions include ruling on unfair labor practices, settling jurisdictional disputes among unions over bargaining rights, and calling for plant elections at the request of workers. These legal changes lent a tremendous impetus to the growth of the union movement and gave unions a favorable environment for pursuing their ends. The major provisions of all the landmark labor relations acts since the 1930s are summarized in Table 3.

TABLE 3	**Landmarks in Union Legislation**	
	This table summarizes the legislation that has shaped the legal environment within which unions function since the 1930s.	

Act/Passage Date	Major Provisions
Norris-LaGuardia Act (1932)	1. Legitimized union activity by limiting the terms of lawful court injunctions against them.
	2. Guaranteed workers "freedom of association, self-organization, and designation of representatives of [their] own choosing to negotiate the terms and conditions of [their] employment." Peaceable assembly also was guaranteed by this provision.
Wagner Act (1935)	1. Strengthened the union position of the Norris-LaGuardia Act by asserting the right of unions to bargain collectively and to engage in "concerted activities for the purpose of collective bargaining or other mutual aid or protection." Set up the National Labor Relations Board to mediate disputes.
	2. Prohibited employers from discriminating against employees on the basis of union activity; required employers to bargain collectively with unions.
	3. Provided for election of union officials by secret ballot.
Fair Labor Standards Act (Federal Wage and Hour Law) (1938)	1. Set minimum wage, maximum hours, overtime pay, equal pay, and child labor standards for employment.
	2. Defined "oppressive child labor" as employment of a child under age fourteen in *any* nonexempt field. (Acting is an example of an exempt field.) Placed limits on workers under age eighteen in "hazardous or detrimental" employments.
	3. Amended in 1966 to include more retail and service businesses and established minimum wage requirements for certain farm workers and others.
Taft-Hartley Act (1947)	1. Passed to eliminate certain "bad" practices of unions, such as (a) secondary boycotts, (b) jurisdictional strikes over work assignments, and (c) strikes to force an employer to fire an employee over his or her union affiliation or lack thereof.
	2. Made collective bargaining agreements enforceable in federal district courts.
	3. Permitted private parties a civil damage remedy when injured by secondary boycotts.
	4. Permitted states to pass right-to-work-laws forbidding coercion of workers to join union.
Landrum-Griffin Act (1959)	1. In general, attempted to protect union members from financial abuses by union officials by giving union members legal remedies for such abuses.
	2. Required financial disclosures by unions and prescribed procedures for electing union officers.

Right-to-work law:
A law that prevents unions from requiring that individual workers join the union as a condition of employment by a particular firm.

The post–World War II era saw much industrial unrest. Unions showed little self-restraint or discipline, so Congress tilted the balance between labor and management back toward management. The Taft-Hartley Act, passed in 1947, allowed states to enact **right-to-work laws,** which forbid unions from coercing workers into their ranks. It added several other constraints on union

FOCUS   Unions and Sympathy Strikes: The Eastern Airlines Case

Contract negotiations between Eastern Airlines and the unions representing the airline's machinists, baggage handlers, and pilots began in October of 1987 under provisions outlined in the Railway Labor Act (RLA). This act governs collective bargaining in the transportation industry and permits secondary boycotts, or "sympathy strikes," in rail and air transport. Any rail or air transport firm's dispute with its unions, then, can threaten the entire transportation system with sympathy strikes. All other unionized laborers follow the guidelines established by the 1947 Taft-Hartley provisions for employees covered under the National Labor Relations Act (NLRA). Critics argue that the RLA is potentially disruptive and should be reconsidered. Are there valid reasons for treating transportation as a special case?

Passed in 1926, when railroads were the backbone of the U.S. transportation system, the RLA established an exhaustive process of negotiations that would prevent disruption of interstate commerce by work stoppages. Under the RLA, agreements between management and labor do not expire until new agreements supersede them. When either side in a dispute determines that no progress is being made, mediation must take place under the auspices of the National Mediation Board (NMB). Until the NMB decides that an impasse has taken place, labor and management must live with the prior contract. In Eastern's case, the NMB waited thirteen months before declaring an impasse. For a number of reasons, including high wages, Eastern lost more than $1 million per day over the thirteen-month period. When Eastern's unions failed to achieve a government-sponsored negotiated settlement, the NMB finally declared an official impasse in Eastern's negotiations. President George Bush could have appointed an emergency board to continue the negotiations—a policy supported by the unions—but instead he chose to pursue a hands-off policy, leaving Eastern free to impose new salary conditions on its machinists. This precipitated the strike. Eastern machinists were prohibited from extending their strike to other carriers and to commuter rail lines only through temporary restraining orders and court injunctions upholding no-strike clauses in other labor contracts.

Air and rail transportation are no longer national monopolies or "public utilities"—if indeed they ever were. The

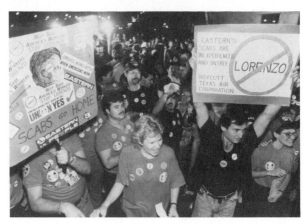

Under the RLA a crippling strike by Eastern Airlines machinists could have spread to other carriers or to commuter rail lines.

transportation system of 1926 is certainly not the system of the 1990s, the present era being characterized by deregulation and oftentimes intense competition. Deregulation in both the rail and airline industries—not to mention the increased use of cars, trucks, pipelines, and barges—suggests to some observers that the RLA is a costly anachronism in the modern competitive environment. While consumers would be inconvenienced by ordinary and isolated labor disputes in transportation, the only real threat is to commuters. Unfortunately, the RLA provisions that make sympathy strikes legal override stricter state laws prohibiting strikes on commuter rail lines. Collective bargaining and the right to strike are as much a part of the competitive process in transportation as they are in other areas of our economy. Critics of the RLA argue that there is no reason for transportation consumers across the country to be threatened with inconvenience or hardship due to a dispute involving a single firm. Further, they argue that consumer welfare is not enhanced when the benefits of deregulation—competition and lower prices in the case of air transport—are reversed by the antiquated provisions of the RLA.

behavior, such as outlawing strikes by government workers and secondary boycotts, by which the union would set up picket lines against other suppliers of the company being struck. (Secondary boycotts are permitted in the transportation industry, however. See Focus, "Unions and Sympathy Strikes: The Eastern Airlines Case.") After the Taft-Hartley Act, charges of union corruption and ties to organized crime led to further legislation to regulate union behavior. The Landrum-Griffin Act, passed in 1959, contained various provisions to ensure that unions were honestly managed. Among other things, this law required the filing of financial reports by union officers and the auditing of union finances.

Even in the face of such restraining legislation, the labor union has assumed a position of influence and power in the U.S. economy. No longer are unions viewed as weak associations of workers fighting for a better standard of living for their members. In some respects, unions are best thought of as strong special-interest groups that are proficient at obtaining special legislative favors such as protective tariffs. On the other hand, union political power is sometimes used to promote general-interest legislation. Civil rights and welfare laws, Social Security, and similar programs have been strongly supported by organized labor.

UNION POWER OVER WAGES: WHAT DOES THE EVIDENCE SHOW?

As we have seen, unions may have an effect on the relative wages of their members, depending on a number of conditions. But what effect have the unions actually had? Several studies have attempted to measure the influence of unions using data on wages and employment in the economy.

H. Gregg Lewis, who made the pioneering study of this issue, estimated that the wages of union members, on average, were 10 to 15 percent higher than those of nonunion members who had about the same marginal productivity as the union members.[2] The airline pilots' union was able to raise members' wages by more than 25 percent compared to the wages of nonunion pilots with the same skill level. In the textile and retail sales industries unionization has had little perceptible influence on members' wages. Craft unions exhibited more strength than industrial unions. Lewis's results square with the economic theory of union power as we have presented it.

Lewis based his estimates on data for the 1940s and 1950s. Similar empirical research using more recent data suggests that unions' power to raise relative wages may be increasing. Holding the characteristics of employees constant, Frank Stafford estimated that the earnings of unionized craft and semiskilled workers were 25 percent higher than those of their nonunion counterparts. Michael Boskin estimated that the union-nonunion wage difference was 15 to 25 percent on average in 1967.[3] Other estimates have shown even higher differentials between union and nonunion members. It is not completely clear why union power has grown over time, but one factor is the

---

[2]H. Gregg Lewis, *Unionism and Relative Wages in the United States* (Chicago: University of Chicago Press, 1963).

[3]Frank P. Stafford, "Concentration and Labor Earnings: Comment," *American Economic Review* 58 (March 1968), pp. 174–81; Michael J. Boskin, "Unions and Relative Wages," *American Economic Review* 62 (June 1972), pp. 466–72.

increasing political power of the union movement. As unions have become more important in politics—for instance, as major suppliers of votes to political parties—their power to increase the demand for union labor and to restrict competing labor supply has increased.

THE IMPACT OF UNIONS ON LABOR'S SHARE OF TOTAL INCOME

The studies just mentioned measure the impact of unions on relative wages—that is, the wages of union members versus those of nonunion members. A broader question concerns the impact of unions on the share of national income that goes to all labor, not just union labor.

Primarily, a general increase in wages requires an increase in the productivity of workers. An increase in productivity can occur in a variety of ways. The quality of tools and other physical capital used by workers can increase, workers' skill levels can be raised through education and experience, innovation or better management can increase worker productivity, and so on. Higher real wages for all workers can be realized only if the output of goods and services in the economy is increased. It would seem to follow that unions can increase the wages of all workers only if they increase the general level of productivity in the economy. While such an impact of unions is not out of the question, it is hard to imagine how it might happen.

Who pays for the benefits that unions obtain through bargaining power, legislation, and other means? The naive answer is that, of course, employers pay, but the evidence suggests otherwise. In fact, economic analysis indicates that consumers and nonunion employees pay for the benefits that unions obtain for their members.

Consumers pay because higher union wages mean higher costs for firms that employ union labor. If these firms produce in a competitive market for their output, output prices will rise to reflect the higher cost of union labor. Basically, the same result holds if the firm that hires union labor has monopoly power, although the monopolist may bargain with the union over the level of monopoly profits earned. In either case, higher costs caused by union wages lead to higher prices for consumers. Consumers thus pay part of the tab for higher union wages.

Nonunion employees pay because higher union wages lead firms to produce less output and to substitute nonhuman capital for union labor. Both these effects cause the level of employment in unionized industries to fall. In other words, as we saw in the models of how unions increase the relative wages of their members, these are cases where union bargaining power leads to a lower employment level for labor in the unionized industry. The workers who do not make it into the union must seek employment elsewhere in the economy. This increases the supply of labor to alternative, nonunion employments and drives down nonunion wages. Thus, nonunion employees also pay part of the tab for higher union wages.

It can be argued on the basis of economic theory that employers do not generally pay for all union gains. Consumers and nonunion employees share the burden because the price of union-made goods rises and the wage rate for

Microeconomics: Key Trends

In this section, we present real data in graphical form to highlight several important economic trends. No less than the student of economics, economists and economic observers benefit from this kind of presentation, one that can reveal at a glance, for example, that the federal government spent over four times as much to service its debt in 1989 than it spent on education. Indeed, it is the task of economists to present, explain, and interpret data in a meaningful and useful way.

Distribution of Government Expenditures

(a) 1989 Federal Government Expenditures
Total $1,197 billion

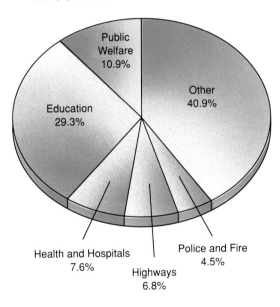

(b) 1985 State and Local Government Expenditures
Total $1,197 billion

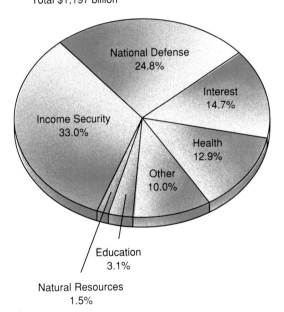

Source: Council of Economic Advisers, *Economic Report of the President* (Washington, D.C.: U.S. Government Printing Office, 1990), p. 385.

Source: Facts and Figures on Government Finance (Washington, D.C.: The Tax Foundation, 1988), p. 168.

On the most basic level, these graphs are a breakdown by category of total expenditures by government at both the federal and the state and local levels for a given year. More broadly interpreted, the graphs are snapshots showing government priorities at a certain point in time; they reveal the relative importance of government's key roles. (a) As revealed in the data for 1989, the federal government is promoter of public goods, corrector of externalities, promoter of competition, distributor of income, and stabilizer of prices, employment, and growth. (b) State and local governments, on the other hand, are the principle providers of police and fire protection, education, highways, and hospitals. As such, state and local governments have a greater impact on our daily lives, although their total expenditures are considerably lower than the federal government's.

The Rise and Fall of Union Membership as a Percent of the Labor Force

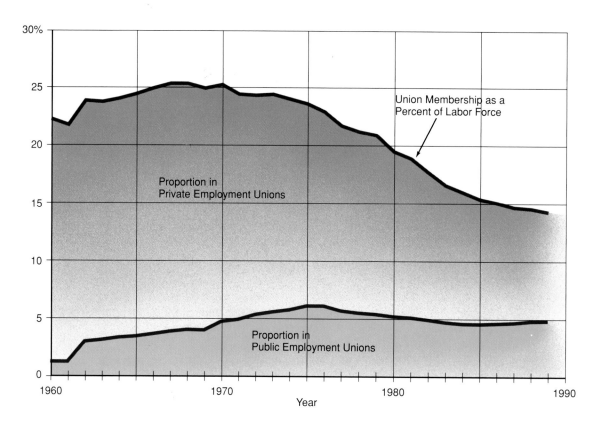

Sources: Troy, Leo, *Union Sourcebook* and *Employment and Earnings,* various issues. Council of Economic Advisers, *Economic Report of the President* (Washington, D.C.: U.S. Government Printing Office, 1990), Table C-32.

The number of workers belonging to unions increased through the 1960s, both in absolute numbers and as a percent of the labor force. In the 1970s, the absolute number increased slightly, but membership as a percent of the labor force began a decline that continued through the 1980s. Since 1985, the absolute number of union members has remained relatively stable, around 17.8 million.

Union members are divided into two groups—those belonging to private employees' unions and those belonging to public employees' unions. The ranks of private employees' unions are composed of what might be termed "traditional" union laborers—autoworkers, steelworkers, carpenters, to name a few. Public employees' unions are organizations of government workers—police officers, teachers, clerical workers. One such union, the American Federation of State, County, and Municipal Employees, is among the ten largest unions in the United States. Overall public employees' union membership has grown both in absolute and in relative terms since 1960.

Exports, Imports, and the Trade Deficit

Billions of Dollars

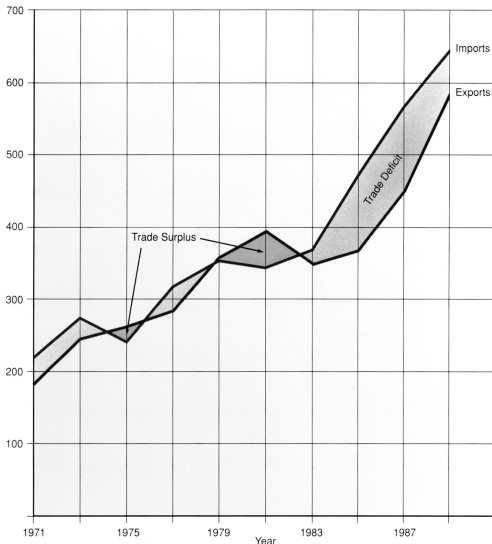

Source: Council of Economic Advisers, *Economic Report of the President* (Washington, D.C.: U.S. Government Printing Office, 1990), p. 297.

The evolution of comparatively isolated national economies into a true global economy over the last two decades is evident in this figure showing U.S. imports and exports during the period. U.S. exports as a percent of GNP nearly doubled between 1971 and 1989, rising from 7.2 percent to 14.2 percent. As shown in the figure, the value of imports nearly tripled over the same period. In absolute terms, the United States is the largest trader in the global economy, importing from and exporting to virtually every nation in the world. Imports consistently outpaced exports in the 1980s, a situation that was frequently attributed to the inability of U.S. firms to compete with foreign manufacturers (especially the Japanese) but that seems more likely to have arisen from a strong U.S. dollar.

Economic Performance of Major Industrial Nations, 1988–1989

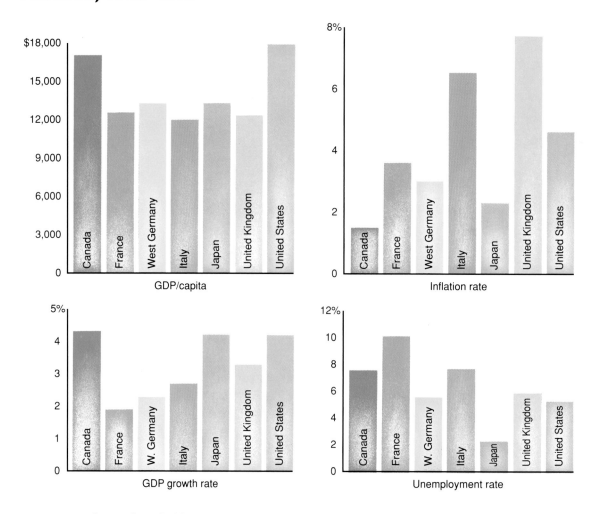

Source: Council of Economic Advisers, *Economic Report of the President* (Washington, D.C.: U.S. Government Printing Office, 1990), p. 45.

When comparing the economic performance of nations, economists examine many variables. Of these, perhaps the most indicative of economic well-being is gross domestic product, which—like gross national product—measures a country's production of goods and services but which excludes income earned from foreign investments. Of the nations shown here, the United States, at $17,843, had the highest GDP per capita in 1988–1989. Economists also look at inflation and unemployment rates to determine economic well-being. High rates of inflation and unemployment are hindrances to economic growth and stability. In 1988–1989, West Germany and Japan had the lowest inflation rates, which is not surprising in that both nations have made maintaining low levels of inflation a priority. Japan also had the lowest unemployment rate. An indication of future economic growth is the GDP growth rate. Canada, Japan, and the United States led in this category in 1988–1989. (A relatively high level of GDP growth in any given year is no *guarantee* of growth the following year; the U.S. economy came to a virtual standstill in 1990.)

nonunion labor falls. The latter effect can be substantial. Lewis estimated that nonunion wages are 3 to 4 percent lower than they would be without unions.[4] Since this effect on nonunion labor covers about three-fourths of the labor force, the resource allocation effects of unions can be substantial in the aggregate.

Table 4 provides some data about the behavior over time of the share of national income that goes to labor. Two ways of measuring labor's share are shown. The second column measures total employee compensation (wage and salaries) plus the employer's share of the Social Security tax as a percentage of national income. This series shows a slight upward trend since World War II, a rise that has been attributed to a decline in the number of self-employed workers over this period, primarily in agriculture.

The third column in the table adds the income of self-employed persons—such as business proprietors, lawyers, and accountants—to employee compensation. Self-employment compensation is clearly income that goes to labor. When we look at this more inclusive concept of labor's share of national

---

TABLE 4

Labor's Share of National Income

The percentage of the nation's real output that labor receives has increased slightly since World War II. This increase is attributed to a decrease in small owner-managed firms rather than to union activities.

Year	Total Employee Compensation (Including Employer Contribution for Social Insurance) (percent of national income)	Total Employee Compensation plus Self-Employment Income (percent of national income)
1935	71.0	84.0
1940	68.0	83.0
1945	68.2	82.4
1950	71.8	82.0
1955	72.2	82.6
1960	74.0	81.8
1965	74.3	82.3
1970	74.2	82.8
1975	74.3	83.4
1980	73.9	82.2
1981	74.6	81.4
1982	76.1	82.5
1983	74.9	79.6
1984	73.1	79.2
1985	74.3	80.4
1986	73.6	81.9
1987	73.4	81.9
1988	73.2	81.4
1989	73.7	82.0

Sources: U.S. Department of Commerce, *Survey of Current Business,* various issues; Council of Economic Advisers, *Economic Report of the President* (Washington, D.C.: U.S. Government Printing Office, 1990), p. 320.

---

[4]Lewis, *Unionism and Relative Wages in the United States.*

income, we see that it has been virtually constant for over fifty years. Thus, during an era when labor union strength grew in the United States, we do not find any evidence that labor's share of national income rose. While labor unions have increased the wages of their members relative to the wages of nonunion workers, there is no evidence to suggest that they have made all workers better off in terms of their share of national income.

The fact is that higher real wages for workers can come about only through increases in worker productivity. Workers in the United States earn high wages because their productivity is high. Their wages can rise only if the output of goods and services in the American economy is increased. All things being equal, it is the level of productivity that explains real wages.

CONCLUSION

The goals of unions are easy to understand. The members want more income, greater income security, and more pleasant working conditions than the market provides. Their ability to achieve these goals is limited by many factors, including the supplies of competing inputs, the monopsony power of employers, and the political power of unions. Unions have provided their members with higher wages and better job security, but they also provide something more.

The union's role extends beyond an economic wage and employment analysis to the plant, where the union provides workers with a set of rules and representation to settle disputes with employers. This presence of the union on the job cannot be discounted as a primary source of nonpecuniary benefits to union members. Such benefits accrue to workers in the form of greater job security, a feeling of power and dignity at work, and less alienation from their work. These are important aspects of work in modern factories and offices, and the union's role in providing workplace representation is a powerful force for creating greater worker satisfaction and thus greater productivity.

There is much concern today over the meaningfulness of work. Workers are said to be alienated and bored by assembly-line types of jobs. In this respect, the role of the union as an arbitrator of workplace rules and procedures will probably become increasingly important. Workers may be willing to trade off some wage gains to obtain changes in the way their work is done. And if workers seek more meaningful jobs and factory arrangements, the union will surely be at the forefront in helping promote such arrangements in future labor contracts.

SUMMARY

1. A labor union is a group of workers in a craft, industry, or government job who organize to gain market power.
2. Labor unions attempt to improve the economic welfare of their members by increasing wages, decreasing the elasticity of demand for their services, and increasing the demand for their members' labor through a variety of activities.

3. Monopsony exists when there is a lack of competition in the employment of labor. A single buyer may force wages below the competitive level.
4. In a bilateral monopoly in a labor market, the wage is determined by the relative strength of the bargainers.
5. A union's ability to achieve its goals is in part determined by its bargaining strength. A union's ability to strike is its strongest negotiating tool.

6. It is estimated that unions have increased the wages of their members relative to nonunion workers in similar occupations.

7. Unions have not increased all labor's share of total income. Gains made by union labor have generally been at the expense of employers, nonunion labor, and consumers.

KEY TERMS

labor union

craft union

industrial union

public employees' union

total wage bill

monopsony

exploitation of labor

bilateral monopoly

collective bargaining

strike

binding arbitration

right-to-work law

QUESTIONS FOR REVIEW AND DISCUSSION

1. How do craft unions increase wages for their members? What happens to the people who are not allowed into a craft union?

2. If industrial unions allow into the union anyone who wishes to enter, how can they increase wages? Could an industrial union in an isolated mining town increase both wages and employment?

3. Suppose the United States exports beef to Japan and imports cars from Japan. If autoworkers persuade Congress to impose a tariff on Japanese cars, what happens to the incomes of cattle ranchers and ranch hands?

4. Why do unions want to decrease the elasticity of demand for their members? How do they do so?

5. What is a monopsony? Does the existence of labor unions promote the existence of monopsonies?

6. It is frequently suggested that firms exploit women in the labor force. Monopsonists' power to exploit is based on the immobility of labor. Are women less mobile than men?

7. In some countries, such as the Soviet Union, there is only one potential employer—the government. Do these countries have the power to exploit their workers? How can their workers avoid exploitation?

8. Why are unions and union employers forced to negotiate wages while nonunion wages are determined without negotiation?

9. Are union wages closer to the monopsony wage or to the wage that maximizes the wage bill?

10. Suppose that a union is successful at organizing only part of the laborers in an industry. Do you predict that the union will be strong or weak? Why?

11. Why do you think unions favor minimum-wage laws?

ECONOMICS IN ACTION
Monopsony in College Athletics

Colleges and universities are virtually the only buyers of high school athletes. This is especially true for football and basketball players, and less so for baseball and tennis players. Baseball has minor professional leagues in which high school players can work and be paid for their services. Many tennis players turn professional at a young age, skipping college competition altogether. In the case of football, however, no players enter the professional ranks directly from high school. The colleges and universities are the sole buyers of high school players' services in football.

College athletics in the United States are governed by rules established by the National Collegiate Athletic Association (NCAA), a collection of colleges and universities that compete in intercollegiate athletics. The NCAA establishes and enforces the rules under which college players can be recruited and compensated for their play. The NCAA rules are very complicated and regulate all aspects of the player's relationship with the school. The bottom line, however, is that the NCAA regulations create a collusive agreement among colleges and universities to act as a monopsony in the purchase of high school athletes' services. In other words, the NCAA has established a buyers' cartel for athletic labor.

Even though a talented college football or basketball player may generate a lot of ticket sales and television revenues for the school, NCAA rules forbid the player from being paid a wage (beyond tuition, room, board, and incidentals) equal to the marginal revenue product of the player. (Marginal revenue product is the increase in school revenues realized by having the particular athlete playing for the school.) Marginal revenue product may be small for a benchwarmer, but it can run into the millions (TV revenue, sold-out stadiums, bowl and post-season tournament revenues, bumper stickers, and so on) for the services of an All-American basketball player or a Heisman Trophy–winning football star. Instead, the player can only be given a scholarship, room and board, and certain other minimal living allowances. Even the details of a player's summer or off-season employment are tightly regulated by the NCAA.

The NCAA system is a monopsony because (1) it is an agreement among schools to create a single system for compensating athletes, and (2) it functions so as to pay athletes less than they contribute to school athletic revenues.

Just like in an output or sellers' cartel, the NCAA agreement to hold down players' wages must be enforced. Individual schools will find it in their interest to cheat on the agreement by offering good players "illegal" inducements (cars, money) to play for them. Clearly, it is advantageous for any given school to behave in this way if all other schools follow the rules. Such a strategy will lead to the recruitment of better players, athletic success, and larger revenues. Cheaters must therefore be rooted out and punished by the NCAA. This is done in a variety of ways, such as taking away valuable bowl, tournament, and TV opportunities from violators or reducing the number of "legal" scholarships the cheating school can offer in the future.

There is no particular reason that college athletics could not be treated like any other form of student employment where the students are paid a wage for their work. What would be so bad about doing this with college football and basketball players? Colleges do not want to pay competitive market wages to their student-athletes, since this would erode their profits from athletic events. Of course, one should not downplay the ideals of amateur athletics and the amateur athlete. However, there is little economic justification for not paying the full value for the work done by student-athletes. A wage scale, for example, for college football players would bring into the open what are currently under-the-table practices, clean up the recruiting process considerably, and allow young college athletes to accrue savings.

In any event, the NCAA has established a monopsony that functions to benefit colleges and universities at the expense of student-athletes and their families (who are often from low-income and minority backgrounds). One would therefore predict that the most vocal defenders of the NCAA buyers' cartel will be college presidents. Students can easily check this prediction by soliciting the view of their president and administration on this matter; college officials will defend their position on the grounds that playing for pay would somehow corrupt the ideals of the amateur student-athlete. However, what is the difference between the basketball player and the student who works the graveyard shift at a local radio station to pay for school? Should all student jobs be banned?

Question

Which type of schools, low-tuition or high-tuition, would you expect to violate the NCAA regulations more often? What will stadium size have to do with NCAA violations? What is the role of coaches in the NCAA cartel?

16

Capital and Interest

Wealthy societies consume, or use, goods and services at an ever-increasing rate. Think, for instance, of the rate at which automobiles have become available in this country. Little more than sixty years ago, relatively few Americans owned cars, and most of these proud owners were happy to keep the same car for years. Today, autos are bought and sold in the millions. Many of us own more than one car; most of us change cars at least every four or five years. Since consumption is possible only through production, the basis of a wealthy society is not its ability to consume but its ability to produce, to transform raw materials into more useful goods and services through the application of human skills and physical capital such as tools and factories. Societies that are better at this transformation are able to reach higher levels of wealth and to consume more.

This chapter is about the role of capital in determining the ability to produce and the level of wealth in a society. The material in Chapter 16 will help you understand

- how roundabout, or less direct, production methods are more productive in creating wealth.
- that the choice between consuming and saving is a key element in producing larger quantities of goods and services.
- how the rate of interest is determined and how inflation relates to it.
- the role of stocks and bonds in saving and investing in our economy.

ROUNDABOUT PRODUCTION AND CAPITAL FORMATION

Economic behavior is forward-looking. The availability of the food we eat today is due to the foresight of farmers in the past who undertook the appropriate productive actions. The food we will eat tomorrow depends on actions farmers take now. A simple analogy illustrates this point.

405

Imagine Robinson Crusoe trying to survive alone on a windswept island in the middle of the ocean. Crusoe's economy is primitive. He lives by fishing with a simple wooden spear that he found on the beach. With his spear Crusoe can catch 5 pounds of fish in about 10 hours of fishing. Suppose that one day Crusoe decides to improve his fishing technique by weaving a fishing net.

Crusoe takes a day off to build the net. His opportunity cost of building the net is the fish that he would have caught during this day by fishing with his spear. Assuming that it takes 10 hours to build the net, the opportunity cost of the net to Crusoe is 5 pounds of fish.

Roundabout production:
The current production of capital goods so that greater amounts of consumption goods can be produced in the future.

Crusoe's purpose in building the net is to catch more fish in the future. That is, he hopes the net will enable him to catch more than 5 pounds in 10 hours. The anticipation of more production and therefore more consumption in the future drives Crusoe to the more **roundabout** method of catching fish.

Of course, Crusoe must have some way to support himself during the period that he stops fishing to weave the net. He provides for his needs during this time by **saving.** If he consumes 5 pounds of fish every 10 hours and it takes 10 hours to make a net, Crusoe must set aside 5 pounds of fish to support himself while making the net. To do so, he could fish extra hours for several days, or he could eat only 4 pounds each day for 5 days. The hallmark of saving is some form of current sacrifice in anticipation of a higher level of future consumption. Extra hours worked means less hours for current leisure; fewer fish eaten in the present mean fewer calories consumed. However Crusoe manages to save fish, his planned one-day abstinence from spearfishing leads to saving and to a greater yield of fish.

Saving:
The act of forgoing present consumption in order to increase future consumption.

What is Crusoe's incentive to abstain? Suppose that with the net he can catch 25 pounds of fish in 10 hours and that the net will last indefinitely. By abstaining from spearfishing for 10 hours, at a cost of 5 pounds of fish, Crusoe is able to raise his daily catch by 20 pounds. The increase is even more significant in the long run: For an investment of a mere 5 pounds of fish, Crusoe raises his weekly catch from 35 pounds to 175 pounds, an increase of 140 pounds per week. This particular act of saving and investment of resources to produce more capital is especially profitable. Indeed, even if the net wears out every so often, Crusoe will be able to afford to take 10 hours to make a new net in anticipation of similar rates of return in the future.

This simple example has relevance to a modern economy. In a modern economy individuals specialize in their activities. They don't spend part of the day fishing and part of the day making rods and reels. But this specialization does not change any of the essential features of what is called *capital formation.*

Capital formation:
An increase in the stock of capital due to roundabout production.

Capital stock:
The total amount of capital goods that exists in an economy at any point in time.

The term **capital formation** refers to the process of building capital goods and adding to the capital stock in the economy. Capital goods are things such as machines and implements that are used to produce final goods and services. The **capital stock** of an economy is the amount of capital goods that exists at a given point in time. To increase capital stock, producers must resort to methods of roundabout production, the use and production of capital goods as a means of achieving greater output in the future. Saving, or the abstinence from present consumption, is required for capital formation to take place. Moreover, the act of saving requires entrepreneurship, a concept involving risk taking, which we discuss in Chapter 17. In the case of capital production, the future is uncertain. Crusoe did not know whether a net would increase his daily catch. He took a chance that it would, and it paid off.

Depreciation:
The wearing out of capital goods that occurs with usage over time.

Capital consumption:
A decrease in the capital stock; occurs when the rate of depreciation is greater than the rate of capital formation.

Another important feature of capital is that it does not automatically reproduce itself. Instead, capital goods are automatically **depreciating;** they decrease in productivity or value over time. This wearing out of capital goods cannot be stopped. If Crusoe does not repair or replace his net, he will ultimately return to spearfishing and to a lower standard of living. The capital goods or capital stock of a society must be repaired and replaced over time if the society is to continue to grow and experience high levels of consumption. This is one of the primary problems of economics: maintaining and increasing the ability to produce.

Capital consumption is the opposite of capital formation. Present consumption is increased temporarily at the cost of a reduction in the future rate of consumption. Suppose that a lumber company owns trees ranging in age from one to twenty-five years. Assume that it cuts down one thousand 25-year-old trees and plants one thousand seedlings each year. As long as external circumstances do not change, this forest can yield one thousand 25-year-old trees annually. For a while, however, the yield from the forest can be increased by harvesting some of the 24-year-old trees in addition to the regular harvest, then dipping into the stock of 23-year-old trees the next year, and so on. Cut in this manner, the amount of timber harvested will increase for a while. Still, the time will come when the total output of the forest will necessarily decline. Capital in the form of younger trees has been used up to increase current output, so the future output of timber must fall. This is capital consumption.

THE RATE OF INTEREST

Saving and capital formation depend on the willingness of individuals to pass up current consumption to achieve greater consumption in the future. In other words, individuals must abstain from current consumption to provide the flow of saving that is used to produce capital goods. Economists stress that an individual's willingness to abstain from current consumption is related to his or her **rate of time preference.** Time preference is the degree of patience that an individual has in forgoing present consumption in order to save. A person with a high rate of time preference has a strong preference for current rather than future consumption. Most individuals have positive rates of time preference; that is, they prefer present to future consumption. Since people prefer to consume now rather than later, they must be paid a price for waiting. This price is called **interest.**

Rate of time preference:
The percent increase in future consumption over present consumption that is necessary to just induce an individual to be indifferent between present and future consumption.

Interest:
The compensation to savers for the act of saving (forgoing present consumption) or the payment made by borrowers; when measured as a percent of the amount borrowed or lent, it is referred to as an interest rate.

The concept of interest has two related meanings. In the first sense, interest refers to returns on investments. A person who saves $100 in a passbook account earns 5¾ percent interest on saving. A firm that invests $1000 in a new piece of machinery earns $200 more in revenue annually because of the resulting improvement in productivity. The firm's investment thus yields 20 percent interest, the firm's reward for roundabout production. In these terms, interest is the amount individuals are willing to *receive* in order to sacrifice current consumption; it is a payment for their abstinence or waiting to consume later.

Interest is also the price that individuals are willing to *pay* to obtain a good or service now rather than later. A consumer who wants a car today might pay 13 percent interest for a loan from the bank. A firm that needs a new plant might pay 10 percent interest to get the necessary financing.

Interest is not just a monetary phenomenon. Whether paid or received, interest is based on the fact that people prefer to consume and invest now rather than later. Moreover, the rate of interest reflects the rate of time preference in the economy. The more impatient people are, the higher the rate of interest must be to induce them to save and to create capital goods.

DEMAND AND SUPPLY OF LOANABLE FUNDS

The rate of interest is determined in the market for loanable funds. It is, in effect, the price of loanable funds. Like other markets, the market for loanable funds has a demand side and a supply side.

The **demand for loanable funds** arises from two sources. Consumers demand loanable funds because they want to consume more now than their current incomes will permit. Loans to these individuals are called *consumption loans*. They are made for myriad reasons. Individuals may want to take a vacation now and pay for it on time, borrow to tide themselves over a temporary decline in income, or borrow to buy cars or household appliances.

The second source of demand for loanable funds is desire for investment loans. Investors borrow to finance the construction and use of capital goods and roundabout methods of production that are expected to be productive. Firms borrow funds to build new plants and to purchase new equipment in the expectation that such investments will increase profits.

A third source of loanable funds demand is the government. Governments at all levels—local, state, and federal—demand funds to cover deficits (when tax receipts do not cover government expenditures), to finance road construction and schools, and to service debt. This demand is added to private demands for loanable funds for consumption and investing purposes.

The sum of the demand for consumption, investment, and government loans equals the total demand for loanable funds. The law of demand applies to the demand for loanable funds just as it does to any other commodity (see Figure 1). The price one must pay to borrow funds for consumption or investment loans is the interest rate. According to the law of demand, the amount of funds demanded is inversely related to the interest rate. As the interest rate falls, the cost of borrowing money to finance the earlier availability of consumption and capital goods falls. Other things being equal, we thus expect to see more borrowing when the interest rate falls. At a lower rate of interest, consumers will expand current consumption, and more investment projects will appear to be profitable.

In Figure 1, the **supply of loanable funds,** S, is provided by savers. These are individuals or firms who are willing to consume less than their present earnings in order to set aside something for the future. As the interest rate—in this case, the return on investment—rises, more and more individuals and firms will be enticed to save; that is, they will forgo current consumption in order to consume even more in the future. Thus, the quantity supplied of loanable funds varies positively with the interest rate offered to savers.

Demand for loanable funds:
A curve or schedule that shows the various amounts individuals are willing and able to borrow at different interest rates.

Supply of loanable funds:
A curve or schedule that shows the various amounts individuals are willing and able to lend or save at different rates.

FIGURE 1

D and *S* are the demand and supply curves for loanable funds. The market for loanable funds reaches equilibrium at *i* and *Q*, where the plans of borrowers and lenders are compatible. That is, for a given interest rate, the amount that borrowers want to borrow and the amount that lenders want to lend are equal.

Determination of Interest Rates

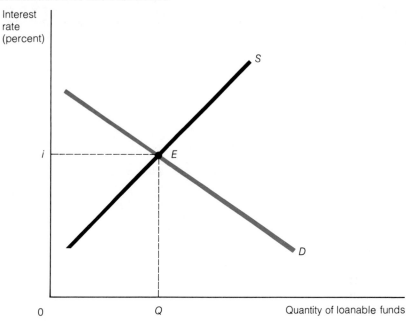

The intersection of the demand and supply curves for loanable funds in Figure 1 yields an equilibrium interest rate and the equilibrium level of loanable funds. At *i* and *Q*, the market for loanable funds is in equilibrium, and the plans of borrowers are compatible with the plans of lenders. At interest rates above *i*, there will be an excess supply of savings, putting pressure on the interest rate to fall. Below *i*, there will be an excess demand for loanable funds, putting pressure on the interest rate to rise. (See Focus, "Usury and Interest Rates: An Application of Price Controls," for an example of the effects of controlled interest rates.)

Stocks and Bonds

Most daily newspapers list the previous day's closing prices of stocks and bonds. These listings show how the market for loanable funds works, coordinating the supply of funds, primarily held by investors and investor groups, with the demand for funds, primarily the desire by corporations to raise capital for future production.

Figure 2 reproduces a listing of stocks, their prices, and other information from the New York Stock Exchange. To the right of the first two columns of numbers, an abbreviation of the stock's name is found. ABdcst, for example, stands for the American Broadcasting Company. Columns one and two give the high and low price of the stock in the previous year (ending at the close of trading the day before). Price information from the latest day is in the last four columns on the right. The latest day's high and low price is reported along with the last (closing) price paid for it. If the high or low price paid for a stock on that day is also a 52-week high or low, a footnote (*u* for up, *d* for down) is attached to the day's high or low price and will be reflected in the

FIGURE 2

Most daily newspapers carry complete listings of stock similar to this portion of a stock listing that appeared in an issue of the *Wall Street Journal*. Among other things, such listings allow stockholders to track—on a daily basis—the performance of companies they own stock in.

Sample New York Stock Exchange Newspaper Listing

52 Weeks High	Low	Stock	Div.	Yld %	P-E Ratio	Sales 100s	High	low	Close	Net Chg.
		— A – A – A —								
39⅞	30¾	Alcoa	1.20	3.8	16	x2283	32	31⅜	31⅜ –	½
25⅝	15½	Amax	.20	1.1	..	523	17⅝	17⅜	17½ –	⅛
42¼	32½	Amax	pf 3	8.8	..	6	34	34	34 –	½
52½	22¾	AmHes	1.10	3.5	16	3877	32¼	31½	31⅝ +	½
2¾	1¼	AmAgr		..	..	70	2⅛	2	2⅛	
19⅝	15⅛	ABakr		..	8	10	18½	18¼	18½ +	⅛
70	53	ABrand	3.90	5.9	9	709	67⅞	66⅛	66⅜ –	1½
27¾	24⅝	ABrd	pf2.75	9.9	..	166	27¾	27⅜	27¾ +	⅜
115	55¾	ABdcst	1.60	1.5	16	899	108⅜	108	108	
26¼	19½	ABldM	.86	3.4	13	12	25½	25½	25½	
27⅛	20⅛	ABusPr	.64	2.5	15	6	26	25¾	25¾ –	⅜
55¾	40⅛	AmCan	2.90	5.5	11	805	53½	53	53⅛ –	⅜
48	36	ACan	pf 3	6.5	..	54	46⅝	46¼	46¼ –	¼
110	103	ACan	pf13.75	12.	..	16	u110¾	109½	110¾ +	1¾
19⅞	16¾	ACapBd	2.20	12.	..	85	19⅜	18⅞	19 –	⅛
33	25⅛	ACapCv	2.51e	9.0	..	13	27⅞	27¾	27¾ –	⅛
11	6½	ACentC		..	11	32	8⅝	8½	8½ –	¼

following trading day's data. The final column gives the net change in a stock's value from the previous closing price. Thus the price of Alcoa (the Aluminum Company of America) stock fluctuated between a high of $32 and a low of $31⅜ , also closing at that value on this day. The net change (from the value of the previous day's closing price) was down by 50¢ a share. Other important stock data is also given in Figure 2. The annual cash dividend is given in the column right of the stock's name. It is based on the rate of the last quarterly payout, and extra dividends are indicated by footnotes following the cash amount. The next column gives yield of the stock by dividing the cash dividend by the closing price. This valuable information permits you to compare the yield with other kinds of financial instruments. The P-E, price-earnings ratio, is found by dividing the latest closing price of the stock by the latest available earnings per share, which is (for the most recent four quarters) the profit of the company divided by the number of shares outstanding. The P-E ratio is an indicator of the stock's performance. The "Sales 100s" column lists the number of shares traded. Thus the number 6 means that 600 shares were traded that day.

Corporations have two means of raising capital: selling shares of stock or issuing bonds. By selling shares of stock, a corporation is effectively selling property rights to itself: The shareholders of a corporation are its owners. Each share of stock permits its holder one vote at meetings that determine the firm's future management. In this way corporate policy is directed by the will of the holders of the majority of the firm's shares—whether one or many individuals. Shareholders do not make operating decisions for the firm, but they are legally responsible for hiring the managers—the board of directors— who do. When shareholders are pleased with the existing management of the firm, they usually assign their votes to the management, which then acts as a proxy for the shareholders in voting on corporate policy.

The stock market is an organized exchange where corporate shares are bought and sold. In the stock market the prices of shares issued by different firms reflect the market's estimate of the future profitability of the firms in

FOCUS   Usury and Interest Rates: An Application of Price Controls

Price controls have been known to all ages and all civilizations. The Roman Emperor Diocletian invoked general price and wage controls prior to the fall of the Roman Empire. During the Middle Ages, church doctrine combined with economic policy to create civil laws related to interest-taking. The laws, called *usury laws,* originated in the belief that an uncontrolled market produced interest rates that were too high. The laws consisted of a legal limit on the amount of interest that lenders could charge or borrowers pay. Such laws survive today in the enactments of certain U.S. state legislatures that protect borrowers and in federal regulations that establish the maximum interest rate allowable on small savings deposits.

The mechanics of the usury laws are simple; we demonstrate them in Figure 3. The figure shows the free-market supply and demand for loanable funds. As market interest rates increase, the quantity supplied of loanable funds rises and the quantity demanded declines. As market rates fall, the quantity of loanable funds supplied falls while quantity demanded rises. Market equilibrium occurs at point E, where quantity demanded equals quantity supplied (Q_E) and where the equilibrium price—the market interest rate—is i_E.

What happens when the government declares that market rate i_E is too high for the poor and that henceforth the maximum rate will be i_C, a ceiling rate below i_E? At rate i_C the quantity of loanable funds demanded, Q_D (point C in Figure 3), exceeds the quantity supplied, Q_s (point B). A shortage of funds, BC, develops at the ceiling interest rate because banks are unwilling to lend the quantity of funds demanded at rate i_C. The available funds, Q_s, must be rationed because of the shortage. In the absence of price rationing, the process can take other forms. Unscrupulous lenders—"loan sharks"—may charge black market rates for the limited funds. Lenders may begin demanding additional collateral or better credit standing for loans at the ceiling rate, reducing their risk and making it more difficult for less creditworthy borrowers to obtain funds. Such borrowers are

FIGURE 3
Interest Rate Ceiling

When a ceiling is placed on interest rates (i_C), a shortage (BC) develops, the difference between the quantity of funds that lending institutions are willing and able to supply (Q_S) and the quantity of funds that borrowers demand (Q_D). Without the ceiling, the forces of supply and demand interact to create equilibrium (E) between the plans of demanders and suppliers of loanable funds.

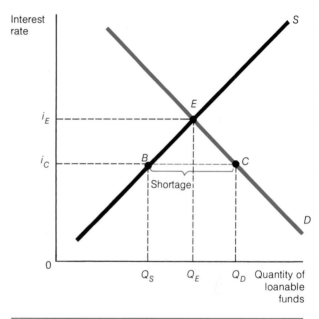

often the poor whom the laws were designed to protect. The poor are often compelled to acquire funds from loan sharks in such circumstances. Usury laws, like all other forms of price controls, have built-in effects that often hurt those who are supposed to be the beneficiaries.

---

question. From the shareholders' standpoint, investing in the stock market means bearing the risk resulting from the uncertain prospects of any given firm. A share of the stock's future value is not guaranteed and can rise or fall with the firm's fortunes, or because of general market conditions such as interest rates.

Corporations and governments also issue another type of obligation—bonds. Unlike shares of stock, bonds do not confer ownership rights; they simply represent IOUs. The firm or government body agrees to pay the bond-holder a fixed sum (the principal that represents the loan to the firm) either on a specific date or in installments over a specified period. Most bonds pay, in addition, a fixed return per year, usually expressed as a percentage of the face value of the bond. For example, a corporation may issue a $10,000 bond (which, if sold, represents a $10,000 loan to the corporation for some specified period) at an interest rate of 5 percent. This bond would pay the holder $500 per year until maturity, when the entire $10,000 is returned to the investor.

Although bonds tend to be issued for long terms (thirty-eight years in the case of some U.S. Treasury bonds), bonds are commonly bought and sold prior to the date of maturity. The bond market is like the stock market; it represents an organized exchange specializing in the buying and selling of bonds.

Interest rates affect the prices of shares of stock indirectly by their impact on the activities and hence the profitability of firms, but interest rates bear a direct relation to the price of bonds. Take, for example, a bond issued with a face value of $10,000 that pays an annual rate of interest of 6 percent. Until maturity, whoever holds the bond is entitled to $600 annually. Suppose, however, that the market interest rate rises to 10 percent. Purchasers of newly issued $10,000 bonds can earn $1000 annually, other things equal. What happens to the price of the 6 percent bonds? Their market value must fall to reflect the new, higher interest rate. No one, in other words, would invest in a bond paying less than 10 percent since they can earn 10 percent on newly issued bonds. The price of the 6 percent bond must fall to $6000 to reflect the new, higher rate of 10 percent. Individuals will not buy the original bonds unless their price falls so as to produce a 10 percent return on a given investment ($600/$6000). The bond will still pay $10,000 at maturity (the firm must pay back what it borrowed), but the sales value of the bond right now is $6000.

The general point to remember about bond price is that the price of a bond varies inversely with the interest rate. When the interest rate rises, the price of a bond falls; when the interest rate falls, the price of a bond rises.

Variations Among Interest Rates

The discussion of the supply and demand for loanable funds might suggest that there is one interest rate in the economy. In reality there is a multiplicity of interest rates: the prime interest rate given to businesses with excellent credit ratings, mortgage rates offered to home buyers, credit card rates, consumer loan rates, and so on. These interest rates tend to be different. For instance, the interest rate on government bonds is generally lower than the interest rate on corporate bonds. What are some of the reasons that interest rates differ?

Risk:
The chance that a borrower will default or fail to repay a loan.

Risk. The **risk** associated with particular borrowers—their likelihood to default on repaying a loan—in part accounts for the differences in interest rates. Creditors go to great lengths to ascertain the degree of this risk, and they adjust the interest rate they charge accordingly. Loans to a government agency will carry a low interest rate because the risk of default is very low. Government can use its power to tax to repay loans. On the other hand, loans to unemployed workers will carry high interest rates because the risk of default is high.

Cost of Making Loans. The cost of making loans differs. Large loans and small loans may require the same amount of accounting and bookkeeping work. The large loan will therefore be less costly to process per dollar loaned; for this reason it will carry a lower interest rate than the small loan. This distinction means, for example, that loans to large companies will carry a lower interest rate than loans to small companies.

Time. The length of time over which a loan is made will affect the rate of interest charged. The longer the term of the loan, the more things that can go wrong for the borrower. Because the risk of default rises with the length of the loan, longer-term borrowers must pay a premium for this rise. Long-term loans will carry higher interest rates than short-term loans, other things being equal. In addition to the risk factor, borrowers are willing to pay a premium for the longer availability of funds.

Nominal and Real Rates of Interest

Nominal rate of interest:
The market-determined rate of interest; usually expressed as a percentage per year of the dollar or nominal amount of the loan.

Inflation rate:
The percent by which the average level of prices in an economy rises; usually expressed as a percent per year.

Real rate of interest:
The nominal interest rate minus the rate of inflation; the interest measured in terms of real buying power.

The **nominal rate of interest** is the interest rate set in the market for loanable funds. With inflation in the economy, the nominal rate of interest can be a misleading measure of how much borrowers pay for consumption and investment loans. Suppose that the **inflation rate,** which is the rate at which the average level of all prices in the economy rises, is 12 percent per year and that the nominal rate of interest is 17 percent. A borrower who borrows $100 will have to repay $117 in a year. However, during the year the average level of prices increases by 12 percent. The $117 paid to the lender at the end of the year will not buy the same amount of goods as the $100 made available to the borrower one year earlier. Since prices have risen by 12 percent, $100 a year ago is equivalent to $112 today. Therefore, the lender of the $100 effectively earns $5 on his or her loan ($117 minus $112), or a 5 percent real rate of return ($5 divided by $100). Thus, when the rate of inflation is factored out, the **real rate of interest** is 5 percent, or 17 percent minus 12 percent.

Lenders and borrowers will not generally be fooled by inflation. The nominal rate of interest will adjust to account for the expected inflation rate. The nominal rate of interest will include a premium to compensate lenders for the expected depreciation of the purchasing power of their principal interest. Lenders will have to be compensated for expected inflation, or they will reduce the amount they are willing to lend. Borrowers will also recognize that they will be repaying loans with dollars of less purchasing power and will adjust the amount of interest they are willing to pay to obtain loans. In the above example, if both borrowers and lenders fully anticipate a 12 percent inflation rate, the nominal rate of interest will adjust to 17 percent. As the inflation rate changes, the nominal rate of interest will also change to reflect the level of expected inflation.

The real rate of interest is the nominal rate of interest minus the expected inflation rate. In the latter part of the 1970s, the nominal rate of interest rose to over 20 percent on some types of loans, but since the expected inflation rate was on the order of 15 percent, the real rate of interest was only 5 percent.

INTEREST AS THE RETURN TO CAPITAL

So far we have considered interest to be the price of loanable funds. Interest may also be viewed as the return that goes to capital as a factor of production. The entrepreneur who buys a machine for $100 and makes $25 a year by using it in production earns 25 percent interest on the investment. Using this concept of interest, we can see how entrepreneurs make investment decisions.

The return earned on capital depends on the quantity of capital in use. In a world with only a few machines, the return on machines would be quite high. As the quantity of machines in use increased, the returns on the margin to each machine would decline. In Figure 4, the marginal return to capital is depicted as MRC. If a capital stock of Q_1 existed, the interest return to capital would be i_1. With a larger capital stock of Q_2, the return would fall to i_2.

To see how entrepreneurs decide how much capital to acquire, consider the marginal return to capital curve in Figure 4 as a demand curve. At an interest rate of i_1, entrepreneurs would prefer to hold Q_1 units of capital. If they initially had less than Q_1 units of capital, it would pay them to borrow funds at an interest rate i_1 and use the money to obtain new capital that earned an interest rate above i_1. New capital would be acquired until the stock of capital rose to Q_1 and the return fell to i_1. Beyond that point it no longer would be profitable to borrow money to obtain additional capital.

If the interest rate fell to i_2, firms would have an incentive to undertake new investment and increase their capital from Q_1 to Q_2 units. Other things remaining unchanged, a decline in the interest rate will lead to an increase in capital stock. A direct link exists between the market for loanable funds and the market for capital goods. An increase in the supply of loanable funds will cause the interest rate to fall, and this will lead to new investment. New in-

FIGURE 4

MRC shows the marginal return to capital. Because of diminishing returns, the return to capital declines as the capital stock increases. The MRC curve can also be viewed as the demand for capital curve, since it shows how large a capital stock entrepreneurs will want at each interest rate. If the interest rate falls from i_1 to i_2, entrepreneurs will undertake additional investment until the capital stock rises from Q_1 to Q_2.

Return on Investment in Capital Goods

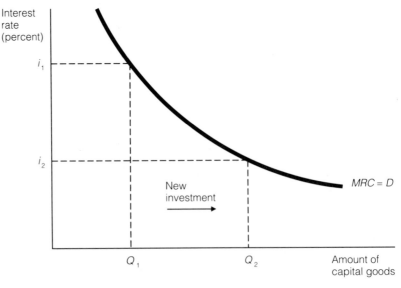

vestment will increase capital stock and lead to future increases in the productive capacity of the economy, causing living standards to rise. This is why there is currently so much concern about the low saving rate and low supply of loanable funds in the United States.

THE NATURE OF RETURNS TO OWNERS OF CAPITAL

Individuals invest in capital goods because they expect to make a rate of return in excess of the cost of capital. The elements of this rate of return can be broken down into three categories: pure interest, risk, and profits and losses.

Pure Interest

Pure interest:
The interest associated with a risk-free loan. The interest rate that produces pure interest is called the risk-free interest rate.

Capital investment yields a return called **pure interest,** the interest rate that must be paid to induce saving when the lender bears little or no risk. Think of pure interest this way: You have a sum of money, and you're trying to decide whether to invest in a piece of capital equipment or a savings account at the bank with a virtually guaranteed return of 5 percent. The 5 percent is a pure interest yield on your money; in a year you will have earned a 5 percent return on your investment in the savings account. Unless you are confident that the alternative investment in the equipment will yield at least 5 percent, there is no incentive for you to invest in it. Investments in capital equipment must pay at least the pure rate of interest, or investors will not provide funds for investments. Again, the pure rate of interest is the rate that must be paid to induce individuals to abstain from current consumption and to save.

Risk

Suppose that you are confronted with the following offer: You can have $100 for sure or you can have a 50-50 chance of receiving $200. The expected value of each alternative is the same. In the second alternative, the probability of receiving $200 is 0.50, and the probability of receiving no money is 0.50. Thus, 0.50 ($200) + 0.50 ($0) = $100. Yet the individual decision-maker is not indifferent between these alternatives. The latter alternative involves risk, while the former does not. Individuals generally view the bearing of risk as a cost and have to be compensated to bear risk.

Risk has a lot to do with capital investment. There is no guarantee of a handsome rate of return on investments in capital goods. Market conditions can change, making the capital goods obsolete or making the things that the capital goods produce less popular with consumers. In other words, capital investments involve risks, so a premium must be paid to induce individual investors to bear risks on their investments. This risk premium is above and beyond the pure rate of interest.

Profits and Losses

Investors in capital goods can earn economic profits or losses. The opportunity cost of fixed capital is the price that must be paid to keep it committed to its present use. This cost consists of the pure interest and any risk premium.

Yet something unexpected can happen in the economy to make the fixed capital more valuable. For example, the demand for the product produced by fixed capital may increase many times over what was expected. In such a case the owners of capital earn economic profits on their investment in addition to pure interest and a risk premium. In a competitive market, these returns will be eliminated by competition as other investors become aware of the excess returns and make capital investments of their own in the industry. Keep in mind, too, that economic profits can be negative; that is, investors in capital goods can incur large and unexpected losses.

These profits and losses are analogous to capital gains and losses to investors in the stock market. A capital gain, for example, derives from an unexpected increase in the value of a firm, its capital stock, and what the capital stock produces.

Summarizing, the rate of return to capital investment embodies three components: a pure interest return, a premium for bearing risk, and a residual component reflecting unexpected changes in the value of capital goods. Each of these components has an important allocative function in the economy. Pure interest induces people to save. The risk premium leads individuals to invest in risky but valuable ventures. Economic profits are the spur to entrepreneurship and innovation in the economy. We have more to say about profits and entrepreneurship in Chapter 17.

THE PRESENT VALUE OF FUTURE INCOME

Present value:
The value today of a payment to be made or received in the future; a future sum discounted by the current rate of interest.

Investment in capital goods and saving balances the needs of tomorrow with the needs of today. Economists find it useful to look at this balancing act in a precise mathematical formula called *present value*. **Present value** refers to the value today of some payment that will be received in the future. This value depends on the current rate of interest and the length of time between the present and future.

How, for instance, would the prospect of making $100 in one year or in two years compare with the prospect of making $100 now, if the rate of interest is 10 percent? The $100 made now would by definition have a present value of $100. But what about the $100 made in one year? What would be the equivalent amount of money made now? That is, what amount invested now at 10 percent would be able to generate a fund of $100 in one year? The answer is $90.91 with simple interest, computed by the formula

$$PV = \frac{\text{receipts in one year}}{(1 + \text{interest rate})^t} = \frac{\$100}{(1 + 0.10)} = \$90.91.$$

where $t = 1$ yr

What sum invested now at 10 percent and compounded annually would produce $100 after two years? Since we are interested in the amount that would yield $100 in *two* years, we *square* the denominator of the formula we used to calculate the present value of money invested for one year:

$$PV = \frac{\$100}{(1 + 0.10)^2} = \$82.64.$$

FOCUS   Present Value and Calculating the Loss from Injury or Death

In many lawsuits the formula for present value is used to estimate the loss of earnings that an individual suffers from an incapacitating injury or premature death. Economists are retained by law firms across the country to make such estimates and to present them to judges and juries.

Consider an instance of premature death. The cost of premature death is treated as the loss of income that would otherwise have resulted over the remaining working lifetime of the deceased. For someone who earned $50 a day and worked 240 days per year, the loss of income would be $12,000 per year, assuming that the individual would have received no raises. If this person died at age sixty but had expected to work five more years before retiring, the total loss of income for the missing five-year period is $60,000. This amount would not be the cost of the premature death. Rather, the cost would be some lesser amount, reflecting the fact that a loss of $100 in the future is not equivalent to a loss of $100 now.

The formula for present value (PV) given in the text is $PV = A_n/(1 + r)^n$. In the case of a person who earned $12,000 per year, A would be $12,000. At a 10 percent rate of interest, what would be the present value of the premature death at age sixty of someone who earned $12,000 per year? Applying the general formula for present value, the answer would be found by solving

$$PV = \frac{\$12,000}{(1.1)^1} + \frac{\$12,000}{(1.1)^2} + \frac{\$12,000}{(1.1)^3} +$$

$$\frac{\$12,000}{(1.1)^4} + \frac{\$12,000}{(1.1)^5} = \$45,521.$$

While a total of $60,000 of income is lost, the present value of this loss is $45,521. For a person who dies prematurely at age sixty, the cost of his death, labeled as premature because it occurred before age sixty-five, would therefore be estimated at $45,521.

The concept of present value thus plays a role in the courtroom. It helps lawyers, judges, and juries establish reasonable bounds for settling lawsuits based on the loss of future income through injury or death.

By extension of this procedure, the present value of any amount at any time in the future can be computed. The formula for doing this is

$$PV = \frac{A_n}{(1 + r)^n}$$

where A_n is the actual amount anticipated in a particular year in the future, r is the rate of interest, and n refers to the particular year in the future.

Note two aspects of present value computations. First, the lower the rate of interest used in making these computations, the higher will be the present value attributed to any given amount of income to be made in the future. Table 1 illustrates this point clearly. The present value of $100 one year from now is approximately $97.10 at a 3 percent interest rate and approximately $89.30 at a 12 percent interest rate. Second, the present value of a given amount to be received in the future declines as the date of receipt advances farther into the future. In Table 1, for any given interest rate the present value of $100 is less the farther it is to be received in the future. To see this relation, simply read down any column in the table. The point is that the present value of future revenues or costs is inversely related to the rate of interest and the distance of the date in the future when payment will be received. Focus, "Present Value and Calculating the Loss from Injury or Death," presents an application of the concept of present value.

TABLE 1

The Present Value of $100 at Various Years in the Future

The farther in the future the $100 is received, reading vertically down the table at any interest rate, the less it is worth now. Reading horizontally across the table, the higher the interest rate, the less is the value of $100 at any year in the future.

Years in the Future	3%	5%	7%	10%	12%
1	$97.10	$92.50	$93.50	$90.90	$89.30
2	94.30	90.70	87.30	82.60	79.70
3	91.50	86.40	81.60	75.10	71.10
4	88.80	82.30	76.30	68.30	63.60
5	86.30	78.40	71.30	62.00	56.70
6	83.70	74.60	66.60	56.40	50.70
7	81.30	71.10	62.30	51.30	45.20
8	78.90	67.70	58.20	46.60	40.40
9	76.60	64.50	54.40	42.40	36.00
10	74.40	61.40	50.80	38.50	32.20
.	.	.	.	.	.
.	.	.	.	.	.
15	64.20	48.10	36.20	23.90	18.30
.	.	.	.	.	.
20	55.40	37.70	25.80	14.80	10.40
.	.	.	.	.	.
30	41.20	23.10	13.10	5.73	3.34
.	.	.	.	.	.
40	30.70	14.20	6.70	2.21	1.07
.	.	.	.	.	.
50	22.80	8.70	2.13	.85	.35

INVESTMENT DECISIONS

The estimation of present value is important to firms because investment decisions involve current expenditures for plant and equipment in the expectation of future revenues from the goods and services produced by the plant and equipment. Two aspects of investment decision making are paramount. First, the future revenues that an investment project will yield are estimated and converted to present value terms. This process provides the firm with an estimate of how much a project is worth now. Second, the firm must know what its cost of loanable funds is; that is, it must know on what terms it can borrow or lend money. This cost is the interest rate that the firm will apply to investment decisions. A simple decision rule follows from these two steps: If the estimated present value of a project exceeds the cost of loanable funds, a profit-maximizing firm will undertake the project. If not, it will turn down the project. For example, if a firm estimates that a project will yield an 8 percent return but money market certificates are currently paying 15 percent, the firm will reject the project and place its funds in the money market.

Here is an example of this reasoning. A firm is contemplating an investment in a $50,000 machine. Its managers estimate that after expenses for maintenance and repair the machine will add $10,000 per year for the next six years to firm revenues. After six years the machine no longer has any value; it has no scrap value. Assuming that the firm can borrow the funds to purchase the machine at a 12 percent rate of interest, it will discount the estimated future revenues at a 12 percent rate. The present value calculations are shown in Table 2.

Discount rate:
The interest rate a firm uses to determine the present value of an investment in a capital good.

By taking the appropriate rate of interest, commonly called the **discount rate** when used in investment planning, from Table 1 and applying it to the estimated future revenue at the end of each year, we derive in the last column of Table 2 how much the flow of future income from the machine for each year is worth today. The total present value of the estimated future income produced by the piece of equipment is $41,200 (the sum of the figures in the last column). This total present value is considerably less than the cost of the machine ($50,000), and so the firm will rationally reject this investment proposal.

Whether an investment project will be undertaken is obviously sensitive to the interest rate that the firm faces. Lower interest rates lead to higher present values. If the discount rate in this example had been 5 percent, the present value calculations would have indicated that estimated revenues would be greater than $50,000. At a 5 percent interest rate, the firm would have undertaken the project.

Will the rates of return on profitable investments differ greatly in a competitive economy? Ignoring differences in risk of different investments, competition will tend to equalize the rate of return to investment projects everywhere in the economy. Where there are profits from investment projects, entry by competing investors in similar projects will occur. For example, in the 1950s Ray Kroc pioneered the concept of a fast-food restaurant by opening McDonald's restaurants across the country. The profits that he earned on this

TABLE 2

The Discounted Present Value of $10,000 for Six Years

Year	Estimated Future Revenue (received at year-end)	Discounted Value (12% rate)	Present Value of Income
1	$10,000	0.89	$ 8,900
2	10,000	0.80	8,000
3	10,000	0.71	7,100
4	10,000	0.64	6,400
5	10,000	0.57	5,700
6	10,000	0.51	5,100
	Total $60,000		Total $41,200

investment attracted many competitors—Burger King, Wendy's, and so on—to make similar investments. Such entry (or exit in the case of losses on investment projects) will drive the rate of return on capital investment to equal its cost. In simple terms, competition will tend to equate the expected future revenues from capital investment to the current cost of the investment. In such a way competition equalizes the rate of return on capital investments in a competitive economy.

THE BENEFITS OF CAPITAL FORMATION

Saving means abstaining from consumption now in the expectation of being able to consume more in the future. Saving thus provides the resources needed to increase the stock of capital goods in the economy. A large stock of capital goods raises the rate of consumption that can be sustained in the future. Saving clearly benefits the saver, but it also benefits those who don't save. Indeed, the benefits from saving are diffused throughout the whole economy. Most of us benefit from advances in computer technology, though few of us contributed to the saving that made such advances possible.

Saving and capital formation also lead to higher wages and incomes for workers. In a competitive economy wages are a function of the productivity of workers, and this productivity is in turn a function of the amount and quality of the equipment and tools that workers use. A worker with a tractor is far more productive than a worker with a mule-drawn plow. Since more-productive workers are paid more, some of the benefits from capital formation are spread to workers who did not necessarily contribute to the saving that made the capital formation possible.

Indeed, those who save and who build capital goods are among the chief benefactors of society. As Ludwig von Mises put it:

> Every single performance in this ceaseless pursuit of wealth production is based upon the saving and the preparatory work of earlier generations. We are the lucky heirs of our father and forefathers whose saving has accumulated the capital goods with the aid of which we are working today. We favorite children of the age of electricity still derive advantage from the original saving of the primitive fishermen who, in producing the first nets and canoes, devoted a part of their working time to provision for a remoter future. If the sons of these legendary fishermen had worn out these intermediary products—nets and canoes—without replacing them by new ones, they would have consumed capital and the process of saving and capital accumulation would have had to start afresh. We are better off than earlier generations because we are equipped with the capital goods they have accumulated for us.[1]

The reverse is also true: Policies that reduce the incentive to save and to produce capital goods, while appearing to harm the suppliers of saving and the owners of capital goods, actually hurt all of us.

---

[1]Ludwig von Mises, *Human Action*, 3rd ed. (Chicago: Henry Regnery, 1966), p. 492.

SUMMARY

1. Wealth can be defined as a high level of sustainable consumption in an economy. The elements of a wealthy society are production, resources, knowledge, capital, technology, and institutions.
2. Roundabout production is the process of saving and investing in capital goods production in order to produce more in the future.
3. Time preference is a measure of an individual's concern for present versus future consumption.
4. Interest is the price that individuals must be paid for waiting to consume later, or the price that individuals are willing to pay in order to consume now rather than later.
5. The rate of interest is determined in the market for loanable funds by the demand and supply of loanable funds.
6. In reality there is a multiplicity of interest rates—such as prime rates, government rates, and credit card rates—determined by the degree of risk, cost, and time allowed for payment. Taking the rate of inflation into account, the real rate of interest is lower than the nominal rate of interest.
7. The returns to capital are composed of pure interest, a risk premium, and economic profits or losses.
8. Present value is the amount of money in the present that is equivalent to a certain amount of money in the future.
9. The discount rate is the interest rate used to discount future amounts of revenues and costs in order to obtain present values.

KEY TERMS

roundabout production	capital consumption	nominal rate of interest
saving	rate of time preference	inflation rate
capital formation	interest	real rate of interest
capital stock	demand for loanable funds	pure interest
depreciation	supply of loanable funds	present value
	risk	discount rate

QUESTIONS FOR REVIEW AND DISCUSSION

1. Give some examples of roundabout production. Describe why going to college is a roundabout method of production.
2. Suppose that you are thinking about investing in a personal computer and laser printer. Your costs will be $2500 and the equipment will last four years. You expect to earn $900 a year typing papers part-time with the computer. The bank will lend you the money at 19 percent interest. Should you buy the computer and printer? Suppose the bank's interest rate was 12 percent?
3. Why is the concept of time preference important in the discussion of interest rate? Explain.
4. How would the following events affect the prime rate of interest in the United States?
   (a) The threat of war in Central America
   (b) An increase in the inflation rate
   (c) The discovery of massive domestic oil resources
   (d) Greater impatience in the general population
   (e) More capricious government intervention in the economy
5. If the interest return that entrepreneurs can earn on capital investments is less than the interest rate paid for loanable funds, how will entrepreneurs behave? What happens to the level of investment in the economy?
6. J. M. Keynes in the *General Theory* suggests that the marginal product of capital can be driven to zero in one generation by increasing the production of capital. Would this ever happen in a free market? If it did, what would this imply about time preference? What would happen to the nation's output? What would be the interest rate?
7. What is the formula for computing present value? How is present value affected by changes in the interest rate used for discounting?
8. What is the present value of your entire future income? Would you consider yourself a millionaire? How much of your future income would a bank be willing to lend you now?

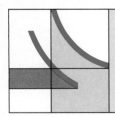

ECONOMICS IN ACTION
The Present Value of Lottery Winnings

In recent years the popularity of state-run lotteries as revenue-raising instruments has increased dramatically. In 1963, New Hampshire became the first state to conduct a lottery since the Civil War. Its success encouraged other states to follow suit; today, nearly thirty states have lotteries.

Initially, state lotteries were quite simple. Lottery players typically were allowed to select numbers between zero and one hundred or, in some states, between zero and one thousand. Daily or weekly drawings were held, with payoffs to winning tickets of about $50 per dollar bet in states using two-digit numbers and of about $500 per dollar bet in states using three-digit numbers. However, as lotteries spread to more states, competition led state lottery commissions to introduce a variety of games. The type that has proven most popular is a "Super Jackpot Game," or "Lotto," in which bettors must match a fairly long sequence of numbers (typically, six numbers out of fifty or sixty) with the sequence drawn. The jackpot continues to grow week to week until there is a winner. Games of this type have generated huge amounts of publicity and have produced frenzied betting, with jackpots rising to over $60 million in some states.

One feature of the jackpot games that has disappointed some lucky winners is the fact that winnings are not paid in one lump sum. Instead, they are typically paid in even installments over a period of years. For example, Florida pays its jackpots in twenty equal annual installments. In the case of a $55 million jackpot recently, the Florida lottery commission put aside enough money to pay twenty installments of $2.75 million. The amount necessary to fulfill this obligation is the present value of $2.75 million in one year plus the present value of $2.75 million in two years and so forth for each of the twenty annual payments. At current interest rates of just over 8 percent, Florida lottery officials were able to meet their obligation by setting aside $26 million. At an interest rate of 5 percent, the obligation could have been met by setting aside about $34.3 million; at a 15 percent interest rate, the obligation would have cost the state only about $17 million. The state has a strong incentive to defer

A winning lottery ticket can bring a single winner upwards of $50 million. Paid in annual installments, however, the jackpot has a substantially lower present value.

payments. In doing so, they can publicize a payout of $55 million, yet meet their obligation at a cost of $26 million.

An understanding of present values makes it clear that a dollar today is worth more than a dollar in the future. Therefore, when we read about a lottery winner who sells a $300,000 winning ticket for $160,000, we should not conclude that the winner is crazy. With the $300,000 being paid at future dates, its present value is substantially less.

Question
A state sold thirty million lottery tickets at $1 each and had to pay for the tickets to be printed and distributed. If the grand prize was $30 million, how could the state collect revenues on such a lottery?

17

Rents, Profits, and Entrepreneurship

Thus far in our study of factors of production, we have looked at labor and capital and their corresponding factor payments: wages and interest. In this chapter we look at two more factors—land and the special form of labor called *entrepreneurship*—and their returns: rents and profits. The vacant lot next door, H. Ross Perot, and Esteé Lauder are as much economic factors of production as are the day laborer and robotic assembly unit.

What was suggested in Chapter 10 about the concept of rent we state here explicitly: Compared with its everyday usage, the term *rent* has a much broader application in economics. In theory, any factor of production, including labor, can earn rents. After we have examined the relation of land supply to rent, we will look at other types of rents and discuss the concept of rent seeking, which refers to the competition for rents among individuals and firms.

In economic terms, rent and profit are closely allied. Profits are the residual payment to capitalist entrepreneurs after all other factor payments—including rents, salaries, and interest—have been made. Every firm and every individual seeks to maximize profits and minimize losses. Competition for profits, or risk taking, involves decision making under uncertainty. We will explore how this process takes place. (An appendix to this chapter shows how *both* input and output markets interact in a general equilibrium process.) When you have completed Chapter 17, you should understand

- how land rents are determined and how they are one species of a more general economic concept of rent.

- the competitive process—rent seeking—by which rents of specialized factors of production are earned and divided.

- the nature of entrepreneurship, the role of entrepreneurs in any economy, and the rewards they get.

TYPES OF RENT

A farmer pays rent to a landowner for the use of an acre of land. A student leases an apartment and pays rent to the landlord each month. A sales representative rents a car to call on customers in a distant city. These examples use the word *rent* in its most familiar sense—payment for the use of something. These rents are all represented in the circular flow of income as the income to property and landowners, a broad category that includes all types of rent payments made according to lease agreements. In 1989, such payments totaled $62.3 billion, or about 1.5 percent of national income. For the economist, **rent** refers to the portion of the payment to any factor of production—land, labor, or capital—that is over and above the factor's opportunity cost. It is the amount a factor is paid that is greater than the forgone value of its next most productive use. Nearly every factor you can name has alternative uses. Farmland could be used as the site of an industrial park. An engineer could be put to use typing correspondence. Again, "payment for lease" stops short of being a complete definition of the economic theory of rent.

Economists distinguish among various types of economic rent. A **pure economic rent** is the payment to a factor of production that has a perfectly inelastic supply curve. In such a case the price of the resource is determined solely by the level of demand for its services because supply is fixed and does not change as price changes. Land in the aggregate is the classic example of a resource whose supply is given and whose return is characterized as a pure economic rent.

Another type of economic rent is received by factors of production whose supply curves are upward-sloping. These rents are called **inframarginal rents.** Inframarginal rent is a payment to a factor of production above and beyond the minimum payment necessary to just induce the factor into the market. This minimum payment is the factor's supply price or opportunity cost. For example, if you are willing to work an hour for $4 but your employer pays you $5, then you receive a $1 inframarginal rent per hour on your job. Virtually all factors of production earn inframarginal rents.

Finally, there are categories of rents that accrue to firms. **Quasi-rents** are returns to a firm owner in a competitive industry above the opportunity cost of the owner's invested capital. Quasi-rents are thus the short-run economic profits of competitive firms, which we analyzed in Chapter 9. **Monopoly rents** are the returns that accrue to the owner of a monopoly firm when the firm restricts output and raises price. Monopoly rents are the profits of the monopolist, which we covered in Chapter 10. Competitive and monopoly profits are recast in this chapter as quasi-rents and monopoly rents to illustrate the relation between economic rent and economic profits.

Rent:
A payment to a factor of production in excess of the factor's opportunity cost.

Pure economic rent:
The total payment to a factor of production whose supply curve is perfectly inelastic.

Inframarginal rent:
That portion of a payment to a factor of production whose supply is upward-sloping in excess of the factor's opportunity cost.

Quasi-rent:
The payment to owners of fixed capital in a competitive industry in the short-run situation that exceeds the opportunity cost of their capital; also called economic profit.

Monopoly rent:
The payment to owners of fixed capital in a monopolized industry that exceeds the opportunity cost of capital; also called monopoly profit.

LAND RENTS

How is land priced? The obvious answer is that the price of land is determined where its demand and supply curves intersect. While this is correct, there are some special aspects of the price-determination process in the case of land. These aspects concern how the supply curve of land is defined. Although the focus in our discussion will be on the supply of land, keep in mind the role of the demand curve for land. As you learned in Chapter 14, this demand curve is based on the marginal productivity of land. In this regard the demand curve for land is the same as the demand curve for any factor of production—it is based on the expected marginal revenue product of land as a factor of production. When land is rented, rent is paid to the landowner. The greater the demand for the land, the larger the rent will be. In equilibrium, where the quantity demanded and quantity supplied of land are equal, the rent to the landowner is equal to the marginal revenue product of the land to the renter.

Pure Economic Rents

To pursue the relation of the supply of land to its price, assume that land is leased by the acre per year. We are concerned with the rent that must be paid to use the flow of services yielded by land for a year. We are not concerned with the related question of the price of a given stock or amount of land, although the two ways of looking at the pricing of the services of land amount to practically the same thing. Land is a resource that yields a flow of services over time. The price of a stock of land will reflect the estimated present value of this future flow of services. Alternatively, the rental price of land will reflect the estimated value of the flow of services for a given period of time. Since our interest is in land rent, we speak in terms of the price of the flow of services from land for a given period of time.

Aggregate supply of land: The total amount of land available for use by the entire economy.

A distinction must also be made between the fixed supply of land and its potential allocation to varying uses. In Figure 1a the supply curve of land is drawn for all land, or the **aggregate supply of land.** The curve is drawn as a vertical line, indicating that land in the aggregate is in fixed supply. In general, the amount of land on earth is given by nature and cannot be changed. Actually, common sense tells us that the assumption of a perfectly inelastic supply of land is not completely true. The supply of usable land can be increased through reclamation of swamps and marshes or reduced through erosion. Nonetheless, it is useful to think of the aggregate supply curve of land as perfectly inelastic, as drawn in Figure 1a.

What are the economic implications of this vertical supply curve for all land? First, the perfectly inelastic nature of the supply of land in the aggregate means that the quantity supplied of land is unresponsive to price. Whether land is priced at \$1 per acre per year or \$1 million per acre per year, the quantity supplied of land in the aggregate will not change. In economic terms this fixed quantity, Q in Figure 1a, means that the rental price of land will be determined solely by the level of demand. Thus, the equilibrium level of rent on the vertical axis depends on where the demand curve for land intersects the fixed supply curve.

The return to land in the aggregate is labeled a pure economic rent. To understand this concept, recall that economic rent is defined as a payment in excess of the opportunity cost of a factor of production. Recall also that a factor's opportunity cost is reflected in its supply schedule because a supply schedule indicates what it takes to bid resources away from their next-best alternative use. A vertical supply curve such as in Figure 1a means that land in the aggregate has no opportunity cost; nothing is given up for its supply, for it has no alternative uses. Very simply, this means that the whole return to land in the aggregate is a pure economic rent. In Figure 1a, land garners $REQ0$ in pure rent.

FIGURE 1

Pure Economic Rent and the Supply of Land

(a) The supply curve for land in the aggregate is perfectly inelastic with respect to rent, which means that the return to land in the aggregate is a pure economic rent. (b) The supply curve of land to competing uses appears as it is normally drawn—sloping upward to the right. This slope reflects the fact that land has competing uses and hence that the price of using land or rent plays an important role in determining the uses to which land is put.

(a) Aggregate

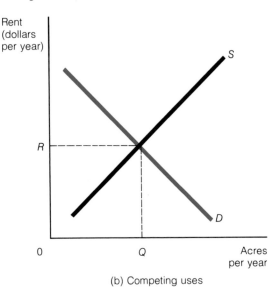

(b) Competing uses

The concept of pure economic rent is normally associated with the supply curve of all land. However, it is possible that other resources will exhibit a range of their supply curve that is perfectly inelastic and that they therefore stand to earn pure economic rents. This characteristic may be true of uniquely talented performers in the worlds of sport and art, a subject to which we will return later in the chapter.

The Supply of Land to Alternative Uses

Since the return to land in the aggregate is a pure economic rent, a price does not have to be paid to call forth a supply of land. The supply of land is fixed and given at Q, and it is not affected by the level of rent, R. Since the supply of all land is independent of its price, we say that price has no allocative function in this case.

If rent does not have to be paid to call forth a supply of land, then why pay it? Or why not tax all rents away as an unearned surplus to landowners? The attractiveness of such a tax is apparent—it raises revenue without affecting the available supply of land. In Figure 1a, for example, a tax equal to the area of pure rents, $REQ0$, would leave the supply of land unaffected at Q.

In 1879, in his book *Progress and Poverty*, Henry George proposed a single tax of 10 percent on land rent on just these grounds. George argued for a single tax on land because he felt that landowners contributed nothing to the land's productivity. Rising land values were determined by general economic growth and by increases in the demand for land. Thus, a tax on land would not affect the amount of land available to the economy and would prevent landowners from getting rich from windfall profits while nonlandowners remained poor. (Windfall profits could occur to lucky landowners with favorable and unexpected changes in economic conditions.) Moreover, George thought a single tax on land rents could finance all the government of his day, eliminating the need for other types of taxes.

George's proposal rests on the assumption of a perfectly inelastic supply curve of land. He was essentially assuming that land has no alternative uses. But this assumption concerns land only in the aggregate. While land in the aggregate has a vertical supply curve, the supply of land to alternative uses does not. Consider what happens, for example, as a city expands. Farmland is converted to sites for houses and shopping centers, as people bid for the right to use the land in other ways. The market process reallocates the land from less valued to more highly valued uses, from farmland to city land.

The supply curve of land for particular uses slopes upward to the right, as shown in Figure 1b. To rent land for a particular use, one must bid it away from competing uses. As more desirable land is rented, the rental rate rises. With a normally sloped supply curve, the rental price paid for land serves to allocate land to competing uses. Those who value the use of a parcel of land more highly will offer higher rents than others. Focus, "Land Rent, Location, and the Price of Corn," discusses this process in more detail. In this sense, rent functions like any other price in signaling the intentions of buyers and sellers in the market for land. Rent for land is not a pure surplus in this case. It serves a useful purpose in the price system, and to tax it away could impose unnecessary shortages and other costs on the economy.

The proper distinction to keep in mind is that while the supply curve of land in the aggregate is approximately vertical, the supply curve of land to alternative uses is positively sloped. Since the latter concept of the supply of land is far more relevant to real-world situations than the former, a proposal such as Henry George's could do much damage to the economy. It was never implemented, although George was a popular politician and twice ran for mayor of New York City.

Whether land is viewed in the aggregate or as a resource of varying desirability and alternative uses, rent does serve a function: It rations land among available bidders.

Land and Marginal Revenue Product

Like the demand curve for any other factor of production, the demand curve for the services of land is a derived demand curve. It is derived from the value of the output that the land, used in conjunction with other factors of production, can produce. Entrepreneurs will therefore employ land in their production processes as long as the marginal revenue product of land exceeds its rental rate. Where the quantity demanded and quantity supplied of land are equal, as shown in Figure 1b, rental payments equal the marginal revenue product of the land. As we stressed in Chapter 14, the principles of marginal productivity theory apply to any factor of production, including land.

The rental rate of land varies greatly from one location to another, depending on the land's productivity. While soil fertility may be identical in two different locations, the rental rates may not be equal because the physical locations of the two plots may account for differences in productivity. To understand this point, consider a straight highway that extends from a large city far into the surrounding rural area. Along this highway farms of equal size produce the same product—corn.

Each farm transports its corn to the city and incurs the costs of transporting each bushel. The distance from each farm to the city is different, and the cost of transportation increases as the distance increases. Thus, farms nearer the city have lower average and marginal costs than farms farther from the city.

Figure 2 shows cost curves of four farms at 50-mile intervals from a city. Farm A is closer to town than Farm B,

B is closer than C, and C is closer than D. The costs of production are lower at locations closer to the city; this land can be described as more productive.

Since each farm is a price taker in a competitive market in town, all farms face the same price, P. Profits are shown by the shaded area in each panel. The land closer to town is more profitable because of its locational advantage and thus is in greater demand. The demand for land decreases as the location is farther from town. Farm D makes no profits; there would be no demand for land by farmers beyond this point. The varying profits bring forth varying demand and thus varying rental rates. The rental rates are bid up by potential farm owners until a normal profit is obtained at each location. The shaded area of profits at each location actually becomes the rental rate. Advantages of a productive location yield income in the form of rents to the suppliers of the land.

FIGURE 2   The Importance of Location in Determining Rents

Figures 2a, 2b, 2c, and 2d show the cost curves for four different farms at four different locations. Farm A is closest to the city; farm D is farthest away. Since costs of transportation increase the farther a farm is from the city, farm A will enjoy lower costs and higher productivity than any of its three competitors.

SPECIALIZATION OF RESOURCES AND INFRAMARGINAL RENTS

An economic rent is defined as a payment to any factor of production—land, labor, or capital—above and beyond its opportunity cost. Rent, in other words, is an excess payment to a resource owner. This concept can easily be applied to resources other than land. For example, a worker provides labor services to a firm. The firm pays the worker the prevailing market wage. The opportunity cost of the worker—her evaluation of her next-best employment prospect—is less than the wage she is paid. The worker thus earns an economic rent in her present job, for she is paid more than it takes to induce her to continue to work in her present employment.

Resource specialization:
A situation in which resources are relatively more adept at one or a few tasks rather than a variety of uses; the result of comparative advantage.

Rents are caused by the specialization of resources. **Resource specialization** simply means that a resource or factor of production is relatively better at working in one occupation or industry than in others. A worker, for example, may be specialized as a welder because he went to technical college to develop welding skills. As a welder, he will supply specialized labor to those industries that employ welders.

In general, we can detect the degree of resource specialization by observing the supply curve of the source. The supply curve of a factor of production measures the willingness of its owner to supply its services at various prices. It therefore gives a measure of the opportunity cost of the resource at different prices.

Examples are given in Figure 3. The supply curve of the resource is flat, or perfectly elastic, in Figure 3a. This means the resource is completely unspecialized with respect to its use in this industry. Any amount of the resource can be purchased at the same price, P_1. The resource's price is determined solely by the level of the supply function. This is the opposite extreme from the case of the perfectly inelastic supply curve of land given in Figure 1a. Whereas the return to land in the aggregate was a pure rent, the resource depicted in Figure 3a earns no rents. Completely unspecialized resources earn no rents.

Many categories of manual labor and jobs that do not require extensive training or experience can be characterized as unspecialized. The supply, for example, of paper carriers, yard workers, and baby-sitters is probably a flat line at the prevailing wage for these services. Given the level of demand for such services, the supply of labor to fulfill them is perfectly elastic.

In Figure 3b, we have drawn a more normal-looking supply curve for a factor of production. In this case, we can say that the upward-sloping supply curve indicates degrees of economic specialization. If the factor is word processors, for instance, some people will be highly specialized at word processing but untrained for anything else. Their next-best alternative would be some low-paying job that requires little skill or training. Such people theoretically would be available as word processors at a relatively low wage—such as P_3 in Figure 3—because their opportunity cost is low. At the upper end of the supply curve are people trained as word processors who are also highly skilled in other areas, such as data programming or legal secretarial work. They can be bid into word processing jobs only by relatively high wages such as P_2 or an

FIGURE 3

Unspecialized and Specialized Resources

(a) The supply curve of an unspecialized resource. Such resources earn no economic rents.
(b) The normal case of economic specialization and an upward-sloping resource supply curve. Inframarginal rents accrue to the resource owners in the amount represented by P_2EP_0

(a)

(b)

even higher wage because the cost of their forgone opportunities—jobs as legal secretaries or data programmers—is high.

Although workers with varying degrees of specialization would thus accept different wages, interaction of supply and demand tends to set an equilibrium wage, P_2, paid to all people or other resources doing the same job. At this price, the more specialized resources on the lower end of the supply curve—those who are relatively better at the work for which they are hired than at anything else—will earn economic rents. Look at the word processors or other resources represented by Q_2 in Figure 3, for example. Their opportunity cost is P_3, which is the price just sufficient to attract them into this industry. Yet because of this market's equilibrium, all units of the resource receive the same price, P_2. The difference between P_2 and P_3, or *ab*, is an economic rent that accrues to the resource depicted by Q_2. It is a payment above and beyond the opportunity cost of the resource. In fact, the whole area below P_2 and above the supply curve, P_2EP_0, represents economic rents earned by suppliers of this resource. The last unit, Q_1, is paid just its opportunity cost, P_2, so we say that Q_1 is the marginal unit of the resource that earns no rents. All the previous units hired earn economic rents by the amount of the difference between their supply prices and their market rate of compensation. Economists call this kind of economic rent an inframarginal rent.

As another example of inframarginal rents, examine the supply curve of volunteer soldiers given in Figure 4. We assume that the army wants to hire Q soldiers per year to maintain its force structure. To do so it finds that it must offer a wage of W. All soldiers hired are paid W, but it is clear from the upward slope of the supply curve that some would have volunteered for lower wages. For example, the very first volunteers would have signed up for a wage slightly

FIGURE 4

S and *D* are the supply and demand curves for volunteer soldiers. Because of the upward-sloping nature of the supply curve, volunteer soldiers earn inframarginal economic rents in the amount represented by *WEA*.

Inframarginal Rents for Volunteer Soldiers

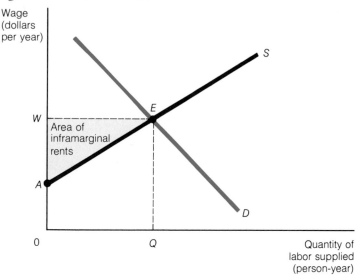

above A. The volunteer army therefore leads to the receipt of inframarginal economic rents by volunteer soldiers. In Figure 4, these rents are given by the area WEA.

The concept of inframarginal rents has general applicability to economic life. Factors of production by their very nature are different, and these differences lead to economic specialization, which in turn leads to inframarginal rents. Yet the prevalence of rents does not suggest that there is something unwholesome about the market process. While these are "excess returns" that do not have to be paid to allocate resources to their most valued uses, it would be a virtual administrative impossibility to tax such returns away. Think of the complexity of determining the opportunity cost of each resource. Moreover, it is the ability to capture such returns that leads to the process of resource specialization in the first place. These rents provide incentives for resource owners to behave in ways that are good for the economy as a whole.

THE ECONOMICS OF ACCOUNTANTS AND SUPERSTARS

It is possible that the same resource can attract both inframarginal and pure economic rents. Such a situation may be created temporarily by a sudden surge in demand for a resource. Consider what happens to the rents earned by accountants if the government unexpectedly passes a new tax law that can be understood and applied only by those with special accounting skills. Prior to the passage of this law, the market for tax accountants would be in equilibrium at a wage of W_1 and a quantity of Q_1 accountants, as indicated in Figure 5. The supply curve of accountants slopes upward to the right, and at the usual wage W_1 accountants earn inframarginal rents represented by W_1BA.

After the passage of the new tax law, the demand for the services of tax accountants increases to D_2. Yet at this point in time, the supply of tax ac-

FIGURE 5

When the demand curve for accountants shifts from D_1 to D_2, the supply of accountants remains constant in the short run at Q_1. Over this period accountants earn both pure economic rents of W_2CBW_1 and inframarginal rents of W_1BA.

Two Kinds of Economic Rent Earned Simultaneously

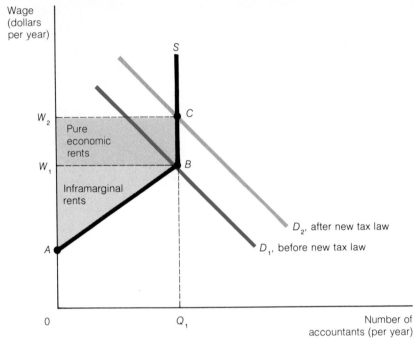

countants is fixed at Q_1. There are just so many tax accountants and their supply cannot be increased overnight. The supply curve of accountants therefore becomes vertical at B for some specified time period. As in the case of aggregate land supply, a vertical supply curve means that the accountants will earn pure economic rents as the demand for their services increases. In Figure 5 these rents are given by the area W_2CBW_1. In such a situation, accountants thus earn two types of economic rent: pure economic rents equal to W_2CBW_1 and inframarginal economic rents equal to W_1BA.

The pure economic rents in this example are only temporary. Over time, these returns in excess of opportunity cost will attract entry into the accounting profession. Entry of new accountants will shift the supply curve for accountants to the right, reducing the price of accounting services and the pure economic rents earned by accountants. During the period in which entry does not occur and the accountants earn pure economic rents, a rising wage for accountants serves to ration their services to the highest bidders.

A supply schedule like that drawn for accountants in Figure 5 can also apply to the income of superstars, such as Madonna or basketball star Michael Jordan. Figure 6 shows a possible supply curve for a superstar. In this case, the next-best alternative to being a superstar is reflected in a price for the star's services of P_1. The job earning P_1 as an alternative to superstardom might be something as ordinary as working in a bank. The supply curve of the superstar becomes vertical at P_1 because he or she possesses unusual abilities that cannot be copied by anyone else. Only "Air Jordan" has certain moves on a basketball court; only Madonna can offer her unique brand of entertainment. Thus the supply curve of the superstar above P_1 indicates that he or she is earning pure

FIGURE 6

The superstar's unique talent cannot be replicated, so it is represented by the vertical portion of the supply curve. The next-best alternative of the superstar is given by P_1. The difference between P_2 and P_1 means that the superstar's income includes a pure economic rent in the amount of P_2ABP_1 as well as an inframarginal rent of P_1BC.

A Superstar's Supply Curve

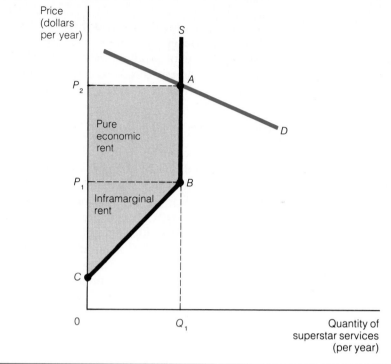

economic rent. As in other cases of vertical supply curves, price rations the services of the superstar among the competing demands of music producers or team owners.

We must be careful, however, in defining economic rents in the case of a superstar. If we define the next-best alternative of a star as being a truck driver, the economic rents that he or she earns will be large. Only if the price for his or her superstar services falls below P_1 in Figure 6 would the star switch to such an alternative job. Suppose, however, that the next-best alternative of the basketball star who earns $1 million per year is to play for another team who would pay him $900,000. In this case, economic rent would be $100,000:

$$\underset{\substack{\text{Resource owner's}\\\text{income}}}{\$1,000,000} - \underset{\substack{\text{Resource owner's}\\\text{opportunity cost}}}{\$900,000} = \underset{\substack{\text{Economic}\\\text{rent}}}{\$100,000}.$$

The measurement of economic rents hinges on how the next-best alternative or the opportunity cost of the resource is defined.

Do the rents that superstars earn affect the future supply of talent in their professions? Are their pure economic rents transitory, like those of the accountants, as new stars rise to compete with them and capture some of their rents? We can surmise that for both questions the answer is yes. Surely, the lifestyle and general level of ability and wealth of superstars provide the incentive for thousands of youngsters to practice hard and to develop extraordinary talents. Over a sufficient period of time, new entry may erode the pure economic rents of superstars.

RENTS AND FIRMS

Firms may also earn rents, and these rents are analogous to the firms' profits. In fact, the concept of economic rent as a return in excess of the opportunity cost of a factor of production is just another way to think about the profits earned by competitive and monopolistic firms. The purely competitive firm can earn quasi-rents, and the pure monopolist can earn monopoly rents.

Quasi-Rents

Quasi-rents are the return to the owner of a competitive firm in the short run. They are called quasi-rents because they are a short-run or temporary return. Figure 7 illustrates a short-run equilibrium for the competitive firm and industry. The firm earns an economic profit in the short run, which we have labeled as quasi-rent. This return is a rent because it exceeds the firm owner's opportunity cost (which by definition is included in the average total cost curve). Quasi-rents are temporary; entry of new firms into the industry will erode these returns over the long run. Quasi-rents can also be negative instead of positive, for the firm can suffer economic losses in the short run. The rents themselves are a return to the owner of the firm for decision making under conditions of risk and uncertainty.

FIGURE 7   **Quasi-Rents**

Quasi-rents are illustrated as the economic profits earned by the owner of a competitive firm in the short run. They are rents because they are a return in excess of the owner's opportunity cost, included in the *ATC* curve. They are called quasi-rents because they are temporary and will be eroded by the entry of new firms in the long run.

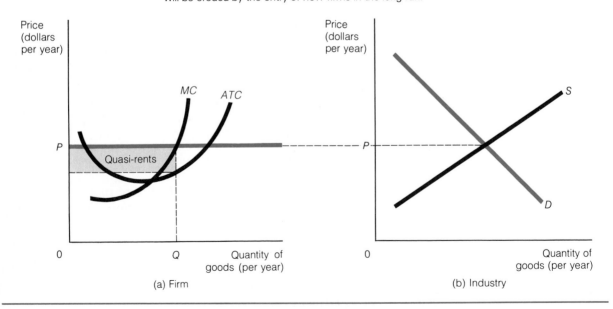

Monopoly Rents

Figure 8 shows the case of a monopolist who makes profits of *PABC*. These profits are sometimes called *monopoly rents* because they are a return in excess of the monopolist's opportunity cost, which is reflected in the average total cost curve. Unlike the quasi-rents earned by the competitive firm, the monopoly rents earned by the monopolist will persist over time. They are permanent, short of an event that would threaten the monopolist's control of an industry. But what happens if the monopolist sells the monopoly? Primarily, the monopolist will sell for the present value of future monopoly rents, as discussed in Chapter 10. Monopoly rents are therefore captured by the original owner of the monopoly; buyers of the monopoly right may earn only a competitive rate of return on their purchase of the monopoly.

RENT SEEKING

When competition is viewed as a dynamic, value-creating, evolutionary process, economic rents play a crucial role in stimulating entrepreneurial decisions and in prompting an efficient allocation of resources. Profit seeking is a normal feature of economic life in a competitive market. The returns of resource owners will be driven to normal levels by competitive profit seeking, as some resource owners earn positive rents that promote entry into the industry

---

FIGURE 8

Monopoly profits can be called monopoly rents. They are returns in excess of the monopolist's opportunity costs, which are reflected in the *ATC* curve. Unlike quasirents, they persist over time because of the monopolist's dominant position in the market.

Monopoly Rents

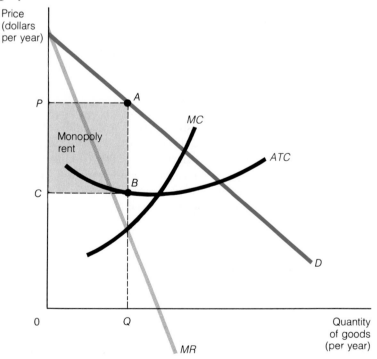

and others earn negative rents that cause exit. In this basic sense, profit seeking in a competitive setting is socially beneficial.

When the setting in which profits are pursued is changed, sometimes through government intervention, problems can arise. Suppose the government wishes to grant a monopoly right in the production of playing cards. In this case, an artificial scarcity is created by the state. As a consequence, monopoly profits or rents are present to be captured by monopolists who seek the government's favor. In a naturally occurring monopoly these rents are thought of as transfers from playing card consumers to the monopolist. Yet this can be the case only if the aspiring monopolists employ no resources to compete for the monopoly rents. To the extent that resources are used to capture monopoly rents by lobbying the government, these expenditures create no value from a social point of view. This activity of wasting resources in competing for transfers is called **rent seeking.** If a potential monopolist hires a lawyer to lobby the government for the monopoly right, the opportunity cost of the lawyer (such as the legal work that he or she does not do while engaged in lobbying) is a social cost of the monopolization process.

Rent seeking:
The process of using scarce resources in an effort to obtain rents or a transfer of wealth.

PROFITS AND THE ALLOCATION OF RESOURCES

As we saw in the discussion of quasi-rents and monopoly rents, rents and profits are closely related concepts. The word *profits,* however, is the term that we usually apply to the earnings of owners of firms. Profits are the last category of input returns we analyze in the circular flow process. Profits are a residual return to those individuals in the economy who provide economic foresight and leadership in an uncertain environment. Profits play an instrumental role in the way the competitive price system works to allocate resources to their most highly valued uses.

Profit Data

For individual firms, industries, or the economy as a whole, profits are not computed directly but are determined by what is left over from revenues after payments have been made to land, labor, and capital. It is in this sense that the profit earner, or the productive factor to which profits are imputed, is referred to as the *residual claimant.* This view of profits as a residual contrasts sharply with the common but misguided notion that employees and other input suppliers are paid only after the entrepreneur has secured profits.

Have levels of profits earned in the economy as a whole grown over the years? Table 1 traces after-tax corporate profits and nonfarm proprietors' income for selected years between 1929 and 1987. Even when taking inflation into account, the absolute level of corporate profits has risen quite steadily over this period, but when measured as a percent of GNP the corporate profit level has remained remarkably stable, ranging between 3 and 6.7 percent since the mid-1950s. In contrast, nonfarm proprietors' income exhibits a strong and continuous downward trend as a percent of GNP, while showing little change from year to year in constant dollar terms. Overall, the data in Table 1

TABLE 1

Corporate Profits and Nonfarm Proprietors' Income, 1929–1987

	Corporate Profits		Nonfarm Proprietors' Income	
Year	After Tax (billions of 1982 dollars)	Percent of GNP	After Tax (billions of 1982 dollars)	Percent of GNP
1929	58.9	8.3	60.2	8.5
1945	60.0	4.4	122.9	9.1
1955	100.0	6.7	123.1	8.2
1965	137.6	6.7	153.2	7.3
1975	141.5	5.3	172.3	6.4
1980	177.7	5.6	191.7	6.0
1981	154.7	4.8	165.1	5.1
1982	106.5	3.4	148.5	4.7
1983	125.5	3.8	161.0	4.9
1984	130.0	3.7	170.4	4.9
1985	117.8	3.3	173.5	4.8
1986	116.9	3.2	190.0	5.2
1987	121.7	3.2	198.5	5.2

Sources: Council of Economic Advisers, *Economic Report of the President* (Washington, D.C.: U.S. Government Printing Office, 1987), pp. 246, 248, and 270–71; *Statistical Abstract of the United States* (Washington, D.C.: U.S. Government Printing Office, 1989), p. 425.

fail to confirm the widely held perception that profits have been growing steadily over time.

Rate of Return on Capital

Rate of return on invested capital:
Profits earned during a period of time divided by the value of invested capital; usually measured as a percent per year.

The profit data given in Table 1 are not relevant to the decisions of firms concerning investments in plant and equipment. What matters for such purposes is not the absolute level of profits but the economic **rate of return on invested capital.** That is, at the margin it will pay to buy an additional dollar's worth of equipment only if the firm expects to earn more than a dollar from the sale of the resulting output from the equipment.

The economic rate of return on capital may be approximated with accounting data by dividing the amount of stock or capital valued at its current replacement cost into profits earned during the year. Historical data indicate that after-tax rates of return on capital have fallen over time. The average annual rate of return between 1955 and 1969 was 10.1 percent, with the highest rates occurring during the 1960s. By contrast, the average annual rate of return on capital between 1970 and 1987 was approximately 8.5 percent. This decline in rates of return has two important implications. The first involves incentives to make capital investments. For investments in capital to be profitable, not only must the rate of return be positive, but the rate of return on capital must exceed the expected return on alternative investments. Since a larger number of competing uses of funds—buying bonds, for example—become attractive as the rate of return on capital falls, the available data suggest that incentives to invest in plants and equipment during the 1970s were lower than in earlier years. Second, the data provide further evidence that the popular view of large and ever-increasing corporate profitability is mistaken.

Accounting Versus Economic Profits

Accounting profit:
Total revenue minus total explicit payments for inputs or out-of-pocket costs.

Economic profit:
Total revenue minus total opportunity costs of production.

As noted in Chapter 8, **accounting profits** tend to overstate the level of **economic profits** because accountants by necessity take a less theoretical view of costs than do economists. Accountants count as costs only those business expenditures involving direct money outlays—wages and salaries, raw materials purchased, rental payments on land and buildings, borrowing costs, advertising expenses, and so forth. Economists identify costs as *all* opportunities forgone, explicit or implicit. If you are self-employed, for example, you must count what you could earn working for somebody else as a cost of your operation.

Accounting profits also tend to be misleading because cost is a subjective, forward-looking concept. That is, insofar as they influence economic decisions, costs are based on presumptions about a future that may or may not materialize. The cost of a particular decision will therefore vary depending on when in time cost is measured. Moreover, what the decision-maker thinks is being sacrificed by a choice cannot be directly observed by someone other than the decision-maker. We are left with the conclusion that accounting profits, based as they are on a restricted concept of costs, provide only a limited guide to the actual level of economic profits in the economy.

Entrepreneurship

Entrepreneur:
An individual who perceives profit opportunities, organizes resources into productive ventures, and bears the uncertain status of residual claimant of the resulting risky economic outcome.

Assuming that economic profits can be measured, what role do they play in the economic process? Economic profits are the return to a particular factor of production, **entrepreneurship.** As such, profits are the residual income accruing to the entrepreneur as a return on the services he or she brings to the productive process. These services include technical abilities in organizing the other factors of production into combinations appropriate for the efficient manufacture of goods. More important, though, is the entrepreneur's alertness to the existence of potential profit opportunities in the economy. In this sense, entrepreneurship consists of linking markets by perceiving the opportunity to buy resources at a lower total cost than the revenue obtainable from the sale of output, or by recognizing that sellers in one market are offering to sell output at a price lower than buyers in another market are willing to pay.

Put another way, entrepreneurship consists of offering the most attractive opportunities to other market participants—perceiving unfulfilled demands, offering higher prices to sellers or lower prices to buyers, improving existing goods or making them more cheaply, finding more effective means of communicating to consumers the availability and attributes of goods. In all of these activities the entrepreneur takes advantage of opportunities that exist because of the initial ignorance of other market participants. But as a result of the entrepreneur's actions, markets move closer to the prices and quantities emerging in equilibrium, the plans of buyers and sellers more closely dovetail, and the knowledge of economic data held by market participants is increased.

In addition to alertness and organizational skills, the entrepreneur brings to the production process a willingness to act in the presence of uncertainty. (We distinguish risk from uncertainty in that risk involves events that occur with known probabilities—the toss of a coin, for example—while uncertainty entails outcomes whose probabilities cannot be specified with precision—for example, war or peace and long-run weather forecasts. There is no guarantee that perceived profit opportunities will materialize. Because it takes time between the purchase of inputs and the sale of output—between the expenditures on resources and the receipt of revenue—intervening events may cause the entrepreneur's plans to be either overambitious or under-ambitious when evaluated with the advantage of hindsight. Entrepreneurs, then, bear responsibility for incorrect anticipations. Profits can be viewed as a return for bearing both risk and uncertainty.

Entrepreneurs and Information: The Austrian View

Economists who work in the tradition of the Austrian economic theorists of the late 1800s are referred to as the modern Austrian school of economics. The modern Austrians include Friedrich A. von Hayek, who won the Nobel Prize in economics in 1972, and Israel Kirzner.

The traditional view of the entrepreneur as a person who discovers and bears the risks of profit opportunities has been expanded in the modern Austrian view.[1] In this view, the entrepreneur must also design and sell partic-ular commodities or specific qualities of commodities that satisfy the desires of consumers or particular groups of consumers. Most products and services, such as dishwashing detergent and automobiles, are sold in a variety of qual-ities, locations, and with a variety of financial terms and warranties. For example, generic and brand name detergents are often found side by side in supermarkets. The entrepreneur not only must perceive profit opportunities in producing and selling such items, but also he or she must develop and fit the *characteristics* of each product or service to a targeted group of consumers. The entrepreneur must discover what consumers are willing to buy and inform them about the wares available for purchase.

One very important aspect of the modern Austrian view of competition is that it is a *rivalrous process,* which contrasts with the traditional view of competition as a static *situation* (as presented in Chapter 9). The old model, which often assumed homogeneous products with perfect knowledge of con-sumers' demand curves, gives the economist an exact account of the course of economic events with the aid of scientific generalizations. But the traditional model of competition has some limitations. Concentrating on some of these limitations, the modern Austrians view competition as the businessperson's rivalry against competitors for a prize. Assuming freedom of entry and *non*-homogeneous products and services, the Austrian view is one of perpetual *dis*equilibrium. Economic profits are created and destroyed perpetually, and products and product qualities change continually as an integral part of the process. In this view, entrepreneurs are constantly experimenting with differ-ent products and informing consumers about these differences.

If consumers received perfect information, there would be no reason to inform them about new products or services, let alone about different qualities of existing products or services. Having perfect information about products or services amounts to having innate wants for products or services. If tastes

---

[1]The Austrian view of the entrepreneur's role in the competitive process is detailed in Israel Kirzner, *Competition and Entrepreneurship* (Chicago: University of Chicago Press, 1973) and in Friedrich A. von Hayek, "The Nonsequitur of the Dependence Effect," in E. Mansfield, ed., *Microeconomics: Selected Readings* (New York: W. W. Norton and Co., 1979). See also Robert F. Hebert and Albert Link, *The Entrepreneur* (Boston: D. C. Heath, 1988).

in music were innate, for example, no amount of advertising by an entrepreneurial promoter could convince someone predisposed to classical music to attend a Madonna concert. Economists such as Hayek argued that very few human wants, except for food, shelter, clothing, and sex, are innate. Human wants, personality, and opinions are shaped by a cultural environment, and one element in this environment is advertising. An entrepreneur may, in a free market, *attempt* to devise products and affect their consumption, but consumers will also be informed about competing products. The success of an individual entrepreneur will depend upon the actions of other producers and many other factors that affect consumers of any particular product. The main point is that consumers cannot react without information. To argue that some tastes and desires are unimportant or irrelevant when compared with desires for food, shelter, and clothing would be to ignore much of cultural history, in Hayek's view.

One role of the entrepreneur, then, is to develop, design, and sell products in the market process. Part of this entrepreneurial role is the ability to advertise products and product qualities. The costs of *selling* output by informing customers of goods and services through advertising and other means are, in other words, part and parcel of entrepreneurship. When the entrepreneur successfully discovers consumer tastes and preferences, and when he or she molds products and services to meet these desires, consumer utility and welfare is enhanced.

The entrepreneur is the prime actor in the economic process. (See Focus, "Entrepreneurs from Edison to Milken.") Entrepreneurs develop products, organize production, and provide necessary capital; they are alert to profit opportunities, willing to act in uncertain conditions, and can inform consumers and potential consumers about the product. Profits are simply a payment to another factor of production, but they are different from the other factors in that the entrepreneur is paid last, claiming the residual after the other factors have been compensated. Profits spur entrepreneurial activity in the economy and thereby encourage the whole competitive process. (See Economics in Action, "Entrepreneurship on the Baseball Diamond" for an example of an unusual type of entrepreneurship.)

GENERAL EQUILIBRIUM

Our study of the essential parts of microeconomic theory is now complete. The basic tools of economic analysis—demand and supply, elasticity, marginal utility, and costs of production—were introduced in Chapters 1 through 8. The pricing and production of goods and services in a variety of market structures ranging from pure competition to pure monopoly were covered in Chapters 9 through 13. In Chapters 14 through 17, the elements of the theory of input markets were presented. We have analyzed each part of the economy in isolation from the other parts. This type of economic analysis is called *partial equilibrium analysis*. Changes in other parts of the economy are held constant while the functioning of a particular market or industry is analyzed.

We are now in a position to understand how all the parts work together. This study of the whole economy, where no part of the system is isolated from the others, is called *general equilibrium analysis*. The appendix to this chapter is devoted to a simple exposition of general equilibrium theory.

FOCUS   Entrepreneurs from Edison to Milken

Entrepreneurship takes many forms. It often springs from ordinary individuals with extraordinary ideas. Although entrepreneurship may be related to innovation and invention, inventors are not necessarily entrepreneurs, and entrepreneurs do not always deal with *physical* objects. Henry Ford was an innovator and an entrepreneur. Ford did not invent the automobile, but his innovation of assembly-line techniques and mass manufacture at the turn of the century permitted Ford Motor Company to dominate the auto business for decades. George Eastman did not invent photography, but he managed to turn his innovations of the folding camera and film in 1888 into the Kodak company. Developments of his famous innovation still account for more than 50 percent of Kodak's profits. Others turn their inventions into successful and profitable businesses. Thomas Alva Edison, perhaps America's most famous inventor, developed early electric light and film companies bearing his name.

Sometimes it takes the right time or situation or the right person to see the potential in already existing inventions and technology. Ideas, inventions, and innovations are often realized by entrepreneurship that deals with marketing techniques or innovations in providing capital to businesses that sell products or services. The financing of huge modern ventures, such as development of fiber optics by communications giant MCI or global broadcasting adventures by Ted Turner, requires entrepreneurship of a different sort. There was no shortage of entrepreneurial vision during the late 1970s and early 1980s; there was a shortage of financing for ambitious ideas, however. Financing from venture funds was limited, and the massive amounts of capital necessary to launch businesses made it difficult for American entrepreneurs to compete with Japanese and other international firms. Enter another kind of entrepreneur—Michael Milken of the Drexel Burnham Lambert investment company. Milken developed a means of acquiring sufficient capital to launch MCI, expand Turner Communications, and boost many other high-tech and creative enterprises. His innovation, which was used earlier in different forms, was the junk bond—a high-yield security that channeled money capital to companies with new ideas and creative innovations. Between 1985 and 1988, Milken earned $1.1 billion for development and sale of the new financing innovation. Shareholders of these innovative companies (and Milken's firm Drexel Burnham Lambert) earned an estimated $400 *billion*.[a] While Milken pleaded guilty to charges of insider trading, and some rivals and commentators have proclaimed him representative of a decade of greed, there is no question

Junk-bond king Michael Milken

that Milken's financial innovations helped change the face of modern capitalism. Because he was so closely associated with the junk-bond market, however, Milken's personal misconduct has sullied the reputation of junk bonds. Yet it seems unlikely that Milken's innovative method of securing financing for new ventures will long suffer the consequences of guilt by association.

Not all inventions are undertaken with entrepreneurship and profits in mind and, needless to say, not all inventions and entrepreneurial activity are successful. For every Edison, Milken, or Donald Trump, there are countless failures. The important thing is that opportunities and potential are not cut off to the ordinary man or woman. In *The Age of the Common Millionaire,* Robert Heller concludes, "Common Millionaires have sprung from a richness in society itself, in its profusion of new tastes, new technologies, and new opportunities, that has given men and women a potential, at work and at leisure, to improve their own fortunes and the lot of humankind to an extent that was once the stuff of dreams."[b]

---

[a]George Gilder, "The Victim of His Virtues," *Wall Street Journal* (April 18, 1989), p. A24.

[b]Robert Heller, *The Age of the Common Millionaire* (New York: D. P. Dutton, 1988), p. 372.

SUMMARY

1. An economic rent is a return in excess of the opportunity cost of an owner of a resource.
2. Land in the aggregate is fixed and has a perfectly inelastic supply curve. Its entire return is a pure economic rent determined by the level of demand for land as a factor of production.
3. The supply of land to competing uses is not fixed. Land must be bid away from competing uses, so the supply curve of land to a specific use is upward-sloping.
4. Proposals to tax land rents away would be costly to the economy. Land is like any other factor of production. It has alternative uses, and it is used in the production process by entrepreneurs and firms up to the point where its marginal revenue product equals its marginal cost.
5. Specialized resources earn economic rents. The degree to which the supply curve of a factor of production is upward-sloping reflects the degree to which it is specialized. Where all units of a resource earn the same market price, the more specialized units will earn economic rents. These rents are called inframarginal rents because all units of the resource except the very last, or marginal, unit earn rents.
6. Superstars earn economic rents because their talents are rare gifts that cannot easily be duplicated. The supply curve of superstar services is vertical, and a great deal of the income of a superstar will consist of pure economic rents.
7. Another way to look at the profits of competitive and monopolistic firms is through the concept of economic rent. Competitive firms earn quasi-rents, or returns in excess of the entrepreneur's opportunity cost. Monopolists can earn monopoly rents, which are equivalent to monopoly profits.
8. Rent seeking is the process of competing for contrived rents created through government intervention in the economy. From society's point of view, expenditures to capture such transfers are wasted.
9. Economic profits are a residual that the entrepreneur receives after the other factors of production have been paid. Profits can be positive or negative (or zero), and the receivers of profits are called residual claimants. Although the absolute level of profits in the economy has grown over time, the rate of return on capital has not. It has declined in recent years. The rate of return on capital is the crucial determinant of firm profitability.
10. Accounting profits differ from economic profits. Typically, accounting procedures understate economic costs and thus overstate economic profits.
11. Profits are the force in the economy that leads to entrepreneurship. They are a return to such activities as decision making under conditions of risk and uncertainty. The concept of entrepreneurship has many dimensions, but perhaps the most basic characteristic is that of being alert to economic opportunities.

KEY TERMS

rent
pure economic rent
inframarginal rent
quasi-rent

monopoly rent
aggregate supply of land
resource specialization
rent seeking

rate of return on invested capital
accounting profit
economic profit
entrepreneur

QUESTIONS FOR REVIEW AND DISCUSSION

1. Distinguish between pure and inframarginal economic rents.
2. At what point in the production process do residual claimants receive their return? Can their return be negative?
3. How does rent seeking lead to the waste of resources?
4. What are the essential things that an entrepreneur does?
5. There is a fixed supply of oil in the world. Is the return to oil producers therefore a pure economic rent? Explain carefully.
6. "Land rent should be completely taxed away." Evaluate.
7. Suppose that all of your earnings were a rent. What implications would this situation have for your behavior where you work? Would you be cantankerous with your superiors or docile and easy to get along with? Why?
8. Explain why a firm making zero economic profit will probably stay in business.
9. Are you earning economic rents as a college student? For example, suppose your college raised tuition.

Would you drop out of school or transfer to another school?

10. Suppose several cable television companies were attempting to obtain an exclusive franchise from your city government to provide cable services. How much would each company be willing to spend in an effort to obtain the franchise? What is the term that describes their activity, and what is the term that describes the winning firm's profits?

11. Suppose a firm is earning economic profits that are greater than the profits of most other firms in the industry because it has a superior business manager. In the long run what happens to the manager's salary? Also, what happens to the firm's production costs and profits?

ECONOMICS IN ACTION
Entrepreneurship on the Baseball Diamond

Most of us think of the entrepreneur as someone who operates in the world of high finance or who starts a business conglomerate in a garage. However, the areas in which the entrepreneur deals can differ greatly. Two economists have produced research that sheds some light on the relative entrepreneurial abilities of some major league baseball managers. Phillip Porter and Gerald Scully examined baseball statistics collected during the 1960s, 1970s, and 1980s to determine which major league team managers got the best efforts from their teams.[a] The manager's job consists of choosing which players on the team play in a game and deciding team strategy, such as when to change pitchers during a game. Some managers even have a large degree of independence in selecting team players. The best on-field baseball entrepreneurs would be those who could produce the most wins for the team from a given pool of hitting and pitching inputs.

To obtain the best measure of a manager's talents, the pitching and hitting "inputs," as well as the number of wins, the team's "output," had to be measured in a very careful manner. Each team's output was measured as the actual number of games won in a season relative to the number of games the team could be expected to win in a season. Hitting performance was measured by the team's slugging percentage—the total number of bases accounted for by all team hits divided by the number of team at bats. Thus, a home run was measured as equal to four singles so as not to bias the results against managers whose teams employ a relatively large number of long-ball hitters. Pitching performance was measured by the ratio of strikeouts to walks of the pitching staff. (These statistics capture pure pitcher per-

formance better than a won-lost record, which would be influenced by the other players on the team.) The pitching and hitting input measures were then compared to league averages in order to filter out the effect on wins of a manager simply having more talented players to work with than other managers.

Results indicated that Earl Weaver of the Baltimore Orioles was the best on-field entrepreneur among all who managed at least five years during the 1960s and 1970s. That is, given the playing talent Weaver had to work with, he outperformed all others in seeing how and when to best use the inputs at his disposal to do his job—winning baseball games. Specifically, Weaver's presence at the helm of the Orioles was estimated to be solely responsible for about ten wins a year—approximately 6 to 7 percent of games played. Many pennant races have been decided by fewer games. In contrast, the late Billy Martin, who managed five teams during the period and was regarded as a superb baseball tactician, ranked tenth among all the managers examined.

It would be impossible to explain fully why certain managers, much less other individuals, seem to do a better job, given what they have to work with, than others. In the baseball manager/entrepreneur case, Porter and Scully suggest that a small part may be played by the manager's experience as well as the number of years with any one team. The larger either of these factors is, the slightly more efficient the manager is at coming up with wins. Whatever the cause, the ability to reap more out of any given set of inputs than out of others can surely be classified as entrepreneurial ability.

Question
How will greater entrepreneurial ability affect a baseball manager's marginal revenue product? His wage rate? Which types of managers would be in favor of establishing a managers' union along the lines of the players' union?

[a]Phillip K. Porter and Gerald W. Scully, "Measuring Managerial Efficiency: The Case of Baseball," *Southern Economic Journal* 48 (January 1982), pp. 642–50.

APPENDIX

Putting the Pieces Together: General Equilibrium in Competitive Markets

At this point each of the components of microeconomics has been introduced and explored. Studying each individually can add a great deal to our understanding of many events that occur in the economy. However, bringing all the parts together can create an overall picture that may help answer the "what," "how," and "for whom" questions introduced in the first chapter of the book. To illustrate, we can describe a situation of general equilibrium and then create a change in an economic variable, tracing its effects throughout the economy.

Consider an economy that has only two goods, wheat and coal. All citizens spend their income on these two goods in a manner that maximizes utility. With limited incomes and diminishing marginal utility, downward-sloping demand curves result. In Figures 9a and 9b, which represent supply and demand conditions in the output markets for wheat and coal, D_{w1} and D_{c1} are the current demand curves for wheat and coal, respectively.

Firms that maximize profits and have diminishing returns will have upward-sloping supply curves for the two goods, S_{w1} and S_{c1}, reflecting the current supply curves for wheat and coal.

The supplies of farm workers and coal miners are determined in part by each individual's maximizing of utility in occupational choice. In Figures 9c and 9d, the equilibrium wage rates W_{f1} and W_{m1} for farm workers and coal miners are determined by competitive forces. There may be a difference in these two wage rates for a variety of reasons. For example, if coal mining is a skilled craft that re-

quires a long training period or if coal mining is especially dangerous, in the long run the wages of coal miners must be greater than the wages of farm workers. The current quantities of labor employed in each industry are L_{f1} and L_{m1}.

P_{w1}, W_1, P_{c1}, and C_1 represent the equilibrium prices and quantities of wheat and coal. In this long-run competitive equilibrium, profits are zero, each firm is forced to operate at minimum average cost, and price is equal to marginal cost. In other words, there is an optimal allocation of resources.

From this initial equilibrium, we can examine a disturbance in the economy. Suppose that consumers permanently decide to spend a larger portion of their income on wheat and less on coal. The demand for wheat shifts to the right to D_{w2} in Figure 9a, and the demand for coal shifts to the left to D_{c2} in Figure 9b. This action will lead to a series of short-run changes and eventually to a new long-run equilibrium.

In the short run the price of wheat will rise to P_{w2} and the price of coal will fall to P_{c2}. These shifts will generate short-run profits for firms in wheat production and losses for firms in coal production. The demand for farm workers increases to D_{f2}, and the demand for coal miners decreases to D_{m2}. The wages for farm workers rise to W_{f2}, while the wages of coal miners fall to W_{m2}. If wages do not adjust to these new levels, there will be a shortage of farm workers and unemployment for coal miners.

As time goes by, firms and resources adjust to the changed conditions. The higher economic profits in the wheat industry will attract new firms. The

FIGURE 9 — General Equilibrium in Output and Input Markets

The current demand curves for wheat and coal are given in (a) and (b) by D_{w1} and D_{c1}. If consumers decide to spend more of their income on wheat and less on coal, the demand curve for wheat shifts to the right from D_{w1} to D_{w2}, and that for coal shifts to the left, from D_{c1} to D_{c2}. The short-run price of wheat will rise from P_{w1} to P_{w2}, and the short-run price of coal will fall from P_{c1} to P_{c2}. In the long run the economy adjusts, and the equilibrium price and quantities become P_{w1}, P_{c1}, W_2, and C_2. The equilibrium wage rates W_{f1} and W_{m1} for farm workers (c) and coal miners (d), respectively, are determined by competitive forces when the demands for wheat and coal shift as in (a) and (b). The demand for farm workers increases, and the demand curve shifts from D_{f1} to D_{f2}. The demand for coal miners decreases, and the demand curve shifts from D_{m1} to D_{m2}. The wages of farm workers rise from W_{f1} to W_{f2} and those of coal miners fall from W_{m1} to W_{m2}. When general equilibrium is reached in the economy, as in (a) and (b), the equilibrium quantities of farm workers and coal miners are L_{f2}, W_{f1}, L_{m2}, and W_{m1}.

(a) Wheat

(b) Coal

(c) Farm workers

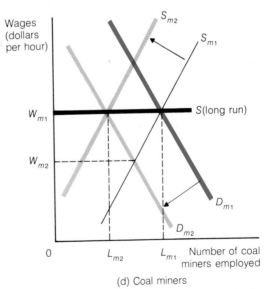

(d) Coal miners

losses in the coal industry will encourage firms to leave the industry. The supply of wheat will begin to increase, while the supply of coal decreases.

In the resource markets, shown in Figures 9c and 9d, let there be only one input—labor. Workers may choose to enter the wheat industry as farm workers or the coal industry as coal miners. The demands for farm workers and for coal miners are derived from the demands for wheat and coal. The higher wages in the wheat industry will attract workers, and the lower wages in the coal industry will discourage the entry of workers. The supply of farm workers increases, while the supply of coal miners decreases.

If resources shift, as they do in this case, the new long-run equilibrium will result in the previously prevailing prices and wages. Profits will return to zero in both industries. The only permanent changes are in the quantities of wheat, coal, farm workers, and coal miners, W_2, C_2, L_{f2}, and L_{m2}, respectively. The long-run supplies of wheat, coal, and labor are infinitely elastic.

This example demonstrates the way in which resources are demand-directed. As consumers' tastes change from coal to wheat, resources shift from coal to wheat. Thus it is said that resources flow to their most highly valued use.

An understanding of what makes this process work is important. Self-interest is the motivating force of individuals; it is also the impelling force that drives the competitive market to the desired result. Self-interest is what attracts firms to profitable industries and leads them away from unprofitable industries. Self-interest is what attracts workers to occupations with high wages and leads them away from those with low wages. Without self-interest the market system would not produce the products that are most highly valued by society.

In actuality, there are many obstacles to long-run competitive equilibrium. Imperfect competition, externalities, or government intervention may inhibit the free flow of resources to the most desired goods.

What would be the result if there had been a monopoly in the wheat industry or a labor union for farm workers? Or what would have happened if government had taxed away the profits of wheat-producing firms and subsidized the coal industry? The most desired quantities of wheat and coal would not have been produced. While both natural and artificial barriers to optimal resource allocation exist, this example should provide the basis for an understanding of the overall workings of the microeconomic system.

18

The Distribution of Income

Are you rich or poor? In what sense? Diane, who is passionately interested in art, may be devoting a long and happy life to painting seascapes, earning no more than five hundred or six hundred dollars a month. John, a stockbroker, may regard himself as one of the walking dead in spite of a six-figure income. Is Diane rich? Is John poor? Surely the question of whether one is rich or poor in an economic sense is different from whether one feels rich or poor in emotional well-being.

While most people, including economists, might argue that it is far better to be rich and unhappy than poor and unhappy, happiness cannot be measured in objective terms or easily be related to income. The equating of rich with happy or poor with unhappy, though tempting, is inadmissible in any scientific sense. Economists cannot measure happiness, but they can measure and analyze differences in income. When you have completed Chapter 18, you should understand

- some of the differences between economic efficiency and social equity in income distribution.
- what income inequality means and how it is measured.
- patterns and characteristics of income distribution in the United States.
- modern policy programs relating to distribution, especially those that address poverty.

EFFICIENCY VERSUS EQUITY

In studying income distribution, economists look at how personal or family earnings are measured and divided among members of society. They try to see how various factors such as individual choice and effort, education, experience, and discrimination influence the distribution of income. Also, they pay close attention to the effects of various government policies on income distribution. The federal government, the president, and Congress devote much time, rhetoric, and effort to the issue of the equity of income redistribution.

Whether the proposal is imposing new gasoline taxes, extending the dairy price support program, or decreasing corporate income taxes, the matter of the equity of such an action is sure to be debated. In following these debates, it becomes clear that there is much genuine disagreement over what constitutes a fair distribution of income. Opponents of higher gasoline taxes will argue that higher taxes on gasoline are unfair to poor Americans who use their cars to commute to work; in turn, advocates of higher gasoline taxes will argue that it is only fair for car users to be taxed, since they cause many of the pollution problems in urban areas. Members of the farm lobby will argue for price supports on milk to increase the incomes of poor dairy farmers; consumer groups will oppose the measure on the grounds that it unfairly transfers income away from milk consumers.

Economists also have strong personal views concerning the equity of various income distributions. However, they recognize that their views are value judgments and therefore tend to focus on other aspects of redistribution proposals. In particular, they pay much attention to efficiency aspects of various proposals to redistribute income. Although it is tempting to imagine that programs such as tax reform simply transfer income from those who need it less to those who need it more without side effects, redistribution never works so simply. Inevitably, some individuals will incur costs to avoid paying higher taxes, while others will adjust their circumstances to qualify for new subsidies. Due to such activity, it almost always ends up costing some groups in society more than a dollar for each dollar that is transferred to other groups. Economists therefore are aware that any program to redistribute income involves a trade-off between equity and efficiency. In part, this explains why economists tend to have greater reservations about redistribution than groups who are willing to ignore the costs of redistribution—namely, politicians.

Economists who oppose a program to pay housing subsidies to all families of below average income, for example, will probably be called "heartless." They will respond by denying this charge and by emphasizing the importance of efficiency. Much of the distance between economists and politicians on the matter of income redistribution can be accounted for by the value each group attaches to equity versus efficiency.

THE INDIVIDUAL AND INCOME DISTRIBUTION

Individual income:
The earnings individuals receive from their labor, from their assets, and from government transfer payments, minus their tax payments.

Labor income:
The payments an individual receives from supplying work time; equal to the wage rate times the number of hours supplied.

The economic question of why one is rich or poor has many facets. Individuals accumulate income from their labor and entrepreneurial skills, from the ownership of assets such as land, or from the receipt of cash or government subsidies called transfer payments. At the same time, most individuals pay a certain portion of income through taxes. We will analyze each factor of **individual income** briefly.

Labor Income

Labor income—income received from supplying labor—is the wage rate received multiplied by the number of hours worked. The supply of labor is by far the largest source of individual income. The supply of labor ordinarily varies according to wage rates, but individuals also differ in their choice of work hours over leisure hours, and wages themselves vary for a number of reasons.

Choices of Work Versus Leisure. Different people with the same skills will often supply different quantities of labor at identical wage rates. The same wage rate affects people differently because they can make choices in the trade-off between work and leisure. Harpo, who has the same skills as Gummo, chooses to play his harp six hours a day for no pay and to work two hours a day for pay. Gummo chooses work and income over leisure, working twelve or fourteen hours a day. The terms *lazy* and *industrious* are certainly relative, but these personality traits do not totally explain different attitudes toward work among those with identical skills.

What else accounts for differences in attitudes toward work? No human being is a machine who can supply labor without limit. At higher and higher wage rates and longer and longer hours worked, we all become leisure lovers (see Chapter 14 on this point). As we choose more work, the costs of losing more and more leisure rise and the rewards of earning more income fall.

The explanation for income-leisure trade-offs also relates to differences in incentives to work. Incentives to work—willingness to supply labor at a given wage rate—are ordinarily thought to result from different doses of the work ethic. The economist must accept this ethic as given and point out that, for some, leisure is freely chosen over income. Unfortunately, the choice of income or leisure is not freely open to all. Disabled persons, the sick, the old, and the unskilled may have few or no choices. Society often compensates by making transfer payments to such individuals, providing them with an income.

Differences in Wage Rates. Wage rates vary widely among occupations. The wage rate you earn is largely a function of the human capital you have built up through education and investments in other skills. Human capital has a lot to do with whether you are rich or poor. Level of schooling attained (a college degree, a high school diploma) is a ticket to enter some occupations. Given government-enforced regulations of the American Medical Association, entry into the physicians' market without a medical degree would almost certainly land you in jail. If education level and achievement are related to the income class one initially comes from, income differences may be somewhat self-perpetuating over time.

Luck also plays a role in the wage rate. At the beginning of the energy crisis in the early 1970s, those entering the labor market with degrees in petroleum engineering received much higher wages than under previous conditions. (The situation was short-lived, since more and more college students were attracted to petroleum engineering by high wages, and, as usual, supply expanded and wages fell.) Others are naturally endowed with rare talents or physical attributes and are rewarded accordingly. P. T. Barnum's midget Tom Thumb was paid a handsome income simply for being abnormally small and talented. For all of us, it is far better to be "lucky than good."

Individuals' or families' incomes are also determined by their stage in the life cycle. Law students at Harvard, Stanford, or the University of Michigan may be poor—students everywhere tend to be poor—but they will not always be poor. Income or earnings tend to rise throughout the period of the active work life. Earnings increase at a fairly rapid pace in early to middle work life. In the latter portion of the work life, earnings still tend to increase, but at a slower pace. After retirement, earnings generally decrease. Other factors also influence the wage rate an individual receives. Without question, race and sex discrimination have been ugly practices affecting wage rates. We look at this matter in more detail later in the chapter.

Broadly speaking, then, an individual's income is determined by his or her choices in the trade-off between work and leisure and by the individual's stock of human capital, current life cycle period, special skills, luck, and degree of discrimination. These factors are major determinants of whether one is rich or poor, but there are other factors related to income, including savings and government benefits or taxation.

Income from Savings and Other Assets

The other major source of income is the return from savings or other assets one owns or has accumulated. We may save as an ingrained habit. Our parents or culture may instill the ethic of frugality in us to "save for a rainy day" or to accumulate wealth or assets for other reasons. Motives for the sacrifice of current consumption are numerous: security, expected future gaps in income, education, retirement, large consumer expenditures, and so forth. In any case, the sacrifice of current consumption for future consumption is rewarded by an interest return or **asset income.**

Asset income:
Earnings from interest on savings, from capital investments, and from land; all result from forgone consumption in the past.

Many people save for future generations. Some current income earners set aside assets for their children's later use, which brings us to another major source of income. Inheritance of money or other assets is related to the luck of having had wealthy parents. Historically, free societies have permitted inheritance and protected the rights of income owners to bequeath gifts at death or while still alive. Most societies have nevertheless taxed the lucky recipients of inheritance on the grounds that such wealth was not due to their own productivity.

The returns from both savings and other wealth and asset accumulations also depend on one's skill at investing. Interest returns on all sorts of investments—monetary, real capital, or land—are determined by the costs of investing and the incentives to maximize income from investments. Small savers and investors often receive lower returns than large-scale investors, partly because of the high costs of gathering information about markets.

Taxes and Transfer Payments

A final source of income is government tax collections and benefit distributions. Economists distinguish between the *ex ante* **distribution** of income, the before-tax and transfer payments distribution, and the *ex post* **distribution,** or after-tax and transfer payments distribution. We all receive goods, services, and benefits from all levels of government, and we all pay taxes in one form or another. National defense, roads, and the local public swimming pool are some of the benefits; property taxes, sales taxes, and income taxes are some of the costs.

Ex ante **distribution:**
The distribution of income before government transfer payments and taxes are accounted for.

Ex post **distribution:**
The distribution of income after government transfer payments and taxes are accounted for.

Most individuals are either net taxpayers or net benefit receivers. In other words, the determination of how rich or poor we are *ex post* depends partly on our position with regard to taxes and benefits. The receipt of government

Transfer payment:
A resource received by an individual from government that is not directly or explicitly paid for by that individual; it may be in the form of money or goods and services such as education or health care.

services and **transfer payments**—such as direct welfare payments, food stamps, subsidized public housing, Social Security, and unemployment compensation—must be added to privately earned income. Transfer payments are all money or real goods or services transferred by government from one group in society (taxpayers) to other groups (transfer recipients). Tax payments of all kinds must likewise be subtracted to help explain *ex post* why we, as individuals, are rich or poor. Most government statistics on income distribution reveal only *ex ante* money distributions of family or household income, but economists have attempted to make some *ex post* calculations as well.

To summarize, we are rich or poor as individuals because of three major factors: our wage income, our income from savings and other assets, and our position with respect to government taxes and benefits. Part of our position in the income distribution depends on luck (health, genetic and financial inheritance, socioeconomic position), part depends on choice (incentives, investments in human capital and skills), and part depends on political decisions—taxes and public benefits—about the justice of the *ex ante* income distribution. With these important distinctions in mind, we turn to the issue of how the government measures income and to the economic tools used to explain income distribution and how it changes over time.

HOW IS INCOME INEQUALITY MEASURED?

Family income:
The total of all incomes from all sources except transfers received by members of a household.

The money income of families (often termed *households*), or **family income,** is calculated in *Current Population Reports* published by the U.S. Bureau of the Census. Table 1 shows family income in the United States for selected years between 1960 and 1987. Total family income is broken down into the percentage received by each fifth of the total number of families over these years,

TABLE 1

Money Income of Families, Percent of Aggregate Income: 1960–1987

These data show an amazing uniformity in pretax income distribution over about thirty years. Special care must be used in interpreting the data, however, since noncash transfers by government also affect income distribution.

Families by Quintile	Percent of Aggregate Income						
	1960	1965	1970	1975	1979	1984	1987
1. Lowest fifth	4.8	5.2	5.4	5.4	5.3	4.7	4.6
2. Second fifth	12.2	12.2	12.2	11.8	11.6	11.0	10.8
3. Middle fifth	17.8	17.8	17.6	17.6	17.5	17.0	16.9
4. Fourth fifth	24.0	23.9	23.8	24.1	24.1	24.4	24.1
5. Highest fifth	41.3	40.9	40.9	41.1	41.6	42.9	43.7
Highest 5%	15.9	15.5	15.6	15.5	15.7	16.0	16.9

Sources: U.S. Department of Commerce, Bureau of the Census, Current Population Reports—Consumer Income, *Money Income of Households, Families, and Persons in the United States: 1984* (Washington, D.C.: 1986), p. 37; *Statistical Abstract of the United States* (Washington, D.C.: U.S. Government Printing Office, 1989), p. 446.

ranked from the lowest, or poorest, fifth to the highest, or richest, fifth. (A fifth of a total distribution is called a *quintile*.) In addition, Table 1 gives the percentage of total money income earned by the top 5 percent of income earners between 1960 and 1987.

Interpretation of Money Distribution Data

We are struck immediately by a feature of Table 1: *The distribution of reported money income did not change significantly between 1960 and 1987,* although in recent years the disparity in income distribution appears to have widened. Reading horizontally across the table, we see that the shares for each quintile stayed roughly the same. The lowest quintile received about 5 percent of aggregate income, and its share is declining, while the highest quintile consistently got the lion's share: over 40 percent. Further, the share of the highest quintile has been rising, as has the share of the top 5 percent of income earners. Before accepting these figures at face value, we should note some limitations of the statistics in Table 1.

1. Money income statistics reported by the Bureau of the Census do not conform to the economist's definition of *income*. Income, in the economist's sense, is what an individual accumulates from labor, assets, or transfer payments minus what is paid in taxes. By contrast, the *Current Population* statistics on income omit all transfer payments, all assets such as capital gains, and all income and payroll taxes.
2. The government statistics report family, not individual, income. Therefore, an increase in the number of family units, income remaining the same, will alter the reported income distribution. In the period 1960–1987, the number of family units increased significantly through later marriages, high divorce rates, and increasing independence of the elderly. The government's statistics do not take this increase into account.

Given these two deficiencies in the Census data, conclusions about the distribution of economic welfare should be deferred until the raw statistics are refined. Before actually making some of these refinements, we turn to the tools economists use to deal with income distribution.

Economists' Measures of Income Inequality

Economists have developed useful methods for describing and analyzing income distribution. The Lorenz curve, the primary tool for measuring income distribution, was developed in 1905 by M. O. Lorenz. A second device derived from the Lorenz curve likewise is named for its inventor: the Gini coefficient, developed by Corrado Gini in 1936.

Lorenz curve:
A curve plotting the actual cumulative distribution of income in percentages; usually compared to a curve showing a perfectly even distribution of income.

The Lorenz Curve. A **Lorenz curve** plots the relation between the percentage of families receiving income and the cumulative percentage of aggregate family income. To understand the Lorenz curve, consider a hypothetical income distribution for some country in the year 2020, as shown in Table 2. Table 2 tells us that the lowest 20 percent of family income earners receive only 5 percent of total income. The next 20 percent of families get 15 percent, so the lowest 40 percent receive a cumulative percentage share of 20 percent. The middle 20 percent get 20 percent of total income, indicating that the lowest

TABLE 2

Hypothetical Income Data for the Year 2020

The second column shows the percentage share of total income received by each quintile of families in this hypothetical country; the third column adds these percentage shares cumulatively. For instance, since the lowest fifth receives only 5 percent of total income and the second fifth receives 15 percent, together these lowest two fifths receive a cumulative share of only 20 percent of total income. The lowest four fifths receive a cumulative share of 65 percent. Data from the third column are plotted on a Lorenz curve in Figure 1.

	Aggregate Income	
All Families by Quintile	Percent Share (year 2020)	Cumulative Percent Share (year 2020)
A. Lowest fifth	5	5
B. Second fifth	15	20
C. Middle fifth	20	40
D. Fourth fifth	25	65
E. Highest fifth	35	100

60 percent of income earners receive only 40 percent of total income. Obviously, 100 percent of income recipients receive a cumulative total of 100 percent of income.

The data in Table 2 may be translated into graphic form. The vertical axis of Figure 1 represents the cumulative percentage of family income, and the horizontal axis shows the percentage of income-earning families. If all families earned equal incomes, the Lorenz curve would be a straight line. Ten percent of all families would earn 10 percent of income; 80 percent of families would earn 80 percent; and so on. Such a curve would actually be a diagonal cutting the square in half, as represented by the line of perfect equality in Figure 1.

A Lorenz curve is constructed from the hypothetical data of Table 2. Point A in Figure 1 corresponds to point A in Table 2—it is the intersection of the lowest 20 percent of families and their cumulative percentage share of total income. Point D in Figure 1 shows that 80 percent of families (the fourth fifth in Table 2) received 65 percent of total income. The combination of points A, B, C, D, and E forms a Lorenz curve.

The distance of the Lorenz curve from the line of perfect equality is a measure of income inequality. The shaded area of Figure 1 is a measure of the degree of income inequality for our hypothetical society. Should the shaded area become larger or more bowed, money income would be more unevenly distributed. A smaller area or a flatter curve would signal a more equal income distribution.

Gini coefficient:
A number between 0 and 1 calculated to estimate the degree of inequality in the distribution of income; the larger the number, the less the degree of equality.

The Gini Coefficient. An economic tool related to the Lorenz curve is the Gini coefficient. A **Gini coefficient** is the ratio of the shaded area of Figure 1 to the total area under the line of perfect equality. The Gini coefficient is simply a number between zero and one. The smaller the number—the closer it is to zero—the more equal the income distribution. A larger Gini coefficient, resulting from a more bowed Lorenz curve, means that income is less evenly distributed. A Gini coefficient of 0.30 for a certain year would indicate the

FIGURE 1

The Lorenz curve shows the cumulative percentage of family income earned by percentages of families. The Lorenz curve indicates that 40 percent of families earned only 20 percent of total income, while 80 percent earned a cumulative 65 percent. This distribution is unequal and falls short of the line of perfect equality. The shaded area in the diagram indicates the degree of income inequality. The farther the Lorenz curve moves away from the line of perfect equality, the less equal the income distribution.

A Hypothetical Lorenz Curve for the Year 2020

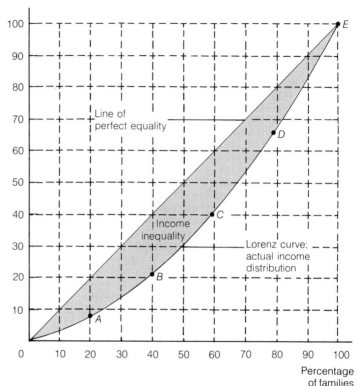

presence of greater income inequality than a year with a coefficient of 0.20. Care must be taken in interpreting both Lorenz curves and Gini coefficients.

Problems with Lorenz and Gini Measures

We have already seen some of the limitations associated with government statistics of money income distribution. Such data are not adjusted for taxes, capital gains, or many kinds of income transfers from government to families. Since the Lorenz and Gini measures are based on these statistics, we must be especially careful in using these instruments. Apart from data deficiencies, the Lorenz and Gini measures have limitations of their own.

1. The Lorenz and Gini income distribution measures are simply mechanical devices and not precise indicators of the relative level of wealth in society. Economists are particularly interested in the effects of policies and programs on income distribution. Yet a change in the Gini coefficient from, say, 0.30 in 1990 to 0.28 in 1995 may not give an accurate enough indication of how distribution has changed. While the lower number does mean more equality overall, it may be that the poorest 20 percent of families received a lower percentage of income and the richest 20 percent received a greater percentage. If economists are concerned with policies to raise the economic welfare at the lower end of the distribution, the mechanically calculated Gini number is a very misleading indicator of social

welfare changes. The actual Gini ratios of 0.376 in 1947 and 0.364 in 1977 tell us little of what the economist wants to know about the component shares in income distribution.

2. Important microeconomic effects may be hidden or neglected by a measure such as the Lorenz curve. Suppose, for example, that policies designed to reduce income inequalities at the top 20 percent are instituted through higher taxes on the rich. The initial *ex ante* effect would be a reduction in after-tax incomes of executives and others earning very high salaries and wages. The Lorenz curve would move closer to the line of perfect equality. But *ex post* factors must also be considered. High income earners might decide to work less, and the labor supply in these areas of the economy would diminish. A reduced supply, given demand conditions, yields higher future returns to workers. The new high returns also signal new entrants into these areas of the economy. These factors may create a new *ex post* bowing out of the Lorenz curve, meaning that the original redistribution policies did not have the ultimate effect of reducing inequalities in income distribution at the upper end.

While changes in both the Lorenz and the Gini measures are suspect for reasons such as these, they remain two of the essential economic tools to measure economic well-being. They are useful so long as we keep their limitations in mind. More important, some of their limitations have been lessened by refinements attached to them by economists interested in problems of economic welfare.

INCOME DISTRIBUTION IN THE UNITED STATES

We have already looked at family income distribution for selected years between 1960 and 1987. We now construct Lorenz curves with the data for the years 1960 and 1987. In Table 3, the cumulative percent share of all families

| TABLE 3 | Share and Cumulative Share in Income Distribution of All Families, 1960 and 1987 |

The data show insignificant changes in the lowest and fourth highest quintiles in income distribution. The second fifth lost almost 1.5 percent of its share—the same percent gained by the highest 20 percent of income receivers; the middle fifth lost about 1 percent.

All Families by Quintile	Percent Share 1960	Percent Cumulative Share 1960	Percent Share 1987	Percent Cumulative Share 1987
Lowest fifth	4.8	4.8	4.6	4.6
Second fifth	12.2	17.0	10.8	15.4
Middle fifth	17.8	34.8	16.9	32.3
Fourth fifth	24.0	58.8	24.1	56.4
Highest fifth	41.3	100.0	43.7	100.0

Sources: U.S. Department of Commerce, Bureau of the Census, Current Population Reports—Consumer Income, *Money Income of Households, Families, and Persons in the United States: 1984* (Washington, D.C.: U.S. Government Printing Office, 1986), p. 37; *Statistical Abstract of the United States* (Washington, D.C.: U.S. Government Printing Office, 1989), p. 446.

by quintiles is calculated from the simple shares for 1960 and 1987. In 1960, for example, the lowest 60 percent of families received 34.8 percent of total income and in 1987 received 32.3 percent. In 1960, the lowest 20 percent received 4.8 percent of money income, but 4.6 percent in 1987, and so on.

Lorenz curves are calculated for these two years in Figure 2. Two important facts may be concluded from these Lorenz curves. First, it appears that money income distribution has changed very little over the twenty-seven year period, as shown by the minute differences between the Lorenz curves. For the lowest and the fourth quintiles of income receivers, the distribution of income remained about the same. In between these two quintiles, income shares declined. The share of the highest quintile rose, although this movement may be insignificant in a statistical sense. (Focus, "Do the Very, Very Rich Get Richer?" analyzes income distribution further.)

What can we conclude from this money income data? Has overall distribution become more unequal over the period 1960–1987? Have the lowest 60 percent of income recipients on balance become worse off? Have the rich gotten slightly richer?

The answers to these questions lie in the taxes and transfers that are not reported in the *ex ante* money income statistics from which the Lorenz curves of Figure 2 were constructed. We have already discussed some of the problems associated with the construction of simple Lorenz curves and Gini coefficients.

FIGURE 2

The Lorenz curves of income distribution for 1960 and 1987 show little change in before-tax income distribution in the United States.

Lorenz Curves for 1960 and 1987

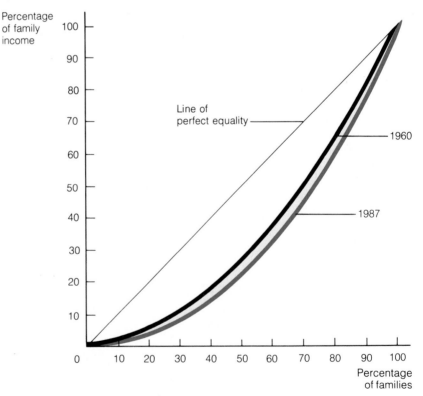

FOCUS   Do the Very, Very Rich Get Richer?

As F. Scott Fitzgerald once remarked to Ernest Hemingway, "You know, Ernest, the very very rich are different than you and I." Hemingway's reply: "I know, they have more money."

How rich are the very rich? The rich in America are not as rich as they were a hundred years ago. Gone are the good old days when Alva Vanderbilt could spend $250,000 1883 dollars on a fancy dress ball or when door prizes consisted of five minutes with a shovel in a sandbox filled with diamonds, emeralds, and rubies. Today, there seem to be fewer huge family accumulations such as those of the Rockefellers, Mellons, Carnegies, or Vanderbilts, although there are some exceptions. But the rich are still among us, as the following table shows.

The percent share of total U.S. wealth (not just income) held by the wealthiest 1 percent of all Americans has changed a good deal since the 1920s. Over the 1920s, wealth holdings concentrated at the top, reaching a high of 36.3 percent in 1929. Since World War II, however, wealth holdings have in general become less concentrated. Tax laws, especially inheritance laws, have probably reduced the concentrations of income in the hands of a few.

The composition of the wealthiest class may have changed, too. Gross statistics on wealth holdings give no indication of who the wealth holders are. With more economic and social mobility in this century than in the last one, membership in the top 1 percent was probably different in 1949, 1972, and 1989. *Forbes* magazine's annual list of the four hundred richest Americans is very revealing in this regard.[a] Of a list of the thirty richest Americans compiled in 1981, only seven or eight names from the same families made it in 1983. Fifteen percent of those making the list in 1989 were not on it in 1988. The minimum net worth required in 1989 was $275 million, up by $50 million over 1988. The typical member of the *Forbes* Four Hundred was a 63-year-old male on his 1.4th marriage, with 3.1 children and a net worth of $672 million.

The interesting feature of the four hundred wealthiest Americans is the diversity of the sources of their wealth. Rather than being frozen in inheritance or traditional economic power, wealth originates in a large variety of occupations, settings, and backgrounds. The 1989 *Forbes* list

Year	Percentage of Personal Wealth Held by Top 1%
1922	31.6
1929	36.3
1933	28.3
1939	30.6
1945	23.3
1949	20.8
1953	24.3
1954	24.0
1956	26.0
1958	23.8
1962	22.0
1965	23.4
1969	20.1
1972	20.7

Sources: 1922–1956: Robert J. Lampman, *The Share of Top Wealth-Holders in National Wealth,* National Bureau of Economic Research, 1962; 1958: James D. Smith and Staunten K. Calvert, "Estimating the Wealth of Top Wealth-Holders from Estate Tax Returns," *Proceedings of the American Statistical Association,* Philadelphia, 1965 (copyright); 1962–1972: James D. Smith, unpublished estimates, the Urban Institute, Washington, D.C., and the Pennsylvania State University (copyright).

includes computer entrepreneurs, TV game show developers, junk bond (a corporate bond with no collateral) sellers, clothing designers, fast-food chicken sellers, candy manufacturers (the Mars family), media moguls (seventy-two of them); less than half the list is composed of purely inherited wealth. Women make up about 14 percent of the 1989 list. It is also the case that high-tech society provides a ripe setting for the rags-to-riches—and riches-to-rags—experience. Big gainers and big losers enter and leave the list from year to year. Given the large amount of economic mobility, tax laws, and incentives of inheritors, the likelihood of families going from shirtsleeves to shirtsleeves in three generations increases.

Ambition, incentive, and intelligence are still winning attributes in U.S. society, in spite of tax laws tending to reduce wealth concentrations. Americans still believe, in the sentiments of the late Duchess of Windsor, that there are two things a person can never be—"too thin or too rich."

[a]"The Richest People in America: The Forbes Four Hundred, 1989 Edition," *Forbes* (Fall 1989).

Consider what happens to income distribution when adjustments are made for such things as income and payroll taxes, capital gains, in-kind transfers, money transfer or welfare payments, and other factors.

Adjustments to Money Income

Two important factors related to money income data must be considered before any conclusions are drawn about recent trends in income distribution in the United States. First, while the reported money income data do reflect the impact of indirect business taxes—excise taxes, property taxes, and corporate income taxes—since these items are paid before money factor payments are distributed, the data in Tables 1 and 3 do not account for payroll and income taxes. Since the U.S. income tax system is progressive, meaning that the higher-income recipients pay higher tax rates, the **adjusted income** distribution is affected in the direction of greater equality.

A second and increasingly important set of items that is not included in the raw money income statistics is transfer payments. These include **in-kind transfers** of benefits other than money—such as food stamps, public housing, Medicare, Medicaid, and other subsidies received largely by lower-income groups—in addition to money transfers or welfare payments. Such in-kind subsidies also tend to equalize income distribution across the various classes.

Economist Edgar K. Browning has attempted to develop a measure of income that conforms more closely to economists' definition. Browning estimated the effects of compensation for taxes, welfare transfers, in-kind transfers (benefits other than money), and other factors for the year 1972, which we reproduce as Table 4. The table shows the distribution of money income in 1972 in billions of dollars, with adjustments for in-kind transfers and other factors added in and with income and payroll taxes subtracted from the raw money income data.

Consider the additions to money income shown in Table 4. In-kind benefits are received largely by the poorest classes in society, whereas capital gains on stocks, bonds, and houses—which are not reflected in money income data—are six to seven times greater for the highest quintile of income recipients than for the lowest.

After these items are added to money income, taxes must be subtracted to obtain an estimate of net income. In the United States the largest burden of income tax—in both percentage terms and total amount—falls on those in the highest quintile. (The U.S. income tax system was more progressive—or more burdensome to higher-income groups—at the time of this study than after the Tax Reform Act of 1986.) In 1972, as the income and payroll taxes line in Table 4 shows, this group paid about $20 billion more in income taxes than all other income earners combined.

What is the net result of these adjustments to money income? Table 4 reports the results in terms of total income adjustment and in unadjusted and adjusted percent distribution. Total income rises for each class after additions to and subtractions from money income are made. But the important point is that the percent distribution among the quintiles is affected. The poorest 60 percent of income recipients all receive increased shares, with the lowest 20 percent receiving a full 7 percent increase in adjusted income.

The effects indicated in the data of Table 4 are summarized in Figure 3 as Lorenz curves. Figure 3 shows a set of three Lorenz curves for 1972. The

Adjusted income: An individual's income after all taxes and all government transfer payments are accounted for.

In-kind transfer payments: Transfer payments that take the form of goods and services such as public housing, veterans' hospitals, or a mass transit system.

TABLE 4

Distribution of Adjusted Income in 1972

Adjusted income distribution statistics for any single year require the addition of in-kind transfer benefits and other items and the subtraction of income and payroll taxes. In 1972, a more equal distribution resulted from these adjustments, as is evident in the comparison between the adjusted and unadjusted distribution figures at the bottom of the table.

Income Item	Families by Quintile (shown in billions of dollars)					
	Lowest	Second	Third	Fourth	Highest	Total
Unadjusted money income	37.1	81.7	120.1	164.1	284.2	687.2
Plus Benefits in kind, capital gains, potential additional earnings, and other adjustments	58.6	54.8	54.1	50.5	102.9	320.9
Minus Income and payroll taxes	1.3	5.8	15.5	26.6	67.5	116.6
Equals Adjusted money income total	94.4	130.7	158.7	188.0	319.6	891.5
Adjusted percent distribution	12.5%	15.8%	17.9%	20.4%	33.3%	100.0%
Unadjusted percent distribution	5.4%	11.9%	17.5%	23.9%	41.4%	100.0%

Source: Edgar K. Browning, ''The Trend Toward Equality in the Distribution of Net Income,'' *Southern Economic Journal* 43 (July 1976), p. 914.

most bowed curve is the unadjusted distribution of money income. Figure 3 also shows a Lorenz curve that is adjusted for payroll and income taxes. The tax adjustment makes the curve less bowed and moves income distribution closer to the line of perfect equality. This shift indicates that a progressive tax system does effect greater equality in income distribution. The inclusion of in-kind transfers and other adjustments pushes income distribution to still-greater equality, as the third Lorenz curve shows. These curves indicate the importance of social programs such as Medicare, food stamps, and public housing in creating greater income equality across the various segments of society.

Historical Changes in Adjusted Income

While a study of adjustments to money income over a given year leads to the conclusion that after-adjustment income is distributed more equally, what about long-range trends? Edgar K. Browning has calculated adjusted net income for 1952, 1962, and 1972 to answer this question. His results are reported in Table 5.

Table 5 indicates that a significant change took place in income distribution over the period 1952–1972. Gains were concentrated in the bottom two quintiles, largely due to the growing importance of in-kind transfers.

FIGURE 3

When taxes are subtracted from before-tax money income and in-kind transfers and other factors are added, the Lorenz curve moves closer to the line of perfect equality.

Source: Figure based on conclusions of Browning, ''The Trend Toward Equality in the Distribution of Net Income,'' *Southern Economic Journal* 43 (July 1976), pp. 912–23.

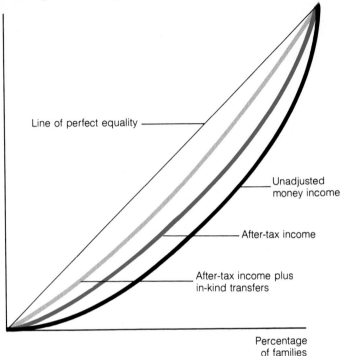

Lorenz Curve Including Income Adjustments, 1972

Cumulative percentage of family income

Line of perfect equality

Unadjusted money income

After-tax income

After-tax income plus in-kind transfers

Percentage of families

These benefits grew in importance over the period, and the benefits were concentrated in the poorest 40 percent of families. The growth in educational expenditures also had an equalizing effect.

The relative positions of the richest two quintiles also changed. A loss of 5.8 percentage points for these groups balanced the gain of 6.1 in the bottom two quintiles. Middle-income families did not fare significantly better or worse over the twenty-year period. These data suggest that a redistribution did in fact take place from richer to poorer families, creating a more equal income distribution between 1952 and 1972. The growth of in-kind transfer payments, moreover, appears to have been the principal means of the redistribution from rich to poor.

The data used in the Browning study are now quite dated. If one were to replicate the study using more recent data, the results would possibly be different. Browning's basic point remains valid, however: In examining changes in income distribution, it is important to account for payments in kind.

The Effect of Single-Parent Families on Income Distribution

Recently, considerable attention has been focused on data that indicate that the share of total *unadjusted* income earned by the poorest quintile of families has declined sharply since 1970. At that time, the poorest fifth of all families earned about 5.6 percent of *unadjusted* income. By 1988, this percentage had

TABLE 5

Adjusted Net Income for 1952, 1962, and 1972

The data spanning two decades from 1952 to 1972 show gains in the poorest 40 percent of income earners and losses in the highest 40 percent. Middle-income families (the third quintile) received about the same proportion of total income.

| Year | Families by Quintile (percent share) | | | | |
	Lowest	Second	Third	Fourth	Highest
1952	7.8	14.8	18.8	23.3	35.3
1962	9.0	15.1	19.1	22.9	34.0
1972	12.6	16.1	18.4	20.9	31.9

Source: Browning, "The Trend Toward Equality in the Distribution of Net Income," *Southern Economic Journal* 43 (July 1976), p. 919.

fallen to about 4.6 percent. In attempting to explain this decline, a number of factors have been considered. Some observers attribute the decline to reductions in spending on government social programs during the Reagan administration. Others have placed the blame on foreign competition, which, in their view, has displaced American workers from high-paying jobs in manufacturing to low-paying jobs in the service sector.

One factor that has received relatively little attention is the growing divorce rate and the resulting increase in the number of single-parent families. Families in the top quintile have always differed from those in the bottom quintile in terms of age, education, and the number of employed adults. In 1970, about 95 percent of families in the top quintile were husband-wife units, and this percentage has changed little since then. What has changed is the percentage of high-income families with an employed wife—it has risen from 50 percent to about 70 percent. As a consequence, the total income of top quintile families has risen sharply. In contrast, the growing divorce rate has brought about a sharp decline in percentage of husband-wife families in the lowest quintile—from 70 percent in 1970 to about 50 percent today. Divorce transforms one family into two—usually resulting in a drop in income for at least one of the two. If income statistics are reported on a per-family basis, increases in the percentage of single-parent families will inevitably lead to increases in income inequality.

Age Distribution and Income

Another useful factor in understanding income distribution is the age structure of the income-receiving population. Take your own situation as an example. Perhaps you are a college student with a part-time job. If so, you are now probably part of the poorest quintile of the population in calculated annual income distribution. But you are not likely to be poor forever. Education and training alone will give you an edge in earning income later. At any point in time, the relative mean income of heads of households tends to peak between ages forty-five and fifty-five. Therefore, annual income figures will either overstate or understate multiyear inequality in income distribution, depending on the age structure of the population.

If the population is heavily populated by young people in the college age group, annual data will overstate actual lifetime or multiyear inequality in income distribution. There is in fact less inequality over multiyear distributions in the United States than there appears to be in any given year. Economists' estimates vary on how much more equal distribution is over the long run, but all agree that there is more equality when age distribution is considered.[1]

Rags to Riches Mobility

Economic mobility:
The movement of individuals among income ranges.

Economic mobility—movements up or down in the quintiles of income distribution—also influences the question of how seriously annual data should be taken. How, for example, do we know that a family in the poorest quintile of income receivers in 1960 was not in the richest quintile in 1990 or vice versa? The answer is that we do not know. To the extent that there is upward (and downward) mobility among income classes, greater equality is achieved over time.

The United States, as a nation of rugged individualists, has historically championed the idea that a hard-working and frugal boy or girl, though poor, could climb to the top. Such economic mobility can promote equality over the long run.

Most studies indicate that there is a high degree of mobility in the United States, especially in the lower quintiles, but there are important statistical problems with identifying mobility over long-run periods.[2] Such problems also extend to measuring age distribution factors and multiyear inequality. While it is safe to say that age distribution factors and economic mobility undoubtedly reduce income distribution inequality over time, economists and policymakers do not yet have the data or the wherewithal to judge the exact amount of the reduction. Annual statistics are nonetheless useful as indicators of certain important trends and characteristics of income distribution.

SOME CHARACTERISTICS OF INCOME DISTRIBUTION

The data collected in population surveys and census reports, though imperfect, reveal a great deal of information about ourselves as a nation.

Family Income Characteristics

Mean income:
A measure of average income; can be computed as per capita, per family, or per earner of income.

Consider Table 6, which shows the total and average incomes of white, black, and Hispanic families by certain characteristics for 1987. The data show that the **mean**—or average—**income** of white families was about $13,000 greater than that of black families and about $9000 greater than that of Hispanic

---

[1]See Alan S. Blinder, "Inequality and Mobility in the Distribution of Wealth," *Kyklos* 29 (1976), pp. 607–38. Also see an estimate by Morton Paglin, "The Measurement and Trend of Inequality: A Basic Revision," *American Economic Review* 65 (September 1975), pp. 598–609.

[2]See Alan S. Blinder, "The Level and Distribution of Economic Well-Being," in *The American Economy in Transition,* ed. Martin Feldstein (Chicago: University of Chicago Press, 1980), pp. 450–54. This entire essay is an excellent nontechnical and modern introduction to the many problems of income distribution.

TABLE 6   The Money Income of Families by Family Characteristics, 1987

The table shows aggregate income and average income by race, age, educational attainment, region, and family size.

Characteristic	All Races[1]		White		Black		Hispanic[2]	
	Aggregate Money Income (billions of dollars)	Mean Income (dollars)	Aggregate Money Income (billions of dollars)	Mean Income (dollars)	Aggregate Money Income (billions of dollars)	Mean Income (dollars)	Aggregate Money Income (billions of dollars)	Mean Income (dollars)
Total	2,927.2	32,144	2,630.7	33,526	211.3	20,743	140.5	24,666
Age of householder								
15–24 years old	102.0	19,504	90.7	20,630	8.5	12,573	10.4	18,601
25–34 years old	621.6	30,200	554.2	31,913	50.0	19,277	40.8	23,493
35–44 years old	763.8	39,529	676.0	41,154	60.4	26,647	39.2	28,737
45–54 years old	597.0	43,796	532.5	45,997	43.6	27,689	25.3	30,631
55–64 years old	447.3	34,818	410.7	36,445	26.7	20,174	16.8	24,474
65 years old and over	395.6	20,333	366.7	21,029	22.2	12,622	8.1	15,332
Region								
Northeast	660.9	34,535	604.2	35,641	40.6	22,937	25.2	22,238
Midwest	691.9	30,886	640.4	31,945	40.7	20,171	9.4	24,470
South	929.2	29,928	808.5	32,130	108.1	19,735	43.4	23,347
West	645.3	34,918	577.6	35,424	21.9	23,776	62.6	26,936
Size of household								
One person	380.1	17,363	340.6	18,048	32.6	12,355	11.4	13,547
Two persons	951.5	32,482	883.2	33,793	50.5	19,860	28.2	22,421
Three persons	608.0	37,615	543.0	39,645	45.2	23,754	29.5	25,663
Four persons	599.6	42,394	536.8	44,326	43.3	26,923	35.5	29,951
Five persons	251.8	41,413	219.5	43,687	21.1	26,588	18.8	27,841
Six persons	84.8	38,981	69.3	41,197	10.0	27,597	9.0	27,861
Seven persons or more	51.4	38,971	38.3	43,241	8.6	25,269	8.1	30,858
Educational attainment of householder								
Elementary school								
Less than 8 years	102.5	15,579	81.2	16,431	17.5	12,494	25.1	16,279
8 years	90.2	17,509	80.0	17,816	8.8	15,143	6.8	17,603
High School								
1–3 years	238.5	21,182	206.1	22,759	28.3	14,112	18.1	19,860
4 years	952.9	29,069	860.9	30,065	75.2	21,139	41.0	26,443
College								
1–3 years	540.6	34,677	482.8	35,646	40.6	26,078	22.7	31,367
4 years or more	1,002.5	50,879	919.7	51,669	40.9	37,700	26.7	46,163

Source: U.S. Bureau of the Census, *Current Population Reports,* series P-60, No. 161, and unpublished data.

[1] Includes other races not shown separately.

[2] Hispanic persons may be of any race.

Per capita income:
Average income per person; the total income of a population divided by the number of people in the population.

families. (If **per capita income**—income per person—were compared for white, black, and Hispanic families, the differences would be even more striking because white families are, on average, smaller than black and Hispanic families.) Some of these differences are undoubtedly the consequence of differences in education, training, and experience, but it is a sad and undeniable fact that some of the differences result from economic discrimination.

Age-distributed income:
The distribution of income broken down by age ranges in the population, usually by ten-year intervals.

Table 6 provides other important information. **Age-distributed income** (mean incomes broken down by the age of the head of the family) rises through all age categories through the 45–54 category. For all age categories, the incomes of white families consistently exceed those of black and Hispanic families.

Table 6 also tells us something about income distribution by family size. Mean income increases as family size increases up to four persons, and then it declines. This is probably because families with more than two children generally have only one adult who is employed, while smaller families more often have two working adults.

Finally, Table 6 shows the relationship between educational attainment and mean income. The data provide striking evidence that income rises with educational attainment. The one exception is black families, for whom mean income is only slightly higher for a family whose head of household completed only eight years of education than for a family headed by a high school dropout. In this particular case, it may be that additional years of work experience are more valuable than additional years of education.

Although the numbers change from year to year, the pattern of income distribution remains stubbornly this: There are striking differences between the mean incomes of white, black, and Hispanic families, not all of which can be accounted for by differences in age, education, or family size.

Poverty

Poverty and economic discrimination are interrelated within our economic system. First we will define poverty; then we will examine various contributing factors to poverty in the United States.

Poverty:
A substandard level of income.

Poverty can be defined as the condition of relatively lower incomes for some individuals or groups compared with others in a society. Defined this way, poverty will always be with us. As long as the Lorenz curve for unadjusted income is not diagonal—in other words, as long as there is not perfect income equality—some families will be better off than others. Moreover, an equitable distribution of income does not necessarily mean perfect equality.

Government measures of poverty are based on a poverty index devised by the Social Security Administration in 1964 and modified by a Federal Interagency Committee in 1969. This is an attempt to define poverty in absolute terms. The index delineates a poverty level according to such factors as size of family, rate of inflation, number of children under age eighteen, and place of residence. Accepting this official definition, we can observe changes in the incidence of poverty over time to different types of families.

Even when measured in absolute rather than relative terms, much poverty still exists in the United States. Many of the poorest families in our society are worse off than the lowest living standards we have deemed to be acceptable. In fact, there is evidence suggesting an increase in poverty between 1974 and 1984 and only a slight decline since 1984. Table 7 provides an overall profile for various types of families for selected years between 1959 and 1987. In 1959, the number of persons living below the poverty line was almost 40 million, or more than 22 percent of all persons in this country. By 1987, the poor had fallen in number to below 33 million, or 13.5 percent of the population; but this progress is somewhat misleading: In 1974, the number of persons living below the poverty line was 23.4 million, or 11.2 percent of the population.

TABLE 7   Poverty by Family Status, Race, and Sex of Householder, 1959–1987

While poverty has declined in absolute numbers and in percentage terms over time, the relative positions of blacks and female householders are still a matter of concern.

Family Status, Race, and Sex of Householder	Number Below Poverty Level (millions)						Percent of Persons Below Poverty Level (millions)					
	1959	1969	1974	1979	1984	1987	1959	1969	1974	1979	1984	1987
All persons	39.5	24.2	23.4	26.1	33.7	32.5	22.4	12.1	11.2	11.7	14.4	13.5
White	28.5	16.7	15.7	17.2	23.0	21.4	18.1	9.5	8.6	9.5	11.5	10.5
Black	9.9	7.1	7.2	8.1	9.5	9.7	55.1	32.2	30.3	31.0	33.8	33.1
Hispanic	(NA)	(NA)	(NA)	2.9	4.8	5.5	(NA)	(NA)	(NA)	21.6	28.4	28.2
Female head of family, husband not present	10.4	10.4	11.5	13.5	16.4	16.9	50.2	38.4	33.6	32.0	34.0	33.6

Sources: U.S. Department of Commerce, Bureau of the Census, Current Population Reports—Consumer Income, *Money Income and Poverty Status of Families and Persons in the United States: 1984* (Washington, D.C.: U.S. Government Printing Office, 1986), pp. 20–24; *Statistical Abstract of the United States* (1989), pp. 452–53.

Although the number of black persons living in poverty has fallen about 25 percent since 1959, the percentage of black families who are poor has remained around 33 percent since 1969. Unemployment rates for Hispanic families have remained at about twice the national average. A third demographic group for which poverty rates have remained high is families headed by single women. In 1987, one-third of such families were living in poverty, and over one-half of all poor families were headed by women.

Poverty also has a geographic dimension. The highest percentage of persons below the poverty level is found in the southern states (16.2 percent in 1984), and the lowest percentage is in the West (13.1 percent in 1984). Connecticut, however, had the lowest percentage of poor in 1980 (8.0 percent); in contrast, 23.9 percent of Mississippians lived in poverty in 1980.

Race and Sex Discrimination in Wages

The overall statistics on poverty since 1960 do show improvement, but the undeniable fact is that there are poor among us and that poverty is often related to race, sex, and family status. What are the reasons for the facts of poverty? Factors are many and often interwoven. Some people are unlucky. Still others are not able-bodied; they are simply unable to work. But these factors cannot explain the existence of all poverty.

Lower incomes also exist for clearly identifiable economic reasons. The poor tend to have lower skills and lower stocks of human capital. These lower stocks of human capital are the result of less education, inferior education, and lower job-related training. Lower productivity means unemployment and lower wages, lower wages mean lower incomes, and lower incomes mean poverty. Environmental factors may make poverty a vicious cycle: Children of the poor often receive less education and training. Moreover, many wage and income differences are the result of outright race and sex discrimination. Indeed, differences in training and education may be related to past and present economic discrimination.

One might object that poverty, race, and sex discrimination are not necessarily related. After all, a black woman may earn $75,000 per year in legal practice but still endure discrimination with respect to her white male counterparts. It is more than coincidence, however, to find such groups as blacks, Hispanics, and women ranking consistently high in poverty statistics.

We must be careful to distinguish between social discrimination and economic discrimination that leads to significantly lower wages and income, although the two are often related. Groups such as Jews, gays, and the handicapped may meet with social discrimination in seeking housing and club memberships but be little affected by economic discrimination.

Economic wage discrimination exists when individuals of equal ability and productivity in the same occupation earn different wage rates. The bald economic facts are that the median income of blacks is only 60 percent of that of whites (in all income classes) and that females earn only about 60 percent of median male income for full-time work. Empirical studies show that about half of this difference is related to educational, productivity, and job-training differences.[3] The remaining half is the apparent result of economic discrimination or other unidentified factors.

Economic wage discrimination:
A situation in which individuals in the same occupation who have the same productive abilities are paid different wage rates by a given employer. The wage-rate differences are based on race, sex, religion, or national origin rather than on productive differences.

The Practice of Discrimination. Economists do not pretend to know the causes of discrimination. Some observers have argued that sex discrimination may originate from historical roles of women that are matters of cultural tradition. Women's biologically unique potential for childbearing may also be a factor in differences in wage rates. Employers may not want to invest in as much job training or pay high wages for women whose work may be interrupted or terminated by childbirth. Both women and blacks receive less formal education and on-the-job training than men and whites, a factor that may be related to past discrimination.

Economic discrimination involves costs to those who discriminate as well as to those against whom discrimination is practiced. An employer who refuses to hire women or blacks of equal productivity to men or whites is discriminating. If the wages of the preferred groups are driven up by these actions, employers must pay a premium for men or whites. In a competitive system, discriminating firms will be at a disadvantage in the marketplace. Employers who do not discriminate in hiring can acquire equally productive labor at lower wage rates and, in the end, will tend to drive discriminating competitors out of business.

Consumer-initiated discrimination:
Wage discrimination arising from consumers' preferences for goods or services produced by individuals of a certain sex, race, religion, or national origin. Consumers must pay a premium in the form of higher prices or lower quality to exercise such discrimination.

Even if employers do not discriminate, consumers may. In a competitive system, **consumer-initiated discrimination** is costly to the discriminator as well as to those discriminated against. Consumers who will deal only with whites or men (avoiding, say, black or female lawyers, doctors, or interior designers) must pay a premium for their prejudice. Prices of goods and services of favored sellers will be higher than prices for the same goods or services available to those who do not discriminate. While higher money prices may not be charged by discriminating sellers, a higher full price may emerge in terms of lower

---

[3]See Dwight R. Lee and Robert R. McNown, *Economics in Our Time: Concepts and Issues* (Chicago: Science Research Associates, 1983), chapter 10, for an excellent analysis of economic issues related to discrimination. Some of the present discussion is drawn from their work.

quality or greater inconvenience of purchase. In sum, the competitive system makes it costly for employers or consumers to discriminate. This economic deterrent has failed to eradicate discrimination in our economy, however, as have government regulations explicitly forbidding discrimination.

Economic Restrictions and Discrimination. The law is clear on one point—employers are to give equal pay for equal work without regard to race, creed, or sex. But employers may simply avoid the hiring of women or blacks. Laws establishing quotas (minimum numbers) of females or racial minorities in employment or educational situations may not have the fully intended results. Reverse discrimination cases have resulted in some instances of quota imposition. In other cases, employers may subtly hide discrimination by reducing the amount of on-the-job training while paying the same money wages. The full wage—both money and training—may not be paid to those against whom discrimination is practiced.

Although there are encouraging statistics on the entry of women and blacks into male- and white-dominated occupations in the past twenty years, a number of factors remain that make the rapid and total elimination of discrimination unlikely. A fully competitive system discourages discrimination, placing extra costs on discriminating employers and consumers, although we do not suggest that discrimination would be eliminated in a perfectly competitive system. Where, then, might we expect to observe more severe discrimination? In markets where regulations or restrictions prevent the competitive process from working. According to the research of economist Thomas Sowell, high degrees of economic discrimination have traditionally been found within labor unions, in regulated industries, and in the professions where legal and government-sanctioned entry restrictions are permitted.[4] In such industries and occupations, nonmarket characteristics—such as color and sex—may be used in deciding whom to employ. Such discrimination may be detected in medicine, law, and dentistry, for example, as well as in those historically regulated areas of our economy such as railroads and the postal service. Government itself has practiced a good deal of discrimination in this century as, for example, in the U.S. military with respect to rank and promotion through World War II and the Korean conflict. However, civil rights legislation and desegregation decisions of the courts have enhanced minority economic opportunities. These laws and rules have effectively reduced artificial impediments to some market activities for blacks and other minorities.

In sum, discrimination appears to be pronounced and long-lived where government-granted regulations and restrictions substitute for freely competitive market forces. Many economists feel that a movement toward a more competitive marketplace would speed reductions in sex and race discrimination. Government regulations and legal rules, where they impede full access to market participation by *all* entrants and potential entrants, should be eliminated. In this sense, deregulation promotes sexual and racial equality. Governments may actively promote equal access to markets with fairness rules that regulate state and local government contracting and employment. Where economic incentives are placed before employers and consumers to avoid discrimination, less discrimination may be confidently predicted.

---

[4]See Thomas Sowell, *Markets and Minorities* (New York: Basic Books, 1981), pp. 34–51.

(Discrimination and minority status are discussed in Economics in Action, "Who Are the Economic Minorities in the United States?" at the end of this chapter.)

Programs to Alleviate Poverty

Poverty is the result of a number of factors—lower productivity, inferior educational opportunities, and economic discrimination. Until full equal economic opportunity for all is a reality, some type of redistribution of wealth is likely to take place.

Contemporary welfare programs (see Table 8) center on the relative needs of the poor. In-kind benefits such as food stamps, Medicare, housing subsidies, and outright money transfers (such as Aid to Families with Dependent Children) are allotted to the poor on the basis of a government agency's determination of need. Benefits, moreover, vary from state to state and among local governments. Without questioning need or the existence of poverty, economists might analyze the costs of fairly and accurately administering such programs. But more important, economists are concerned with the effects of such programs on the incentives of the poor.

While there will always be poor unfortunates who for health or other reasons cannot work, the contemporary welfare system historically has discriminated against most of the poor in one respect: It has tended to discourage any effort on the part of the poor to better themselves by earning income additional to their subsidy and perhaps acquiring job training in the process. Take a highly stylized example: Rita, a widow with three small children, could earn $4000 a year to supplement her modest welfare subsidy of $7000 per year. Such work would surely not be in her interest, however, since under the welfare system in some circumstances her subsidy would be taxed at a rate of

TABLE 8   Summary of Principal Welfare Programs

U.S. welfare programs include both cash subsidy and in-kind benefits. Welfare programs, moreover, are aimed at various segments of society and are administered at all levels of government.

Program	Level of Administration	Purpose	Beneficiaries
Aid to Families with Dependent Children (AFDC)	Federally mandated; administered by state and local governments	Income maintenance, often used in conjunction with in-kind subsidies	Poor families with unemployed heads of household
Unemployment compensation	State governments	To aid the unemployed for limited periods	Directly benefits the unemployed and their families
In-kind benefits, housing subsidies, food stamps	Federal, state, and local governments	Supplements to nutrition and to the quality of housing of the poor	Poor families and the children of poor families
Social Security, including Medicare and Medicaid	Federal government	To provide retirement insurance	Insurance for survivors, welfare for the aged poor, medical care for the elderly (Medicare) and the poor (Medicaid)

Negative income tax:
An income tax system that pays a subsidy, or a negative tax, to individuals with incomes below a certain level. Below this level, as income increases, the subsidy decreases—but by less than the amount income increases.

100 percent. By "taxed" we mean that Rita would lose her welfare benefits if she works. In other words, Rita would have less incentive to work if her subsidy were reduced by an amount equal to what she earned and still less incentive if she were to lose the entire subsidy by working.

Consider another possibility, one supported by a large number of economists interested in public policy relating to poverty: the **negative income tax.** The negative income tax originates from the observation that welfare recipients such as Rita will react to economic incentives if such incentives are provided. Under a negative income tax system Rita would be taxed for working but not at a rate of 100 percent.

Suppose that Rita and her children are guaranteed a minimum income subsidy of $7000; an income of $14,000 is determined by some agency calculation to be adequate for her situation—a widow with three children to support. (The figures given here are wholly hypothetical.) Further suppose that rather than being taxed at a rate of 100 percent, as in the current welfare system, Rita is taxed at a lower rate, say 50 percent of all additional private earnings. What happens when Rita works and earns income?

As Table 9 shows, Rita now has an incentive to enter the marketplace. If she earns $4000, she does not lose $4000 in subsidy but instead gains $2000. In other words, if Rita earns $4000, she pays only 50 percent of it in taxes, which, in effect, reduces her subsidy by $2000. Her total income would climb to $9000. Should Rita be able to earn $8000 by job advancement, she would pay in taxes only $2000 of the additional $4000 earned. Her subsidy would be reduced, in effect, to $3000, giving her a total income of $11,000. Should she be able to earn $14,000, her minimum acceptable income, Rita would receive no subsidy (paying, in effect, an additional tax of $3000). If Rita earns an income over $14,000 per year she would become a net taxpayer.

The point is that Rita would have positive incentives in this system to work and be self-supporting. While the numbers in this example—such as a 50 percent tax rate—are completely hypothetical (progressivity or regressivity may be built into the plan), the principle is clear. If the poor could improve their lot by working, economists predict that such incentives would encourage

---

TABLE 9

Negative Income Tax for a Hypothetical Welfare Recipient

If Rita could earn $4000 per year from working, her subsidy would be taxed only at a rate of 50 percent, giving her a total income of $9000. At a marginal or additional negative income tax rate of 50 percent, she would have an incentive to work and earn additional income. After she earns an income greater than $14,000, Rita becomes a net taxpayer.

Rita's Income from Working or Other Sources	Rita's Subsidy (Negative Income Tax)	Rita's Total Income (Private Sources plus Subsidy)
$ 0	$7,000	$ 7,000
4,000	5,000	9,000
8,000	3,000	11,000
14,000	0	14,000
16,000	−1,000	15,000
20,000	−3,000	17,000

work effort. While a negative income tax plan has not received much political support, many economists have strongly urged its implementation in preference to much of the contemporary welfare system. Indeed, some of the principles of the negative income tax are finding their way into the overall system of income transfers.

The Family Support Act of 1988

From an economic point of view, at least, it is important that the welfare system serve as a tonic rather than an impediment to the progress of the poor. In November 1988, the first major welfare reform legislation in 53 years, the Family Support Act of 1988, was signed into law. As a major revision in the rules affecting the approximately eleven million people receiving Aid to Families with Dependent Children (AFDC) (see Table 8), the program attempts to institute economic incentives into the welfare system. It is specifically addressed to the problem created by the tremendous increase in the number of households headed by women. By 1985, for example, women were 51 percent more likely to be living in poverty than men. In 1986, there were 3.5 million single mothers on the welfare rolls. In fact, almost 95 percent of the welfare recipients in the United States are members of families headed by single mothers.

In the past, welfare recipients could not remain on the rolls if they earned income. Under the new system, working does not disqualify the welfare recipient from receiving assistance. The Job Opportunities and Basic Skills (JOBS) program requires welfare parents with children over age three to enroll in basic education, work experience, job search, and community service programs provided and paid for by state and federal governments. Prior to the Family Support Act, cash benefits were not extended to two-parent families in most states. The act directs states to pay support to two-parent families whose principal earner is unemployed. This provision prevents families from intentionally breaking up to be eligible for welfare benefits as a single-parent family. The new welfare system focuses principally on the requirement that one parent engage in intensive job search. If a job is not found, one parent in each unemployed two-parent household must put in sixteen hours per week of mandatory service in a state-organized job or in job training.

The Family Support Act aids recipients in the transition from welfare to market work. Single parents who begin working will be provided with one year of day-care assistance. Medicaid health insurance eligibility for the family will also be assured for one year. Transportation, often a problem for single-parent and other welfare families, will be provided to and from job-training sites. In all, these provisions are positive economic incentives during the transition from welfare to market work. The new welfare act requires employers to deduct court-ordered child support payments automatically from the paychecks of absent parents. States receive federal assistance for computerized monitoring systems for these activities.

No foolproof welfare system has ever been devised, and the new system is no exception. Critics have charged that single parents who have market jobs and are not currently on the welfare rolls may have an incentive to quit their jobs temporarily. Provision of day-care benefits and health insurance for one year after starting a new job may encourage intentional periodic "temporary unemployment" by workers who seek to use the system to receive benefits in spite of their ability to find market work. But most observers emphasize the fact that the law recognizes the problem for what it is—a problem of unemployment. Many economists have hailed the Family Support Act of 1988 as providing economic incentives to a complex welfare structure that historically has simply sustained the poor and offered little hope of betterment.

THE JUSTICE OF INCOME DISTRIBUTION

Economists have attempted—not always successfully—to avoid advocating any given distribution of income or any redistribution of income. In other words, economists have tried to avoid normative statements about what should be and have taken a more positive stance—what income distribution is and how it might be changed to produce greater incentives to work and produce, while maintaining some politically derived concept of justice. The proposal that a negative income tax plan be instituted in place of the contemporary system of welfare transfers is an example of a positive economic solution related to income distribution. The Focus, "Pareto Movements and Income Distribution," considers further the role of economists.

Justice itself is not part of the positive economist's vocabulary, but the effects of some concepts of justice are within the economist's purview. For example, some concepts of justice could create extreme income redistributions that would make income distribution more equal at the expense of working and producing members of society. This notion of extreme redistribution is condemned in some popular literature as putting too many people in the wagon with too few pulling the wagon. In economic terms, such redistributions and the high tax rates involved would probably create disincentives to work. If so, total real output of goods and services available to all citizens would decline. As a result, a shrinking segment of a smaller pie would be available to all classes of economic society, including the poor.

More than a hundred years ago, the classical economist John Stuart Mill observed that two kinds of equality are involved in questions of distribution: *ex ante* equality and *ex post* equality. *Ex ante* equality is a situation where "all start fair"—where, through educational opportunities, the absence of discrimination, social and economic mobility, and so on, every individual is given an opportunity to maximize his or her potential. *Ex post* equality is a guarantee that through redistributive policies all end up at the same place. While Mill championed *ex ante* equality, he believed that differing incentives, innate talents, luck, and so on meant there would and must be differences in income distribution in the end. To guarantee all citizens *ex post* equality would stultify incentives, which are the very mode of economic progress. Enforced *ex post* equality would surely shrink the total economic pie.

Modern economists concerned with income distribution face the same problem. The trick is to evaluate the contemporary system and to propose means that provide that all start fair (akin to golfing or bowling handicaps) but that do not force redistributions that significantly reduce incentives to produce. The modern economist is as much on a razor's edge as were past writers dealing with the questions of income distribution. The issues of fairness, justice, and equality will always be matters of dispute. The economist, as a maker of positive statements and proposals, will always be a contributor to this important debate.

FOCUS   Pareto Movements and Income Distribution

Are there any rules governing the ability of an economist to make statements concerning income distribution? Practically speaking, can an economist say anything about whether a housing subsidy or a new dam would make people better off, all things considered?

A famous turn-of-the-century economist, Vilfredo Pareto (1848–1923), had something to say on these matters. His view, sometimes called Pareto optimality, was that the economist could pronounce one distribution of income or wealth preferable to another if and only if the change made one group better off without leaving another group worse off. "Better off" is expressed as satisfaction or utility, so judgment depends on the ability of the economist to measure welfare.

It is almost impossible to think of distributional changes that do not help one group without simultaneously making another group worse off. The provision of food stamps ob-

viously aids the recipients, but it reduces the welfare of those who pay taxes to support such expenditures. While it is tempting to argue that a dollar's worth of something provides more satisfaction to a poor person than it takes away from a rich person, the positive economist (one who attempts to avoid value judgments) cannot make this leap because utility cannot be measured. Support for a progressive income tax on this basis is invalid for the same reason. It would involve what economists call an interpersonal utility comparison—a judgment about the relative utility of, say, a dollar to a rich person and to a poor person. The economist can measure rich or poor but cannot measure happy or unhappy. Thus the economist depends on the political process to decide on a particular distribution made through taxes and expenditures. The economist is then concerned with the effects of specific taxes and specific expenditures on economic efficiency.

SUMMARY

1. Economists deal with positive, not normative, aspects of income distribution, for the economist's view of "who should receive what" is only as good as anyone else's. The economist therefore does not normally deal with questions of justice or fairness but focuses instead on the facts of income distribution and on the possible effects of alternative welfare programs.

2. Money income distributions differ for a number of reasons: Some persons choose leisure over work and income, while others earn lower incomes because of bad luck, poor health, lower educational opportunities and productivity, and race or sex discrimination.

3. A Lorenz curve and the related Gini coefficient are measures of income inequality. Ordinarily, the more bowed the Lorenz curve or the larger the Gini coefficient, the more inequality there is in a society's income distribution.

4. Lorenz curves showing money income distribution for a given year overstate actual inequality when in-kind benefits, income and payroll taxes, and other factors are considered. Age distribution of the population and income mobility also create greater long-term equality in income distribution.

5. Poverty and economic discrimination are interrelated features of our economic system. Economic discrimination exists when individuals of equal productivity are paid different wages on the basis of sex or racial differences.

6. Economic discrimination exists against blacks and women in our society in the sense that only half of the difference between black-white and male-female earnings is explainable on the basis of productivity differences.

7. Economic discrimination cannot be practiced by employers or consumers without costs in a competitive environment. Government-sanctioned regulations and restrictions on competitors appear to account for a large amount of observed economic discrimination in the United States.

8. Contemporary welfare programs, such as the Family Support Act of 1988, provide positive incentives for the poor. Many economists support a formal negative income tax structure to provide work incentives to the poor.

KEY TERMS

individual income	Lorenz curve	age-distributed income
labor income	Gini coefficient	poverty
asset income	adjusted income	economic wage discrimination
ex ante distribution	in-kind transfer payments	consumer-initiated discrimination
ex post distribution	economic mobility	negative income tax
transfer payment	per capita income	
family income	mean income	

QUESTIONS FOR REVIEW AND DISCUSSION

1. What are the components of an individual's income? Which of these are matters of choice by the individual?
2. How does an individual obtain asset income?
3. What does a Lorenz curve show? What does it mean if the Lorenz curve moves closer through time to the line of perfect equality?
4. What is the difference between income as measured by government and adjusted income as reported by some economists?
5. What is economic wage discrimination? Give an example of wage discrimination that fits the description.
6. What are the problems associated with the use of Gini coefficients to report income distribution?
7. Why do young people have lower incomes than older people? If average lifetime incomes rather than annual incomes could be used to construct Lorenz curves, would the Gini coefficient be lower?
8. If every married couple in the United States obtained a divorce, would the Lorenz curve move away from the line of perfect equality? Would this alteration change the actual distribution of income?
9. Suppose all people were born with the same amount of natural abilities and the same amount of inherited money wealth. Under these circumstances, what would the sources of income differences be?
10. Do income redistribution programs affect the supply of labor? How does a negative income tax compare to other transfer programs in its effect on work effort?

ECONOMICS IN ACTION
Who Are the Economic Minorities in the United States?

Who are the economic minorities in the United States, and on what does their relative position in the income distribution depend? Economist Thomas Sowell has suggested answers to these questions in an extensive investigation of the characteristics of a number of minorities in America.[a] While Sowell's arguments are controversial, his thesis is that discrimination is not a good single explanation for why some minority incomes are above or below the national average. Other factors—some of them brought out in this chapter—must figure prominently in any explanation of income differences.

A part of Sowell's intriguing explanation is revealed in the following table. The table ranks ethnic origin (or ethnicity) with the ethnic group's average income compared to the average per capita income of the U.S. population as a whole. The average income of white, Anglo-Saxon, Protestant Americans is not reported in the table, but it amounts to 104 percent of national average income.

What factors explain the differences? According to Sowell, genetic color differences are not much of an answer. The income of the average black West Indian American (also not reported in the table) is 94 percent of the mean U.S. income,

[a]Thomas Sowell, *Markets and Minorities* (New York: Basic Books, 1981).

Ethnicity	Relative Income (percent of national average)	Median Age	Children per Woman
Jewish	172	46	2.4
Japanese	132	32	2.2
Polish	115	40	2.5
Chinese	112	27	2.9
Italian	112	36	2.4
Irish	102	37	3.1
Mexican	76	18	4.4
Puerto Rican	63	18	3.5
Black	62	22	3.7
American Indian	60	20	4.4

Source: Adapted from Thomas Sowell, *Markets and Minorities* (New York: Basic Books, 1981), Tables 1.1, 1.2, and 1.3, pp. 8, 11, and 16.

and the average Japanese American earns 132 percent as much as the average American. Contrast these relatively high earnings for some dark-skinned minorities with the earnings of light-skinned Puerto Ricans: only 63 percent of the mean income. Color alone cannot be a big factor explaining ethnic income differences.

According to Sowell, at least three factors explain differences in average incomes: (1) median age in the ethnic group, (2) locational concentrations, and (3) the fecundity of women (children per woman) within the ethnic group. The table above shows, in general, that the older the median age and the fewer children per woman in the ethnic group, the higher the median income of that group. In all groups, income earned varies with age differences. Income earnings generally peak between the ages of forty-five and fifty-five and perhaps at higher ages. We would thus expect those ethnic groups with the lowest median ages to earn less income than those with higher median ages. This age differential in part explains, for example, why Mexican Americans—with a median age of eighteen—earn 63 percent of average national income and why Jewish Americans—with a median age of forty-six—earn 172 percent.

In these age distribution statistics lie hidden signs of hope for the condition of ethnic minorities. Attitudes toward minorities are clearly changing, but the effects of attitude changes on equal education and job opportunities are being felt largely by the younger members of ethnic minorities. As Sowell reports, African Americans over forty-five years of age earn less than 60 percent of the sum earned by their age-peers in the population, but African Americans aged eighteen to twenty-four earn 83 percent of their age-peers' income.

The number of children per woman is also a factor explaining the relative economic position of minorities. In general, those with lower relative incomes have a higher fecundity rate. The number of children can also have an impact on differences between family and per capita incomes among minorities. In family income terms, for example, Mexican Americans earn significantly more than African American families. But in per capita terms, when the number of children per woman becomes a factor, the more fecund Mexicans earn lower incomes than African Americans. Age and fecundity factors lead to other surprising statistics. For example, half of all Mexicans and Puerto Ricans in the United States are below the age of eighteen.

Geographic differences also account for relative income differences. Greater poverty exists in the southern part of the United States. The same fact pertains to comparisons of ethnic incomes and poverty. As Sowell notes and as the table indicates, Mexican Americans and Puerto Ricans earn more than African Americans nationally, but African Americans outside the South earn more than both those groups. The place one lives also makes a difference. Native Americans living in Chicago or New York earn more than twice as much as those living on reservations. Mexican Americans living in Detroit earn more than twice the amount of those living in cities in the Rio Grande Valley of Texas.

With arguments such as these, Sowell questions the extent to which discrimination is a function of others' sins. A number of factors explain the relative position of minorities, including age, number of children, and geographic differences. Discrimination cannot explain all differences. How, for example, could we explain Jewish and Japanese relative incomes in spite of rampant discrimination against these groups in the past and to a certain extent in the present as well?

Question

Why must most generalizations about income distribution and minority incomes be carefully analyzed and dissected?

Thomas Malthus

Gary Becker

Thomas Malthus and Gary Becker: The Economics of Population Growth

THOMAS MALTHUS (1766–1834) was born in Surrey, England, during the Industrial Revolution. It was widely believed at the time that the effects of industrialization, such as increased trade and specialization of labor, would eventually improve the quality of human life. When anarchist and pamphleteer William Godwin published his utopian outlook for society in his book, *Political Justice,* in 1793, an argument developed between Malthus and his father. Malthus's father was inclined to agree with Godwin's views, but the younger Malthus believed that society was caught in a trap in which population would increase more rapidly than the food supply, leaving the standard of living at a subsistence level at best. In 1798, the same year he became a minister of the Church of England, Malthus published his views of population and the economy in his treatise, *An Essay on the Principle of Population.* It was this pessimistic treatise on the future of humanity that led essayist Thomas Carlyle to label economics "the dismal science."

Malthus went on to become the first professor of political economy in England at the East India College in 1805. His work on population influenced his friend and critic David Ricardo as well as Charles Darwin.

GARY BECKER (b. 1930), currently University Professor of Economics at the University of Chicago, gained international recognition for his work in applying microeconomic theory to areas such as marriage, crime, and prejudice. His book, *The Economics of Discrimination* (1971), introduced prejudice and discrimination as forces that can be analyzed and

measured in their effect on the economy. In *The Economics of Human Behavior* (1976), Becker argues that all human behavior, even selection of a marriage partner, is based on economics.

In 1965, Becker authored his famous treatise on the concept of human capital. In *Human Capital,* Becker treats the individual as a "firm" that makes investment decisions (such as education or on-the-job training) on the basis of rate of return. Soon after the publication of *Human Capital,* Becker was awarded the John Bates Clark medal by the American Economic Association for excellence in research by an economist under the age of forty.

THE CHECK OF MISERY

Malthus's theory of population growth is strongly pessimistic. In *An Essay on the Principle of Population,* Malthus wrote that the world's population will increase at a rate that will ultimately test the limits of our available food supply and other subsistence goods. As the supply of food increases through additional labor and agriculture, population will increase as well, with the result that per capita income—the fruits of labor—will never exceed bare subsistence standards for the population as a whole. The threat of widespread famine will persist indefinitely. Only the lucky will survive.

An alternative way of stating Malthus's proposition is that children are what economists call normal goods, demand for which rises and falls in response to changes in income. Any increase in income to parents will increase their demand for children, other things being equal. At the point when an additional child will actually reduce living standards below subsistence—a point Malthus called the "check of misery"—parents will cease reproducing.

475

Given this gloomy scenario, it is not surprising that Malthus, a parson, would urge "moral restraints" on parents. Such restraints included abstinence and postponing marriage. It is interesting to speculate about whether Malthus would urge modern forms of birth control. The morality of contraceptive use, forced sterilization, and abortion is one of the burning issues of our times.

Malthus's theory of population growth seems today most applicable to the exploding populations of China, Mexico, Bangladesh, and other developing countries. In the industrialized nations, including the United States, the last century has seen actual declines in average family size, while average family incomes have risen well above the level of bare subsistence. Many economists, including Gary Becker, have sought reasons why the theory has not, fortunately, held true.

THE PRICE OF CHILDREN

Becker's theory of human capital helps explain both the power and the limits of the Malthusian theory. For Becker, the choice of whether to reproduce has a second rationale, one beyond a simple change in income. Parents' demand for children will be influenced not only by changes in income but also by the relative "price" of children. This price is partly the direct costs of raising the child, but it also includes the opportunity costs that additional children represent. As the parents' income increases, the opportunity cost of children will also tend to increase. In other words, the sacrifices borne by increasing the size of a family will increase with income. To take one example, if an executive forsakes a high-paying job to stay home with the children so that his or her spouse can pursue a career, the cost of that decision is the wages and income the executive receives now and the higher income he or she could expect to receive in the future.

As the costs of children increase, the quantity demanded will decrease, other things being equal. As a result, parents may substitute quality for quantity in their decisions to raise children. Instead of feeding an additional child, parents might decide to spend additional income on housing, education, or any of a host of goods that improve living standards for the children they already have.

Becker's approach to the costs of children helps explain why parents in developed countries, with relatively high incomes, have fewer, better-educated children than parents in developing countries with relatively low incomes. In less-developed, largely subsistence agricultural countries, children represent direct labor inputs—even small children can do useful work on a subsistence farm—thus lowering the price of children. Where the price of children is lower, we expect to see more children produced, other things being equal. Thus we see the law of demand at work.

According to Becker, then, Malthus failed to take into account relative prices in his theory of population. While rats or horses may tend to breed up to the limit imposed by the available food supply, the behavior of human beings will also reflect the influence of opportunity costs and the rational choices such costs inspire.

PART FOUR

Microeconomics

and

Public Policy

19

Regulation and Public Policy

Natural monopoly:
A combination of market demand and cost conditions that results in only one firm in an industry being able to produce output profitably; occurs when decreasing long-run average costs exist up to the level of total industry demand.

Antitrust policies:
Regulations established by laws and government agencies that attempt to preserve business competition.

Regulatory policies:
Administrative or legal attempts to influence the behavior of firms or industries when competitive goals cannot be realized or when positive goals are to be pursued.

Our market economy has grown in ways that Adam Smith could never have imagined. Smith believed that market forces, operating under a laissez-faire form of government, would eventually bring us to a point of perfect competition among firms, what Smith termed "a nation of shopkeepers." Our economy, however, has followed a different path, and its market structures range from nearly pure competition to nearly complete monopoly. In the process, a few of our "shopkeepers" have managed to capture huge shares of their markets. In 1882, for example, John D. Rockefeller's Standard Oil Trust controlled 95 percent of the oil refineries in the United States, virtually eliminating all competition. Such amassing of market power may temporarily allow lower prices through economies of scale and coordination of production—characteristics often necessary to undermine competitors. But, once such a monopoly is created, some believe that it can dominate the industry at the consumers' expense. Responding to public alarm, the U.S. government began late in the nineteenth century to pass laws designed to thwart the growth of monopolies. These laws have slowed, but not eliminated, the trend toward monopoly power. When U.S. authorities intervened and broke up Rockefeller's Standard Oil Trust, it created several firms in its place. Today one of those firms, Exxon, is still one of the largest industrial corporations in the world.

The government's failure to eliminate monopoly power led economists and policy-makers to suspect that monopoly in the U.S. economy might be the *natural* outcome of competitive forces. **Natural monopolies,** according to some economists, can lead to such practices as price discrimination, quantity reductions, and other abuses if left unchecked. Electrical and power suppliers, municipal water distribution, airlines, and railroads have all been characterized as natural monopolies at one time or another in the twentieth century. Public policy in the area of monopoly is two-pronged. Some policies are designed to restore and maintain competition where viable competition can exist. These **antitrust policies** control "unfair" business practices such as anticompetitive mergers, cartels, price discrimination, and deceptive advertising. **Regulatory policies,** on the other hand, establish and manage the behavior of firms and industries where competition cannot exist or where positive goals—for ex-

478

ample, health and safety—are pursued. Here, the government imposes on natural monopolies and other businesses rules and regulations that substitute for competition and undesirable behavior in markets. After you read Chapter 19 you should know

- how government has dealt with monopoly and large-scale enterprise through antitrust and regulatory policies.
- how regulation may have *created* more monopoly power than it has dispersed.
- whether deregulation of natural monopolies helps economic efficiency and enhances consumer welfare.

PUBLIC POLICY: ANTITRUST

Purely competitive industries represent the ideal in market performance. In industries characterized by imperfect competition, the ideal is not obtained—profits may be greater than normal, production costs are not necessarily minimized, and welfare losses can occur. If these losses to society are significant, then there is a call for social action in the form of government regulation of some businesses' activities.

Public regulatory policies affecting business performance take many forms. Variety in policies is desirable because the imperfections in markets are caused by many diverse conditions. For example, the market conditions affecting a natural monopoly differ significantly from those that promote a trust company or cartel. Even though the conditions vary, the final consequences of these market structures are indeed the same—monopoly price, restricted output, and welfare loss.

Public solutions to the monopoly problem take four basic forms.

1. Antitrust laws basically designed to prevent the creation of monopolies.
2. Price regulations designed to allow the existence of monopolies but to control prices and profits.
3. Government ownership that removes the firm from the private sector and thus places its performance directly in the hands of the public.
4. Laissez-faire policy that allows the market to determine the fate and performance of firms with no government interference.

Antitrust Law

The late 1800s was a time of great change in the American economy. A significant merger wave led to the creation of very large firms with nationwide operations—the first modern corporations. Some of these firms engaged in questionable business practices, such as **predatory pricing** (the act of selling goods below cost as a method of destroying competitors), price fixing, and collusion.

Antitrust policies are aimed at preventing firms from engaging in such anticompetitive activities. During the 1870s and 1880s, an antitrust movement sprang up, primarily among American farmers. Facing falling prices for

Predatory pricing:
The temporary pricing of goods or services below cost in order to reduce or eliminate competition.

their products and stable prices for the goods they bought, they became fearful that monopolies or trusts were wielding unwarranted economic power. Through organizations such as the National Grange and the National Anti-Monopoly Cheap Freight League, the farmers successfully influenced the two major political parties to add antimonopoly planks to their 1888 election platforms. Antitrust legislation was enacted soon after, with subsequent revisions to strengthen the government's ability to fight monopolistic practices in court.

Sherman Antitrust Act. The Sherman Antitrust Act of 1890, the first anti-monopoly law passed by Congress, provided that "every contract, combination in the form of trust or otherwise, or conspiracy, in restraint of trade or commerce among the several states, or with foreign nations, is hereby declared to be illegal. . . ." The Sherman Act also declared "every person who shall monopolize, or attempt to monopolize . . . guilty of a misdemeanor, and subject to fine or imprisonment." The statute did not spell out what would constitute an illegal restraint of trade. Its main purpose was to place the antitrust issue under federal law and to provide a means of penalizing monopoly whenever it was discovered.

Clayton Antitrust Act. Believing that the Sherman Act was ineffective in preventing monopoly, Congress passed the Clayton Act in 1914. The Clayton Act clarified what Congress considered to be illegal under the Sherman Act. This act sought to limit a firm's acquisitions of the stock of another firm "where in any line of commerce in any section of the country, the effect of such acquisition may be substantially to lessen competition, or to tend to create a monopoly." Unfortunately, the Clayton Act was silent on the legality of mergers through acquisition of physical assets, leaving a large loophole for avoiding antitrust prosecution.

The Clayton Act also enumerated some specific restraints of trade that could be challenged if their effects lessened competition substantially or created a monopoly. These included (1) price discrimination—selling the same product to different customers at different prices not related to cost differences; (2) tying arrangements—making the sale of one good contingent on the purchase of some other goods; (3) interlocking directorates—the same person's serving on the boards of competing companies; and (4) exclusive dealing—selling to a retailer only on the condition that the firm not carry rival products.

Federal Trade Commission Act. Section 5 of the Federal Trade Commission (FTC) Act, also passed by Congress in 1914, contains the broadest statutory language, declaring illegal "unfair methods of competition in commerce." The act established a five-member commission independent of the executive branch, with the idea that the FTC would be a repository of economic and antitrust expertise not available to the federal courts.

Other Antitrust Statutes. The Clayton Act has been amended twice. In 1936, the Robinson-Patman Act revised the provisions relating to price discrimination and added language prohibiting predatory pricing (see Focus, "Cutthroat Competition"). In 1950, the Celler-Kefauver Act closed the Clayton Act loophole relating to mergers through the acquisition of physical assets.

FOCUS Cutthroat Competition

Predatory pricing was declared illegal in the Robinson-Patman amendment to the Clayton Act. Predatory pricing—sometimes known as "cutthroat competition"—exists when a firm lowers its price below its competitors' cost of production with the intention of driving competitors out of business. If the firm is able to do this, it may eventually become the only firm in the industry. It can then raise prices, and its subsequent monopoly profits can compensate for the losses it incurred during its predatory pricing period.

This activity was made illegal to prevent monopolies from arising in industries where competition could presumably exist. However, economic theory suggests that predatory pricing will not result in a monopoly unless the market conditions for a natural monopoly already exist. The only way that a single large firm can survive with no entry of new firms is to have lower average cost of production than the potential entrants. Otherwise, it must continually incur losses to prevent new firms from entering.

When a natural monopoly evolves in a market, one firm becomes larger, its price falls, and smaller firms go out of business. The term *predatory pricing* seems to describe these circumstances fairly accurately, but making cutthroat competition illegal does not change the market conditions that create a natural monopoly. Antitrust laws do not change the cost of production or the demand for the product.

Laws prohibiting predatory pricing are at best temporary hindrances to the emergence of a natural monopoly. Such prohibitions may indeed postpone the emergence of monopoly long enough for market conditions to change. Otherwise, outlawing price competition can have undesirable effects. For example, if a firm is prevented by law from charging a price below its competitors' average cost, then the law in effect may be protecting inefficient firms. Price competition is what forces the survival of only low-cost firms and thus low prices for consumers. Preserving competition by protecting firms from low prices ensures high prices for consumers.

The FTC Act has been revised even more often. First, in 1938 the Wheeler-Lea Act added "unfair or deceptive acts or practices in commerce" to the behavior declared illegal. In the late 1970s, the Hart-Scott-Rodino Antitrust Improvement Act established a premerger notification system by which firms contemplating a merger would notify the FTC and the Department of Justice prior to consummating the acquisition.

Antitrust Agencies

The United States has a dual system of antitrust enforcement whereby two government agencies—the Federal Trade Commission and the Justice Department's Antitrust Division—share responsibility for policing the antitrust laws. Both agencies can enforce the Clayton Act, and, since 1948, the FTC has had the power to bring charges against behavior that violates the Sherman Act.

In addition to the two government agencies, complaints charging Sherman and Clayton antitrust violations can be brought by private parties. Private plaintiffs can sue for treble damages; that is, guilty defendants can be required to pay penalties of up to three times the value of the actual injury caused by their illegal conduct. Because private suits offer such potentially large rewards for successful plaintiffs, in any given year the number of private antitrust actions is many times higher than the number of cases brought by government.

The Value of Antitrust Policies

The antitrust laws and agencies have provided a means to control anticompetitive behavior in industries. Initially they were promulgated to prevent firms from organizing into trusts or cartels designed to increase members' profits by decreasing price competition. Antitrust policies have since been extended to prevent other activities that decrease consumers' surplus, such as price discrimination and tying arrangements. Under most circumstances, the free market prevents these forms of competition. However, when concentration of market power is high, the market can fail to prevent such practices. Antitrust laws and agencies have therefore extended government control over industry with the goal of preventing increases in concentration.

Many factors external to firms can increase concentration, however. A fall in industry demand or a change in either input prices or technology that increases the optimal plant size can cause increases in concentration. These changes are beyond the control of the firms in the industry, and a decrease in the number of firms is indeed socially optimal under these circumstances. Thus, antitrust policies designed only to promote low concentration can be detrimental to economic efficiency.

Enforcement of Antitrust Policies

Antitrust policies are carried out in the courtroom. Antitrust officials, policymakers, and court officials face difficulties in distinguishing between behavior that is a conscious intent of firms to decrease competition and behavior that is the result of firms' responding to external changes. For this reason, the Justice Department and the FTC treat every market situation as unique. Before either agency takes action in altering market activities, it examines the individual firms and their activities. Firms judged to be in violation of antitrust laws may be ordered to stop their anticompetitive practices or to divest themselves of some of their assets by splitting the monopoly into several smaller competing firms. Sound economic theory is not always well represented in these court decisions. We will consider some specific cases that have been tried and the consequences of the decisions.

Cartel Policies. In 1927, the Supreme Court in the Trenton Potteries Case[1] held that price-fixing conspiracies were per se illegal under the Sherman Act, even though the act did not specifically prohibit price fixing. That is, attempts by competitors to fix prices would be found illegal regardless of whether the fixed price was actually above the competitive level.

The case involved the activities of the Sanitary Potters Association (SPA), a Trenton, New Jersey, trade association, whose twenty-three member firms produced 82 percent of the U.S. output of bathroom sinks, tubs, and commodes. The SPA published price lists that included suggested discounts and surcharges for six geographic regions; members following the SPA lists charged identical prices.

The question addressed by the Supreme Court was whether a lower court judge was correct in directing the jury not to consider the reasonableness of the particular prices charged. The Court held that "uniform price-fixing by those controlling in any substantial manner a trade or business in interstate commerce is prohibited by the Sherman Law, despite the reasonableness of the particular prices agreed upon."[2] Economic theory would support the

---

[1]*United States* v. *Trenton Potteries Co.,* 273 U.S. 392 (1927).

[2]See Phillip Areeda, *Antitrust Analysis: Problems, Text, Cases,* 3rd ed. (Boston: Little, Brown, 1981), p. 165.

Court's decision. If a large percentage of the firms in an industry agree on price, then it is likely that price competition has been abolished.

Merger Policy.   As we noted earlier, the Clayton Act, as amended by the Celler-Kefauver Act, seeks to limit corporate acquisitions that "tend to create a monopoly." Under the Hart-Scott-Rodino premerger notification system, most large firms contemplating a merger are required to apprise both the FTC and the Justice Department's Antitrust Division of their intentions. The agency chosen to handle the merger must decide whether to challenge it by seeking a preliminary injunction in federal court or to allow the merger to proceed without opposition. In the case of relatively small mergers, the antitrust authorities may become involved after the fact. In particular, a firm that is later found to have acquired another company in violation of the Clayton Act may be required to divest itself of the acquired assets in order to restore the premerger status quo.

An important aspect of merger law enforcement is the use of guidelines to establish which particular acquisitions will be challenged. For example, vertical and conglomerate mergers are not often challenged, but horizontal mergers that significantly decrease competition are. The merger guidelines issued by the Justice Department contain numerical standards that identify markets thought to be "unconcentrated" or "concentrated" prior to a merger. The guidelines set limits on the amount that concentration will be allowed to rise in each case before antitrust action is initiated. In 1968, concentration ratios were established for this purpose; in 1982, these ratios were supplanted by the Herfindahl index.

In 1966, before these indexes were in use, the Supreme Court considered the legality of a merger between two Los Angeles retail grocery chains, Von's Grocery Company and Shopping Bag Food Stores.[3] At the time of the acquisition, 1960, Von's was the third largest grocery chain in Los Angeles; Shopping Bag was the sixth largest. Together, the two grocery retailers accounted for only 7.5 percent of sales in the Los Angeles area, however. Despite the relatively small market shares involved in the merger, the Court held that Von's had violated the Clayton Act. The decision placed great weight on the fact that the number of owners operating single grocery stores in Los Angeles had declined from 5365 in 1950 to 3818 in 1961. This decline, the Court alleged, indicated a trend toward concentration.

In his dissenting opinion, Justice Potter Stewart called the Court's decision "a requiem for the so-called 'Mom and Pop' grocery stores . . . that are now economically and technologically obsolete in many parts of the country." He went on to say that the Court,

> through a simple exercise in sums, . . . finds that the number of individual competitors in the market has decreased over the years, and, apparently on the theory that degree of competition is invariably proportional to the number of competitors, it holds that the historic reduction in the number of competing units is enough under Section 7 of the Clayton Act to invalidate a merger . . . with no need to examine the economic concentration . . . , the level of competition . . . , or the potential adverse effect of the merger.[4]

---

[3]*United States* v. *Von's Grocery Co.,* 384 U.S. 270 (1966).

[4]Areeda, *Antitrust Analysis,* pp. 961–64.

X

If the number of firms in an industry is declining because of technological changes, economic theory suggests that the optimal size of firms is increasing. This change will naturally lead to an increase in concentration. According to economic theory, therefore, the merger probably should not have been prevented, especially since the two firms constituted such a small percentage of the market.

Price Discrimination.   Charges of price discrimination may also require subtle distinctions. In a private suit, the Utah Pie Company charged Continental Baking Company,[5] Carnation Company, and Pet Milk Company with price discrimination in the sale of frozen pies. Utah Pie, located in Salt Lake City, alleged that its three California-based competitors sold pies shipped to Salt Lake City at prices below those charged for pies sold nearer their own plants.

The evidence before the Supreme Court pointed to a highly competitive pie market in Salt Lake City. The price discrimination evidence appeared superficially correct in the sense that, given the cost of transportation, one would not expect the prices of the California firms to be lower in Salt Lake City. Accordingly, the Supreme Court found in favor of Utah Pie.

Some feel that the Court's decision does not square with some of the facts, however. For one thing, it can be argued, the prices charged by Utah Pie were consistently lower than the prices of its rivals throughout the price discrimination episode. Second, Pet Milk Company suffered substantial losses on its Salt Lake City sales. Third, Utah Pie consistently increased its sales volume and continued to make a profit while facing the alleged anticompetitive practices of its rivals. Finally, prior to the entry of Continental, Carnation, and Pet, Utah Pie enjoyed a 67 percent market share in Salt Lake City, and while the new competition cost Utah Pie a portion of its market, at the end of the price discrimination period the Salt Lake City firm still accounted for 45 percent of the pies sold in the area.[6] It appears to some observers that Utah Pie could have been using the antitrust policy to eliminate price competition and to gain a larger share of the market.

Natural Monopoly and Antitrust Cases.   Antitrust policies may also be inappropriately applied to natural monopolies. The Aluminum Company of America (Alcoa) was involved in antitrust litigation as early as 1912 on allegations that it had violated the Sherman Act by, among other charges, monopolizing deposits of bauxite (the crucial ore in aluminum production), conspiring with foreign aluminum firms to fix world prices, and entering into exclusive contracts with power companies guaranteeing that the power companies would not supply electricity to any other aluminum producers. In 1945, the U.S. Circuit Court of Appeals finally rendered its decision on charges brought by the government that Alcoa had monopolized the production and sale of virgin aluminum ingot.

The appeals court decision, written by Judge Learned Hand, is one of the most celebrated in American antitrust history.[7] Judge Hand, in overturning

---

[5]*Utah Pie Co.* v. *Continental Baking Co.,* 386 U.S. 685, 699 (1967).

[6]Areeda, pp. 1070–75.

[7]*United States* v. *Aluminum Co. of America,* 148 F.2d (2nd Cir. 1945).

a lower court decision favoring Alcoa, wrote that even though Alcoa's monopoly was "thrust upon it" and the firm "stimulated demand and opened new uses for the metal," the firm should not increase production in anticipation of increases in demand. He contended that Alcoa prevented new firms from entering by increasing its capacity as demand increased and that because of Alcoa's lower cost, no new firms could effectively compete.

Although the court found Alcoa guilty, it refused to dissolve "an aggregation which has for so long demonstrated its efficiency." The "problem" of lack of competition in the aluminum industry was solved at the end of World War II, when the government sold to Reynolds Metals and Kaiser Aluminum the aluminum production plants it had set up for the war effort.

This evidence shows that Alcoa had a natural monopoly and that **divestiture**—breaking the company into several smaller firms—was undesirable. Indeed, antitrust policies are generally ineffective when a natural monopoly exists. Antitrust legislation is best suited to stopping cartels, trusts, and conspiracies from eliminating competition when competition is the natural order.

Divestiture:
The breaking up of a single firm into two or more smaller, independent firms as a result of a legal decree.

An Economic View of Antitrust Cases

How well enforcement of the antitrust laws agrees with economic principles is a complex question with no simple answers. On the basis of our brief sketch of laws, agencies, and court interpretations, we can draw the rough conclusion that economic theory has not made a large impression on legal thinking. In the words of George Stigler, "Economists have their glories, but I do not believe that the body of American antitrust law is one of them."[8]

In particular, the courts seem to equate the degree of competition with the number of firms in an industry and to seek to protect competition by protecting competitors. This focus on the number of firms in an industry ignores the other dimensions of competition (number of buyers, entry and exit conditions, degree of product homogeneity, number of close substitute goods, and so forth). More important, the numbers game neglects the possibility that firms can grow relative to their rivals not because they use unfair methods of competition or expand by buying out their competitors but because they can serve consumers better at lower cost.

Multinational Firms

The economies of the world are becoming increasingly interdependent. Events outside our borders have an important impact on our economy—so much so that the U.S. economy should be viewed as but one component in the global economy. This global setting has important implications for U.S. antitrust and regulatory policies.

Many firms in the global economy operate as multinational corporations. These firms operate simultaneously in a number of countries. Many business arrangements fall under the heading of the multinational corporation. Firms may locate production facilities abroad to obtain lower labor and production costs; Ford Motor Company, for example, has production facilities in Mexico.

[8]George Stigler, "The Economists and the Problem of Monopoly," *American Economic Review* 72 (May 1982), pp. 1–11.

Other firms, such as RCA, make arrangements with foreign suppliers to produce products abroad for sale in the United States under the American firms' respective brand names.

Globalization of business firms and increased international competition will make the U.S. economy more competitive. If U.S. producers have high costs, they will lose market share to foreign competitors. The rise of imported cars in the United States aptly illustrates this point. Similarly, the presence of excess profits in the U.S. economy will attract the entry of foreign competitors. To some extent, then, international competition is a substitute for U.S. antitrust policy.

The proliferation of multinational firms is not without its troubling aspects, however. Multinational firms owe allegiance to no particular country; they can operate wherever they please, holding out the prospect of jobs and incomes to competing countries for promises of a less strict regulatory and antitrust environment. Moreover, these large firms may find it easier to collude and to behave oligopolistically across international markets. In short, multinational firms may be better equipped to undermine competition.

Multinational firms are a mixed economic blessing. Their impact on competition must be assessed on a case-by-case basis. However, one cannot adequately assess the role of competition and competitive policy in the U.S. economy without considering these firms.

PUBLIC POLICY: REGULATION

Antitrust policies are basically designed to maintain competition when competition can exist. Therefore, the antitrust policies are not very effective when a natural monopoly exists. How does the public avoid the potential problems of monopoly when only one firm can survive in an industry? Price regulation is offered as a solution to some of the problems that can arise under these circumstances. Governments may attempt to regulate prices to keep them low for consumers' sake or may even establish agencies controlling the activities of specific industries. But like antitrust litigation, these regulatory efforts may have unwanted economic effects.

Regulatory Agencies

Broadly, regulation is any administrative or legal attempt to influence markets for goods and services. Government at any level can create regulation, which takes the form of subsidies to businesses, municipal zoning commissions, rate regulation of telephone and electricity services, legal support of occupational licensing, or any other attempt to intervene in markets.

In the United States, regulation by administrative tribunals, or commissions, is a compromise between outright government ownership and free-market functioning. Since legislative bodies (Congress, state legislatures, city councils) are ill-equipped to directly regulate industries themselves, the regulatory commissions they set up deal with monopolistic imperfections such as natural monopoly and market failure. The first such commission at the federal level was the Interstate Commerce Commission, established by the

Act to Regulate Commerce to regulate the rates and practices of interstate railroads (see Table 1). The ICC and all other administrative commissions at all levels of government extend the legislative power of government with members appointed by the administrative branch (the president, governors, mayors, or city councils).

Within the limits set forth by the respective legislative bodies that create them, commissions do a good deal of rule making and "quasi-judicial" decision making. On some major points of law, commission decisions may be brought before state or federal courts, but the regulatory commissions regulate industries or services for the most part autonomously.

What are the industries and services that have been subjected to commission regulation in the United States? As you can see from Table 1, electricity, gas, and telephone services followed the railroads into regulation early in this century. A surge of new federal regulations in the 1930s brought interstate commerce in electricity, natural gas, broadcasting, telephone, ocean shipping, airlines, and securities issuance under the regulatory umbrella. This period produced the Securities and Exchange Commission (SEC), the Federal Communications Commission (FCC), and the Food and Drug Administration (FDA), among others. Recent federal regulatory activity has focused upon such matters as industrial health and safety, automobile safety and fuel economy, air and water pollution, and the safety of consumer products. When state and municipal regulations—of occupations, zoning, rents, sanitation, highway safety, funeral homes, milk producers—are added to federal regulations, practically no area of the economy remains untouched by regulation.

OSHA [handwritten margin note]

The Purpose of Regulation

Economists hold varying interpretations of how and why regulatory policies emerge. In a natural monopoly the market fails to provide goods and services in quantities and at prices that would prevail under competitive conditions. However, there are many regulations in businesses and professions where the market does seem to provide goods and services at competitive prices and quantities. Why, for example, are physicians, lawyers, nurses, and hairstylists subject to extensive regulations?

Some economists argue that regulation promotes the public interest by correcting market failures and improving economic efficiency. This is the **public interest theory of regulation.** Some consumer advocates and economists also think that regulation should be used to redistribute income—that is, to tax away income from wealthier to poorer consumers. However, most regulators (and legislators) shy away from this goal.

Other groups of economists believe that in many cases regulatory agencies are captured by the industry or profession they are supposed to regulate. This is the **capture,** or **interest group, theory of regulation,** wherein groups interested in the suppression of competition lobby legislatures and press regulatory agencies to obtain particular goals. Electricians, carpenters, barbers, and construction firms typically lobby at local or municipal levels for "standards restrictions" that limit entry into their lines of work. Physicians, lawyers, veterinarians, nurses, and architects have engaged in similar efforts at state and federal levels. Such occupational licensing has important economic effects—notably, to restrict entry into the profession and carefully limit competition. Unions, of course, have similar effects. On a larger scale, some

Public interest theory of regulation:
Maintains that regulations are contrived so as to promote the public interest by correcting market failures and improving economic efficiency.

Capture, or interest group, **theory of regulation:**
Argues that regulations are constructed so as to further the interests of the existing firms within a particular industry.

economists argue that whole industries have at times "captured" the agencies that regulate them: namely, railroads, the trucking industry, television networks, airlines, and coastal water transportation.

Regulatory agencies are said to be captured when an industry or a subset of firms within an industry can influence agency activity to the benefit of the industry. This might be accomplished by agency employment of industry partisans or "experts," by hiring agency staff within the industry *after* their agency tenure, by bribes, or by other means. Administrative bodies are appointed to balance the benefits and costs of imposing regulations. Regulations always benefit some industry or some consumers and impose costs on others. Legislators frequently must weigh the benefits they receive from proponents of regulation (in terms of votes, money, and other perquisites) against the costs they incur from imposing regulation (also in terms of votes and support). Proponents of the capture theory argue that this process redistributes wealth based upon politicians' self-interest. They argue, further, that consumers, who do not have a large pro rata stake in legislation and regulation, often get shortchanged. The stronger interests of industry tend to dominate.

TABLE 1   Major U.S. Regulatory Agencies

A great deal of industry regulation was passed in the 1930s, including that related to telephone service, pipelines, and broadcasting. More recent regulation has centered on health, safety, and the environment.

Agency	Year Established	Jurisdiction
Economic Regulation		
Interstate Commerce Commission (ICC)	1887	Interstate railroads (1887) Interstate trucks (1935) Interstate water carriers (1940) Interstate telephone (1910–1934) Interstate oil pipelines (1906–1977)
State regulatory commissions	35 states 1907–1920; 50 states by 1973	Local electricity (46 states by 1973) Local gas (47 states in 1973) Local telephone (48 states in 1973)
Federal Communications Commission (FCC)	1934	Interstate telephone (1934) Broadcasting (1934) Cable television (1968)
Federal Power Commission (FPC) Federal Energy Regulatory Commission (FERC)	1935 1977	Interstate wholesale electricity (1935) Interstate natural gas pipelines (1938) Field price of natural gas sold in interstate commerce (1954) Oil pipelines (1977) Intrastate gas and gas pipelines (1978)
Federal Maritime Commission (FMC)	1936	Ocean shipping (1936)
Civil Aeronautics Board (CAB)	1938	Interstate airlines (1938)
Postal Rate Commission	1970	Established classes of mail and rates for these classes; set fees for other services (1970)
Federal Energy Administration (FEA) Energy Regulatory Administration (ERA)	1973 1974	Petroleum prices and allocation (1973)
Copyright Royalty Tribunal	1976	Copyright material (1976)

Sponsors of the capture theory tend to oppose most regulation. They argue that regulation may initially be directed at improving economic efficiency, but that politics will likely thwart the best intentions of regulators. Whether this is a correct assessment in all cases is questionable, but the capture theory does seem to apply in a number of instances, especially in occupational licensing. There are other reasons for opposing regulation, apart from the political problems identified by capture theorists. Regulation may be inherently inefficient at addressing market failures. An imperfectly functioning market, in other words, may produce better results than an imperfectly functioning regulatory apparatus. Consider some common forms of regulation and their attendant problems.

Price Regulation. Public utilities, such as firms that provide local electricity, telephone, gas, and water services, are often considered natural monopolies because their provision is usually associated with economies of scale. In this case, Figure 1 illustrates the relation between demand for and cost of these services.

TABLE 1   **(Cont.)**

Agency	Year Established	Jurisdiction
Environmental, Safety, and Health Regulation		
Food and Drug Administration (FDA)	1906	Safety of food, drugs (1906), and cosmetics (1938) Effectiveness of drugs (1962)
Animal and Plant Health Inspection Service	1907	Meat and poultry packing plants (1907)
Federal Trade Commission (FTC)	1914	False and misleading advertising (mainly after 1938)
Securities and Exchange Commission (SEC)	1934	Public security issues and security exchanges (1934) Public utility holding companies (1935)
CAB Federal Aviation Administration (FAA)	1938 1958	Airline safety (1938) (flight standards program only)
Atomic Energy Commission (AEC) Nuclear Regulatory Commission (NRC)	1947 1975	Licensing of nuclear power plants (1947)
National Highway Traffic Safety Administration (NHTSA)	1970	Automobile safety (1970), automobile fuel economy (1975)
Occupational Safety and Health Administration (OSHA)	1971	Industrial safety and health (1971)
Environmental Protection Agency (EPA)	1972	Air, water, and noise pollution (various environmental laws were enforced by several agencies 1963–1972)
Consumer Product Safety Commission	1972	Safety of consumer products (1972)
Mine Enforcement Safety Administration (MESA) Mine Safety and Health Administration	1973 1978	Safety and health in mining, especially coal mines (1973)

Sources: Dennis W. Carlton and Jeffrey M. Perloff, *Industrial Organization* (Glenview, Illinois: Scott, Foresman, 1990), chapter 23; Leonard W. Weiss, "Introduction: The Regulatory Reform Movement," in Leonard W. Weiss and Michael W. Klass, eds., *Case Studies in Regulation: Revolution and Reform* (Boston: Little, Brown, 1981); and Paul W. MacAvoy, *The Regulated Industries and the Economy* (New York: W. W. Norton, 1979).

FIGURE 1

An unregulated natural monopoly might charge the profit-maximizing price P_m, at which it would sell the quantity Q_m. With average cost price regulation, the price would be set equal to the firm's average cost, P_{AC}, increasing the quantity sold to Q_{AC}. Marginal cost pricing would result in even lower price and higher quantity: Price P_{MC} and output Q_{MC} result where the demand curve intersects the marginal cost curve. But such a policy would force the firm to operate at a loss, for the marginal cost is lower than the firm's average cost of production.

Two Forms of Price Regulation

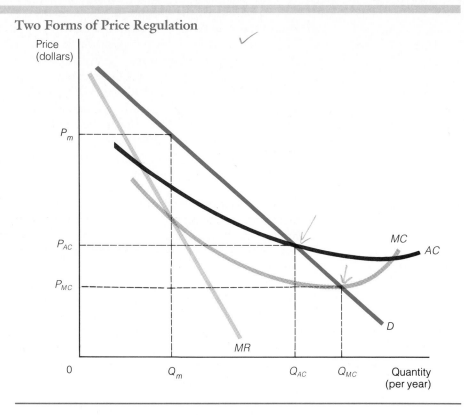

With no regulation, a firm holding a natural monopoly chooses the profit-maximizing price and output P_m and Q_m, which result in profits. If the local government chooses to regulate the firm to eliminate profits, it may force the firm to charge a price that just covers its average cost of production.

This price regulation is achieved through an agreement between the firm and the local government—the government allows the firm to exist as the sole provider of services, and in return, the firm agrees not to allow profits to rise above a normal rate of return and also agrees to meet the total demand for the product. The resulting price and output, P_{AC} and Q_{AC}, occur where the industry demand crosses the average cost curve. Economic profits are zero, since price equals average cost.

Average cost pricing:
A regulatory policy that causes a firm to charge a price equal to average cost, inducing the firm to produce an output such that economic profits are zero.

Marginal cost pricing:
A regulatory policy that forces a firm to charge a price equal to marginal cost, resulting in a socially optimal allocation of resources.

This **average cost pricing** is indeed a very popular form of price regulation. It seems to eliminate one of the problems of regulating a monopoly. However, it does not result in the optimal level of output. Many economists believe that price should instead be set equal to marginal cost, in what is called **marginal cost pricing**. The price and output that result from the intersection of the demand curve and the marginal cost curve, P_{MC} and Q_{MC}, are optimal. That is, when price equals marginal cost, the benefit to society of one more unit of output is just equal to the extra cost of that unit. However, as in the case shown in Figure 1, marginal cost pricing may result in losses for the firm. One of the basic problems of price regulation is that natural monopolies cannot be forced into the ideal competitive solution where $P = AC = MC$. Since marginal cost pricing may result in losses, average cost pricing may be the preferred form of price regulation.

Another problem with price regulation is that when firms are forced to earn only a normal rate of return, their incentive to achieve efficiency is diminished. Maintaining low costs of production is not rewarded with higher profits. For this reason we may see public utilities allowing costs to rise.

In spite of the potential problems of price regulation, direct control of industry prices became popular in the late 1800s. It was believed that government regulation beyond antitrust legislation could promote more efficient behavior than could market forces.

Problems with Price Regulation. Direct regulation of prices to achieve economic efficiency and to improve consumer welfare often proves to be self-defeating. When rates are inflexible over a period of time, surpluses or shortages are likely to occur with changes in demand or cost. The inability of a board of commissioners to accurately predict market forces can cause great inefficiencies in some regulated markets. Consumers in these markets do not pay prices that are based upon costs and, at times, are unable to obtain the amounts desired.

Rate of return regulation: A cap imposed by a regulatory commission on the allowable percentage that a utility can earn on its investments in capital and other resources.

In an attempt to establish prices that reflect costs, state and federal regulatory agencies have resorted, with regard to telephone and electric rates especially, to **rate of return** (ROR) **regulation.** Instead of setting the prices charged by utilities, regulators attempt to control prices and output *indirectly,* by placing maximum allowable rates of return on capital and other investments. Rate of return regulation is a direct attempt by state and federal regulatory commissions to limit to competitive levels the aggregate return that a utility makes on its operations. In calculating the allowable rate of return for a utility firm, a commission must estimate what a "competitive" rate would be for a comparable firm in the marketplace. For example, if an electric utility is earning 14 percent on its investment in capital and the allowable rate (computed from returns to similar businesses) is 11 percent, the regulatory commission will order price adjustments to increase the welfare of the utility's consumers. Calculations of an allowable or competitive return will differ among various commissions and jurisdictions for a number of reasons, including regional differences in costs and technology. Unfortunately, rate of return regulation may induce regulated firms to behave inefficiently. If the allowable rate of return exceeds the firm's cost of acquiring capital, the firm may overinvest in capital to increase the basis for its allowable return. Consumers might have to pay higher prices to support this overinvestment.

Product Quality and Price Regulation. To add to the problems of price regulation, it is impossible to regulate *all* dimensions of a market. For many years, the Civil Aeronautics Board regulated airline rates as well as entry into the airline services market, but the CAB did not regulate service quality. Since regulated airlines could not compete on the basis of nominal price, they competed by constantly changing and improving quality. Costs rose because of better meals, better in-flight service and more flights for more departure-arrival time choices, even though planes were seldom filled to capacity. Costs increased to equal (and sometimes exceed) the regulated rates imposed by the CAB. Deregulation of rigid rates—in this case, their elimination—was necessary for the survival of some airlines, and the policy was supported by many competing carriers. Presently, in the era of deregulation, airlines have better control over nominal rate schedules and are able to offer consumers many alternative price-quality "packages" of airline services. Deregulation, the relaxation or elimination of legal price or entry controls on firms or industries, is discussed later in this chapter.

What if the Monopoly Is Not "Natural"? Many modern economists have questioned the usefulness of regulation. In part, doubts about regulation are related to concerns that many markets may be mislabeled "natural monopolies." That is, they may not experience the constantly downward-sloping average cost curve shown in Figure 1.

The important issue for public policy is whether and to what degree a firm can sustain its monopoly power. If a monopoly can completely forestall entry in the absence of regulation, it is a **sustainable monopoly.** Such a firm is able to restrict output and, therefore, to reduce economic welfare; the firm might properly be the subject of regulation. On the other hand, if entry into any of the firm's markets is viable, the market is said to be **contestable.** If the firm's cost curves are U-shaped over the range of demand, unlike those in Figure 1, the need for regulation does not exist; market forces will ultimately generate competitive results. With a U-shaped cost curve, the average or unit cost of producing the good or service does not decline over the entire range of demand. If one firm can satisfy all demanders at lower and lower unit costs, entry by other firms is, if not impossible, far less likely.

If regulators are "captured" by the industry they serve, they may bar entry into an otherwise contestable market. Alternatively, captured regulators may permit the regulated firm to charge prices in excess of costs. The latter practice alone, however, merely encourages entrants. As technology changes, the regulated firm may encounter a great deal of competition from unregulated sectors in the market. If the regulated industries are not natural monopolies with falling average cost curves, in other words, regulation is probably unnecessary and *creates* inefficiency.

Sustainable monopoly:
A monopoly that can forestall the entry of competitors in the absence of regulation.

Contestability:
Characteristic of a market in which the entry of competitors is possible.

Health and Safety Regulation

As Table 1 reveals, much of the recent economic regulation deals with product safety and safety in the workplace. Such externalities are discussed in detail in Chapter 20. Here, we briefly consider the issue of safety in the workplace.

If employers are not liable to employees for accidents that result from unsafe work conditions, employers may have an incentive to scrimp on safety; safety equipment tends to be expensive. This does not mean, however, that employers will have no economic incentive to provide safety. The employer whose place of work is unusually dangerous will be at a competitive disadvantage in recruiting workers and must compensate by offering higher wages. The issue, then, is the degree of safety provided.

Theoretically, there are several ways employers could be induced to improve safety. The government could subsidize installation of safety procedures and equipment, but this would burden taxpayers. Alternatively, tax penalties could be imposed on employers with bad safety records. Or the liability for accidents due to negligence could be placed solely on the employer; this solution would require changes in current workers' compensation laws, which limit the employer's liability.

Most modern health and safety regulations do not employ any of these methods. The Occupational Safety and Health Administration (OSHA) and the Environmental Protection Agency (EPA) instead rely on a system of imposing standards for safe behavior, and the burden of maintaining these standards are on businesses. While health and safety standards have changed the behavior of business firms, they are costly to enforce, since each place of business must be inspected regularly by an OSHA employee. In addition, there is reason to believe that there are much cheaper ways to provide equal levels of safety.

To comply with government standards, employers might be required to provide hard hats for each employee, even though employees have little use for hard hats and generally refuse to wear them. As a consequence, money spent to comply with OSHA's standards often adds little to safety. If, instead, employers were provided with incentives to improve safety records (either by fines or by strict assignment of liability), they would have an incentive to spend money wisely to reduce accidents. Some safety measures currently required by OSHA would be eliminated, but other measures not currently required would be implemented. Although there is much dissatisfaction with OSHA's current safety standards, the current system is clearly preferable to one alternative—conflicting standards by various states.

Government Ownership

Socialization:
Government ownership and operation of a firm or industry.

An alternative to antitrust policy or regulation is government ownership, or **socialization.** When monopolies exist and their performance is less than socially optimal, government may choose to own and operate the firm in the interests of the public. We see this happen occasionally, more often at the state or local level than at the national level. For example, many public utilities such as electric services, water, and natural gas are owned and operated by local governments.

Socialization of firms is a solution to the monopoly problem, but is it an efficient solution? Ideally, the firm should approximate the competitive equilibrium. It should minimize its costs of production and charge a price equal to marginal cost. However, the performance of the firm depends on its managers. The managers must operate within the bounds allowed by the politicians who employ them, the voters, and the buyers of their services.

The efficiency of publicly owned firms is questioned by many economists. Many suggest that there is a lack of incentive for efficiency because there are no residual claimants. That is, no one may receive any profits acquired by the socialized firm, so managers have no reason to ensure low costs of operation or product quality.

To judge the efficiency of publicly owned firms, it is possible under some circumstances to compare their price, costs, and quality of service to those of privately owned firms in the same industry. For example, we can compare a locally owned electric firm's price and service to a privately owned electric firm's price and service. Many industries have both privately owned and publicly owned firms, such as education, medical care, telecommunications, television, garbage services, and employment agencies. However, in most situations we must compare government-owned firms with government-regulated firms, as in the case of electricity.

The U.S. Postal Service is a socialized firm that we cannot compare directly to a private firm, for the government prohibits the delivery of first-class mail by anyone except the U.S. Postal Service. However, there are many firms wishing to enter the mail delivery market, and occasionally they do so illegally. The suggestion that private firms could make a profit at the same price whereas the U.S. Postal System does not is an indication that the Postal Service is run inefficiently. Indeed, many government-owned firms must be subsidized by tax dollars.

Despite its lack of incentives for efficiency, socialization is still considered by some supporters to be an appealing alternative to trust busting or regulation in monopoly-prone industries. The price of medical services has been rising, and socialized medicine has been offered as a solution. AT&T (American Telephone and Telegraph) was divested through an antitrust case, but an alternative could have been to socialize telephone services. The possible consequences of such actions can be predicted by observing the prices and quality of services of similar industries that have been socialized in other countries.

Franchise Bidding Under Natural Monopoly

When government seeks to improve the efficiency of certain businesses, it may not be necessary for the government to regulate or operate the facility itself. As a compromise the government may acquire the property rights to supply the good or service and then **franchise,** or lease, the right out to private businesses. Cities as diverse as New York City and Scottsdale, Arizona, use this system to provide garbage collection, fire protection, and other public services. The practice, first formalized by the utilitarian philosopher Jeremy Bentham and his associate Edwin Chadwick, has been employed in European cities for centuries. (See Focus, "Franchising Funerals in Nineteenth-Century London and Paris.")

The idea of franchising is simple: Let noncollusive potential suppliers bid for the exclusive right to supply some good or service (garbage pickup or electrical utility services) by offering to provide the service at the lowest price. With enough bidders vying for the job, prices will fall to average cost, mimicking a competitive outcome. In terms of Figure 1, bidders would offer successively lower bids to supply the service until the price reached P_{AC}. The winning bidder would then sign a contract with the government for a specified period of time and with certain conditions mandated for the exclusive supply of the good or service. Theoretically, the government would not have to worry about the supply of the good until the contract expired and another bidding period was invoked.

Is this scenario likely? One of the problems with price regulation by a commission is that demand and costs change over time. Demand and costs will also change in markets where the good is "franchised" by government. If and when demand or costs change, the winning supplier will be making economic losses or gaining economic profits. Either way, the socially optimal price will not be charged and shortages or surpluses will appear. Allowances may be made for such changes in the initial contract, but negotiations between the government and the franchisee will likely be necessary. Such negotiations are akin to price regulations by the standard administrative commission, however, effectively nullifying the advantages of franchising over commission regulation.

Many other problems exist with franchising utility services through contract. Suppose you win a contract to supply ambulance services to the neigh-

Franchise bidding:
The privatization of traditionally governmental responsibilities via a bidding process.

FOCUS   Franchising Funerals in Nineteenth-Century London and Paris

Franchising is often presented as an alternative both to government ownership or operation and to more traditional forms of regulation. The argument is usually illustrated by natural monopolies such as gas, electricity, and cable TV services, but by no means is it limited to these cases. The most ardent proponent of franchising was nineteenth-century English social reformer Sir Edwin Chadwick (1800–1890). Practically no industry escaped Chadwick's scrutiny. Chadwick wanted the government to take over property rights to sell the good or service (milk, beer, police services, prisons) and then auction the rights to private businesses as a franchise wherever there was waste, or inefficiencies.

Consider Chadwick's case for franchising funerals in London. He estimated that between six hundred and seven hundred undertakers in London performed over a hundred funerals per day, so that about six undertakers competed for each funeral. Though the market situation appeared to be noncollusive and roughly competitive, Chadwick alleged that the funeral suppliers acted as monopolies. They could charge exorbitant prices because demanders were faced with high information and search costs when shopping for a funeral supplier. Such high costs, moreover, encouraged home funerals, which led to health and sanitary hazards— all the more reason to make funeral supply a fit object of franchising.

Parliament ignored Chadwick's proposals, but Munich, Frankfurt, Berlin, and Paris implemented his principle. Chadwick estimated the total cost of 28,000 interments in Paris at £80,000 in 1843, while the estimated cost of 45,000 interments in London under open competition was £626,000.[a] Under the Paris rate system, Chadwick estimated that London funerals would have cost £166,000, a saving of £460,000, which would be directly attributable to uniform rates within the various classes of services. Thus, in Chadwick's logic, monopoly power created by high information costs could be eliminated by franchising.

How good was Chadwick's case? In the first place, it is doubtful whether funeral service directors, then or now, have significant monopoly power. At the time of bereavement, most individuals rely on recommendations by friends and family when selecting a funeral home. (Most funeral homes today allow you to plan ahead.) Experience and reputation are important in the business, and long-standing firms represent high or acceptable quality levels.

Franchising funeral services by contract would entail— whenever implemented, even today—policing, enforcing, and contracting costs. If you lose the franchise, what happens to the "horses and carriages" and how would they be transferred? How long will the contract run? What happens if costs or demand change within the period of the contract, forcing losses on the funeral suppliers or abnormal profits? What happens to private property? Chadwick's proposals would apply whenever "waste" occurs in markets. It would apply not only in natural monopoly (or regular monopoly) situations, but also when *competitive markets are in disequilibrium,* as may have been the situation in the funeral example Chadwick describes. Chadwick failed to recognize that a real-world competitive system always operates with some friction. Even so, it is usually preferable to regulation, franchising, or government operations.

[a]Edwin Chadwick, "Results of Different Principles of Legislation and Administration in Europe; of Competition for the Field, as Compared with Competition within the Field of Service," *Royal Statistical Society Journal* 22 (1859), pp. 389–90. Few essays in the history of economics are more interesting.

borhood in which you live. Who will provide the ambulances? If the contract is of fixed length and you might not win the contract again, you may be stuck with ambulances if you cannot reach agreement with the new contract holder, or you may be forced to sell them at prices below their actual value. This kind of uncertainty means that you probably will not employ the optimal number of ambulances. If, on the other hand, the city supplies the ambulances, you will have little incentive to maintain them. Inefficient upkeep will mean that consumers will (eventually) pay more for services than they would under free and open competition. Since it is virtually impossible to devise optimal contracts that account for every detail, every eventuality, critics of franchise bidding argue that commission regulation might be preferable in natural monopoly situations.

Laissez-Faire

Antitrust policies, regulations, and government ownership are not the only alternatives to the monopoly problem. Under many circumstances, the forces of the market are capable—given enough time—of eliminating the undesirable performances of monopolies, cartels, and trusts. Over a long enough period of time, for example, entry and new competition will emerge, perhaps through technological innovation, to challenge existing monopolies. Leaving an industry alone so that it can be cleared of monopolist inefficiencies and high prices is called **laissez-faire** (allow to do) policy.

Laissez-faire:
A public policy of not regulating to any degree or interfering with market activities (from the French, meaning, roughly, "allow to do").

Natural Shifts in Market Power. To understand how markets can be self-correcting, let us examine the circumstances facing a natural monopoly.

Natural monopolies exist because of the special relation between industry demand and the firm's average cost. In an industry in which the demand curve intersects the firm's average cost curve at a point where average cost is still declining due to economies of scale, as in Figure 2, only one firm will survive, and profits will exist. These monopoly profits motivate competition from other firms.

New firms will want to reap the potential profits, and their profit-seeking activities can limit the welfare loss due to monopoly. For example, many entrepreneurs may attempt to discover and produce substitutes for the monopolist's product, or they may attempt to create a new technique of production

FIGURE 2

The monopoly with no threat of entry charges price P_M and sells quantity Q_M. However, the threat of entry of new firms may be diminished if the monopoly charges a price, such as P_E, below the potential entrant's average cost. The entry-limiting price is still above the monopoly firm's average cost, which is kept low through economies of scale. Limit pricing in effect maximizes the firm's long-run profits and diminishes the adverse social effects of a monopoly.

Limit-Entry Pricing

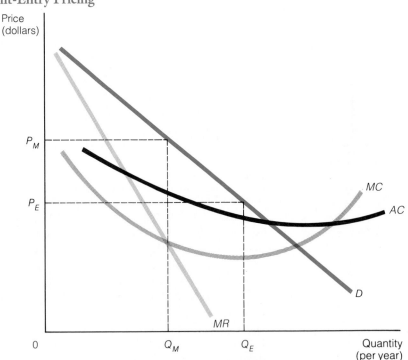

Contestable mkts

that allows them to produce the same product on a smaller scale of production with equally low cost.

Limit-entry pricing:
A pricing strategy of a firm that discourages entry by setting price below the short-run profit-maximizing price.

Without the threat of entry, the monopolist may charge price P_M, the typical profit-maximizing price. However, if new firms are on the verge of entry, then the monopolist may engage in **limit-entry pricing.** The monopolist may drop to a price lower than P_M, such as P_E in Figure 2. The entry-limiting price P_E must be low enough that new firms are not able to survive. Though designed to squeeze out potential rivals, this activity in effect allows the monopoly to maximize its long-run profits, since demand is infinitely elastic at price P_E in the long run. If the firm raises prices above P_E, it will lose customers through time to new entrants.

$\uparrow D_{IND} \Rightarrow$ entry) $\downarrow$ in
$\downarrow$ input p $\Rightarrow$ opt$^{\ell}$
Δ tech^y $\Rightarrow$ plant
(k-int^{ve}) size

The monopoly power of a firm may diminish in the long run anyway. The monopoly exists because of the particular demand-cost relation. Through time we expect demand and costs to change. New firms can enter and survive if industry demand increases or if prices of inputs and technology change in such a way that the optimal plant size decreases. Because the economy is truly dynamic, we expect to see the optimal number of firms and concentration ratios rise and fall in many industries, including monopolistic industries. Just because a monopoly exists now does not imply that it will be there forever. According to laissez-faire thinking, there may be no need to intervene in certain monopolized industries because the monopolies may eventually disappear anyway.

The situation illustrated in Figure 2, with the demand curve intersecting the average cost curve where there are economies of scale (*AC* is falling), represents the usual natural monopoly. The figure also represents the situation believed to exist for public utilities such as electric companies. If there are economies of scale, then firms with low rates of output, such as electric companies in small towns, should have higher average costs and thus higher prices than electric companies in larger towns with high rates of output. If we do not observe this relation, then natural monopolies no longer exist, and the firms are monopolies only because the local authorities grant them monopoly rights. Indeed, it is difficult to find a free-market monopoly—one that exists without monopoly rights granted by government.

THE MOVEMENT TO DEREGULATION

Deregulation:
The removal of some or all government regulations from a previously regulated industry in an effort to improve the allocation of resources.

In addition to simply leaving monopolized industries alone, a laissez-faire policy might dictate removing previous regulations—**deregulation** of the industries. Firms in regulated industries often attempt to use regulatory agencies to promote the firms' profits. Government regulation has often protected the very companies that antitrust laws and regulations are intended to suppress. In particular, regulatory limits on the entry of new firms into an industry and on the prices charged by existing companies can give the existing firms a degree of market power they could not otherwise achieve.

That regulation is more costly to society in many cases than the benefits it produces or that regulation has only negative effects was first perceived by economists in the 1960s and early 1970s. Nobel Prize–winner George Stigler demonstrated that state electrical utility regulation had done little to reduce prices and price discrimination and to suppress monopoly returns in that industry.[9] Glaring inefficiencies and misallocations of resources on railroads and airlines also brought the public's attention to the problem. During the Carter and Reagan administrations, portions of the transportation, banking, telecommunications, and natural gas industries were deregulated. Table 2 shows the major deregulation decisions.

Two examples of limited deregulation have occurred in the interstate trucking and airline industries. Until 1980, the Interstate Commerce Commission severely restricted entry of new firms into the trucking industry, as well as price competition among firms. The Motor Carrier Act of 1980 decreased the ICC's ability to restrict new entry, and the number of firms has increased by several thousand; prices have fallen 20 percent. In the airline industry the Civil Aeronautics Board set passenger fares and restricted entry until the Airline Deregulation Act in 1978. From then until the CAB's demise in late 1984, the CAB's ability to restrict price competition and entry was severely limited. Deregulation results in the airline industry have been similar to those in trucking. The number of firms has increased and prices have fallen. Since deregulation, some trucking and airline firms have also gone bankrupt—exactly what one would expect of inefficient firms facing competition. Concentration has decreased in both industries.

Deregulation has also had distributional effects—some parties or firms benefit, while others must bear new costs. Problems may emerge when only *part* of an industry is deregulated. The partial deregulation of railroads and the distributional effects of realigned price policies have led to self-interested pressures on Congress for *reregulation* of these transport firms. (See Economics in Action, "Captive Shippers and Attempts to *Re*regulate the Railroads.") Most of these efforts, however, pit particular interests against the public interest. Whenever public policies are debated in a political arena, some interests will be overrepresented.

CONCLUSION

A purely competitive free market is impersonal and unforgiving. It forces efficient behavior by eliminating firms that are not able to achieve the minimum cost of production. No special-interest groups can reap profits because a competitive market acts as an impartial arbitrator in the task of resource allocation. However, certain market conditions can lead to the survival of only a few firms. In such cases, pure competition cannot exist, and firms are not forced into the socially optimal solution.

We have examined several forms of public policy that are aimed at preventing poor market performance. Each of these—antitrust, regulation, socialization, and laissez-faire—has its merits, but no public policy can achieve the efficiency generated by a competitive market. When imperfect competition exists, our best solutions are themselves imperfect.

Not only are our best solutions theoretically imperfect, but actual government policies appear to be schizophrenic. One action attempts to increase

---

[9]George J. Stigler and Claire Friedland, "What Can Regulators Regulate? The Case of Electricity," *Journal of Law and Economics* 5 (1962), pp. 1–16.

TABLE 2 Major Deregulation Decisions, 1968–1989

Major deregulation initiatives with respect to communications, transportation, and the financial industry have spanned five administrations.

1968	The Supreme Court permits non-AT&T equipment to be connected to the Bell System.
1969	MCI is permitted to connect its long-distance network with local phone systems.
1970	Interest rates are deregulated on bank deposits of $100,000 or more.
1972	The Federal Communications Commission (FCC) establishes a domestic satellite open skies policy.
1975	The Securities and Exchange Commission ends fixed brokerage fees for stock market transactions.
	Rate bureaus for railroads and trucking firms are prohibited from protesting independent rate filings.
1976	The Railroad Revitalization and Regulatory Reform Act of 1976 partially deregulates railroads and makes rate setting more cost-based.
1977	Deregulation of air cargo gives airlines more freedom in pricing.
1978	Congress partially decontrols natural gas.
	The Occupational Safety and Health Administration revokes 928 "nit-picking" rules.
	The Civil Aeronautics Board is phased out, eliminating controls over airline entry and prices.
	The Environmental Protection Agency permits emissions trading.
1980	The FCC removes most federal regulation of cable TV and of equipment in consumers' premises.
	The Motor Carrier Act eliminates barriers for new entries and permits operators to establish fares and routes with little oversight by the Interstate Commerce Commission.
	The Depository Institutions law phases out interest rate ceilings and permits savings and loans and banks to offer interest-bearing checking accounts.
	The Staggers Rail Act enables railroads to adjust rates without government approval and enter into contracts with shippers.
1981	President Reagan decontrols crude oil prices and petroleum allocations.
	The FCC removes many radio regulations.
1982	A new bus regulatory statute allows intercity bus companies to change routes and fares.
	The Garn-St. Germain Act allows savings and loans to make more commercial and consumer loans and removes interest rate differentials between banks and savings and loans.
1984	As part of an antitrust settlement, AT&T agrees to divest local operating companies.
	Individual ocean shipping companies are allowed to offer lower rates and better service than shipping "conferences."
1986	Trading of airport landing rights allowed.
1987	Sale of Conrail.
	The FCC eliminates fairness doctrine.
1989	Natural Gas Wellhead Decontrol Act.

Sources: Dennis W. Carlton and Jeffrey M. Perloff, *Industrial Organization* (Glenview, Illinois: Scott, Foresman, 1990), chapter 23; Murray Weidenbaum, *The Benefits of Deregulation* (Contemporary Issues Series 25, Center for the Study of American Business, Washington University, December 1987); Tenpao Lee, C. Phillip Baumel, and Patricia Harris, "Market Structure, Conduct and Performance of the Class I Railroad Industry, 1971–1984," *Transportation Journal* 26 (1987), pp. 54–66; and Robert N. Hahn, "Regulation: Past, Present, and Future," *Harvard Journal of Law and Public Policy* 13 (Winter 1990), p. 183.

competition and reduce profits, while other actions promote monopolies and their profits. The reason for these contradictions is that public policies are formulated in a political arena and not by impartial economic theorists or forces. An understanding of public choice theory—to be explored in Chapter 22—can tell us more about public policies in monopolized industries.

SUMMARY

1. Antitrust laws are basically designed to promote and maintain competition in the economy.
2. Price regulation allows the existence of monopoly but attempts to decrease the social loss by imposing a particular pricing policy. However, price regulation may decrease the firm's incentive to maintain efficiency. Regulation of competitive industries has resulted in government-managed cartels.
3. Government ownership as an alternative to monopoly can prevent higher-than-normal profits. However, a government-owned business is not forced by the market to maintain efficiency.
4. Franchise bidding is an attempt to assure that competitive prices will be charged without destroying incentives for efficiency.

5. Economic regulation has the potential to achieve results in the public interest. However, economic groups that are harmed by or that could benefit from regulation have an incentive to capture the regulatory process and frustrate regulations conceived in the public interest.
6. Since regulation is inevitably imperfect, the existence of a less-than-perfect unregulated market does not necessarily justify regulation.
7. A laissez-faire system is an alternative to active public policy. Under some circumstances this policy to leave the market alone is clearly preferable.

KEY TERMS

natural monopoly
antitrust policies
regulatory policies
predatory pricing
divestiture
public interest theory of regulation

capture, or interest group,
    theory of regulation
average cost pricing
marginal cost pricing
rate of return regulation
sustainable monopoly

contestability
socialization
franchise bidding
laissez-faire
limit-entry pricing
deregulation

QUESTIONS FOR REVIEW AND DISCUSSION

1. Why does government regulation sometimes act to enforce a cartel? Why do voters and consumers put up with such programs and policies? What effect would deregulation have on such an industry?
2. Blue laws outlaw Sunday sales in a given locality. From the point of view of economic regulation, explain who gains and who loses from such legislation.
3. How does rate-of-return, or profit, regulation affect firm behavior? Does this regulation promote production efficiency? Do we achieve the optimal output with average cost pricing?

4. Are local television companies natural monopolies? How could the answer be determined? If they are, would they want to be regulated?
5. Can public policy change an industry characterized as a natural monopoly into a competitive industry that results in competitive equilibrium?
6. Suppose that your university decided to have its cafeterias operated under a franchise bidding arrangement. Could the university assure that the franchisee maintained adequate standards in the food served?

Might the franchisee actually improve the quality of food served? Explain.

7. States uniformly require teachers of primary and secondary schools to be licensed, but they do not require the licensure of college professors. Between students and professors, which group do you think would be more likely to make demands for the licensure of professors? What does your answer say about your confidence in the capture theory of regulation versus the public interest theory?

8. Businesses and workers often have conflicting interests about worker safety. Can you think of some safety standard that both workers and businesspersons would oppose? One that they both would support?

9. Some economists argue that there is a trade-off between safety regulations and employment in a particular industry. Is it likely that tighter safety standards in, say, the textile industry will lead to fewer textile jobs? Explain.

ECONOMICS IN ACTION
"Captive Shippers" and Attempts to Reregulate the Railroads

Large portions of railway regulation were dismantled by the Staggers Act of 1980 in the face of the threatened collapse of the railway industry. The Penn Central had declared bankruptcy in 1970, and by the end of the decade, almost one-third of U.S. railroads were being managed by bankruptcy courts. Since passage of the Interstate Commerce Act in 1887, the railroads were professedly regulated in the public interest. In reality, railway regulation took on the nature of a rent-seeking game played by competing private interests. Some of these interests included the competing trucking and inland waterway transport industries, farming interests, regional interests—including those related to mining and port facilities—as well as the competing railway carriers themselves. Private interests were able to "capture" regulation and subvert the public's interest in a sound and viable rail transport system. Use of railway regulation to carry out social and distributional policies resulted in a nearly complete breakdown of rail profits, investment, and capital maintenance by the end of the 1970s. The Staggers Act of 1980 was in part an attempt to avoid an extremely costly alternative—nationalization of American freight lines.

The key provisions of the Staggers Act permit the railroads to set their own rates, within limits, and to engage in confidential contracts with shippers and purchasers of rail transport services. After 1980, rails could raise some artificially low regulated rates and lower other rates to attract new business. Prior to passage of the Staggers Act, the ICC often protected competing transport modes (such as trucking and intercoastal barge traffic) by imposing artificially high rates on the railroads. In short, the Staggers Act allowed rail line pricing to become more competitive, with rates more accurately reflecting costs of doing business. In addition, by permitting rails to enter confidential long-term contracts with shippers, the act allowed the rails to plan and conduct efficient capital investment.

The Staggers Act was not the immediate salvation of the railroads, but the industry has made significant economic progress since its passage. Improved cash flow and major cost reductions have resulted in increased profits, even in the face of lagging revenues. Maintenance and rail safety have improved, and industry expenditures for research and development are at record highs. Most important, federal subsidies to freight lines fell from $500 million in 1980 to $66 million by mid-decade.

Wealth redistribution is inevitable with deregulation. Private interests associated with the coal and utilities industries—among those who lost out in the deregulation of the railroads—have made demands on Congress for reregulation. The Staggers Act did not completely deregulate the railroad industry. The ICC retained rate-making authority in cases in which rail carriers are declared to have "market dominance" (an absence of effective competition), as demonstrated by revenues that exceed their variable costs by a prescribed percentage. Some shippers may be captive and subject to monopoly power if served by a single railroad with no alternative means of transport. Certain mining interests in Pennsylvania and West Virginia and electric utility companies who use coal for generating power in the eastern United States claim that they are captives of the railroads in this respect.

The case for reregulation is not particularly strong, however. Monopoly behavior is no longer assumed when only one supplier exists. Trucking and barge traffic are alternatives to shipping by rail. Extensive pipelines can transport coal and coal products in the form of slurry. Failing both intramodal (competition between rails) and intermodal competition (competition between rails and other transport modes), railroads are still subject to product competition. An electric utility is not a captive shipper unless it cannot substitute one input for another and has no *make or buy options*. A make or buy option is the decision to generate one's own electricity or to buy it from another utility, who—due to lower input costs—can generate it more cheaply. When confronted by high transport rates or other high input costs, a utility may "import" electricity from lower-cost plants for resale to its own customers. Such substitution often severely constrains railways' pricing.

Since deregulation, average freight rates on *all* goods have declined. Freight rates on coal have declined, but not by as much as on products such as farm goods. In spite of these facts, rent-seeking contests have developed to get Congress to force the rails to again artificially lower prices to utilities. Most proposals would amount to reregulation of the railroads, which likely would represent merely the first step toward nationalization. For that reason, the best solution is to let warring parties fight it out under the rules of competitive markets.

Question

Suppose a merger between competing brick companies ends competition in the industry. Will home builders be subject to exploitation by brick sellers?

20

Market Failure and Public Policy

Chapter 19 addressed some of the ways that private markets can fail to achieve ideal economic results. Monopoly was the primary culprit, with its attendant restriction of output and high prices causing a reduction in the economic welfare of society. Monopoly is a form of market failure—that is, a failure of private markets to provide goods and services in the right quantities at the right prices.

Market failure often arises from problems of incomplete or nonexistent ownership rights to basic resources. Owners of private property bear directly the economic results of the use of property and are therefore motivated to use resources efficiently. In contrast, when property is held or used by everybody, users do not bear the full costs of its use. Common ownership creates a conflict between the pursuit of self-interest and the common good.

Consider some examples. We are all familiar with the problem of litter in public parks or along city streets. Littering occurs because each individual is not directly assigned property rights for the use of common property. We do not ordinarily allow litter to pile up in our living rooms or automobiles because we are forced to bear the costs of our actions. We are not completely forced to bear the costs of public littering, however.

In this chapter we review the approaches to market failures. To improve on situations of market failure we must carefully weigh the costs and benefits of alternative policies. After reading Chapter 20 you should understand

- the nature of market failure and how market failures such as pollution and overfishing can be corrected.
- how calculation of costs and benefits of methods to improve market failure works as an economic tool.
- how the legal system—specifically assignment of rights to use property—might be used in market failure situations.
- the nature of public goods, their relation to market failure, and the means for promoting efficiency in government programs and policies.

Our discussion begins with analysis of the problem of commonly owned resources and how this problem is approached in three concrete cases: acid rain, the common stock of fish in international waters, and the oil pool.

Market failure:
A situation in which the socially optimal amount of a good or service does not get produced by the private market; usually stems from unclear property rights assignments.

THE ECONOMICS OF COMMON PROPERTY

Common ownership:
An arrangement whereby the property rights to a resource are nonexistent or poorly defined; by default, anyone may use or consume the resource.

The fundamental economic disadvantage of **common ownership**—the right to the use of a resource by anyone or by competing users—is the lack of incentive to invest in the productivity of the common property. Rather, each person with access to the resource has an incentive to exploit it and neglect the effects of his or her actions on the resource's productivity. This principle applies to both renewable resources such as air and fish and nonrenewable resources such as oil.

Global Pollution Problems

The most difficult and far-reaching market failures in the world today have been created by the progress of humanity itself. The Industrial Revolution brought economic development and progress to many, but it has also had an especially ugly side effect—pollution. Pollution stems from by-products of the production and consumption of goods and services. The problem, basically, is this: Gaseous by-products of industrial and agricultural production, such as carbon dioxide, methane, nitrous oxide, ozone, and chlorofluorocarbons, have collected in the atmosphere. At best, the collection of these gases has become undesirable; it may be, however, that our failure to control pollution in the past will have catastrophic effects now and in the future.

We know that the residue of the gaseous by-products of production returns to earth as acid rain. Acid rain kills trees, streams, even whole lakes. Besides damaging the ecosystem, acid rain speeds the deterioration of bridges and buildings. Even worse, many scientists warn of a "greenhouse effect," or global warming, which could have drastic effects upon weather, food production, sea levels, and the environment. Evidence shows a 25 percent increase in carbon dioxide levels over the past century, and these greenhouse gases will continue to grow. The warming effect could be an increase of between three and nine degrees Fahrenheit in mean temperature by the mid twenty-first century. This seemingly minor temperature change would have dramatic effects. Melting glaciers would raise the level of the seas, causing whole islands to disappear and altering coastlines everywhere. Shifts in regional weather patterns, brought about in part by warmer sea water, would bring drought to some areas and greater than normal rainfall to others, with profound implications for agricultural production. The ozone layer in the upper atmosphere is also being depleted by gaseous by-products. Holes in the ozone layer caused by pollution let in rays of the sun that encourage skin cancer, eye diseases, and immune system deficiencies.

Naturally, these problems have caused a great deal of debate among scientists, politicians, producers, and consumers. While the *extent* of the problem is hotly disputed, no one denies that a market failure of some magnitude does exist. In other words, the socially optimal amount of some good—in this case, clean, noxious gas–free air—is not being produced. Incomplete or nonexistent property rights to air have resulted in the failure of individuals, acting in their own self-interest, to conserve this resource.

Identifying the problem is simpler than solving it, however. Since pollution controls—such as automobile emissions standards or requirements that smokestacks be outfitted with scrubbers—are not free, resistance by producers and consumers to new and more severe regulations can be expected. Strong resistance is likely when the suggested solutions entail huge costs, particularly when the scientific evidence is under dispute. Further, the global nature of market failure and the potentially discriminatory effects of radical temperature change have not encouraged international cooperation. Some regions and countries may actually benefit from potential temperature changes. Countries whose pollution causes acid rain may not themselves bear the costs due to prevailing wind patterns in the atmosphere. Air pollution is a most complex common ownership problem. Everyone agrees that world governments should do something, but there is much disagreement on what should be done and on who should bear the costs. By comparison, problems associated with fishing and oil drilling seem easy to deal with.

Fishing in International Waters

In international waters anyone may acquire exclusive ownership of a fish by catching it, and no one has rights to the fish until it is caught. This system causes each fisherman to ignore the effect of the well-known biological law that the current stock of a species of fish determines its reproduction rate. Thus, fish harvested today reduce today's stock and thereby affect the size of tomorrow's stock and tomorrow's harvesting costs and revenues. Overfishing results because no single fisherman has an incentive to act on this bioeconomic relation. If all fishermen would cooperate to restrain themselves now, tomorrow's stock would be larger and future harvesting cheaper and more profitable. However, under competitive conditions, each individual knows that if he or she abstains now, rivals will not, and much of the effect of abstention is lost. Further, the reduction in future costs would accrue to everyone, not just to the abstainer. Hence each person has little reason to abstain, since the major effect is to lower others' future costs at some immediate present cost to the abstainer.

Sole ownership removes this dilemma. If only one person is fishing, he or she need not worry that rivals will not abstain. Alternatively, all the people involved could negotiate an agreement to abstain, and all would benefit. The fact that such agreements are not usually successfully negotiated is due to the costs of dealing with all current and potential people who will fish and the difficulty of ensuring that all abstain as agreed. A third method of dealing with this dilemma is government regulation.

Such regulation usually sets an annual catch quota. To allocate the quota, regulators rely on restrictions on technology or simply close the season when the quota is taken. Both means create difficult enforcement problems and potential economic waste. If the season is closed when the quota is taken, for example, excess profits are dissipated in competition among fishermen to buy bigger, faster boats and thus get a larger share of the quota. The season progressively shrinks, and resources stand idle or are devoted to inferior employments.

Drilling for Oil

Oil presents another version of the same common ownership dilemma (see Figure 1). Unlike fish, oil is technically nonrenewable. However, oil does move about, so pumping one well lowers the entire reserve and affects the pressure

FIGURE 1   The Problem of Common Ownership in Oil Drilling

If a fixed reserve of oil is owned in common, and the co-owners cannot agree to share the reserves, then each owner will likely try to pump as much oil as possible from the reserve. Doing so reduces the available reserves at a rate disadvantageous to both owners.

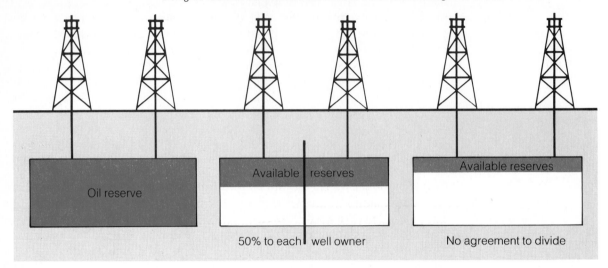

below other wells. These characteristics create a problem when more than one person has rights to the same oil reserve. For example, if the land above a reserve of oil is owned by two people, each has the right to drill for oil. But the only way to own the oil is to pump it to the surface. Oil in the ground belongs to the landowner only when that person pumps it. Herein lies the crucial lack of private ownership rights to oil reserves.

It may be more economically efficient to exploit an oil reserve with a single well than with two wells—not only because it costs more to drill two wells than one, but also because the existence of one well interferes with the other's technical ability to pump. If one person owned the property rights to all the oil, he or she would probably use only a single well. Likewise, if two landowners with rights to a common oil pool negotiate, both can be made better off by agreeing to split the proceeds of a single well rather than both drilling.

If they cannot negotiate, perhaps because of legal restrictions, or if a larger number of owners causes difficulties in communication, each may go ahead and drill. Once two wells are in production, there is an economically efficient rate of pumping for each well that a single owner would adopt to maximize his or her wealth. Nevertheless, if the two owners cannot agree on efficient exploitation, each will be tempted to pump oil at too high a rate, a tendency reinforced by the fear that the other is doing the same thing. In fact, even if negotiations are successful, it may be costly to monitor each other's pumping, and the agreement might dissolve in mutual cheating. The costs of negotiating and enforcement probably rise in proportion to the numbers of owners, as do the incentives for each to overpump because others are likely to do so.

The problems of market failure and common property resources encountered in modern society are not unique to contemporary modes of production, nor are they based on greed (a term that has no meaning in economics). There is evidence that overexploitation of resources was a common feature of primitive peoples. For example, the Anasazi Indians of the Southwest developed settlements in Chaco Canyon, Arizona, but failed to manage the forest product resources in the vicinity by replanting or employing conservation techniques. As a result, according to one account, the community's size and progress were limited and it was ultimately abandoned. The woolly mammoth disappeared from the North American continent as a result of rapid population growth and the absence of private property rights thousands of years ago.[1] In New Zealand, scientists have linked the disappearance of the moa, a huge flightless bird, to the overzealous exploitation by natives in search of food. The lessons of these and the modern problems of market failure, such as acid rain and overfishing, are clear. They are not the result of good or bad behavior, so blaming any population, ancient or modern, is unproductive. The lesson regarding common property resources is straightforward: What belongs to everyone belongs to no one; the deterioration and rapid exploitation of common property resources are clear implications of economic theory.

EXTERNALITY THEORY

Externality:
Benefits or costs of an individual's activity that the individual does not receive or bear.

Under certain circumstances, an individual's pursuit of his or her self-interest results in costs or benefits to others. This kind of market failure is called an **externality;** the costs and benefits are external to the individual who caused them. Obviously, any economic entity can create an externality, including firms, government agencies, and individuals.

Negative and Positive Externalities

A common example of an externality is a factory's emission of smoke as a by-product of production. If the factory is able to avoid responsibility for the consequences of its smoke—such as the expenses for painting soot-covered buildings nearby or laundering sooty clothes—the output of the factory will be excessive, in that the value of additional output is less than the additional costs of the additional output plus the damage. If the factory were held responsible for the damage done by its smoke, its costs would rise, its product would become more expensive, and it would produce less. This example illustrates a **negative externality,** a situation in which production entails costs for others, such as those living near a factory. Other potential examples of negative externalities are the exhaust emissions of automobiles, a neighbor's excessively loud stereo, low-flying jet airplanes landing at an airport, cigarette smoke in a crowded elevator, drunk drivers, the contamination of underground water by toxic chemical dumps, and so on.

Negative externality:
A situation that arises when an individual or other economic entity imposes costs on others without first compensating them.

---

[1]On these fascinating issues see two articles by Jared Diamond, "The American Blitzkrieg: A Mammoth Undertaking," *Discover* (June 1987) and "The Golden Age That Never Was," *Discover* (December 1988).

Positive externality:
A situation that arises when an individual or other economic entity creates benefits for others without receiving any compensation in return.

Positive externalities are benefits accruing without costs to the beneficiaries. Suppose a beekeeper and the owner of an apple orchard have adjoining land. The beekeeper's bees fly into the orchard and pollinate the apple blossoms, making the orchard more productive. If the beekeeper were to reap the consequences of the increased value of the orchard, the yield on his investment in bees would rise, and he would raise more bees. But as it is, his bees' social service is provided free. For both illustrations the point is identical: Externalities arise when one person's activities affect the well-being of others, either positively or negatively. Some other examples of positive externalities are the impact of public education on literacy rates, personal hygiene and health care, inoculation against contagious disease, charity, and invention.

Determining the Need for Government Intervention

To promote the general economic well-being through a more socially efficient allocation of resources, an ideal government would intervene to encourage the production of goods that generate positive externalities and retard the production of goods that yield negative externalities. These inducements to alter production may be indirect in that they focus on the side effects of production, but they nonetheless work to change the amounts of output produced, which generated the externalities to begin with. In the preceding examples, government might intervene to reduce the amount of smoke emitted by the factory or to increase the number of bees kept by the beekeeper. Intervention is not always called for, however. Individuals might settle such matters privately because the costs of intervening might be prohibitive.

To enhance the bees' contribution to the orchard's productivity, the orchard owner could contract with the beekeeper to supply more bees.[2] Alternatively, the orchard owner could raise his own bees. As long as the beekeeper's marginal costs of raising additional bees are less than the value the bees contribute to the orchard owner, it will be possible for both parties to reach an agreement that will leave each better off. Such private contracting in effect eliminates the apple-bee externality and makes public intervention unnecessary.

In addition to the possibility of private settlements, a second consideration when determining the need for government intervention in externalities is whether the externality is irrelevant or relevant. Externalities are trivial when the situation is not worth anybody's effort to do anything about it. The world is full of trivial externalities. You may not like the way a friend dresses, but not enough to say anything about it. Some people's unfailingly gracious and friendly behavior creates external benefits, and yet they are rarely complimented or rewarded for such behavior. The same goes for an attractive lawn. Neighbors reap external benefits from a well-kept lawn, but not so much that they would offer a subsidy to support the yard work.

Externalities are termed irrelevant when the externality generates a demand, but not a sufficient demand, by the affected party to change the situation. Your neighbor's messy yard may disturb your sense of propriety. You would be willing to pay her $50 a year to clean up the mess, but her price to

---

[2]See Steven N. S. Cheung, "The Fable of the Bees: An Economic Investigation," *Journal of Law and Economics* 16 (April 1973), pp. 35–52.

clean it up is $600 a year. In this event her yard will not be cleaned up, and the externality will persist. The messy yard is a nuisance but not enough of a nuisance to cause sufficient demand to get the yard cleaned up. In principle, the best thing to do with an irrelevant externality is to leave it alone because it costs more than it is worth to correct the problem.

A relevant externality creates sufficient demand on the part of those affected by it to change the situation. The neighbor's yard is messy, and the neighbor will supply a cleanup for $10. You are willing to pay as much as $50. In this case you can make an effective offer to correct the externality and reach a deal with your neighbor. With relevant externalities, it is worthwhile to correct the situation because the benefits of correction exceed the costs.

Correcting Relevant Externalities

Economic theory suggests that correction of relevant externalities can be approached in a number of different ways. In general, these can be categorized as defining property rights, taxing negative externalities or subsidizing positive ones, selling rights to create an externality, and establishing regulatory controls.

Establishing Ownership Rights. Externality problems generally persist because of the presence of some element of common ownership. The beekeeper's and the apple grower's ownership rights are clearly established and easily transferable. In such a situation it will be in the interest of both parties to conclude an agreement that places resources in their most highly valued uses. But in the case of the polluting factory, does the factory have the right to use the air as it pleases, or do the people in the surrounding community have the right to clean air? Air-use rights are indefinite and nontransferable: It is generally impossible for people to buy and sell rights to the use of air. In this case, there is no reason to believe that the pursuit of individual interest will promote the use of air in its most highly valued manner.

The establishment of ownership, then, is one way of eliminating problems associated with externalities. Since nonownership is a source of market failure, the creation of ownership is a means of correcting market failure. (See Focus, "An Exotic Common Pool–Externality Problem: A Bite of the Iguana?" for examples.)

An important analysis of the economics of establishing ownership rights was first introduced by R. H. Coase.[3] Coase posed the question, Does the legal assignment of property rights to one party or the other in an externality relationship make any difference to the observed market outcome? To keep the analysis simple, Coase assumed that the costs of bargaining and transacting among the parties were zero.

We will apply the Coase analysis to an example of air pollution—a factory belching smoke over a nearby community.[4] Figure 2 illustrates the analysis.

---

[3]R. H. Coase, "The Problem of Social Cost," *Journal of Law and Economics* 3 (October 1960), pp. 1–44.

[4]More subtle, widespread damages such as the loss of fish and trees to acid rain and the loss of work time to health impairment are not dealt with here. For the sake of simplicity, we consider only obvious costs to the local community. But if claimants organize and the source of pollution can be clearly pinpointed, the same analysis can be applied to the more subtle costs of air pollution.

FIGURE 2

In this graph depicting the Coase theorem, *MC* represents the externality imposed by the firm's pollution, and *MB* represents the profits to the firm from producing various levels of output (*Q*). The Coase theorem states that regardless of who is assigned ownership rights to the air, costless bargaining between the parties will result in the same market outcome at *Q*.

The Coase Theorem

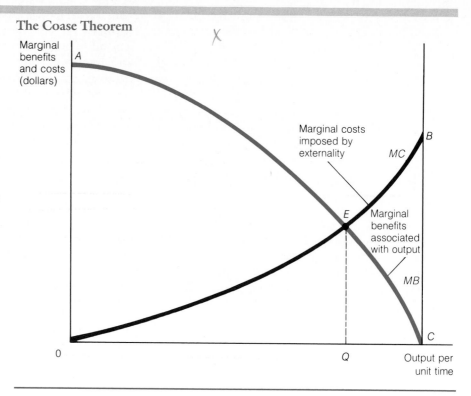

Firm output per unit of time is given along the horizontal axis. The marginal benefits (*MB*) to the firm of producing this output are given in dollar terms on the vertical axis. For the sake of this analysis, marginal benefits can be thought of as the net profits of producing additional units of output. The *MB* schedule therefore declines with increases in output because the rate of return on additional production generally declines (see Chapter 8). The marginal cost (*MC*) curve represents the externality caused by the firm's production and is also given in dollar terms along the vertical axis. The *MC* function measures the additional cost created at each output level by additional smoke. (Assuming that the amount of smoke the firm produces is directly related to its rate of output, more production will cause more smoke.) The *MC* curve rises as output increases.

Now we apply Coase's analysis. As an experiment, we give the ownership right to clean air to the homeowners in the surrounding neighborhood. Assuming that bargaining costs nothing, we can predict what will happen with the help of Figure 2. For rates of output up to *Q*, we observe that *MB* > *MC*. The firm's profits on additional units are greater than the additional pollution costs borne by the neighborhood; this means that the firm would be willing to buy and the neighborhood willing to sell the right of using the air to produce these units. Since the total cost of the externality caused by this output is represented by the area under the *MC* curve, 0*EQ*, a bargain can be struck between the firm and the neighborhood to produce *Q* by agreement on how to divide the surplus marginal benefit, *AE*0. Beyond *Q*, *MC* > *MB*. A bargain to produce these units cannot be reached between the firm and the neighborhood because the firm would not be willing to bid enough to obtain

FOCUS   An Exotic Common Pool–Externality Problem: A Bite of the Iguana?

The property rights regime that evolves or is chosen (common or private) has much to do with the scarcity of the resource. Common ownership—the right of anyone to use resources in unrestricted quantities—has a profound impact on the incentives of individuals to neglect conservation. Property rights systems tend to evolve at the point when increases in demand for a resource held in common begin to exceed the supply of that resource. In the case of *renewable resources* such as timber, shrimp, or fish, overfishing or timber stripping can have negative effects on future harvests. In many cases, however, the market devises means that alter property rights and save the resource. Consider an exotic actual example of renewable reptile resources that are being saved through the market evolution of property rights.

Travelers to Central America or to Mexico's Yucatan Peninsula may recall seeing the three- to six-foot-long common iguana for sale in markets or on the roadside. The locals so favor the flavor (much like chicken or alligator) of these reptiles that their populations prior to 1986 were being decimated. These forest creatures were being overhunted in rural areas because they were a common property resource. Overhunting by each individual (who had no incentive to conserve) imposed costs on all individuals by depleting the stock, principally through a reduction in the reproductive capacity of iguanas.

The iguana has met a brighter fate through the intervention of science and an alteration of property rights. Biologist Dagmar Werner, an East German scientist of the Smithsonian Tropical Research Institute in Balboa, Panama, and an expert on iguanas and their reproduction, is teaching Central Americans to cultivate iguanas.[a] By intensive *private* cultivation and nest modification, the hatching rate of iguanas can be improved from 2½ percent to 95 percent. High-protein diets of soya and fish meal cause iguanas to grow more rapidly than in the wild. Werner's work is encouraging the *campesinos* to grow and harvest iguanas for food, just as chicken is grown and harvested. While Central Americans are learning conservation and preservation of the wild iguana, the reptiles are disappearing over large sections of South America due to disappearing forests and hunting.

The economic lessons from such reproducible resources are clear. In the case of the iguana, an *economic value* must be given the resource for market forces to (at least partially) internalize the externality created by common property. Growing scarcities, moreover, are often the cause of a change in property rights systems from common to private, as in the modern private pond cultivation of food fish and certain crustaceans.[b] Finally, although there are many difficult details attached to specific cases, it is a general rule that the survival of many renewable resources is contingent on the assignment of an economic value and private property rights to them.

Iguana burgers, anyone?

[a]See "How to Have Your Iguanas, and Eat 'Em Too," *Discover* (November 1986), p. 7.

[b]Another interesting example of the (partial) private internalization of externalities (and the partial adoption of private property rights in production) is the case of crayfish (or crawfish) farms in Louisiana. Crayfish, long a staple in the diet of Louisiana Cajuns, underwent an enormous increase in demand over the 1970s and 1980s, primarily due to the popularity of Cajun cuisine. The result has been the same as for iguana—privately owned crayfish ponds augment the overfished catch in common waters. See Frederick W. Bell, "Mitigating the Tragedy of the Commons," *Southern Economic Journal* 52 (January 1986), pp. 653–64.

the right to produce these units. So Q, where $MB = MC$, is the equilibrium outcome when the neighborhood is given the transferable right to use of the air.

Suppose that a judge decided instead to award the firm the right to use the air as it chooses. What happens in this case? We go through the same analysis, but now we see that the neighborhood must pay the firm to produce less output. For up to Q units of output, $MB > MC$, which means that the neighborhood cannot offer a large enough sum of money to induce the firm to reduce its output and its smoke. Beyond Q, the situation is changed: The firm would be willing to accept an offer of money to reduce its output. Beyond Q, the smoke causes $EBCQ$ in damage to the neighborhood, and the benefits to the firm of this output are only ECQ. The neighborhood is therefore willing to make it worthwhile to the firm to reduce pollution to the point where $MB = MC$ at Q.

Provided that we have been logical, we have shown a simple but powerful result: No matter who has the legal right to the use of the air, the amount of pollution is the same. When the firm must pay to pollute, it produces Q. When the firm has the unfettered right to pollute, it produces Q. This is the central insight offered by the **Coase theorem:** In a world in which bargaining costs nothing, the assignment of legal liability *does not matter.* A certain equilibrium level of output and its resulting level of pollution will exist regardless of whether firms or consumers own the air.[5] Under the stated conditions of the Coase theorem, government intervention—in the form of pollution guidelines, tax penalties, and the like—cannot improve upon a settlement negotiated by those parties who are directly involved with the externality problem.

Coase theorem:
States that the amount of an externality-generating activity will be the same regardless of the assignment of property rights if the bargaining costs are small.

The Coase theorem provides a benchmark for analyzing externality problems. It shows what would happen in a world of zero bargaining and transaction costs. Many real-world externality problems can be analyzed with the Coase theorem, as long as the bargaining and transaction costs are low.

Nevertheless, using the establishment of ownership to correct externalities cannot always be relied upon to eliminate the difficulties of market failure because it may be exceedingly difficult, if not impossible, to establish ownership in some instances. Many externality problems do not fit the assumption of zero or low transaction and bargaining costs. In the factory smoke example, the neighbors of the plant are likely to be numerous, difficult to organize, and diffuse in their interests with respect to the air pollution problem. The widely dispersed sufferers of the smoke damage would face insuperable costs if they had to organize to purchase the agreement of the factory to reduce its emissions. If the firm had the right to pollute, it is not likely that the neighborhood could overcome these problems, get organized, and offer the firm money to cut pollution back to Q in Figure 2. Looked at the other way around, if the neighborhood owned the air space, the firm would find it costly to track down all homeowners and arrange for the purchase of their consent to produce up to output Q.

No matter who held the right to use of the air, bargaining costs would be high, and the likelihood is that nothing would be done to correct the situation. Some homeowners, for example, would seek to hold out for a larger payment from the firm where the neighborhood had the property rights to the air. This would jeopardize the possibility of a bargained agreement. The costs of defining and enforcing a system of ownership can be so high that some system of taxation or administrative control would be more effective than reliance on the definition of property rights and any contractual arrangements.

Taxing or Subsidizing Externalities. A seemingly simple way of dealing with externalities is to tax activities such as pollution that create negative externalities and to subsidize activities such as beekeeping that create positive exter-

---

[5]The Coase theorem also marked the beginning of a new field in economics called *law and economics,* which studies the impact of legal rules and institutions on the economy; the Coase theorem, for example, analyzes the role of legal liability assignment in an externality problem. Many law schools have specialized fields in law and economics, and much of the literature in this area is published by the *Journal of Law and Economics* and the *Journal of Legal Studies.*

nalities. Many complexities surround such a simple-sounding prescription, however. How could a negative externalities tax be levied? Against the product the factory produces? Against the amount of smoke it emits? Either solution might create burdens on the industry and on consumers that are not necessary in cleaning up the environment. Similarly, how would a subsidy for positive externalities be worked out? Based on the honey produced by the beekeeper? Based on the number of bees kept? Despite such complexities, the essential idea of taxing the negative externality and subsidizing the positive has a rich tradition in economic theory.[6]

Marginal private cost:
The change in total cost that only the firm bears when output changes by one unit.

Marginal social cost:
The change in total cost borne by the economy as a whole (the firm plus all others, or society) that results from a one-unit change in the firm's output.

To understand the effects of taxation, consider the pollution problem in terms of output decisions facing individual firms. In deciding what output to produce, the competitive firm compares marginal cost and marginal revenue. Marginal cost in this context means **marginal private costs** (MPC), the extra costs that the firm must pay to increase its output. These costs do not include externalities. By definition, an externality imposes costs on others that are not reflected in the private costs of the firm. The full costs to society of an increase in the firm's operations are summarized as **marginal social costs** (MSC). MSC are equal to MPC plus the externality costs (E): $MSC = MPC + E$. When there is no externality at the margin ($E = 0$), then $MSC = MPC$.

This analysis can be applied to the competitive industry. Consider the situation depicted in Figure 3. These are the same types of graphs that we used in Chapter 9. Figure 3b shows that an industry is initially in equilibrium at E_1 where industry demand (D) and supply (S_1) intersect. Under these conditions the firm (Figure 3a) reacts as a price taker to P_1 and sets its MPC curve equal to P_1 ($= d_1 = MR_1$). The competitive firm, acting on the basis of marginal private costs, produces q_1 units of output.

Notice, however, that the firm's MSC curve lies above the MPC curve at all levels of output; for example, it exceeds MPC by ab at q_1 units of output. The MSC curve traces the externality that the firm's operations impose, such as the amount of damage that the firm's air pollution causes in the surrounding neighborhood.

Our question is this: What can government do to improve the situation? Basically, government must get the firm to behave as if its marginal cost curve is MSC, not MPC. In this way the competitive firm would equate MSC to price, and the externality would be "internalized" in the firm's output decision; that is, the firm will produce the output where $MSC = P$, which is the correct output from society's point of view. (As we saw with the Coase theorem, the socially optimal level of pollution is not zero. At some point, clean air costs more than it is worth.)

This solution can be obtained by imposing a tax on the industry's output that reflects the degree to which MSC and MPC diverge. Such a tax is illustrated in Figure 3 as an excise tax imposed on the firm of ab per unit. The impact of the pollution tax is to shift the marginal cost curve of the firm from MPC to MSC. This change is reflected at the industry level by a shift in the industry supply curve from S_1 to S_2. The tax forces the competitive firm to account for the externality in choosing its output level. It thus chooses the socially efficient output level where $MSC = P_2$, or where marginal social costs are equal to marginal private benefits.

---

[6]The tax-subsidy approach to externalities is often called *Pigovian*, after A. C. Pigou, author of *The Economics of Welfare* (London: Macmillan, 1920).

FIGURE 3   X   **The Effects of a Tax on an Externality**

(a) A pollution excise tax of *ab* per unit is placed on the output of the firm to correct the externality. The marginal private costs facing the firm are given by *MPC,* and marginal social costs are given by *MSC.* The tax raises the *MPC* curve to become identical with the *MSC* curve. In such a way the firm is made to account for the externality in its decision about how much output to produce. (b) At the industry level, the pollution tax reduces industry supply to S_2, and the pollution tax is paid by both consumers and producers, though the proportions need not be equal, as depicted in Figure 3b.

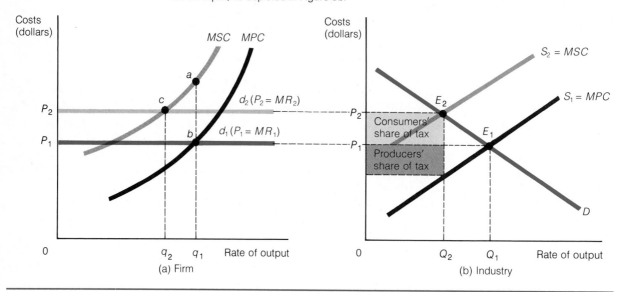

Who pays the pollution tax? As we see in Chapter 21, part of the tax will be paid by producers and part by consumers. Consumers will face a higher price for the industry's output, but the price will not rise by the amount of the tax. The producer thus absorbs some of the pollution tax.

Selling Rights. A simple alternative to the tax example is to establish a market for externality rights such as the right to pollute. In this approach, government sets an allowable level of pollution and sells the right to pollute. In theory, this market works like any other market. Those who value the pollution rights most highly will buy and hold them. Firms will make decisions about whether it is less costly to install pollution-control equipment or to buy pollution rights. Government does not tell industry how to clean up the air. It sets the allowable level of pollution and lets firms decide how to control their pollution. This marketlike approach to pollution control has the virtue of ensuring that the acceptable level of pollution is reached at least cost.

Difficulties arise in such a scheme, however. Indeed, whether it chooses to tax pollution or sell pollution rights, government must somehow estimate what the "optimal" level of pollution is. The relevant knowledge in this case is economic rather than technical; the government's interest is less in determining the damage done by varying degrees of air pollution than it is in determining the values individuals attach to the different degrees of damage. Such knowledge is not easy to come by. Moreover, both a tax scheme and a pollution rights scheme must be monitored and enforced by government. Without such actions tax evasion and pollution without permit will be serious problems.

Setting Regulations. For such reasons government has most often not adopted an economic approach to control externalities such as pollution. More typically, government has sought to control pollution and other externality problems through direct regulation of industry. In the case of pollution, regulation generally consists of detailed rules about the technology that firms must adopt to control pollution. Firms in certain pollution-prone industries must install special pollution-control equipment as a condition of being able to stay in the industry. This is a practical way to control pollution. Each firm must clean up its emissions in the prescribed manner. In contrast to the pollution-rights approach, however, direct regulation does not allow firms to choose the most efficient means of staying below the allowable level of pollution. Firms cannot choose to pollute or not pollute or select among different types of pollution-control technologies. They must follow the rules laid down by government. Moreover, these rules can affect different firms in an industry in different ways. Large firms, for example, may be better able to adapt to the technology required by government than small firms. Some small firms may be driven out of the industry as a result, and the large firms will benefit through higher prices and profits. Additionally, specific equipment and method requirements lessen the degree of flexibility firms have in responding to changes in pollution-control device prices and innovations in pollution-control technology. What may be an efficient method of pollution control at the time government regulations are established can turn out to be an economically inefficient method due to some new variable such as equipment price changes or the invention of a superior cleanup method. Getting the government rules changed may take time and be costly. With these considerations in mind, it is difficult to say whether the government-regulation or the selling-of-pollution-rights approach is the best way for society to deal with this problem.

Each approach to the problem of externality control that we have discussed—the establishment of property rights, taxation or subsidy, selling of rights, and direct regulation—has costs and benefits in different applications. In some cases, the establishment of property rights may resolve the externality. In other cases, like automobile pollution, some form of government taxation or regulation may be used to control the externality of pollution. No approach will yield a perfect solution to these problems. There will still be disputes among property owners about where one's property ends and another's begins. And government will not always act to resolve an externality in the most cost-effective way. There may, for example, be very little air pollution in Wyoming, which has fewer cars or industries, but new cars purchased there will nonetheless be required to have the same pollution control equipment as new cars purchased in smog-ridden New York.

Politics and Externalities. The attempted solution to real-world externalities problems often directly involves the political process. Solutions dictated by political forces do not necessarily produce economic efficiency. Consider, for example, the attempt to save several species of Gulf Coast sea turtles, particularly the Kemps Ridley turtle. Some environmentalists claim a major reason for the disappearance of the turtles is that many are killed in shrimpers' nets.

This alleged externality has been at the center of a protracted debate between fishermen, environmental groups, state governments, federal agencies, and legislators. Over the years, environmentalists have supported a technological solution to the problem—the use of turtle exclusion devices to be attached to shrimpers' nets. Sewn into shrimp nets, the cagelike devices are designed to permit accidentally snagged turtles to escape. Fishermen charge that the devices are ineffective and, more important, that they reduce the shrimp catch by up to 20 percent.

The debate became politicized, with some U.S. senators and representatives from coastal states arguing that the proposed devices would put unnecessary financial hardship on shrimpers. Most state legislators and state fishery commissions opposed mandatory use of the devices. The National Marine Fisheries Service (an agency of the Department of Commerce) has enforced implementation of the device, although Congress initially disapproved of the agency's spending federal money to enforce the proposed regulations. High costs of government enforcement due to the large number of shrimpers has meant spotty implementation of the exclusionary devices. Meanwhile, the turtle population continues to decline.

PUBLIC GOODS THEORY

As we discussed in Chapter 3, government affects the economic well-being of a society in two essential ways. Government provides and maintains a system of laws to protect and enforce property rights and to permit the free flow of goods through markets. And government provides various goods and services that are not ordinarily provided through the free-market system.

Public good:
A good such that, once produced, one individual's consumption of the good does not reduce or exclude the ability of other individuals to consume the good.

These government-provided goods and services fall into the broader category of **public goods**—goods such as radio broadcasts and highways that, once provided to one person, are available to all on a noncompeting or nonrivalrous basis. It is difficult or impossible to exclude anyone from the use of a public good, and its use by one person does not prevent its use by another. A nuclear submarine, for example, provides national defense as a public good for all members of a society. One member's consumption of national defense does not preclude another's consumption. The use of a lighthouse beam by one ship does not stop other ships from using the same beam. The consumption of a public good by one consumer does not impose an opportunity cost on other consumers; all can consume the public good at the same time.

A private good is consumed exclusively by the person who buys it. Its consumption by one individual precludes consumption by others. When Benny eats a cheeseburger, Barbara cannot eat the same cheeseburger. The concern here is not with the fact that Benny bought the cheeseburger and owns it in the sense that he has legal title to it. The concern is with a technical characteristic of consumption—that when one person is consuming a private good, it cannot be simultaneously consumed by other people. The consumption of a private good carries an opportunity cost: Consumption of the same good is denied to other consumers.

A mixed good embodies attributes of both private and public goods. An outdoor circus, for example, would seem to be a pure public good. Two people can watch the circus at the same time without interfering with each other's consumption. If the crowd gets large enough, however, the circus can become more of a private good because congestion detracts from each person's view. In other words, rather than being equally available to all, consumption becomes rivalrous; some people's consumption of the circus detracts and may even prevent other people's consumption. We say then that the outdoor circus is a mixed good. It has characteristics of both private and public goods.

It is important to keep in mind the difference between public goods and goods that are publicly provided. The concept of a public good refers to the attributes of the good and not to whether it is produced by government. Indeed, the public sector produces many private goods such as first-class mail delivery, and the private sector produces many public goods such as beautiful architecture. In other words, the supply of public goods comes from both the public and the private sector. As we will see, it is largely the costs of excluding nonpayers that determine whether a public good is privately or publicly provided.

Public Provision of Public Goods

How can a free-market system provide national defense? Once a defense system is provided, it is equally available to all consumers or citizens. Since individuals cannot be excluded from the benefits of military defense, who would voluntarily contribute to its provision? Most individuals would hold back in the expectation that someone else would provide the necessary funds, and then they would reap the benefits of military defense for free.

Lighthouses provide another illustration of market failure to provide public goods. A lighthouse's beam is available to all ships passing by, regardless of whether a particular ship pays for the light. Since it is difficult or impossible to exclude nonpayers from using the beam, individual shipowners probably will not contribute to the lighthouse, even though it provides an obviously valuable service for all shippers. To overcome this market failure, government assumes responsibility for the lighthouse. Through its power to tax, government can raise enough revenue to build and maintain the lighthouse.[7]

Public health services also illustrate the need for government to overcome market failure to provide a public good. At certain times when the public health seems in danger, such as the swine flu outbreak in the late 1970s, the government provides inoculations against disease. Individuals who are inoculated protect themselves against the disease. Their inoculation also protects those who are not inoculated. As a person becomes inoculated, the sources of contagion for the disease are reduced, so person A's inoculation reduces the odds that B and C, who have not been inoculated, will catch the disease. B and C theoretically owe A something for the protection, but would they pay for it? Obviously not, since they cannot be excluded from A's protection. Government's providing such a public health service is a way of overcoming the market failure in this case.

Not all goods provided to a number of people at once require government provision. In some cases, the costs of excluding noncontributors are low

---

[7]While the lighthouse has long served as an archetype of a public good, the private provision of lighthouses is a historical fact. See R. H. Coase, "The Lighthouse in Economics," *Journal of Law and Economics* 17 (October 1974), pp. 357–76.

enough that private firms will produce goods enjoyed cooperatively by many people. For example, a movie, a football game, and a concert are goods that are jointly provided to many consumers at once. In this respect these goods are like the lighthouse and national defense. The difference is that it is feasible for the producers of these goods to exclude those who do not pay for their provision, and so they can be supplied by private producers within the free market.

Free Riders

Free rider:
An individual who receives the benefit of consuming a public good or service without paying for it.

Sellers of private goods can exclude nonpayers from using the goods by charging a price for their use. Once a public good is produced, however, it is equally available to all consumers, regardless of whether they contribute to its production or not. Individuals who do not contribute to production and yet enjoy the benefits of goods are called **free riders.**

The problem facing producers of public goods is that free-riding behavior makes it difficult to discover the true preferences of consumers of a public good. Individuals will not reveal their true preferences for public goods because it is not in their self-interest to do so. For example, if a neighborhood tried to organize a crime-watch group, many neighbors might not contribute but would still appreciate any protection provided, thus concealing their true preferences for the service. On the other hand, some who do not contribute voluntarily might be totally disinterested in the service. The possibility of free riding makes it difficult to determine the true level of demand for the public good.

If everyone free rides and no one contributes to the production of public goods, then everyone will be worse off as a result. No public goods will be produced, even though each individual would like some provision of public goods. Herein lies a rationale for government provision of public goods. Government has the power of coercion and taxation, and it can force consumers to contribute to the production of public goods. Citizens cannot refuse to pay taxes and thus contribute to the costs of public sector output. When the cost of excluding nonpayers is high, government can produce public goods through tax finance.

Pricing Public Goods

Should a price be charged for use of public goods? In a sense, the correct price of a public good is zero. Take the example of a bridge. Once the bridge is built, the marginal cost of one more car going over it is approximately zero. If we follow the rule in Chapter 9 for optimal pricing, we should set price equal to marginal cost. Since the marginal cost of an additional bridge crossing is effectively zero, price should be zero according to the $P = MC$ rule. According to this logic, public goods should be free.

This rationale is fine as far as it goes, but it does not go far enough. In rationing the use of the good among demanders, zero is the correct price. Except for cases of congestion, a public good presents no rationing problem; by definition, additional individuals can consume a public good at zero marginal cost. But rationing is not the only function of price. A second important function of price is to achieve the right quantity of the public good by relating quantity to demand. Without information about what people are willing to pay to cross the bridge, authorities are left in the dark about the desired amount of bridge construction to undertake. After all, public goods involve the expenditure of scarce resources, and prices for public goods help public officials develop information about the demand for these goods.

How then should a price be set for a public good? Suppose a defense alliance is formed by two countries, A and B.[8] The alliance provides for a common defense policy through a treaty agreement. National defense is a public good for the alliance, and the problem facing the two countries is how to reach an agreement on the amount of national defense to be produced by the alliance. Figure 4 illustrates the problem.

We assume that each country faces the same marginal cost curve (MC) for providing defense. MC rises because additional scarce resources devoted to defense come at an increasing cost to the two countries.

Each country has a demand curve for national defense, D_A and D_B. The consumption of private goods is mutually exclusive. When A gets a unit of a private good, there is one less unit available for B to consume. In Chapter 4, this condition meant that to derive a market demand curve for a private good, the demand curves of individual consumers had to be summed horizontally. National defense, however, is not a private good. It is a public good, and this makes the nature of the "demand curves" in Figure 4 quite different.

Consumption of a public good is not mutually exclusive among consumers. All the units along the horizontal axis in Figure 4 are equally available to both demanders for simultaneous consumption. Both A and B receive benefits from, for example, Q_1 units of military protection. Thus, the total protection benefits offered by Q_1 to A and B are equal to the vertical sum of their demand prices for this quantity or output. At Q_1 the benefit that each country places on alliance protection is read vertically off its demand curve. A derives aQ_1, B derives bQ_1, and both countries together place a value of cQ_1 (equal to $aQ_1 + bQ_1$) on Q_1 units of alliance output.

This point applies to all public goods. The **market demand curve for a public good** is obtained by vertically summing all individuals' demand curves. The demand curves are summed vertically rather than horizontally because all demanders can consume any given unit of output along the horizontal axis at the same time. In Figure 4, then, market demand is given by $D_A + D_B$, which is the vertical sum of D_A and D_B.

At points along the horizontal axis less than Q_T, marginal benefit exceeds marginal cost ($D_A + D_B > MC$), and production will be expanded. At points beyond Q_T, marginal benefit is less than marginal cost ($D_A + D_B < MC$), and production will be cut back. Equilibrium output is at E, where $D_A + D_B = MC$. The equilibrium defense output in the alliance is Q_T, and the alliance defense budget is $P_T \times Q_T$.

How should this budget be divided between the two countries? One way to apportion the costs is in proportion to the benefits received. P_B represents the benefit that accrues to country B from consuming Q_T units of defense, and P_A is the benefit that country A receives from consuming the same amount. Country B pays more because it benefits more from alliance output. B, for example, may be a larger country, with more income, capital, and population to defend.

Market demand curve for a public good:
Obtained by summing vertically, instead of horizontally, all individuals' demands for the public good. Vertical summation is used because consumption is noncompeting.

---

[8]See Mancur Olson and Richard Zeckhauser, "An Economic Theory of Alliances," *Review of Economics and Statistics* 47 (August 1966), pp. 266–79.

FIGURE 4

MC is the marginal cost curve for production of military protection under an alliance. D_A and D_B are the individual country demand curves for national defense. The appropriate "prices" for national defense for each country are P_A and P_B. D_A + D_B is the vertical sum of D_A and D_B. Optimal output for the alliance is Q_T, where D_A + D_B = *MC*.

Sharing the Costs of Defense

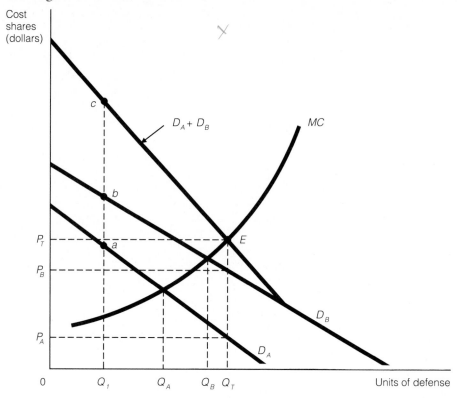

This is an idealized presentation of alliance behavior. For example, what happened to the concept of free riding? Basically, we ignored it to depict a perfect outcome for the alliance. But free riding will be a thorn in the alliance's side. Look at the individual equilibrium positions of the two countries in Figure 4. Given the marginal cost of providing defense, the small country prefers Q_A as its defense output; the large country prefers Q_B. When the treaty to form the alliance is signed, *A* gains access to the benefits of *B*'s production. *B*'s production more than satisfies *A*'s demand for national defense. In group alliances, small countries like *A* will therefore have strong incentives to reduce their defense spending and to free ride on the defense expenditures of larger countries such as *B*. This tendency will lead to much bargaining and many debates about contributions to alliance output, with the large countries complaining about the efforts and contributions of the small countries. The problem of free riding will be more pronounced the more countries there are in the alliance.

COST-BENEFIT ANALYSIS

Externalities and public goods require government intervention in the economy. Unless private ownership can be established, externalities call for government regulation or taxation of private activities that create externalities. The need for public goods calls for government provision of certain goods and services such as national defense. Up to this point we have assumed that government officials can obtain the necessary information about how to correct externalities and to provide public goods in more or less the correct quantities. This is a questionable assumption. Government decision-makers face tremendous practical difficulties in obtaining information to guide their decisions. For example, since consumers will rationally not reveal their true preferences for a public good, how does government decide how much of the good to produce? This is not an easy question to answer, but the technique of cost-benefit analysis has been applied to help government officials answer such questions.

Cost-benefit analysis:
A procedure used to estimate the difference in costs and benefits, or the net benefits, of a project.

   Cost-benefit analysis is just what the term implies: It is a procedure by which the costs and benefits of government programs are weighed so that decisions can be made about which programs to undertake. Clearly, a wise use of public resources is to rank programs from highest to lowest in their benefit-cost ratios and undertake those programs with the highest ratios.

   Cost-benefit analysis emerged as a result of efforts to find more systematic information on which to base government decisions about investment in physical resources. While cost-benefit analysis can be traced to the 1920s, it was first used after World War II for various water resource investments under the aegis of the Army Corps of Engineers and the Bureau of Reclamation. Military applications became important in the early 1960s in the Department of Defense, although these applications were referred to as systems analysis. Eventually, cost-benefit analysis was applied throughout the government budget process. Investments in human resources and proposed changes in legislation were added to investment in physical resources as reasonable subjects for cost-benefit analysis.

   Government cost-benefit analysis can be divided into two main categories, according to purpose. In the case of public investment, the goal of cost-benefit analysis is efficiency—to help choose more efficient over less efficient dams, for example. The other main category is the use of cost-benefit analysis to determine the merit of government intervention in private sector activity. The application of cost-benefit analysis in such areas as penalizing alcohol abuse, determining health effects of smoking, breaking up monopolies, regulating drugs, discouraging disposable containers, analyzing food additives, and promoting automobile safety are illustrations. Cost-benefit analysis in such instances provides evidence about the desirability of particular government interventions or public policies.

   Although cost-benefit analysis is equally applicable to firms and governments, its development has been inspired mainly by an interest in promoting efficiency in government. Careful comparisons between the costs and benefits of a proposed dam, for example, help discipline government decisions, since market forces are not present to reward good or discourage bad government decision making. Estimating anticipated costs and benefits resulting from a particular government program helps decision-makers select the most efficient programs from among those that could be adopted. Cost-benefit analysis is forward-looking; it seeks to assess the consequences of various proposed courses of action.

   Prior to conducting any cost-benefit analysis, planners must agree on a desired objective and array the various means of attaining the objective. Cost-benefit analysis does not propose a course of action. It is simply a technique for helping to evaluate proposed courses of action. The proposals themselves come from outside the framework of the analysis.

Once the goals of a government program are stated and the possible ways to reach these goals are described, the primary task of cost-benefit analysis is to measure the anticipated benefits and costs of the project. The relevant benefits fall into two categories: direct benefits and indirect benefits. Direct benefits accrue to users of the project after its completion, such as the benefits that a new subway system provides to its users. Indirect benefits might occur if the subway system reduces congestion on the highways and highway users save travel time. Estimating the benefits, even the simple direct benefits, of a program is a difficult task. It requires much judgment because hard evidence of real benefits is often impossible to develop.

In addition to measuring or estimating benefits, a cost-benefit analysis must measure or estimate the anticipated costs of a proposed project. The cost of a project is the value of the benefits from other potential uses of resources that must be sacrificed to undertake the project. If the costs of a dam are determined to be $10 million, this $10 million represents the value of the other services that could have been produced in place of the dam. This is why economists typically use the term *opportunity cost* synonymously with *cost;* cost represents a sacrificed opportunity.

As with benefits, there will be direct and indirect costs associated with public programs. Moreover, the same inherent problems that plague benefit estimation plague cost estimation. As in the case of benefits, prices of programs often are not available to estimate the value of alternative uses of public resources. And what is forgone when specific alternatives are adopted is not easily observable. Cost and benefit estimations are therefore likely to be only crude approximations of real values—even under the most favorable circumstances.

A ROLE FOR GOVERNMENT

The presence of externalities and public goods means that government has an important and productive role to play in the economy. Externalities lead to a regulatory role for government. Public goods imply a role for government as a direct producer of some goods and services. In this case, in order to pay for such public goods and services, government levies taxes on citizens to raise revenue. It is to this important area of government activity—taxation—that we turn in the next chapter.

SUMMARY

1. Market failure occurs when the private market system fails to allocate resources in an optimal or ideal fashion. Externalities and public goods are two categories of market failure.
2. Owners of private property bear the economic results of its use. When property is held in common, users do not bear the full costs of its use. Common or undefined ownership creates a conflict between

the pursuit of self-interest and the common good. The implication is that common resources will be overused and exploited.
3. An externality occurs when an economic unit does not bear all the value consequences of its actions. Externalities can be positive or negative, trivial, irrelevant, or relevant. A relevant externality creates an effective demand to correct the externality.

4. The Coase theorem assumes that in a world of zero transactions and bargaining costs, the amount of an externality such as pollution is independent of who has legal liability for pollution damage.

5. Where transaction and bargaining costs are high, other routes to externality control become feasible. A per unit pollution tax would force a firm to act as if its marginal cost curve were identical to its marginal cost curve plus the cost of the externality, or the marginal social cost curve. Other approaches include establishment of a market for pollution rights and direct regulation of firm technology.

6. Public goods are goods that are nonrivalrous in consumption, with high costs of excluding nonpayers. Whereas a private good is consumed exclusively by one individual, a public good can be simultaneously consumed by all consumers. A mixed good has both private and public characteristics.

7. To "free ride" means to reap the benefits of a public good without bearing its costs. If everyone free rides, no public good is produced by the private sector, even though each individual values its production. Such behavior means that public goods typ-ically have to be produced by government through its power to tax.

8. Public goods are not free; they cost real resources. In terms of rationing a public good among consumers, a zero price is the correct price because additional consumers can consume a public good at near-zero marginal cost. However, a zero price for a public good offers no guidance for public officials about how much of a public good to produce. There is thus a trade-off regarding whether public goods should be priced.

9. Individual demand curves for public goods are summed vertically to arrive at total demand for a public good. Optimal output of a public good occurs where the vertically summed individual demand curves intersect the marginal cost curve. Optimal prices for this output are read off the individual demand curves.

10. Cost-benefit analysis is an analytical tool for evaluating and promoting efficiency in government programs and policies. Cost-benefit analysis does not set goals; it evaluates the costs and benefits of attaining goals in alternative ways.

KEY TERMS

market failure
common
   ownership
externality
negative externality

positive externality
Coase theorem
marginal private cost
marginal social cost
public good

free rider
market demand curve for a public good
cost-benefit analysis

QUESTIONS FOR REVIEW AND DISCUSSION

1. Are whales an example of a common property resource? If so, what sort of behavior would you predict among whale hunters?

2. What is an externality? Name the various types of externality. Why is an externality considered a market failure?

3. Suppose that pollution is controlled with a pollution tax on polluting firms. Who will pay the tax? Firms? Consumers?

4. Define a public good. What is the difference between a private and a public good? How will individuals behave when asked how much they will contribute toward payment for a public good? What does this mean for the nature of the demand curves for public goods?

5. "Museums should be free." Evaluate.

6. Describe how you would apply cost-benefit analysis to the evaluation of an addition to the football stadium at your college or university.

7. Are all public goods produced by government? If not, name some goods that fit the definition of a public good that are produced by private producers.

ECONOMICS IN ACTION
Is Urban Mass Transit Worth the Cost?

Several U.S. cities have new public transit systems, and others have systems in the construction or planning stage. Between 1984 and 1989, cities (and the federal government) spent roughly $14 billion for construction and repair in an effort to overcome traffic congestion, air pollution, and the economic decline of downtown metropolitan areas.

For the most part, urban mass transit systems represent a large subsidy to their ridership, who typically bear only a fraction of a system's true cost in the fares they pay. It was estimated that in 1982 fares in the New York City subway system failed to cover $1.3 billion in total operating expenses. But mass transit advocates argue that investment in these systems is nevertheless justified because the positive externalities of these systems more than make up for typical operating losses. A question faces voters and politicians: Is urban mass transit worth its cost?

Backers of mass transit point to three main categories of positive externalities generated by large-scale bus and subway systems. First, population density increases in urban areas because new residents are attracted by the reduced cost of transportation. This increase in population brings more tax income to hard-pressed local governments. The second positive externality is economic development. Businesses will concentrate in or near the denser population centers to reduce the costs of business transactions and to take advantage of a large, accessible labor supply. The Bay Area Rapid Transit (BART) in San Francisco has been credited with stimulating $1.4 billion of construction since it opened. Third, mass transit may reduce traffic congestion and pollution levels as commuters switch from cars to buses or the subway. Mass transit proponents argue that the positive externalities generated by such systems are high enough to equal or exceed the costs of construction and operation.

Others argue that large-scale investment in bigger and more modern mass transit systems is not necessary to solve many metropolitan transportation problems. Instead of building more subways and urban rail lines, these "demand-siders" suggest that in many cases the existing system is more than sufficient to carry the load *if highway use is properly priced.*

With drivers not paying a fee for road use, the cost to the individual driver of using the highway during the rush hour is only a few extra minutes spent in a traffic jam. But the rush-hour commuter pays, through gasoline taxes, only a small fraction of the social costs generated by rush-hour traffic—the fouling of the air, additional police services necessary to unsnarl traffic, and so on. Nonetheless, the level of rush-hour traffic plays a major role in determining highway

capacity in many areas. This is so even though rush-hour traffic constitutes less than one-third of all traffic on most metropolitan highways.

The demand-side alternative to more mass transit is to charge a fee for using the highway, with the fee higher at peak times and low or nothing at off-peak times. Faced with paying a larger share of the full cost of using the highway, some drivers will respond by carpooling, riding in buses, and staggering work and travel hours to avoid the high-priced travel times. As a result, remaining vehicles would face less congestion and travel faster. Road maintenance and police expenditures would be lower also. Air pollution would decrease, and taxpayers would save the expenses of new mass transit investment.

Some toll roads already exist in certain areas. Opponents of the highway user fees argue that toll booths would slow traffic considerably, defeating the purpose of the user fee. However, technology has advanced tremendously from the toll booth era. Since 1975, Singapore has required a simple auto-license sticker for low-occupancy cars to enter the center city at peak traffic times. Enforced by a small police force, the sticker fees have reduced traffic on the previously congested city highways by about 40 percent. In 1983, Hong Kong experimented with an electronic license plate. The license plate sent a signal to a computer when a car entered a given stretch of road and the computer sent a bill to the driver each month for highway use. Other entities, such as the State of Oregon, the New York–New Jersey Port Authority, and CALTRANS (the California State Transportation Agency) have found optical scanners and electronic toll collectors to be efficient means of pricing highway and bridge use so as to reduce congestion.

Technological advances mean that market-oriented substitutes for large mass transit projects can be applied to existing transportation systems. The hard part may be convincing motorists of the social benefits of pricing highway use.

Question
Houston, Texas, is a large urban center. Voters in that city, however, have turned down several proposals for mass transit systems. Is this proof that the costs of such systems outweigh the benefits to the city of Houston? Upon what economic considerations should such decisions be made?

Sources: David M. Stewart, "Rolling Nowhere," *Inquiry* (July 1984), pp. 18–23; and Jonathan Marshall, "How to Break Up Traffic Jams," *Wall Street Journal* (September 15, 1986), p. 34.

21

The Microeconomics of Taxation

When government finances the provision of public goods or services—a local sewer system, a research program looking into the cause of acid rain, a nuclear warhead, a presidential limousine—it uses taxes to help pay the bill. In the United States, about 82,000 governmental bodies at the federal, state, county, city, school district, municipal, and township levels have the power to establish and collect taxes.

Unpopular as they may be, taxes are a necessary part of life in a mixed economy such as the United States. Every tax has a purpose; directly or indirectly, tax revenues finance government expenditures. The private market fails to provide the optimal amounts of public goods, such as national defense, police and fire protection, and education, or to deal with externalities through programs such as environmental protection. Traditionally, federal, state, and local governments have taken an active role in providing or influencing the production of such goods and services. **Public finance** is the study of government expenditures and revenue-collecting activities. When you finish this discussion of public finance, you should understand

Public finance:
The study of how governments at the federal, state, and local levels tax and spend.

- the overall tax structure in the United States.
- some of the effects of specific taxes upon various groups in society.
- the principles underlying taxation and their relation to questions of fairness and equity.
- the nature of Social Security taxes within the tax structure.

FINANCING GOVERNMENT EXPENDITURES: THE U.S. TAX STRUCTURE

Chapter 3 reviewed some of the major categories of government expenditures and gave some statistics on the rate of government growth. There are two basic types of government expenditures: (1) direct purchases of goods and services and (2) transfer payments, the redistribution of income from one group of people to another. Direct purchases involve spending on such items as defense, fire and police protection, and wages and salaries of government employees. Transfer payments include such expenditures as Social Security payments, Aid to Families with Dependent Children, and unemployment insurance.

The two basic methods of financing public expenditures are taxing and borrowing. State and local governments usually borrow by selling bonds, or IOUs, to finance special projects such as highways, schools, or hospitals. The federal government has come to use borrowing as a routine means of financing its burgeoning debt. Nevertheless, the largest portion of government expenditures is still financed by taxes. Table 1 shows the total tax receipts of the federal government from 1980 to 1991 from each tax source. The largest single source of federal revenues is the personal income tax, followed closely by Social Security taxes.

Property taxes and sales taxes are the two largest contributors to state and local government tax revenues, which are broken down in Table 2. The statistics reveal a recent trend in state and local financing: Property tax revenues have not been rising as rapidly as sales and income tax revenues. This indicates that property owners are being taxed relatively less over time than other groups. Many state governments have implemented weekly lotteries as an alternative to raising taxes. Focus, "Tax Freedom Day," discusses a little-known effect of taxation on individuals.

The Effects of Taxes

The nature of the U.S. tax system effectively eliminates total tax avoidance. Since the federal government enacts excise and income taxes and state and

TABLE 1

Tax Revenues of the Federal Government

The federal government obtains most of its tax dollars from personal income taxes and Social Security taxes. Total revenues increased by over $600 billion between 1980 and 1991. (1991 figures are projections.)

Source	Tax Revenues (billions of dollars)							
	1980	1982	1984	1986	1988	1989	1990	1991
Individual income taxes	244.0	297.7	298.4	348.9	401.2	455.7	489.4	528.5
Corporate income taxes	64.6	49.2	56.9	63.1	94.5	103.6	112.0	129.7
Social Security taxes	157.8	201.5	239.4	283.9	334.3	359.4	385.4	421.4
Excise taxes	24.3	36.3	37.4	32.9	35.2	34.1	36.2	37.6
Estate and gift taxes	6.4	8.0	6.0	7.0	7.6	8.7	9.3	9.9
Customs duties	7.2	8.9	11.4	13.3	16.2	16.3	16.8	18.6
Miscellaneous receipts	12.7	16.0	17.0	19.9	19.9	22.8	24.4	24.6
Total revenues	517.1	617.8	666.5	769.1	909.0	990.7	1073.5	1170.2

Sources: Council of Economic Advisers, *Economic Report of the President* (Washington, D.C.: U.S. Government Printing Office, 1989), pp. 398–99; *Economic Report of the President* (1990), p. 385.

"Welcome aboard. You are now exempt from federal, state, and local taxes."

Drawing by Schoenbaum; © 1990 The New Yorker Magazine, Inc.

local governments levy sales, excise, and occasionally income taxes, essentially everyone who spends money or earns income pays taxes, even though such payments do not always show up as taxes. Taxes are intended to eliminate free riders and thus should be unavoidable. Yet the burdens of taxes and attempts to avoid them do influence individuals' activities. Altering economic behavior is sometimes intentional and desirable for society as a whole; other times it leads to undesirable economic inefficiency.

Taxes that have no effect on behavior are called **neutral taxes.** Taxes are rarely neutral. Typically, by affecting price, taxes affect the quantity of goods supplied and demanded and the allocation of resources. Furthermore, the burden of taxes is frequently shifted away from the group that was intended to pay the taxes. Taxes are necessary to obtain desired public goods, but taxation can have a detrimental effect on the quantity of goods produced or the amount of resources supplied.

Resource Allocation: The Effect of Taxes on Price and Output

There are many different types of taxes, all of which have a particular base. The **tax base** is the item or transaction upon which taxes are levied. For example, property taxes are based on the value of property owned by an individual or a business. Likewise, **sales taxes** are based on retail sales revenues;

Neutral tax:
A tax that has no effects on the production or consumption of goods.

Tax base:
The item or action—such as the amount of a good produced, the sales of a good, the income of a business or household, or the wealth of an individual—upon which a tax rate is applied in order to determine total tax liability.

Sales tax:
A tax that is based on the total expenditures on a particular product.

TABLE 2

State and Local Tax Revenues

Unlike the federal government, state and local governments' largest share of tax revenues is collected in the form of property taxes. Property taxes are falling in relative importance, while sales and income taxes are rising.

Source	Tax Revenues (millions of dollars)						
	1960	1965	1970	1975	1980	1985	1988
Property taxes	16,405	22,583	34,054	51,491	68,499	103,757	132,240
Sales and gross receipts taxes	11,849	17,118	30,322	49,815	79,927	126,281	156,257
Individual income taxes	2,463	4,090	10,812	21,454	42,080	70,097	88,349
Corporation income taxes	1,180	1,929	3,738	6,642	13,321	19,158	23,741
Revenue from federal government	6,974	11,029	21,857	47,034	83,029	106,193	117,602
All other	11,634	17,250	29,971	51,735	95,466	172,233	208,956
Total	50,505	74,000	130,754	228,171	382,322	597,719	727,145

Source: Council of Economic Advisers, *Economic Report of the President* (Washington, D.C.: U.S. Government Printing Office, 1989), p. 405.

Social Security taxes are based on businesses' payrolls; and individual income taxes are based on household income.

The primary effect of a tax based on a product or a resource is that a wedge is driven between the price that buyers pay and the after-tax price that sellers receive. Consider, for example, the price tag on a necklace. The price shown represents the store's receipts when you purchase the necklace. However, it is not the price you pay if sales tax must be added. The price you pay is greater than the price the store receives, since sales tax receipts are eventually collected by state or local governments. Just as a sales tax drives a wedge between the price customers pay and the price stores receive for retail commodities, a payroll tax such as Social Security drives a wedge between the wage businesses pay and the wage workers receive for labor. Most other taxes have a similar effect on prices even when they are not explicit, but rather are figured into the price tag. For this reason, taxes alter the prices of various tax bases and, consequently, the amounts purchased.

To understand how taxation affects price and quantity, consider a simple per unit tax—that is, an **excise tax.** Let D and S in Figure 2 represent, respectively, the demand and supply of gasoline in the United States with no taxes. P_0 and Q_0 represent the original price and quantity. Then assume that the federal government imposes an excise tax of t cents per gallon for every gallon sold. This tax effectively increases the cost to the suppliers of producing and selling gasoline.

What happens? The supply of gasoline decreases. The supply curve shifts upward by the amount of the tax. Before the tax, producers were willing to offer quantity Q_0 at price P_0; after the tax, producers are willing to offer Q_0 only at a higher price, P_0 plus the tax t. The tax results in a new equilibrium, E_t. The price increases, but probably not by the full amount of the tax.

Excise tax:
A tax that is based on the quantity of a good sold; a per unit tax.

FOCUS Tax Freedom Day

The average American worker spends a great deal of time earning income just to pay taxes. Not only does the federal government tax the worker directly in the form of income tax, but state and local governments collect taxes in many other forms. How much time does the average worker spend earning money to pay all these taxes?

In 1948, Dallas L. Hostetler decided to estimate how long the average worker spent each year working to pay taxes, beginning on January 1. Bringing his calculations up to date, the Tax Foundation, Inc. yearly estimates "tax freedom day," the day of the year that the average worker begins to earn take-home pay. Figure 1 represents the foundation's estimates.

In 1930, the average worker devoted only 43 days per year to pay all taxes. In 1989, 124 days—one-third of a year's work—were required to pay taxes.

Compared with other wealthy countries, the United States celebrates its tax freedom day earlier than some but later than others. For example, Sweden's tax freedom day falls around July 10, while France, the Netherlands, and Belgium celebrate tax freedom in June. In England, West Germany, and Canada tax freedom arrives in late May, while Japanese begin earning money for themselves around April 25.

FIGURE 1   Tax Freedom Day

"Tax freedom day" is the day of the year on which the average worker is able to begin earning take-home pay.

In this example, if the original price was $1.30 and the tax is 20 cents, then the price to consumers, P_c, rises by only 10 cents, to $1.40. In this case, the price that producers receive after paying the tax is $1.40 minus 20 cents, or $1.20. The price the producers receive, P_p, may be found on the original supply curve at the new reduced quantity, Q_t.

The tax thus has two primary effects on the market for the taxed item. First, it changes the relative prices that sellers and buyers face. In fact, it lowers the price that sellers receive and raises the price that buyers pay. Second, the quantity exchanged falls—the lower price to sellers usually induces them to offer less gasoline. Likewise, the higher price to buyers encourages them to buy less. The decrease in quantity depends on the size of the tax and on the elasticities of supply and demand.

The elasticities of demand and supply are an indication of buyers' and sellers' responsiveness to price changes. Since an excise tax raises the price to buyers, an elastic demand for gasoline would result in a relatively large decrease in the quantity of gasoline purchased. For example, consider Figure 3.

FIGURE 2

An excise tax shifts the supply curve upward by the amount of the tax. This shift increases the price paid by consumers from P_0 to P_c and lowers the net price received by the sellers from P_0 to P_p. The tax also lowers the amount produced and consumed from Q_0 to Q_t. The shaded areas represent tax revenues for the government and the welfare loss to society, discussed later in this chapter.

Effects of an Excise Tax

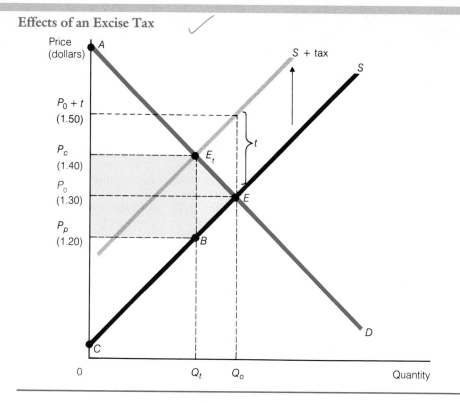

With the same pretax price, quantity, and supply as illustrated in Figure 2, an excise equal to t (20 cents) results in a larger decrease in quantity (Q_0 to Q_1) because the demand is more elastic. In general, we may say that the more elastic the demand for a product, the greater the decrease in quantity for a given excise tax rate. Alternatively, the less elastic the demand, the smaller the decrease in quantity. Recall from Chapter 5 that the elasticity of demand varies directly with the number of substitutes and the percent of income spent on a good.

Just as the elasticity of demand influences the effects of an excise tax, the elasticity of supply contributes to the determination of equilibrium quantity. The pretax price, quantity, and demand in Figure 4 are the same as those in Figure 2; however, the supply curve is more elastic. With the more elastic supply, the same excise tax rate (20 cents) has a greater impact on the quantity exchanged. In general, the more elastic the supply, the greater the impact on quantity; the less elastic the supply, the smaller the impact of an excise tax on quantity.

If the supply or demand for a good or resource is totally inelastic, a tax will not affect quantity and is therefore neutral. Taxes are rarely neutral, since demand and supply typically have some elasticity; but elasticity does vary across markets, so the impact of taxes on resource allocation varies from one good to another. There is, however, one rule of thumb: Taxing the production or purchase of a particular good or resource or increasing existing taxes will decrease the amount exchanged. This bit of information is useful if taxes are to be used as an instrument for influencing the allocation of resources; if

FIGURE 3

The more elastic the demand for a product, the greater the impact on equilibrium quantity for a given tax rate t. Notice that the price to consumers rises by a smaller amount $(P_c - P_0)$ than the price to producers falls $(P_0 - P_p)$.

The Effects of an Excise Tax with Elastic Demand

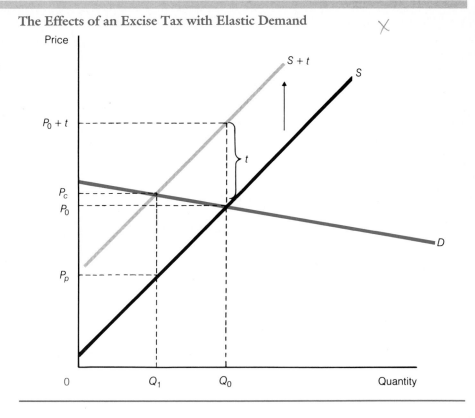

government wishes to alter the relative levels of production of various goods or the employment of resources, it may do so through a properly devised tax system.

The basic effect of taxing a good or service is a decrease in production. In Figure 2 the imposition of the excise tax caused the equilibrium quantity of gasoline to fall from Q_0 to Q_t. The decrease in production and consumption represents a loss to society that can be measured in terms of consumer and producer surplus.

The consumers' surplus at the original price is represented by the triangle AEP_0, and the producers' surplus by P_0EC. Recall from Chapter 10 that consumers' surplus represents the net benefits that consumers receive from buying a particular quantity of a good at a particular price; it is the difference between the amount of money that consumers would be willing to pay for a particular quantity and the amount they actually have to pay. Producers' surplus is the inframarginal rents received by the suppliers of resources; this includes the payments in excess of opportunity cost to suppliers of land, labor, capital, and entrepreneurial talents. When the tax causes an increase in the price to consumers, consumers' surplus falls to AE_tP_c; when the tax lowers the price to producers, the producers' surplus falls to P_pBC. The loss to producers and consumers is represented by the area $P_cE_tEBP_p$. The area $P_cE_tBP_p$ represents tax revenues for the government (t times Q_t). This revenue is not lost to society as a whole; it is transferred to government. But the area E_tEB is lost. It is a deadweight loss to society that is similar to the welfare loss

FIGURE 4

The more elastic the supply, the greater the impact on equilibrium quantity for a given tax rate t. Notice that the price to consumers rises by a larger amount $(P_c - P_0)$ than the price to the producers falls $(P_0 - P_p)$.

The Effects of an Excise Tax with Elastic Supply

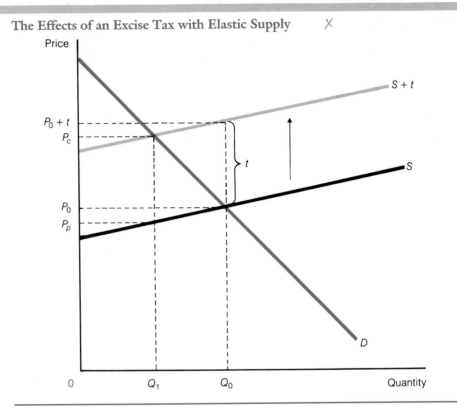

due to monopoly. No one captures this income; it vanishes from the economy as lost income and product.

In some cases, a decrease in quantity may be socially desirable. For example, if government wants people to consume less liquor or tobacco, an excise tax may be imposed to discourage drinking and smoking. Or government may actively encourage the consumption and production of some goods by not taxing these goods and taxing all others. If government wants to increase consumption of agricultural products relative to other goods, for example, then agricultural products may be exempted from a general sales tax.

Tax policies may have unintended allocative effects; that is, they may result in a decrease in the production, consumption, or employment of some goods or resources. For example, property taxes may cause geographical shifts in population and industry. The aggregate supply of land, many people believe, is perfectly inelastic. However, the current property tax system is not neutral in its effects because the demand for land is elastic. State and local governments tax land according to market value, which varies according to demand. Owners of land in the center of cities and other strategic locations must therefore pay higher taxes than owners of less valuable land. These high property tax rates may drive firms and homeowners out of such areas in search of lower taxes, other things being equal.

To summarize, the allocative effect of a tax depends on the size of the tax and the elasticity of supply and demand for the product. In general, the larger the tax, the greater the reduction in production and consumption of the good.

Also, the more elastic the supply or demand for the good, the greater the reduction in production due to the tax. Conversely, when demand or supply is perfectly inelastic, the tax has no effect on the quantity of the taxed good; the tax is said to be allocatively neutral.

Tax Revenues

While taxes have an allocative effect, they are most often enacted as a source of tax revenues to finance government expenditures. The amount of revenues collected from a particular tax depends on the tax rate, the charge per unit, and the tax base—the amount of the taxed good sold. As mentioned previously, the tax revenues from the gasoline excise tax in Figure 2 are equal to the tax rate, t, times the tax base, Q_t, or the area $P_cE_tBP_p$. The level of tax revenues may be altered by changing the tax rate. For example, a tax rate higher than t may result in greater tax revenues, or a lower tax rate may result in lower revenues. However, we should not assume that there is strictly a direct relation between tax rates and tax revenues. Remember that tax revenues are equal to the tax rate times the tax base, and an increase in the tax rate results in a decrease in the tax base.

To understand the relation between tax rates and tax revenues, consider Figure 5. Figure 5a represents the demand and supply of gasoline. The quan-

---

FIGURE 5   **Tax Rates and Tax Revenues: The Laffer Curve**

Various tax rates result in different levels of tax revenues. As the tax rate rises from t_0 to t_1 to t_2 in Figure 5a, the tax base falls from Q_0 to Q_1 to Q_2. Total tax revenues (the tax rate times the tax base) rise, reach a maximum, and then fall as tax rates rise in Figure 5b. Tax rate t_1 maximizes tax revenues.

(a)

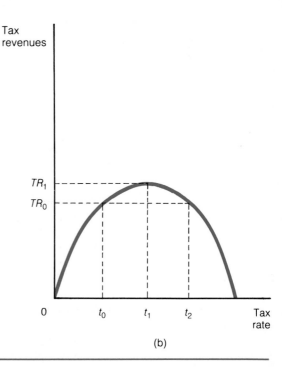

(b)

tities illustrated represent equilibrium tax bases that result from various excise tax rates, t_0, t_1, and t_2. Notice that as the tax rate rises, the tax base falls from Q_0 to Q_1 to Q_2. Figure 5b shows the level of tax revenues (t times Q) that result from all possible tax rates. As the tax rate rises from 0 to t_0, tax revenues initially increase; at t_1, tax revenues are maximized, and at rates higher than t_1, such as t_2, tax revenues begin to fall. This relation between tax rates and tax revenues was brought into focus in the early 1980s by economist Arthur Laffer—for whom the curve in Figure 5b, the **Laffer curve,** is named.

Laffer curve:
A curve that shows the relation between tax rate and tax revenues; it demonstrates graphically how as the tax rate rises, tax revenues rise, reach a maximum, and then fall.

The Laffer curve illustrates two important concepts. First, it shows that higher tax rates do not always result in higher tax revenues—an increase in tax rates may so erode the tax base that lower total receipts result. Second, there is a tax rate that maximizes the tax revenues generated from a particular tax base. Consequently, if legislators wish to maximize tax revenues from a particular source, they must choose the revenue-maximizing rate and not simply a very high rate. The tax rate that maximizes revenues results in a price to consumers identical to a monopolist's profit-maximizing price. In other words, legislators can enact taxes in a competitive market that yield a monopoly-level price and output, and the rents that are created are transferred to the government in the form of tax revenues.

Tax Incidence

The effect of taxes on price and quantity is clear—they raise price and lower quantity. In this respect, taxes are a burden to the buyers and sellers of taxed goods and services. One question arises from this realization: Who receives the greater burden from taxes, buyers or sellers? At a basic level, we know that the buyers of goods in competitive markets cover the entire cost to producers—production costs plus any and all taxes. However, we can determine the actual burden of the tax—the **tax incidence,** or final resting place of the tax—by observing the relative change in price to producers and consumers. Notice that in the excise tax example in Figure 2 the price received by producers fell by 10 cents ($P_0 - P_p$) and the price paid by consumers increased by 10 cents ($P_c - P_0$) after imposition of the tax. These changes indicate that the tax incidence was shared equally by the buyers and sellers—each faced a price change of 10 cents.

Tax incidence:
The burden, or final resting place, of a tax or loss of welfare due to a tax.

The incidence of a tax is not always shared equally by buyers and sellers—indeed, we suspect that an equal incidence is a rare event—but it is most often shared to some degree. It is most unusual for the entire burden of a tax to be shifted forward to the buyers or backward to the sellers. In other words, the price to consumers does not usually increase by the full amount of the tax or decrease to producers by the full amount.

Tax shifting depends on the elasticity of demand and supply. In general, the more elastic the demand for a product, the greater the incidence of tax shifted backward to the sellers. Conversely, the more elastic the supply, the greater the incidence shifted forward to the buyers (for example, see Figures 3 and 5). In some circumstances, the tax incidence may be shifted entirely to one group or the other. In particular, if demand is perfectly inelastic or if supply is infinitely elastic, the entire burden is shifted to the buyers. The entire burden is shifted to the sellers if demand is infinitely elastic or if the supply is perfectly inelastic. Such extremes of elasticity are not common.

Regardless of whether a tax is shared or is borne entirely by the buyer or the seller, it drives a wedge between the price that buyers pay and the price that sellers receive. This chunk claimed by the government occurs whether the tax is an excise tax, a payroll tax, a property tax, or an income tax. For example, the Social Security tax drives a wedge between the wage that employers pay for labor and the wage employees receive for their services. The burden of the Social Security tax is shared by employers and employees, although it may not be equally shared. If, for example, the supply of labor were relatively inelastic, then the burden of the tax would shift mostly to the employees. Conversely, if the demand were inelastic, then more of the burden would shift forward to the employers.

THEORIES OF EQUITABLE TAXATION

Given the government's need for tax revenues, how should taxes be levied among the people? Our society attempts to find an equitable way of distributing the tax burden, but there are no easy formulas for determining what is truly equitable. In theory, however, two basic criteria are used to determine who should be taxed and by how much: the benefit principle and the ability-to-pay principle.

Benefit Principle

Benefit principle:
The notion that people who receive the benefits of publicly provided goods or services should pay for their production.

According to the **benefit principle,** individuals who receive benefits from government-produced goods and services should pay for their production, and the rate of payment should be according to the level of benefits received. Many taxes arise from this principle.

When government is the sole provider and nonbuyers can be excluded, government can directly tax the users of its goods and services. People who ride on public transportation facilities such as buses or subways are charged a tax in the form of a fare. Electrical power companies owned by local governments charge individuals according to the amount of electricity they use and thus the amount of benefits they receive. By means of tolls, highway users may be taxed directly for their use of a road. Certain other taxes attempt to force users to pay indirectly for categories of benefits they enjoy. For example, the revenues collected from excise taxes on gasoline, tires, automobiles, and automobile batteries are used to build highways, roads, and bridges.

The benefit principle is not easily applied to all taxes, however. For one thing, benefits are not always obvious. With some goods, such as highways and education, direct users receive the greatest benefits, but others receive indirect benefits. A Milwaukee resident who has no car may still buy fruits trucked across highways from California, Texas, and Florida. Families with no children to educate benefit from an educational system that increases worker productivity and raises the standard of living.

A second problem with the benefit principle is that individuals who receive government benefits cannot always afford to pay an equitable share of taxes. For example, welfare recipients are not likely to have the ability to pay for all the benefits they receive. For these reasons, many taxes are based on the ability-to-pay principle.

Ability-to-Pay Principle

Ability-to-pay principle:
The notion that tax bills should vary directly with income levels or the capacity of individuals to pay taxes.

According to the **ability-to-pay principle,** individuals who are more able to pay should pay more taxes than those less able. Under this principle, levels of an individual's income or wealth are measures frequently used for determining the level of tax obligations. The higher the level of income or wealth, the greater the tax liability, regardless of the benefits an individual receives. For example, income taxes and property taxes are higher for people with a greater ability to pay.

When taxes are levied according to the ability-to-pay principle, the equity of taxation is theoretically measured in two dimensions. The ideal of **horizontal equity** suggests that people with equal abilities to pay should pay equal amounts of taxes. For example, all people who earn $10,000 income should pay the same amount in taxes—perhaps $2000. The ideal of **vertical equity** suggests that people with greater ability to pay must pay a higher absolute amount of taxes than people with less ability to pay. For example, if those who earn $10,000 pay $2000 in taxes, anyone who earns more than $10,000 must pay more than $2000 in taxes. Ideally, taxes levied according to ability to pay exhibit both horizontal and vertical equity.

Horizontal equity:
A tax structure under which people with equal incomes pay equal amounts of taxes.

Vertical equity:
A tax structure under which people with unequal incomes pay unequal taxes; people with higher incomes pay more taxes than people with lower incomes.

One of the problems with establishing an equitable tax is defining ability to pay. Income is the most common measure used to determine ability to pay, but two families with the same income may have dramatically different abilities to pay. One family might have four children, huge medical bills, and no stored wealth. Another family with the same income might have no children, few medical bills, and a great store of wealth. Wealth itself is sometimes proposed as a better measure of ability to pay, but wealth is very hard to measure: Is it the value of a house, of a work of art, of a portfolio of stocks and bonds? A family with enormous wealth in this sense may find itself with very little income.

There is general agreement that the wealthy should pay more taxes than the poor, but the question of how much more is not easily resolved. Three concepts are used to describe the relation of taxes to ability to pay. The following discussion illustrates these three concepts with reference to an income tax, but they also can be applied to other taxes. Figure 6 illustrates the effects of the three types of taxes.

Proportional income tax:
A tax based on a fixed percentage of income for all levels of income.

Proportional Tax.   A tax that requires individuals to pay a constant percentage of their income in taxes is a **proportional income tax.** If the proportion is 10 percent, a taxpayer earning $50,000 a year would pay $5000 in taxes. If a taxpayer earned $5000, his or her tax bill would be $500. A proportional income tax can result in both horizontal equity, where all people with equal incomes pay equal amounts in taxes, and vertical tax equity, where people with higher incomes pay more than people with lower incomes. The advantage of a proportional income tax is its simplicity. Some states have a proportional income tax.

Progressive income tax:
A tax based on a percentage of income that varies directly with the level of income.

Progressive Tax.   A progressive income tax requires that a larger percentage of income be paid in taxes as income rises. If the tax structure is based on this principle, an individual with a $15,000 income may pay only 5 percent of income in taxes, while an individual with a $30,000 income pays 15 percent. A progressive income tax is also capable of meeting the vertical and horizontal equity conditions.

FIGURE 6

With a progressive tax, individuals pay a larger percentage of their income in taxes as their income rises. A proportional tax takes a constant percentage of income for taxes. A regressive tax takes a smaller percentage of income as income rises.

Progressive, Proportional, and Regressive Taxes on Individual Income

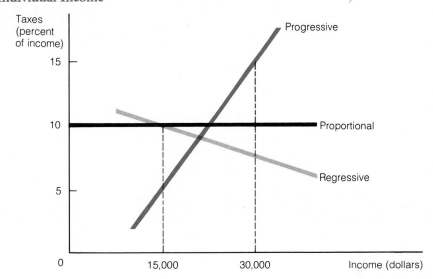

Regressive income tax:
A tax based on a percentage of income that varies inversely with the level of income.

Regressive Tax. With a **regressive income tax** a lower percentage of income is paid in taxes as income rises. An individual with a $15,000 income may pay 10 percent in taxes, while an individual with a $30,000 income may pay 8 percent in taxes. While a regressive tax results in a lower percentage of income paid in taxes as income rises, people with higher incomes may pay higher taxes in absolute amounts. According to our example, the individual with a $15,000 income pays $1500 in taxes, while the individual with a $30,000 income pays $2400 in taxes. For this reason, regressive taxes can be vertically equitable. Further, these taxes can be horizontally equitable, as long as people with equal incomes pay equal taxes.

TYPES OF TAXES

Dozens of different taxes are imposed by federal, state, and local governments on individuals and businesses. These taxes are usually based on income, wealth, or particular activities.

Personal Income Taxes

The federal government receives more tax revenues from personal income taxes than from any other single source. An individual's **taxable income** is found by subtracting tax exemptions and deductions from total income. The remainder is subject to a tax rate that is used to determine total tax liability. Figure 7 illustrates some of the details for determining personal taxable income.

Taxable income:
The amount of income that is subject to income taxes; total income minus deductions and exemptions.

FIGURE 7

Estimating Taxable Personal Income

This chart demonstrates the basic method of determining personal income subject to federal income taxes. Notice that total income is not taxable. Individuals are allowed to exempt some income for each dependent. Also, certain other expenses are deducted from total income regardless of whether or not the taxpayer itemizes expenses.

Source: Abbreviated from IRS form 1040, 1983.

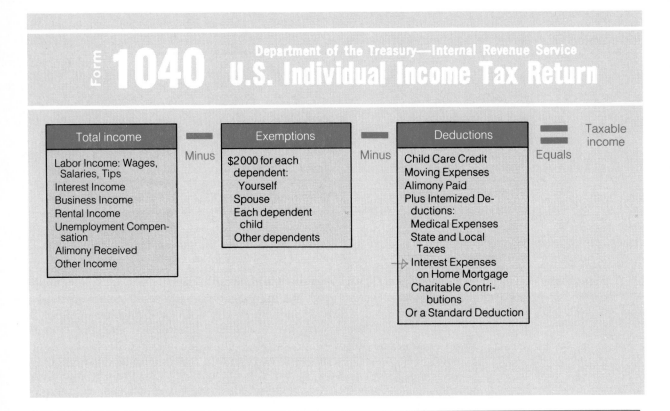

Average tax rate:
The percentage of income paid in taxes; total tax liability divided by total income.

Marginal tax rate:
The percentage of an increase in income that must be paid in taxes; change in tax liability divided by change in taxable income.

Tax liability is determined by applying tax tables with a progressive tax rate to taxable income. Table 3 shows a sample of the pretax year 1988 tax table for a married taxpayer filing a joint return. Taxable income in column (1) is divided into the tax obligation in column (2) to yield the **average tax rate** in column (3)—the percentage of income paid in taxes.

The **marginal tax rate** in column (6) is the percentage of a small increase in income that must be paid in taxes. It is the change in taxes (column 5) divided by the change in taxable income (column 4). For example, if a worker normally earned $29,750 a year but had the opportunity to earn an extra $5000 in overtime pay, then 15 percent of that extra income would have been paid in taxes; that is, $750 of the $5000 would be used to pay taxes and only the remaining $4250 would be take-home pay. For incomes below $171,090, the marginal tax rate is higher than the average tax rate. Therefore, until that income level is reached, average tax rates rise.

Some economists believe that the federal income tax system does not result in vertical or horizontal equity. Some people with higher incomes pay

TABLE 3

Income Tax Rates

The average tax rate rises until income reaches $171,090. The marginal tax rate rises to 33 percent over the $149,250 to $192,930 income range because personal exemptions and the 15 percent tax rates are phased out until a 28 percent average tax rate is reached.

(1) Taxable Income (dollars)	(2) Taxes (dollars)	(3) Average Tax Rate (%) (2) ÷ (1)	(4) Change in Taxable Income (dollars) (1)	(5) Change in Taxes (dollars) (2)	(6) Marginal Tax Rate (%) (5) ÷ (4)
0	0	0	0	0	0
29,750	4,462.50	15	29,750	4,462.50	15
71,900	16,264.50	22.6	42,150	11,802.00	28
149,250	41,790.00	28	77,350	25,525.50	33
171,090	48,997.20	28.6	21,840	7,207.20	33
192,930	55,112.40	28.5	21,840	6,115.20	28

Tax avoidance:
Legal means—tax shelters and loopholes—by which individuals can reduce tax liabilities.

lower taxes than others with lower incomes. Also, people with equal incomes do not always pay equal taxes.

Income tax inequities occur because many people engage in **tax avoidance.** This is a legal activity in which individuals can reduce tax liability by using what are commonly called tax loopholes or tax shelters. One means of avoiding taxes is obtaining income from nontaxable sources. For example, the interest income received from municipal bonds (bonds issued by city governments) is nontaxable, whereas the interest income received from bonds issued by businesses is taxable.   IRA's,

Individuals also may avoid taxes by spending their money in a particular way. For example, interest paid on a home mortgage is deducted from total income. Therefore, borrowing the money to purchase a house rather than renting can lower tax obligations. Deductions and exemptions such as these may result in tax inequities. Even though the Tax Reform Act of 1986 closed many loopholes, vertical and horizontal inequities still occur.

Corporate Income Tax

The federal government charges incorporated businesses an income tax on their accounting profits. The corporate income tax is progressive, with a maximum marginal rate of 34 percent for profit income over $100,000. The after-tax profits can be distributed to the shareholders (owners) of a corporation in the form of dividend payments, which are themselves taxed. The shareholders' incomes are also subject to personal income taxes. Thus corporate profits are taxed twice, once from corporations and once from shareholders.

Social Security Taxes

Social Security taxes, the second largest source of federal tax revenues and the fastest-growing revenue source, represent taxpayers' contributions to federal programs that support the elderly, ill, and disabled. The Social Security tax is a payroll tax in which the employer and the employee each pay 7.65 percent of the employee's income up to $51,300 (as of 1990).[1] The marginal tax rate is zero for income above $51,300. Nonlabor income, such as rental or interest income, is not subject to Social Security taxes. These features lead to a vertically and horizontally inequitable tax. For example, an individual with wage income of $51,300 pays $3924 in Social Security taxes, and an individual who earns $75,000 in wage income pays the same amount because income over $51,300 is not taxed. Since unequals are not treated unequally, vertical inequity results. As currently structured, the Social Security tax is also horizontally inequitable: Equals are not treated equally because interest income is not taxed. An individual who earns $51,300 in interest from bonds pays no Social Security tax.

Even though the Social Security tax is inequitable, the Social Security system may not be inequitable. The benefits that people receive from Social Security in the form of retirement and disability benefits are based on labor earnings and contributions. In this sense, the Social Security system roughly operates on the basis of the benefits principle. (See Focus, "Social Security: A Bad Investment?")

Property Taxes

The largest source of state and local government tax revenues is property tax. Owners of land and permanent structures are charged a tax based on the assessed value of their property. The assessed value is usually a percentage of the market value—that is, the selling price of the buildings and land.

A property tax is actually a tax on wealth rather than on income. Individuals who hold their wealth in the form of property pay more taxes than people who hold their wealth in other forms, such as gold, art, or bonds. For example, people who hold bonds are taxed on the income from bonds—just as property owners are taxed on rental income—but they are not taxed on the value of the bonds, as property owners are taxed on the value of their property. From this perspective, the property tax may be regarded as inequitable.

Sales and Excise Taxes

Sales and excise taxes also account for a large portion of state and local tax revenues. They are levied on the purchase of consumer goods. A sales tax is a specific percentage of the price of a good; an excise tax is a per unit tax. For example, a sales tax may be 5 percent of the price of a good regardless of the price. Under a sales tax, as the price of a good rises, the amount of the tax per unit rises. However, an excise tax may be 5 cents per unit of good. The amount of the tax per unit does not change as the price rises or falls.

Sales taxes levied by state and local governments vary from state to state. In many locations, items such as food and medicine are exempt from sales

---

[1]As a consequence of legislation passed in 1983, the maximum income on which Social Security is collected will continue to rise yearly by a percentage equal to average increases in wages.

FOCUS   Social Security: A Bad Investment?

Is the Social Security system going broke? Are you going to pay Social Security taxes all of your working life only to discover that upon retirement there is no money left for you? The answer to these questions is an emphatic no. The Social Security system is not a business—it will not go broke. Basically it operates on a pay-as-you-go basis. In this sense, the Social Security system is relatively better off than many other government agencies. There is, however, another aspect of the system that concerns some economists.

Most private retirement systems effectively operate as personal savings programs. While people work, they contribute to a trust fund, from which deposits are invested in low-risk, interest-bearing accounts. This system allows for growth in retirement funds for the workers and retirement benefits exceed payments, since individuals receive all that they paid in plus interest.

Social Security, however, does not operate in the same manner. The benefits paid out to the retired this year are paid by people working this year. This method of operation does not allow for growth in retirement funds through the accumulation of interest. If retired workers receive more in retirement benefits than they paid in, then current workers are paying more into the system than previous workers. Current workers could pay more into the system than previous workers because of three reasons: There may be more workers, current workers may be earning higher wages, or Social Security taxes may be increased. Social Security is simply a transfer payment; income is transferred directly from the working to the retired. In effect, one generation of retired people is supported by the next generation of workers.

Currently, and throughout the past, the Social Security program is a good deal for retired workers; that is, they receive and have received more in Social Security retirement benefits than they paid in Social Security taxes and are receiving a relatively high rate of return on their investment. Until recently, the transfer payment method of financing the system worked well for two reasons: First, through the years, workers' productivity and wages have increased; and second, the labor force has grown substantially relative to the number of retired people.

For people entering the work force today, however, the transfer system may not be as lucrative. Before, Social Security contributors received a high rate of return on their donations. Some economists predict that today's contributors will receive a much lower rate of return—perhaps as low as 2 percent. Under the current method of taxation and payment, the average young worker may pay almost as much into the system through the years as he or she will receive upon retirement. If this does not seem like such a bad deal, consider all the lost interest receipts that could have been earned if an alternative retirement system were in effect—one that pays interest on contributors' payments.

One of the reasons today's young workers may receive a lower rate of return is that throughout their working lives they are likely to carry a heavier burden of retired workers than previous working generations. There will be larger numbers of retired people in the years 2000–2010 because of the increased life expectancy and the baby boom years of the 1940s and 1950s. Also, the birth rate decreased in the 1960s, 1970s, and 1980s, causing an increase in the retired-to-worker ratio. The inequities that have arisen in the system seem unavoidable. Today's young workers could be offered a better deal by lowering their annual contributions, thereby lowering payments to the current generation of retired workers. This would not eliminate the inequities, but it would transfer the inequity from the young workers to the retired workers. Alternatively, current workers could be offered greater retirement benefits, but this would increase the tax burden to future generations.

A pay-as-you-go retirement system will inevitably have inequities as long as population and worker productivity fluctuate through the years. Slight variations in the rate of return on Social Security contributions could be eliminated by an accumulated fund that serves as a buffer between the fluctuations in Social Security tax receipts and Social Security retirement payments. In fact, the founders of the Social Security system planned the program with a buffer fund in mind. However, the fund was not large enough to buffer the profound benefit payments of recent years. The loss of the buffer has diminished the system's ability to offer a constant rate of return. As the Social Security system stands now, some generation is likely to be forced to earn a low rate of return: either the present generations of young workers or retired workers or even a future generation of workers.

Source: Peter J. Ferrara, "Social Security: Bad Deal for Young Workers," *Cato Policy Report,* May/June 1985.

taxes. Excise taxes are levied both by federal and by state and local governments, but only on selected items. For example, liquor, tobacco, gasoline, and certain sporting goods have excise taxes. Frequently these tax revenues are earmarked for specific government projects.

The purchase of financial assets such as stocks and bonds is not subject to a sales tax. This feature of sales taxes may create a horizontally inequitable tax distribution when people with the same income spend their money in different ways. An individual can pay less in sales taxes by spending more on investment goods or savings than on consumption goods. Furthermore, since higher-income families invest or save a larger percentage of their incomes than lower-income families, a smaller percent of their incomes is subject to sales taxes. This feature of sales taxes makes them regressive—higher-income families pay a smaller percent of income in sales taxes than lower-income families.

THE AGGREGATE EFFECT OF TAXES

By changing quantities demanded and supplied and thus reallocating resources, taxes have a strong impact on the economy. Some economists are concerned that the impact of taxes may stunt the growth of the economy. For example, payroll taxes lower real wages to workers and thus may decrease the participation of workers in the labor force (a phenomenon discussed in Economics in Action at the end of this chapter). If this occurs, then the nation's total output will fall because of the tax.

Taxes on savings also can affect the overall performance of the economy. Interest obtained from bonds or savings accounts is subject to the personal income tax. The tax lowers the interest rate received from savings, so people tend to save less. With a decrease in savings, fewer funds are available for business purchases of capital. The tax on interest income can therefore diminish the rate of capital formation, which is an essential ingredient for economic growth.

To encourage growth, the government sometimes cuts taxes on certain activities. The government may, for example, encourage productive behavior by lowering the tax rate for businesses or individuals engaged in activities that increase the supply of resources. For example, an investment tax credit lowers the tax liabilities for firms that invest in new production equipment. Moving expenses are also deductible when people relocate for new jobs. Such tax credits and deductions can improve the productive capacity of the nation and thus increase real output.

The overall effect of taxes on production in the United States is not certain. However, the burden of taxes is growing, and the notion that their effect is detrimental to economic performance is gaining popularity. Many people are calling for decreased taxes and for tax reform. Some economists even believe that when tax rates get too high, tax revenues to the government actually fall. The important issue is whether the net effect of taxes encourages or discourages productive efficiency or, more specifically, whether we have the optimal amounts of public goods and whether our methods of taxation result in the most efficient use of resources.

TAX REFORM

Growing displeasure with federal tax policy among taxpayers, politicians, and economists reached a critical point in the mid-1980s. By 1986, the U.S. tax system had become so complex that the federal tax code, the textbook of federal tax regulation, contained more than 40,000 pages. Individual tax liabilities were difficult to determine, since deductions and exemptions had become so numerous and complex that tax specialists were often needed to determine routine household tax obligations. Compliance costs are what individual taxpayers must pay to maintain records and calculate tax liabilities; these costs were soaring. Adding to the concern was the understanding that, over and above the federal income tax, taxpayers are subject to a maze of sales, excise, property, and payroll taxes. And an unknown portion of the incidence of business taxes is passed on to taxpayers in the form of higher prices or lower wages. (See Focus, "Business Taxes: Who Pays?")

Economists were concerned with the inequities brought about through the numerous loopholes and the effects of high marginal tax rates on labor force participation and tax avoidance (see Economics in Action, "If You Are Taxed More, Will You Work Less?"). Also, government tax officials were concerned with the administrative costs of the old tax system.

The tax rates shown in Table 3 reflect significant changes in tax law enacted in 1986. Previously, there were fourteen tax brackets, and marginal tax rates ranged from 11 percent in the lowest bracket to 50 percent for incomes in excess of $175,000. Now there are only three tax rates, the highest one being 33 percent. The tax law changes in 1986 not only reduced the progressivity of the tax system, but they also eliminated many deductions. In particular, interest payments on consumer loans are no longer deductible. As a consequence, some taxpayers pay substantially more than before tax reform, while others pay less. Although there is much debate about the fairness of the new system, it is simpler than the previous tax laws.

The Tax Reform Act of 1986 may have decreased the complexity of personal and business taxes, but households and businesses continue to employ resources, both labor and capital, in an effort to minimize tax liability. Keeping records and receipts throughout the year and staying abreast of new tax loopholes are not trivial tasks. Several hundred million dollars is spent on professional tax services each year. Not only is bookkeeping labor employed for tax purposes, but many industries employ lobbyists in an effort to obtain new tax loopholes from Congress. While these resources are employed in the production of a valuable service to recipients of the tax reductions, they are not necessarily employed in the production of goods and services that benefit all of society.

Inefficient tax:
A tax that decreases the overall productive capacity of the economy; a tax that decreases the supply of resources or decreases the efficiency of resource use.

Figure 9 on page 545 shows the effects of an **inefficient tax** system on the productive capacity of the nation. Point A shows the level of output of publicly produced goods, G_1, and privately produced goods, P_1, with an inefficient tax system—that is, one that suppresses the supply of resources to the production of goods and services. Tax reform that encourages a more efficient tax system could increase the supply of resources and thus shift the production possibilities curve rightward. More of all goods—public and private—could be produced with a more efficient tax system.

FOCUS   Business Taxes: Who Pays?

Businesses are subject to many taxes, including corporate income taxes and license fees. When tax reforms or tax increases are considered, legislators are often encouraged to increase business taxes instead of personal income taxes. Many people believe this action shifts the tax burden away from individuals and places it on businesses. In the final analysis, however, businesses do not pay taxes: People pay taxes. All business taxes are either shifted to consumers in the form of higher prices or to resource suppliers in the form of lower prices. The resource suppliers who are affected include workers, shareholders, and suppliers of intermediate inputs.

Suppose that the government raises taxes by imposing a per unit tax on the sale of automobiles. This increases the cost of producing cars and causes the supply to decrease.

In Figure 8a, the supply curve is shifted from S_0 to S_1, causing the price to rise from P_0 to P_1 and the equilibrium quantity to fall from Q_0 to Q_1. However, the tax causes the net price to producers to fall from P_0 to P_p, where P_p is P_1 minus the per unit tax. This decrease in the after-tax price of the car causes the demand for inputs to fall. In Figure 8b, the effect of the tax on autoworkers is shown as a decrease in demand for their labor services. As a consequence, their wage rate falls from W_0 to W_1, and fewer of them remain employed. The tax will have a similar effect on demand for steel, tires, and all other inputs used in car production.

This business tax ultimately is divided among individuals who buy the cars and individuals who supply inputs to the auto producers. How this tax burden is divided among these groups depends on the elasticities of supplies and demands.

FIGURE 8   The Incidence of Business Taxes

(a) A tax on firms that produce automobiles decreases the supply of cars and raises the price to consumers. The net price that producers receive for cars falls, resulting in a decrease in the demand for inputs such as autoworkers. (b) The price (wage) that input suppliers receive falls as a consequence of the tax.

(a)

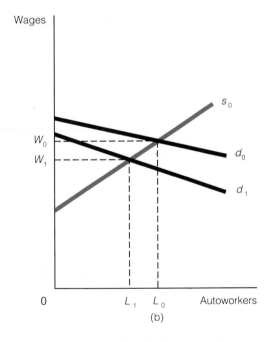

(b)

FIGURE 9

The Effect of Tax Reform

An inefficient tax system can depress the supply of resources. Point *A* shows a low level of production with an inefficient tax system. If tax reform results in a more efficient tax, then there will be greater production of both public and private goods— point *B* on the shifted production possibilities curve.

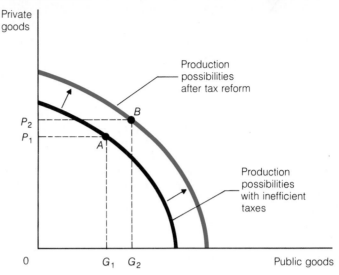

Political pressures can threaten the relative efficiency of any tax system. Concern over persistent federal deficits forced President George Bush to reconsider an oft-repeated campaign promise—No new taxes. Seeing a need for additional tax revenues is one thing; determining the best source of tax revenues is quite another. The President's change of heart was met with a number of proposals from members of both parties. Some Democrats proposed increasing the marginal tax rate on the highest incomes from 28 percent to 33 percent. Others, both Democrats and Republicans, suggested increases in "sin taxes"—excise taxes on cigarettes and alcohol—as well as increases in federal gasoline taxes to help cover the shortfall between expenditures and income. There was also some talk of a national sales tax. Clearly, shifting priorities in the 1990s could compromise earlier attempts to improve the equity and efficiency of the tax system.

SUMMARY

1. Taxes are payments for the support of government that are required of people to finance public goods. Although some taxes are levied directly on the users of public goods, in many cases beneficiaries cannot be explicitly defined, so general taxes must be used to diminish free ridership.
2. Most existing taxes effectively drive a wedge between the price that buyers pay and the price that sellers receive for a product or resource. The resulting price change decreases the size of the tax base, since demanders and suppliers respond to price changes, and thus affects the allocation of resources.

3. The amount of tax revenues is determined by the tax rate and the tax base, the amount of the taxed good. Raising the tax rate decreases the tax base, which means tax revenues may rise or fall.
4. The incidence, or final resting place, of a tax is usually shared by the buyers and sellers of the taxed good or resource. The relative elasticities of supply and demand determine whether or not the tax incidence is shared equally by sellers and buyers.
5. Taxes are levied according to two basic principles: the benefit principle and the ability-to-pay principle. The benefit principle suggests that the people who

receive the greatest benefit from public programs should pay the most taxes. The ability-to-pay principle suggests that people with the greatest ability to pay taxes should pay the most.

6. The ideal of equity, or fairness, in taxation has both a horizontal and vertical dimension. An equitable tax takes greater revenues from higher-income groups than from lower-income groups and also taxes people with equal incomes equally.

7. In general, the relation of tax liability to level of income falls into one of three categories: a proportional tax takes a constant percentage of income regardless of the size of that income; a progressive tax takes a larger percentage of income as income rises;

and a regressive tax takes a smaller percentage of income as income rises.

8. The marginal tax rate is the increase in tax liabilities, or tax bill, that results from an increase in income. With a progressive income tax, the marginal tax rate is greater than the average tax rate.

9. The U.S. government imposes a progressive income tax. Because of loopholes—exemptions and deductions—the federal income tax has both horizontal and vertical inequities.

10. The Tax Reform Act of 1986 decreased income tax progressivity and eliminated many deductions and exemptions.

KEY TERMS

public finance	benefit principle	taxable income
neutral tax	ability-to-pay principle	average tax rate
tax base	horizontal equity	marginal tax rate
sales tax	vertical equity	tax avoidance
excise tax	proportional income tax	inefficient tax
Laffer curve	progressive income tax	
tax incidence	regressive income tax	

QUESTIONS FOR REVIEW AND DISCUSSION

1. Draw the demand curve for a product with a perfectly inelastic supply curve. Show the effect of an excise tax. Who bears the burden of the tax? Is the tax neutral?

2. Does an income tax decrease the amount of labor supplied? If the supply of labor were perfectly inelastic, would an income tax decrease the level of employment? Who would bear the entire tax burden?

3. Some states have a competitive market for alcoholic beverages in bottles, but they charge an excise tax. Other states have state-owned and -operated liquor stores that are profit-making monopolies. Under which of these two systems would a state maximize revenues? Could a state make more money by selling the monopoly right to the highest-bidding firm?

4. Does the government use valuable resources to prevent tax avoidance? When state and federal agents attempt to detect and prevent bootlegging, are they attempting to protect a tax base? If there were no tax on liquor, would the government prevent bootlegging?

5. The current Social Security tax requires that both employers and employees pay 7.65 percent of the worker's gross income as Social Security tax. If the

law were changed so that the whole 15.30 percent were charged to the employee, would the burden of the tax shift?

6. What principle of taxation does a user tax follow? What principle does a property tax follow?

7. Which principle of taxation does the U.S. income tax follow? Is the U.S. income tax horizontally and vertically equitable? If a tax is not horizontally equitable, can it be vertically equitable?

8. When is a regressive income tax vertically equitable? With a regressive income tax, is the marginal tax rate greater than the average tax rate?

9. If consumption expenditures rather than income were taxed, would the after-tax wage still fall? Would a consumption tax decrease the amount of labor supplied? Would a consumption tax decrease the amount of capital supplied?

10. What would happen to the amount of capital in the United States if the interest income from savings were not taxed? Describe a tax that could increase the supply of capital.

11. What are the benefits of eliminating tax loopholes? How can tax loopholes be used to improve the productivity of the economy?

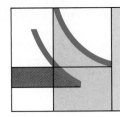

ECONOMICS IN ACTION
If You Are Taxed More, Will You Work Less?

Just about everyone has heard someone complain about the high tax rates, especially with regard to earning extra income, such as overtime pay. The percentage of extra income taken in taxes is determined by the marginal tax rate. With a progressive income tax, the marginal tax rate rises, so extra income is taxed at a higher rate than the rate at which the first dollars earned are taxed. This system may make people who have the opportunity to earn extra income resent the higher tax rate, but does it actually affect work decisions? Specifically, does a progressive tax rate have a more detrimental effect on the supply of labor than a proportional tax rate?

Any tax based on labor income effectively decreases a worker's wage. A proportional tax decreases the wage by a constant amount per hour regardless of the hours worked. For example, if a worker earns $10 per hour, a 20 percent income tax would lower the after-tax wage to $8 per hour regardless of the number of hours worked. A progressive income tax results in a lower hourly wage as the number of hours worked increases. For example, if the worker chooses to work 15 hours in a week, he or she may be taxed at a 10 percent rate, whereas 25 hours of work may be taxed at a 20 percent rate and 40 hours at a 30 percent rate. Figure 10 shows the relative effects of progressive and proportional tax rates. Both lower after-tax income and thus lower the wage rate, but by different amounts at different numbers of hours worked.

What effects do these two patterns of taxation have on the amount of labor supplied? A decrease in wages has an income effect and a substitution effect, which work in opposite directions. The income effect suggests that a wage decrease lowers real income and thus encourages individuals to work more. The substitution effect suggests that a wage decrease lowers the price of leisure and encourages individuals to buy more leisure—that is, to work less. Because these two effects work in opposite directions, the combined effect of a wage decrease on the amount of labor supplied cannot be determined. However, we may suggest the following: If per hour wages decrease because of the income tax, workers with an upward-sloping supply curve of labor will work fewer hours and workers with a downward-sloping supply curve will work more hours. Furthermore, if the aggregate supply of labor is upward-sloping, an income tax will decrease the overall amount of labor supplied.

The relative effects of proportional and progressive tax rates on the supply of labor also can be determined. In Figure 10, the two tax rates result in equal tax revenues at 40 hours of work per week. At this level, the income effect of the two tax rates is therefore identical, for they both decrease

---

FIGURE 10
Before- and After-Tax Income with Proportional and Progressive Tax Rates

The Y curve represents the level of income earned before tax withholdings. The Y_p curve shows after-tax income with a proportional tax rate, and Y_r shows after-tax income with a progressive rate. As workers increase the number of hours they work, their after-tax hourly wage falls. The decline is steady with a proportional tax, but not with a progressive tax. In this example, both tax schedules result in identical tax revenues at 40 hours of work per week: $80 for the government, with $320 left as take-home pay.

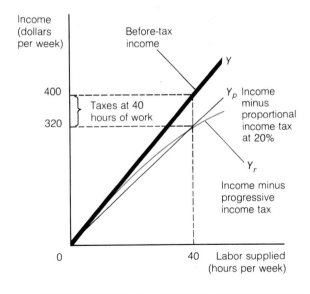

income by the same amount. However, the substitution effects are not the same under both tax systems. The progressive income tax has a stronger substitution effect than the proportional tax because it lowers the wage at the margin by a greater amount. This difference suggests that the progressive income tax will have a more detrimental effect on the amount of labor supplied than the proportional tax when both taxes bring in the same amount of tax revenues.

Question

If as a result of an increased tax rate John works more, what can be concluded about John's income and substitution effects—in other words, which is larger—if leisure is a normal good?

22

Public Choice

The discussions of public goods and externalities in Chapter 20 and taxation in Chapter 21 were based in part on the concept of market failure. When or where markets do not produce ideal outcomes, government can and often does play a role in correcting the situation. In Chapter 20 we assumed that government is capable of making these corrections. The overall capability of government to compensate for market failure, however, is itself an issue. Democratic governments act through a unique set of institutional arrangements, such as majority voting, representative democracy, political parties, bureaucracies, and special-interest groups. The theory of **public choice** attempts to use economics to understand and to evaluate how governments operate. A central precept of public choice theory is that government is not perfect; like markets, governments can fail to achieve ideal outcomes. Appropriate solutions to economic problems in the economy are frequently a choice between markets that are not perfect and government programs that are not perfect. The costs and benefits of alternative institutional arrangements must be carefully examined case by case.

The fundamental premise of public choice is that political decision-makers (voters, politicians, bureaucrats) and private decision-makers (consumers, market intermediaries, producers) behave similarly: They follow the dictates of rational self-interest. In fact, political and economic decision-makers are often one and the same person—consumer and voter. The individual who buys the family groceries also votes in an election. If the premise of public choice is correct, we can learn a lot about such issues as why people take the time and trouble to vote by applying the same logic to the voting decision that we have applied to the grocery-buying decision. As we do so, keep in mind that the institutions and constraints facing political decision-makers are different from those facing private decision-makers. For example, the benefits of buying groceries are fairly obvious, but what are the benefits of voting? We will be careful to specify such differences between private and public choices throughout our analysis.

Public choice, like the rest of economics, has both a normative and positive side. **Normative public choice** involves judgments about the desirability of certain political situations. In the design of voting procedures, for

Public choice:
The economic analysis of political decision making, politics, and democratic process.

Normative public choice:
Economic analysis that determines shortcomings and failures of the political process and suggests improvements.

example, how does majority rule compare with other voting rules in reflecting the true preferences of voters? Is there a better voting rule or process through which to make political decisions? Normative public choice looks at the way political institutions work from the standpoint of how we might make them work better.

Positive public choice seeks to explain actual political behavior. Why do high-income individuals vote more often than low-income individuals? How do committees and legislatures work? What is the impact of special-interest groups on government? In this chapter we will examine both normative and positive aspects of public choice after first exploring how self-interest affects decision making.

Positive public choice:
Economic analysis of political decision making and other political behavior that aims to understand, explain, and predict such behavior.

When you finish Chapter 22 you should understand

- some of the consequences of treating government decision-makers as rationally self-interested individuals.
- how the process of voting may not lead to optimal choices by individual voters.
- how self-interested groups affect government.
- the nature of bureaucratic behavior and its relation to government growth.

SELF-INTEREST AND POLITICS

The public choice approach to politics is based on the idea that political actors are no different from anyone else: They behave in predictable ways and seek to obtain their goals efficiently.

Proprietary:
Relating to private ownership and profit motivation; individuals directly bear consequences of their decisions.

Nonproprietary:
Relating to nonprivate ownership; entails motivations other than strictly profit motivations; individuals do not always or fully bear the consequences of their decisions.

Nevertheless, market behavior and political behavior differ in the constraints facing decision-makers. The market is a **proprietary** setting—one in which individuals bear the economic consequences of their decisions, which either enhance or decrease their wealth. In the market economy, a firm that produces a new product stands to make profits or losses depending on the quality of its efforts. The political arena is a **nonproprietary** setting—one where individuals do not always bear the full economic consequences of their decisions. For example, the political entrepreneur who comes up with a new political program does not bear the full costs of the program if it is a failure and does not reap all the benefits if it is a success. Behavior will therefore differ in market and in political settings, not so much because the goals of behavior are different but because the constraints on behavior are different.

We can distinguish the economic constraints at work in a market or proprietary setting and in a political or nonproprietary setting by analyzing the roles of agents and principals in each case. In both settings the agent, whether a firm or a politician, agrees to perform a service for the principal, whether a consumer or a voter. Because the agent and the principal are both self-interested, the agent will not always act in the interest of the principal, particularly if the agent's behavior is costly to monitor.

The agent-principal problem has been analyzed primarily in a private setting. For example, the corporate manager is an agent, and stockholders are principals. How do the stockholders get the manager to act in their interest? They do so primarily through economic incentives. Managers of private firms have incentives to control costs in their firms because increased costs cause a decrease in the firm's profitability. Stockholders, through such mechanisms as stock options and takeover bids, can discipline managerial behavior toward maximizing wealth.

Managers of political "firms," or bureaucracies, do not face a similar incentive to control costs. They cannot personally recoup any cost savings that they achieve for their agencies, and the means available to voters to curtail poor performance by political managers are minimal and costly to implement. This does not mean that public officials can do anything that they want to do. Like any other economic actors, they are constrained by costs and rewards.

The main point about the agent-principal problem is that political agents face different constraints on their behavior than do private agents because political principals face different incentives to control the behavior of the agents. This difference is the focus of public choice analysis.

One reason majoritarian democracy tends to waste resources is that the people who commit resources to particular uses need not bear the value consequences of their decisions. In contrast, within market processes those who make allocation decisions about resources do bear the value consequences of those decisions. Consider the case of an entrepreneur who sees many possibilities for recreation and camping at a nearby lake. The entrepreneur assembles the necessary resources, including land, utility hookups, boats, water slides, and so on in the belief that this commitment of resources will be profitable. If she is correct, the resources will generate services that are valued more highly than the other possible uses for the same resources. Should the entrepreneur's decision prove wrong, or should she make a loss, other members of society will be worse off because of the entrepreneur's error; in this case, the employment of resources generates services of lesser value than some other employment could have yielded. No one can guarantee that a particular employment of resources will prove profitable. However, the entrepreneur's responsibility for the value consequences of her actions will concentrate her attention on decisions more than if she did not bear this responsibility.

Suppose, instead, that some government agency, perhaps a Department of Parks and Recreation, decides to provide a campground and water-oriented recreation area. Government would probably plan to levy some admission fee, but the project would also receive support from the public treasury. Assume, for purposes of illustration, that 60 percent of the population enjoys camping and water recreation, while the other 40 percent has little use for such activities. Further assume that the average income is the same for both categories; if government is financed by an income tax, users would pay 60 percent and nonusers would pay 40 percent of the funds budgeted for the recreation facility.

The private entrepreneur's decision about what kind of facility to create depends on her judgment about what people will pay for different types and sizes of facilities. The more she thinks they are willing to pay, the larger the investment that will seem warranted. Suppose people would support a two-hundred-acre facility but not one with four hundred acres. What users would be willing to contribute in admission fees would not be enough to bid, or buy, the additional two hundred acres of campground and park away from others who would employ the resources differently. The creation of the two-hundred-acre facility where none had existed before would shift resources from less-valued to more-valued uses, but the creation of a four-hundred-acre facility would represent a shift from more-valued to less-valued uses. Suppose, however, that the government agrees to pay 40 percent of the admission fee. A five-dollar ticket could be bought for three dollars because the other two dollars would be paid by government subsidies. Under this arrangement, facility usage would rise, possibly enough to justify a four-hundred-acre facility. But where does the two-dollar discount come from? With tax financing by government, the money would come both from users and from nonusers of the facility. If the cost per user-day is five dollars, and if the usage is concentrated among 60 percent of the taxpayers, users receive a 40 percent subsidy from taxes paid by the public. The 60 percent majority is able to place a portion of the facility cost on nonusers. So the winners—actual users of the park—on the issue will choose a larger facility than if they had to bear all of the costs themselves.

Compared with a two-hundred-acre facility, four hundred acres represents a shift of resources from more-valued to less-valued uses. However, no entrepreneur loses wealth from deciding to commit resources to the larger facility. Instead, the loss of wealth is diffused over all of the taxpayers, whose tax payments to finance the facility exceed the value of the facility to them. When responsibility for the value consequences of decisions concerning resource usage can be avoided, as when tax financing takes the place of market prices, less care will go into decisions concerning resource usage.

Our example merely illustrates a potential problem with majority voting. Parks may not even be a good example, since there may be externalities associated with the public provision of park services. Despite the presence of externalities from the public provision of parks, however, our point is simple: Private entrepreneurs and public officials face different patterns of costs and gains from failure to keep their biases in check. Because public officials need not bear the consequences of their decisions to commit resources, they will be less restrained in pursuing their natural bias. Compared with private entrepreneurs, public officials will tend to commit resources to unprofitable uses more often than to profitable uses; they have different incentives.

But is it proper to compare the decisions of private entrepreneurs and public officials according to some standard of profitability? Some might wonder whether the single-minded promotion of economic calculation elevates the marketplace to the focal point of ultimate value. This sentiment reflects a belief that monetary concerns can be contrasted with human concerns. In this perspective, assessing different institutions in terms of ability to promote economic calculation—that is, to employ resources profitably—would, if pursued too far, elevate budgets over people.

There is undoubtedly some truth in this point of view. Making money is not always harmless or socially productive. Drug dealers and bank robbers make money in ways that harm society. But is there an intrinsic conflict between money and people? In a well-ordered society, Samuel Johnson noted, "people are seldom so innocently engaged as when they are making money." As a corollary, it might be added that in a well-ordered society people are seldom so destructive as when they are losing money. What does it mean when a particular commitment of resources makes a loss? Simply that resources are committed to wants that are valued less highly than those wants that could have been satisfied with an alternative employment of the same resources. To make a profit, by contrast, means that resources have been employed in a way that satisfies more highly valued wants.

The key to comparative institutional analysis is good judgment. Some activities are best left to market processes to organize and perform, and some are best left to governmental processes. Public choice theory helps us sort out the two categories.

PUBLIC CHOICE ANALYSIS OF VOTING

Normative public choice theory analyzes the performance of political institutions in serving voters. In this section we illustrate the usefulness of this approach by examining the process of voting by majority rule and by introducing the problem of constitutional choice.

Majority Voting[1]

In a democracy, public choices are typically based on a majority vote: If candidate A wins even one vote more than candidate B, then candidate A is elected to office. Particularly when more than two choices are available, majority rule does not always accurately reflect voter preferences.

Imagine a three-person nominating committee that must choose from among three alternatives—Smith, Jones, and Tobin—the nominee for club president. Each committee member ranks the three candidates in order of preference (first, second, third), and the winner is to be selected by majority vote (two out of three committee members in favor). Table 1 shows the rankings of the three candidates by the committee members (A, B, and C). Member A, for example, prefers Smith to Jones and Jones to Tobin. Note that each member has consistent preferences; that is, each member is able to rank the three candidates in order of preference.

Now let the voting begin. To find the preferred nominee, the committee pairs each candidate against one of the other two until a winner is found. Suppose they start with Smith against Jones. Who wins? A votes for Smith, B

TABLE 1   A Voting Problem

The committee must choose among Smith, Jones, and Tobin. The candidate receiving a simple majority (2 votes) wins. When each candidate is paired against another (Smith versus Jones, Jones versus Tobin, Tobin versus Smith), no clear winner emerges. Smith beats Jones, Tobin beats Smith, but Jones beats Tobin. This is a problem of simple majority voting on more than two candidates two at a time. Individual voters can clearly rank candidates, but majorities cannot. Majority voting in this case leads to a repetitive cycle of winners.

Committee Member	Smith	Jones	Tobin
A	1	2	3
B	2	3	1
C	3	1	2

[1]The origins of this analysis can be found in Kenneth Arrow's *Social Choice and Individual Values* (New York: Wiley, 1951) and in Duncan Black's *The Theory of Committees and Elections* (London: Cambridge University Press, 1958).

votes for Smith (*B* prefers Tobin overall, but between Smith and Jones prefers Smith), and *C* votes for Jones. Smith wins by a majority vote of 2 to 1. Can Smith now beat Tobin? *A* votes for Smith, *B* votes for Tobin, and *C* votes for Tobin. Tobin wins that round. Now, how does Tobin fare against Jones? Since Smith previously beat Jones, we would also expect Tobin to dominate Jones because Tobin dominated Smith. But notice what happens: *A* votes for Jones, *B* votes for Tobin, and *C* votes for Jones. This time, Jones wins! Thus in three rounds of voting, a different candidate wins each round.

The committee's stalemate points up a problem with majority voting. Under majority voting each individual voter can have consistent preferences among multiple candidates or issues, and yet voting on candidates two at a time can lead to inconsistent collective choices. In other words, individuals can make clear choices among Smith, Jones, and Tobin, but majorities cannot. Majorities will choose Smith over Jones, Tobin over Smith, Jones over Tobin, and on and on in a repetitive voting cycle until a way is found to stop the voting. Either Smith, Jones, or Tobin will win when the voting is stopped, but only because the voting stopped at a particular point, not because one candidate is a clear winner over the other two.

This simple proof strikes at the rationality of majority voting procedures. Although individual choices will be clear and rational, majority choices will be inconsistent and cyclical. Where does such a paradoxical result lead us? First, it leads us to look for a better voting procedure than simple majority rule when voting on two issues or candidates at a time. (See Focus, "A National Town Meeting," which discusses a proposal for national computer voting.) Second, the problem of voting cycles is mitigated to some extent by the institutions of democracy. Our legislatures and committees do not cycle endlessly among alternative proposals without reaching a decision. Votes are taken and decisions are made. Attempts to reach agreement do not go on forever. Powerful committee chairpersons, for example, can call for votes on legislation and see to it that the legislature produces new laws. While such legislative procedures do not solve the problem of inconsistent choices in majority voting, they do keep the tendency toward voting cycles in check.

Constitutional Choice

In a constitutional democracy there are two levels of political decision making: day-to-day decisions about running the government, which are made under given rules and procedures, and decisions about rules and procedures themselves. The first level of decision making takes place under given political constraints. The second involves the choice of the constraints themselves, which amounts to a constitution of the set of rules under which day-to-day government operates. For example, the choice of whether to employ simple majority voting or some other system would be a constitutional choice, while voting on current issues with the chosen voting system would be part of the day-to-day process of running the government.

Public choice theory can be applied to an analysis of **constitutional decision making.**[2] As an illustration, we will analyze the choice of a voting rule

Constitutional decision making:
The process of choosing which set of rules (voting rules, for example) society will adopt for its use.

---

[2]This analysis was first developed by James M. Buchanan, the Nobel laureate in economics for 1986, and G. Tullock, *The Calculus of Consent* (Ann Arbor: University of Michigan Press, 1962).

FOCUS   A National Town Meeting

Direct or participatory democracy, in which each citizen has the opportunity to cast his or her vote on all public issues, is often held up as the ideal method of reaching a political consensus. The use of such a voting process has been limited historically—the Athenian agora and the New England town meeting are the prime examples—chiefly because of the costs of meeting in large groups. But the advent of personal computers makes a direct voting system conceivable in the near future.

James C. Miller III envisions personal computers being used in conjunction with cable television or other data transmission systems to register and tally the votes of millions of individuals on legislative issues now decided by elected representatives. One can imagine that voters would spend a portion of each evening sitting in front of their computers examining the legislation that had been brought up for consideration, casting their votes, and soon after learning the results of the night's balloting.

Although the computer would vastly reduce the costs of registering and counting votes, it would not appreciably lower the cost to the public of becoming informed about issues. Miller's proposal consequently allows voters to assign proxies to experts or specialists. The proxy could be general, giving the proxy holder permission to cast a vote on all proposed legislation, or it could be confined to particular topics. For example, a voter could assign a proxy to an economist to vote on economic matters, to an expert in military affairs for votes on defense issues, and so forth.

Voters would assign proxies to individuals who would be expected to cast ballots in the same way the voter would if the voter were informed about the proposed legislation. The assignment of a general proxy would be similar to electing a congressional representative or senator except that proxy holders would represent the views of each voter and not just the views of the majority. Moreover, the speed of computers would allow proxy assignments to be made for as long as each voter wished—perhaps only an hour—instead of for fixed terms of two to six years.

Under Miller's system a role would exist for a legislative assembly to propose bills or to debate important issues. He suggests that the "house of representatives" be composed of the four hundred individuals wishing to serve there who have the largest number of proxies and that the "senate" be constituted from the one hundred largest proxy holders. The possibility of quick recall would assure that each representative would exercise the proxy exactly as voters wish.

The three main elements of Miller's proposal—direct registering of citizen voters, proxy assignments, and a bicameral legislative body—are not far removed from the current system established by the U.S. Constitution. The main difference is that technological development makes it possible for the democratic ideal of a small town meeting to operate on a national scale.

Source: James C. Miller III, "A Program for Direct and Proxy Voting in the Legislative Process," *Public Choice* 6 (Fall 1969), pp. 107–13.

for the legislature. We assume that the constitutional decision-makers are unbiased and impartial (a large assumption). Figure 1 illustrates the analysis.

The horizontal axis measures a number of people *N*, all the voters of a hypothetical society. The vertical axis is a measure in dollars of the expected costs of the various voting rules that could be selected for the society. Examples of these costs will be presented shortly.

Constitutional decision-makers face the following problem: How do they choose the voting rule that minimizes the expected cost of collective decision making in this society? The answer to the question can be found by examining the *D* curve and the *E* curve. The *D* curve measures the costs of collective decision making. As the voting rule is made more inclusive—requiring, for example, a two-thirds vote rather than a simple majority for approval or defeat of an issue—the costs of reaching collective decisions increase. In fact, as more people are required for agreement, the *D* curve increases at an increasing rate. This is a logical result in any group decision process. More people require more discussion, larger meetings, more bargaining, and so on. Agreement is more costly to obtain in a larger group.

FIGURE 1

Curves D and E represent the expected costs facing the constitutional decision-maker. D represents the costs of collective decision making; as the number of voters increases, D increases at an increasing rate. E is the cost of a decision rule requiring less than unanimity. Summing the two curves (D + E) and taking the minimum point gives the optimal voting rule chosen by the constitutional decision-maker. N_1 represents the optimal number of individuals in the society of N persons who must agree before a collective decision is made. N_1 may be any number. Here, it is a simple majority, $(N/2) + 1$.

Constitutional Choice

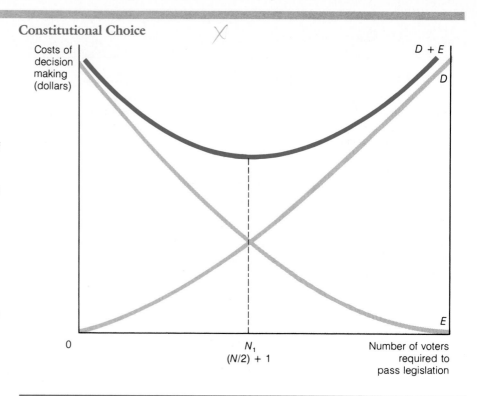

Costs of decision making (dollars)

D + E

D

E

0

N_1
$(N/2) + 1$

Number of voters required to pass legislation

The E curve reflects the potential costs that a collective decision can impose on the individual affected by the decision. If very few people are required to agree on a measure, agreement will occur more frequently and E-type costs will be high. In other words, a small number of people could get together and pass measures that benefit them at the expense of other voters. If a unanimity rule prevails, however, requiring that all members of the legislature agree before a tax can be passed, then E-type costs to any individual will be zero. Under these conditions, no collective decision can be made unless every voter consents. Unanimity means that one person can block a collective decision.

We have, then, the two major categories of costs related to the choice of a voting rule by constitutional decision-makers. The minimum of the two costs can be found by vertically summing the D and E functions and picking the minimum point on that curve. This occurs at N_1 in Figure 1. In this society, the two types of voting costs are minimized where N_1 persons are required to agree before a collective decision is made. N_1 may be any number. It may, for example, be a simple majority voting rule—$(N/2) + 1$ in Figure 1—or it may be a stricter voting rule in which more than a simple majority agreement is required before a collective decision is made. The analysis in Figure 1 leads to a more inclusive voting rule than simple majority. Though stricter voting rules involve higher D-type costs, the prospect of lower E-type costs could easily make stricter voting rules an important route to the improvement of collective decision procedures. What would happen, for example, if every proposal for a public expenditure had to carry with it a proposal for the taxes to finance it and, moreover, had to pass the legislature with a majority of seven-eighths?[3]

PUBLIC CHOICE ANALYSIS OF POLITICS

Positive public choice analysis is like positive economics: It consists of the development of models of political behavior that can be subjected to empirical testing. A positive theory can be wrong; it can fail to be supported by the evidence. A positive theory can never be proved; it can just fail to be refuted by the evidence. In this case, a positive theory will hold its ground against alternative theories until a theory comes along that offers a better explanation of the process. This is the spirit in which we outline positive public choice theory in this section. We present some positive propositions about government and political behavior that seem to be supported by evidence from the world around us.

Political Competition

Have you ever wondered why by election time the two major parties' candidates sound like Tweedledum and Tweedledee, and you cannot see any difference in the views espoused by either? Perhaps more important, why do we have only two major political parties in the United States? If we had only two firms in every market, antitrust authorities would become alarmed and might intervene to increase competition. The following model helps us answer these and other questions about political competition in a democratic setting.

Assume that voter preferences on issues can be distributed along an imaginary spectrum running from radical left (perhaps the Socialist Workers) to radical right (perhaps the John Birch Society), as in Figure 2. Further assume that voters vote for the candidate closest to their ideological position. The normal distribution of voters holding different ideological positions is split down the middle by M. The total area under the curve in Figure 2 represents 100 percent of the voters. We call the voter at M the median voter. If either candidate in a two-party race adopts a middle-of-the-road position such as M's position, he or she is guaranteed at least a tie in the election; he or she will receive at least 50 percent of the vote, since 50 percent of the votes lie to the left of M and 50 percent lie to the right. If the other party's candidate adopts any other position, such as R, he or she will get less than 50 percent of the vote. Remember: Voters follow the rule of voting for the candidate closest to their ideological position; fewer than half the voters in Figure 2 are closest to R. With one candidate at R and one at M, the candidate at R receives the percent of total votes to the right of the line at b, while the candidate at M receives the larger percent equal to the area under the curve to the left of b. Point b represents the ideological stance midway between M and R. The best strategy for each candidate is to adopt position M and hope that random

Median voter theorem

---

[3]A famous Swedish economist named Knut Wicksell proposed such a scheme more than ninety years ago.

FIGURE 2

The distribution of voters in this example is single-peaked, ranging from radical left to radical right. *M* represents voters at the middle, or median, of the distribution. The total area under the curve represents 100 percent of the votes. Two-party political competition leads to middle-of-the-road positions, similar to those held by voters at *M*. Points *a* and *b* represent ideological positions midway between points *L* and *M* and *R* and *M*, respectively.

Ideological Distribution of Voters

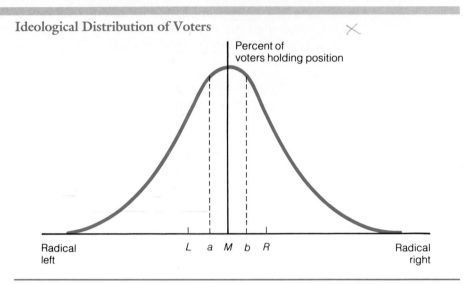

error (pulling the wrong lever) by voters will make him or her a winner. *M*, the median position, is the vote-maximizing position for both candidates; by election time, therefore, both candidates are virtual carbon copies of each other.

What happens if a third candidate enters the race? If he or she adopts a position such as *R* while the other two are at *M*, he or she will get all votes to the right of *b*, thereby beating both candidates at position *M*. Such an entry would probably induce one of the other two candidates to move away from *M*, perhaps to *L*. The remaining candidate at *M* would be isolated with a small fraction of the vote, those between *a* and *b*, where point *a* represents the ideological stance midway between *M* and *L*. The candidate at *M* would have an incentive to move outside of the *LR* segment, thereby trapping one of the other candidates, and so on. Starting from a position in which all candidates are at the center, at least one candidate in a three-party or larger system will have an incentive to move away from the center. But this spreading-out process has its limits. As long as the peak of the distribution of voters remains at *M*, a candidate can increase his or her percentage of the vote by moving toward *M*. With three candidates at *L*, *M*, and *R*, the two outside candidates can increase their votes by moving toward *M*.

This model of political competition is oversimplified, but it does offer some insights into political behavior. Where the distribution of voter preferences is single-peaked, as at *M* in Figure 2, there are strong tendencies toward median outcomes. This holds true for virtually any type of collective decision process, from a committee consensus to a public election. Middle-of-the-road policies are vote-maximizing; therefore, we expect middle-of-the-road candidates and policies to be winners. In addition, the analysis underlying Figure 2 gives some clues as to why we have only two major parties in the United States. If parties can enter on either the left or right flank of parties at *M*, such entry jeopardizes control of government by the center parties. We can expect that the *M*-type parties will do their best to place barriers to entry in the way of noncenter parties, such as making it costly and difficult for a new party to get on the election ballot.

Finally, this discussion assumes that parties know what the distribution of voters is. If there is uncertainty or lack of information about what voters want, then political parties will have to spend resources and take risks to better understand voter desires. Uncertainty about the distribution of voters explains why political parties commission polls, spend money on campaigns and advertisements, and engage in a host of activities to try to attract voters.

Logrolling

Logrolling:
The exchange of votes by legislators, usually in order to gain support for particular legislation.

Positive public choice also takes into account the behavior of officials once they are in office. A typical political behavior is **logrolling,** a term used to describe the process of vote trading. Representatives in a legislature are constantly making deals with one another. One wants a dam in his district; the other wants a new courthouse in hers. They agree to trade votes on issues: You vote for my dam; I'll vote for your courthouse.

There are many beneficial aspects of logrolling. Mainly, it enables representatives to register the intensity of their preferences across issues. For example, a minority representative who feels strongly about animal rights can trade his votes on issues about which he does not feel so intensely for support on the animal rights issue. Logrolling also helps mitigate the problem of indifferent majorities winning over intense minorities. In essence, logrolling, or vote trading, is a form of exchange, and economists usually view exchange as a productive and efficiency-enhancing process.

We must be careful, though, in assessing logrolling. Its general efficiency depends on the political setting. Most legislatures, for example, are formed on the basis of geographic representation, under which a representative's constituents have one thing in common: They all reside in the same area. Any bill the representative can get through the legislature that benefits the members of her district should win votes at election time. In effect, a geographically based system provides the legislator with incentives to represent local interests in the national legislature at the expense of broader national issues.

Most individuals in a community share an interest in the vitality of the community's economy. In many instances, a bloc of voters from a single voting district may receive income from a single firm or industry, as in a company town or in geographically concentrated industries like the steel, automobile, lumber, defense, and regional agricultural industries. When economic activity is concentrated, representatives can win political support by serving the economic interests of their respective home districts. Tariffs, industry- and company-oriented tax concessions and subsidies, local public works projects, and defense contracts are all examples of issues that often are decided, in part, on the basis of their economic impact on certain regions.

Representatives therefore trade their support on national issues, such as air pollution control, for support on amendments or separate bills that serve their local interests. National legislation often becomes a vehicle for local support, and the result is pork-barrel legislation that carries rich rewards for specific locales. Logrolling, which attempts to redistribute income toward certain regions and industries, generally does not lead to a more productive economy. Rather, it leads to legislation such as individual industry tariffs, unnecessary and costly public works legislation, and special-interest tax "reform" bills. This form of logrolling at the national level is unproductive, not because it reveals relative intensities of preferences on national issues, but because in its most blatant forms it reveals relative intensities of preference on essentially local issues. When restricted to national issues, however, logrolling can be a beneficial means for revealing voter preferences. For example, the voters of one senator's state may prefer more foreign aid for Latin America, while the voters in another's state may strongly favor increasing Social Security benefits to the elderly. The necessary legislation for both issues may be passed with the exchange of the senators' votes, thereby indirectly promoting voters' preferences.

Voting. In Chapter 6 we discussed whether voting was rational. Simply put, one voter out of many has very little impact on any election. Therefore, even if the marginal costs of voting—the time it takes to register and go to the polls—are very low, they may make it too costly for the average voter to vote. The voter is rational; he or she will vote when the marginal benefits exceed the marginal costs of voting. If an election is predicted to be close, the marginal benefit of voting will rise, and voter turnout will rise.

In this section we examine the act of voting in more detail by discussing some of the relevant differences between the market and voting as means to allocate resources. We compare consumer behavior within market institutions and voter behavior within political institutions.

In markets, consumers make marginal choices; in politics, voters must evaluate package deals. When you buy carrots or hot dogs, you can buy one more or one less; that is, you engage in marginal decision making. When you vote for a politician or a party, you vote not for a single issue but for a package or a platform—all-or-none decision making. Politicians do not offer voters a little more or a little less of this or that public program. They offer package deals. This feature of voter choice makes voting complex and costly. Moreover, when people are forced to make package choices, they are likely to end up choosing a lot of items that they really do not want in order to get a few things that they do want.

Elections generally involve the choice of numerous candidates and issues. In addition to the packaged nature of political choice, the voter has to make a variety of choices at the same time; many candidates and issues are on the ballot. To some extent, this is efficient. It is better to vote on many things at once than to vote on a lot of individual matters in separate elections. Clearly, economies of scale accrue in voting. But having numerous candidates and issues on the ballot also leads to greater complexity and cost in voter choice.

Consumption is frequent and repetitive; voting is infrequent and irregular. The consumer goes grocery shopping weekly or daily; the voter votes every year or every two or four years. This infrequency makes it more difficult for the voter to find reliable policies and candidates. Imagine how the grocery-buying decision would be altered if you bought groceries once a year. Your ability to discard bad products and try new ones would be reduced dramatically.

The primary difference between voting and the market, deriving from the above three factors, is that voters have little incentive to be informed. Voting is more complicated than market choice. This means that voters have little incentive to gather information about their public choices. In market choice, consumers have direct and strong incentives to gather information and to search for useful, reliable products. In public choice, voters have difficulty evaluating candidates and issues. The costs of being informed are high. Suppose the Defense Department argues for an expensive new missile system on the grounds that it is needed to deter a Soviet threat. How can the average voter hope to obtain the information needed to make a rational choice? The same is true for proposals for dams, foreign aid, welfare, relations with China, the money supply, jobs, and so on. Voters are quite rationally uninformed about such matters; they estimate that the costs exceed the benefits of being fully informed. Indeed, they may free ride by not gathering information, not voting, and letting those who do vote make the choices for them. If the choices of other voters happen to be beneficial to nonvoters, the nonvoters benefit without bearing any of the costs. This behavior leads to a fifth and final implication.

4.

Since voters are not well informed, the information transmitted to politicians by elections is not very useful in helping politicians determine what voters want. Politicians predictably have great difficulty assessing the implications of an election with respect to what voters want them to do. Politicians who are good at reading the public's pulse will survive and be reelected. Nevertheless, the transmission of information is not direct. In markets, if consumers want more carrots, they can effectively transmit this information to producers and get more carrots. In voting, if consumers want more butter and fewer guns, it is costly and hard to make this preference known to politicians through voting.

In sum, private and public choices differ in important ways. Political markets are more imperfect than private markets. This is a positive proposition derived from the way our political institutions are designed. (For more on the act of voting, see Focus, "The Rationality of Voting.")

Interest Groups

Interest groups:
Collections of individuals with one or more common characteristics, such as occupation, who seek collectively to affect legislation or government policy so as to benefit members of the group.

The behavior of **interest groups** helps explain a significant amount of government activity. To see how interest groups affect government policy, consider the process by which a statewide group of barbers might organize to advance their interests.

The most fundamental problem that the barbers face is how to get organized. Specifically, each barber has incentives to stay outside the interest group, for if the interest group is successful in, say, obtaining higher prices for haircuts, a free-riding barber—one who does not pay dues to the barbers' association—can benefit without incurring any costs. Free-riding behavior makes the formation of interest groups difficult but by no means impossible. For such reasons, interest groups seek ways to limit the benefits of their activities to members only.

Assume that the barbers organize. The group's representatives go to the state legislature and seek a legally sanctioned barbers' cartel. The purpose of this cartel is to protect barbers from new competition by erecting barriers to entry into barbering, thereby allowing barbers to raise the price of a haircut above the costs of providing a haircut. In other words, the barbers petition the state government to raise their wealth at the expense of haircut consumers. Put another way, they are demanders of a wealth transfer from the state.

Who are the potential suppliers of wealth transfers? The suppliers are those—in this case, consumers of the barbers' product—who do not find it worthwhile to organize and to resist having their wealth taken away by the

FOCUS   The Rationality of Voting

You know that where *N* is the total number of voters, each individual vote represents a 1/*N* chance of affecting an election. Hence, when *N* is large, it really is not rational to vote on the grounds of having one's vote count or tipping the election one way or the other.

People do vote in substantial numbers in statewide and national elections in the United States, however, so the idea that it is not rational to vote is not taken very seriously. Voting tends to vary positively with such variables as an individual's income and education. Higher-income citizens are more likely to vote and to participate in politics than lower-income citizens. Even though their votes do not count more—don't carry any more weight in the 1/*N* sense—and it is more costly for higher-income people to take time off to vote, they vote in greater proportions than lower-income citizens.

Higher-income citizens consider voting both an act of investment (getting one's candidate elected) and an act of consumption (doing one's patriotic duty). Voting may be irrational in the investment sense, but it is quite rational in the consumption sense. Doing one's duty gives one tangible economic benefits. Hence, there is no paradox when voting is analyzed as an act of investment *and* consumption.

Source: R. D. Tollison and T. D. Willett, "Some Simple Economics of Voting and Not Voting," *Public Choice* 16 (Fall 1973), pp. 59–71.

---

barbers. This is an unusual concept of supply, but it is a supply function nonetheless. The attitude that will prevail among suppliers is that it would cost them more to protest the barbers' proposal than any benefits they would derive from protesting. For example, the average consumer might spend $100 to defeat the barbers' proposal, the net result of which would save $10 in haircut costs. Why spend $100 to save $10?

This example describes a "demand" and a "supply" of wealth transfers in the case of barbers. How does the market for wealth transfers work? Politicians are brokers in this market and in the **market for legislation** generally. The politician's job is to pair demanders and suppliers of wealth transfers. If they transfer too much or too little wealth, they will be replaced at the next election by more efficient brokers.

Market for legislation: The interaction between interest groups acting as demanders of legislation beneficial to the group and legislators acting as suppliers of legislation; legislation generally entails some type of wealth transfer.

The outcome for the barbers is shown in Figure 3. The barbers start out as a purely competitive industry, producing Q_c haircuts per year at a price of P_c. When their interest group forms, they persuade the legislature to grant them cartel status. This persuasion is not very difficult because the consumers who are harmed by the cartel do not find it worthwhile to protest to the legislators. The barbers are the only ones to be heard, and perhaps by putting their arguments for a cartel in public-interest terms ("higher prices mean higher quality," "barbers must be licensed to ensure an orderly marketplace," and so on), they carry the day with the legislature.

The legislators assess the costs and benefits of creating a barber cartel. In Figure 3, the barbers seek $P_g ABP_c$ in cartel profits at the expense of consumers' welfare; haircut consumers incur an additional loss equal to ACB. (Area ACB represents the welfare loss due to monopoly discussed in Chapters 10 and 13.) The per capita gains to barbers, who are a relatively small number of producers, exceed the per capita costs to the more numerous haircut consumers. The result: The legislature passes a law giving the barbers a cartel.

However, this discussion is highly stylized. Interest groups do not always work as producers versus consumers. Technically, any group can organize and act as an interest group, and we find that interest groups represent many overlapping segments of society. There are labor unions; women's rights groups; religious groups; trade associations; organizations for doctors, lawyers, hunters, environmentalists, farmers. Moreover, not all of these groups are small. Many large groups, such as farmers, are effectively organized as an interest group. The basic point is that you can begin to explain why a certain law is passed if you try to answer two questions: Who wins? and Who loses?[4] Focus, "Interest Groups and the British Factory Acts," presents a historical example of how the demands of interest groups result in legislation.

Ideology

Ideology:
A set of beliefs or preferences that are held by the legislator independently of his or her constituents' self-interest.

What role does ideology play in explaining the voting behavior of legislators? In this case, **ideology** may be defined as a set of beliefs or preferences held by the legislator independently of his or her constituents' self-interest. The legislator may believe in a balanced budget and so may vote against a new post office for the district. In doing so, the legislator's conservative fiscal ideology overrides the constituents' preference for a new post office. Public choice theory poses our original question about the role of ideology slightly differently: How much legislator behavior is explained by ideological preferences and how much by responsiveness to the local interests of constituents?

Research on this issue finds that both ideology and the self-interest of legislators in supporting local projects matter in voting behavior. In other

FIGURE 3

P_c is the competitive price that the industry—in this case, barbers—charges, and P_g is the price established by the group after it is granted cartel status. After the cartel is formed, it stands to gain P_gABP_c in profit from consumers, and consumers stand to lose ACB in welfare. In some cases, the former wealth transfer dominates the latter welfare loss, and a law is passed sanctioning the cartel.

How an Interest Group's Demands Are Met

[4]For more analysis of interest groups, see R. E. McCormick and R. D. Tollison, *Politicians, Legislation, and the Economy* (Boston: Martinus Nijhoff, 1981).

FOCUS   Interest Groups and the British Factory Acts

The interest-group theory of government evaluates legislation in terms of who benefits and who loses. Not only is this framework a useful way to analyze present-day laws and regulations, but it is also helpful in the study of economic history.

The British Factory Acts of 1833–1850 placed restrictions on employment of children and women in the English textile industry. Most historians have analyzed this legislation by accepting at face value the rhetoric of those who agitated to get it enacted. This rhetoric was couched in humanitarian terms, but suppose that we go behind what the reformers said and apply the interest-group theory to this legislation. Who won and who lost as a result of the Factory Acts?

Two groups stood to gain from restrictions on children and women in the labor force. Skilled male workers would gain because children and women were competitors for their jobs. If competing labor could be outlawed, male wages would rise. There is, in fact, evidence that male workers were the primary agitators for the factory legislation (predictably, according to interest-group theory). Males presented their lobbying efforts in terms of doing a favor for women and children and serving the public interest.

The other group that may have gained from restrictions on women and children was the owners of steam textile mills. Mills in the 1830s were water- or steam-powered. Steam mills could run all the time, but water mills were subject to droughts. Water mills typically made up for time lost during droughts by operating for long hours when water power was available. The restrictions on women's and children's hours of work made this catching-up process more difficult. Textile prices rose as a consequence, and the wealth of the steam mill owners increased because their operations were less hampered by the law.

Who lost? Obviously, the women and children who lost jobs and income suffered. Yet one would have to count against this loss the extent to which the law led to better working conditions, especially for children. Women were particularly vocal about their loss, but since women could not vote, politicians could ignore their wishes at low cost. The other losers were the owners of water-powered mills.

Interest-group analysis goes beyond what people say they want and evaluates the costs and benefits that actually result from government action. In this light, the Factory Acts appear to have been primarily an example of wealth transfer and sexism.

Sources: G. M. Anderson and R. D. Tollison, "A Rent-Seeking Explanation of the British Factory Acts," in David Colander, ed., *Neoclassical Political Economy* (Cambridge, Mass.: Ballinger, 1984), pp. 187–201; Howard P. Marvel, "Factory Regulation: A Reinterpretation of Early English Experience," *Journal of Law and Economics* 20 (October 1977), pp. 379–402.

Carding, drawing, and roving in a Lancashire, England, cotton mill, 1834

words, the role of legislators in voting extends beyond representing the interests of voters.

The debate over ideology generally takes this form: A model of representative voting behavior is specified that includes constituent interest and ideological measures such as the Americans for Democratic Action (ADA) or the American Conservative Union (ACU) ratings of legislators. If the ideological measures have a statistically significant impact on the model, ideology influences the behavior of politicians. Some challenge this conclusion: They argue that the model should include better measures of the "economic" variables that affect voting behavior; including these variables would tend to reduce the statistical significance of the ideological variables.

The whole issue is mired in difficulties. Consider a simple example. Representative *A* is from an oil-rich district and yet votes no on an oil import fee bill. The vote gives the representative a higher ACU rating, but did the representative express an ideological preference in this case? Because the representative is probably voting no in exchange for votes on other issues, it is not clear that the vote was on ideological grounds. Logrolling obscures the role of ideological voting on *single* issues. Many post offices and dams owe their existence to logrolling; these structures are capable of generating at least the level of local political benefits for a sponsoring representative as the oil import fee in our example.

In voting across all issues, ideology plays an economically rational role, according to Douglas Nelson and Eugene Silberberg.[5] Narrowly focused bills where the final destination and distribution of funds are well known make ideological voting more costly; hence, less is observed. More general bills that have unknown or unpredictable effects make ideological voting less costly; hence, more such behavior is observed. Ideological voting obeys the law of demand—more occurs when such behavior is cheaper. Nelson and Silberberg presented evidence from voting on defense appropriation bills to show that this approach to ideology and voting is useful.[6]

Bureaucracy

Bureaus:
The arms of government that serve to implement and enforce legislation and to administer programs created by legislation.

While legislatures enact laws and authorize levels of public spending, the actual implementation of those laws is delegated to a variety of agencies, commonly referred to as **bureaus.** Created by the legislature, bureaus are generally supportive of the legislature's interests. Bureau employees generally fare better as the bureaus' budgets expand because, among other things, opportunities for promotion expand and, with them, salaries. With expansion, bureaus become more effective as vehicles for imposing their version of the public interest on the citizenry. At the same time, legislators have strong interests in the enactment of legislation that will be implemented by bureaus. Consequently, bureaus and the legislative committees with which they deal generally have similar interests.

---

[5]See Douglas Nelson and Eugene Silberberg, "Ideology and Legislator Shirking," *Economic Inquiry* 1 (January 1987), pp. 15–25.

[6]Nelson and Silberberg used ADA ratings as well as several other variables, including the per capita value of defense contracts, as indicators of legislator ideology and measurements of constituent interests. The authors compared individual senators' voting records to their constituents' interests for twelve roll call votes in the United States Senate during the 97th Congress.

As organizations engaged in the supply of services, public bureaus differ from private firms in two important respects. These differences in turn lead to important differences between the conduct of bureaus and the conduct of firms.[7]

1. Bureaus derive revenue from legislative appropriations, which in turn come from tax collections. By contrast, firms derive revenue from the voluntary buying decisions of customers.
2. There are no transferable ownership rights to public bureaus. In bureaus, there is no status comparable to that of stockholders, the residual recipients of differences between revenues and expenses. Although there may be profits in the operation of bureaus, these profits do not show up as residual income to residual claimants or owners. Rather than being converted to personal use, any differences between revenue and expense disappear through added expenditures. For example, at the end of each fiscal year in Washington, bureaus with funds left over try to find ways to spend the funds—which goes a long way towards explaining why many large research grants are made at the end of the fiscal year.

The difference in incentives between private and public decision making yields many familiar results. It is often more difficult to register a car, get a passport, or buy alcoholic beverages in a state that has state-franchised stores than it is to buy automobiles, plane tickets, or wine from private suppliers. Under government operation, a bureau's hours of operation are usually shorter than those of private businesses and, hence, less convenient to customers. There is also a reluctance on the part of bureaus to accept checks and credit cards.

In addition to these common observations, empirical studies have shown that public bureaus have higher costs of doing business than private firms. To cite a few examples, Roger Ahlbrandt has estimated that the cost of providing the same type of fire protection is about 88 percent higher when it is provided by public bureaus rather than by private firms. David Davies has estimated that a private airline in Australia was 104 percent more productive in carrying freight and mail and 22 percent more productive in carrying passengers than a public airline. Robert Spann estimated that refuse collection is 43 percent more expensive when done by public bureaus than when done by private firms.[8]

Without the profit-maximizing incentives of private business, there are numerous ways that the indirect appropriation of excess funds through higher expenditures can take place within bureaus. Different public bureaus face

---

[7]See, for example, Ludwig von Mises, *Bureaucracy* (New Haven: Yale University Press, 1944); Gordon Tullock, *The Politics of Bureaucracy* (Washington, D.C.: Public Affairs Press, 1965); Anthony Downs, *Inside Bureaucracy* (Boston: Little, Brown, 1967); and William A. Niskanen, *Bureaucracy and Representative Government* (Chicago: Aldine-Atherton, 1971).

[8]Roger Ahlbrandt, "Efficiency in the Provision of Fire Services," *Public Choice* 16 (Fall 1973), pp. 1–16; David G. Davies, "The Efficiency of Public Versus Private Firms: The Case of Australia's Two Airlines," *Journal of Law and Economics* 14 (April 1971), pp. 149–65; and Robert M. Spann, "Public Versus Private Provision of Governmental Services," in *Budgets and Bureaucrats,* ed. Thomas E. Borcherding (Durham, N.C.: Duke University Press, 1977), pp. 71–89.

different opportunities for appropriating profits. A public hospital, for instance, may overinvest in equipment that is underutilized. A highway department may award contracts without competitive bidding and pay higher prices than necessary. Since excess funds cannot be appropriated directly, they are appropriated indirectly, as profits dissipated through expenditures.

One main difference between a private firm and a public bureau lies in the identification of the customer. For private firms, the people who use the good or service are the customers whose continued favor is essential for the firm's success. The public bureau's customers, however, are not the people who queue up for space at a public campground or who try to get efficient service at the motor vehicle department. Although the bureau provides services to those people, the public bureau's customer actually is the legislature because it is responsible for the bureau's existence through legislation and funding. To remain in existence and to be successful, the bureau must please the legislature.

To some extent, of course, the legislature reflects the interests of citizens. But we must distinguish between the special interests of particular citizens and the interests of citizens in general. In cases where a bureau's performance pursues special interests, those special interests may represent a quite different set of people from those who use the bureau's service. For legislation to reward some special interests, it must penalize other, general interests. The often poor performance of public bureaus is another feature of a special-interest approach to government; this performance may not be so poor viewed from the perspective of the bureau's true customers—the special interests that demanded the legislation.

The theory of public choice represents an expansion of normal economic analysis into the realm of politics. This area of research will undoubtedly attract the attention of economic researchers in the future. Hopefully, work in this area will enhance our understanding of how the political process works and how it can be made to better serve the interests of the average citizen.

SUMMARY

1. Public choice analysis is the study of government with the tools of economics. It treats government decision-makers like private decision-makers—as rationally self-interested actors.

2. Public choice theorists assume that government officials maximize their individual interests, not the "public interest." In the process, they face different constraints than private decision-makers, and so they behave differently.

3. Normative public choice analysis evaluates the effectiveness with which political institutions represent the preferences of voters, focusing on the evaluation of voting rules.

4. Voting on issues two at a time by majority rule can lead to a voting cycle where there is no clear winner, even though each individual voter knows clearly which candidate he or she prefers.

5. Constitutional decision-making analysis considers the choice of rules in the political arena. In other words, it asks how disinterested decision-makers design such things as a voting rule for legislatures.

6. Positive public choice analysis seeks to present testable theories of government behavior. It is analogous to positive economics applied to politics.

7. In political competition the median voter is the controlling force. Parties and candidates compete by taking middle-of-the-road positions.

8. Logrolling, or vote trading, reveals relative intensities of preference across issues. When combined with geographic representations, however, logrolling can lead to an overexpansion of local public projects.

9. Voting and the market are two different means of allocating resources. For a variety of reasons, voters

have little incentive to be informed in making voting decisions. As a result, voting is an imperfect mechanism for allocating resources.

10. Interest groups seek wealth transfers from government. Successful interest groups win transfers at the expense of general efficiency in the economy.

11. Bureaucracy is the production and management side of government. Unlike private production, govern-

ment production takes place in a not-for-profit environment. As a consequence, bureaucrats behave differently from private decision-makers.

12. The ideology of legislators may have an impact on choices made in the political arena. These choices may be independent of the legislator's constituency.

KEY TERMS

public choice
normative public choice
positive public choice
proprietary

nonproprietary
constitutional decision
    making
logrolling

interest groups
market for legislation
ideology
bureaus

QUESTIONS FOR REVIEW AND DISCUSSION

1. What is a voting cycle? What conditions cause a voting cycle?

2. What is logrolling? What are the benefits and costs of logrolling?

3. Name three differences between voting and the market as mechanisms for allocating resources.

4. What is the difference between a public bureau and a private firm as a productive unit?

5. Discuss three experiences you have had in dealing with government that can be explained by the not-for-profit nature of government production.

6. Suppose that the size of government is declining relative to the size of the economy. Apply public choice theory to explain how this might happen.

7. Using the median voter model of voter preferences discussed in the chapter, explain why Democratic presidential candidates are more liberal in the primaries than in the general election.

8. Why do we not observe voting cycles in the U.S. House of Representatives?

ECONOMICS IN ACTION
The Growth of Government

A particularly important problem for public choice analysis is to explain why government changes size over time. As Table 2 shows, the size of government in the United States has grown substantially over the period from 1929 to 1989. As the data clearly show, this growth has occurred in both absolute and relative terms. There are ways to measure the size of government other than total spending or spending as a percent of GNP. The absolute or relative size of public-sector employment could be used. However, even though

any measure of government size has its drawbacks and advantages, many economists feel comfortable using expenditure measures. The relative size of government at all levels stood at 10 percent of GNP in 1929, compared to 34 percent in 1989.

Explanations for the growth of government are easy to find in some periods. Expenditures for World War II clearly explain the high percentage of GNP accounted for by government expenditure over the period 1940–1945. Likewise,

TABLE 2
The Growth of Government Expenditures in the United States Since 1929

Total government expenditure is measured as expenditure by all levels of government: federal, state, and local.

Year	GNP (billions of dollars)[a]	Total Government Expenditure (billions of dollars)[a]	Percentage of GNP
1929	103.9	10.3	9.9
1933	56.0	10.7	19.1
1939	91.3	17.6	19.2
1944	211.4	103.1	48.8
1949	260.4	60.0	23.0
1954	372.5	97.5	26.2
1959	495.8	131.9	26.6
1964	649.8	177.8	27.4
1969	963.9	290.2	30.1
1974	1472.8	467.4	31.7
1976	1782.8	587.5	33.0
1978	2249.7	694.8	30.9
1980	2732.0	889.6	32.6
1982	3166.0	1111.6	35.1
1984	3765.0	1275.2	33.9
1985	3998.1	1401.7	35.1
1986	4208.5	1484.1	35.3
1987	4524.3	1575.0	34.8
1988	4880.6	1658.8	34.0
1989	5233.2	1778.7	34.0

Source: Council of Economic Advisers, *Economic Report of the President* (Washington, D.C.: U.S. Government Printing Office, 1990), pp. 294, 387.

[a]Dollar amounts have not been adjusted for inflation.

the figure for 1969 in Table 2 is high due in no small part to expenditures on the Vietnam War. However, the general upward march of government expenditures has many complex causes. For public choice theorists, the growth of government poses both positive and normative issues.

On the positive side is the fundamental question, Why does government grow? Part of the answer rests with the various forces that we have discussed in this chapter. Those who pay for and elect government officials do not pay close attention to what government is doing; interest groups and government expand in size and scope as a consequence. Politicians are happy to accommodate the interest groups and bureaus so long as voters remain uninterested. The increases in the share of GNP taken by government expenditure since the mid-1970s may be partly explained by changes within the political structure. In the mid-1970s, the U.S. Congress underwent certain structural changes in the way committee chairs were decided. The old seniority system of assigning chairs was disposed of in favor of a more democratic elective system. This tended to make agreement on spending bills among representatives more difficult, and thus more costly. Logrolling became a relatively more important method of doing business in the Congress, resulting in larger expenditures.

Such things can come to an end, however. Government and independent bureaus in government can become so large or controversial that they attract the voters' attention. In this case, citizen reaction can lead to a reduction in government or bureau size: In the late 1970s, California voters approved a proposition on the statewide ballot leading to a radical reduction in local property taxes. Government growth is not inevitable. Our basic argument has been that government is a more imperfect mechanism for allocating resources than the market is. This does not mean that government is out of control; it just means that it takes longer to effect changes in the size of government.

Government has also grown because the problems that it addresses have grown. These include the greater capacity of the private sector to create negative externalities, the perceived need for expensive defense technology, and the importance of such public goods as basic research and education.

On the normative side, scholars have addressed the issue of how to contain government expansion. The basic thrust has been to suggest fiscal constraints on government. That is, in recognition of the incentive of politicians and bureaus to expand government, the way to check such expansion would be to impose a system of fiscal discipline on political decision-makers. For example, many states in the United States operate under state constitutions that require state governments to run balanced budgets. Unlike the federal government, these states are not permitted to borrow if the legislature or governor wishes to spend more than the available tax revenues. Other states allow governors to veto certain parts of proposed total expenditures in budgets passed by legislatures. This fiscal constraint can retard state government expenditure by allowing only a part of a proposed budget to be rejected rather than the entire budget. The U.S. Constitution could be amended to require that the annual budget be balanced or that government expenditure not exceed a given percentage of gross national product. This approach recognizes the incentives of politicians and bureaucrats, and it seeks to design constitutional rules that will enhance the degree to which the political process reflects the underlying desires of voters.

Question

Different cities provide different levels of public goods such as education, street repair, and police and fire services. Individual citizens, however, do not value different "packages" of public goods in the same manner. One response to the situation is to move to other cities when those cities offer a more satisfactory package. Under what conditions of local public goods supply might you prefer one city to another?

A. C. Pigou

Ronald Coase

A. C. Pigou and Ronald Coase: Solving the Problem of Social Costs

ARTHUR CECIL PIGOU (1877–1959), an English economist, succeeded Alfred Marshall in the chair of political economy at Cambridge University in 1908. Like Marshall, Pigou had been drawn to economics because of its social importance. Both men were deeply interested in improving the living standards of the poor. Both had great faith in the power of economics to improve the welfare of all members of society. Pigou and Marshall disagreed, however, on the proper role of government. Like his neoclassical peers, Marshall advocated laissez-faire policies, whereas Pigou felt that government's power to tax and redistribute wealth among all members of society was a crucial ingredient of general economic prosperity.

Pigou held his prestigious position at Cambridge for more than thirty-five years. During this period he wrote several books, including *Wealth and Welfare*, *The Economics of Welfare*, and *The Theory of Unemployment*. His students at Cambridge included Joan Robinson and John Maynard Keynes. Pigou continued to be productive after his retirement from Cambridge in 1943. For many, his death in 1959 marked the end of the English neoclassical tradition in economics, a tradition begun in the 1870s.

RONALD COASE (b. 1910) has earned international recognition for his papers "The Nature of the Firm" (*Economica*, November 1937) and "The Problem of Social Costs" (*Journal of Law and Economics*, October 1960). Modern theories of the firm and of externalities owe much to the work of this English-born economist. Coase's novel economic analysis of institutions, particularly the law of business, has helped spawn a new area of economic inquiry, much of which has challenged traditional views of how government and government regulations affect the behavior of firms. Coase himself has written extensively on utilities, broadcasting, and other government-regulated monopolies. He is generally critical of the effects of regulatory law, believing that solutions to market failure can and do exist outside of government intervention. Coase is Professor Emeritus of Economics at the University of Chicago. He has held posts at the University of Buffalo and the University of Virginia.

TAXING THE SMOKE

Pigou pioneered the modern microeconomic theories of externalities and market failure. In *The Economics of Welfare* he distinguished between private costs of production—the operating and maintenance costs of producers—and social costs of production—the expense or damage to society that results from the producer's activity. There are many possible illustrations of social costs. A nuclear power plant's social costs include the potential danger of radiation to the surrounding community—a reality after the Chernobyl incident in the USSR. A railroad's social costs might include the danger of fire caused by sparks from its wheels. Pigou's own example of private and social costs is a smoke-belching factory. The factory owner's private costs derive mainly from the people and machines that make up the factory. The social costs of the factory derive from the smoke the factory produces as a by-product of its operation. The smoke from the factory soils clothing and property nearby, creates a noxious odor, and poses a health risk to the community.

Pigou pointed out that there is nothing in the economic forces of market supply and demand to prevent the factory owner from continuing and even increasing the pollution. Since the market, in essence, permits the owner to shift part of the costs (the smoke) onto others, the owner will likely protect this advantage.

Pigou also sought to prove that market failure resulted in inefficient resource allocation. According to Pigou's theory, the factory owner will try to manage production so that the marginal private costs of the factory equal the price of the product. Pigou pointed out that by doing so, however, the owner is not responding to the true costs of production. Since the owner's private costs are less than the full (private plus social) costs of production, the owner will produce "too much" output. If, however, the owner managed production so that private plus social costs equaled price, the excess output would be eliminated, and all resources would be allocated according to their true opportunity cost.

To remedy the inequities and inefficiencies of market failure, Pigou proposed a tax on polluters and other sources of social costs. In the case of a smoke-belching factory, the tax would depend on the amount of smoke produced and would force the owner to restrict pollution to the point at which the benefits of production were equal to its true costs. Such a tax would also likely restrict output. In this way, both producers and consumers would share the costs of the tax.

ASSIGNING LIABILITY

In his 1960 article "The Problem of Social Costs," Ronald Coase challenged Pigou's major assumption that social costs always move in one direction—from producer to society. In fact, Coase argued, the issue of social costs poses potential harm to both parties. On the one hand, society may be harmed by the unwanted by-products of production, and on the other hand, producers may be harmed by society's attempt to correct the market failure through taxation. In terms of Pigou's example, should the factory owner be allowed to pollute the local community, or should the local community be allowed to drive up the factory's costs of production by forcing it to cease polluting? The issue is especially pertinent today in the debate over acid rain and toxic waste.

Coase argued that an efficient solution to the problem of social costs would involve negotiation between the polluter and those affected by the pollution. If it were possible for both sides to negotiate, then a market might be created between them. The two sides could "trade" for the right to the pollution: Either the factory would pay the local community for the right to pollute or the community would pay the factory not to pollute. Coase showed that the actual outcome of such negotiations would be the same regardless of which side had the "right" to use the atmosphere as it saw fit.

In the real world, such negotiations between parties help solve a variety of potential social cost problems. For example, restaurant customers have influenced restaurants to segregate smokers from nonsmokers, eliminating the social cost of tobacco smoke. Home buyers shopping for a house near an airport can negotiate for a lower price to offset the social cost of airplane noise.

Often, both sides in the dispute face enormous transaction costs to enter such negotiations. A community, for instance, might find it very costly to organize into a bargaining unit with a nearby factory. The millions of people affected by acid rain and the hundreds of producers responsible for the pollution could hardly transact freely. In such instances Coase suggested that the parties look to the courts, not the legislature, for a solution. Courts could determine the relative costs involved and could assign liability, or responsibility, to the party whose costs of adjusting to the social cost are lower.

For example, who should be responsible for injuries and death resulting from the use of defective products? For a long time, the rule of *caveat emptor*, or "let the buyer beware," prevailed among courts, and the consumer was fully responsible for the safe use of products. Such a rule worked reasonably well in times when products were relatively simple in design and use. However, as products become more complex, consumers may not be able to judge their safety and reliability. As a result, the courts have gradually increased the range of cases in which producers are held liable for shoddy and dangerous merchandise. This shift in the legal posture of the courts is an illustration of the Coase idea at work: The legal system alters liability assignment in response to the relative costs of adjusting to social costs.

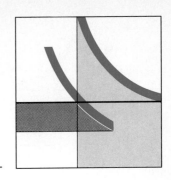

PART FIVE

Private-Sector

and Public-Sector

Macroeconomics

23

Macroeconomics: Contemporary Problems and Issues

Today's local newspaper or the evening television newscast is likely to contain much economic news. There might be stories on conditions in microcomputer markets or on the migration of agricultural labor from Minnesota to South Dakota. By far the most consistently reported economic news relates to the overall health of the economy.

The media pay careful attention to monthly and quarterly statistics on such measures as the inflation rate, the unemployment rate, and the growth rate in gross national product (GNP). Government economic policies to remedy macroeconomic problems are also heavily reported.

Topics such as the real rate of growth in the economy may seem abstract and distant, but they do have an immediate and lasting impact on individual economic well-being. Economists have spent more than two hundred years seeking to understand how the macroeconomy—the large-scale economy—shapes our lives.

Think for a moment about how the major macroeconomic issues—inflation, unemployment, and growth—are likely to influence your future. Will economic conditions affect your ability to repay your college loan? Will you enter the job market during a time of high unemployment? Will your hopes for a high-paying job, a comfortable home, a promising future for your children be realized? The study of macroeconomics certainly cannot answer these questions for you, but it can better equip you to plan for the future, whatever the future may hold. Likewise, this chapter is not intended to begin our formal study of macroeconomics. Instead, we present an overview of basic macroeconomic policy goals and introduce much of the terminology employed by macroeconomists. When you complete Chapter 23 you should understand

- the overall goals of macroeconomic policy and the trade-offs between goals.
- the nature of unemployment and inflation and their effects on economic growth.
- how, in general terms, fiscal and monetary policies are used to achieve the goals of macroeconomic policy.
- the essential tools of aggregate demand and aggregate supply that economists use to analyze the macroeconomy.

THE GOALS OF MACROECONOMICS

In Chapter 1 we defined *macroeconomics* as the analysis of the economy as a whole. When working with macroeconomic theory, the focus is on whole quantities, or what economists call aggregate quantities. Macroeconomics concerns not just one market but all markets; not just one price change but all price changes; not just one firm's employees but all employment.

As with any discipline, the field of macroeconomics is made up of many specialized areas, competing theories, and ongoing debates. Consistent throughout macroeconomics, however, is a shared set of goals. Both macroeconomists and the politicians who heed (or disregard) their advice are interested in achieving three separate, sometimes conflicting, objectives: full employment, price stability, and economic growth. We discuss each of these goals separately, but you will soon see they are closely intertwined.

The Full-Employment Goal

Full employment is a primary goal of any economic society for obvious reasons. The more fully resources are employed, the greater the levels of output of goods and services, and the higher the prosperity.

Social Concern over Unemployment. Not only does high unemployment threaten to bring poverty to millions of citizens, but it also can lead to political upheaval. During the Great Depression of the 1930s, for example, signs of social and political unrest appeared in the United States. Farmers marched on Washington, D.C., makeshift camps of the poor and out-of-work dotted the nation's cities, and mass migrations of the jobless from the Dust Bowl of the Midwest to the Promised Land of California took place. When World War II mobilized the economy, full employment was restored before serious political and social upheaval could erupt.

Other nations of the world have not been spared such upheavals. Witness the frequent changes of government and political systems in developing nations, where poverty—much of it caused by widespread unemployment—is rampant. Increased crime and even violent revolution can result from failure to attain the macroeconomic goal of full employment.

The purely human costs of unemployment on individuals, families, and society itself can be devastating. Unemployment is a primary cause of poverty, dislocations of families, and, in extreme cases, homelessness. It puts extraordinary pressure on social and welfare services that are funded with taxes. More important, unemployment represents resources *not used* to produce goods and services—perhaps the ultimate inefficiency.

In recognition of the social and political implications of unemployment, the U.S. government passed the Employment Act of 1946 on the heels of the Depression and World War II. The act recognized and enshrined maximum employment as a macroeconomic goal of the federal government. The meaning of the term *maximum employment* has been modified in the intervening years, but policy-makers still respect the intent, if not the letter, of the law. Unemployment rates of 10 percent and more, for example, which characterized the U.S. economy in 1982 and 1983, brought great concern to the U.S. Congress and to the Reagan administration. Unemployment rates also ran high in Europe during the early 1980s, reaching over 13 percent in England and close to 10 percent in Italy by 1984. In all nations, the goal of full employment is critical. Social programs such as unemployment compensation and food stamps ease the burden of unemployment, but they cannot substitute for the economic benefits of full employment.

Defining the Levels of Employment and Unemployment. Some unemployment in specific markets is always expected. In a dynamic economy, demand grows for some goods and services and declines for others. In recent years, for example, the demand for high-technology outputs such as microcomputers, lasers, and fiber optics has outpaced demand for the products of heavy industry, and temporary unemployment in heavy industries such as steel and machine tools has been very high. Some workers may develop new skills, however, and temporarily unemployed resources may flow into new areas of production.

From an economic perspective, there is little reason to be concerned with the temporary periods of unemployment that workers in specific fields experience as the economy undergoes change. In such cases, **unemployed** workers generally remain out of work for relatively brief periods of time before they succeed in obtaining a job. However, there *is* reason for concern when numerous workers in many different industries simultaneously become unemployed. When this happens, output levels fall far below potential, and families of the unemployed workers experience real hardship over extended periods of time. For this reason, the federal government keeps close tabs on the **unemployment rate** each month.

A random sample from 55,800 household units is surveyed each month to calculate unemployment. Household members who are under sixteen years of age are not counted as members of the labor force, nor are nonworking full-time students, the hospitalized, or the incarcerated. Qualifying individuals are asked a series of questions to determine whether they are employed, unemployed, or not in the labor force. A person is considered to be employed if, during the survey week, he or she did any work at all as a paid employee or for a personally owned business or a profession. Unemployed persons are all civilians who had no employment during the survey week, who were available for work (except, perhaps, for temporary illness), and who had made specific efforts to find employment some time during the prior four weeks. Persons who are neither employed nor unemployed (those not working and either unable to work or not looking for employment) are not deemed to be members of the labor force.

The labor force is therefore defined as the total of employed and unemployed persons. To calculate the unemployment rate, the number of unemployed persons is divided by the total labor force. This method of measuring unemployment is not without problems. During periods of high unemployment, unemployed workers become discouraged and stop searching for jobs. Once they stop looking, they are no longer considered members of the labor force. This behavior causes measured unemployment to fall. (The opposite is true during periods of unusually low unemployment, when people are enticed into the labor market.) For reasons such as these, the unemployment rate may not provide a perfect picture of what is happening in the economy.

Unemployed:
A labor-force status characterized by an individual who is actively seeking employment but is not working.

Unemployment rate:
The percentage of the labor force without jobs.

Figure 1 shows the growth of the labor force and the fluctuations in employment and unemployment since 1950. Table 1 presents data on the unemployment rate, the number of unemployed workers, and the size of the labor force since 1975.

The Bureau of Labor Statistics also breaks down the unemployment rate into rates for various demographic groups to show the *differing rates* of unemployment for particular groups in the economy. Figure 2 shows the total unemployment rate in the U.S. economy for the period 1960–1989 and the corresponding unemployment rates by race, sex, and age. Some facts about the composition of the unemployment rate are apparent: (1) Minority groups

---

FIGURE 1   **The Labor Force, Employment, and Unemployment**

The national labor force is the sum of the employed and the unemployed. The labor force has increased steadily because of population growth, but the level of unemployment has fluctuated with changes in the overall economy.

Sources: U.S. Board of Governors of the Federal Reserve System, *Historical Chart Book* (Washington, D.C.: Board of Governors of the Federal Reserve System, 1984); Council of Economic Advisers, *Economic Report of the President* (Washington, D.C.: U.S. Government Printing Office, 1990), pp. 330, 338.

TABLE 1

Unemployment, Unemployment Rate, and the National Labor Force, 1975–1989

Year	Unemployment Rate (percent)	Unemployment (thousands of persons)[a]	Civilian Labor Force (thousands of persons)[a]
1975	8.5	7,929	93,775
1976	7.7	7,406	96,158
1977	7.1	6,991	99,009
1978	6.1	6,202	102,251
1979	5.8	6,137	104,962
1980	7.1	7,637	106,940
1981	7.6	8,273	108,670
1982	9.7	10,678	110,204
1983	9.6	10,717	111,550
1984	7.5	8,539	113,544
1985	7.2	8,312	115,461
1986	7.0	8,237	117,834
1987	6.2	7,425	119,865
1988	5.5	6,701	121,669
1989	5.3	6,528	123,869

Source: Council of Economic Advisers, *Economic Report of the President* (Washington, D.C.: U.S. Government Printing Office, 1990), p. 330.

[a]Age sixteen and over.

Full employment:
A situation in which unemployment exists only because of normal market adjustments to changing demand or supply or to outmoded skills of workers; also a numerical federal government goal for the unemployment rate.

Natural rate of unemployment:
A theoretical concept; the unemployment rate that coexists with macroeconomic stability or labor-market equilibrium in the long run.

have experienced a higher unemployment rate than whites, (2) teenagers in the 16–19 age group have experienced a higher unemployment rate than any other age group, and (3) women over twenty years of age have generally experienced higher unemployment rates than men of the same age.

Despite the presence of unemployment, **full employment** remains a political goal. As we have seen, the Employment Act of 1946 charged the federal government with the responsibility of promoting maximum employment. In 1978, Congress passed the Full Employment and Balanced Growth Act, which committed the government to full employment, defined as an unemployment rate of 4 percent. The goals of the act have been modified in the intervening years, with the goal being adjusted upward over the 1970s and 1980s.

How can full employment be defined as allowing for any unemployment? Some economists feel that there is a **natural rate of unemployment** (or employment), the rate that would exist under long-run equilibrium conditions because of the time needed for adjustments in the labor market, the lag in matching vacancies and workers, the costs of hiring and firing and of changing jobs, regulations affecting structural changes in labor markets, and so forth. Market forces and institutions, not individuals, determine the natural rate of unemployment at any given time. The actual rate of unemployment can be compared to the theoretical concept of the natural rate, as in Figure 3. Note that the actual unemployment rate has fluctuated around the natural rate, with cycles of business activity producing unemployment below the natural rate in some periods and above the rate in other periods. In the most direct sense, macroeconomics deals with why the actual rate of unemployment differs from the natural rate and with what might cause the natural rate to change over time.

Economists debate, sometimes hotly, what the appropriate level of full employment is. In fact, the unemployment rate has not fallen below 5 percent

FIGURE 2

Unemployment Rates

The unemployment rate (the number of persons unemployed divided by the labor force) rises and falls with other economic activity. However, blacks and teenagers consistently have higher rates of unemployment than other groups.

Source: Council of Economic Advisers, *Economic Report of the President* (Washington, D.C.: U.S. Government Printing Office, 1990), p. 338.

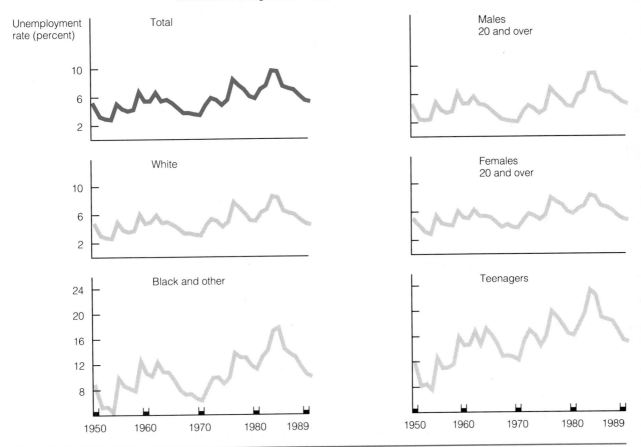

since 1973, and many economists now think that the "full-employment" unemployment rate should be in the 5–7 percent range, a range close to the theoretical concept of the natural rate of unemployment. Unemployment is a familiar problem in economies, even in rapidly growing countries (see Focus, " 'Floating Waves' of Unemployed in Japan").

The Goal of Price Stability

Price stability:
A situation of no inflation or deflation in the economy; no change in the overall level of prices of goods, services, and resources.

The second major macroeconomic goal is **price stability**—the absence of inflation or deflation in the overall level of future prices. Inflation is a process of price level increases that take place over time. Inflation can be stable and predictable or unstable and unanticipated—in either case, bringing higher costs to consumers and producers, and to buyers and sellers. Inflation is far more disruptive when it arrives unannounced, however.

FIGURE 3

Rate of Unemployment, 1890–1989

The actual rate of unemployment has fluctuated widely since 1890. The unemployment rate rose to dangerous levels during the 1930s but has stayed within narrower limits since World War II. The actual unemployment rate has fluctuated around the natural rate of unemployment, a theoretical concept that depends on the situations and institutions surrounding the demand and supply of labor.

Source: Robert J. Gordon, *Macroeconomics,* 5th ed. (Glenview, IL: Scott, Foresman, 1990), p. 14.

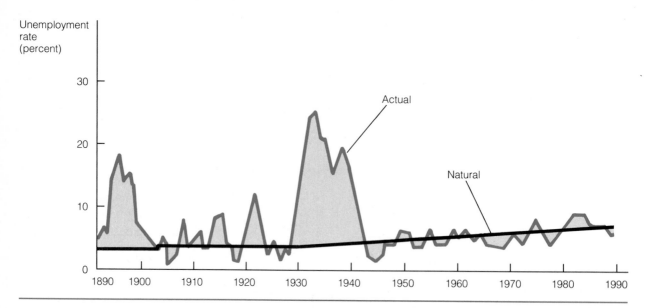

Rate of inflation:
The percentage change in the average level of prices over a period of time; the speed at which prices in general are rising.

Inflation is not simply a rise in the price of gasoline or chicken. Rather, inflation is a macroeconomic situation characterized by sustained and continuous increases in the overall level or average of all prices. One way to measure inflation is to look at the average of prices for some representative collection, or market basket, of goods and services that people buy. An increase in this average, or general, level of prices over some given time period (a month or a year) indicates the presence of inflation in the economy.

Suppose that food was the only good people bought. A 2 percent increase in the average level of food prices during the month of March means that the consumer must spend $1.02 at the end of March to buy the same market basket of food items that $1.00 would purchase in February. Never mind that bacon prices actually fell in March and that potato chip prices rose by 10 percent. Inflation is measured by considering the average prices of some representative bundle of goods at some given level—such as the retail, wholesale, or producer level.

If the cost of some market basket of goods and services was, say, $200 in one month and $210 in the next month, then prices in general would have risen by 5 percent during the month. When the change in prices over any period of time (a month here) is expressed as a percentage, the number calculated is called the **inflation rate.** The inflation rate is the speed at which

FOCUS   "Floating Waves" of Unemployed in Japan

Popular wisdom has it that Japan's postwar economic "miracle" provides jobs and prosperity for all in society. Although formal unemployment does exist in Japan, a generous social safety net provides for the unemployed. A recent article disputes the conventional wisdom about the magnitude of unemployment in Japan.[a] The *furosha*, or "floating waves" of homeless street people, wander day and night through the parks, streets, and rail stations of Japan's major cities—despite free medical care from the government, subsidies of up to $1000 per month per person for food and shelter, and subsidized housing. How is such homelessness to be explained in a prosperous and growing nation?

As in the United States, many who find their way to the streets are old, infirm, or addicted to alcohol or drugs; they are unable to raise themselves to a level of self-support. Many of the unskilled day laborers who helped build the infrastructure of Japan in the 1960s are now too old to find work. In addition, residents of outlying areas often move

[a]Neil Gross, " 'Floating Waves' of Homeless in a Sea of Prosperity," *Business Week* (September 12, 1988), p. 50.

into the cities, hoping to secure a job with a salary that will allow them to send money back home.

Important cultural differences between Japan and the United States may explain why the Japanese homeless problem may be more entrenched, despite the considerable social safety net provided. The rigid employment track, where job entry to retirement is carefully planned within an employment "family," means that job mobility is not as fluid as in the United States. On-the-job skills are important; older workers may find it difficult to secure new jobs if employers think there is a need for significant retraining and projected work years for the workers are few. Japanese unable to find work have access to welfare and social services but apparently do not use them. The shame associated with failure—losing one's job, falling into debt, or the simple inability to find work—is far more culturally ingrained in Japanese than in Americans. In Japan, a governmental investigation into family finances is required before subsidies will be paid. In the United States, this kind of scrutiny would represent merely a minor structural impediment to the unemployed; in Japan, the impediment is cultural and moral as well, and of great importance in explaining the *furosha*.

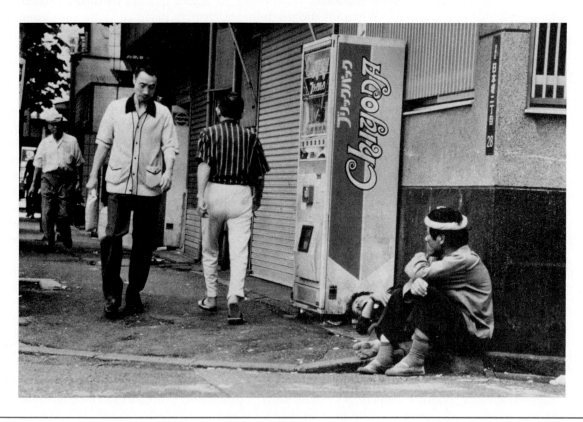

prices in general are increasing. In this example, the inflation rate calculated is 5 percent per month. If prices continued to increase at the same speed for an entire year, the inflation rate would be 80 percent per year (5 percent per month compounded for 12 months). A statistic calculated by the federal government's Bureau of Labor Statistics called the consumer price index (CPI) is used to measure the overall average level of prices in the United States. By calculating the percentage changes in the CPI, the inflation rate in the U.S. economy can be measured. (The CPI will be explained and discussed fully in Chapter 24.)

Deflation is a decrease in the general price level. Since World War II, price instability has been due to inflation rather than deflation. During the 1970s, for example, the United States experienced double-digit inflation rates reaching almost 14 percent per year in 1980.

Certainly we have plenty of evidence that inflation can get out of hand. Like severe unemployment, runaway inflation can wreak havoc in a society, causing social and political disintegration. A classic example occurred in post–World War I Germany when the inflation rate was as high as thousands of percentage points *per day*. Eventually, the German mark was worth more as paper—it was actually used as wallpaper—than as money. As a result, goods disappeared from markets and people starved. Looking farther back in time, economic historians claim to have evidence that runaway inflation was partly responsible for the breakdown of the Roman Empire's economic and political institutions.

Many of the costs of inflation and deflation can be traced to the inability of various economic institutions to adjust quickly to unanticipated price changes. When inflation is fully anticipated, personal savings for education, retirement, or vacations; tax codes; and financial contracts may be adjusted. But when inflation is unanticipated, adjustments become costly and difficult. People who live on fixed incomes—many of them elderly and poor to begin with—are particularly hard hit by inflation, as we will see in Chapter 34.

Historically, inflation has been a problem in the United States during postwar periods. Even then, as Figure 4 shows, the inflation rate has seldom risen above 10 percent per year. In the period of inflation following the Vietnam War, the inflation rate rose to 13.5 percent in 1980, before falling sharply. Increases in the inflation rate late in the 1980s again generated fears of serious inflation. Other countries have had much worse inflation problems in recent years. For example, the inflation rate in Argentina and Brazil reached annual levels in excess of 1000 percent during the 1980s. In Bolivia, the annual inflation rate exceeded 20,000 percent in 1985. Mexico had inflation rates in excess of 150 percent but has since adopted policies that sharply reduced the inflation rate to less than 25 percent per year.

Even when the rate of inflation stands at relatively modest levels, it can pose problems for the economy. First of all, inflation has peculiar redistributive effects. That is, it enhances some people's real incomes at the expense of others'. **Real income** is the quantity of goods and services that can be bought with an individual's **nominal,** or money, **income.** In other words, real income is the real purchasing power of one's nominal income. For example, if a person was earning $10,000 per year in 1975 and continued to do so in 1990, a modest inflation rate of 6 percent per year from 1975 to 1990 would mean that the person's real income, or purchasing power, would have fallen by more

Deflation:
Sustained decreases in the average level of prices.

Real income:
The purchasing power of money income; the quantity of goods and services that money income can buy.

Nominal income:
Income measured in terms of money, not in terms of what the money can buy.

FIGURE 4

The inflation rate is measured by calculating the yearly percentage changes in the CPI. Inflation rates varied greatly over the period 1950–1989, although the trend since 1950 has been toward average higher rates. Notice, however, the downward trend in the inflation rate since 1980.

Source: Council of Economic Advisers, *Economic Report of the President* (Washington, D.C.: U.S. Government Printing Office, 1990), p. 364.

The Rate of Inflation, 1950–1989

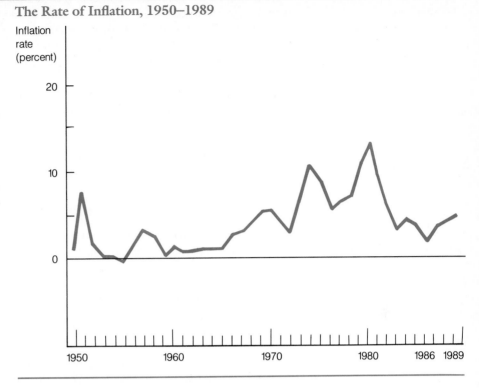

than 50 percent, despite the fact that the nominal income remained the same. This loss of real income is all too familiar to people on fixed money incomes—those on fixed pension plans, for example. When prices of the goods and services consumed by these groups rise, but their nominal incomes remain the same or do not rise as fast as prices, the real income of these consumers falls. Naturally, consumers whose income is rising at a faster rate than prices are better off during inflationary periods. Under such circumstances, arbitrary redistributions take place, with those on fixed incomes bearing the costs.

Uncertainty about future prices also results from price instability. Debtors and creditors, for instance, must guess at future prices and charge or pay interest rates that may or may not cover the real change in the value of money. Inflation also disrupts decisions of producers and consumers. Consumers' expectations about future prices and future real incomes are especially important. Consumers may adjust to their expectations, buying today if they expect prices to push higher tomorrow or if they think that inflation will reduce purchasing power in the future. (Likewise, if consumers expect deflation at some point in the future—far less likely, given U.S. experience—they would be more likely to postpone purchases, especially of durable goods.) While fully expected inflation may cause some transaction costs, unanticipated inflation and an unstable, unpredictable inflation rate greatly disrupt the plans of buyers and sellers. Before 1981, consumers also faced the possibility of real income erosion due to the tax structure. When nominal income increased as a result of attempts to maintain real income, income earners were forced into higher

Tax indexation:
The basing of income taxes on real income instead of nominal income.

tax brackets. This "bracket creep" occurred because tax rates have been levied on money income received, not on real income earned. **Tax indexation** is one way to curb this detrimental effect of inflation. Under tax indexation, the federal tax tables are tied to the inflation rate. Tax indexation was first implemented in 1981 and was preserved in the Tax Reform Act of 1986.

Producers are also profoundly affected by unanticipated inflation. With uncertainty about inflation, producers may withhold output of goods and services from the market. Under extreme uncertainty, the plans of investors and business entrepreneurs can be badly upset, causing postponement or abandonment of projects that enhance employment and economic growth. High, unpredictable rates of inflation help explain the low rates of capital formation and slow economic growth in some developing nations.

The Objective of Economic Growth

Economic growth:
A sustained increase in the overall productive capacity of an economy over time.

The third major macroeconomic issue is growth in the economy. **Economic growth** refers to any increase in the productive capacities of the economy, whether as a result of an increase in the labor supply, an increase in the productivity of labor (the output per worker), or a net increase in the quality or quantity of the nation's capital stock, the wherewithal of production.

The labor supply grows through increases in population, immigration, or the number of people willing to work. Increased productivity of labor in output per worker is achieved through improvements in education and human capital or through a higher quantity and quality of capital stock supplied to labor. Writers and secretaries, for instance, may increase their productivity by switching from typewriters to word processing systems. Additions to the nation's capital stock are made through new investment in capital goods—word processors in offices, robots in factories. This investment arises from another macroeconomic variable, private saving. To save, individuals must forgo present consumption. Under favorable economic conditions, when the two goals of price level stability and full employment are achieved, any given rate of private saving is more likely to generate new investment, capital formation, and economic growth than would otherwise be the case.

Gross national product (GNP):
The value of all the final goods and services produced in an economy during a year.

Real economic growth, measured in terms of changes in **gross national product (GNP)**, has averaged about 3 percent per year in the United States over the past hundred years. However, this rate of growth has slowed somewhat in the last two decades. Another related problem in recent U.S. experience has been slowed growth in productivity—a reduction in the ratio of total output to the number of employed workers. While the reasons for a slowdown in productivity growth are complex—as are the relations between economic growth and changes in productivity—one major problem has been a reduced rate of technological development in the United States. Reduced productivity may translate into much slower economic growth in the future and a lessened standard of living for Americans.

Although politicians often express concern over the slow rate of productivity growth and the somewhat lessened rate of economic growth over the past few decades, this issue tends to be given low priority in policy decisions. After all, the effects of these slower growth rates are not immediately apparent. However, the cumulative effect of a slower growth rate can become staggeringly large in just a generation. For example, if a country's rate of growth is 8 percent per year instead of 10 percent per year, real GNP will be only half as large within thirty-six years as it would have been at the slightly higher annual rate. Except for the period of the Great Depression, for over one hundred years each generation of Americans has had reason to believe that it would have a markedly higher standard of living than the preceding generation. If U.S. productivity and economic growth fall to low levels, this expectation may no longer be realistic for many Americans. Figure 5 shows two measures of aggregate economic growth between 1950 and 1988. One line measures **nominal GNP;** the other line, **real GNP.** Nominal GNP for each of the years is measured in terms of prices that prevail in that year. Therefore, increases in nominal GNP can be caused either by increases in output or by increases in prices. Real GNP is a measure of the economy's output adjusted for general price level changes. The measures of real GNP in Figure 5 reflect the quantities of goods that are produced in the various years in constant dollars, or in prices that existed in some given year (1982 in Figure 5).

Nominal GNP:
The economy's total production of final goods and services measured in dollars unadjusted for changes in the price level.

Real GNP:
The total production of final goods and services measured in dollars that have been adjusted for changes in the price level.

FIGURE 5

Real and Nominal GNP

The black line shows the rising level of GNP. Most of this increase is caused by rising prices. The colored line shows the trend of real GNP by removing the effects of inflation on prices. GNP, in other words, rises less rapidly in terms of constant 1982 dollars.

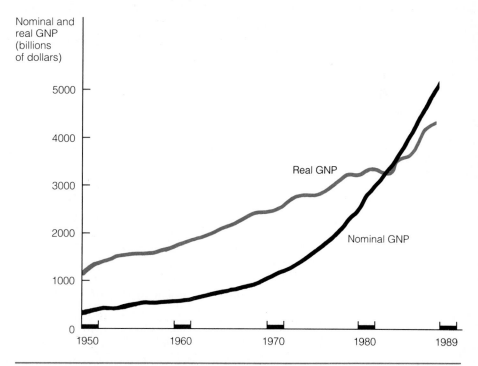

The distinction between real GNP and nominal GNP is important: Price changes cloud the picture of the value of output over time. Nominal GNP can increase between any two years even if production levels fall because the effect of rising prices can offset the effect on nominal GNP of falling levels of production. Therefore, we focus on real GNP, not nominal GNP, in measuring the rate of economic growth.

ECONOMIC STABILITY AND BUSINESS CYCLES

Economic stabilization:
A situation in which the price level and the unemployment rate vary from desired levels only temporarily and by small amounts.

The overall goal of macroeconomic policy is to achieve **economic stabilization.** By stabilization, we do not mean *no* economic growth. Instead, the term describes an environment in which price changes (resulting either from inflation or from deflation) are moderate and in which the unemployment rate differs little from the full-employment level. In such an environment, the prices of individual goods will change, leading to changes in employment levels, as existing industries grow and contract and as new industries arise. However, neither a persistent change in the price level nor excessive unemployment will upset overall consumption and production and disrupt economic growth under stabilization.

Economic stability thus means the achievement of full employment under inflationless or near inflationless conditions to attain maximum economic growth in the present and future. Stabilization is a tall order in a modern economy, where economic activity is subject to fluctuations. These fluctuations, called **business cycles,** are the result of severe variations in the plans of buyers and sellers beyond those variations necessary for changes and improvements in production and consumption.

Business cycles:
Recurrent, systematic fluctuations in the level of business activity; usually measured by changes in the level, or rate of growth, of real GNP over time.

Business cycles are made up of, at one extreme, peaks and, at the other extreme, recessions or depressions. At the peak of a business cycle, the economy is expanding rapidly, with employment at or near capacity. In a recession or depression, resources—especially human resources—are grossly underused. In the expansionary phase of a cycle, increased demand for goods and services causes rapidly increasing demand for all resources, putting pressure on the supplies of labor, capital, and raw materials. One signal that the economy is in the expansionary phase is that business inventories are rapidly being depleted. This period of a business cycle is often characterized by increased inflation, as business activity and employment expand. After the peak of the cycle, the economy enters a contractionary phase. As production of goods exceeds demand for them, inventories build up—one signal of contraction. This phase is characterized by stable or falling prices, excess production capacities, and unemployment. When depression or recession is reached, the economy experiences negative real economic growth rates and stagnation. When recovery is relatively quick in arriving, the period of stagnation is termed a *recession*. A *depression* is a longer, more damaging period of stagnation. Eventually, however, growing demand for goods and services will pull the economy out of any slump. Figure 6 shows cycles of business activity as measured by real GNP growth rate since 1950. Figure 7 illustrates a typical business cycle. (In Chapter 36 we examine a number of explanations for the nature of and turning points of business cycles.)

The goals of macroeconomic policy are to even out or counterbalance the opposing forces of the business cycle. Such policy is therefore called countercyclical policy. Its role is to counter the business cycle to produce inflationless economic growth with full employment. The role of macroeconomic and monetary theory is to understand the causes of changes in business activity—that is, the causes of the business cycle.

AGGREGATE DEMAND, AGGREGATE SUPPLY, AND MACROECONOMIC POLICY

Identifying goals is only the first step. Questions abound: How can full employment be reached? How can inflation be tamed? How can economic growth be sustained? Questions such as these require both theoretical and political answers. In this section we briefly introduce two of the most important macroeconomic theoretical tools—aggregate demand and aggregate supply—and the two most important types of macroeconomic policy.

FIGURE 6

Cycles of Real Annual Growth Rates in GNP, 1950–1989, in Constant (1982) Dollars

Periods of economic expansion and contraction have varied a great deal in this century. Note the roller-coaster path since 1960, punctuated by sharp recessions in 1974–1975, 1980, and in 1981–1982.

Sources: U.S. Board of Governors of the Federal Reserve System, *Historical Chart Book* (Washington, D.C.: Board of Governors of the Federal Reserve System, 1984), p. 12; Council of Economic Advisers, *Economic Report of the President* (Washington, D.C.: U.S. Government Printing Office, 1990), p. 297.

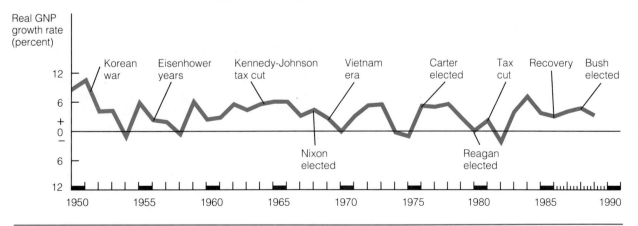

FIGURE 7

Most business cycles vary in length and intensity. A typical cycle includes an expansionary phase of rising business activity and growth, a peak of activity, a contractionary phase of falling activity, and a low point, usually referred to as a recession or depression.

A Typical Business Cycle

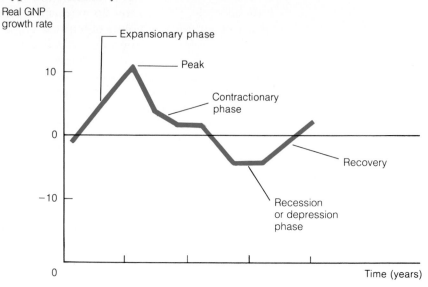

Aggregate demand:
The total spending that occurs in an economy at various price levels during a specified period of time.

Aggregate supply:
The total output that will be produced by an economy at various price levels during a specified period of time.

Aggregate Demand and Aggregate Supply

In examining macroeconomic phenomena, it is often useful to conceive of aggregate demand and aggregate supply curves. In the abstract, **aggregate demand** represents all components of expenditure on domestically produced goods and services. Like an ordinary demand curve, which shows the quantity of a particular good or service that buyers as a group are willing to purchase at each possible price, an aggregate demand curve shows the value of all goods and services that buyers (domestic consumers, business firms, government agencies, foreign buyers) are willing to purchase at each price level over a specific period of time. Similarly, the **aggregate supply** curve shows the time-specific value of all goods and services that producers as a group are willing to offer for sale at each possible price level. In drawing an aggregate demand or supply curve, price level is measured on the vertical axis, and aggregate output is measured on the horizontal axis. Typical aggregate demand and supply curves are depicted in Figure 8.

Although the analogy between demand and supply in an individual market (such as the market for CDs) and the aggregate demand and supply of all goods and services is not perfect, the concepts are similar. Both the demand curve for an individual product and the aggregate demand curve are negatively sloped; as price declines, quantity of goods and services demanded rises. Several factors lead to larger aggregate demand at lower price levels. One of the most obvious is an increase in export sales to foreign buyers. A decrease in prices in this country is likely to make American goods more attractive to foreign buyers, causing the foreign component of aggregate demand to rise. Spending by domestic buyers is also likely to increase, for reasons we will detail in Chapter 28.

FIGURE 8

Like the demand and supply curves for a single good, the aggregate demand and aggregate supply curves for all goods and services determine a price level and a level of output for all goods produced and consumed. Equilibrium is achieved at the point where aggregate demand equals aggregate supply.

Aggregate Demand and Aggregate Supply Curves

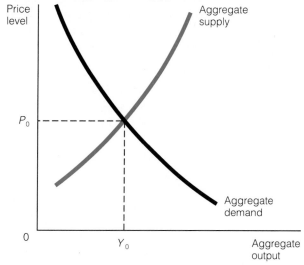

Like a typical supply curve in an individual market, the aggregate supply curve shown in Figure 8 is positively sloped. Producers as a group are revealed in Figure 8 to be willing to supply larger quantities of goods and services at higher price levels, presumably because higher price levels yield higher rates of profit. A detailed discussion of the forces underlying aggregate supply will also be presented in Chapter 28.

Equilibrium occurs where aggregate demand equals aggregate supply. This occurs at a price level of P_0 and an output level of Y_0 in Figure 8. At price levels above P_0, aggregate supply of goods and services exceeds aggregate demand. This surplus of goods and services in aggregate exerts downward pressure on prices, causing the price level to fall to P_0. At price levels below P_0, aggregate demand is greater than aggregate supply. General shortages of goods and services cause prices to rise, driving the price level up to the equilibrium at P_0.

Aggregate demand and supply curves are useful for examining the issues of unemployment, price stability, and economic growth. Depending on the positions of aggregate demand and supply, the equilibrium level of output can be at high or low levels. Unemployment becomes a serious problem when the equilibrium level of production is too low, causing many workers to lose their jobs.

To consider the goal of price stability, it is necessary to consider shifts in aggregate demand and supply over time. Such shifts can lead to price instability—changes in the equilibrium price level above or below P_0 in Figure 8. Price stability occurs if neither of the curves shifts or if both shift rightward or leftward at the same rate. However, suppose aggregate demand increases more rapidly than does aggregate supply. In this case, the economy will experience inflation, as the price level rises to an equilibrium level above P_0. Similarly, the economy would experience deflation if aggregate supply rose relative to aggregate demand.

Comparing the equilibrium level of output over time provides a picture of economic growth. Shifts to the right in either aggregate demand or aggregate supply will cause economic growth, the pace depending on the rate at which aggregate demand or supply increases.

MACROECONOMIC ISSUES: ACHIEVING GOALS IS NOT EASY

Unfortunately, policies to achieve full employment, price stability, and economic growth often fail. One explanation for this is that macroeconomic policies that might work beautifully in isolation sometimes can conflict with each other. For example, policies that shift aggregate demand rightward to attain full employment will tend to cause price increases rather than price stability. Also, certain policies to contain inflation will increase unemployment. In such cases, decision-makers are faced with a **policy trade-off;** they are forced to decide which of the economic goals is more important to attain.

Additional problems in implementing macroeconomic policy arise from political considerations. Certain policy changes, such as reductions in government spending or tax increases, are politically unpopular. Therefore, such policies tend not to be implemented or tend to be delayed, even when economically desirable.

Policy trade-off:
A situation in which a policy that promotes the attainment of one macroeconomic goal necessarily implies that the attainment of another macroeconomic objective becomes more difficult.

Can Discretionary Macroeconomic Policy Work?

A more fundamental macroeconomic issue relates to the advisability of using **discretionary policies** (monetary or fiscal adjustments in the economy). Some economists question whether the economy can be managed at all by fallible public officials who possess imperfect information. **Fiscal policy**—taxing and spending policy—is controlled by Congress and the president. **Monetary policy**—control over the growth in the money stock—is controlled by the politically appointed Federal Reserve Board. The issue is whether these groups could ever know enough about the economy or react quickly enough to disturbances to direct and control the economy in discretionary fashion. If mistakes are possible, could not discretionary policies create so much uncertainty and confusion that they might sometimes have the opposite effects to those intended?

Some contemporary macroeconomists believe that, for reasons such as conflicting goals and imperfect information, discretionary fiscal and monetary policies have built-in side effects that make them worse than useless. These economists call for the use of policy rules such as predetermined growth in the money supply and balanced federal budgets instead of discretionary control of the macroeconomy. Rules and balanced budgets would, in the view of some, take policy out of error-prone human hands, leading to more certain expectations among consumers, producers, and investors in the economy.

Underlying a faith in establishing rules rather than discretion in enacting policy is the belief, held by early classical economists and upheld by their

Discretionary policy:
A policy or change in policy that is determined by choices or decisions of policy-makers.

Fiscal policy:
The use of government spending and taxation to effect changes in aggregate economic variables.

Monetary policy:
The use of money supply changes to effect changes in aggregate economic variables.

followers today, that the economy, if left undisturbed by government, will automatically achieve the goals of full employment, price stability, and maximum economic growth. Much of the policy controversy discussed in ensuing chapters centers on issues such as these. Can discretionary policy work? How automatic are free-market forces in achieving macroeconomic goals? Are rules preferable to continual alterations in fiscal and monetary policies?

Demand-Side Versus Supply-Side Policies

Most contemporary macroeconomic theory and policy, originating in the 1930s in the writing of John Maynard Keynes, is directed toward manipulating aggregate demand, either in discretionary fashion or with rules designed to produce full employment, price stability, and growth. This approach is now referred to as **demand-side policy.**

Demand-side policy:
Fiscal or monetary policy intended to alter the overall level of spending, or aggregate demand.

Some economists, notably those associated with the Reagan administration, have focused instead on some of the factors related to output response or to aggregate supply changes. As noted earlier, output response is largely determined by factors related to resource supply and to investment and capital accumulation. The **supply-side** view of the macroeconomy emphasizes the possible effects of taxes on work effort, labor supply, and investment. High tax burdens on consumer-workers and on investors mean that the economy's output response is constricted. A lower output response creates rigidities in the economy, limiting the attainment of macroeconomic goals. Indeed, one of the goals of the Tax Reform Act of 1986 was to stimulate output by lowering the federal income tax rates individuals and businesses face. Institutional changes surrounding the work decision—such as an increase in the number of women in the work force—plus government social programs and minimum-wage laws may also play a role in influencing aggregate supply.

Supply-side policy:
Fiscal or monetary policy intended to directly alter the incentives to produce output; policies designed to shift aggregate supply.

A focus on aggregate supply should not be taken to mean that aggregate demand theory or policy is unimportant. As we will see, both aggregate demand and aggregate supply play critical roles in explaining success or failure in obtaining macroeconomic goals.

MODERN MACROECONOMICS: A MIXED APPROACH

Our brief look at the confusing and often conflicting issues surrounding the attainment of macroeconomic goals should not discourage you. Rest assured that modern economists can lay claim to a practical understanding of the basic functioning of the aggregate economy.

Still, economists often take different policy positions based on alternative outcomes—and different magnitudes of outcomes—predicted by different theories. One rather unsettling fact will become clear as we go on: No single theory tells us everything we want to know. Rather, there is some truth in a number of theoretical approaches that may be viewed as alternative or complementary to each other.

SUMMARY

1. Macroeconomics studies the effects of the interplay between aggregate demand and aggregate supply on inflation, unemployment, and economic growth, whereas microeconomics is concerned with the functioning of supply and demand in specific markets.
2. The overall goal of macroeconomic theory and policy is economic stabilization. Specifically, macroeconomic policy aims at an inflationless and fully employed economy with maximum economic growth. Some unemployment is expected in any fluid, dynamic economy, as individuals change jobs and other resources adapt to changing market conditions.
3. Inflation and unemployment are the enemies of economic growth because they create an environment within which private saving and new investment are reduced. A reduction in new investment means lower capital formation and reduced growth prospects.
4. Runaway inflation can have disastrous social and economic effects in an economy. Redistributions of real income from those on fixed incomes, often the poor and elderly, extreme variations in buyers' and sellers'

plans, and arbitrary increases in taxes required by government are among the problems created by inflation.
5. Trade-offs may exist between the achievement of two or more economic goals such as inflation and unemployment.
6. Fiscal policy and monetary policy are the two major means for manipulating aggregate demand and aggregate supply. Fiscal policy is the alteration in tax or spending activities by government. Monetary policy is control of the money supply and interest rates.
7. Economists have differing opinions about whether discretionary macroeconomic policy is stabilizing or destabilizing in promoting economic goals. In the view of some economists, rules should be substituted for authority in the quest for economic stabilization.
8. Supply-side economists have shifted attention to the factors affecting output response in the economy, such as the effect of taxation on work effort, new investment, and labor productivity.

KEY TERMS

unemployed
unemployment rate
full employment
natural rate of
   unemployment
price stability
rate of inflation
deflation
real income

nominal income
tax indexation
economic growth
gross national product
   (GNP)
nominal GNP
real GNP
economic stabilization
business cycles

aggregate demand
aggregate supply
policy trade-off
discretionary policy
fiscal policy
monetary policy
demand-side policy
supply-side policy

QUESTIONS FOR REVIEW AND DISCUSSION

1. What is price stability? Is a constant rate of inflation at 10 percent less harmful to people than an inflation rate that randomly fluctuates between 2 percent and 8 percent?
2. What are the three major goals of macroeconomic policy? Why have politicians in the past been less concerned with policies aimed at achieving sustained long-run growth than achieving the other two goals?
3. Why do economists disagree on macroeconomic policies? Does this imply that economists do not understand macroeconomics?
4. What is discretionary-demand management policy? Can discretionary fiscal policy eliminate swings in the business cycle?

5. Suppose that the economy is experiencing less than full employment. Utilizing the aggregate demand and aggregate supply theory developed in this chapter, explain the possible trade-offs that would have to be made to attain full employment.
6. What is necessary to achieve economic growth? Do inflation and unemployment hinder this process?
7. Can discretionary-demand management cause aggregate supply problems? What other trade-offs exist for policy-makers?
8. Which do you suppose is better for the economy, an increase in aggregate demand or an increase in aggregate supply? What is the difference?

Macroeconomics: Key Concepts

We have culled some of the most important principles of macroeconomics from the pages of this book for presentation in this section. Separating these important concepts from the text and presenting them as a group serves two purposes. First, it gives beginning students an idea of the scope of macroeconomics and sets them on the road toward an economic way of thinking. Second, it provides students who are familiar with the basics of macroeconomics an opportunity for review and—with an expanded use of color, especially—an opportunity to see new relationships.

Aggregate Supply and Aggregate Demand

The aggregate supply curve shows the relation between real output and the price level. The slope of the aggregate supply curve depends on economic conditions. The horizontal portion of the curve, called the *Keynesian range,* represents supply during times of severe unemployment and underutilization of resources. In this range, an increase in output will not be accompanied by an increase in the price level. The upward-sloping portion of the curve, the *intermediate range,* represents supply under normal or nearly normal conditions. The economy has not reached its production possibilities frontier (represented by Q_F, full employment), but neither is it depressed. In this range, any real increase in output will be accompanied by higher price levels. The vertical portion of the curve, the *classical range,* represents the economy at full employment. In this range, output cannot increase, and supply is perfectly inelastic in relation to the price level.

One goal of macroeconomic policy is maintaining full employment. If aggregate demand is not sufficient to achieve full-employment output, depicted by AD_1 in the figure, then demand-increasing monetary or fiscal policies may be used. An easy money policy or an expansionary fiscal policy may shift aggregate demand from AD_1 to AD_2. The movement from AD_1 to AD_2 will increase output from Q_1 to the full-employment level and increase price from P_1 to P_2.

The Federal Reserve System

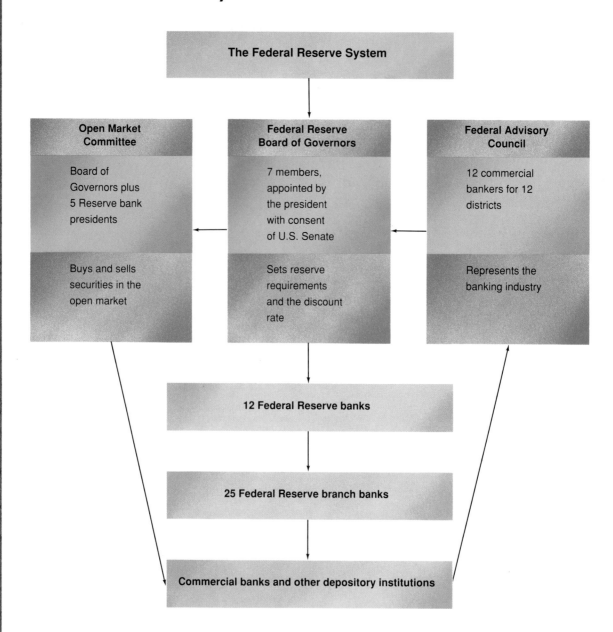

The Federal Reserve System

Open Market Committee	Federal Reserve Board of Governors	Federal Advisory Council
Board of Governors plus 5 Reserve bank presidents	7 members, appointed by the president with consent of U.S. Senate	12 commercial bankers for 12 districts
Buys and sells securities in the open market	Sets reserve requirements and the discount rate	Represents the banking industry

12 Federal Reserve banks

25 Federal Reserve branch banks

Commercial banks and other depository institutions

The commercial banking system and other financial institutions that issue checkable deposits are regulated and controlled by the Federal Reserve System, which is composed of twelve Federal Reserve banks and twenty-five branch banks. Monetary control is exercised through the Board of Governors in Washington, D.C., by means of reserve requirements and the discount rate. The major tool of monetary policy, open market operations (the buying and selling of securities on the open market), is overseen by the Federal Open Market Committee. The Federal Advisory Committee is the banking industry's voice in the monetary policy-setting process.

Keynesian and Monetarist Transmission Mechanisms

(a) The Keynesian monetary transmission mechanism

(b) The monetarist transmission mechanism

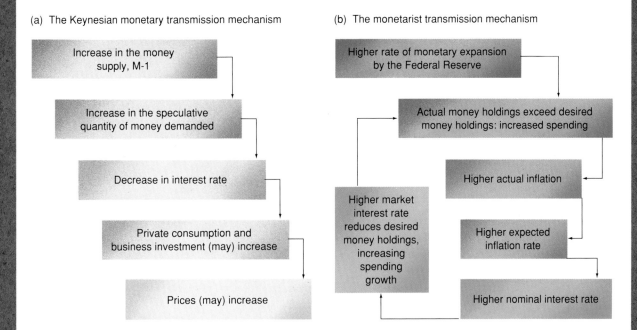

Keynesians and monetarists differ on the effects of an increase in the money supply on prices. Despite a shared starting point—the increase in M-1—and shared focus (both approaches focus on money holders and the uncertainty that drives money holders to act), the monetarist model predicts inflation, while the Keynesian model predicts modest or negligible price increases.

Economists differentiate between types of demand for money: transactions demand, precautionary demand, and speculative demand. With regard to M-1 and inflation, Keynes was interested primarily in speculative demand. Speculators are constantly reevaluating their holdings—deciding sometimes to hold money, while opting at other times to hold less-liquid assets, such as bonds. (a) In Keynes's view, an increase in the money supply will decrease interest rates and increase bond prices, thereby increasing the speculative demand for money. Since people may tend to hold money rather than to spend it in uncertain economic times, speculative demand short-circuits the normal cause-and-effect relation between money supply and prices. In a depressed economy total expenditures and, therefore, prices may not rise—or may rise only slightly—along with the money supply. Individuals and businesses may view the higher bond prices as abnormal and so may avoid capital losses when bond prices drop by holding money instead. (b) Monetarists ignore distinctions between types of money demand. Instead, they view money as something held in response to independent variables such as real income and interest rates. In the monetarist view, the increase in money supply will be spent away in an attempt by individuals and businesses to restore equilibrium between quantity demanded of money and quantity supplied. The increased spending will push up prices, or increase the actual rate of inflation. Eventually, the public will accept the new rate of inflation and adjust expectations accordingly. Since nominal interest rates are the sum of the constant real rate of inflation and the expected inflation rate, nominal interest rates rise. Higher interest rates will prompt businesses and consumers to again rid themselves of cash balances. (Money is a poor store of value in inflationary periods.) The monetarists see the process as continuing until the Fed stabilizes the rate of monetary growth.

The Effects of a Tariff

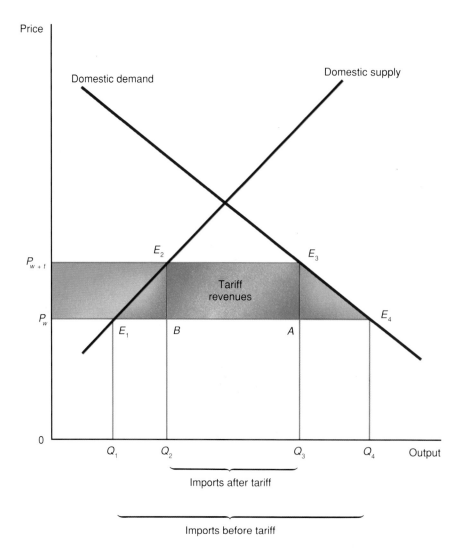

The world price of a good or service is determined by global supply and demand. Consumers and producers in individual countries may buy or sell all they wish at the world price. Here, we show the domestic demand and supply curves. A world price of P_w results in domestic production of Q_1 and domestic consumption of Q_4, with the difference, $Q_4 - Q_1$, made up by imports. A tariff on imports in the amount of t per unit of output effectively raises the world price to P_{w+t}. At the higher price, producers increase their output to Q_2, and consumers decrease their purchases to Q_3. Imports of the foreign-made good fall to $Q_3 - Q_2$; government receives tariff revenue in the amount of t times the amount imported, $Q_3 - Q_2$ (represented here by E_2E_3AB); producers' increased benefits are represented by the area $P_{w+t}E_2E_1P_w$. The gains received by producers and government come at the expense of domestic consumers; the total loss to consumers is represented by $P_{w+t}E_3E_4P_w$. Imposition of a tariff results in a net loss to society equal to the sum of the areas E_2BE_1 and E_3E_4A.

24

Measuring the Macroeconomy

Chapter 23 presented recent data on the American economy, including statistics on gross national product, unemployment, and inflation. In this chapter we look at these measures in more detail, examining the components of gross national product, the relation between GNP and national income, and the methods through which economists derive these aggregate data. We also look at the methods for measuring inflation in the economy and at how a price index is compiled. Statistics such as GNP and the rate of inflation are the bread and butter of macroeconomic study and of policy debate. Price changes are revealed monthly and real GNP performance is revealed quarterly. Consumers and businesses, not to mention many world markets, react to each announcement of the data. When you complete Chapter 24 you should recognize

- what aggregate measures of economic well-being include (and what they do not include).
- why no measure of an economy's progress is perfect and why all measures must be qualified.
- the methods upon which economists and statisticians build the national income accounts.
- how price changes and inflation or deflation relate to aggregate measures of economic progress.

AGGREGATE ACCOUNTING AND THE CONCEPT OF GNP

National income accounting—and macroeconomics itself—was born in the seventeenth-century endeavor to develop a "political arithmetic." Chief among the writers in this tradition were Sir William Petty (1623–1687) and his follower Charles Davenant (1656–1714). "By Political Arithmetick," wrote Davenant, "we mean the art of reasoning by figures upon things relating to government. . . . The art is undoubtedly very ancient. . . . But Petty first gave it that name and brought it into rules and methods."[1] Petty tried to estimate the national income of England as early as 1665, and economists have attempted to measure the economic performance of economies ever since.

Although economists have long been interested in aggregate economic statistics, it was not until the 1930s in both the United States and Great Britain that economists and government agencies began to collect such data. At that time, Congress instructed the Department of Commerce to assemble and report on the national accounts. Modern **national income accounting,** or the statistical measuring of the nation's economic performance, was officially born.[2] These principles were, in large measure, the legacy of two Nobel Prize–winning economists—Simon Kuznets in the United States and Sir Richard Stone in Great Britain. (See Focus, "Pioneers in Social Accounting: Kuznets and Stone.")

Before we examine the process of national income accounting, consider the concept of **gross national product (GNP)** in more detail. GNP is the most comprehensive national income statistic, and the one that usually gets the most public attention. Gross national product is the market value of all the final goods and services produced in an economy over a given period. As we shall see in more detail later, the word *gross* means that the total market value of all goods produced, including the production of capital goods, is included in GNP. GNP therefore does not account for the wear and tear on physical assets—called depreciation—that takes place during a given period. The word *national* means that GNP covers the whole economy. The word *product* refers to the market value of final goods and services. We cannot sum physical amounts of goods because many goods simply cannot be added together. What, for example, is the total of ten haircuts plus thirty hamburgers? Also, there are goods and services for which data on the total number of units produced do not exist. We can, however, sum the money or market values of different goods and services because businesses keep records of their receipts for tax purposes. GNP is thus the sum of the final market values of all goods and services sold.

Two other elements of the definition are important. First, only sales of *final* goods and services are counted in GNP. To do otherwise would be to double-count. The value of McDonald's or Burger King's purchases of raw meat would be added to consumers' purchases of hamburgers and thus be double-counted if all purchases of goods and services sold in the economy were used to calculate GNP. The flow of inputs and outputs in the economic system that creates double-counting problems also permits an alternative means of calculating GNP, as we shall see presently.

A second point involves the time period. GNP ordinarily refers to final sales over the period of a year. GNP and other national income accounts are measures of what economists call *flows.* Flows are processes taking place

 cross out

National income accounting: The process of statistically measuring the nation's aggregate economic performance.

Gross national product (GNP): The market value of all final goods and services produced in an economy over a given period of time, usually a year.

[1]Charles Davenant, quoted in Joseph A. Schumpeter, *History of Economic Analysis* (New York: Oxford University Press, 1954), pp. 210–11.

[2]Economists use the term *national income* both as a generic term encompassing all of the national income accounts (gross national product, net national product, national income, and so on) and as a specific term referring to the total compensation of all the factors of production (labor, capital, and so on) in the economy over some period.

FOCUS   Pioneers in Social Accounting: Kuznets and Stone

Prior to World War I very little was known about income and output (GNP), although the quest among economists for an accurate measure of national economic performance goes back several centuries. One of the first to fill in the facts and figures about the aggregate economy was Simon Kuznets (1901–1985). In a series of studies from the mid-1920s until the 1950s, the Russian-born Kuznets developed and made estimates of total output (GNP) and income, measured by final product, industry of origin, and type of income. Further, Kuznets provided methods of estimating savings and capital formation and a means for estimating the income distribution between the rich and the poor. The Great Depression of the 1930s, the development of Keynesian economics in the 1930s, and World War II spurred Kuznets's inquiries into aggregate consumption, savings, and investment statistics, which he developed under the auspi-

ces of the National Bureau of Economic Research. For his work on business cycles and comparative economic growth among nations, Kuznets was awarded the Nobel Prize in 1971. Sir Richard Stone (b. 1913), who won the Nobel Prize for economics in 1984, is another innovator in the area of national income accounting. Along with collaborators, Stone was the first economist to officially estimate British national income and expenditure (in 1944). More important, he provided a theoretical model and specified a scrupulously accurate statistical method for calculating his integrated system of balanced national income accounts on a worldwide basis.

No one would argue that the actual numbers produced through the social accounting system are perfect. Economists make constant refinements, but they build on the enormous advances of pioneers such as Kuznets and Stone.

---

through time and, as such, are measured per unit of time. GNP is the total output of an economy *per year*. A stock, such as the capital stock of an economy, is the total amount of something in existence at a point in time. Additionally, economists also discuss the rates at which variables such as GNP are changing. These growth rates are measured by calculating percentage changes of the variables from one period to the next.

What GNP Does Not Count

Official statistics on GNP are far from perfect. The most serious shortcoming is that they fail to include the value of certain types of production. Goods and services produced for home consumption are omitted, for example. This category includes such activities as backyard vegetable gardens, do-it-yourself home repair, and the myriad services provided by homemakers. Since the value of such goods and services is so hard to estimate, national income accountants omit the value of this kind of production in their calculations of GNP.

A second category of production that does not appear in official GNP estimates is the underground economy. Various goods and many services, such as yard work or maid service, are paid for in cash and are not reported for tax purposes. Also, some business firms avoid paying taxes by not recording all sales. GNP accountants elect to omit such transactions because it is so difficult to estimate their magnitude. (See Focus, "The Underground Economy.")

The third major category of omitted production is illegal goods and services. As you know, profits from illegal drug sales run into the billions worldwide each year. These transactions are omitted from official statistics—again, because the magnitude of drug sales is difficult to judge; but there is also a reluctance to view the production of illegal goods as an addition to national income.

FOCUS The Underground Economy

The underground economy refers to all the transactions between individuals and firms that are not officially recorded in the government's national income accounts. Unrecorded transactions are not limited to illicit transactions such as gambling, prostitution, and the drug trade. They also include the summer yard work that children and teenagers do for pay, baby-sitting and daytime child-care services that are paid for in cash and not reported to the Internal Revenue Service (IRS), the many kinds of barter transactions that occur, and a multitude of other exchanges that take place in economies that simply do not get entered on the official books. Most of us have participated in the underground economy at one time or another.

One factor responsible for the existence of the underground economy is the income tax and all other taxes levied at all levels of government. Individuals act in their own self-interest, and some will choose to evade paying a portion of their taxes in order to increase their wealth. Some professionals, for example, simply do not declare all their earned income on their income tax forms. Waiters and waitresses occasionally understate their tips to the tax authorities. One result is that the value of these services does not enter the government's official income accounts. Nonetheless, the services these people perform make the economy wealthier and should be reflected in GNP. Quite often these unreported transactions are purely cash transactions. Checks or credit cards leave a paper trail, whereas cash is much harder for income tax auditors to trace.

Income tax rates have traditionally played a major role in determining the extent and size of the underground economy. When people barter or swap goods and services, the value of the transaction goes unreported in GNP but still enhances the barterer's economic welfare. When all relevant tax rates that individuals face are lower, the incentive to barter is diminished, and the underground economy will shrink in size. Indeed, this was one of the reasons that the top federal income tax rate was reduced from 70 percent in 1981 and further reduced from 50 percent in 1986. (The top rate in 1990 was 33 percent.) Other taxes at all levels, including Social Security taxes, have been rising over recent years, however.

A third explanation for the existence of the underground economy is that artificial entry barriers exist in many occupations. Factors such as a person's age, immigrant status, union status, or other legal requirements may prevent employment in the regular economy. Illegal aliens may work as domestics for unreported income in order to avoid detection and deportation. Hundreds of "gypsy cabs" operate in New York City; these private automobiles that ferry passengers about the city are driven by people unable to obtain a license for an official taxicab. Doubtless, many such transactions go unreported. These people work in the underground economy because they can earn larger incomes than they could by working in the official economy.

Just how big is the underground economy? No one knows for sure, but some economists have used various techniques to measure its size. One method is to compare Department of Commerce data on GNP to the IRS's income data. Another approach looks at government-reported data concerning the proportion of the population that is officially reported as employed. This figure can be compared to the number that could reasonably be expected in calculating the size of underground income earned. A third method tracks the total amount of cash, as well as the amount of "large" bills, circulating in an economy and compares it with total checking accounts and credit purchases. Unusually large amounts of cash or large bills indicate a large underground economy.

Estimates on the size of the underground economy in the United States for the late 1970s range from 4 to 25 percent of GNP. If 10 percent of all economic activity were hidden from official view in 1989, then underground GNP would total more than $500 billion. While this is large in absolute terms, some have estimated Italy's underground economy to amount to about 35 to 40 percent of that country's official GNP. Japan, however, appears to produce only about 1 to 2 percent of its total output in an underground economy. Clearly, such factors as tax rates, cultural attitudes, laws, and resources devoted to uncovering the underground economy will influence the extent of such activity across countries.

There are positive and negative aspects to an underground economy. Government clearly loses tax revenue that could be used to finance social goods and national defense. Additionally, macro variables calculated by the government, such as the unemployment rate, are not as accurate as economists would like them to be. On the other hand, the underground economy provides jobs and income for literally millions of people. Some of these jobs constitute full-time employment, while some represent only moonlighting and part-time work. Either way, many households benefit from income earned underground.

Such glaring omissions caution against making sweeping statements about international comparisons of GNP. In developing countries a huge percentage of all production may be used by the large rural population for home consumption. In other countries, a majority of all production may be sold in the underground economy. Official GNP statistics understate actual levels of production in all economies, though not necessarily to the same degree. Official statistics showing the GNP of the United Kingdom to be slightly larger than the GNP of Italy are not conclusive evidence that actual production is larger in the United Kingdom. It may simply be that a smaller proportion of Italian production is included in GNP statistics.

Other transactions are excluded from GNP calculations because they do not represent purchases of current goods or services. For example, the purchase of stock or other securities is not included because it represents a transfer of assets and not production of goods or services. Similarly, real estate transactions involving old homes are not counted. However, any fees paid to stock brokers or real estate agents would be included, since they represent payment for current services.

GNP as a Measure of Economic Welfare

It is tempting to use readily available GNP statistics to measure economic welfare. Even if the problem of uncounted production were solved, however, GNP still would not accurately measure worldwide economic welfare. GNP statistics do not account for pollution and congestion costs, which go hand in hand with economic growth in most developed countries. Also, the average work week in industrial countries has declined markedly in this century, but GNP statistics do not capture the value of increases in leisure time. Actually, GNP never was intended to be a measure of economic welfare. GNP is a measure of production—without any indication of who gets the goods and services produced or what the goods and services are. GNP is indifferent between the provision of handguns or health care. Nonetheless, some economists have attempted to compute a **measure of economic welfare (MEW)** based on GNP statistics (see Economics in Action, "GNP, Leisure, and Social Welfare," at the end of this chapter).

Measure of economic welfare (MEW):
A concept of social and economic well-being that accounts for the production of all goods and services, not just those transacted for in markets.

Final goods:
Goods sold to the final consumers of the goods.

Intermediate goods:
Goods used as inputs in the production of final goods.

Final-Goods Versus Value-Added Approaches

GNP may reflect either market values of all final goods and services or the value added at each stage of production because both sums are identical. **Final goods** and services are end products in the economy; **intermediate goods** go into the production of end products. McDonald's meat purchases to produce hamburgers are purchases of intermediate goods. In the final-goods approach, the purchases of intermediate goods are excluded from GNP to avoid the problem of double counting. For example, cigar making is a multi-step operation. If we counted the value of the tobacco sold by the farmer to the cigar maker and the value of the cigar sold to the cigar store by the cigar maker, as well as the price consumers pay for the finished cigars, we would have counted the value of the tobacco three times. This is an example of double counting or, we should say, triple counting. The value of the tobacco should be counted

Value added:
The increase in value or market worth of a good associated with each stage of production.

only once. One way to avoid double counting is to count only the price of the final good; the other is to count only the value added at each stage of production. **Value added** is the difference between the revenues the firm receives from selling its product and the cost of inputs that it has purchased from other firms.

To better understand value added, consider the making of a cigar in more detail. Suppose that the farmer sells a quantity of tobacco to the cigar maker for $3. The value added by the farmer is thus $3, which covers the farmer's costs of producing the tobacco (wages, rent, interest, and profit). In the second stage, the cigar maker sells a certain number of cigars, produced from the quantity of tobacco, to the cigar store for $8. Since the cigar maker paid the farmer $3 for the tobacco, the value added at the second stage by the cigar maker is $5 ($8 − $3). In the final stage, the cigar store sells the cigars to smokers for $15. Since the cigar store paid $8 for the cigars, the value added in the third stage is $7 ($15 − $8). Table 1 illustrates the value-added approach to GNP with the example of cigars.

Summing the value added at each stage of production, we find that $15 equals the market price of the final good. If we had instead added the sales price at each stage of production ($3 + $8 + $15), we would have double-counted. The correct measure of GNP is $15, not $26. The value-added approach is logically equivalent to using the market price of final goods and services to estimate GNP. The final-goods approach is easier to calculate, but the value-added approach serves as a useful check on other methods of estimating GNP.

NATIONAL INCOME ACCOUNTING

Although we have thus far spoken only of the market value of goods, aggregate value in the economy can actually be derived either by summing all expenditures for final goods or by summing all income received. The following sections explain why these constructs should yield identical results and what factors must be taken into account to arrive at identical sums.

TABLE 1

Value-Added Approach to GNP

When GNP is estimated by the value-added approach, the extra value added at each stage of production is summed. At the first stage, the farmer adds $3 in value; at the second stage, the cigar maker adds $5 in value; and, finally, the cigar store adds $7 in value. The sum of the three values added is $15, which is identical to the final sale price.

Stage of Production	Seller	Buyer	Sale Price of Good	Value Added
First	Farmer	Cigar maker	$3	$3
Second	Cigar maker	Cigar store	$8	$5
Third	Cigar store	Smoker	$15	$7
				$15

The Circular Flow of Economic Activity

Flow of expenditures:
Total spending of consumers, businesses, and government on final goods and services during any given time period.

Flow of earnings:
Total income received by resource suppliers during any given time period.

National income (GNP) can be measured in two ways: the flow of expenditures approach and the flow of earnings, or income, approach. The **flow of expenditures** approach looks at national income as the total amount spent on final goods and services. The **flow of earnings,** or income, approach looks at national income as the amount earned by factors of production (land, labor, capital, and the entrepreneur).

Logically, the two approaches have to yield the same figure for national income: All income earned by all factors in the production of goods and services is spent on those goods and services. Figure 1 is a circular flow diagram for an economy with only two sectors—a household, or consumer, sector and a firm, or business, sector. In the inner loop of the upper part of

FIGURE 1   The Circular Flow of Economic Activity

The circular flow diagram is portrayed with only a business and a household sector. The upper loop is the flow of final output and expenditures on final output. The lower loop is the flow of input factors of production and the return flow of factor incomes. By definition, the value of the upper and lower loops must be equal. Therefore, GNP as measured by the flow of expenditures approach and GNP as measured by the flow of earnings approach must be identical.

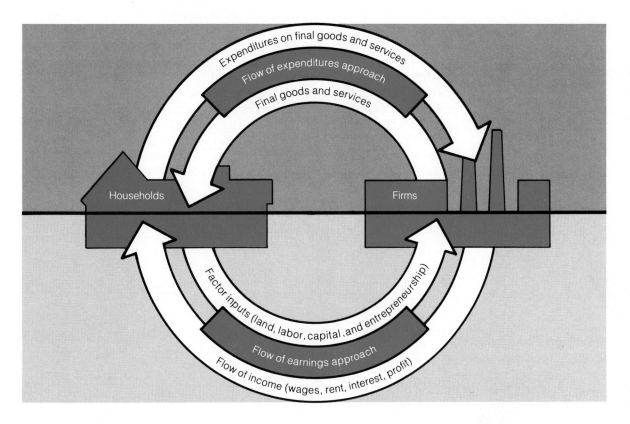

the diagram, firms (suppliers) produce goods for sale to consumers (demanders). The flow of goods to households is matched by a return flow of expenditures, indicated by the outer flow line. Businesses use the revenue from final sales to cover their costs of operation.

The inner part of the lower loop shows businesses or firms (demanders) employing factors of production from the household sector (suppliers). The factors of production are paid incomes that reflect their productivity in producing final output. Firm revenues are exhausted by factor payments because any left over, or residual, portion accrues to the entrepreneur or owners of the firm in the form of profit, which is a type of income.

The upper and lower loops of the circular flow diagram illustrate the identity of the two approaches to measuring national income. The revenues from producing final goods and services are transformed into payments to cover the costs of producing the output. Total revenues from producing goods break down into profits, wage payments, interest, and land rent. By necessity, the dollar value of the expenditure flow on goods and services equals the dollar value of the income, or earning, flow to the factors of production. The important point is that national income can be measured with either approach, and the results will be identical. The flow of expenditures approach is formally identical to the flow of earnings, or income, approach.

Leakages and Injections: Some Complications

Before using these equivalent approaches to national income, consider some complications. The simple case described by Figure 1 excludes such features as saving and other important sectors of the economy such as government or the foreign sector. Without them, the flow of income to factors of production matches the flow of expenditures on final goods and services to firms. But since the excluded features and sectors are part of the economy, Figure 1 does not account for certain leakages out of and injections into the simple flow of expenditures and receipts. A leakage occurs when spending is diverted from the income stream. Household or business saving is a leakage from the expenditure stream. When processed through banks and other financial institutions or intermediaries, such saving becomes investment, an injection or addition to the expenditures flow.

Likewise, government expenditures are injections into the simple flow of expenditures, since the government, like households and businesses, makes expenditures on goods and services. Government transfers income to recipients through welfare and other programs as well. All such expenditures are injections into the circular flow. Financing such expenditures, however, requires the taxation of households and businesses. Taxation represents a leakage from the expenditure stream of the private economy.

The U.S. economy is also heavily involved in international trade and exchange, but the simple flows shown in Figure 1 do not include exports and imports. Exports—the sale abroad of goods and services produced in the United States—are an injection into the circular flow of expenditures and income, while imports—expenditures on goods and services produced abroad—are leakages from the simple income-expenditure flow.

In short, the simple income-expenditure model of Figure 1 does not account for certain leakages and injections. Government expenditures and exports must be counted as injections into the expenditure stream of private household and business spending. Likewise, household and business savings, along with government taxes and imports, are leakages from the simple circular flow of economic activity (see Figure 2).

The Flow of Expenditures Approach

National income accounting puts into practice the principles of the simple, two-sector circular flow diagram as amended by injections and leakages. The national income accountants apply the flow of expenditures approach to measuring GNP by breaking the economy down into four sectors: household, business, government, and foreign. Individuals in the economy are assigned among the four sectors, and GNP is estimated by adding the amount spent on final output by individuals in each sector. Table 2 gives the 1989 data on spending in each sector. Figure 3 compares the flow of expenditures to the flow of earnings.

FIGURE 2   **Leakages from and Injections into the Circular Flow**

The simple two-sector economy portrayed in Figure 1 does not include the leakages represented by savings, taxation, and imports and injections represented by investment, government purchases, and exports. When these additional concepts are included, economists speak of a four-sector economy, including firms, households, government, and foreign markets.

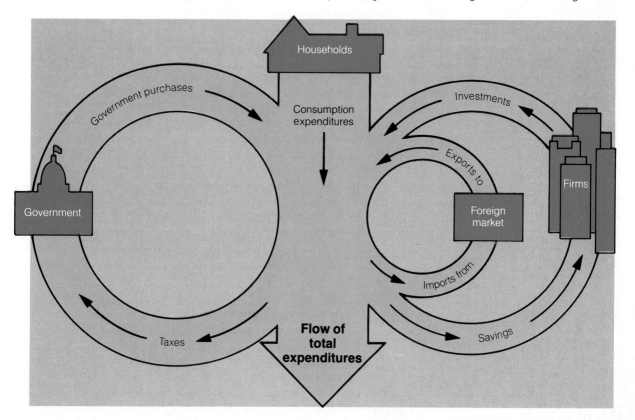

TABLE 2

Gross National Product, 1989: The Flow of Expenditures

Total expenditures in the economy are broken down into four basic groups: private consumption expenditures; private domestic investment expenditures by businesses; government expenditures; and net exports (foreign purchases of U.S. goods minus U.S. purchases of foreign goods).

		Expenditures (billions of dollars)
Personal consumption expenditures (C)		
Durable goods >3 yrs	473.6	
Nondurable goods	1122.6	
Services	1874.1	
Total		3470.3
Gross private domestic investment (I)		
Fixed investment	747.7	
Change in business inventories	29.4	
Total		777.1
Government purchases (G)		
Federal (no transf payments)	404.1	
State and local	632.5	
Total		1036.7
Exports and imports of goods and services		
Exports (X)	624.4	
Imports (M)	675.2	
Net total (X − M)		−50.9
Total expenditures in GNP		5233.2

Source: Council of Economic Advisers, *Economic Report of the President* (Washington, D.C.: U.S. Government Printing Office, 1990), p. 294.

Note: GNP is in 1989 nominal dollars. Subcategories may not total because of rounding.

Personal consumption expenditures (C):
Total spending by households on final goods and services.

Personal Consumption Expenditures. Expenditures by individuals and non-profit institutions are called **personal consumption expenditures (C).** These expenditures are broken down into spending on durable goods, on nondurable goods, and on services. Durable goods are items such as refrigerators that are expected to last for more than three years. Nondurable goods are such things as food and clothes that are not expected to last for more than three years. Services are intangible items such as travel, car repair, entertainment, and medical care. Personal consumption expenditures represent the largest expenditure component of GNP ($3470.3 billion in 1989).

Gross private domestic investment (I):
Total spending by private businesses on final goods, including capital goods and inventories.

Gross Private Domestic Investment. Expenditures on final output by private business firms (including resource-owning households) are called **gross private domestic investment (I).** Investment expenditures include spending on capital goods such as machinery and warehouses, new residential construction, improvements to existing houses, farm investments, and inventories. These expenditures were 777.1 billion in 1989. The qualifier *gross* is used because these expenditures include spending on new plant and equipment as well as on the replacement of worn-out plant and equipment. Business inventories are an investment in the holding of finished goods, semifinished goods,

FIGURE 3

Total Expenditures Equal Total Income Plus Adjustments

In any given year, total expenditures, composed of consumption, investment, government, and net foreign spending, must equal the income to the factors of production plus corrections. This income is composed of wages, rents, interest, proprietors' income, and corporate profits. The flow of total expenditures must equal the flow of total earnings.

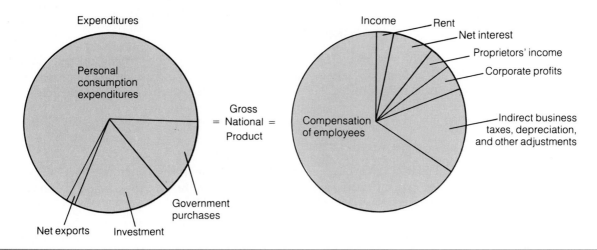

or raw materials by business firms. Investment in business inventories can vary greatly; that is, inventories can be built up or drawn down. For example, firms often draw down the level of their inventories in a period when business is bad, such as a recession. They hold fewer goods in inventory in the anticipation of decreased demand for the goods by consumers. Conversely, businesses will add to inventories in anticipation of sales increases and prosperous times.

Government Purchases. The third component in the expenditure approach to GNP is **government purchases (G)** on final goods and services at the federal, state, and local levels. Government spending was $1036.7 billion in 1989. Government transfer payments, such as Social Security and veterans' benefits, are not included in this figure because such payments are not made to individuals for current productive activities.

Net Exports. The final category of spending in the expenditure approach to GNP is **net exports (X − M). Exports (X)** are domestic goods purchased by foreigners. **Imports (M)** are foreign goods purchased by U.S. citizens. The purpose of GNP accounting is to measure current production in the economy. Thus, we must add the value of domestic goods purchased by foreigners and subtract the value of foreign goods purchased by Americans in calculating GNP by the expenditures approach. In other words,

Net exports = total exports (X) − total imports (M).

Net exports can be negative or positive. Obviously, if we spend more on imports than we sell in exports, net exports are going to be negative. In 1989, net exports were negative. We imported more than we exported by $50.9 billion.

Government purchases (G):
Total spending by federal, state, and local governments on final goods and services.

Net exports (X − M):
Total spending by foreigners on domestically produced goods and services minus total spending by domestic residents on foreign-produced goods and services.

Exports (X):
Total spending by foreigners on domestically produced goods and services.

Imports (M):
Total spending by domestic residents on foreign-produced goods and services.

The flow of expenditures approach to measuring GNP is quite simple.

$$GNP = \text{personal consumption expenditures } (C)$$
$$+ \text{ gross private domestic investment } (I)$$
$$+ \text{ government purchases } (G)$$
$$+ \text{ net exports } (X - M), \text{ or}$$
$$GNP = C + I + G + (X - M)$$

By this method, GNP was $5233.2 billion (over 5 trillion dollars!) in 1989, as shown in Table 2. Keep in mind that the expenditures approach is the national income accounting measure of the upper loop in the circular flow model of economic activity.

The Flow of Earnings Approach

The flow of earnings approach should give us the same value for GNP as does the expenditures approach. Table 3 gives the categories used in the flow of earnings approach. (Refer also to Figure 3.)

National income (NI):
Total earnings of resource suppliers during a given period of time.

National Income. The most inclusive figure in the flow of earnings approach to GNP is specifically called **national income (NI).** NI is determined by adding the income earned by factors of production (land, labor, capital, and entrepreneurship) used to produce final goods and services during a given period. Table 3 shows national income of $4265.0 billion for 1989, the sum of income items 1 through 5: compensation of employees, proprietors' income, rental income of persons, corporate profits, and net interest.

TABLE 3

Gross National Product, 1989: The Flow of Earnings

GNP can be calculated by summing the incomes received by suppliers of resources. Labor income, interest income, rental income, and profits are all summed—with adjustments for indirect business taxes and depreciation—to obtain the same level of GNP as found by the expenditures approach.

	Earnings (billions of dollars)
1. Compensation of employees	3145.4
2. Proprietors' income	352.2
3. Rental income of persons	62.9
4. Corporate profits	298.2
5. Net interest	324.0
National income (NI) (total of 1–5)	4265.0
6. Indirect business taxes and other adjustments	434.2
Net national product (NNP)	4699.2
7. Capital consumption allowances (depreciation)	552.2
Gross national product (GNP)	5233.2

Source: Council of Economic Advisers, *Economic Report of the President* (Washington, D.C.: U.S. Government Printing Office, 1990), pp. 318–21.

Note: GNP is in 1989 nominal dollars. Subcategories may not total because of rounding.

Compensation of Employees. Compensation of employees is the largest component of national income. It is the sum of wages and salaries paid to employees plus employer contributions to Social Security and employee benefit plans. In 1989, this category amounted to $3145.4 billion.

Proprietors' Income. Proprietors' income is the net income earned by sole proprietorships and partnerships. Both proprietorships and partnerships are mainly small businesses that are not incorporated. Proprietors' income in 1989 amounted to $352.2 billion.

Rental Income of Persons. Rental income of persons is the income of individuals from renting property, like a house or a car, as well as returns to individuals who hold patents, copyrights, and rights to natural resources, such as an oil or timber lease. National income accountants also estimate a rental value to owner-occupied houses. In other words, home ownership is treated like a business that produces a service sold to the owner. All these forms of rental income yielded earnings of $62.9 billion in 1989.

Corporate Profits. Corporate profits are the net income of private corporations, including profits on foreign operations. The total of corporate profits was $298.2 billion in 1989.

Net Interest. Net interest consists of the interest received by U.S. households and governments minus the interest paid by these households and governments. Some interest payments are not counted as a part of national income because they are not considered payment for current production. Net interest totaled $324.0 billion in 1989.

From National Income to Gross National Product. The figure for national income in Table 3—the sum of income items 1 through 5—does not equal the 1989 figure for gross national product in Table 2 figured by the flow of expenditures approach. Yet we know by the principle of the circular flow model that both approaches to measuring GNP must yield the same result. The problem is that there are two items—items included in total expenditures that are not income to anyone—that must be added to national income to obtain GNP. Let us examine these adjustments in detail.

Indirect Business Taxes and Other Adjustments. Indirect business taxes and other adjustments must be added to national income to determine GNP because such taxes are part of the total expenditures on goods and services but are not received by anyone as income. These include sales and excise taxes paid by purchasers of goods and services; property taxes; business transfer payments such as corporate donations to charitable institutions; government subsidies; and other minor statistical adjustments.

Capital Consumption Allowances. Capital consumption allowances, or depreciations, are an adjustment made for the wearing out of capital goods such as plant and equipment during the current production period. Capital consumption allowances, like indirect business taxes, enter the flow of earnings approach to calculating GNP even though they do not truly represent earnings. They do represent, however, part of the resource cost of producing

GNP, but not an expenditure on final output. For this reason, these items are included in the flow of earnings calculation of GNP. In Table 3, depreciation is equal to $552.2 billion. With adjustments for indirect business taxes and capital consumption allowances, GNP figured by the flow of earnings approach is $5233.2 billion, the same estimate derived from the flow of expenditures approach given in Table 2. Using the flow of earnings method of accounting, GNP is, in short, the sum of returns to the factors of production (wages, proprietors' income, rents, interest, and corporate profits) plus indirect business taxes and depreciation.

Net National Product

Net national product (NNP):
GNP minus capital consumption allowances (depreciation); the value of total output less the value of the capital used up in producing output.

Another useful national income concept can be derived from the statistics of Table 3. Net national product is equal to GNP minus depreciation, the value of the capital consumption allowances. In Table 3, the net national product for 1989 can also be determined by adding to the national income of $4265.0 billion the indirect taxes and other adjustments of $434.2 billion. Net national product in 1989 was $4699.2 billion. **Net national product (NNP)** is the net market value of goods and services produced in any economy in a given period. It tells us the value of all cars and houses and such produced during a certain period minus the value of the capital, plant, and equipment used up in this production. Since such capital is constantly being used up or transformed into current production of goods and services, it must be subtracted to get the net value of current production.

Other National Income Concepts

Macroeconomics is often concerned with the amount of income that goes to the household sector in an economy. By adjusting the figure derived for national income—income earned by factors of production—we can arrive at the concepts of personal income and disposable personal income.

Personal income (PI):
Total earnings resource suppliers actually receive during a given period of time plus transfer payments.

Personal Income. Personal income (PI) is the amount of income that households receive during a certain period. There is a difference between income earned and income received. A writer, for example, may not receive royalties on the great American novel until years after writing the book because of the time lags in the production and marketing processes. Current production does not necessarily translate instantly into current income. The major categories of situations in which household earnings do not coincide in time with household income are given in items 1, 2, and 3 in Table 4.

To determine personal income, items 1, 2, and 3 must first be subtracted from national income because they represent income earned but not directly received by households in the current period. Corporate profits do not flow directly to individuals, but instead to firms. Net interest, because it refers to interest earned by businesses, also must be subtracted from national income in calculating personal income. Contributions for social insurance ($479.3 billion)—such as payroll deductions for Social Security—are also excluded from personal income because they are earned but not received by workers in the current period.

TABLE 4

National Income, Personal Income, and Disposable Personal Income, 1989

National income minus income not received (items 1, 2, 3) plus income received (items 4, 5, 6, 7) yields personal income. Subtracting personal taxes from personal income yields disposable personal income.

		Value (billions of dollars)
National income		4265.0
1. Minus: Corporate profits[a]	−298.2	
2. Minus: Net interest *(business)*	−461.1	
3. Minus: Contributions for social insurance	−479.3	
4. Plus: Government transfer payments	+600.3	
5. Plus: Personal interest income	+657.8	
6. Plus: Personal dividend income	+112.4	
7. Plus: Business transfer payments	+31.8	
Personal income		4428.7
8. Minus: Personal taxes	−513.4	
Disposable personal income		3780.0

Source: Council of Economic Advisers, *Economic Report of the President* (Washington, D.C.: U.S. Government Printing Office, 1990), pp. 319, 324.

[a]Includes inventory valuation and capital consumption adjustments.

Note: Disposable personal income is in 1989 nominal dollars.

Items 4 through 7 are received by households in the current period and are therefore counted as part of personal income. These include government transfer payments, such as Social Security payments, personal interest income, dividends, and business transfer payments.

Depending on the magnitudes of the minuses and pluses, national income can be larger or smaller than personal income. In a period of declining business activity, for example, national income can fall below personal income because corporate profits go down while government transfer payments go up. Personal income in 1989 was $4428.7 billion, an amount greater than national income.

Disposable personal income:
Personal income minus taxes; income available to spend.

Disposable Personal Income. Disposable personal income—what income receivers have left to spend or save after taxes—is found in Table 4 by subtracting certain personal taxes from personal income. These personal taxes include income and property taxes. In 1989, disposable personal income was $3780.0 billion.

Personal Saving

Personal saving:
Disposable personal income less personal consumption expenditures.

Personal saving, another important economic statistic, represents the funds provided for investment by the saving of individuals and unincorporated businesses in the economy. Their choice to refrain from spending all they receive is a crucial ingredient in economic growth. Table 5 shows the calculation of personal saving as $206.3 billion in 1989.

TABLE 5	**Personal Saving, 1989**

Disposable personal income may be saved or spent by households. In 1989, households chose to save $206.3 billion and spend $3573.7 billion of their disposable personal income.

	Value (billions of dollars)
Disposable personal income	3780.0
Minus: Personal outlays	−3573.7
Personal saving	206.3

Source: Council of Economic Advisers, *Economic Report of the President* (Washington, D.C.: U.S. Government Printing Office, 1990), p. 324.

Note: Personal savings in 1989 nominal dollars.

THE MEASUREMENT OF PRICE CHANGES

Was GNP in 1989 greater than in 1980? To answer this question, we might simply compare GNP for 1980 and 1989. Yet changes in prices make such comparisons difficult. Think of a simple world in which only chocolate fudge is produced. The fact that total expenditures on fudge rose from $5 million in 1980 to $10 million in 1989 tells us very little. Total expenditures will increase if (a) more fudge is produced, (b) the price of fudge rises, or (c) both (a) and (b) happen at the same time. The same facts hold for changes in GNP. GNP can change over time because total output increases, prices increase, or both happen at the same time. Thus, since we are interested in comparing differences in aggregate output over time when using national income statistics, a means has to be found to adjust GNP data for changes in prices. (The more difficult issue of changes in the type and quality of goods over time is treated in Focus, "GNP and Economic Change.") The **price level** is the average of the prices of all goods and services. It is not to be confused with relative prices, which show the price of one good in terms of another.

Economists and national income statisticians approach the problem of detecting price level changes by constructing **price indexes.** All indexes use a base year, against which subsequent changes in prices are measured. The most common method of measuring price change uses base-year quantities as weights for the price indexes of ensuing years.[3] Any price index compares the

Price level:
The average of the prices of all goods and services in the economy; used for calculating the inflation rate and for converting nominal into real values.

Price index:
A statistic used to calculate the price level and the rate of inflation.

---

[3]An understanding of the base-year index calculation can be reached with a simple example. Assume that the consumer price index is composed of only two goods, beer and pizzas, and that the relevant data on prices, outputs, and expenditures are as follows.

Commodities	Price (per unit)	Quantity Sold	Total Expenditures
Beer (six-packs)			
1989	$2.00	2 million	$ 4 million
1990	$3.00	3 million	$ 9 million
Pizza (each)			
1989	$4.00	3 million	$12 million
1990	$5.00	5 million	$25 million

FOCUS   GNP and Economic Change

Comparisons of GNP over time are even more complicated than controlling for price changes with a price index. Such comparisons are fundamentally difficult because entrepreneurs introduce new and improved goods and services to the economy. For example, how useful is it to compare GNP in 1890 with GNP in 1990? The United States at these two time periods comprised two different economies. In 1990, there were cars, fast-food restaurants, televisions, computers, and liver transplants. These goods and services did not exist in 1890. On the other hand, there was a great deal of open land, a relatively low crime rate, and little or no acid rain in 1890. These conditions largely no longer existed in 1990.

The goods available to consumers—that is, the final outputs of the economy—change over time. Even someone with a lot of money in 1890 could not have purchased what the average middle-income family purchases today. The point is simple but profound. An economy changes across time, and comparisons of GNP therefore lose much of their relevance.

So, while we know that the U.S. economy has grown remarkably over its history, the fact that the bundle of goods available to consumers has changed over time makes the measurement of this growth difficult. For example, real per capita GNP in 1950 was $3535. In 1980, it was $6645. Does this mean that workers in the United States produced roughly twice the amount in 1980 as they produced in 1950? The problem is that GNP cannot give a clear answer to this type of question. (Remember: A change in GNP does not necessarily measure a change in welfare.) The goods pro-

duced in each period have changed. We do not now produce twice the amount of the *same* goods produced in 1950. Our capacity to produce goods and services has increased, no doubt, but the exact amount of this growth is not measured by the growth of real GNP.

The farther apart in time that comparisons of GNP are made, the more severe is the problem caused by the differences in economies in the two periods. However, even over a short period, GNP comparisons are difficult because of changes in the quality of existing goods. In a span of a little more than ten years, consumers in the United States have gained access to improved goods such as cable television and more efficient computers. Do these improvements in quality mean growth in the value of the economy? If so, how could it possibly be measured? These complications indicate that GNP comparisons over time are useful, but not perfect.

Finally, exactly the same point can be made about the difficulty of comparisons of GNP across countries. Countries obviously produce different bundles of goods, and for the reasons just given, international comparisons of GNP are difficult and subject to interpretation. Different tastes for goods and services likely exist across countries, further complicating simple GNP comparisons intended to reflect differences in economic well-being. None of this argues that comparisons of GNP are meaningless. The point is that such comparisons should be made carefully and conclusions drawn about economic growth only after a careful study of all the relevant information about the economy or economies concerned.

Assume that the base year is 1989 and that we are interested in how prices have changed in 1990; that is, has there been inflation or deflation? A base-year quantity weight index for beer and pizza can be expressed

$$\text{Price index} = \frac{q_b^{89} p_b^{90} + q_p^{89} p_p^{90}}{q_b^{89} p_b^{89} + q_p^{89} p_p^{89}}.$$

The superscripts denote the relevant year (1989 or 1990), and the subscripts denote beer (b) or pizza (p). Price is p and quantity is q. Using this price index formula with 1989 as the base year, the price index is equal to 1.31. That is,

$$\text{Price index} = \frac{\$(6 + 15) \text{ million}}{\$(4 + 12) \text{ million}} = 1.31.$$

The value of the index is always equal to 1.0 in the base year (try the calculation). When the index is greater than 1.0, it tells us that prices are, on average, higher than they were in the base year. When the index is less than 1.0, the average of prices is lower than it was in the base year. The inflation rate is the percent by which the index changes from one year to the next. In this example, the inflation rate in the beer-and-pizza economy was 31 percent (1.31 minus 1.00 divided by 1.00).

average level of prices at a given point in time (be it today or 1947) to the average level of prices at some specific point in the past (the base year or period). If the ratio is greater than 1, then prices in general are greater at the time for which the index is calculated than they were in the base year. If the ratio is less than 1, then prices are generally lower than in the base period. (The consumer price index formula is multiplied by 100.)

Price indexes serve two very important functions. Above all, they give us a measure of what is happening to the overall level of prices. By calculating the percentage change in a price index, the inflation rate over any given time period is measured. Additionally, a price index can be used to convert nominal variables, such as GNP, to real variables. Suppose the price index is based in 1982. Dividing nominal GNP in 1990 by the price index in 1990 (based in 1982) gives a measure of the total output of the economy in 1990 measured in 1982 prices. This allows more accurate comparisons of GNP between years, comparisons that are not biased by price changes. This gives a more accurate picture of how aggregate output changes over time. Almost all nominal variables can be converted to real variables by dividing by a price index. Government statistics calculate several indexes for the American economy.

The Consumer Price Index

Consumer price index (CPI):
A price index that uses the prices of goods and services consumers generally buy to calculate the price level and the rate of inflation.

The **consumer price index (CPI)** measures price changes in a typical market basket of goods purchased by urban wage earners and clerical workers. This "market basket" was developed from a survey of about 20,000 families, who provided information on their buying habits. The market basket includes food, housing (rental costs), apparel, transportation, health and recreation, and miscellaneous services. To measure price changes in the market basket, the Bureau of Labor Statistics at the Department of Labor collects data every month from a wide variety of retail stores and service establishments. The CPI is issued monthly, and its base period is 1982–1984. Current prices are compared to average base-period prices. In the CPI, 1982–1984 = 100.

Figure 4 shows the movement of the CPI for the period 1970–1989. Notice that the CPI for all items has been broken down into two categories: food and rent. Each of these categories fluctuates over time; one may be rising while another is falling during a given period.

The Producer Price Index

Producer price index (PPI):
A price index that calculates the general level of prices and the rate of inflation of goods businesses purchase.

The Bureau of Labor Statistics also publishes statistics known as the **producer price index (PPI),** previously known as the wholesale price index. This index excludes consumer prices and instead covers about 2800 industrial commodities, from raw materials to finished goods. For the PPI the Bureau of Labor Statistics collects about 10,000 price quotations each month from companies that sell goods to producers.

The Implicit Price Deflator

Implicit price deflator:
A price index that uses the most comprehensive set of prices to calculate the level of prices and the rate of inflation facing households, businesses, and government; also called the GNP deflator.

The final major index is the **implicit price deflator,** often called the GNP deflator. This index goes to the heart of the problem of measuring price changes over time. As we have seen, it is impossible to add the different outputs

FIGURE 4

The Consumer Price Index, 1970–1989

The consumer price index measures the average change in price of a bundle of consumer goods. The prices of goods in the categories of food or rent change at different rates. However, the overall CPI has increased fairly consistently. The base period for constructing the price indexes measured on the vertical axis is 1982–1984 (1982–1984 = 100).

Source: Council of Economic Advisers, *Economic Report of the President* (Washington, D.C.: U.S. Government Printing Office, 1990), pp. 359–60.

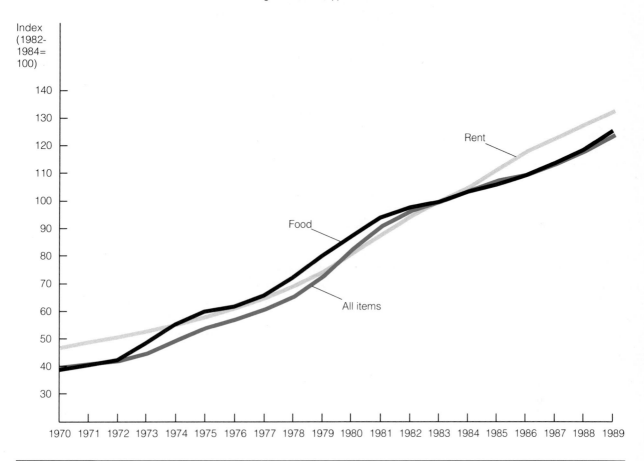

of goods over time. Rather, we add the dollar amounts spent on commodities. But since both prices and quantities of commodities can change over time, the comparison of GNP at different points in time is difficult. Remember that the economist is interested in measuring the economy's real output. Therefore, the GNP statistician must be careful to distinguish current or nominal GNP, which is evaluated in current dollars, from real or constant GNP, which is evaluated in constant dollars. The implicit price deflator is a means to convert nominal GNP values into real GNP values.

The GNP deflator is similar to the CPI in that it is a price index. However, the GNP deflator is a broader index of prices than the CPI. The CPI pertains only to goods and services purchased by consumers; the implicit price deflator also takes into account goods and services generally consumed by producers and government. A major weakness of price indexes is the noncompatability of base years. Government agencies that collect and publish various statistics often change the base year used, causing potential confusion. Nominal GNP is converted to real GNP by use of the GNP deflator—by dividing nominal GNP by a constant GNP value for the same base-year prices. For example, Table 6 shows that in 1989 the GNP implicit price deflator was 1.263. This number tells us that, on average, prices were 26.3 percent higher in 1989 than in 1982 (1982 being the base year). Nominal GNP for 1989, $5233.2 billion, divided by the GNP deflator for 1989 gives the real GNP for 1989—$4143.5 billion ($5233.2/1.263). This figure reveals what the value of GNP would have been in 1989 if prices had not changed since 1982. Put another way, it measures the value of the output of final goods and services in terms of 1982 prices. (For examples of price changes for selected goods, see Focus, "Price Changes from Truman to Bush.")

Table 6 shows GNP in both constant-dollar and current-dollar, or nominal, terms, using the varying implicit price deflator for GNP for the years 1972 to 1989. One interesting aspect of these data is that between 1973 and 1975 and again between 1981 and 1982, GNP in current terms was rising but real GNP was falling. In other words, growth in the GNP was due to inflation in prices rather than to increases in output. The proper measure of the real performance of the economy is the movement of real GNP over time.

TABLE 6

Nominal GNP, GNP Deflator, and Real GNP, 1972–1989

The GNP deflator is used to convert nominal GNP into real GNP. By dividing any year's GNP by that year's GNP deflator, one can estimate real GNP in terms of 1982 dollars.

Year	Nominal GNP (billions of dollars)	÷	GNP Deflator (1982 = 1)	=	Constant GNP (billions of 1982 dollars)
1972	1212.8		0.465		2608.1
1973	1359.3		0.495		2746.1
1974	1472.8		0.540		2727.4
1975	1598.4		0.593		2695.4
1976	1782.8		0.631		2825.4
1977	1990.5		0.673		2957.7
1978	2249.7		0.722		3115.9
1979	2508.2		0.786		3191.1
1980	2732.0		0.857		3187.9
1981	3052.6		0.940		3247.4
1982	3166.0		1.000		3166.0
1983	3405.7		1.039		3277.9
1984	3772.5		1.077		3502.8
1985	4014.9		1.109		3620.3
1986	4231.6		1.138		3718.5
1987	4524.3		1.174		3853.7
1988	4880.6		1.213		4023.6
1989	5233.2		1.263		4143.5

Source: Council of Economic Advisers, *Economic Report of the President* (Washington, D.C.: U.S. Government Printing Office, 1990), pp. 296, 298.

Note: Nominal GNP is in billions of dollars, the GNP deflator is 1982 = 1, and constant GNP is in billions of 1982 dollars.

FOCUS   Price Changes from Truman to Bush

Are historical contrasts valid or misleading? A recently released movie has grossed over $100 million and now ranks ahead of such classics as *Gone with the Wind* in terms of all-time box-office receipts. The average salary among major league baseball players is now more than three times as high as the highest salary ever paid to Babe Ruth. A house in California purchased at the end of World War II for $10,000 sells for $885,000. When adjustments to reflect changes in purchasing power are made, prices such as the $15 million paid for the Louisiana Purchase may not be so surprising.

Let's focus on Babe Ruth's salary. In 1933, he earned a salary of $90,000. By 1988, the average major league salary stood at about $270,000. Using the implicit price deflator to measure average price changes, prices in 1988 were about 11.1 times as high as in 1933. In other words, Babe Ruth's 1933 salary had roughly the purchasing power of $1,000,000 in 1988. Although he was not paid as much as modern stars, Ruth's real pay was nearly four times as high as today's average player's. To compare the total receipts of *Gone with the Wind* and, say, *Raiders of the Lost Ark,* it would be necessary to ascertain annual sales since each was released before making appropriate adjustments.

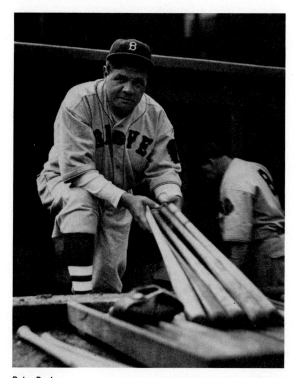

Babe Ruth

TABLE 7
Prices of Selected Goods in 1949 and 1989

While the price of each of the selected goods increased between 1949 and 1989, the rate of increase was far from uniform. Had the price of flour risen at the same rate as prices in general over the forty-year period, ten pounds of flour would have cost $4.34 in 1989. The actual price in 1989 was $2.99.

Item	1949 Price (Truman Dollars)	Equivalent Number of Bush Dollars	1989 Price (Bush Dollars)
Flour (10 lb)	$.83	$4.34	$2.99
Eight O'Clock coffee (1 lb)	$1.15	$6.01	$8.39
Lean ground beef (1 lb)	$.45	$2.37	$1.69
Dozen eggs (large)	$.57	$2.98	$1.03
Coca-Cola (12 oz)	$.05	$.26	$.50
Wool suit	$39.75	$207.89	$210.00
Muffler	$4.95	$25.89	$39.95
Movie ticket (adult)	$1.32	$6.96	$4.50
Washing machine (Hotpoint)	$119.95	$627.33	$439.00

Price indexes reflect average price level changes, but it is important to realize that the prices of all goods do not change uniformly over time. Using the implicit price deflator to measure price level changes, prices were about 5.23 times as high at George Bush's presidential inauguration in 1989 as they were in 1949, when Harry Truman took the same oath of office (the index had risen from 23.6 to 123.6, using 1982 as the base year). In other words, the *Truman Dollar*—the purchasing power of the dollar in 1949—had 5.23 times as much purchasing power as the *Bush Dollar.* Table 7 shows the 1949 prices of selected goods, the equivalent number of Bush Dollars, and the actual prices of the goods in 1989. Prices were taken from advertisements in local newspapers on the inaugural dates discussed. While all prices increased over the period, the rate of increase was not, as you might expect, a uniform 5.23 percent.

SUMMARY

1. National income accounting is concerned with the measurement of the aggregate performance of the economy.
2. Gross national product (GNP) is the market value of all the final goods and services produced in an economy during a given period. It includes only currently produced goods and services, and it excludes such items as illegal transactions and household production.
3. GNP is not a measure of economic welfare. It does not count social costs such as pollution, which lowers economic welfare, or such goods as leisure, which raises economic welfare.
4. Gross national product can be measured by the value-added approach, the final-goods approach to expenditures, or the income paid to factors of production to produce final outputs. The latter two methods are the most useful.
5. Gross national product can be computed in two ways: by adding expenditures on final goods and services produced during a given period or by adding the earnings or incomes of the factors of production used to produce final goods and services during the period. The two approaches, subject to a statistical discrepancy, yield the same result for GNP.

The Flow of Expenditures Approach

Personal consumption expenditures (C) + gross private domestic investment (I) + government purchases of final goods and services (G) + Net exports (X − M) = GNP

The Flow of Earnings Approach

Wages + proprietors' income + rents + net interest + corporate profits + indirect business taxes + depreciation = GNP

The flow of expenditures approach focuses on buyers' evaluations of goods produced during a year. The flow of earnings approach concentrates on the cost of production of goods and services. The circular flow of economic activity, therefore, ensures that the two approaches are identical. That is,

$$\text{Dollar spending on final outputs} = \text{GNP} = \text{dollar costs of producing final outputs.}$$

6. Other important national income accounting concepts are personal income, disposable personal income, and personal saving. Each provides important information for the macroeconomist in analyzing economic stability and growth.
7. To compare GNP in different time periods, some method must be used to control for price changes. The government uses various price indexes, including the consumer price index, the producer price index, and the implicit price deflator for GNP.

KEY TERMS

national income accounting
gross national product (GNP)
measure of economic welfare (MEW)
final goods
intermediate goods
value added
flow of expenditures
flow of earnings

personal consumption expenditures (C)
gross private domestic investment (I)
government purchases (G)
net exports (X − M)
exports (X)
imports (M)
national income (NI)
net national product (NNP)

personal income (PI)
disposable personal income
personal saving
price level
price index
consumer price index (CPI)
producer price index (PPI)
implicit price deflator

QUESTIONS FOR REVIEW AND DISCUSSION

1. Why does GNP count only the production of final goods and services? Why aren't intermediate goods and services counted?
2. What are the relations among gross national product, net national product, national income, personal income, and disposable personal income?
3. List three reasons GNP should not be considered an overall indicator of society's well-being.
4. What are the three approaches used to estimate GNP?
5. American society has become more urbanized and industrialized since 1930. Other things being equal, do you think this means that our measurement of GNP is more or less precise? Why?
6. What is GNP in constant dollars and how is it calculated?

7. Why might GNP be a misleading statistic with which to compare the economy of the United States with that of the Soviet Union?
8. Which of the following are counted in the calculation of this year's GNP: (a) the services provided by a homemaker; (b) the wage paid to a maid; (c) Sam's purchase of an antique desk; (d) Joan's purchase of ten shares of stock; (e) Social Security checks received by the elderly; (f) Social Security taxes paid by workers?
9. Can a price index be calculated for the commodities in Table 7 of this chapter? If so, make up some numbers and calculate an index.

PROBLEM

Suppose that nominal GNP in 1995 totals $8475 billion and rises to $12.5 trillion ten years later. If the GNP deflator for 1995 is 1.85 and for 2005 is 2.75, in what year is real GNP greater? By how much?

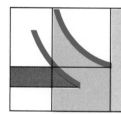

ECONOMICS IN ACTION
GNP, Leisure, and Social Welfare

As you know, GNP is not a perfect measure of economic well-being. GNP statistics exclude the value of goods produced for home consumption, the value of increases in leisure time, and the value of goods produced in the underground economy. In addition, some of the costs that are often associated with economic development, such as pollution and congestion, are not subtracted from GNP in measuring economic well-being. If one is willing to assume that all such omissions are proportional to measured GNP, then changes in GNP can be considered an excellent measure of changes in economic well-being. However, if this assumption is viewed as unrealistic, then there is reason to have serious reservations about using measured GNP to determine economic progress.

Some scholars have tried to overcome these problems in measuring GNP by proposing alternative measurements of an economy's performance that would more closely re-

flect the underlying welfare or happiness of its people. William Nordhaus and Nobel laureate James Tobin have proposed the use of measure of economic welfare (MEW) as such a measure. Their MEW would modify the traditional measurement of GNP in the following ways.

1. Measures of the value of leisure time and household production and consumption would be added to GNP.
2. The costs of pollution and congestion would be subtracted from GNP.
3. Expenditures on goods produced by government, such as national defense and police protection (which are intermediate goods that are inputs to other end-product activities), would be subtracted from GNP.

By their calculations, MEW has grown slower than GNP since 1965, which implies that official GNP statistics have overstated the rate of economic improvement. This is largely attributable to rapid increases in the costs of pollution in recent years.

The use of MEW by national income scholars remains controversial, although it represents a step toward more accurate measurement of the macroeconomy. However, it should be noted that MEW does not attempt to adjust GNP figures to account for goods produced in the underground economy. Although it is extremely difficult to obtain any reliable estimates concerning the size of the underground economy, many observers believe that it has grown in relative importance in recent years, as Americans have increasingly become a nation of tax evaders. If this observation is true, then official GNP statistics would tend to understate the extent of economic progress in recent years.

In comparing official measures of economic production across countries, it is important to keep in mind that all countries (even totalitarian ones) have underground economies. Therefore, some goods and services that are produced and consumed will not be included in official statistics. Accordingly, some differences in measured GNP among countries may be caused by differing abilities to record production. This problem was made clear at the July 1989 summit meeting between the five leading free-market countries (the United States, France, Japan, West Germany, and Great Britain). Government leaders in Italy were offended by being excluded from the meeting, arguing that they, not Great Britain, deserved an invitation. The Italians claimed that production in Italy was greater than in Great Britain, despite official statistics to the contrary. According to the Italian officials, the amount of output that was omitted in Britain's official GNP statistics was quite small, since the British are meticulous record keepers and, further, a nation of law-abiding citizens not given to tax evasion. In contrast, omitted output in Italy was large, Italy being a country with a lax system of records keeping and massive tax evasion. Therefore, since official statistics indicated that Britain's production was slightly larger than Italy's, it must be the case that Italy in fact outproduced Britain. Although the dispute was never settled, Italy was invited to a follow-up meeting.

If the problem of uncounted output creates confusion in comparing the success of the economies of highly developed countries, the problem is much greater for Third World countries. In developing countries, the economic system is based on production for home use, and a huge proportion of total production takes place in the uncounted underground economy. Official GNP statistics for such countries can be highly misleading.

Question

How would one go about estimating the value of leisure or the extent of production for home consumption?

Source: William Nordhaus and James Tobin, "Is Growth Obsolete?" in *Economic Growth,* Fifteenth Anniversary colloquium (New York: National Bureau of Economic Research, 1972).

25

Classical Theory

Measuring the rise and fall of macroeconomic variables such as the rate of inflation, GNP, and unemployment is only a first step toward understanding why these economic indicators fluctuate and what measures, if any, are needed to maintain stability and growth.

The next four chapters survey some of the major theoretical tools of macroeconomics to discover the conditions under which the economy can achieve stability and growth. We concentrate on both aggregate demand—the spending side of the economy—and aggregate supply—the producing side of the economy. This chapter and Chapters 26 and 27 develop economic principles pertaining to aggregate demand. Chapters 28 and 29 deal with the interaction of aggregate demand and aggregate supply.

Some simplifications are necessary to understand how aggregate demand and supply interact to sustain full employment, economic growth, and low levels of inflation. This chapter and the next concentrate on two views of consumer and business spending—the private or nongovernment part of aggregate spending. The first view is the classical notion of a self-regulating aggregate economy; the second is the perspective of John Maynard Keynes, who focused attention on how spending changes cause prosperity and depression. To simplify our development of aggregate demand and supply theories, we only briefly cover here important but complicating variables such as the money supply. We defer our in-depth analysis of money until Part Six.

The classical view sees the economy as self-regulating, without need of large-scale government intervention. A full appreciation of the classical view is the starting point for understanding how and why Keynes and others modified macroeconomic theory. When you complete Chapter 25 you should understand

- why the classical writers had faith that a nonregulated economy could fully employ all resources in the long run.
- the four essential components of the classical view that the economy would function at or near full employment over time.
- the basic classical view that government intervention should be minimized in the private economy.
- how classical macroeconomic theories and their policies interrelate.

617

CLASSICAL THEORY

Can the economy remain as close as possible to its production possibilities frontier? Can it manage to keep all resources, human and nonhuman, fully employed? More fundamentally, can the economy automatically produce full employment, a maximum GNP, and price stability? If not, what actions are necessary to maintain these important goals?

Historically, economists have given many different answers to these difficult questions. **Classical macroeconomic theory** stems from Adam Smith's pioneering work, *An Inquiry into the Nature and Causes of the Wealth of Nations,* published in 1776. Smith and those who followed in the classical tradition believed that, given laissez-faire government policies and enough time, the economy would achieve the goals of price stability, full employment, and economic growth through its own ability to correct short-run unemployment and inflation. In other words, the classical theorists believed that unemployment and inflation were temporary phenomena. In the long run (a period of time that is hard to specify), the economy would remain close to or on its production possibilities frontier and enjoy a stable level of prices. This classical tradition lasted for well over 150 years (the last great neoclassical economist, A. C. Pigou, died in 1959). The theory that grew from Smith's faith in a self-adjusting market mechanism was the work of many economists who wrote at different times in response to different conditions. The following simplified discussion of classical macroeconomics is a composite of various individual contributions. First, consider the classical engine of economic growth.

Classical macroeconomic theory:
A view of the macroeconomy as being self-adjusting and capable of generating full employment and maximum output in the long run without government intervention; dominant from the late eighteenth century through the early twentieth century.

The Classical Blueprint for Economic Growth

The classical economists were writing at a time of rapid technological advance. Attitudes toward the Industrial Revolution—the catchphrase for the technological advances of the eighteenth and early nineteenth centuries—undoubtedly colored the classical economists' conception of how the economy works and grows. The **classical process of economic growth** conceives of a circular flow of human activities leading to growth in per capita output and economic well-being for the average citizen of the economy. The circular flow of this classical process of economic growth—like the one considered in Chapters 3 and 24—focuses on the real factors and activities leading to economic growth.

The heart of Adam Smith's view of economic progress is the natural tendency for society to divide tasks. The **division of labor** in producing some output creates enormous advantages for society. A modern assembly line or fast-food production by McDonald's, Wendy's, or Burger King are excellent examples of the division of labor. Given enough time, a single worker could certainly build an automobile from scratch. Only the hobbyist would approach car building this way, however. Adam Smith hit on the critical idea (from observation) that the division of tasks (in the context of automobile manufacture, fitting parts, welding motor parts, installing windshields) educates workers in some critically important ways. The repetition of specific tasks in production leads to increased skill and dexterity in every worker, thereby increasing human capital and productivity. The repetition of specific tasks also fosters invention and creativity in workers—an advantage encouraged by the

Classical process of economic growth:
A process based on the division of labor but also involving increases in saving, investment, capital accumulation, and, ultimately, growth in real GNP.

Division of labor:
An economic principle whereby individuals specialize in the production of a single good, service, or task, thereby increasing overall productivity and economic efficiency.

narrow focus of the individual's attention on particular job tasks. Moreover, while training and retraining for specific tasks takes time, on balance the application of the division of labor saves time in that workers need not move from task to task.

Figure 1 shows, in simplified form, how the division of labor leads to the growth of real output as it works its way through production processes in an economy. As the circular flow progresses, increased real GNP creates higher real wages and higher per capita incomes. Higher wages and incomes permit individuals to consume and save more annually. But, as we will see in more detail later in the chapter, saving by some individuals is translated directly into investment by other individuals. At low interest rates, individuals want to invest more, and savers want to save less. High rates encourage savers and discourage investors. There is a point at which the desires of savers and of investors are in equilibrium.

The process depicted in Figure 1 is continuous; there is no starting point. Each element is equally important to the process, and each can serve as the "first step." For ease in understanding, however, we may think of the process as beginning with increased demand (consumption) for goods. The saving of consumers permits, through the link to investment, additional capital accumulation. An increase in the (net) capital stock raises the productivity both of labor and of natural resources, permitting more division of labor. The result of greater application of capital and enhanced division of labor is higher real GNP. Wages rise, as do per capita incomes, leading to more consumption, saving, and investment. The process continues until, in Adam Smith's words, the extent of the market is reached—that is, until domestic and international markets are saturated with goods and services.

It is worthwhile to remember that, in this simple process, savings are translated *automatically* into the exceptionally important mechanism of investment. Through investment, capital is accumulated. Capital—broadly defined to include factories, machinery, tools, and human skills—is a force for

FIGURE 1

Enhanced division of labor in the classical growth process leads directly to increased output of goods and services. The division of labor is directly fueled by capital accumulation in the circular flow.

The Classical Process of Economic Growth

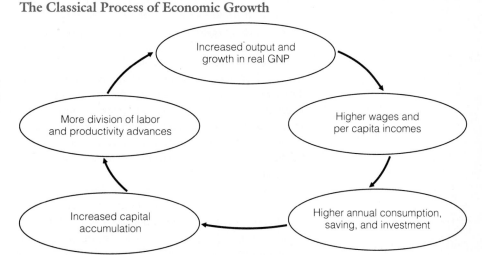

growth because it permits and facilitates the division of labor. Increased capital accumulation, as shown in the circular flow of Figure 1, allows division of labor and, along with it, *productivity of labor and capital*. Using Smith's words again, the "wealth of a nation"—GNP—is the annual product of the raw materials, land, and labor of a society, assisted, critically, by the accumulation of capital goods and the division of labor.

Many of the classical economists' predecessors equated the accumulation of gold and other precious metals with the wealth of a nation. Instead, according to the classical economists, human capital and resource development, assisted by growing capital and the division of labor, produced the wealth of the nation and contained the keys to economic growth. The division of labor gives rise to increased output and economic growth. Higher per capita wages and incomes result from increased real output. Higher incomes produce higher consumption and savings. Additional savings lead to additional investment in capital and in capital accumulation. Capital accumulation enhances and facilitates a greater division of labor, and the process continues.

Limits to Growth. The process depicted in Figure 1 is neither instantaneous nor limitless. As we already mentioned, the growth process may be limited by the "extent of the market." Profitable investment outlets may dry up as demand, both foreign and domestic, for goods and services becomes saturated. The classicals knew that the economy's maximum attainable output is limited by its actual supply of human and nonhuman resources, the state of technology, productivity, and population. The classical view of the macroeconomy was a **long-run equilibrium** conception. In other words, classical theory was concerned with how an economy adjusts to some hypothetical equilibrium given some actual supply of resources, level of population, technology, or state of specialization.

Classical long-run equilibrium:
The hypothetical adjustment of an economy to full employment given an actual supply of resources, population, technology, and degree of specialization.

The classicals believed that mechanisms within the economy were self-adjusting—in other words, that self-adjusting mechanisms automatically brought full employment in the long run. Full employment of resources in the long run is, of course, tantamount to being on the economy's production possibilities curve (see Figure 2a). Society's choice between capital and consumer goods in the present has an effect on future economic growth. In the classical context, a choice of more capital goods relative to consumer goods means encouraged investment and capital accumulation, which produces a greater division of labor and more rapid future economic growth. The point to remember, however, is that the attainment of any point such as A on PP in Figure 2a is the result of self-adjusting forces in the economy in the long run. The exact point chosen on any production possibilities curve also depends on society's relative demands for present and future consumption. The society that chooses more capital goods at the expense of consumer goods will enjoy more future growth potential. The society that chooses more consumer goods in the present will enjoy more goods and services now but will have less growth potential.

Points such as A on PP_0 in Figure 2a also imply that *all* resources are fully employed in the economy. At the risk of getting a little ahead of ourselves, we should note that later economists, including Keynes, challenged the belief that automatic, self-adjusting forces could be relied upon to get the economy to points such as A on PP_0. They believed that certain short-run factors, such as wage and interest-rate inflexibility inhibited the classical mechanism. For

FIGURE 2

Production Possibilities and the Aggregate Supply Curve

In the long-run adjustment mechanism of classical economics, attainment of points such as *A* on production possibilities curve *PP*$_0$ of Figure 2a translate to vertical aggregate supply curves, such as *AS*$_A$ at output level *Y*$_0$ in Figure 2b. In the classical model, there is no unemployment in the long run. Technological advances or discovery of new resources could be part of the long-run economy-wide adjustments that shift the production possibilities frontier and aggregate supply curve rightward.

(a)

(b)

now, just keep in mind that points such as *A* in Figure 2a are attained only after adjustments take place in the long run and full employment is reached in the entire economy.

Economic Growth and Aggregate Supply. Economic growth, as summarized by a production possibilities model, may also be related to the aggregate (economy-wide) supply curve developed in Chapter 23. If production possibilities curve *PP*$_0$ is drawn under assumptions of constant technology, possibilities for the division of labor and economic growth are limited. The attainment of point *A* in Figure 2a may be viewed as equivalent to a level of income, *Y*$_0$, that defines the aggregate supply curve *AS*$_A$ in Figure 2b. At any given moment, then, the growth process is limited by, among other things, the state of technology. The maximum amount of output that can be had out of the economy, irrespective of the price level, is designated *AS*$_A$ or *Y*$_0$. Note that the vertical supply curve of Figure 2b differs from the upward-sloping aggregate supply curve in Chapter 23 because the attainment of any point on production possibilities curve *PP*$_0$ means that consumer and capital goods production is maximized. The upward-sloping aggregate supply curve indicates that some unemployment of resources exists—in other words, that the outer limits of the production possibilities curve have not been reached.

A change in technology or the augmentation of resources (perhaps through international trade or through resource discoveries) would shift the production possibilities curve rightward. Attainment of a new equilibrium point such as B in Figure 2a through long-run, economy-wide adjustments would shift the aggregate supply curve rightward. All points on new production possibilities frontier PP_1 contain higher total production of consumer and capital goods than on PP_0. In terms of Figure 2b, aggregate supply shifts to AS_B at output level Y_1. In short, the aggregate supply curve of any economy is based on the "possibilities" of attaining maximum production. A vertical aggregate supply curve means that society has reached the production possibilities curve of the economy. We must now investigate how the classicals arrived at the rather startling conclusion that the economy would adjust itself to full employment in the long run if left unassisted by an outside force such as government.

Cornerstones of Classical Macroeconomic Theory

Classical economic theory primarily concerned itself with how economies grow and prosper. Imbedded within the elements of economic progress they described, however, is a theory of macroeconomic functioning. Taken as a group, the classicals developed an exact theory of how the economy adjusts in the long run to reach a point on the production possibilities or aggregate supply curve. The classical economist's belief that the economy self-adjusts in response to short-run disturbances and produces full employment and economic growth without government interference rests on four cornerstones:

1. Say's law;
2. Interest rate flexibility;
3. Price-wage flexibility; and
4. Quantity theory of money.

The first three cornerstones deal with the flexibility of the macroeconomy in maintaining full employment. The fourth concerns the determination of the price level and the control of inflation.

Say's law:
A proposition of the classical economists that the production of goods and services will generate incomes sufficiently large that those goods and services will be purchased.

Say's Law. Say's law is an economic principle first attributed to Jean Baptiste Say (1767–1832). According to Say's law, diagrammed in Figure 3, the act of supplying goods, or total real output, is the equal but opposite side of demanding goods, or total real expenditures. Say's law implies that full employment is a permanent, built-in feature of the macroeconomy. Resource unemployment is impossible because the act of producing goods is the same act as demanding goods. In other words, supply creates its own demand.

Say's law is most easily understood in a barter economy, where goods are exchanged for goods. Suppose, for example, that a chicken farmer supplies eggs and demands auto parts. If a deal can be worked out with an auto parts supplier, the farmer's act of supplying eggs is simultaneously the act of demanding auto parts. Likewise, the auto parts supplier's demand for eggs is reflected in his supply of auto parts. What is true for the farmer and the auto parts supplier is also true for all traders in the economy.

Say's law also applies to an economy using money. When money is used as a common denominator or as a medium of exchange for all goods and services, the egg supplier does not deal directly with the auto parts seller, but he or she does exchange goods indirectly through the use of money. Money in this system is merely a veil that hides the real workings of the economic system.

FIGURE 3

In the circular flow of income and output, the act of supplying goods and services is necessarily equal to the act of demanding goods and services.

Say's Law

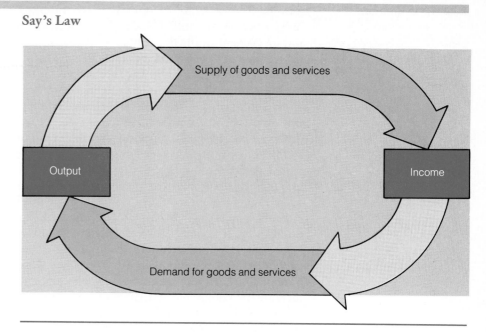

Say believed that in a money economy the aggregate demand for goods and services is financed through the earning of income, as in the circular flow diagram in Figure 1 of Chapter 24. How do productive factors earn wages, rents, interests, and profits? They do so by producing goods and services. In this system, as in a barter system, the act of producing specific goods and services results in the demand for other goods and services.

According to Say, supply creates its own demand, since the income generated in the act of producing (or supplying) goods would always be used to buy (or demand) goods of equal value. Say's law may seem perfectly sensible, but what happens when consumers choose to save part of their income? The act of saving—the sacrifice of present consumption for larger future consumption—disrupts the perfect balance between income and output.

Saving is a leakage, or withdrawal, from the circular flow of income and spending. If this withdrawal from spending is not matched by an injection—another form of spending to compensate for the saving withdrawal—underconsumption and unemployment result and Say's law does not work. Investment spending is one form of injection into the circular flow to make up for a savings leakage. But how do private saving—the leakage—and investment—the injection—become linked? Can Say's law be vindicated? The answer, the classical economists thought, lay in the mechanism of interest rates.

Interest Rate Flexibility. People save, or postpone current consumption, because of a reward for doing so. Interest paid on savings is their reward, enabling savers to consume more goods later. This important relation may be expressed

$$S = s(r),$$

or saving (S) is a function of the real rate of interest (r). The rate of interest is both the percentage that savers earn annually on their savings and the percentage that borrowers must pay to use funds deposited in savings insti-

Real rate of interest:
The nominal interest rate minus the inflation rate; the interest rate that measures the true incentives and costs that savers and investors face.

tutions. The **real rate of interest** is the nominal rate of interest minus the annual rate of inflation. The real rate reflects the fundamental forces of saving and investment in the economy.

Classical economists believed that saving was positively related to the real interest rate: A rise in the interest rate increased the amount saved. For example, when the real interest rate increases from r_0 to r_1, depicted in Figure 4, consumer-savers in the economy are encouraged to save more for future consumption. The higher the interest rate, the less you must sacrifice today in order to increase consumption by a given amount in the future for a new car, a college education, a new house. A high interest rate encourages savers to devote greater amounts to saving out of current income because future goods become "cheaper" relative to current consumption. Any increase in attitudes encouraging saving would cause the S curve in Figure 4 to shift to the right, indicating more saving at all rates of interest. If attitudes toward thrift become discouraged, of course, the whole curve would shift to the left.

Keep in mind that increases in saving are accompanied by simultaneous decreases in current consumption. In other words, according to the classical model, aggregate demand falls by the amount that saving increases. Will an increase in saving mean that aggregate supply will not call forth enough aggregate demand? Will goods remain on shelves, inventories pile up, and thousands of workers be laid off? To both of these questions, the classical economists answered no—with the qualification that the economy must be allowed to reestablish its equilibrium. Not only does the interest rate paid to savers determine their choices, but the interest rate charged on loans determines the behavior of investors. Investment is a flow of expenditures to repair or replace capital goods or to make additions to the capital stock of the nation. Investment spending, just like consumption spending, generates income and employment.

In classical theory, a lower rate of interest makes more investment projects—such as expenditures for warehouses and machinery—profitable. Since interest payments factor into the cost of new investment, higher interest rates make new investment more costly, other things being equal. Investments become more attractive when the interest rate falls. The interest rate may be thought of as the price of loanable funds to investors (whereas the price level is the price of commodities to consumers). As this price (the interest rate) rises, investors are discouraged from engaging in new investment projects. As it falls, investors spend more on capital goods. Technically, this relation can be expressed

$$I = i(r),$$

or investment (I) is a function of the real rate of interest (r). However, unlike the relation between saving and interest, investment and the real rate of interest are negatively related. Rises in r cause declines in the amount of I, and reductions in r provoke increases in the amount of I.

This inverse relation is depicted in Figure 5. As the real rate of interest declines, the investment spending represented by curve I increases. Conversely, when the rate of interest rises, fewer and fewer investment projects become profitable, and investment spending declines. Increases in the productivity of capital—through inventions or improvements in technology—would increase the level of investment at every rate of interest, shifting the whole curve to the right.

FIGURE 4
The Classical Concept of Saving

Saving and interest rates are positively related. As the real rate of interest rises, from r_0 to r_1, the level of saving in the economy rises from S_0 to S_1. An increase in the amount saved means that present consumption, or demand, is diminished by an equal amount.

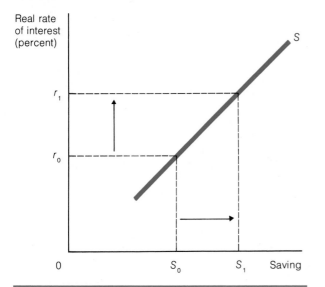

FIGURE 5
The Classical Concept of Investment

The amount invested (I) and the real rate of interest (r) are negatively related, given a constant rate of return on investment in capital goods. As the rate of interest falls from r_0 to r_1, businesses invest more in capital goods. The increase in investment expenditures from I_0 to I_1 represents a net increase in demand.

According to the classical system, saving and investment are balanced by means of the interest rate. Figure 6 reproduces the saving and investment curves already discussed. An initial economy-wide equilibrium is established where saving equals investment at interest rate r_0. At interest rate r_0, in other words, the amount that individuals in society wish to direct from consumption to savings is S_0. Real interest rate r_0 is the savers' reward for their thrift. At interest rate r_0, moreover, investors find I_0 worth of investment projects to be profitable—no more, no less. Given curves S and I, no other interest rate is compatible with equilibrium. Why? Because an interest rate lower than r_0 would create a shortage of investment funds, and one higher than r_0 would mean a surplus of funds. In the former case, according to the law of supply and demand, investors' demand would force the interest rate up to r_0; in the case of a surplus of funds, savers' demand would force the interest rate down to r_0. To put the matter formally, macroeconomic equilibrium requires that the amount of saving equals the amount of investment, or, in terms of the above expressions, that

$$S = I.$$

What happens if the whole saving curve or investment curve shifts, reflecting a sudden change in society's underlying attitudes toward thrift (increased saving for retirement or expectations of hard times) or a technological

FIGURE 6

The Relation Between Rate of Interest, Saving, and Investment in the Classical System

Initial equilibrium E_0 is established at interest rate r_0 with saving and investment curves S and I. An increase in thrift will cause the saving function to shift rightward from S to S_1, lowering the rate of interest from r_0 to r_1. As the interest rate declines, the amount of investment spending increases. Reduction in the amount of consumption spending brought about by increased saving is therefore accompanied by a counterbalancing increase in the amount of investment spending.

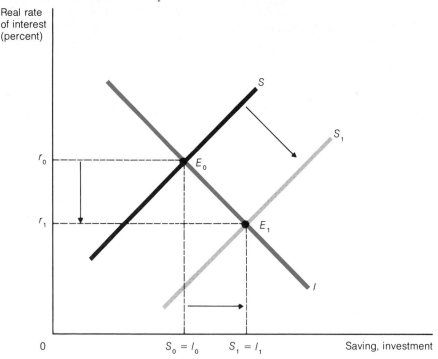

breakthrough that increases the productivity of investments? Suppose, for example, that individuals wish to save more at every rate of interest, shifting the saving function rightward from S to S_1, as shown in Figure 6. A surplus of saving develops at interest rate r_0, forcing the rate of interest down. As the rate falls, investors take advantage of new, profitable investments. Finally, at the new equilibrium interest rate, r_1, a new higher quantity of savings, S_1, equals a new, higher level of investment expenditures, I_1.

If Say's law is true, all leakages from the income stream must be replaced by injections. According to classical economics, increases in saving (leakage) are replaced by increases in investment (injection) through the mechanism of the real rate of interest. Aggregate demand for goods and services would fall short of aggregate supply were it not for the mechanism of interest rates. In other words, the classical economists believed that Say's law is valid if the interest rate is able to adjust freely upward or downward without regulations or restrictions. Consumption spending plus investment expenditures will be sufficient to purchase all of the output produced by the economy.

Price-wage flexibility:
An economic principle whereby prices and wages can fluctuate with changing economic conditions; thus the economy will be self-adjusting toward full employment even in response to shocks in supply and demand.

Price-Wage Flexibility. The validity of Say's law requires another cornerstone of classical thought: **price-wage flexibility.** To understand this second concept, suppose that future economic conditions appear very uncertain. There might be expectations of war, of a coming depression, or even of an overall decrease in prices. In response to this uncertainty, individuals seek greater immediate economic security. A drastic increase in saving at such a time of crisis will have the effect of lowering the interest rate; the price of loanable funds is reduced to investors, encouraging more investment and additions to the capital stock and making up the difference for the reduction in consumption. But in the event of a sudden surge of saving, investors might not be able or willing to adjust their spending quickly enough to make up the difference in total spending. Aggregate demand would be insufficient to carry off the aggregate supply of goods and services and Say's law (temporarily) would not hold; supply would not be creating its own demand. Unemployment would increase disastrously, leaving the economy vulnerable to collapse. According to classical theory, however, any such reduction in demand would also provoke another mechanism—price-wage adjustment.

With a (temporary) reduction in total spending, prices and wages would be expected to fall in the economy in proportion to the size of the reduction. As the prices of shoes, pizzas, hair stylings, and all other goods and services decline, additional quantities of goods will be demanded, and all excess production will quickly be bought up by consumers. Wages of laborers and the prices of all raw materials and other inputs will also decline, encouraging their employment by businesses. Nominal wages and the price level (for commodities) will both decline, helping to preserve the purchasing power of the new, lower nominal incomes. The flexibility of prices and wages in a competitive market helps guarantee full employment, even in the event of a sharp and protracted reduction in aggregate demand.

It must be emphasized that the classical cornerstone of price-wage flexibility applies when aggregate demand is insufficient to maintain full employment for *any* reason. Natural disasters and wars were thought to pose no threat to full employment in the long run, as long as prices and wages were allowed to adjust. The purely competitive market system—an assumption of classical economists—is the fail-safe mechanism through which unemployment over long periods of time was thought to be impossible. For the system to operate properly, of course, there could be no restrictions on prices (such as price controls) or wages (such as a minimum wage) in either product or resource markets.

The Quantity Theory of Money. In the long run, real GNP and employment would be maximized in a laissez-faire economy. Thrift, the productivity of capital investment, and Say's law guaranteed maximum output in the classical economist's theoretical system. The price level and the nominal wage level were explained in the classical system by a theory that, in the long run, viewed output and employment as independent of the money supply—the **quantity theory of money.** The quantity theory of money simply states that, in the long run, there is a clear and proportional relation between the money supply and the price level in the economy.

While we postpone a detailed discussion of money and prices until Part Three, it is useful at this point to understand some of the principles that underlie the formation of prices and inflation. The classical economists (like modern economists) used certain relationships in the real world to explain and predict how the price level is formed. Specifically, they began their argument by noting that the following relationship existed:

Money supply × velocity = the price level × real GNP.

Quantity theory of money: A theory stating that in the long run with output and velocity fixed, changes in the money supply cause proportional changes in the price level.

In symbols,

$$MV = PY,$$

where M = the money supply, consisting of currency in the hands of the public plus all checkable deposits (all checkbook money) used in transactions by the public (in the U.S. monetary system, M is determined by the Federal Reserve System, an agency of the federal government);

　V = velocity, or the average number of times a unit of money changes hands per year (or other time period) in financing the purchase of real output by the public;

　P = the price level of all output (goods and services); and

　Y = the final real output of goods and services produced and sold in the economy over some time period. (Y, in other words, is real GNP.)

If money is defined as currency plus checkable deposits held by the public, the public, at any given time, will hold a certain portion of their wealth in the form of money, in addition to houses, goods, and other types of assets. They will demand money (currency and checkable deposits) to facilitate transactions as a proportion of their total income. For example, if income in the economy was $900 billion in 1990 and the public demands one-third of this amount to facilitate all transactions in the economy, the average dollar exchanged hands or "turned over" three times in the economy in 1990. This means that **velocity** (necessary to facilitate the purchase of yearly GNP) was 3. The classical economists thought that this proportion was a constant over specific time frames, such as a year, and that velocity changed slowly due to (slow-changing) institutions in the economy.

If we consider the above equation and believe, along with the classical economists, that money serves individuals only as a medium of exchange, we may understand that increases in the *supply* of money will cause the price level to rise in the same proportion. That is, by assuming velocity and real GNP constant, the equation $MV = PY$ becomes an expression of the quantity theory of money. If the money supply, M, were to double, the equation indicates that the price level, P, also would double. More money in the hands of individuals means that too much is being held to facilitate their level of goods and services transactions. What will people do? They will increase their demands for these goods and services by offering larger amounts of money for them. But recall from the other three foundations of the classical system that *real* output of these goods and services is always (over the long run) at a maximum. When no more goods can be obtained, prices must rise. If the velocity of money, which is another way of expressing individuals' money demand behavior, is constant, and if real income is already at a maximum, the only possible effect of an increase in the money supply is to cause an increase in the price level.

 If resources were for any reason unemployed in the short run, and if, as this implies, real output (real GNP) were not at a maximum, increases in M with constant velocity would imply that real output and employment could be brought to a maximum. New spending created by increases in M would increase society's real output of goods and services and employ the resources

Velocity:
The average number of times a unit of money changes hands per year in financing the purchases of GNP.

necessary to produce them. This means that velocity is a key to understanding why increases in the money stock could be used in a short-run situation of unemployment to return the economy to full employment. The classical economists assumed that the public's money demand (which determined velocity) was stable and did not change when the money supply was altered. Thus, the strict quantity theory relationship—for example, a doubling of M causing a doubling of P—held only in the long run, when real output and employment were at a maximum and velocity was constant.

Throughout the nineteenth century and into the twentieth, the size of the money supply was, in the main, determined by gold and silver stocks. The discovery (or hoarding) of precious metals had a profound impact on the price level at any time (and on the rates of inflation or deflation). In the modern U.S. system, the money supply is independent of the amount of gold or silver in the economy. It is controlled by the Federal Reserve System, an agency of the federal government. The Federal Reserve directs the money supply by regulating lending and other activities of banks in our economy. All of these matters will be carefully discussed in Part Three, but it is useful to remember that the classical writers thought that resources were fully employed and real output was maximized in the normal state of the world.

CLASSICAL THEORY AND POLICY: THE MEANING OF A SELF-ADJUSTING ECONOMY

The cornerstones of classical macroeconomic theory imply that self-adjusting forces in the economy will guarantee full employment. Long-run unemployment is simply not possible if the economy functions as the theory predicts. Consider the meaning of the **classical self-adjustment mechanism** in a real-world context.

Classical self-adjustment mechanism:
The theory that, through Say's law, full employment will be reached given interest rate flexibility and price-wage flexibility.

The classical economists knew that adjustments due to supply "shocks" such as rapid technological change or new inventions, weather conditions, or wars were not instantaneous. Suppose, for example, that a drought occurs. A sharply reduced supply of grain and other foodstuffs means that the price of food will rise (given some inelasticity of demand). But given the logic of the quantity theory of money, the prices of other goods that are consumed in the economy must fall! Adjustments of nominal prices in all of the various markets of the economy will be accompanied by changes in the nominal wage rates associated with each production. While all of these prices and wages are changing, the economic system will be in disequilibrium, with temporary surpluses and shortages of some goods and with excess demand for or supplies of labor in various markets. Unemployment of labor and other resources, as a temporary *and necessary* phenomenon, will take place, a fact the classical economists freely acknowledged. If wages and/or prices were "sticky"—that is, if they were not allowed to rise—unemployment would be more persistent. A critical question is, How long will the economy have to endure this temporary phenomenon in actual time? Two months? One year? Ten years?

While never directly answering this question, the classical economists did offer some important insights, based on the understanding that any interference by government or private coalitions would make the problem of adjustment worse. In other words, although natural and unfettered market forces would not restore equilibrium instantaneously, reliance on market forces was the best choice in an imperfect world. The setting of wage or price controls of any kind, such as minimum wages or union-controlled wage rates, would only impede flexibility in the marketplace. Market forces would eventually conquer the controls, extending the time period for adjustment. Unemployment would last longer if wages, prices, and interest rates were not permitted to adjust through unregulated market forces. The long run over which the market will adjust to changing underlying conditions in the economy (a drought, perhaps, or technological changes) was an indeterminate period of time that was minimized by the absence of controls in the economy.

John Maynard Keynes took exception to classical economic theory's conception of the nature of actual conditions in the economy—specifically, the issue of how rigid or flexible prices and wages are in the real world. The logic of classical economics led to the conclusion that market forces, in and of themselves, are the best means of providing adjustments in prices, wages, employment, and output. All adjustments take time, of course, but in the classical view free-market adjustments minimize the time necessary for full employment of resources to take place.

Classical Policies for Rapid Self-Adjustment

The classical economic policy recommendations fit hand in glove with the theoretical cornerstones. If the logic of their system required full flexibility of prices, wages, and interest rates—as well as the encouragement of industry— then their economic policy had to promote free markets. On practically every point of economic policy, the classicals supported economic freedom. Consider some of the chief tenets of their economic policy.

Balance the Budget. Classical economists emphasized the need for a balanced government budget for a number of reasons. If government is allowed to spend more than it receives in taxes, the government will be forced to compete with investors to borrow available funds. Such competition will tend to increase real interest rates, choking off private investment, capital formation, and economic growth. Financing deficits by printing money—an attractive option when governments have access to the presses—would have equally bad effects on the private economy. As we will discuss in Chapter 34, increases in the money supply can create inflation, which is tantamount to a tax on the private sector.

Keep Government Small. High levels of taxes necessary to finance big government reduce incentives to private saving from which new investments are made. Big government, in the classical view, short-circuits the mainspring to progress.

Moreover, large-scale government includes domestic or international regulations that tend to reduce trade, productivity, and consumers' well-being. In the classical laissez-faire view, the government should be restricted to providing national defense, a legal system, and few other functions. Over the past two centuries, a number of policy-makers have pursued these classical economic conclusions, as described in Economics in Action, "Macroeconomic Theories and Policies in Classical and Modern Economics."

Laissez-faire. Capitalism requires well-defined property rights. The classical economists underscored this belief by promoting policies that encouraged individual ownership and increased incentives to save and invest. These were primarily "hands-off" policies, or laissez-faire. The theory is that most regulation in the workplace, business, and in financial markets should be dismantled; also, all newly proposed regulations should be viewed with extreme skepticism. The classicals also adhered to the belief that much regulation was inspired by interest groups who wanted to capture the political process for their own gain. A good example of this is the factory legislation of early nineteenth-century England, which, supposedly, was passed to protect children from exploitation. (See Focus, "The Factory Acts and the Macroeconomy of Nineteenth-Century England.") Any laws or regulations that reduced saving, investment, or capital formation—domestic or international—were opposed by classicals.

Free Foreign Trade. The self-adjusting macroeconomy and economic growth were also believed to be fostered by international free trade. The free-trade philosophy espoused by nearly all classical economists brought about calls for the elimination of all barriers to free exchange, such as tariffs and quotas. A major strand of classical economic policy, then, was the removal or reduction of all impediments to both internal and external trade—in other words, anything in the way of the gains from specialization and comparative advantage.

Classical Theory and Policy: Summary

The classical cornerstones of macroeconomic theory were part of a long-run view of economic activity. Yet the classical writers never stated the actual time period needed for the economy to self-adjust. They merely emphasized that any short-run government tinkering with the private economy in either a macroeconomic or a microeconomic sense would have negative long-run effects. In their view, the best long-run economic hope for all members of society—laborers, households, consumers, businesspeople, investors, savers—was to let unfettered market forces work in the private economy, unassisted by government.

Recessions, depressions, or periods of high unemployment caused by massive shifts in consumption spending, natural disasters, or wars all could wreak short-run havoc and temporary unemployment in the economy, as all classical economists knew. Society's members, however, would all be better off to suffer the temporary consequences rather than demand that government intervene. In the classical view, nearly all short-run actions of government in the aggregate economy only made problems worse, prolonged recessions or depressions, and created built-in instabilities in the macroeconomic system. Capitalism was not perfect, but society's inability to endure the short-run pains of recession and unemployment (reflected in demands for government to do something) meant that there would be greater economic pain in the long run.

FOCUS The Factory Acts and the Macroeconomy of Nineteenth-Century England

In general, policy recommendations of the classical economists were based on the notion of a self-adjusting economy. The vehemence of the classical economist Nassau Senior's (1790–1864) objections to factory legislation is not unusual.

The Factory Acts, enacted between 1833 and 1850, were a series of restrictions on the employment of women and children in the British textile industry. While many historians believe that these acts were passed for humanitarian reasons, Senior saw more rhetoric than genuine concern for working women and children. He identified an interest group—primarily, male workers—as the real agitator for factory legislation. If competing suppliers of labor—women and children—were eliminated from the work force and if hours of work were shortened or regulated, the wages of male workers would rise. Senior believed that the actual efforts to pass factory legislation had little to do with the "public interest."

Senior's second reason for opposing the Factory Acts rested on the impact on the macroeconomy of legislatively mandated reductions in work hours and labor participation in the textile industry. Senior interviewed mill owners on the matter of the proposed restrictions, quoting one as having said, "When a laborer lays down his spade, he renders useless, for that period, a capital worth eighteen pence. When one of our people leaves the mill, he renders useless a capital that has cost 100 pounds."[a] In other words, restrictions on labor contracts idled capital and reduced the marginal efficiency of capital, thereby reducing the efficiency of resource allocation. Senior knew that a legislated reduction in the efficiency of capital would lower the rate of return on capital investment in the textile industry below that which

could be earned outside the industry. Higher-cost producers would leave the industry, reducing employment and granting a competitive advantage to foreign producers not subject to legislated restrictions on work hours and labor participation. Senior therefore complained that "the English capitalist using his machinery for only 10 hours a day will be undersold by the German or the American who employs his for 12, 13, 14 and even 15," and that "the factories which work for the foreign market must be closed, and with them the means of clothing, feeding, and supporting many hundreds of thousands of workpeople [in England]."[b]

Senior's point, shared by most classical economists, was that regulations that had negative effects on investment, capital formation, and domestic employment were detrimental to maximizing society's total income. A modern parallel of this argument is the U.S. Environmental Protection Agency's regulations on the sulphuric content of coal. This legislation has adversely affected the demand for coal extracted in Appalachia by coal demanders such as electrical utilities in the northeastern United States. The response of these utilities has been to import coal (of lower sulphuric content) from western Canada (via the Panama Canal) and from Latin American countries. Economists, of course, do not dispute the fact that clean air has value or that some humanitarian purpose might have been accomplished by the Factory Acts. Rather, they point out that rules and regulations have costs—costs that are often ultimately reflected in the self-adjusting character of the economy and in the economy's attainable output and income potential.

[a]N. W. Senior, *Selected Writings on Economics* (New York: Augustus Kelley, 1966), p. 14.

[b]N. W. Senior, *Industrial Efficiency and Social Economy,* vol. 2 (New York: Henry Holt, 1928), p. 309. Also see Gary M. Anderson, Robert B. Ekelund, Jr., and Robert D. Tollison, "Nassau Senior as Economic Consultant: The Factory Acts Reconsidered," *Economica* 56 (February 1989), pp. 71–81.

SUMMARY

1. The classical blueprint for economic growth consists of progressive extensions of the division of labor, private savings and investment, and capital accumulation.
2. Economic growth in any economy is limited by, among other things, the economy's actual supply of human and nonhuman resources, the state of technology, productivity, and population.

3. Given the factors that limit growth at any one point in time, the best the economy can attain is a point on the production possibilities curve. The point of attainable possibilities corresponds to a vertical aggregate supply curve for the economy.
4. Classical macroeconomics consists of four cornerstones: Say's law, price-wage flexibility, interest rate flexibility, and the quantity theory of money. From

these foundations, classical economists concluded that the economy would self-adjust to reach a full-employment level of production and income.

5. Say's law states that the act of supplying goods creates an automatic demand for the goods. The act of saving or hoarding does not mean that overproduction will occur. If prices and wages are flexible downward, price and wage declines will ensure that all units of production will be sold. Further, the linkage between the rate of interest and saving and investment guarantees that what is removed from the income stream (saving) will be returned in a different form of spending (investment). The quantity theory of money indicates that the price level is proportional to the nominal money supply and suggests an avenue by which prices change when the money supply changes.

6. Classical economic policy, in the main, reflected the classical economists' theoretical view of the macroeconomy. They supported policies that promoted the flexibility of prices, wages, and interest rates in the face of ever-changing conditions.

7. In the classical view, maximum price and wage flexibility would be promoted by the reduction both of internal and external regulations and by minimal government involvement in the economy and a balanced budget.

8. Classical macroeconomic theory was a long-run theory that emphasized the self-adjusting character of the economy as the least-cost means for arriving at the economy's production possibilities curve. In the classical view, all economies must go through adjustments, and the best way to let all markets adjust is through reduction or elimination of government interference.

KEY TERMS

classical macroeconomic theory
classical process of economic growth
division of labor
classical long-run equilibrium
Say's law

real rate of interest
price-wage flexibility
quantity theory of money
velocity
classical self-adjustment mechanism

QUESTIONS FOR REVIEW AND DISCUSSION

1. According to Say's law, under what circumstances would the quantity of goods demanded be less than the quantity of goods supplied?

2. Will people be willing to save money when the real rate of interest is equal to zero? What is the real rate of interest on a passbook savings account if the inflation rate is 7 percent and the bank pays 5½ percent interest?

3. According to the classical view, why does an increase in the level of saving not decrease the total level of spending? Would this be true if interest rates were not flexible?

4. What is the importance of price and wage flexibility under the classical system? What would be the consequence of rigid wages or prices if the macroeco-

nomic system were disturbed by, say, poor grain crops?

5. Does the self-adjusting mechanism of classical economics indeed guarantee full employment of labor and other resources at all times? (Remember the distinction between the short run and the long run.)

6. How were classical macroeconomic theories and economic policy recommendations related?

7. Why did classical economists recommend small balanced budgets for government? Why did they suggest that large budget deficits would lead to lagging economic growth?

8. Why did the classical economists oppose regulations on business behavior? What did laissez-faire mean to classical economists?

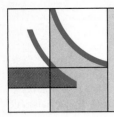

ECONOMICS IN ACTION
Macroeconomic Theories and Policies in Classical and Modern Economics

Numerous parallels exist between classical and modern macroeconomic theory and policy. The self-adjusting economy is a major tenet of several modern schools of thought. The monetarists and new classical economists, whose theories we will develop at length in Chapters 34 and 35, both hold to the classical idea that government interventions in markets will, at best, do little good and, perhaps, will reduce output potential in the economy. While these theories of how the economy functions are complex extensions on classical ideas, they are based on the persistent notion that maximum output results from free-market functioning with minimal government interference.

Classical writers and policy-makers insisted on balanced budgets and minimal government intervention. Consider the policies of William Gladstone, appointed vice-president of the Board of Trade in England under the Conservative government of Prime Minister Robert Peel in 1841. Designed to eliminate as much government intervention in the private sector as possible, Gladstone's policies included a reduction in import tariffs and the abolition of the income tax. Before Gladstone's reductions, approximately four hundred products were subject to import tariffs, a form of excise tax on imported goods; Gladstone removed the tariffs on all but about fifteen items.

Major tariff reductions resulted in a temporary government deficit. To balance the budget, Gladstone called for a 10 percent income tax. The income tax rate was reduced in subsequent years, before being eliminated altogether. The income tax was a temporary measure and disappeared from the budget after its aims had been achieved.

Certain more recent policies bear a resemblance to Gladstone's. President Jimmy Carter's administration achieved significant deregulation in the economy—for example, in the airline industry. President Ronald Reagan's *original* economic proposals emphasized less total government spending and lower taxes to increase private saving and investment, although lower total spending proved to be unfeasible politically. Reagan, like Carter before him, sponsored reductions in domestic regulation in, notably, the transportation and communications industries. Reagan's policies, moreover, had a long-run orientation; the slogan employed at the midway point of Reagan's first term—"Stay the Course"—implied both a direction for and the duration of his administration's economic policies. Certainly, the Reagan administration's so-called trickle-down theory (the idea that prosperity follows a downward course from increased in-

dustry to the poor) is a long-run view with origins in classical macroeconomics.

The supply-side economics that surfaced in the 1980s also has its origins in classical ideas. Stated simply, supply-side economics means that taxes and/or restrictions on individuals and markets must be eliminated to increase aggregate supply of goods and services in the economy. Higher tax rates on individual work effort reduce the incentive to work and produce. Higher tax rates on capital investment mean less investment and less capital accumulation. The Tax Reform Act of 1986 was inspired in large part by the classical principle that lower tax burdens on individuals mean greater work effort. Similarly, the Bush administration's calls for a reduction in the capital gains tax (a lower tax rate on capital gains from investments than on ordinary income) are consistent with the classical notion that investment and capital accumulation are key elements leading to the increased wealth of a nation.

Despite the ongoing goal of marginally lower levels of government involvement in the economy, total federal government outlays grew between 1980 and 1990, partly as a result of a large defense buildup, partly as a consequence of the increased burden of social programs. At the same time, huge deficits began to worry financial markets and citizens.

A key to classical laissez-faire policy is the denial of permanent political access to tax revenues—this to guard against entrenched government intervention. Today, the role of government in the economy—efficient or inefficient—is so pervasive that even marginal changes are considered radical. Recent administrations' policies aimed at lowering the financial base of the federal government have been less successful than those aimed at deregulating some critical industries and transferring control over resources from the public to the private sector and from federal to state and local governments. Whether modern economic policies filtered through a political process can achieve, have achieved, or will achieve critical macroeconomic goals and objectives in an efficient manner remains a matter of great debate.

Question

This discussion has depicted the Reagan administration and others as having reduced the scope of government. Is there any evidence that the scope of government has in fact declined?

26

Introduction to Keynesian Economics

Classical economic theory, the topic of the previous chapter, dominated the economic debate until the early twentieth century, when a series of catastrophic events sorely tested economists' faith in a self-adjusting economy and the validity of Say's law. After the extraordinarily prosperous 1920s, the United States and the rest of the world fell into the deepest and most prolonged depression in modern history.

In September 1929, the market for stocks and other securities began to fail. On what has come to be known as Black Thursday, October 24, 1929, stock prices plummeted and thousands of investors lost hundreds of millions of dollars' worth of securities. The stock market crash ushered in (though it did not necessarily cause) steep declines in industrial production, real income, and civilian employment. For more than a decade, between 1929 and 1940, industrial production in the United States failed to exceed its 1929 level. Real GNP (expressed in 1982 dollars) was about $700 billion in 1929, a level unmatched until 1939. Most important, civilian unemployment rose to more than 30 percent by 1933.

The exact causes of the Great Depression are still a matter of debate among macroeconomists, but the prolonged economic chaos is a matter of fact. The Depression and the unemployment that accompanied it brought ruin for millions of Americans and similar hardships around the world. The classical self-adjusting macroeconomic system did not appear to work. In this chapter we present the theory of John Maynard Keynes, which was a reaction to the apparent failure of the macroeconomic system to adjust to the problems of the Depression. After reading Chapter 26 you should understand

- Keynes's criticisms of the self-adjusting classical principles of macroeconomics.
- how Keynes evaluated classical ideas to construct his own model of macroeconomics.
- how total private expenditures by consumers and businesses form the basis for Keynes's model of income determination.
- the role of saving and investment interactions in producing equilibrium income in the private economy (with no government assumed).

KEYNES AND THE CLASSICALS

Economists were among the first to recognize that the catastrophic events of the Great Depression appeared to overwhelm theory. In particular, some economists at Cambridge and Oxford universities in England began to question and analyze the cornerstones of classical economics. Economists Richard Kahn, Joan Robinson, R. G. Hawtrey, Roy F. Harrod, Friedrich Hayek, and John Maynard Keynes met regularly during the early 1930s to discuss reasons for the apparent failings of the classical system.

J. M. Keynes (1883–1946) was particularly vocal. In open letters to President Franklin D. Roosevelt, published in the *New York Times,* Keynes advocated the use of government spending and taxation policies to supplement private spending as a cure for the ailing economy. (Roosevelt, clinging to more traditional thinking, heeded Keynes's advice guardedly and hesitantly.) Keynes was firmly convinced that, contrary to classical theory, private market forces would not be sufficient to regain full-employment equilibrium in the depressed economy. He dismissed the long-run self-adjustment theory of the classical economists with scorn. As he said in another context, "In the long run we are all dead." The economy could be stuck at some equilibrium characterized by high levels of unemployment for an extended period of time, as it seemed to be in the early 1930s.

Since the classical theory, in Keynes's view, did not offer rescue from the Depression, Keynes sought a better model from which to interpret events. In 1936, Keynes published his *General Theory of Employment, Interest and Money,* which established a new theory of how the economy functions—a new macroeconomics. In proposing this theory, Keynes had to counter the foundations of the classical macroeconomic system.

Keynes's Evaluation of Classical Theory

Recall that Say's law states that supply creates its own demand if savings (a leakage) can be transformed into investment expenditures (a compensating injection) through a flexible interest rate and if prices and wages are flexible when aggregate demand is exceeded by aggregate production. Keynes took exception to Say's law and to the two other cornerstones that support it—the belief that price-wage flexibility and interest rate flexibility will cure any temporary disruptions in the economy.

First, Keynes argued that saving and investment are determined by a host of forces in the economy in addition to the rate of interest. In Keynes's view, savers and investors are different groups with different sets of motivations and interests. Savers, he thought, are more responsive to their amount of personal disposable income than to the rate of interest in deciding how much to save. Higher interest rates, thought Keynes, might even mean less saving if people were saving toward a particular goal—such as some fixed retirement income—since a high interest rate means that less saving is required per period.

Similarly, investment was not very responsive to the short-run interest rate, in Keynes's view. Much investment, especially in large projects, takes place over long periods. Once investment decisions are made, the investment is autonomous, unrelated to the interest rate or other variables. The point is that the different motivations of savers and investors mean that saving and investment plans could become unlinked. A flexible interest rate, responsive to the desires of savers and investors, would not guarantee that the saving leakage would automatically be turned into the investment injection. There was no built-in assurance that savings would equal investment at a full-employment, growth-maximizing level of economic activity.

Second, Keynes argued that in reality the internal structure of the economy was not competitive enough to permit prices and wages to fall in response to insufficient aggregate demand. To Keynes, the existence of monopoly and union pressures in the economy had to be taken into account. If demand fell off, monopolies would let output fall rather than accept price reductions. Workers, moreover, would refuse to take cuts in their money wages, thereby creating unemployment and layoffs by businesses. Even if workers did take money wage cuts, the reduction in income would further reduce the demand for goods and services, probably reducing output and employment even more. The conclusion: *Classical self-adjusting mechanisms in the private economy would not lift us out of a depression.*

The Relative Unimportance of Money

Money does not play the same role in relieving economic distress in the Keynesian system as it does in classical economics. The classical economists believed that the quantity theory mechanism could, in the event of short-run unemployment of resources, help return the economic system to full employment and maximum income. Their view was premised upon a constant demand for money that resulted in constant velocity. With constant velocity, aggregate spending would increase with increases in the money supply. This would increase the production of goods and services in the economy and the employment of resources that would be necessary to produce them.

Keynes had no such faith in the use of money to cure recessions or depressions characterized by low production and low employment. He did not adhere to the classical notion of the quantity theory—that there was a predictable relation between the money supply and prices in the long run or between money and output and employment in the short run. His reasoning was somewhat complex, but it depended on the notion that money was not simply held by individuals to act as a medium of exchange (as the classicals believed). People held money for other purposes—for a "rainy day" or in order to take advantage of profitable investments in the present or future. This meant that under conditions of short-run economic distress, an increase in the money supply would not necessarily increase total spending and create new production and employment. Money, or the intentional alteration in the quantity of it, was, to Keynes, relatively unimportant.

In the terms of classical economics, an increase in M could be accompanied by a fall in V or, what is the same thing, a rise in the demand for money. To Keynes, people might simply hold more money when economic conditions were poor, meaning that the average dollar would circulate more slowly as the money stock increased. These effects, according to Keynes, would short-circuit the link between money supply increases and increases in real GNP. Monetary policy could not cure unemployment problems; it could not increase the aggregate demand for goods and services. Only government, in

Keynes's view, was powerful enough to affect aggregate demand by changes in spending or taxing policies to restore the economy to full employment. Before we consider government's role in the Keynesian model, we will examine the Keynesian theory of spending—specifically, the interrelation of income, consumption, saving, and investment—in more detail.

The Importance of Income

Keynes believed that a prolonged depression proves that the economy can establish equilibrium at less than full employment. The classical economists, as we have seen, placed their confidence in a flexible price system—flexible prices, wages, and interest rates—as the self-adjusting mechanism that would assure full employment when aggregate demand got out of kilter with aggregate supply.

Income-expenditures model:
A theory suggesting that private expenditures are basically determined by the level of national income and that these expenditures in turn determine the levels of output and employment in the economy.

Keynes argued instead that aggregate demand and economic activity in general were determined by income and by changes in income. He thereby developed an **income-expenditures model** of macroeconomics. The income-expenditures model shows that private expenditures (the same as aggregate demand) are primarily determined by the level of national income and that such expenditures, in turn, establish equilibrium (or nonequilibrium) levels of output and employment in the economy. Other factors, as we will see, may help determine expenditures, but they are unimportant as short-run determinants of what people spend.

In the Keynesian view, equilibrium output would occur when demand for goods and services just equaled the production of goods and services. At lower output levels, production would fall short of demand, and this would lead to increases in production until the equilibrium level was reached. If production temporarily took place at a level above the equilibrium level, production would exceed demand, inventories of unsold goods would accumulate, and businesses would contract production. Again, the level of production would adjust to the equilibrium level. However, unlike the classical system, in which the equilibrium level of production implied full employment, the Keynesian model allowed for equilibrium at any level of production. Should conditions arise under which demand was low, the equilibrium level of production would coincide with high unemployment.

THE INCOME-EXPENDITURES MODEL

Keynes focused on aggregate demand or spending because he viewed rapid aggregate demand changes as the villain in recessions and depressions. Keynes believed that aggregate supply factors—large-scale changes in productivity, such as new technology and inventions and changing incentives to work and produce—changed slowly and could therefore be neglected when considering short-run macroeconomic problems. (Aggregate supply factors will be considered in Chapters 27 and 28.) In the short run, the time period most relevant to Keynesian macroeconomics, the economy's production or supply of goods and services seemed to react passively to changes in total expenditures.

Assumptions of the Income-Expenditures Model

The Keynesian view of total spending is quite complex. In its most complete form, total spending for goods and services is viewed as coming from domestic households, domestic business firms, domestic units of government, and from foreign buyers. Therefore, in the complete Keynesian model, the equilibrium level of production occurs when production equals the spending by these four groups of buyers. We will develop the Keynesian model in steps. Initially, for example, buyers will be assumed to consist only of domestic households and business firms. We make several other assumptions.

1. Government spending and taxation as well as foreign trade (exports and imports) are excluded from the basic model of private spending. Taxes, transfer payments (such as Social Security payments), and any other government activities are not considered. Depreciation is also ignored. Income or output is produced and consumed only in the private sector of the economy. This simplification also means that national income and disposable after-tax income are the same.
2. The purely monetary side of the economy is excluded from the basic model. The interest rate and any possible effects of interest rate changes are therefore excluded from consideration. This assumption makes sense if we accept Keynes's basic point that real income, not the interest rate, is the principal determinant of both consumption and saving. (Keynes did believe that money and interest rates play some role in explaining total spending in the economy, but we will defer discussion of these factors for the time being.)
3. We assume that, over the short run, prices and wages remain constant. This assumption means that total income or output will increase or decrease solely in response to changes in aggregate spending and not to price or wage changes. This also means that we do not need to distinguish nominal from real income, consumption, saving, or investment. With the price level fixed, changes in the nominal values of these variables are identical to changes in their real values.

In subsequent chapters these simplifying assumptions will be dropped, and a complete model will be developed.

Given these assumptions, the equilibrium level of output will occur when production equals household spending (consumption) plus business spending (investment). An understanding of consumer spending behavior and business spending behavior needs to precede any effort to understand how the equilibrium level of output is determined.

$Y = C + I$

Private Consumption Expenditures

The classical writers, as we saw earlier, placed primary emphasis on the real rate of interest in determining the relation between savings (income reserved for future consumption) and expenditures (income used in current consumption). One of Keynes's basic criticisms of classical theory was that the rate of interest could not always enable us to predict how much of current income an individual would choose to save or to spend. Keynes believed that current income was the most reliable and predictable determinant of consumption expenditures. Private saving, the residual of income after consumption, was also a function of, or was explained by, income. The simple Keynesian model of consumption and saving, in other words, does not account for any factors other than current income. Consider how these relations between consumption and income and between saving and income might be expressed and analyzed.

Consumption and Saving Functions and Schedules

Keynes constructed consumption and saving functions and schedules based on income. The consumption function and the saving function can be expressed simply as

$$C = C(Y) \quad \text{and} \quad S = S(Y).$$

In other words, consumption (C) is a function of income (Y), and saving (S) is a function of income, which simply means that consumption and saving are related to income in some way. Both consumption and saving, as we will see, are positive functions of income, meaning that an income increase will increase both consumption and saving, and an income decrease will decrease both consumption and saving.

Consumption and saving relations can also be regarded as schedules. A consumption-income schedule shows the amount that households would desire or plan to consume at every level of income. Likewise, a saving-income schedule shows the desired or planned level of saving that households would undertake at various levels of income.

In the basic Keynesian model, income can be disposed of by households in only two ways: They may consume it or save it. This observation means that

$$Y = C + S,$$

and it also means that consumption and saving are related in a unique way.

Numerous studies have attempted to relate saving and consumption to family income. The evidence provided by these studies shows that as income increases, families increase both saving and consumption. Further, richer families tend to save a higher proportion of income than do poorer families.

The Marginal and Average Propensity to Consume and Save. Macroeconomists are often interested in knowing how consumption or saving will change with a change in income. The two concepts that give us this answer are the marginal propensity to consume and the marginal propensity to save. The **marginal propensity to consume (MPC)** is defined as the ratio of the change in consumption (ΔC) to the change in income (ΔY) that causes the change in consumption, or

Marginal propensity to consume (MPC):
The percent of an additional dollar of income that is spent on consumption; change in consumption divided by change in income.

$$MPC = \frac{\Delta C}{\Delta Y} = \frac{\text{change in consumption}}{\text{change in income}}.$$

Marginal propensity to save (MPS): The percent of an additional dollar of income that is saved; change in saving divided by change in income.

The **marginal propensity to save (MPS)** is the ratio of a change in saving (ΔS) to a change in income that causes the change in saving, or

$$MPS = \frac{\Delta S}{\Delta Y} = \frac{\text{change in saving}}{\text{change in income}}.$$

Since households in the simple Keynesian model dispose of income only by consuming or saving, any change in income will be completely exhausted by the resulting changes in consumption and saving. This means that because the *MPC* measures the change in consumption resulting from a change in income and the *MPS* the change in saving arising from the same change in income, the *MPC* plus the *MPS* must add to 1:

$$MPC + MPS = 1.$$

Economists are also interested in how much, on average, households consume and save at various income levels. The **average propensity to consume (APC)** is the proportion of income consumed at any income level, or *C/Y*. Likewise, the **average propensity to save (APS)** is the ratio of saving to income at any level of income, or *S/Y*. Since consumption and saving are the only two ways that households can dispose of income, a unique relation exists between the *APC* and the *APS*:

Average propensity to consume (APC): The percent of a particular level of income that is spent on consumption; total consumption divided by total income.

Average propensity to save (APS): The percent of total income that is saved; total saving during any given period divided by total income in the same period.

$$1 = \frac{\text{consumption}}{\text{income}} + \frac{\text{saving}}{\text{income}},$$

or

$$1 = APC + APS.$$

Keynes's Theoretical Model of Consumption and Saving

The features of actual household consumption and saving behavior can be translated into a theoretical model of consumption and spending for the entire economy—how the country as a whole would choose to spend or save at different levels of national income. (Using hypothetical data for the entire economy, we abstract essential information from the actual behavior of households.) To make this model easier to comprehend—with no important loss in accuracy—we will assume that the consumption-income and saving-income relations are in the form of straight lines. This assumption means that the *MPC* and the *MPS* are constant. No matter what the level of income, the *MPC* will be the same number. If, for example, the *MPC* were 0.8 at the $100 billion level of income, it would be 0.8 at the $300 billion and the $750 billion levels also. The same relationship holds for the *MPS*. This simplifying assumption does no damage to our conclusions, and it greatly facilitates understanding of these crucial ideas.

Hypothetical information about economy-wide consumption and saving is given in Table 1. The hypothetical data of Table 1 show, in billions of dollars, what private consumption and private saving would be at alternative levels of income. Consider, for instance, a year in which national income is $100 billion. How would households plan to divide this income between purchases of consumption goods and saving? Consumption expenditures at a $100 billion

---

TABLE 1 Hypothetical Consumption and Saving Data for the Economy

The economy consumes and saves more as income increases. Further, the average propensity to consume declines and the average propensity to save rises with increases in income. For the sake of simplicity, the MPC and the MPS are assumed to be constant.

National Income (billions of dollars) (Y)	Planned Consumption Expenditures (billions of dollars) (C)	Planned Savings (billions of dollars) (S)	Average Propensity to Consume (APC = C ÷ Y)	Marginal Propensity to Consume (MPC = $\Delta C \div \Delta Y$)	Average Propensity to Save (APS = S ÷ Y)	Marginal Propensity to Save (MPS = $\Delta S \div \Delta Y$)
0	40	−40	—	0.8	—	0.2
100	120	−20	1.2	0.8	−0.2	0.2
200	200	0	1.0	0.8	0	0.2
300	280	20	0.93	0.8	0.07	0.2
400	360	40	0.90	0.8	0.10	0.2
500	440	60	0.88	0.8	0.12	0.2
600	520	80	0.87	0.8	0.13	0.2
700	600	100	0.86	0.8	0.14	0.2

Dissaving:
Occurs when consumption is greater than income; the use of previous years' savings or borrowing to finance consumption expenditures that are greater than income.

Autonomous consumption:
Consumption expenditures that are independent of the level of income.

Consumption function:
The positive relationship between levels of consumption expenditures and levels of income, holding all other relevant factors that determine consumption constant.

level of national income would exceed income by $20 billion. This − $20 billion would be **dissavings.** To consume $120 billion at an income level of $100 billion, in other words, households would have to draw down $20 billion in previous savings. A special interpretation is given to dissaving at a zero income level. Note that all households would consume at the level of $40 billion even if no income were earned; this $40 billion is independent of income. Such **autonomous consumption** expenditures are independent of income. At levels of income higher than zero, consumption expenditures increase until they are equal to income. If national income were $200 billion, all income would be devoted to consumption. At income levels higher than $200 billion, consumption expenditures fall short of current income, and the remainder is devoted to saving.

Consumption and the 45-Degree Line. An important method for understanding how consumption is related to income is to compare historical consumption levels with a hypothetical relation in which consumption spending is always equal to income. When consumption spending always equals income, graphing the two variables yields a straight 45-degree line like that in Figure 1. The positive slope of the consumption schedule graphed in Figure 1, $C(Y)$, reflects Keynes's basic notion that the larger our income, the larger will be our consumption expenditures.

Examine Figure 1, on which national income levels are displayed on the horizontal axis and consumption expenditures on the vertical axis. At every point on the 45-degree line in Figure 1, total spending—in this case, consumption spending—*equals* total income. The extent to which actual consumption levels for particular periods differ vertically from this 45-degree line indicates the degree to which consumption does not equal income. Points along the **consumption function** above the 45-degree line indicate dissavings;

FIGURE 1

The consumption function C(Y), shows that the level of consumption expenditures rises as income rises. When income is $100 billion, consumption spending is $120 billion; when income is $200 billion, consumption is $200 billion; and when income is $300 billion, consumption is $280 billion. Along the hypothetical 45-degree line, consumption expenditures are exactly equal to income. The degree to which consumption differs from income indicates dissaving or saving by society as a whole. In this example, consumption spending is equal to income only at the $200 billion income level. Along the consumption function and above the 45-degree line, society dissaves; along the consumption function and below the 45-degree line, positive saving takes place.

The Level of Consumption as a Function of the Level of Income

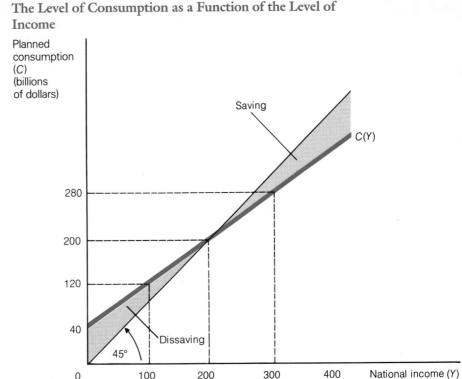

points below it indicate savings. In Figure 1, actual consumption is equal to income only at the $200 billion income level. At a national income below this break-even point, society would go into debt or dip into past savings; above it, society would save some of its income.

The Consumption Schedule. Household consumption is the major factor in total spending, spending that creates jobs and production in the economy. Macroeconomists are therefore very interested in how much household consumption will change with changes in national income. The value of the marginal propensity to consume tells us how much more will be consumed out of an additional dollar—or an additional 100 billion dollars—in national income.

The marginal propensity to consume is of course different for different individuals and for different groups in society. Some of us are more likely than others to spend every dollar we have. In this example, we simplify the variations by choosing an *MPC* value of 0.8 for society as a whole and by holding this value constant across varying national income levels. In Figure 2, an increase in national income from $300 billion to $400 billion will increase the level of consumption spending from $280 billion to $360 billion, an increase of $80 billion. Likewise, an increase from $400 billion to $500 billion will cause

FIGURE 2

Along a straight-line consumption function, $C(Y)$, the MPC is constant. In this graph, $MPC = 0.8$. Each time income rises by $100 billion, the level of consumption rises by $80 billion. Or, for every $1 increase in income, consumers increase expenditures by $0.80.

Marginal Propensity to Consume

consumption spending to increase by another $80 billion. The MPC is, therefore, the ratio 80/100 or 80 percent or 0.8, as indicated in Table 1.

Though the actual relation of the MPC to national income is a matter of debate, we know that the average propensity to consume changes as income levels change. In general, as income rises, the APC, or the ratio of consumption to income, falls. At a $300 billion income level, for instance, consumption expenditures are $280 billion and the APC equals 280/300 or 0.93. On average, the population would be spending 93 percent of its income. But if national income rose to $600 billion, households would spend only 87 percent of their income (520/600).

The Saving Schedule. Like consumption, saving is a positive function of income. That is, the more income we have, the more we save; the lower our income, the less we are able to save. In the hypothetical **saving function** in Figure 3, at a national income level of $400 billion, desired saving is $40 billion. In fact, saving becomes positive rather than negative at all levels of income greater than $200 billion in this example.

The marginal and average propensity to save are also illustrated in Figure 3. Remember, the MPS is the ratio of a change in saving to a change in income. As shown in Figure 3, incremental changes of $100 billion change saving by $20 billion, so

$$MPS = \frac{20}{100} = 0.2.$$

Saving function:
The positive relationship between levels of current saving and levels of income, holding constant all other relevant factors that determine saving.

FIGURE 3

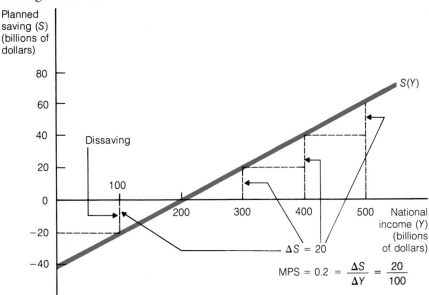

A Saving Function

The saving function, $S(Y)$, shows that the desired or planned saving is positively related to the level of national income. At a low level of income (below $200 billion), there is dissaving. As the level of income rises from $200 billion to $300 billion, the level of saving rises from $0 billion to $20 billion. At $Y = 400$, $S = 40$, and at $Y = 500$, $S = 60$. The figure also illustrates the marginal propensity to save. Along a straight-line saving function, the *MPS* is constant. Here the *MPS* is equal to 0.2. For each increase in income of $100 billion, the level of saving increases by $20 billion.

$$MPS = 0.2 = \frac{\Delta S}{\Delta Y} = \frac{20}{100}$$

The average propensity to save is the ratio of savings to income at any level of income. The *APS* rises as income rises, as you can see in Table 1, from which the data in Figure 3 are taken.

Assuming straight-line consumption and saving functions and the use of all income as either saving or spending,

$$1 = MPC + MPS \quad \text{and} \quad 1 = APC + APS,$$

or

$$MPS = 1 - MPC \quad \text{and} \quad APS = 1 - APC.$$

The values of *MPC*, *MPS*, *APC*, and *APS* are very important for economic policy. A high *MPC* means that increases in income will generate a large amount of additional private spending. A low value for the *MPC* (or, exactly the same thing, a high *MPS*) means that increases in income will generate only small increases in consumption. (Keep in mind that the values of *MPC* and *MPS* given in Figures 2 and 3 are based on hypothetical data.) These features of the consumption function will have an extremely important impact on the model of total expenditures developed in the following chapters.

Nonincome Factors Influencing Consumption and Saving

Although Keynes's basic argument involved the effects of income levels, income is not the only factor affecting consumption expenditures. A host of nonincome factors also determine the amount of planned consumption spending by all households. If any nonincome determinant of consumption spending changes, the entire consumption function shifts upward or downward. The amount of planned consumption changes at every income level when a nonincome element affects consumption changes. In contrast, a change in income simply changes the amount of income consumed, expressed graphically as a movement along a given consumption function.

In Figure 4, assuming an initial consumption function $C_0(Y)$, a change in any nonincome factor affecting consumption will shift the consumption schedule either upward to $C_2(Y)$ or downward to $C_1(Y)$. (The break-even level of income, where consumption spending equals income—on the graph, the point where the consumption function intersects the 45-degree line—also changes to Y_2 with consumption C_2 or to Y_1 with consumption C_1.) By contrast, if income increases from Y_0 to Y_2, consumption increases along consumption function $C_0(Y)$ from point A to point F.

In this section, we address seven of the most important nonincome factors that may affect consumption: wealth; the price level; price and income expectations; credit and the interest rate; taxation; age, geographic location, and population; and the distribution of income.

Wealth or the Stock of Assets. People consume not only on the basis of the flow of current income but also on the basis of a previously accumulated stock of wealth. Purchase of real goods—such as precious stones or a painting by Andrew Wyeth—takes place at a given time. As the money value of such assets increases over time, people feel richer and consume more, even though their incomes do not increase. Conversely, reductions in the money value of assets

FIGURE 4

Any change in nonincome factors affecting consumption spending will shift the consumption function, $C_0(Y)$, either upward or downward. An increase in consumption means that consumption spending rises for every level of income (from A to B); a decrease in spending creates a fall from A to D in the figure. By contrast, a change in income, all other factors being equal, moves consumers along a given consumption function. For example, increasing national income from Y_0 to Y_2 would move consumption from point A to point F in the figure.

Shifts in the Consumption Function

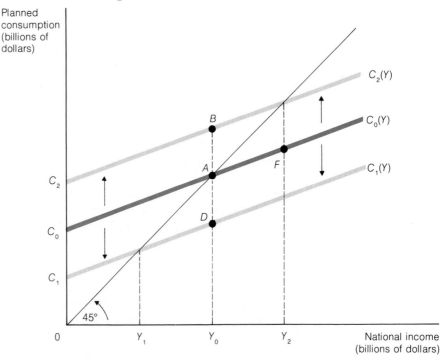

reduce wealth and tend to reduce consumption at every level of income. (Wealth effects are treated in detail in Chapter 28.)

The Price Level. Some assets—money or assets denominated in money terms, such as bonds—change value with changes in the price level. If you hold a given stock of money, a halving of the price level would double the real value or purchasing power of the money assets you hold. Since you would then be richer, your desired consumption would increase. For the opposite reason, rising prices reduce consumption expenditures.

Price and Income Expectations. We all have anticipations about our economic lot in the future. If we expect prices to be higher in some future period, we will tend to increase consumption expenditures in the present to beat price hikes. Expectations of lower prices will reduce present consumption. Likewise, if we expect higher future incomes, our present consumption will rise. Expectations of harder economic times will reduce present consumption and increase present saving.

Credit and the Interest Rate. Two closely interrelated factors affecting consumption are the availability of credit and the interest rate. The number of institutions offering credit in the economy has increased dramatically since World War II. The overall effect of increased credit availability, along with improved terms of credit (longer payback period, lower down payment), is to make consumption higher at any given level of income.

Along with credit availability and improved credit terms, an important factor affecting consumption is the cost of credit, determined by the interest rate. As the interest rate rises or falls, other things such as credit terms being equal, consumers will reduce or increase their present consumption expenditures. A higher rate of interest, moreover, will mean a higher level of saving in the present because reduced consumption will lead to increased saving. As indicated earlier, Keynes did not believe that the interest rate had predictable effects on consumption and saving. His view was in direct contrast to the classical writers, who thought that the interest rate was central to explaining saving and consumption behavior.

Taxation. As we will see more fully in Chapter 27, consumption and saving behavior are also affected by taxation and government transfers. An increase in income taxes, for example, reduces the amount of income available to a family and thereby tends to reduce both consumption and saving. Similarly, an increase in government transfer payments such as Social Security payments has the effect of increasing spendable income and raising both consumption and saving.

Population, Age Distribution, and Geographic Location. An increase in population will obviously shift the consumption schedule upward over time. The age distribution of the population—the proportion of young, middle-age, and older citizens to the total population—is a slowly changing but important factor affecting consumption. (For details, see Economics in Action, "The Life Cycle and Consumption Behavior," at the end of this chapter.) Both the young and the old have a tendency to spend a larger portion of their income than do people in their middle years. An age distribution shift to the middle years will therefore tend to reduce consumption and increase saving.

Factors such as geographic location may also affect consumption spending. A large population movement from rural to urban areas may increase present consumption, for example, if city dwellers have a higher tendency than country dwellers to consume their income.

Distribution of Income.   A final factor affecting planned household consumption is how income is distributed among different income levels. Low-income, middle-income, and high-income households may have different marginal propensities to consume and to save. Specifically, low-income families may have generally higher *MPCs* than high-income families. In the Keynesian analysis of consumption, a permanent redistribution of income from high-income families to low-income families may cause an increase in total consumption; that is, it may shift the consumption schedule upward, because low-income families have higher marginal propensities to consume than high-income families.

Although Keynes envisioned differences in the *APC* between income groups, empirical evidence on actual consumption functions over the long run suggests that a long-run proportionality exists between consumption and income; society seems to consume the same proportion of income at low as well as at higher levels of income, indicating a more or less constant *APC*. A number of economists have attempted to reconcile data showing short-run nonproportionality with long-run proportionality, although explanations vary. At bottom, it is not clear how a redistribution of income from rich to poor families would affect aggregate consumption spending at any one time or over a long period of time.

Consumption spending is affected by a large number of nonincome determinants. A change in any one of them will shift the consumption function either upward or downward. A single consumption function, however, is constructed by holding all the factors constant and by varying income.

Investment Expenditures

So far, we have looked at household consumption and its relation to income. Private spending in the economy also includes investment spending. In a macroeconomic context, **investment spending** means spending by the private sector—mainly businesses—on capital goods. Public investment in goods such as schools, water reclamation projects, or dams is not included in private investment expenditures. Public investment expenditures are categorized as government spending and will be covered in Chapter 27. Rather, private investment refers to the national income category gross private domestic investment, defined previously as including fixed investment in plant and equipment, all private-sector residential and nonresidential construction, and changes in business inventories (increases or decreases in stocks of finished goods, semifinished goods, or raw materials).

Clearly, there are two effects on the capital stock of the nation at any given time: Some of it is being used up or depreciated, and new net investment

Investment spending:
Expenditures made by businesses on capital goods plus any change (positive or negative) in business inventories.

is creating additions to it. Businesses usually replace their worn-out capital stock and add to their stock of capital with new investments.

Autonomous Short-Run Investment Spending

Short run

Keynes argued that in the short run, investment expenditures could be viewed as autonomous—independent of the level of income, profit expectations, the interest rate, and all of the other factors possibly affecting investment. The idea that investment could be autonomous in the short run stems from the fact that most investment expenditures in any current period have been determined by past investment decisions.

Businesses, in fact, make investment decisions from a long-run perspective. The building of new plants and the installation of sophisticated equipment typically take a number of years to complete. During the investment period, planned investment expenditures are often carried out regardless of current business conditions. Planned investment expenditures are those that businesses desire to undertake. (Planned investment expenditures may not be the same as actual expenditures, as we will see later in this chapter.) These investment expenditures are then independent of the level of income.

Autonomous investment:
Investment expenditures that are independent of the level of income.

The concept of **autonomous investment** spending can be analyzed within the framework of the simple Keynesian model of private spending. If I stands for investment spending by businesses, autonomous investment is simply described as some constant level, I_0, or

$$I = I_0,$$

where the subscript 0 means that expenditures are constant at some specified level—$20 billion, $50 billion, $100 billion—during the period under consideration.

If we assume that autonomous investment expenditures are constant at $20 billion, we can express investment this way:

$$I = I_0 = \$20 \text{ billion.}$$

Figure 5 shows the relation between income levels and autonomous investment. Autonomous investment is constant at every level of income. An increase or a decrease in autonomous investment shifts the flat **investment function** upward or downward, respectively, by the amount of the increase or decrease.

Investment function:
In the income-expenditures model, all investment is autonomous, or independent of the level of income. The investment function is horizontal when plotted against income.

In short, planned investment expenditures, while volatile and changing from period to period, may be assumed constant over any given short-run period. They provide, in addition to consumption spending, the means of arriving at the Keynesian concept of total expenditures in a purely private economy.

Long-Run Factors Affecting Investment. While investment is considered autonomous in the Keynesian context, it is subject to a number of rapidly changing factors, including the rate of interest, the cost of capital, and current and expected sales.

Rate of Interest and the Cost of Capital. Ultimately, profitability—or expectation of future profits—determines the amount of investment that bus-

FIGURE 5

The horizontal investment function, *I*, shows that the level of planned investment expenditures is independent of the level of income. As income changes, the level of investment remains constant. An increase in investment caused by factors such as a change in interest rates is shown as a parallel shift upward.

Autonomous Investment Expenditures

inesses will undertake. Profitability is, in simple terms, the difference between a firm's revenues and its costs.

The cost of capital investment is heavily dependent on the rate of interest. Whether a business uses its own internal funds or borrows to make an investment, it incurs an opportunity cost in the form of interest lost. An increase in the interest rate, other things being equal, will reduce the amount of investment; a reduction in the interest rate will increase investment. The cost of the capital equipment itself is also important in determining the amount of desired investment. An increase in costs, other things being equal, reduces the amount of investment.

Current Sales and Expected Sales. The other side of the profitability of business investment is sales. If a large capacity to produce already exists, an increase in current sales will not encourage new investment expenditures very much. If businesses are operating close to the limits of their ability to produce, an increase in current sales will cause current investment spending to rise.

Expectations are also a central feature of Keynes's theory of investment. Sales expectations require estimates of future business conditions and tend to vary greatly and quickly over time. Optimism concerning future sales and business conditions will mean increases in capital investment in the present. Pessimism will have the opposite effect.

As we will see in later chapters, the volatility of profit expectations is a principal cause in the creation of unstable income levels, unemployment, and cycles of business activity. Before turning to these issues, however, we must first understand how income equilibrium is defined in a purely private economy.

PRIVATE INCOME-EXPENDITURES EQUILIBRIUM

The classical economists argued that full employment would be achieved automatically simply through the activity of supplying goods in an essentially private economy, an economy theoretically free of government intervention. Should difficulties in adjustment to this full-employment equilibrium take place, prices, wages, and interest rates would change to bring the aggregate output of goods in line with aggregate expenditures.

For reasons already outlined, Keynes did not agree that wages, prices, or interest rates would change in any predictable way to bring the demand for goods in line with the supply of goods. How could a depression economy reach equilibrium with high unemployment? Keynes argued that levels of private spending (consumption and investment) determine the output of goods produced in the economy. In other words, businesses react to any level of total expenditures by producing the quantities demanded. If households want more kitchen appliances, they are produced; if businesses demand less computer software, less is produced. Since it obviously takes more or less labor and other resources to produce more or less total output, the level of employment is also affected.

Keynes's theory of output and income determination can be expressed in symbolic terms using the tools of private spending analysis developed previously. Since total private expenditures are a function of income, and since these total private expenditures consist of consumption and investment spending, we can express the Keynesian equilibrium as follows:

$$Y = C + I = \text{total expenditures.}$$

Private-sector equilibrium:
A situation of equality between total private expenditures and output. In this equilibrium, there is no unplanned investment and no tendency for the level of output to change.

Private-sector equilibrium, or equilibrium output, occurs when $C + I$ equals income. In other words, equilibrium output in the economy exists when total expenditures equal what is produced.

An alternative way to define the establishment of equilibrium output involves the relation of income to expenditures. We know that income received by all factors of production may be disposed of in two ways, or

$$Y = C + S.$$

That is, income may be used for consumption spending or for savings, the residual of consumption spending. Equilibrium will occur when income received is equal to total expenditures:

$$C + S = C + I, \quad \text{or} \quad S = I.$$

Total Expenditures Equal Total Output

Keynes's theory—that equilibrium income (or, its mirror image, equilibrium GNP or output) is a function of total expenditures—can be expressed numerically and graphically using tools already at our disposal. All of our previous consumption, investment, and income figures are reproduced in Table 2. Total expenditures, shown in the fourth column, are equal to the sum of consumption and investment expenditures. Recall that planned consumption depends di-

TABLE 2   **Planned Total Expenditures Determine Total Output and Equilibrium Income**

For equilibrium in the private economy, planned total expenditures, $C + I$, must equal total income or output, Y. In this example, equilibrium is reached at a national income (or output) level of $300 billion. At national incomes less than $300 billion, total expenditures exceed total income. At national incomes higher than $300 billion, total expenditures are less than total income.

	(1) National Income or Output (Y)	(2) Planned Consumption Expenditures (C)		(3) Planned Investment Expenditures $(I = I_0)$	(4) Desired or Planned Total Expenditures $(C + I_0)$	(5) Difference Between Total Expenditures and Total Output $(C + I_0 - Y)$
	100	120	+	20	140	+40
	200	200		20	220	+20
Equilibrium	300	280	+	20	300	0
	400	360		20	380	−20
	500	440		20	460	−40

Note: All values are in billions of dollars.

rectly on the level of national income, reported in column (1). According to the circular flow model, the first column represents both the total output of goods and services in the economy as well as national income. Total expenditures may be greater or less than total production or output. The amount by which income or output exceeds expenditures is shown in the last column.

At an income level of $100 billion, for example, total expenditures are greater than total output by $40 billion. This situation is possible only if businesses draw down on inventories of goods. Producers react to such a situation by producing greater quantities of goods and services, thus generating additional income to workers and to the other factors of production. The resulting increases in income will change consumption plans. At incomes higher than $100 billion, households will spend greater amounts on goods and services, indicated in the second column of Table 2 and in Figure 6, which merely reproduces the information of Table 2 graphically. (Note in Figure 6 that investment is added vertically to the consumption function at an autonomous level of $20 billion in order to obtain the $C + I$ line.)

A new, higher level of output produced and income received at $200 billion creates higher total spending, but there is still an excess of total expenditures over output (amount FG in Figure 6). Inventories continue to be drawn down and production stepped up until an **equilibrium level of national income** of $300 billion is reached. Only at this level of income will production plans be in line with the plans of households and businesses to consume and invest.

What would happen at an income level greater than $300 billion, say $400 billion? If an income level of $400 billion were temporarily established, total output would temporarily exceed total expenditures by $20 billion, or AB in Figure 6. Unwanted inventories of goods would pile up unsold, and producers would cut back the rate of production. Since a cutback in production would reduce income, consumption plans of households would be revised downward. Equilibrium would again be achieved when the level of income dropped to $300 billion.

Equilibrium level of national income:
In the income-expenditures model, the level of income at which total private expenditures equal total output.

FIGURE 6

The equilibrium level of income exists when total private expenditures are just great enough to purchase the total output of the economy. At equilibrium, expenditures and output will meet at the point along the 45-degree line where they are exactly equal. At income level $Y = 300$, the economy is at equilibrium, E. At an income or output level of 400, desired total private expenditures at point B are insufficient to purchase the total output generated at point A. Inventories of goods will pile up, causing reductions in the rate of output and a lowering of income. These reductions will take place until income and output again equal the equilibrium level of 300. At this level, total expenditures equal total output produced in the economy. The reverse analysis applies to income and output levels that are less than the equilibrium level.

Private-Sector Equilibrium

It is always worth remembering that the simple Keynesian model of total private spending is a short-run model. Prices, wages, and interest rates do not adjust as they do in long-run classical theory. The only factors that are adjusting are the real quantities of goods and services produced in the economy.

Desired Saving Equals Desired Investment: An Equivalent Method

An equivalent method for determining private-sector equilibrium is to equate private saving and private investment. This method is based on the fact that private saving is what is left over after planned private consumption is determined for various income levels.

Desired saving and desired investment concern the plans of households and businesses. Over any period and at alternative income levels, businesses plan to invest some amount—in the foregoing model, $20 billion worth of investment at every level of income. Households, likewise, plan to save some amount out of income for every level of income; but unlike business investment, household saving varies with income. Desired saving at an income level of $400 billion in our numerical example is a positive $40 billion. But it is a negative $20 billion at an income level of $100 billion; that is, $20 billion will be dissaved.

In other words, at an income level of $100 billion (see Table 3), businesses plan or desire to invest $20 billion. But because total expenditures draw down inventories by $40 billion, they actually end up with a negative $40 billion worth of unplanned investment. Recall that economists include business inventories in the measure of gross private domestic investment. Thus, in this example, when inventories are reduced by $40 billion, the $40 billion represents an unplanned reduction in investment. What do businesses actually invest? Actual investment is the sum of desired (planned) investment plus unplanned investment. In the numerical example of Table 3, actual investment is a negative $20 billion at the income level of $100 billion ($20 billion planned plus a negative $40 billion unplanned). In this situation of falling inventories (negative unplanned investment), businesses respond by increasing output. The increases in output drive up incomes, and thus saving, and move the economy toward its equilibrium level of output.

At the $500 billion level of income, consumption expenditures fall short of income-producing unplanned investment (inventory increases) of $40 billion. Total investment at the $500 billion level of income will then be $60 billion ($40 billion unplanned plus $20 billion desired). Businesses will cut back on production with the effect of lowered incomes. These lower incomes reduce saving, and once again, the economy moves back toward an equilibrium output, one at which planned saving and investment are equal. (For a discussion relating saving to economic progress, see Focus, "The Low Saving Rate in the United States.")

At alternative income levels, therefore, actual investment may diverge from desired or planned investment, but whenever this occurs, producers will change their rate of production. The important point is that actual investment will always equal the actual amount of savings. But when the plans or desires of savers and investors differ, income and output will increase or decrease. The only possible equilibrium will take place when the plans of both household savers and business investors are identical. As Table 3 and Figure 7 show, this equilibrium income occurs when $300 billion of output is consumed by consumers and investors.

TABLE 3   Equilibrium Income

The actual levels of investment and saving are accountings of the difference in total expenditures and total income. If total expenditures are greater than total income, then actual investment is below desired investment. In such cases, businesses increase output until their actual investment equals their desired investment. If total expenditures are less than total income, then actual investment is greater than total income, and businesses decrease output. Equilibrium occurs where desired and actual saving equals desired and actual investment.

	National Income (Y)	(Planned) Desired Saving	(Planned) Desired Investment	Unplanned Investment	Actual Investment	Actual Saving	Income Adjustment
	100	−20	20	−40	−20	−20	increase
	200	0	20	−20	0	0	increase
Equilibrium	300	+20	20	0	+20	+20	—
	400	+40	20	+20	+40	+40	decrease
	500	+60	20	+40	+60	+60	decrease

Note: All values are in billions of dollars.

FOCUS   The Low Saving Rate in the United States

According to the Council on Competitiveness, the greatest challenge facing the United States is reversing the decline in the national saving rate. This concern is based on the notion that a country's savings determines how much it has to invest in new plant and equipment. A decline in the saving rate therefore leads to less investment, which in turn reduces the ability of the economy to produce goods and services.

Although there is some controversy concerning the importance of the saving rate as a determinant of economic growth, two things are clear: The saving rate in the United States has declined sharply over the last fifteen years, and this decline has brought the U.S. saving rate to a level far below that of other major economic powers. In 1973, Americans were saving about 10 percent of their disposable income; this percentage fell to under 3 percent in 1987. Since then, the trend has reversed, and the saving rate reached 6 percent by 1989.

In explaining the difference between the saving rate in the United States and in other countries, much attention has been paid to the way that interest income is taxed in the United States. In the United States, interest earnings are taxable income. If a family has accumulated, say, $20,000 in savings that yields 9 percent interest, the $1800 in annual interest is an addition to taxable income. Assuming the family to be middle income, each additional dollar of taxable income will lead to a twenty-eight cent increase in federal taxes owed by the family. In addition, the interest earnings are also subject to state taxation. While the rate varies among states, this family probably would pay about five additional cents in taxes for each additional dollar in interest earnings. When state and federal taxes are combined, $600 of the $1800 earned in interest will go to pay taxes—in effect reducing the interest rate to 6 percent. By taxing interest income, the tax system in this country reduces the returns to saving and presumably causes the saving rate to be lower than it otherwise would be.

In addition to discouraging saving, the U.S. tax system subsidizes borrowing. If a family in this country borrows $100,000 to buy a new home, any interest that the family pays is tax-deductible. Assuming mortgage interest payments of $9000 per year on the loan, this debt enables the family to reduce taxable income by $9000, which lowers state and federal taxes by about $3000. In effect, the loan costs the family only 6 percent in interest. Until recently, all interest paid on consumer loans was tax-deductible. However, this deduction has been phased out, explaining in part the recent upturn in savings. Nonetheless, tax policy in this country still has the effect of reducing the return to saving and reducing the cost of borrowing.

In many countries, individuals do not pay taxes on interest earnings, nor can they use interest payments as a tax deduction. Many economists feel that the U.S. should adopt a similar tax policy.

Only where desired saving comes in line with desired investment does the process of adding to (or subtracting from) inventories stop. Only at an income level of $300 billion does desired saving of $20 billion equal desired investment of $20 billion. At this level, and only at this level, producers' motivations to increase or decrease production will cease. That is why it is called the equilibrium level of income. Only at an income of $300 billion is the behavior of savers or, more properly, consumer-savers, consistent with that of investors. Not only does $S = I$ in the actual accounting sense, but the desired economic behavior of savers and investors is mutually consistent. Thus, for equilibrium,

$$\text{Desired } S = \text{desired } I = \text{actual } S = \text{actual } I.$$

The condition that in equilibrium desired saving equals desired investment is equivalent to the condition stated earlier that total expenditure ($C + I$) equals total income for an equilibrium level of income to exist. Anytime desired saving and investment are not equal, unintended investment in the form of inventory changes is taking place. From our earlier discussion, unintended investment occurs only when total expenditure does not equal total income. Thus, to say that intended investment equals intended saving in equilibrium is also to say that total expenditure equals total income in equilibrium.

FIGURE 7

Saving-Investment Equilibrium

When $C + I = Y$ (at an equilibrium output equal to $300 billion in Figure 6), saving is equal to investment. The equilibrium level of income occurs where the saving function intersects the autonomous investment function (I_0)—in this case, at 300.

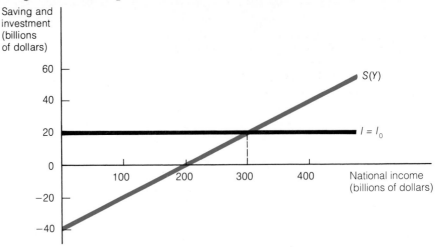

Private Equilibrium in the Keynesian System

Unlike the classical economists, who believed that the economy would self-adjust until full employment was reached, Keynes thought that the economy could adjust to an equilibrium level with widespread unemployment. In terms of the situation depicted in both Figure 6 and Figure 7, the $300 billion level of income is not necessarily the full-employment level of income. This unfortunate state of affairs, in Keynes's view, either was permanent or would last a long time. In either case, some action was demanded in the economy. That action, as we will see, was a role for the government.

SUMMARY

1. Theory clashed with events when, in the 1930s, a decade-long depression in output and employment took hold of the United States and other Western countries. The response of economists was to provide a new version of how the macroeconomy functions. The principal developer of the new macroeconomics was the English economist John Maynard Keynes.

2. Keynes criticized classical theory as being an inadequate description of events in the real world. For example, Keynes did not believe that prices, wages, and interest rates were flexible enough to create a permanent and sufficiently rapid tendency to private-sector full-employment equilibrium.

3. Keynesian economics is predicated on a model of total expenditures. In the simple private-sector model, consumption and investment spending determine equilibrium output and income.

4. Keynes argued that consumption was primarily a function of current income and that the marginal and average propensities to consume were related to in-

come in a stable and predictable manner. Investment, the other kind of private spending, was related to expectations and to a number of factors but could, in the short run, be considered autonomous of income.

5. The income-expenditures model of equilibrium output/income determination employs Keynes's arguments concerning the relationship of certain macroeconomic variables. The level of consumption spending is positively related to the level of income. The marginal propensity to consume (*MPC*) measures the change in consumption expenditure that results from a $1 change in income. The marginal propensity to save (*MPS*) measures the change in saving that results from a $1 change in income. Other factors, such as the price level, wealth, and taxation, help determine consumption and saving. Investment spending is assumed to be autonomous.

6. The level of equilibrium income or output in the private-sector model can be derived by either of two approaches, each yielding the same answer. In the

income-expenditures approach, the equilibrium level of income exists when total expenditure equals total income or output in the economy ($Y = C + I$). In the desired saving–desired investment approach, the equilibrium level of income exists when desired saving equals desired investment output in the economy ($S = I$).

7. Whenever total expenditure does not equal total income or whenever desired saving does not equal desired investment, unintended investment in the form of inventory changes exists. The unintended investment will drive income or output toward its equilibrium level. However, the equilibrium level of income may not be a level of income at which full employment occurs.

KEY TERMS

income-expenditures model
marginal propensity to consume
   (*MPC*)
marginal propensity to save
   (*MPS*)
average propensity to consume
   (*APC*)
average propensity to save
   (*APS*)

dissaving
autonomous consumption
consumption function
saving function
investment spending
autonomous investment
investment function
private-sector equilibrium
equilibrium level of national income

QUESTIONS FOR REVIEW AND DISCUSSION

1. How does Keynes's view of saving differ from the classical view of saving? How does Keynes's view of wage-price flexibility differ from the classical view?
2. Define marginal propensity to consume and average propensity to consume. What is the essential difference between the two?
3. If the *MPC* is 0.75 and national income increases by $200 billion, then by how much will consumption expenditures increase?
4. Can you think of any nonincome factors not listed in the text that might affect consumption decisions?

5. What is autonomous investment spending? Does it change as the level of income changes? Do you think that this is an accurate interpretation of how businesses make investment decisions?
6. When does equilibrium occur in the Keynesian income-expenditures model? What adjusts to obtain equilibrium?
7. Why does the level of actual investment always equal the level of actual saving, while the level of desired investment may not equal the level of desired saving?

PROBLEM

Consider a basic income-expenditures model (with no government sector and where $Y = C + I$) in which Y is real national income, C is real consumption expenditures, and I is real autonomous investment expenditures.

Let $C = \$40$ billion $+ (MPC)Y$ and $I = I_0$. If $I_0 = \$50$ billion and $MPC = 0.5$, compute the equilibrium levels of national income, Y; consumption, C; and saving, S.

ECONOMICS IN ACTION
The Life Cycle and Consumption Behavior

The Keynesian consumption function used in this chapter is often called the absolute income hypothesis concerning the consumption behavior of members of society. The absolute income hypothesis suggests that current income determines the amount of household consumption. Keynes, however, did not base his theory of consumption on budget studies or on extensive economic reasoning about how and why individuals exhibit such behavior. Since Keynes, economists have developed a number of alternative theories about why individuals and households consume and save as they do. One of the most interesting concerns the human life cycle and our perception of it.

Originally developed by economists Albert Ando, R. E. Brumberg, and Nobel laureate Franco Modigliani, the life-cycle hypothesis is based on the idea that household income and wealth (income plus all accumulated assets) change through time.[a] Individuals and households, further, recognize

[a]Franco Modigliani and R. E. Brumberg, "Utility Analysis and the Consumption Function: An Interpretation of Cross-Section Data," in *Post-Keynesian Economics,* ed. K. K. Kurihara (New Brunswick, N. J.: Rutgers University Press, 1954); and Albert Ando and Franco Modigliani, "The 'Life-Cycle' Hypothesis of Saving: Aggregate Implications and Tests," *American Economic Review* 53 (March 1963), pp. 55–84.

this fact and consume and save depending on their life-cycle income and wealth, and, of course, on how long life is expected to be. Figure 8 depicts the notion graphically.

The average individual's income flow, in Figure 8, is much lower in early age (age t_0 through t_1) and in "old" age (t_2 through death, D) than in middle age (age t_1 through t_2). The consumption stream of the individual (as shown in Figure 8) is constant (or rising slightly) over time. This means that individuals (and households) consume more of the value of their (expected) lifetime income/wealth flow in early age and old age and less in middle age. In early age, individuals are net borrowers and dissavers. In middle age, they build up savings (consume less than their incomes) to pay off debts from early age and to provide "nest eggs" for retirement. In old age, the individual is again a dissaver. That is, he or she spends assets accumulated during middle age.

Students, for example, have some perception of the present value of expected lifetime income from property and from labor. This expected income is conditioned by many factors, such as educational level (or the one you hope to attain), the average expected earnings in the job or profession you expect to go into after graduation, expectations about longevity, probable inheritance, unexpected bequests, and so on. Consumption in the present is conditioned by the present value of this expected income. (Present value

---

FIGURE 8   Hypothetical Life-Cycle Consumption Behavior

The figure depicts a stylized profile of income, consumption, and savings. In the life-cycle theory, individuals consume and save on the basis of expected income over the life cycle. This implies that consumption is at a higher level than income in early age, is less than income in the middle years, and is again greater than income (people dissave) in retirement. In the figure, time t_2 represents retirement. After t_2, during retirement, the source of income becomes interest earnings from accumulated assets.

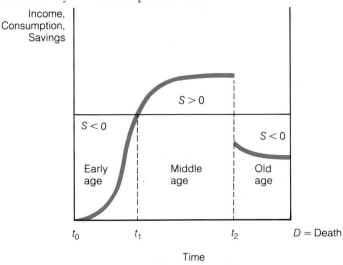

is today's value of income received in the future, or it is future income discounted by the rate of interest.) Some medical, law, or MBA students buy BMWs, Porsches, and fine wardrobes; these students are dissaving out of current income. They are, however, consuming in response to expected income over the life cycle.

The importance of the life-cycle hypothesis for macroeconomic theory is that it explains some rather apparent empirical contradictions. The consumption function, estimated over some short-run period, such as a year, shows that consumption is not proportional to income. People and households with lower incomes tend to consume a *larger* proportion of their incomes, whereas higher-income individuals and households consume a smaller proportion. How-

ever, when the consumption function is estimated over long periods of time, we find that, in the aggregate, consumption is proportional to income. This means that a relatively constant proportion of aggregate income is consumed from year to year. The life-cycle hypothesis explains this apparent anomaly by maintaining that consumption is a function of the present value of *lifetime* income and wealth, not short-term yearly income.

Question

How might a changing age distribution of the U.S. population toward (a) older citizens or (b) younger people affect consumption expenditures in the present?

APPENDIX

An Algebraic Treatment of Keynesian Theory

The tables in the text of this chapter provide useful information for several levels of national income. But what if the information you need cannot be obtained from these tables? At times, an algebraic version of the Keynesian model of equilibrium will prove useful to you.

Using the simplifying assumption that the marginal propensity to consume is constant regardless of level of income, a general consumption function can be expressed as

$$C = a + b(Y),$$

where b is the marginal propensity to consume and a is the consumption spending that would occur if national income were zero.

It is therefore reasonable to assume that a is some positive number and that b is a fraction. For example, the consumption function presented in numerical form in Table 1 in the text could be expressed as

$$C = 40 + 0.8(Y).$$

If some income level (say, $400 billion) is substituted into the equation, then the equation can be

solved for C to determine that planned consumption is $360 billion when income is $400 billion— exactly the answer provided in Table 1.

Similarly, an algebraic equation can be derived to express the saving function. Since, by definition,

$$Y = C + S,$$

S can be expressed as

$$S = Y - C.$$

However, $C = a + b(Y)$. Substituting in the previous equation yields

$$S = Y - [a + b(Y)],$$

or

$$S = Y - a - b(Y).$$

Rearranging terms,

$$S = -a + Y - b(Y),$$

or

$$S = -a + (1 - b)Y.$$

Here, $(1 - b)$ is interpreted as the marginal propensity to save, and $-a$ is the level of saving when income is zero.

The specific saving function presented in Table 1 is

$$S = -40 + (1 - 0.8)Y.$$

If specific numbers are substituted for Y, the above equation can be used to determine the level of planned saving at each income level. Doing so yields numbers identical to those presented in Table 1.

Finally, it is also possible to develop an algebraic expression of the equilibrium income. In the simple case presented in the text of this chapter, where demanders of goods and services are domestic households and business firms, the equilibrium level of production occurs when

$$Y = C + I_0,$$

or when

$$Y = a + b(Y) + I_0.$$

Rearranging,

$$Y - b(Y) = a + I_0,$$
$$Y(1 - b) = a + I_0,$$

or

$$Y = \frac{(a + I_0)}{(1 - b)}.$$

If we know the appropriate consumption function (the values of a and b) and the investment function (the value of I_0), we can substitute the values into the equation and solve for the equilibrium income level. For example, using the numer-

ical example presented in Table 1, where $a = 40$, $b = 0.8$, and $I_0 = 20$, in equilibrium,

$$Y = \frac{40 + 20}{1 - 0.8},$$

$$Y = \frac{60}{0.2},$$

or

$$Y = 300.$$

We can see that at a production level of $300 billion, consumers will be willing to buy $280 billion of goods and services—$280 = 40 + 0.8(300)$—with the business sector preferring to buy the remaining $20 billion of goods and services. At that production level, total spending is equal to production.

We can also employ an algebraic approach to determine equilibrium income, using the savings and investment approach. At the equilibrium level of income,

$$S = I_0.$$

Since $S = -40 + (1 - 0.8)Y$ and $I = I_0 = 20$, then, in equilibrium,

$$-40 + 0.2(Y) = 20,$$
$$0.2Y = 60,$$

or

$$Y = 300.$$

With simple examples, the equilibrium level of income can be depicted with either numerical charts or with graphs. However, as the model is made more complete and realistic, these two approaches become cumbersome. The use of an algebraic equation can therefore be quite helpful.

27

Output Fluctuations and the Public Sector

The last chapter focused on how equilibrium in the private economy is reached in the Keynesian model. In the classical view, discussed in Chapter 25, equilibrium was conceived from a long-run perspective, a period of time that could encompass short-run swings in income and employment. From a short-run perspective, however, equilibrium seems an illusive concept, for we commonly observe fluctuations in real GNP, employment, and inflation whenever the government releases its latest statistics on the economy. An essential part of the Keynesian model and Keynes's critique of classical economics was an explanation of how and why the economy in the short run increases or decreases its output in response to changes in spending. Keynes sought, in other words, the reasons for short-run economic instability and what can be done to correct it. In essence, Keynes argued that spending in the private economy would normally be insufficient to produce an economy characterized by full employment and little or no inflation. He felt that the public sector—the government—must pursue spending and taxation policies to ensure full employment and economic growth. After reading Chapter 27 you should understand

- the process through which changes in private spending are translated into changes in output and income.

- how the impact of spending changes on income described by Keynes is important in explaining cycles of business and economic activity.

- how foreign trade and government act as components of spending in the economy.

- how government spending and taxation in a Keynesian system are called upon to alleviate downturns and to modify inflationary pressures in the private economy.

FLUCTUATIONS IN THE PRIVATE SECTOR

Before we analyze the mechanics of the Keynesian model, let's review briefly. The private-sector equilibrium discussed at the end of Chapter 26 was based on Keynes's central assumption that total expenditures determine output and income. (Keep in mind that the terms *output* and *income* are used interchangeably in macroeconomics. In the circular flow of goods and services, one person's expenditures on output always represent another person's income. The final or total value of output must therefore equal the level of income in the economy.)

In the Keynesian model, output and income can increase or decrease in response to any change in the components of total expenditures. For example, if autonomous consumption or investment increases, income will increase. If the economy-wide marginal propensity to consume increases, income will increase. Table 1 summarizes possible changes in private expenditures and their effects on income and output.

To see how changes in these factors actually affect income and output, consider an increase in autonomous investment spending. Recall that autonomous investment spending is independent of income and depends instead on factors such as the cost of capital, expected sales, and business profits. What happens to income when investment spending increases? In the example illustrated in Figure 1, the initial level of income of $300 billion is determined by the private spending level $C + I_0$. Assume that investment spending then increases by $20 billion because of an increase in expected future profits. The total spending curve shifts upward to $C + I_1$ by the amount $\Delta I = \$20$ billion. Desired spending then exceeds the output of goods and services by $20 billion (distance AB in Figure 1). To meet the demand, inventories are drawn down, producers step up the rate of output, and income rises. The question is, What effect does a $20 billion increase in autonomous investment spending have on equilibrium income? Does income increase by $20 billion exactly or by a greater or lesser amount? As you may have noticed in Figure 1, income increases by $100 billion with an investment spending increase of $20 billion. Why does such a relatively small increase in investment result in such a relatively large increase in income?

TABLE 1

The Sources of Income and Output Changes in the Private Economy

Increases or decreases in autonomous consumption or investment spending or in the marginal propensity to consume (and save) will cause increases or decreases in the level of income and output in the economy.

Component Change	Change in Income and Output
↑ Autonomous consumption spending	Increase
↓ Autonomous consumption spending	Decrease
↑ Marginal propensity to consume	Increase
↓ Marginal propensity to consume	Decrease
↑ Autonomous investment spending	Increase
↓ Autonomous investment spending	Decrease

FIGURE 1

When the level of autonomous investment increases by $20 billion, from $60 billion to $80 billion (*AB*) in the figure, and the marginal propensity to consume is 0.8, equilibrium income rises by $100 billion— in this case, from $300 billion to $400 billion. The multiplier effect causes the level of income to rise by more than the amount of the increase in investment.

The Effects of an Increase in Investment Expenditures

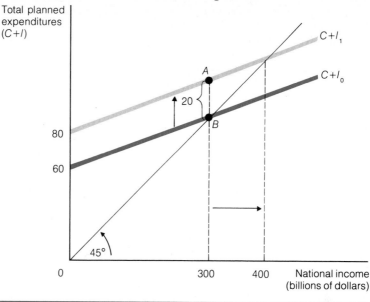

Investment multiplier:
The multiple by which equilibrium income will change given a change in autonomous investment expenditure; 1/*MPS*.

The Investment Multiplier

The answer to this question is given by the value of the multiplier, a number found by dividing the change in income by the change in autonomous spending that caused the change in income. In Figure 1, we are looking at a change in autonomous investment spending. Thus the **investment multiplier** is found by dividing $100 billion by $20 billion or, if k_I represents the investment multiplier,

$$k_I = \frac{\Delta Y}{\Delta I} = \frac{100}{20} = 5.$$

If autonomous investment spending increases by ΔI, or $20 billion, the initial expenditure first generates an addition to income of $20 billion ($\Delta Y$) because expenditures on investment goods create returns (or income) to resources. However, the process does not end here, for all resource owners, laborers, holders of capital or land, and so on, are consumer-savers. New income will cause the consumer-saver to spend some and to save the rest. The *MPC*—the marginal propensity to consume—and the *MPS*—the marginal propensity to save—will always add to 1 out of total income. (What is consumed is not saved; what is saved is not consumed.) Consumption expenditures on goods and services, then, create additional income out of which another set of income recipients spend a portion and save the rest. In this process, the initial increase of $20 billion is multiplied at each stage.

This multiplier process is illustrated in Table 2. The initial injection of $20 billion in autonomous investment spending creates an addition to income (ΔY) of $20 billion. Assuming that the *MPC* is 0.8 and the *MPS* is 0.2, income recipients will spend 80 percent and save 20 percent of the new income. The new consumption thus creates an addition to total income of $16 billion on

TABLE 2   The Workings of the Investment Multiplier

Any change in autonomous investment spending changes equilibrium income by some multiple, depending on the value of the *MPS*. In this example, *MPC* = 0.8 and *MPS* = 0.2. The simple multiplier is the reciprocal of the *MPS*—in this case, 1/0.2 = 5. In a simple Keynesian framework, the change in equilibrium income is equal to the multiplier times the original change in spending, or 5(20) = 100.

Round of Spending	Increase in Autonomous Investment Spending (ΔI)	Increase in Income (ΔY)	Increase in Consumption (ΔC)	Increase in Saving (ΔS)
1	20	20	0.8(20) = 16	0.2(20) = 4
2		16	0.8(16) = 12.8	0.2(16) = 3.2
3		12.8	0.8(12.8) = 10.24	0.2(12.8) = 2.56
4		10.24	0.8(10.24) = 8.19	0.2(10.24) = 2.04
•		•	•	•
•		•	•	•
•		•	•	•
All others		40.96	0.8(40.96) = 32.96	0.2(40.96) = 8.19
		100	0.8(100) = 80	0.2(100) = 20

Note: All values are in billions of dollars.

the first round of consumption spending. The recipients of the $16 billion consumption spending in turn spend part of it—80 percent of $16 billion, or $12.8 billion—and save part of it—20 percent of $16 billion, or $3.2 billion. The multiplier process goes on until the total change in income equals $100 billion, of which $80 billion is composed of new consumption and $20 billion of new saving. It is no accident that the new savings are exactly equal to the initial amount of new autonomous investment spending. Why? Because only when the increase in desired investment is matched by an equal amount of additional desired saving will the initial disequilibrium caused by the new investment be corrected and equilibrium be restored.

The Multiplier Formalized

The value of the multiplier is determined by the *MPC* or *MPS*. A quick method of determining the multiplier, therefore, is to divide 1 by the *MPS*.

$$k_I = \frac{1}{(1 - MPC)} = \frac{1}{MPS}$$

Using an *MPC* of 0.8,

$$k_I = \frac{1}{(1 - 0.8)} = \frac{1}{0.2} = 5.$$

Any change in income caused by a change in an autonomous expenditure may then be determined by multiplying the autonomous expenditure change by the multiplier or, in the example,

$$\Delta Y = k\Delta I = \frac{1}{MPS}(\Delta I) = 5 \times \$20 \text{ billion} = \$100 \text{ billion}.$$

A change in the *MPS,* which also means a change in the *MPC,* will obviously change the value of *k,* the multiplier. The multiplier is the reciprocal of the *MPS.* If the *MPS* is 0.1, the multiplier is 10. Under these circumstances, a $20 billion injection of autonomous expenditures would increase income by $200 billion. Or, if Americans saved one-half of every additional dollar received in income, the multiplier would take on a value of 2. (On a piece of scratch paper, demonstrate to yourself why this is so.) In this case, a $20 billion increase in investment spending would raise equilibrium income by only $40 billion.

The Autonomous Consumption Multiplier

Autonomous consumption multiplier:
The multiple by which equilibrium income will change given a change in autonomous consumption expenditure; 1/*MPS*.

The **autonomous comsumption multiplier** applies to the autonomous portion of consumption, that portion of consumption spending independent of income and determined instead by variables such as thrift attitudes and the rate of interest on savings.

If autonomous consumption increases, income also increases by some multiple. If, for example, the autonomous component of consumption increases from $40 billion to $50 billion in a society with a marginal propensity to save of 0.2, equilibrium income would rise to $450 billion from its previous level of $400 billion. The change in income can be expressed as follows:

$$\frac{\Delta \text{Autonomous consumption}}{MPS} = \frac{\$10 \text{ billion}}{0.2} = \$50 \text{ billion.}$$

Thus the autonomous consumption multiplier, like the investment multiplier, is the reciprocal of the *MPS* (in this example, 1/0.2 = 5). The higher the *MPC* (or, what is the same, the lower the *MPS*), the higher the consumption multiplier and the higher the income change from a given change in autonomous expenditures.

To summarize, income will rise or fall by an amount greater than the expenditure change because of a multiplier process. The multiplier, which is simply the reciprocal of the *MPS,* magnifies the change in autonomous expenditures that creates the change in equilibrium income. Stated another way, changes in equilibrium income are calculated by applying the multiplier to changes in autonomous expenditures.

These concepts are of great importance for practical policymaking. The most significant effect of the multiplier is that very small changes in spending may be greatly magnified in resulting income and employment changes. For example, a small change in private spending could precipitate a relatively large economic contraction or reduction in employment and business activity. As we will see later in this chapter, Keynes recommended that government's fiscal actions be used to counteract the instabilities generated by the multiplier effects of private spending on GNP, employment, economic growth, and inflation.

The Multiplier and Private Income Equilibrium

Before turning to more elaborate models of the macroeconomy and the impact of prices in the Keynesian framework, it is useful to reflect on some crucial assumptions about the multiplier process and about the basic Keynesian private-sector model in general.

The multiplier process just described is a simplification. No time horizon is placed on the rounds of spending, and the process requires that income receivers who spend and save do so in the exact amounts given by the *MPC* and the *MPS*. In the simple model there are no other deductions from income except saving. Since there is still no role for government in the model, income receivers do not have to pay taxes on income received or on income spent, such as excise or consumption taxes. (As we will see later in this chapter, taxes are a leakage from income that has the effect of reducing the numerical value of the multiplier.)

In addition, the simple private model does not consider spending injections into the macroeconomy other than autonomous consumption and investment spending. As we will see in the next section, investment can be accelerated by changes in income, and there are other injections, such as government spending, to account for. Such additional spending tends to increase equilibrium income. In general, then, leakages—deductions from income such as savings and taxes—reduce equilibrium income, while injections—additions to spending—increase equilibrium income. Most of these factors are fully integrated into the basic macroeconomic model later in this chapter.

THE MULTIPLIER AND THE BUSINESS CYCLE

The income-expenditures approach to macroeconomic theory establishes an explanation for equilibrium levels of GNP and employment. As we have seen, the multiplier process explains how changes in autonomous consumption or investment spending change the equilibrium level of income. These models are extremely useful in organizing our understanding of how GNP and employment of resources are determined. However, data on unemployment, GNP fluctuations, and inflation suggest that our economy undergoes cycles of business activity. As indicated in Chapter 23, the business cycle consists of observed upswings and downswings in the production of goods and services and in the employment of resources to produce goods and services.

The Business Cycle

Business investment in a particular period is determined by the level of autonomous expenditures and by the growth or decline of sales. If sales are growing at a steady rate (for example, 3½ percent per year), only autonomous factors will affect investment. If all other factors affecting income growth remain constant, the economy will grow at a steady rate. Businesses, however, will seek to maintain additions to net investment (and hence their capital stock) in some proportion to the levels of their output of goods and services. These additions, above and beyond the ongoing autonomous investment spending that takes place in the economy, will rise when the amount of capital falls below the amount that businesses wish to maintain in proportion to their current output. When does this happen? This additional "kicker" of net investment can rise when actual sales of goods and services grow beyond some expected and predictable steady rate or when some other factor affecting new additions to net investment changes.

Consider some actual and potential reactions of businesses to increases or reductions in the demand for their products. In the short run, businesses with a relatively fixed capacity must either add labor and other variable resources when sales increase or lay off labor and other resources when sales decline (in which case business capital simply depreciates). In the short run, businesses have relatively few options. Decreases in sales will create unemployment of labor and other resources, as well as unused capacity; increases in output demand may lead to pressure on labor and other resources, accompanied possibly by a high rate of inflation. The result: In the short run, businesses may alter the rate of output of their plants, but actual increases in output are severely constrained because of the impossibility of adding capacity by building warehouses and plants or purchasing sophisticated equipment over a short-run period.

Figure 2 shows the path of real GNP through time; the straight line depicts a constant and steady growth rate in output. This straight-line path in output (about 3 percent growth, on average, over the past hundred years in the United States) would occur steadily and smoothly when all factors affecting the growth in investment spending remain the same. For example, when sales are assumed to be growing at a steady rate, as between hypothetical time periods t_0 and t_1 in Figure 2, income also grows at a steady rate. But what happens if actual sales outpace expected sales at some hypothetical point in time, t_1, and actual sales increases are expected to continue? Investment expenditures of the autonomous type will rise initially, raising income; but rising demand for and sales of goods and services will also signal new additions to net investment because businesses will want to maintain some desired ratio of capital stock to total sales volume.

This accelerated growth in investment expenditures in response to rising sales creates a business cycle. As income is increased through the multiplier

FIGURE 2

A jump in investment spending at time period t_1 due to an unexpected rise in sales of goods and services creates a business cycle; output rises sharply due to the multiplier effect. Eventually, the growth in output slows, and a peak is reached as resources such as labor and raw materials become scarce. Investment may then return to lower levels, causing the economy to contract. Since expectations about future business conditions change constantly, business cycles are a fact of life in market economies.

Changes in Autonomous Investment and the Business Cycle

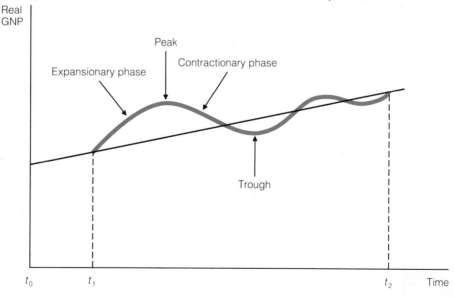

process, investment expenditures are magnified in the system *because* of the increased growth rate of output and sales. Additional capital investment creates an expansionary phase of the business cycle (again, see Figure 2). The expansionary phase is characterized by the struggle to hire more labor and other inputs in order to expand business activity and production; in addition, there are new net additions to investment and the capital stock.

If the economy is producing close to capacity—where labor, raw materials, and available capital goods are scarce—higher prices may accompany this phase (which is why the vertical axis of Figure 2 shows *real* GNP). With no influence other than a new, higher expected growth in sales, the rate of growth in real GNP eventually slows owing to these resource scarcities, and new investment expenditures slow. As actual sales of goods and services grow at a slower rate, businesses desire smaller new net additions to the capital stock and hence reduce investment spending. A peak of the cycle is reached, and business activity, measured in real GNP, begins to decline. Workers are laid off and plant production is reduced in this contractionary phase of the cycle. Existing capital depreciates, or "wears out" with no new net investment. At some point, the decline in real GNP finally slows down; a bottom, or trough, of the business cycle is experienced, and the process starts over again.

Figure 2 shows the cycle of output swings getting smaller, ultimately reaching stable equilibrium at hypothetical time t_2. However, is the steady state of GNP growth outcome likely in the real world? The answer is no; there is too much uncertainty about investment and income. The likely scenario is an economy in a perpetual state of flux, with recurring cycles of business expansion (and possible inflation) and contraction. In the Keynesian view of the world, even the act of saving may produce economic contractions.

Contractionary and Expansionary Gaps

Contractionary gap:
The amount by which total planned expenditures at the level of full-employment income fall short of the level required to generate full-employment income; also called a recessionary gap.

Expansionary gap:
The amount by which total planned expenditures at the level of full-employment income exceed the level required to generate full-employment without inflation; also called an inflationary gap.

Failure of the private economy to provide stable growth and predictable, stable levels of full employment led to Keynes's fundamental criticism of classical economics. Though Keynes himself did not discuss a business cycle, in his view the private economy was erratic and subject to long-run periods of large-scale unemployment and low production levels. In terms of Figure 2, the contractionary phase of the cycle would engender more and greater pessimism about future business conditions, keeping the economy in a contractionary phase of the cycle for a very long period of time. Only accident, not dependable market forces as the classical economists had maintained, would produce a stable equilibrium at full employment with no inflation.

For our more familiar income-expenditures approach to the macroeconomy, Keynes envisioned the economy as reaching, and remaining in, either a contractionary gap or an expansionary gap. A **contractionary gap** (sometimes called a recessionary gap) exists when equilibrium output is less than full-employment output. This is so because the level of total expenditures that would exist at full employment would be insufficient to purchase total output. Inventories would pile up, and the level of output would adjust to a lower equilibrium level as businesses cut back production. An **expansionary gap** (sometimes called an inflationary gap), the opposite situation, means that total private expenditures exceed those expenditures necessary to produce a full-employment level of income without inflation.[1] Excess expenditures, in other words, put pressure on the employment of resources. Since the economy cannot push output beyond its production possibilities frontier, inflation is created.

These gaps can be illustrated graphically. Figure 3 shows the two possible equilibrium positions for the private economy. In Figure 3a, private spending results in an equilibrium at point E. Private consumption and investment spending produce an equilibrium income (and level of employment) Y_E. Income level Y_E is not, however, a full-employment level of income. Workers are laid off and other resources are unemployed, as indicated by the spending or contractionary gap represented at income level Y_F, the level needed for full employment without inflation. The contractionary gap in the private economy (AB in the figure) presents the amount of additional consumption and investment spending that would be necessary to bring the economy to a full-employment equilibrium.

Figure 3b depicts the opposite situation. Consumption and investment spending produce equilibrium and a level of employment at Y_E. Full employ-

---

FIGURE 3

(a) A contractionary, or recessionary, gap exists when private spending is insufficient to bring the economy to full employment without inflation. Y_E is the equilibrium income reached by private spending and investment. Unemployment is high and production is low, however, with a contractionary gap AB represented at Y_F, the level needed for full employment without inflation. (b) An expansionary gap results when private spending exceeds the resource capabilities of the economy. Such excess spending creates inflation. Equilibrium at Y_E is in excess of the level Y_F needed for full employment without inflation. The excess spending creates pressure on the economy to expand, usually causing inflation.

Contractionary and Expansionary Gaps

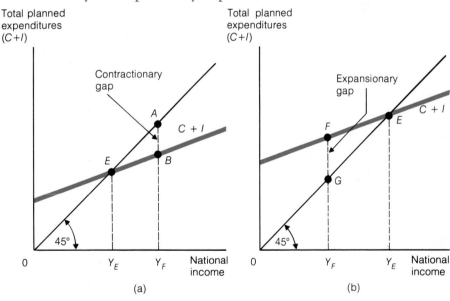

(a)   (b)

---

[1]The expansionary gap is also called an inflationary gap, but the amount of inflation produced by excess spending depends on how close the economy is to maximum capacity. When the economy is on its production possibilities frontier, no additional output is possible and the excess spending produces pure inflation.

ment without inflation occurs at the lower income level Y_F, however. Spending in excess of what is needed for the full-employment income level Y_F creates pressures on the economy to expand. Because resources are limited, these pressures usually create inflation, a general rise in prices. An expansionary gap exists in the amount represented by FG at full-employment income level Y_F. This gap represents the amount of excess consumption and investment that causes inflation at full employment.

GOVERNMENT SPENDING AND TAXATION

Keynes believed that the invisible hand—those forces that would return the economy to full-employment equilibrium without inflation—was seriously arthritic. Even if such forces on private spending did exist, in Keynes's opinion they would probably be unendurably slow in restoring equilibrium. Keynes argued that society should not have to endure contractionary or expansionary gaps of long duration. Since automatic forces were unreliable, he saw discretionary government interventions as necessary. Keynes felt that macroeconomic management should be entrusted to the central government, which theoretically has the ability to adjust aggregate spending in line with national economic goals by the use of its two major budget weapons: government spending and taxation. Changes in one or both of these areas constitute fiscal policy, the object of which is the manipulation of total spending in the economy. In this section we will examine the macroeconomic effects of government spending, taxation, and foreign trade; in the final section of the chapter, we will analyze how leakages and injections to total expenditures can be manipulated to control the whole economy.

Government Expenditures

In the context of the basic Keynesian income-expenditures model, government spending (G) is an addition to total private spending, represented graphically by raising the $C + I$ curve to account for the new source of spending. (In adding government spending, we are relaxing one of the simplifying assumptions of our basic model discussed in Chapter 26.)

Once a government sector is incorporated into the model, the equilibrium production level is that at which output is equal to consumption (demand from households) plus investment (demand from businesses) plus government spending on goods and services (demand from the government sector). Previously, we had operated under the assumption that the level of government purchases of goods and services was zero. Then, total spending consisted of household spending (consumption) plus business spending (investment).

$Y = C + I + G$

Government spending can take many forms and have many (sometimes conflicting) objectives. For example, in one sense the government behaves like a business, purchasing inputs used in its daily operations, such as labor, machinery, and buildings. In another sense, the government acts like a consumer, purchasing products for its own use, such as missile systems, tanks, ammunition, and airplanes. An extensive and controversial type of government spending does not result in the outright purchase of goods and services:

transfer payments or "negative taxes" that redistribute income among various groups in society—from rich to poor, from able to disabled, from healthy to sick, from employed to unemployed. These transfer payments are not included in our definition of government purchases of goods and services; government spending, which we will designate as G, thus includes only purchases of goods and services.

Keep in mind that a government's decision about how much to spend is somewhat different from private decisions to consume or invest. A major difference is that the government is a not-for-profit sector of the economy. Its decisions are often not motivated by private profit or economic efficiency. Furthermore, its spending is not constrained by its income in tax receipts. Congress can, and often does, spend far more than it takes in in the form of taxes, issuing government bonds or creating money to cover the difference. Because government spending is not constrained by government tax collections, enormous budget deficits have built up in recent years, causing much concern among the electorate and in Congress. One reflection of this concern is the broad support for a balanced budget amendment to the Constitution (see the Economics in Action at the end of this chapter). It is dangerous to ignore the consequences of budget deficits, but in this first approach we will do so to keep the model simple.

Autonomous government expenditures:
Government expenditures that are independent of the level of income.

To further simplify the analysis, we will assume that government expenditures to purchase goods and services actually are **autonomous government expenditures;** in other words, they do not depend in any predetermined way on national income. Thus we may write, as we did previously for investment, $G = G_0$ to indicate that government expenditures are independent of income. Total spending can now be redefined as follows:

$$C + I + G_0 = \text{total expenditures.}$$

Graphically, the addition of autonomous government spending, G, results in a parallel upward shift of the total spending function. In Figure 4a, the $C_0 + I_0 + G_0$ curve is higher than the $C_0 + I_0$ curve at each level of national income by whatever amount of G_0 government decides to spend. Notice that the addition of government spending to the total expenditures curve has the effect of moving the total spending curve to an intersection point higher up the 45-degree line. In other words, government expenditure, taken by itself, is expansionary; it leads to a higher level of equilibrium income.

Government expenditures are also an injection into the expenditures stream. In Figure 4b, government expenditures in the amount of G_0 are added vertically to private investment expenditures of I_0. Since there are no leakages in this simple model other than private saving, equilibrium occurs where saving—the leakage from the income-spending stream—is equal to the sum of investment and government spending injections into the income stream. The equilibrium level of income and output is equal to that produced in the total expenditures approach to income determination shown in Figure 4a.

The Effects of Taxation

To introduce the concept and effect of government spending, we merely acknowledged the impact of an injection of new spending on the macroeconomy. In fact, government spending decisions are rarely made in a budgetary vacuum. Decisions about taxes—both their level and their structure—almost always

FIGURE 4

The introduction of government spending increases total spending and the equilibrium level of income. (a) With government spending of G_0 added to autonomous consumption and investment, $C_0 + I_0$, total income rises from Y_0 to Y_1. (b) An equivalent level of income appears in a leakage-injection analysis. The saving leakage, S, is equated to the investment and government spending injections, $I_0 + G_0$, to determine an equilibrium level of income.

Effects of Government Expenditures on Total Spending

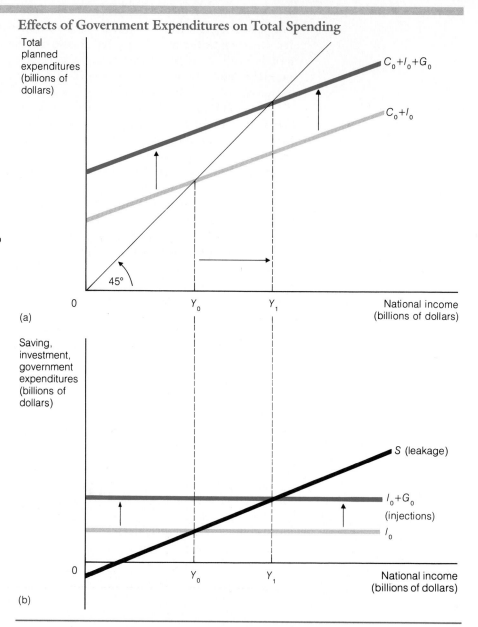

accompany decisions about government spending. We will disregard changes in tax structure and concentrate on the effects on output and employment of changes in the level of taxes. Taxes represent a leakage from the income-expenditures flow. In this respect they are like savings and for analytical purposes can be treated in the same way as savings. (You might think of taxes as "public saving" in conjunction with the private decision to withhold from spending a part of national income.) The fact that taxes represent involuntary saving does not concern us for the moment because the macroeconomic effects do not depend on whether saving is voluntary or involuntary.

To determine the effect of taxes on the macroeconomy we must ask, Who pays taxes? The answer, of course, is that consumers (and, to a lesser extent, businesses) do. The effect of taxes, therefore, is primarily to lower planned consumption insofar as taxes reduce the disposable income received by households, the income left after taxes. We must refine another assumption in light of government spending. As we saw earlier, when government is not a factor in the economy, several of the aggregate income measures are identical to each other. But once we subtract taxes from the national income, national income and disposable income are no longer the same. Disposable income is equal to national income minus the amount of taxes paid. Total spending is, therefore, a function of disposable aggregate income once taxes are admitted into the analysis. However, the purpose of the analysis is to determine equilibrium national income. As such, all of the figures and graphs we use measure national income on the horizontal axis. When the difference between national income and disposable income changes as a result of tax changes, the result is to alter consumption at every level of national income (and therefore total spending). When taxes change, the consumption function shifts when it is plotted against national income. This same explanation is, of course, applicable to the saving function.

Exactly how do taxes affect spending and saving levels? Let us assume for convenience that taxes are paid out of household income only and that businesses are not taxed. In Chapter 26 we saw that any increase in household income will be distributed between consumption and saving and that once we know the marginal propensity to save (*MPS*), we know the percentage of the change in income allocated to each use. What works for injections to household income works in reverse for leakages from household income. That is to say, facing a higher tax bill (a lower disposable household income), households will finance the higher level of taxes partly at the expense of current consumption and partly at the expense of future consumption, or saving. This is true of any kind of tax increase. But the effect of the tax on the shape of the consumption and saving curves depends on the type of tax levied.

Lump-Sum Taxes. In order to concentrate on the effect that taxation has on equilibrium output, assume that the type of tax the government levies is a **lump-sum tax,** whose effect is straightforward: Every income earner is taxed the same amount, say $100. Each dollar increase in lump-sum tax revenue collected by government results in a dollar lost from household disposable income. An increase in the lump-sum tax therefore shifts the consumption curve downward, but the curve does not shift downward by the full amount of the tax because the saving schedule is also shifted downward. If *MPC* equals 0.8 and *MPS* equals 0.2, then every dollar increase in the lump-sum tax will reduce consumption by 80 cents and reduce saving by 20 cents. The downward shifts in consumption and saving curves will be parallel; a lump-sum tax means that the tax amount is the same regardless of the level of income. Figure 5 shows the shifts in consumption and saving curves resulting from the imposition of a lump-sum tax.

In Figure 5a, the imposition of a lump-sum tax on each household causes household consumption to decline by 80 percent of the tax because the *MPC* is 0.8. (Given any level of nominal income, disposable income, *DI,* falls by the amount of the tax. Since consumption is dependent on disposable income, consumption falls by $MPC \times \Delta DI$.) If the lump-sum tax is $100, the shift from $C_0 + I_0 + G_0$ to $C_1 + I_0 + G_0$ represents an $80 cut in household expenditures at every level of aggregate income. In Figure 5b, the shift of the

Lump-sum tax:
A fixed level of total taxes; total taxes do not change as the level of income changes.

FIGURE 5

Effects of a Lump-Sum Tax on Aggregate Household Spending and Saving

A lump-sum tax decreases both consumption and saving. (a) The decrease in consumption from C_0 to C_1 is determined by the MPC. If $MPC = 0.8$, a lump-sum tax reduces consumption by 80 percent of each tax dollar paid. A lump-sum tax reduces equilibrium income—in this case, represented by the shift from income level Y_0 to Y_1. (b) Imposition of the lump-sum tax reduces saving by an amount equal to the MPS times the tax paid, T. The saving function shifts downward from S_0 to S_1. The total tax leakage, T, is then added vertically to saving function S_1, making the total leakage $S_1 + T$. When equated to the investment and government injections, $I_0 + G_0$, equilibrium income shifts to Y_1.

saving curve from S_0 to S_1 represents a $20 reduction of household saving ($MPS \times \Delta DI$) at each level of aggregate income.

The effect of a tax increase, taken by itself, is contractionary. It causes a reduction in aggregate income and output. This point is readily seen in Figure 5a, where the effect of the tax is to reduce national income equilibrium from Y_0 to Y_1. Likewise, in the leakages-injection approach illustrated in Figure 5b, a new equilibrium is attained where the sum of the leakages, $S_1 + T$, equals the sum of the injections, $I_0 + G_0$. Equilibrium occurs at income level Y_1.

The Effects of Foreign Trade on Equilibrium Income

Exports:
Expenditures by foreigners on domestically produced goods.

Previously, we have operated under the assumption that all goods produced in the United States are sold here and that all goods purchased by American households, business firms, and government agencies are made in the United States. There was a time when the foreign sector could be ignored without sacrificing believability; the United States used to be relatively self-sufficient. No more. Now, any realistic economic model must include a foreign sector. Fortunately, incorporating a foreign sector into our basic Keynesian model is easy to do. First, the notion of equilibrium income must be modified slightly. With foreign trade, equilibrium occurs when domestic production of goods and services is equal to total spending for those goods and services, including spending by foreign buyers. In other words **exports** (X), defined as spending by foreign households, business firms, or government agencies on goods produced in the United States, must be added to $C, I,$ and G as a component of total spending. At the same time, the model must be altered to take imports into account. A portion of consumption spending, business spending, and government spending may be on goods produced abroad, and such expenditures do not represent demand for domestically produced goods. Therefore, if we define **imports** (M) as total spending on foreign goods, we must subtract M from total spending. Total spending, then, is equal to $C + I + G + (X - M)$, and the equilibrium level of national income is that level at which Y is equal to $C + I + G + (X - M)$.

Imports:
Expenditures by domestic residents on goods produced in foreign countries.

It is also possible to use the injections and leakages approach to determine the equilibrium level of income in a model that contains a foreign sector. Total injections equal $I + G + X,$ and total leakages equal $S + T + M.$ Equilibrium income is where $(I + G + X) = (S + T + M).$

The concept of a foreign trade component of total domestic spending is intuitive. The import of cashmere sweaters by consumers, computer chips by business investors, or titanium by the U.S. government replaces domestic spending by these groups and represents increased demands on *foreign* producers. Increased demand by U.S. consumers, investors, and by the U.S. government generates income in foreign countries. On the other hand, exports of American wheat, machinery, and airplanes represent demand for domestic products. These components of total spending (both positive and negative) must be compared before we can determine whether the trade sector contributes to or detracts from total expenditures in the United States. When imports exceed exports, total spending declines at home. The opposite occurs when our exports of goods and services exceed our purchases abroad.

In recent years, the United States was a net importer of goods and services to the tune of over \$100 billion per year. This means that Americans collectively spent over \$100 billion more on goods and services produced abroad than foreigners spent on U.S. products. In terms of the Keynesian model, this means that total domestic expenditure on all goods and services was billions of dollars less than it would have been had our exports equaled our imports. This international trade deficit has a number of implications for the U.S. economy, but we postpone a more complete discussion of foreign trade and its effects until Chapters 38 and 39, where both real and financial aspects of international transactions are considered.

Total Expenditures: A Recap

In summary, equilibrium income (and, by implication, the amount of employment hired to produce it) may be determined either by examining total expenditures, $C + I + G + (X - M)$, or by equating leakages to injections, $S + T + M = I + G + X$. Total income, the result of total planned or desired expenditures, can be viewed schematically in Figure 6 as subtractions from or additions to, leakages from or injections to, private consumption expenditures. The net effect of these leakages and injections from private consumption is that a specific level of total spending is determined, which in turn determines a specific level of income. This level of income is produced by some quantity of resources, including labor usage. Total employment or jobs filled is therefore the product of consumer spending modified by leakages and injections.

Countercyclical fiscal policy:
Changes in government expenditures or taxes that are designed to reverse changes in private expenditures or savings that produce unemployment or inflation.

COUNTERCYCLICAL FISCAL POLICIES

Having reached an understanding of how the presence of a government sector influences the economy, we now move the discussion toward a fuller understanding of the Keynesian prescriptions for **countercyclical fiscal policy.** Fiscal policy, as we have already noted, means budget actions: government expendi-

FIGURE 6

Total Planned Expenditures Determine Total Income and Employment

The Keynesian model of total spending can be viewed as a series of injections into and leakages from the flow of income. Savings, taxes, and imports are subtracted from private consumption expenditures; investment, government, and export spending injections are added, yielding total planned or desired expenditures. These expenditures determine an equilibrium income and output, at the level of income at which $S + T + M = I + G + X$.

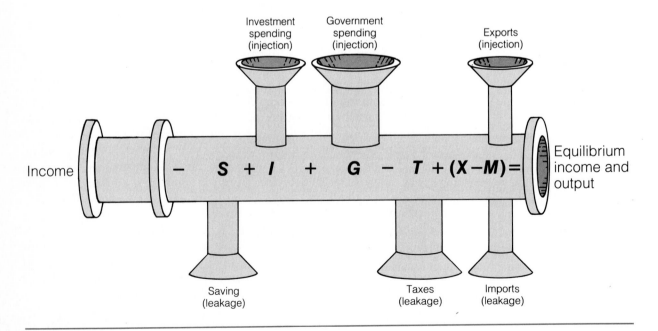

ture changes, tax changes, or a combination of the two. To say that a policy is countercyclical means that the policy seeks to correct whatever phase of the business cycle—contractionary or expansionary—the economy happens to be in. In a recession, for example, total spending, output, and employment are below the full-employment equilibrium level. In such circumstances, counter-cyclical fiscal policy would seek to raise the level of total expenditures to the full-employment level. During inflation, a countercyclical fiscal policy must try to induce a lower level of total spending. But knowing the appropriate direction of budgetary changes does not guarantee that the exact equilibrium target will be achieved. To do that, policy must be guided by knowledge of the relevant expenditure multipliers. Expenditure multipliers play a major role in the following analysis. Any autonomous expenditure is subject to the mul-tiplier process; thus it is possible to identify consumption multipliers, invest-ment multipliers, government spending multipliers, export multipliers, import multipliers, and so on.

Fiscal Policy to Deal with a Recession

To see how fiscal policies are used to change the direction of the business cycle, let us first suppose that the economy is in a recession. Imagine that government economic policy-makers have determined that the actual level of aggregate income-output is $50 billion below the full-employment level. In Figure 7, the government's problem can be seen as that of moving the economy from an income level of $2.50 trillion to one of $2.55 trillion (an increase of $50 billion). What is required in this case is an increase in G or a decrease in T, either of which would lead to an increase in total spending, $C + I + G + (X - M)$. If government simply increases G by $50 billion, it will overshoot

---

FIGURE 7

Government Spending to Eliminate a Contractionary Gap in Income

If total spending, $C_0 + I_0 + G_0 + (X_0 - M_0)$, is not great enough to achieve full employment, then an increase in government expenditures may restore full employment. In this example, initial expenditures, $C_0 + I_0 + G_0 + (X_0 - M_0)$, are insufficient to create a full-employment level of income. Government expenditures are increased to $C_0 + I_0 + G_1 + (X_0 - M_0)$, and, through a multiplier process, the contractionary gap, AB, is eliminated.

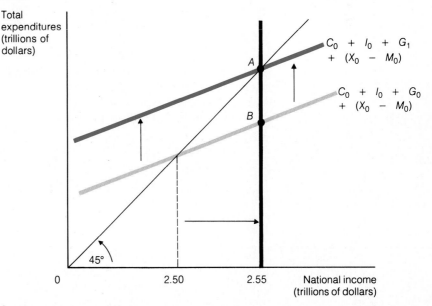

the desired target because the new additional expenditure of $50 billion will be multiplied through various rounds of spending into a much larger increase. What, then, is the appropriate fiscal stimulus?

The answer depends on the size of the contractionary gap, whether households or businesses are the ultimate recipients of government expenditures, and the value of the relevant multiplier. In the following analysis, assume (1) that only households will receive the government expenditures and (2) that *MPC* equals 0.8. We can determine the size of the contractionary gap, *AB*, and design a fiscal policy to eliminate it.

Since we know the value of the *MPC*, we can compute the consumption multiplier (the only relevant multiplier in this case):

$$k = \frac{1}{1 - MPC} = \frac{1}{0.2} = 5.$$

We know the size of the income gap ($50 billion), and we know that whatever increase in government spending occurs will be multiplied by 5. Therefore, we can determine the size of the contractionary gap, *AB*, by the formula

$$\text{Contractionary gap} = \frac{\text{income gap}}{k} = \frac{\$50 \text{ billion}}{5} = \$10 \text{ billion.}$$

In this case, an increase in total expenditures of $10 billion will, via the multiplier, produce an increase in aggregate income of $50 billion, thereby moving the economy to its full-employment equilibrium level.

There are two ways that fiscal policy could produce the additional $10 billion expenditure. The most direct way is to increase government expenditures, *G*, by $10 billion. We assume that this direct injection to the spending stream is not subject to any leakages. Therefore, the full $10 billion enters the expenditure flow at once.

An indirect way to accomplish the same thing is to cut taxes to stimulate consumption spending, as shown in Figure 8. Remember, however, that tax changes do not produce expenditure changes of the same dollar amount because taxes are paid partly at the expense of consumption and partly at the expense of saving. Against a contractionary gap of $10 billion, a lump-sum tax cut of $10 billion will only induce additional consumption of $8 billion ($MPC \times \Delta T$). To raise consumption spending by $10 billion requires in this instance a tax cut of more than $10 billion to offset the leakage of saving that occurs when household disposable income increases. A lump-sum tax cut of $12.5 billion, given that $MPC = 0.8$, would be required to raise aggregate consumption by $10 billion and thereby eliminate the $10 billion contractionary gap.

Government expenditure changes are more direct and more powerful, dollar for dollar, than tax changes of the same amount. This must be kept in mind when expenditures and taxes are changed simultaneously.

Fiscal Policy to Deal with Inflation

Once full employment is reached, further increases in total spending will tend to drive the price level upward, creating an expansionary gap. An expansionary gap develops because raw materials, labor, and inputs of all kinds become increasingly scarce. GNP, the economy's output, can be pushed only so far by excessive spending and only at the cost of causing inflation to accelerate. The

FIGURE 8

If total spending, $C_0 + I_0 + G_0 + (X_0 - M_0)$, is not great enough to achieve full employment, then total expenditures may be increased by a tax cut. In this example, if taxes fall, then consumption increases from C_0 to C_1 to achieve full employment. A tax cut increases the disposable income of consumers, causing them to spend more.

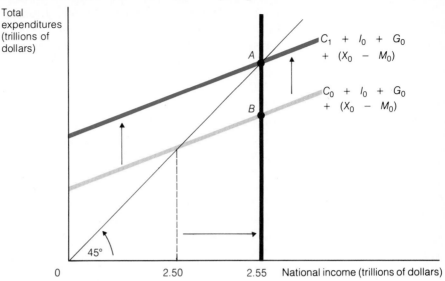

Taxation to Eliminate a Contractionary Gap

reverse of a given policy that works in one phase of the business cycle works for the opposite phase of the cycle. If the economy is characterized by inflation and full (or "overfull") employment, the appropriate fiscal response would be a decrease in government expenditures or an increase in taxes.

An expansionary gap, as discussed earlier, is the difference between the existing level of total spending and the desired level. The trick is to bring the actual level of total expenditure, $C + I + G + (X_0 - M_0)$, in line with the desired full-employment level. As in the case of contractionary gaps, the correction can be achieved in one of two ways: either a change of government expenditures or a change of taxes.

Assume that the economy is operating at a level of nominal output-income too high for full employment. (Since we are talking about the effects of inflation, the concepts of real and nominal come into play.) In what sense could the nominal level of income be too high? "More is better than less" when it comes to economic output, but there are two factors to consider. First, by definition, aggregate real output in the macroeconomy cannot increase after full employment has been reached because the economy is already at a point on the production possibilities frontier. Second, income measures beyond the full-employment level mean that a constant amount of goods and services is valued at higher unit prices, the effect of inflation. When the newspapers say that the economy is "overheating" they mean that a lower level of national income is preferred to the present higher one. Too high a level of total spending produces inflation.

The problem posed by inflation, then, is how to reduce the level of nominal income by some amount, say by $50 billion. With a multiplier of 5, a reduction in spending of one-fifth the observed income gap will produce the desired effect. This result can be achieved by cutting government expenditures by $10 billion, leaving taxes unchanged. Likewise, it can be achieved by leaving government expenditures unchanged and raising lump-sum taxes by $12.5 billion (to reduce the consumption component of aggregate demand by $10 billion). The mechanics of these changes are exactly the reverse of those used in the contractionary-recessionary situation. Changes in taxes or government expenditures therefore composed Keynes's arsenal of methods for counteracting severely contractionary or inflationary swings of the business cycle.

Keynesian Economics in Historical Context

Was Keynes right about the ability of government to use countercyclical fiscal policies to counteract extreme phases of the business cycle? Although the policy and theoretical issues are complex, it is probably the case that certain theoretical and political effects unforeseen by Keynes have inhibited the ability of government to control the business cycle and thereby guarantee continuous inflation-free levels of full employment and maximum economic growth.

Keynes was primarily concerned with the economic and human costs of economic depression (or, if you prefer, an extreme contractionary phase of the business cycle). His advice, though not fully implemented in Western democracies during the Great Depression of the 1930s and early 1940s, was at least partially responsible for the increased economic role of government at the time and, perhaps, for the absence of prolonged and serious depressions after World War II. But problems other than depression became paramount in the U.S. economy of the late 1960s, 1970s, and 1980s—particularly high rates of inflation combined with slowed economic growth. Keynesian economics was not explicitly designed to deal with these problems. Further, U.S. fiscal history since the beginning of the Vietnam War may have contributed greatly to contemporary difficulties. (In this regard, see Focus, "Deficits and Democracy.")

How could actual fiscal policy have caused these problems? The use of Keynesian countercyclical fiscal policy means that balancing government expenditures and receipts—a balanced budget—takes on secondary importance. The cumulative effect of unbalanced budgets is ignored by this approach. As we have seen, antirecessionary fiscal policy requires raising government expenditures or reducing taxes, either of which tends to produce a budget deficit. For reasons that will be explained more fully in Chapter 30, the history of fiscal policy in the United States has been one in which, since World War II, annual deficits have outnumbered annual surpluses by a margin of almost twenty to one, a policy that Keynes probably would not have supported. A deficit implies that government expenditures exceed revenues, further implying the need for creation of money and credit. Credit creation, in turn, has implications in the money markets of the macroeconomy, the most important of which is inflation.

A major deficiency of the income-expenditures model we have employed to this point is that it excludes monetary variables, particularly prices. Therefore, it does not tell all of the macroeconomic story. Prices affect both consumption and investment spending, which in turn affect macroeconomic activity. In other words, simple Keynesian economics leaves us ill-equipped to adequately analyze recent experience with unemployment and inflation. A more complete Keynesian theory of total expenditures, one including prices and other monetary factors, will help us better understand today's macroeconomic problems. This expanded theory will be presented in Chapters 28 and 29.

FOCUS Deficits and Democracy

Deficits occur when government expenditures exceed government income from taxation in any given fiscal year. The national debt is the sum at a certain point in time of all prior deficits. During the 1980s, huge deficits—on the order of $100 billion to $180 billion per year—were incurred by the federal government, which pushed the national debt over $2 *trillion* in 1990. Nondemocratic countries do not appear to experience deficits and debt to this degree.[a] Were these deficits, and the debt they created, the product of overt discretionary action to eliminate contractionary gaps as supported by Keynes or were they simply the products of institutions peculiar to democracy? While Keynes likely would not have supported such deficits, it may be that they are inevitable given the nature of the democratic political process; in other words, there may be an incentive to supply and demand deficits in a democracy.

The right to supply government products of all kinds is temporary, subject to renewal at election time and open to competition (Democrats versus Republicans). Once in office, a politician is confronted with a choice for financing the desired output of the public sector between raising taxes or borrowing funds and creating deficits. Naturally, this choice will be influenced by the preferences of voters, but there may be reasons for supplying deficits that are *independent* of voter choice. The key to understanding politicians' preferences for debt finance is the fact that responsibility for the

physical facilities (roads, buildings, bombers, national parks) owned by the community at large is assigned to politicians only temporarily. These temporary suppliers can issue outstanding claims (debt) without being personally liable for such debts—other than each politician's minimal *pro rata* share of the national debt as a taxpayer. Deficit finance may be preferred because it is less costly than the alternative—the decidedly unpopular tax increase.

Why would some voter-demanders of political products and services reveal a preference for deficit finance? Those who earn little or no income and who receive large net benefits from the government have little incentive to demand restraint from politicians. The taxes required to finance deficits and to fund the government's debt are applied either to human capital or to nonhuman capital. Since taxes fall disproportionately on human capital (in the form of income taxes) in most democracies, including the United States, some voters, especially *older* voters, have an incentive to support deficit finance over direct pay-as-you-go taxation to finance new government expenditures. In effect, these voters are electing to pass part of the burden of financing government expenditures on to succeeding generations of taxpayers.

There are incentives for both politicians and voters to prefer deficits over increased taxes to finance new expenditures. Politicians naturally want to get reelected; voters—some voters at least—would like to pass the bill for present enjoyment on to succeeding generations. Without an effective balanced budget constraint on federal politicians or on the financing process, democracies seem to have a built-in tendency to run deficits.

[a]See W. Mark Crain and Robert B. Ekelund, Jr., "Deficits and Democracy," *Southern Economic Journal* 44 (April 1978), pp. 813–28.

SUMMARY

1. A multiplier is calculated by dividing a change in income by the change in autonomous expenditures that caused the change in income. The multiplier is the reciprocal of the marginal propensity to save, or $1/MPS$.

2. A multiplier may be applied to any change in autonomous expenditures. For example, if the autonomous portion of consumption expenditures increases, income changes by the value of the expenditures multiplied by the reciprocal of the MPS.

3. Fiscal policy consists of budgetary action taken by the central government. More specifically, fiscal policy means congressional action to adjust either the level of taxes or the level of government expenditures to achieve a stable level of growth.

4. An increase in government expenditures, G, is expansionary. A decrease in government expenditures is contractionary.

5. An increase in the level of taxes, T, is contractionary. A decrease in the level of taxes is expansionary. Insofar as tax changes affect private spending only indirectly, a tax change is less effective than the same dollar amount of change in government expenditures.

6. Output effects from changes in G or T are multiplied. Although the value of the consumption multiplier ($1/MPS$) is the same in both cases, the output effects are different because a $1 change in taxes affects consumption less than a $1 change in government expenditures does.

7. Keynes's macroeconomic theory and his remedies for macroeconomic ills, while probably appropriate for periods of contraction and widespread unemployment, omitted crucial monetary variables, especially prices, from primary consideration. A modern and useful theory with a more complete ability to explain inflation and other contemporary macroeconomic problems requires the consideration of such factors.

KEY TERMS

investment multiplier
autonomous consumption multiplier
contractionary gap

expansionary gap
autonomous government expenditures
lump-sum tax

exports
imports
countercyclical fiscal policy

QUESTIONS FOR REVIEW AND DISCUSSION

1. What effect will a $30 billion decrease in autonomous investment have on total expenditures if the MPC is 0.9?
2. What is the essential implication of the investment multiplier? What is multiplied when autonomous investment changes?
3. How does the consumption multiplier differ from the investment multiplier? Will a $50 billion change in autonomous consumption expenditures have the same effect as a $50 billion change in autonomous investment expenditures when the MPS is 0.2?
4. Suppose autonomous consumption expenditures are $50 billion, autonomous investment expenditures are $20 billion, and the MPC is 0.8. What is the equilibrium level of income? What happens to the equilibrium level of income if autonomous consumption falls to $20 billion?
5. Does the full effect of changes in investment occur instantly? How long should it take?

6. What determines the level of investment expenditures? Does the level of investment expenditures determine the level of income or does the level of income determine the level of investment?
7. What was Keynes's basic dispute with the classical economists? What were his recommendations for smoothing out the business cycle?
8. What fiscal policy would Keynes recommend for large-scale unemployment? What would he recommend for inflation?
9. What can government do to offset a leakage from the income-expenditures flow? What can it do to offset an expansionary injection into the flow?
10. What effect does a lump-sum tax of $20 billion have on total expenditures if the MPC is 0.9? Would it have a greater effect if the MPC were 0.8?
11. Does an increase in government expenditures of $20 billion have the same effect on total expenditures as a $20 billion tax cut? Why?

PROBLEM

Suppose that total expenditures are $250 billion short of the full-employment level of income and that MPC = 0.7. In the Keynesian framework, by how much would government expenditures have to increase to bring the economy to full employment?

ECONOMICS IN ACTION
Should Congress Be Forced to Balance the Budget?

There is much grass-roots support for a constitutional amendment to balance the budget. Since 1977, thirty-two states (two short of the required number) have called for a constitutional convention to consider such an amendment.

In August 1982, the Senate approved the amendment by a vote of 69–31 with all senators present, but it was rejected in the House, 236–187, only 46 votes short of the two-thirds majority needed to amend the Constitution. In 1986, a Senate balanced-budget resolution came within one vote of passage (66–34). However, not until the summer of 1990 did the matter again reach the floor of either chamber for a vote.

In July 1990, the House rejected a balanced-budget amendment 271–150, seven votes short of approval. The House did approve a balanced-budget statute, which would require the president and the House and Senate budget committees to at least *present* a balanced budget every year (they could present unbalanced budgets as well). Support for a constitutional amendment persists, however, fueled by frustration and anxiety over Congress' seeming inability to do anything about budget deficits. What would be the economic effects of such an amendment? Consider the diverse views of three economists, all past members of the Council of Economic Advisers.[a]

William A. Niskanen, member of President Ronald Reagan's council, defends a constitutional amendment as appropriate and workable. It is appropriate, in Niskanen's view, as simply another economic rule like those already enshrined in the Constitution regarding property rights. A balanced budget rule is defensible, moreover, to help prevent the economic excesses of deficits and deficit finance. Niskanen argues that a constitutional amendment would not necessarily lead to a total abandonment of countercyclical fiscal policy by Congress; a supermajority in Congress could override the balanced budget in certain economic conditions, but violation of the balanced budget rule would require broad support in Congress. As Niskanen has argued: "Fiscal rules . . . are like a dam or like a fence—they can be valuable even if they have some openings."

James V. Tobin, Yale University professor and 1981 Nobel laureate in economics who served on President John F. Kennedy's Council of Economic Advisers, argues against the proposed amendment. How, asks Tobin, could the mid-1980s yearly budget deficits of approximately $200 billion be corrected without creating another Great Depression? Aside from the immediate problem of eliminating big contemporary deficits, Tobin believes that the amendment would actually increase economic instability. Escape valves to a strictly balanced budget would be open, but delays could be caused by minorities in Congress, which could be very costly for the economy. Tax receipts fall during business cycle contractions as incomes fall, and they rise during expansions as incomes rise, creating built-in stabilization in the economy. These stabilizers would tend to become ineffective over the business cycle, as deficits or surpluses would force Congress to enact procyclical spending and taxing policies. Def-

icits and surpluses, in other words, are themselves affected by business cycles. Tobin, in sum, thinks that abandonment of discretion in the use of fiscal policy would eliminate the insurance that has guarded the economy against depressions since the end of World War II.

Hendrik S. Houthakker, Harvard professor and economic adviser to President Richard M. Nixon, agrees with Tobin that a balanced budget amendment would be useless in view of the size of present deficits, but he argues that deficits must be harnessed. To Houthakker, broad-based public support for an amendment is merely an indication that the public is disenchanted with fiscal policy as it has been conducted over the past twenty-five years. Constant stimulus of the economy—witnessed by only one budget surplus (in 1969) in the previous twenty-eight years—has been self-defeating. Like overprescribed antibiotics, deficits will not work now when we really need them. As Houthakker says: "We have tried to prime the pump even when it was already working overtime."

The problem, in Houthakker's view, is that the federal budget does not follow sound budgetary principles. For one thing, it makes no distinctions between capital and current budgets. For example, on the assumption that bridges and highways will last forever, no provisions have been made for maintenance of the nation's capital stock. Budget reform is needed with respect to both revenues and expenditures. Both Social Security and Great Society income transfers and entitlements have grown dramatically without adequate provisions for financing. Fiscal reform, in other words, must take place before any sort of constitutional amendment could be successfully implemented.

In essence, economists are not in agreement as to the desirability of a balanced budget amendment or with respect to how such an amendment would affect the macroeconomy. Some are in favor of effective legal constraints, rules that allow little or no legislative or executive discretion concerning spending or taxes. One such rule was the Gramm-Rudman-Hollings Deficit Reduction Act, which attempted to force the Congress and the president to reduce the federal budget deficit. Others argue that these strict rules on spending and taxation will, by reducing the flexibility of policymakers to respond to changing economic conditions, impede the attainment of the macroeconomic goals of full employment and stable prices.

Question

Would the passage of a balanced budget amendment likely lead to a smaller total size of the federal budget? Would politicians, in other words, be apt to find less support if they voted for policies and programs that must be immediately financed through taxation?

[a]These views are reported in "At Issue: The Balanced Budget Amendment," *Fiscal Policy Forum* (Washington, D.C.: Tax Foundation, January 1983).

28

Aggregate Demand and Aggregate Supply

After World War II, a moderate inflation rate held off a doubling of the price level for twenty-five years. Less than ten years later, the price level doubled again. Since 1981, the acceleration of the inflation rate has slowed, but many economists believe there is a prospect of double-digit inflation in the future. By international standards, the United States has an enviable record of avoiding inflation. Peru, Mexico, Brazil, and Israel have experienced annual inflation rates in excess of 100 percent in recent years. In each case, runaway inflation has devastated the country's economy. Such experiences should teach us the importance of avoiding economic policies that lead to excessive inflation.

When we began our discussion of macroeconomics in Chapter 23, we included price stability in our list of primary macroeconomic goals. (The other two were full employment and economic growth.) Subsequent chapters developed a model that explained how the level of national income was determined. This model was used to explain unemployment and inadequate economic growth. However, in that model the price level remained unchanged; the model did not address the problems of inflation and deflation. This chapter develops a model of aggregate demand and aggregate supply in which the interaction of these two forces determines both the level of national income and the price level. We will show how shifts either in aggregate demand or in aggregate supply can cause inflation or deflation. After you complete Chapter 28 you should understand

- how price level changes cause changes in total real expenditures by consumers and businesses.
- how the aggregate demand curve relates national income and output to price level changes.
- how the aggregate supply curve is constructed and how its shape is determined by production and capacity levels.
- how shifts in aggregate demand and supply affect output and price levels.

PRICE CHANGES AND AGGREGATE DEMAND

We have defined the function $C + I + G + (X - M)$ as total expenditures. But an important distinction must be made between total expenditures and aggregate demand once the price level is explicitly recognized. The term *aggregate demand* refers to the relation between the price level of all output and the total quantity of all goods and services demanded. In other words, from here on, as we discuss contractionary and expansionary phases in the economy and proper macroeconomic policies to remedy such phases, we will be tying total real expenditures to a specific price level, a composite index of all prices in the economy. We will then vary the price level to see how such changes affect equilibrium output or income, since price level changes will affect total real expenditures.

The simple Keynesian model we have used up to this point assumes, correctly, that total expenditures are a function of national income. But it is also true that the price of something affects the amount that people choose to buy, so expenditures are determined by prices in addition to income. The factors affecting demand and supply for some particular good—textiles, Wendy's hamburgers—and the aggregate demand and supply for *all goods* are analogous. Both individual demand and aggregate demand are inversely related to price; both curves, therefore, are downward-sloping. In dealing with aggregate demand, however, we consider the effects of a declining price *level* on the aggregate demand, where each price level is associated with a different possible equilibrium of total expenditures and income. In contrast, the market for hamburgers shows how supply and demand interact to produce one possible equilibrium price and quantity in the hamburger market (see Chapter 4). Aggregate demand, as we will see in this chapter, is a locus of different points of equilibrium associated with different price levels. Aggregate supply of all goods and services produced in the economy is also shown as a function of the price level. Just as the interaction of supply and demand for hamburgers gives the equilibrium price and quantity of hamburgers, the interaction of aggregate demand and supply determines a unique price level and equilibrium quantity of *all* goods and services produced in the economy.

Price Changes and Changes in Purchasing Power

Chapter 23 defined the difference between nominal, or money, income—the income we receive in dollar terms—and real income—the purchasing power of those dollars. In times of inflation, nominal incomes may increase, yet real incomes may remain the same or even fall. Since inflation erodes the purchasing power of each dollar received, real income, or income adjusted for changes in the price level, is a more accurate measure of how the economy is performing.

Inflation affects more than income, unfortunately. It also affects wealth. The term *income* is usually taken to mean the sum of weekly, monthly, or annual earnings. **Wealth,** on the other hand, is the sum of all assets. Income is a flow variable; wealth is a stock variable. Flow variables are measured per unit of time. Speed, for example, is a flow variable—it is measured in feet per second

Wealth:
The total value of monetary plus nonmonetary assets in existence at a point in time; a stock variable.

or miles per hour. By contrast, weight is an example of a stock variable; it is defined independently of time. It is meaningful to say that someone weighs one hundred pounds without making any reference to time.

Wealth may be pecuniary (dollar-denominated, such as a savings account) or nonpecuniary (non-dollar-denominated, such as a house, auto, or Persian rug). The distinction between pecuniary and nonpecuniary wealth is important because the value of each type of wealth is affected differently by changes in the price level. Compare a $10,000 Persian rug with a $10,000 deposit in a savings account. When the price level doubles under 100 percent inflation, what happens to the real value of these two kinds of wealth? Dollar-denominated assets such as the $10,000 deposit in a savings account or a bond with a face value of $10,000 have a fixed dollar value. With a 100 percent increase in the price level, the value of a dollar-denominated asset has been cut in half, in terms of purchasing power. However, the higher price level implies that the nominal value of all non-dollar-denominated assets, including the Persian rug, has increased, assuming that prices of collectibles keep pace with the general price level. But the rug is still a rug: In real terms it is worth as much as it was before. It would now fetch $20,000 in the marketplace instead of $10,000, but the higher dollar amount would merely purchase the same amount of goods and services as $10,000 would have previously. In other words, the real value of many nonpecuniary assets (real estate, paintings, jewels) is unaffected by changes in the price level.[1]

Now contemplate the unfortunate effects of the same degree of inflation on the $10,000 savings deposit. Except in the unlikely case that the interest rate has kept pace with the 100 percent rate of inflation, the real value of the deposit will have declined. Assuming *no* interest return, the same $10,000 that would have purchased $10,000 worth of goods and services before inflation will purchase only $5,000 worth of goods and services now. In other words, price level changes bring about changes in the real value, or purchasing power, of pecuniary assets.

The Real Balance Effect

As inflation erodes the purchasing power of the money in our bank accounts and of our holdings of other dollar-denominated assets, we have to economize—buy fewer books, try to keep the old car running instead of buying an expensive new one. This change in consumption behavior that results from a change in the price level is sometimes called the **real balance effect.**

Real balance effect:
The effect on investment and consumption spending of a change in the price level that alters the real value of pecuniary assets.

If we let *MS* stand for society's entire stock of pecuniary, or dollar-denominated, assets and *P* for the aggregate price level, then the value of real balances can be expressed as *MS/P*. The level of real household consumption expenditures will be determined by the value of real balances as well as by the level of disposable income.

The relation between consumption and real money balances is positive, just as the relation between consumption and income is positive. If prices fall,

---

[1]The real value of nonmonetary assets can change. The belief, for example, that the purchase of Persian rugs would protect investors from inflation might mean brisk real demand increases. If the prices of Persian rugs were rising faster than the inflation rate, their real value would be increasing. Their increased real value would mean that they could be sold to purchase more goods and services than they did before the inflation.

assuming that MS remains the same, the value of real balances rises and consumers experience an enhanced wealth effect; that is, their money assets will purchase more goods and services than before. Thus, consumption will rise in response to greater real wealth. Graphically, the consumption function will shift upward, establishing a higher equilibrium level of output and employment. Conversely, if prices rise, the value of real balances declines, the consumption curve subsequently falls, and lower output and employment result. Changes in real balances are capable of inducing the same kinds of changes in total expenditures as fiscal policy manipulations (ΔG and ΔT).

We have already encountered this important concept. Recall that classical economists before Keynes generally believed that wage-price flexibility would automatically bring about total expenditure changes that would correct the cyclical swings of the macroeconomy. The logic behind this self-correcting view was as follows: If the economy slides into a recession and unemployment occurs, labor markets will be faced with an excess supply of workers. In competitive labor markets, this excess of workers will create downward pressure on wages. As wages fall, so will the unit costs of production; prices will therefore decline as well. The general decline in prices will sooner or later raise the real value of money balances, thus inducing consumers to spend more. The increased spending will thereby stimulate output and employment, lifting the economy out of the recession. In a similar fashion, the presence of inflation will eventually lead to a reduction in real balances and a consequent decline in total spending, thereby eliminating the inflationary tendencies. For the classical economists, the real balance effect on consumption helped explain the self-adjusting nature of the economy.

This important process can be fixed more precisely in graphical terms. In Figure 1, three total spending functions are shown for three alternative price levels. Given some price level P_0 and some constant level of pecuniary assets in the economy, real balances will produce some level of consumption, C_0. Consumption function C_0 and given levels of investment, government, and net foreign expenditures, I, G, $(X - M)$, produce an equilibrium level of real income Y_0.

What happens in the event of a price decline? A price reduction will increase the real value of pecuniary balances, causing an increase in the consumption component of total spending. In Figure 1, the original total spending function shifts upward to $C_1 + I + G + (X - M)$ at the new, lower price level. This new, higher total expenditures function is associated with a higher level of equilibrium income, Y_1. By the same reasoning, a rise in the price level above the initial level brings a reduction in equilibrium income to Y_2.

The Interest Rate Effect

We have seen that changes in the price level affect the purchasing power of our pecuniary assets and equilibrium income. Price level changes also affect income through the mechanism of interest rates.

Interest rates are always in the news. Consumers are highly interested in whether interest rates are high or low, rising or falling. Interest rates to some extent determine purchasing decisions—whether to buy a new car or to mortgage the purchase of a new home. Businesses are also very watchful of interest rate levels when deciding whether to make capital investments—build a warehouse, acquire new machinery, expand their inventories.

FIGURE 1

How Price Level Changes Alter Consumption Spending and Real Income

Any change in the price level from the initial level, P_0, will create a real balance effect on consumption, shifting the total spending curve upward or downward. A lower price level, P_1, is associated with a higher level of equilibrium real income, Y_1, and the total spending curve shifts upward to $C_1 + I + G + (X - M)$. A price level P_2 higher than the initial price level would, for similar reasons, be associated with a lower level of equilibrium income, Y_2, and a spending curve that shifts downward to $C_2 + I + G + (X - M)$.

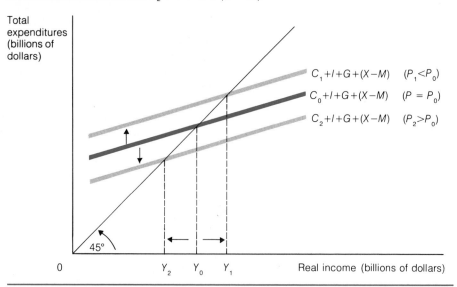

In general, interest rates depend on changes in the price level. When the price level rises, interest rates tend to rise; when the price level falls, interest rates tend to fall. As with all other goods, individuals will want to hold equilibrium quantities of real money—balances for transactions, for investments, or simply as a precautionary ("rainy day") measure. In other words, people are interested in the real value, or purchasing power, of their money balances, not in their nominal holdings of money. The value of dollar-denominated assets is inversely related to the price level, since these assets are fixed in money terms. The real supply of money is also altered by price level changes. The purchasing power of each dollar we hold rises when the price level falls and declines when the price level rises. In part, interest rates are the product of the demand for real money balances and their supply in real terms. Thus, as the real supply of these balances increases with reductions in the price level, the interest rate tends to fall. And, as the real supply of money balances declines with increases in the price level, the interest rate tends to rise. The details of this process are discussed in Chapter 34; at this point it is important to recognize that these interest rate changes affect the investment and consumption components of expenditures.

Figure 2 shows the effect of changes in the price level on interest rates. Investors react to these changes because the interest rate change alters the cost and profitability of investment projects; consumers react by changing expenditure plans, especially for durable goods (such as refrigerators) or homes. These changes in expenditures in turn cause changes in income and employ-

FIGURE 2

A rise in the price level may be related to a decrease in real income and employment via the process of investment and consumption spending. Conversely, a fall in the price level can lead to an increase in income. The lower half of the diagram shows that declines in the price level tend to lower the interest rate and expand investment and consumption expenditures. Increased production and jobs result.

The Interest Rate Effect

Interest rate effect:
The effect on investment spending that results from a change in the interest rate produced by a change in the price level.

ment. As prices rise (and the value of real money balances falls), output and real income decline; as prices fall, output and real income increase.

The **interest rate effect** can be viewed in the income-expenditures model depicted in Figure 3. With the price at some initial level, P_0, total expenditures equal $C + I_0 + G + (X - M)$. A decrease in the aggregate price level to P_1 will lower interest rates. Other things being equal, lower interest rates will lower the cost of all new investment projects. The consequent effect in the total expenditures model is to raise the investment function, thus stimulating the economy to a higher level of output and employment, Y_1.

Conversely, higher aggregate price levels tend to drive up interest rates. Now all new investment projects will be more costly than before, so a decline

FIGURE 3

Decreases in the price level from P_0 to P_1 lower interest rates and increase investment from I_0 to I_1. The higher level of investment increases real income from Y_0 to Y_1. Increases in the price level to P_2 increase interest rates and decrease investment to I_2 and income to Y_2.

The Price Level and Investment Spending

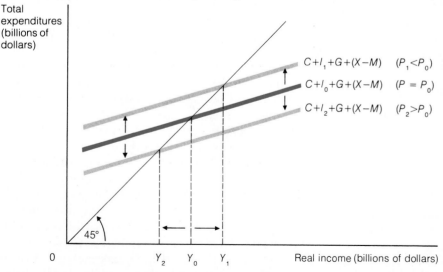

in the investment schedule can be predicted. In Figure 3, the total expenditure schedule will shift downward to $C + I_2 + G + (X - M)$ and establish a lower level of national income at Y_2.

To summarize, changes in the aggregate price level are likely to affect aggregate consumption (the real balance effect and the interest rate effect) and aggregate investment (the interest rate effect). The macroeconomy, viewed realistically, is a complex structure of relations in which the level of total expenditures is determined by the aggregate levels of income, wealth, and prices.

AGGREGATE DEMAND

Aggregate demand curve: Graphical relation showing the different levels of national income that exist at different price levels.

In Chapter 4, we saw that all demand functions relating prices and quantity demanded are downward-sloping. This also applies to the **aggregate demand curve,** which captures the relation between the aggregate price level and real national income. The aggregate demand curve basically tells us that as the price level falls in the macroeconomy, other things being equal, households and businesses tend to buy more. Conversely, as the price level rises, other things being equal, households and businesses tend to decrease their spending. Again, a contrast between microeconomic supply and demand relations and the macroeconomic concepts is instructive. Recall from Chapter 4 that the demand curve for a particular good or service slopes downward because a price decrease for some good—say, football tickets—alters its *relative* price compared to all other goods. A lower relative price causes the student to substitute football tickets for all other goods in her budget; this substitution explains the negative slope of the demand curve. The negative slope of aggregate demand in macroeconomic theory does not depend on changes in relative prices but on changes in the price level—a relation that can be shown with the Keynesian income-expenditures model.

Deriving the Aggregate Demand Curve

Examine Figure 4, assuming that the macroeconomy is in equilibrium at Y_0. The $C_0 + I_0 + G + (X - M)$ curve in Figure 4a is constructed for a given price level, P_0 in Figure 4b. Starting from this point, we can hypothetically vary the price level up and down in Figure 4b, observing the corresponding income level produced. Matching pairs of P and Y will trace out the aggregate demand curve. For example, assume the price level falls from P_0 to P_1. The effect of this price decline will be to raise household consumption (the real balance effect) and to raise business investment (the interest rate effect). Thus, total expenditures will shift upward, establishing a higher income level at Y_1. A lower price level, P_1, therefore, matches a higher level of real income, Y_1. This matched pair of variables is plotted in Figure 4b as point F.

We can continue the conceptual experiment by raising the price level from P_0 to P_2. Inflation causes the consumption function to shift downward (the interest rate effect), moving the equilibrium income to Y_2. The combination (P_2, Y_2) is shown in Figure 4b as point B. The aggregate demand curve (AD) is the locus of all points generated in the manner of points B, A, F. The curve is downward-sloping, as stated at the beginning of this section.

FIGURE 4

A decrease in the price level from P_0 to P_1 creates an increase in consumption and investment spending. (a) A decrease from P_0 to P_1 increases real income from Y_0 to Y_1. Increases in the price level decrease C and I, so real income falls from Y_0 to Y_2. (b) The price and income combinations trace out the aggregate demand curve: Greater quantities of goods and services are demanded at lower prices.

Derivation of Aggregate Demand from Total Expenditures

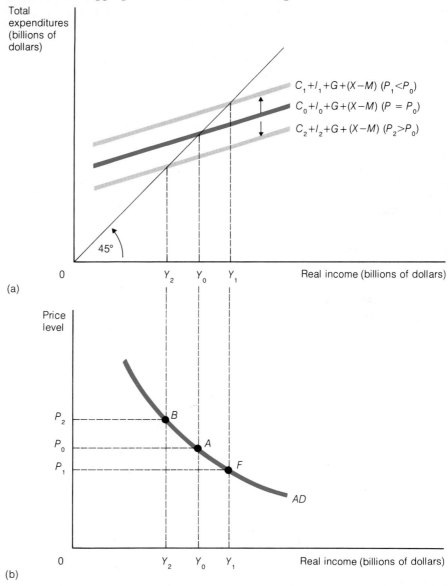

(a)

(b)

The Shape of the Aggregate Demand Curve

Both the real balance effect and the interest rate effect cause the level of aggregate demand to increase as the price level falls and to decrease as the price level rises. The shape of the aggregate demand curve depends on the magnitude of the two effects. If in Figure 4 a price level reduction from P_0 to P_1 causes a large increase in consumer wealth (perhaps because consumers have large holdings of dollar-denominated stocks), the total spending function will shift upward by a large amount. This in turn will result in a level of aggregate demand much greater at price level P_1 than at P_0. Accordingly, income level Y_1 will lie far to the right of Y_0, causing the aggregate demand curve to be flat. On the other hand, if consumers have few dollar-denominated assets, a fall in the price level will have little effect on total spending and the aggregate demand curve will be steep. In a similar fashion, the stronger the interest rate effect, the more elastic the aggregate demand curve.

The shape of the aggregate demand curve is important. With flat aggregate demand curves, shifts in aggregate supply will primarily affect the level of output, having little impact on the equilibrium price level. With steep aggregate demand curves, a shift in aggregate supply will have a large impact on price level but little impact on production level.

Shifts in the Aggregate Demand Curve

In tracing out the relation between the aggregate price level and the aggregate level of income, certain variables other than price are assumed constant. These constants are numerous. They involve all of those things that shift the demand function either rightward or leftward. The following list of factors capable of shifting aggregate demand is representative but not exhaustive.

household consumption (C): autonomous component
business investment (I): autonomous component
government expenditures (G)
saving (S): autonomous component
net exports ($X - M$)
the money stock (MS)
taxes (T)

A change in any of these factors will result in a different level of national income at the same level of prices. Graphically, a change in any of these factors will create a rightward or leftward shift in the aggregate demand function. Table 1 summarizes the effects on aggregate demand for each change listed, and Figure 5 shows the shifts graphically.

To test our understanding of the principles involved, assume some change in total expenditures, such as an increase in the net export balance. Spending increases at every price level, creating higher real income for every possible price level. In Figure 5, the aggregate demand curve shifts to the right from

---

TABLE 1

Shifts in the Aggregate Demand Function

A change in any of the listed variables will shift the aggregate demand function rightward or leftward, depending on whether the variable increases ($\uparrow$) or decreases ($\downarrow$).

Rightward Shift	Leftward Shift
Autonomous consumption $\uparrow$	Autonomous consumption $\downarrow$
Autonomous investment $\uparrow$	Autonomous investment $\downarrow$
Government expenditures $\uparrow$	Government expenditures $\downarrow$
Net exports ($X - M$) $\uparrow$	Net exports ($X - M$) $\downarrow$
The money supply $\uparrow$	The money supply $\downarrow$
Saving $\downarrow$	Saving $\uparrow$
Taxes $\downarrow$	Taxes $\uparrow$

FIGURE 5

Any change in a nonprice factor affecting total expenditures will shift the aggregate demand curve rightward or leftward. An increase in savings, for example, will reduce total expenditures and aggregate demand at each price level, causing a leftward shift from AD_0 to AD_2. A decrease in taxes or an increase in government expenditures will shift the curve rightward from AD_0 to AD_1, reflecting greater spending on goods and services at every price level.

Shifts in Aggregate Demand

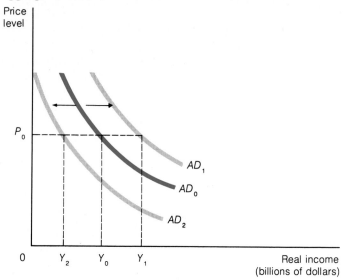

AD_0 to AD_1, illustrating that the real income at each price level increases. The same effect would occur with an increase in consumption (a reduction in saving), investment expenditures, or government expenditures.

Leftward shifts in the aggregate demand curve are likewise caused by both private-sector and government-controlled factors. Reductions in consumption (increases in saving), investment, or net exports would cause a leftward shift in the aggregate demand curve, from AD_0 to AD_2 in Figure 5, for example. An increase in taxes or a reduction in government spending would also shift the function leftward. These shifts occur due to a reduction in spending at every possible price level, meaning that the level of real income associated with any given price level falls.

As we have seen, many economic variables are capable of altering aggregate demand in the macroeconomy, thereby also altering the equilibrium levels of output, income, and employment. Some of these variables—such as household consumption and business investment—are determined by millions of decentralized, individual decisions. Others are determined by highly centralized government directives—decisions such as the appropriate level of government expenditures and taxes and the money supply. Among the latter set are various policy actions to combat the ups and downs of the business cycle.

The point of discretionary budget policies—manipulating taxes or government spending—is to stimulate the economy during periods of economic contraction and unemployment and to cool down the economy during periods of rapid expansion and inflation. Such efforts by the government to steer the economy are known as **discretionary fiscal policies.**

Discretionary fiscal policies: Government policy actions that attempt to influence aggregate demand.

Before we can discuss the possible effects of fiscal policy on aggregate demand, however, we must look at aggregate supply, the other major force determining the quantity of goods and services produced in the economy. We cannot determine the actual quantity of output produced through demand factors alone; we must also know what all businesses in the economy are willing to produce at alternative price levels.

AGGREGATE SUPPLY

Although higher price levels reduce the level of aggregate demand, they tend to have the opposite effect on aggregate supply. When producers receive higher prices for output, their profits rise, giving them an incentive to increase production. Furthermore, when producers attempt to increase production levels, they use existing resources more intensively, which drives up production costs. Producers are forced to charge higher prices to recover increased costs. The **aggregate supply curve** traces the relation between the price level and the aggregate level of production. A typical aggregate supply curve is shown in Figure 6.

Aggregate supply curve: A graph showing the different levels of aggregate output produced at different price levels.

The Shape of the Aggregate Supply Curve

The shape of the aggregate supply curve depends on the state of the economy. When the economy is operating far below capacity with large quantities of unemployed resources, production can be increased without having much effect on input prices. Not only is it possible to employ workers of nearly all

---

FIGURE 6

The Aggregate Supply Curve

The aggregate supply curve, *AS,* shows the relation between real output, measured on the horizontal axis, and price level, measured on the vertical axis. The slope of the aggregate supply curve depends on economic conditions. The horizontal portion of the curve, called the Keynesian range, represents supply during times of severe unemployment and resource underutilization. In this range, any increase in output will not be accompanied by an increase in the price level. The upward-sloping portion of the curve, termed the intermediate range, represents supply under normal or near normal conditions. The economy has not reached its production possibilities frontier (represented by Y_F, full employment), but neither is it depressed. In this range, any real increase in output will be accompanied by higher price levels. The vertical portion of the curve, labeled the classical range, represents the economy at full employment. Output cannot increase and supply is perfectly inelastic in relation to the price level.

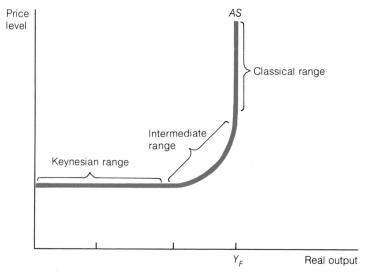

types, but productive inputs such as land and machinery are also readily available. This means that firms can hire more inputs without having to compete for them and that output can be expanded without much increase in average production costs. Therefore, small increases in the price level will lead to large increases in the level of production. This portion of the aggregate supply curve in Figure 6 is called the **Keynesian range,** reflecting Keynes's attention to large-scale unemployment in an economy.

When the economy is producing fairly close to capacity, the aggregate supply curve will be much steeper, as depicted in the **intermediate range** in Figure 6. In this range, attempts to increase production lead to shortages of certain inputs. Average production costs will rise, as firms are forced to pay more for scarce inputs. While it is possible to expand production, additional output can only be obtained at substantially higher price levels.

In the **classical range**—named for the classical economists, who described a full-employment economy—resources are fully employed and the economy is producing at some point on the production possibilities frontier. Since all available resources are employed, an individual producer can expand production only by bidding resources away from competing producers. The effect is to drive the price level up without increasing overall production. In this range, the aggregate supply curve becomes vertical.

Shifts in the Aggregate Supply Curve

In drawing an aggregate supply curve, certain variables other than price level are held constant. Should any of these variables change, the entire aggregate supply curve will shift. A complete list of variables that *might* cause aggregate supply to shift would be lengthy, but a relatively small number of variables have the greatest impact on aggregate supply—in particular, productive resource supply, technology, tax rates, and freedom to respond to economic incentives.

Resource supply often affects aggregate supply in obvious ways. For example, the discovery of new energy resources will cause energy prices to fall and productive capacity to rise; at all price levels, firms will have an economic incentive to increase output. Increases in resource availability, then, shift the aggregate supply curve to the right; decreases will cause a leftward shift. Let's consider a less obvious example—the recent criticism of the educational system in the United States and the many proposals for educational reform. Proponents of reform argue that improved education is necessary for the country to remain competitive in world markets. In terms of aggregate demand and supply, this proposal is an economic policy to increase the stock of human capital and, therefore, aggregate supply. (For an analysis of the effects of a decrease in the supply of a particular resource, see Focus, "Aggregate Supply Shifts: OPEC in the 1970s and 1980s.")

An improvement in technology affects aggregate supply in a way similar to an increase in resource availability. It also reduces production costs and increases the economy's capacity, shifting the aggregate supply curve to the right.

To understand how a change in tax rates affects the aggregate supply curve, keep in mind that in a free society aggregate supply is determined by the willingness of producers to produce, not just by the ability to produce. With high marginal tax rates, producers must pay a substantial portion of

Keynesian range:
A horizontal segment of the aggregate supply curve; shows that output can increase with no change in the price level because of some unemployment of resources.

Intermediate range:
A positively sloped segment of the aggregate supply curve; indicates that aggregate output and the price level will both change in the same direction.

Classical range:
A vertical segment of the aggregate supply curve; indicates that attempts to increase aggregate output will result only in a higher price level, since resources are fully employed.

FOCUS   Aggregate Supply Shifts: OPEC in the 1970s and 1980s

When the supply of any resource or the level of technology changes, the production possibilities of the economy expand and the aggregate supply curve shifts. In effect, for any given level of labor employment, more or less output can be produced. Supplies of resources can change for a variety of reasons. For example, the reduction in oil supplies imposed by the Organization of Petroleum Exporting Countries (OPEC) in the 1970s decreased the amount of oil available for the production of goods and services in the United States. Labor and other productive factors suddenly had less energy to work with, indicating that the productive effects of labor and other resources were lower, which in turn reduced the demand for labor. OPEC's action thus caused a "supply shock"—an unexpected, once-and-for-all leftward shift in aggregate supply, as illustrated in Figure 7.

A shift in aggregate supply from AS_0 to AS_1 in Figure 7, given a stable aggregate demand curve AD_0, meant that the price level rose permanently and output and employment declined. The emergence of the OPEC cartel contributed to the inflationary and recessionary pressures observed in the United States and in the world economy over the 1970s.

The 1980s witnessed a reversal of the OPEC supply shocks of the 1970s. Owing partially to price cutting by OPEC members and an inability to maintain and police output restrictions, the cartel lost much of its power. As a result, there was an increased availability of oil at lower prices to United States producers and consumers, as represented by the rightward shift in aggregate supply to AS_2 in Figure 7. To the extent that the formation of OPEC contributed to the inflationary and recessionary trends of the 1970s, its partial dissolution fostered lower inflation rates and higher output levels in the 1980s. The economy may respond to supply shocks by developing alternative resources. Part of the rightward shift to AS_2 has been due to the adaptation of production to the initial supply shock. New resource development,

FIGURE 7
Reduced Availability of Oil Shifts Aggregate Supply Leftward

The reduction in oil supplies in the early 1970s diminished the productive capacities of the United States with a supply shock, a sudden leftward shift in the aggregate supply curve. The effects were an increase in the price level from P_0 to P_1 and a reduction in real income and output from Y_0 to Y_1.

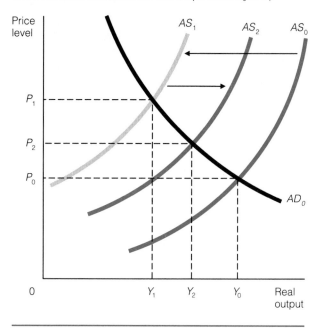

such as solar energy, and alternative production techniques also reduced the impact of the initial OPEC-induced supply shock.

their incomes in the form of taxes, and this reduces the incentive to produce. Workers in high tax brackets may chose to work shorter hours or retire earlier. Reductions in tax rates remove disincentives to work and shift the aggregate supply rightward. Similarly, many economists believe that certain governmental regulations form a barrier between individuals and the business activities in which they have economic incentives to engage. For instance, a teenager may see an opportunity to use his car as a taxi during rush hours, but he is prohibited from doing so because a government license is necessary. Removal of such regulation would increase the incentive to produce and cause aggregate supply to shift to the right. Much of the deregulation policy initiated during the Carter and Reagan administrations attempted to increase aggregate supply by reducing government red tape and, in Reagan's case, taxes.

THE EQUILIBRIUM LEVEL OF PRICES AND PRODUCTION

Since both the aggregate demand curve and the aggregate supply curve are plotted with real output on the horizontal axis and the price level on the vertical axis, both curves can be plotted on the same graph. In Figure 8, we see that AD_0 and AS_0 intersect at price level P_0 and output level Y_0. At any price level above P_0, the quantity of goods producers are willing to supply will exceed the quantity demanded by households, business firms, and so on. The excess demand for goods will cause prices to fall and drive the price level down to the equilibrium level, P_0. Aggregate demand and aggregate supply jointly determine the level of prices and output. Furthermore, any change in the equilibrium price level or output level can be viewed as being caused by a shift in either aggregate demand or supply. If, in Figure 8, the aggregate demand curve were to shift to AD_1 because of a change in one of the variables affecting aggregate demand, both the price level and the level of production would increase—to P_1 and Y_1, respectively. Had the aggregate supply curve been in the Keynesian range, output would have risen with little effect on the price level. The same increase in aggregate demand would have led to inflation but no increase in real output if aggregate supply had been in the classical range.

As depicted in Figure 8, an increase in aggregate supply would lead to an increase in equilibrium output and a decrease in the equilibrium price level. Decreases in aggregate supply have the opposite effects. Chapter 29 discusses specific government policies designed to shift either the aggregate demand curve or the aggregate supply curve.

FIGURE 8

With aggregate supply AS_0 and aggregate demand AD_0, the equilibrium price level will be P_0 and the equilibrium level of output will be Y_0. A change in any of the variables affecting aggregate demand that leads to increased aggregate demand shifts the curve rightward—in this case, to AD_1. This increase in aggregate demand increases the equilibrium price level to P_1 and raises the equilibrium level of real output to Y_1.

Equilibrium Price and Output Levels

SUMMARY

1. The simple income-expenditures model is limited because it ignores monetary variables and price changes. These factors have become increasingly important since the late 1960s owing to inflation.
2. Price level changes affect household consumption by changing the real value of money balances held by consumers. This real balance effect means that price increases will decrease consumption spending and that price decreases will increase consumption spending. These spending changes affect the level of real income and employment, meaning that price changes may be related to the aggregate demand for output.
3. Price changes also alter business investment expenditures via the mechanism of interest rates. Investment spending will increase with declines in interest rates and decrease with increases in interest rates. The interest rate effect means that real income and employment are negatively related to prices through investment spending.
4. The aggregate demand function relates national income and output to changes in the price level; it is a downward-sloping function, like the demand curves discussed in Chapter 4.
5. Changes in both private and public nonprice variables (autonomous consumption, imports, government spending, taxation) cause the aggregate demand curve to shift rightward or leftward.
6. The aggregate supply curve relates the production of goods and services to the price level. It is a positively sloped function because higher prices increase the incentive to produce goods.
7. The shape of the aggregate supply curve depends on the level of production. At production levels that are low relative to capacity, the aggregate supply curve will be flat; its slope will increase until it becomes vertical as the production level reaches capacity.
8. The interaction of aggregate demand and aggregate supply determines the equilibrium level of output and the equilibrium price level, much like demand and supply for a particular good determine its equilibrium price and quantity.

KEY TERMS

wealth	discretionary fiscal policies	classical range
real balance effect	aggregate supply curve	
interest rate effect	Keynesian range	
aggregate demand curve	intermediate range	

QUESTIONS FOR REVIEW AND DISCUSSION

1. What macroeconomic goal does the simple Keynesian model of aggregate demand ignore? Why was this goal disregarded in the years immediately following World War II?
2. What effect does an increase in the price level have on the interest rate and, therefore, on the level of investment? Is this change in investment an example of the real balance effect?
3. Suppose that relatively small changes in the interest rate lead to large changes in business investment. Does this have any effect on the shape of the aggregate demand curve?
4. Moving from one point to another along the aggregate demand curve, what happens to exports? To government spending?
5. Can you think of two specific changes that would lead to a rightward shift of the aggregate demand curve? Two that would lead to a decrease?
6. As price level rises, what is likely to happen to business profits? To production levels?
7. Is it possible to solve major macroeconomic problems by inducing the aggregate supply curve to shift to the left?
8. If the government wanted to reduce the price level, would a reduction in aggregate demand be necessary?
9. What variable is likely to affect both aggregate demand and aggregate supply?
10. Under what circumstances is an increase in aggregate demand most likely to cause inflation? Least likely?

ECONOMICS IN ACTION
The Opening of the Iron Age: A Supply Shock in Ancient Greece

Americans had a number of long-run reactions to the energy crisis precipitated by the OPEC cartel in the 1970s. Initially, the supply shock caused a mass movement away from enormous, gas-guzzling American cars to small, fuel-efficient cars. After OPEC lost some of its power to control prices, gas prices stabilized, and larger automobiles were again in favor. Things were not the same after the supply shock, however, and will never be the same again. Today's full-size cars are relatively fuel-efficient; solar and other alternative forms of energy have found new uses; and production processes have adjusted permanently to oil shortages and to the possibility of future shortages. In sum, the doomsdayers who claim society will have to learn to live with less were not accurate. In fact, OPEC's supply shock may have had extremely beneficial effects on the American economy.

Two economists have taken the doomsdayers to task, examining a large number of supply shocks throughout 10,000 years of recorded history.[a] Supply shocks, they argue, never permanently reduce aggregate supply; instead, adjustments to supply shocks produce beneficial effects that reverse leftward shifts in aggregate supply.

Consider, for example, a supply shock in ancient Greece that marked the transition from the Bronze Age to the Iron Age. Why did our Greek ancestors switch from bronze to iron tools and weapons around 1000 B.C.? The reasons often given—that the Greeks didn't invent iron until 1000 B.C. and that iron was a much better metal than bronze—are questionable. People in ancient Greece had a knowledge of iron making as early as 3000 B.C. What's more, hammered bronze tools and weapons are almost as hard as iron ones and will hold an edge almost as well as iron tools. Since neither of these explanations is satisfactory, what other factor may have ushered in the Iron Age?

Consider some conditions existing during the Bronze Age. From trading records, we know that iron was extremely expensive during the Bronze Age. Records from the nineteenth century B.C. indicate that the exchange ratio of iron to silver was 1:40; in other words, one unit of iron cost 40 units of silver. Bronze is an alloy of about 90 percent copper and 10 percent tin. At the time, copper was abundant, especially relative to iron—the trading ratio of copper to silver was 200:1. Tin was not so abundant and was probably imported into Greece from Iran, for there is practically no tin in the eastern Mediterranean area. During the Bronze Age, tin exchanged for silver at between four and ten units of tin to one unit of silver. Everything considered, the components for a bronze tool cost about 0.05 percent of what an iron tool would have cost. Small wonder the Greeks used bronze.

What happened to alter this situation? Around 1000 B.C. tin became extremely scarce in the Aegean. The Greeks experienced a supply shock of enormous severity owing to

Greek shoemaker's shop, 520–510 B.C. Black figured amphora. By the early 6th century B.C., the use of iron in toolmaking and weaponry had become commonplace.

[a]See S. Charles Maurice and Charles W. Smithson, *Doomsday: 10,000 Years of Economic Crises* (Stanford: Hoover Institution Press, 1985), pp. 95–105.

the wartime disruption of trade caused by the invasion of the Sea Peoples (the Philistines) into the eastern Mediterranean. These invasions, lasting from about 1025 to 950 B.C., led to the collapse of the major Bronze Age civilizations—Mycenean Greece, New Kingdom Egypt, and the Hittite Empire.

With tin no longer available, the price of bronze rose precipitously. Old bronze was melted down for its tin content and, because iron now became cheaper relative to bronze, ancient smiths began to forge iron tools and weapons. The Greeks responded to the tin crisis by ushering in the Age of Iron. Even when trade was reestablished and bronze prices fell, iron continued to be used. The crisis encouraged the smiths to learn ways to produce iron more cheaply. Iron continued to be used, even though the Greeks reverted in part to the use of bronze. In short, when resource crises or supply shocks occur, alternatives become cheaper and more attractive. Leftward shifts in aggregate supply create new circumstances that may mean vastly increased aggregate supply in the future. Within crises are the seeds of undreamed-of future economic possibilities.

Question

Assume that fires and disease destroy three-quarters of America's timber stock. What might be the effects of the catastrophe upon alternative resource development in the short run? Over a longer period of time?

29

Aggregate Demand and Aggregate Supply Shifts: Fiscal and Supply-Side Policies

Contemporary macroeconomic theory and policy contain a large measure of both the classical and the Keynesian world views. Reserving an extended treatment of macroeconomic policy for Part Seven, here we will briefly discuss how aggregate demand and aggregate supply can be used to understand macroeconomic policies. The major Keynesian prescription uses policies designed to manipulate aggregate demand to correct imbalances of employment and income growth in the economy. But in the debate over policy today, more and more attention is being paid to the concerns first expressed by Adam Smith and other classical economists. Labor productivity and capital accumulation were major concerns of the classical writers—the supply side of the economy. Supply-side economics, popular early in the Reagan administration, is based on the idea that overreliance on aggregate demand management, in the form of taxation and spending policies, has had ill effects on the growth of aggregate supply and has fostered much economic instability. This chapter considers the relation between aggregate demand and aggregate supply from both of these policy perspectives. When you complete Chapter 29 you will have insight into

- the role of government spending and taxing policies (fiscal policy) in Keynesian and new classical views of macroeconomics.
- using discretionary tools to affect the business cycle.
- how changes in fundamental factors affect the supply side of the economy on aggregate output and income.
- the interaction between policies designed to affect aggregate demand and the institutions and mechanisms that underlie aggregate supply.

POLICIES DESIGNED TO SHIFT AGGREGATE DEMAND

In large part, macroeconomic policy is an attempt to correct perceived failures in the private laissez-faire economy. When markets do not adjust automatically or adjust too slowly to correct imbalances in employment or economic growth, macroeconomic policies such as changes in taxes, government spending, or

701

supply-side stimulation may be used as correctives. To assess the effects of macroeconomic policies, however, it is necessary to understand both the classical and Keynesian views of how the economy functions to correct imbalances.

Classical and Keynesian Perspectives

The classical economists' perspective on adjustments in the economy was long-run. Prices and wages were assumed to be flexible when there was an excess demand for or excess supply of labor in the labor market. These adjustments were not given an equivalent "clock time"; rather, classical theory assumed instantaneous adjustments. The result, as we noted in Chapter 25, was a vertical supply curve.

This classical supply curve can be matched with an aggregate demand curve, as in Figure 1. The elegant simplicity of the classical argument is revealed when aggregate demand is either increased or decreased from an initial equilibrium. Suppose, as in Figure 1, that the economy experiences a reduction in aggregate demand due to a fall-off in some component of private spending—the autonomous component of consumption, investment, or expenditures on exports. This reduction of aggregate demand is shown as a shift in the demand function from AD_0 to AD_1.

Equilibrium was established initially at E_0, where the economy was producing full-employment output (experiencing the natural rate of unemployment) at price level P_0. With the decrease in aggregate demand, we can think of the economy as moving to point A, where supply ceases to create its own demand. Demand is insufficient to purchase Y_F worth of output at price level P_0. Contraction of production and employment temporarily sets in, since prices (and money wages) will not totally and immediately adjust downward. Once prices start to fall from P_0 toward P_1, additional spending will result in

---

FIGURE 1

In the classical view, when aggregate demand decreases, as from AD_0 to AD_1, the level of output temporarily falls from Y_F to Y_0, causing the level of employment to fall as well. The price level then falls from P_0 to P_1, and output rises back to Y_F. With flexible wages and prices, the economy returns to full employment.

The Classical Long-Run Self-Adjustment Mechanism

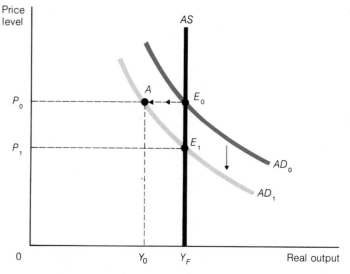

increased output back to the full-employment level. As noted in Chapter 28, falling prices will increase consumption spending *and* investment spending through increases in the real balances and decreases in the rate of interest.

When spending declines, unemployment is initially created. But in the classical version of events, wages also decline, so that all laborers seeking work find work, but at a lower nominal wage. In terms of Figure 1, prices and wages fall, so the economy rapidly ends up at a new full-employment equilibrium, E_1 at Y_F, but at a lower price level, P_1. In fact, the key to understanding the basically noninterventionist policies of the classical writers in macroeconomic affairs is the point that price, wage, and interest rate adjustments take place very rapidly.

Keynesians and the new classical theorists differ on many policy issues. One of the central differences rests upon the time required for automatic macroeconomic adjustment to take place. This difference is conceptualized in Figure 2. Once more, assume that autonomous consumption, investment, or export expenditures decline, causing the aggregate demand curve to shift from AD_0 to AD_1. Demand is again insufficient to purchase the full-employment output Y_F and to sustain full employment at price level P_0. In this case, the economy is in disequilibrium; aggregate supply, represented by point E_0, exceeds aggregate demand at point A for price level P_0. The degree and speed of wage and price level flexibility determines how quickly the economy will adjust to the excess supply at price level P_0. In the classical view, prices will

---

FIGURE 2

Demand Deficiency Unemployment: Short-Run Keynesian and New Classical Views

If aggregate demand falls from AD_0 to AD_1, unemployment will result. If prices and wages do not adjust at all, the short-run Keynesian view, a movement from point E_0 to point A takes place. The economy will produce a level of output equal to Y_1. The difference in employment levels at Y_F and Y_1 is the measure of demand deficiency unemployment. In the classical view, prices will adjust quickly to point B. Demand deficiency unemployment will be less—the difference between employment levels at Y_F and Y_0.

Demand deficiency unemployment:
A short-run situation in which the level of employment is less than if the full-employment level of output were produced; arises when aggregate demand is insufficient to purchase the full-employment output given the price level.

quickly adjust downward to point B, but Keynesians believe that downward adjustments in prices and wages can be slow, unpredictable, "sticky." Either drop—to A or to B—creates a certain amount of **demand deficiency unemployment,** unemployment that results whenever aggregate demand is insufficient to purchase the quantity of goods and services produced under full employment.

Under rigid Keynesian assumptions, prices and money wages are totally inflexible, meaning that the economy would move to point A with a relatively large amount of demand deficiency unemployment. Demand deficiency unemployment is measured as employment at the full-employment output, Y_F, minus the employment that will exist if the economy produces a level of output equal to Y_1. If prices and wages were somewhat flexible over a short period of time, however, a movement from E_0 to a point such as B on the short-run aggregate supply curve AS_0 would result. In this case, demand deficiency unemployment would equal the level of employment at Y_F minus the level of employment at Y_0.

Short-run unemployment of labor and reductions in real output are a fact of life for both modern Keynesians and for new classical theorists. But they differ widely in the kind of policies they would recommend. Keynesians favor the use of discretionary fiscal policy—the use of government expenditures and taxation or, to a lesser degree, discretionary monetary policy—to force the aggregate demand rightward from AD_1 back to AD_0 in Figure 2. According to Keynesian analysis, the economy is quasi-permanently stuck at point B, where unemployment exists. Government must do something about it.

By contrast, new classical economists believe that attempts to manipulate aggregate demand are doomed to fail. They feel that the discretionary actions of government—through fiscal and monetary policy—are unsettling and disruptive; they heighten fears about inflation and the economy in general, making the restoration of equilibrium even more difficult to achieve. They would prefer that government refrain from countercyclical fiscal policies except under certain conditions. Building on the simple concepts just outlined, we can describe some important aspects of the nature and practice of fiscal policy.

Fiscal Policy and Demand Management

Ordinarily, the economy's aggregate supply curve is positively sloped, meaning that, like the supply curves of individual products, higher price levels for all output are associated with higher levels of production. The positively sloped aggregate supply curve is midway between traditional classical assumptions and rigid Keynesian assumptions about the speed of price and wage adjustments to changes in the aggregate economy. In Figure 3, such a supply curve is reproduced along with the negatively sloped aggregate demand curve developed in the previous chapter.

Equilibrium output occurs initially at the intersection of the aggregate demand curve AD_0 and the aggregate supply curve AS along the ordinary, upward-sloping intermediate range of the supply curve. A level of real output or income is produced within the economy in the amount of Y_0 at a price level P_0. However, aggregate demand level AD_0 is insufficient to provide a level of

FIGURE 3

Fiscal Policy Shifts the Aggregate Demand Curve to Combat Recession

Assuming a positively sloped aggregate supply curve, *AS,* an increase in government spending or a decrease in taxes will shift the aggregate demand curve rightward from AD_0 to AD_1. The increase causes prices to rise as real income and employment rise to the full-employment level.

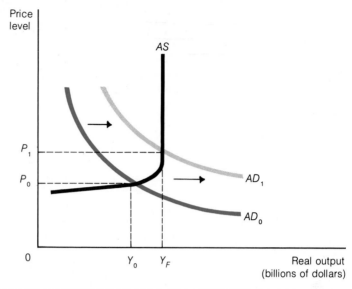

(handwritten margin notes:) For AD to shift rightward:

↑ govt exp
↓ tax on C & I

↑ X by subsidy
↓ M by trade barriers

full-employment output, designated Y_F. What kind of macroeconomic policy would be called for? For fiscal policy, the government would attempt to stimulate spending by reducing taxes and thereby increasing consumption, by increasing government spending, or by stimulating consumption and investment spending. Demand management consists of manipulation of these politically controlled variables (the tax system and government spending) to shift AD_0 to AD_1, or to move demand in the opposite direction to combat rapid expansion and inflation. Fine-tuning the economy by shifting aggregate demand either rightward (to stimulate economic activity) or leftward (to cool down economic activity), the government thus manages aggregate demand to achieve economic goals of full employment and maximum economic growth. For an overview of the federal government's budgetary process, the method by which the federal government implements aggregate demand management policy through expenditure determination, as well as some suggestions for streamlining the process, see Economics in Action, "The Federal Budget: Process and Problems," at the end of this chapter.

Many government policies other than tax or spending changes and practices affect aggregate demand. Federal policies relating to international trade, for example, can affect aggregate demand. As noted in Chapter 11, *net* foreign spending—the difference between exports and imports—is a component of aggregate demand. Anything that affects either imports or exports, such as the erection or elimination of trade barriers, will shift the aggregate demand curve either to the right or to the left. Trade agreements with Japan to limit the American importation of automobiles or computer components will, for example, increase domestic aggregate demand by increasing *net* foreign spending (exports *minus* imports). Likewise, policies that encourage exports of American products will shift the aggregate demand curve rightward.

FOCUS   Politics and Fiscal Policy

In any discussion of government economic policy, some allowance must be made for the possibility that policy-makers will not make the "right" response—namely, the policy change consistent with accepted countercyclical economic theory. Experience tells us that in the world of interest-group politics, economic considerations are not always uppermost in the minds of policy-makers. There is every reason to believe that, like everyone else, elected politicians are self-interested individuals. What is it that the self-interested politician seeks to maximize? Is it the public interest or job security (the probability of future reelection by voters)? Many economists believe it is the latter, so they recognize that knowledge of economic theory on the part of government policy-makers does not guarantee justifiable decisions. Political motives, in other words, frequently dominate fiscal policy decisions.

Consider the accepted "cure" for inflation, according to economic theory. In the Keynesian view, the appropriate fiscal response is a cut in government expenditures, an increase in taxes, or some combination of the two. But how many elected officials have the courage to vote for a tax increase in an election year? By the same token, reductions in government expenditures are politically unpopular with interest groups that receive these expenditures. What are politicians to do? If they wish to curry favor with the electorate—and what politician doesn't?—they will vote against unpopular fiscal measures, even though such measures may be sound countercyclical actions. Proof of this principle

is the fact that the United States has incurred budget deficits in every year but two since World War II. If economic theory had dictated the deficits, their existence would imply that the U.S. economy has been in a quasi-perpetual state of recession, with Congress continually trying to spend us out of the slump. We know that this has not been the case. For many of the postwar years, Congress has actually pursued procyclical rather than countercyclical policy because politicians were unwilling to pay the political price for an unpopular though analytically sound economic policy.

One possible solution to this dilemma is to reduce the degree of autonomy that politicians have over fiscal policy, to take decisions out of their hands to a degree by placing fiscal constraints on the executive branch and the Congress. One such fiscal constraint is a balanced budget rule imposed by a constitutional amendment. This would prevent Congress and the president from spending amounts larger than tax revenues allow—in other words, no budget deficits. While a legal balanced budget requirement (or the pegging of government expenditures to a percent of GNP) could be procyclical, some argue that there would be less inflationary bias than under the current political system. Some type of constraint, the argument goes, would force Congress and the president to choose more carefully how to spend a more limited source of funds. A legal fiscal constraint may prevent, during periods of inflation, pork-barrel spending legislation; it might remove some of the built-in incentives politicians have to cast economically unsound votes.

Demand and Supply Interaction

Figure 3 shows that an increase in aggregate demand and an increase in real income and employment accompanies an increase in the price level. Whether or not prices will rise with increases in aggregate demand depends on the shape of the aggregate supply curve.

Figure 4 depicts aggregate demand shifts under alternative economic conditions summarized in the shape of the aggregate supply curve. With widespread unemployment of resources, as in the Depression of the 1930s, the economy is performing well within its production possibilities frontier. In Figure 4, an increase in aggregate demand from AD_0 to AD_1 through government fiscal policies will have the effect of increasing real output and employment *without* creating inflation by raising prices. Why? Because widespread resource availability permits increased real output without putting pressure on resources and output prices. This situation is close to the one Keynes described for the Depression world of the 1930s and 1940s. Under these extreme conditions, fiscal policy could achieve increases in output and employment without inflation.

The opposite extreme is also possible. When resources are fully and most efficiently employed, the economy is operating at or very near the production

FIGURE 4

The Effects of Demand Management and Alternative Shapes of Aggregate Supply

The effects of equal changes in aggregate demand on prices and output will be determined by the shape of the aggregate supply curve. Given the Keynesian case of depression and widespread unemployment, an increase in demand will increase real income with no increase in the price level. In a classical world of fully employed resources, an identical increase in aggregate demand will simply cause inflation with no increase in income. In the classical case, output cannot increase in real terms; it can, however, increase in nominal terms. In other words, the economy suffers inflation with no increase in output. In the intermediate case, both the price level and real income respond somewhat to aggregate demand increases.

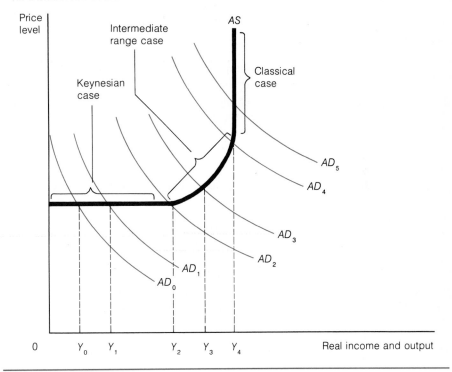

possibilities frontier. Given the state of technology, resources, and institutions, there is some maximum possible amount of real output and employment. If the economy is at this maximum point, the aggregate supply curve is vertical, as represented by the vertical section of the supply curve, the "classical case" in Figure 4. With a vertical supply curve, an increase in aggregate demand created by monetary or fiscal policies will be inflationary. In an increase of aggregate demand from AD_4 to AD_5, for example, real output would remain at a level Y_4 no matter what sort of discretionary demand management policies are followed. Demand management is unnecessary in the classical case because, as we saw in Chapter 25, the economy is self-adjusting and will produce full employment and maximum output automatically. Economists who adhere to classical principles or to modern versions of classical macroeconomics argue that discretionary demand management by government is unnecessary and possibly harmful to the economy.

Between the two extremes lies an intermediate case. Increases in aggregate demand will put some pressure on prices along with some increase in real national income and employment. This situation was depicted in Figure 3 and is shown as the intermediate case in Figure 4. An increase in demand from AD_2 to AD_3 will create some increase in prices, but real output and employment will also rise, from Y_2 to Y_3. However, shortages will develop in some resource markets, creating production bottlenecks and price increases. As the economy approaches full employment and the production possibilities frontier, prices will ordinarily rise at a faster rate and output increases will be smaller and smaller as resource shortages become more acute.

In sum, the effectiveness of managing demand by monetary or fiscal means depends in part on the shape of the aggregate supply curve. In the Keynesian case, reflecting depression conditions, demand changes will have their full impact on real income and employment with no effect on prices. In the classical case, demand management is virtually useless in affecting employment or output: Its sole effects are on the price level. The intermediate case contains elements of both Keynesian and classical conclusions. Aggregate demand changes will change real output and employment as well as the price level. The government's ability to adjust spending and aggregate demand to contractionary or expansionary gaps—to control unemployment and inflation and to promote economic growth—is therefore partially limited by the shape of the aggregate supply curve.

Possible Limits to Discretionary Demand Management

In addition to extreme shapes of the supply curve or the presence of stagflation, demand management by the government may be limited in its effectiveness by the realities of private decision making. About two-thirds of annual total expenditures in the economy come from the private sector—households and businesses. The private sector may have an ability to spend roughly equivalent to its income and wealth, and its desire to spend is not subject to direct government control. Thus it is possible for any governmental policy designed to accelerate or decelerate total expenditures to be thwarted by cumulative individual decisions to reduce or increase spending. In the context of the simple Keynesian model, for example, an increase in government spending could be partially or totally offset by a decrease in some autonomous component of private expenditures. By and large, the limits of discretionary demand management are related to expectations in the private economy and to the supply behavior of workers and other resource suppliers in the economy.

AGGREGATE SUPPLY POLICIES

Policies affecting the aggregate demand for goods and services in the U.S. economy are only one important part of macroeconomic policy. Throughout the 1970s and 1980s there was growing recognition that prolonged use of demand management might adversely affect aggregate supply. Many academic economists, for example, have been investigating the effects of tax rates on work incentives, the labor supply, and productivity. Some economists believe that tax rates, tax rate changes, and unpredictable changes in government spending affect the aggregate supply curve and thus employment and prices.

Others emphasize the impact of institutional factors, such as minimum-wage laws and income maintenance programs, on raising the natural rate of unemployment. This means that discretionary aggregate demand changes brought about by altering tax rates (as well as legislatively mandated institutional changes) might be partially offset by adverse shifts in aggregate supply. In that event, macroeconomic policy might be self-defeating.

Aggregate Supply and Resource Employment

Full employment:
To the classical economist, a situation in which all workers willing and able to work at the current market real wage rate are employed.

As Chapter 28 stressed, aggregate supply in the economy is related to the cost and availability of resources, especially labor resources. To classical economists, **full employment** meant that everyone who wanted a job had one; in other words, there was no excess demand for labor. In this view, the real wage established by the interaction of supply and demand for labor is the full-employment wage. Some unemployed workers would work for wages higher than the equilibrium real wage, but they are not considered unemployed because they voluntarily take themselves out of the labor force. All who would accept lower than equilibrium real wages are employed.

Today, economists prefer to talk of a natural rate of employment or unemployment. A certain amount of unemployment is expected in an economy at any given time. Because of changing demand conditions, resources constantly shift among producers. As Chapter 23 explained, a certain rate of unemployment arises from "friction" in the economic system, although the precise rate has changed over time and is a topic of debate among economists.

Natural rate of unemployment:
The rate of unemployment due to frictional unemployment plus structural unemployment; the rate of unemployment that will exist when expectations of inflation reflect actual inflationary conditions and all short-run macroeconomic adjustments have been made.

The **natural rate of unemployment** is easier to define than to measure: It is the rate of unemployment that exists when all unemployment is either frictional or structural unemployment. These two types of unemployment primarily result when there is imperfect labor market information, when the job search requires time, and when there is no match between the skill and location requirements of job openings and those of unemployed workers. The natural rate of unemployment stems from fundamental market and institutional changes that affect the decisions of workers to supply and employers to demand labor. Specifically, changes in minimum-wage laws, tax laws (especially income tax laws), and the availability and scope of retirement benefits affect workers' incentives to supply labor and thus the natural rate of unemployment. Another important factor is the increased participation rate of women in the labor force over the last twenty years.

The business environment also affects the natural rate of unemployment on the demand side of the resource markets. Taxes and tax laws affect business investments in capital and resources, including labor resources. Changes in tax laws or business regulations will affect the real demands for labor and other resources and ultimately affect the natural rate of unemployment in the economy.

Once these institutional factors are accounted for, the natural rate of unemployment may be interpreted as the rate of unemployment that occurs when full employment exists. This implies that the level of full-employment real output, Y_F, will be produced when the natural rate of unemployment exists. Any change in these institutional factors that affects either the supply of or the demand for resources will shift the aggregate supply curve either rightward or leftward. Supply-side economics, therefore, attempts to shift the aggregate supply curve rightward by changing policies and institutions that reduce the natural rate of unemployment. A rightward shift, for example, would enhance economic growth in terms of actual employment of resources and higher output.

The effects of supply-side or aggregate supply shifts may be shown utilizing the aggregate demand–aggregate supply apparatus from previous chapters. In Figure 5, long-run vertical aggregate supply curves are shown with an aggregate demand curve AD_0. Assume that initial equilibrium is associated with the intersection of the aggregate demand curve, AD_0, and aggregate supply curve AS_0. If the full-employment level of income produced by this intersection, Y_{F_0}, is insufficient, policy-makers might choose policies to increase income and employment growth. Policies that affect the natural rate of unemployment and aggregate supply will shift the aggregate supply curve rightward to new equilibrium positions. Two of these positions are shown in Figure 5. Tax reductions or deregulation in labor or product markets will decrease the natural rate of unemployment and increase the equilibrium income potential in the economy. In terms of Figure 5, policies designed to increase aggregate supply would increase the output potential of the economy from Y_{F_0} to Y_{F_1} or Y_{F_2}. These supply-side policies have been the concern of politicians and policy-makers in Congress for over a decade.

Supply-Side Economic Policies

Macroeconomic policy over recent political administrations (those of Presidents Carter, Reagan, and Bush) has been shaped by the recognition that excessive and prolonged use of demand management might have adverse effects

---

FIGURE 5

The Effects of Increases in Aggregate Supply

If government policies such as tax cuts and deregulation reduce the natural rate of unemployment, the aggregate supply curve will shift rightward—in this case, from AS_0 to AS_1 to AS_2. As a consequence, the price level will fall (below P_0) and real output will rise, from Y_{F_0} to Y_{F_2}.

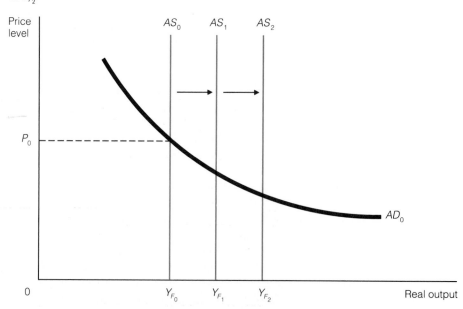

on the economy. Over the 1970s and 1980s, economists and policy-makers perceived that discretionary aggregate demand changes may have produced offsetting shifts in aggregate supply. Specifically, there was a realization that certain fiscal and legislative measures, particularly tax measures and regulatory changes, could alter incentives. Do businesses and workers respond to tax decreases by increasing investment in and production of goods and services? The Reagan administration made **supply-side economics**—the attempt to stimulate real production by providing new incentives to workers and businesses— a hallmark of its economic policy. (Although George Bush labeled Reagan's supply-side theory "voodoo economics" during the 1980 presidential campaign, Bush promised to embrace a similar approach as president.) Consider the nature of some of these policies.

Supply-side economics: Policy designed to stimulate production by altering incentives of producers; policy that has the purpose of shifting the aggregate supply curve to the right.

Policies to Increase Work Effort and Savings. Americans tend to save a smaller portion of their incomes compared to income earners in most other industrialized countries. However, Americans are not simply spendthrifts who live only for the present: We have been encouraged by the design of fiscal policies to borrow more and save less. Interest income from savings is taxed as ordinary income, while for many years interest *payments* were tax deductible. Under present law, interest earnings are still taxed as ordinary income, although deducting interest payments on loans for consumer goods purchases is no longer allowed. (Interest on home mortgages and home equity loans remains deductible.)

Policies enacted during the 1980s were directed at upgrading American saving and work habits, especially among low-income groups. Interest rate restrictions paid to small savers by banks and other financial institutions were loosened or removed, thereby encouraging private saving. The largest income tax cuts in recent history were passed in 1981 and 1986 to increase both saving and work incentives. Individual Retirement Accounts (IRAs), which allowed income earners to shelter some income from taxes for retirement purposes, were also instituted in the early 1980s. IRAs clearly encourage private saving, especially among lower- and middle-class income earners, although the tax deductibility of these instruments was limited by the Tax Reform Act of 1986. Policies to enhance saving may be working: Gross private personal savings rose (in real 1982 dollars) from $109.6 billion in 1986 to $158.7 billion in 1989.

Policies to Encourage Business Investment. Higher saving rates usually translate into higher investment rates by businesses. Institutional restrictions, such as high capital gains taxes and output-lowering regulations, have hampered productive investment in the past (and continue to do so today). Capital gains taxes are taxes on profits from the sale of stocks, real estate, and other investments. Prior to the Tax Reform Act of 1986, capital gains were taxed at a *lower* rate than ordinary income to encourage productive investment by small and large investors alike. These investments are an essential vehicle for creating higher employment and output growth.

The Tax Reform Act of 1986 increased the capital gains tax by treating capital gains from investments as ordinary income. That is, after 1986, capital gains were taxed at the same rates as earned income (15, 28, or 33 percent). Critics of this action claim that it had a chilling effect on investment—reducing the aggregate supply curve of the economy and thereby reducing economic growth potential. Institutional rigidities—in this case, a tax on investment—

may have a negative impact on aggregate supply and on economic performance.

Deregulation of Markets.   Red tape and unnecessary regulations hamper economic performance in markets for goods and services or inputs, including labor. In the late 1970s, the federal government took steps to deregulate several industries, including the banking and financial services industry. The financial system that has emerged is more flexible and efficient, although the result has been tempered by widespread bankruptcies in the savings and loan industry, which may or may not be the result of deregulation.

Partial deregulation of transportation, including airlines, railroads and interstate trucking, began under President Carter and continued through the Reagan administration. Deregulation of these industries gave consumers lower prices, larger output, and greater choice of services. Elimination of institutional restrictions on businesses by government agencies, including the Occupational Safety and Health Administration (OSHA), increased the productivity of business capital and encouraged new investment during the 1980s. Recent changes in labor markets were also supply-oriented. For instance, modification of the minimum-wage law included a general increase in the minimum hourly wage but permitted the hiring of teenagers in need of job experience at lower-than-minimum wages for a limited "training period." The intended effect was an enhancement of aggregate supply and an improvement in long-run labor productivity.

There are indications that such institutional changes have produced a more efficient use of resources, but this is not to say that all supply-oriented changes have been beneficial. Because of federal deposit insurance, taxpayers are going to have to bail out the savings and loan industry—at a cost of perhaps $500 billion. Also, certain Reagan-Bush supply-side policies—for example, the elimination of job training programs and cuts in educational grants and loans—may have adversely affected labor-market institutions and skill levels of workers.

Trade Policies and the Supply Side.   Protectionism has contradictory and self-defeating effects on the economy. The imposition of import tariffs or other trade restrictions may temporarily benefit the economy by providing a temporary increase in aggregate demand. However, the imposition of tariffs or other less formal trade restrictions will simultaneously reduce the long-run growth potential of the economy by reducing competition for domestic firms, input availability, and aggregate supply. While formal tariffs and quotas on goods and services are presently low (see Chapter 39), foreign cartels such as OPEC and "voluntary" trade agreements to restrict importation of foreign products or raw materials, which are more plentiful, have the same effects. As shown in a Focus of Chapter 28, the OPEC cartel created a negative supply shock in the U.S. economy, although its effects were mitigated somewhat over the 1980s. Likewise, import restrictions on inputs to protect domestic industries such as the computer and textile industries will reduce aggregate supply and the growth potential of the economy. While some protectionist agreements were reached during the 1980s, other trade agreements, such as the free-trade agreement concluded with Canada, will have significant effects on the aggregate supply curve.

The Impact of Supply-Side Policies

The results of supply-side policies enacted since the late 1970s have so far been mixed. A recession in the early 1980s, possibly precipitated by inflation-control measures, dampened enthusiasm for some such policies, although growth rates in real output and employment rose in 1983 and 1984. The economic growth rate in terms of real GNP was at a two-decade high in 1984 (6.8 percent); the rate has slowed to a little over 3 percent per year since 1984. Unemployment rates fell steadily after 1984. In 1988, Americans experienced the lowest unemployment rate (around 5½ percent) since 1972. Inflation was brought down from 18 percent in 1979 to little more than 6 percent in 1983 and ranged from about 2 percent in 1986 to a steady 4–5 percent in the late 1980s. Indeed, the U.S. economy suffered only one sharp but brief recession—in 1981–1982—throughout the 1980s.

DEMAND AND SUPPLY INTERACTION: PROBLEMS AND PROSPECTS

By the early 1980s, the ill effects of decades of countercyclical demand policies on aggregate supply were apparent to many economists. From the perspective of these economists, government at all levels tended to overspend and the increased taxation or inflationary tendencies created by deficit finance constrained work effort and private business investment. Aggregate demand policies by government may have worked faster than supply policies to alter inflation or unemployment, but their negative long-run effects on the economy's aggregate output of goods and services could no longer be ignored. Many economists now feel that quick-fix aggregate demand policies do not get at the long-run problems of economic growth and productivity. Aggregate supply policies—especially those relating to labor productivity, long-run business investment, and institutional change—will be more effective, but they also take more time. In this view, demand policies should receive consideration, but supply issues should be raised to equal importance.

Unfortunately, demand- and supply-side policies are enacted within a political process that often prevents or hampers coordination of macroeconomic policy goals. During the 1980s, tax cuts were enacted—a reasonable supply-side policy to enhance work effort, savings, and productivity. But at the same time, government expenditures were not reduced enough to cover increasing deficits in the federal accounts. These huge federal deficits were tantamount to an enormous Keynesian demand-side boost to total expenditures, which might explain the economic growth and general prosperity of the 1980s. But the federal deficit leads to uncertainty in private markets, which has a negative impact both on aggregate demand and aggregate supply. The deficit signals to potential savers and investors that inflation and/or government competition for private funds might soon be on the way. Deficits, then, have a dual impact: They increase the government portion of aggregate expenditures while reducing private expenditures through the creation of adverse expectations. These effects, and other economic impacts of deficits and debt, are the subject of Chapter 30.

SUMMARY

1. The interplay of aggregate supply and aggregate demand, in the long-run perspective of classical economists, produces full employment and economic growth at stable prices. Fiscal policy as a discretionary tool of government is largely unnecessary in the context of classical supply and demand interactions.
2. The Keynesian view of macroeconomics is that concerted discretionary policy is necessary to alleviate imbalances in aggregate demand and supply, since the private economy cannot produce equilibria at full employment with output growth.
3. Fiscal policy is the taxing and spending power of government. It can affect aggregate demand by increasing total government spending in the economy or by stimulating private consumption and investment spending (via tax cuts, for example). In the event of inflation, fiscal policy may also be used to reduce aggregate demand—that is, it can be contractionary as well as expansionary.
4. Policies other than tax and spending changes can also affect aggregate demand in the economy. Since *net* foreign spending is a component of aggregate demand, any policy change that affects imports or exports will shift the aggregate demand curve rightward or leftward.
5. The effects of fiscal policy by government depend on the shape of the aggregate supply curve. In the Keynesian range, demand increases cause increases in real income but not in prices; in the classical range, demand increases are inflationary, with no increase in income and employment; in the intermediate range, both prices and real income increase with increases in demand.
6. Supply-side economics is based on the idea that overreliance on aggregate demand management, in the form of tax policy, has had ill effects on the aggregate supply side of the economy.
7. Aggregate supply is related to the cost and availability of resources in the economy, especially labor resources. It is also related to the natural rate of unemployment, which exists when all unemployment is either frictional or structural in nature.
8. The natural rate of unemployment is dependent upon the institutions surrounding decisions to supply or demand labor. These institutions include but are not limited to tax policies on work and investment, the amount of government regulation, and trade policies.
9. Supply-side policies are designed to enhance work incentives, to increase productive investment, to eliminate regulations on businesses and workers, and to reduce formal or informal trade barriers.
10. Macroeconomic policies relating to both aggregate demand and to aggregate supply have been hampered by the existence of huge federal deficits.

KEY TERMS

demand deficiency unemployment
full employment

natural rate of unemployment
supply-side economics

QUESTIONS FOR REVIEW AND DISCUSSION

1. Discuss the classical long-run adjustment mechanism with regard to a decrease in aggregate demand.
2. What is demand deficiency unemployment? How might it arise in a short-run Keynesian context?
3. What, exactly, is demand management?
4. Why do modern Keynesians favor discretionary fiscal policies to address short-run unemployment problems?
5. In general, why do new classical or supply-side economists oppose demand management to address short-run problems of unemployment?
6. How would the elimination of all trade barriers with Japan affect aggregate demand and aggregate supply in the United States?
7. Suppose that demand management policies are effective in reducing aggregate demand. How will the price level be affected? Does your answer depend on the shape of the aggregate supply curve?
8. Define the natural rate of unemployment. How do market and institutional changes affect the natural rate?
9. How do policies related to saving and business investment affect output growth and employment in the economy?
10. Does the political process ever prevent or hamper the achievement of macroeconomic policy goals? How?

ECONOMICS IN ACTION
The Federal Budget: Process and Problems

Currently, federal government spending (including transfer payments) comprises nearly 25 percent of the United States' approximately $5 trillion GNP. The budget submitted to Congress by President Reagan in January of 1987 was the first ever to exceed $1 trillion. Clearly, expenditures of such magnitude will affect aggregate demand. The process by which the level of federal government expenditures is determined each year is complicated. These expenditures are not simply set by the president and implemented immediately; they must be proposed, debated, and approved in a complex budget process. This is a history of the technical budgetary process (the legal process by which federal government expenditures for any given year are established) up to the present. Some of the problems associated with the current process are discussed, as well as some popular suggestions for reform.

Prior to 1921, each major federal agency, such as the State Department, Department of War (now the Defense Department), the Treasury, and so on, submitted its own funding request to Congress for approval. In essence, there was no all-encompassing "federal" budget, but many federal budgets. Congress would either approve or modify and approve separate agency budgets through the voting actions of various committees. Determination of total federal government expenditures was a disjointed and uncoordinated process.

The Budget and Accounting Act of 1921 required, for the first time, that the president submit an executive budget to Congress for approval. All agencies were to submit their spending requests to the president. The newly created Bureau of the Budget, under the control of the president, would coordinate the various agencies' requests and prepare the president's expenditures requests. Thus, proposed agency spending became a direct responsibility of the president. The act also created the General Accounting Office (GAO) to provide Congress with an analysis of the president's budget. The Congress would then pass, with majority votes in both houses, a spending budget (usually the president's budget with some modifications). The president would either approve the federal spending legislation, thereby determining government expenditures, or veto the legislation and start the spending determination process anew.

With minor modifications, this process remained intact until the early 1970s. President Nixon, a Republican, faced Democratic majorities in both the House of Representatives and the Senate, hindering his ability to formulate and implement legislation. Differing philosophies of the two parties

resulted in much disagreement over both the proper level of government expenditures and their composition. As a result, Congress often passed spending bills that contained items President Nixon did not want. Facing the options of vetoing congressional budgets (and starting the long budget process again) or accepting budgets for expenditures he did not want, President Nixon discovered a third alternative: He signed budget legislation passed by Congress but ordered agencies in the executive branch not to spend some of the funds appropriated by Congress. In short, he impounded funds that Congress voted to be spent, effectively altering the congressional budget to be more in line with his own budget, but without congressional approval.

These episodes resulted in the passage of the Congressional Budget and Impoundment Control Act of 1974. The stipulations set out in this act are still in effect today. The major effects of the 1974 act are to deny the president the authority to refuse to spend congressionally appropriated funds and to establish a specific timetable for all the steps of the budgetary process (see Table 1). The act also established the Congressional Budget Office (CBO) to specialize in budgetary analysis for the Congress. The GAO by this time had acquired so many other duties, and federal budgets had become so very large and complicated, that Congress felt better economic analysis of federal spending could be provided by an office for which this was the sole task.

Though the reforms established by the 1974 act were intended to make the budget process more efficient and streamlined, they had the opposite effect. Deadlines are seldom reached, deficits have ballooned, and, frequently, special temporary budgets have been approved to prevent the government from running out of money and ceasing operations. A number of proposals have been suggested for overcoming these problems.

Among the most popular is the line-item veto, a power given to most state governors. This would allow the president to veto specific parts, or line items, of budgets passed by Congress. One of the current problems with the budget process, as some see it, is that the president faces an all-or-nothing situation. The budget passed by Congress must be accepted intact or vetoed. This provides an incentive to attach special-interest spending bills, known as riders, to major spending bills. With a line-item veto, the president could dispose of riders and leave the major budget legislation intact; it also would provide greater flexibility in pinpointing federal spending the president would prefer to cut. Opponents of the line-item veto point out that it would alter

TABLE 1 Timetable for the Congressional Budget Process

To pass a federal budget for government expenditures, the Congressional Budget and Impoundment Control Act of 1974 requires that these specific legal actions be taken by the president and Congress each year. The act also sets deadlines for each step.

Deadline	Action to Be Completed	Deadline	Action to Be Completed
November 10	President submits current services budget	Seventh day after Labor Day	Congress completes action on bills and resolutions providing new budget
Fifteenth day after Congress meets	President submits budget	September 15	Congress completes action on second required concurrent resolution on the budget
March 15	Committees submit reports to budget committees	September 25	Congress completes action on reconciliation bill or resolution, or both, implementing second required concurrent resolution
April 1	CBO submits report to budget committees		
April 15	Budget committees report first concurrent resolutions to their houses	October 1	Fiscal year begins
May 15	Committees report bills and resolutions authorizing new budget authority; Congress completes action on first concurrent resolution on budget		

the balance of constitutional power between the president and Congress by giving the president effective total control over federal government spending.

Other proposals consist of a two-year instead of a one-year budget, as well as dividing the budget into a current expense budget and a capital budget. With a two-year budget, Congress would go through the budget process only once every two years, rather than annually. Since the budget process has become a costly, drawn-out affair, this proposal has some merit. However, it reduces the flexibility and the ability to time federal fiscal policy properly. Dividing the budget into a capital budget for public goods, investment outlay,

(for example, highways), and a current expense budget for yearly operating expenses also may provide for greater fiscal flexibility as well as greater opportunity for the president and Congress to agree on compromise federal expenditures.

Question

If the federal government adopted a capital and a current expense budget, under which budget should federal spending on education be included?

Source: Budget Reform Proposals (Washington, D.C., American Enterprise Institute, 1985).

30

Public Finance and the Debt

Chapter 29 examined how fiscal policy could shift aggregate demand and supply curves to attain important macroeconomic goals. While fiscal policy may be a recommended stabilizing device, political pressures have led systematically to deficit spending. Since 1960, the U.S. government has run a surplus in only one year—1969. Government deficits were as large as $200 billion during the 1980s and could go even higher in the early 1990s. Despite political promises to balance the budget, the national debt has risen tenfold since 1960, to about $3 trillion in 1990. The Gramm-Rudman-Hollings legislation enacted in 1986 mandated that government deficits be eliminated over time. Nonetheless, it has failed to eliminate high deficits. The public, politicians, and economists are anxious about the effects of deficits and debt. This chapter examines the political foundation of federal deficits and debt. After reading Chapter 30 you should understand

- the proposed effects and the results of fiscal policy.
- features of government finance that automatically help control business cycles of recession and inflation.
- basic principles of public finance, especially as related to taxation.
- why deficits and debt concern economists and the public.

FISCAL POLICY IN PRACTICE

Fiscal policy is often difficult to implement—primarily because it must work through a political process. Inherent in this process are impediments to the smooth functioning of discretionary fiscal policy. It is often difficult to forecast economic downturns accurately or to implement appropriate fiscal policies in a timely fashion. In addition, political motives often cause politicians to favor fiscal measures. For now, though, we will focus on other aspects of fiscal policy that cause difficulties.

How Much Is Discretion?
How Much Is Automatic?

Governments continually levy taxes and make expenditures on a variety of goods and services, and all taxes and expenditures have fiscal effects. But most government taxes and expenditures are positioned in the budget no matter what the particular phase of the business cycle happens to be. The *level* of these tax receipts and expenditures varies with phases of unemployment and inflation in the economy, however, and these changes, called **automatic stabilizers,** are a part of fiscal policy.

In order to understand the role of automatic stabilizers, consider the nature of certain types of taxes and expenditures. Prior to 1986, the personal income tax code in the United States was highly progressive (as opposed to proportional or regressive). Although we will explore the differences among types of taxes later in this chapter, it is important to recognize the nature of a progressive tax. A progressive tax taxes additions to income at higher and higher rates. For example, if Sam earns $15,000 per year, he pays 10 percent in taxes, or $1500. If Judy earns $30,000 per year, she would pay a greater total tax than $3000 (2 times $1500) in a progressive system. If Judy's total tax bill is $4500 on income of $30,000, her tax rate is 10 percent on the *first* $15,000 of earnings and 20 percent on the second $15,000 of income.

The advantage of a progressive structure (and other tax systems) is that it can act as a built-in stabilizer against inflation and recession in the economy. As money income rises—pushing the economy against its production possibilities frontier and fully employing resources—rising money incomes would push people into higher and higher income tax brackets. This, in turn, would withdraw some inflation-producing consumption expenditures from the economy. (This effect assumes that government does not spend the increased tax revenues.) As income falls, the total tax bill of individuals declines with lower and lower tax rates placed on declining incomes, causing unemployment-reducing purchasing power to be automatically injected into the economy. (In this case, the tax bill will also fall with a proportional tax, but it will fall faster with a progressive tax.)

Certain types of government expenditures, such as transfer payments from entitlement (aid) programs, also constitute an automatic stabilizer in the economy. Social Security payments, Aid to Families with Dependent Children, food stamps, unemployment compensation, and other such income security programs automatically inject purchasing power into the poorer and older segments of the economy in case of recession and unemployment. At federal, state, and local levels—but especially at the federal level of government—larger amounts of support flow through these programs during periods of unemployment, and smaller amounts are paid out during periods of fuller employment (and often inflation). Thus, both the tax structure and expenditure programs can be designed and set in place to act as moderating influences on adverse swings in the business cycle of unemployment and inflation.

What, then, is discretionary fiscal policy? If the Congress (with the help of the president) has previously decided the rules under which individuals will receive transfer payments and the rules under which individuals will be taxed, what is left to discretion? One obvious answer is that setting up the

Automatic stabilizers: Taxes and government expenditures whose levels do not depend on decisions by policy-makers for change but instead change counter-cyclically in response to changes in the level of economic activity.

automatic stabilizers is itself an act of discretion. The Tax Reform Act of 1986 changed the automatic tax stabilizers that were part of the previous tax system, reducing the number of **marginal tax rates** from sixteen to three. The marginal tax rate is the percentage rate that applies to some additional amount of taxable income; it is figured by dividing the change in taxes by the change in taxable income. Welfare or entitlement program eligibility also may be changed periodically by Congress, and this has an impact on the countercyclical effectiveness of automatic stabilizers. Congress ordinarily decides on these matters from time to time by creating changes in the automatic stabilizers, but at any given time or phase of the cycle, many tax and expenditure programs are fixed.

At any point in time, some expenditures (and tax sources) are controllable and some are not. Approximately 25 to 35 percent of federal expenditures are fully discretionary—that is, not tied to ongoing, in-place programs such as Social Security, unemployment compensation and other income security programs, and interest payments on the federal debt. The bulk of these fully discretionary expenditures includes a large portion of national defense expenditures, public works programs, and appropriations to federal agencies and to state and local levels of government. Without question, Congress has the power and the responsibility to set up all tax and expenditure programs over the long run, but once many of these programs are set, room for short-run discretion is narrowed considerably. Over the short run, discretionary fiscal policy in the hands of Congress and the president is limited by the conditions attached to automatic stabilizers already in place. Some expenditures in the short run are controllable; some are uncontrollable.

Fiscal Policy and the Budget

As we have seen, discretionary fiscal policy suggests **budget surpluses** during periods of inflation and **budget deficits** over periods of unemployment and recession. While some classical economists advised strict balance in government accounts, the Keynesians argued that the budget should be balanced over the business cycle. A **cyclically balanced budget** in theory requires that budget surpluses run during periods of inflation match budget deficits run during periods of economic distress and unemployment. That is, economic contractions demand budget deficits that expand aggregate demand, and inflation demands a surplus in the federal accounts to reduce total spending on goods and services.

Unfortunately, the fiscal process has not worked exactly in this fashion over the past three decades. Deficits, which are supposed to be cyclically counterbalanced by surpluses, have been run by the federal government in twenty-nine of the past thirty years. These deficits have fiscal ramifications of their own. As we will see later in this chapter, a pile-up of deficits since 1960 pushed the **federal debt** over $3 trillion in 1990. It is most unlikely that such debt will bankrupt the United States, since the federal government has the power to tax and (unlike any individual or other unit of government) to create money. Economists do worry about other effects of deficits and debt. Such effects include adverse impacts on private spending in the present and possible reductions in economic growth and production possibilities in the future.

Marginal tax rate:
The tax rate, in percentage terms, that applies to additional taxable income; additional taxes divided by the additional income taxed.

Budget surplus: 1969
The amount by which government's tax revenues exceed government's expenditures in a year.

Budget deficit:
The amount by which government's expenditures exceed government's tax revenues in a year.

Cyclically balanced budget:
A long-term view of the budget, in which surpluses generated during expansions match deficits created during recessions over a period of years.

Federal debt:
The total value of federal government bonds outstanding; arises from both current and past budget deficits.

PUBLIC FINANCE

Government expenditures obviously require some means, such as taxation, to finance them. When government finances the production of public goods or services—a local sewer system, a research program looking into the cause of acid rain, a nuclear warhead, a presidential limousine—it uses taxes to help pay the bill. In the United States, about 82,000 governmental bodies at federal, state, county, city, school district, municipal, and township levels have the power to establish taxes. As we saw in Chapter 3, the market fails to provide the optimal amounts of public goods such as national defense, police and fire protection, and education. In response, federal, state, and local governments traditionally have taken an active role in providing or influencing the production of such goods and services. In macroeconomic stabilization, government expenditures and taxation (especially at the federal level) take on new roles and new significance. Since the impact of fiscal policy is felt in the economy through government expenditures and taxation, it is important to understand some of the history and foundations of **public finance,** which is the study of government expenditures and revenue-collecting activities. Each and every government expenditure, along with the various tax schemes to finance it, has fiscal effects in terms of helping or hindering economic stabilization.

Public finance:
The study of how governments at the federal, state, and local levels tax and spend.

Government Expenditures

Chapter 3 reviewed some of the major categories of government expenditures and gave some statistics on the rate of government growth. There are two basic types of government expenditures: direct purchases of goods and services, and transfer payments, which are the redistribution of income from one group of people to another. Direct purchases involve spending on items such as defense, fire and police protection, and wages and salaries of government employees. Transfer payments include such expenditures as Social Security payments, Aid to Families with Dependent Children, and unemployment insurance.

The size of all government expenditures, adjusted for inflation, is shown in Table 1 for selected years from 1950 to 1989. Total government expenditures have increased dramatically since 1950 and are expected to rise even higher. These expenditures are ultimately determined by legislative decision, but about 70 to 80 percent are part of ongoing programs such as funds for police protection, water and sewer services (at the local level), military salaries, welfare entitlement programs, Social Security, and interest on the federal debt.

Trends in Government Expenditures. In Table 1, total expenditures are broken down into federal government expenditures and state and local government expenditures. Federal expenditures (which include grants-in-aid—cash distributions—to state and local governments) exceed state and local expenditures by a fairly constant proportion. Up to the early 1900s, local government expenditures exceeded the sum of federal and state expenditures. The Reagan administration attempted to return the provision and financing of many government goods and services to state and local entities, which caused many state and local governments to reorient their fiscal activities. This policy was dubbed the "New Federalism" because it sought a return to the fiscal system that existed prior to the 1930s in the United States.

TABLE 1

Real Federal, State, and Local Government Expenditures, 1950–1989

All government expenditures have increased over the past four decades, with real state and local expenditures increasing at about the same rate as real federal expenditures. This increase is not totally due to population growth; per capita real expenditures increased more than three-fold between 1950 and 1989.

Year	Expenditures (billions of 1982 dollars)			
	All Governments	Federal	State and Local	Total Per Capita
1950	266.5	172.4	94.1	1753
1960	465.4	303.9	161.5	2576
1965	594.1	370.7	223.4	3058
1970	813.8	494.8	319.0	3969
1975	1010.8	614.2	396.6	4680
1980	1141.5	717.7	423.8	5012
1981	1164.6	748.2	416.4	5060
1982	1195.5	781.2	414.3	5141
1983	1228.2	804.5	423.7	5231
1984	1273.5	831.6	441.9	5373
1985	1354.6	888.7	465.9	5661
1986	1403.8	908.6	495.2	5810
1987	1429.0	913.8	515.2	5982
1988	1459.3	921.9	537.4	5924
1989[a]	1502.4	947.3	555.1	6039

Source: Council of Economic Advisers, *Economic Report of the President* (Washington, D.C.: U.S. Government Printing Office, 1990), pp. 298, 387. Conversion to constant dollars provided by authors through use of the GNP implicit price deflator.

[a]Preliminary data.

Per household and per capita government expenditures at all levels have increased in the last few decades. Not only has the absolute level of expenditures increased, but the level of government expenditures as a percentage of GNP has simultaneously increased. Government expenditures at all levels increased from 21.3 percent of GNP in 1950 to 26.9 percent in 1960, 31.3 percent in 1970, and 35.3 percent in 1986; the percentage declined slightly in the late 1980s (see Figure 1).

Since the 1950s, federal government expenditures have increased most in the area of transfer payments, a trend that was sharply reinforced in the 1960s under the Great Society policies of the Lyndon Johnson administration. These Great Society policies expanded the welfare system, setting such expenditures at a sharply increasing rate of growth. As shown in Figure 2, the trend in federal expenditures on national defense declined as the percentage of outlays on social programs rose. Figure 2 also shows that the trend in these two broad expenditure classes reversed slightly under the Reagan administration, which emphasized defense readiness and military parity, or equality, with the Soviet Union.

Direct purchases of goods and services by the federal government also have increased in absolute terms but have decreased as a percentage of total expenditures. Direct purchases at state and local levels exceed those of the federal government. Such a result is not surprising when you consider the

FIGURE 1

Government expenditures at all levels have grown to well over 30 percent of GNP, although they have fluctuated widely—especially during wartime; note, for example, the huge increase during the World War II era due to defense spending.

Source: Council of Economic Advisers, *Economic Report of the President* (Washington, D.C.: U.S. Government Printing Office, 1990), pp. 294, 387.

Government Expenditures as a Percent of GNP, 1939–1989

Total government expenditures as a percent of GNP

programs offered. Most streets, roads, and highways, police and fire protection, hospitals, education, and sewage and garbage disposal are provided by state and local governments. Indeed, state and local governments probably have a greater fiscal influence on our daily lives than does the federal government.

Discretionary Policy and the Level of Government Spending.   Aspects of government finance at the various levels are critical to understanding the expenditure side of discretionary fiscal policy. Unquestionably, the expenditures of states, counties, townships, and cities have an impact on cycles of inflation and unemployment. Emphasis on the effectiveness of discretionary fiscal policy must be placed on *federal* policies, however, and the reason is not hard to understand. State and local governments, in most cases, *must* rely on tax sources to finance government expenditures. Most states and lower units of government, for example, are constitutionally forced to balance their budgets. (The predicament of states is this: A state cannot use its fiscal policy to help the country out of a recession, and it is difficult for a state to recover from a recession while the country is in one.) Although some governmental entities may borrow (largely through bond sales) to finance longer-term projects and budget deficits, their ability to sustain large debt is limited. Unlike the federal government, they do not have the power to print money and to engage in massive levels of debt. The result is that budget policy at the state and lower levels of government tends to be procyclical in character—expenditures are reduced on the downswing due to reduced tax collections and increased on the upswing when tax revenues are rising. In periods of economic distress and widespread unemployment, for example, these levels of government are forced

FIGURE 2

Defense and Social Programs as a Percent of Government Expenditures, 1920–1989

Expenditures in these two categories of government finance have fluctuated through time. In percentage terms, social programs have grown dramatically since the mid-1950s and the Great Society programs of the 1960s, while defense has generally declined since 1950.

Source: Council of Economic Advisers, *Economic Report of the President* (Washington, D.C.: U.S. Government Printing Office, 1990), p. 389.

National
defense and
social programs
as a percent
of total
government expenditures

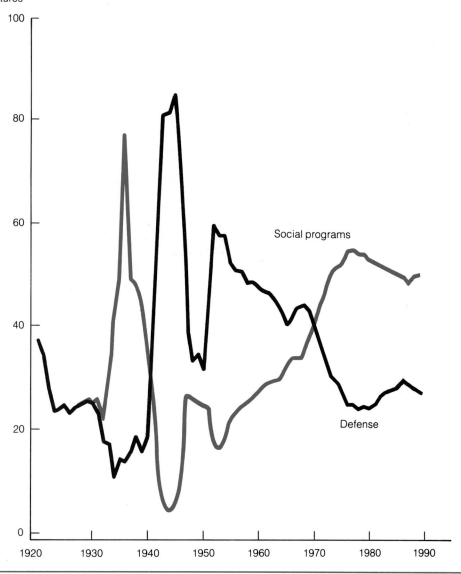

to cut back on all kinds of goods purchases and services. For example, the weakening of OPEC in the early 1980s and the consequent fall in oil prices caused recessions and reduced tax revenues in Texas, Louisiana, and Oklahoma. These states' response was, at least in the short run, to reduce expenditures on goods and services, such as road repair, public education, and county and city services of all types. This response is said to be procyclical rather than countercyclical in character because discretionary policy would call for increased government expenditures and/or reduced taxes in the face of recession and unemployment. Indeed, the fact that state and local fiscal policy tends to be procyclical in nature is itself important for the conduct of discretionary policy at the federal level.

Tax Revenues

Bonds:
Financial instruments that create future obligations on the part of the issuers to make principal repayments and, in most cases, interest payments.

The two basic methods of financing public expenditures are taxing and borrowing. State and local governments usually borrow, as we have stated, by selling **bonds** to finance special projects such as highways, schools, or hospitals, but their access to such funds is limited by their ability to meet future obligations—that is, by their financial soundness and the faith that they will be able to pay off debt in the future. The federal government has come to use borrowing as a routine means of financing its burgeoning deficit, a practice that might eventually create economic problems of its own. Nevertheless, the largest portion of government expenditures is still financed by taxes. Table 2 shows the actual total tax receipts of the federal government from 1987 to 1989 and estimates for 1990 and 1991 from each source. The largest single source of federal revenues is the personal income tax, followed closely by Social Security taxes.

Property taxes and sales taxes are the two largest contributors to combined state and local government revenues, which are broken down in Table 3. The statistics reveal a recent trend in state and local financing: Property tax

---

TABLE 2

Actual and Estimated Tax Revenues of the Federal Government, 1987–1991

The federal government obtains most of its tax dollars from personal income and Social Security taxes. Total revenues are expected to increase by $180 billion between 1989 and 1991.

| | Total Revenues (millions of dollars) | | | | |
| | Actual | | | Estimated | |
Source	1987	1988	1989	1990	1991
Individual income taxes	392,557	401,181	445,690	489,444	528,489
Corporate income taxes	83,926	94,508	103,583	112,030	129,665
Social Security taxes	303,318	334,335	359,416	385,362	421,449
Excise taxes	32,457	35,227	34,084	36,154	37,634
Estate and gift taxes	7,493	7,594	8,745	9,279	9,809
Customs duties	15,085	16,198	16,334	16,785	18,615
Miscellaneous receipts	19,307	19,910	22,809	24,397	24,572
Total budget revenues	854,143	908,954	990,691	1,073,451	1,170,232

Source: Council of Economic Advisers, *Economic Report of the President* (Washington, D.C.: U.S. Government Printing Office, 1990), p. 385.

TABLE 3

State and Local Tax Revenues in 1977 and 1988

Unlike the federal government, state and local governments do not obtain the largest share of their tax revenues from individual income taxes. Since 1977, income and property taxes have fallen in relative importance, while sales and other miscellaneous taxes have risen.

| | Tax Revenues (millions of dollars) | | | |
| | 1977 | | 1988 | |
Type of Tax	Total Dollars	Percent of Total	Total Dollars	Percent of Total
Individual income	30,852	16.9	88,349	12.2
Corporation net income	9,709	5.3	23,741	3.3
Property	64,164	35.1	132,240	18.2
Sales and gross receipts	38,740	21.2	156,257	21.5
All other	39,307	21.5	326,558	44.9
Total tax revenues	182,772	100.0	727,145	100.0

Source: Council of Economic Advisers, *Economic Report of the President* (Washington, D.C.: U.S. Government Printing Office, 1990), p. 391.

revenues have not been rising as rapidly as sales and income tax revenues. This indicates that property owners are being taxed relatively less over time than other groups.

Equitable Taxation: Theories About Who Should Pay. Given the government's need for tax revenues, how should taxes be levied among the people? While voter-taxpayer resistance to specific forms of taxation is always a factor to consider since incumbent politicians must face voters after tax increases, the issue of tax equity is also important. Our society attempts to find an equitable way of distributing the tax burden, but there are no easy formulas for determining what is truly equitable. Theoretically, there are two basic methods by which we may determine who should be taxed and by how much: the benefit principle and the ability-to-pay principle. While these principles are not directly concerned with the impact of discretionary fiscal policy, they are worth mentioning briefly here.

Benefit principle:
A method of determining individuals' tax burdens on the basis of the beneficiaries of the expenditures that are financed by taxes; an example is a gasoline tax.

Many taxes arise from the **benefit principle,** which means simply that individuals who receive the most benefits from government goods and services should pay the most for their production. Public transport facilities such as buses or subways, publicly owned electrical, water, and gas utilities, and toll roads charge users for the services provided. Many goods, such as national defense, interstate highways, and some educational facilities, provide indirect benefits to citizens that are not easily calculated. Some individuals receiving government benefits cannot always afford to pay an equitable share of taxes, even if the benefits they receive could be calculated exactly. For these reasons, most taxes are based on the ability-to-pay principle.

Ability-to-pay principle:
A method of determining individuals' tax burdens on the basis of those most capable of paying taxes.

According to the **ability-to-pay principle** of taxation, those who are more able to pay should pay more taxes than those less able to pay. Under this principle, levels of an individual's income, wealth, or expenditures are measures frequently used for determining the level of tax obligation. There is general agreement that the wealthy should pay more taxes than the poor, but the question of how much more is not easily resolved.

Taxes and Ability to Pay. Three methods of relating taxes to ability to pay have been used in the past. Here, these methods of determining ability are applied to an income tax, but they also can be applied to other taxes.

Proportional income tax:
A tax that is a fixed percentage of income for all levels of income.

Proportional Taxes. A tax that requires individuals to pay a constant percentage of income in taxes is a **proportional income tax.** If the proportion is 10 percent, a taxpayer earning $50,000 per year would pay $5000 (or 10 percent) in taxes. If a taxpayer earned $5000, his or her tax bill would be $500 (or 10 percent). Some states, such as Michigan, Illinois, and Indiana, levy a proportional income tax (with deductions and exemptions allowed).

Progressive income tax:
A tax that is a percentage of income and that varies directly with the level of income.

Progressive Taxes. A **progressive income tax** requires that a larger percentage of income be paid in taxes as income rises. If the tax structure is based on this principle, an individual with a $15,000 income may pay only 5 percent of income in taxes, whereas an individual with a $30,000 income may pay 15 percent. Both the new and the old federal income tax systems are based on the principle of progressive taxation.

Regressive income tax:
A tax that is a percentage of income and that varies inversely with the level of income.

Regressive Taxes. With a **regressive income tax,** a lower percentage of income is paid in taxes as income rises. An individual with a $15,000 income may pay 10 percent in taxes, whereas an individual with a $30,000 income may pay 8 percent in taxes. While a regressive tax results in a lower percentage of income paid in taxes as income rises, people with higher incomes may pay higher taxes in absolute amounts. State and local sales taxes are good examples of regressive taxes, as are the more selective excise taxes on tobacco and alcohol.

FEDERAL TAXATION, TAX REFORM, AND FISCAL POLICY

All taxation at federal, state, and local levels alike has a direct impact on the overall economy through its effect on individuals. The very *fact* of taxation means that income is withdrawn from the private sector of the economy, reducing aggregate demand. On the other side, the very *fact* that governments at all levels spend has an effect on aggregate spending. A *change* in government spending or taxation also will have effects on economic stabilization, *whether or not the effects are intended.*

When examining discretionary fiscal policy, however, we may provisionally ignore taxing and spending systems that are procyclical in nature and concentrate instead on those types of expenditures and taxes that may be used intentionally to affect aggregate demand. State and local spending and taxing policies certainly affect the economy. But such taxes and expenditures may be downplayed when discussing discretionary changes in the fiscal accounts because they tend to be procyclical in nature. Likewise, some taxes collected at the federal level, such as Social Security taxes, will clearly affect aggregate demand in the economy. But they are not, in the usual case, the taxes used to conduct discretionary policy in dealing with cyclical swings in unemployment and inflation.

Income and Corporate Taxes

Federal taxes both on individuals and on corporations were significantly altered in 1913 with the passage of the Sixteenth Amendment. This amendment allowed the federal government to levy income taxes on U.S. citizens. After its inception, the income tax system grew rapidly in size and complexity. By 1986, there were thousands of provisions for exemptions and deductions and sixteen income brackets, with marginal tax rates of 50 percent for the highest bracket. In the same year, taxes on corporate income stood at 46 percent of all business profits in excess of $100,000.

Beginning in 1966, the issue of tax reform was uppermost in some political rhetoric. In 1976, President Carter called the U.S. tax system "a disgrace to the human race" due to its confusing and complex provisions. The major criticism of the tax system was the number and kinds of items allowed both individuals and corporations as deductions from income. Rather than viewing the tax system as primarily a means of generating revenue, federal taxation was used for a number of other purposes. Special breaks were given to individuals and to corporations, for example, for investment purposes. The **investment tax credit** was instituted (in the early 1960s) on the principle that the tax code should encourage industrial modernization. Accelerated depreciation of business investments also was featured for the same purpose. Other deductions for both individuals and businesses were introduced, creating a tax code of incredible complexity and inequity.

Most economists believed that the tax code was inequitable and that it established counterproductive incentives for individuals and businesses. Tax "shelters" were sought and used to generate income losses to deduct from regular reportable income. The availability of tax shelters led to investments that generated loss potential rather than economic growth, which in turn weakened the economy. High marginal tax rates, moreover, may have caused individuals to work less or to work in an underground (untaxable) economy. Further, huge quantities of resources were employed in finding loopholes (tax provisions that generated tax-lowering deductions) in the tax laws.

Investment tax credit: A percentage or amount of new investment expenditure that is directly subtracted from the investor's tax bill in calculating total taxes.

The 1986 Tax Reform Act

In the largest tax overhaul since World War II, Congress passed the Tax Reform Act of 1986. One major thrust of the reform was to scale down both individual and corporate tax rates and to reduce tax complexity. Three tax brackets replaced the sixteen in place previously, with a maximum marginal tax rate of 33 percent. Under the reformed tax law, the top corporate income tax rate was reduced to 34 percent. (Figure 3 summarizes tax rates from 1913 to 1990.) Another major accomplishment of the new tax law was the reduction and standardization of exemptions. (overall exempts)

While both individual and corporate rates fell under the 1986 legislation, more income was taxable. Many deductions—both for individuals and for businesses—were eliminated. The notorious "three-martini lunch" became a "2.4-martini lunch," since only 80 percent of business entertainment expenses could be deducted.

The new tax law was also designed to provide more equity. Partly as a result of increased personal exemptions, millions of low-income families were

FIGURE 3

Individual and corporate tax rates have varied widely since 1913, with individual rates reaching a maximum marginal rate of 90 percent. After the Tax Reform Act of 1986, the maximum marginal rate on individuals is 33 percent, and corporations pay a maximum rate of 34 percent (with fewer deductions both for individuals and corporations).

A Summary of Individual and Corporate Tax Rates, 1913–1990

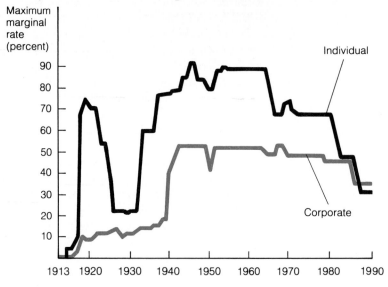

completely removed from the tax rolls. In addition, the elimination of many tax loopholes forced more well-to-do Americans to pay their fair share of taxes.

Economic Criticisms of the Tax Reform Act. The 1986 tax bill has been criticized on a number of fronts. First and foremost, the bill was designed to be revenue-neutral, meaning that the decrease in income tax collections of $121 billion (estimated over five years) would be exactly counterbalanced, or neutralized, by increased corporate and excise taxes of $120 billion. The shift in burden to corporations is incorrectly perceived, however, by the average citizen and journalist. Corporations do make tax payments, but corporations are simply legal entities owned by people who hire labor and other resources and sell output to customers. While corporations make tax payments to government, it is the owners, resource suppliers, and customers who bear the burden of the corporate tax. While economists cannot be certain of the exact shares of taxes shifted from corporations, the ultimate incidence of the "new" tax burden will not be on corporations, as it has never been, but on individuals (as workers, consumers, or stockholders).

Second, the revised tax code provided some simplification, but it fell short of the simplification that would pertain to a proportional tax, also called a flat-rate tax. While many deductions and exemptions were eliminated in the 1986 tax code, most economists point to the 2000-page (plus) document and argue that reform has not made the tax law much less complicated to adhere to or administer. As many resource costs—such as accounting costs and costs associated with preparing tax returns and keeping records—pertain to the new as to the old tax code.

Third, what Congress (and the president) does, it can undo. There is no guarantee that Congress will not alter the tax law again in coming years, perhaps reinstating pre-1986 complexities and inequities. Cynics view the 1986 tax law as little more than the foundation for new political campaign financing boondoggles. Nobel Prize–winning economists Milton Friedman and James Buchanan have argued that tax law changes have cleaned the slate so that future changes in the tax code will be available in return for political contributions from constituencies who would benefit from tax law changes.[1]

4   A final criticism of the tax reform act is that it provides no help in reducing the huge federal deficits, since it is revenue-neutral in character. Indeed, the likelihood that the law will be changed may be increased by the simple fact that it has not, at least in the short run, generated any help with high federal deficits.

DEFICITS, DEBTS, AND FISCAL POLICY

High deficits in the 1980s alarmed voters, economists, and politicians. Just what are the effects of huge deficits and the growing federal debt they have created?

Growing Deficits

As we have shown, deficits are created when government expenditures exceed taxation. Figure 4 provides a disturbing portrait of the emerging deficit situation. Since local and state governments tend to have balanced budgets, the

---

FIGURE 4   Deficits over Time and as a Percentage of GNP

While the size of deficits has grown over time, the federal deficit as a percent of GNP has remained fairly stable. This result is not surprising, since GNP is growing also.

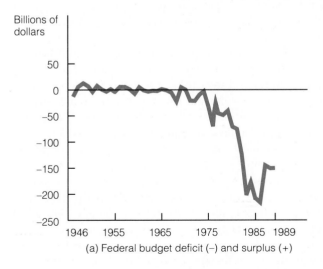

(a) Federal budget deficit (–) and surplus (+)

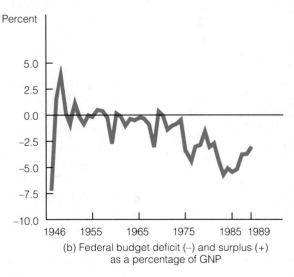

(b) Federal budget deficit (–) and surplus (+) as a percentage of GNP

---

[1]See, for example, Milton Friedman, "Tax Reform Lets Politicians Look for New Donors," *Wall Street Journal* (July 7, 1986).

overall government deficit is created primarily at the federal level. Large deficits have been a feature of federal finance since 1960, but in the mid-1970s, their magnitude mushroomed. From the middle to late 1970s, but especially in the 1980s, the federal deficit raced on uncontrolled. The deficit reached $200 billion in 1986 and has remained alarmingly high since then. Deficits of these magnitudes did not emerge overnight. The fiscal pressures of the Vietnam War, the social programs of the Great Society of the 1960s, the modernization of national defense by the Reagan administration, and so on—all added to contemporary deficit problems. There would be no deficit if Congress and presidential administrations were willing to tax in order to pay for government goods. Their unwillingness to do so means that the resulting deficits, or additions to the total federal debt, must be financed.

Deficits, Fiscal Policy, and Crowding Out

What other means might the federal government use to finance a deficit in its accounts? Since the federal government is allowed to print money, it could simply create money to finance the shortfall between expenditures and receipts. The creation of money, which will be discussed in the next four chapters, would erode the purchasing power of individuals' money holdings. Resources would be shifted from the private sector to the public sector due to the reduction in purchasing power in the private sector. The effect would approximate taxation, since resources are shifted to government from the private sector without the explicit consent of the governed.

The federal deficit is financed primarily through the sale of bonds to individuals and to privately owned commercial banks. Predictably, increases in the supply of bonds resulting from deficit financing lower bond prices. As the price of a bond declines, however, its interest rate rises. Thus, increases in the supply of bonds raise interest rates and channel private saving from private investment into government expenditures. When bonds are sold directly to individuals (EE or HH savings bonds, Treasury bills and notes, and such) or to commercial banks, pressure is placed on private investment if additional funds are not saved. This phenomenon, known as **crowding out,** means that, depending on the reaction of savers and investors to the rise in interest rates, government borrowing may crowd out private investment. If private investment is discouraged, the rise in the interest rate may reduce the long-term growth prospects of the economy—unless individuals react to the increased deficit by saving more for future generations. (See Focus, "Do Deficits Matter? The Ricardian Equivalence Theorem.")

The high interest rates that result from government deficits may also lead to another type of crowding out—the displacement of domestically produced goods by foreign goods. As we will explain in more detail in Chapter 39, high interest rates in the United States make U.S. dollars attractive to foreign investors. This increase in demand for the dollar causes its price to rise in world markets; that is, the amount of a foreign currency that can be obtained for one dollar increases. For example, instead of getting 130 yen for a dollar, high interest rates in the United States may make it possible to obtain 140 yen. As a consequence, foreign goods become cheaper to Americans, but American goods become more expensive to foreign buyers. This leads to an increase in U.S. imports and a decrease in U.S. exports—both of which cause

Crowding out:
The competitive pressure exerted on private investment by government expenditures.

FOCUS   Do Deficits Matter? The Ricardian Equivalence Theorem

Precipitously high deficits throughout the 1980s raised alarm in U.S. political and economic circles. Such deficits—yearly shortfalls in tax receipts necessary to finance yearly government expenditures—add considerably to the federal debt—the sum of past years' deficits. Do these deficits—for several years during the 1980s on the order of $150 billion to $200 billion per year—constitute or foretell a major economic crisis? Many observers and commentators have issued such warnings, despite reasonable annual economic performance. The inflation rate, the employment rate, industrial production, and other signals of economic growth were within tolerable limits between 1983 and 1990. So what is the issue—if indeed there is an issue?

For centuries, economists have debated the nature of deficits in government finance. Nineteenth-century economist David Ricardo argued that the effects of budget deficits and taxation were approximately the same. This idea—called the Ricardian equivalence theorem—suggests that individuals are indifferent between paying taxes in the present and paying taxes in the future (by incurring deficits and debt in the present to pay for government goods and services).

The best-known modern version of the theorem was presented by economist Robert Barro in 1974.[a] Barro argues that each individual has an "infinite" time horizon. This "infinite" time horizon assumes that the preferences or utilities of heirs in future generations are equal to those of the present generation. When the government issues bonds (or debt) to cover deficits in the present, the present generation compensates the next generation (one's heirs) with an increase in its bequest to cover the expected *future* tax liability. In other words, the present generation increases saving to make up for the future tax liability. In this sense, present taxation and budget deficits are equivalent because both result in a reduction in consumption in the present generation. A tax cut financed by an increase in the deficit will not shift aggregate demand or raise interest rates, in this view. The increase in demand for loanable funds by the govern-

ment—through issuing bonds to finance the deficit increase—is exactly matched by increased saving on the part of the present generation (an increase in the supply of loanable funds). Since government spending and consumption spending remain the same, moreover, aggregate demand is unaffected.

Other economists, including 1986 Nobel laureate James M. Buchanan, oppose Barro's thesis on the basis that the present generation does not fully account for the future tax liability at the time debt is issued.[b] Present members of the economy behave as if government bonds add to net wealth. This perceived net wealth increase leads people to increase consumption and to reduce saving, which lowers capital accumulation and harms the heirs of the present generation. There is some empirical support for the view that taxation and debt are not equivalent and that the effects of bond-financed deficits are discounted in comparison with present taxation.[c]

Economists do not yet have a definitive answer concerning the full effects of deficits and debt. For many reasons, deficits and taxation might not be equal. Indeed, deficits may be the preferred method of financing federal expenditures by many groups in society. The age profile of U.S. citizens is an important component of this complex analysis. Older citizens are apt to prefer debt finance (bond issuance) to current taxation, as are single individuals and childless couples. Those in or expecting ill health (early death) might show similar preferences. In short, deficits may not be equivalent to taxation and may shift significant costs onto future generations of Americans. For some economists, debt and taxation are not equivalent, and the choice of more debt over higher present taxes must be carefully weighed.

To summarize: Deficits *do not* matter if our heirs are provided the financial wherewithal to pay them in the future. They *do* matter if Americans do not increase their bequests to future generations to cover the tax liability of current deficits.

[a]Robert J. Barro, "Are Government Bonds Net Wealth?" *Journal of Political Economy* 82 (November/December 1974), pp. 1095–1117; and "Budget Deficits: Only a Minor Crisis," *Wall Street Journal* (January 16, 1987), p. 22.

[b]James M. Buchanan, "Barro on the Ricardian Equivalence Theorem," *Journal of Political Economy* 84 (April 1976), pp. 337–42.

[c]Randall G. Holcombe, John D. Jackson, and Asghar Zardkoohi, "The National Debt Controversy," *Kyklos* 34 (1981), pp. 186–202.

aggregate demand to shift to the left. In this way, an increase in the government's budget deficit crowds out private spending by both domestic and foreign buyers.

Often when the Treasury finances a government deficit, the Federal Reserve attempts to prevent interest rates from rising by simultaneously buying bonds on the open market. This might temporarily keep interest rates down and prevent crowding out, but it causes the money supply to rise, which ultimately leads to inflation and higher interest rates.

Deficits and the Federal Debt

Large deficits have created a total federal debt on the order of $3 trillion in 1990. In order to assess its importance, it is instructive to see who owns the debt.

Table 4 shows the composition of debt ownership in 1988. Ownership of the federal debt is dispersed among private individuals, banks, and foreigners. Most of the debt is thus **internally held debt,** with a sizable portion held by individuals and banks outside the United States. (The importance of this **externally held debt**—claims or IOUs against U.S. resources by foreigners—is discussed in Focus, "Who Bears the Burden of the Debt?")

The Effects of the Federal Debt

Many economists, citizens, and politicians argue that the growing federal debt is a grave present and future problem for the economy and for economic growth. Their concerns relate to (1) the supposed relation between the size of the debt, inflation, and interest rates and (2) the possible burden of the debt on present and future generations.

Debt, Inflation, and Interest Rates. Depending on how government debt is financed, it tends either to raise interest rates or to cause inflation. When the

Internally held debt:
The amount of a country's total federal debt that is owned by the country's various governments, businesses, and individuals.

Externally held debt:
The amount of a country's total federal debt that is owned by foreign governments, businesses, and individuals.

TABLE 4

Ownership of the Federal Debt in 1988

The federal debt is owned, or held, by various groups. This table shows distribution of ownership of the federal debt as of the third quarter of 1988. All figures are in billions of dollars.

Type of Holder	Amount (billions of dollars)		
Total federal debt:	2602		
Total U.S. government ownership:		779	
U.S. government agencies			550
Federal Reserve			229
Total private ownership:		1823	
Commercial banks			203
Other U.S. financial institutions			232
Individuals			180
Foreign ownership			334
Other, including state and local governments			874

Source: Federal Reserve Bulletin (May 1989), p. A30.

FOCUS   Who Bears the Burden of the Debt?

Deficits occur when government expenditures exceed the taxes necessary to finance them. When the government borrows to finance these deficits, debt is created. The federal government has created debt from the very beginnings of the nation. Likewise, the debate over such policies is an ancient one among economists, politicians, and voters. In the nineteenth century and for part of our own, sizable debt was issued before and during wartime, with repayment effected through taxation after war's end. Modern times have witnessed the explosion of bond-financed deficits and a federal debt reaching more than $3 trillion in 1990. Does this seemingly astronomical debt matter to Americans? Does the sheer size of the debt forebode disaster? Are we burdening our children, grandchildren, and more remote descendants with the disastrous prospect of having to pay our debts back?

As a way to begin answering these questions, we again point out that it is most unlikely that the federal government of the United States will ever have to declare bankruptcy. Since the federal government is permitted (by the Constitution) to print money, the debt could be covered, if necessary and perhaps with ill consequences, in this fashion. Further, since the rate of growth in GNP exceeds the growth rate of the debt, the economy is (in a real sense of productivity) able to "stand" the growth in the debt. But problems associated with bankruptcy are not what economists contemplate when discussing the burden of the debt.

Economists usually think in intergenerational terms when discussing the possible effects of debt. They are concerned with whether government debt is borne solely or only partly by present or future generations. One idea prevalent in the post-Keynesian period is that "we owe the debt to ourselves" and that, therefore, it is not a problem to be very concerned about. A simplified version of this view, attributed to economist Abba Lerner, asks the questions, "Who owns the debt?" and "Who owes the debt?" Since the answer in both cases is "Americans," Lerner concluded that we owe the debt to ourselves.[a] While some of our children will inherit debt through taxation, others (or the same individuals) also will inherit claims (government bonds) to offset these debts.

However, a number of matters arise when we consider Lerner's proposition. In the first place, what if foreign individuals and governments hold some of our debt? Some $400 billion of the U.S. debt was so held in 1990. These foreign-held bonds represent real claims against the resources and output of the United States. The foreign-held proportion of the debt is small, however.

Another important matter is that the issue of debt by the federal government may have distributional effects over time. Bonds are usually purchased by high-income groups in our economy, but taxes are paid by all income ranges. Total economic well-being may be affected when a burden is placed on some Americans to the benefit of other Americans. Depending on propensities to consume, total private expenditures may be biased downward when debt is repaid from overall taxation to the upper-income groups over time.

Then there is the necessity of paying interest on the bonds that comprise the debt. Short of a declaration of bankruptcy, interest payments must be paid. They are, as Social Security has become, an untouchable area of the federal budget. During periods of high interest rates, this burden can become especially acute, putting demands on the tax system *or* on new debt finance. (In 1989, these interest payments were $174.4 billion, a significant part of the total federal budget.)

Nobel laureate James M. Buchanan argues that the effects taxation and debt have on present and future generations are *not* equivalent due to the fact that interest payments place a burden on present and future taxpayers.[b] When debt is created, buyers and sellers engage in voluntary exchange and therefore cannot be made worse off. But when it becomes necessary to pay interest on government bonds, taxation is required, and it is not voluntary. Future generations, therefore, do bear at least a portion of the burden of the debt.

Economists disagree over the question of where the burden of debt should be placed. The issue of whether our grandchildren will bear a portion of the burden of present government expenditures is an open one, but at least some effects of debt are passed on.

[a]Abba P. Lerner, "The Burden of the National Debt," in *Income, Employment, and Public Policy* (New York: W. W. Norton and Company, 1948).

[b]James M. Buchanan, *Public Principles of Public Debt* (Homewood, Ill.: Richard D. Irwin, 1958).

U.S. Treasury places bonds up for sale, it has no control over who the purchaser will be—that depends on who is willing to pay the most for the bonds. When the highest bidders are individuals, business firms, or financial institutions, the deficit will drive up interest rates by the amount necessary to attract these buyers. At other times, the bonds will be purchased by the Federal Reserve, the central banking authority in the United States. (The details of such purchases will be made much clearer in Chapter 33.) Purchase by the Federal Reserve tends to keep interest rates down (at least in the short run), but it can lead to higher inflation in the future. (Again, Chapters 31–34 will make it clear why this is likely.) The upshot is that financing the deficit inevitably leads to higher interest rates, inflation, or both—something to consider when such deficits are recommended.

Are Deficits and Debt a Burden on Future Generations? Economists are divided on the issue of whether the federal debt is a burden on future generations. The preponderance of opinion is that it is not, although the issue is far from settled.

How can this opinion be justified? First, the U.S. government will go bankrupt only if the government cannot meet all the debt claims that it issues. This is unlikely. If economic growth and the tax receipts that it brings continue at vigorous levels, the government will have no trouble meeting its obligations.

Other troublesome features of a large public debt are more subtle. Economic growth may be retarded if deficit and debt crowd out private investment expenditures. If private-sector expenditures are directed to more efficient and cost-effective investments, as they are under the revised tax system, productive expenditures might be crowded out by less-productive government expenditures through government bond sales.

Ownership of the debt, moreover, might create other problems. A portion of the debt is owned by middle- to high-income families, although pension funds, which tend to be owned by low- to middle-income families, also invest heavily in government bonds and notes. To the extent that future generations must finance present debt through tax payments, the burden of the debt will fall upon *all* future taxpayers. In other words, that portion of the debt owned by upper income groups will be paid for by *all* income groups in society in the future; some income will be intergenerationally redistributed from poor to rich.

Debt Management, Interest Payments, and Fiscal Policy. Discretionary fiscal policy may be influenced in several ways by the existence of a large federal debt. In 1989, almost 16 percent of total federal expenditures was composed of interest payments on the federal debt. A growing proportion of interest payments to total federal expenditures creates a growing problem with both the size of the annual deficit and the ability of Congress to manipulate expenditures and taxes to control periodic swings in the business cycle. At times, growing interest payments may help create larger deficits, which, in turn, create larger debt, and so on. The debt, in this view, may be self-perpetuating.

Can the Federal Deficits and Debt Be Controlled?

While it is easy to become unduly alarmed over deficits and the mounting federal debt, some real problems do exist. Economic growth and income distribution may be influenced in undesirable ways by growing debt and the problems (such as interest payments) that accompany it. Moreover, if discretionary fiscal policy is destabilizing, as some economists argue, efforts to balance the budget may bring some stability to the economy.

In late 1985, the U.S. Congress passed the Balanced Budget and Emergency Deficit Reduction Control Act (or Gramm-Rudman-Hollings) to deal

WHAT *YOU* CAN DO

Drawing by R. Chast; © 1984 The New Yorker Magazine, Inc.

with growing deficits and debt. Gramm-Rudman-Hollings "prorates," or automatically reduces, federal government expenditures when Congress does not come within preset deficit guidelines for the period 1986–1991. (For details, see Economics in Action, "Gramm-Rudman-Hollings and the Future of Macro Policy," at the end of this chapter.) While part of Gramm-Rudman-Hollings—the movement of congressional authority over spending to the executive branch of government—was challenged successfully in the legal system, the vigorous support and passage of the bill in the House and Senate by both political parties (and its legislative reassertion in 1987) may indicate a changing attitude toward the status of balanced budgets and discretionary fiscal policy in Congress. The entire question of whether discretionary fiscal policy can or will be effective in controlling unemployment and inflation is intimately bound to tax, spending, and budget policies, as well as to constraints at the federal level of government.

SUMMARY

1. Fiscal policy is the intentional manipulation of government expenditures and receipts to control cycles of unemployment and inflation in the economy. Its role is to help provide, along with monetary policy, stable growth in the economy without inflation.

2. While from a Keynesian perspective budgets are to be balanced over the business cycle, perennial deficits have been a feature of federal finance for the past thirty years. The mounting debt that these yearly deficits have produced has been a cause of concern.

3. Automatic stabilizers exist within the framework of government finance, wherein the levels of tax receipts and expenditures vary with rising and falling incomes in the economy, although they do not replace discretionary actions on the part of the president and Congress. They are not sufficient to produce a cyclically balanced budget.

4. Tax and spending policies of states, counties, townships, and cities have an impact on cycles of inflation and employment, but these entities have a limited

ability to engage in deficit finance. Budgets at these levels tend to be balanced and procyclical in character.

5. There are two basic principles of taxation: the benefit principle and the ability-to-pay principle, where those who are more able to pay actually pay more in taxes.

6. With a progressive tax, individuals pay a larger percentage of their income in taxes as their income rises. A proportional tax takes a constant percentage of income for taxes. A regressive tax takes a smaller percentage of income as income rises.

7. The Tax Reform Act of 1986 has simplified many aspects of the tax structure, including reducing the number of income tax brackets to three—with the highest marginal tax rate being 33 percent—and reducing the complexity of tax deductions.

8. Many economists and politicians warn that the growing federal debt created by massive deficits will create serious problems for economic growth and the distribution of income.

KEY TERMS

automatic stabilizers
marginal tax rate
budget surplus
budget deficit
cyclically balanced budget
public finance

federal debt
bonds
benefit principle
ability-to-pay principle
proportional income
    tax

progressive income tax
regressive income tax
investment tax credit
crowding out
internally held debt
externally held debt

QUESTIONS FOR REVIEW AND DISCUSSION

1. Mention and discuss three automatic or uncontrollable expenditures in the federal budget. How large are controllable or alterable federal expenditures relative to those that are less easy to change?

2. What are the major principles of discretionary budget policy?

3. Name and discuss two important trends in spending at the federal level. At the state and local levels of government.

4. What is public finance? Are the principles of public finance the same as those of personal finance? If not, how do they differ?

5. Clearly distinguish between progressive and regressive taxation, giving examples of each.

6. What are some of the economic advantages to society of the Tax Reform Act of 1986 over the previously existing tax code?

7. Economist Abba Lerner once observed that we owe the federal debt to "ourselves." Explain whether you agree or disagree with this proposition, and why.

8. How would you control deficits and debt at the federal level? Is a constitutional amendment the answer? Why or why not?

ECONOMICS IN ACTION
Gramm-Rudman-Hollings and the Future of Macro Policy

No economic issue has received more attention in the media recently than growing federal deficits. Deficits have long been a part of the American political and economic scene; the federal government ran a surplus in only two years out of the past thirty, as federal expenditures grew as a percent of gross national product. The problem became

critical after 1982, with an actual deficit in excess of $200 billion in 1986 and a projected deficit of over $250 billion in 1991.

In late 1985, in what some economists and observers branded an act of desperation, the U.S. Congress passed the Balanced Budget and Emergency Deficit Reduction Control Act (hereafter Gramm-Rudman-Hollings or GRH). While portions of the Gramm-Rudman-Hollings act were successfully challenged on grounds that it illegally transferred spending-cut authorization to the executive branch, the vigorous support of the bill throughout the House and Senate may be one indication of a changing attitude toward the status of discretionary fiscal policy in Congress. In fact, Congress passed a bill in 1987 that resolved the constitutional problems of the 1985 bill and set new deficit targets.

In essence, GRH prorated federal government expenditure cuts in the event that Congress itself did not come within deficit guidelines over the period 1986–1991. Actual deficits must, in any year, equal allowable deficits. Budget deficit limits were to be reduced by $36 billion per year in each fiscal year until the limit reached zero in 1991. Cuts were to be made automatically, when necessary, by the Office of Management and Budget, an agency of the executive branch. Gramm-Rudman-Hollings exempted some expenditures relating to the "social safety net" such as Medicare, food stamps, Aid to Families with Dependent Children, Social Security, and nutrition programs, as it did interest payments on the federal debt. Cutable expenditures include defense, transportation (Amtrak), education, foreign aid, agriculture, environment, and energy. To meet the GRH limits, Congress would either have to reduce expenditures or increase taxes.

Passage of GRH attempted to shift the mandatory and legal authority to cut budget deficits to the president when Congress cannot agree to do so. Opponents of the bill argued that it was unconstitutional because it violated the separation of powers. The Supreme Court agreed in 1986 and struck down the provisions mandating spending cuts by an appointee of the executive branch. No longer are cuts mandated by the Office of Management and Budget (OMB), a part of the executive branch, but violation of the limits imposed by GRH requires explicit congressional approval.

The passage of GRH carries some unmistakable implications. First, the act revealed that the political process is unable to balance the budget without some external constraint. Second, while some opponents argue that budget balancing would create economic instability, passage of the bill indicates that a majority of Congress believes that deficits per se have little or nothing to do with the business cycle. As Senator Phil Gramm (R., Texas) noted, deficits have coexisted with all phases of the business cycle—with falling interest rates, rising interest rates, growth in real income and employment, reductions in real income and employment, and so on.

The widespread support of GRH is consistent with the growing belief, both in and out of Congress, that there is a deficit bias in the political process. The persistence of pork-barrel legislation—where representatives and senators swap votes to provide vote-getting (but less necessary) projects for home constituents—and the unwillingness of politicians to raise taxes (for obvious political reasons) means that the probability of a balanced budget by an unconstrained Congress is virtually nil. In this view, supporters of GRH were trying to improve their reelection prospects by "passing the buck" to the executive branch of government, confident that the budget act would be rescinded or become ineffective, enabling them to return to spend and spend again.

An even more cynical interpretation is that Congress was trying to forestall a convention that could amend the Constitution to provide for a balanced budget—an event that many believe will be necessary in the long run. Since 1977, thirty-two states (only two short of the required number) have called for a constitutional convention to consider the matter. The passage of GRH could be an indication that politicians and those who elect them are losing confidence in the possibilities of discretionary policy implemented by the U.S. Congress and in the present fiscal system itself. Keynes believed that the private economy was unstable and required discretionary policies to moderate business cycles. In this system, budgets would be balanced over the business cycles (not necessarily in every year). Passage of GRH indicates the opposite conclusion—that governmental manipulations may be creating instability in the economy. Passage of GRH highlights the fact that, at one point in time, the vast majority of Americans, acting through their representatives, favored clear limits to the size and functions of the federal government.

At present, Congress is morally bound to the goals of GRH, although a vote could override the targets. Since, as many believe, Congress passed GRH to look as if it was addressing the problem without actually cutting spending or increasing taxes, such an override might not be politically popular. Other observers believe that GRH, while no panacea for the problem of deficits, at least defines the problem for Congress and the American people. Gramm-Rudman-Hollings might have been, as one observer put it, "a bad idea whose time had come."

Question

Do you believe it is possible to balance the federal budget given the "realities" of the reelection process, and given the fact that a large number of American voter-taxpayers would prefer reductions in government expenditures (on defense, domestic spending, and so on) to increases in taxes?

John Maynard
Keynes

Joseph A.
Schumpeter

J. M. Keynes and Joseph Schumpeter: Intervention or Innovation?

JOHN MAYNARD KEYNES (1883–1946) was the son of John Neville Keynes, a famous logician and writer on economic method. Educated at Eton and later at King's College, Cambridge, the younger Keynes developed interests in literature, mathematics, and, later, economics. One of his teachers at Cambridge, the neoclassical economist Alfred Marshall, was much impressed with Keynes's precociousness and strongly urged him to become an economist.

As an undergraduate, Keynes became an integral part of a small coterie of British intellectuals known as the Bloomsbury Group. Its members included novelist Virginia Woolf and biographer and literary critic Lytton Strachey. The group provided Keynes with an arena for intellectual debate, but he still had to decide on a career. Self-confidently, he wrote to Strachey, "I want to manage a railway or organize a Trust." Neither option materialized, and Keynes entered London's India Office of the British civil service in 1907.

Soon bored with civil service duties, Keynes returned to Cambridge and became editor of the prestigious *Economic Journal,* a post he held for thirty-three years. He joined the British treasury in 1915 as a monetary expert and became a key figure representing Britain at the Versailles Peace Conference at the end of World War I. In 1919, he wrote *The Economic Consequences of the Peace,* a condemnation of

the Versailles Treaty, which brought him international recognition. He went on to write a *Treatise on Probability* (1921) and to amass a personal fortune in the risky game of speculating in foreign exchange markets.

In the late 1920s, Keynes's interest turned increasingly to the theory and practice of macroeconomics. His productivity was enormous: Major works of the period include the *Treatise on Money* (1930), *Essays in Persuasion* (1931), and *Essays in Biography* (1933). In 1936, Keynes published the work for which he is most famous, *The General Theory of Employment, Interest, and Money.* In this book, Keynes rejected the idea of automatic adjustment in the economy and maintained that public policy and government expenditure are required for the prevention of economic stagnation and excessive unemployment. During World War II, Keynes negotiated lend-lease programs and was a leading figure in plans to restore the international monetary system. He died of a heart attack soon after the war ended.

JOSEPH A. SCHUMPETER (1883–1950) and Keynes were born only a few months apart. Schumpeter was raised in a provincial town in Austria (then Austria-Hungary) and studied law at the University of Vienna, where he also attended seminars on economics led by Carl Menger and Frederick von Weiser, two founders of the neoclassical Austrian school of economics. In 1906 Schumpeter earned his law degree and practiced law for a short time before deciding to devote himself to economics. At age twenty-eight he produced a brilliant doctoral dissertation, *The Theory of Economic Development* (1911), which brought him recognition as a first-rank theorist. After World War I and the breakup of the Austro-Hungarian monarchy, Schumpeter served as Austria's minister of finance. Throughout the 1920s he lectured throughout Europe. In 1932, as Fascism began its rise in Central Europe, he emigrated to America and became the senior economics faculty member at Harvard, where he remained until his death.

Schumpeter stands out as an extremely innovative thinker. He rejected many contemporary approaches to macroeconomic theory partly because they were based on pure mathematical insight. Schumpeter preferred to base his theory of economic change on the creative force of the individual, whose social, historical, and psychological dimensions are largely ignored by strict mathematical formulas. Schumpeter is also known for his broadly historical views of the discipline itself, which are presented in the posthumously published *History of Economic Analysis* (1954). Another work, *Capitalism, Socialism, and Democracy* (1942), is famous for its prediction that capitalism will eventually destroy itself, not because of its failures (as a Marxist would contend) but because of its successes.

FINE-TUNING THE ENGINE OF DEMAND

Keynes's central work, *The General Theory of Employment, Interest, and Money,* shared one important characteristic with the work of economist Alfred Marshall: a love for abstraction. Robert Heilbroner calls the *General Theory* "an endless desert of economics, algebra, and abstraction, with trackless wastes of the differential calculus, and only an oasis here and there of delightfully refreshing prose."[a] Beneath the calculus, however, were ideas capable of influencing an entire generation of economists and affecting the economic fortunes of millions of people.

Keynes's great insight rested upon his central abstraction, aggregate demand—in shorthand, $C + I + G + (X - M)$. Unlike his classical and neoclassical forebears, Keynes believed that insufficient demand, or spending, by consumers would leave the economy in disequilibrium, stagnating permanently below full employment. Accordingly, Keynes focused on means to increase demand through government policies and interventions in the economy.

In Keynesian terms, the economy is inherently unstable yet manageable. Guided by economic variables such as national income and business investment, government policy-makers can rely on fiscal measures to increase or decrease aggregate demand in amounts sufficient to restore equilibrium. Individual, or microeconomic, decisions to spend, invest, or save could predictably follow whatever course the fiscal and monetary planners design.

Despite the increased role he recommended for government, Keynes was mistrustful of overreliance on central planning. He was not attempting to redraw capitalism but to rescue it. (When the *General Theory* appeared, unemployment in the United States was close to 25 percent.) Keynes wrote the following in response to criticisms by economist Friedrich Hayek that an overplanned economy represents tyranny.

> Moderate planning will be safe enough if those carrying it out are rightly oriented in their own minds and hearts to the moral issue (of tyranny).[b]

CREATIVE DESTRUCTION

Whereas Keynes could be said to honor the economist's role in rescuing a stagnant economy, Schumpeter honored the entrepreneur's role. In many respects Keynes viewed the economy from above, from the heights of abstraction. Schumpeter looked from below, from the vantage point of individuals whose risk-taking and profit-seeking behavior spurred innovations and new growth opportunities. Accordingly, Schumpeter looked for ways to ensure free enterprise, not manage it.

To Schumpeter, the tendency of an economy to fall below levels of full employment resulted from shrinking opportunities for profits. As breakthroughs in technology or production occur, inspiring new investment and greater opportunities for profit, the economy generates growth. Schumpeter called the process *creative destruction* of profit opportunities, the continual rebirth of production frontiers.

Schumpeter naturally argued against government intervention and central control of the economy. He was much more mistrustful of the results of fiscal management than Keynes and felt that governmental tyranny would be its inevitable result. The first victim of such tyranny, in Schumpeter's mind, would be the entrepreneurial spirit. As Schumpeter summarized the matter: "The problem that is usually being visualized is how capitalism administers existing structures, whereas the relevant problem is how it creates and destroys them."[c]

[b]Heilbroner, p. 244.

[c]Joseph A. Schumpeter, *Capitalism, Socialism, and Democracy,* 3rd ed. (New York: Harper & Row, 1950), p. 81. Also see the excellent article by Peter Drucker, "Schumpeter and Keynes," *Forbes* (May 23, 1983), pp. 124–28, on which some of the themes of this section are based.

[a]Robert Heilbroner, *The Worldly Philosophers,* rev. ed. (New York: Simon & Schuster, 1961), p. 235.

PART SIX

Money:

Its Creation

and Management

31

An Introduction to Money and the Banking System

As suggested in our discussion of macroeconomic theory, money is a vital link in our economy. This chapter and the three that follow it explore the nature of money and its economic role. We look at how economists define money, how money functions within the economy, and the reasons people hold and use money. Further, we see how money is related to the banking system and how the banking system itself is regulated by the government.

Money and monetary control are intimately related to the major goals of economic stabilization. Conversely, lack of monetary control can contribute to a society's economic downfall. Before we delve into these issues, our goal in the present chapter is to lay the groundwork for an understanding of money.

Familiar quotations point up the fascination—and the suspicion—that surrounds money. Shakespeare wrote that the person who wants money, means, and content is without three good friends. George Bernard Shaw noted, contrary to a certain religious teaching, that the *lack* of money is the root of all evil. And, in a cynical reversal of the notion that money cannot buy happiness, it has been said that happiness cannot buy money either.

Economics, of course, is not interested in the moral questions that money provokes, but it is interested in the nature of money and its role in our individual and collective lives. When you complete Chapter 31 you should understand

- why money emerged in economic life.
- the various ways in which money functions to increase specialization, the division of labor, and economic growth.
- the definition of money and the role of commercial banking and other financial institutions in the monetary system of the United States.
- the structure and basic economic functions of the Federal Reserve System.

FUNCTIONS OF MONEY

Barter economy:
An economy in which money is not used to facilitate exchange between individuals and firms; goods trade directly for other goods.

To understand the essential functions of money, try to imagine what a society would be like without it. Without the use of money all goods or services would be traded for other goods or services—a **barter economy** would exist. A visit to a psychiatrist, for example, would require a trade of some good or service for an hour on the couch. Suppose that you are the psychiatrist and three potential clients are waiting for your services, each with his or her own item of specialization to trade. Sam offers four hours of typing services, Bill three Persian kittens, and Judy, a farmer, one fully dressed hog. Will the demanders of psychiatric services be able to trade with you?

The result would depend on whether you, the psychiatrist, demand those goods or services in exchange for your own skills and on whether a price—a certain quantity of pork or kittens per hour of psychiatry—could be agreed on. In other words, a **double coincidence of wants**—a cat breeder wanting psychiatry and a psychiatrist wanting cats—would be required for a mutually satisfactory exchange to take place. It may be that, although not a cat lover yourself, you know someone who would be willing to exchange cassette tapes for Persian cats. In that event, a more complicated set of exchanges might be arranged. But these sorts of trades would require either luck or a great deal of information gathering. Transaction costs—the costs of getting buyers and sellers together for mutually advantageous exchanges—are astronomical in a barter economy. Many mutually beneficial transactions in a money economy could never take place in a barter economy due to high transaction costs.

It is not surprising that where barter is practiced, specialization and trade tend to be at relatively low levels. The high transaction costs associated with barter inhibit specialization and trade. A modern free-trade economy could not be founded on a system of barter because of the system's limiting effects. Money emerged to overcome these limitations. (The spontaneous emergence of money in a prisoner of war camp is the subject of Economics in Action at the end of this chapter.) In economic terms, money serves four separate functions: as a medium of exchange, as a unit of account, as a standard of deferred payments, and as a store of value.

Money as a Medium of Exchange

The evolution of money as a **medium of exchange,** or means of payment, came about from the desire to avoid the transaction costs associated with barter and to achieve greater economic efficiency. The need for a coincidence of wants between traders is avoided by the introduction of money. Once money is generally accepted as a means of payment, the hog or kitten owners sell their output in hog and kitten markets. They are willing to accept money in exchange for their products or services because they know that psychiatrists and sellers of all other items they consume are willing to do likewise. No longer is the psychiatrist required to search out demanders for psychiatric services who are simultaneously suppliers of goods or services that the psychiatrist demands. Use of money as a means of exchange fosters specialization and economic efficiency.

Commodity Money. Virtually anything can serve as money if it is generally accepted as a means of exchange or payment. Historically, an incredible assortment of items has served as **commodity money** within different societies, including horses, cowrie shells, elephants, stone wheels, cigarettes, colored beads, slaves, gold and other precious metals, cows, paper, and feathers. Most of the items that various societies have adopted to use as commodity money have had some common characteristics. Generally, commodities that have served as money have been scarce relative to other commodities. Scarcity

Double coincidence of wants:
A situation in trading in which each party to the trade has what the other wants and wants what the other has.

Medium of exchange:
An item that is generally acceptable as payment for goods and services.

Commodity money:
An item that serves as a medium of exchange and that is also a good itself.

744 An Introduction to Money and the Banking System

ensures that only a fairly small quantity of the commodity money will be needed to make most purchases. Such items also were easily authenticated or readily identifiable as the commodity that actually served as money. Commodity monies also were divisible, so that a variety of sizes of transactions could take place, as well as highly portable, so that buyers and sellers were not severely limited in geographical market area. Physical durability is a characteristic common to the vast majority of commodities that have served societies as a money. Also, any commodity serving as money would need to be comparatively stable in supply; large fluctuations in supply of a commodity money would result in large fluctuations in the prices of other goods and services. (For a discussion of a somewhat unusual commodity money still in use today, see Focus, "The Stone Money of Yap.")

Most important, a commodity serving as money should be relatively scarce. The feathers of the extremely rare and beautiful quetzal bird would not have made a good medium of exchange in pre-Columbian Central America if the birds and their feathers had been in abundant supply. A sudden growth in the quetzal population would have produced inflation in the feather prices of goods—too many feathers available to exchange for too few goods. (Indeed, this is what inflation means—that money becomes overabundant in relation to the goods and services it can purchase.)

Yet another and possibly more important problem associated with all commodity monies, including quetzal feathers, is that there is an opportunity cost to using any commodity as money. A moment's reflection tells us what that cost is. Use of a commodity as a monetary medium of exchange means that it cannot simultaneously serve other uses. If quetzal feathers are used as money, they cannot simultaneously be used in headdresses.

Gold is perhaps the most familiar commodity money. The opportunity cost of using gold as money is particularly important. Most societies have valued gold highly as decoration, as an object of possession, and, more recently, in industrial or medical uses such as dentistry. Gold that is used for money cannot simultaneously be used to produce jewelry or to serve any other purpose. The value of gold in nonmoney uses is precisely the value given up when gold is used as money. When this opportunity cost rises above the value of gold in use as a medium of exchange, gold will be converted—coins melted down—to the uses of higher value.

History is peppered with such conversions resulting from changes in the opportunity cost of using gold or other precious metals as money. And social visionaries, seeking to abolish the "tyranny" of gold as money, have naively sought to demonetize gold by decree. Lenin once said that the first goal of his revolution would be to use gold in the manufacture of toilets. It does not appear that there are any gold-plated toilets in the Soviet Union today, and opportunity cost provides the explanation.

Fiat Money. Two problems—the opportunity cost of using commodities as money and instabilities in the exchange value of the commodity used as money—contributed to the emergence of fiat money. **Fiat money** is paper (or some other inexpensive, low-cost item such as lead or nickel) that is certified by government decree, or fiat, to be money. Dollars, pesos, rubles, and yen are all fiat money. Fiat money is not backed by a commodity such as gold; that is, it is not freely and perfectly convertible into that commodity. A system of paper backed by a commodity functions exactly the same as commodity

Fiat money:
Money, usually paper, that is made acceptable in exchange by law; usually not backed by any commodity such as gold.

FOCUS The Stone Money of Yap

Yap is a tiny, thirty-seven-square-mile island in the South Pacific about 500 miles southwest of Guam. In the past, like many other peoples, the Yapese used commodity monies in order to facilitate trade among themselves and with the occasional foreign trader. Unlike in most parts of the world today, commodity money still plays a major role in expediting exchange among the Yapese. Such items as *yar* (pearl shell), *gau* (shell bead necklaces), *mbul* (woven mats), and bottles of beer all serve the citizens of Yap in making trades. U.S. dollars also circulate in Yap and are widely used in daily commerce.

In Yap, however, one commodity has served people as a money for some two thousand years and continues to do so today. A *rai* is a circular piece of limestone with a hole in the center; it looks like a washer. *Rai* range in size and weight from a few inches across and several ounces to twelve feet across and more than a thousand pounds. A very large *rai* can be carried only by nearly a dozen men shouldering a pole placed through the center of the stone.

Until the twentieth century, the stone money of Yap was used in many types of transactions, ranging from everyday trade to paying for tribal feasts and financing island wars. Today, its use has dwindled but has not disappeared. *Rai* have been used in modern times as partial payment for house construction and for some large purchases such as land transactions. Their use also seems rooted deep within Yapese culture and traditions. Yapese men still offer payments of *rai* for the right to marry to the fathers of prospective brides. An offer of dollars would be considered bad manners and an insult. The stone money also is used in making payments to settle disputes that have arisen among the islanders. It is by no means merely ceremonial, however. *Rai* still trade for many goods and services. This is, of course, the major reason that *rai* still actually functions as a money rather than a mere historical artifact.

The exchange value of any particular stone is unusually determined. Size is not the only factor determining what any particular stone will command in the Yapese marketplace. The age of the stone seems to matter most. The first *rai* were transported to Yap from the neighboring island of Palau by raft. Generally, these are the most valuable in terms of their command over goods. In the 1870s, a shipwrecked sailor transported a large number of *rai* to the island. Today,

Limestone money used on the island of Yap

these stones are worth about half as much as the earlier ones. Currently, there are about 6500 stones used as money in Yap.

The stones have, at first glance, some characteristics that a good commodity money would not possess. For example, *rai* are not easily transported. The Yap islanders avoid this nuisance by simply assigning ownership rights to the stones. The stones therefore need not be physically moved in facilitating exchange; only the ownership rights are transferred. Divisibility does pose a problem sometimes, which is the reason that other commodity monies have developed in Yap and the *rai* are used today in a limited range of transactions.

There are advantages, though, that go along with the stone money. The money is easily identified. Counterfeit *rai* do not pose a problem, nor do pickpockets. *Rai* are also fairly stable in supply as well as relatively scarce. Perhaps most important, they have served as a means of preserving the culture and customs of the Yapese. In fact, as a goodwill gesture, a representative from Yap has even offered a *rai* to the United States government as a contribution to help reduce the budget deficit.

Sources: Art Pine, "Fixed Assets, Or: Why a Loan in Yap Is Hard to Roll Over," *Wall Street Journal* (March 29, 1984); and Cora Lee C. Gillilland, *The Stone Money of Yap: A Numismatic Survey* (Washington D.C.: Smithsonian Institution Press, 1975).

money: The commodity must be stored for instant convertibility, thereby incurring an opportunity cost.

Even though fiat money is not backed by a commodity, governments have various ways of giving the money a generally accepted value as a medium of exchange. Fiat money sponsored by government is issued under closely enforced monopoly restrictions by the state. As long as the state does not allow the quantity of fiat money to grow too rapidly, the public generally remains willing to accept the money. Each individual remains confident that any fiat currency received will be accepted by others as payment for goods and services. The government contributes to the general acceptability of fiat money by declaring that debts are forgiven if the creditor refuses to accept fiat money as payment and by accepting fiat money as payment for taxes.

Use of fiat, nonconvertible paper money has one great benefit: It releases valuable resources—gold, silver, or other items—to other uses. But like all commodities, paper is not perfect money. Although it is easily transferable, divisible, and portable, it is less durable than some other forms of money such as gold. Paper money must be periodically replaced by the government, so replacement is a cost of using it. Another important cost is that the government monopoly might overissue paper money relative to the demand for it, thereby creating inflation. However, the widespread use of fiat money indicates that the benefits from using it outweigh the costs.

The reader may object: Is not paper a commodity and is there not an opportunity cost to using paper as fiat money? Paper is a commodity, but the price and thus the opportunity cost of using paper as money is extremely low relative to other possible forms of money. The important point is that the paper money must be generally acceptable as a medium of exchange. If a base metal or anything else meets this criterion, it also can serve as money.

A Medium of Exchange in International Markets.   To understand how the use of a common medium of exchange facilitates exchange, it is useful to consider transactions between citizens of different countries. What is commonly accepted as a medium of exchange in one country is unlikely to be used in another. An American merchant offered payment in Japanese yen is in the same position as the psychiatrist offered payment in Persian kittens. The merchant will accept the yen only if there is a direct use for them (something that can be obtained in exchange for yen) or if the yen are easily converted to dollars. For this reason, transaction costs tend to be higher on international sales than on domestic ones—a situation that would be eliminated with the adoption of a common currency. At various times, certain currencies have come to be widely accepted in world markets. The British pound played such a role earlier in this century, but it was replaced by the U.S. dollar after World War II. However, rapid inflation in the United States in the late 1970s eroded some of the world's confidence in the dollar, and it became less widely accepted. As the U.S. dollar declined, currencies such as the German mark and the Japanese yen rose in importance. As part of the economic unification of Western Europe, plans are underway for a common currency—the European Currency Unit, often referred to as the European dollar. While there is a strong economic incentive for the European countries to use a common currency, nationalist forces in several of the participating countries actively oppose a common currency. Though unlikely to be adopted in the near future, a common European currency would be a strong candidate for an international medium of exchange.

Money as a Unit of Account

Money transactions are preferred to barter partly because money reduces the cost of economic transactions. To illustrate, a leathersmith in a small-scale barter economy produces tanned leather in exchange for blankets, gunpowder, food, alcohol, and metal traps. Without a money serving as a unit of account, the leathersmith (and anyone else who trades) must calculate relative prices of goods in terms of other goods in order to make rational trades. To allocate exchanges rationally, the leathersmith must consult four separate markets to find out the leather price of blankets, of food, and so on. Each trader must do the same. As the number of traders and the number of goods rises, the number of calculations rises exponentially.

Unit of account:
A standard measure, such as the dollar, that is used to express the values of goods and services; a function of money.

The use of money as a **unit of account** helps solve such problems. When money is introduced, all goods are valued in a common measure. Thus, if Jane knows that leather coats cost $4 each and that alcohol costs $2 a bottle, she will also automatically know that her can of gunpowder, worth $8, will trade for two leather coats or four bottles of alcohol or any other combination of goods equaling $8. The function of money as a unit of account means that the number of mental calculations required to determine the relative prices of all traded goods is vastly reduced. This function of money was called the *numeraire* by the French economist Léon Walras (1834–1910). The numeraire is the unit in which the prices of all other goods are stated. Prices are ordinarily stated in the society's monetary unit, such as dollars, sous, or pounds, but there is no reason why any other commodity could not serve as the numeraire. Prices may be reckoned through a leather unit of accounting or through an alcohol standard. The important point is that some *thing* serves to reduce the number of mental calculations required for rational trade. Money has often served in this capacity.

Money as a Standard of Deferred Payments

Money not only helps us keep track of the relative prices of goods, it also serves as a standard for payments that are deferred from the present to the future. When we borrow money for a Caribbean vacation, a home, or a new car, we are using money as a **standard of deferred payment.** Money is used as a standard of deferred payment when a debt or obligation is expressed in terms of dollars, pounds, or any other medium of exchange.

Standard of deferred payment:
A standard measure for expressing contractual values over time, such as the future payments associated with loans and debts; a function of money.

Contracts to buy or sell in the future use money as a standard of deferred payment, and there are potential costs in doing so. One of them is inflation—a reduction in the value of money. When money is used as a standard of deferred payment, there are potential gainers and losers. A contract to pay for a new car two years hence means an inflation risk for the lender. If the inflation rate depreciates the value of money by 10 percent in two years, the lender would receive dollars that would buy 10 percent fewer goods and services. Lenders will therefore try to protect themselves by charging interest to cover the risk of inflation.

Money as a Store of Value

Store of value:
The ability to own wealth in the form of some item, such as money; a function of money.

Individuals who want to save must store wealth, and one way to store it is in the form of money. Money's role as a **store of value** is its least exclusive function. Virtually all commodities, including furniture, houses, stamps, Pekinese puppies, and money, serve as temporary storehouses of wealth or value. But there are better and worse keepers of value. Commodities such as perishable foods are used up relatively quickly. Other commodities, such as land, precious metals, works of art, or buildings, tend to change value relatively slowly.

Liquidity:
The ease with which any asset or commodity can be converted into money with little or no risk of loss to the holder.

While any commodity is a store of value, not all commodities are instantly salable. The salability of commodities is called **liquidity,** the ease or rapidity with which any commodity can be converted into a medium of exchange. Money is the most liquid asset—the one most readily accepted in exchange for other goods and services. All other commodities take varying amounts of time to be converted into money. When cash is needed, land or warehouses cannot easily be converted into cash, but stocks and bonds (which are not money) can. Land is therefore less liquid than stocks and bonds.

Money has its own advantages and disadvantages as a store of value. It may retain its value over long periods, but during periods of inflation it may be a poor store of value. Under extreme conditions, as when a nation at war is forced to make huge expenditures to defend itself, money may lose its value or purchasing power very rapidly through inflation. Such was the case during the American colonial period, when paper money was known as Continentals. The phrase "not worth a Continental" refers to a rapidly depreciating store of value. In fact, inflation, or currency depreciation, has occurred during or after every American war, including the Vietnam War.

In general, money has served fairly well as a store of value in the United States, although its performance over the last several decades has been uneven. The holding of money, therefore, is both safe and risky. Money is instantly convertible to other goods and services, but it may lose its value more or less rapidly than other commodities. When a person holds any other asset (an interest-bearing savings account, IBM stock, a Picasso painting), liquidity is sacrificed.

THE OFFICIAL DEFINITION OF MONEY

Money:
Anything that is generally acceptable as a medium of exchange.

Transactions accounts:
Demand deposits or other checkable accounts that allow the transfer of funds by writing a check.

Demand deposit:
A type of transaction account with virtually no restrictions as to the size, timing, or number of checks that can be written on the account.

Checkable deposits:
Demand deposits plus other types of transaction accounts that pay interest but that may carry some restrictions on use, including minimum balance and limits on the number of checks that can be written per month.

Now that we have gained some understanding of money by examining its various functions, we can define more carefully what we mean by the word *money.* Of the various functions that money serves, its use as a medium of exchange is of greatest economic importance. Therefore, our definition of **money** was along these lines: Money is anything that is generally acceptable as a medium of exchange. Since coins and currency and checkbook money are widely accepted for payment, they must be considered money. To these, we want to add all close substitutes. Since how close a substitute certain assets are to currency is a matter of judgment, various official definitions of the money supply have emerged.

Possible confusion caused by the terminology surrounding checkbook money can be avoided by remembering that any accounts from which payments or funds transfers may be made are called **transactions accounts.** These include all demand deposits and checkable deposits managed by banks and other financial institutions. **Demand deposits** are those transactions accounts against which an unlimited number of checks may ordinarily be written. **Checkable deposits** often carry restrictions on transferability—a maximum number of checks may be written per month without penalty, and so on. Both demand deposits and checkable deposits are "checkable" in the sense that either may be utilized as a medium of exchange.

Though the "general acceptability" definition is reasonably clear-cut, a number of assets, such as noncheckable savings accounts, may have important effects on the behavior of investors and consumers and, therefore, on the economy. These less-liquid assets, sometimes called "near-monies," are therefore included in some statistical compilations. Thus the nation's money supply is officially measured in a number of ways.

Four major measures of money developed by the Federal Reserve System, the nation's central bank, are described in Table 1. Notice that the M-1 measure corresponds to the definition of general acceptability. M-1 is composed of coins and currency in the public's hands and most checkable deposits.

The measures are arranged from M-1 to L in order of decreasing liquidity. Small savings deposits, included in M-2, are ordinarily more liquid than large-denomination time deposits, included in M-3, since convertibility of the latter into cash often requires advance warning to the financial institution. U.S. government securities, included in measure L but not in M-3, are less liquid still, and so on. Conceptually there is no limit to these distinctions (Is the Brooklyn Bridge a more or less liquid asset than the Hoover Dam?), but these three measures plus M-1 are sufficient for most important economic calculations.

You may be wondering why credit card balances have not been included in any of our definitions of the money supply. After all, if money is viewed as *anything* that is generally acceptable as a medium of exchange, credit card balances should qualify. Having $500 in unused credit card balances is as useful in making purchases as having $500 in a checkable account. Albeit indirectly, unused credit card balances are included in each of our money supply definitions. One component of M-1 (and therefore of the other money supply measures) is deposits in checkable accounts. Credit cards operate this way: The issuing company maintains checkable balances that are transferred to the merchant's account whenever the merchant accepts one of the company's cards as payment. It would be double counting to include both these deposits and the unused balances held by cardholders.

Definitions of *money* and *near-monies* evolve with new developments, like the recent emergence of checkable accounts at nonbank financial institutions such as credit unions. Various items in the Federal Reserve System's definitions are lumped together because they are more alike than other possible groupings. Each definition has its own strengths and weaknesses as a tool for measuring the nation's money stock. M-2, for example, may be used in analyzing economic problems where a broader view of liquidity is appropriate.

Lest the reader get the impression that money is the economist's elusive cat in the hat, calculation of the various measures produces real numbers. Figure 1 graphically presents money supply data for October 1989. These figures, calculated in billions of dollars by the Federal Reserve System, correspond to the definitions given in Table 1. The figure shows that M-2 is almost four times the size of M-1, and L, the broadest definition of money, is almost six times the size of M-1. In general, however, economists consider "money" or the "money supply" to be M-1, which consists of assets that are generally accepted as a medium of exchange.

MONEY AND THE BANKING SYSTEM

The largest components of M-1 are bank deposits. As indicated in Figure 1, commercial bank demand deposits were worth $280.4 billion at the end of October 1989. Checkable deposits at other financial institutions accounted for another $280.3 billion. Together these bank deposits are more than two

TABLE 1   Four Measures of the Money Stock

Federal Reserve System classifications of money stock range from M-1 to L, in order of decreasing liquidity. The most liquid measure is M-1, which includes currency in the public's hands, most checkable and demand deposits at financial institutions, and travelers' checks. Although L is many times greater than M-1, as shown in Figure 1, economists often identify money as only assets that are generally accepted as a medium of exchange—that is, M-1.

Measure	Components	Definitions
M-1	Currency, including coins and paper money held outside banks *←min bal ←no restr^ns at all*	
	Checkable and demand deposits at commercial banks, savings institutions, and credit unions	
	NOW and super-NOW accounts	NOW (negotiable order of withdrawal) account: Interest-earning account on which owner may write checks; super-NOW account: NOW account with higher interest and additional restrictions on withdrawals.
	ATS accounts	ATS (automatic transfer savings) account: Interest-earning account, the contents of which are automatically transferred to an individual's checking account when the checking account falls to a minimum level.
	Travelers' checks	
	Checkable money market accounts	
M-2	M-1	
	Savings deposits and small-denomination time deposits in both commercial banks and savings institutions	Time deposit: Large savings deposit requiring notification (usually 30 days) or interest penalties for early withdrawal.
	Certain money market mutual funds	Money market mutual funds: Investment funds managed by banks or investment companies whereby investors' money is pooled and used to buy or sell bonds or other interest-earning investments; investors generally can write checks against their fund balances under some restrictions.
	Overnight Eurodollars	Overnight Eurodollars: Short-term dollar-denominated deposits held in foreign banks.

and a half times the size of the holdings of currency (including coins) by the nonbank public. We are all accustomed to accepting currency and coin as money. But how did bank money—that is, checkable deposits—evolve?

The Evolution of Banking

The emergence of banks and checkable deposits was intimately linked with the origins of fiat money. Before the Renaissance and the emergence of a modern market society, commodity money, usually gold or silver, circulated as a medium of exchange.

Use of gold, for all its advantages as a medium of exchange, had some drawbacks in actual trade. As Eastern and Western trade routes expanded and as exchange became less localized, merchants were forced to transport gold overland and overseas. A sale of goods by a merchant in Constantinople to

TABLE 1   **(Cont.)**

Measure	Components	Definitions
	Overnight repurchase agreements	Overnight repurchase agreements: Overnight loans of idle funds, in which Treasury bills serve as collateral.
M-3	M-2	
	Large-denomination time deposits ($100,000 or more) at commercial and savings institutions	
	Term repurchase agreements	Term repurchase agreements: Short-term loans of idle funds, in which Treasury bills serve as collateral.
	Eurodollar deposits held by U.S. individuals	Eurodollars: Deposits denominated in U.S. dollars held by individuals and nonbank businesses in banks located abroad (mostly in Europe), as opposed to overnight Eurodollars.
L	M-3	
	U.S. savings bonds	
	Short-term U.S. government securities _upto 6mths_	
	Bankers' acceptances	Bankers' acceptances: Notes that are issued by businesses to obtain short-term credit and that are accepted by a bank or other financial institution. Acceptance by the bank indicates that the bank stands ready to pay the principal of the note to the holder at maturity. At maturity the bank pays off the note, charges the business issuer's account, and charges a fee for its services.
	Commercial paper	Commercial paper: Short-term (up to six months) financial obligations (notes) of large corporations traded among finance companies and companies dealing in installment loan credit. Commercial paper may be placed in the market by corporations directly or through specialized dealers.

buyers in Venice required a corresponding payment in gold. But traders soon recognized the safety and convenience of not actually transporting gold at all.

Gold "warehouses" developed, often run by people whose job it was to certify the gold or silver content of coins and to stamp the coins accordingly. These warehouses were a primitive though essentially complete form of the modern bank. Goldsmiths stored the precious metal for traders, issuing a receipt representing the quantity of gold on deposit. These warehouse receipts, which were claims to gold, soon became acceptable as the medium of exchange in both local and international commerce.

This acceptability was a giant leap toward the development of nonconvertible, nonredeemable fiat money, although a commodity standard was still in existence at the time since these receipts were instantly convertible into gold or silver. Traders acquired faith in the goodness or ready convertibility of their warehouse receipts into gold, and with general acceptance, the receipts

FIGURE 1

Numerical Measures of the Money Stock, October 1989

The Federal Reserve System has calculated numerical measures of the money supply for October 1989. As the numbers indicate, L includes the largest numbers and amounts of assets, and the range from M-1 to L is in order of decreasing liquidity of assets. M-1, consisting of currency, all demand and checkable deposits except money market mutual funds, and travelers' checks, is the most useful measure of money. The *Federal Reserve Bulletin* does not report numerical values of all components of a measure; those reported for M-2, M-3, and L are thus selected portions of the measures.

M-1 787.7	**M-2** 3176.5	**M-3** 4027.1	**L** 4852.8
Currency (held outside banks) 219.7 Demand Deposits 280.4 Travelers' Checks 7.3 Other Checkable Deposits 280.3	M-1 + Savings Deposits 301.6 Small-denomination Time Deposits 882.5 Money Market Mutual Funds 241.0	M-2 + Large-denomination Time Deposits 436.6	M-3 + U.S. Savings Bonds, Short-term Government Securities, Bankers' Acceptances, Commercial Paper and European Deposits Held by U.S. Individuals

Note: Amounts in billions of dollars. Totals do not necessarily sum due to the provisional nature of the data.

themselves became money. Currency had thus arrived; and modern checkbook money was only a small step away.

Accepting deposits is one of the two essential functions of banks, and the early goldsmith-warehousers originated the practice. A second major role of commercial banks is to make loans, a profitable but sometimes dangerous practice that was also devised by early bankers. In the beginning, the warehouser undoubtedly earned some income solely by guarding the deposited gold and charging a fee for risk and insurance. The warehouser's receipts were backed by 100 percent of the deposited gold. Soon, however, the primitive banker recognized that not all depositors presented receipts for payment at the same time. On the average, perhaps half the receipt holders demanded their gold during any given day or week. The ever-present profit motive took over. Gold (or gold receipts) could be lent to borrowers at some rate of interest, as long as some "safe" percentage of gold holdings was kept in reserve

Fractional reserve banking system:
A banking system in which banks hold only some percentage of deposits as reserves.

for conversion on demand. In this way, a **fractional reserve banking system,** in which banks maintain only a fraction of cash reserves against deposits, was born. The early goldsmiths issued more receipts than the actual value of gold in their vault. They kept a fraction of gold reserves in their vaults against the likelihood that depositors would demand their specie (gold and silver). The rest was lent at interest, creating another source of profit.

In performing the banking functions of accepting deposits and making loans, early goldsmith-bankers also encountered dangers similar to those inherent in modern fractional reserve banking. Greed in the form of lending too much money for profit—that is, underestimating the fraction of total gold reserves demanded by depositors at any given time—brought disaster. Bank runs occurred when customers became fearful that the goldsmith's deposits were not safe and immediately sought to withdraw their funds.

Two crucial points related to early banking are central to understanding modern banking systems: (1) The practice of lending at interest in a fractional reserve system meant that goldsmiths could actually alter the money supply, expanding it by lending, reducing it by calling in loans; and (2) goldsmiths could place all deposits and banks in jeopardy by misjudging the fraction of depositors' liabilities that would be presented for payment at one time. The first matter—multiple expansion and contraction of checkable deposits by commercial banks in a modern fractional reserve system—is the subject of Chapter 15. The second issue—the safety of the banking system and its regulation by the Federal Reserve System—is treated in Chapter 16. Before investigating these topics in detail, we take a brief overview of the contemporary banking system.

The U.S. Banking and Financial System

Commercial bank:
Chartered financial institution that accepts deposits of various types, especially demand deposits, and that makes commercial and consumer loans.

There are currently about fifteen thousand commercial banks in the United States. **A commercial bank** is a privately owned but publicly regulated financial institution whose primary role is accepting checkable deposits and making business and consumer loans. For years, there was a clear distinction between commercial banks and other financial institutions: Only banks could issue checkable accounts. However, during the 1970s, other financial institutions found ways to circumvent rules preventing them from offering checking privileges. Since then, regulations have been changed so that checking services can now be offered by the seventeen thousand credit unions and the three thousand savings and loans in this country. Since 1980, regulatory changes have brought these nonbank institutions increasingly under the control of the Federal Reserve System.[1] Today, the primary difference between banks and nonbanks lies in the types of loans in which they specialize (see Table 2). However, it is still informative to focus on commercial banks in discussing the role of financial institutions in money and money creation.

---

[1] Do not confuse the Federal Reserve System with the U.S. Treasury Department. The U.S. Treasury handles the budget, issues U.S. government bonds and securities to make up the difference when the budget is in deficit, and issues small amounts of money, mainly coins. The Federal Reserve System does not issue securities and does not act as the fiscal agent for government. It is primarily responsible for control and stability of prices and employment in the economy through control of the money stock.

TABLE 2

Major Types of Selected Financial Institutions in the United States and Assets, 1987

Type of Institution	Major Activities	Total Number[a]	Total Assets (billions of dollars)
Commercial banks	Accepting checkable deposits; making business loans	14,473	2743
Savings and loan associations	Accepting time deposits and NOW accounts; making residential mortgage loans	3513	1263
Life insurance companies	Issuing insurance policies; buying corporate bonds; and making commercial mortgage loans	2125	1000
Private pension funds	Issuing pension plans; buying corporate stocks and bonds	Not known	986
Money market funds	Issuing shares in fund; buying short-term liquid securities	670	316
Mutual savings banks	Accepting time deposits and NOW accounts; making residential mortgage loans	393	263
Credit unions	Accepting savings deposits and NOW accounts; making consumer loans	15,877	184
Mutual funds	Issuing shares in fund; buying corporate stock	1026	453

Source: Data from *Statistical Abstract of the United States,* 1989 (Washington, D.C.: U.S. Government Printing Office, 1989), p. 487.

[a]Data for 1984.

Federal Reserve System: The central bank of the United States; regulates financial institutions and establishes and conducts monetary policy.

Both the individual states and the federal government charter, or license, privately owned commercial banks. National bank charters are issued by the Comptroller of the Currency (an official of the U.S. Treasury Department), while state banking commissions or similar bodies issue state bank charters. By law, all national banks must belong to the **Federal Reserve System,** whereas state banks may elect membership in "the Fed" subject to the approval of the Federal Reserve System. The basic role of the Federal Reserve System, a system of banks organized by geographic region, is to regulate member banks and other financial institutions. About two-thirds of all banks do not belong to the Federal Reserve System, but as we will see, this limited membership does not prevent the Federal Reserve System from overseeing and regulating the activities of all banks.

Statistics on commercial bank assets and liabilities provide an idea of the overall importance of the commercial banking system in our economy. Table 3 shows the balance sheet (total assets equal total liabilities plus net worth) of all domestically chartered commercial banking institutions in the United States as of the end of May 1990.

A glance at Table 3 reveals that the major functions of the U.S. commercial banking system—accepting deposits and making loans—are identical to those of the early gold warehousers. Modern U.S. banking follows the same

TABLE 3

The Balance Sheet of All Commercial Banks, May 1990

The aggregate balance sheet of all commercial banks highlights the major assets and liabilities of commercial banks. Major assets are cash and income-earning loans and securities. Major liabilities include demand, savings, and time deposits. Double-entry bookkeeping guarantees that total assets equal liabilities plus capital or net worth. Aggregate data include all Federal Reserve System member and nonmember commercial banks, mutual savings banks, and non-deposit trust companies in the United States, except branches of foreign banks.

Total Assets (billions of dollars)		Total Liabilities and Capital (billions of dollars)	
Total cash assets	245	Total deposits	2288
Currency and coin	30	Transactions	618
Reserves with the Federal Reserve banks	28	Savings	554
		Time	1117
Balances with depository institutions	32	Borrowing	543
Cash items in process of collection/other cash assets	155	Other liabilities	235
Loans and securities	2831		
Loans, excluding interbank loans	2037		
U.S. Treasury securities	417		
Other securities	377		
Other assets	202	Residual assets (assets less liabilities)	212
Total assets	3278	Total liabilities and capital	3278

Source: Federal Reserve Bulletin (August 1990).

tradition, but it is far more complex in that many financial instruments—variants of the early bankers' warehouse receipts—have evolved. Regulations to prevent problems in the banking system have also evolved; in the United States the Federal Reserve System, which was created by the Federal Reserve Act of 1913, makes and enforces such regulations.

Assets. Many of the assets and liabilities of the commercial banking system are self-explanatory, but some require comment. In Table 3, total commercial bank cash assets in May 1990 were $245 billion. The first but smallest category of cash assets is vault and till cash (currency and coins). The second and third cash assets are currency deposits that commercial banks have in other banks, including the Federal Reserve banks. Commercial banks often have financial arrangements with other commercial banks (and other depository institutions, such as savings and loans). These are called correspondent relations with correspondent banks. A special type of correspondent relation exists between commercial banks and the Federal Reserve banks: Commercial banks are required to keep a percentage of their deposit liabilities—a fractional reserve—available at all times. Some of this reserve is deposited in the Federal Reserve banks. The last cash asset, cash items in process of collection, refers to temporarily uncleared checks held by banks that, when cleared, will give the banks control over cash assets.

Loans and purchases of government securities and other interest-bearing instruments are the two most important means by which commercial banks earn returns and, presumably, profits. Loans include commercial, industrial, and private loans. Other assets ($202 billion in Table 3) include accrued interest on notes and securities, Federal Reserve bank stock (a required purchase by member banks), and real estate—bank premises, furniture and fixtures, and long-run real estate mortgages.

Liabilities. The major liabilities of commercial banks are deposits of several kinds. Transaction and demand deposits are checkbook money—generally acceptable orders by one business or individual depositor to pay another. Recall that such checkable deposits are included in M-1 and are therefore money as we have defined it. Savings deposits and time deposits include passbook savings deposit accounts, time deposits of various long-run durations, and interbank deposits (deposits held by one bank at another bank). Most time deposits require notification of intended withdrawal or invoke interest penalties for early withdrawal. If savings accounts are checkable or instantly transferable to checkable deposits, they are money in the M-1 sense.

The borrowing category includes borrowings from other banks, financial institutions, or the Federal Reserve System. Commercial banks often borrow from each other and from the Federal Reserve to invest in interest-earning assets such as loans or securities.

The Federal Reserve System

The Federal Reserve System is the basic regulatory agency in the business of commercial banking and other financial intermediaries. Its relation to the banking system is similar to that of the Federal Communications Commission and the radio and television industry. One might assume that the main purpose of the Federal Reserve System is to harness the activities of overzealous bankers, who might act in the manner of overzealous gold warehousers—that is, lending out too much money at interest and thereby being unable to meet commitments to depositors. Bank and depositor safety, however, is not a primary or even essential function of the Federal Reserve.

The Federal Reserve System, or any other modern central bank such as the Bank of England or the Bank of Sweden, has two essential functions. One is the older function of serving as a lender of last resort to commercial banks and other lending institutions—to respond quickly and adequately to bank runs, panics, or liquidity crises by providing currency or specie to meet withdrawals. The other, more modern function is to control the money supply to affect the business cycle and economic activity—to produce significant short-run effects on the rates of employment, inflation, and real income growth. This latter function developed slowly and has come into prominence only since the Great Depression of the 1930s, but it is now the major purpose of the Federal Reserve System. The Federal Reserve also conducts other service functions such as issuing currency and holding deposits of the federal government and its agencies.

The following chapters discuss monetary economics in detail—how the Federal Reserve controls the money supply and how changes in the money supply affect employment, inflation, and real income. As an introduction, we consider now the structure and membership of the Federal Reserve System.

Structure. Failure of the old National Banking System, established in 1863, to act as the lender of last resort led to the creation of the modern Federal Reserve Banking System in 1913. The system began operation with the following purposes: (1) to provide an elastic currency to help eliminate panics and bank runs: (2) to supervise the banking system at the federal level; (3) to provide facilities for the buying and selling of financial assets, a means of providing funds to banks at an interest rate called the discount rate; and (4) to enlarge facilities for check clearance. A formal structure within which these functions were to be performed was also established. The original structure survives almost unchanged today, although concentrations of power over monetary policy have developed within the system over the years of its existence. These power concentrations will become apparent in our discussion of the formal structure.

The structure of the Federal Reserve System is shown in Figure 2. The Federal Reserve System is composed of two basic units: the decentralized twelve Federal Reserve banks (see Figure 3 for their locations) and the central node of power, the Board of Governors in Washington, D.C. The Board of Governors consists of seven members appointed by the president, with six

---

FIGURE 2

The commercial banking system and other institutions issuing checkable deposits are regulated and controlled by the Federal Reserve System, which is composed of twelve Federal Reserve banks and twenty-five branch banks. Monetary control is exercised through the Board of Governors and the Federal Open Market Committee in Washington, D.C. The seven members of the board, including its chair, are appointed by the president, subject to Senate approval.

The Federal Reserve and Commercial Banking Systems

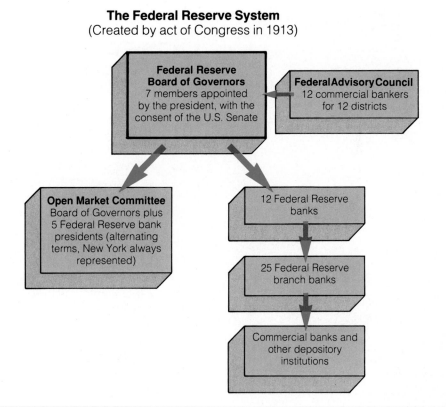

The Federal Reserve System
(Created by act of Congress in 1913)

Federal Reserve Board of Governors
7 members appointed by the president, with the consent of the U.S. Senate

Federal Advisory Council
12 commercial bankers for 12 districts

Open Market Committee
Board of Governors plus 5 Federal Reserve bank presidents (alternating terms, New York always represented)

12 Federal Reserve banks

25 Federal Reserve branch banks

Commercial banks and other depository institutions

Federal Open Market Committee (FOMC):
A committee of the Federal Reserve System made up of the seven members of the Board of Governors of the Federal Reserve System and five presidents of Federal Reserve district banks; directs open market operations (buying and selling of securities) for the system.

governors serving staggered fourteen-year terms; the chair of the board serves a four-year term. The board in general and the chair of the board in particular are almost solely responsible for the establishment of national monetary policy.

The **Federal Open Market Committee (FOMC)** consists of the seven members of the board plus five Federal Reserve bank presidents; the president of the New York bank is always on the committee because of the amount of major financial activity that takes place in New York City. Virtually all monetary policy is carried out by the board and the Open Market Committee. The board must approve any changes in regulations that directly affect the supply of money.

In contrast to the centralization of power and action in the hands of the board and the FOMC, the actual structure of the Federal Reserve System is elaborate and decentralized. As Figure 3 shows, the system is organized into twelve districts with one Federal Reserve bank and a varying number of branch

FIGURE 3   **The Twelve Districts and Branches in the Federal Reserve System**

The Federal Reserve System is geographically decentralized to service banks and other financial institutions throughout the United States. Services include the provision of an elastic currency supply to prevent bank runs, the discounting of paper, and check-clearing facilities. The major purpose of the Federal Reserve System is to help provide full employment, economic growth, and price stability by control of the money supply.

Source: Federal Reserve Bulletin (November 1986).

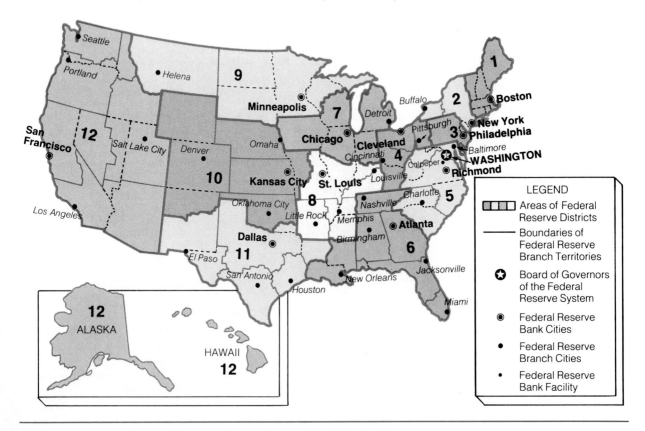

banks for each district. The Federal Reserve bank for the sixth district is in Atlanta, for example, and branch banks for that district are in Miami, Jacksonville, New Orleans, Birmingham, and Nashville. The Federal Reserve banks and their branches are geographically dispersed to service and inspect member banks and other depository institutions in their areas.

Membership. Membership in the Federal Reserve System has fluctuated over the years. Assets and deposits of member banks declined between the mid-1960s and 1980, especially during the late 1970s. The major reason for this decline was the increasing regulatory cost of belonging to the federal system in contrast to looser regulations over banks at the state level. Shifts therefore occurred from national bank charters to state charters. In response, Congress gave the Federal Reserve System sweeping new powers over all banks and over nonbank depository institutions with the passage of the Depository Institutions Deregulation and Monetary Control Act of 1980 (discussed in Chapter 33). The Financial Institutions Reform, Recovery, and Enforcement Act of 1989 gave the Federal Reserve System additional regulatory powers over both banks and nonbanks. Despite declining membership in the Federal Reserve System, the system directly controls all checkable deposits in all U.S. financial institutions, the largest component of the money supply. This control, as we will see in the following chapters, enables the Federal Reserve System to control the overall money supply and greatly influence the course of economic growth.

THE IMPORTANCE OF MONEY: A PREVIEW

Individually, we might take the use of money for granted, for some form of money has always been and always will be part of our lives. However, most economists historically have regarded the control of money as central to sound economic policy. The basis for this belief is the quantity theory of money (discussed briefly in Chapter 25), an idea that is well over two hundred years old and is now the basis for modern monetarist thought. Before turning to the intriguing conflicts over monetary policies, we must more closely investigate how bank money is created, how the Federal Reserve System affects money creation, and how monetarists view the world of aggregate economic activity.

SUMMARY

1. Money was invented to avoid the transaction and information costs of barter, which required a coincidence of wants among traders and imposed limits on the division of labor and specialization.

2. Money serves as a medium of exchange, a unit of account, a standard of deferred payments, and a store of value. Money's most important function is its general acceptability among traders as a means of ex-

change or payment. Virtually anything may serve as a medium of exchange, and there are costs and benefits attached to any item chosen.

3. Fiat money is paper or other low-cost money that is nonconvertible to gold or other commodities. Fiat money is certified by governments, and its general acceptability is fostered by its acceptance by the government as payment for taxes.

4. Money has a number of alternative official definitions, but the one most commonly used by economists is the classification M-1, which consists of all currency and coins in circulation and all checkable deposits at banks and other financial institutions. Currency and checkable deposits are the only two items that are generally acceptable as media of exchange.

5. The major functions of commercial banks are accepting checkable deposits (also called demand deposits) and making loans.

6. The Federal Reserve System was formed in 1913 to regulate and control the banking system. Its functions are to prevent bank collapse and to control the money supply to promote full employment and economic growth and to prevent inflation.

7. The structure of the Federal Reserve System includes twelve geographically dispersed Federal Reserve banks and twenty-five branch banks to serve the commercial banking and financial system. Decision-making power rests with the Board of Governors and the Federal Open Market Committee, both located in Washington, D.C.

KEY TERMS

barter economy	standard of deferred payment	checkable deposits
double coincidence of wants	store of value	fractional reserve banking system
medium of exchange	liquidity	commercial bank
commodity money	money	Federal Reserve System
fiat money	transactions accounts	Federal Open Market Committee (FOMC)
unit of account	demand deposit	

QUESTIONS FOR REVIEW AND DISCUSSION

1. Explain the functions of money. Does inflation rob money of some of its functions?

2. Explain why a money system of exchange is better than a barter system.

3. For money to lower the costs of transactions and to perform its other functions well, it must have some particular physical characteristics. List and explain the desirable physical characteristics and also explain why paper makes better money than M&M's or stamps.

4. Would using gold as a medium of exchange solve the problems of constant changes in the level of prices? Explain your answer.

5. Define money and then discuss why each of the following is not considered money: IRAs, savings accounts, certificates of deposit, and gold.

6. What is the major feature that distinguishes M-1 from M-2, M-3, and L?

7. Essentially, what is a bank and what is the value to society of banks?

8. What is the major purpose of the Federal Reserve System? How does it achieve this purpose?

9. Why might the Federal Reserve be considered a system of decentralized banks rather than one central bank?

ECONOMICS IN ACTION

The Spontaneous Emergence of Money: The Prisoner of War Camp

Stalag 17, a highly acclaimed play and movie, depicted everyday life in a German prisoner of war camp. Seth, the antihero entrepreneur, ran rat "horse races," sold schnapps fermented in his own distillery, and seemed to be able to obtain almost anything for a price. Money in the form of coins and currency did not exist, but trades were conducted by the prisoners with another form of money—cigarettes. This part of the fictionalized account of prison life has basis in fact, as reported by an economic observer, R. A. Radford, who was a POW in Germany and Italy.[a] Radford's report tells us much about the relation between economic activity and the spontaneous emergence of money.

POWs in Stalag 17 did not do paid work, but they were allotted weekly rations of goods from the Red Cross and other private sources. These rations consisted of such items as tinned milk, jam, butter, biscuits, chocolate, sugar, and cigarettes. Tastes differ among individuals, and with everyone receiving roughly equal amounts of the same commodities, prisoners would barter among themselves for the items they preferred. As time passed, trade expanded and the relative price of one item in terms of others became well known. Trade became increasingly complex, and a generally accepted medium of exchange developed in the form of cigarettes, a commodity in common use. With the camps and their residents becoming semipermanent, prices of items in terms of cigarettes quickly became widely known. An exchange and mart board listing desired trades was set up: a pound of cheese for seven cigarettes, two cigarettes for a drink of schnapps. Unlike the case of Yap money, where stones are not standardized (see Focus, "The Stone Money of Yap," in this chapter), the use of cigarettes as a standardized commodity greatly reduced the transaction and information costs of trade and thus increased the volume of trade.

Additional economic issues were made easier by the new medium of exchange. Price fluctuations from Mondays, when the provisions were handed out, until a new shipment of rations came in on the following Sunday were smoothed out through voluntary exchanges between prisoners that smoothed fluctuations in supplies over time. Speculators would buy on Mondays when the price of toothpaste and food was low. As supplies diminished through the week and prices rose, speculators would sell their hoarded goods for profit. Relative price differences for goods between Mondays and Sundays were thus narrowed.

The POW camp did not avoid the economic problems of inflation and deflation. Periodic injections of higher quantities of cigarettes produced inflation. Scarcity of cigarettes caused the price levels to fall.

As all economists know, prices are also affected by psychological factors. Air raids, good or bad war news, and the

[a]R. A. Radford, "The Economic Organization of a P.O.W. Camp," *Economica*, n.s. (November 1945), pp. 189–201.

Prisoners of war playing poker for cigarettes at Stalag Luft III, Germany, 1944

weather all affected the prices because these events clearly changed the nonmonetary demand for cigarettes. The prisoners would smoke cigarettes rather than save them. All commodity money standards are influenced by such factors. Altered demand for quetzal feathers as decoration or for gold in dentistry or industry would clearly affect the price level in economies using feathers or gold as money.

The POW camp experience illustrates the naturalness or spontaneity with which money as a medium of exchange emerges. The liberation of prisoners by the U.S. infantry created chaos for the cigarette standard. When commodities are no longer relatively scarce, there is no need for economic organization or activity. The POW economy, as Radford reports, simply collapsed. The lesson to be learned is that scarcity, coupled with the recognition by traders of the costs of barter, will inevitably lead to the use of money.

Question

Money, in order to function efficiently, must be portable, durable, divisible, easily recognized, stable in supply, and relatively scarce. How well do cigarettes conform to these characteristics? Can you think of any other goods likely to be found in a POW camp that would be preferable to cigarettes as money?

32

Money Creation

Chapter 31 defines *money* as anything that is generally acceptable as a medium of exchange—all currency, coins, and checkable deposits in the hands of the public. The most important part of our generally accepted money is checkbook money, called demand deposits or checkable deposits. In fact, in October 1989, the value of checkable deposits was more than two and a half times the value of dollars and coins in circulation—$560.7 billion in checkable deposits compared to $219.7 billion in currency.

Checkable deposits are money because of our faith that others will accept our checks—our orders to transfer funds—as currency and the faith of others that we will do likewise. This means that when the amounts kept in checkable deposits expand or contract, the economy's money supply also expands or contracts. In this chapter we explore how the process of money creation and destruction works through the commercial banking system. In the next chapter we will look at how the Federal Reserve System regulates the deposits to maintain economic stabilization.

Historically, commercial banks were exclusive issuers of checkbook money, and other nonbank financial institutions, also called thrift institutions—savings and loan institutions, mutual savings banks, credit unions, and the like—limited their services to transferring funds from savers to investors such as home buyers. But nonbank financial institutions are competing strongly for such accounts. The general blurring of the roles of banks and nonbank institutions reflects the dynamic character of the financial side of our economy. For ease of understanding, we discuss money creation from the perspective of commercial banks.

Among the key issues concerning commercial banking you should understand after reading Chapter 32 are

- the important process through which banks create and destroy deposits and money in the banking system.
- the critical role of required reserves—regulated by the Federal Reserve System—in the process of money creation and destruction.
- the impact of currency drains on the money and deposit creation process.
- how banks as privately owned institutions are motivated to make profits and, at the same time, to function in the money creation and destruction process in the interests of society as a whole.

MONEY CREATION BY A SINGLE BANK

The major functions of any commercial bank are to accept deposits and to make loans and investments—the same functions as the early banker-warehousers. We present a simplified balance sheet for a hypothetical individual bank in Table 1 to show how these roles interact. A balance sheet uses the accounting identity, the convention that the sum of all bank assets must equal the sum of all liabilities plus capital or net worth. The assets of the hypothetical bank are listed on the left side and liabilities and net worth on the right side. Double-entry bookkeeping—in which every asset creates an equal liability, and vice versa—guarantees that the balance sheet always balances.

Major bank liabilities are sums that the bank owes to others. These obligations include checkable, or demand, deposits, which depositors can draw on by writing checks, as well as savings, time, and interbank deposits. Liabilities also include the bank's borrowings from other commercial banks and from the Federal Reserve bank. Capital accounts, funds raised from the sale of stocks, are placed on the right side of the balance sheet, along with the liabilities.

The items that balance these figures are all the things the bank owns—cash, notes representing loans to consumers and businesses, securities, bank buildings, equipment, and so on.[1]

Balance sheets give a snapshot of banking activities. To better understand the importance of banks and their role in the expansion and contraction of the money supply, we need to step back for a moment and look at the process of how a bank gets started.

TABLE 1

Simplified Bank Balance Sheet

Capital investments of $2 million permit the formation of the Second Bank of Show Low. The left side of the balance sheet gives the bank's assets—cash, notes representing loans to its customers, securities, and buildings and equipment. This balance sheet shows that the bank's entire initial investment was used to purchase the building and furnishings. The right side of the balance sheet gives the bank's liabilities—all deposits (checkable, time, and savings), its borrowings from other banks, and capital invested in it. Double-entry bookkeeping is used, so every asset creates an equal liability, and vice versa.

Second Bank of Show Low Balance Sheet			
Assets (thousands of dollars)		Liabilities and Capital Accounts (thousands of dollars)	
Cash	0	Deposits	0
Loans	0	Borrowings	0
Securities *bank buys*	0	Capital *bank sells stocks*	2000
Plant and fixtures	2000		
Total assets	2000	Total liabilities and capital	2000

[1]Throughout this chapter we will be using the word *cash* to refer to currency and coin held in the bank's vaults or tills plus cash balances held with the Federal Reserve.

How a Bank Gets Started

Suppose that a group of investors organizes and decides that the town of Show Low, Arizona, needs a new bank and that such a bank would be profitable. They apply for and obtain a state charter and pledge $2 million in capital investment. With these funds they purchase a building, elect directors, and christen their bank the Second Bank of Show Low. The balance sheet of the bank after the purchase of the plant and equipment is given in Table 1.

Note that the accounting identity is satisfied in the balance sheet. Total assets are $2 million worth of plant and fixtures (all of the original asset, cash, was converted into the bank building and furnishings). These assets are equal in value to the sum of total liabilities and capital stock because at this point of bank organization, the initial investors have claim against the value of the bank's plant and fixtures. There are no other assets besides the building and no liabilities, but this situation cannot last if investors hope to earn a return on their capital, which they certainly do. The bank must begin to function by accepting deposits.

Assume that an entrepreneur, Josephine Eccentric, is a citizen of Show Low. Josephine has made a fortune as a fast-food restaurant organizer. She deposits $1 million in cash in the Second Bank of Show Low. The bank's new balance sheet appears as Table 2.

The Second Bank has now acquired $1 million in cash and a counterbalancing demand deposit liability. As a result of Josephine's deposit, the total money supply has not changed in amount, but it has changed in composition. Josephine gave up currency for a checking account deposit. The checkable deposit is counted as money, however, so Josephine's deposit simply altered the composition, not the amount, of the money supply. But this act of putting money in the bank as a deposit to be drawn at a later time allows the bank to create more money by means of the fractional reserve banking system.

The Fractional Reserve System

The *fractional reserve banking system*—in which banks keep only a percentage of funds deposited with them available for withdrawals—is a vital aspect of banking behavior regulated by the Federal Reserve System. We will briefly examine how Josephine's cash deposit in the Second Bank becomes part of the money creation process.

TABLE 2   **Recording a Deposit on the Balance Sheet**

A deposit of $1 million creates liabilities of $1 million for the bank and cash assets of an equal amount. Total assets remain equal to total liabilities plus capital.

Second Bank of Show Low Balance Sheet			
Assets (thousands of dollars)		Liabilities and Capital Accounts (thousands of dollars)	
Cash	1000	Deposits	1000
Loans	0	Borrowings	0
Securities	0	Capital	2000
Plant and fixtures	2000		
Total assets	3000	Total liabilities and capital	3000

Cash reserves: R
Commercial banks' and other depository institutions' holdings of vault cash or deposits at the Federal Reserve district banks.

Required reserves:
Reserves against checkable deposits that banks and other depository institutions are required by the Federal Reserve to keep in the form of cash reserves; equal to the required reserve ratio times checkable deposits; also called legal reserves.

Reserve ratio:
The percentage of checkable deposits that banks and other depository institutions hold as reserves.

Excess reserves:
Total reserves minus required reserves.

Cash assets of commercial banks held in their own vaults or at the district Federal Reserve bank are called **cash reserves.** The Federal Reserve specifies that banks and other deposit-issuing institutions must keep a certain percentage of their cash reserves on hand or with a Federal Reserve bank at all times. These **required reserves,** sometimes called legal reserves, can be expressed as a percentage of checkable deposits or as a **reserve ratio:**

$$RR = r \times D,$$

where r is the reserve ratio, D is the amount of demand deposit liabilities, and RR is the amount of required reserves for demand deposits. (Different reserve ratios apply to the various kinds of savings and time deposits.) If, for example, the deposit liabilities at a commercial bank are $1,000,000 and r is 10 percent, or 0.10, required reserves equal $100,000. If r is 5 percent, 0.05, required reserves are $50,000.

Depending on business conditions or expected loan demand, the bank may well decide to hold more than the required percentage of deposits as cash reserves. The total quantity of cash reserves held by a bank or the banking system consists of required reserves and excess reserves. **Excess reserves** are cash reserves over and above those reserves required by the Federal Reserve. If total reserves were $1,000,000, the required reserve ratio were 10 percent, and deposit liabilities were $1,000,000, excess reserves would total $900,000 ($1,000,000 − $100,000 = $900,000). Some of these excess reserves could be desirable for the bank—an extra cushion against the possibility of default, of its being unable to meet its depositors' demands for cash. Some excess, however, may be undesirable, for the bank is holding funds that it could use to earn profits through loans or purchases of securities. Generally, banks try to minimize the amount of excess reserves they keep on hand.

Assume that the bank in Show Low puts all of its cash (Federal Reserve notes) on deposit with the district Federal Reserve bank in San Francisco. Our assumption that the bank keeps none of its deposits in its own vaults is unrealistic, of course, but we are simplifying matters for clarity. The balance sheet of the Second Bank of Show Low now appears as Table 3. The balance

---

TABLE 3

Depositing a Cash Reserve in a Federal Reserve Bank

The Second Bank of Show Low deposits cash in the amount of $1 million in the San Francisco Federal Reserve bank. These cash deposits are called cash reserves or simply reserves and are recorded as cash reserve assets rather than cash on the balance sheet. Bank cash reserves are sometimes physically held in the bank's own vaults.

Second Bank of Show Low Balance Sheet			
Assets (thousands of dollars)		Liabilities and Capital Accounts (thousands of dollars)	
Cash	0	Deposits (demand)	1000
Cash reserves RR+ER	1000	Borrowings	0
Loans	0	Capital	2000
Securities	0		
Plant and fixtures	2000		
Total assets	3000	Total liabilities and capital	3000

sheet of the San Francisco Federal Reserve bank appears as Table 4. The composition of the Second Bank's assets has changed—its cash is now listed as cash reserves—but the structure as well as the total amount of liabilities and net worth remain the same as in Table 2. The Second Bank's cash reserves can be instantly converted into cash disbursements as long as the legal reserve requirement is still met. Assuming that the reserve ratio (r) is 10 percent (0.10), legal required reserves against deposits of $1,000,000 are 0.10 × $1,000,000, or $100,000. Excess reserves are $1,000,000 − $100,000, or $900,000.

Table 4 shows the change in the San Francisco Federal Reserve bank's balance sheet after accepting the Show Low bank's cash deposit. In acquiring the cash deposit, the Federal Reserve bank reduces its Federal Reserve note liabilities but incurs equivalent liabilities in the form of claims against the reserves that the Federal Reserve bank holds for the commercial bank.

Advantages and Disadvantages of Fractional Reserve Banking

An alternative to fractional reserve banking would be a system in which banks are required to hold 100 percent of their deposits on reserve. Such a system compares unfavorably to the current fractional reserve system in several respects. To begin with, 100 percent reserve banks would be unable to make loans—their role would consist solely of holding deposits for safekeeping. As a consequence, their only potential source of revenue would be a charge to depositors for the service of protecting deposits. In effect, interest rates on deposits would be negative, since depositors would be charged a fee instead of being paid interest—an unattractive prospect to depositors accustomed to earning substantial interest on deposits.

A second disadvantage of 100 percent reserve banking is that it would increase the costs of coordinating potential lenders and borrowers. Today, fractional reserve banks very ably play the role of intermediary between these two groups—without having to match each desire for a loan of particular size and maturity with a desire to lend that particular sum of money for that time period. Instead, banks gain flexibility with regard to borrowers by pooling the deposits of those with funds to lend.

TABLE 4

The Federal Reserve Bank's Balance Sheet

By accepting the Second Bank's deposit, the San Francisco Federal Reserve bank acquires cash in the amount of $1 million, thereby reducing Federal Reserve note liabilities, and incurs an equal amount of liabilities to the Second Bank in the form of reserves. Reserves are assets to the Second Bank but are liabilities to the Federal Reserve bank.

San Francisco Federal Reserve Bank Balance Sheet	
Assets (thousands of dollars)	Liabilities and Capital Accounts (thousands of dollars)
	Federal Reserve notes outstanding −1000
	Claims against reserves (Second Bank of Show Low) 1000

Despite the clear advantages of fractional reserve banking, there is one disadvantage—a lack of overall liquidity. During the normal course of business, an individual bank or all banks as a group can operate with only a small percentage of their deposits on reserve. Each day, customer deposits and withdrawals result in relatively small increases or decreases in the reserves that are available to the bank. However, should all depositors simultaneously choose to withdraw their deposits (perhaps as a consequence of a loss of confidence in the bank), the bank would not have sufficient cash to meet the demands. A single bank might be able to stop a bank run by borrowing reserves from other banks, but a widespread loss of confidence would take away this option; the practice of fractional reserve banking entails some risk of large-scale bank failure. A primary responsibility of the Federal Reserve System is to minimize this risk by making loans to banks when extra reserves are needed to meet deposit demands.

How Checks Clear

What happens within the banking system when a depositor in one bank sends a check to a depositor in another bank? Currency is not trucked from one bank to another; rather, the transaction involves bookkeeping shifts known as check clearance, orchestrated by the Federal Reserve district banks and by other clearing facilities provided by commercial banks.

Suppose Josephine, the initial depositor in the Second Bank of Show Low, plans to expand her restaurant business and requires additional inputs and equipment. She has found bargains at a restaurant supply shop in Needles, California, called Roberto's Restaurant City. A purchase of $400,000 worth of restaurant equipment is arranged, and Josephine writes a check in that amount to Roberto's that is drawn on the Show Low bank.

After Roberto's receives Josephine's check, it deposits the check in the Needles National Bank—a member of the Federal Reserve System with deposits in the Federal Reserve bank in San Francisco. Figure 1 traces the movement of the check. Needles National Bank incurs a new demand deposit liability to Roberto's, but it also acquires a matching asset—cash reserves—after the check is cleared through the San Francisco Federal Reserve bank. When Needles National Bank forwards Josephine's check to the San Francisco bank, the Federal Reserve bank balances its books by increasing its reserve liabilities to Needles National Bank and simultaneously decreasing its reserve liabilities to the Show Low bank. The Federal Reserve bank then "clears" the check by sending it on to the Second Bank of Show Low, which adjusts its own accounts by reducing cash assets by $400,000 and deposit liabilities to Josephine by the same amount. These changes are all summarized in Figure 1.

Check clearance is not a mysterious activity. The simple example of Josephine and Roberto's describes what happens every day for the millions of checks written and cleared. The example actually is one of intradistrict check clearance, where the two banks are in the same Federal Reserve district but in different and distant cities. Check clearinghouse facilities often exist within cities, in which case the services are called intracity clearing. When a check is written to someone who holds an account with the same bank, the check is cleared *intrabank,* or within the bank: Deposit liabilities are simply shifted with a change in the accounting entries on the bank's balance sheet. The principles of clearance are the same whether the writer and the receiver of the

FIGURE 1

Josephine writes a check to Roberto's in the amount of $400,000, and Roberto's deposits the check in the Needles National Bank. Needles National Bank in turn deposits the check in the San Francisco Federal Reserve bank, obtaining reserve assets. The Show Low bank loses reserve assets in the amount of $400,000, as does Josephine's account when the check is cleared and all books are balanced.

Clearing a Check

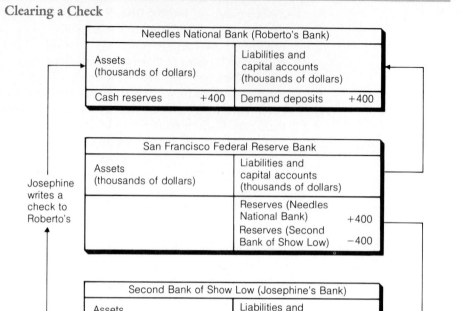

check live in the same city or in separate Federal Reserve districts (interdistrict clearing). In the latter case, all Federal Reserve banks have deposits in other Federal Reserve banks, which permits interdistrict clearing. Bookkeeping entries are adjusted without the necessity for cash to change hands. One bank gains cash reserves, another loses them. Note that the two banks involved both gain and lose reserves and deposits in equal amounts. This point is crucial in describing the process of money creation by a commercial bank or by the banking system as a whole.

Loans and Money Creation

Banking, like any other business, seeks to maximize profits. Banks earn income by investing in various private and government securities, but the most important means of earning income is making loans and earning interest on them. In a fractional reserve banking system, banks are able to make additional loans equal to the amount of their excess reserves. This important principle can be expressed symbolically as

$$L = R - rD,$$

where L is the credit or loan creation potential of a single commercial bank, R is the total reserves of the single bank, r is the legal reserve requirement on demand deposits, and D is total demand deposit liabilities.

New loans, L, cannot exceed the value of excess reserves. Consider the Second Bank of Show Low, whose cash reserves and deposit liabilities have dropped to $600,000 after Josephine's check to Roberto's for $400,000 clears (Table 5). If the Federal Reserve bank's required cash reserve ratio (r) is 10

TABLE 5

Losing Deposits and Reserves on the Balance Sheet

After Josephine's check for $400,000 has cleared, the Second Bank of Show Low loses deposit liabilities in that amount and cash reserves in the same amount.

Second Bank of Show Low Balance Sheet			
Assets (thousands of dollars)		Liabilities and Capital Accounts (thousands of dollars)	
Cash reserves	600	Demand deposits	600
Loans	0	Borrowings	0
Securities	0	Capital	2000
Plant and fixtures	2000		
Total assets	2600	Total liabilities and capital	2600

percent, $60,000 of the cash reserves must be kept on hand, leaving excess reserves of $540,000. Suppose that the Show Low bank lends this $540,000 to one borrower, Madge's Greenhouse, in demand deposits (for simplicity, we assume that no currency is withdrawn). Madge is creditworthy and will pay interest on the loan, providing the bank with returns and, presumably, profits. No one borrows money to let it sit in the bank. Madge promptly writes checks on her demand deposit account for $540,000. These transactions are summarized in Figure 2, beginning with the initial situation of the Second Bank of Show Low.

By lending Madge its excess reserves of $540,000, the bank changes its balance sheet to number 2 in Figure 2, with new loan assets and deposit liabilities. Madge then purchases $540,000 worth of goods and services, so in balance sheet number 3 of Figure 2, $540,000 of the bank's demand deposits and reserves are "checked away" to another bank or banks. In the final accounting, the balance sheet of the Second Bank of Show Low appears as number 4 in Figure 2.

The Second Bank of Show Low has created money in the process of making loans to Madge. It traded a demand deposit, which is money, for a promissory note, Madge's debt, which is not money. The money supply expands by exactly $540,000 (until, of course, the loan is paid off by Madge).

The single bank can lend out only the amount of its excess reserves because it faces the legal reserve requirement as well as the loss of both reserves and deposits. In Figure 2, for example, the Show Low bank is fully committed with loans after Madge's check has cleared (the bottom balance sheet). One more dollar loss in deposits and reserves would force the bank below the legal reserve requirement.

MONEY CREATION IN THE COMMERCIAL BANKING SYSTEM

The single commercial bank can lend only up to the amount of its excess reserves, but what of an entire banking system? How much money can be created by all of the depository institutions under control of a central bank such as the Federal Reserve System? To simplify the answer to this important

FIGURE 2

The Second Bank of Show Low creates money when it accepts something that is not money—a note pledging future payment from Madge's Greenhouse—and provides something that is—a checkable demand deposit. The bank is fully committed with loans when Madge's deposit, created by the loan, is checked away because $60,000 in reserves is required to support demand deposits of $600,000 when the required reserve ratio is 10 percent.

A Single Bank Making a Loan and Creating Money

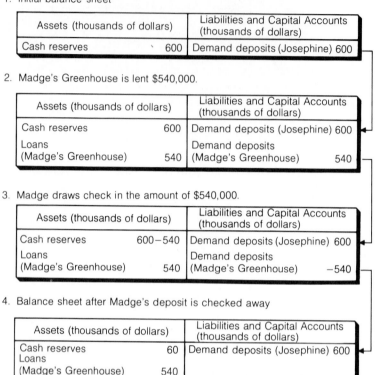

Second Bank of Show Low Balance Sheet

1. Initial balance sheet

Assets (thousands of dollars)		Liabilities and Capital Accounts (thousands of dollars)	
Cash reserves	600	Demand deposits (Josephine)	600

2. Madge's Greenhouse is lent $540,000.

Assets (thousands of dollars)		Liabilities and Capital Accounts (thousands of dollars)	
Cash reserves	600	Demand deposits (Josephine)	600
Loans (Madge's Greenhouse)	540	Demand deposits (Madge's Greenhouse)	540

3. Madge draws check in the amount of $540,000.

Assets (thousands of dollars)		Liabilities and Capital Accounts (thousands of dollars)	
Cash reserves	600−540	Demand deposits (Josephine)	600
Loans (Madge's Greenhouse)	540	Demand deposits (Madge's Greenhouse)	−540

4. Balance sheet after Madge's deposit is checked away

Assets (thousands of dollars)		Liabilities and Capital Accounts (thousands of dollars)	
Cash reserves	60	Demand deposits (Josephine)	600
Loans (Madge's Greenhouse)	540		

question, we initially assume that there is only one bank to service the entire economy—a monopoly bank, in effect. This assumption is farfetched, but it will help us understand the principles of money creation in a multibank context.

Deposit Expansion by a Monopoly Bank

We call our hypothetical monopoly bank the Universal Monopoly Bank. We initially assume that it is under the control of a central bank and that its balance sheet appears as in Table 6. If the reserve requirement imposed by the central bank is 10 percent, then Table 6 indicates that the Universal Monopoly Bank is fully committed with loans. Universal Monopoly Bank holds $150 million in cash reserves against deposit liabilities of $1.5 billion; in other words, cash reserves are exactly 10 percent of total deposits. Universal Monopoly Bank has no excess reserves and therefore no lending capacity.

Suppose that for stabilization purposes, the central bank wishes to buy $50 million of the securities from Universal. (These securities are promises to pay back the principal, or face value, at maturity plus interest over specified time periods.) How does the central bank induce the Universal Monopoly

TABLE 6

Universal Monopoly Bank's Initial Balance Sheet

With deposit liabilities of $1.5 billion and a cash reserve requirement of 10 percent, the Universal Monopoly Bank is fully committed with loans because it holds exactly $150 million in cash reserve assets. The Universal Monopoly Bank does not face the possibility of losing deposits and reserves to other banks, however, because there are no others.

Universal Monopoly Bank Balance Sheet			
Assets (millions of dollars)		Liabilities and Capital Accounts (millions of dollars)	
Cash reserves	150	Deposits	1500
Loans	250	Borrowings	0
Securities	1000	Capital	500
Plant and fixtures	600		
Total assets	2000	Total liabilities and capital	2000

Bank to sell its securities? It goes into the open securities market and increases its demand for securities. The increase in demand raises the price of such securities, provoking a sales response from the monopoly commercial bank, which seeks to earn a capital gain. (For simplicity, the capital gain is omitted in our analysis.) If we assume that Universal Monopoly Bank sells $50 million worth of its previous total of $1 billion in securities, its new balance sheet appears as in Table 7.

In Table 7, securities have been converted into cash reserves, meaning that the monopoly bank now has excess reserves of $50 million. The question now is, What quantity of demand deposit liabilities will this $50 million support?

If the Universal Monopoly Bank lent out all its excess reserves, loans would expand by $50 million, as would deposit liabilities. But what of cash reserves? Since the bank is a monopoly, it cannot lose reserves to other banks in the system via check clearance, for there are no other banks in the system. Cash reserves therefore will remain at the same level—$200 million—after an

TABLE 7

Selling Securities and Creating Excess Reserves

A sale of $50 million worth of securities (such as U.S. Treasury bills) for cash increases Universal Monopoly Bank's reserves by $50 million. These cash reserves of $50 million are excess reserves because they are greater than the amount ($150 million) required against $1.5 billion in deposit liabilities.

Universal Monopoly Bank Balance Sheet			
Assets (millions of dollars)		Liabilities and Capital Accounts (millions of dollars)	
Cash reserves	200	Deposits	1500
Loans	250	Borrowings	0
Securities	950	Capital	500
Plant and fixtures	600		
Total assets	2000	Total liabilities and capital	2000

initial loan and deposit creation of $50 million. Since reserves cannot be checked away, the Universal Monopoly Bank will still hold excess reserves after the loan. Under a 10 percent reserve requirement, deposit liabilities of $1.550 billion require only $155 million in legal cash reserves. The bank still holds excess reserves in the amount of $45 million ($200 − $155 = $45). Suppose it lends that amount. Lending out $45 million in deposits will create still another income-earning asset (loans), and new deposit liabilities will now be $1.595 billion and required reserves will be $159.5 million (10 percent). Excess reserves still remain in the amount of $40.5 million. If the bank continues to lend excess reserves to new borrowers who hold demand deposits (and no currency), the creation of money through **deposit expansion** will be many times the initial amount of excess reserves. Deposit expansion is the total amount of money created above some initial amount of excess reserves.

The total amount of deposits that can be supported by cash reserves can be conveniently expressed as

$$D = R\left(\frac{1}{r}\right),$$

where D is the total amount of deposits and demand deposit money created, R is the total amount of cash reserves, and r is the required reserve ratio.[2]

The reciprocal of the reserve ratio $(1/r)$ is sometimes referred to as the **simple money multiplier**—the number multiplied by reserves to obtain total deposit expansion. In the example of the Universal Monopoly Bank, the money multiplier is 10 $(1/0.10 = 10)$. The lower the required reserve ratio, the larger the money multiplier; the higher the ratio, the smaller the multiplier. For example, a value of r of 20 percent would reduce the value of the multiplier to 5 $(1/0.20 = 5)$.

To see the effects of the money multiplier, consider the final position of the monopoly bank after all excess reserves have been eliminated from the system. The monopoly bank is again fully committed in loans, as shown in Table 8. Reserves of $200 million support $2 billion in deposits (money). This value is calculated from the deposit expansion equation, $D = R(1/r)$, or $2000 = $200(10)$. The change in deposits and the money supply can be calculated using a slight variation of the earlier expression:

$$\Delta D = \Delta \text{ reserves}\left(\frac{1}{r}\right),$$

or, in the case of the Universal Monopoly Bank,

$$\$500 = \$50\left(\frac{1}{0.10}\right).$$

Deposit expansion:
The total amount of additional money or checkable deposits created by some given amount of excess reserves.

Simple money multiplier:
The reciprocal of the reserve ratio.

---

[2]There is a clear parallel between the investment (or autonomous expenditures) multiplier discussed in Chapter 13 and the money multiplier. Recall that the autonomous expenditures multiplier is equal to the reciprocal of the marginal propensity to save (*MPS*). It is the multiple by which income changes when autonomous (investment or consumption) spending changes. The money multiplier is calculated in similar fashion, but it is the reciprocal of the required reserve ratio. It is the percentage by which money expands or contracts with increases or decreases in excess cash reserves in the banking system. The *MPS* is the leakage from the income expansion process, while the required reserve ratio is the leakage from the deposit expansion process.

TABLE 8

Increasing Deposit Liabilities and Loans

Initial excess reserves of $50 million can support an additional $500 million in deposit liabilities in the monopoly bank when the money multiplier is 10. A monopoly bank, unlike a single commercial bank, cannot lose deposits or reserves to other banks.

Universal Monopoly Bank Balance Sheet			
Assets (millions of dollars)		Liabilities and Capital Accounts (millions of dollars)	
Cash reserves	200	Deposits	2000
Loans	750	Borrowings	0
Securities	950	Capital	500
Plant and fixtures	600		
Total assets	2500	Total liabilities and capital	2500

By selling $50 million in securities, the monopoly bank actually increased the money supply by $500 million, the amount of deposits that the cash it receives will legally support.

A crucial principle emerges from this example of the monopoly bank: Single commercial banks, like the Second Bank of Show Low, can lend and create checkbook money only in an amount equal to their excess reserves, whereas a monopoly bank can lend and create money by a multiple $(1/r)$ of its excess reserves. Now we will see how this principle translates into the real world of the U.S. multibank competitive banking system.

Money Expansion in the Multibank System

Just as the monopoly bank cannot lose reserves when deposits are checked away, the banking system as a whole can lose neither reserves nor deposits. **Money expansion** through the loan process is the same for the fractional reserve multibank system used in the United States as for the simple monopoly bank we just described. Once again, we will analyze the process of money creation in the multibank system with the use of balance sheets.

As with the Universal Monopoly Bank case, we must begin with some simplifying assumptions. First, we assume that the entire banking system is initially fully committed with loans. There are initially no excess reserves in the system. Second, all borrowers at all commercial banks are assumed to want their loans in demand deposits rather than in currency. Third, as in the previous balance sheets, savings deposits are assumed not to exist. Fourth, we assume that banks are solely profit maximizers and do not wish to hold any excess cash reserves. In other words, banks do not hold any reserves in excess of legally required reserves. Finally, to simplify matters even further, we assume that in each transaction, the bank granting a loan lends its entire excess reserves to a single borrower who places the loan in another bank, which then does the same thing. We assume that excess reserves work their way through the banking system in this simplified manner.

Initially, we assume that Cut and Shoot National Bank and all other commercial banks are fully committed with loans. Now suppose that Monica, a wealthy miser, deposits $1 million in cash in Cut and Shoot National Bank. The balance sheet change for Cut and Shoot is shown in Table 9a. The bank

Money expansion:
The increase in the money supply created by some given amount of excess reserves.

TABLE 9   Money Creation in the Commercial Banking System

Money is created as loans and demand deposits are created in the banking system. In this example, as before, the reserve requirement is 10 percent. (a) Cut and Shoot National has excess reserves of $900,000, which it lends to Jonathan. (b) When Jonathan checks his new deposit away to Yvonne, a customer of Altoona State Bank, Cut and Shoot loses deposit liabilities and cash reserve assets of $900,000 to Altoona State Bank. (c, d) Altoona State Bank, with excess reserves of $810,000, lends the entire amount to Chris, creating new money in the amount of $810,000 in demand deposits. (e) Chris checks his deposits away to a third bank (not shown), leaving Altoona State Bank fully committed with loans. As excess reserves and deposits move through the financial system, money is created.

(a) Cut and Shoot National Balance Sheet

Cash reserves	+ 1000	Deposits (Monica)	+ 1000

(b) Cut and Shoot National Balance Sheet

Cash reserves	+ 1000	Deposits (Monica)	+ 1000
Loans (Jonathan)	+ 900	Deposits (Jonathan)	+ 900

(c) Cut and Shoot National Balance Sheet

Cash reserves	+ 100	Deposits (Monica)	+ 1000
Loans (Jonathan)	+ 900		

(d) Altoona State Bank Balance Sheet

Cash reserves	+ 900	Deposits (Yvonne)	+ 900

(e) Altoona State Bank Balance Sheet

Cash reserves	+ 900	Deposits (Yvonne)	+ 900
Loans (Chris)	+ 810	Deposits (Chris)	+ 810

(f) Altoona State Bank Balance Sheet

Cash reserves	+ 90	Deposits (Yvonne)	+ 900
Loans (Chris)	+ 810		

Note: Balance sheet figures in thousands of dollars.

acquires cash reserve assets and demand deposit liabilities (to Monica) of $1 million. Cut and Shoot is now in a position to lend dollar for dollar with its excess reserves. Given the assumptions described and a legal required reserve ratio of 10 percent, excess reserves exist in the amount of $900,000. Total reserves in the bank are $1 million, and required reserves are $100,000. $(R - rD) = \$1,000,000 - (0.10 \times \$1,000,000) = \$900,000.$

Cut and Shoot finds a borrower, Jonathan, for the entire amount of its excess reserves. Table 9b reflects the position of Cut and Shoot after it makes the loan. The asset category Loans is enhanced by $900,000, as are deposits of a like amount. Jonathan, however, does not let his demand deposit lie idle. He has been in debt to Yvonne of Altoona State Bank on a business deal and wishes to pay back $900,000 of the debt. Jonathan writes a check to Yvonne, who deposits it in her bank. When Jonathan's check is cleared through the Federal Reserve System's interdistrict clearinghouse, Cut and Shoot loses cash reserves of $900,000 and Jonathan's deposit liabilities of the same amount. Simultaneously, Altoona State Bank gains cash reserves and deposit liabilities of $900,000. Cut and Shoot is left with an interest-earning asset (the loan to Jonathan), but its cash reserves have been checked away to another bank. At a 10 percent legal reserve ratio, Cut and Shoot is fully committed with loans.

Not so at Altoona State Bank. After Yvonne's deposit, Altoona State Bank has excess reserves in the amount of $810,000 [$900,000 − (0.10 × $900,000)]. These reserves may be lent to provide income for the bank. A borrower, Chris, wants the entire proceeds of the loan in the form of a demand deposit so that he can pay off a debt to Susan, a creditor who lives in Buffalo. Susan accepts Chris's check and deposits it in her bank (Buffalo Bank and Trust, not shown in Table 9). After Chris's deposit is checked away to Buffalo, Altoona State Bank loses deposit liabilities of $810,000 and cash reserves of the same amount. Altoona State Bank is fully committed with loans (Table 9f) when it holds $90,000 in legally required reserves against Yvonne's deposit of $900,000.

Excess reserves make their way through the banking system in the manner described in Table 9. Each individual bank can lend only an amount that is within its excess reserves, but part of these reserves becomes excess to some other bank in the system.

Naturally, the process described in the balance sheets of Table 9 does not end with Altoona State Bank. Reserves are checked away to Buffalo and may stay in Buffalo, be checked away to some other bank, or return to Cut and Shoot. Given our assumptions about the continuous movement of excess reserves through the system, the money creation process stops only when there are no more excess reserves within the commercial banking system. Table 10 summarizes this process.

The initial $1 million deposit of cash creates $9 million worth of new loans and deposits. As the individual commercial banks make loans, they are accepting something from borrowers that is not money—a private note payable to the bank—and are providing the borrower with a demand deposit that is money. Individual banks can lend dollar for dollar with excess reserves only

TABLE 10

Creating Money as Excess Reserves Work Their Way Through the Banking System

The money multiplier, the reciprocal of the required reserve ratio, determines the amount by which the money supply can increase. With a required reserve ratio of 10 percent and initial excess reserves of $900,000, demand deposits and the money supply can be increased by $9 million.

Bank	Reserves and Deposits Acquired	Required Reserves	Excess Reserves	Bank Loans	Increase in Demand Deposits	Increase in Money Supply
Cut and Shoot	1000	100	900	900	900	900
Altoona State	900	90	810	810	810	810
Buffalo Bank and Trust	810	81	729	729	729	729
.	.	.	.	.	.	.
.	.	.	.	.	.	.
.	.	.	.	.	.	.
All other banks	7290	729	6561	6561	6561	6561
Totals	10,000	1000	9000	9000	9000	9000

Note: All numbers are in thousands of dollars.

because they face the possibility of losing both cash reserves and deposits, but reserves and deposits cannot be lost to the multibank system as a whole. We may think of this system as closed, just as the monopoly bank could not lose deposits and reserves. In fact, the expression for deposit expansion that applies to the monopoly bank applies to the commercial banking system as well. In both cases, deposit expansion is expressed as

$$\Delta D = \Delta \text{ reserves} \left(\frac{1}{r}\right),$$

or, in this case,

$$\$10,000,000 = \$1,000,000 \left(\frac{1}{0.10}\right).$$

Deposits expand by $10 million when reserves of $1 million are introduced into the system. However, the money supply expands by only $9 million because Monica no longer holds $1 million in cash. Do not forget that the initial cash deposit of $1 million (Monica's deposit) merely altered the form of the money supply from currency outstanding (in Monica's possession before her deposit) to demand deposits. The money supply was not increased by Monica's cash deposit, although Cut and Shoot Bank had to hold a legal cash reserve of $100,000 against it. The money supply increased by $9 million through the process of deposit expansion *after* the initial deposit of $1 million. Thus, the change in the money supply, ΔM, is expressed as

$$\Delta M = \Delta \text{ excess reserves} \left(\frac{1}{r}\right), \text{ or}$$

$$\$9,000,000 = \$900,000 \left(\frac{1}{0.10}\right).$$

Money is expanded on the basis of excess reserves, and money expansion takes place at the same rate as the expansion of loans and deposits. In fact, money expansion is equivalent to demand deposit expansion. The process of money expansion can also work in reverse. Contraction of the money supply is possible within the fractional reserve commercial banking system.

MONEY SUPPLY LEAKAGES

Two important sources of leakage from the money expansion process are cash withdrawals and idle reserves. In the previous section, we eliminated both situations for simplicity. Here we examine how either cash withdrawal or idle reserves can slow or even reverse the process of money expansion.

Currency Drain

In the example described in the previous section, if a depositor had withdrawn cash from his or her account in the Cut and Shoot Bank, a chain of deposit destruction could have been brought about. While the act of currency withdrawal by itself does not initially alter the money supply, the bank's cash reserves—the raw material that it draws on to make loans—would be depleted. Especially if Cut and Shoot Bank fell below its legal reserve requirement, it would be forced to call in or not renew loans. This action would cause reductions in cash reserves in other parts of the commercial banking system. In the limit, deposits could be reduced by

$$\Delta D = \Delta \text{ reserves} \left(\frac{1}{r} \right).$$

Note that the money supply would fall by *less* than deposits fall, since the initial withdrawal of cash from the Cut and Shoot Bank does not alter the money supply. Cash (a part of the money supply) is increased and deposits (also a part of the money supply) are reduced in equal amounts in the initial transaction between bank and depositor.

A normal demand for cash is to be expected, even in a modern system of electronic transfers and at-home computerized bill payment. (For a discussion of the effects of new technology on demand for cash, see Focus, "The Future of Cash.") Currency and coin are still necessary to accommodate day-to-day transactions—coins for a candy bar or soda from a machine or currency to pay for a subway ride or lunch. Economists express this demand for cash through the **currency-deposit ratio,** which is simply the desired ratio of currency holdings to demand deposit holdings, on average and for all money holders. In the United States, the ratio has fluctuated widely through history, from high levels during bank panics and depressions to lower levels with the advent of federally insured and closely regulated commercial banking, as well as with modern computerized credit card payment schemes. In recent years, the ratio has been around $1 in currency desired for every $3 or so in demand deposits.

Let us assume that the currency-deposit ratio approximates 30 percent. What is the significance of a currency-deposit ratio of 30 percent for money expansion in a commercial bank? Any currency drain from the system is a leakage that reduces the ability of the commercial banking system to create deposits and money. If a bank acquires cash reserves of $1 million and lends to the limit with a 10 percent reserve requirement, the bank will lend $900,000. But if the average borrower's desired currency-deposit ratio is 30 percent, the borrower will want 30 percent of the loan, or $270,000, in cash, taking the remainder, $630,000, in demand deposits. (Actually, the person or persons paid by the borrower will hold the cash—a complication we ignore for now.) If this currency leakage continues to circulate and the cash does not find its way back into banks—a likely event—the deposit- and money-creating potential of the banking system is reduced.

Currency withdrawals, then, are a leakage that reduces the ability of the commercial banking system to create deposits and money. They are like required reserves in their ability to restrict deposit and money expansion. A slightly more complicated expression for deposit and money expansion or contraction gives us an idea of the effect of this currency leakage:

$$\Delta M = \Delta \text{excess reserves} \left(\frac{1 + c}{c + r} \right),$$

where c is the currency-deposit ratio, r is the reserve-deposit ratio (the legal

Currency-deposit ratio:
The percentage of total deposits held that people also wish to hold in the form of currency; currency holdings expressed as a decimal fraction of checkable deposit holdings.

FOCUS   The Future of Cash

A generation ago, regulation of the banking industry was much tighter than it is today. Most states strictly limited the hours during which banks could be open for business, and many states prohibited banks from opening branch offices. In addition, banks were legally prohibited from competing by offering higher rates of interest to depositors. Someone once quipped that to succeed in that era, bankers only had to obey the "3-6-3 rule" of banking—pay 3 percent on deposits, charge 6 percent on loans, and close at 3:00 in the afternoon to go golfing. If there was ever any truth in that statement, it certainly doesn't hold for today's bankers; changes both in bank regulation and bank technology have had dramatic effects on the day-to-day operation of commercial banks. One consequence of these changes is that it is now much more convenient for depositors to withdraw cash. In the past, withdrawals could be made only during the regular and quite limited business hours. With limited branch banking, this generally meant arranging a visit to your bank's sole location in the central business district during business hours. Because of the inconvenience of such trips, individuals had an incentive to withdraw relatively large sums on each bank visit. Many customers, therefore, maintained high average cash holdings.

Today, bank hours have been greatly extended, and branch banks have sprung up everywhere—even inside supermarkets. Changes in technology have enabled banks to offer automated teller services. A large bank is likely to have dozens of automated teller machines (ATMs) located throughout its service area, giving customers convenient access to cash twenty-four hours a day. ATMs have also been linked in nationwide networks, making it possible for customers to obtain cash quickly in other cities. Banks are also offering a variety of services by which funds can be transferred electronically from a depositor to a business establishment. Are cash holdings becoming obsolete?

Given the changes we've mentioned and the growing use of credit cards, you might expect the currency-deposit ratio to have decreased dramatically in recent years. However, this has not yet proven to be the case. As Table 11 shows, the currency-deposit ratio in the United States rose fairly steadily from 1960 until 1984. It dropped sharply between 1984 and 1986 and then increased again. The technology for transferring funds electronically already exists, but most retailers and consumers appear reluctant to abandon cash; for one thing, with electronic transfers every transaction is recorded—a departure from cash transactions that, for a variety of reasons, lacks universal appeal.

One factor that undoubtedly has affected the currency-deposit ratio is the growth of the underground economy. Many of the activities in the underground economy are legal, although income often is not reported or is underreported. Waiters and waitresses, bartenders, hairstylists, and cab

TABLE 11
Changes in the Currency-Deposit Ratio, 1960–1989

The ratio of currency to deposits held by the public rose steadily from 1960 to 1984, dipped in 1986, and began to rise again. Growth in the underground economy—for example, in the drug trade—tends to increase the ratio.

Year	Currency-Deposit Ratio
1960	0.257
1962	0.258
1964	0.269
1966	0.284
1968	0.273
1970	0.294
1972	0.293
1974	0.326
1976	0.354
1978	0.371
1980	0.393
1982	0.390
1984	0.400
1986	0.335
1988	0.371
1989	0.386

Source: Council of Economic Advisers, *Economic Report of the President* (Washington, D.C.: U.S. Government Printing Office, 1990), p. 372. Computed from data in Table B-68.

drivers are among those who may not report tips they receive; and, especially among service providers, a certain amount of bartering goes unreported. However, as confirmed by news reports featuring pictures of piles of money recovered in drug arrests, illegal activities play a significant part in the underground economy. Since illegal transactions are almost always conducted with cash, rapid growth in the underground economy will tend to increase the currency-deposit ratio.

It appears that cash is falling into disuse in the traditional economy but that it still plays a major role in the underground economy. The direction of the currency-deposit ratio in the future depends on many factors, one of which is our country's drug policy. Therefore, the Federal Reserve should be alert to any changes in drug policy that might affect cash holdings and, therefore, the money multiplier. If the Fed believes that the "war on drugs" is being waged successfully, it should anticipate a rise in the money multiplier due to a reduction in cash holdings and should be prepared to take offsetting actions to prevent undesired increases in the money supply.

required reserve ratio), and M is money created.[3] If we give a value of 10 percent to r, 30 percent to c, and excess reserves increase to \$900,000 in an otherwise fully committed banking system, how might the money supply expand? The result will be

$$\Delta M = \$900{,}000\left(\frac{1.30}{0.40}\right), \text{ or } \$2{,}925{,}000 = \$900{,}000(3.25).$$

Deposits and the money stock expand by \$2,925,000, much lower than the \$9 million expansion when no currency drain was considered. The money multiplier in this case is $(1 + c)/(c + r)$, or 3.25, whereas it was $1/r$, or 10, when no currency drain was considered. The existence of a currency drain, therefore, lowers money expansion possibilities in the U.S. fractional reserve banking system because it lowers the money multiplier. It is a leakage in the money creation process.

As Chapter 33 will show, the Federal Reserve System could stem this contraction by supplying supplementary cash reserves to the banking system. Indeed, one of the reasons the Federal Reserve System was created was to stem semihysterical currency drains or bank runs by acting as a lender of last resort. You should be aware nevertheless that the money supply can be shrunk as well as expanded through the banking system.

Idle Reserves

In earlier examples we assumed that banks did not wish to hold idle reserves above those that were required by the central bank. This assumption is clearly not the case, especially during periods of high economic uncertainty. Banks are privately owned, profit-maximizing institutions, but they also tend to be prudent. As we indicated earlier, a bank totally committed with loans will fall below its legal required reserve if so much as \$1 in cash reserves is withdrawn. Banks will not ordinarily let this happen because of the resulting embarrassment and possible repercussions from the Federal Reserve System or from other lenders or clients. Commercial banks therefore usually hold an additional amount in cash reserves. It should be clear that any holding of idle reserves by commercial banks further reduces the possibilities of money and

---

[3]This more complex expression is obtained in the following way. If in addition to demand deposits the public holds cash, then the money stock equals demand deposits plus currency held by the public. Any change in the money supply is equal to the sum of changes in D and C, or $\Delta M = \Delta D + \Delta C$. However, with a currency ratio of c, $C = c(D)$. Any change in the public's currency holdings can be written as $\Delta C = c(\Delta D)$. Substituting into the equation above, $\Delta M = \Delta D + c\Delta D$, so $\Delta M = (1 + c)\Delta D$.

The equation $\Delta D = \Delta$ reserves $(1/r)$ holds only if all new reserves are used to support new deposits. If a portion of the new reserves come to be held as cash, then that equation must be rewritten $\Delta D = (\Delta$ reserves $- \Delta C) (1/r)$, since ΔC represents the new reserves that cannot support deposits. Rearranging, $r\Delta D = \Delta$ reserves $- \Delta C$, and $\Delta C + r\Delta D = \Delta$ reserves. Substituting $c\Delta D$ for ΔC in this equation yields $c\Delta D + r\Delta D = \Delta$ reserves. Therefore, $\Delta D (c + r) = \Delta$ reserves, and $\Delta D = \Delta$ reserves$/(c + r)$.

We have seen that $\Delta M = (1 + c) \Delta D$. If for ΔD in this equation we substitute Δ reserves/$(c + r)$, we obtain $\Delta M = (1 + c) \Delta$ reserves/$(c + r)$. Rearranging, $\Delta M = \Delta$ reserves $\left(\dfrac{1 + c}{c + r}\right)$.

Even this money multiplier is a simplification. For example, if we consider the possibility that financial institutions may hold excess reserves or if we account for noncheckable deposits on which reserves must be held, the money multiplier becomes even more complex. The true multiplier involves approximately forty variables.

deposit expansion. In other words, the holding of idle reserves, like the currency drain, acts as a brake to increases in the money supply as well as a cushion against decreases.

While other, more complex money multipliers involving savings and government deposits could be considered, it is sufficient here simply to understand the major factors affecting money expansion and contraction. By now you may suspect a deeper theme to money creation and destruction than the simple mechanical exercises of this chapter. Another actor in addition to the commercial banks and the public lurks backstage. The Federal Reserve System pulls the strings that control deposit and money expansion within the commercial banking system. We have only indirectly hinted at the tools of the Federal Reserve in manipulating the money stock. The details of this process will be discussed in Chapter 33.

THE BOTTOM LINE: TO MAKE MONEY BY CREATING MONEY

Commercial banks and some other financial institutions are basically no different from firms that sell shoes or hamburgers. (Indeed, banks may take on unusual forms; see Economics in Action, "How Does a Pub Become a Bank? The Modern Case of Ireland," at the end of this chapter.) They are in business to make a profit. Yet they also perform an essential macroeconomic role in that they create money. The proper management of these institutions is crucial to achieve three interrelated goals: (1) pleasing stockholders with adequate—that is, competitive—returns on their investments; (2) keeping the bank solvent and liquid; and (3) reacting to the implementation of ever-changing government (Federal Reserve) regulation over banking activity.

Returns on Investment

Bank management is tricky business. Think about how banks make profits. Banks and other depository institutions sell services such as savings, checking, and money market savings accounts. As any bank customer knows, these services come in a variety of packages. Some checking accounts are interest-bearing, offering limited checking privileges without cost, while others do not bear interest but offer unlimited checking with minimum balances. NOW accounts and super-NOW accounts available at various financial institutions are examples of interest-bearing checking services.

In addition to the costs of supervising many different kinds of accounts, depository institutions must bear the interest costs associated with savings accounts. Interest must be paid on all passbook and other types of savings and time deposits. These institutions have been allowed to pay unlimited interest on money market savings accounts since 1983, with competition for depositors' money leading to higher interest costs to banks and other financial institutions.

Demand deposits and all other deposits form the raw material from which financial institutions can earn income by lending. These institutions make loans for many purposes, but specialization in certain types of loans has occurred. Thrift institutions such as savings and loans and mutual savings banks have traditionally given long-term home and property mortgage loans, while commercial banks have concentrated on short-term consumer and business loans. Many of these institutions also earn interest returns from investments in securities.

The difference between a bank's costs and returns determines the profit to its stockholders. The spread between interest paid and interest received is an indication of the profitability of a bank, but banks incur costs other than interest. Labor costs in the servicing of deposit liabilities are a significant factor, so a spread of 14 percent interest received and 7½ percent interest paid is not necessarily an indication of great profitability. In more specific terms, the profitability of a financial institution depends on management of the bank's portfolios of assets and liabilities. The profit-maximizing structure of the portfolio changes constantly with changing market conditions and Federal Reserve regulations or deregulations.

Solvency and Liquidity

As with any other business, the bank or financial institution must maintain both liquidity, the ability to meet current depositor liabilities in cash, and solvency, the ability of all assets to cover all liabilities. In an attempt to make high returns, an incautious bank manager may develop an unwise or unsafe loan policy, perhaps by lending to speculative or high-risk borrowers. Although longer-term and higher-risk loans typically earn higher interest and income, both liquidity and solvency may be threatened by such loans. To further complicate the problem, variability in deposits and shifts within a bank between types of deposits are not exactly predictable. The possibility of coming up short when depositors demand repayment in cash is always very real for a bank or depository institution. As a result, these institutions have developed sophisticated methods of portfolio management.

Government Regulations

Banks are for-profit, privately owned institutions, but they are also regulated by government. Their major function of creating or destroying money is of the highest importance to economic society. The regulatory umbrella over the entire banking system includes a multiplicity of state and, particularly, federal regulations. The maintenance of legally required reserves is but one of the Federal Reserve System's regulations. Indeed, the U.S. constitutional authority to print and control money is carried out through the Federal Reserve System. The manner in which the Federal Reserve conducts its activities through a privately owned banking and financial system is the subject of Chapter 33.

SUMMARY

1. A bank gets started by accepting capital through selling stock to investors. After purchasing a bank building and equipment, the bank begins to perform the major functions of accepting deposits and making loans.
2. Through double-entry bookkeeping, the deposit of cash by an individual or business means that the bank's cash assets are counterbalanced by a corresponding amount of demand deposit liabilities.
3. The Federal Reserve System requires that all banks and financial institutions accepting checkable deposits must hold a certain percentage, called the required reserve ratio, of cash reserves against deposit liabilities.
4. All reserves above required reserves are called excess reserves. Banks can lend and create demand deposit money on the basis of their excess reserves.
5. An individual commercial bank can lend dollar for dollar with its excess reserves, but a single monopoly bank can lend and create money by a multiple of its

excess reserves because its reserves and deposits cannot be checked away to other banks. The commercial banking system, like the monopoly bank, can lend and create money by a multiple of its excess reserves.
6. The multiple of excess reserves by which the banking system can create money is called the money multiplier. The simple money multiplier is the reciprocal of the required reserve ratio ($1/r$). Deposits and the money supply will expand or contract by an amount equal to the multiplier times the change in excess reserves.
7. A currency drain resulting from an increased demand for cash and coin or the maintenance of idle reserves by banks will reduce the value of the money multiplier.
8. Banks create or destroy money in an attempt to make profits. Commercial banks and other financial institutions, though privately owned and motivated to make profits, are nonetheless controlled in the public interest by the Federal Reserve System.

KEY TERMS

| cash reserves | reserve ratio | deposit expansion | money expansion |
| required reserves | excess reserves | simple money multiplier | currency-deposit ratio |

QUESTIONS FOR REVIEW AND DISCUSSION

1. Are commercial banks the only creators of money in the market?
2. What are the options for a bank if it finds that its actual reserves have fallen below its required reserves?
3. Explain how checks are cleared within a bank, between two banks in the same Federal Reserve district, and between two banks in different Federal Reserve districts. Look on the backs of some cleared checks. Are there clues as to whether these cleared between banks in the same district or in different districts?
4. By how much can a single bank increase the money supply from a deposit of $1 million of new cash? By how much can the entire banking system increase the money supply from such an injection?
5. If a bank purchases U.S. government securities from the Federal Reserve, does this purchase increase the money supply? Does the money supply change if an individual purchases a government bond from the Federal Reserve?
6. If $2 million were stolen from a bank's vault, would this theft increase or decrease the money supply?
7. What is a currency drain? If the currency drain increases, does it increase the money supply? Why?
8. "Banks do not like to hold excess reserves." Is this statement true? Explain.
9. What is the money multiplier? What does it show?
10. Why would anybody want to own a bank? What is the output of a bank? What is the essential input that banks must purchase to produce this output?

PROBLEM

If the reserve requirement is 15 percent and the currency-deposit ratio is 0, what happens to the money supply if the Federal Reserve injects $150,000 in cash into the banking system? How would this number change with a currency-deposit ratio of 5 percent?

ECONOMICS IN ACTION
How Does a Pub Become a Bank? The Modern Case of Ireland

The proportion of hand-to-hand currency relative to checkbook money is low in most advanced societies. Historically, Americans' use of currency is only one-third the amount of checkable deposits, though the ratio changes over time. Other countries have even lower ratios of currency to demand deposits. Ireland's ratio, for example, was 18 percent in 1966, 15 percent in 1970, and 14 percent in 1976. But Ireland is unique in that its banks close frequently and for longer periods of time than banks of any other relatively advanced nation in the world. In fact, Irish banks closed for varying periods during 1966, 1970, and 1976 because of industrial disputes. For almost seven months (May 1–November 17) during 1970, citizens of the Republic of Ireland were deprived of the services of the Associated Banks, their branches, and their clearing facilities, which controlled virtually all of Ireland's demand deposits. Without 85 percent of its money supply, could Irish society function? Did the Irish resort to barter and to the reduced economic activity associated with barter? In 1979, Antoin E. Murphy of Trinity College, Dublin, presented some intriguing evidence on all of the bank closures, especially the long 1970 closure.[a]

Money did not totally disappear after the bank closures. Irish currency and coin continued to circulate, and some major companies were provided with account facilities and clearing services by North American and non-Associated banks. The Central Bank of Ireland transferred currency to government departments at the beginning of the closure to pay wages and salaries of government employees and to continue welfare payments, but at the end of the closure there was only a net addition of £4 million to the currency supply.

The increased demand for currency was partially offset by the summer tourist trade. Currency freely circulates in Ireland, and from April to November currency in circulation grew from £5 million to about £40 million. The North American and non-Associated banks provided some demand deposit transactions with means of alternative payment, but the aid was very limited because these banks had no branch facilities and were physically incapable of handling the volume of new business. By the end of May most of these banks refused to handle new accounts. In November 1970, according to Murphy's estimate, there was a total of £52 million in new demand deposits to facilitate consumers' money demands. This was less than one-twelfth of the closed Associated Banks' demand deposit accounts! How, then, did the Irish manage to transact?

People simply continued writing checks against pre-closure deposits and against checks received from other parties. During the bank closure, checks were written not against known accounts, but against the value of other uncleared checks along with the check receiver's assessment of the writer's creditworthiness. In such circumstances, default risk increased. Further, there was uncertainty about when the banks would reopen. Credit was therefore undated.

In this situation a personalized transaction system substituted for an institutionalized one. The nature of the Irish economy helped. A high degree of personal contact exists in the Irish population of about 3 million. Where personal information was lacking, credit information often existed at the 12,000 retail shops and at the more than 11,000 pubs in the Republic. One pub exists in Ireland for every 190 citizens over eighteen years of age. A pub keeper does not serve ale to a customer for years, as Murphy put it, "without discovering something of his liquid resources." Thus, pubs and shops provided goods, services, and currency for their customers against undated checks. They in fact formed the nexus of a substitute banking system.

Economic activity actually grew over the period at a somewhat reduced rate. There were no significant differences in retail sales and no significant deflationary trends. The important point is that information was the key to the emergence of a substitute medium of exchange. The Irish economy did not collapse or even cease growing when deprived of over 80 percent of its money. It simply and naturally fell back on or invented new and alternative forms of transacting.

Question

Suppose all banks closed in the United States. Who would experience more difficulty in finding bank substitutes—city dwellers or citizens of small towns? Who would most likely assume the role of banker—your local power company or your local hairstylist?

[a]Antoin E. Murphy, "Money in an Economy Without Banks: The Case of Ireland," *Manchester School of Economics and Social Studies* 46–47 (1978–1979), pp. 41–50.

33

Money Regulation by the Federal Reserve System

The economic power of the Federal Reserve Board is awesome. Changes in Federal Reserve policy or even general comments on the health of the economy by the chairman of the Federal Reserve Board frequently send the stock market plunging or soaring. Fed-watching—anticipating the Federal Reserve's next change in policy—is so important to investors that some major investment banking houses pay experts more than $200,000 a year, three times the salary of the Federal Reserve Board chairman, to monitor Federal Reserve activity.

Until 1980, the Federal Reserve System had extensive regulatory control only over banks that were members of the Federal Reserve. The Fed had less authority over nonmember banks or over financial institutions such as credit unions and savings and loans. Federal Reserve controls over nonmember banks did include some regulation of the sorts of liabilities they could issue and the kinds of businesses that could be owned by bank holding companies. However, the Fed could not determine reserve requirements or monitor and control the risk-taking behavior of nonmember banks. As a consequence of two separate developments during the 1970s, this lack of control by the Fed came to be viewed with alarm. The first development was the entry of nonbanks into the checking market—previously, the exclusive domain of banks. The second development was a large-scale withdrawal of banks from the Federal Reserve System. By 1980, then, a large portion of all checkable accounts was held in financial institutions outside the control of the Federal Reserve. Concern was expressed by Federal Reserve chairman Paul Volcker and others over the Fed's growing inability to control the money supply. This concern led to passage of the Depository Institutions Deregulation and Monetary Control Act of 1980, which required all financial institutions to comply with the required reserve ratio established by the Fed. This effectively gave the Fed regulatory control over the entire financial market. Due to large-scale failures of savings and loans (for a discussion of those failures, see the Economics in Action at the end of this chapter), the Financial Institution Reform, Recovery, and Enforcement Act of 1989 was passed, and this legislation further increased the Fed's regulatory powers.

In Chapter 31, we examined the institutional structure of the Federal Reserve. Recall that the Federal Reserve System is made up of twelve Federal branch banks operating in all regions of the country. Overseeing the activities of these banks is the Federal Reserve Board of Governors, appointed by the president and based in Washington, D.C.; the board's role is to establish and oversee the nation's monetary policy. In this chapter we will see how Federal Reserve policy is carried out to control the size of the money supply. After reading Chapter 33 you should understand

- the nature of the tools that the Federal Reserve uses to control the money supply and, indirectly, interest rates in the economy.
- the central nature of one such tool—open market operations—in accomplishing the Federal Reserve's economic objectives.
- how the Federal Reserve influences the monetary base to achieve money supply or interest rate changes.
- how the monetary base and the real-world money multiplier interact to produce a money supply in the economy.
- some of the issues surrounding the debate over how "independent" the Federal Reserve System should be in our economy.

THE FEDERAL RESERVE SYSTEM'S BALANCE SHEET

The Federal Reserve System's basic activities in the banking system are concisely illustrated in its balance sheet, shown in Table 1. Its assets and liabilities are reported in the monthly *Federal Reserve Bulletin,* which compiles statistics on the activities of the central bank and on the financial system in general. The following is a brief description of the major assets and liabilities of the Federal Reserve System, each of which totaled $280 billion in February 1989.

The Federal Reserve's Assets

The first asset listed in Table 1 is gold certificates. The Federal Reserve System no longer holds gold, and since 1968 all ties between gold and Federal Reserve notes (dollars or currency) and other deposit liabilities have been abandoned.

TABLE 1

Basic Setup of the Federal Reserve System Balance Sheet

Generally, increases in the Federal Reserve's assets will increase member commercial bank reserves, while increases in its liabilities—except for the reserves deposited with the Federal Reserve by banks themselves—will decrease member bank reserves. Changes in bank reserves have important effects on the overall money supply.

Assets	Liabilities and Capital Accounts
Gold certificates *(issued by Treasury dept before 1968)*	Federal Reserve notes (outstanding)
Loans and securities (earning assets)	Total deposits *(req. reserves)*
	All other liabilities
Bank premises	
All other assets	Capital accounts

Before 1968, the U.S. Treasury issued and sold gold certificates to the Federal Reserve, which was required by law to hold a percentage of these certificates against currency and other liabilities. Some of these gold certificates remain on the Federal Reserve books as assets.

The next and largest group of items, loans and securities (earning assets), is the most important for understanding the Federal Reserve System's role in regulating bank reserves and the money supply in general. These assets consist of loans to banks and other depository institutions and securities, including federal agency obligations (various kinds of bills and notes) and U.S. government bonds. The Federal Reserve, as we will see, may purchase these securities from banks or from the nonbank public. Lumped together, loans and securities assets (along with other smaller items) are sometimes called **reserve bank credit** because increases and decreases in these assets affect member institutions' reserves—the raw material of money creation. We will explain this process later in the chapter.

Reserve bank credit:
The total value of loans and securities owned or held by the Federal Reserve System. Changes in Reserve bank credit affect member institutions' reserves.

The Federal Reserve's Liabilities

Table 1 shows two major liabilities of the Federal Reserve System. One is Federal Reserve notes (currency or dollars) held outside Federal Reserve banks. The dollar bills in circulation are part of this liability because they represent claims against the assets of the Federal Reserve. Cash issued by the Federal Reserve and kept on hand is neither an asset nor a liability: It is paper.

The liabilities also include deposits, such as member institutions' reserves—the required reserves of banks and other depository institutions discussed in Chapter 32 as well as other commercial bank funds deposited at the Federal Reserve. As liabilities to the Federal Reserve, they are assets to the commercial banks, and any excess reserves may be instantly converted by the banks into cash. Recall that money can be created within the fractional reserve system on the basis of such excess reserves.

Other deposits listed as liabilities in Table 1 include checking account privileges to the U.S. Treasury and to foreign countries and their residents. The capital accounts include several liabilities, notably the stock deposits of financial institutions that are members of the Federal Reserve System.

THE MONETARY BASE: RAW MATERIAL OF MONEY CREATION

Our enumeration of the Federal Reserve's major assets and liabilities is more than an accounting exercise. The Federal Reserve balance sheet illustrates how it controls the money supply.

Basically, the Federal Reserve achieves control over the money supply by manipulating member institutions' reserves. Recall from Chapter 32 that banks can lend by a multiple of their excess reserves, thereby expanding or contracting the money supply. By increasing assets, either through new loans to member institutions or by purchasing securities from members, the Federal Reserve makes additional reserve funds available to member banks.

While increases in Federal Reserve assets increase bank reserves, increases in its liabilities other than commercial bank reserves reduce the banks' reserves. Increases in the Federal Reserve's stock of securities would increase bank reserves, for example, while decreases in loans to banks would decrease reserves. The difference between the value of the factors increasing bank reserves and those decreasing reserves is called reserve bank credit outstanding. This statistic is deemed so important that it is reported on a weekly basis in the *Federal Reserve Bulletin.* Changes are often viewed as an indicator of whether the Federal Reserve is increasing bank reserves (and therefore increasing the money supply) or limiting bank reserves (and therefore decreasing the money supply).

Monetary base:
The sum of depository institutions' reserves plus currency held by the public.

The Federal Reserve attempts to control the money supply by controlling the **monetary base,** the sum of banks' reserves (including the reserve in their own vaults as well as the reserves deposited with the Federal Reserve) and currency in the hands of the public. Controlling the monetary base is the object of Federal Reserve control because of the direct relation between the monetary base and M-1, the money supply. Naturally, the public decides how much currency it wishes to hold relative to demand deposits. To control the money supply, then, the Federal Reserve must control bank reserves—the stuff of demand deposit money creation—and adjust for the changes in currency holdings of the public, which also affect the ability of banks to create money.

We know from Chapter 32 that currency withdrawals limit the amount of money that commercial banks can create. Sharp increases or decreases in the public's currency demands could have far-reaching effects on the total quantity of bank reserves in the system and thus on the ability of such reserves to support a certain total money supply. Factors such as currency withdrawals are said to be outside the system's control, which does not mean, however, that the Federal Reserve cannot estimate and predict them. It does mean that overall Federal Reserve control of reserves and the money supply is a complicated business.

METHODS OF FEDERAL RESERVE CONTROL

The Federal Reserve can control the money supply in a number of ways. Some methods, such as open market operations (discussed below), affect the monetary base directly. Others, such as changes in the reserve requirement, affect the ability of depository institutions to lend and affect the monetary base indirectly. The major tools of the Federal Reserve, sometimes called **credit controls,** are the following:

Credit controls:
The method or tools that the Federal Reserve System uses in efforts to control the monetary base and the money supply, including reserve requirements, open market operations, the discount rate, and other selective credit controls.

1. Open market purchases and sales of securities; OMO
2. Changes in the discount rate;
3. Alterations in the reserve requirement;
4. Changes in the margin requirement and, on occasion, imposition of consumer credit controls.

The Federal Reserve can also exercise warnings, generally verbal, to banks—an option called moral suasion, discussed later in this chapter.

Open Market Operations

The most important and flexible tool available to the Federal Reserve in its attempt to control the monetary base is the **open market operation**—the buying and selling of securities on the open market. The Federal Reserve uses this tool daily to directly affect member banks' reserves. Again, when the Federal Reserve increases its securities holdings by purchasing government-issued bonds, the reserves of banks are increased, meaning that banks have greater capacity to lend money, thus increasing the money supply. When the Federal Reserve sells its securities, the reserves of banks are decreased and the money supply contracts. Open market operations are used to correct short-run, predictable fluctuations in the money supply or to expand or contract the money supply over longer periods. If, for example, the Federal Reserve purchases government securities directly from the portfolio of commercial banks, the bank acquires reserve assets and loses securities assets in an equal amount. The bank will want to turn these reserves into interest-earning assets (loans), a process that creates deposits and expands the money supply. If the Federal Reserve purchases securities from nonbank individuals, the result is essentially the same. Individuals receive the proceeds of the sale in a check, deposit the check in commercial banks, thereby providing the banking system new reserves on which to lend.

Some alterations in the monetary base take place owing to seasonal currency drains, such as the withdrawal of cash in December for Christmas purchases. These drains predictably increase the demands of the public for checkable deposit money. The Federal Reserve intervenes to compensate for these predictable drains. Other currency drains are less predictable and would contract the money supply were it not for the Federal Reserve's attempts to compensate by purchasing securities. When currency needs have passed, the Federal Reserve again compensates by selling securities, depending on business conditions. It may also purchase or sell securities in a concerted effort to expand or contract the money supply, to alleviate recession and unemployment, or to control inflation.

The Role of the Federal Open Market Committee (FOMC). The Federal Open Market Committee, introduced in Chapter 31, is the principal operating arm of the Federal Reserve System. It is responsible for Federal Reserve Board decisions to buy or sell securities. This committee ordinarily meets every three or four weeks to set trading policies, which are kept secret to avoid upsetting the plans of buyers and sellers. In these sensitive, closed-door sessions, the FOMC considers such factors as the inflation rate, the economy's growth or real income (GNP), the unemployment picture, the size of excess reserves and borrowings from the Federal Reserve, probable currency drains, and the international balance of payments. It then decides on a monetary base, or reserve target, and a federal funds rate target to shoot for.

The **federal funds rate** is the interest rate commercial banks charge on overnight and short-run loans to other banks. Banks often lend excess reserves overnight and short term in order to earn interest returns; the rate is basically determined by the supply of and demand for these reserves. The key point here, however, is that the Federal Reserve attempts to influence this rate by altering the supply and demand for reserves through open market operations.

Open market operations: The purchase or sale of securities by the Federal Reserve System in order to affect the monetary base and the money supply; the major tool of monetary policy.

Federal funds rate: A market-determined interest rate on loans and borrowings of bank reserves among commercial banks and other depository institutions.

When the Federal Reserve targets changes in the federal funds rate, it is attempting, in effect, to change all interest rates, such as the prime interest rate and mortgage rates.

After the FOMC decides how it would like to alter reserves, the money supply, and the federal funds rate, the decision is transmitted to the open market account manager, an officer of the Federal Reserve Bank of New York. This individual, who controls the open market desk at the New York Federal Reserve and deals directly with commercial securities and investment houses on Wall Street, then implements the intentions of the FOMC. According to 1979 rule changes, the account manager has only narrow latitude in affecting monetary aggregates (such as bank reserves, the monetary base, and the money supply), but the account manager is still given a specific target for the federal funds rate.

As of February 1989, the Federal Reserve System held almost $225 billion worth of securities on its balance sheet. In January 1989, it acquired $94 billion, and it also sold $94 billion. Let us see how these open market transactions affect the condition of the banking system, expanding or contracting the money supply. There are two open market channels through which the Federal Reserve can affect bank reserves and the money supply: It can deal directly with banks or with the nonbank public.

Purchase of Securities from Banks. First consider a Federal Reserve purchase of securities (bonds, notes, or bills) from commercial banks. The effects of a $5 billion purchase are summarized in Table 2, which shows only changes in accounts. The Federal Reserve acquires $5 billion in assets (+ securities) but creates a new reserve liability to the banks to pay for the securities in exactly the same amount (+ reserves). On the other hand, the commercial banks lose a securities asset on the asset side of their balance sheet but gain an asset—reserves—of equivalent amount. The crucial point is that the monetary base rises as excess reserves—those above required reserves—are created in the banking system. Banks cannot lend on the basis of securities, but they can lend on the basis of excess reserves. After the Federal Reserve's purchase of securities, these excess reserves are ready to be lent. Given a specific reserve

---

TABLE 2

Purchase of Securities from Banks

When the Federal Reserve purchases securities from commercial banks or other depository institutions, it provides them with reserves on which the banks may make new loans, increasing the money supply. The Federal Reserve's purchase of $5 billion in securities from commercial banks changes those assets from a securities entry to a reserves entry in the commercial banks' aggregate balance sheet.

Federal Reserve System		Commercial Banks	
Assets (billions of dollars)	Liabilities and Capital Accounts (billions of dollars)	Assets (billions of dollars)	Liabilities and Capital Accounts (billions of dollars)
+ Securities 5	+ Reserves 5	− Securities 5 + Reserves 5	

requirement, the banking system's desired reserve holdings, and a desired ratio of currency to deposits on the part of the public, money creation may proceed apace. In theory, as the Federal Reserve buys securities and as the banks begin supplying new loan funds, interest rates tend to fall initially, encouraging consumers and investors to borrow. (A securities sale would have the opposite effect.) In reality, the monetary expansion also depends on general business conditions and expectations for the future.

Purchase of Securities from the Public.   Another method by which the Federal Reserve conducts open market operations pumps demand deposits in or out of the monetary system directly. Suppose that instead of purchasing $5 billion worth of securities from commercial banks, the Federal Reserve buys them directly from the nonbank public. The results of such a purchase are summarized in the balance sheets of Table 3.

When the Federal Reserve buys securities from the public and pays for them with, in effect, checks written on itself, the public gains demand deposit assets and loses securities assets in equal amounts. Note that the commercial banks gain new reserve assets and new deposit liabilities of $5 billion if the public deposits all of its proceeds from the sale into banks. In such a case, the money supply is increased directly by $5 billion by the very act of the public sale. Monetary expansion will depend on banks' desired idle reserves, the legal reserve ratio, the public's desired currency holdings, and, more broadly, general economic conditions. The extent of monetary expansion due to a securities purchase does not depend on the seller of securities to the Federal Reserve—commercial banks or the public.

TABLE 3	Purchase of Securities from the Public

When the Federal Reserve buys securities from the public and the public deposits the proceeds in banks, the public gains demand deposit money and commercial banks acquire new reserves. Banks may then lend additional money on the basis of their excess reserves.

Federal Reserve System Balance Sheet			
Assets (billions of dollars)		Liabilities and Capital Accounts (billions of dollars)	
+ Securities	5	+ Reserves	5

Public Balance Sheet			
Assets (billions of dollars)		Liabilities and Capital Accounts (billions of dollars)	
− Securities	5		
+ Demand deposits	5		

Commercial Banks' Balance Sheet			
Assets (billions of dollars)		Liabilities and Capital Accounts (billions of dollars)	
+ Reserves	5	+ Demand deposits	5

These open market operations take place daily and are the most flexible and efficient tool in the Federal Reserve's arsenal. But how can the Federal Reserve be sure that banks or the public will be willing to sell or buy securities on demand? Simple supply and demand analysis provides the answer. When the Federal Reserve sells securities, it increases the supply of securities on the open market in quantities large enough to affect the interest rate. When the Federal Reserve buys securities, demand for them is increased. An increase in supply lowers the price and increases the interest return on securities, making security holdings an attractive investment for banks or the public. Likewise, when the Federal Reserve places an order to buy on the open market, the demand increase causes security prices to rise and the interest return from holding them to fall. Selling securities to the Federal Reserve then becomes attractive to banks and the public because of the possible capital gains from selling and because of the reduced yield from holding the securities. Supply and demand conditions thus assure the Federal Reserve that there will be a response to its actions in the open market.

Who gets the interest return on the large quantity of securities held by the Federal Reserve? The Federal Reserve itself does. Congress permits the Federal Reserve to use this income to finance its operations. Historically, the Federal Reserve has been able to pay its own way out of its earning assets. Excess income is turned over to the U.S. Treasury. Remember, however, that the Federal Reserve is not supposed to be in business to make profits but to control the money supply for purposes of economic stabilization. The same is true of the other earning assets on the Federal Reserve balance sheet such as loans to depository institutions. Like securities, these assets are used to affect monetary policy and are not for profit. (See Focus, "The Quasi-Independence of the Federal Reserve System," for a discussion of the Fed's relationship with the U.S. Congress.)

Loans to Banks: The Discount Rate

Discount rate:
The interest rate charged by the Federal Reserve to depository institutions on loans of reserves from the Federal Reserve.

The process of lending to banks at some interest rate, called a **discount rate,** is the oldest function of a central bank. The discount rate is an interest rate (expressed as a percentage) charged by the Federal Reserve to depository institutions for loans backed up by some form of collateral—securities, notes, or commercial paper. This loan process was originally related to the status of a central bank as a lender of last resort—an institution that provided liquidity and currency to the banking system in times of sudden currency demands. Many of these bank crises or panics took place in the United States prior to the establishment of the Federal Reserve System in 1913. Yet modern banks are not immune to crises. In 1984, the massive Continental Illinois National Bank and Trust Company of Chicago, the nation's largest business and industrial lender, narrowly avoided closing its doors. The Federal Deposit Insurance Corporation (FDIC) and the Federal Reserve came to the rescue, the latter through loans and through the discounting of notes for the bank.

Initially, the discount rate was perceived to be the Federal Reserve System's major tool to avert crises. In modern times, loans to member banks and other financial institutions have performed another function as well—to control expansions and reductions in money and credit. Several discount rates are charged by the Federal Reserve depending on the kind of collateral put up by the banks and the purpose and duration of the loans. The rate for short-run

FOCUS The Quasi-Independence of the Federal Reserve System

The Federal Reserve System is unique among government regulatory agencies in one important respect: The Federal Reserve enjoys relative freedom from the oversight of Congress or the executive branch. This unique status is called quasi-independence and has been a source of much conflict among politicians, economists, and the investment community.

The Federal Reserve System was created by Congress in 1913 to administer and manage the money supply as directed in the Constitution. As an agency of Congress, the Federal Reserve Board represents or is an extension of Congress, but Congress set up the Federal Reserve to be quasi-independent—that is, at some distance from the control of the president and from direct congressional involvement. For example, Federal Reserve Board members other than the chair are appointed for fourteen-year terms by the president, which means that they can remain on the job regardless of which party controls the White House. The chair is also appointed as a member of the Board for a fourteen-year term. The appointment as chair lasts four years but may be renewed. Independence is also reflected in the fact that the Federal Reserve is not dependent on congressional and administrative budget appropriations. The Federal Reserve finances all of its own operations, mainly through interest earned on government bonds. This independence from congressional appropriations and from the typical auditing procedures applied to all other U.S. regulatory agencies has gone far in placing the Federal Reserve out of the grasp of Congress or the president.

Is the Federal Reserve too independent? Should it be brought under closer scrutiny of Congress or the president, or is its current position appropriate to its intended function? Critics argue that the loose connection between the presi-dent and the Federal Reserve System creates discoordination between fiscal and monetary policy. Monetary policy, in this view, should be under the direct control of the executive branch of government so that it is tied closely to the democratic wishes of voters. Such criticism is especially vocal during periods of high interest rates and tight money.

Defenders of quasi-independence claim that there are very good reasons for the special status of the Federal Reserve. In this view, monetary policy is far too important to the well-being of society to be left to self-interested politicians; control of the money supply and other aspects of monetary policy should be insulated from politics. Defenders of the Fed argue that quasi-independence permits monetary policy-makers to have a longer-run perspective, to be able to see beyond the next election. They point out that the Federal Reserve is a creation of Congress and that it can be abolished at any time by an act of Congress. (During the 1980s, when many members of Congress actively opposed the Fed's tight monetary policy, Congress amended the Federal Reserve Act and limited the Fed's ability to change reserve requirements—an action widely interpreted as a symbolic gesture to remind the Fed that too much independence would not be tolerated.)

The Federal Reserve Board chair is required to present periodic reports to Congress, some in person, relating to the management of M-1 and interest rates. To go beyond this level of accountability, some say, might tempt politicians into inflating the money supply to cover budget deficits, unwise government spending, or political ambition. It may be that, despite the periodic criticisms and threats, both the president and Congress have an incentive to keep the Fed relatively independent: The Federal Reserve gives them a place to pass along blame when economic troubles develop.

---

or seasonal credit is lower than that for extended credit to institutions whose loans extend beyond 150 days. These differential rates reflect the Federal Reserve's policy toward banks' motivations for borrowing. A commercial bank may borrow because of seasonal cash drains, to cover very short-run deficiencies in legal reserves, or because it sees the Federal Reserve discount loans as a source of profit. If there is a wide spread between the discount rate paid for borrowing excess reserves at the Federal Reserve and the interest rate banks receive on lending out these excess reserves, banks may seek to borrow from the Federal Reserve to enhance their profits. The Federal Reserve discourages borrowing for this reason by charging higher rates for longer-run credit. In fact, the Federal Reserve may stop this sort of borrowing entirely.

Whatever the reason for borrowing, lending by the Federal Reserve swells the quantity of reserves at the disposal of the banking system. Table 4, for example, shows the Federal Reserve balance sheet and that of a single com-

TABLE 4

Lending to the First Bank of Nome

When the Federal Reserve lends at interest to a commercial bank, the commercial bank acquires reserves as a new asset and a new liability to the Federal Reserve. The bank may now create new demand deposit liabilities along with new loan assets, thereby expanding the money supply.

Federal Reserve System		First Bank of Nome	
Assets (billions of dollars)	Liabilities and Capital Accounts (billions of dollars)	Assets (billions of dollars)	Liabilities and Capital Accounts (billions of dollars)
+ Loans (First Bank of Nome) 2	+ Reserves 2	+ Reserves 2	+ Due Federal Reserve 2

mercial bank, the First Bank of Nome. This process of discounting a note for $2 million from the Bank of Nome has the clear effect of increasing the bank's stock of reserves. If any or all of these new reserves are in excess of the required reserves, money creation may proceed in multiple fashion, again depending on banks' required and desired excess reserves, currency drains, and general economic conditions.

The Federal Reserve has several ways of encouraging or discouraging borrowing: (1) it alters the rate or rates charged; (2) it changes the form of collateral required; and (3) it always retains the option to lend or not to lend. Loans to depository institutions and acceptances (another form of short-run lending with different collateral required) make up a relatively small percentage of the Federal Reserve's financial transactions compared to open market operations. But the ultimate importance of the discount rate hinges not so much on the quantity of loans as on the information the rate conveys concerning the intentions of the Federal Reserve. Commercial and consumer interest rates, such as the prime rate (the rate that banks charge to their lowest-risk commercial borrowers), tend to follow the discount rate. Along with the Federal Reserve's changing monetary base targets, the discount rate is seen by the banking and business community as one indicator of whether the Federal Reserve is following an expansionary or contractionary monetary policy. A higher rate indicates a tightening of credit and a contractionary policy. A lower rate indicates the reverse. The stock market, for one, is apt to react sharply to changes in the Federal Reserve discount rate. Thus, while the discount rate is not the major mechanism of Federal Reserve control over the monetary base, it is often considered the principal messenger of the Federal Reserve's policy intentions.

Changing the Reserve Requirement

Changing the legal reserve requirement is potentially the most powerful tool at the disposal of the Federal Reserve, but it is seldom used. To understand this seeming contradiction, remember that an alteration in the legal reserve ratio affects the ability of any given amount of excess reserves to support new money, and it increases or decreases the amount of excess reserves held by depository institutions. A simple example, utilizing the simple money multiplier without a currency drain, illustrates the importance of the legal reserve requirement for the money supply. If we assume that excess reserves in the banking system are $5 billion and that the legal reserve requirement is 15 percent, the potential expansion in the money supply, neglecting currency drains and other factors, is

$$\Delta M = \Delta D = \text{excess reserves} \left(\frac{1}{r}\right),$$

or

$$\Delta M = \Delta D = \$5 \left(\frac{1}{0.15}\right) = \$33.3.$$

The increase in the money supply M equals the increase in deposit expansion, $33.3 billion. The money multiplier $1/r$ is equal to $1/0.15$, or 6.66. As indicated in Chapter 15, the money multiplier is the number by which excess reserves are multiplied to determine potential change in the money supply. It is the reciprocal of the reserve requirement.

A reduction in the reserve requirement from 15 percent to 10 percent would have dramatic effects on the money supply. Suppose that the banking system initially had $500 billion in deposits and $80 billion in reserves. With a reserve requirement of 15 percent, the banks would initially have $5 billion in excess reserves. If the reserve requirement were then lowered to 10 percent, banks would be required to hold only $50 billion as reserves, so their excess reserves would amount to $30 billion. The potential increase in money and demand deposits would be $300 billion.

$$\Delta M = \Delta D = \$30 \left(\frac{1}{0.10}\right) = \$300 \text{ billion}$$

Small changes in the required reserve ratio can bring about large increases or decreases in the money supply.

Actually, banks must observe several reserve requirements, depending on the size of their deposit liabilities. Table 5 provides a summary of reserve requirements in force in May 1989. After implementation of the Monetary Control Act of 1980, reserve requirements apply uniformly to all depository institutions according to the size of checkable, savings, and time deposit liabilities. As Table 5 shows, transactions accounts—all checkable accounts— less than $41.5 million at depository institutions carry a reserve requirement

TABLE 5

Contemporary Reserve Requirements of Depository Institutions

Reserve requirements have been made uniform for all institutions issuing demand, savings, or time deposits. The total amount of reserves required for an individual bank or savings and loan, for example, depends on the type and amount of deposits issued by the institution.

Net Transaction Accounts	Nonpersonal Time Deposits
3% up to $41.5 million 12% over $41.5 million	3% on less than 1½ years maturity 0% on more than 1½ years maturity

Source: Federal Reserve Bulletin (March 1987).

of 3 percent, while 12 percent must be held on deposits over $41.5 million. Some large ($100,000 or more) nonpersonal time deposits, such as certificates of deposit, and savings deposits (less than one and one-half years maturity) now carry a requirement of 3 percent. All in all, these reserve requirements are more uniform and lower than in the past.

Reserve requirements limit the profitability of banking and depository institutions and so are regarded as a necessary evil by the financial system. Changes in the requirements (especially increases) can cause massive disruptions and large-scale adjustments in the portfolios of member banks and other institutions required to hold legal reserves. Even small changes might create financial crises for some institutions, depending on their profitability. When banks are fully committed with loans—that is, have low amounts of excess reserves—an increase of only one-quarter or one-half percent in the legal reserve could reduce lending and money creation by billions of dollars, creating tight money and possibly bank failures. The Federal Reserve is therefore reluctant to make sudden large changes in the reserve requirement. Open market operations are far more flexible in operation and predictable in effect. The reserve requirement will always be a part of monetary control, but it will likely be used sparingly.

The Margin Requirement and Other Selective Credit Controls

Stock margin requirement: The percentage of the price of a stock purchase that must be paid in cash rather than borrowed.

Other tools sometimes available to the Federal Reserve through congressional action are selective credit controls, which include credit restrictions on stock market purchases and consumer borrowing for durable goods and home purchases. At present, the Federal Reserve controls only the **stock margin requirement,** which is the percentage of the total price of a stock that must be paid in cash. A margin requirement of 40 percent means that only 60 percent of the purchase price of stock can be borrowed; 40 percent must be paid in cash. The Federal Reserve acquired the power to demand a margin requirement through the Securities and Exchange Act of 1934, allegedly to stem the rampant stock speculation that was thought to have contributed to the stock market crash of 1929 and the ensuing Depression. The purpose of the margin requirement is thus to provide a brake in what is regarded as unwise stock speculation. Alterations in the required margin selectively affect credit for stock market purchases and, therefore, also affect the volume of such purchases. Since 1968, the rate has varied between 80 percent and 50 percent, the latter rate being in force since 1974.

Finally, during periods of potential and real economic crisis, Congress has in the past given the Federal Reserve powers over the terms of home mortgages and consumer credit for the purpose of buying durables. The rationale for restrictions on the amount of down payment and the period of repayment is simple: During periods of all-out war, resources must flow into military spending. Simultaneously, however, the overfull employment that accompanies a war effort means high nominal incomes, which create huge demands for consumer durables and new housing. Consumer credit controls tend to suppress these demands, having the dual effect of releasing real resources to the war effort and keeping a temporary lid on domestic price inflation. Between 1941 and 1947 and again during the Korean War, Congress authorized the Federal Reserve to impose restrictions on consumer credit. The Federal Reserve does not especially like the discriminatory impact of these controls because they affect only particular markets, such as home building and automobile manufacturing. At present and for the foreseeable future, the only selective control maintained by the Federal Reserve is the stock margin requirement. Under the Credit Control Act passed by Congress in 1969, the president was given the power to institute consumer credit controls, administered through the Federal Reserve System. With one minor exception, these controls have been unused, probably for some of the reasons given above. The act was not renewed by Congress in 1980.

Moral Suasion

Moral suasion:
The use of advice and suggestion, rather than concrete policy actions, by the Federal Reserve to induce depository institutions to follow a certain course of action.

Another tool of the Federal Reserve—alluded to earlier—is **moral suasion,** the ability to persuade banks that some course of action is desirable or undesirable. For example, during a period of rapid credit and money expansion—deemed undesirable by the Federal Reserve—banks may be warned subtly or not so subtly that continued expansionary behavior will result in implementation of policies that will force banks to cut back on money expansion. As we have seen, these threatened actions could be a raising of the discount rate, the selling of securities, or possibly increases in reserve requirements. To the extent that such suasion achieves the desired results, it could be a tool of the Federal Reserve. Sometimes, however, admonitions do not work, and the threatened action becomes necessary. Thus, the effects of moral suasion, while real, are not exactly predictable.

The Federal Reserve is always on sounder ground if it can affect the nature of banks' portfolios directly. Table 6 summarizes the Federal Reserve's major tools for money control and their likely effects.

TABLE 6   Major Federal Reserve Controls and Their Probable Effects

Alterations in any one of the three major credit controls of the Federal Reserve will affect the monetary base of the financial system, bank reserves, and the money supply.

Federal Reserve System Tools	Effects					
	Bank Reserves	Money Supply	Monetary Base	Excess Reserves	Money Multiplier	Currency
Open market operations:						
Federal Reserve buys bonds	Increase	Increases	Increases	Increase	Remains same	Increases
Federal Reserve sells bonds	Decrease	Decreases	Decreases	Decrease	Remains same	Decreases
Discount rate:						
Raise rate	Decrease	Decreases	Decreases	Decrease	Remains same	Decreases
Lower rate	Increase	Increases	Increases	Increase	Remains same	Increases
Reserve requirement:						
Raise requirement	Decrease	Decreases	Remains same	Decrease	Decreases	Decreases
Lower requirement	Increase	Increases	Remains same	Increase	Increases	Increases

MONETARY CONTROL: RESERVES, THE MONETARY BASE, AND THE MONEY SUPPLY

We have seen that the Federal Reserve has numerous means of altering the stock of reserves and the monetary base. It remains to be shown how the monetary base—the sum of bank-held reserves and currency in circulation—is related to the money supply. In October 1989, for example, the monetary base was $278 billion, while the M-1 measure of the money supply was $787 billion. These figures indicate a money supply on the order of 2.83 times the value of the monetary base. The **M-1 money multiplier** is the number by which the monetary base is multiplied to obtain the M-1 measure of the money supply. This number can change over both short-run and long-run periods. We must understand why and how it changes because the very ability of the Federal Reserve to control the money supply through the monetary base depends on the predictability of the money multiplier.

> **M-1 money multiplier:**
> The multiple by which the money supply will change given a change in the monetary base.

The Exact Relation Between the Money Stock and the Monetary Base

To understand the forces determining the money stock, M-1, we must come to a more exact formulation of the money multiplier. In simplified terms the money stock may be expressed as

$$\text{M-1} = \text{monetary base} \times \text{M-1 money multiplier}.$$

We have already seen that the Federal Reserve controls the monetary base by pumping reserves into or withdrawing them out of the banking system through its credit control powers. But recall that bank reserves are only one part of the monetary base. Currency in public circulation is the other part of the monetary base, and currency holdings by the public are determined by the desires of the public. An individual may, at his or her discretion, convert demand deposits into cash by writing a check at the bank or some other place that cashes checks. The individual's decision to hold cash has an impact on the banking system's ability to expand the money supply. It would reduce the money-expanding capabilities of the system if an individual made a permanent decision to hold more cash than checkbook money.

The money multiplier discussed earlier in this chapter is actually a simplification, as shown in Chapter 32. The simple multiplier is the reciprocal of the reserve requirement. While we will not account for every factor contributing to the multiplier, a more realistic way of determining the money multiplier must take into account the desires of the public to hold currency in relation to demand deposits. The components of a more realistic money multiplier can be defined as follows:

c = Desired currency holdings of the public relative to demand deposits;
r = Holdings of reserves required by the Federal Reserve and desired by depository institutions relative to demand deposits.

If, on average, people wish to hold 35 cents in cash or coin for each dollar in demand deposits, the value of c is 0.35. If the sum of required and desired (or idle) reserves in the banking system is 15 cents for every dollar of demand deposits issued, the value of r is 0.15. For obvious reasons, c is sometimes called the currency-deposit ratio, and r is called the reserve-deposit ratio.

A slightly more complicated expression for the money multiplier, then, is

$$\text{Money multiplier} = \left(\frac{1 + c}{c + r}\right).$$

This equation differs from the simple money multiplier in its inclusion of the currency-deposit ratio in both the numerator and the denominator. In practical terms, the addition of c reduces the value of the simple multiplier. Using only the reserve-deposit ratio of 0.15 produces a money multiplier of $1/r = 1/0.15$, or 6.66. Use of a multiplier that includes the impact of the public's desire to hold currency gives a money multiplier of 1.35/0.50, or 2.7.

We are immediately able to understand the actual relation mentioned above for October 1989 between an M-1 of $787 billion and a monetary base of $278 billion.

$$\$787 \text{ billion} = \$278 \text{ billion } (2.83)$$

The monetary base of $278 billion is only one factor in explaining the money supply. The composition of the money multiplier, equal to $(1 + c)/(c + r)$, or 2.83 in our real-world example, is the other factor influencing Federal Reserve monetary control.

Federal Reserve Controls

In practice, it is often difficult to tell what the Federal Reserve is attempting to control—the money supply or interest rates. Although the Board of Governors of the Federal Reserve has at various times in the past stated clear objectives concerning the size of the money supply or the level of interest rates, the board has often failed to hit its targets. These failures have raised the question of whether the Fed is able to control the money supply or—through controlling the money supply—interest rates.

Any change in the money supply is caused by either a change in the monetary base or in the money multiplier; if these remain the same, the money supply in the preceding example will remain at a level of $787 billion.

Can the Fed control the size of the monetary base? The answer to this question is yes, though with some difficulty. As we saw earlier (see Table 6), the monetary base changes when the Fed engages in open market operations or when banks borrow additional reserves from the Fed or repay loans previously taken from the Fed. Since the Fed is in total control of open market operations, it can regulate any changes in the monetary base that originate from this source. However, the Fed has only indirect control over bank borrowing at the discount window. For example, the Fed may lower the discount rate to discourage banks from reducing their borrowed reserves, but the Fed cannot prohibit banks from repaying these loans, thereby reducing the monetary base. While this complicates the Fed's control over the monetary base, it does not make control impossible. If banks insist on repaying a certain amount (say $2 billion) in borrowed reserves, the Fed can counter this by purchasing exactly $2 billion in bonds on the open market. In this manner, the Fed can control the overall size of the monetary base regardless of independent action by banks.

If we consider changes in the money supply caused by changes in the money multiplier, we find that the money multiplier can, with difficulty, be controlled by the Fed. Since the money multiplier equals $(1 + c)/(c + r)$, a change in either the currency-deposit ratio or the required reserve ratio will change the size of the money multiplier. The Fed has control over r, but not over c. Should the public elect to reduce the currency-deposit ratio, the money multiplier will rise. To offset this change in c, however, the Fed can increase r by the amount necessary to return the money multiplier to its initial level.

Independent actions by banks or by the public can cause the money supply to change—perhaps in a way not desired by the Fed. However, by making appropriate changes in the required reserve ratio, the discount rate, or in open market operations, the Fed can offset these undesired changes in the money supply—which is another way of saying that the Fed does exercise some control over the money supply.

Real-World Multipliers, the Monetary Base, and the Money Stock

The actual M-1 money multiplier, calculated since 1959, has tended to decline except for a minor upturn from the late 1970s to the mid-1980s. As shown in Figure 1, the real-world multiplier has fluctuated widely since 1960. A brief analysis of variations in the multiplier gives us some valuable information on trends in our banking system.

In general, both the banks' desired holdings of idle reserves and the required reserve ratio set by the Federal Reserve have declined over the period, helping to explain the decline through the late 1970s. The Federal Reserve has very gradually lowered the reserve requirements and has, at the same time, applied them more uniformly to all financial institutions accepting deposits.

FIGURE 1

The actual M-1 money multiplier has, in general, declined over the past three decades in the United States. Reductions in the required reserve ratio (*r*) over the period would have increased the multiplier, but increases in the currency-deposit ratio have been the primary cause of the overall decline shown in the figure.

Source: Federal Reserve Bulletin, various issues.

The Real-World Money Multiplier, 1960–1989

Other things being equal, the reduction in the r ratio would have increased the money multiplier rather than reducing it. But other factors have not remained equal. Since 1960, the ratio of the public's desired holdings of currency to its demand deposits has steadily risen, causing a reduction in the money multiplier. The increase in the public's desired holdings of currency relative to checkable deposits has been accompanied by a shift to money substitutes, notably to the numerous forms of savings and time deposits, many of them new. The Federal Reserve, of course, has been aware of this overall decline and has attempted to adjust the monetary base to fit its money supply policy intentions.

Since deregulation of the financial system, beginning in 1980, holdings of checkable deposits have become more attractive relative to currency. The availability and attractiveness of these deposits has caused a long-term decline in the currency-deposit ratio. The increased holding of large quantities of checkable deposits relative to currency was a major cause of the decrease in the money multiplier over the 1980s.

Month-to-month and week-to-week changes in the money multiplier render Federal Reserve control of the money stock through changes in the monetary base more difficult. Constantly changing market rates of interest on time, savings, and checkable deposits, as noted earlier, are a devilish factor in the Federal Reserve's calculations. But since 1979, the Federal Reserve has made a concerted effort to control the money supply by controlling a monetary aggregate—the monetary base and bank reserves. Before 1979, an interest rate target—the federal funds rate—was the principal means used by the Federal Reserve to direct money and credit conditions. Despite short-run alterations in the money multiplier, the Federal Reserve is perfectly able to control the money supply within fairly narrow bounds by following monetary aggregate targets. The question that concerns macroeconomists is whether any discretionary control over the money stock would be adequate medicine for the macroeconomic ills of inflation, unemployment, and lagging growth in GNP.

SUMMARY

1. Major activities of the Federal Reserve System are summarized in its balance sheet. On the asset side, the Federal Reserve holds a portfolio of earning assets such as loans and securities. Increases in these earning assets indicate an increase in the commercial banking system's reserves, the monetary base, and the nation's money supply.
2. Liabilities of the Federal Reserve System include Federal Reserve notes (currency) in the hands of commercial banks and domestic and foreign governments. An increase in any liability item, except bank reserves themselves, will reduce the monetary base and the nation's money supply.
3. Reserve bank credit outstanding is an important statistic in that it shows the difference between factors increasing reserves and factors decreasing reserves of the commercial banking system.
4. The monetary base is the sum of banking system reserves and currency in the hands of the public. The Federal Reserve attempts to control the monetary base, which is the basis of expansions and contractions in the M-1 money supply.
5. The monetary base is controlled by the Federal Reserve's use of major credit controls: open market operations, loans or discounts to commercial banks, and changes in the required reserve ratio.
6. Purchases of securities from commercial banks or the public, lowering of the discount rate, and lowering of the required reserve ratio all have the effect of increasing bank reserves. Sales of securities, raising of the interest or discount rate charged to banks for loans, and increases in the required reserve ratio decrease bank reserves and the monetary base.

7. Less important controls over bank reserves and lending are sometimes used by the Federal Reserve. Selective credit controls include special powers over consumer credit, mortgage loans, and stock margin requirements. Moral suasion, attempts to alter bank behavior through nonformal nonbinding means, may also be used by the Federal Reserve.

8. Federal Reserve control over the money supply is made trickier by changes in the money multiplier, $(1 + c)/(c + r)$. A change in the money multiplier may be caused, in both the short run and the long run, by changing desires on the part of the public to hold currency relative to demand deposits.

KEY TERMS

reserve bank credit	open market operation	stock margin requirement
monetary base	federal funds rate	moral suasion
credit controls	discount rate	M-1 money multiplier

QUESTIONS FOR REVIEW AND DISCUSSION

1. How does the Federal Reserve System control the money supply through the banking industry? What tools does the Federal Reserve use? How does it control the money supply without using the banking system?

2. What is the monetary base? Is this the same thing as the money supply?

3. "The Federal Reserve can control the minimum amount of reserves that the banking system holds but not the maximum amount." Is this statement true or false? Explain.

4. If the statement in question 3 is true, does it mean that the Federal Reserve can limit increases in the money supply but cannot stop the money supply from falling?

5. What are the things that determine the "powerfulness" of the monetary base?

6. "If the Federal Reserve purchases securities from the nonbank public rather than the banking system, it has a different effect on the money supply." True or false? Explain.

7. Why would a bank want to borrow money from the Federal Reserve and pay the discount rate rather than just accept demand deposits and pay no interest?

8. Is moral suasion an effective monetary tool of the Federal Reserve?

9. Does the reserve-deposit ratio or the currency-deposit ratio have anything to do with the monetary base?

10. "The Federal Reserve is just a big cartel that is operated by the government to make greater profits for the banking industry." Give some arguments that may support this view and some that may refute it.

ECONOMICS IN ACTION
Federal Reserve Policy and the Savings and Loan Crisis

By early 1989, the full extent of the problems faced by the U.S. savings and loan industry became clear to the American public; although estimates differ, taxpayer subsidies of at least $100 billion and perhaps as much as $500 billion will be required to bail out insolvent S&Ls. The cost of this bailout may amount to $1400 for each American. However, it is still

a mystery to most Americans how the situation could have developed into a crisis; how could so many loan institutions have gotten so far into debt?

Prior to 1980, the savings and loan industry was subject to extensive government regulations. In particular, S&Ls were prohibited from offering checking services, they were

"AS A MATTER OF FACT, I'D LIKE TO SEE SOME IDENTIFICATION FROM YOU, TOO."

not permitted to pay interest rates of more than 5.5 percent to depositors, and they were precluded from making speculative loans (such as loans to real estate developers). In addition, nearly all the S&Ls in the country were members of the Federal Savings and Loan Insurance Corporation (FSLIC), a governmental agency that insured deposits at member S&Ls. Member savings and loans were charged an insurance fee equal to one-twelfth of one percent of their deposits for insurance coverage protecting all depositors against loss on accounts containing up to $40,000.

In the early 1980s, regulations on maximum interest rates for S&Ls were gradually phased out. As a consequence, S&Ls began offering higher interest rates to attract depositors. At the same time, other regulations that enabled S&Ls to make loans for a variety of risky ventures from which they previously had been excluded were lifted. In addition, insurance coverage by the FSLIC was expanded to cover deposits of up to $100,000.

As a consequence of these regulatory changes, managers of S&Ls found themselves operating in an environment totally different from the one to which they had grown accustomed. Aggressive institutions pursued new deposits by offering higher interest rates, which forced even conservative S&Ls to match the rates or risk losing business. In paying higher interest on deposits, the S&Ls put themselves in the position of having to generate higher interest rates on their loans in order to turn a profit. As a consequence, they turned increasingly to loans to high-risk ventures and to investors willing to borrow at high interest rates. Soon the S&Ls found that their loan portfolios, previously comprised primarily of loans to local customers for the purpose of financing homes and autos, now contained billions of dollars in loans to high-risk ventures in real estate, energy, and farming. Inexperience in making these kinds of loans was one of the factors that eventually led to insolvency.

The ability of S&Ls to attract deposits was greatly enhanced by the existence of federal deposit insurance. Had deposits not been insured, depositors would have become alarmed at the particularly risky loans S&Ls were taking on and would have protected themselves against loss by diverting deposits elsewhere. Because deposits were insured, however, depositors were indifferent about the financial status of the neighborhood S&L. S&Ls on the brink of financial disaster had no trouble attracting additional deposits—right up to the day they were finally shut down by FSLIC examiners. This enabled the S&Ls to run up debts of unprecedented magnitude.

The ongoing financial difficulties of the S&Ls greatly complicate things for the Fed. The survival of many S&Ls depends on repayment of their delinquent loans. If economic growth can be sustained, the default rate on these loans may turn out to be surprisingly low, and relatively few additional S&Ls will fail. This means that the Fed is under unusually great pressure to carry on a monetary policy that leads to continued economic growth. On the other hand, the survival of S&Ls also depends on future interest rates. Many of the loans held by insolvent S&Ls are long-term loans at fixed interest rates; if interest rates rose rapidly, S&Ls would find themselves paying more on their deposits than they receive from their loans, and failure would be inevitable. Whether the Fed will be able to perform this balancing act remains to be seen.

Question

If the Federal Reserve's monetary policy brought interest rates down by 2 to 3 percentage points in the next two years, would you expect the number of savings and loan failures to increase or decrease? Explain.

34

Money and Inflation

Money clearly matters. The Federal Reserve Board announces weekly changes in M-1, the nation's basic money supply, and that announcement—which can suggest the possibility of loose or tight credit in the future—creates optimism or pessimism along Wall Street. Investors react by buying or selling stock. Buyers and sellers of home mortgages and all other financial instruments also anxiously observe the weekly changes in M-1 in an attempt to predict changes in interest rates and the future profitability of their financial investments.

The main reason for all of the attention paid to M-1 is the relationship—understood by most Americans—between M-1 and price inflation. Inflation has been perhaps most aptly described as "too much money chasing too few goods," and although economists have constructed elaborate theories to explain inflation, it is still best understood in these simple terms. When the production of real output (bananas or personal computers or hair stylings) does not grow as fast as the M-1 medium of exchange, inflation sooner or later is the result. And most people readily understand that when their nominal money income does not grow at the same rate that prices increase, they are worse off.

In the preceding three chapters we investigated the nature of money, how it is created in the commercial banking system, and how the supply of money is regulated by the Federal Reserve System. In this chapter we take a brief look at monetary theories, specifically at the relation between the money supply—M-1—and the price level. When you finish reading Chapter 34, you should understand

- the three components of the demand for money and their importance for monetary theory and policy.
- how classical, Keynesian, and modern monetarist writers interpret the relation between money, prices, and the real output of goods and services in the economy.
- who wins and who loses from inflation.
- some of the causes of and cures for inflation.

THE DEMAND FOR MONEY

How do economists explain the relation between M-1 and inflation? Economists argue that, like the value of other goods, the value of money—the price level of all output—depends on its demand and supply. However, when discussing how money supply and demand interact to determine the price level, we need to be particularly careful with the terms we use. When economists talk about the demand for money, they are implicitly talking about **real money demand.** Real money demand is a demand to hold or own purchasing power in the form of money (cash and checkable deposits), not just the demand to hold pieces of paper. Thus, real money demand should always be interpreted as a purchasing-power concept. (The purchasing power of a dollar changes with alterations in the price level.) The money supply, though, is a nominal variable unrelated to purchasing power. When economists speak of the supply of money, they simply mean the total current number of dollars that the amount of cash plus checkable deposits in the economy add up to. Throughout the remainder of this chapter, we will use these meanings for money demand and supply.

We have seen that the Federal Reserve controls the nominal money supply, but the Federal Reserve does not control real money demand. People in their roles as money holders determine what real money demand is and what specific quantity of real money they wish to hold. Economists have singled out three reasons or motives for holding purchasing power in the form of money—in other words, for the existence of real money demand. These motives, which may exist simultaneously, are described as the transactions, precautionary, and speculative demands for money.

Transactions Demand

People hold or demand money, the medium of exchange, as a simple means of carrying out transactions—to buy chewing gum, dinner at a fancy restaurant, or a personal computer. Businesses demand money to pay for labor, materials, and other inputs. The amount of real money holdings that accommodates transactions of businesses and consumers is referred to as the **transactions demand** for money.

The transactions demand for money is related to the real income of consumers and businesses. As real incomes rise, the demand for more and more money to carry out transactions also rises. For example, a family with an income of $30,000 will have a greater transactions demand for money than a family with an income of only $15,000. This general relation is true of the economy as a whole as well. As real income rises throughout the economy, the transactions demand for money will also increase.

Precautionary Demand

A second reason for holding money is the "rainy day" motive. People usually want to keep some money readily available to meet unforeseen emergencies such as illness or car repair. Likewise, firms generally exercise caution in how much money they hold.

Real money demand:
Demand on the part of individuals and businesses to hold purchasing power in the form of cash and checkable deposits.

D_M : Real

S_M : Nominal.

Transactions demand:
Money demand that arises from the desire of businesses and consumers to facilitate exchange with the use of money.

Precautionary demand:
Money demand that arises from the desire of businesses and consumers to hold money in order to facilitate unexpected purchases.

Speculative motive or demand:
Money demand arising from uncertainty of future interest rates and the fact that people can substitute between holding money and holding bonds.

The **precautionary demand** for money is simply the amount of money that households and firms want to hold to meet unforeseen events. Ordinarily, the amount of money that people wish to hold against unforeseen contingencies rises with income. Precautionary demands may therefore be included with transactions demands as being directly related to income.

Speculative Demand

A final explanation for money demand is the **speculative motive or demand.** Like precautionary demand, the speculative motive for holding money is based on uncertainty: Some individuals will want to hold money to speculate in the markets for bonds or other liquid assets whose price and interest return vary. These speculators have to choose between holding money and holding interest-bearing bonds. To make the choice, they consider the present interest rate and the degree of uncertainty about future conditions.

To money holders, the nominal interest rate is the opportunity cost of holding money. It is the return we give up by holding money and not investing it in some other asset (a savings account, a share of a firm's stock, or a bond) that would yield interest. Holding money means keeping or owning some quantity of cash and/or checkable deposits over a period of time. Economists theorize that high interest rates make people want to hold bonds. The price of a bond and its interest yield are inversely related, so high interest rates mean that bond prices are relatively low. Under these conditions, bonds are a good deal for two reasons. One obvious reason is the high interest return; in addition, if the price of bonds rises in the future, bond holders would experience a capital gain. A capital gain occurs when bond buyers purchase bonds at a low price and then bond prices increase. In the event of rising bond prices—which occurs with falling interest rates—selling bonds becomes more attractive. With high bond prices and low interest rates, people generally prefer to hold more money and fewer bonds. Conversely, low bond prices and high interest rates mean that people will hold less money and more bonds.

The speculative motive for holding money means that real money demand is inversely related to the interest rate. As the interest rate rises, bonds are a more attractive asset, and the real quantity of money demanded declines. As the interest rate falls, bonds are less attractive and money is more attractive.

Figure 1 graphically expresses the preceding ideas. The curve labeled L_s is the speculative demand for money (L is demand for money, or "liquidity"). At any time, money holders have formed some expectations about what interest rates and therefore bond prices will be in the future. Given expectations about future bond prices and interest rates, a present interest rate of r_0 means that the real quantity of money demanded for speculative purchases is L_{S_0}. A lower interest rate, such as r_1, means that actual bond prices rise and, as discussed above, the amount of money that individuals will want to hold for speculative reasons will rise. In Figure 1, the real quantity of speculative balances demanded rises to L_{S_1}.

Liquidity preference theory:
A theory stating that the interest rate is determined by the interaction of real money demand and supply, and that interest rate changes due to real money demand or supply changes produce changes in real economic activity.

The speculative demand for money is concerned with *liquidity preference*—how liquid people want to be. The speculative motive for holding money also forms the basis of the **liquidity preference theory,** which states that the rate of interest is determined by overall money demand and supply. As we will see later in this chapter, this theory implies that economic activity, including price changes, flows from changes in the rate of interest.

FIGURE 1

Individuals hold money for speculative purposes—that is, to take advantage of good deals in the bond market. A low interest rate, r_1, means relatively high bond prices and increased real money holdings, L_{S_1}, means relatively high bond prices and increased real money holdings, L_{S_1}. A higher interest rate, r_0, indicates higher bond holdings and lower holdings of money for speculative purposes, L_{S_0}.

The Speculative Demand for Money

Money Demand: Summary

We now summarize the three influences on the demand for money. Table 1 lists the three types of money demand with the chief factors affecting them and the effects of a change in the factors on the quantity of money demanded. As Table 1 indicates, the total real demand for money is related to income and the rate of interest. As income rises or falls, the transactions and precautionary demand for money rises or falls. If income is held constant, a rise in the interest rate reduces money holdings for speculative purposes. Conversely, a fall in the interest rate produces a rise in the holdings of speculative money.

TABLE 1

The Three Motives for Demanding Money

Both the level of real income and the rate of interest determine the total demand for money. The real quantity of money demanded by all consumers and businesses varies directly with income and inversely with the actual rate of interest, given some level of expectations about future bond prices.

Type of Money Demand	Factor Affecting Demand	Effects on the Quantity of Money Demanded
Transactions To buy and sell goods and services	Rising real income	Higher money demand
	Lowering real income	Lower money demand
Precautionary To save money for unforeseen circumstances	Rising real income	Higher money demand
	Lowering real income	Lower money demand
Speculative To invest in money instruments	Rising interest rates	Lower money demand
	Falling interest rates	Higher money demand

But this information is only half the story. Just as the price of potatoes is the product of both supply and demand, the price level is a product of both money supply and real money demand. On this fact all economists agree. But there are two different theories about how money demand and supply interact to produce a given price level, inflation or deflation, and employment and real income. One theory, the quantity theory of money, places primary emphasis on transactions demand; the other, the liquidity preference theory, highlights the influence of the speculative demand for money.

THE QUANTITY THEORY OF MONEY

Quantity theory of money:
A hypothesis suggesting a predictable positive relationship between the money supply and the price level; specifically, that money supply changes cause price level changes.

Equation of exchange:
An identity used to derive the quantity theory of money; $MV \equiv PQ$.

One of the essential ingredients of classical economic theory and policy, developed toward the end of the eighteenth century, was the **quantity theory of money.** This theory maintains that there is a direct and predictable relation between the money supply, M-1, and prices, given a constant transactions demand for money. If the number of real dollars demanded to carry out everyday transactions (referred to by the classical economists as the income velocity) remains constant, then an increase in the nominal money supply will increase prices.

The quantity theory is derived from an identity (an equation that must be true) called the **equation of exchange.** In economic shorthand, the equation of exchange is written

$$MV \equiv PQ,$$

where M = the nominal money supply, M-1, consisting of currency in the hands of the public and checkable deposits;

V = the income velocity, or the average number of times dollars (the medium of exchange expressed in M-1) are used per year (or week or month) to finance the final purchase of goods and services;

P = the price level of all goods and services; and

Q = the final real output of all goods and services produced and sold in the economy over some period (a year, a month, a week).

Income velocity:
The average number of times that a unit of money (a dollar) is used, or changes hands, in purchasing nominal GNP.

The concept of **income velocity** is crucial to our understanding of the quantity theory of money. M-1 in 1989 was approximately $788 billion. In that same year, GNP, which is expressed as the price level P times final output Q, was $5233 billion. For $788 billion to pay for $5233 billion worth of output, the average dollar must finance at least $6.64 worth of goods ($5233 ÷ $788 = $6.64). We say that the average dollar turned over at least 6.64 times in the course of the year, or that the income velocity of one dollar in 1989 was 6.64. If we know the value of GNP and the quantity of money (M-1) at some point in time, velocity is easily calculated from the equation of exchange as

$$V \equiv \frac{PQ}{(\text{M-1})} \equiv \frac{\text{nominal GNP}}{(\text{M-1})}.$$

While the equation of exchange is useful in some respects, it does not help the economist predict how M-1 is related to P and therefore to inflation. Economists need a theory to do that. To make the equation of exchange a theory, we must specify something about $V, Q, P,$ or M in advance. That is, we must make something in the expression variable and then predict cause and effect on the basis of some hypothetical value of the variable or variables. This is exactly what the classical and neoclassical economists did in converting the equation of exchange into a quantity theory of money.

The Simple Quantity Theory

The simple quantity theory is expressed in exactly the same fashion as the equation of exchange except that the equivalence sign is not given as ≡, which means "must be equal," but as =, which means "is predicted to be equal." The simple quantity theory

$$MV = PQ$$

is stated so that it possibly can be falsified—shown to be untrue—and is therefore a theory.

One of the oldest commonsense macroeconomic propositions is that inflation is "too much money chasing too few goods." The quantity theory explains why that is true. First note that, in general, V and Q were assumed to be constant and predictable. Income velocity—the turnover of money— was thought to be relatively constant over the short run and predictable over the long run. Although the velocity of money, or its average turnover time, for money holders varied from individual to individual, its average remained constant and stable for all money holders taken together.

Why didn't early quantity theorists worry about the level of Q, the final output of real goods and services? They simply assumed that real output was at a maximum. In fairness to these early theorists, we should point out that theirs was a long-run view. Economic disasters created by financial panics, wars, famines, supply shocks, or other disruptions were certainly as much a part of their world as ours, as were beneficial economic events such as inventions and improvements in technology and labor productivity. These events obviously caused reductions or increases in real output. Early monetary theorists such as Adam Smith, David Ricardo, Alfred Marshall, and Irving Fisher neither were unattuned to real-world events nor were they fools. They knew that there would always be short-run fluctuations in output and in the employment of resources—what economists call business cycles. Adjustments were always taking place. The classical economists assumed that output and therefore income were at a maximum because they believed there is a persistent tendency to have economy-wide full employment of resources, implying maximum Q.

As we saw in Chapter 25, the classical and neoclassical economists were believers in Say's law, a principle given expression by Jean Baptiste Say, an early French follower of Adam Smith. Briefly, Say's law states that supply creates its own demand. In other words, the act of producing and supplying goods creates the wherewithal to purchase these goods from the market. Gluts of goods or shortages of goods would not ordinarily take place, but if they did, prices of final goods and services and of labor and other inputs would quickly adjust. This classical assumption of price and wage flexibility meant that adjustment time to full employment would be brief. Should prices and wages fail to be flexible, interest rates would adjust to save the day, according to the classical economists.

The significance of assuming V and Q to be constant or predictable is that the quantity theory of money becomes a theory of cause and effect. Money supply is the cause; prices are the effect. In a modern context, if income velocity and real income are constant, increases in M-1 will increase prices; decreases in M-1 will decrease prices. But by how much do prices increase with increases in M-1? And, more pointedly, how exactly do "too many dollars" end up "chasing too few goods"? A feature of the relation between money and prices assumed by many early economists answers both questions.

Money and Relative Prices

Early economists advanced a proposition called the **neutrality of money,** which means that the relative prices of all goods and services (how many computer games trade for rock concert tickets, for example) are independent of the overall price level.

The neutrality of money can be easily understood with a simple example. Suppose that, starting from some stable equilibrium money supply that produces an equilibrium price level—that is, where money demand equals money supply—the money supply is suddenly doubled. That is, we wake one morning to find that the banks will redeem every $1 bill with $2 and will double the value of all of our checkable deposits. The quantity theory predicts what will happen:

$$MV = PQ,$$

so

$$2MV = 2PQ.$$

If consumers' tastes remain the same, the price level will exactly double in the long run when the excess balances created by a doubling of the money supply are spent, but relative prices of goods and services will not change.

What does this mean in practical terms? At first, individuals perceive the increase in their money holdings to be a bonanza. Their new real money holdings exceed their real demand for money. What do these individuals do to restore a balance between money demand and supply? They spend their excess money holdings in the attempt to acquire more goods. If their tastes do not change, their relative expenditures on shoes, candy, and gasoline do not change. But—and here is a major point—there are no more goods to be had. The economy is already at a full-employment level of real output. The only effect of these increased money expenditures is to drive all prices up. The price level doubles, but relative prices remain unchanged if money is neutral. Once the price level has doubled in response to the doubling of the nominal money supply, people find themselves with the same real holdings of money. Their attempts to spend excess real money stop because there no longer is excess real money. The process ends with the price level exactly doubled but no change in relative prices.

We will investigate this process with a numerical example. Consider a simple, three-good world where quantities of beer, pretzels, and pizzas are produced at certain base prices. Table 2 gives data showing the final output of the three goods and an initial set of prices, indicated as P_0. GNP in this simple world is measured by price multiplied by the quantities of goods produced, an initial sum of $80. Now suppose that the money stock doubles

TABLE 2

Effect of Doubling the Nominal Money Stock in a Three-Good World

If money is neutral—that is, if it does not affect relative prices—a doubling of the nominal money stock doubles the price level from P_0 to P_1, though relative prices and output do not change. The price of beer per case in terms of pretzels is the same before and after the price increase.

Good	Final Output Produced (Q)	Initial Price (P_0)	$P_0 \times Q$	P_1	$P_1 \times Q$
Beer	2 cases	$10 per case	$20	$20	$ 40
Pretzels	10 bags	$1 per bag	$10	$ 2	$ 20
Pizzas	5 large	$10 each	$50	$20	$100
Nominal GNP			$80		$160

and that the new nominal GNP equals $160. If money is neutral, the price of each good produced before the money stock increase must exactly double. This means that relative prices of all the goods traded both before and after doubling of the money stock must remain the same. And, in the example of Table 2, they do. One case of beer still trades for ten bags of pretzels and for one large pizza.

Thus, if money is neutral, relative prices are independent of the price level and of the nominal prices of all goods and services traded in the economy. Neutrality means that money is the oil of trade, not the wheel of trade.

The Simple Quantity Theory: Transmission Mechanism

We summarize the cause-and-effect relation between money and prices in Figure 2. Increases in M-1 initially create excess amounts of real money in the hands of consumers and businesses. Their demand for money is unchanged as a proportion of income, but they now actually hold larger real quantities of money. Their spending attempts are met with frustration since real output is already at a maximum. The effects of this attempt to acquire more goods and services simply drive the money price of goods and services upward. The process ends only when prices have risen to the point where money demanders are again holding real balances equal to their real demands for money.

The classical mechanism relating changes in the money supply to aggregate demand—the classical transmission mechanism—is shown graphically in Figure 3. The line from the origin in Figure 3a shows points of equilibrium between MV and PQ—points where the quantity of money (depicted on the vertical axis), given a constant velocity (V) and a constant *real* full-employment level of output and income (Q_f), produces some *nominal* level of income (P times Q), or GNP (depicted on the horizontal axis). The slope of the line from the origin in Figure 3a is given by a constant, k, which is the reciprocal of velocity, or $1/V$. As velocity rises, k falls, and vice versa. Given some value for M, say M_0, a unique value of nominal income, P_0Q_f is produced, since real output and velocity are assumed constant. If the money supply (M-1) is

FIGURE 2   **The Simple Quantity Theory of Money**

Increases in the nominal money stock initially create excess amounts of real money balances, causing consumers and businesses to attempt additional purchases of goods and services. Assuming a constant output and full employment of resources, price level increases result.

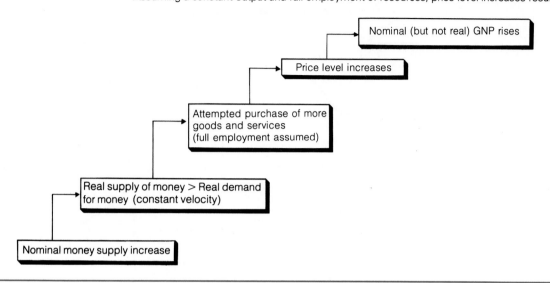

increased to M_1, a new level of *nominal* income, P_1Q_f, is produced. But what happens to the real output of goods and services in the economy?

In Figure 3b, the aggregate supply curve is vertical at full employment. If we now designate Y as real output of goods and services, Y_f represents the full employment of all resources. An increase in the money supply from M_0 to M_1 has the effect of shifting the aggregate demand curve rightward from AD_0 to AD_1. In the classical view of the macroeconomy, an increase in the money supply (assuming full employment at Y_f) has *no* effect on real output; for a time, the real supply of money is greater than the demand for it. People attempt to purchase more goods and services, but these attempts are thwarted by the fact that full employment exists. The result is a rise in the price level, as shown in Figure 3b, from P_0 to P_1. At the new point of equilibrium—E_1 in Figures 3a and 3b—money demanders are again holding actual balances equal to their desired balances. In the classical transmission mechanism, the only impact of a change in the money supply in the long run is to cause an increase in the price level.

SPECULATIVE MONEY DEMAND AND PRICES: KEYNES'S PERSPECTIVE

We now consider a second important theory about the relation between money supply and prices. The classical economists, as we have seen, emphasized the transactions and precautionary motives for holding money and related money demand solely to real income. John Maynard Keynes emphasized a third motivation for holding money—to speculate in bond and other asset markets

FIGURE 3
The Classical Transmission from Money to Prices

An increase in the money supply has no effect on any "real" variables in the economic system such as real output or income. In the long run, prices rise as aggregate demand shifts upward from AD_0 to AD_1.

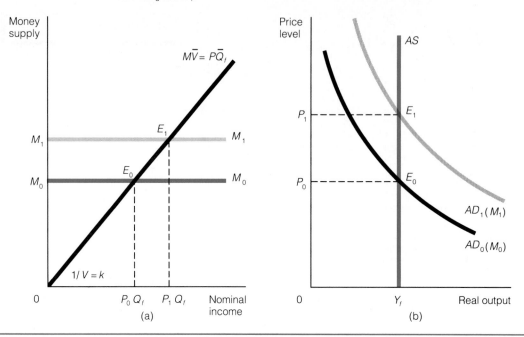

(a)

(b)

where price and interest rates vary. Recall also that this speculative demand for money varies inversely with interest rates: When interest rates rise, the quantity of money demanded for speculative purposes declines, and vice versa.

The Importance of Speculative Demand

In the Keynesian view of macroeconomics, speculative demand plays a special and important role. Assuming that transactions and precautionary demands are satisfied, the rate of interest is the product of the demand for speculative balances and their supply. This is called the liquidity preference theory of money and interest. More important, *economic activity is determined by changes in the rate of interest.*

The importance of the speculative demand for money becomes apparent when we examine the effects of increases in the money supply on the rate of interest and of changes in the rate of interest on economic activity. Figure 4a shows that the rate of interest is a product of the interplay of speculative balances demanded, L_s (reproduced from Figure 1) and the supply of money devoted to speculation, M_s. (Transactions and precautionary money demands are assumed to be satisfied.) The interplay of speculative demand and supply produces an equilibrium interest rate r_0 when supply is M_{s_0}. As Figure 4a shows, an increase in the supply of money available for speculative purposes— in this case, to M_{s_1}—drives interest rates down. The higher bond prices that result from lower interest rates cause asset holders to opt for fewer bonds and more speculative money balances. In other words, lower interest rates create a preference for the liquid asset, money, over the less-liquid asset, bonds.

FIGURE 4   Money Supply, Interest Rates, and Investment Spending

In the Keynesian framework, an increase in the money supply for speculative balances *may* succeed in lowering the interest rate (a), which *may* increase investment spending in the economy (b). Keynes thought these events unlikely in a depression economy, however.

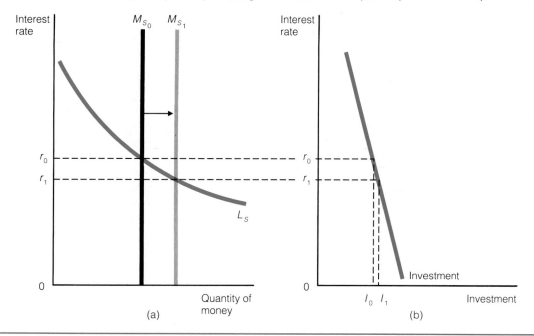

The key to understanding the importance of speculative demand is to observe that investment and consumption might be affected by changes in the interest rate, as the classical economists had suggested. As discussed in Chapter 8, a rise in the interest rate reduces desired investment and increases desired saving, whereas a fall in the interest rate has the effect of increasing both investment and consumption. In the classical approach, lower interest rates ordinarily mean higher spending, higher output, and higher employment. In the event of unemployed resources, monetary policy—altering the quantity of money—could be used to lower interest rates, to increase consumption and investment spending, and to help bring the economy back to full-employment equilibrium if it ever veered from that level.

Keynes rejected the classical assessment. He did not believe that interest rate reductions would necessarily have much impact on investment and consumption. In his view, consumption and investment were largely insensitive to interest rate changes, being autonomous or more responsive to change in income. In Figure 4b, increases in the speculative component of the money supply from M_{S_0} to M_{S_1} produce a small reduction in the rate of interest from r_0 to r_1. These reductions in the interest rate *may* have an impact on investment, but this effect depends on the responsiveness of investment to changes in the interest rate. Keynes believed that individuals would be hesitant to invest in bonds (or in durable consumption goods—big-ticket items) in periods of economic distress. Uncertainty about economic conditions would cause people to hold money even though bond prices were falling (making bonds "a good deal"). Likewise, businesses would exercise extreme caution about investments in new capital in the midst of recessions or depressions. In short, investment would not be very responsive to reductions in the interest rate. Figures 4a and 4b show that interest rate reductions would increase investment only slightly, from I_0 to I_1. Monetary policy, in Keynes's view, would not be a very effective way to nudge the economy toward full employment.

Money and Prices: The Keynesian Transmission Mechanism

What does Keynes's view mean for the short-run relation between the money supply and prices? The addition of speculative demand to the transactions and precautionary demand for money short-circuits the cause-and-effect relation between the money supply and prices. Increases in the money supply may have little or no effect on the price level if the spending generated by an interest rate decrease is small or nonexistent.

Figure 5 illustrates Keynes's scenario. An increase in M-1 creates an excess supply of money. The resulting reductions in interest rates (and concurrent increases in bond prices) cause increased holdings of idle money. Consumption and investment spending increase little, meaning that aggregate demand increases only slightly. Even if resources are fully employed, prices cannot be much affected. If there is widespread unemployment, prices are not affected. The liquidity preference theory, based on the speculative demand for money, therefore implies an uncertain and unpredictable relation between the money supply and prices.

Keynes's view of the transmission from money to prices is depicted in Figure 6. *If* increases in M-1 actually do cause interest rates to fall and *if* the

---

FIGURE 5   Money and Prices: Liquidity Preference View

According to Keynes, an increase in M-1 has an uncertain effect on the price level. A declining interest rate, for instance, may not encourage additional total demand. Even if demand increases, prices may not increase if the economy is experiencing widespread unemployment.

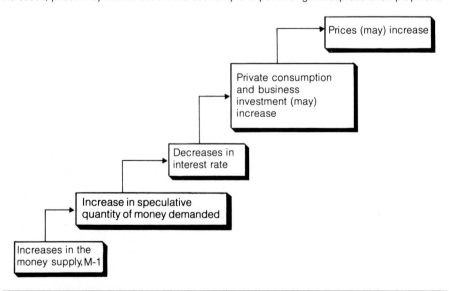

FIGURE 6

Keynes did not have much faith that monetary expansion could increase real output and employment during recessions or depressions. As the money supply increases, investors (and consumers) *might* increase spending *if* the interest rate actually falls. Aggregate demand increases, however, would likely be insignificant.

The Keynesian Transmission Mechanism

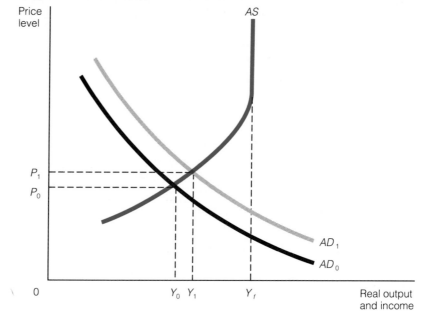

fall in interest rates causes investment and consumption to increase, total expenditures would increase and aggregate demand would shift rightward. As we have seen, Keynes believed that in the presence of uncertainty about economic conditions money holders, consumers, and investors would hold on to speculative money balances and postpone purchases of consumer and investment goods. We show these effects with a minimal increase in aggregate demand and small increases in real output in the economy in Figure 6. Clearly, the Keynesian prescription for economic recovery had to rely on other factors affecting total spending and aggregate demand—namely, increases in government spending and/or reductions in taxes.

MONETARISM: A MODERN APPROACH TO MONEY AND PRICES

The quantity theory of money predicts a positive long-run relation between the money supply and the price level, whereas the liquidity preference approach explains a possible link between money and prices in the short run through the effects of money supply changes on interest rates. A widely accepted contemporary explanation of inflation and deflation—**monetarism**—combines elements of both views along with a new perspective on the inflation process.

Monetarists are concerned with both short-run and long-run adjustments of the economy to different rates of change in the money supply. The monetarist view of inflation emphasizes the uncertainty people feel about what inflation rates will be in the future and the effects this uncertainty will

Monetarism:
A theory that centers on money supply growth, real money demand, nominal and real interest rates, and inflationary expectations in explaining the process of inflation or deflation.

have on present behavior. These expectations have a short-run impact on employment and real income, as well as on prices. We focus here on a simple monetarist explanation of the inflation process, which contains three basic elements: a monetarist explanation of the demand for money, a distinction between the market or nominal interest rate and the real interest rate, and the impact of people's expectations concerning future prices and the inflation process.

Money Demand

One of the foundations of modern monetarism is the formulation of a short-run demand for money. Milton Friedman developed a short-run money demand model in the mid-1950s as a direct extension of both the simple quantity theory and the liquidity preference or speculative money demand approach. Earlier economists argued that people hold money for transactions, precautionary, and speculative purposes. Friedman makes no such distinctions, simply accepting the fact that money is held in response to several independent variables. The most important of these variables are real income and the nominal interest rate.

Like the quantity theorists and Keynes, Friedman argues that some money holdings for transactions depend partly on income.[1] Also in the manner of Keynes, the monetarists find that the nominal interest rate affects real money holdings. While other variables affect money demand in the monetarist model, we neglect them in the following discussion of the monetarist view of inflation and concentrate only on y, current real income, and i, the nominal interest rate, as the factors influencing money demand. A shorthand version of money demand can thus be expressed as

$$L_d = L_d(y, i).$$

In this expression the real demand for money is determined only by current income and the nominal interest rate.

The Nominal Interest Rate and Price Expectations

Real interest rate:
The nominal interest rate minus the expected rate of inflation.

Market, or nominal, interest rate:
The interest rate computed from the money values of a borrowing or lending arrangement, such as a savings account; the interest rate unadjusted for expected inflation.

The classical economists had written extensively about the determinants of the real rate of interest. The **real interest rate**—the nominal rate minus the expected rate of inflation—is determined by the real and fundamental forces of thrift (saving) and productivity (investment) in the economy. But this fundamental rate is generally not the rate of interest that one would pay to borrow money at a bank. The **market,** or **nominal, interest rate**—the rate actually paid at banks and lending institutions—has two components: the real rate of interest and a dynamic element based on price expectations. Consider why the market rate includes both elements.

If you decide on January 1 to borrow $100 from a bank for one year, how will the interest rate be determined? Put another way, on what basis will banks decide to make loans? If the real rate of interest, reflecting basic forces of

---

[1]Friedman's assumption rested on permanent income—the income expected over a lifetime—rather than current income. In our simple discussion of inflation, however, we retain current income as a determinant of money demand, neglecting Friedman's more complex measure of permanent income.

saving and investment, is 4 percent, the bank will certainly charge at least 4 percent. But will the bank charge more? If the rate of inflation expected over the year is 8 percent, the bank would lose real income on a 4 percent loan. It would be lending at a return of 4 percent, but the value of the money returned at the end of the year will have also lost 8 percent of its purchasing power. Thus, after the fact, the bank would have made a bad bargain at any loan rate below 12 percent.

The nominal interest rate is thus influenced by the **expected inflation rate** as well as the real interest rate. When inflationary expectations rise, the nominal interest rate also rises. When the inflation rate is expected to fall, nominal rates tend to fall. When actual, realized rates of inflation are different from those expected, borrowers and lenders adjust in the following period. The effect of inflationary expectations on market rates of interest is a stock-in-trade of modern monetarist thought. Through inflation rate expectations, a dynamic period-to-period element is brought into modern interpretations of the quantity theory of money.

How do we form expectations about future prices? A well-known and currently used theory about this matter is the **adaptive expectations theory,** which states that present price expectations about the future are adapted to the public's most recent experience with prices. The basic premise of adaptive expectations is that it takes time for individuals to adjust to changed circumstances. Expectations about occurrences in the future hinge primarily on present knowledge and present experiences. Consistent experiences in the present ("the sun rose in the east every day this week") tend to create the same expectations about future events ("the sun will rise in the east tomorrow"). The adaptive expectations theory simply asserts that our expectations about future price conditions are formed on the basis of actual past price experience, with the most recent experience having the greatest influence. There are other theories about the formation of expectations (some of which will be explored in the following chapters), but the simple adaptive expectations idea goes far in explaining the modern monetarist connection between monetary expansion and the inflation rate.

Expected inflation rate:
The rate of inflation that consumers and businesses expect to exist over a relevant future period, such as the coming year.

Adaptive expectations theory:
A proposition suggesting that consumers and businesses form expectations of future inflation on the basis of actual inflation from the recent past.

MODERN MONETARISM AND INFLATION

The simple tools of the old quantity theorists combined with a modern version of the demand for money and the adaptive expectations theory provide a monetarist explanation for the process of inflation. Before turning to this concept, it is important to recall exactly what inflation is. Inflation is a rate of increase in prices, not a simple rise in the price level. In a static framework, it is sometimes convenient to say, as we did using the simple quantity theory, that a doubling of M produces a doubling of P and to identify this once-and-for-all change as inflation. In a dynamic real-world setting, however, the money supply is constantly being increased or decreased by the Federal Reserve Board at some rate per week, month, or year. Likewise, prices are rising or falling at some rate. Real income is also changing, by values typically expressed in terms of growth rates such as 3½ percent per year, although in the present simple discussion of the inflation process we assume a constant income growth rate. To arrive at the modern conception of inflation, therefore, we must adapt the static quantity theory to a dynamic setting.

The Process of Inflation

The simple process of inflation is best understood by starting from a dynamic equilibrium position in the economy. In this initial position, the economy is characterized by the following conditions.

Rate of monetary expansion:
The annual percent by which the nominal money supply is changing.

1. A constant **rate of monetary expansion** (whether 3 percent or 50 percent growth in the money stock, M-1, per year—the actual percentage is not important as long as it is constant).
2. Expected and actual inflation rates are equal, and further, market participants will expect the inflation rate to be exactly what it has been in the present and recent past.
3. The nominal rate of interest equals the real rate of interest plus the constant inflation rate. Since the inflation rate has been assumed constant in the most recent past experience, according to the adaptive expectations theory the inflation rate (and therefore the nominal rate of interest) is expected to be the same in the future.
4. People are actually holding real cash balances equivalent to their desired holdings of money balances. The quantity demanded of money is equal to the quantity supplied of money in real terms.
5. Real income or real GNP is growing at a constant rate.

If we numerically express the percentage rates of change of the items in the quantity theory, we can calculate a rate of change in prices. If, for example, the monetary expansion rate, which we now designate with a dot on top of M, or $\dot{M}$, is 12 percent, and the constant growth rate in real income, $\dot{Q}$, is 4 percent, and velocity V is constant ($\dot{V}$ is thus zero), the inflation rate $\dot{P}$ is easily calculated. The dynamic quantity theory becomes

$$\dot{M} + \dot{V} = \dot{P} + \dot{Q},$$

or, given the hypothetical numbers,

$$12\% + 0\% = \dot{P} + 4\%,$$

$$\dot{P} = 12\% - 4\% = 8\% \text{ inflation rate.}$$

The inflation rate is thus calculated as 8 percent.

The exercise of casting the quantity theory into rates of change might seem mechanical so far, but it is invaluable in providing a simple understanding of inflation as a process. To initiate the inflation process we need simply to suppose that the Federal Reserve, through its powers over the monetary base, suddenly increases the rate of monetary expansion from 12 percent to 15 percent. Further, the Federal Reserve maintains the rate of monetary expansion at 15 percent from that point forward and forever.

Figure 7 illustrates what happens. The new, higher growth rate in the money supply initially creates disequilibrium among money holders. After the expansion, but before prices begin rising faster, money demanders find themselves holding more real money balances than they want to hold, given the previous state of equilibrium. Consumers and businesses will attempt to rid themselves of these excess balances by spending more on all goods and services.

What, however, is the long-term impact of the increased spending on real income and employment? The answer in real terms is "nothing." Since output and employment were already growing at a constant full-employment

FIGURE 7

The process of inflation begins with an increased rate of M-1 expansion by the Federal Reserve. Excess money holdings are spent, creating higher actual inflation and higher expected inflation. Higher expected inflation causes higher market interest rates, further increasing spending and inflation. The process continues until the Federal Reserve stabilizes the rate of growth in M-1.

How the Fire of Inflation Gets Fanned

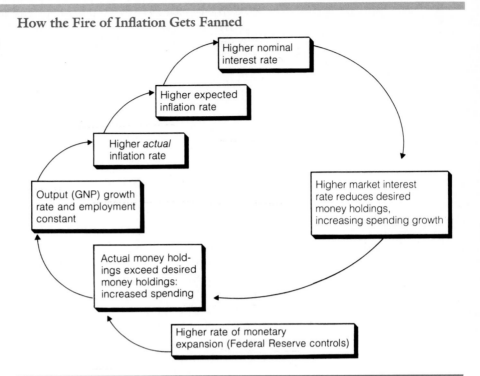

rate, the attempt to purchase more goods will only drive up prices and money income more rapidly. Thus the actual inflation rate begins to rise. Since it takes time for higher actual inflation rates to be translated into expectations of higher inflation—that is, for the adaptive expectations theory to come into play—higher expected inflation rates will lag behind the actual rate.

It is easy to predict what will happen next. Since the nominal interest rate equals the real interest rate (which we assume to remain constant) plus the expected inflation rate, nominal rates begin to climb. This rise in the nominal rate affects the desired real holdings of money. Since the real demand of money is partially a function of the nominal interest rate (the opportunity cost of holding money), the higher interest rate generated by higher inflation expectations leads to lower desired money holdings. This effect reinforces the attempt of money holders to rid themselves of cash balances. That is, the higher nominal rate further fans the rise in the inflation rate.

When does the process stop? When is a dynamic equilibrium reattained? The process will stop only if the Federal Reserve sticks to a constant rate of monetary expansion (15 percent in our example). The process of increasing inflation rates will continue only if the Federal Reserve continues to increase the rate of money creation. If the Federal Reserve holds the rate to 15 percent, for example, equilibrium will be reattained at a new constant inflation rate, a new nominal interest rate, and a new rate of price expectations equal to the actual inflation rate. In the numerical terms of our example, equilibrium will take place when

$$\dot{M} + \dot{V} = \dot{P} + \dot{Q},$$
$$15\% + 0\% = 11\% + 4\%.$$

Prices must rise, in other words, so that *actual* real money holdings are equivalent to *desired* real money holdings. Spending and the inflation rate will rise until real money demand equals money supply.

Some Preliminary Lessons About Inflation

The monetarist view of inflation contains certain explicit and implicit lessons. First and foremost, monetarists argue that inflation is always a monetary phenomenon. Milton Friedman and Anna Schwartz[2] have supported this proposition with massive hundred-year empirical studies of the quantity theory in the United States and England. As we note in Figure 3, the villain in the monetarists' inflation scenario is expansionist policies of the monetary authority that controls the money stock. For a discussion of alternative monetary policies and the rate of inflation in Europe, see Focus, "European Inflation Under a Common Currency Agreement."

To keep ROI down, govt ↑Mss.
But ↑Mss ⇒ infl'n ⇒ ↑nom ROI

In the monetarist version of events, for example, high interest rates do not *cause* inflation; rather, they are the *result* of inflation. What we did not mention in our simplified treatment is that one short-lived initial effect of the Federal Reserve's monetary expansion is a temporary decline in market interest rates. Of course, the market rates begin to rise as expectations of higher inflation take hold of borrowers and lenders. Observers and politicians often make the mistake of arguing that the money stock growth rate should be expanded to lower the interest rates. As we have seen, however, the monetarists show that such a shortsighted policy will have the opposite effect: Increasing the rate of expansion of the money supply will soon raise nominal interest rates. Higher interest rates follow higher inflation rates, but higher monetary expansion is necessary for both events to occur.

Many people also think that inflation is self-generating. Higher nominal interest rates do affect desired money balances and spending. But in the monetarist view, this process must come to an end if the central bank holds the money expansion to a constant rate. It may, of course, take time for inflationary expectations to adjust between consumers and producers, borrowers and lenders, and employers and employees, but when the market adjusts, a dynamic equilibrium will be attained.

It is very important to note that an increased rate of monetary expansion *will* have some short-run effects on the economy. Specifically, the Federal Reserve can temporarily lower both the nominal and the real rates of interest, thereby creating a *temporary* surge in total spending. This might have short-term effects on output and employment as well if employment is not growing at a full-employment rate (or if overfull employment is a temporary possibility). If the economy is at or near full employment, however, the inevitable result in the monetarist view is a higher rate of inflation. A contemporary school of macroeconomics called *rational expectations theory* goes one step further than monetarism on the matter of even the short-run possibility of monetary policy having any real effects on the economy. In an extreme view of this theory, monetary policy can have *no* effects on real output or employment because all of the effects of policy are fully anticipated. We will turn to these considerations in Chapters 35 and 36 after looking at some of the problems caused by inflation.

---

[2]Milton Friedman and Anna J. Schwartz, *A Monetary History of the United States* (Princeton, N.J.: Princeton University Press, 1963).

FOCUS   European Inflation Under a Common Currency Agreement

One of the stated goals of the European Community is to establish a common currency in 1992. On the surface, this proposal appears to have several advantages without any serious disadvantages. Nonetheless, the proposal has become quite controversial.

The major advantage of adopting common currency is reducing transaction costs and thereby increasing the opportunity for trade between the various European countries. It is easier for British firms to do business with firms in France if both countries use a common currency than if the British use the pound and the French use the franc.

However, in agreeing to a common currency system, the European nations are also agreeing to a unified monetary policy. Some type of European central bank (which could be modeled after the U.S. Federal Reserve System, with branch banks in each member country) would be created with the authority to conduct open market operations and set discount rates, among other things. Depending on the policies pursued by the central bank, the money supply within the European Community would rise at some particular rate. However, it would not be possible for member nations to independently control monetary growth within their borders.

If each of the member countries were in agreement over appropriate monetary policy, this would not present a serious problem. However, such a consensus does not exist. Currently, most of the European countries have linked their respective currencies to the deutsche mark (the currency of Germany), but some of the countries, particularly France and Italy, are unhappy with the anti-inflation policies

previously pursued by the West German government. The Germans' experience with hyperinflation in 1923 sensitized them to inflation. The German central bank has responded to this sensitivity by pursuing policies to keep inflation rates down. French and Italian objections to a common currency amount to a dispute over control of the central bank. Should France and Italy gain control, there is reason to expect that the rate of inflation in Europe would rise more rapidly than under German control.

Although Germany has publicly supported the proposal for a unified currency, there are signs that the Germans are hesitant to trust their monetary fate to others. Even Switzerland, which is not a member of the European Community, has announced that it would not participate in a common currency agreement because of fears that it would lead to a policy of inflation.

Margaret Thatcher has similarly been reluctant to commit Britain to the monetary union. Instead, she has proposed a system of competing currencies, with all Europeans free to choose the currency they want to use. Prime Minister Thatcher believes that such a system would lead to dominance by the least inflationary currency and would thus discipline the various central banks to vigorously pursue anti-inflationary policies.

Since the various members of the European Community differ with regard both to economic priorities and to economic philosophies, it is difficult to predict what monetary policies would be pursued by a unified European central bank. This uncertainty will prove to be a major obstacle in obtaining participation by the member countries.

INFLATION

Several measures of inflation are used in the real world to guide policymaking. As we mentioned in Chapter 24, a consumer price index and a producer price index are calculated by the Bureau of Labor Statistics. A third major index is the implicit price deflator, a means of converting nominal GNP values into real GNP values. No matter what measure is used, the presence of higher indexes over time indicates a rising price level. Actual U.S. inflation rates are shown in Table 3.

The Effects of Inflation

The statistical presence of inflation in the economy tells us little about the costs and other distortions it inflicts there. Runaway inflation of 80 or 2000 percent per month or per year, such as that sometimes experienced in war-torn or developing countries with low or severely restricted stocks of goods

TABLE 3

Two Measures of Inflation, 1960–1989

Two popular measures of inflation used in the United States are the implicit price deflator, a means for converting nominal GNP into real values, and the consumer price index, which bases the inflation rate on price changes in some hypothetical market basket of consumer goods. The numbers given for both indexes are annual rates.

| Year | Inflation Rate, as Measured by | | Year | Inflation Rate, as Measured by | |
	Implicit Price Deflator	Consumer Price Index		Implicit Price Deflator	Consumer Price Index
1960	1.6	1.6	1975	9.8	9.1
1961	1.0	1.0	1976	6.4	5.9
1962	2.2	1.1	1977	6.7	6.5
1963	1.6	1.2	1978	7.3	7.7
1964	1.5	1.3	1979	8.9	11.3
1965	2.7	1.7	1980	9.0	13.5
1966	3.6	2.9	1981	9.7	10.4
1967	2.6	2.9	1982	6.4	6.1
1968	5.0	4.2	1983	3.9	3.2
1969	5.6	5.4	1984	3.7	4.3
1970	5.5	5.9	1985	3.0	3.6
1971	5.7	4.3	1986	2.6	1.9
1972	4.7	3.3	1987	3.2	3.6
1973	6.5	6.2	1988	3.3	4.1
1974	9.1	11.0	1989	4.1	4.8

Source: Council of Economic Advisers, *Economic Report of the President* (Washington, D.C.: U.S. Government Printing Office, 1990), pp. 301, 363.

and services, can reduce an economy to barter or cause it to collapse altogether. Milder inflation—3 to 15 percent per year—also creates economic costs in any advanced economy. The full effects of increases in inflation rates may take some time to be fully realized, so inflation has both short- and long-run effects.

Inflation, Fixed Incomes, and Assets. The most publicized effect of inflation is the redistributive impact it has between specific groups in society. Inflation affects those who can least afford to pay for it—the sick, the poor, and especially the elderly and others on fixed incomes—through erosions of purchasing power. Congress, in recent years of inflation, indexed or "tied" Social Security and other welfare benefits to a price level index, thereby alleviating some of the problems inflation causes for the retired or the aged. Nevertheless, inflation is a constant threat to the most economically vulnerable groups in society.

Inflation also adversely affects holders of assets denominated in nominal, or money, terms as opposed to real terms. Suppose you purchase a house—a real asset—and hold it for five years, over which time the price level doubles because of inflation. What happens to the nominal value of your investment? Excluding the real factors of natural appreciation and depreciation that might take place over the five years (resulting from the location, deterioration of property, and so on), the money value of your house should closely follow the inflation rate over the period, doubling at the end of the five years.

While the value of real assets tends to follow inflation, the value of money-denominated assets may not. Suppose that you lend a friend $10,000, to be paid at the end of a five-year period, and that your friend issues you a promissory note attesting to the loan. Again suppose that the price level doubles over the five-year span because of inflation. Aside from any interest paid by your friend, what has happened to the real value of your asset? Although the nominal value of the note remains at $10,000, the real value is only half of what it was at the beginning of the five-year period. You will now be able to purchase only half the goods and services that you could have bought before you made the loan. Capital gains or losses—changes in real value—are always associated with holding any kind of asset in the face of unanticipated inflation. Real assets generally gain in value, whereas money assets—those expressed in fixed money terms—generally lose value.

Asset holders also experience transaction and information costs as they move into and out of inflation-prone assets. It is costly, in other words, to find out which real assets will best follow the price level—a Picasso or a Jackson Pollock, a house or IBM stock.

Disruptive Expectations. A second major effect of inflation is that it distorts expectations of inflation, wage rates, and interest rates. When the inflation rate is not perfectly anticipated, workers and employers, buyers and sellers of goods and services, and borrowers and lenders will be uncertain of future real values. Since these transactors will generally make mistakes in forecasting the effects of inflation in specific markets, there will be continuous and unanticipated transfers of wealth among workers and employers, buyers and sellers, borrowers and lenders.

Market participants try to protect themselves, of course. Workers belonging to labor unions often bargain for **escalator clauses** in their contracts, provisions that tie future wages to some index of the price level as a hedge against inflation.

Inflation and expectations of the rate of inflation also affect nominal interest rates. When the inflation rate fluctuates, so do expectations of inflation as well as nominal and real interest rates. These changes can have severe effects on the economic well-being of various groups and individuals in the economy by altering the real value of indebtedness. In the late 1970s, for example, unexpected inflation worked to the benefit of many homeowners by substantially reducing the real value of their mortgage payments, the real value of the indebtedness incurred when they borrowed money to buy houses. Of course, there is the other side of this coin. Lenders were being paid back, in real terms, much less from homeowners than they had originally agreed to. The presence of volatile inflation and interest rates not only transfers wealth among groups in society, but also will serve to make credit markets function less efficiently. (See Focus, "The Winners and Losers from Unexpected Inflation.")

Inflation as a Tax. Inflation also levies two different kinds of "taxes" on people, taxes that are not directly imposed through the traditional democratic process of taxation by legislation. The first of these is the **pure inflation tax.** No one fills out an inflation tax form and writes a check, but the pure inflation tax is nonetheless very real. The taxpayers are those individuals and businesses who hold money. Anyone who holds money over, say, a month will see the purchasing power of that money decline due to inflation. The amount by which the purchasing power of an individual's money holdings declines is the pure inflation tax.

Escalator clause:
Provision of a labor contract that ties changes in nominal wages to changes in some price index.

Pure inflation tax:
The reduction in purchasing power of an individual's nominal money holdings due to inflation.

FOCUS The Winners and Losers from Unexpected Inflation

Just as price changes for a particular commodity can benefit one group and simultaneously harm another, the financial positions of debtors and creditors also can be modified by unexpected changes in the inflation rate. Expectations of the future inflation rate are built into nominal or money rates of interest. The nominal rate of interest at the time money is borrowed or lent not only reflects the real interest rate, but also the inflation rate that the borrower and lender expect will persist over the term of the loan. If, after the loan is made, the rate of inflation that actually occurs turns out to be different from that expected, the purchasing power of the interest and principal repayments turns out to be different from what both parties to the loan expected it to be. The result is an unexpected wealth transfer between the debtor and the creditor. The direction of the transfer depends on whether inflation was "overanticipated" or "underanticipated."

Consider the more familiar case of underanticipated inflation first. This occurs when the rate of inflation that actually exists turns out to be higher than the rate the debtor and creditor expected when the loan was made. For simplicity, assume that a student wishes to borrow $3000 from a rich aunt for one year to finance college expenditures. Both agree that the real interest rate on this family loan will be 0 percent. Suppose that both expect no inflation—an inflation rate of 0 percent—over the year. The student then promises (a loan contract) to repay $3000 at the end of the year. Since both parties to this agreement expect no inflation over the course of the year, both parties expect the $3000 repayment to have the same purchasing power at the end of the year that the $3000 loan had at the beginning of the year. The promise (or the loan contract) is to repay 3000 nominal dollars. The expectation implicit in the loan agreement is that the 3000 nominal dollars will purchase the same amount of goods and services at the end of the year that they were able to purchase at the beginning of the year.

At the end of the year, suppose that the price level had doubled; that is, suppose that the inflation rate had been 100 percent. The student would be obligated to pay back $3000, but each dollar would purchase only one-half as much as it did at the beginning of the year. In essence, the student would pay back only 1500 constant-purchasing-power dollars. The inflation rate was actually 100 percent,

but the debtor and creditor expected 0 percent. Hence, inflation was underanticipated, and as a result, a wealth transfer of 1500 constant-purchasing-power dollars from the creditor (the rich aunt) to the debtor (the student) has taken place.

No matter what the levels of the actual and expected inflation rate, if inflation is underanticipated, debtors win and creditors lose from inflation. The people who borrowed to buy homes in the 1950s and 1960s benefited from the high and underanticipated inflation rates of the 1970s. Their real mortgage payments turned out to be much lower than either they or the lenders thought they would be due to underanticipated inflation. The lenders of mortgage funds, on the other hand, were financially hurt, as was evidenced by the bankruptcy of a number of savings and loan associations during this period. The federal government, as well as state and local governments, probably also benefited from underanticipated inflation. With much debt outstanding that was issued under fairly low expected rates of inflation, the real interest and principal repayments ended up lower than expected. Of course, the holders of these bonds—individuals and businesses who lent funds by buying bonds—saw their real wealth drop as a result of underanticipated inflation. Whenever inflation is underanticipated, debtors win and creditors lose.

The direction of the wealth transfer is not always from creditors to debtors, however. It is quite possible for it to be in just the opposite direction. Consider the fictitious student loan discussed above. Suppose, though, that both parties expect a 100 percent inflation rate over the year. The student will be agreeable to paying back $6000 at the end of the year because it is expected that each dollar paid back will be worth half as much as each dollar borrowed. A constant-purchasing-power payback of 3000 beginning-of-the-year dollars is expected. If the actual inflation rate during the year turns out to be 0 percent, who wins? The rich aunt expected a purchasing-power repayment of $3000 ($6000, but at a doubled level of prices). But with zero inflation, she will receive 6000 nominal dollars that have a purchasing power of 6000 beginning-of-the-year dollars. The wealth transfer here goes from the student (debtor) to the rich aunt (creditor) because both overanticipated inflation when the loan was made.

 A second way in which inflation acts as a tax is more direct. In many countries, including the United States, a progressive income tax exists. Higher tax rates are applied to higher incomes. However, when the tax rate that a person is subject to depends on the person's nominal income, inflation has the effect of pushing people into higher tax brackets even though their real incomes have not changed or have even fallen. The individual ends up paying a larger fraction of income in income taxes solely because of inflation, not because of any increase in real income or any direct change in the tax laws.

This phenomenon, sometimes called "bracket creep," became prevalent in the United States during the inflationary years of the 1970s. In 1981, however, the Congress voted to include **tax indexation** as a feature of the federal income tax code. Beginning in 1985, tax indexation eliminated bracket creep due to inflation by adjusting the income tax brackets yearly to account for any inflation that has occurred during the year. This actually makes the U.S. income tax a tax on real, rather than nominal or money, income.

Tax indexation:
Periodic adjustment of the tax brackets of a progressive income tax so as to base taxes on real, not nominal, income; eliminates bracket creep and increased income taxes due solely to inflation.

THEORIES OF INFLATION

Theories about the cause of inflation can be broadly divided into two categories: cost-push and demand-pull. In brief, **cost-push inflation** results from monopoly or union power pushing prices up. Either unions may respond to rising monopoly output prices by demanding higher wages or output monopolists may respond to union demands for higher wages by raising prices. A variant of the cost-push explanation is the supply shock theory of inflation, which explains inflation as the result of a sudden increase in production costs caused by some resource scarcity, such as that created by OPEC or by crop failure.

Demand-pull inflation is a rise in prices owing to increases in expenditures on goods and services. When actual holdings of cash balances exceed consumers' and investors' desired holdings, they begin to spend. Such spending drives prices upward until they rise enough to reduce actual real money holdings to desired real holdings. In other words, increases in demand pull prices up.

Monetarists adhere to the demand-pull explanation of inflation. In their view, long-run inflation is the result of the Federal Reserve's pumping the money supply above the level necessary to keep its growth in line with the growth in the public's desired real holdings of money. Most Keynesians view inflation as a combined result of demand-side and supply-side forces in the economy.

Cost-push inflation:
Increases in the price level caused by monopoly and/or union power or by shocks to the economy that reduce aggregate supply.

Demand-pull inflation:
Increases in the price level caused by increases in aggregate demand.

Cost-Push Theories of Inflation

Cost-push explanations place the blame for inflation on pressures from monopolies or unions or from sudden shortages of natural resources. The corresponding theories of how these factors can cause inflation are called the monopoly power/wage-price spiral argument and the supply, or resource, shock explanation.

The Monopoly Power/Wage-Price Spiral Theory. Some economists argue that one cause of inflation is that the prices of goods and services are pushed up by monopoly power. There are two variants of this argument, depending on the source of monopoly power—output monopolies in product markets or input monopolies, such as labor unions, in resource markets.

Concentration of monopoly power in input or output markets causes rigid constraints on the ability of prices and wages to move downward in response to falling aggregate demand. Output monopolies are able to resist cutting prices by controlling output—by supplying lower quantities in an effort to maintain their revenues. Rather than accept lower wages, input monopolies such as giant labor unions curtail labor's supply in an effort to counteract falling demand for labor. The rigidities imposed by output and input monopolies mean that prices and wages are not freely adaptive to changes in demand. When aggregate demand falls, the result is lower output and employment rather than falling prices and wages.

Further increases in the degree of monopolization or of union membership will create new price and wage rigidities in the economy and, with them, reductions in output and employment. These increases will have the effect of shifting the aggregate supply curve leftward over time. The rate of output and employment will decline and prices will rise.

Another version of this argument is that, at any point in time, the price demands of monopolies or the wage demands of unions will create a **wage-price spiral** of inflation. If monopolies can set prices and make higher prices stick, the wage demands of unions will escalate; erosions of real purchasing power will cause union members to demand higher nominal wages. Either increased monopoly price demands or union wage demands will reduce the short-run aggregate supply of output because both market activities have the short-run effect of temporarily reducing the hiring of labor.

The process may also be viewed from a different perspective. Union demands may create cost increases for business. These cost increases, where output markets are monopolized, are passed on to the buying public by monopolies in the form of price increases. A wage-price spiral may develop, and the result is the same whether the original cause is unions or monopolies.

Some economists discount the wage-price spiral explanation of inflation based on monopoly and union power. In the first place, the argument *assumes* the existence of monopoly and union influence on the price level. In the automobile industry, however, industry and union forces often counteract each other's influence, settling on wage bargains and prices that are roughly competitive. Union wage increases cannot automatically be passed on to consumers; sellers, even monopoly sellers, still face a demand curve of a certain elasticity.

More important, any wage-price spiral must ultimately be **accommodated** by the Federal Reserve. Unless the Federal Reserve validates price and wage increases by increasing M-1, unemployment and reduced output will occur. Pressured by unions and monopolies, discretionary monetary and fiscal authorities may stand their ground, forcing unions and monopolies to endure unemployment until prices and wages fall and the economy is brought back to equilibrium at full employment. Or the Fed may accommodate cost-push pressures by increasing the money stock, thereby validating inflation. At most, argue critics of the wage-price spiral, unions and monopolies can force a once-and-for-all increase in nominal wages and prices—unless the Federal Reserve accommodates these pressures in the economy. The rise in prices will not be continuous—that is, inflationary—unless the Federal Reserve permits it to be so.

Wage-price spiral:
The process whereby increased prices of final goods cause increased wage rates and other resource prices, which in turn result in still-higher prices of final goods; for the spiral to continue, the money supply must continually increase or real output must continually fall.

Accommodation of cost-push inflation:
Increases in the money supply designed to offset a decrease in aggregate supply caused by monopoly or union action or by an aggregate supply shock; increased aggregate demand results, preventing decreases in real output.

Supply shock inflation:
Price level increases stemming from a decrease in aggregate supply; decreased aggregate supply usually occurs because of sudden increased scarcity of essential resources.

The Supply Shock Theory of Inflation. Another cost-push explanation of inflation is related to **supply shocks**—natural or artificial reductions in the supply of vital natural resources. The Iraqi invasion of Kuwait in August 1990, which gave Iraq control over nearly 20 percent of the world's oil reserves, constitutes such a supply shock. A worldwide embargo of Iraqi oil and Iraqi-held Kuwaiti oil effectively removed four million barrels of oil from the market each day, instantly pushing up the costs of producing and transporting final goods everywhere. (For an account of how the global economy absorbed this latest oil shock, see Focus, "Economic Repercussions of Iraq's Invasion of Kuwait.")

The United States has experienced oil price shocks before. In the 1970s, the OPEC nations progressively monopolized the oil export industry and raised prices. Since oil-based energy was an important input in U.S. manufacturing and other uses, some observers argued that increases in costs were passed on to consumers in the form of higher prices. OPEC's price demands were seen as ushering in a higher rate of inflation. (Between 1974 and 1980, the average inflation rate was approximately 9 percent.)

While it is certainly correct that oil and energy-related prices rose during the 1970s and, further, that the period witnessed high rates of inflation, it is by no means clear that OPEC *caused* inflation, viewed as a continuous rate of price increase. OPEC lost much of its cartel power in the 1980s, an event that coincides with moderate inflation. Does this mean that OPEC's partial dissolution *caused* the reduction in inflation?

For the supply shock to inflict a continuous increase in prices, other forces must be at work in the economy. For instance, in the 1970s the Federal Reserve Board steadily increased the growth in the money supply, partly in response to the rising prices of oil-related goods brought about by OPEC. By increasing money supply growth, the Federal Reserve not only accommodated OPEC's higher prices but fueled inflation for all other goods as well. As a trading partner with the United States, OPEC nations soon faced higher prices for their imports and responded by increasing the price for their oil. This sequence—higher costs leading to higher prices leading to higher costs, and so on—is a **cost-price spiral,** a variant of a wage-price spiral. Naturally, other forces contributed to the pressure on prices; monopoly and union rigidities complement the effect of a supply shock.

Cost-price spiral:
The process whereby increased production costs lead to increased final goods prices, which lead to further increases in resource prices and production costs; for the spiral to continue, the money supply must continually increase or real output must continually fall.

In determining who was to blame for the inflation of the 1970s, then, some economists might begin with the oil sheiks. Others believe that the supply shock scenario just described would have been impossible without the cooperation of the Federal Reserve's expansionary monetary policy. Not every OPEC-dependent country suffered the same inflationary consequences. Switzerland, for example, whose central bank followed a much more conservative policy, seemed to suffer least from the OPEC supply shock.

Demand-Pull Theories of Inflation

The theories we have discussed so far—monopoly power, wage-price, and supply shock—focus on the supply side of inflation. These theories predict inflation on the basis of shifts in the aggregate supply curve.

Inflation, of course, also has roots in the demand side of the economy. Any rightward shift in the aggregate demand curve, given an upward-sloping supply curve, will create or increase inflationary pressures. Monetary expansion on the part of the Federal Reserve will shift the aggregate demand curve

FOCUS   Economic Repercussions of Iraq's Invasion of Kuwait

Iraq's August 1990 invasion of Kuwait sent shockwaves through the U.S. economy, many of which seemed to arrive simultaneously with news of the invasion. Less than a day after Saddam Hussein's forces poured over the border into neighboring Kuwait, service stations across the United States were posting higher gasoline prices, prompting concern about an already shaky economy and recollections of the 1974 and 1979 oil shocks. In the days and weeks following the invasion, oil prices were up sharply, despite occasional retreats. The effect at the pump: By Labor Day 1990, U.S. consumers were spending nearly twenty-five cents per gallon more for a fillup.

The United Nations embargo of oil from Iraq and Iraqi-held Kuwait took four million barrels off the world market every day. A majority of OPEC oil ministers eventually voted to allow cartel members to expand production, which reduced the shortfall to between 500,000 and one million barrels a day. Even so, as oil industry experts pointed out, the additional production was not of the same quality as the previously available crude; in other words, the additional crude would yield less gasoline when refined. This, coupled with the loss of 600,000 barrels a day of refining capacity in Kuwait, placed upward pressure on gasoline prices. There were calls for tapping the 586 million barrels of oil in the United States' Strategic Petroleum Reserve to soften the supply shock, but higher prices would have persisted even if President Bush had immediately authorized dipping into the reserves—at least in the short run. U.S. reserves consist entirely of crude, crude that would have had to be refined by facilities that were barely able to meet demand for high-quality refined products before the crisis.

As higher oil prices worked their way through the economy, the inflation rate was expected to jump between 1 and 2 percentage points. The oil shock was also certain to lop at least half a percent off the rate of economic growth, which stood at an anemic 0.4 percent in the second quarter of 1990. Immediately following the invasion, many economists thought the economy would escape recession, but consumers weren't so sure: Both leading measures of consumer confidence declined in August. Since consumer spending makes up two-thirds of GNP, this lack of confidence in the economy loomed large; the ranks of economists who predicted a recession-free 1990 had thinned considerably by September.

Had events in the Middle East not complicated matters, the Federal Reserve might have eased monetary policy in response to generally depressed business conditions and rising unemployment in the fall of 1990. Even after the level of the U.S. military commitment had become clear and hopes had faded for a decline in gasoline prices as dramatic as their rise, some observers urged the Fed to increase the

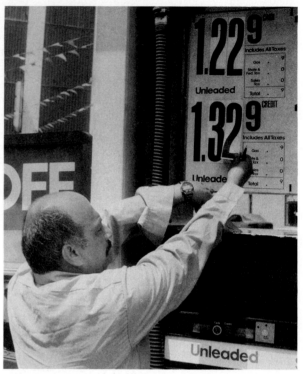

Supply shock: Consumers were faced with almost daily increases in the price of gasoline in the days and weeks following Iraq's August 1990 invasion of Kuwait.

money supply in the belief that the sluggish economy would put the brakes on inflation. Unwilling to risk setting off a 1970s-style inflationary spiral, however, and fearful of further upsetting an inflation-wary bond market, the Fed did not immediately ease.

The 1990 oil shock jolted the U.S. economy, but the United States and other industrialized nations benefited from having experienced this kind of shock before. Brazil, Chile, Thailand, and South Korea were less prepared, having developed successful but oil-dependent economies mostly since the earlier shocks. The economies-in-transition of Eastern Europe, which had been shielded from the 1970s shocks by a now-defunct barter arrangement whereby the Soviet Union would supply all the oil they wanted at subsidized prices, watched helplessly as higher oil prices forced double-digit inflation rates still higher.

Sources: David E. Rosenbaum, "Economic Uncertainties Are Intensified for U.S. Policy Makers," *New York Times* (August 4, 1990), p. 6; Allana Sullivan, "Renewed Jitters Boost Prices of Oil, Products," *Wall Street Journal* (August 31, 1990), p. A3.

and drive the price level up. (The effects of demand shifts depend on the shape of the aggregate supply curve.) Other factors that can shift the aggregate demand curve include increased government spending, investment spending, and consumer demand.

Money-Supply Growth and Inflation. Monetarists and other economists believe there is a direct relation between expansionary monetary policy on the part of the Federal Reserve and inflation. In other words, inflation—a continuously rising price level—cannot take place without a continuously rising money supply.

This demand-pull theory of inflation is based on an updated version of the quantity theory of money. Briefly stated, the monetarist demand-pull model assumes that monetary expansion on the part of the Federal Reserve will merely increase the cash holdings of individuals without affecting output. If individuals rid themselves of excess money holdings by spending, but output is constant, then prices will go up. Price increases will fuel expectations of higher prices as well as higher nominal interest rates. Higher interest rates will increase pressure on the Federal Reserve to increase the money supply, and so on.

Monetarists believe that this cycle of inflation can be halted only when the Federal Reserve maintains a steady growth rate in the money supply. Such a policy will stabilize money demand, price expectations, and interest rates and permit steady growth in output.

The Relation Between M-1 and Inflation. Does the monetarist demand-pull theory correspond with actual inflation rates? Milton Friedman, the leading proponent of the monetarist position, argues that M-1 growth rates and inflation should be tracked for a number of years. The relation is fairly consistent: Inflation generally follows an increase in M-1 growth, with about a two-year lag between the change in M-1 and the change in prices. In the early 1980s, M-1 grew at a fairly steady rate of about 8 percent annually. This brought inflation rates down sharply—from above 12 percent in 1980 to less than 2 percent in 1986. Between 1985 and 1986, however, the growth rate in M-1 increased to about 17 percent per year, and the inflation rate increased to over 4 percent annually from 1987 to 1989. Since 1986, the growth rate in M-1 has decreased sharply, which monetarist theory predicts will curtail future inflation.

Inflation and the Deficit. Politicians are fond of blaming high inflation on growing government deficits. Economists, however, are quite unsure of the effects of deficits on the inflation rate. For one thing, deficits are not always caused by increasing government expenditures. They may also result from decreasing revenues. Therefore, the deficit may be increasing at a time when the economy is in a recession and prices are not under inflationary pressure. Deficits can affect inflation, however, if the government finances them in certain ways. When the government borrows money from the Federal Reserve System, it spurs growth in the money supply, setting off the inflationary spiral. Reserves and deposits are added to the banking system with no withdrawals, which would have occurred with taxation. When the government borrows from private sources, it contributes to higher interest rates, another source of inflationary pressure. The relation between federal deficits and inflation is further discussed in Economics in Action at the end of this chapter.

CURES FOR INFLATION

Solutions to inflation—policies that might bring about price stability—are always being hotly debated. Just as there is no single agreed-upon cause for inflation, there is no single accepted cure. When policy-makers attempt to resolve the inflation problem, moreover, they may bring about other, perhaps worse, consequences. Many blame the Federal Reserve's anti-inflationary policy of 1979–1980 for the severe recession that followed almost immediately.

Strategies to combat inflation can be placed in two broad categories: nondiscretionary policies and discretionary policies.

Nondiscretionary Cures

Those who believe that inflation is directly attributable to monetary expansion urge restraint on the Federal Reserve. This restraint may take several forms. Monetarists urge that the Federal Reserve avoid policies that disrupt the price expectations of the public. Sudden expansions or contractions of the money supply, for example, usher in cycles of rising and falling prices. Such changes affect future prices and interest rates and require future discretionary actions. The roller-coaster path of high inflation followed by debilitating recessions is not caused by a destabilized economy but by a destabilizing stop-and-go policy on the part of the Federal Reserve. Monetarists urge that the Federal Reserve adopt a money supply growth rule. Such a rule, they believe, can allow the economy to reach a proper, long-run equilibrium rate of GNP growth with stable prices.

Discretionary Cures

Discretionary policies to combat inflation are varied. The first step in proper policymaking is accurate diagnosis: Is the inflation a supply-side or demand-side phenomenon? If the inflation is caused by excessive demand, the proper fiscal cures involve budget cuts or higher taxes to dampen the growth in expenditures. Such policies are obviously not very popular with politicians or voters, so inflation-fighting measures are often left to the Federal Reserve. The Federal Reserve's proper monetary policies include reductions in M-1 growth rates and higher interest rates. Both actions tend to choke off consumption spending and investment, reducing the pressure on prices (and meanwhile risking a recession).

Policies to combat inflation caused by supply factors such as monopoly or union pressures and the wage-price spiral are also varied. We briefly look at two such policies: price and wage controls and tax-induced policies.

Price and Wage Controls: Gain Without Pain?   Under price and wage controls, price and wage increases are forbidden by Congress, with penalties for non-compliance. Direct price and wage controls are a familiar, staple policy of governments. From the Roman emperor Diocletian (and probably earlier) through the Nixon years, governments have tried to put a ceiling on price levels by legal means or by the use of price and wage "guidelines," with means of enforcement ranging from fines to death by firing squad. Two basic beliefs underlie the modern advocacy of price and wage controls: (1) Structural rigidities—monopolies and unions—are the cause of inflation, and (2) fiscal and monetary policies are at times insufficient for dealing with the inflation problem.

Price and wage controls usually fail because they cannot be enforced or because they are too costly to enforce. Black markets develop in both output and input markets where there is excess demand for goods or input services (see Chapter 4). Rationing output through coupons and other devices usually fails to overcome these problems. After the OPEC oil crisis, the Carter administration initiated plans for an emergency rationing program for gasoline. The program sparked much controversy and was eventually dropped.

Relaxation of controls opens the floodgates to price increases. After the price and wage controls accompanying World War II were lifted, for example, huge levels of pent-up demand for consumer goods and services—especially durable goods such as autos—were unleashed on insufficient quantities of these goods. The same effects were felt in 1973 after the Nixon price and wage controls were lifted.

Presidential guidelines are another "voluntary" form of price and wage controls. Congressional arm-twisting of businesses and unions to back off from price or wage demands has the same purpose as legally imposed price and wage controls, but with less strict and even unannounced penalties.

Most economists are opposed to price and wage controls because they distort production and economic relations between transactors in the market. If the government is successful as an enforcer of controls, which is itself a costly and difficult job, short-run price expectations may be somewhat stabilized, helping to contain inflationary pressures. Most often, however, a simultaneous and politically popular increase in monetary expansion takes place along with the price and wage controls, turning expectations in the other direction and creating more difficulties. Many economists believe that announced and concrete action on the part of government to control money and fiscal growth has proved to be of greater benefit in containing and stabilizing expectations and, therefore, inflation. Most economists believe that wage and price controls attack the symptoms of inflation but not the cause.

Tax-Induced Policies. Tax-induced policies for fighting inflation are a recent variant of direct price controls. They were first proposed in the United States in the late 1970s. Institution of tax-induced policies would mean the establishment of price guidelines for businesses and labor. These guidelines would not be legally enforced but would carry penalties for violation in the form of higher taxes. Lower taxes would be applied to price or wage changes that did not exceed the guidelines.

The major advantage in using tax-induced policies is that nonprice rationing, such as long waiting lines that discourage consumers, is eliminated. Those willing to pay higher prices or higher wages get the goods or the resources. The disadvantage of tax-induced policies is also a potential disadvantage of price and wage controls. If inflation is not caused by monopoly-union pressures, but rather by increases in the rate of money expansion, imposition of tax-induced policies will not stop inflation.

SUMMARY

1. There are three basic demands for money: transactions demands, precautionary demands, and speculative demands in the bond or securities market.

2. Transactions and precautionary demands are directly related to income. An increase in income, for example, would cause an individual to hold a proportionately greater amount of money for transactions and precautionary purposes.

3. The public also holds money to speculate on the bond market. Expectations of higher bond prices (lower interest returns) would mean that individuals would choose to hold money rather than bonds, whereas low bond prices (higher interest returns) would mean that individuals would prefer to hold bonds rather than money. Speculative money demands are therefore inversely related to the interest rate.

4. The simple quantity theory of money is a macroeconomic theory of how the price level is formed. When transactions demands are considered proportional to income, velocity is assumed constant. Since real output and income are also assumed to be at a maximum, increases in money supply, M-1, cause proportionate increases in the price level.

5. The modern monetarist theory of inflation integrates the transactions, precautionary, and speculative demands for money into a dynamic view of the inflation process. In the monetarist conception, money demands depend in part on the nominal interest rate, which in turn depends on both the real rate of interest and inflationary expectations.

6. The monetarists view inflation as a dynamic process originating with higher rates of M-1 expansion by the Federal Reserve System. Increased spending leads to higher actual and expected inflation rates (real GNP being constant) and therefore to higher nominal interest rates. Higher nominal interest rates lead to lower money demand, more spending, and more inflation.

7. In the monetarist explanation of inflation, the inflationary process does not end until the Federal Reserve stabilizes growth of the money supply.

8. Inflation is a process of price increases. Inflation redistributes income in society away from those on fixed incomes and those holding dollar-denominated assets. Inflation also disrupts expectations and amounts to a tax that is imposed without having been voted on.

9. Nonmonetary theories of inflation feature structural problems in the economy such as the existence of or increases in monopoly and union power. In this view, unreasonable demands can create a wage-price spiral that can be stopped only through government intervention or through price and wage controls.

10. Monetarists argue that the ultimate cause of inflation is monetary expansion in excess of the economy's ability to produce goods and services. They feel that only rules pertaining to the conduct of both fiscal and monetary policy can create stability in the macroeconomy.

KEY TERMS

real money demand
transactions demand
precautionary demand
speculative motive or demand
liquidity preference theory
quantity theory of money
equation of exchange
income velocity

neutrality of money
monetarism
real interest rate
market, or nominal, interest rate
expected inflation rate
adaptive expectations theory
rate of monetary expansion
escalator clause

pure inflation tax
tax indexation
cost-push inflation
demand-pull inflation
wage-price spiral
accommodation of cost-push inflation
supply shock inflation
cost-price spiral

QUESTIONS FOR REVIEW AND DISCUSSION

1. Why do people hold money? What effect does the level of income have on the amount of money people hold?

2. What is the cost of holding money? If bond prices fall, does the cost of holding money rise or fall?

3. What is the difference between the quantity theory of money and the equation of exchange? When does the quantity theory of money hold true and when does the equation of exchange hold true?

4. What is the income velocity of money, V? How does V relate to the transactions demand for money?

5. If the rate of growth of the money supply is equal to 10 percent, the velocity of money is constant, and real output is falling by 2 percent, what will be the rate of inflation according to monetarist theory?

6. What effect does an increase in the rate of monetary expansion have on the total level of spending? The actual rate of inflation? The expected rate of inflation?

7. According to monetarists, what causes inflation? How is inflation stopped?

8. How does inflation decrease individuals' wealth? How can people protect themselves from inflation?

9. In what sense is inflation a tax? Do government tax revenues increase when inflation occurs?

10. How might monopolies or unions cause inflation? Can monopolies cause inflation without the assistance of monetary expansion?

11. Why do wage and price controls fail to stop inflation when monetary expansion continues?

PROBLEM

Suppose that the rate of monetary expansion is 10 percent per year, the growth rate in real income is 3 percent, and velocity is constant. Calculate the inflation rate through the "dynamic" quantity theory. Now suppose that the rate of monetary expansion rises to 15 percent per year, all else remaining the same. What is the rate of inflation? Clearly explain the process by which the increase in monetary expansion changes the inflation rate.

ECONOMICS IN ACTION
The Impact of Budget Deficits on Inflation

The effects of federal budget deficits on inflation are complex and controversial. As noted in the text, increasing deficits may result from declining tax revenue during periods of recession and falling prices. In the view of many economists, however, deficits may also be associated with inflation.

Take a look at budget deficits and surpluses throughout U.S. history[a] (see Figure 8). Between the establishment of the U.S. Treasury in 1789 and the year 1990, there have been 199 budgets, of which 96 have been in deficit and 103 in surplus. Between 1789 and 1930, the budget was in deficit 32 percent of the time, but between 1931 and 1990 the government ran deficits more than 86 percent of the time. The White House deficit projection for 1991 was $232 billion, which included the cost of the savings and loan bailout but did not take into account the costs of the enormous military buildup in response to Iraq's invasion of Kuwait. With the addition of defense costs and the costs associated with a slowdown in the U.S. economy, the deficit for 1991 appeared likely to soar to between $250 billion and $300 billion.

Since the deficit is simply the difference between what the government spends and what it takes in as taxes, the difference must be made up somewhere. Roughly, the government has two alternatives to finance the deficit: (1) having the Treasury sell bonds to the Federal Reserve System, which in effect means "to print more money," and (2) selling government bonds on the open market, thus competing with businesses for private savers' funds. Though it is difficult to determine the extent to which the money supply increases as a result of deficit financing, most economists (and most citizen-taxpayers) view such financing as inflationary.

If the government finances deficits by selling newly printed bonds in the private markets, interest rates will rise, causing private investment to decline. The rise in interest rates caused by the price-lowering effects of the government's bond sale will also reduce consumption spending. In this view, deficits will crowd out private investment and consumption expenditures, reducing the production and consumption of private goods and services and permitting an increase in the production of public goods and services. Either method of financing deficits forces resources from the private sector into production in the public sector.

Critics of this position on the economic effects of deficits point out that there is no clear correlation between deficits and the money supply. The Federal Reserve, after all, is not required to purchase bonds from the U.S. Treasury. Indeed, the Federal Reserve may attempt to neutralize the impact of deficit financing on M-1 through compensating open mar-

[a]An excellent survey on the effects of deficits is "The Deficit Puzzle: Fitting the Pieces Together," *Economic Review,* Federal Reserve Bank of Atlanta Special Issue (August 1982).

FIGURE 8   **Federal Budget Surplus or Deficit as a Percentage of GNP,
1790–1990**

Sources: James R. Barth and Stephen O. Morrell, "A Primer on Budget Deficits." *Economic Review,*
Federal Reserve Bank of Atlanta Special Issue (August 1982), pp. 10–11; Council of Economic Advisers,
Economic Report of the President (Washington, D.C.: U.S. Government Printing Office, 1990), pp. 294,
384, 385.
Note: 1990 is estimated.

ket operations or with the use of its other monetary policy tools. Still other economists believe that deficits have no long-run effects if they are financed through the sale of bonds in private markets. Why? Because government bonds are "wealth" to those who buy them, but they are an equivalent and corresponding liability to future taxpayers who must pay taxes to finance the principal and interest on the original issue. In the main, however, most economists and citizens believe that deficits are inflationary and that they crowd out private expenditures.

Question

In what ways do budget deficits inhibit long-run economic expansion? Does the existence of a huge deficit affect expectations of how high interest rates or inflation rates will be?

Milton Friedman

James Tobin

Milton Friedman and James Tobin: How Important Is the Money Supply?

MILTON FRIEDMAN (b. 1912) is best known for his strong and eloquent defense of capitalism and the free market, for his support of monetarism, and for his arguments against government intervention in the economy.

Born in Brooklyn, New York, Friedman was the son of immigrant parents. His mother was a seamstress; his father, the owner of a small retail dry goods store. When his father died, fifteen-year-old Friedman and his mother were left with very little money. The teenager showed great aptitude in mathematics in high school and won a scholarship to Rutgers University in 1929. While a student at Rutgers, Friedman waited tables to support himself, passed exams to become an accountant, and then became increasingly interested in economics. His professor, Arthur Burns, who later became chairman of the Federal Reserve Board, taught him the importance of empirical research in economics, and another professor, Homer Jones, encouraged Friedman to apply for a scholarship to graduate school at the University of Chicago. Friedman went on to receive his M.A. from Chicago and, in 1946, a Ph.D. from Columbia University. During the 1930s he worked as a statistician for the National Bureau of Economic Research, and in 1938 he married economist Rose Director, a fellow graduate student at the University of Chicago.

Friedman taught economics at Chicago until his retirement in 1977, when he moved his scholarly base to the Hoover Institute at Stanford University. Winner of the Nobel Memorial Prize in Economics in 1976, Friedman has authored many highly acclaimed books, in addition to contributing a regular column to *Newsweek*. In *Capitalism and Freedom* (1962), Friedman argues that market forces are sufficient in both individual and aggregate markets to direct resources and to establish steady growth in the economy. Government fiscal policies, Friedman believes, often bring about results contrary to those that policy-makers intend and disrupt planned expenditures in the private sector. In his classic work, *A Monetary History of the United States* (1963), coauthored by Anna Schwartz, Friedman claims that money velocity—related to the demand for money—is stable enough to make the money supply an excellent barometer of inflation, output, and economic growth. His views provided the basis for modern monetarist theory.

JAMES TOBIN (b. 1918), winner of the 1981 Nobel Memorial Prize in Economics, grew up during the Depression with an awareness that many of the world's problems were economic in origin. He made the decision to become an economist while taking an introductory economics course during his sophomore year at Harvard University in 1936. One of his major influences at that time was his teacher, Spencer Pollard, who suggested he read Keynes's *General Theory,* which had just been published. According to Tobin, *The General Theory* "was a difficult book, but when you are 19 you don't know what's difficult and what's not. You just plow into it."

Describing himself as a "very, very, shy, noncompetitive individual" during his undergraduate years, Tobin went on to obtain his Ph.D. from Harvard in 1947 and was appointed Sterling Professor of Economics at Yale University in 1957. He faithfully carried Keynesian principles into the public policy arena when he was appointed to President John F.

Kennedy's Council of Economic Advisers in 1961. He was one of the architects of the Kennedy-Johnson tax cut of 1964 and has consistently advocated a loose reign on the money supply. He has also played a key role in the recent effort to join Keynesian macroeconomics and neoclassical microeconomics.

Tobin received the Nobel Prize primarily for his analysis of portfolio selection and financial markets. He was president of the American Economic Association in 1971 and continues to support modern activist economic policies.

KEEPING WATCH OVER THE MONEY SUPPLY

Friedman and Tobin certainly represent different views on monetary and fiscal policies. For Friedman, control of the money supply is the main determinant of economic stability. For his part, Tobin emphasizes the effects of government spending, taxation, and stable interest rates on economic performance. Juxtaposed, the views of each man illustrate the difference between monetarist and Keynesian approaches to the economy.

Are money supply fluctuations a cause or effect of changes in real income? This question may be impossible to answer definitely, but Milton Friedman has consistently argued that money supply growth is the best barometer we have of economic expansion and contraction. Friedman cites a variety of statistics to back his claim. For example, since the turn of the century, fluctuations in rates of growth in real GNP have strongly coincided with annual growth rates in the nation's money supply. Prior to recession and depression, the money supply growth rate has fallen dramatically; prior to expansions and a booming inflationary economy, the money supply growth rate has shown marked increases.

To explain this statistical marriage of money supply and economic activity, Friedman argues that money velocity is a stable variable. Therefore, interest rates, which may vary up or down in response to government spending, do not contribute to economic fluctuations as many economists believe. They are merely a sideshow to the growth patterns in the money supply.

If Friedman's premise is correct, then the government's attempts to fine-tune the economy through spending and taxation policies are largely misdirected. For the sake of stability, Friedman argues, government should concern itself with a stable growth rate in the money supply. By doing so, he believes, the roller-coaster ride of business cycles, of temporary boom followed by temporary bust, can be leveled out and the economy can achieve consistent, measured growth for the future.

There are many complicated issues surrounding Friedman's proposal. For instance, can government officials afford to sit idly by in times of high unemployment, believing that over the long run a stable monetary policy will rescue the economy? Experience in the 1960s and 1970s suggests that Friedman's proposal is perhaps politically unfeasible. A second issue involves the definition of money supply. For Friedman, the only significant money supply definition is M-1—currency plus demand deposits. Recently, however, changes in the banking system have created uncertainties over what exactly constitutes money in the traditional sense of M-1. If the Federal Reserve policy-makers cannot rely on a firm definition of the money supply, efforts to control its growth may be frustrating or even futile. Friedman strongly believes that the concept of M-1, for all its apparent weaknesses, is the Federal Reserve's best measure of money supply. Larger aggregates, such as M-2 or M-3, are far beyond the control of the Federal Reserve System.

FISCAL ACTIVISM AND STABLE INTEREST RATES

For James Tobin, the issue of what determines ups and downs in the economy is not nearly so straightforward. In essence, Tobin believes that consumption and investment activity are the true determinants of economic performance. Controlling or directing such activity, however, is much more complicated than simply monitoring the money supply. On the one hand, it involves spending and taxation policies to counterbalance the rise and fall of aggregate demand. On the other hand, it involves monetary policies to keep interest rates at acceptable levels.

Unlike Friedman, Tobin believes that the velocity of money is unstable. If this assumption is correct, then interest rates are much more important in economic policy than M-1 growth rates because interest rates determine the shifting demand between different kinds of money assets, leading to greater or lesser consumption and investment activity. Tobin argues that the "strict monetarist regime" he believes to have been in effect at the Federal Reserve between 1979 and 1982 was a failure. He blames the recession and high unemployment between 1981 and 1983 on the Fed's attempt to place limits on M-1 growth.[a] Rather than target M-1 or the money base, Tobin believes the Fed should target broader economic aggregates such as the growth rate in nominal GNP and adjust its monetary policy according to its best estimate of where the economy is headed. (Friedman disputes the idea that monetarism has ever been tried by the Federal Reserve System.)

Tobin's position not only admits the need for politicians to do something in times of high unemployment, but it argues for such action. His activist stance, however, can be a two-edged sword. Spending policies can adversely affect interest rates, and therefore fiscal and monetary policies can conflict with one another. The current debate over high government deficits reflects this conflict, for many economists argue that growing deficits drive up interest rates.

[a]For details on Tobin's position see his "Monetarism: An Ebbing Tide?" The Economist (April 27, 1985), pp. 23–25.

PART SEVEN

Monetary and

Macroeconomic

Problems and

Policy

35

Macroeconomic Theory and Policy

As we have seen in previous chapters, economists find it hard to agree on where the economy is heading and what should be done about it. How many times have you heard different predictions of future macroeconomic events by government economic advisers, academics, and business economists? Economists often are equally at odds over the proper policy to correct or sustain economic forces. These differences over policy often arise from differences in theory, particularly whether the economy is seen as inherently stable or unstable. Earlier we discussed how specific theories of the economy, such as early classical theory and Keynesian theory, have led to quite different policy prescriptions. In the view of most economists, these older theories have not fully explained events or predicted accurately.

Over the past two decades new theories have arisen that build upon older ideas and that are currently being tested. In this sense, macroeconomic theory is in a state of flux and in search of new ideas, which might include combinations of older theories. Two major schools of modern thought may be labeled new Keynesian and new classical theories of the macroeconomy, both of which build upon some of the ideas we have already encountered. The reader must be warned, however: Divisions and categories of theories in this chapter by no means encompass every economic view. Many contemporary Keynesians share one or more of the monetarists' views, for instance. As a road map to policy debates, however, the distinctions drawn here are useful. When you complete Chapter 35, you should understand

- how macroeconomic policy prescriptions designed to alleviate inflationary or unemployment situations depend on theories about how the economy functions.
- how new Keynesians and new classical writers—those who lean toward monetarist or "rational expectationist" theories—view fiscal and monetary policy.
- some of the elements in the debate between macroeconomists on the issues of discretionary versus nondiscretionary policies.

POLICY ALTERNATIVES

The purpose of macroeconomic policy is to ensure economic stability—full employment, price stability, and steady growth. There are, of course, various interpretations of exactly what full employment, price stability, and steady growth mean in percentage terms, but most economists and policy-makers would agree, for instance, that persistent unemployment rates of 12 or 14 percent or inflation rates of 15 or 20 percent are unacceptable. Likewise, most economists and observers would agree that unemployment rates of 5½ to 7½ percent, inflation rates of 2 to 4 percent, and real GNP growth rates of 3 percent are "in the ballpark" as acceptable macroeconomic policy goals. These ballpark figures are about the right percentages for a well-functioning economy.

In previous chapters on macroeconomic and monetary theory, we saw that there are a number of interacting monetary and nonmonetary factors that affect prices, real income, and employment. Figure 1 summarizes these various forces. As the figure shows, the nonmonetary factors are consumption, investment, real interest rates, and net foreign trade expenditures on the private

FIGURE 1

Both monetary and nonmonetary variables determine whether the goals of economic policy are achieved. Of these determinants only government spending, taxation, and the money supply may be directly altered in discretionary fashion (also see Figure 2).

Determinants of Price Stability, Full Employment, and Economic Growth

Goals of Macroeconomic Policy:

Price stability

Full employment

Economic growth

Statistics to Watch:

Prices

Income

Employment

Private and Public Variables That Determine Goals

Nonmonetary variables	Monetary variables
Consumption expenditures	Money demand
Investment expenditures	Money supply
Real interest rates	
Government spending and taxation	
Net foreign trade	

side and government spending and taxation on the public side. The monetary factors are money supply and money demand.

A subset of these variables can be manipulated through discretionary government policy. Fiscal policy—manipulation of government spending or taxation by Congress and the president—is one means of ensuring overall stability. One organization used by Congress to develop fiscal policy is discussed in Focus, "Fiscal Policy in Action: The Congressional Budget Office." Monetary policy—actions of the Federal Reserve Board to alter the money supply or interest rates—is another means of achieving macroeconomic goals. Table 1 summarizes these two types of policy.

Fiscal and monetary policies differ according to the amount of time each takes to implement, the magnitude of their effects, and the direction of their effects. For example, by using one of its specific tools the Federal Reserve can act quickly to alter the money supply when there is a perceived employment downturn or inflation upsurge, but Congress usually requires a bit more time to enact fiscal correctives. Fiscal policies, moreover, may have more immediate effects on the economy, but the effects of monetary policies may be longer lasting. In the following sections, we consider different views of these possible effects.

NEW KEYNESIAN THEORY AND POLICY

Early Keynesian economics, developed in the 1930s and 1940s, was a product of the era in which it was born: It was primarily oriented toward the problems of depression and unemployment. New Keynesians retain a belief that the economy, left to itself, is unable to adjust to falling aggregate demand and restore the equilibrium level of income and full employment. In this view, fundamental instabilities pervade the economic system. In the broadest sense, the role of policy is to overcome the forces of instability in the economy.

TABLE 1

Types of Macroeconomic Policies

Fiscal policy is controlled by the president and Congress. Monetary policy is directed by the Federal Reserve Board.

Type of Policy	Scope	Tools
Fiscal policy	Changes in government taxation, spending	Alterations in income tax rate or other tax rates
		Changes in government spending on goods and services or for transfer payments
Monetary policy	Changes in money supply, interest rates	Open market operations
		Changes in discount rates
		Changes in reserve requirements

FOCUS   Fiscal Policy in Action: The Congressional Budget Office

In the give-and-take of politics, Congress has a major role in setting fiscal policy. Individual members, who are often greatly affected back home by spending and taxing decisions, find the job of keeping track of the megabillion-dollar federal budget almost impossible. Few if any members know, or could know, what is going on at all levels of fiscal policy and implementation. The difficulty of congressional monitoring of a growing federal budget led, in 1921, to the establishment of a Budget Bureau under President Warren Harding. The Budget Bureau has evolved into the administration-directed Office of Management and Budget. OMB and the president limit items in the budget through limits on procedures of federal agencies and, of course, the veto power. Congress, however, retains fundamental control over the establishment of all revenue (taxation) measures and expenditures associated with the budget. Clearly, Congress as a whole, as well as individual members of Congress, must be able to track the budget as a tool of overall fiscal policy and for the impact that it might have on constituents.

An agency has evolved to assist Congress in these matters. The Congressional Budget Office (CBO) was the creation of the Congressional Budget and Impoundment Control Act of 1974 (which itself was the product of disputes over the president's and OMB's power to "impound" the funds of federal agencies, possibly thwarting the intentions of Congress). The CBO was created along with House and Senate budget committees, and its role is to work with these committees. It is administered by a director, who is appointed for a four-year term by the Speaker of the House and the President Pro Tempore of the Senate, in consultation with the chairpersons of the House and Senate budget committees. CBO makes staff and resources available to *all* congressional committees, with priority given to the budget committees.

CBO is designed to keep both congressional committees dealing with budget matters and individual members of Congress abreast of all matters related to the budget. Specific responsibilities include economic forecasting and fiscal policy analysis; cost projections; annual reports on the budget; and special studies, such as those projecting the economic impact of actual or proposed budget changes on the economies of specific congressional districts or on states.

Importantly, CBO gives Congress the experts and the computer assistance to understand and analyze the president's budget. Indeed, under former CBO director Alice Rivlin, the organization took a more activist stance in working for the entire Congress. Part of this role has included the submission of an alternative budget to the one submitted by the president and OMB. In its budget projections, CBO uses its own economic models and forecasts, which often are at variance with the administration's. (The OMB and the CBO budgets reflect administration and congressional priorities, respectively.) Fiscal policy is hammered out in the ebb and flow of politics. Personalities and shifting political powers are critical in establishing policies that affect microeconomic well-being for some and the macroeconomic health of the entire nation.

An Unstable Economy

Sharp fluctuations in GNP, unemployment, and inflation can occur for a variety of reasons. Investment spending can initiate cycles of rising and falling business activity. Supply shocks, caused by natural disasters or international upheaval, can disrupt domestic markets. Autonomous consumer spending, magnified by the multiplier, can drive GNP and unemployment up or down. (For the macroeconomic consequences of a sudden shift in our international relations, see Focus, "The Macroeconomic Consequences of Peace.")

Our analysis of aggregate demand shifts in Chapter 28 helps illustrate graphically the effects of such disturbances. Figure 2 shows aggregate demand and aggregate supply of a hypothetical economy. Along curve AD_0, the economy reaches full employment, Y_F. Assume, however, that investment spending, in response to a sudden change in profit expectations, drops. As a result, unemployment increases and real output falls. Figure 2 shows the effect: a shift in aggregate demand from AD_0 to AD_1 and a fall in income from Y_F to Y_1. The gap in employment caused by the shift in aggregate demand is usually

FOCUS   The Macroeconomic Consequences of Peace

The widespread abandonment of Soviet-style socialism in 1989 and 1990 marked the true end of the Cold War. U.S. policy-makers found themselves all at once in a brand-new world; it was a time for discarding established ways of thinking made suddenly obsolete, a time for reordering priorities. When the changes took on an air of permanence, even the staunchest cold warrior could not deny the opportunity for substantial reductions in U.S. defense spending. But what should be done with this windfall, this "peace dividend"?

In the debate over what to do with the potential reduction in defense spending, politics took its usual prominent place. Various political groups expressed greatly differing views concerning both the best use of these dollars and the proper magnitude of the spending reductions. The Bush administration initially proposed defense spending reductions of about $8 billion. Others suggested initial cuts of about $30 billion and future reductions of up to $150 billion. The proposed uses of these dollars also varied. There was some support for applying the reductions in defense to reducing the size of the government's deficit; an opposing view was that taxes should be reduced or that government spending on either investments in infrastructure (roads, bridges, mass transit systems) or on various social programs should be increased. Another proposal earmarked defense savings for foreign aid programs to ease the transition to democracy and free markets.

Many economists argued that defense spending should be allowed to fall with no offsetting increases in government spending or reductions in taxes. Such a deficit-reducing act would lower interest rates and increase private investment. The subsequent buildup of the nation's capital stock would lead to future increases in production. However, other economists held the view that any reduction in government defense spending would decrease aggregate demand and would surely lead to a recession. Therefore, they argued that the reduction in defense spending should be offset by a roughly equivalent increase in government spending on infrastructure or on various social programs such as housing and day-care. According to these economists, failure to offset reductions in defense spending with increases in other types of government spending would run the risk of leading to high unemployment rates, since so many former military personnel would be entering the labor market. Defense contractors would be hard hit by spending cuts, as would the communities that have come to depend on the companies for jobs and revenues. One proposal attempted to stave off the devastating effects of widespread defense cutbacks by involving defense contractors in environmental cleanup efforts. Still other economists argued that at least a portion of the peace dividend should be used to reduce the tax burden on working Americans.

As we have seen, Washington reacted to the prospect of a peace dividend with a number of proposals. While all of these proposals were rendered premature by the 1990 invasion of Kuwait by Iraq—at least temporarily—the peace dividend may eventually materialize. At that time, the powerful economic consequences of a final decision on allocation of the windfall will prove difficult to ignore.

---

referred to as demand-deficiency unemployment. With resources idle and a gap in demand, policy-makers are left with the questions, Will the economy be able to self-correct the deficiency? and How long will it take to do so? In the long run, as we have noted, theory predicts that prices and wages will fall in response to a shift in aggregate demand. But what about the short run? Can the economy or the unemployed afford to wait for the natural market forces to restore full employment?

Countercyclical Fiscal Policy

In the Keynesian view, time is at the heart of the problem and, to Keynes, the short run could last a long time. While the economy might be self-correcting in the long run, the adjustment would be painful and time-consuming. In the short run, prices and wages would not fall sufficiently to restore full employment. Unnecessary economic disruption—in product and labor markets— would occur if the economy were allowed to establish its own natural rate of

FIGURE 2

A decrease in real expenditures causes aggregate demand curve AD_0 to shift downward to AD_1, also causing a shift from full employment, Y_F, to Y_1. This gap in income caused by a shift in aggregate demand produces demand-deficiency unemployment. Keynesians suggest that this unemployment can be eliminated through the use of fiscal policy, returning aggregate demand, income, and employment to their original levels.

The Keynesian Stand on Demand-Deficiency Unemployment

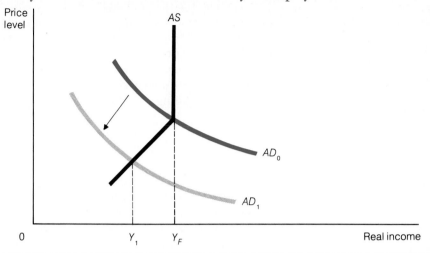

income and employment growth. Keynesians' recommended cure for macroeconomic problems is to apply countercyclical fiscal policy. Proper macroeconomic policy in the event of recession and unemployment is to run budget deficits—that is, to keep government expenditures greater than tax revenues. And, though the advice has seldom been taken, inflation calls for budget surpluses—that is, for tax receipts to exceed government expenditures.

Table 2 simplifies and summarizes the Keynesian position. During recession or depression, Congress, the administration, and state and local governments should increase spending and/or reduce taxes. Inflation calls for the opposite policies.

TABLE 2

Keynesian Prescriptions to Control the Business Cycle

In the fiscal arena, budget deficits should be employed to cure unemployment and lagging economic growth, while inflation should be controlled by budget surpluses. Throughout all phases of the cycle, stable interest rates should be maintained by the Federal Reserve in money markets.

Economic Problem	Keynesian Corrective	
	Fiscal Policy	Monetary Policy
Recession (unemployment and slow income growth)	Budget deficits ($G > T$) (government spending greater than taxation)	Increase M-1 and keep interest rates low and stable
Inflation	Budget surpluses ($G < T$) (taxation greater than government spending)	Reduce M-1

Keynesian Monetary Policy

Note in Table 2 that monetary policy is also included in the Keynesian approach to economic instability. Most Keynesians advocate that the Federal Reserve Board respond to inflationary or recessionary pressures in the economy by keeping order in financial markets. That is, the Federal Reserve should use its discretionary power over the M-1 money supply to stabilize interest rates, which, left unchecked, can rise to levels that discourage or even choke off private spending.

The early 1980s witnessed an application of the Keynesian approach to monetary policy. At that time, the Federal Reserve, in response to severe inflation, initiated dramatic cuts in the M-1 supply. Such cuts, many Keynesians felt, were unwise, since they brought about a sharp rise in interest rates. The economy lurched from high inflation to a costly recession with a high level of unemployment. The Keynesians blamed the recession on the Federal Reserve's failure to maintain low interest rates.

As outlined in the discussion of the liquidity preference curve and the speculative demand for money in Chapter 34, the Federal Reserve might be unable to increase or decrease interest rates at will. Changes in the money supply can affect interest rates, but only if money demanders cooperate. If, for example, money demanders want to hold additional balances for speculative purposes due to dim expectations about bond prices or about the economy in general, an addition to the money supply will not have much effect on interest rates. Alternatively, if the Federal Reserve wanted to increase interest rates by lowering the supply of money, individuals might simply reduce their holdings of money for speculative purposes in roughly equal proportions, which again would result in little or no change in interest rates. Further, any change in interest rates—large or small—might not translate into changes in consumption or investment spending if expectations are that future investment profitability and economic conditions will not be good.

The use of an interest rate target, therefore, is an unpredictable method of changing total spending because the Federal Reserve is constrained by the liquidity preference curve. Since speculative demands for money are based on expectations, liquidity preference is likely to change without much notice. The role of the Federal Reserve, therefore, is to attempt to maintain order in financial markets and, if possible, to keep interest rates low to encourage consumption and investment spending.

Direct Versus Indirect Policy. Given recurring short-run instabilities in the economy, Keynesians consider fiscal policy a more direct and more immediately effective tool to manage aggregate demand than monetary policy. In the Keynesian model, there is no solid link between changes in M-1 and changes in aggregate demand. If M-1 increases, the larger holdings of money by individuals and businesses might not all be spent on more goods and services; some of these funds will be channeled into speculative holdings.

Problems with M-1. In addition, the money supply is less suited to discretionary policy. The Federal Reserve is sometimes unable to keep interest rates within specified targets by manipulating M-1. One reason for this problem is the recent emergence of close money substitutes such as money market mutual funds (a type of checkable deposit not included in M-1), which have tended to blur the definition of M-1 money. Without a reliable measure of the money supply, the Federal Reserve is potentially unsure of the effects of its M-1 policy.

For these reasons and others, Keynesians believe that tax and spending policies can give policy-makers greater discretionary control over the business cycle than can monetary policies. The effects of monetary adjustments, especially on interest rates, are a second, unpredictable line of defense to ensure economic stability.

More important, perhaps, than the issue of whether fiscal or monetary policy is the preferred tool of policy-makers is the issue of whether such policy does what it is supposed to do—correct the instabilities caused by shifts in aggregate demand. Keynesians obviously believe that ignoring such instabilities in the short run would inflict greater potential harm on the economy. As we will see, however, not all economists believe that countercyclical discretionary policy is the best way to ensure stability.

NEW CLASSICAL ECONOMICS: MONETARIST THEORY AND POLICY

New classical economics (NCE) is an alternative view of the macroeconomy that predicts that, in the extreme, monetary policy will have *no* effect on real magnitudes of output and employment and that fiscal policy will not have the effects on output and employment that Keynes had predicted. It combines elements of a number of older theories—classical, supply-side, monetarist—to produce a theory of market behavior based on perceptions and learning by market participants. Much of new classical economics is based on the assumption of rational expectations—the assumption that rational market participants (investors, consumers, taxpayers) learn to anticipate the effects of monetary and fiscal policy changes and act to neutralize them. Because new classical economics takes monetarism one step further, let us again consider the monetarist policy position, aspects of which were treated in Chapter 34. The monetarist, like the classical economist but unlike the Keynesian, views the economy as inherently stable.

A Self-Stabilizing Economy

Figure 3 analyzes demand-deficiency unemployment from the monetarist perspective. Assume there is a reduction in autonomous consumption or investment, shifting the original aggregate demand curve from AD_0 to AD_1. The reduction in autonomous spending is accompanied by an increase in consumers' and businesses' holdings of real money balances. Initially, the economy is in equilibrium at point E_0. The price level is P_0, and the full-employment level of output, Y_F, is being produced. The rate of unemployment in the economy is the natural rate of unemployment that will exist when Y_F is produced. The drop in aggregate demand moves the economy to a new equilibrium at point E_1 in the short run where the level of real income produced is Y_1, less than the full-employment level of income. The rate of unemployment is higher than the natural rate of unemployment, or, what is the same thing, the level of employment is less than full employment. Then the economy self-adjusts to a

FIGURE 3

Monetarist Policy on Demand-Deficiency Unemployment

The economy will self-adjust to the natural rate of unemployment, Y_F, in the event of a decline in aggregate demand. Price and nominal wage reductions occur when aggregate demand declines from AD_0 to AD_1, creating increased real balances, which in turn increase consumption and investment spending. Such price reductions also create, through adaptive expectations, rightward shifts in short-run aggregate supply from $SRAS_0$ to $SRAS_1$. The economy finally readjusts to the full-employment level of output, Y_F, at equilibrium E_2 with lower price level P_1.

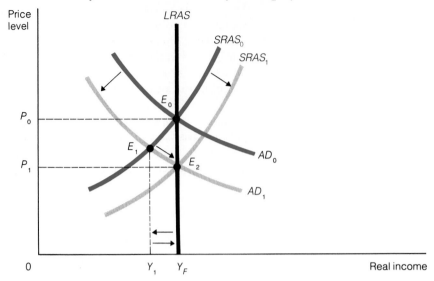

new long-run equilibrium at E_2. Real income rises back to Y_F. The level of employment returns to the full-employment level, and of course, the rate of unemployment falls back to the natural rate of unemployment.

Errors in Real Wage Perceptions: Friedman's View

How might we explain the important process of movement from E_0 to E_1 and then from E_1 to E_2? When aggregate demand falls from AD_0 to AD_1, the level of prices and, to a lesser degree, nominal wages also fall. Employers correctly perceive an increase in real wages and respond by reducing the amount of labor employed. Although the price level has fallen somewhat, workers' price expectations have yet to adjust downward. They still perceive the price level as being P_0. This means that workers believe their real wage has fallen. They will consequently reduce their work effort.[1] The economy will move along the short-run aggregate supply $SRAS_0$ to point E_1, and real income falls to Y_1. Temporarily, unemployment exists in the economy equal to the level of employment associated with real output level Y_F minus that associated with output level Y_1. This unemployment is demand-deficiency unemployment.

From the monetarist perspective, the demand-deficiency unemployment that occurs when the economy produces Y_1 cannot exist permanently. In the monetarist view of the macroeconomy, dynamic forces are at work assuring a return to the full employment of resources at some new equilibrium, E_2. If we assume that no fiscal or monetary actions are undertaken by Congress or the Federal Reserve to deal with unemployment, two sets of automatic changes will dominate. First, falling prices will affect the aggregate demand for goods

---

[1]The expectations-adjusted aggregate supply curve is related to unemployment and inflation in Chapter 19.

and services through the real balance effect. As described in Chapter 28, a decline in the price level will increase real holdings of money, leading to increased consumption and, through lower interest rates brought about by the increased real money supply, to increased investment.

A second effect will act on the short-run aggregate supply curve. When workers' expectations adapt to the lower price levels, their perceptions of the real wage they receive will change. Specifically, they will adapt their expectations to falling actual prices, which signal an increase rather than a decrease in real wages. Time is required, in short, for workers to perceive the actual decline in prices. They will begin to supply more, not less, labor at every wage level. This adaptation in expectations has the effect of shifting the short-run aggregate supply curve rightward from $SRAS_0$ to $SRAS_1$.

Given pressures on prices, where will equilibrium finally reemerge? Downward pressure on nominal wages and prices will exist as long as there is unemployment in the system. As price expectations adjust to lower price levels, the $SRAS$ curve shifts rightward because of unemployed workers' desires to regain work even at lower nominal wages. After effects from the drop in prices have taken place and after expectations have finally adjusted to the lower prices, equilibrium will reemerge at E_2. The economy moves along aggregate demand curve AD_1 and the relevant short-run supply function will be $SRAS_1$. Due to the initial decrease in consumption and investment spending, prices will fall to P_1, a level to which both employers and workers will again adjust.

In the monetarist view, the interplay between price changes and aggregate demand and between price-wage changes and short-run aggregate supply is sufficient to return the economy to full employment at E_2. However, the monetarist result hinges crucially on the *absence* of interventions by Congress or the Federal Reserve. In the monetarist view, such interventions interfere with the adjustment of price level expectations. As a result, they complicate and prolong the adjustment process.

Destabilizing Effects of Fiscal and Monetary Policies

Monetarists adhere to the belief that the market economy will stabilize at full employment. But we observe alternating swings in recession and inflation, as we did over the 1980s. How, then, do monetarists explain the facts of instability?

Like Keynesians, monetarists admit that shifts in aggregate demand can cause waves, or cycles, of unemployment and inflation. Monetarists, however, believe that the primary cause of aggregate demand shifts is not the movement of investment or consumption spending but the actions of government fiscal and monetary policy-makers. According to monetarists, the destabilizing element in the macroeconomy is the shifting expectations of market participants—laborers, businesspeople, consumers, and producers—created by erratic alterations in government expenditures, taxation, and the money supply.

The Effects of Financing Government Expenditures. In the monetarist view, increases in government expenditures—one of the primary tools of fiscal policy—come at the expense of private expenditures. If government spending is financed through taxation, private consumption and investment spending are

Govt sells securities ⇒
↓ bond p's & ↑ ROI

reduced by the amount of the tax. If government spending is financed through borrowing in private markets, its demand for loanable funds will likely raise real interest rates, and higher interest rates will tend to choke off investment, depending on the responsiveness of investors to the increase. This competition for private funds is termed the crowding-out effect. If government spending is financed through the selling of Treasury bonds to the Federal Reserve, the result is potentially inflationary (Chapters 33 and 34 explain why this is so). In sum, the effects of financing government expenditures may offset any gain those expenditures offer a demand-deficient economy. In addition, such policies may create destabilizing effects.

2.

Lags in Fiscal Policy. Another problem with fiscal policy often cited by monetarists concerns legislative frailties. Given the nature of public policy and the competing demands of political interest, fiscal policy-makers are often slow to recognize and act on economic distress signals. **Recognition lags** are the time it takes the president and Congress to identify impending or existing economic conditions. Predicting economic events is both a science and an art. There are often compelling interpretations offered by both sides to a debate over policy.

Recognition lag:
The amount of time it takes policy-makers to realize that a destabilizing economic event has occurred.

In addition to the difficulties of recognizing a problem, there are administrative lags with fiscal policy. **Administrative lags** are the length of time between politicians' recognition of a business cycle problem and their enactment of legislation to correct the problem. (The lag is even more properly called a *decision lag*—the time it takes to decide what to do.) We cite two examples of such lags. The Kennedy-Johnson tax cut of 1964 to stimulate economic growth was proposed as early as 1961 and 1962; its not being enacted until 1964 indicates an administrative lag. Likewise, a jobs bill passed in 1982 to deal with unemployment was debated for months and, when finally passed, was scheduled to go into effect more than a year later. Monetarists emphasize that economic conditions may change before the effects of these legislative acts take place. This would mean that fiscal policy could be procyclical rather than countercyclical in effect, buttressing inflation or recession as the case may be.

Administrative lag:
The amount of time between recognition of a destabilizing economic event and the implementation of a policy designed to correct it.

Once fiscal policy is enacted, it also takes time for its full impact to be realized—an impact lag, if you will. Estimates vary, but it is thought that tax or spending changes may take from one to two years to have their full impact on income and employment. Recognition and administrative lags make monetarists dubious about the effectiveness of fiscal policy. The unpredictability of how long it may take even well-intentioned fiscal policy to have an effect means that market participants' expectations about prices and future incomes are thrown into uncertainty in the meantime.

3.

Effects of Monetary Policy. Discretionary monetary policy has its own problems in the monetarist view. Like fiscal policy, the attempt to control the money supply in countercyclical fashion is also subject to recognition and administrative lags. In the case of monetary policy, it is the quasi-independent Federal Reserve Board and its Federal Open Market Committee, not politicians, who must recognize macroeconomic problems and then enact and administer a change in policies affecting interest rates or the money supply. While problems of recognizing signs of recession or anticipating unemployment or assessing inflationary pressures may be as great as with fiscal policy, they are somewhat easier to handle because of the small number of Federal Reserve Board or Open Market Committee members. Concerted discretionary recognition and action is probably quicker than with the larger numbers of participants in the fiscal setting.

Despite the quicker response, the time between enactment of monetary policy and when it takes effect is as unpredictable as the time related to fiscal manipulations. Some economists believe that the lag between growth in the money supply and the rate of inflation is at least two years long. These same economists view the effects of monetary growth on income and employment as somewhat more immediate. Other studies appear to show that most of the effects of monetary growth on prices, income, and employment take place rapidly, perhaps within six months. A third body of evidence seems to indicate that changes in aggregate demand induced by monetary growth will first have an impact on employment and income and will affect prices later, when expectations catch up. Such competing evidence illustrates the present uncertainty over the effects of discretionary monetary policy. The short run, in other words, may be shorter than the lag time between the money supply and policy variables.

The monetarist conclusion is that, on balance, discretionary fiscal and monetary policy will not be able to control swings of the business cycle. Indeed, in some regard, business cycle alterations are *caused* by destabilizing attempts to control cycles of inflation and unemployment. Stop-and-go policies that accelerate, decelerate, or otherwise interfere with private saving and spending are seen as the primary causes of aggregate demand instability, leading to prolonged recession and unemployment. The solution to the problems created by discretionary political or quasi-political attempts to control the business cycle is to establish rules through which fiscal and monetary policy is carried out.

Monetary Rules, Government Restraints, and Market Deregulation

In general, monetarists advocate that both fiscal and monetary policy be taken out of the hands of discretionary authorities—Congress and the Federal Reserve Board. On the fiscal side, government's budget should be balanced at all levels—local, state, and federal—through fiscal restraint or through a balanced budget amendment. Along with balanced budgets, the monetarists and other economists urge that government regulations supporting monopoly should be eliminated or modified. Deregulation in some industries and some occupations would create greater price and wage flexibility. Greater price and wage flexibility would in turn encourage a faster adjustment to both demand-deficiency unemployment and to inflation when the economy is disturbed.

Monetary rule:
A monetary policy consisting of a fixed rate of growth of the money supply.

Monetarists, led by Milton Friedman, also advocate the use of a **monetary rule** over the money supply growth rate.[2] In a study of the effects of monetary growth, Friedman and Anna Schwartz argue that depressions in the United States and other nations have always been preceded and accompanied by severe reductions in the money stock and that all inflations have been precipitated

---

[2]Milton Friedman, *A Program for Monetary Stability* (New York: Fordham University Press, 1960).

by sharp increases in the money stock.[3] With regard to the Great Depression of the 1930s, which was accompanied by a one-third drop in the money stock, Friedman and Schwartz conclude:

> The Great Depression in the United States, far from being a sign of the inherent instability of the private enterprise system, is a testament to how much harm can be done by mistakes on the part of a few men when they wield vast power over the monetary system of a country.[4]

Stop-and-go policies of the Federal Reserve Board—raising the monetary growth rate 16 percent one month and lowering it to a negative 6 percent the next—create uncertainty among market participants. The monetarists' solution: Take discretionary policy out of the hands of the Federal Reserve and institute an announced and constant growth rate in the money stock of 3 to 5 percent per year. Why 3 to 5 percent? Because the average rate of growth in the American economy through increases in labor productivity and technology has been on the order of 3 percent per year for more than a hundred years. In the monetarists' view, a growth rate in the money supply of 3 to 5 percent is consistent with a stable price level and a healthy rate of economic development. Moreover, a monetary rule would create much-needed stability and correspondence between expectations and actual price experience.

Critics of the new classical monetarist notion that there should be a rule for monetary policy point out that such a conclusion rests heavily on the short-run and long-run stability of velocity—the inverse of the demand for money, a process described in Chapter 34. Further, critics argue that adherence to monetary rules would result in unstable interest rates. Dissenters also criticize both Friedman's test methods and his results. The outcome of this debate is far from clear. The monetarists' tracking of inflation to changes in M-1 (with a two-year lag) has nevertheless persuaded a number of macroeconomists that the dog (money supply growth or declines) wags the tail (faster or slower inflation rates).

NEW CLASSICAL ECONOMICS: RATIONAL EXPECTATIONS

Some of the new classical economists are concerned with the ability of the economy to adjust to the policy actions of Congress or the Federal Reserve. In the opinion of traditional classical writers such as A. C. Pigou, market participants (buyers, sellers, consumers, investors) could not be consistently manipulated by government. Their "rationality" was based on an assumption of perfect information, although classical models did not formally take ration-

---

[3]Milton Friedman and Anna Schwartz, *A Monetary History of the United States, 1867–1960* (Princeton, N.J.: Princeton University Press, 1963).

[4]Critics of the Friedman-Schwartz analysis of the Depression (and of monetary policy generally) argue that they have simply shown a *relation* between money and prices but that they have not proved that changes in the rate of money stock expansion or reduction *cause* inflation or deflation. See Peter Temin, *Did Monetary Forces Cause the Great Depression?* (New York: Norton, 1976).

ality into account. This strand of thought is evident even in the earliest classical literature. Consider the following quotation from Adam Smith's *Theory of Moral Sentiments,* published in 1759.

> [The economic planner] seems to imagine that he can arrange the different members of society with as much ease as the hand arranges the different pieces upon a chessboard; he does not consider that the different pieces upon the chessboard have no other principle of motion besides that which the hand impresses upon them; but that, in the great chessboard of human society, every single piece has a principle of motion of its own, altogether different from that which the legislator might choose to impress upon it.[5]

Smith's view conforms well to the new classical belief that expectations occupy a central role in the economic system. We have seen, however, that "adaptive" expectations are central to the monetarist view of the effects of policy. What is the difference between the monetarist conception and the newer theory of rational expectations?

In Chapter 34 we presented the adaptive expectations theory, which holds that market participants form expectations about the future course of the inflation rate by tracking past rates of inflation. To use a simple example, suppose that people expect inflation this year to be what it was last year. If it was 10 percent last year, people expect it to be 10 percent this year, but if the inflation rate turns out to be 5 percent this year, people adapt and expect it to be 5 percent next year. At each period the public adjusts its expectations according to the differences between the actual inflation rate and the predicted inflation rate. It takes time and many readjustments of expectations for people to become convinced that any inflation rate (be it 6 percent or 106 percent) is permanent.

The Rational Expectations Hypothesis

Over the past two decades, a group of new classical economists has developed a new theory of expectations to challenge and amend the adaptive expectations hypothesis. It was founded on a pioneering contribution by economist John Muth in 1961.[6] Although much of this work—called **rational expectations theory**—is extremely technical, the major thrust of the idea is simple, straightforward, and intuitively appealing. According to the rational expectations view, people are rational in the sense that they make use of both past and present relevant information in forming expectations of the future. Here, information includes not only the current values of important policy variables such as government expenditure and money growth; it also includes knowledge of the structure of the relationships among variables such as that between

Rational expectations theory:
A theory of behavior that assumes that people make efficient use of all past and present relevant information in forming expectations; implies that people's reactions to policy may neutralize the intended effects of the policy.

---

[5]Adam Smith, *The Theory of Moral Sentiments* (1759; reprint, Indianapolis: Liberty Classics, 1976), p. 325.

[6]See John Muth, "Rational Expectations and the Theory of Price Movements," *Econometrica* (July 1961), pp. 315–35. Other innovators in this area include macroeconomists Thomas J. Sargent, Neil Wallace, and Robert E. Lucas; see Thomas J. Sargent, "Rational Expectations, the Real Rate of Interest, and the Natural Rate of Unemployment," *Brookings Papers in Economic Activity* 2 (1973), pp. 429–72; Thomas J. Sargent and Neil Wallace, "Rational Expectations and the Theory of Economic Policy," *Journal of Monetary Economics* (April 1976), pp. 169–84; and R. E. Lucas, "An Equilibrium Model of the Business Cycle," *Journal of Political Economy* (December 1975), pp. 1113–44.

the inflation rate and the nominal interest rates. It suggests that, after some learning, individuals begin to understand some of the fundamental workings of the economy. For example, they will learn through experience that increases in the rate of monetary expansion by the Federal Reserve are generally followed by increases in the inflation rate, which are then followed by higher nominal interest rates. Knowing something of the basic structure of the economy as well as the current values of key policy variables, individuals will be able to form expectations of likely future outcomes in the economy.

Does this mean that market participants will always be correct in their anticipations? In a world filled with uncertainty, outcomes will depend on an enormous number of random occurrences. Individuals will not always be right in their expectations about future economic events, but they will be correct on average.

If people can anticipate discretionary policy and its effects, they are in a position to neutralize the purpose of the policy. For example, if the Federal Reserve Board increases M-1 to increase employment but workers and firms perfectly anticipate the resulting increase in prices, then workers will instantly demand a proportionately higher nominal wage. Firms, anticipating higher nominal revenues, would be willing to pay the higher nominal wage, thus leaving the real wage and the level of unemployment unaffected. In this contest, policy-makers are pitted against market participants, and policy-makers will not win continuously and certainly will not win over time. Policy-makers may attempt to surprise the public, but they cannot do so forever. People catch on to, say, the effects of federal deficits on inflation, anticipate the change, and neutralize or counteract the effects of the change. In the long run, when a model of macroeconomic behavior is learned and actions are correctly anticipated, fiscal or monetary policy is totally ineffective in producing intended alterations on the demand side of the economy. Paradoxically, to have any purposeful effect fiscal and monetary policy would have to be random. If it is not—if policy-makers act in any systematic manner—learned behavior over time will neutralize the policy.

Rational Expectations and Monetary Policy

As with Keynesians and monetarists, time is an important factor in rational expectations. Short-run and long-run effects of rational expectations will depend on whether monetary policy—or any event affecting the macroeconomy—is anticipated.

Anticipated Monetary Policy. We can imagine the (non)effects of rational expectations as a result of the increases or decreases in monetary expansion with the aid of Figure 4. Note that with *adaptive* expectations, an increase in monetary expansion shifting the aggregate demand curve rightward to AD_1 from AD_0 would increase income above the full-employment level, Y_F, because it would take time for the price expectations and perceptions of workers and employers to adjust to the full effects of monetary expansion. In other words, there would be an upward-sloping short-run aggregate supply curve through E_0 in Figure 4, as there is in Figure 3.

But this is not the case under an assumption of rational expectations of anticipated policy. Figure 4 shows no short-run expectations-adjusted aggregate supply curve because all effects are perfectly anticipated by all market

FIGURE 4

According to the rational expectations approach, wages, interest rates, and prices adjust in anticipation of changes in aggregate demand caused by upward or downward adjustment of the money supply. For this reason there is no short-run aggregate supply curve. The economy simply moves along the long-run aggregate supply curve *LRAS*, with prices rising as the money supply is increased, shifting the demand curve from AD_0 to AD_1, or falling as the money supply is decreased, shifting aggregate demand to AD_2.

Rational Expectations and Monetary Policy

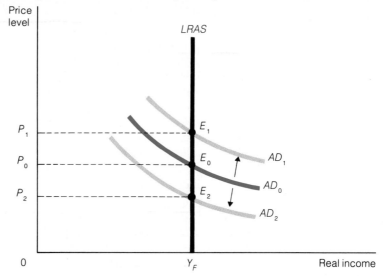

transactors. An increase in aggregate demand from AD_0 to AD_1 caused by a preannounced increased rate of monetary expansion (or a decrease from AD_0 to AD_2 caused by reduction in monetary expansion) simply creates a new equilibrium at E_1 (or at E_2) with all adjustments perfectly worked out instantaneously. In this case, the inflation or deflation is perfectly accounted for by all market transactors, and the full-employment level of income, Y_F, is left undisturbed by policy changes. Only prices change. This principle also applies when, for example, employment falls below the natural rate, due perhaps to some reduction in private autonomous expenditures that reduces aggregate demand. Any attempt on the part of monetary authorities to remedy the situation will be met with counteracting reactions on the part of market participants, leaving the unemployment rate unchanged.

Unanticipated Monetary Policy and Random Shocks. The preceding conclusions apply as long as policy changes aimed at correcting aggregate demand are fully anticipated and expected. When the expectations of market participants about aggregate demand management are fully realized, no change in real income or employment can occur. But the rational expectationist argument also allows for surprises or random events in the short run. If, for example, the Federal Reserve Board changes the M-1 growth rate erratically or if it alters its target, short-run changes in income and employment will occur until all market participants catch on and acknowledge the new policy. Unless Federal Reserve policy is continuously random, expectations will adjust in the long run.

Surprises such as crop failures caused by climatic changes or timber losses caused by a volcanic eruption will also disrupt production and market plans in the short run. The rational expectations theory predicts, however, that all market participants will adapt and adjust behavior to the new conditions in the long run. In sum, the rational expectations idea does not preclude short-run fluctuations in output and employment due to policy or natural surprises. It does predict that policy changes will be neutralized in the long run unless policy is implemented in a random manner.

Rational Expectations and Fiscal Policy

When fiscal policy encounters rational expectations, it may not leave the supply side of the macroeconomy unchanged, especially in the long run. Consider Figure 5, for example, and assume that the economy is initially in equilibrium at full-employment level of income Y_{F_0}. Further assume that Congress enacts increases in government expenditures financed by increases in taxes or by borrowing in private markets.

In the classical, monetarist, or rational expectationist view of the economy, the increase in government expenditures is closely matched by reductions in private consumption, investment, or imports. Such a reduction would leave the aggregate demand curve of Figure 5 stationary. With no further effects, it would appear that equilibrium would remain at E_0, and the level of income as well as employment would remain constant at Y_{F_0}. However, rational expectations theorists assert that fiscal policy would likely have effects on aggregate supply as well as on the public versus private composition of aggregate demand.

Changes in tax rates will affect work incentives. Any reduction in work incentives may reduce the total equilibrium labor input, shifting the aggregate supply curve leftward. Moreover, increased taxes on business investment could adversely affect the demand for labor. Both of these possible effects would reduce the natural level of employment, increasing the natural rate of unemployment. This means that the rate of employment consistent with equilibrium, given all factors (such as taxes) that affect hiring and labor-supply conditions, is lower than before. In Figure 5, the aggregate supply curve shifts

---

FIGURE 5

If rational expectations exist in the long run, fiscal policy has no effect on aggregate demand. Furthermore, fiscal policy can cause reductions in labor input or business investment, causing the long-run aggregate supply curve to shift to the left.

Rational Expectations and Fiscal Policy

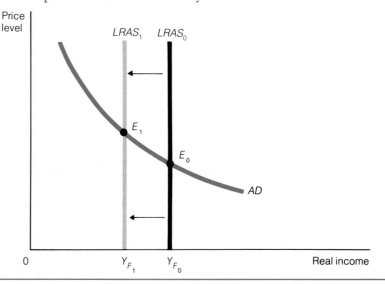

(or drifts) leftward, reducing equilibrium income with a tendency toward higher prices. Fiscal policy therefore may have effects on aggregate supply as well as on aggregate demand.

At base, the theory of rational expectations reinforces the classical-monetarist position: The private economy, while not perfect in providing full employment and maximum income at all times, is superior to fiscal and monetary authorities in providing a relatively stable economy. But rational expectations theory goes further and proposes that over time the effects of fiscal and monetary manipulations can be fully anticipated and therefore neutralized. Policies related to aggregate demand will either have no effect or in the longer run will actually produce reductions in aggregate supply. In short, there is little or no room for discretionary macroeconomic policy. Robert Lucas, a leading proponent of the rational expectations hypothesis, has therefore offered this advice: "The Administration and Congress should stop thrashing around pretending to know better than the economy how much can be produced. And the Federal Reserve should move as quickly as possible to a 4 percent monetary growth."[7]

NEW KEYNESIAN CRITICISMS OF NEW CLASSICAL ECONOMICS

The rational expectations approach, or, more accurately, nonapproach, to policy has generated an enormous amount of interest. Much of the contemporary research has been devoted to the question of whether or not and under what conditions the policy-neutral implications of new classical economics hold. A good deal of sophisticated econometric testing has left open the answer to the question, Does discretionary policy work? Much of the evidence does not support the major positions of the rational expectationists.[8] Until testing yields consistent results, the matter of policy neutrality and the theoretical foundations of the new classical economics will form a lively debate between the rational expectationists and those championing the efficacy of discretionary policy and those with differing theoretical perspectives. Chief among the critics of new classical economics are the new Keynesians.[9]

While many new Keynesians see value in more sophisticated theories of expectations, they retain a belief in the efficacy of discretionary government action in the economy. Policy, to the new Keynesians, is nonneutral and necessary in an economy that is inherently and endogenously unstable over nontrivial clock-time periods. The basic dispute is over the form of the

---

[7]Robert E. Lucas, quoted in "The New Economists," *Newsweek* (June 26, 1978), p. 60. Copyright 1978 by Newsweek, Inc. All rights reserved. Reprinted by permission. For a nontechnical explanation of the rational expectations idea, see "The Rational Expectations Model," *Wall Street Journal* (April 2, 1979).

[8]See, for example, Michael C. Lovell, "Tests of the Rational Expectations Hypothesis," *American Economic Review* (March 1986), pp. 110–24.

[9]For two critical evaluations of the new classical economics, see Robert J. Gordon, "Recent Developments in the Theory of Inflation and Unemployment," *Journal of Monetary Economics* (April 1976), pp. 185–220; and James Tobin, "Are New Classical Models Plausible Enough to Guide Policy?" *Journal of Money, Credit and Banking* (November 1980), pp. 788–99.

expectational assumptions of the rational expectationists and over the related issue of the efficiency of market functioning.

New Keynesians (and others) object that the new classical economics requires market participants to be more sophisticated than they really are in their abilities to predict. How might we expect buyers of VCRs and sellers of rental properties to utilize intricate and sophisticated theories of economic functioning in order to accurately predict prices, outputs, interest rates, or any other economic variable into the future and to quickly and accurately act on the prediction in the present?

Rational expectationists counter with the point that market participants are correct, *but only on average* and only after a "learning" period. If, in other words, policy itself is not random (which would be a peculiar manner of conducting it), those who consistently come up with inaccurate predictions would be severely punished in the market through losses on exchanges. In their own self-interest market participants would attempt to learn the probable effects of policy. Armies of economists in the "think tank" or "prediction service" business are hired by market participants to help them learn or to give them rational information about the future. It would be strange, indeed, for markets not to react in this manner.

Importantly, new Keynesians argue that rational expectations theory fails to explain prolonged periods of unemployment and depression. New Keynesians regard the economy as inherently unstable (especially with regard to investment spending) and characterized by institutionalized sticky prices and wages (from monopolies and other imperfections in both product and labor markets). Rational expectationists do *not* believe, as the old classical writers did, that full production and employment *always* characterize the economic system. Unanticipated policy and price surprises cause real variables such as employment and income to diverge from their natural rates. Once market participants discover the "true" nature of the policy change, expectations catch up with actual economic magnitudes (such as prices) and the economy returns to the rational expectations equilibrium. An important question is, How long does this take?

New Keynesians point to events such as the Great Depression of the 1930s, with its prolonged periods of unemployment and reduced growth rates in real GNP, as proof that market participants do not react in the manner described by the rational expectationists. To restate the question, even if expectations are "rational" and even if they eventually return the economy to the natural or full-employment level of output and employment, aren't the sacrifices unacceptable? (Note the modern version of the "all dead in the long run" precept of early Keynesian economics.)

The question is, of course, a good one. The actual situation of the 1930s economy has proved difficult to gauge. New Keynesians believe that factors such as reduced aggregate demand and sticky nominal wages and prices due to effective rigidities in both product and labor markets are the essential explanation for the prolonged depression of the 1930s. Rational expectationists counter by arguing that that depression was prolonged, if not fostered, by wrongheaded government policies. Price changes failed to clear product and labor markets due to the *continuous* and *persistent* policy and institutional changes by the government. Discouragement of business investment and unanticipated policy "surprises" were the result of the government's increased participation in the private market system. Blame for the origins and length of the Great Depression is also placed at the door of the Federal Reserve System, which failed to perceive and correct for the precipitous decline in the real stock of money.

The debate between the new Keynesian and the rational expectationist views of the proper role of policy will, of course, continue. Whether discretionary policy or "rules" give the best results will not be decided by theory or opinion, but by facts, illuminated by econometric testing.

THE MAJOR POLICY POSITIONS: A SUMMARY

We have now evaluated three major policy positions based on three theories of the functioning of the aggregate economy. Some theoretical or policy views are contrasting and some are complementary, as Table 3 reveals.

New Keynesians hold that the private economy is inherently unstable and unable to correct itself during periods of inflation and unemployment. In their view, government should take a primary role in managing fiscal and monetary policy for economic stabilization. Of the two major arms of policy, new Keynesians advocate discretionary fiscal policy as the primary weapon in controlling unemployment and inflation. Fiscal policies, they believe, have

TABLE 3   **Alternative Positions on Macroeconomic and Monetary Policy**

A simplified menu of economic policy choices includes various recommended roles for fiscal and monetary policy. The new Keynesian position places primary emphasis on fiscal policy, while the monetarist defends a rule for monetary policy and balance in the budget. The rational expectations theory predicts that, over the long run, neither fiscal nor monetary policy will have a positive effect on the aggregate economy.

Policy Position	Role of Monetary Policy	Predicted Effects of Monetary Policy	Role of Fiscal Policy	Predicted Effects of Fiscal Policy
New Keynesian	Maintain orderly and low interest rates through discretionary adjustments in money supply	Possible destabilizing effects on interest rates if Federal Reserve only attempts to control money supply	Primary tool of macroeconomic stabilization; discretionary changes in government spending and taxation	Discretionary fiscal policy capable of ensuring full employment
Monetarist	Maintain a 3% to 5% growth rate in M-1	Discretionary policy will destabilize decision making in private markets; monetary rule will stabilize expectations	Provide stable environment for private economy through balanced budgets	Discretionary policy will bring erratic effects on income, employment, and prices; such policy creates an unstable economy
Rational expectations theory	Same as monetarist	In the long run, rational expectations will neutralize discretionary policy	Same as monetarist	Possible adverse long-run aggregate supply effects

" . . . First I was a Keynesian . . . Next I was a monetarist . . . Then a
supply-sider . . . Now I'm a bum . . . "

© Bill Schorr, 1982 *Los Angeles Herald Examiner*

direct effects on spending in the private economy, whereas monetary policy
(control of the money stock) has only indirect results. Monetary policy should
maintain the order or stability of interest rates, keeping them low or moderate.

Monetarists and rational expectationists view the economy as essentially
stable and self-correcting. Both views envision the private decisions of laborers, employers, money demanders, and consumer-savers and investors as producing a natural equilibrium constituting some natural rate of output and
employment (or unemployment). In the monetarist view of this process, discretionary policy of any sort produces instabilities in private markets that
distort, exaggerate, or accentuate any natural changes. In the monetarist view,
discretionary fiscal or monetary policy contributes to instability in the private
economy. That is, discretionary policy (consciously taken direct government
action) either creates inflation and unemployment of itself or it has erratic
effects on the private economy's ability to establish economic stability. The
solution: Conduct monetary and fiscal policy so as to minimize disturbances
of private market participants' expectations and decisions. In the monetarist's
policy views, such stability can be achieved by invoking a monetary rule, such
as fixing the money supply growth rate, with balanced government budgets.

In the rational expectations variant of macroeconomic theory, the recommended role of fiscal and monetary policy is identical to that espoused by
monetarists. Differences between these two positions lie rather in the rational
expectationists' view of the probable effects of monetary and fiscal policy. As
market participants gain sufficient information about the effects of economic
policy through time, policy can have no effects on the private economy. Participants learn the effects of anticipated policy and act more and more quickly
to counteract them. The rational expectations approach might be regarded as
an extreme view within the monetarist position.

The important point is that *macroeconomists have not reached a consensus on exactly how the macroeconomy works*. Under such circumstances we expect to see a variety of policy views, as Table 3 shows. One of the problems with establishing a consensus among macroeconomists is the difficulty of proving one view with a statistical test that all would accept. The economist, like the meteorologist, is faced with a kaleidoscope of ever-changing conditions; hard-and-fast answers are difficult to come by.

SUMMARY

1. Macroeconomic policies—those prescribed to solve macroeconomic problems such as inflation and unemployment—rest on alternative versions of macroeconomic theory.
2. The tools of policy-makers include changes in taxes, government spending, and the money supply to effect changes in total spending.
3. The new Keynesians argue that fiscal policies—government spending and taxation policies—have direct and predictable effects on the private economy. Discretionary fiscal policies should be used to cure economic problems such as demand-deficiency unemployment and inflation. Money supply changes may affect spending indirectly through their impact on interest rates.
4. Monetarists advocate a stable, nondiscretionary fiscal and monetary approach to economic stabilization. Monetarists assert that lags in the recognition of economic problems on the part of both fiscal and monetary authorities, as well as lags between policy

implementation and the effects of policies, are potentially disruptive in controlling the macroeconomy. Monetarists advocate a balanced budget on the fiscal side and a rule fixing money supply growth for the Federal Reserve's conduct of monetary policy.
5. Rational expectations theorists argue that, rather than ignore useful information, market participants use all learned information to predict the outcome of policy-makers' discretionary decisions. Decision-makers with rational expectations are not always right, but they learn through time and are able to predict outcomes over the long run. The result is that when the discretionary decisions of policy-makers are perfectly anticipated, monetary and fiscal policy will have no effect on aggregate demand. Unanticipated policy or events will have short-run effects, which are eventually overcome through natural adjustments. Fiscal demand-side policies, moreover, may result in long-run adverse shifts in aggregate supply.

KEY TERMS

recognition lag   monetary rule
administrative lag   rational expectations theory

QUESTIONS FOR REVIEW AND DISCUSSION

1. Explain how fiscal and monetary policies differ with respect to the amount of time necessary to implement them and the amount of time required for their full force to be realized.
2. Under what conditions is Keynesian fiscal policy most effective? What fiscal policies are called for during times of recession? During inflation?
3. What role do the monetary authorities play in Keynesian policies? In the monetarists' view, what is the proper role of the monetary authorities?
4. According to monetarists, what variables adjust to maintain full employment? What effect do discretionary demand management policies have on the economy?
5. According to monetarists, what effect does increased government spending have on aggregate demand? What effect do recognition and administrative lags have on the cycles of inflation and unemployment?
6. Why do monetarists suggest that monetary rules be followed rather than discretionary policies?

7. What is the difference between rational expectations and adaptive expectations? If individuals have rational expectations rather than adaptive expectations, would discretionary monetary policy be more effective in diminishing swings in the economy?

8. According to the rational expectations view, what are the probable effects of discretionary monetary and fiscal policies?

9. What theoretical conditions would have to exist before discretionary fiscal or monetary policies could completely eliminate the cyclical swings in inflation and unemployment?

ECONOMICS IN ACTION
Economists in Control of Economic Policy? The Role of the Council of Economic Advisers

President Harry S. Truman is reputed to have once remarked that he would have been willing to pay a princely sum for a one-handed economist. After the Council of Economic Advisers gave their economic policy recommendations, Truman bemoaned, his economists would always end up saying, "But on the other hand. . . . "

What is the Council of Economic Advisers, and what exactly does it do? The Council of Economic Advisers (CEA) was established as an office in the executive branch of the federal government by the Employment Act of 1946. The CEA's basic duties are to supply the president with economic analysis and advice in order to assist in the development and implementation of national economic policy. Outstanding economists such as James Tobin, a Nobel laureate (1981) appointed by President John F. Kennedy, have served as members of the CEA.

The CEA consists of three members who are appointed by the president, with approval of the Senate, one of whom serves as chair of the CEA. The professional staff of the CEA is made up of eleven senior and six junior economists, as well as a statistician. The staff economists specialize in fields of expertise such as macroeconomics, international finance, labor, public finance, taxation, monetary policy, regulation, and agriculture. In most cases, the senior staff economists are on leave of absence from major universities, research institutions, or other government agencies.

By far, the CEA's most important duties are to provide the president with sound economic analysis concerning areas where policy decisions, either legislative or regulatory, are to be made. These areas include, of course, the broad area of national macroeconomic policy. The CEA not only assists the president in formulating macroeconomic policy, but also assists in designing the necessary programs through which such policy is carried out. Forecasts and projections of critical macroeconomic variables such as the deficit, inflation, real GNP growth, and foreign exchange rates are all prepared by the CEA. In addition, the CEA has prepared economic analyses of such microeconomic issues as farm credit, airline and trucking deregulation, banking deregulation, space shuttle pricing, immigration, and antitrust legislation.

At the end of each January, the CEA submits an annual report to the president. This report, together with the president's own report, is then transmitted to Congress. These are then published yearly as the *Economic Report of the President*. The *Report* is not only an informative analysis of recent economic events and current problems, but it is also one of the better sources of economic statistics. Data on everything from budget deficits to farm income to unemployment are reported here, some going as far back as 1929. The CEA also is responsible for data contained in a more up-to-date monthly publication called *Economic Indicators*.

The Council of Economic Advisers, in short, does not decide economic policy. This is the duty of the president and Congress. However, the CEA is in a position to strongly influence economic policy. The CEA chair and members are usually chosen on the basis of shared philosophy with the president, as shown by President George Bush's selection of Stanford University economist Michael Boskin, a moderate, to head his CEA. Like other administration officials dealing with economic questions and problems—the Secretary of the Treasury, the head of the Office of Management and the Budget—CEA members influence decision-making by force of personality, reputation, and personal relationship with the president.

Question

If you were a faculty member at your university, what *economic* factors would enter your decision to accept or turn down a position offered to you on the CEA? Remember that the salary of a CEA member is generally less than what the appointee could earn at a university.

36

Unemployment and Business Cycles

The real GNP of any economy fluctuates up and down over time. Such fluctuations were defined in Chapter 23 as business cycles. In previous chapters we have examined classical, Keynesian, and monetarist theories of the economy to gain insight into why these periodic expansions and contractions take place. In this chapter we will consider business cycles in more detail. We will examine how business cycles are measured, consider some of the costs associated with business cycles, and present various theories of the causes of business cycles. We will also consider some of the tools used by economic forecasters to predict changes in the business cycle and reexamine economic policies designed to prevent or moderate business cycles.

Some critics of capitalism base their criticism on the notion that business cycles are an inherent, undesirable consequence of the operation of a market system. In fact, advocates of central economic planning often contend that government intervention is necessary to prevent frequent and extreme economic downturns. However, evidence from centrally planned economies such as China and the Soviet Union indicates that business cycles are also an economic fact of life in centrally planned economies. Serious recessions in the Soviet Union, East Germany, and in Poland hastened disenchantment with central planning and led to adoption of free-market policies and alternative political systems. After you complete Chapter 36 you should understand

- the fundamental nature of business cycles.
- how economists attempt to predict or forecast cycles on the basis of fundamental economic indicators.
- the role of expectations and labor market adjustments in providing one explanation for short-run cycles of unemployment and inflation.
- how politics might be related to business cycles.

DEFINING AND PREDICTING BUSINESS CYCLES

Over any period of time, economic capacity to produce goods and services tends to increase because of factors such as technological change, growth in labor supply (population), and discovery and development of natural resources. Within the overall trend of long-run growth, economies fluctuate in aggregate output and employment (see Figure 1).

Business cycle:
A recurrent pattern of fluctuations in the level of economic activity as measured by the growth rate of real GNP; or the variation through time of the level of real GNP around its long-term trend.

A **business cycle** is a downward or upward fluctuation in the real GNP of an economy that repeats itself over time. Three points should be kept in mind about this definition. First, business cycles recur over time, but not necessarily in a predictable pattern. Recurrent and predictable seasonal variations in business activity—such as the purchase of more firewood in winter than in summer—are not business cycles. For example, everyone is aware of the upsurge in the purchase of goods and services every December as Christmas approaches. This seasonal change in business activity is a short, predictable fluctuation that is fully accounted for and therefore is not a business cycle.

FIGURE 1

Annual U.S. GNP Growth Rates, 1929–1989

The percentage change in a country's real GNP tends to fall and rise over time; economists refer to these fluctuations as business cycles. Cycles of expansion and recession have characterized the U.S. economy throughout most of its history. Despite these fluctuations, between 1929 and 1989 the average growth rate has been about 3 percent per year.

Sources: Council of Economic Advisers, *Economic Report of the President* (Washington, D.C.: U.S. Government Printing Office, 1966, 1987, 1990); *Federal Reserve Bulletin* (September 1984).

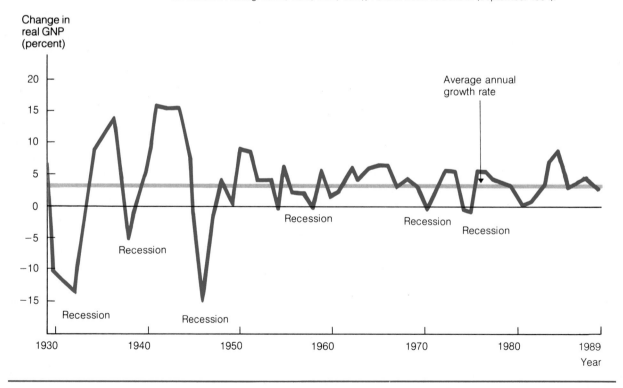

Second, the term *business cycle* normally refers to overall business activity as measured by real GNP. There can also be cycles in the component parts of GNP. Spending on consumer durables, such as refrigerators and cars, exhibits cyclical behavior over time, whereas consumer spending on nondurable items, such as food, does not. Cyclical patterns are also observed in retail sales, business profits, business incorporations, interest rates, residential construction, and many other reported statistics. For our purposes, however, we take business cycles to refer only to the movement of real GNP.

Third, there can be different types of business cycles, depending on the length of time over which a given business cycle runs. Short cycles last less than two years; intermediate cycles extend five years or more; and long-run cycles run over ten years. Indeed, some students of the business cycle have identified cycles that extend over several decades or even centuries.

The Language of Business Cycles

A business cycle includes expansions and contractions of business activity. An expansion is a cumulative increase in real GNP, while a contraction is a cumulative decrease. Contractions are often called recessions or depressions. A **recession** is a decline in real GNP that lasts for six months or more. **Depression** is a more ambiguous term, but it generally refers to a serious and persistent decline in economic activity lasting several years, accompanied by an unemployment rate of 15 percent or more. Depressions are preceded by recessions, but not all recessions are followed by depressions.

The period, or length, of a business cycle can be measured in two ways: from peak to peak or trough to trough. Figure 2 illustrates the alternative measurements. Peaks are upper turning points in a cycle where an expansion finally peters out. Troughs are the opposite of peaks; they are the lower turning points of a cycle where contractions bottom out. The length of a business cycle differs depending on whether it is measured from peak to peak or trough to trough.

The trend line in Figure 2 measures a hypothetical long-run growth path of the economy. The extent of deviations from the trend line, at either a peak or a trough, indicates the intensity of a business cycle. Business cycles have no set patterns. They recur over time, but each one is slightly different. Each business cycle varies in length and intensity.

Recession:
A contraction in overall economic activity, usually defined as a decrease in real GNP over a period of at least six months.

Depression:
A severe, persistent recession that may last several years.

Business Cycles in the United States

Using statistical analysis, researchers have identified numerous business cycles in U.S. economic history. Table 1 presents some data on business cycle activity in the United States since the turn of the century. The statistics show that business cycles are recurrent but have different lengths. Nineteen cycles were identified from 1900 to 1981. Measured peak to peak, the average duration of these cycles was approximately 51 months, or a little over four years. The shortest business cycle (January 1980–July 1981) lasted 18 months. The longest (April 1960–December 1969) lasted 116 months.

Moreover, the business cycles exhibited varying degrees of intensity. In the two-year expansion from April 1958 to April 1960, real GNP rose by 8 percent. By contrast, in the expansion from July 1980 to July 1981, real GNP rose by only about 2 percent. Each business cycle and its phases possess a

FIGURE 2

Hypothetical Business Cycle

The curve represents the phases of a hypothetical business cycle. One phase is contraction or recession, when aggregate output and employment fall. The trough occurs when this part of the cycle bottoms out. The expansion or recovery phase occurs when the economy exhibits expanding output and employment. The peak occurs when general business activity and employment stop rising. When the next recession begins, the economy starts another business cycle. The period of the cycle is measured from peak to peak or trough to trough. This cycle has a period of $t_1 t_2$, measured peak to peak. The intensity of the cycle is given by the deviation of the peak or trough from the trend line of long-run growth.

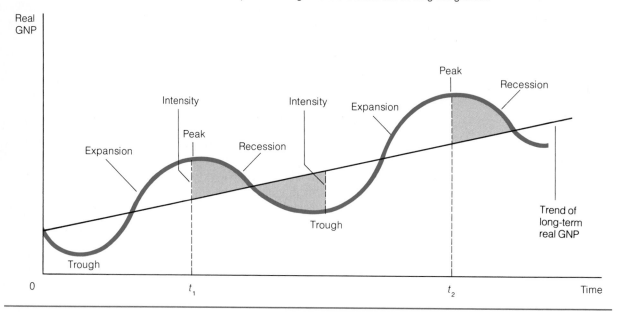

unique character. Since 1982, the business cycle pattern has diverged somewhat from its traditional look in that it has not shown a traditional fluctuating pattern.

Forecasting Business Cycles

Some economists specialize in forecasting business conditions. These individuals are often called econometricians because they are highly trained in the use of statistics, called **econometrics,** to predict events in the economy. Some well-known economic forecasters are Lawrence Klein of the University of Pennsylvania, who won the Nobel Prize in economics in 1980; Michael Evans, who has his own forecasting firm; and Alan Greenspan, who was chairman of the Council of Economic Advisers under President Ford and who was appointed chairman of the Federal Reserve Board in 1987.

Forecasting is both a science and an art. The science of forecasting involves the construction of statistical models of the operation of the economy and of economic indicators that predict the future level of such variables as GNP. The art of forecasting is the use of past experience and commonsense judgment about what types of variables are important in predicting how the economy will behave, since no two business cycles are precisely alike.

Who are some of the users of economic forecasts? Business decision-makers and government policy-makers need reliable data on the future course

Econometrics:
The combined use of economic theory and formal statistical techniques to analyze, explain, and predict economic phenomena.

TABLE 1

U.S. Business Cycles, 1900–1990

Trough	Peak	Length of Cycle (peak to peak in months)
December 1900	September 1902	39
August 1904	May 1907	56
June 1908	January 1910	32
January 1912	January 1913	36
December 1914	August 1918	67
March 1919	January 1920	17
July 1921	May 1923	40
July 1924	October 1926	41
November 1927	August 1929	34
March 1933	May 1937	93
June 1938	February 1945	93
October 1945	November 1948	45
October 1949	July 1953	56
May 1954	August 1957	49
April 1958	April 1960	32
February 1961	December 1969	116
November 1970	November 1973	47
March 1975	January 1980	74
July 1980	July 1981	18
November 1982	. . .[a]	. . .

Source: Department of Commerce, Bureau of Economic Analysis, *Business Conditions Digest* (July 1986), p. 104; U.S. Bureau of the Census, *Statistical Abstract of the United States* 1989, p. 534.

[a]In September 1990, many observers felt that this expansion would end with a recession in the fourth quarter of 1990.

of GNP to plan their activities. When business executives make decisions about investments in plant and equipment that will lead to increased output in the future, they need to have some idea of what the state of the economy will be when this output comes on the market. Overall tax revenues will usually depend on the level of national income and consumer spending in the future. To plan government spending, policy-makers need estimates of future tax revenues.

To produce a forecast, the forecaster seeks information about what changes in the economy today are a good indication of what the state of the economy will be tomorrow. For this purpose economic forecasters have developed **economic indicators,** key economic statistics that provide clues about the state of the future economy.

Economic indicators come in three basic varieties. Leading economic indicators anticipate a business cycle. They tend to turn down before a general economic downturn and up before an expansion. A coincident indicator runs in step with a business cycle, and a lagging indicator follows changes in the business cycle. Of these three sets of indicators, the most attention is paid to leading indicators because they give decision-makers clues about the future course of the business cycle.

The commonly used leading indicators are listed in Table 2. Data on these statistics are published quarterly by the Department of Commerce, and the trend of leading indicators is usually reported in the press. The leading indicators tend to change together over time, and a particularly useful sum-

Economic indicators:
Important data, or statistics, such as the money supply, investment spending, unemployment, and inventories that are used to help forecast economic activity and business cycles; these indicators are classified as leading, lagging, and coincident indicators.

TABLE 2	Leading Economic Indicators

Indicator
New business orders
Unfilled orders
Construction approvals and starts
New company formation and vacancies
Average hours worked
Average profits
Inventory change and level
Production bottlenecks
Stock prices
Changes in raw materials prices
Tendency surveys of expected production

Source: Department of Commerce, *Survey of Current Business* (August 1989), p. 24.

mary statistic is the composite or combined index of leading indicators. The behavior of this index since 1948 is shown in Figure 3.

How reliable is the composite index of leading economic indicators in predicting downturns? Compare the path of this index to the occurrence of recessions, represented by the shaded areas in Figure 2. Prior to each recession, the index of leading indicators dropped. Sometimes, however, it dropped more than a year before a recession started (as in the 1957–1958 recession), and at other times it dropped just months prior to a recession (as in the 1953–1954 recession). Moreover, the index dropped several times during the 1960s and no recession ensued. Economist Paul Samuelson once quipped that economic indicators "have correctly predicted nine of the last five recessions."

No predictive model of the future is perfect, but the fact that the leading indicators are widely used by economists, government officials, and businesspeople is a testimony to their usefulness as inputs to economic forecasts.

THE COSTS OF BUSINESS CYCLES

Business cycles have received much attention from economists and politicians because they entail genuine economic costs. When the economy goes into a recession or depression, the production of goods and services falls, causing living standards to fall. It may seem that these reductions in living standards are only temporary and that rapid increases in production during the recovery stage of the business cycle will counteract them. However, much of the lost production can never be regained. An economic downturn results in unemployment of economic resources of all types. Plants are closed down, farmland may lie idle, and workers with all types of labor skills remain out of work. Although all of the idle resources may become employed when the economy recovers, the lost production cannot be regained; a worker unemployed for a year cannot make up for lost production during the ensuing year. Production that is lost due to idle resources is production that is lost forever.

FIGURE 3

A Comparison of Business Cycles with the Composite Index of Leading Economic Indicators, 1948–1988

The shaded areas represent business downturns or recessions. The composite index of leading economic indicators dropped before each recession. However, the lag between the drop and the subsequent recession varied. In addition, the index sometimes forecast a recession that did not materialize.

Source: Department of Commerce, *Business Conditions Digest* (various issues).

Composite index of leading economic indicators (1967=100)

The second way in which business cycles reduce living standards is by depleting the capital stock. At any point in time, a society's ability to produce goods and services depends crucially on the size of its capital stock. As we saw in Chapter 2, a society's production possibilities curve is shifted rightward when capital accumulates and leftward when the capital stock declines. During an economic recession or depression, existing capital continues to depreciate, which lowers the capital stock. In a normal business environment, business firms have an incentive to replace and even add to depreciating plant and equipment; in a recession, firms are less likely to replace depreciating capital. Sales are so low that existing firms have idle capital and little incentive to replace equipment that becomes worn out. As a consequence, business downturns tend to erode the stock of productive capital and to reduce future production ability.

Similar choices by individuals also lead to a decline in the stock of another kind of capital—human capital in education and on-the-job training. In a recession, individuals have less incentive to invest in human capital: Why study to become a welder if there are no jobs for welders? This is precisely what happened in the United States and elsewhere during the Great Depression of the 1930s. Some of the anti-depression policies implemented by the Roosevelt administration were designed to prevent the nation's stock of both human and nonhuman capital from declining. Programs such as the PWA and the WPA hired unemployed workers to construct bridges, highways, and public buildings. In doing so, they provided job skills for workers (human capital) and improved the nation's infrastructure. Despite these programs, the United States entered World War II with a greatly reduced stock of capital goods, which hampered U.S. military mobilization at the outset of the war.

Who Pays for Business Downturns?

In the preceding section we saw that business downturns are costly, since downturns lower living standards both in the short run and in the long run. This does not mean that the burden is borne evenly by all citizens in terms of uniformly lower real incomes. Since U.S. firms tend to respond to downturns in business by laying off a portion of their labor force instead of reducing the hours of all workers (a practice common in Japan), the experiences of workers will vary. Workers who are laid off experience huge reductions in incomes, while other workers are barely affected. Table 3 indicates that the overall unemployment rate has risen on average by more than two percentage points during each of the eight recessions since World War II. In a typical recession, the unemployment rate has risen from about 4 percent to just over 6 percent.

TABLE 3

Changes in Unemployment Rates During Recessions

During the eight recessions that have occurred in the United States since World War II, the overall unemployment rate increased by an average of over two percentage points. However, increases in the unemployment rates for teenage workers and for black workers were substantially higher over the recession periods.

Recession Year	Unemployment Rate			
	All Workers	Females	Blacks	Teenagers
1947	3.8%	4.1%	5.9%	9.2%
1948	5.9	6.0	8.9	13.4
1952	2.9	3.6	5.4	8.5
1954	5.4	6.0	9.9	12.6
1957	4.2	4.7	7.9	11.6
1958	6.6	6.8	12.6	15.9
1960	5.4	5.9	10.2	14.7
1961	6.5	7.2	12.4	16.8
1969	3.4	4.7	6.4	12.2
1971	5.8	6.9	9.9	16.9
1973	4.8	6.0	9.0	14.5
1975	8.3	9.3	13.8	19.9
1979	5.8	6.8	11.3	16.1
1980	7.0	7.4	13.1	17.8
1981	7.5	7.9	14.2	19.6
1982	9.5	9.4	17.3	23.2

Source: Council of Economic Advisers, *Economic Report of the President* (Washington, D.C.: U.S. Government Printing Office, 1989), p. 353.

While the unemployment rate for most types of workers rises during a business downturn, it rises much more for some types of workers than for others. The data in Table 3 indicate that, during recessions, unemployment rates for teenage workers and for black workers tend to rise about 60 percent more than the overall unemployment rate. However, the unemployment rate for female workers generally rises a little less than the overall rate. Statistics for workers in different industries or in different parts of the country also reflect the uneven burden of unemployment among workers. During recessions, sales of consumer durables like new homes and cars generally fall sharply, causing extremely high unemployment for workers in building trades and in the auto industry. Since the auto industry and its suppliers are concentrated in certain parts of the United States, some states—Michigan, in particular—are hit harder by economic downturns. The unemployment costs of recessions therefore tend to be borne disproportionately by workers in such states.

Inflation and the Business Cycle

The economic disadvantages of business cycles are not necessarily limited to the costs associated with high unemployment. There is also evidence that business cycles are a cause of inflation. During economic "booms," when demand for goods and services grows rapidly, bottlenecks in the production process are likely to arise. Rapid economic growth often frustrates the economy's ability to quickly match unemployed workers with job openings; the newly created jobs may arise in geographic areas or in industries with relatively few unemployed workers. The consequence of production bottlenecks is that wages and prices are bid up, causing inflation. (Such bouts of inflation are examples of the demand-pull theories of inflation discussed in Chapter 34.) Consider the economic experience of the United States since World War II. The average postwar inflation rate is about 5 percent per year. Inflation rates of over 6 percent correspond to upturns in the business cycle; the figure for downturns is less than 3 percent.

INFLATION AND UNEMPLOYMENT: IS THERE A TRADE-OFF?

Most vexing for policy-makers is the possibility that there may be a trade-off between inflation and unemployment. If so, achievement of price stability would require unemployment, or full employment would require inflation.

British economist A. W. Phillips published an important paper related to inflation and unemployment in 1958,[1] in which he used actual data to show that there may be a long-run trade-off between inflation and unemployment.[2]

---

[1]See A. W. Phillips, "Relation Between Unemployment and the Rate of Change of Money Wage Rates in the United Kingdom, 1861–1957," *Economica* 25 (November 1958), pp. 283–99.

[2]Actually, neoclassical economist Irving Fisher was the first to notice the inverse relation between inflation rates and unemployment rates. See Irving Fisher, "A Statistical Relation Between Unemployment and Price Changes," *International Labor Review* (June 1926), pp. 785–92. Reprinted posthumously as "I Discovered the Phillips Curve," *Journal of Political Economy* (March–April 1973), pp. 496–502.

Phillips's data are based on money wage rates; since they follow the inflation rate, money wage changes may serve as a proxy for inflation. Phillips's data showed an almost hundred-year (long-run) inverse relation between inflation and unemployment for the United Kingdom. The data also indicated that the cost of less unemployment is higher inflation rates or, conversely, that the cost of lowering the inflation rate is a higher unemployment rate.

Phillips's study caused a great stir among macroeconomists because an inverse relation between unemployment rates and inflation rates means that the long-run aggregate supply curve is positively sloped, not a vertical line. In other words, higher levels of output and employment are invariably associated with higher price levels. (Alternatively, a long-run curve relating unemployment rates with inflation rates would be negatively sloped.) This means that long-run income and employment growth must come at the expense of inflation. If Phillips is right, the promise of achieving one economic goal (price stability or full employment) means that the other economic problem cannot be solved simultaneously. The policy-maker must choose between problems in a no-win trade-off.

Phillips Curves: Hypothetical and Actual

Phillips curve:
A graph showing the relation between the rate of inflation and the unemployment rate.

Before analyzing American experience with inflation rates and unemployment, examine a hypothetical **Phillips curve** and what it means. Figure 4 depicts a hypothetical relation between the unemployment rate and the inflation rate that Phillips's long-run data suggested. Note that in place of the level of income or employment, the unemployment rate appears on the horizontal axis. When these data are displayed against the inflation rate, a curve of negative slope results.

Phillips's basic argument is straightforward: A reduction in unemployment comes at the expense of higher inflation. The degree of the inverse relation, however, depends on the initial rate of inflation. At higher rates of inflation, the trade-off is less severe. For instance, as Figure 4 shows, a reduction of 2 percent in inflation from an initial rate of 16 percent causes unemployment to rise by only 1 percent (from 4 to 5 percent), whereas a similar reduction at a lower inflation level (from 10 to 8 percent) may force unemployment to rise by a full $3\frac{1}{2}$ percent (from 8 percent to $11\frac{1}{2}$ percent).

In the analysis of the Phillips curve, inflation is a necessary evil. Resource scarcities are such that higher and higher inflation rates are required to coax the resources into use. Likewise, lower and lower rates of inflation are insufficient to put large quantities of labor resources to work. The economy requires inflation to achieve high rates of employment and real income growth. Alternatively, the cost of price stability at low rates of inflation is high unemployment, low income, and lower growth rates.

Neither new Keynesian nor new classical economists believe that there is a *long-term* trade-off between inflation and unemployment, but what is the evidence for a short-run Phillips curve for the United States? Figure 5 relates the inflation rate to the unemployment rate for the years 1960–1989, using the GNP price deflator as the measure of inflation. From looking at the raw data of Figure 5, it appears that trade-offs are indeed a fact! Note, for example, that a reduction in the unemployment rate between 1967 and 1969 was accompanied by a rise in the inflation rate.

FIGURE 4

According to A. W. Phillips, there is an inverse relation between the inflation rate and the rate of unemployment. At an inflation rate of 16 percent, the unemployment rate is 4 percent. If the inflation rate falls to 14 percent, unemployment rises to 5 percent. At zero inflation, unemployment is very high.

A Hypothetical Phillips Curve Relating Inflation and Unemployment

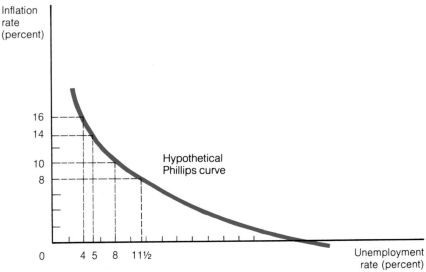

As we get closer to the present, the trade-off still appears to hold for some time periods. Look at the movements between 1972 and 1973, between 1976 and 1979, and between 1981 and 1982. In the latter case, a reduction in the inflation rate from 9.4 to 6.0 percent was accompanied by an increase in the unemployment rate from 7.6 to 9.7 percent, a dramatic increase with all sorts of economic and political consequences. The inverse relation appeared as recently as 1986–1989, with gradual increases in the inflation rate (from 2.6 to 4.1 percent) contrasted with a gradual reduction in the aggregate unemployment rate (from 7.0 to 5.3 percent).

Consider, however, the relation between the unemployment rate and the inflation rate for other recent time periods. Between 1969 and 1970, 1971 and 1972, 1973 and 1974, 1975 and 1976, 1979 and 1981, and 1982 and 1986, it appears that a positive rather than inverse relation existed between the unemployment rate and the inflation rate. Does this positive relation mean that Phillips's theory is wrong, or does it mean that the sometimes positive relation indicates a movement of the trade-off to higher and higher rates of unemployment and inflation? The answer given by some economists—mostly new classical and new Keynesian—is that the Phillips relation must be viewed from both short-run and long-run perspectives and that expectations play a major role in explaining cycles of inflation and unemployment.

A Phillips Curve Adjusted for Expectations

When the Phillips relation is analyzed both from short- and long-run views, the expectations of consumers and producers regarding the inflation rate become important. Suppose that the inflation rate is zero, the unemployment

FIGURE 5

Combined Unemployment and Inflation Rates, 1960–1989

The Phillips relation—the theory that increases in inflation rates are associated with decreases in unemployment rates, and vice versa—appears to hold over selected years in the United States. Shaded areas represent possible Phillips trade-offs between inflation and unemployment.

Source: Council of Economic Advisers, *Economic Report of the President* (Washington, D.C.: U.S. Government Printing Office, 1990), pp. 299, 338.
Note: Inflation data based on GNP price deflator; unemployment rates apply to civilian workers.

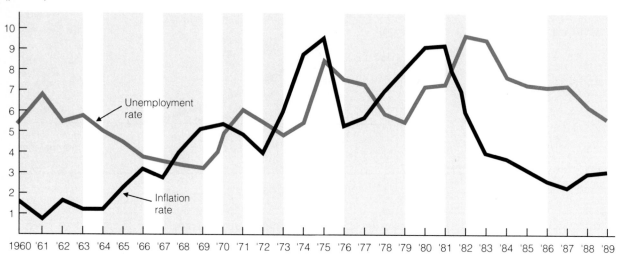

Short-run Phillips curve:
A downward-sloping curve indicating an inverse relation between the rate of inflation and the unemployment rate, holding constant the inflation expectations of workers.

rate is at the natural rate U_N, and that people do not anticipate any inflation. In terms of Figure 6, the initial state of the economy is depicted by point a on the **short-run Phillips curve** ($SRPC_0$). Now suppose that a sudden increase in aggregate demand causes some shortages to develop and drives the inflation rate up to 3 percent. The economy will move to point b on $SRPC_0$, and the unemployment rate will temporarily fall to U_1. The reason for this temporary decrease in unemployment is that workers who anticipate zero inflation remain willing to work for the initial nominal wage, since they do not anticipate inflation. Employers who correctly perceive that inflation reduces the real wage are then willing to employ more workers.[3]

Once workers adjust their expectations to the new inflation rate of 3 percent, the unemployment rate will again rise to the natural rate U_N. Workers will no longer be willing to work for the old nominal wage but will remain willing to work only at a new nominal wage, which is 3 percent higher. Employers will then have no incentive to retain the additional workers. In terms of Figure 6, the Phillips curve will have shifted upward from $SRPC_0$ to

---

[3]The so-called "fooling model" of expectations adjustment was developed in large part by Milton Friedman in "The Role of Monetary Policy," *American Economic Review* (March 1968), pp. 1–17.

FIGURE 6   **Short-Run and Long-Run Phillips Curves**

Each short-run Phillips curve shows the trade-off between the inflation rate and the unemployment rate when expectations are fixed. If people expect zero inflation and the inflation rate rises to 3 percent, the unemployment rate will fall to U_1. Once expectations adjust to an inflation rate of 3 percent, the short-run Phillips curve shifts upward, from $SRPC_0$ to $SRPC_3$, and the unemployment rate rises back to U_N. The long-run Phillips curve, $LRPC$, assumes fully anticipated inflation. It indicates that the natural rate of unemployment will exist in the long run no matter what rate of inflation occurs—as long as the rate of inflation is anticipated.

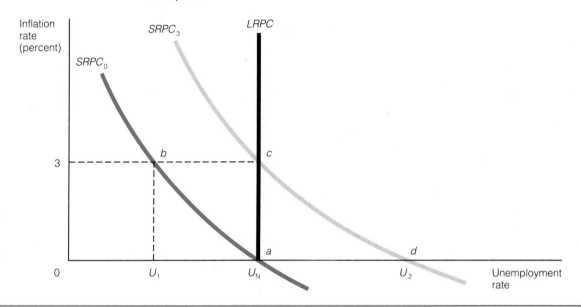

$SRPC_3$. This upward shift will equal the 3 percent increase in the anticipated rate of inflation. In Figure 6, the economy will move from point *a* to point *c* by way of point *b*. When the actual inflation rate exceeds the expected inflation rate, unemployment will temporarily drop below the natural rate. Then, when workers' expectations of inflation rise to the new inflation rate, the unemployment rate will rise from U_1 to U_N.

By similar logic, we can see that an unanticipated decrease in the inflation rate will temporarily lead to an increase in unemployment. Suppose that after workers adjust their expectations to the new inflation rate of 3 percent, a decrease in aggregate demand causes the inflation rate to fall to zero percent. Workers who fail to realize that inflation has ceased will continue to demand 3 percent annual increases in their nominal wages; they view these increases as necessary to keep their real wages from falling. With constant prices, real wages will rise, causing employers to reduce the number of workers they employ. The economy will temporarily move to point *d* in Figure 6. The unemployment rate will remain above the natural rate until workers adjust their inflation expectations downward to the actual level of inflation. This will shift the Phillips curve downward from $SRPC_3$ to $SRPC_0$.

This suggests that whenever the actual inflation rate differs from the anticipated rate, the unemployment rate will move away from the natural rate. Higher-than-anticipated inflation will cause unemployment to fall temporarily below the natural rate. A lower-than-anticipated rate of inflation will push unemployment above the natural rate.

If we make the assumption that workers eventually come to anticipate existing inflation rates, we see that *in the long run,* there is no trade-off between unemployment and inflation. As the economy moves from a low inflation rate to a higher rate, unemployment falls but then returns to the natural rate. In the long run, unemployment will be unaffected by changes in the inflation rate, as illustrated in Figure 6 by the vertical **long-run Phillips curve** (*LRPC*).

Long-run Phillips curve:
A vertical line at the natural rate of unemployment; indicates that if there is enough time for workers' expectations to adjust to the actual rate of inflation, then changes in the inflation rate produce no change in the rate of unemployment.

Prices, Wages, and Employment Adjustment: A Keynesian Perspective

Some economists, notably new Keynesians, argue that misconceptions or "fooling" of laborers is not necessary to explain the slow adjustment of nominal wages to changed aggregate demand conditions over the short run. Price level changes, such as inflation, are felt immediately at the grocery store or at the gas pump—and confirmed, certainly, in countless media reports. Workers, in short, catch on quickly.[4]

Although workers may be temporarily fooled into supplying more or less labor due to misconceptions about real wages, other reasons may be stressed for the slowness of nominal wages to adjust to changed demand conditions. Certain forces work on firms and on workers to avoid frequent or unnecessary job changes. Employers typically spend considerable time and money for on-the-job training specific to their needs. These trained workers are paid a premium (over untrained workers), a premium that workers might lose by moving to another job or occupation. For this reason, during periods of rising demand and lagging nominal wages, workers will hold out and actually work harder in anticipation of future nominal wages adjustments to an increased price level.

Additionally, a large number of industrial workers are covered by union contracts—often lasting up to three years—that also contribute to sticky wages. These union contracts are designed to avoid strikes and costly and frequent negotiations with workers. They remain in force whether aggregate demand rises or falls. Though these contracts often contain escalator or cost-of-living clauses that provide for nominal wage increases over the contract period (often through some tie with an index of prices), they seldom provide for a full increase. Individual firms will not ordinarily agree to tie fully the wages paid their laborers to a price index, since the increase in aggregate demand that precipitated the higher price level may not materialize for their own product. A computer firm that made such an agreement, for example, might find itself with higher wage costs and no increase in the nominal demand for computers.

Wage contracts are not tied to aggregate demand conditions, and nominal wages are only partially adjusted to changing demand and price conditions. Aspects of the employer-worker relationship and long-run wage contracting, in addition to short-run misconceptions of workers, help explain the stickiness of nominal wages over short-run periods. Just as expectations catch up with actual price behavior, workers will also request that nominal

---

[4]A fuller discussion of these issues may be found in Robert J. Gordon, *Macroeconomics,* 5th ed. (Glenview, IL: Scott, Foresman, 1990), pp. 195–99.

wage increases match price level increases when union and other bargaining contracts come up for renegotiation, especially during expansionary or boom periods of high output and employment. Workers will also be convinced to negotiate nominal wage cuts during periods of recession and low employment. Ultimately, real wages readjust to equilibrium levels of employment and output.

CAUSES OF BUSINESS CYCLES

Eighty years ago, the primary goal of some economists was to gain an understanding of the business cycle and its causes. Although many economists at the time believed that economic science would one day arrive at a single explanation for business cycles, this has not yet proven to be the case. Instead, we now have many competing theories of business cycles. The first set of theories can be described as investment theories because they suggest that the causes of the business cycle can be traced to variations in the level of private investment spending. Recall that Keynesians emphasize destabilizing tendencies in the economy, especially the uncertainty of profit expectations on the part of business investors.

The second group of theories examines a wide variety of causal factors, all of them external to the private economy. For instance, monetary theorists emphasize the unpredictability of the money supply process and its impact on the economy. Theories of a political business cycle emphasize the effects of political institutions on the general economy. We devote the remainder of this chapter to an examination of the various theories of the causes of business cycles.

Investment Theories

The central proposition of the various investment theories of the business cycle is that any change in the level of private investment spending will have a significant impact on the level of GNP. Investment theories include many of the ideas of Keynes and his followers, particularly the concept of the investment multiplier (see Chapter 27). In a simple Keynesian model of the economy, the investment multiplier is expressed as the reciprocal of the marginal propensity to save.

$$k_I = \frac{1}{1 - MPC} = \frac{1}{MPS},$$

where k_I is the investment multiplier, MPC is the marginal propensity to consume, and MPS is the marginal propensity to save. The investment multiplier enables statisticians and economic forecasters to determine how much a given change in autonomous investment spending, I, will affect an overall change in GNP, Y.

$$\Delta Y = k_I \Delta I = \frac{1}{MPS} \Delta I.$$

What does this mean in practical terms? Suppose that the economy is initially in equilibrium at an output level of $500 billion when business investors' expectations about future profits suddenly change for the worse and businesses reduce investment spending by $10 billion. By how much will GNP fall from its initial equilibrium level of $500 billion? By $10 billion or by more than $10 billion?

In Chapter 27, we saw that a reduction in investment spending causes an initial decline in income, which in turn reduces both consumption and saving. The reduction in consumption spending reduces income, which further reduces consumption and saving, and so on until a new, lower level of GNP is reached. The amount of the reduction in GNP depends on the values of the *MPC* and the *MPS*. As seen above, the multiplier is equal to the reciprocal of the *MPS*. For example, if the *MPS* is one-fourth, or 0.25, the reduction in GNP will be the multiplier ($1 \div 0.25 = 4$) multiplied by the initial reduction in autonomous spending, $10 billion. The initial GNP of $500 billion will fall to $460 billion, a new equilibrium level.

Combining the notion of the investment multiplier with the possibility of volatile investment spending results in a potential explanation of business cycles. A group of economists associated with Keynes argued that business firms typically adjust their capital stock in response to changes in sales. In an industry experiencing rising sales, business firms respond by increasing investment. The increases in investment then, through the multiplier process, lead to increases in sales, which bring about additional increases in business investment and national income. This view of the world suggests that even a minor increase in aggregate demand can lead to a major economic upswing, as can a minor business downturn lead to recession. In the case of a business downturn, these economists argued that business firms would respond to decreased sales by canceling orders for new plant and equipment, a decline in investment spending that would then lead to a larger decrease in national income.

Today, relatively few economists view the relationship between business sales and business investment in such rigid terms. Nonetheless, many economists still attribute business cycles to changes in business investment. The following sections discuss various causes of business investment fluctuation.

Business Expectations. Many economists have concluded that the level of investment spending in the economy depends largely on expectations of future economic conditions. Will the economy grow or stagnate? Will interest rates go up or down? Will inflation increase or decrease? All of these questions weigh heavily on business decision-makers. In Chapter 34, we mentioned the concepts of adaptive expectations and rational expectations. Both concepts have been used to explain the investment behavior that leads to business cycles. Pessimistic forecasts naturally lead to less and less investment spending, while optimism about the future leads to more investment. Keynes even spoke of "animal spirits"—unexplained changes in business investors' decisions leading to large overall changes in spending.

Supply Shocks. Sudden changes in the supply of certain resources owing to natural disasters or international conflicts may also initiate business cycles. In addition to their effect on the costs of production, these supply shocks may drastically alter business expectations. The OPEC supply shock in the 1970s is a case in point. The sudden cutback in the availability of oil drove up prices for gasoline and all other petroleum products and affected output around the world. The OPEC crisis also shook investor confidence, contributing to the recessionary conditions that plagued many economies for several years afterward. (A more recent oil shock is discussed on page 400.)

Creative Destruction.   Another theory focuses on the role of the entrepreneur, the person whose new ideas and new products offer expanding opportunities for profit. According to Joseph Schumpeter, the contributions of entrepreneurship to the economic process—the new commodity, the new technology, the new source of supply, the new type of organization—spur economic growth by "destroying" old ways of doing things.[5] Innovators who succeed at cutting costs or fulfilling previously unmet demands earn economic profits, and these profits attract entry by new firms that rush to emulate the discovery. In the scramble to obtain a share of the profits, however, overinvestment by new entrants occurs, and the market becomes saturated. Some of the firms go bankrupt, and a period of reversal follows, precipitating a downturn in economic activity. In microcosm, the recent upheaval in the computer industry in which a temporary boom has been followed by lagging profits and a rash of bankruptcies illustrates the sequence. The cycle finally turns up again as new ideas and new profit opportunities arise. To Schumpeter, the business cycle—a cycle of creation and destruction of profit opportunities—is a necessary accompaniment to capitalist development. This point of view has been called the **creative destruction theory.**

Creative destruction theory:
A business cycle theory that emphasizes the role of the entrepreneur as an innovator supplying new products and services, thereby creating new profit opportunities and destroying old ones; competitors follow the innovator's lead, which creates business cycles.

Monetary Theories

Monetary theories of the business cycle are based on the idea that business cycles arise from attempts by government to fine-tune the macroeconomy. In the case of monetary policy, decisions by the monetary authority (the Federal Reserve) made in the presence of implementation lags, in error, or in a conscious attempt to influence political outcomes destabilize the economy in one direction. A period follows during which the Federal Reserve takes necessary corrective action. The business cycle is thus thought to be generated by a stop-and-go monetary policy cycle.

To see how monetary policy might generate a business cycle, we return to the concept of a Phillips curve. The short- and long-run Phillips relations are depicted in Figure 7. In the short run there is a trade-off between inflation and unemployment, and in both Figure 7a and Figure 7b this trade-off is represented by a family of negatively sloped Phillips curves, each corresponding to a different expected rate of inflation.

Recall that the long-run Phillips curve is a vertical line at the natural rate of unemployment, U_N. When the expected rate of inflation is equal to the actual rate, the economy will be in long-run equilibrium with an unemployment rate equal to U_N. In other words, there is no trade-off between inflation and unemployment in the long run, and many possible inflation rates are consistent with long-run equilibrium.

Consider now the effects of an unforeseen increase in the rate of monetary expansion. In Figure 7a, the economy was initially in equilibrium at E_1

---

[5]Joseph A. Schumpeter, *Capitalism, Socialism, and Democracy,* 3rd ed. (New York: Harper & Row, 1950), esp. pp. 81–86.

FIGURE 7

Monetary Policy and the Business Cycle

The economy's long-run Phillips curve is *LRPC,* and several short-run Phillips curves (*SRPC*) are also shown. (a) An unexpected increase in money supply causes the unemployment rate to fall for a while from U_N to U_1, but ultimately its impact is to increase the rate of inflation that is consistent with the natural rate of unemployment. (b) An unexpected decrease in the money supply causes the opposite process of adjustment. Through these processes, uneven performance by money supply authorities can lead to cyclical behavior in the economy.

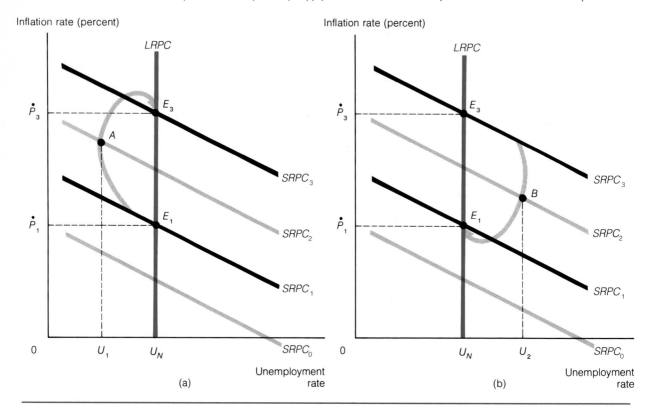

on the short-run Phillips curve $SRPC_1$, with unemployment at the natural rate and an inflation rate of $\dot{P_1}$. If individuals form their expectations about inflation adaptively, they will continue to expect an inflation rate of P_1 for a time. Because unexpected monetary expansion pushes the actual inflation rate higher than $\dot{P_1}$, however, some workers will believe that their real wage has risen, while employers will begin hiring additional workers in the mistaken belief that the demand for their products has increased. As a result, individuals will accept jobs for which the real wage will eventually turn out to be too low. Unemployment nevertheless falls, and the economy moves leftward along $SRPC_1$.

As workers and employers begin to recognize the more rapidly rising price level, they revise their expectations about inflation, and as a result, the short-run Phillips curve begins shifting to the right to $SRPC_2$. At some point, say A on $SRPC_2$, the unemployment rate reaches its lowest level at U_1 but then begins to rise again as individuals' expectations about inflation begin to catch up. A new equilibrium is eventually reached at E_3, when the expected rate of inflation is equal to the higher actual rate, $\dot{P_3}$. The unemployment rate returns to the natural rate. In the long run, the expansionary monetary policy did nothing more than raise the inflation rate from $\dot{P}_1$ to $\dot{P}_3$. In the short run, however, what looks like the expansionary phase of a business cycle was generated.

Suppose that the inflation rate $\dot{P}_3$ is viewed as too high, inducing the Federal Reserve to take corrective measures. In particular, suppose that the Federal Reserve adopts a policy of reducing the rate of growth in the money supply. The adjustment process now operates in reverse. Beginning from E_3 in Figure 7b, the inflation rate starts to fall, but workers and employers continue to expect inflation rate P_3. Some workers will be fooled into thinking their real wage has fallen as employers begin laying off workers in response to a mistaken belief that demand has fallen. Individuals will refuse job offers for which the real wage will eventually turn out to have been acceptable. Unemployment rises, and the economy moves rightward along $SRPC_3$.

Downward revisions in the expected inflation rate shift the short-run Phillips curve downward and to the left. The unemployment rate reaches its highest level, U_2, at B on $SRPC_2$ and then falls again until a new equilibrium is attained at E_1, when inflationary expectations catch up. When that occurs, the unemployment rate is again at the natural rate, U_N, and the expected and actual inflation rates have fallen from $\dot{P}_3$ to $\dot{P}_1$. The short-run adjustment process looks like the contractionary phase of a business cycle. Using historical data, monetarists have argued that mistaken money supply adjustments by the Federal Reserve have been responsible for business cycle swings, including the Great Depression, as described in Focus, "The Monetary Explanation of the Great Depression."

It is important to keep in mind that some degree of surprise is required for monetary policy changes to generate a business cycle. As discussed in Chapter 35, if individuals form their expectations about the effects of monetary policy rationally rather than adaptively, then monetary policy will have a milder impact on the levels of the real variables in the economy. Consumers, workers, savers, and investors will adjust if expectations are rational, but cycles of unemployment and income may be generated until expectations are fully adjusted to new conditions.

POLITICAL BUSINESS CYCLES

Political business cycle:
A business cycle that results from the manipulation of policy tools by incumbent politicians hoping to stimulate the economy prior to an election and thereby improve their reelection chances.

Some economists have suggested that there is a **political business cycle.**[6] Incumbent politicians pursue economic policies that promote their reelection, and as a consequence the economy goes through a business cycle every four years. In an attempt to enhance their reelection prospects, incumbent politicians promote expansionary policies prior to election day—tax cuts, increased government spending, and greater money supply growth. These policies have politically popular consequences in the short run: lower unemployment and interest rates, along with increased real income (output). Immediately after the election, the politicians often reverse course. To limit the higher inflation rates that the reelection strategy fosters, they raise taxes and cut spending, and money supply growth is reduced. The result of these political moves is a business cycle whose length is roughly equal to the interval between elections.

---

[6]The political business cycle idea is usually attributed to William Nordhaus, "The Political Business Cycle," *Review of Economics and Statistics* 42 (April 1975), pp. 169–90.

FOCUS   The Monetary Explanation of the Great Depression

The Great Depression, occurring over the decade of the 1930s in the United States and abroad, was a period of record low levels of employment, industrial production, and real income.

Monetarists Milton Friedman and Anna Schwartz lay the blame for the Great Depression on a series of blunders by the Federal Reserve Board.[a] Between August 1929 and March 1933, the Federal Reserve allowed the money supply to decrease by 35 percent. In defense of the Fed, the monetary base did grow during that period, but rapid decreases in the money multiplier led to a decrease in the money supply. Some historians have argued that the Fed thought that its policies during that critical period were expansionary. However, other Fed decisions during the period seemed to be designed to prolong the economic crisis. For example, the board allowed the New York Federal Reserve Bank to lower the discount rate—a proper countercyclical policy—only if the district bank ceased its purchases of securities on the open market, a decision that prevented the New York Federal Reserve Bank from using its primary tool for increasing the money supply. Moreover, the Board of Governors voted in early 1933 to reduce the monetary base by $125 million, and twice in 1937 the board raised the reserve requirements it imposed on member banks. The latter action was sufficient to choke off an economic recovery that had begun in late 1934. Friedman and Schwartz cite additional evidence to support their main point that the actions of the

[a]Milton Friedman and Anna Schwartz, *A Monetary History of the United States, 1867–1960* (Princeton: Princeton University Press, 1963). For some different perspectives on the cause of the Great Depression, see Karl Brunner, ed., *The Great Depression Revisited* (Boston: Kluwer-Nijhoff, 1981).

monetary authority during the 1930s helped prolong and deepen the worst economic contraction in U.S. history.

Other, less technical reasons might be offered for the passivity of the Federal Reserve System during the banking panics of the early 1930s. One possible reason is that the Federal Reserve Board did not understand the critical impact that bank failures might have on the money supply and economic activity. Bank failures feed on themselves by lowering confidence in all banks. The rush to acquire "safe" currency on the part of money holders will increase the currency-deposit ratio (see Chapter 33) and further reduce the ability of the entire banking system to expand loans and the money supply. The effect is to strongly discourage business activity and consumer spending. The Federal Reserve System chalked up small bank failures to "bad management," not realizing that such failures put big-city banks in jeopardy. Another reason offered for the apparent failure of the Federal Reserve System to soften the jolt of the Great Depression was internal jealousy between the Board of Governors in Washington, D.C., and the Federal Reserve Bank of New York. Until 1928, the New York Bank was the dominant political force within the System. The New York Bank strongly argued for large open market purchases of securities to stave off bank panics (a policy that might have been effective), but to no avail. The Board of Governors, in a fight to obtain control of the monetary system, resisted the policy.

Citing such poor historical performance by the Federal Reserve, Friedman has argued that a rule governing the rate of growth of the money supply over time would be superior to the present system of discretionary monetary management. Friedman's policy proposal for a monetary rule is discussed in Chapters 34 and 35.

Do Political Business Cycles Exist?

Three main arguments have been raised against the concept of political business cycles. First, the model is said to be naive because it assumes that voters in a presidential election care only about inflation and unemployment. The critics note, correctly, that election results turn on a variety of issues, including foreign relations, the distribution of income, and the personalities of the candidates. A second criticism raises the question of timing. Monetarists in particular argue that monetary policy lags are long and unpredictable. Since the repercussions of a change in the rate of monetary expansion are not felt immediately but occur over a period of perhaps two years, it may be difficult for incumbents to chart an economic course that ensures their political support within the confines of a four-year election cycle.

Macroeconomics: Key Trends

In this section, we present graphs of real data to highlight several important macroeconomic trends. Students of economics, economists, and economic observers benefit from this kind of presentation, which can show at a glance, for example, that in the 1980s high federal deficits seem to have pushed up interest rates and prevented their decline. Indeed, it is the task of economists to present, explain, and interpret data in a meaningful and useful way.

Labor Productivity and Investment

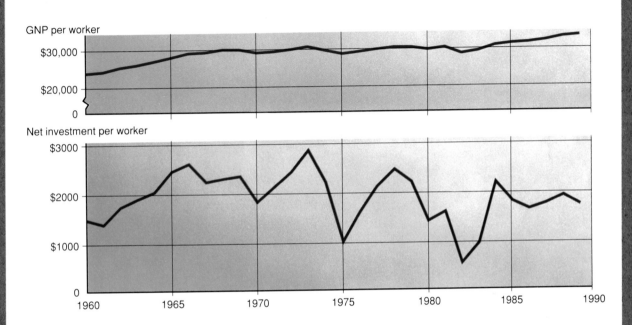

Source: Council of Economic Advisers, *Economic Report of the President* (Washington, D.C.: U.S. Government Printing Office, 1990), calculated from Tables C-2 and C-32.

One measure of labor productivity is output per worker, which is real gross national product divided by the number of persons in the labor force. GNP per worker in the labor force in 1989 was $33,443. Considerable productivity gains in the 1960s gave way to a fifteen-year period of stagnant growth. Since 1985, the productivity picture has improved somewhat, but what accounted for its earlier, persistent flatness? One factor, certainly, was the increased participation of women in the labor force over the period. Another factor was an erratic, generally low level of investment per worker in the United States.

Workers using newer equipment will be more productive than workers using older equipment. You can think of net investment per worker as the amount of new tools or equipment available to each worker. Net investment per worker is found by subtracting the amount of depreciation of existing capital from gross private domestic investment in new capital equipment and then dividing by the number of persons in the labor force. In 1989, net investment per worker was $1745. High interest rates throughout the decade and the 1980 and 1982 recessions are cited as reasons for the low rates of investment per worker in the 1980s.

Real Interest Rates and the Deficit

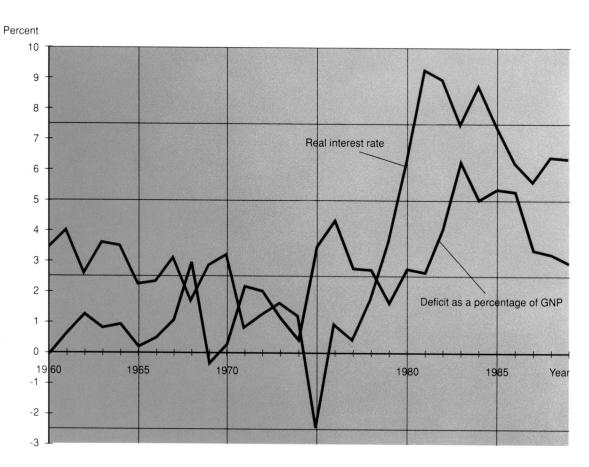

Percent

Source: Council of Economic Advisers, *Economic Report of the President* (Washington, D.C.:
U.S. Government Printing Office, 1990), Tables C-7 and C-76.

Some economists believe that the enormous deficits run by the federal government in the 1980s pushed up interest rates and kept them high, effectively blocking business borrowing for investment purposes. Federal deficits are financed primarily through the sale of bonds to individuals and commercial banks. Increases in the supply of bonds push bond prices down and simultaneously drive interest rates up; in this way, government borrowing to finance deficits is said to crowd out business investment.

Is there proof of a relation between federal deficits and interest rates? Real interest rates—prime interest rates (the rates banks charge their business customers for loans to purchase new capital equipment) minus the rate of inflation—were relatively stable during the 1960s, volatile in the 1970s, and sharply higher in the 1980s. Since 1960, federal budget deficits—the amount by which government expenditures exceed tax revenues in a given year—have occurred in every year except 1960 and 1969; although deficits have generally risen as a percentage of GNP over the period, the biggest increases came during the 1980s. As the graph shows, the picture prior to 1980 is muddy, but real interest rates did seem to follow federal deficits as a percentage of GNP throughout the last decade.

Gross National Product and Its Components

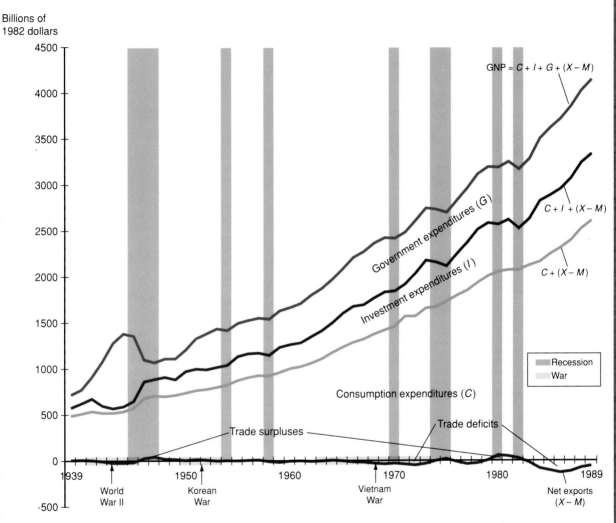

Billions of 1982 dollars

GNP = $C + I + G + (X - M)$

Government expenditures (G)

$C + I + (X - M)$

Investment expenditures (I)

$C + (X - M)$

Consumption expenditures (C)

Trade surpluses

Trade deficits

Recession
War

1939   1950   1960   1970   1980   1989

World War II   Korean War   Vietnam War   Net exports $(X - M)$

Source: Council of Economic Advisers, *Economic Report of the President* (Washington, D.C.: U.S. Government Printing Office, 1990), Table C-2.

Gross national product (GNP) is the dollar value of all final goods and services produced in an economy in one year. GNP is made up of four components: consumption expenditures, investment expenditures, government expenditures, and net exports (exports minus imports). Consumption expenditures are by far the largest component of GNP in the United States, accounting for 64.4 percent in 1989. In that same year, government expenditures accounted for 19.5 percent, investment expenditures for 17.4 percent, and net exports for −1.3 percent.

Here, we track GNP in the United States over a fifty-year period, 1939–1989. The top line represents the level of GNP in 1982 dollars over the period. The graph also breaks down GNP into its component parts. As you can see, GNP has increased dramatically since 1939, though not without interruption. Declines in GNP, called *recessions,* occurred—at least one per decade—in four of the five decades shown.

The Emergence of the European Community

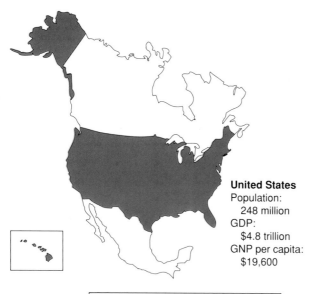

United States
Population:
248 million
GDP:
$4.8 trillion
GNP per capita:
$19,600

European Community
Iceland
United Kingdom
Denmark
Netherlands
Belgium
Germany
France
Luxembourg
Portugal
Spain
Greece
Italy

European Community
Population: 325 million
GDP: $4.5 trillion
GNP per capita: $13,770

U.S. Exports to the European Community	
Machinery and Transport	49.1%
Manufactured Goods	6.2%
Chemicals	11.3%
Mineral Fuels	3.2%
Crude Material	8.8%
Beverages and Tobacco	2.1%
Food and Live Animals	5.2%
Others	14.1%

Source: U.S. Department of Commerce, International Trade Administration, *Industrial Outlook,* p. 31.

The European Community, comprised of Belgium, Denmark, France, Germany, Greece, Iceland, Italy, Luxembourg, the Netherlands, Portugal, Spain, and the United Kingdom, is a coalition of nations working toward full economic and monetary union by 1993. The European Community treaty will remove all remaining trade barriers and restrictions on mobility of labor and capital between member nations, creating the largest market in the world. National borders will be no greater a barrier to trade than state borders are in the United States. Plans also call for the designation of a single currency, the European Currency Unit (ECU), within the twelve-nation bloc and the establishment of a central bank, a "EuroFed," to administer monetary policy. The latter goal may materialize first; the European central bank is scheduled to begin operating January 1, 1993, but the United Kingdom has proposed retaining the various national currencies for a time, believing that competition with these currencies will make the ECU stronger.

What effects will the creation of this unified market have on the U.S. economy? American exporters are understandably anxious about the potential for enormous changes in international trade patterns in the coming years. Such a dramatic reorganization of the world market likely will alter at least the composition of U.S. exports. The EC treaty represents a threat to domestic producers because free trade among EC nations will open new markets for member nations. Should the EC collectively pursue protectionist policies, U.S. exporters could find themselves shut out of previously dependable markets. However, the treaty also represents potential opportunities. Given access to the new market, U.S. exporters would benefit from following a coordinated set of trade regulations, and demand for U.S. goods (for *all* goods) is likely to rise in the wake of the community's expected spurt in economic growth.

The most important question, of course, is whether voters can be systematically fooled. If individuals are in fact shortsighted, then the political business cycle hypothesis would seem to be plausible. Under the rational expectations thesis, however, no such policy cycles can be manufactured because voters will foresee the consequences of reelection macroeconomic manipulation. Individuals would quickly revise upward their expectations about inflation when confronted with a higher rate of monetary expansion, thus deflating the political gain the incumbent had hoped for.

A number of attempts have been made to test various aspects of the political business cycle theory. Most of the direct tests consist of searches for patterns in unemployment rates or other macroeconomic variables during the periods surrounding congressional or presidential elections. The studies concerning the existence of a political business cycle have so far been inconclusive. This is not really surprising given the relatively few opportunities for observation and the ambiguous effects of election years in which different parties control the White House and Congress. Nonetheless, there is evidence on both sides of this issue, and the idea continues to intrigue economists. In this regard, Economics in Action, "Can Economics Help You Predict the Next Presidential Election?" at the end of this chapter offers a unique perspective on the Federal Reserve's possible involvement in the political business cycle.

The Austrian Theory of the Political Business Cycle

Economists who work in the tradition of the Austrian economic theorists of the late 1800s (Menger, Von Weiser, Böhm-Bawerk) are referred to as the neo-Austrian school of economics. These modern Austrians or neo-Austrians include Friedrich A. von Hayek, who won the Nobel Prize in economics in 1972.[7]

Following the lead of Hayek, the modern Austrians have presented a special theory of the political business cycle. The **neo-Austrian political business cycle** theory stresses two basic points. First, the inspiration for a political business cycle is microeconomic, not macroeconomic. Politicians do not manipulate aggregate economic variables such as the unemployment rate; rather, they seek to influence specific markets and industries, a process that in turn has aggregate economic consequences. To take just one small example, a subsidy to the domestic steel industry benefits steelworkers directly by providing jobs. It also represents a large expenditure on the part of government. If such legislation is carried out for many industries or for many separate economic groups, the government will incur huge costs, leading to a large deficit and subsequent macroeconomic problems.

The second neo-Austrian point is that real economic distortions and reductions in income result from politically inspired monetary expansions and contractions. In essence, the Austrians argue that politically inspired expansions and contractions in the money supply upset production plans by changing the nominal rate of interest. The process works in the following way: An unexpected and politically motivated expansion in the money supply creates

Neo-Austrian political business cycle:
A business cycle that results from political action to influence specific markets and industries rather than broad macroeconomic variables; microeconomic manipulation distorts industry-specific investment decisions and leads to a business cycle.

---

[7]Friedrich A. von Hayek, *Monetary Theory and the Trade Cycle* (New York: Harcourt Brace, 1932).

an artificially low rate of interest. In the division of labor between production for present and future consumption, the interest rate, which reflects the forces of real saving and investment, is the price that coordinates production plans efficiently. A low interest rate leads to an overinvestment in capital goods in the economy. In effect, the lower interest rate misleads investors; it provides them with a signal that is not compatible with the real plans of consumers and savers in the economy. The overinvestment in capital goods leads to huge losses on the part of investors and then to an economy-wide reduction in income and employment, or to what we normally call a recession. The recession will not end until the plans of producers of capital goods and producers of consumer goods are coordinated again—that is, until they plan according to the same relative price and interest rate data. The cycle bottoms out when the excess capital equipment caused by the overinvestment is depreciated and the accompanying economic losses cease.

The essential problem that the Austrian theory of the business cycle addresses is the distortion in relative prices and the loss of economic efficiency that results from a political manipulation of the money supply. The aggregate economic effects of this manipulation, such as inflation, are merely incidental to its impact on relative prices.

Moreover, the Austrian theory of the political business cycle focuses on groups of voters, not on voters in the aggregate. The question is not whether voters in general will respond positively or negatively to the inflation rate; it is how certain groups in the electorate will react to specific changes in public policies.

It is safe to say that there is no single theory of the business cycle. None of the hypotheses we have reviewed in this chapter provides a completely satisfactory explanation for the recurrent fluctuations in the general level of economic activity. At most, economists have developed a rich statistical and factual knowledge of business cycles. It remains to find a generally acceptable theory to explain these facts.

The Role of Government in Regulating the Business Cycle

In this chapter we have pointed out many of the costs associated with business cycles and discussed alternative theories about the cause of business cycles. One topic of ongoing debate among economists is the proper role of government in moderating business cycles. Essentially, there are two schools of thought. One group of economists advocates an active interventionist role by the government. Activists consider stabilization to be the primary economic role of government. Furthermore, they feel that economic policy should be modified frequently to take account of the latest changes in economic conditions. They advocate continuous fine-tuning of taxes, government spending, and interest rates to offset destabilizing changes that arise in the private sector. These activists feel that only the proper use of discretionary economic policy will assure a reasonably stable economy.

In contrast, many other economists feel that frequently changed government policy ends up having a destabilizing impact on the economy. Nonactivists advocate steady and predictable long-term policies by the government. For example, they would prefer that the central bank pursue a policy of steady monetary growth instead of making constant adjustments. Although there are several differences between the two groups, one essential difference is the confidence the groups place in economic forecasts.

Earlier in the chapter we discussed leading economic indicators. We saw that economic forecasters have had mixed success using these measures to predict upturns and downturns in the economy. Those who believe that future changes in the economy can be accurately predicted tend to advocate a more activist role for the government. They feel that it is irresponsible for the government to sit idly by when economic difficulties are apparent. In contrast, economists who are skeptical about the ability to make accurate forecasts tend to be less inclined to advocate government intervention. The fear is that forecasting errors will compromise any activist policy, as likely leading to destabilization as to stabilization.

SUMMARY

1. A business cycle is a recurrent but not predictable fluctuation in GNP. No two business cycles are exactly alike.

2. The four phases of a business cycle are expansion, peak, recession, and trough. The length of a cycle can be measured from peak to peak or from trough to trough. The intensity of an upturn or downturn in business activity is measured by the degree to which a peak or trough deviates from the long-run growth path of real GNP in the economy.

3. Economic forecasters try to predict economic upturns and downturns. Economic indicators are an integral part of the forecaster's tools. Leading economic indicators, economic variables that tend to turn up or down before a general business upturn or downturn, are key statistics for forecasters.

4. Investment theories of the business cycle stress the instability of private investment spending as a primary cause of economic fluctuations.

5. Other investment theories of the business cycle are the creative destruction theory of Joseph Schumpeter and those relating to business expectations. The expectations of businesspeople are also emphasized as an important determinant of investment spending in Keynesian theories of the business cycle.

6. The monetary theory of the business cycle sees the uneven and unpredictable management of the money supply by the Federal Reserve Board as the basic cause of economic fluctuations. Concern over Federal Reserve behavior has led some monetarists, such as Milton Friedman, to propose that discretionary authority over the money supply of the Federal Reserve be replaced with a rule to govern the growth of the money supply.

7. Some economists have identified the possibility that business cycles are politically inspired. Given short-sighted voters, incumbent politicians win reelection by inflating the economy prior to an election, driving down unemployment, and then allowing unemployment to rise and inflation to recede after the election. Each four years, the cycle is repeated, and so we say that there is a political business cycle. The evidence for this type of manipulation of the economy by politicians is inconclusive.

8. The modern Austrian theory of the political business cycle is that politicians intervene in specific markets and industries to affect specific groups of voters. Relative prices and interest rates in the economy are thus distorted, leading to an overinvestment in capital goods industries. This overinvestment must subsequently be wrenched out of the economy. These cyclical effects are caused by political manipulation of the money supply.

9. Economics has developed a rich factual understanding of business cycles, but no single plausible theory of the cycle has yet emerged.

KEY TERMS

business cycle	econometrics	short-run Phillips curve	political business cycle
recession	economic indicators	long-run Phillips curve	neo-Austrian political business cycle
depression	Phillips curve	creative destruction theory	

QUESTIONS FOR REVIEW AND DISCUSSION

1. Why do we say that business cycles are recurrent but not predictable?
2. To which theory of the business cycle would you attribute cycles caused by the following events?
   a. The Federal Reserve Board increases the money supply dramatically.
   b. Sales in the garment industry fall.
   c. The French suddenly change governments and close their doors to American goods.
   d. Major new oil reserves are discovered in Alaska.
3. An increase in the unemployment rate can be caused either by an increase in the number of persons who become unemployed during a year or by an increase in the average duration of unemployment. Which of

these two factors do you think best explains rising unemployment rates during recessions?
4. How can the Federal Reserve Board cause a business cycle?
5. In a modern economy, information about the motives and activities of politicians is relatively easy to obtain, much easier than it was years ago. Does the availability of information mean that a political business cycle is presently more or less likely than in the past?
6. Do changes in leading economic indicators actually cause the changes in GNP?
7. What would macroeconomic policy-makers need to know in order to eliminate the business cycle?

ECONOMICS IN ACTION
Can Economics Help You Predict the Next Presidential Election?

Political pollsters, TV commentators, special-interest groups, and especially political candidates would like to know what it takes to win a presidential election. Many believe that presidential elections are won through political organization, TV advertising, good luck, and charisma. Others are more likely to view economic variables such as personal income and inflation as critical variables. Some have tried to determine which economic variables are the most reliable indicators of success or failure for an incumbent candidate.

Ray Fair concluded that both the inflation rate and growth in real GNP are concerns to voters in presidential elections.[a] It is the *change* in these variables prior to the presidential election that matters, not their level. Incumbents who can boast of strong growth rates in GNP and low inflation rates usually remain in office; those who cannot, are voted out.

However, another predictor of election outcomes may be the Federal Reserve's handling of the money supply, M-1,

before the election. Although the Federal Reserve was designed as a semi-autonomous branch of government, some economists and political observers believe that the Federal Reserve behaves politically to protect its own interests and those of the party in power. David Meiselman has presented evidence that monetary expansions and contractions are possibly politically inspired. Figure 8 shows the rate of growth in M-1 prior to the last eight presidential elections. The vertical axis in each graph shows the six-month rate of change in M-1. The rates shown are annual percentages.

In four of the eight cases, money supply growth rapidly accelerated for six to twelve months prior to the election and contracted soon after.[b] In 1960, when Vice-President Richard Nixon lost to John Kennedy, and in 1976, when incumbent Gerald Ford lost to Jimmy Carter, money supply growth did not accelerate very rapidly in the year before the election. Interestingly enough, in the year prior to Ronald Reagan's landslide victory over Walter Mondale, money growth declined significantly. The rate declined six months prior to George Bush's election in 1988 and fell dramatically after the election. These elections emphasize the critics' contention that money growth prior to an election is not the only factor influencing election results.

Tracking economic variables such as the growth rate in per capita GNP and the rate of M-1 growth may not always

[a]See Ray C. Fair, "On Controlling the Economy to Win Elections," Cowles Foundation Discussion Paper No. 397, 1975; and "The Effect of Economic Events on Votes for President," *Review of Economics and Statistics* 60 (May 1978), pp. 159–73. For an excellent survey of the evidence, see Friedrich Schneider and Bruno S. Frey, "Politico-Economic Models of Macroeconomic Policy: A Review of the Empirical Evidence," in Thomas D. Willett, ed., *Political Business Cycles* (Durham, N.C.: Duke University Press, 1988), pp. 239–75.

[b]David I. Meiselman, "The Political Monetary Cycle," *Wall Street Journal* (January 10, 1984), p. 32.

FIGURE 8

These graphs show the relation of the growth rate of the money supply, M-1, to presidential elections between 1960 and 1988. Notice that in most cases, the money supply increased sharply before the election. This finding suggests that there may be a link between monetary policy and elections.

Sources: David I. Meiselman, "The Political Monetary Cycle," *Wall Street Journal* (January 10, 1984), p. 32; and *Federal Reserve Bulletin,* various issues.

Money Supply and Presidential Elections

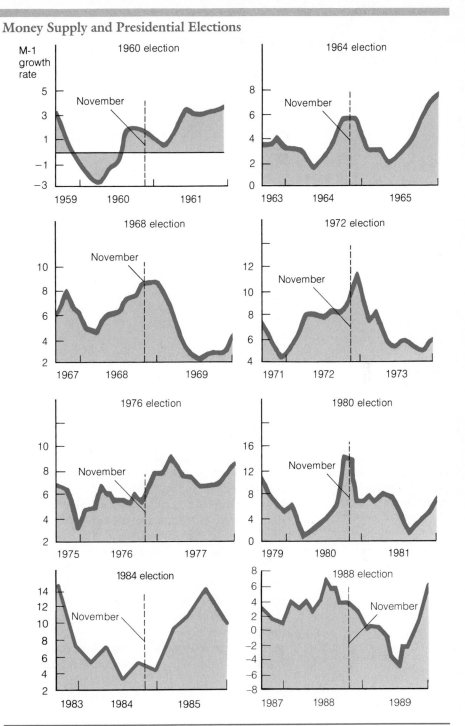

allow for accurate predictions of presidential election outcomes. However, such an analysis does provide interesting evidence of how closely our economic health is related to the four-year cycle of presidential elections.

Question

How might the unemployment rate be a predictor of election outcomes? Would it likely be more important in congressional contests or in presidential elections?

37

Economic Growth and Productivity

A full-employment economy without inflation is the major goal of macroeconomic policy. But achievement of this goal does not necessarily mean that an economy is growing over the long run. Full employment and price stability surely affect long-run economic growth prospects, but factors such as population, natural resources, capital growth, and improvements in technology also determine the economy's future.

Standard of living:
The real value of the quantity of goods and services consumed by the average member of the economy.

Long-run growth has been the key to the United States' prosperity. The **standard of living,** usually defined as the quantity of real goods and services that the average citizen is able to consume per year, has risen by an average of 2 to 3 percent per year for more than 150 years in America. Other nations have not experienced such good fortune. Many developing nations in Asia, Africa, and Latin America, for example, are stymied in their growth prospects because of a lack of productive labor or capital equipment or because population is growing as fast as or faster than output of real goods and services.

Unfortunately, there is some evidence of a slowdown in long-run growth rates in the United States. Is this slowdown temporary or is it a permanent state of affairs owing to the fixed or dwindling supplies of some of our natural resources? Will future generations of Americans suffer the effects of a shrinking economy, or are there economic policies that might ensure steady prosperity? This chapter attempts to provide insight into such questions. After reading Chapter 37 you should understand

- how economic growth is defined and some of the factors that lead to growth.
- the insights of the classical economists into the growth process.
- how aggregate demand and labor productivity are key elements in explaining economic growth.
- some of the features of U.S. economic growth, past and present.

THE MEANING OF ECONOMIC GROWTH

Economic growth:
Increases in real GNP or real per capita GNP over time.

Economic growth actually has two definitions. It may simply refer to increases in real GNP, the value of the annual output of final goods and services in the economy adjusted for inflation. While this measure certainly tells us whether overall economic performance has improved, it does not tell us much about whether the average citizen is better or worse off than at some previous time.

Real per capita GNP:
Real GNP divided by the population size; real output per person in the economy.

An increase in **real per capita GNP** is a more accurate measure of economic growth. If real GNP increases by 4 percent over some period and population increases by 2 percent, real economic growth per capita has taken place. By contrast, a population increase of 6 percent with 4 percent growth in real output means that the average citizen is worse off, that economic decline has occurred in per capita terms.

Both measures are useful for understanding growth processes. For example, a statement that Mexico's real GNP grew at a rate of 3 percent last year tells us that some of the prerequisites for growth exist in Mexico. Likewise, to say that per capita GNP grew at only 1½ percent last year indicates that Mexico may be having population problems, since per capita income growth depends on population growth. Both measures, however, are merely statistical concepts; economists generally recognize that neither measure, no matter how useful for comparison purposes, can tell us definitively about the quality of life or the distribution of wealth in a society.

The Causes of Growth

The causes of economic growth are complex. We have already pinpointed some of the important short-run requirements of economic growth: Adequate employment of productive resources, price stability, efficient allocation of resources, and other such conditions generally ensure a rising standard of living.

To sustain long-run growth in real GNP, however, an economy must enjoy steady growth in population, natural resources, productivity of labor and resources, capital formation, human capital, and technological improvement, encouraged by a free-market environment and free-trade policies.

Population. Population may be detrimental to growth in real per capita GNP in many modern nations, but under certain conditions, an expanding population may be essential to growth. During the industrialization of the United States in the nineteenth century, rapid population growth, much of it achieved by immigration, fueled a phenomenal economic growth rate. On the supply side, growth in population and labor supply led to increased efficiency in production through higher productivity in the use of machinery and natural resources. Mass production such as assembly-line techniques greatly improved the productivity of labor through increased specialization. On the demand side, higher population led to increased demand for all goods and services, making possible mass production and greater consumption. Population growth is therefore an ingredient in growth, but increases in population by themselves are insufficient for sustained economic growth. As we will see later in this chapter, rampant or unrestrained population increases may retard, halt, or even reverse any progress in per capita GNP.

Natural Resources. Every society is endowed with some quantity of land and natural resources such as fresh water, forests, and minerals. The United States, the Soviet Union, and many developing countries have large quantities of both. Possession of land and natural resources may make growth easier, but it will not guarantee growth; nor will lack of natural resources prevent growth. Japan has a small quantity of land and natural resources, yet Japan's post–World War II growth rate has been greater than that of most other countries.

By themselves, natural resources are valueless. They must be developed by labor and capital. Improvements in technology, moreover, may make resources more productive—as in fertilizing land—or even contribute to the development and invention of new resources. Aluminum, for example, is an invented alloy. It is a common misconception that the quantity of certain natural resources is absolutely fixed in supply. For example, as technology develops, it becomes possible to tap oil reserves at previously unreachable depths. New technology also may create opportunities to profitably extract oil from shale. Should the supply of oil ever begin to run short, new technology would likely bring alternative fuel sources to the market. Technological change continuously alters the relative scarcity of natural resources.

Productivity of labor:
Output per worker over any given period of time.

Productivity of Labor. Economic growth is very closely tied to the **productivity of labor**—how much output per hour, week, and so on, results from labor input. Labor's productivity depends on a number of factors, including the quantity (population size) and quality (degree of education and skill) of the labor supply, the stock of capital and other resources each laborer has to work with, and the technology available for production. Educational development and on-the-job training of laborers—growth in human capital—is a rather obvious requirement for productivity increases, but productivity increases are also closely linked to capital formation and technology.

Capital Formation and Infrastructure. A fourth ingredient of economic growth is growth in the size and quality of the capital stock—productive assets like buildings, machinery, and equipment used in production and the infrastructure, the roads, bridges, and communications systems used in moving goods and disseminating information. (For a discussion of the importance of infrastructure as a determinant of economic growth, see Economics in Action, "Infrastructure and Economic Growth," at the end of this chapter.) Labor productivity—output per worker—is enhanced when the stock of capital available grows faster than the labor supply. When capital is growing faster than the labor supply, capital is said to be deepening. **Capital deepening** has occurred throughout most of the economic history of the United States. In contrast, many countries experience rapid population growth and little capital accumulation, which causes labor productivity to fall and adversely affects the growth potential of these countries.

Capital deepening:
Increases in the total stock of capital in conjunction with increases in the ratio of the capital stock to the labor force; occurs when the capital stock grows at a faster rate than the labor force.

Increases in capital stock are costly, however. Resources, including time, must be sacrificed to produce capital goods that are not directly consumable, so capital growth requires saving or abstention from current consumption. For new investments in machinery, buildings, and equipment to grow, society's ability to save must grow. The reward for saving is greater future growth in either consumable goods or in more capital stock. In the latter sense, economic growth is cumulative: It feeds on itself by using capital to produce more capital.

Improvements in Technology. Technological growth and invention—improvements in the methods by which goods and services are produced and sold—is another key to economic growth. The Industrial Revolution of the eighteenth and nineteenth centuries in Europe and the United States ushered in the age of mechanization, increasing the productivity of labor and natural resources. The result has been the highest standards of living for the greatest numbers of people in the recorded history of humanity. Such living standards would be unthinkable without the invention of items such as the steam engine, the spinning jenny, assembly-line production, and indoor plumbing. Who could have imagined twenty or thirty years ago, for example, that a high-speed digital computer no larger than a breadbox would be within the reach of the average American to calculate income taxes, store recipes, or play games on? Technology and invention have been responsible for nothing less than the modern world.

The Market Environment. Most Western economists believe that the market environment surrounding the growth in, among other things, natural resources, labor productivity, and capital formation is a large contributing factor to economic growth. A competitive market system, many believe, encourages invention and rapid innovation. Those holding this view generally argue that free-trade policies also enhance a country's ability to grow economically; such policies enable the country to specialize in the production of the goods and services at which it is most efficient. However, Japan's experience shows that growth can also occur in a restrictive environment; despite the Japanese government's elaborate system of barriers to internal and external trade, the country has achieved a remarkable record of economic growth since 1950.

The Production Possibilities Frontier Revisited

All the fundamental elements of long-run economic growth may be summarized in terms of a production possibilities frontier. A production possibilities frontier, introduced in Chapter 2, shows the choices available to society in producing two goods given a fixed quantity of resources—labor, capital, and natural resources—and assuming a given state of technology. If society is positioned on the production frontier, it is fully employing and efficiently allocating all resources and utilizing technology to its best advantage. However, most societies, even highly efficient ones, are at times positioned inside the frontier because of unemployment or underemployment of resources. Societies cannot advance beyond the frontier because of absolute limits at any given time in the quantity and quality of resources.

Figure 1 shows production possibilities frontiers for two economic societies—country X and country Y, respectively—both of which must choose production levels for consumption goods and capital goods. Each country is assumed to possess a similar resource base and the same technology. Country X's initial choice between capital goods and consumer goods is labeled A in Figure 1a; country Y's choice in Figure 1b is labeled B. Country X has devoted a higher proportion of its resources to capital goods production in year 1 than has country Y. The net result—and the key to understanding the principles underlying economic growth—is that country X's choice results in a higher production possibilities frontier in some future year, say year 2. In year 2, societies X and Y will again choose some capital–consumer goods combina-

FIGURE 1

Economic Growth and the Production Possibilities Frontier

Growth is assumed to result from increases in the stock of capital goods. (a) If an economy forgoes a relatively large amount of consumption goods to obtain more capital goods, then the production possibilities frontier will shift outward by a larger amount than the economy that does not make the sacrifice. (b) Country Y's preference for consumer goods in year 1 results in significantly less growth by year 2.

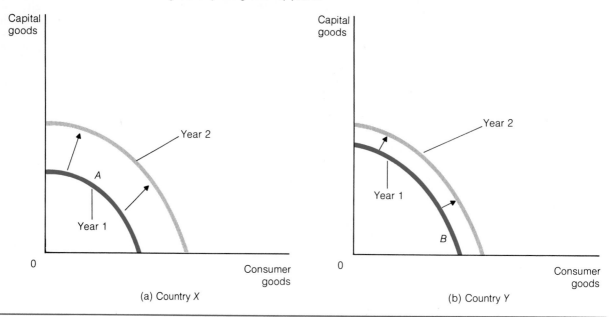

(a) Country X

(b) Country Y

tion on a new frontier, but if both countries remain fully employed, country X's economy will have grown to a higher level of output and presumably to a higher level of real GNP per capita.

Economic growth, in other words, is determined by society's choice of future goods over present goods. This fact does not mean that the capital stock is the only element in growth. Capital combines with labor and natural resources to increase society's growth possibilities, even with a constant state of technology.

Different forms of resource growth would have similar effects on the production possibilities frontier. Consider Figure 2, which shows an economy based on two products—computer hardware and food. An equal growth rate in all resources, or in all nonspecialized resources, would shift the curve uniformly out, as in Figure 2a, whereas faster growth rates in resources specialized in computer hardware or in food production would enhance the production possibilities of either computers or food, as in Figure 2b.

The Law of Diminishing Marginal Returns

As always, the law of diminishing marginal returns (or of increasing marginal cost) applies. The law states that as more and more units of any variable resource are combined with some fixed amount of another resource or resources, successive applications of the variable input will increase total output by smaller amounts. Consider the farmer who has planted a field of corn. If

FIGURE 2   **Technological Change and the Production Possibilities Frontier**

The hypothetical economy is based on just two products—computer hardware and food. An improvement in technology shifts the production possibilities frontier to the right. (a) A change in technology that affects both products equally causes an increase in output of both products. (b) A change that affects either one product or the other but not both equally increases the output of one but not the other.

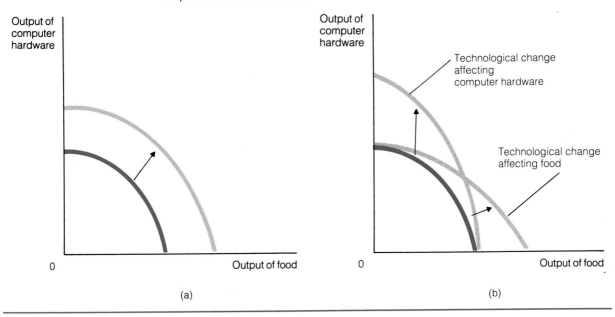

(a)   (b)

the farmer could spend only one day during the growing season tending the field, his efforts during that day would be devoted to the activities that yield the greatest return. It is likely that production in the field with one day's labor would exceed production in an untended field by a substantial amount. Should the farmer apply an additional day tending his field, output would again rise, but by a smaller amount; the activities available to the farmer on the second day would be less imperative than those of the first day. Similarly, additional days of labor would raise production by successively smaller amounts. The law of diminishing marginal returns explains the shape of short-run production and cost curves to any firm producing any sort of goods or services. The law also explains some macroeconomic aspects of growth.

As we know from experience, resources, talents, and training are not all alike and are not perfectly adaptable to alternative uses. Given any state of technology and level of knowledge, one good cannot be transformed with equal facility into another good. As we learned in Chapter 2, orange groves cannot be converted into peanut farms at constant opportunity costs. The same applies to any two goods or classes of goods: The most adaptable resources are transformed first. As less adaptable resources are transformed, total additions to output get smaller and smaller. This fact explains the concave shape of the typical production possibilities curve.

The law of diminishing marginal returns also applies to growth in the following way: In the event that any factor affecting growth is fixed or grows at slower rates than the others, output possibilities will increase, but at slower rates. Successive incremental applications of expanding resources to fixed production factors will result in smaller and smaller additions to output. If labor supply is fixed, for example, progressive increases in all other resources, excluding technology, will increase output potential, but at slower and slower rates. Technological change may enhance possible increases in output by "economizing" on the necessity to use labor. The gain would only be temporary, however. Given any state of technology, the point of diminishing marginal returns will be reached in time.

Comparative Growth Rates

Countries' economies are growing at different rates, for various reasons. Diminishing marginal returns when one or more resources is fixed or growing slowly is a major feature of theories featuring limits to growth. For instance, bottlenecks may be predicted when all arable land and freshwater resources in a country are already being used intensively for food production. Regardless of whether there are absolute or relative limits to long-run economic growth, it is clear that growth is an extremely complex matter. Further, it is clearly the case that even small differences in growth rates matter a great deal over time.

Table 1 presents actual average growth rates in real GNP between 1984 and 1989 in seven industrialized nations. The growth rates vary from 4.58 percent in Japan to 1.93 percent in the Soviet Union. These growth rates are then applied to a hypothetical $500 billion GNP in each of the countries in 1990 to project real GNP in each of the countries in future years. With these differences in growth rates, the Japanese GNP will grow to a level almost twice that of the Soviet Union by 2010. Relatively small differences in the growth rate will produce huge differences in real income in the not-too-distant future.

A warning about the determinants of growth in different nations: Many cultural and institutional factors heavily influence actual growth rates. Significantly different growth rates even in highly developed nations may ultimately be explained only in terms of a particular society's cultural, government, and institutional structures, areas where the economist may not be able to analyze key differences. Why, for example, has the Japanese economy grown recently at a faster rate than that of most other industrialized nations of the world?

Economists are accustomed to focusing on measurable factors such as the saving rate or the level of net investment—hard data. Trying to get at the reasons for Japan's success puts economists on less familiar ground; contributing factors mentioned include the rigorous Japanese work ethic and the practice of providing employees with what amounts to guaranteed life employment. While workers in other cultures might be inclined to exploit job security by shirking and reducing productivity, company loyalty and peer pressure seem to be a powerful motivating force in the Japanese workplace—especially compared with the United States. The tremendous loyalty that workers in Japan display to their employers is one factor that has enabled the Japanese to reach such high quality standards in the production of many goods. Attempts to apply Japanese techniques to production in the United States have been made, but economists have no special insight into how to successfully transplant these techniques to an alien culture—or even into whether such a transplant is possible.

TABLE 1   Cumulative Effects of GNP Growth

Different growth rates applied to the same hypothetical GNP in 1990 will produce dramatic changes in real GNP in the future. GNP will double in twenty years with an approximate growth rate of 3.5 percent per year.

Country	Actual Growth Rate of Real GNP, 1984–1989 (annual percent change)	Hypothetical Real GNP, 1990 (billions of dollars)	Projected Real GNP, 1995 (billions of dollars)	Projected Real GNP, 2000 (billions of dollars)	Projected Real GNP, 2005 (billions of dollars)	Projected Real GNP, 2010 (billions of dollars)
United States	4.00	500	610	740	900	1095
Canada	4.43	500	620	770	960	1190
Japan	4.58	500	625	780	980	1225
France	2.37	500	560	630	710	800
Italy	3.05	500	580	675	785	910
United Kingdom	3.42	500	590	700	830	980
Soviet Union	1.93	500	550	605	665	735

Source: Council of Economic Advisers, *Economic Report of the President* (Washington, D.C.: U.S. Government Printing Office, 1990), p. 419.

To understand the economic development of any nation, we must look to cultural and institutional factors, as well as the quantifiable features of growth.

THE CLASSICAL DYNAMICS OF GROWTH

More than any other economists before or since, the classical writers of the period 1776–1848 were interested in why economies grow, stagnate, or decline. Of the classical writers, David Ricardo (1772–1823) and Thomas Robert Malthus (1766–1834) were notable for their predictions about growth. Both Ricardo and Malthus predicted that society would reach some stationary state because of diminishing marginal returns in agriculture and severe population pressures.

Diminishing Marginal Returns and the Malthusian Population Principle

Malthus and Ricardo wrote about a hypothetical, purely agrarian economy with fixed quantities of land and natural resources and only one output, food. They also assumed that technology was fixed. They reasoned that as more and more capital and labor were applied to land of any given quality, marginal output of food would decline, for two reasons: (1) diminishing marginal returns—as more capital and labor were applied to any given quantity of land, marginal output would decline; and (2) scarcity of fertile land—as capital and labor were applied to agriculture, lower and lower grades of land would be used, yielding smaller quantities of food per acre.

At the same time that the marginal productivity of land was falling, society's demand for more and more food to feed a growing population would

Malthusian population principle:
The notion that the population has the capability to grow geometrically while the food supply can only grow arithmetically; leads to the concept of the subsistence wage.

Subsistence wage:
A real wage rate that is only high enough to allow for a zero rate of population growth.

be rising. The **Malthusian population principle,** developed by Malthus in 1798 in his book *On Population,* states that population tends to increase geometrically over successive generations (1, 2, 4, 8, 16, 32, . . .), while the food supply is capable of increasing only at an arithmetic rate through the generations (2, 4, 6, 8, 10, 12, . . .).

Related to the population principle is another Malthusian idea—that real wages are always tending toward the subsistence level. A **subsistence wage** was defined by classical economists as a wage sufficient for a husband and wife to reproduce themselves—to bring two children to adulthood. A wage above the subsistence level would lead to larger families. This would shift the labor supply to the right and eventually depress wages to the subsistence level.

The population–subsistence wage mechanism is presented in simple terms in Figure 3, which shows labor supply and demand curves and an initial equilibrium at E_0. We assume that the population, as well as the input of labor, is at level N_0 and receives a subsistence wage W_S. If the demand for labor increases from D_1 to D_2, a new equilibrium is established along the labor supply curve S_1 at E_1, and a new wage rate W_0 is established that is higher than subsistence. This shift occurs slowly—it may take a generation or more to reach the higher wage rate. If, as Malthus assumed, individuals react to a higher-than-subsistence wage rate by increasing family size and population to N_1, the supply curve of labor will shift rightward, bringing society back to the subsistence wage. If the increased economic well-being of workers ($W_0 - W_S$) is squandered in increased population, there is little hope for the progress of society. According the Malthus's theory, the subsistence wage will always

---

FIGURE 3

Malthus's analysis starts from equilibrium E_0, where the quantity of labor N_0 calls for the subsistence wage W_S. An increase in the demand for labor increases the wage to W_0, a level above the subsistence wage, and equilibrium is established at E_1. This surplus for workers, however, is eventually squandered through increased population. As the population increases from N_0 to N_1, the labor supply increases, and in the long run the wage returns to the subsistence level, at E_2.

The Classical Population–Subsistence Wage Mechanism

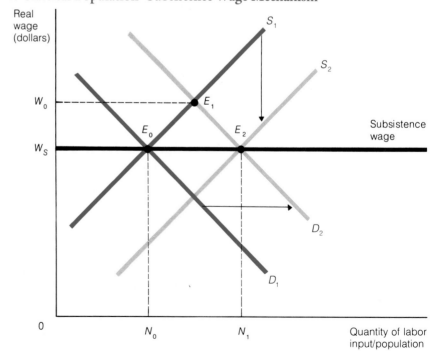

tend to prevail over the long run. If unrestrained, population will grow from N_0 to N_1, returning the per capita income of workers to subsistence.

Malthus also considered a worse possibility. If population and labor supply overreacted to the high wage rate W_0 and increased beyond S_2, wages would temporarily fall below the subsistence wage. Starvation would result for some, and Malthus predicted all sorts of dire consequences, including famine, plague, wars, and urban crowding. In Malthus's view, abstinence was the only "moral" way in which population could be restrained.

Deficiencies in Classical Growth Theory

While this classical theory is a marvelous simplification of the growth process, it suffers from several oversimplifications. The first is the Malthusian population theory. Does the population mechanism operate as Malthus described it? Do individuals squander increases in real income by increasing population growth rates? Evidence since the days of Malthus does not give a great deal of support to his idea, especially in industrialized countries. Massive growth in real GNP per capita has been made possible largely because increases in real income did not create an urge to procreate. Growth rates in the U.S. population have remained at relatively low levels since 1940 and, as indicated in Table 2, have actually declined since the early 1960s. Some developing nations have had population problems, however. Indeed, Malthus's model may be more applicable to countries with rapidly expanding populations, such as India or Ethiopia.

TABLE 2

Population Growth in the United States, 1961–1990

The U.S. growth rate has shown a dramatic decline since the 1950s baby boom, when population growth averaged between 1.7 and 1.8 percent per year.

Year	Population (millions)	Percent Change	Year	Population (millions)	Percent Change
1961	183.7	1.7	1976	218.0	1.0
1962	186.6	1.5	1977	220.2	1.0
1963	189.2	1.4	1978	222.6	1.1
1964	191.9	1.4	1979	225.1	1.1
1965	194.3	1.3	1980	227.7	1.2
1966	196.6	1.2	1981	230.1	1.0
1967	198.7	1.1	1982	232.5	1.0
1968	200.7	1.0	1983	234.8	1.0
1969	202.7	1.0	1984	237.0	1.0
1970	205.1	1.2	1985	239.3	1.0
1971	207.7	1.3	1986	241.6	1.0
1972	209.9	1.1	1987	243.9	1.0
1973	211.9	1.0	1988	246.1	1.0
1974	213.9	0.9	1989	248.6	1.0
1975	216.0	1.0	1990	251.1	1.0

Source: U.S. Bureau of the Census, *Statistical Abstract of the United States,* 1989 (Washington, D.C.: U.S. Government Printing Office, 1989), p. 7.

Note: Years 1989 and 1990 are authors' estimates.

A second major deficiency in the classical theory of economic growth is the classical theorists' mistaken belief that technology, especially related to food production, was a relatively constant factor in growth. In the early nineteenth century, one farm worker could feed only three or four nonfarm workers. Today, one farm worker in the United States is able to feed more than eighty people. While it is true that agriculture today is more mechanized—farm workers have more capital with which to work—a portion of the increase in productivity can be explained by technological advances. For example, farmers planting disease-resistant hybrid seeds can expect dramatically larger yields than farmers of just a generation ago. The tremendous increase in technology and invention in the nineteenth and twentieth centuries has been the mainspring of real per capita GNP growth, and it has accrued on an unprecedented scale. The steam engine in transportation, highly sophisticated mass production processes, modern electronics, and a host of other technological breakthroughs have all helped forestall what Malthus perceived to be an inevitable decline in growth.

GROWTH AND MODERN MACROECONOMIC THEORY

Modern economic theory has much to say on the issue of growth. Foremost in current analysis is the importance of capital formation and improvements in technology. According to modern analysis, growth potential also depends on the ability of an economy to absorb growth.

The Demand Side of Growth

Growth absorption:
Increases in total spending sufficient to purchase additional output generated by increases in productive capacity.

Growth absorption means keeping up with the expanding productive capacity of the economy through increasing total expenditures. Recall that aggregate demand must always be sufficient to create full employment at any point in time. The same must hold true to create full employment and maximum economic growth over time.

Figure 4 shows total expenditures on the vertical axis and the output capacity of the economy over time on the horizontal axis. Along the 45-degree line, total expenditures equal the total output capacity of the economy. A central requirement for sustainable economic growth is that total expenditures, private and public, must keep the economy on or near this 45-degree line through time; otherwise, unemployment and slower growth will result. If output capacity is Y_0 in 1970, total expenditures must be at the level of TE_0 to achieve maximum income and income growth. A given level of net investment and capital formation in 1970 creates a larger output capacity in 1980, Y_1, which in turn requires a rise in total expenditures in 1980 to realize the growth potential of the 1980 economy.

Ensuring adequate aggregate demand for maximum growth is one of the goals of short-run macroeconomic theory. New Keynesians argue that the economy should be managed in discretionary countercyclical fashion to keep aggregate demand at full-employment levels. Monetarists and new classical economists argue that adequate growth in aggregate demand can be achieved only through stable rules for Congress and for the Federal Reserve System.

FIGURE 4

In this simple model, increases in total expenditures must keep up with expanding resources and population to bring about maximum economic growth. If the economy grows from an output capacity of Y_0 in 1970 to Y_1 in 1980, the aggregate demand curve must shift from TE_0 to TE_1 by 1980 to keep resources fully employed. Total output equals total expenditures along the 45-degree line.

Growth in Total Expenditures Required for Economic Growth

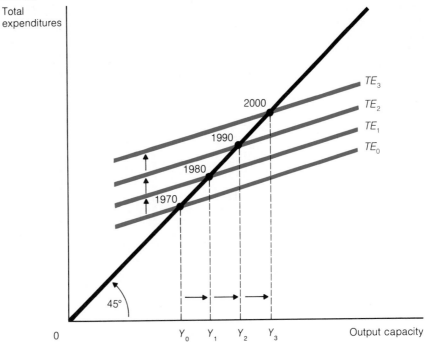

However one looks at the matter, policies to ensure adequate aggregate demand are essential in maintaining a sustained high rate of economic growth.

The Supply Side of Growth

The other facet of economic growth involves the factors that enhance or enlarge the productive capacities of the economy. All the factors—capital growth, technological improvements, growth in natural resources—discussed earlier in this chapter create growth in supply. We call these supply-side factors because they have the effect of shifting the aggregate supply curve of real output to the right.

In Figure 5, we assume that the economy's demand for goods and services will be sufficient to absorb the increased output of goods and services made possible by growth. The question we ask instead is, What factor or factors underlie rightward shifts in the aggregate supply curve? The long-run supply of goods and services is influenced by certain variables—capital accumulation, the productivity of labor, taxation, and so on. For purposes of discussion, however, there are two major economic factors to watch in predicting the growth rate in the productive capacities of any economy:

1. Growth in private saving and investment, which leads to capital formation; and
2. Growth in the numbers of laborers, in laborers' participation in the work force, and in labor's productivity.

FIGURE 5

Over time, the level of technology or the supply of resources may increase, shifting the long-run aggregate supply curve to the right and increasing full-employment income.

Economic Growth and Rightward Shifts in Long-Run Aggregate Supply

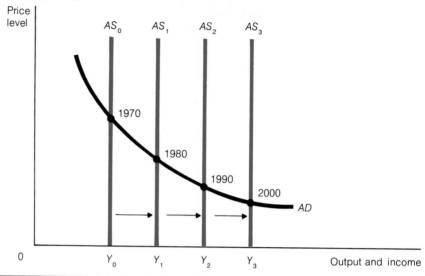

Any variable, policy, or institutional factor that affects these two factors will affect economic growth through its effect on the long-run aggregate supply curve. Consider some recent trends in the United States of these components of economic growth.

RECENT U.S. ECONOMIC GROWTH AND PRODUCTIVITY

The various growth rates in real GNP and per capita GNP in industrialized nations reported in Table 1 have numerous causes. Short-run economic stabilization—the ability of an economy to provide full employment of resources—will naturally affect long-run growth prospects. But the supply-side features of economic growth are of greatest importance in explaining U.S. growth trends.

Capital Formation

Capital formation:
The process whereby the stock of capital in an economy increases.

A useful measure of **capital formation** is net investment as a percent of GNP. This shows the proportion of total output being put into new plant and equipment—an indicator of future productivity. As Table 3 shows, net investment fell to $64 billion in 1982, barely 2 percent of GNP. Since then, the investment rate has risen sharply—to levels more in line with historical norms.

Saving

Personal savings are the primary source of new investment and capital formation in the United States. However, corporations also engage in saving, as do governments when they run government surpluses. In recent years, foreign

TABLE 3

Net Private Domestic Investment, 1970–1987

Net investment as a percentage of GNP remained fairly steady between 1970 and 1987, though there were dips in 1982 and 1983.

Year	Net Private Domestic Investment	Percentage of GNP
1970	60.0	5.91
1975	57.8	3.62
1980	133.1	4.87
1981	167.7	5.49
1982	64.1	2.02
1983	105.7	3.10
1984	249.4	6.61
1985	205.9	5.13
1986	210.0	4.95
1987	233.0	5.15

Source: U.S. Bureau of the Census, *Statistical Abstract of the United States,* 1989 (Washington, D.C.: U.S. Government Printing Office, 1989), pp. 421, 533.

capital has flowed into the United States, providing an additional source of savings. Figure 6 shows that while, historically, Americans have saved about 7 percent of their disposable income, the rate in the late 1970s and for most of the 1980s was lower—at times, significantly so.

The dip in personal savings coincided with an era of enormous government deficits. To finance these deficits, the government has been forced to

FIGURE 6

Personal Saving Rate in the 1980s

The personal saving rate moved up to 5.5 percent in 1989, rebounding from an average 1987 low of 3.2 percent of disposable income but still considerably lower than the 7.2 percent average for the period 1950–1979.

Source: Council of Economic Advisers, *Economic Report of the President* (Washington, D.C.: U.S. Government Printing Office, 1990), p. 41.

compete with private investors. Accumulated savings drained to finance government deficits greatly reduce the funds that are available for private capital formation.

Productivity

The declines in net investment and saving combined to reduce U.S. productivity in the early 1980s (see Table 4). After 1982, total output and output per hour rose dramatically; the 8.3 percent rate of output growth in 1984 was the highest since 1950. Since 1984, the growth rate has moderated somewhat, and while the rate remains much higher than it was in the late 1970s and early 1980s, productivity growth remains low compared with what it has been throughout most of U.S. history.

Small differences in productivity growth rates and in the rates of investment and capital formation that cause them may seem inconsequential. Over the long run, however, they are critical to growth. As the Council of Economic Advisers pointed out in 1983,

> The consequences of reduced productivity growth for our standard of living over the long run are greater than those of any other current economic problem. In 1981 the American economy produced approximately $12,780 worth of output per capita. Had productivity growth continued at the 1948–67 rate during the 14 years subsequent to 1967, output per capita would have reached $16,128 in 1981, 26 percent higher than the actual value.[1]

Small changes in growth rates in productivity, investment, and capital formation can have a major impact on economic growth. Increasing the annual productivity growth rate by only 2 percentage points, for example, would more than double the standard of living in terms of goods and services by the year 2020.

TABLE 4

Output and Productivity Growth Rates in Nonfarm Business Sector, 1980–1989

The output growth rate fluctuated throughout the 1980s, with growth in productivity (output per hour) lagging stubbornly behind.

	Growth Rates (percent)										1980–1989 (average)
	1980	1981	1982	1983	1984	1985	1986	1987	1988	1989	
Output per hour	−0.4	1.1	−0.9	3.0	2.1	1.3	2.0	1.1	2.0	0.8	1.2
Output	−1.2	1.7	−3.3	5.0	8.3	3.9	3.0	4.4	5.4	3.0	3.0

Source: Council of Economic Advisers, *Economic Report of the President* (Washington, D.C.: U.S. Government Printing Office, 1990).

Note: Figures for 1989 are averages of the first three quarters of 1989.

---

[1]Council of Economic Advisers, *Economic Report of the President* (Washington, D.C.: U.S. Government Printing Office, 1983), p. 83.

DENISON'S STUDIES

The somewhat disappointing picture of growth in the U.S. economy over the last fifteen years has many interrelated causes. Unfortunately, economists cannot pinpoint the exact causes of the slowdown. More important, once the causes of the slowdown in productivity are identified, are policies available to reverse the trend?

The slowdown in labor productivity has been attributed to, among other things, lower research and development expenditures; a transition to a high-technology economy; higher energy prices; swings in the business cycle; increased regulation affecting saving, investment, and labor markets; changing composition of the labor force; and changing attitudes of workers. Some experts place responsibility for the decline of labor productivity on the reduction in capital formation.[2] Discrimination against private capital formation has taken a number of forms, including tax policies, destabilizing inflation created by expansionist monetary policies, and the competition for investment funds by the federal government through government budget deficits. Public policies of the Reagan administration, for example, were aimed at countering some of these trends in hopes of increasing capital formation and thus promoting growth. Increases in both saving and investment beginning in 1984 are encouraging, although the large federal deficit could choke the recovery.

A more comprehensive accounting for productivity declines and for slower overall growth must be found in the identification of the sources of economic growth itself. Since the early 1960s, economist Edward F. Denison has sought to account for the relative importance of all of the major ingredients of economic growth by using index numbers. Denison has converted trends in total output (national income) and in various factor inputs (labor, capital, legal and human environment, and so on) for the period 1929–1982 into index numbers (see Figure 7).

According to Denison's estimates, U.S. national income rose at an average annual rate of 2.9 percent per year over the period 1929–1982. Of the factors contributing to this rise, increases in factor inputs—labor and capital combined—were most significant. Increase in the labor supply consisted partly of increased education and partly of an increased rate of employment. Recall that new net capital growth is the result of growth in savings and in net investment. The remaining major factors contributing to growth, in order of importance, are advances in technology (knowledge), economies of scale, and improvements in resource allocation.

Note that changes in the legal and human environment actually reduced economic growth. The latter statistic makes sense because investments in environmental protection, for example, do not increase the quantity of the output of goods and services but do increase the quality. To the extent that quality is important in assessing economic growth and well-being, output per worker is understated because capital investments in environmental and pollution production do not ordinarily result in more real salable output but

---

[2]See, for example, John A. Tatom, "The 'Problem' of Procyclical Real Wages and Productivity," *Journal of Political Economy* 88 (February 1980), pp. 385–94.

FIGURE 7   **Denison's Estimates of U.S. Growth Factors, 1929–1982**

In addition to the growth in factor inputs themselves, Denison estimated that advances in technology or in knowledge accounted for the largest contribution to economic growth. Environmental restrictions reduced the output rate by 0.03 percent, but the quality of output may have increased.

Source: Edward F. Denison, *Trends in American Economic Growth* (Washington, D.C.: Brookings Institution, 1985), p. 30. Reprinted by permission.

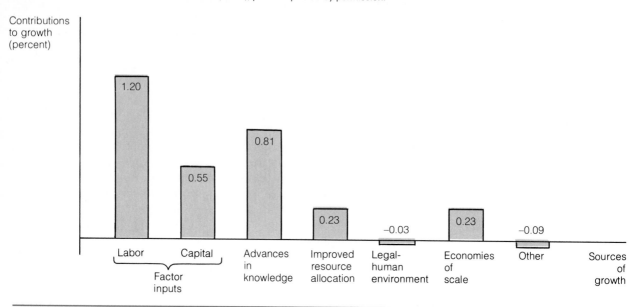

simply in output with fewer by-products. Naturally, a number of interrelated factors contribute to growth. Focus, "The Rise and Fall of Nations: Growth and the Age of Economies," discusses a new and provocative thesis relating economic growth to an economy's age.

LOOKING AHEAD

Denison's careful studies of the sources of growth point out the complexities of trying to identify causes of growth and then trying to stimulate them. Factor growth and, with it, technological change—the importance of which was downplayed in classical economics—are the two essential causes of growth. The long-run benefits and the possible short-run costs of rapid technological change have received a great deal of attention from politicians, economists, and the media in recent years, creating a rather muddy picture.

It is clear that the United States is experiencing a transformation from traditional smokestack industries (coal, steel, heavy machinery) toward high-technology industries (computers, communications). This transformation was clearly evident in the 1982 recession, when there were 25,346 business bankruptcies but 566,942 new companies opened. There were massive worker layoffs in the automobile, steel, and shipbuilding industries and in most heavy industries, while engineers and computer scientists were able to choose between high-paying jobs.

FOCUS   The Rise and Fall of Nations: Growth and the Age of Economies

An interesting and controversial theory of economic growth, developed by economist Mancur Olson, relates the relative economic growth of societies and regions to their age and the respective levels of bureaucratic controls created within their governmental processes.[a] In this view, industry, business, and labor unions (or any other organization) will lobby for legislation or rulings that will allow them to act monopolistically to influence prices or wages to benefit themselves. While success is often difficult to predict, ordinarily the smaller the group, the greater the success of collective action. Large groups, such as taxpayers, consumers, the poor, and the unemployed, are most often not in a position to combine in order to achieve group objectives.

Comprehensive organization of all common interest groups will not be possible in any society, but those who are successful tend to persist. As time goes on, some of these organizations will persist and new ones will emerge if the conditions for monopolization are favorable. Organizations receiving special rewards (higher prices or wages) through collective action have no incentives to disband. Their elimination would spread benefits across the society, but the benefits would be small to group members, smaller than those they can receive from cartelization and collective group action.

The straightforward implication of Olson's thesis is that "new" societies or "younger" societies are at an advantage because they carry less "excess baggage" in the form of efficiency-reducing organizations. Older societies, such as England or France, have had slower growth rates over the past two hundred years, or in the past twenty-five, than the United States. Some societies are destroyed through war, revolution, or totalitarianism and thus may be considered "new." This fact may help explain the experience of high post–World War II growth rates in Germany and Japan relative to other developed nations.

Other testable implications of the theory relate to the economic development of regions. Olson argues that his theory helps explain the relatively high economic development rates in the South and the more recently settled and more westerly states than in the Northeast and the older midwestern states of the United States.[b] Long-settled areas have had more time to accumulate special-interest organizations, and Olson points to the relative lack of labor organizations and to other factors as contributing to an explanation of higher relative economic growth rates in other regions since World War II. Naturally, the factors influencing economic growth are as numerous as they are complex. Olson's thesis provides an interesting possible explanation for economic growth.

[a]Mancur Olson, *The Rise and Decline of Nations: Economic Growth, Stagflation, and Social Rigidities* (New Haven: Yale University Press, 1982).

[b]Mancur Olson, "The South Will Fall Again: The South as Leader and Laggard in Economic Growth," *Southern Economic Journal* 49 (April 1983), pp. 917–32.

The political blame for much of this economic change has been placed on foreign competition. The United States is no longer a self-sufficient economy; it imports more than twice as many goods now as in 1970. For example, the United States now imports 28 percent of its autos, 18 percent of its steel, 55 percent of its consumer electronic products, and 27 percent of its machine tools.

The two major reasons for heightened foreign competition are the lower wage rates and the swift spread of technology to foreign countries. Labor costs in South Korea and Taiwan are about one-fifth those in the United States. Japan, relying greatly on automation, uses approximately six times as many industrial robots as the United States. Some economists and business leaders fear that more automation in the United States will lead to higher unemployment, while other economists feel there will be a shift into other jobs.[3]

According to projections, new jobs are being created in the service industries. The Labor Department has predicted employment in 1995 of 28.5 million people in **service industries**—those offering teaching, health care, and

Service industries:
Those industries whose major, or sole, output is a consumer service, such as banking, entertainment, and health care.

[3]See, for example, "The New Economy," *Time* (May 30, 1983), pp. 62–70, from which the discussion in this section is developed.

food service, for example, rather than manufactured goods—compared to 27 million in 1989. There has been a 53 percent increase in the number of service industry workers since the mid-1970s. By contrast, the number of employees in manufacturing has dropped 2.7 percent since 1973, and predictions are that only 22 million workers will be employed in manufacturing industries in 1995, considerably fewer than the 28.5 million service workers. An example of the increase in service industries compared to heavy industries is the fact that McDonald's now employs more workers than USX (formerly U.S. Steel).

The United States is not alone in its transition from heavy industry to high-technology and service industries. European industrial nations are also having difficulty with changing economies. Even Japan is experiencing some decline in heavy industry, but Japan, unlike Western countries, encourages changes in the economy. Japanese companies diversify greatly in areas of production. One company produces products ranging from foodstuffs to nuclear power plants. This diversity allows workers whose jobs become unnecessary to move into other branches of production within the same company. The setup requires large-scale retraining programs within the companies.

Rather than following the Japanese model, politicians, businesspeople, and workers in the United States have demanded protection for the old smoke-stack industries against foreign competition. During the late 1970s and through the mid-1980s, the United States experienced its worst outbreak of protectionism (the establishment of legal artificial trade barriers and restrictions such as tariffs and import quotas) since the 1930s. The United States has tried to reduce imports and place quotas on autos, steel, and many other products, as we will see in Chapter 38. However, trade restrictions could well do more harm than good to the United States. The United States now exports more than twice the quantity of products it exported ten years ago, and retaliation (in the form of trade restrictions on U.S. goods set in place by foreign governments) by other nations in response to U.S. restrictions is always a possibility. Such reactions inevitably reduce economic growth and well-being among all traders.

It is not likely that the United States will meet the challenge of economic growth by increasing restrictions and regulations on competition or on capital formation but rather by adapting to new technology through competition and human capital development. The management of change in a complex economy is a difficult matter. It often amounts to a balancing of the present interests of workers and other resource suppliers against the overall interests of consumers and economic growth. American prosperity is clearly the result of earlier technological challenges that were met head-on within the context of vigorous and open competition, with due regard for the temporary distortions that new trade and technology might create.

SUMMARY

1. Economic growth is defined as growth in real GNP or in real GNP per capita.
2. The sources of economic growth are complex, but they certainly include growth in population, labor productivity, capital accumulation, and technology.

3. The classical writers envisioned an economy progressing to a stationary (no-growth) state. A Malthusian population mechanism with a long-run tendency to a subsistence wage was a cause of the stationary state, as was a diminishing return to food production.

4. The classical economists also viewed technology as being constant, but modern economists have pointed to growing technology as the mainspring of the economic growth of the Western world.
5. Economic growth requires increases not only in the productive capacity in the economy but also in aggregate demand, which must keep pace with increases in potential output.
6. An essential feature of slower U.S. economic growth in the 1980s was the decline in the growth rate of the productivity of labor—in output per worker. Though numerous factors caused the decline, the major factor appears to be a reduction in capital formation.

7. A lower saving rate, which has led to a lower growth rate in investment expenditures, is a major factor in explaining the lower rate of capital formation.
8. The United States is faced with a high-technology challenge to economic growth—a movement away from heavy industries such as steel, automobiles, and shipbuilding to industries based on electronics and other advanced technologies and to service industries. America's response to this challenge will determine growth prospects for many decades to come.

KEY TERMS

standard of living	capital deepening	capital formation
economic growth	Malthusian population principle	service industries
real per capita GNP	subsistence wage	
productivity of labor	growth absorption	

QUESTIONS FOR REVIEW AND DISCUSSION

1. What is the difference between growth in real GNP and growth in real GNP per capita? Would it be accurate to suggest that the percent change in real GNP per capita is equal to the percent change in real GNP minus the percent change in the population?
2. Do increases in population cause increases in real GNP per capita? Would an increase in the labor force participation rate (the percentage of the population that is in the labor force) increase real GNP per capita?
3. Would it be accurate to suggest that a developing country with an abundance of natural resources has the potential for a high growth rate? What must occur in such countries before a high rate of growth can occur?
4. What is the cost of capital? What happens to real GNP per capita when the number of machines increases?
5. What changes occurred during the Industrial Revolution that resulted in large increases in real GNP per capita? Are similar changes necessary to obtain growth in developing countries?
6. Explain what economic growth means in terms of production possibilities curves. What causes this growth? Is this identical to increases in aggregate supply?
7. Suppose that 1000 tractors were added to a nation's stock of capital every year. Would total farm output rise by the same amount every year? Why or why not?
8. What did Malthus predict about the real GNP per capita? Explain why this prediction has not occurred in the United States. Does his theory appear accurate for some countries?
9. If growth causes an increase in aggregate supply, what must happen to the price level to achieve the higher level of output? Does this suggest that increases in aggregate demand must accompany increases in aggregate supply to maintain price level stability and full employment?
10. What has happened to the rate of growth in real GNP per capita in the United States since the late 1960s? What has caused or accompanied this trend?
11. If you had to choose between price and employment stability and sustained growth in real GNP per capita, which would you choose?

ECONOMICS IN ACTION
Infrastructure and Economic Growth

Discussions of economic growth typically focus on the impact of private investment and capital formation, but the size and condition of government's capital stock is also critical to growth. What is the society's capital stock? In the United States, society's share of the capital stock is approximately one-quarter of the total and is composed of highways, schools, streets, bridges, sewers, and other public goods. The bulk of the nonmilitary government capital—or infrastructure—is owned by state and local governments, although some of the original investments were federally provided. Often, as in the case of highways, maintenance and upkeep expenditures are shared by federal and the other government entities.

The value of infrastructure in economic growth tends to be undervalued and underappreciated in the United States; government investment in goods such as highways, schools, and airports is not generally subject to a market test of profitability, as are investments in the private sector. The value of an investment in computer chip production or in building new privately provided student apartments soon becomes apparent as investors make or lose returns on the difference between revenues taken in and costs incurred. Such measures of profitability are difficult or impossible to apply to new investments in public university buildings or city streets. It would be a mistake, however, to take the absence of a market test for these kinds of goods to mean that infrastructure is not critical to private sector productivity and economic growth.

That this nation's infrastructure is deteriorating is undeniable. Water main breaks are an almost daily occurrence in New York City, and bridge closures (or, worse, collapses) are common everywhere. Over the past two decades, according to the President's Council of Economic Advisers, there has been a dramatic decline in the growth in state and local infrastructure investments.[a] Growth in infrastructure investments at state and local levels fell from an average rate of 4.9 percent per year in the 1950s and 1960s to 2.2 percent in the 1970s and to only 0.9 percent in the 1980s. Completion of the interstate highway system and a decline in the size of the school-age population (the petering out of the post–World War II baby boom) explains some of the decline in infrastructure investment, but certainly not all of it. To many observers, failing local government services, underinvestment in real education plant and equipment, outmoded air-port facilities, and overcrowded streets and poor or failing rapid transit systems suggest that there is an infrastructure crisis in America and that investments are far from adequate. Critics also point out that rapidly growing countries such as Japan and Taiwan are devoting huge amounts of resources to infrastructure to complement increased productivity in the private sector.

As usual, the issue of infrastructure provision comes down to this: Who pays? In general, the federal government has shifted the financial burden for infrastructure provision to state and local governments under the Reagan and Bush administrations. State and local governments complain that access to new taxes for infrastructure items is limited and that the federal government is acting irresponsibly by refusing to shoulder more of the tab for maintaining and expanding facilities. The void left by slashes in federal funding has largely been filled with a controversial mix of privatization schemes and user fees.

For their part, economists concur that "taking advantage of productive opportunities to maintain and improve the infrastructure is an important part of federal, state, and local government policies to raise economic growth."[b] Economists warn, however, that maintenance priorities as well as new projects must be carefully weighed according to costs and benefits. Since governmentally provided infrastructure does not have to meet a market test, detailed estimates of the net benefits of any project (new or continuing) are critical if waste is not to be incurred. There are some classic cases of government miscalculation. Anxious to encourage movement of its population westward from coastal urban cities such as Rio de Janeiro, Brazil built a new inland capital—Brasília. The problem has been that few people want to live there; billions of dollars' worth of infrastructure and facilities lies grossly underutilized and deteriorating. While these kinds of costly miscalculations are possible in infrastructure provision or in maintenance priorities wherever market signals cannot be used, maintenance and expansion of the nation's capital stock is indisputably a necessary condition for increased productivity in any nation that aspires to higher economic growth.

Question

Can the investment returns on the privately financed construction of a new movie theater and the publicly financed construction of a new school building be compared? Why or why not?

[a]Council of Economic Advisers, *Economic Report of the President* (Washington, D.C.: U.S. Government Printing Office, 1990), pp. 122–23.

[b]*Economic Report of the President* (1990), p. 123.

Paul Samuelson

Robert E. Lucas, Jr.

Paul Samuelson and Robert Lucas: Do We Need Discretion or Discipline in Policy?

PAUL SAMUELSON (b. 1915) " . . . has done more than any other contemporary economist to raise the level of scientific analysis in economic theory." So announced the Swedish Academy of Sciences in 1970, when Samuelson became the first American recipient of the Nobel Memorial Prize in economics. Although he has been called on frequently by presidents and Congress for his advice on economic matters, Samuelson has never held an official policy role in any administration. He has worked principally in the service of his profession: as a professor of economics at M.I.T., as president of the American Economic Association, and as a frequent contributor to journals and magazines. Born in Gary, Indiana, Samuelson received his Ph.D. in economics from Harvard in 1941. His doctoral dissertation, titled *Foundations of Economic Analysis,* was published in 1947 and became one of the definitive technical treatises on neoclassical economics. Today, Samuelson is one of the most widely respected Keynesian economists. He is known as a policy activist, one who recommends the use of fiscal and monetary policy to counter recessionary and inflationary cycles of economic activity.

ROBERT E. LUCAS, JR. (b. 1937), credited with introducing rational expectations theory into macroeconomics, has helped change the way economists view the role of macroeconomic policy. Born in Yakima, Washington, Lucas received his Ph.D. in economics in 1964 from the University of Chicago, where he gained a firm background in Keynesian economics. One of the texts he found particularly influential at that time was Paul Samuelson's *Foundations of Economic Analysis,* which he believes is "a great book for first-year graduate students."

After graduate training, Lucas became increasingly disillusioned with Keynesian interpretations of the macroeconomy. His article "Econometric Testing of the Natural Rate Hypothesis," published in 1972, is one of many that discuss the implications of rational expectations theory. This theory assumes that people will make rational and intelligent economic decisions based on their knowledge of economic policy, their past experiences, and their expectations of future events. In theory, such rational behavior can distort or even neutralize the effects of well-publicized fiscal and monetary policies. According to Lucas, he and his early followers were initially regarded as "very far out" by colleagues for their nontraditional views. However, appreciation of rational expectations theory has grown so that Nobel Prize–winner George Stigler has suggested that Lucas himself may soon share the award. Lucas has held academic posts at Carnegie-Mellon University, the Ford Foundation, and the University of Chicago, where he currently teaches.

THE CASE FOR ACTIVISM

In 1964, the unemployment rate stood at 5.2 percent and GNP was $638 billion. The economy was near the end of a bitter recessionary period. Government policy advisers, following Keynesian theory, called for direct intervention in the form of a massive tax cut. Congress responded by passing the 1964 Revenue Act, which slashed personal income taxes by almost 20 percent and corporate taxes by almost 8 percent.

The tax cut, aided by a strong surge in the money supply, ushered in several boom years. Over the next four years, GNP grew over 11 percent and unemployment dropped to 3.8 percent. Policy activists such as Paul Samuelson cite the 1964 tax cut as good evidence of the usefulness of well-planned fiscal and monetary actions. Although the evidence since the 1960s has been somewhat less clear-cut, the case for activism rests on the assumption that the economy cannot easily readjust to full employment without some form of countercyclical policy, whether in the form of monetary growth, monetary restraint, fiscal cutbacks, or fiscal spending. The fiscal actions are generally preferred by activists because they can exert a direct impact on the flow of expenditures. Monetary policy works somewhat more slowly and less directly on expenditures, through the mechanism of interest rates.

Defending the need for activism, Samuelson and other economists focus on the terrible social costs of economic downturns and sudden shocks to the system. Left to correct itself, a shrinking economy could inflict insufferable damage on millions of people before prices and aggregate demand readjust to full-employment levels.

The record of policy activism gives some support for this view. For the past thirty years, the United States has suffered several recessions, but depressions seem to be a thing of the past. "Another depression on the order of the 1930s just doesn't seem possible," says Samuelson. The government nowadays "will do what it has to do" to avert economic disorder. "There's no longer the sense that we must somehow sweat these things out."[a]

Although activist policy has eased the severity of business cycles, it has not found a means to avoid them altogether. Indeed, there are many who argue that the economy's boom-and-recession pattern since World War II has been more the effect of discretionary policy than the cause. Also, there are many economists who point to the accelerating inflation suffered over these years and the failure of government to apply the appropriate countercyclical fiscal medicine: budget surpluses.

THE CASE AGAINST ACTIVISM

For Robert Lucas, the attempts on the part of policy-makers to unbend the business cycle through discretionary, countercyclical policy are based on some unexamined assumptions. For such a policy to work, individuals and firms must

[a]Quoted in "Economists Don't See Threats to Economy Portending Depression," *Wall Street Journal* (October 12, 1984), p. 1.

respond cooperatively; when the government tries to close a recessionary gap, they must respond as though such actions will have no effect on prices.

Lucas believes that expectations about prices will always direct behavior, whether one is speaking in microeconomic or macroeconomic terms. If individuals and firms believe that government policy will drive up prices, they will act to protect themselves: Wage earners will demand higher wages, investors will seek higher interest rates, and so on. When such expectations are considered, Lucas deems most countercyclical policy to be futile and counterproductive. For instance, if policy-makers try to reduce unemployment through deficit spending, wage earners who have experienced the effects of such spending in the past will anticipate higher inflation. They will naturally try to keep the wages they have and to increase them. In the face of such demands, employers will find it more and more difficult to hire additional labor, and unemployment will remain despite the increase in aggregate demand. Rather than bend the recessionary cycle, the policy-makers will have managed to foster inflationary pressures, perhaps ushering in high unemployment and high inflation, or what is known as stagflation.

The checkered performance of macroeconomic policy in the early 1980s provided Lucas plenty of ammunition to blame discretionary policy for a variety of economic ills. To Lucas, appropriate macroeconomic policy would try neither to fool nor to ignore the expectations of individuals and firms. Instead, Lucas calls for some fixed limits for policy that recognize the long-run patterns of growth in the economy, which have been in the range of 3 to 4 percent for GNP over the past one hundred years. He also advocates a monetary rule proposed by Milton Friedman that would keep the growth rate of the money supply to approximately 3 percent.

Economists who accept the rational expectations hypothesis have begun the large task of accumulating evidence in its behalf. In the meantime, many find the rational expectations model extreme in its assumptions. How is it, they ask, that citizens can adopt an accurate set of expectations about the effects of policy when even competent observers of the economy are often misjudging the rate or even direction of economic change? Moreover, what happens when fiscal or monetary policies are overwhelmed by a supply shock? Will government then be required to overcome the instability? Questions such as these have brought lively debate over the future course of policy. The issue of activism versus nonactivism in policy is certain to occupy economists for years to come.

PART EIGHT

International

Trade and

Economic

Development

38

International Trade

$\mathbf{W}$e do not often stop to ponder all the ways in which imported goods enrich our lives and improve the material well-being of all nations of the world. On a typical day, for example, an American student's consumption patterns are clearly global. She awakes on sheets made in England and prepares breakfast on a hot plate made in Taiwan. Donning a cotton dress made in India and shoes made in Mexico, she catches the morning news on a TV with components manufactured in Japan. She drives to campus in a Japanese-made Honda Civic.

The desirability of a diverse array of available goods and services and the interrelation of the U.S. economy with the economies of other nations present us with issues and problems we have left unexamined until now. The issue of the competitiveness of U.S. firms in world markets may have directly affected you or your family. The large foreign trade deficit that arose in the 1980s spawned much debate in business, labor, and government circles on the desirability of a new U.S. trade policy with countries such as Japan and Canada. Large swings in the value of the U.S. dollar overseas can alter not only vacation plans but consumption patterns and employment as well.

To this point, we have simplified our analyses of the national economy by treating it as closed—as isolated and with no international interchange. In the next three chapters, we focus exclusively on international trade, finance, and development, with special attention to U.S. involvement.

Today's revolutions in technology are enabling nations to become more and more economically interdependent. In a sense, the whole world is now an economic system. International economics is the study of this world economy with the tools of economic theory. The concepts of supply and demand and production possibilities are quite useful in discussing worldwide trade, the international finance system, and the problems facing the developing economies of the world. These chapters examine the organization and functioning of national economies such as those of the Soviet Union and Eastern Europe that are replacing organized central planning by government with systems in which private property and markets play larger roles.

International economics is composed of both microeconomic and macroeconomic elements. This chapter focuses essentially on the microeconomics of trade. After reading Chapter 38 you should understand

- the reasons for and the advantages of specialization and trade.
- the factors that determine actual amounts and directions of trade between countries.
- how artificial interferences with trade, such as tariffs and quotas, affect the prices and quantities of goods and services sold in importing countries.
- how historical and contemporary trade policies and international integration, such as that contemplated by Western European nations, affect world trade.

THE IMPORTANCE OF INTERNATIONAL TRADE

All nations have particular talents and resources; like individuals, whole nations can specialize in one or many activities. For example, the islands of the Caribbean have abundant sunshine and good weather year round, and so these islands specialize in tourism. **Specialization** enables nations to emphasize the activities at which they are most efficient and at the same time gain certain advantages through trade.

Specialization:
An economic entity's (an individual's or a nation's) producing only one good or service, or the performance of a single task in a production process by an individual.

Examples of international specialization and trade abound. France has a favorable climate and specialized land for wine growing, so it exports wine to Colombia and the United States and imports Colombian coffee and U.S. machinery. Likewise, both Colombia and the United States specialize and trade products that best utilize their qualities and quantities of resources.

Trade and specialization take place within a given economy as well as among economies. The former type of trade is called intranational or interregional trade; the latter is called international trade. In principle, the two types of trade are the same. As we saw in Chapter 2, Canada may specialize in lumber production and Mexico may specialize in silver production. Each meets its wants for the commodity it does not produce through international trade. Likewise, Texans import potatoes from Idaho, while residents of Idaho import beef produced in Texas. Such intranational or interregional trade is common—so common in fact that most of us do not even think of it as interregional trade. This process is not fundamentally different from the trade of U.S. wheat for Japanese television sets.

In practice, important differences exist between interregional and international trade. Resources—climate, fertile land, and work forces with specialized skills—cannot easily be moved between countries or regions. What distinguishes international trade from interregional trade is *lower* factor mobility between nations than within countries. A nation generally trades with the products and services of its resources, not with the resources themselves. Beyond this basic point, countries have different currencies and political systems and values. (See Focus, "1992: Dawn of the European Community.") For such reasons, international trade is different from interregional trade and therefore merits special study by economists.

FOCUS   1992: Dawn of the European Community

The goal of eliminating economic barriers and creating new levels of integration in Western Europe is set for 1992. The European Community (EC)—forged largely from the European Economic Community, or Common Market—will become a unified market of twelve member nations, making trade within Europe almost as easy as trade between states in the United States. (The twelve countries are the United Kingdom, France, Denmark, Belgium, Greece, Italy, Luxembourg, The Netherlands, Portugal, Ireland, Spain, and a recently reunified Germany.) In economic terms, this means that all tariff and nontariff trade barriers will eventually fall to zero, making the EC market the largest and most populous in the world.

The economic advantages of the union to the well-being and progress of the countries involved are outlined in the theory presented in this chapter. Specifically, the free flow of goods and services and the unrestricted migration of labor and capital will be the central forces propelling economic growth in the whole region. The advantages of specialization and trade by comparative advantage *with no artificial impediments to trade* will be enormous. Just as Texas trades oil and gas for Idaho potatoes without barriers, so Ireland will be able to freely trade finished textiles for Italian shoes. EC countries have begun the process of eliminating barriers in telecommunications, life insurance, and auto production (the EC's biggest employer). Deregulation and free trade in many of these areas will mean (sometimes) painful relocations of production.

European union also raises many larger questions.[a] How, and in what sense, will the EC evolve in terms of monetary and political union? There is much debate (and some dissension) among member nations about these two issues. An elected European Parliament and Council of member country representatives meet in Strasbourg to discuss and approve decisions about future policies of the EC, but the real power is based in Brussels with the European Commission and with the European Court. These permanent (and unelected) bureaucracies make binding rules on the member countries to further integration.

[a]See Peter Brimelow, "The Dark Side of 1992," *Forbes* (January 22, 1990), pp. 85–89, upon which some of this discussion is based.

Just how far political and monetary integration will go is debatable. For example, a European central bank and a common currency might evolve over time, but enforced central banking with a common currency is unlikely to be accepted by all member nations at the outset. Countries that have typically taken a hard line on inflation, such as West Germany, are unwilling to relinquish control over their respective monetary units. Likewise, common policies such as uniform welfare subsidies to citizens of all EC countries could actually reduce the comparative advantage of some regions. This would occur if specialization were based upon low-priced labor or real wage differences. Of even more fundamental difficulty in achieving full integration are the different political traditions and legal systems within EC countries. Great Britain, for example, has a long history of independence and self-government, while some Continental nations have traditionally embraced centrist or Catholic socialist traditions—France and Italy, respectively. The actual outcome of EC integration is, for these reasons and others, most unclear.

The benefits and costs of European integration in 1992 is of great concern to EC trading partners. Will full economic integration of these twelve nations restrict or shut out American, Canadian, or Japanese exporters of goods such as beef and automobiles? In other words, will the EC become a giant protectionist monster with new monopoly powers to restrict U.S. and world trade? While the United States has been an ardent supporter of European union in the past, its motivations have been chiefly military, not economic. The remarkable "decentralization" in the Soviet Union and Eastern Europe that began in 1989 and the reduced threat of armed aggression has caused the United States to rethink a united Europe. On the one hand, protectionism by the EC would reduce world trade and welfare. On the other hand, an *external* policy of free trade by EC nations along with similar policies from other major trading nations could expand world specialization and economic well-being. Open access to the EC consumers (along with reciprocal access to American consumers) could provide an enormous and revitalized world market for America's goods and services and significant economic growth. Only time will tell.

National Involvement in International Trade

The overall magnitude of international trade and countries' shares in this trade can be measured in a variety of ways. The value of goods in international trade is given in Table 1 by major areas of the world. In 1988, world trade totaled almost $3 trillion, measured in exports or imports.

TABLE 1	World Trade: Exports and Imports, 1987–1988		
	Area	Exports (billions of dollars)	Imports (billions of dollars)
	Industrial countries	1988.1	2067.7
	Developing countries	699.8	701.6

Source: International Financial Statistics (Washington, D.C.: International Monetary Fund, 1990).

Table 2 lists the foreign trade of eleven nations as a percentage of gross national product for 1988; the percentages vary widely. Exports accounted for over 30 percent of West Germany's total output but less than 10 percent of Brazil's or the United States's output. Imports were about one-fourth to one-third of the real consumption of such countries as South Africa, West Germany, Sweden, and Switzerland.

Percentage figures do not tell the whole story, of course. In absolute terms the United States was the world's largest trader in both exports and imports in 1988. The value of merchandise exports totaled $319.3 billion and the value of merchandise imports was over $446.5 billion. The United States trades with virtually every nation of the world, the primary sources of imports being Canada (19 percent in 1988) and Japan (20 percent). The main destinations of U.S. exports in 1988 were Canada (23 percent), Japan (12 percent), and Western Europe (27 percent). In terms of products, the three main U.S. imports are crude oil, motor vehicles, and food, and the three main exports are machinery, motor vehicles, and grain.

Why Trade Is Important: Comparative Advantage

The reason for all this trading is that all nations benefit from some degree of specialization and trade. Suppose two nations produce computer components and food with an equal expenditure of time and resources. Trade between the two countries will likely emerge because each can specialize at what it does

TABLE 2	Exports and Imports as a Percentage of GNP in 1988		
	Country	Exports as a Percentage of GNP	Imports as a Percentage of GNP
	United States	8.8	11.0
	United Kingdom	23.0	26.8
	Switzerland	34.5	34.2
	Sweden	33.0	30.9
	Japan	13.0	10.1
	Italy	18.2	18.4
	West Germany	32.4	26.7
	Canada	27.0	26.5
	Brazil	9.5	6.2
	South Africa	29.8	24.4
	Venezuela	22.5	28.2

Source: International Financial Statistics (Washington, D.C.: International Monetary Fund, 1990).

better—emphasizing the production at which it is more efficient—and trade with the other country for the other good. As we will see, both countries will be better off because specialization and trade lead to increases in production and therefore to increases in the attainable consumption levels of both goods in both countries.

Comparative advantage:
An economic entity's (an individual's or a nation's) ability to produce a good at a lower marginal opportunity cost than some other entity.

According to the principle of **comparative advantage,** countries will specialize in producing those goods and services in which they have relatively lower opportunity costs than their trading partners. For example, a hilly, rocky country will not be able to raise as many sheep per acre as a country with fertile grasslands, but the rocky land cannot support any production other than sheep raising, whereas the grassland will support more lucrative cattle production. Even though the grassland is absolutely more productive at raising both sheep and cattle, the rocky land has a comparative advantage in sheep growing because the opportunities forgone are very small. The rocky country will therefore tend to specialize in sheep, the grassy country in cattle.

Consider the simplicity and power of the idea that each country produces those products that it can produce with relatively greater efficiency—at a lower relative opportunity cost. Countries that have relatively lower opportunity costs of producing certain goods and services have a strong incentive to produce those goods and services. Production across the world will thus come to reflect the principle of comparative advantage at work. The large amounts of fertile U.S. farmland combined with advanced farm technology have made the American farmer the most productive in the world. America has a clear comparative advantage in certain farm products and raw materials. America's skilled labor force and high rate of technological advance through huge investments in private and public research and development have helped make the United States relatively efficient in producing highly sophisticated machinery and equipment. Trading partners of the United States, especially Japan, have specialized in routinized productions such as automobiles and steel. Energy regulations and increased demand have forced the United States to import immense quantities of petroleum. The pattern of United States imports and exports therefore shows the process of economic specialization and comparative advantage at work.

Production Possibilities Before Specialization. To demonstrate more precisely how all trading partners benefit by exercising their comparative advantages, we must look at what happens in each country before and after specialization and trade. Suppose that both the United States and Japan, in isolation, produce just two goods: computer components and food. Further assume that the production possibilities schedules facing the United States and Japan are depicted in Table 3, which gives the alternative combinations of food and computer components that could be produced in the United States and Japan if resources are fully employed. The United States, for example, may choose to produce 60 units of food and no computer components, 40 units of food and 10 units of computer components, 20 units of each, or 30 units of computer components and no food. With fully employed resources, Japan may choose between 45 units of computer components and no food at one end of the production spectrum and no computer components with 30 units of food at the other, or combinations between these extremes, as shown in Table 3.

TABLE 3

U.S. and Japanese Production Possibilities Schedules for Food and Computer Components

Within the United States 2 units of food cost 1 unit of computer components. Within Japan, ⅔ unit of food costs 1 unit of computer components. The relative opportunity cost of food production is lower in the United States, and the relative opportunity cost of computer component production is lower in Japan.

	Production Possibilities (at full employment)			
	1	2	3	4
United States				
Food	0	20	40	60
Computer components	30	20	10	0
Japan				
Food	0	10	20	30
Computer components	45	30	15	0

These production alternatives are merely the trade-offs that are implicit in the countries' production possibilities curves. For the United States, the extreme choice is between producing 60 units of food (F) or 30 units of computer components (CC). That is, if the U.S. produces 60F, it will have to forgo 30CC. Within the United States, then, the opportunity cost of producing 1F will be ½ a unit of CC. Alternatively, the cost to the United States of producing 30CC is 60F, or 1CC costs 2F. In summary, within the United States,

60F costs 30CC to produce, or
1F costs ½CC to produce, or
1CC costs 2F to produce.

These costs measure how many units of food must be given up to obtain a unit of computer components, or how many units of computer components must be given up to get an additional unit of food. In either case, what is being measured is the relative opportunity cost of producing food or computer components in the United States—that is, what must be given up to increase the production of food or computer components.

Exactly the same analysis can be applied to Japan. For Japan, the production possibilities schedule indicates that, in the extreme, either 45 units of computer components and no food or 30 units of food and no computer components can be produced. The opportunity cost of producing 1F in Japan is then 1½CC. Likewise, 1CC costs ⅔ a unit of F. In Japan, the opportunity cost of production is summarized as

30F costs 45CC to produce, or
1F costs 1½CC to produce, or
1CC costs ⅔F to produce.

Gains from Specialization and Trade. The concepts of production possibilities and opportunity costs provide a perspective for understanding the benefits of trade. Continuing our example of trade between the United States and Japan, first look at the U.S. and Japanese production possibilities curves in Figure 1. Notice that these production possibilities curves are straight lines. In practical terms, this means that resources can be transformed from food production to computer component production at constant opportunity cost, that resources are perfectly adaptable to one production process or the other in both economies. The simplicity of this assumption does not compromise the argument for specialization and trade.

The important part of the argument for gains from specialization turns on the pretrade opportunity costs of producing the two goods that face Japan and the United States. Before trade, consumers in the United States must sacrifice 2 units of food to produce 1 unit of computer components, while Japanese consumers must sacrifice only ⅔ unit of food to produce the same amount of computer components. On the other side of the coin, American consumers must sacrifice only ½ unit of computer components to obtain 1 unit of food, while their Japanese counterparts must give up 1½ units of computer components to get 1 unit of food.

Both countries can gain from trade. Since the United States produces food at an opportunity cost of ½CC and Japan produces computer components at an opportunity cost of ⅔F, we know that the Americans would gain if trade gave them more than ½CC for 1 unit of food, and the Japanese would gain from ⅔F for a single unit of computer components. These differences in relative opportunity costs of producing food and computer components yield a basis for specialization and trade between the two countries.

FIGURE 1

Prespecialization Production Possibilities Curves

The straight-line production possibilities curves for the United States and Japan indicate that resources can be transferred from computer component production into food production at constant opportunity cost. The different slopes of the two curves indicate that different opportunity costs provide the basis for both countries to benefit from specialization and trade. The United States has a comparative advantage in food production, whereas Japan is relatively more efficient at producing computer components.

(a) United States

(b) Japan

Terms of trade:

The number of units of one good that exchange in the market for one unit of some other good; a relative price.

Consumption possibilities curve:

All the possible combinations of two goods that could be consumed by first specializing according to comparative advantage and then trading at the terms of trade.

At what price will trade take place? The **terms of trade**—the ratio at which two goods can be traded for each other—will settle somewhere between the relative opportunity cost ratios for each country. For example, terms acceptable to both Japan and the United States will fall between $\frac{2}{3}F = 1CC$ (Japan) and $2F = 1CC$ (United States). We might say that the two countries bargain to set the terms of trade, and the bargaining range is determined by each country's internal opportunity cost trade-off. For simplicity, let us assume that the terms of trade settles at 1 unit of food for 1 unit of computer components, or $1F = 1CC$.

Figure 2 illustrates the potential outcomes of this agreement in terms of the production possibilities curves and each country's posttrade **consumption possibilities curve.** If the countries choose to specialize totally according to comparative advantage, the United States produces 60 units of food and Japan produces 45 units of computer components. Each country can now trade for the product it no longer produces; each country is no longer restricted to consuming a combination of goods on its production possibilities curve. Without trade, a country is restricted to consuming whatever it produces. In

FIGURE 2

Production and Consumption Possibilities Curves

The production possibilities curves for the United States and Japan are the dark straight lines. The United States specializes in food, producing 60 units; Japan specializes in computer components, producing 45 units. Once trade can take place at the terms of trade of 1F for 1CC, the consumption possibilities curves become relevant. The United States exports 25F and imports 25CC, increasing its consumption (over the pretrade situation) of food by 15 units and computer components by 5 units. Japan exports 25CC and imports 25F, increasing its consumption (over the pretrade situation) of food by 5 units and computer components by 5 units.

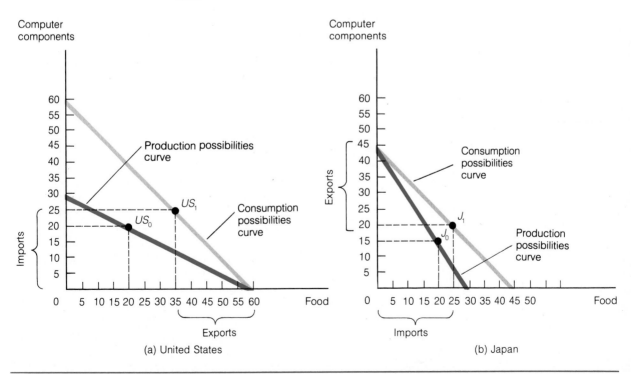

(a) United States

(b) Japan

the absence of trade, its production possibilities curve and its consumption possibilities curve would be one and the same.

With trade, however, each country's consumption opportunities are determined by how much of its specialized output is produced and the terms of trade. A country's consumption possibilities curve shows all the possible combinations of the two goods that could be consumed if production were specialized (according to comparative advantage) and trade could take place at the given terms of trade. Of course, only one combination can actually be consumed, so the consumption possibilities curve should be viewed as a menu of alternatives open to the country. The consumption possibilities curve with trade will always lie beyond the production possibilities curve, indicating that specialization and trade will leave the country economically better off. Remember, without trade the country's consumption opportunities are identical to its production opportunities.

Given that each country specializes and can now trade (at a price or terms of trade of 1F = 1CC) for the product it no longer produces, the consumption possibilities curves in Figure 2 become relevant. In contrast to a domestic opportunity cost of 60F for 30CC, the United States now enjoys a situation in which production of 60F could be traded for 60CC. Japan enjoys a similar expansion of consumption opportunities with specialization and trade. By specializing and trading, both countries are made economically better off. Each has the ability, with trade, to consume a bundle of goods beyond its production possibilities curve. This would be impossible, given each country's resources and technology, without trade. Specialization does not even have to be complete for the two countries to gain from trade. We have used the example of complete specialization here for simplicity.

If we assume that U.S. consumers originally consumed the bundle of food and computer components labeled US_0 in Figure 2a, we can note the improvement in their well-being by considering a new, posttrade consumption bundle, US_1, on their consumption possibilities curve. More of both goods are consumed after specialization and trade. A similar conclusion arises for Japan if we compare hypothetical pre- and postspecialization and trade consumption bundles, J_0 and J_1, respectively. Specialization and trade enlarge the consumption possibilities of the trading nations so that both countries can consume more of both goods after trade occurs.

Note that trade between the United States and Japan in this example takes place according to the principle of comparative advantage. Figure 3 shows the explicit pattern of trade. The United States exports food (25 units) because it has a comparative advantage over Japan in food production. This is so because 1F costs the United States only ½CC to produce, whereas 1F would cost Japan 1½CC to produce. Japan exports computer components for the same reason. It has a comparative advantage in producing them over the United States. Each country imports the good for which it is at a comparative *dis*advantage—that is, the good for which its trading partner possesses a comparative advantage. Gains from trade accrue to producers and consumers. In this example, American consumers of computer components benefit from the lower prices made available by imports, while American food producers benefit by obtaining a price for the food they export higher than the price they could obtain by selling it in the United States—which is not to suggest that no one is harmed by free trade. U.S. food consumers must pay higher food prices as a result of the decision to export some U.S. production. Similarly, U.S. pro-

FIGURE 3

Japan has a comparative advantage in computer component production; the United States, in food production. This means that Japan will export computer components and import food, whereas the United States will export food and import computer components. The terms of trade, 1F for 1CC in this example, must be between the two countries' opportunity costs of production.

The Pattern of U.S.-Japan Trade

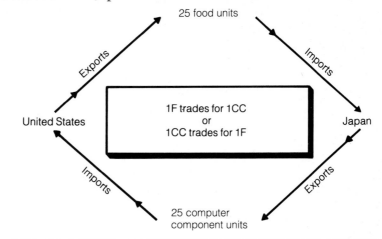

25 food units

Exports

Imports

United States

1F trades for 1CC
or
1CC trades for 1F

Japan

Imports

Exports

25 computer
component units

ducers of computer components are harmed when Japanese supplies enter the market and cause prices to fall. On balance, however, gains from free trade exceed losses; free trade leads to improved standards of living.

Our discussion has been based on a simple example of how the principle of comparative advantage works. In discussing two-good trade between Japan and the United States, we assumed that each country was absolutely more efficient than the other at producing one of the two goods. What if one country is absolutely more efficient in producing both goods? Suppose that productivity in the United States tripled—production of computer components increasing to 90 units and production of food increasing to 180 units. U.S. production capacity in this case would outpace Japan two to one in computer components and six to one in food. Nonetheless, the opportunity cost to the United States of producing each computer component would still be 2 units of food, which is higher than Japan's opportunity cost. It would still be mutually advantageous for the United States to specialize in food and to obtain computer components from Japan through trade. Remember, the argument for free trade is based on the principle of *comparative* advantage. Trade between two countries is mutually beneficial whenever the countries bear different opportunity costs of producing goods. This is true even if one of the countries is absolutely more productive at both goods.

Tariffs and Quotas

Despite the advantages of specialization and trade, certain barriers to trade exist in the real world. Some are natural costs of exchanges, such as negotiating and transportation costs, and cannot be avoided. Other barriers to trade are artificial, contrivances of governments designed to raise revenues or protect domestic producers from foreign competition. The major examples of artificial trade barriers are tariffs and quotas. A **tariff,** or import duty, is simply a tax levied on particular imported goods. For example, the United States imposes a tariff on imported shoes and steel. A **quota** is a partial or absolute limitation on the quantity of a particular good that can be imported. For example, until

Tariff:
A tax or levy on imported goods.

Quota:
A restriction or limit on the quantity of an imported good.

1972 the United States imposed a quota on the importation of foreign oil and permitted oil refiners to import only the allowed amount of oil. Both tariffs and quotas reduce the extent of specialization and trade and, therefore, the gains that consumers obtain from free trade. Both raise the prices of imported and domestically produced goods and restrict imports. In these respects, tariffs and quotas are similar. For an analysis of the similarities and differences of quotas and tariffs that concentrates on the quotas the Reagan administration imposed on Japanese automobiles in 1981, see Economics in Action, "Voluntary Export Restraints: A Quota Is a Quota Is a Tariff," at the end of this chapter.

THE EFFECTS OF ARTIFICIAL TRADE BARRIERS

Though tariffs and quotas presumably are adopted by governments out of national self-interest, they usually do not benefit most citizens in the long run. Tariff duties on imports were an essential source of U.S. government revenues from the Revolution until the late nineteenth century, and the use of tariffs to protect domestic industries is still being promoted. The effects of tariffs and quotas have long been debated. Adam Smith made the definitive economic statement on the matter in his *Wealth of Nations* in 1776.

> To give the monopoly of the home-market to the produce of domestic industry, in any particular art of manufacture, is in some measure to direct private people in what manner they ought to employ their capitals, and must, in almost all cases, be either a useless or a hurtful regulation. If the produce of domestic industry can be bought there as cheap as that of foreign industry, the regulation is evidently useless. If it cannot, it must generally be hurtful.[1]

Smith knew that individual traders, such as tailors and shoemakers, could gain from specialization and trade. But he went further and argued that the principle applied no less to nations.

> What is prudence in the conduct of every private family, can scarce be folly in that of a great kingdom. If a foreign country can supply us with a commodity cheaper than we ourselves can make it, better buy it of them with some part of the produce of our own industry, employed in a way in which we have some advantage. The general industry of the country, being always in proportion to the capital which employs it, will not thereby be diminished.[2]

Free trade:
The exchange of goods between countries without the presence of artificial trade barriers such as tariffs and quotas.

With very few exceptions (to be discussed later in the chapter), **free trade**—trade without artificial barriers—leads to maximum economic welfare among nations. Free trade and specialization expand consumption possibilities and deliver goods to consumers at the lowest possible costs. Yet given all

---

[1]Adam Smith, *An Inquiry into the Nature and Causes of the Wealth of Nations,* ed. Edwin Cannan (1776; reprint, New York: Modern Library, 1937), pp. 423–24.

[2]Smith, *Wealth of Nations,* p. 424.

the benefits of free trade, the world does not often seem to allow it to work, at least not completely. The reason is that some parties are harmed by free trade. Pressures are brought to bear on governments by producer groups for protection from foreign competition. Sometimes these groups win political favors, such as tariffs or quotas, to reduce the competitive threat. In this section we use economic theory to show how these interferences with free trade reduce the overall economic welfare of a country.

Trade and Tariffs: Who Gains? Who Loses?

To understand who really gains and loses from a tariff, consider Figure 4. It shows two possible prices facing domestic suppliers of automobiles: the free-market world price of autos, P_w, and the free-market world price plus some per unit tariff on autos imported to the United States, P_{w+t}.

Imposition of a tariff on imported autos clearly benefits domestic automobile manufacturers. Since imported cars are now more expensive, domestic suppliers can raise their prices, without any increase in costs. The higher price P_{w+t} encourages domestic auto producers to increase output from quantity Q_0 to quantity Q_1, increasing domestic suppliers' profits by the shaded area $P_{w+t}E_1E_0P_w$. This increase in profits is often described as an increase in producer surplus. Naturally, because the tariff increases domestic production, it also increases domestic employment in the industry producing the tariffed good. We must be careful, though, not to generalize that a tariff on a specific good or set of goods will increase the overall level of employment in a country. The tariff is likely to have economic repercussions that are felt in the markets for other goods and services and that tend to reduce employment in those markets.

What if the auto tariff were reduced? A reduction in the tariff would reduce producers' profits (their producer surplus) as well as domestic em-

---

FIGURE 4

Imposition of an import tariff on imported automobiles allows U.S. producers to raise the prices of their automobiles from the free-market world price, P_w, to P_{w+t}. The higher prices encourage them to increase the quantity of automobiles they produce from Q_0 to Q_1. Their profits are therefore increased by the shaded area $P_{w+t}E_1E_0P_w$. This increase in profits is also referred to as an increase in producer surplus. Employment of domestic resources increases because domestic production rises from Q_0 to Q_1.

Domestic Producers' Supply Schedule for Automobiles

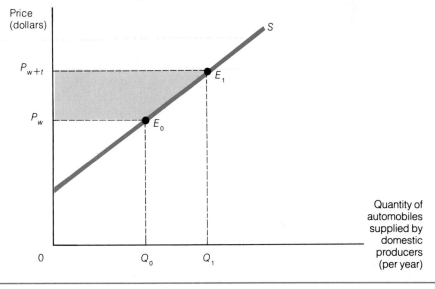

ployment in the auto industry. But before we can present an economic assessment of tariffs, we must investigate their effects on consumers.

The effects of a tariff on consumers are shown in Figure 5. The figure shows an initial price, P_w, and an initial quantity of autos, Q_0, purchased by consumers. Imposition of a tariff on imported cars increases the price to P_{w+t} and reduces consumption of autos from Q_0 to Q_1. A reduction in benefits to consumers accompanies the increase in price. (Previously, we have equated these benefits with consumer surplus.) The shaded area $P_{w+t}E_1E_0P_w$ in Figure 5 represents the reduction in consumer surplus caused by the tariff on automobiles. This concept will be elaborated in the following sections.

The Benefits of Free Trade

Using the concepts of consumer and producer surplus, we can now see the benefits of free trade. We will first examine an industry in which the United States is an importer—the automobile industry. Then we will look at the effects of free international trade on an industry in which the United States is an exporter—the wheat industry.

Consider Figure 6, which shows the U.S. domestic supply curve for automobiles, S_{US}, the curve S_F, which shows the supply of cars to the U.S. market by foreign producers, and the American demand curve, D. The domestic supply curve and the foreign supply curve for automobiles are added together horizontally to produce S_T, a curve showing the total supply of cars to the U.S. market by domestic and foreign producers.

If no cars were allowed to be imported, the domestic price of cars would be P_D, and the quantity bought and sold would be Q_D. However, if cars were imported without restriction, the market would clear at E_1, where the price is P_T and the quantity is Q_T—the point at which domestic demand for cars

---

FIGURE 5

A tariff on imported automobiles causes the price to increase from P_w to P_{w+t}, which in turn causes a reduction in the quantity of automobiles demanded by consumers from Q_0 to Q_1. Benefits to consumers are reduced by the amount represented by the shaded area $P_{w+t}E_1E_0P_w$. This loss is referred to as a reduction in consumer surplus.

Effects of Tariff on Consumer Demand

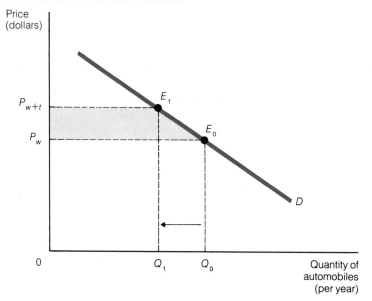

FIGURE 6

The total supply curve S_T is the horizontal summation of domestic (S_{US}) and foreign (S_F) supplies of automobiles. In the pretrade situation, when consumers purchase only domestic automobiles, equilibrium E_0 is established at price P_D and quantity produced Q_D. Under free trade, imports lower prices from P_D to P_T and increase quantity consumed in the domestic market from Q_D to Q_T, with equilibrium established at E_1. Consumers benefit from free trade in the amount represented by $P_D E_0 E_1 P_T$.

The Benefits of Importing Freely

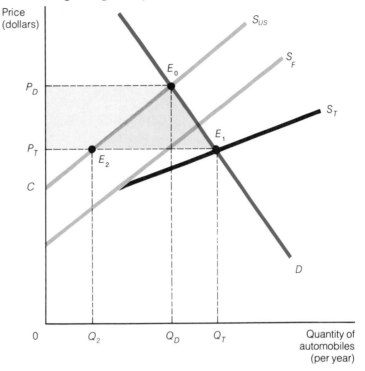

equals total supply of cars. If we compare the equilibrium under free trade with the equilibrium under no trade, we see that the consumer surplus is larger by an amount $P_D E_0 E_1 P_T$. However, under free trade and a price of P_T, domestic producers produce only Q_2 cars and receive a producer surplus that is smaller by the amount $P_D E_0 E_2 P_T$ than the surplus they previously received. In other words, domestic car producers are harmed by free trade, since they sell fewer cars (Q_2 instead of Q_D) at a price of P_T. However, the gain that consumers receive by moving to free trade, $P_D E_0 E_1 P_T$, is larger than the cost of free trade to U.S. producers by an amount equal to $E_0 E_1 E_2$.

Figure 7 shows the effects of free trade in an industry like the wheat industry in which the United States is an exporter. In Figure 7, D_{US} and S_{US} show domestic demand and supply of wheat, respectively. D_F shows foreign demand for U.S. wheat, and D_T shows the horizontal total of U.S. and foreign demand for wheat. If wheat is not permitted to be sold abroad, the wheat market in the United States will clear at E_1, with a price of P_D and with Q_D units bought by U.S. consumers from U.S. producers. However, if the United States allows free trade, the market will clear at E_2. The equilibrium price of wheat will rise to P_T and the equilibrium quantity will rise to Q_T. Of the Q_T units sold by domestic producers, Q' will be sold to domestic consumers, and the remainder ($Q_T - Q'$) will be exported. As a consequence of free trade, U.S. producers will experience an increase in producer surplus of $P_T E_2 E_1 P_D$. U.S. consumers will find that their surplus has fallen by $P_T E_3 E_1 P_D$. The gain to producers exceeds the loss to consumers by $E_3 E_2 E_1$.

FIGURE 7

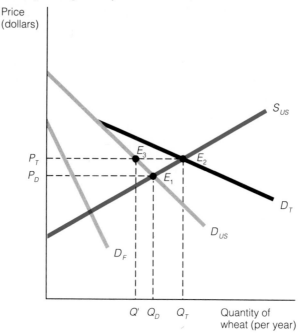

The Benefits of Exporting Freely

The total demand curve, D_T, is the horizontal sum of domestic demand (D_{US}) and foreign demand for U.S. wheat (D_F). In the pretrade situation, the equilibrium is at E_1. If exports are permitted, the price rises from P_D to P_T. Domestic producers increase sales from Q_D to Q_T, but domestic consumers reduce purchases from Q_D to Q'. As a consequence, the increase in the producer surplus of domestic producers is larger than the decrease in the consumer surplus.

We see that, as a group, consumers and producers benefit from free trade. Although some parties are harmed, the gains by others more than offset these losses. There are net gains from trade both for an import industry and an export industry.

Welfare Loss from Tariffs

We have now seen how trade creates net benefits to domestic consumers and producers. Let us now look at the effects of a protective tariff on the society as a whole, using a hypothetical market for television sets.

Figure 8 represents the domestic market for TV sets, including the domestic supply of the product and the U.S. demand. Prior to the imposition of a tariff, American consumers buy Q_4 units at the world price P_w. Of this quantity purchased, Q_1 are sold by domestic manufacturers and Q_1Q_4 are imported from abroad.

Assume that a tariff is imposed in the amount t, causing the price of TVs to American consumers to rise to P_{w+t}. (For clarity, we have assumed that the foreign TV supply curve is horizontal. This totally elastic supply curve could arise from TV production in the world being a constant-cost industry or from the idea that the United States buys such a small share of total world TV output that it is a price-taker country.) American TV producers gain additional profits in the amount represented by $P_{w+t}E_2E_1P_w$ because of the increased domestic output permitted by the higher price. Imports are reduced to Q_2Q_3, and the total number of sets sold decreases to Q_3. Consumers lose total benefits in the amount of $P_{w+t}E_3E_4P_w$. At the same time, the tariff on

FIGURE 8

The Effects of a Tariff

Gains in producer profits and government revenue do not equal consumer losses from tariff imposition. Net consumer losses are shown in the shaded triangles in the figure. Before a tariff on TV sets, consumers purchase Q_4 units at price P_w. The tariff causes the price to rise to P_{w+t}, imports to decrease from Q_1Q_4 to Q_2Q_3, and the total number of TVs sold to decrease to Q_3. Consumers' total loss is represented by $P_{w+t}E_3E_4P_w$, but producers gain $P_{w+t}E_2E_1P_w$, and government tariff revenues are E_2E_3AB. The net loss to society is therefore the sum of the areas E_2BE_1 and E_3E_4A.

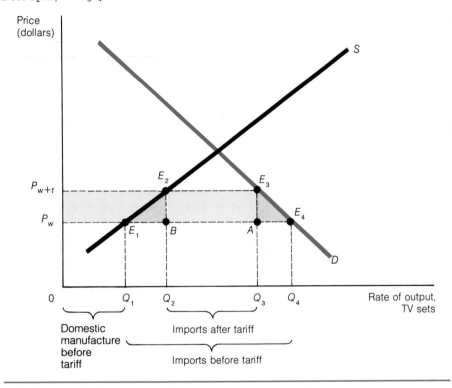

imported TV sets creates government revenues. These revenues are composed of the per unit amount of the tariff multiplied by the units of TV sets imported after the tariff is imposed (area E_2E_3AB in Figure 8).

Economists typically assume that the government revenue is used in a manner that produces benefits equivalent to those lost by consumers of TV sets. However, the tariff causes a net loss in benefits to society, of which TV consumers are a part, represented by the sum of the two areas E_2BE_1 and E_3E_4A. The sum of these triangles represents a loss that is not counterbalanced by the sum of producers' gains and government revenue resulting from the tariff. Economists call this loss a **welfare loss to society.**

Welfare loss to society: The *net* loss to an economy resulting from the imposition of an artificial trade barrier; government revenues plus producer gains minus consumer losses.

Why Are Tariffs Imposed?

If tariffs create a welfare loss to society, why are they imposed? Certainly tariff revenue to the federal government is minuscule when compared to other sources of government revenue. More than two hundred years ago, Adam Smith identified the real cause of protective tariffs:

Merchants and manufacturers are the people who derive the greatest advantage from this monopoly of the home-market. . . . Manufactures, those of the finer kind especially, are more easily transported from one country to another than corn or cattle. It is in the fetching and carrying manufacturers, accordingly, that foreign trade is chiefly employed. In manufactures, a very small advantage will enable foreigners to undersell our own workmen, even in the home market. . . . They [merchants and manufacturers] accordingly seem to have been the original inventors of those restraints upon the importation of foreign goods, which secure to them the monopoly of the home-market.[3]

The source of tariff protection is to be found in the urgings of "merchants and manufacturers" as well as from labor in domestic import-competing industries, today as it was in Smith's day. Consumers of TV sets and of any goods that actually bear a tariff could conceivably convince both producers and the government not to impose tariffs because, as we have shown, consumers lose more than producers and government gain from tariffs. Practically, however, the world does not work this way. Consumers, the gainers from free trade, are widely dispersed and costly to organize in any fight for free trade. Interest in fighting a tariff or quota is also apt to be low among consumers because their pro rata share of losses from artificial barriers to trade is generally small. To an individual consumer, for example, the tariff is a small proportion of the total price of an automobile. The incentive to organize and fight protective tariffs is therefore small.

Not so for producers. The pro rata, or proportionate, share of the effects of tariff protection is much higher among manufacturers, for they are far fewer in number than consumers. Manufacturers thus have stronger incentives than consumers to form an interest group, and, being fewer in number, their costs of organizing are lower. For such reasons, the consumer interest in free trade is often thwarted.

Nontariff Barriers to Trade

Nontariff trade barriers: Alternative (to tariffs and quotas) means of restricting trade; examples include domestic content legislation and health and safety regulations.

Historically, tariffs and quotas have been the most important types of artificial trade restrictions. In recent years, other types of restrictive practices, which are generally called **nontariff trade barriers** (NTBs), have taken on increased importance. Examples of nontariff trade barriers include domestic content legislation (laws that require a certain portion of goods sold in a country to be produced there) as well as safety or health regulations designed to discriminate against foreign products. NTBs have grown rapidly in recent years because many countries have enacted trade legislation that forbids tariffs or quotas; NTBs represent an alternative form of protectionism. The use of NTBs varies greatly among countries. In the United States, NTBs exist for about 25 percent of imported goods. The corresponding percentage for Japan is about 12 percent. Within the European community, percentages vary but average about 20 percent.

Although it is difficult to determine the specific effects of nontariff trade barriers, the general effects are quite similar to those of tariffs. Figure 8 shows how a tariff artificially raises the price of imported goods and causes the

---

[3]Smith, *Wealth of Nations*, pp. 426, 429.

quantity of imports to fall. NTBs have similar effects. If, for example, the United States were to enact legislation requiring that cars sold in this country have a 50 percent domestic content, the Japanese could continue exporting cars to the United States only if at least half of the parts and the assembly were American. The cost of compliance would be higher production costs to the Japanese, but it would be very difficult to determine how much costs would rise. The effect therefore would be identical to the imposition of some specific tariff. Without knowing by how much this legislation would increase production costs, it would be impossible to determine what an equivalent tariff would be.

Nontariff trade barriers have become a major issue in the United States, particularly with regard to the economic unification of the European community. There is some concern that a unified Europe will implement technical standards that discriminate against foreign firms. Some observers have suggested that U.S. exports to Europe would fall sharply as a result of any such barriers. Although it is impossible to predict what economic policies the unified European community will pursue, the economic unification of Europe is sure to present certain advantages to U.S. exporters. For one thing, U.S. firms will no longer have to contend with different NTBs in each of the European countries nor have to meet different standards by producing a different product for each country.

THE CASE FOR PROTECTION

Throughout history numerous arguments have emerged in defense of protection from free trade. Some arguments are well constructed; others are but thin veils for producers' interests. All the arguments—both the well-constructed and the questionable ones—deserve careful scrutiny.

National Interest Arguments for Protection

The two oldest and best-formed arguments in defense of protection and against free trade are the national defense argument and the "infant industries" argument. Both arguments contain a grain of truth, but each should be closely scrutinized before serving as a base for protectionist policies.

National Defense. The oldest argument for protection—and the one with superficially the best justification—is that such restrictions are necessary for national defense. As military technology has changed, steel, gunpowder, manganese, uranium, and a host of other inputs have all been commodities essential to making war at various times, and they have been the subject of tariffs and quotas to keep domestic production of these commodities strong.

The logic of protection for defense is clear: Since the ultimate function of government is national defense, any possible threat to national defense, such as the unavailability of some resource during a crisis, must be avoided. A loss in consumers' benefits from protection is thus justified for a greater benefit—the availability of essential materials to be prepared for war. Artificial barriers to trade in these materials are used to protect domestic industries considered essential for national defense.

The national defense argument is plausible for some industries and some products, but consider that cheese, fruit, and watch manufacturers and other, non-defense-related industries have all resorted to the argument. History seems to prove that patriotism is the last and best refuge of a producer seeking protection from foreign competition. The national defense argument has seen double duty as an argument for maintaining unprofitable routes on railroads and protecting truck, air, and railroad companies by setting legalized cartel rates. The telephone industry was long protected on similar grounds.

Other ways can be devised to handle the national defense issue besides imposing tariffs and quotas. A tariff is nothing but a hidden subsidy or cash grant to domestic producers. Thus, if an industry is to be protected for national defense reasons, an explicit subsidy may be more straightforward than tariff protection. That way the national defense issue is made clear, and voters know how much defense actually costs them. If, for example, it is deemed vital to national security that the United States have a certain capacity to produce iron and steel, an alternative public policy would be to subsidize domestic iron and steel producers rather than to protect them against foreign competition with a tariff or quota.

Protection of Infant Industries. Possibly the most frequently heard argument for protection, especially in developing nations, is the so-called **infant industries** argument. Discussed by Adam Smith and supported by Americans such as Alexander Hamilton, the infant industries argument reached its highest expression in the mid-nineteenth-century writing of German nationalist Friedrich List (1789–1846). List sought to unify and develop the German states against the incursions of British imports. He argued that protective tariffs were necessary in the transition from an agricultural-manufacturing to an agricultural-manufacturing-commercial stage of development. His reasoning was clear: Specific tariffs were necessary to maintain fledgling industries until they could compete with foreign imports on their own. After the "infancy" period of industrial development was over, protective tariffs would be lifted, forcing the businesses to meet the rigors of competition.

The infant industries argument is related to the idea of economies of scale. Economies of scale exist when, as plant size increases up to a point, long-run unit costs decline. This occurs because individual workers become more proficient at narrowly defined tasks, and machines are more closely tailored to individual processes. Scale economies may also occur because both workers and managers "learn by doing" and acquire more experience as output grows. Often, moreover, production of certain manufactured goods results in an enormous initial setup cost. As firm and industry output grow larger, these setup costs are spread over larger and larger numbers of units produced. A number of developing nations use this economies of scale or infant industries argument today in their quest for unilateral tariff protection. One-crop economies, whose foreign earnings are heavily dependent on a single export, seek to use an umbrella of protectionist policies to buy time for diversification.

As much as one might be concerned for the economic plight of poor nations, great care must be exercised in applying the infant industry argument to them. At best, the argument is one for allowing domestic industry to gain a foothold in international competition. Protection for any reason, as we have seen, means lost benefits for consumers. Obviously, any gains from ultimate

Infant industry:
A new or developing domestic industry whose unit production costs are higher than those of established firms in the same industry in other countries.

independence must be balanced against the costs of lost consumer benefits over the period of protection.

A final question that should be applied to the infant industries argument concerns the vagueness of the goal of removing protection "when the industry grows up." It is hardly legitimate to apply the infant industries argument to the present-day steel industry in the United States and Western Europe, but the argument is still being used. Entrenched protectionist interests will always attempt to prolong the "infancy" of any industry. The dangers of giving protectionists a general legal foothold negate any merit the argument might have in limited and specific cases.

Industry Arguments for Protection

A number of other arguments for protection crop up from time to time, usually put forward by domestic firms and industries seeking protection for protection's sake. We characterize these arguments as wrong because they are assaults on the very principle that gains may be realized from trade. They are all variations on the theme that special-interest groups deserve protection from international competition.

The "Cheap Foreign Labor" Argument. A common argument for tariff or quota protection is that labor or some other resource is cheaper abroad, enabling foreign manufacturers to sell goods at lower prices than U.S. manufacturers. The defenders of this argument are often producers or workers displaced by imports and foreign competition. During the early 1980s, for instance, U.S. producers and workers bitterly complained through their union representatives that imports were creating unemployment.

While the argument may be correct—foreign producers may be more efficient combiners of resources—this truth in no way denies the benefits to free trade. The *absolute* level of wages in any other country does not matter. As we have seen, gains from trade derive from *comparative* advantage. Indeed, the request for protection from cheap labor turns the gains from trade position on its head: The reason *for* trade becomes a reason to limit or restrict trade. Open trade is beneficial precisely because resources may be cheaper or combined more efficiently elsewhere. The opening or extension of trade creates a temporary disruption of markets, including the unemployment of resources. To impose tariffs or quotas on the grounds that some groups of U.S. laborers are temporarily thrown out of work or that some U.S. stockholders are losing wealth is to subsidize special interests at a greater cost to all U.S. consumers of the subsidized product or service. Moreover, the domestic economy may actually gain from the movement of domestic resources into new fields of comparative advantage. For example, resources released from domestic steel production may be reallocated to computer production.

Side issues arise in the cheap foreign labor argument. One common complaint is that foreign governments subsidize the production of exported goods to shore up their domestic industries and prevent unemployment. This complaint is used as a plea for protection from cheaper imports. But to argue for tariffs on these grounds is to look a gift horse in the mouth. The benefits from trade are independent of the reasons that imports are cheaper. If governments choose to subsidize their exports, they in effect tax their own citizens to benefit foreign consumers.

Dumping:
The selling of goods in foreign markets at prices lower than those charged in domestic markets.

Dumping, selling goods abroad at a lower price than in the home market, is also related to the cheap foreign labor argument for protection. The practice, an example of price discrimination (see Chapter 10), means that foreign buyers gain greater benefits from consuming the commodity or service than domestic consumers. In practice, it is often difficult to determine whether goods are being dumped. As defined by U.S. trade policies, dumping occurs when a foreign producer sells in the American market either below costs or at a price below that charged to the foreign producer's domestic customers. In real-world cases, then, a producer could be selling to his or her own customers at monopoly rates and be prohibited from selling to American consumers at lower rates (even though they more than cover costs). Such restrictions, if enforced by trade authorities, could work against American consumers.

Special interests in the favored country often complain that dumping constitutes "unfair competition," but the argument for free trade remains intact nonetheless. Consumers in the favored nations are able to purchase goods at lower prices, and overall welfare in the consuming country is enhanced.

It should not matter why foreign prices are low, as long as the foreign supplier who is dumping goods in U.S. markets has no monopoly power. If the producers of Japanese television sets undersell U.S. producers with an eye to putting them out of business and subsequently raising their price to a monopoly level, dumping does pose an issue for public concern. This is not usually the case, however. More often, alleged dumping by foreign producers is simply a reflection of their lower costs of production and puts competitive pressure on U.S. producers.

The "Buy American" Argument. The "buy American" argument, a call to patriotism, means to keep money at home. More specifically, "buy American" means that imports should be restricted so that high costs or inefficient producers and their employees may be protected from foreign competition.

This well-known argument is fallacious on several counts. First, it asks consumers to pay higher prices for goods and services than are available to them through trade, thereby negating the potential expansion of trade benefits. Second, when money is kept at home, foreign consumers are unable to purchase domestic exports, reducing the welfare of domestic export producers and their workers and other input suppliers.

"Terms of Trade" Advantage. A final argument applies to countries that have monopoly or monopsony power in international markets. It suggests that a country employ its power to increase its share of the gains from international trade. Thus, if the United States is the world's largest supplier of computers, putting restrictions on computer exports will drive up the price of computers in the international market. Although the United States will then sell fewer computers, it will get a higher price per computer and possibly higher computer sales revenues. In effect, by restricting computer exports, the United States would alter the terms of trade in international transactions in its favor.

Terms of trade argument:
Defending the use of artificial trade barriers combined with monopoly or monopsony power in international markets in order to produce an improvement in a country's terms of trade.

The **terms of trade argument** suggests that countries exercise monopoly and monopsony power where possible. Doing so is a means for a country to increase its revenues from international trade. The argument founders, however, on a simple point: the possibility of retaliation by other countries. If all countries seek terms of trade advantages, the trading nations of the world *collectively* may be made worse off. The exercise of monopoly or monopsony power to improve the terms of trade for all countries could mean a shrinking of total world production for exports. This negates the gains possible from comparative advantage and from the division of labor and reduces specialization within nations.

Perhaps the greatest flaw in all arguments for protection lies in the implicit assumption that other nations will lose export markets and will not retaliate. It is improbable that a country could win permanent terms of trade advantages on a unilateral basis while its trading partners sit idly by. U.S. history is peppered with examples of tariff wars. One of the fiercest tariff wars in history took place in the midst of the Great Depression of the 1930s, discussed in the next section. Tariffs or other forms of trade barrier retaliation can only create a reduction in worldwide economic welfare and massive and inefficient allocations of resources. Whatever the initial reasons for protective tariffs, consumers ultimately suffer the costs.

U.S. TARIFF POLICY

U.S. tariff history has been punctuated by cycles of free trade and of protectionism, with a move toward free trade in the past fifty years that may be more apparent than real. The average tariff rates for the years between 1821 (the year of the first good statistics) and 1989 are shown in Figure 9, along with some highlights of our tariff history. Import duties as a percentage of the value of all imports subject to duty ranged from almost 60 percent in the early 1930s to a mere 3.5 percent in 1989.

Why has the average tariff fluctuated so widely during U.S. history? Before turning to a specific analysis of changing conditions, one broad issue will help us answer the question. With the minor exception of tariffs imposed for revenues to fight wars or to apply foreign policy pressures, the average tariff has varied with business conditions, falling in periods of prosperity and rising during prolonged recessions or depressions. During periods of rising prosperity, manufacturers and workers displaced by free trade find little political support for the imposition of tariffs. When general business conditions turn downward, creating reduced demand for products and increased unemployment, the cry for protection grows louder in the political arena.

Early Tariff Policy

Tariffs were a major source of revenue for our republic in its early years, as they are for some developing countries today. Post-1820 tariffs tended to vary with business conditions, rising during recessions and falling during more prosperous periods of business activity. On the eve of the Civil War, tariff revenues stood at about 19 percent of the value of imports, the lowest level in American history up to that time. In 1861, the Morrill tariff passed Congress under the pretext of generating much-needed revenue for the Union treasury. Whatever the initial intention, the Morrill tariff set off a wave of protectionism

FIGURE 9

Level of Tariffs

The United States today has lower tariffs, as measured by the ratio of tariff fees collected to the value of imports, than at any time in its history. Since the establishment of the General Agreement on Tariffs and Trade (GATT) in 1947, tariffs have followed a downward trend.

Sources: U.S. Bureau of the Census, *Historical Statistics of the U.S.,* 1976; *Statistical Abstract of the United States,* 1985, p. 823; Tax Foundation, *Facts and Figures on Government Finance* (Baltimore: Johns Hopkins University Press, 1990), p. 91.

in U.S. policy that lasted until the second decade of the twentieth century. Tariffs declined dramatically during the Wilson administration, standing at only 16 percent in 1920.

The dramatic downturn in the economy beginning in the late 1920s had a stark and lingering effect on protectionism in the United States. Manufacturing and commercial interests, coinciding with a willing political climate, produced the Smoot-Hawley Act of 1930, which legislated the highest peacetime tariff in U.S. history. Average tariff levels were raised to almost 60 percent of the value of imports, setting off a frenzy of protectionist retaliations in other nations. The result of what was perceived as American self-interest was falling real incomes, sharply reduced consumer welfare, and a deepened and prolonged worldwide depression in the major world-trading countries.

Modern Tariff Policy

Contemporary tariff policy may be viewed as an attempt to overcome the disastrous effects of protectionism embodied in the Smoot-Hawley Act. The first Roosevelt administration, under the aegis of Secretary of State Cordell Hull, acted swiftly to counteract the protectionism of the Smoot-Hawley tariff. In 1934, the Reciprocal Trade Agreements Act was passed, giving the president power to negotiate bilateral tariff reductions of up to 50 percent with other countries. This act was the important first step in establishing the character of modern U.S. tariff policy. It established a framework within which free trade is envisioned as a goal of policy, and to a large extent it stripped Congress of its tariff-making power (but not the power to set nontariff barriers). While Congress could legally remove the tariff-setting powers of the president, these powers have been renewed and strengthened a number of times since 1934.

In the post–World War II era, the powers of the president have been expanded to include multilateral negotiations for tariff reductions—that is, negotiations with all nations simultaneously. A manifestation of America's multilateral policy was its support of the multinational organization called GATT (General Agreement on Tariffs and Trade) in 1947. Originally a twenty-two-member body, GATT now includes more than eighty world nations representing about 80 percent of world trade. GATT sets rules and conditions for tariff reductions and oversees bargaining with all participating nations simultaneously.

Modern U.S. trade policies evolve through GATT, and tremendous gains and expansion of world trade have occurred since the formation of this multinational body. Moreover, Congress has expressed some willingness to move toward free trade. In 1962, a Trade Expansion Act was passed, permitting the president to negotiate tariff reductions on all commodities simultaneously rather than commodity by commodity. This act led to the so-called Kennedy round of tariff reductions (1964–1967), which produced huge concessions on manufactured and industrial products, with special concessions for poor or developing countries.

Where Does the United States Stand in the Battle for Free Trade?

Given the rhetoric of the Reagan and Bush administrations and recent changes in U.S. tariff policy, one can be forgiven for concluding that the U.S. unabashedly supports free trade. Beyond a doubt, there has been movement toward free trade in recent years. The United States has forcefully worked toward lowering tariffs worldwide in a series of GATT negotiations and, through these same channels, has actively supported measures to free up trade in agricultural products. In addition, the United States and its largest trading partner, Canada, removed all trade barriers between the two countries in 1989. Efforts to reduce trade restrictions between the United States and Mexico have been made. Finally, the disintegration of the Soviet bloc made long-standing trade and finance restrictions against Eastern European countries obsolete—virtually overnight.

The United States is a long way from having completely free trade, however. With two exceptions—Canada and Israel—no country escapes having certain of its imports taxed by the United States. For Cuba, South Africa, and China, the current policy essentially prohibits trade. The U.S. tariff policy for the European Community after 1992 is indeterminate, but creation of a free trade zone with the member countries appears unlikely. In fact, many observers foresee trade restrictions on the European Community greater than those used against members of the European Common Market.

In terms of nontariff barriers, the United States has been moving away from a policy of free trade. Since the authority to enforce laws against dumping was transferred to the Department of Commerce in 1980, the number of dumping cases has risen sharply. In the last ten years, the United States initiated about 30 percent of all the antidumping cases worldwide—a percentage exceeded only by Australia. The United States has applied pressure on other countries to enter into "voluntary" agreements to limit exports of various products to the United States. In addition to the well-known agreement with Japan to limit the number of cars sold in the United States, voluntary export agreements have been negotiated with other countries to limit the amounts of textiles, steel, and various agricultural products that enter the United States. In short, the United States is actively protectionist in its use of nontariff barriers to trade.

SUMMARY

1. All individuals possess talents that give them advantages in trade. Nations, like individuals, benefit from specialization and trade. Nations trade not resources but rather the products and services created with resources. Differing resource endowments are the basis for trade in products because products are ordinarily more mobile than the resources that produce them.

2. Specialization and trade may take place between countries of vastly differing degrees of economic development. The reason is the law of comparative advantage, which states that trade is possible when the relative opportunity cost of producing two goods differs between two countries.

3. Specialization according to the law of comparative advantage permits the production possibilities and hence the rate of sustainable consumption of nations to expand. That is, the parties to trade may obtain more of both traded goods after specialization and trade.

4. There are both natural and artificial barriers to trade. Natural barriers are all exchange costs, including transportation costs of moving goods from one country to another. Artificial barriers include taxes on imports of goods, or tariffs, and limitations or prohibitions on imported items, or quotas.

5. Tariffs on imports increase the profits of domestic producers and the revenue of government, but consumers lose more than producers and governments gain. This net welfare loss is the reason most economists oppose protectionist policies.

6. Though tariffs carry a net loss to society, they are imposed whenever domestic producer-competitors are strong enough to supply gains to politicians. Consumer groups may oppose tariffs but are seldom well enough organized or vocal enough to oppose them successfully.

7. Two substantive arguments are made for protection: the national defense and infant industries arguments. Most economists, however, question the adequacy of these arguments in actual operation. Other arguments—such as "cheap foreign labor" or "buy American"—are regarded by most economists as only thinly veiled protectionist fallacies.

8. U.S. trade policies have historically waxed and waned with prosperity and depression, becoming more protectionist during economic downturns. Although import tariffs have been reduced dramatically in the past fifty years, freer trade has not necessarily resulted. Protectionism lives on in the form of quotas and nontariff trade barriers.

KEY TERMS

specialization
comparative advantage
terms of trade
consumption possibilities
    curve
tariff

quota
free trade
welfare loss to society
nontariff trade
    barriers
infant industry

dumping
terms of trade argument

QUESTIONS FOR REVIEW AND DISCUSSION

1. Evaluate and discuss the following statement: "Trade across international boundaries is essentially the same as trade across interstate boundaries."
2. How can two countries simultaneously gain from trade? Under what circumstances can two countries not gain from trade?
3. What is the difference between natural barriers and artificial barriers to trade? Was the development of the Panama Canal an artificial encouragement of trade?
4. What does a tariff do to the terms of trade? Are consumers in both countries hurt by a tariff?

5. What are the differences and similarities between tariffs and quotas? Would consumers prefer one of these barriers to the other?
6. Who is hurt by a tariff? Who is helped? Who encourages government to impose tariffs?
7. What is the purpose of protective tariffs? Who or what is protected?
8. Evaluate the following statement: "Tariffs discourage the movement of goods between countries; therefore, they encourage the movement of resources such as capital and labor between countries."

PROBLEMS

Nations Alpha and Beta have the following production possibilities for goods X and Y.

Alpha	X	0	3	6	9
	Y	12	8	4	0
Beta	X	0	4	8	12
	Y	15	10	5	0

1. Draw the production possibilities curves for both countries. What does 1 X cost in Alpha before trade? What does 1 Y cost in Beta? If these countries traded, which would export X and which would export Y?
2. If some country Omega can produce 100 units of X with all its resources or 60 units of Y, how much does 1 unit of Y cost? If another country, Gamma, can produce 60 X or 40 Y, what does 1 unit of X cost in Gamma? Which country has a comparative advantage in the production of X?

ECONOMICS IN ACTION
Voluntary Export Restraints: A Quota Is a Quota Is a Tariff

Voluntary export restraints (VERs)—quota agreements between two countries to voluntarily limit exports from one country to the other—have become a popular alternative to tariff controls. In 1990, for example, President Bush used the device to restrict imported steel through 1992, but a precedent for this had been established during the Reagan administration with VERs on automobiles. On April 1, 1981, an international trade agreement between the governments of Japan and the United States was put into effect. Under the VERs, the government of Japan would prevent Japa-nese automakers from exporting as many cars as they would like to the U.S. market. Japanese car manufacturers were restricted to shipping only 1.68 million cars to the U.S. market per year from 1981 to 1984. What was the economic effect of the VERs on U.S. automobile producers and consumers?

In order to answer this question, we must first recognize that this "voluntary" restraint was nothing more than a quota of 1.68 million cars. The U.S. government effectively restricted imports from Japan to a level of 1.68 million cars.

The next question to answer is, What effect has the imposition of an import quota had on the domestic (United States) market for automobiles?

Figure 10 will help answer this question. In Figure 10, P_W is the price of a car in the United States before the quota. Domestic producers sell Q_1 cars, and imports equal Q_4 minus Q_1 autos. Once the quota, equal to Q_3 minus Q_2, is imposed, how does the domestic market move to a new equilibrium? Recall that an equilibrium price is one at which quantity demanded equals quantity supplied. Part of quantity supplied is supplied by foreign producers, the amount of the quota in this case. To find what equilibrium price will be under the quota, we need only find a price at which the horizontal distance between the demand and supply curves equals the quota. At price P_{W+Q} domestic output, Q_2, plus the quota, Q_3 minus Q_2, equals total quantity demanded, Q_3. Thus, at price P_{W+Q} quantity demanded equals total quantity supplied. P_{W+Q} will then be the domestic price of a car if a quota of Q_3 minus Q_2 is imposed.

Figures 8 and 10 are similar in many respects because tariffs and quotas are similar in many respects. They both raise domestic price and reduce imports, but the tariff works initially by affecting price and letting quantity adjust, whereas the quota directly affects quantity with the result that prices adjust. Whichever method is used to restrict trade, higher domestic prices and fewer imports result.

Economist Robert Crandall of the Brookings Institution in Washington, D.C., has studied the Reagan administration's VERs in an attempt to gauge the economic effects on consumers and producers of automobiles.[a] He estimated that in 1984 the price of a Japanese car sold in the United States was about $2500 more than it would have been without the VERs. Additionally, the higher prices of Japanese imports allowed U.S. automakers to charge about $1000 more per car than they would have been able to in the absence of quotas. The stockholders of U.S. auto companies and the employees of these companies clearly benefited from the VERs. Crandall also estimates that American auto consumers paid approximately $16 *billion* more for cars in 1984–1985 than they would have in the absence of the quotas.

Although Figures 8 and 10 suggest that tariffs and quotas yield identical results in the domestic market, there can be

[a]Robert W. Crandall, "Detroit Rode Quotas to Prosperity," *Wall Street Journal* (January 29, 1986), p. 30.

FIGURE 10

The Effect of a Quota on the Domestic Market

When the quota is imposed, it is still necessary for quantity demanded to equal quantity supplied for the domestic market to be in equilibrium. Only at price P_{W+Q} will total quantity demanded, Q_3, equal total quantity supplied. Total quantity supplied equals quantity supplied domestically, Q_2, plus imports, Q_3 minus Q_2. The quota raises price, increases domestic producers' profits, and produces welfare losses—just as a tariff does.

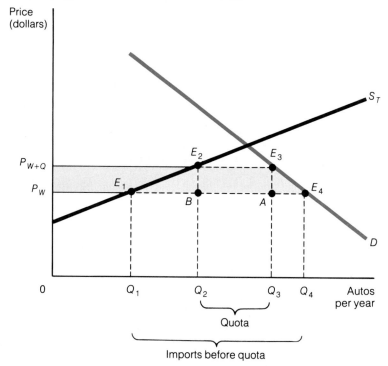

differences. In Figure 10, if a tariff had driven domestic price up to P_{w+a}, the U.S. government would have collected tariff revenue in the amount of area E_2E_3AB. However, under the VERs, no tariff revenue was collected from Japanese automakers. In fact, the United States government merely allowed the Japanese government and Japanese automakers to decide for themselves which companies would fill the quota of 1.68 million units. With the import rights left specifically unassigned (and not charged for) by the U.S. government, the area E_2E_3AB became revenue to Japanese producers (and their U.S. dealers) rather than tariff revenue for the United States. Crandall estimates this area to have been on the order of $10 billion over the 1984–1985 period. This is one of the wealth transfers, from American consumers to Japanese producers, of a quota designed in this fashion.

An interesting alternative study expands on the effects of U.S.-Japanese VERs on autos by calculating the impact of third parties on American consumers. Producers in Germany, Sweden, and France, though *not included* in the VER arrangement, were very much affected by it. These European auto exporters also were able to increase prices—by about one-third over the pre-VER level, according to economists Elias Dinopoulos and Mordechai Kreinin.[b] This price hike, which is a direct transfer from U.S. consumers to European producers, added considerably to the total welfare loss in the United States. Dinopoulos and Kreinin reveal a threefold welfare loss: "the loss to Japan (estimated at $2.3 billions in 1982 and $2.4 billions in 1984); the loss to Europe (estimated at $1.5 billions in 1982 and $3.4 billions in 1984); and a small social loss within the United States, over and above the pure internal transfer from consumers to producers ($208 millions in 1982)."[c] Further, they put the total cost of the auto VER in 1982 at $4 billion. The automobile VER may have saved 22,358 auto-related jobs in 1982, but American consumers had to pay $181,000 for each of those jobs, many times each autoworker's average annual compensation. The Bush administration appears determined to maintain and extend such VERs as a basis for trade policy.[d] In 1991, for instance, VERs on steel will be set at 20.14 percent of the total U.S. steel market—meaning, on balance, more losses to American consumers.

Question

If you had designed the voluntary export restraints, how could you have designed them so as to eliminate the $10 billion wealth transfer from American consumers to Japanese producers?

[b]Elias Dinopoulos and Mordechai E. Kreinin, "Effects of the U.S.-Japan Auto VER on European Prices and on U.S. Welfare," *Review of Economics and Statistics* 70 (August 1988), pp. 484–91.

[c]Dinopoulos and Kreinin, p. 491.

[d]See Peter Truell, "U.S. Agrees to Quotas on Steel Imports with EC and 16 Other Major Suppliers," *Wall Street Journal* (December 13, 1989), p. A2.

39

The International Monetary System

When a car dealer in Virginia buys cars from a Detroit manufacturer to sell in Virginia, both use the same medium of exchange—U.S. dollars. Suppose, however, that the dealer buys cars from Japanese or German manufacturers to sell in Virginia. The Japanese firm will likely want payment in yen; the German firm, in marks. The car dealer thus confronts an international monetary problem. Are the prices stated in yen and marks fair? This question brings up others. How are dollars converted into yen and marks? Is there a fixed rate for currency exchange or does it vary? How would changes in exchange rates affect import prices in the United States? How do fluctuating exchange rates influence foreign investors seeking to buy real estate or stocks and bonds in the United States? U.S. exporters face the same questions from a different perspective. They sell to citizens in foreign countries and seek payment for their goods and services in U.S. dollars. They must be careful, therefore, to pay attention to exchange rates because these rates can determine the prices and profits of their foreign sales.

The monetary, or financial, side of international trade concerns the ways in which countries pay for the goods and services they exchange. In this chapter we examine many aspects of the relations among the currencies of the world, relations that reflect a kaleidoscope of changing conditions in each country, from interest rates and inflation rates to exports and imports of goods and capital. When you finish Chapter 39 you should understand

- how international trade takes place when transactions must be made in terms of other countries' currencies.
- how currency transactions are determined when governments fix their respective currencies' value and when the market determines the relative value of currencies.
- how macroeconomic fiscal and monetary policies both affect and are affected by foreign trade and international exchange rates.
- the meaning of the balance of payments, its relation to exchange rates, and its importance for economic growth.

THE FOREIGN EXCHANGE MARKET

Foreign exchange:
The monies of countries that are used to facilitate international trade in goods, services, and financial assets.

International sellers and buyers usually prefer to deal in the currency of their own country. American sellers prefer U.S. dollars for their products, and Japanese sellers prefer yen. The currency of another country that is required to make payment in an international transaction is called **foreign exchange.** Foreign exchange is bought and sold in **foreign exchange markets**—typically, large brokers and banks scattered about the globe.

Foreign exchange markets:
The interaction of the suppliers and demanders of foreign exchange, through which exchange rates are determined in a flexible exchange rate system.

Sometimes consumers demand foreign exchange; for example, when travelers land in a foreign airport, they often exchange dollars for the local currency. Large firms dealing in international transactions simply keep bank deposits in foreign currencies to cover their foreign transactions. An American importer of French wine will likely pay for it by writing checks on an American bank that holds an account in a French bank. The American bank will use the importer's dollars to purchase the francs needed for payment.

The demand for foreign exchange arises because a country's residents want to buy foreign goods. Conversely, the supply of foreign exchange arises because foreign customers want to buy U.S. goods. For example, we have a demand for francs by the U.S. importer who wishes to purchase French wine and a supply of francs by French customers who wish to purchase U.S. personal computers.

Exchange Rates

Exchange rate:
The (relative) price of one national currency in terms of another national currency.

One is the inverse/reciprocal of the other.

An **exchange rate** is the price of one country's money in terms of some other country's money. It is a relative price, much the same as the relative price concept discussed in Chapter 4, except that it is the relative price of one national currency expressed in terms of another national currency. Like the relative prices of goods, exchange rates can be expressed in one of two equivalent ways. We can talk about one U2 concert ticket "costing" five pizzas, or we can say that one pizza costs one-fifth of a concert ticket. Either way, the relative price of one good in terms of another good (one concert ticket in terms of pizzas or one pizza in terms of concert tickets) is expressed. Which expression we choose is simply a matter of choice or convenience.

So it is with exchange rates. Because they are relative prices of one money in terms of another money, the way we choose to express the exchange rate is a matter of choice and convenience. For example, in 1989, one U.S. dollar traded on the foreign exchange market for about six French francs (ff), the national currency of France. (The actual rate was 6.3802 to one dollar.) One U.S. dollar cost six French francs to buy, or one U.S. dollar sold for six French francs. This exchange rate is the relative price of the U.S. dollar in terms of French francs. Alternatively, it would be just as accurate to say that one French franc cost, or would buy, sixteen and two-thirds cents. This would be the relative price of the French franc in terms of the U.S. dollar. One is nothing more than the inverse or reciprocal of the other.

Exchange rates are often expressed both ways. An American in France must use French francs to make purchases. Starting out the vacation, the traveler may have a budget, say $500, that she wishes to spend on meals. By using the U.S. dollar in terms of French francs exchange rate (6 per dollar), she can calculate that she will have 3000 ff (6 ff per **dollar** × $500) to spend on meals in France. Once in France, if our tourist pays 100 ff for a lunch, she may wish to know how many dollars the lunch cost. A quick calculation using the French franc in terms of the U.S. dollar exchange rate will give the answer ($0.1667 per ff × 100 ff = $16.67).

Of equal importance are changes in exchange rates, for such changes can alter the prices of imports and exports. Suppose that a bottle of French wine sells for 100 ff. Ignoring transportation costs and any tariffs, with a dollar-franc exchange rate of $0.1667 per French franc, the wine will cost $16.67 in the United States. But suppose the exchange rate were to change to $0.20 per French franc? The same bottle of wine would still cost 100 ff in France, but its cost in the United States would rise to $20. Changes in exchange rate can alter the prices of foreign goods in home markets, as well as the prices of domestic goods in foreign markets.

Just as tourists must pay attention to exchange rates in order to make plans and informed decisions, so must businesses and governments. International trade, like interpersonal trade, requires the use of money. The prices of these monies relative to one another are important economic variables. A sudden change in an exchange rate can alter the actual values of any business transaction, making it more or less profitable than at first thought. Such changes influence business decisions and can alter the volume of international trade. At issue, then, is what determines exchange rates. Why, in 1989, did a dollar buy (cost) six French francs and not about four or ten French francs? What has caused the U.S. dollar price of French francs, or for that matter German marks, Japanese yen, Mexican pesos, or any other country's money, to change from day to day and year to year?

Exchange Rate Systems

Exchange rates, like any other price, are determined in markets by the forces of supply and demand. However, exactly who suppliers and demanders are, and under what constraints the market operates, determines the type of system within which the exchange rate will be determined. One type, the **flexible,** or **floating, exchange rate system,** is a system whereby the exchange rate is determined solely by the interaction of private demanders and suppliers of foreign exchange. This is the type of system most major trading countries employ today to determine the world market value of their respective currencies. Of course, government fiscal and monetary policies can help determine the exchange rate under such a system by influencing the behavior of private market participants. But government policies usually are not specifically designed to directly influence the exchange rate.

A second system of exchange rate determination is called a **fixed exchange rate system.** A fixed exchange rate system was in existence from the late 1940s until 1971. A few countries today still fix the value of their currencies on world markets in terms of U.S. dollars. Under a fixed exchange rate system, government intervenes directly in the foreign exchange market, either as a buyer or as a seller, in order to fix the exchange rate at some level. Some European countries combine elements of both the fixed- and flexible-rate systems. The values of these European currencies are fixed relative to one another, but all float against the U.S. dollar.

Flexible, or floating, exchange rate system:
An international monetary arrangement in which exchange rates are determined by private suppliers and demanders without government intervention.

Fixed exchange rate system:
An international monetary arrangement in which exchange rates are set by the government, which then must intervene in the foreign exchange market in order to maintain the pegged exchange rate.

Since 1973, the exchange rate system determining the relative prices of national currencies has been a blend of these two systems. By and large, the flexible-rate system is in use for the currencies of the United States and other major industrial countries. No country, however, allows its exchange rate to float freely all the time. Wide swings in the exchange rate are controlled by government intervention in the foreign exchange market. For this reason, the present international monetary system is called a **managed flexible-rate system.** In the next two sections we analyze how floating exchange rates and fixed exchange rates work.

Managed flexible-rate system:
Primarily a flexible exchange rate system, but with occasional government purchases or sales of foreign exchanges intended to influence the exchange rate.

FLEXIBLE EXCHANGE RATES

As we pointed out earlier, U.S. demand for foreign currency arises because U.S. citizens wish to buy foreign products, travel in foreign countries, invest in foreign companies, and carry on other international activities. The supply of foreign currencies to the United States arises because foreigners want to buy U.S. goods, travel in the United States, send their children to school in the United States, invest in this country, and so on. All of these forces of supply and demand affect the exchange rate between the U.S. dollar and other currencies. In effect, they form the basis of the supply and demand schedules in the foreign exchange markets.

Exchange Rates Between Two Countries

We begin our analysis with a simple model of the determination of floating, or flexible, exchange rates. For simplicity, we assume that international trade takes place only between two countries, the United States and Switzerland. The U.S. demand for foreign exchange is thus a demand for Swiss francs; the supply of foreign exchange is a supply of Swiss francs.

Supply, Demand, and the Market for Foreign Exchange. Before beginning our analysis of the factors that determine, and change, exchange rates, some preliminaries are in order. The exchange rate is determined in the foreign exchange market. It is the relative price of one money in terms of another. As we have indicated, the actions of both the Americans and the Swiss are manifested in this market. But any action on the part of residents of one country is mirrored in the actions of residents of the other. For example, Swiss exports are American imports, and vice versa. This means that technically we would want to look at both the supply and demand of dollars and the supply and demand of Swiss francs to the foreign exchange market in order to examine exchange rate determination. But because the dollar-franc exchange rate is just the inverse of the franc-dollar exchange rate (so that changes in one are mirrored by changes in the other), and because Swiss imports are American exports, we can simplify matters. We need only examine the supply and demand for either francs or dollars on the foreign exchange market in order to be able to discuss exchange rate determination. We will look at the supply and demand for Swiss francs, the foreign exchange in our discussion.

Figure 1 depicts the supply and demand for foreign exchange, Swiss francs. What establishes the supply and demand for francs on the foreign exchange market? Consider the demand for franc foreign exchange first. American importers of Swiss goods must pay Swiss producers with francs. Thus, American imports from Switzerland are the basis of foreign exchange demand. The demand for foreign exchange slopes downward because, other things constant, a higher exchange rate (more dollars per franc) implies higher import prices, fewer imports, and a smaller quantity demanded (by Americans) of foreign exchange.

The supply of foreign exchange arises from Swiss import activity and, therefore, American export activity. Swiss importers must pay for goods produced in the United States (American exports) with dollars. In order to obtain dollars, they must buy them with francs in the foreign exchange market. The supply of foreign exchange originates with Swiss imports or, what is the same thing, American exports. It is upward-sloping because, other factors considered, a rise in the dollar price of the franc (the exchange rate measured on the vertical axis) means that one franc now buys more dollars, making American goods cheaper to the Swiss. This implies an increase in the desire of the Swiss to import from the United States. They will then offer more francs for sale at the higher exchange rate to obtain additional dollars. The additional dollars are then used to purchase the larger quantity of imports.

The equilibrium exchange rate, like any other price, is one that equates quantity demanded with quantity supplied. In Figure 1, this equilibrium exchange rate is $0.50 per Swiss franc. Suppose, for some reason, the exchange rate were below equilibrium, at $0.20 per franc. The quantity demanded of foreign exchange would then exceed the quantity supplied of foreign exchange.

FIGURE 1

The exchange rate—in this case, the dollar price of one Swiss franc—is measured on the vertical axis. The quantity of francs is measured on the horizontal axis. The equilibrium exchange rate is $0.50 per Swiss franc because this is the only exchange rate that equates quantity demanded with quantity supplied. At the exchange rate of $0.75 per franc, there exists a surplus of francs, and the exchange rate will fall. At the $0.20 exchange rate, a shortage of francs on the foreign exchange market exists, which will drive the exchange rate back to $0.50.

A Two-Country Foreign Exchange Market

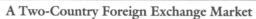

There would be a shortage of francs on the foreign exchange market. As in any other market, a shortage in the foreign exchange market will tend to drive price back toward equilibrium.

Given the fundamental economic factors determining exports and imports in both countries, an exchange rate below the equilibrium exchange rate ($0.20 per franc in Figure 1) creates a situation in which Americans wish to import much more from Switzerland than the Swiss wish to sell. At this exchange rate, Swiss goods are "too cheap" to Americans because the dollar price of the franc is "too low." On the other side of the coin, American goods are "too expensive" to the Swiss. Swiss imports are too low, and thus the quantity supplied of foreign exchange is also too low. To stimulate the quantity of Swiss imports and increase the quantity supplied of foreign exchange, as well as to reduce the quantity of U.S. imports and reduce the quantity demanded of foreign exchange, an increase in the exchange rate is necessary. The movement to equilibrium from $0.20 to $0.50 results from the bidding up of the dollar price of francs by American consumers eager to obtain Swiss goods. (Americans demand Swiss francs and *simultaneously* supply U.S. dollars.) The actions of American consumers tend to elevate the price of Swiss francs in terms of dollars, returning the dollar-franc market to equilibrium. Naturally, the rise in the dollar price of francs reduces the quantity demanded of Swiss goods and services by Americans as equilibrium is approached. (The Swiss are willing to supply the additional francs because of the higher price of their currency expressed in dollars.)

Likewise, the exchange rate of $0.75 per franc is too high for equilibrium, creating a surplus of foreign exchange. At $0.75 per franc, Swiss products are very expensive for Americans and American products are relatively inexpensive to the Swiss. As the Swiss demand dollars to get American goods, the price of dollars in terms of francs rises and the price of francs in terms of dollars falls. Simultaneously, with Americans wanting to import less than the Swiss wish to export to the United States, a surplus of franc foreign exchange exists. A fall in the dollar price of the franc will increase American imports and the quantity demanded of foreign exchange. This same fall will also make American goods more expensive in Switzerland, reduce imports, and thus reduce the quantity supplied of francs to the foreign exchange market. Equilibrium is restored, as shown in Figure 1, when the dollar price of francs returns to $0.50.

Changes in Flexible Exchange Rates

The foreign exchange market is much like any other market studied in economics. Supply and demand determine price, whereas surpluses and shortages of foreign exchange will move the exchange rate toward its equilibrium value. We now examine why the supply of or demand for foreign exchange might change, producing a change in the equilibrium exchange rate in a flexible exchange rate system.

Appreciation and Depreciation. The dollar price of the Swiss franc, or any other currency, fluctuates from day to day and even minute to minute. Trying to explain every small fluctuation in the exchange rate would be a fruitless exercise. However, broad and significant changes in exchange rates have occurred since the collapse of the fixed-rate system and subsequent inception of

Depreciation:
A decrease in the equilibrium exchange market value of a country's currency in a flexible-rate system; an increase in the number of units of a country's money required to purchase one unit of a foreign country's money.

Appreciation:
An increase in the equilibrium exchange market value of a country's currency in a flexible-rate system; a decrease in the number of units of a country's money required to purchase one unit of a foreign country's money.

the managed flexible-rate system in 1973. The late 1970s was a period of dollar **depreciation.** A depreciation of a country's currency on world markets means that the equilibrium exchange rate has changed such that it requires more of the currency to purchase other money. An increase in the equilibrium dollar price of the Swiss franc from $0.50 to $0.70 constitutes a depreciation of the dollar. It takes more dollars to buy a franc than previously, or equivalently, one dollar buys fewer francs. Another term used frequently by the financial press to describe a depreciation is a "weakening" of the currency on the foreign exchange market. The early 1980s was a period of dollar **appreciation.** An appreciation is the opposite of a depreciation; less of the money is required to buy other monies on the foreign exchange market. A fall in the equilibrium exchange rate from $0.50 to $0.30 per franc signifies a dollar appreciation (and a franc depreciation). A currency that has appreciated is said to have "strengthened" on world currency markets or is a "strong" currency. The basic reasons and fundamental causes of currency appreciations and depreciations are addressed in the following sections.

Price Levels, Money Supplies, and Inflation Rates. One factor that can cause the exchange rate to change is a change in the price level of either country. Suppose that the price level in the United States were to increase by 20 percent while the general level of prices in Switzerland was stable. Figure 2a depicts the effects this would have on the foreign exchange market and the exchange rate. Other things equal, higher U.S. prices would reduce Swiss import demand for American goods. This would, in turn, cause a decrease in the supply of foreign exchange, shown as a shift of the supply curve of francs from S to S_1. The rise in the prices of U.S. goods also would make Swiss goods relatively more attractive to Americans. American import demand would increase, and the demand for foreign exchange also would then increase. In Figure 2a, the demand for foreign exchange shifts from D to D_1.

The effect is to increase the dollar price of the franc. The equilibrium exchange rate rises from e_0 to e_1, or the dollar depreciates on the foreign exchange market. Of course, one could also say that the franc has appreciated. Had the price level in Switzerland risen by 20 percent with the price level in the United States constant, just the opposite would have occurred. Swiss goods would have become more expensive to Americans, reducing American import demand and the demand for foreign exchange from D to D_2 in Figure 2b. Swiss import demand would increase as American goods become cheaper in Switzerland, causing the supply of foreign exchange to increase from S to S_2. The equilibrium exchange rate would fall from e_0 to e_2, and a dollar appreciation (franc depreciation) would have taken place.

If in our first example the dollar had depreciated by 20 percent in response to the U.S. price level increasing by 20 percent, our model of exchange rate determination would reflect the **purchasing power parity (PPP) theory** of exchange rates. Formulated by Gustav Cassel around 1917, PPP is an intuitively appealing notion. Basically, PPP theory implies that if a dollar can buy a certain basket of goods in the United States, then converting that dollar into francs at the market exchange rate should yield enough francs to buy the same basket of goods in Switzerland.

If in Figure 2a the change in the exchange rate from e_0 to e_1 is a 20 percent change, then PPP holds. The dollar has lost purchasing power at home

Purchasing power parity (PPP) theory:
A theory that predicts that the equilibrium exchange rate will adjust so as to equate the purchasing power of a unit of each country's money.

FIGURE 2   **Price Level Changes in the Flexible Exchange Rate System**

S and D are the initial foreign supply and demand curves. In Figure 2a, an increase in the U.S. price level, holding the Swiss price level constant, causes the supply of foreign exchange to shift to S_1, while the demand for foreign exchange shifts to D_1. This causes the Swiss franc to appreciate from e_0 to e_1. This can also be described as a depreciation of the dollar. If the Swiss price level increased while the price level in the United States remained unchanged, the supply and demand curves would shift to S_2 and D_2 in Figure 2b. This would cause the exchange rate to fall from e_0 to e_2.

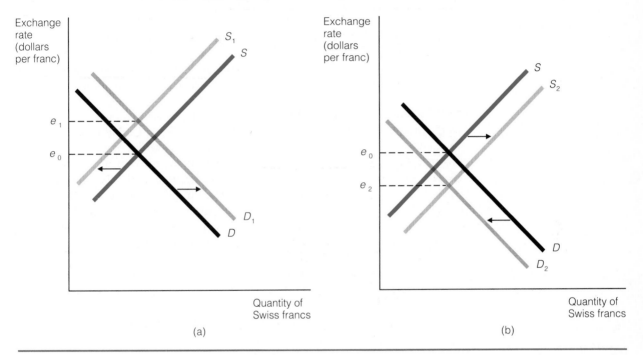

(a)   (b)

to the tune of 20 percent. It buys 20 percent fewer goods and services in the United States. A depreciation on the foreign exchange market of 20 percent guarantees that one dollar will buy 20 percent fewer Swiss goods also and that the franc's purchasing power over United States goods is maintained. According to PPP theory, the exchange rate adjusts to reflect changes in the purchasing power of currencies. While the PPP theory seems to do a fair job of describing long-term movements in exchange rates (given other determinants), it has not proved a very powerful explanation of short-term exchange rate fluctuations during the recent floating-rate period.

Note that in the long run, given other factors, if the Federal Reserve had increased the money supply, the price level in the United States would have risen. Because price level increases in the United States will depreciate the dollar on the foreign exchange market, and because money supply increases can cause the price level to rise, increases in the U.S. money supply can cause the dollar to depreciate on the foreign exchange market. In fact, some economists believe that money supply changes are one of the prime sources of exchange rate changes. Of course, an increase in the foreign money supply, *ceteris paribus*, will cause the dollar to appreciate.

Consider the possibility that both countries experience continuous increases in their price levels or positive, but constant, inflation rates. Assume that the rate of inflation differs between the United States and Switzerland. In such a scenario, the supply and demand for foreign exchange would be constantly changing, causing the equilibrium exchange rate to change continuously. We can make a statement about the direction of the change in the exchange rate if we know something about the relationship between the two inflation rates. Suppose that the rate of inflation in Switzerland is greater than the rate of inflation in the United States. Under these circumstances, the Swiss price level is rising faster than the U.S. price level. We would then see the dollar price per franc continuously falling on the world market. The dollar would be appreciating. If the U.S. inflation rate were larger than that of Switzerland, just the opposite would happen. The dollar would then continuously depreciate on the foreign exchange market.

Real Income, Exports, and Imports. Other factors also can cause a currency to appreciate or depreciate on world currency markets. Consider the effect of an expansion in the Swiss economy that results in an increase in Swiss real income. As Swiss real income increases, the demand for imports from the United States also increases. More francs are supplied to the foreign exchange market at any given exchange rate, and the supply of foreign exchange increases. In Figure 3, the foreign exchange supply curve shifts from S to S_1 and the equilibrium exchange rate falls from e_0 to e_1. The increase in Swiss real income has caused the dollar to appreciate on the foreign exchange market or, equivalently, the franc to depreciate.

Should real income in the United States rise, the dollar would depreciate on the foreign exchange market. Larger U.S. real income would cause a desire

---

FIGURE 3

An increase in real income in Switzerland has the effect of shifting the supply of foreign exchange from S to S_1. This appreciates the dollar in the foreign exchange market, causing the exchange rate to fall from e_0 to e_1. Should U.S. real income rise, the effect will be to increase the demand for foreign exchange to D_1 and depreciate the dollar, moving the exchange rate from e_0 to e_2.

Real Income Changes and the Exchange Rate

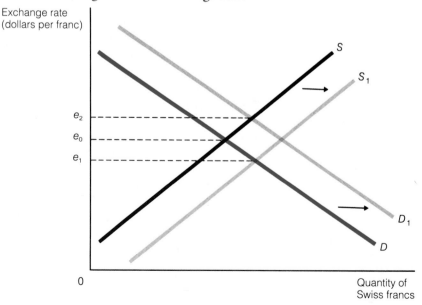

for greater imports from Switzerland. The demand for francs would increase in Figure 3 from D to D_1. Given the initial supply of foreign exchange, S, the rise in U.S. real income causes a depreciation of the dollar (appreciation of the franc) on the foreign exchange market. In this case, the exchange rate rises from e_0 to e_2.[1]

Changes in factors that directly affect exports and imports can also cause changes in exchange rates. Should consumer tastes in the United States change in favor of goods produced at home, for example, the demand for foreign exchange would decrease, causing an appreciation of the dollar. Government policies aimed at restricting imports or encouraging exports tend to reduce the demand for foreign exchange and appreciate the country's currency on world markets.

Interest Rates. So far, we have discussed the supply of foreign exchange as arising from the desires of foreigners to buy goods and services produced in the United States. But foreigners purchase real estate and financial assets in the United States as well; for instance, Rockefeller Center in New York was purchased by Japanese investors. Stocks and bonds of U.S. businesses and governments (state, local, and federal) are other, less-publicized examples of such purchases by foreign businesspeople. Both such examples are foreign investments in the United States. Just as the purchase of U.S. goods by foreigners creates a supply of foreign exchange, so does the purchase of financial assets or real assets such as automobile or computer assembly plants. Likewise, U.S. citizens purchase the financial assets of other countries, adding to the demand for foreign exchange. Our next task is to determine how changes in the purchases of financial or real assets may affect the exchange rate.

An increased desire on the part of the Swiss to invest in the United States, to buy more U.S. financial or real assets, signals an increased supply of foreign exchange. More francs are supplied to the foreign exchange market to purchase the dollars necessary to buy U.S. assets. In Figure 4, the supply of foreign exchange increases from S to S_1 and the exchange rate falls from e_0 to e_1. What would cause this to happen?

Investors everywhere look at many different variables in deciding how to allocate their investment funds among particular firms, industries, or countries. Such factors as risk, liquidity, and the degree of political stability are all important. However, a primary factor that goes into any investment decision is the real rate of interest those funds earn.

The real interest rate, recall, is the rate of interest earned adjusted for inflation. Suppose that the real interest rate in the United States rose. That would make U.S. financial assets more attractive to own and would increase the demand by foreigners to purchase U.S. financial assets. This increase in the U.S. real interest rate would have caused the increase in the supply of francs to the foreign exchange market depicted in Figure 4. The effect of a rise in the real interest rate in the United States is dollar appreciation, a decline in the dollar price of the Swiss franc on the foreign exchange market from e_0 to e_1.

Alternatively, should the real interest rate increase in Switzerland, the demand for francs on the part of Americans would increase, from D to D_1 in

---

[1] We are assuming that as real income rises, the money supply increases enough to accommodate the extra demand for money.

FIGURE 4

When the U.S. real interest rate rises, the Swiss wish to invest more in the United States, to buy more financial assets. The supply of foreign exchange increases to S_1, and the exchange rate falls to e_1. Higher U.S. real interest rates cause dollar appreciation. When the real interest rate in Switzerland rises, Americans wish to buy more Swiss securities and the demand for foreign exchange increases. The exchange rate moves from e_0 to e_2, and the dollar depreciates.

Real Interest Rate Effects on the Exchange Rate

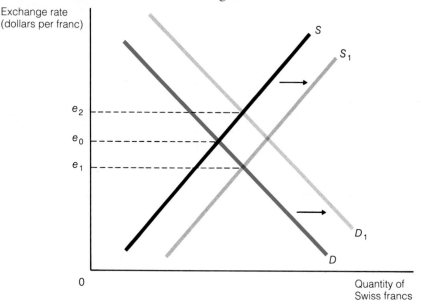

Figure 4. Given the supply of franc foreign exchange of S, the exchange rate would rise to e_2. An increased Swiss real interest rate causes the dollar to depreciate, or the franc to appreciate, on the foreign exchange market.

FIXED EXCHANGE RATES

As we have seen, a system of flexible exchange rates allows the foreign exchange market to determine the prices at which currency will change hands. By contrast, a fixed exchange rate system does not allow exchange rates to float in a free market. Government intervenes in the foreign exchange market to fix the international price of its currency. Once fixed exchange rates are established, governments stand ready to protect the rates through intervention in the foreign exchange market.

The Operation of a Fixed Exchange Rate System

Undervalued:
A term describing the foreign exchange market value of a country's money; occurs when the number of units of a country's money that purchases one unit of a foreign currency is *greater* than the equilibrium exchange rate.

Although the United States and Switzerland no longer trade on the basis of a fixed exchange rate, imagine what would happen if they did. Figure 5 illustrates what happens when a fixed exchange rate between francs and dollars does not happen to correspond to ever-shifting market conditions. If the current market equilibrium rate is e_0, but the U.S. government seeks to maintain an exchange rate of e_1, the official or fixed rate is above the equilibrium rate. In this case, the dollar is said to be undervalued relative to the Swiss franc. The dollar is **undervalued** because at exchange rate e_1 each dollar will buy fewer francs than it would at the lower equilibrium exchange rate, e_0. Of course, if the

FIGURE 5

If the government sets an exchange rate below equilibrium, such as e_2, a shortage of foreign exchange develops, and the central bank must continuously sell foreign exchange from its exchange reserves to keep the rate at e_2. If the rate is set at e_1, a surplus of foreign exchange is created, and the central bank must continuously buy foreign exchange, adding to its exchange reserves, in order to maintain the fixed rate.

Fixed Exchange Rates Above and Below Equilibrium

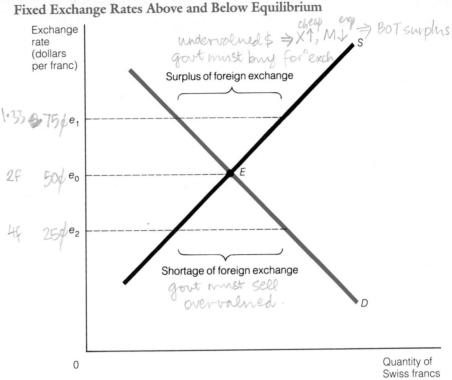

[handwritten annotations on figure:]
undervalued \$ ⇒ X↑, M↓ ⇒ BOT surplus
(cheap) (exp)
govt must buy for'exch

Surplus of foreign exchange

Exchange rate (dollars per franc)

1·33 75¢ e_1
2F   50¢ e_0 E
4f   25¢ e_2

Shortage of foreign exchange
govt must sell
overvalued.

S

D

0   Quantity of Swiss francs

Overvalued:
A term describing the foreign exchange market value of a country's money; occurs when the number of units of a country's money that purchases one unit of a foreign currency is *less* than the equilibrium exchange rate.

Foreign exchange market intervention:
Purchases or sales of foreign exchange by government, usually a central bank, with the goal of maintaining a fixed exchange rate or influencing the exchange rate in a flexible-rate system.

Foreign exchange reserves:
The stock of a foreign exchange held by a central bank that is available for use in exchange market intervention.

dollar is undervalued, then the franc is overvalued. Similarly, if the government were to fix the exchange rate at e_2, each dollar would purchase more francs than it would at the equilibrium exchange rate, e_0. In this case, the dollar (franc) would be **overvalued** (undervalued).

Suppose that the government decides to fix the price of its currency in the foreign exchange market at e_1. In order to do so, the government must not merely decree that all currency trades take place at an exchange rate equal to e_1. The government, usually the central bank, must instead become a big enough player in the market to make the exchange rate e_1. To do this, the central bank must continuously engage in **foreign exchange market intervention.**

When the government fixes the exchange rate at e_1 even though fundamental foreign exchange market forces dictate an equilibrium exchange rate of e_0, a surplus of francs on the foreign exchange market is created. At the high dollar price of the franc, quantity supplied of francs will exceed quantity demanded. Without exchange market intervention, as described earlier, the exchange rate would fall back to its equilibrium value, e_0. The central bank can prevent this fall, and maintain exchange rate e_1 only if it intervenes in the exchange market by buying up the franc surplus. The buying of francs, in this case, by the central bank builds up the central bank's **foreign exchange reserves,** its holding of foreign currencies. Such an intervention is not a one-time affair. Each month or year that the exchange rate is fixed above its equilibrium value, the central bank must purchase the surplus of francs in order to maintain the fixed rate. Fixing the rate above equilibrium tends to make a country's exports cheaper and its imports more expensive. Hence, such a policy may be used by governments in an attempt to reduce imports and encourage exports.

Sometimes central banks fix the exchange rate below the market equilibrium exchange rate, such as rate e_2 in Figure 5. This creates a shortage of foreign exchange, since quantity demanded at exchange rate e_2 is greater than quantity supplied. Again, without continuous exchange market intervention, the exchange rate would move back toward its equilibrium level, e_0. In this case, foreign exchange market intervention takes the form of sales of foreign currency (Swiss francs) from the central bank's foreign currency reserves. Setting such an exchange rate, one that deliberately overvalues the country's currency in world markets, is not a policy that most countries could pursue indefinitely. Sooner or later the central bank would run out of reserves and be unable to support the fixed exchange rate. Fixing the exchange rate below equilibrium tends to encourage imports and discourage exports.

Fixed Exchange Rates

The fixed exchange rate set by government can stray significantly from the equilibrium exchange rate. A country will therefore experience persistent problems in international trade; namely, it will confront persistent surpluses or deficits in its foreign trade. In the balance of trade between exports and imports, a country whose exports have greater value than its imports is said to have a **balance of trade surplus;** one whose imports' value exceeds its exports' value has a **balance of trade deficit.** What are the options under a fixed-rate system for alleviating such situations?

Changes in Domestic Macroeconomic Policy. Consider first the example of Figure 5, where the dollar price of the franc is maintained at e_1 while the equilibrium price is e_0. The dollar is undervalued, and the United States experiences a balance of trade surplus, while Switzerland runs a persistent deficit, importing more than it exports. The Swiss will demand that something be done.

One option is to change domestic macroeconomic policies in the two countries. Suppose the United States allows its money supply to rise and Switzerland lets its money supply fall. In the United States the increase in money supply will lead to higher prices and costs. In Switzerland the opposite effects will occur: There will be lower prices and costs. Thus, U.S. exports will fall because they are now relatively more expensive on world markets, and U.S. imports will rise because foreign goods are now cheaper and income is higher. In Switzerland exports will rise because Swiss goods are now relatively cheaper, and imports will decline because U.S. goods are more expensive and Swiss GNP has fallen. The basic tendency in both countries, then, is toward adjustments that erase the surplus of exports over imports in the United States and the corresponding deficit in Switzerland.

An important point emerges from this discussion. In a fixed exchange rate system, where the government chooses to defend the fixed rate at all costs, imbalances in foreign trade must be resolved through macroeconomic adjustment of entire domestic economies. To keep one price—the foreign exchange rate—fixed, the United States and Switzerland manipulate the level of all the

Balance of trade surplus:
Occurs when the value of a nation's exports exceeds the value of a nation's imports; also called a trade surplus.

Balance of trade deficit:
Occurs when the value of a nation's exports is less than the value of a nation's imports; also called a trade deficit.

other prices in their economies. A flexible-rate system, by contrast, changes one price—the foreign exchange rate—to resolve balance of trade problems.

Devaluation and Revaluation. The second option facing two fixed-rate countries with a trade imbalance is to change the official exchange rate. In this way, the two governments can avoid costly manipulation of their domestic economies to restore foreign trade equilibrium. There are two possible changes in this regard.

Devaluation:
An official change in a country's exchange rate in a fixed-rate system; the number of units of a country's money that purchases one unit of another country's currency is *increased* by the government.

One is **devaluation** of one country's currency. When the dollar is overvalued (e_2 per franc in Figure 5), the United States suffers a trade deficit and Switzerland a trade surplus. With Switzerland's agreement, the United States can lower the official exchange value of its currency. In this case, we say that a devaluation has occurred. In Figure 5 this means that the dollar price of francs is moved upward, closer to its equilibrium value. This change in the exchange rate changes the relative prices of each country's imports and exports so as to help erase the U.S. deficit and the Swiss surplus without each country's having to resort to costly deflation and inflation of its domestic economy.

Where the official rate is above the equilibrium rate (such as e_1 per franc in Figure 5), the opposite process can be applied. In this case, the United States has a trade surplus and Switzerland a deficit. The two countries can support this exchange rate if the United States buys francs or if Switzerland sells dollars or some combination of both. However, to avoid inflation in the United States and deflation in Switzerland to correct the balance of trade situation, the two countries might agree to revalue the dollar. A **revaluation** occurs when the official price of a currency is raised. This means that the dollar price of francs would move downward in Figure 5, closer to its equilibrium value. The value of the dollar is thus raised, or revalued, and the corresponding value of the franc is lowered, or devalued.

Revaluation:
An official change in a country's exchange rate in a fixed-rate system; the number of units of a country's money that purchases one unit of another country's currency is *decreased* by the government.

Adjustments in official exchange rates seem less costly than the manipulation of whole economies. However, as we will see later, such adjustments are not always easy to accomplish. The Swiss may reap advantages from a balance of trade surplus and may resist efforts to devalue the dollar or to implement a domestic economic policy that chips away at their surplus. Complex international negotiations are inherent in a fixed-rate system.

Changes in Trade Policy. A third option for resolving balance of trade difficulties under a fixed-rate system is for a deficit country to erect barriers to international trade. Tariffs, quotas, and other barriers to the free movement of people and goods across international borders can be established to try to solve a trade problem. This is not an option that would find much favor among economists, however. As detailed in Chapter 38, such impediments to international trade cost the worldwide economy economic efficiency and gains from specialization.

Instead of erecting trade barriers, another policy is pressuring trading partners to abolish current import restrictions. This strategy has been advocated as a means of reducing the persistent trade deficit between the United States and Japan.

Both floating and fixed exchange rate systems have been used in the past. The most economically powerful countries presently operate essentially on a floating system and have done so since early 1973. Before that, starting shortly after World War II, a fixed exchange rate system governed international monetary relations. For an analysis of the balance of trade problems as they persist in the 1990s, see Economics in Action, "Trade Deficits, Flexible Exchange Rates, and the Competitiveness of the U.S. Economy," at the end of this chapter. We will discuss the historical evolution of the international monetary system later in the chapter.

MACROECONOMIC POLICY, EXCHANGE RATES, AND TRADE BALANCE

Foreign trade can have dramatic effects on a government's macroeconomic policy. We consider briefly how monetary policy and fiscal policy are affected by foreign trade.

Monetary Policy

The link between the foreign exchange market and monetary policy depends on whether trade takes place under a system of fixed or floating exchange rates. In the former case, the central bank fixes the exchange rate and allows the money supply to be determined by the economic system; in the latter case, the central bank lets the exchange rate be determined in the market for foreign exchange and manipulates the domestic supply of money.

The Case of Fixed Exchange Rates. To support a fixed exchange rate, the central bank must be prepared to buy and sell whatever foreign exchange is necessary to keep the exchange rate at the fixed level. Suppose there is a surplus in the balance of trade: At the current exchange rate, the quantity of foreign exchange supplied by exporters exceeds the amount of foreign exchange demanded by importers. In this case, the central bank must purchase foreign exchange by an amount equal to the excess supply to eliminate the tendency for the exchange rate to fall. The central bank purchases foreign exchange by printing more domestic currency, and this increase in the supply of money sets forces in motion that tend to restore equilibrium. Other things being equal, domestic prices rise with a larger money supply, and these higher prices will discourage exports and encourage imports, thus diminishing the trade surplus. In the case of a trade deficit, the central bank will be selling foreign exchange (in effect decreasing domestic currency) to keep the exchange rate from rising. This action will lower the domestic money supply, and the accompanying lower domestic prices will tend to discourage imports and encourage exports. The important point is that to fix one price—the exchange rate—the central bank must give up other money supply controls and allow all other prices to adjust.

The Case of Flexible Exchange Rates. If the government instead is using a flexible exchange rate system, the central bank can use its domestic monetary policy tools, allowing the exchange rate to be determined by the market. Starting from equilibrium, an increase in the domestic money supply tends to raise prices, and these higher prices tend to encourage imports and discourage exports. Thus, there is a trade deficit (an excess demand for foreign exchange) at the old exchange rate. For individuals to be willing to supply the extra foreign exchange to finance these trade movements, the exchange rate must rise by whatever amount is necessary to eliminate the excess demand. The result of an increase in the domestic money supply is therefore a rise in the exchange rate by exactly the same proportion.

Fiscal Policy

The effects of a government's fiscal policy initiatives on exchange rates depend largely on how the changes in government spending are financed. If we assume, for simplicity, that all increases in government expenditures are financed by borrowing, then expansionary fiscal policies stimulate aggregate demand, including the demand for imports on the one hand, and raise government borrowing on the other. The increased demand puts upward pressure on the exchange rate because of the additional foreign currencies required to finance the increased imports. But the increased government borrowing tends to raise interest rates, attracting foreign capital and placing downward pressure on the exchange rate. The net change in the exchange rate owing to the expansionary policy depends on which of the two effects dominates.

Similarly, contractionary fiscal policies may raise or lower the exchange rate. A lower level of government spending will reduce aggregate demand, reduce the demand for imports, and, at the same time, lower government borrowing. The lower import demand will tend to lower the exchange rate by fostering an excess supply of foreign currencies. But with less government borrowing, interest rates tend to fall. Capital outflows increase, putting upward pressure on exchange rates. Again, the net change of the exchange rate depends on which event—the fall-off in imports or the decline in interest rates—has greater effect.

THE GOLD STANDARD

Gold standard:
An international monetary system in which currencies are redeemable in gold at fixed rates or prices.

The **gold standard** is a type of fixed exchange rate system with a long history in international trade. David Hume (1711–1776), a Scottish philosopher and friend of Adam Smith, was the first person to analyze the workings of an international gold standard. The world economy functioned on a gold standard as recently as World War I. Many observers today wistfully call for a return to the gold standard.

Under a gold standard, all trading nations are willing to redeem their currencies for gold. With each currency linked to gold, the precious metal becomes, in effect, a world currency.

Price-specie flow mechanism:
The channels by which gold inflows or outflows would cause price level increases or decreases in a country on the gold standard, thereby eliminating trade surpluses and deficits.

A key element of the gold standard is that each country links its money supply to its holdings of gold. Both foreign and domestic citizens are allowed to redeem currency for gold in a country at a fixed rate. This action creates a natural equilibrating mechanism (Hume called it the **price-specie flow mechanism**), which keeps the imports and exports of countries in balance. Suppose that while operating on a gold standard, the United States imports more than it exports over a given period of time. This differential of purchases has to be paid in gold. Since money supplies are tied to gold, the gold payment causes the money supply of the United States to fall and the money supplies of trade surplus countries to rise. Prices and costs in the United States would thus fall, and prices and costs in the trade surplus countries would rise. Deflation in the trade deficit countries such as the United States would stimulate exports and dampen imports, and inflation in trade surplus countries would dampen exports and stimulate imports. Balance of trade equilibrium is thus restored in both types of countries under a gold standard.

The gold standard is very much like the fixed exchange rate system. However, a gold-based standard is not necessary to operate a fixed exchange rate system. What is required is that countries act as if they are on the gold standard. When a country runs a trade surplus, it increases its money supply, and its domestic prices and costs rise; ultimately, exports decrease and imports increase. When a country has a trade deficit, it decreases its money supply, prices and costs fall, and thus exports increase and imports decrease. In both cases, a country is required to manipulate its whole economy to maintain equilibrium in its balance of trade with a fixed exchange rate.

The crucial difference between the gold standard and modern fixed-rate systems managed by government intervention in the foreign exchange market is that under a gold standard the domestic authorities do not have a choice about changing the money supply, thereby inflating or deflating currency. No international negotiations are required; the system works automatically. A modern fixed-rate system requires that countries agree to follow the appropriate domestic monetary and fiscal policies or to devalue or revalue the official rates when disequilibrium exchange rates lead to persistent deficits and surpluses. To reach such agreements requires complex and costly international negotiations. Modern fixed-rate systems are thus at the mercy of individual action by each country. Countries may or may not follow the rules of the game. The gold standard left no such discretion to political authorities. (Focus, "Should We Return to a Gold Standard?" details the advantages and disadvantages of the gold standard.)

THE BALANCE OF PAYMENTS

Countries keep track of the flow of international trade and periodically publish a report of their transactions, called the **balance of payments.** The balance of payments is essentially an accounting record of a nation's foreign business. It contains valuable information about the level of exports, imports, foreign investment, and the transactions of government such as purchases and sales of foreign currencies.

The balance of payments, as an accounting statement, is kept according to the principles of double-entry bookkeeping. The concept of double-entry bookkeeping is simple: Each entry on the credit side of the ledger implies an equal entry on the debit side.[2] Thus, each international transaction creates both a debit ($-$) and a credit ($+$) item in the balance of payments ledger.

only def

Balance of payments:
An official accounting record of all the foreign transactions of a nation's residents, businesses, and governments.

---

[2]Double-entry bookkeeping is discussed in Chapter 7.

FOCUS   Should We Return to a Gold Standard?

The relatively high inflation rates experienced by the United States during the late 1970s and early 1980s led to a variety of proposals for a return to a gold standard. Proponents of the gold standard argued that linking the nominal money supply to gold would prevent large increases and decreases in the money supply that lead to inflations and deflations. Congress established a U.S. Gold Commission to study the question, and the members not only debated the desirability of again tying the dollar to gold but also considered how to implement a new gold standard.

Proponents of a return to the gold standard argue that the Federal Reserve has neither the willingness nor the ability to follow monetary policies that promote price stability and that some constraint on excessive monetary expansionism is necessary. What are the advantages and disadvantages of gold-backed dollars?

Under a gold standard, currency is freely convertible into gold at some fixed rate, such as $35 per ounce, which was for many years the official U.S. price of gold. Thus, a nation's currency supply is directly related to its supply of gold. The supply of currency can be expanded relative to the supply of gold only by devaluing the dollar in terms of gold—that is, by raising gold's dollar price. A gold standard therefore enforces monetary discipline. In the absence of devaluation, the currency supply can be increased only at a rate equal to the increase in the output of gold, an expansion that has occurred historically at about 1.5 to 2 percent annually. Such a monetary policy would foster price stability with little or no inflation in the economy.

There are several major drawbacks to a gold standard. Real resources are tied up in money production—gold must be mined, stored, and transported. Also, the supply of gold is relatively inelastic. Expansion in the demand for money as economic growth occurs will generate downward pressure on the general price level. If the supply of gold rises more slowly than the demand, a gold standard will bring about persist deflation. Discovery of new gold sources or improvements in the technology used to extract gold from existing mines would likely bring about rapid inflation.

Even though the dollar price of gold is fixed, a variety of demand-side factors can cause the market price of gold to diverge from its official price. Indeed, it would be the sheerest coincidence for the two prices to be equal. Cooperation among nations is required to maintain the official price in such circumstances. For instance, during the late 1960s, a two-tier system evolved in which a world price of $35 per ounce was supported through sales among Western central banks and by an agreement between governments not to buy or sell gold in the open market. Prior to that time, a group of countries had formed a gold pool for the purpose of using their gold reserves to intervene periodically to stabilize the open market price at the official price.

Finally, incentives to engage in monetary expansionism are not completely eliminated by a gold standard. Increases in the stock of currency can be purchased for a time by a willingness to suffer a drain on gold reserves. That is, domestic inflation tends to create a trade deficit, which under a gold standard is balanced by shipments of gold to trade surplus nations. However, the inflating country's currency becomes overvalued, and pressures to devalue gradually become irresistible. In fact, persistent monetary expansion by the United States ultimately led to the collapse of the earlier world gold standard.

There is a simple rule to follow in classifying debits and credits: Any foreign transaction that leads to a demand for foreign currencies (or a supply of dollars) is treated as a debit, or a minus, item. The act of importing is a debit entry in the balance of payments. Any foreign transaction that leads to a demand for dollars (or a supply of foreign currency) is entered as a credit, or a plus, item. The act of exporting is a credit entry in the balance of payments.

Suppose a U.S. firm exports computers to France, and the French importer of the computers pays for the purchase with an IOU. The French IOU is entered on the credit side in U.S. balance of payments bookkeeping because the French importer must ultimately demand dollars to pay off its IOU to the U.S. firm. The sale of computers is entered on the debit side as the offsetting part of the transaction. The U.S. firm must give up a computer in return for the French importer's payment. Since each transaction implies an equal debit and credit, the balance of payments must always balance. In this respect, the balance of payment is like any other accounting balance sheet.

Of course, although the total balance of payments of a country must always balance (debits minus credits equal zero), its component parts need not balance. For example, the imports and exports of specific merchandise such as automobiles do not have to balance. But overall, surpluses in one part of the balance of payments must be canceled out by deficits in other parts. This is not to say, of course, that countries do not experience balance of payments problems. Problems arise, as we will see, from persistent surpluses or deficits in the component parts of the balance of payments. (See Focus, "Debtor Nations in the 1990s," for a discussion of the consequences of persistent deficits.)

Exports and Imports: The Balance of Trade

Table 1 presents the data on the U.S. balance of payments for 1988. Items 1 and 2 represent exports and imports of goods and services. The difference between the sums of these aspects of the balance of payments—exports contrasted with imports—is the balance of trade. Note that trade in merchandise is only one facet of this balance. Merchandise trade figures are the result of a country's international trade in physical goods, such as books, cars, planes, and computers—the visible exports and imports. The data in Table 1 show that in 1988 merchandise exports (1a) were less than merchandise imports (2a) by $127.2 billion. This figure is sometimes called the merchandise trade balance and is equal to merchandise exports minus merchandise imports. If the figure is positive, there is a merchandise trade surplus. It was negative in 1988, so there was a merchandise trade deficit.

Many imports and exports are invisible. U.S. citizens and firms supply various services to foreigners, such as transportation, insurance, and telecommunications. Payments are received for these services just as in the case of visible exports. Items 1b and 2b represent invisible exports and imports in the balance of payments. When both visible and invisible exports and imports are considered in Table 1, U.S. exports were still substantially less than U.S. imports, yielding a trade deficit of $111.8 billion.

Net Transfers Abroad

Net unilateral transfers abroad are one-way money payments from the United States to foreigners or United States citizens living abroad. Included in this category are such items as foreign aid and pension checks to retired U.S. citizens living abroad. Nothing tangible comes back to the United States for these transfers, but they do give rise to a demand for foreign exchange. They thus are entered as a debit item in the balance of payments. In 1988, the United States made $14.7 billion worth of such transfers.

Current Account Balance

The balance on current account is equal to exports of goods and services minus imports of goods and services minus net unilateral transfers abroad. The United States had a deficit on current account in 1988 of $126.6 billion.

TABLE 1

U.S. Balance of Payments, 1988

U.S. exports enter the balance of payments with plus signs because buyers of these exports must pay U.S. firms with dollars. Dollars thus flow into the United States and are recorded as a plus, or credit, in the balance of payments. U.S. imports receive a minus sign, indicating that to pay for foreign goods U.S. buyers must supply dollars to foreign countries. Dollars thus flow out of the United States, and imports are then treated as a minus, or a debit, in the balance of payments. Similarly, outflows of U.S. capital and inflows of foreign capital are treated as debits and credits, respectively. To classify an item as a debit or a credit, think of whether dollars are leaving or entering the country. If they are leaving, the item is a debit; if they are entering, the item is a credit.

Item		Amount (billions of dollars)
1. Exports of goods & services		+529.8
a. Merchandise, excluding military	+319.3	
b. Other goods & services	+210.5	
2. Imports of goods & services		−641.7
a. Merchandise, excluding military	−446.5	
b. Other goods & services	−195.2	
3. U.S. government grants		− 10.4
4. Remittances, pensions, and other transfers		− 4.3
5. U.S. assets abroad, net (capital outflow)		− 82.1
a. U.S. official reserve assets, net	− 3.6	
b. Other U.S. government assets, net	+ 3.0	
c. U.S. private assets, net	− 81.5	
6. Foreign assets in the U.S., net (capital inflow)		+219.3
a. Foreign official assets, net	+ 38.9	
b. Other foreign assets, net	+180.4	
7. Statistical discrepancy		− 10.6
8. Total		0

Source: U.S. Department of Commerce, *Survey of Current Business* (December 1989), p. 22.

Note: Total does not add to zero due to rounding.

Net Capital Movements

When U.S. residents purchase foreign stocks and bonds, they obtain a claim to foreign capital (buildings, factories, future foreign government payments, and so forth). Funds that would otherwise be invested in the United States are exported, or, to put it another way, capital is exported. When foreign citizens purchase the stocks and bonds of U.S. businesses and governments, foreign capital is imported into the United States. In 1988, capital outflows were $82.1 billion, whereas capital inflows were $219.3 billion.

Note what happens in bookkeeping terms when capital flows into and out of a country. Capital outflows are treated as a debit item in the balance of payments because they constitute a payment; they give rise to a demand for foreign exchange with which to make foreign investment. Capital inflows are a credit item because they consist of receipts by U.S. residents from foreigners; they generate a supply of foreign exchange necessary to obtain dollars with which to purchase U.S. financial assets.

FOCUS   Debtor Nations in the 1990s

In recent years, much concern has been expressed concerning international indebtedness. To take but one example, Mexico alone owed U.S. banks more than $20 billion in 1988. In this discussion, there is a tendency to view international debt as an economic evil. Those who hold this view advocate any policy designed to eliminate such indebtedness. However, a more careful examination of the issue shows that debt is not the result of sinister forces but of choices made by individuals and business firms within a country. Further, the acquisition of debt often is a sensible way for a country to undertake economic growth.

In examining this issue, it is useful to draw an analogy between countries that become indebted and individuals or families who do the same. Many college students elect to go into debt. Fully capable of entering the labor force and being self-sufficient, many high school graduates opt instead for more education, taking out student loans and incurring significant debts. This choice will not necessarily prove to be profitable for every student; some will choose majors of questionable value in the job market and these same majors may not even yield any personal satisfaction. Still, most students find borrowing to pay for a college education worthwhile. Enhanced earning power in the future will enable the college student both to pay off student loans and to have a better standard of living.

Of course, paying for tuition and room and board is not the only way to go into debt. Perhaps you have borrowed money to buy a car or run up your credit cards to pay for clothes and vacations. Again, however, your indebtedness is the consequence of your own choices. In most cases, the decision to borrow will prove to be a wise one; it is usually "worth it" to have less in the future in order to have more now. Only when the repayment of debts involves great future sacrifices can the decision to borrow be considered positively unwise.

The reasons students incur debts and the reasons countries incur debts are of a kind. In many cases, poor countries with growth potential obtain loans from abroad to build plants, office buildings, highway systems. Often, these turn out to be wise investments, much like most educational loans and for a similar reason: The future productivity of the country is enhanced, which enables the debt to be easily repaid. Sometimes, countries borrow huge sums but fail to use them in a way that enhances future productivity. During the past two decades, Argentina, Peru, Mexico, and Chile have all incurred huge debts but have failed to achieve much in the way of economic growth. Hence, the loans now represent a real burden to the countries, as repayment will require marked decreases in living standards. Debt forgiveness for these countries is possible—most likely in exchange for lower tariffs and elimination of other trade barriers against U.S. goods.

As a consequence of large trade deficits since 1982, the United States has also become a debtor nation. This position is a manifestation of the choice to consume foreign goods far in excess of any willingness on the part of other nations to buy American goods—not the consequence of any sinister forces. This choice has enabled Americans to enjoy a higher standard of living during this period than would have been possible otherwise. The consequence will be a somewhat lower living standard in future years than would have been the case without so much borrowing. This does not mean that it is a mistake for the United States to have gone into debt. The United States resembles a well-to-do family with large credit card bills—bills easily paid in the future.

Transactions in Official Reserves

Items 5a and 6a in Table 1 reflect the activities of government in the foreign exchange market. The official reserve assets of a country are its holdings of gold and foreign exchange. Also included in reserve assets are special drawing rights (SDRs) with the International Monetary Fund, an international central bank located in Washington, D.C. SDRs are supplementary reserves of purchasing power that a country can draw on to pay international debts. SDRs are simply bookkeeping entries that member countries may draw against to settle an international payments deficit. They are not money in any physical sense, but SDRs may be used as a means of payment. Suppose that Mexico experiences a balance of payments deficit and is without dollars to repay Canada for its purchases of capital goods. Mexico, as a member of the IMF, may opt to settle the debt by transferring some of its special drawing rights credit to Canada. In this way international reserves and liquidity are increased without any actual transfer of funds. After the transfer, Canada may utilize the increased credit to settle some international obligations.

A government can finance an excess of imports over exports by drawing down its holdings of official reserves. Countries experiencing surpluses may want to add to their official reserves. During the 1947–1973 period of fixed exchange rates, these reserve accounts were quite important because countries used the reserves to stabilize their exchange rates. Deficit countries used reserves to defend the value of their currency, and surplus countries accumulated valuable international reserves.

Item 5a is U.S. holdings of official reserve assets. In 1988, these holdings increased by $3.6 billion. This item enters the balance of payments as a debit because an increase in official reserve holdings means an increase in the demand for foreign exchange. Item 5a is thus treated like a merchandise import.

Item 6a is net investments of official agencies of foreign countries, such as the OPEC countries, in the United States. Since these investments represent demand for dollars, they are treated as a credit item in the balance of payments.

In 1988, the United States increased its net position in international reserves by $35.3 billion, the sum of items 5a and 6a.

Statistical Discrepancy

Item 7 in Table 1 is called statistical discrepancy, an accounting fudge factor. When all the data were collected and debits and credits computed, the credits outweighed the debits by 10.6 billion. The negative statistical discrepancy is added to make the balance of payments balance by compensating for imperfections in data gathering. Some debits have apparently gone unrecorded in computing the balance of payments. These could include hidden imports or unrecorded capital outflows. Most experts think that the former is the source of most of the discrepancy, which is clearly quite large.

The Balance of Payments and the Value of the Dollar

The last entry in Table 1 is zero, indicating that the balance of payments must balance. This is the way any double-entry accounting system works.

The balance of payments, however, is an aggregate record of a country's international payments for one year. Behind this record are the myriad transactions of U.S. citizens and firms with foreign citizens and firms. These transactions determine how the U.S. dollar fares in the foreign exchange market. If, over time, the value of the dollar rises against other currencies, we say that the dollar is strong. This is precisely what happened over the period 1982–1985, although the dollar generally depreciated in the latter half of the 1980s. The dollar appreciated in the range of 10 to 15 percent against most major foreign currencies between 1982 and 1985. Most observers feel that this appreciation of the dollar reflected high U.S. interest rates that attracted an inflow of foreign capital into the United States.

This capital inflow led to a higher demand for the dollar and thus to its appreciation. There are obviously costs and benefits associated with large inflows of foreign capital into a country. Foreigners thereby own more U.S. assets and firms, but the United States has an expanded supply of capital as a consequence. The important point is that the dollar appreciated in currency markets during the early 1980s, and though this fact is not directly reflected in the balance of payments, it indicates that the U.S. foreign economic position might loosely be described as a surplus. That is, the impact of all our foreign transactions over time has been to cause the dollar to rise in value. Since 1986, the dollar has been on a path of depreciation vis-à-vis most major foreign currencies. While dollar depreciation can be expected to turn our loosely described balance of payments surplus around, such reactions are usually relatively slow in occurring. It is still too early to gauge the impact of this latest dollar depreciation on the overall balance of payments, although the trade deficit decreased between 1986 and 1988.

THE EVOLUTION OF INTERNATIONAL MONETARY INSTITUTIONS

Major world trading nations today rely on floating exchange rates. These governments will occasionally intervene in the foreign exchange market when exchange rate changes are significant, but generally currency prices are free to adjust according to the forces of supply and demand. We briefly review the developments over the past hundred years that led the major trading nations to adopt floating exchange rates in 1973.

The Decline of the Gold Standard

In the period before World War I, dating back to the 1870s, most currencies in the world economy were tied to gold. This means that each country was prepared to redeem its currency at a fixed price in gold to both its own citizens and foreigners. The United States, for example, stood ready to exchange an ounce of gold for $20.67 over this period. In addition, countries on the gold standard linked their money supplies to their holdings of gold bullion.

The gold standard worked reasonably well in eliminating balance of trade surpluses and deficits over the period 1870–1914. Nonetheless, for a variety of reasons the gold standard broke down after World War I. There were attempts to return to the gold standard in the 1920s, but the shock to the international economy caused by the Great Depression in the 1930s brought the gold system down once and for all.

Bretton Woods and the Postwar System

Not until after World War II were the problems of the international monetary system addressed in a concerted way. Negotiators for the free-world countries met in Bretton Woods, New Hampshire, in 1944 to develop a new international monetary order. The **Bretton Woods system,** which lasted almost thirty years, consisted of a system of fixed exchange rates and an international central bank, called the **International Monetary Fund** (IMF), to oversee the new system.

We have already discussed the economics of fixed exchange rates. The basic idea of the Bretton Woods system was that, over time, countries would obtain or pay for their imports with their exports. However, there might be

Bretton Woods system:
The fixed exchange rate system established among Western countries after World War II.

International Monetary Fund:
An international organization, established along with the Bretton Woods system, designed to assist in the efficient functioning of the Bretton Woods fixed exchange rate system.

temporary periods over which a country might wish to run a trade deficit to obtain more imports than its current level of exports allowed it to obtain. Under the Bretton Woods system the country could do so by borrowing international reserves from the IMF. Over time, the country was expected to return to a trade surplus, out of which the earlier loan of reserves could be repaid.

The IMF was the bank that held the reserves that allowed the system to operate in this way. When the IMF was formed, each member country was required to contribute reserves of its currency to the bank. The bank thus accumulated substantial holdings of dollars, marks, francs, pesos, and so on, and when member nations ran into balance of trade deficits, the bank would lend them reserves. Each time a loan was made, the debtor nation was encouraged to reform its economic policies to avoid future deficits. Sound economic management might also lead to a trade surplus and a source of funds to repay the IMF loan.

The Bretton Woods system sounds fine in principle, and indeed it functioned tolerably well for a number of years. However, as we saw earlier, fixing the price of a currency is like fixing the price of any other good or service—it is very likely to cause surpluses and shortages in the currency market. As the conditions affecting imports and exports across countries change, the demand and supply of currencies will shift. Countries can find themselves with overvalued fixed exchange rates, which means that they will face persistent balance of trade deficits. Under the IMF system the deficit country could draw on its IMF reserves to settle the deficits, but it could not do this forever because it would exhaust its reserves. Chronic deficit countries with overvalued exchange rates were thus said to be in fundamental disequilibrium.

In our discussion of the theory of fixed exchange rates, we reviewed the various courses of action that a country in fundamental disequilibrium could take. First, it could devalue its currency as a step toward restoring equilibrium in its balance of trade. Once its currency was devalued, the exchange rate would again be fixed and defended. Second, the country could attempt to improve its trade balance by imposing tariff and quota barriers to imports and perhaps by subsidizing exports. In other words, the country could move away from free trade to balance its imports and exports. Third, the country could behave as if it were on the gold standard. This would mean adopting restrictive monetary and fiscal policies designed to promote domestic deflation and high interest rates in the hope that such changes would restore the balance of trade to equilibrium. This, of course, is a problematic course of action for any country. For example, if the country's unemployment rate were already high, it is hard to believe that the nation's leaders would be sufficiently disciplined to undertake a deflationary course of action.

Speculation by buyers and sellers of currencies also undermines a fixed exchange rate system. Suppose Great Britain is running chronic trade deficits, and everyone, including speculators, expects that the pound will be devalued (even though British central bankers will deny such rumors vehemently). In effect, speculators are in a no-lose position. Will they continue to hold pounds? Clearly, they will not; pounds are about to become less valuable relative to other currencies. Speculators will sell their pounds for other currencies, increasing the supply of pounds to the foreign exchange market and putting additional downward pressure on the pound. By selling the weak

Speculation:
The buying and selling of currencies on the foreign exchange market with the intent of profiting from possible devaluation or revaluations in a fixed-rate system or from possible future movements in the exchange rate in a flexible-rate system.

currency and buying a strong currency, speculators make it more difficult for authorities to find a new fixed value for the pound. This is why speculation in a fixed exchange rate system is often termed destabilizing.

In the early period of the Bretton Woods system, the United States ran a large trade deficit, and this deficit provided a means of supplying dollar reserves to the rest of the world. It was thought that this deficit was a temporary problem that would soon be replaced by a U.S. trade surplus. This was the premise of the Bretton Woods system. Yet the dollar was overvalued, and the U.S. deficits continued and grew larger into the 1950s and 1960s. The United States was in a difficult position. It was hard for it to devalue the dollar because the dollar was held by virtually every nation as an international reserve asset. A U.S. devaluation would have decreased the wealth of all those countries holding dollars. Several times, the United States tried to impose a restrictive macroeconomic policy to correct its balance of trade. However, when unemployment rose as a consequence, such policies were rapidly abandoned, as political pressures were brought to bear on policy-makers. U.S. deficits continued to grow, and foreign holdings of dollars rose.

Speculators entered again. Many holders of dollars became concerned about what the United States was going to do. There were various runs on the U.S. gold stock, as dollars were traded in by foreigners. In 1950, the United States had 509 million ounces of gold; by 1968, this stock had fallen to 296 million ounces. Confidence in the dollar fell further, and the stage was set for a drastic change in the international monetary system.

The Current International Monetary System

The present international monetary system was born in 1971. In the face of continuing large trade deficits and mounting speculation against the dollar, President Nixon broke the link between the dollar and gold in August 1971. No longer would the United States stand ready to exchange gold for dollars at $35 an ounce. In effect, the dollar was set free to fluctuate and seek its own level in the foreign exchange market. As a result, the overvalued dollar depreciated substantially against other major currencies. There were interim attempts to fix the price of the dollar again, but they failed. By early 1973, all the major currencies were floating.

The international monetary system that has been in effect since 1973 is a managed flexible-rate system. Exchange rates are allowed to seek their free-market values, as long as fluctuations are within an acceptable range. If fluctuations fall outside this range, governments may intervene with their reserve holdings to dampen the fluctuations in their currencies. Thus, exchange rates are not completely free; government intervention in the foreign exchange market will be forthcoming if a country's currency falls dramatically in value. In 1978, for example, the dollar fell sharply, and the Carter administration intervened to restrict this decline with international reserves and loans from West Germany and Japan. The central banks of major trading countries also have stepped up intervention activity since September of 1985. It should be remembered, though, that under the managed flexible-rate system, the ranges within which governments consider exchange rate fluctuations acceptable are not well defined as a matter of policy. As a result, it is difficult to tell how far a nation's currency would have to appreciate or depreciate before central bank interventions would occur.

Although the new system abandoned fixed exchange rates, it did not abandon the IMF, which still exists as an international monetary organization. The role of the IMF under the managed flexible-rate system is still evolving, and to this point it has consisted of helping countries that have persistent balance of payments problems by giving them loans and policy advice about how to conduct domestic macroeconomic policy to overcome these problems. The World Bank, which is part of the IMF system set up by the Bretton Woods agreement, has also played an increasing role in the new system. This sister institution of the IMF makes long-run development loans to poor countries.

Advantages of the Current System. The consensus view seems to be that the new system has worked very well under difficult circumstances. The following are the major advantages of the flexible-rate system.

1. It allows countries to pursue independent monetary policies. If a country wants to inflate its economy, it can do so by letting its exchange rate depreciate, thereby maintaining its position in international markets without sacrificing its preferred monetary policy.
2. Under the fixed-rate system, a country sometimes had to deflate its economy to solve a balance of trade deficit. With floating rates it only has to let its exchange rate depreciate. Clearly, it is easier to change one price than to change all prices to resolve balance of trade difficulties.
3. The current exchange rate system has proven capable of handling large economic disturbances. When the OPEC countries dramatically raised the price of oil in 1973–1974, the world economy experienced a tremendous shock. The greatest achievement of the flexible-rate system is the way it handled this shock. Oil-importing countries developed large trade deficits; huge trade surpluses built up in OPEC countries. These deficits and surpluses were accommodated by floating rates. Moreover, the huge oil revenues of the OPEC countries were recycled into Western investments. Though exchange rates changed significantly over the period, the new system weathered the storm and got the job done.

Disadvantages of the Current System. The flexible-rate system is not, however, without its critics.

1. Some observers point out that flexible rates can be very volatile, and this volatility creates considerable uncertainty for international trade. Thus, exchange rate flexibility leads to conditions that can retard the amount of international trade and therefore the degree of specialization in the world economy. Table 2 lists the exchange rates for several major currencies from 1973 to 1989. It is clear that some rates have changed significantly—the Swiss franc and the yen appreciated strongly, while the value of the French franc dropped considerably. The strength of the dollar against all these currencies is evident from 1982 through 1984. Since 1985, as noted earlier, the general trend has been one of dollar depreciation against the major world currencies shown. Do these changes impede international trade? Several studies suggest that they have not. They have found basically that the volume of a country's trade is not very sensitive to fluctuations in its exchange rate.[3]

---

[3]See Leland B. Yeager, *International Monetary Relations* (New York: Harper & Row, 1976), chapter 13.

TABLE 2

Foreign Exchange Rates, 1973–1989 (currency units per U.S. dollar)

Year	French Franc	German Mark	Japanese Yen	British Pound	Swiss Franc
1973	4.4534	2.6714	271.30	0.408	3.1687
1974	4.8106	2.5867	291.84	0.427	2.9804
1975	4.2876	2.4613	296.78	0.450	2.5839
1976	4.7824	2.5184	296.45	0.554	2.5001
1977	4.9160	2.3236	268.62	0.573	2.4064
1978	4.5090	2.0096	210.38	0.521	1.7906
1979	4.2567	1.8342	219.02	0.471	1.6643
1980	4.2250	1.8175	226.63	0.439	1.6772
1981	5.4396	2.2631	220.63	0.494	1.9674
1982	6.5793	2.4280	249.06	0.572	2.0327
1983	7.6203	2.5539	237.55	0.660	2.1006
1984	8.7355	2.8454	237.45	0.748	2.3500
1985	8.9799	2.9419	238.47	0.771	2.4551
1986	6.9257	2.1705	168.35	0.681	1.7979
1987	6.0122	1.7981	144.60	0.610	1.4918
1988	5.9595	1.7570	128.17	0.561	1.4643
1989	6.3802	1.8808	138.07	0.610	1.6369

Source: Council of Economic Advisers, *Economic Report of the President* (Washington, D.C.: U.S. Government Printing Office, 1990), p. 418.

2. A second criticism of floating rates is that they promote increased world inflation rates. Under a fixed-rate system, countries experience a balance of trade deficit if they inflate their respective economies. This link is severed under a flexible-rate system. Hence, domestic political authorities can more easily give in to those interests who benefit from inflation. Some proponents of the gold standard argue for its return to guard against domestic inflation.

3. Some countries that have relied primarily on adjustments in exchange rates to resolve trade imbalance problems have found that the solution has been a long time in coming. For example, despite depreciation of the dollar, the U.S. deficit with Japan has persisted for years, causing some observers to conclude that it never will solve the problem. Indeed, in certain cases, depreciation of the dollar will not improve the U.S. trade deficit. When the dollar depreciates against the yen, Japanese goods become more expensive to Americans, so Americans buy less from Japan. However, this does not necessarily mean that Americans will spend fewer dollars overall. If the price of a Japanese car rises by 10 percent and U.S. consumers reduce the quantity of Japanese cars purchased by less than 10 percent—if our demand for Japanese cars is inelastic—then Americans end up spending more dollars on Japanese cars, which tends to make the U.S. deficit worse. As more time is allowed to pass and our demand increases in elasticity, the devaluation is more likely to work. However, those interested primarily in an exchange system's ability to quickly eliminate trade deficits have become disillusioned with the current system.

4. Some regard the present system of various international monies as an anachronism. These critics argue that it would be more beneficial for the world to adopt a single currency and to become a unified currency area.

Such a system would allow various benefits to the world economy and would do away with the need to convert one currency to another in international trade. Although monetary unification has been tried on a modest scale in some areas of the world—notably, the recent monetary cooperation of the European countries in seeking to establish a European currency unit—a single global currency seems to be some distance in the future. After all, the forces of national autonomy are still strong, and virtually no government would lightly give up its power to control its money supply.

In sum, there are pros and cons with respect to the present international monetary system, but in general the system seems to have worked well over a difficult period in the international economy. Growing problems in the international payments system, however, call for the prospect of still further reform of the system.

SUMMARY

1. Foreign exchange is the currency of another country that is needed to make payment in an international transaction.

2. Foreign exchange can be obtained in the worldwide foreign exchange market. The demand for foreign exchange arises from the desire to buy foreign goods. The supply of foreign exchange arises from the desire of citizens of one country to buy the goods of another country.

3. A foreign exchange rate is the price of one currency in terms of another. A currency's value appreciates when its purchasing power in terms of other currencies rises. It depreciates when its purchasing power falls.

4. The demand for foreign currency in one country depends largely on income and relative price levels in the two countries.

5. Under a floating, or flexible, exchange rate system, a country allows its exchange rate to be set by the forces of supply and demand in the foreign exchange market. Flexible exchange rates change in response to changes in countries' money supplies, price levels, inflation rates, real interest rates, and fundamental factors such as technology, consumer rates, and government export and import policies. Under a flexible-rate system, exchange rate movements act to alleviate balance of trade surpluses and deficits.

6. Under a fixed exchange rate system, governments intervene in the foreign exchange market to set and defend the value of their currency. When a country's currency is overvalued relative to the equilibrium rate, the country will run a balance of trade deficit. It can seek to cure this deficit by deflating the domestic economy, establishing trade barriers, or devaluing its currency to a new, lower, fixed rate of exchange. When the fixed exchange rate is below its equilibrium value, a country will experience a balance of trade surplus and will sometimes revalue its currency upward.

7. Under a gold standard, a historical form of a fixed exchange rate system, each country makes its currency redeemable in gold and ties its money supply to its stock of gold. When a surplus of imports over exports appears, gold is shipped to foreigners to settle the balance of trade deficit, causing deflation in the domestic money supply of the deficit country and inflation in the surplus country, restoring equilibrium.

8. An important difference between floating- and fixed-rate systems is that the former changes one price to maintain equilibrium in the balance of trade, while the latter changes all prices in the economy to maintain a fixed exchange rate.

9. The balance of payments is a record of the international transactions of a country's economy. It follows the principles of double-entry bookkeeping and must therefore always balance in an accounting sense. Transactions that give rise to a demand for foreign exchange are entered as debits; transactions that give rise to a supply of foreign exchange are treated as credits.

10. The modern history of the international monetary system began with the gold standard, followed by a system of fixed exchange rates managed by the International Monetary Fund. The present international monetary system is a managed floating-rate system. Exchange rates are set by supply and demand, but governments can and have intervened if exchange rate movements are too large.

KEY TERMS

foreign exchange
foreign exchange markets
exchange rate
flexible, or floating, exchange rate system
fixed exchange rate system
managed flexible-rate system
depreciation
appreciation

purchasing power parity (PPP) theory
undervalued
overvalued
foreign exchange market intervention
foreign exchange reserves
balance of trade surplus
balance of trade deficit
devaluation

revaluation
gold standard
price-specie flow mechanism
balance of payments
Bretton Woods system
International Monetary
   Fund
speculation

QUESTIONS FOR REVIEW AND DISCUSSION

1. Suppose that the British pound is worth $1.50, and that $1 is worth about 6.5 Swedish kronor. How much would a Jaguar automobile cost in U.S. dollars if the British price is 20,000 pounds? How much would a Volvo cost in U.S. dollars if the Swedish price is 84,000 kronor?

2. The following exchange rates came from a newspaper report for February 1, 1987.

	U.S. Dollar per Currency Unit	
	Wednesday	Tuesday
Swiss franc	0.6656	0.6696
Italian lira	0.0007849	0.0007874

	Currency per U.S. Dollar	
	Wednesday	Tuesday
Swiss franc	1.5025	1.4935
Italian lira	1274	1270

   a. Did the Swiss franc rise or fall from Tuesday to Wednesday?
   b. What about the Italian lira?
   c. What happened to the dollar value of the franc?
   d. What about the dollar value of the lira?

3. Suppose the United States and Sweden are on a floating exchange rate system. Explain whether the following events would cause the Swedish krona to appreciate or depreciate.
   a. U.S. interest rates rise above Swedish interest rates.

   b. American tourism to Sweden increases.
   c. Americans fall in love with a newly designed Volvo, and Volvo sales in the United States skyrocket.
   d. The U.S. government puts a quota on Volvo imports.
   e. The Swedish inflation rate rises relative to the U.S. rate.
   f. The United States closes a military installation in Sweden at the urging of the Swedish government.

4. What happens to the floating exchange rate of a country that has a higher inflation rate than other countries? Show your answer graphically.

5. How would you treat the following items in the balance of payments? In other words, would you enter them as debits or credits?
   a. An American travels to Canada.
   b. A U.S. wine importer buys wine from Italy.
   c. A California wine grower sells wine to England.
   d. An Austrian corporation pays dividends to American stockholders.
   e. General Motors pays dividends to French investors.
   f. Several Japanese visit Hawaii on an American cruise ship.
   g. A Swedish citizen invests in a U.S. company based in Houston.

6. Explain why capital inflows are a credit entry in the balance of payments and capital outflows are a debit entry.

7. When we say that the gold standard required that all prices but one be changed to overcome a balance of trade deficit, what do we mean?

8. What are the primary advantages and disadvantages of the present international monetary system?

ECONOMICS IN ACTION
Trade Deficits, Flexible Exchange Rates, and the Competitiveness of the U.S. Economy

Two of the concepts explored in this chapter cropped up again and again in the financial news during the 1980s. The value of the dollar abroad during the flexible exchange rate period has fluctuated significantly. Depreciation was the order of the day during the late 1970s, whereas the early 1980s saw a record strengthening of the dollar. (In general, the dollar has depreciated since 1985, although there was some appreciation between 1988 and 1989.) The United States has not only seen merchandise trade deficits every year since 1976, but this deficit was at an all-time high of approximately $150 billion in 1987. These events have provoked much debate concerning the worldwide competitiveness of U.S. producers, the desirability of new tariffs and quotas to stem the deficit, and suggestions to return to a fixed exchange rate system. A clearer focus on the concepts involved in the debate, as well as a review of their behavior in the 1970s and 1980s, can lead to a better understanding of the current problem.

The merchandise trade balance is, for most people, the most familiar international economic statistic. This is the number that we usually hear or read in the media as representing the trade deficit. As pointed out in this chapter, however, the merchandise trade deficit only measures the amount by which the value of imported goods exceeds that of goods exported.

A truer measure of trade flows and imbalances includes trade in services along with trade in goods. Both goods and services are traded among nations, and trade in both goods and services is subject to the same fundamental economic forces. In discussing trade, there is little reason to exclude trade in such services as travel and telecommunications, just as there would be little reason to exclude the value of services consumed by an individual from a measure of the individual's economic well-being.

Figure 6a shows both measures of the trade balance since 1971. While the balance on merchandise trade has been in deficit since 1976, once trade in services is included (military transactions have been excluded) serious balance of trade deficits did not appear until 1983. In fact, as Figure 6a shows, the balance on goods and services was in surplus for most of the flexible exchange rate period.

Since 1983, however, even the surpluses on the services trade account have not prevented large deficits in the overall trade balance. What has caused such large deficits, however measured, in the last few years? Unfortunately, no simple answer exists, much less a cure. Economists have

focused attention on a number of possible causes and have offered suggestions for possible cures.

One explanation for trade balance movements is the exchange rate. Figure 6b depicts the movement of an index of the average dollar price of the currencies of ten of the major trading partners of the United States. As Figure 6b indicates, the period of the middle to late 1970s was a period of dollar depreciation on foreign currency markets. The dollar price of foreign exchange rose by approximately 17 percent from 1976 to 1980. While the merchandise trade balance remained fairly level in this interval, the balance on goods and services went from deficit to surplus. Notice, however, that the goods and services balance responded a year or so after the beginning of the exchange rate movement.

From 1980 through 1985, the dollar appreciated significantly vis-à-vis other major currencies. As the average dollar price of foreign currency fell, imports became less costly to Americans, while the prices of American-produced goods and services abroad rose. This strengthening of the dollar in the early 1980s, some economists believe, was a major factor in explaining the burgeoning trade deficit. Again, the balance on goods and services responded to dollar appreciation with a lag of about one year.

As the trade deficit ballooned, the issue of American "competitiveness" in international markets arose. Merchandise exports of the United States actually decreased from 1981 to 1986, while imports climbed steadily. A popular explanation was that American industry could no longer compete with more efficient foreign manufacturers, resulting in high prices of U.S.-made goods. Opponents of this argument noted that between 1980 and 1985, unit labor costs rose by 11 percent in the United States but by 16 percent in other major countries.

Thus, it does not appear that U.S. firms lack the ability to compete on world markets. Smaller increases in unit labor costs imply production efficiency gains. However, the reduction in the world relative prices of U.S. exports that would have occurred from these relative productivity gains were more than wiped out by appreciation of the dollar. As a result, the prices of U.S. exports on world markets rose, while the prices of foreign goods in the United States fell or did not rise as much. American firms did not lose their ability to compete; they were instead the victims of exchange rate appreciation.

Large government budget deficits undoubtedly contributed to the continued strength of the U.S. dollar on world

FIGURE 6   Trade Balances and Exchange Rates, 1971–1988

(a) Both the balance of merchandise (goods) trade and goods and services trade are shown. While the balance of merchandise trade was in deficit throughout most of the period, the goods and services balance did not go into significant deficit until 1983. The difference between the two lines is the surplus in services trade. Both measures exclude military purchases. (b) The index of exchange rates is an average of the dollar prices of ten major U.S. trading partners' currencies. Increases in the index signal general dollar depreciation and rising import (falling export) prices. Decreases in the index indicate dollar appreciation and falling import (rising export) prices for Americans.

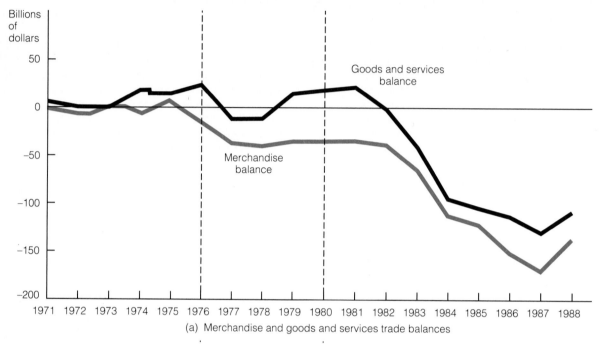

(a) Merchandise and goods and services trade balances

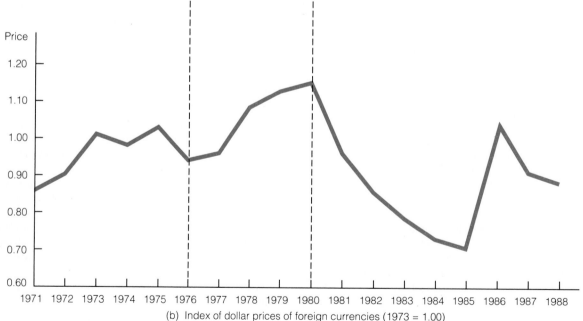

(b) Index of dollar prices of foreign currencies (1973 = 1.00) markets during the 1980s. In 1982, the budget deficit rose to over $100 billion, and it remained there through the end of the decade. Actions by the U.S. Treasury to finance these deficits kept real interest rates high in the United States compared to other countries. As we saw in this chapter, a rise in the real interest rate in a country will lead to an appreciation of the currency of that country on world markets. Therefore, we can see that there is a link between the "twin deficits"—the trade deficit and budget deficit. The large budget deficit brought about high interest rates, which led to an appreciation of the dollar. With the dollar remaining strong, American business firms found it difficult to compete in world markets, so the large U.S. trade deficit persisted.

In 1990, real interest rates in West Germany and Japan began to rise relative to those in the United States. If the trend continues, reductions in the U.S. trade deficit may not be far behind. As Figure 6 suggests, the generally lowered price of foreign exchange between 1986 and 1988 has been associated with a gradual improvement in both the merchandise and goods and services balances.

Question

With trade deficits come foreign capital inflows into the United States—that is, investment in U.S. plant and equipment by foreigners. In the long run, is this good or bad, economically, for the United States?

Sources: Council of Economic Advisers, *Economic Report of the President* (Washington, D.C.: U.S. Government Printing Office, 1987), pp. 358, 365; U.S. Department of Commerce, *Survey of Current Business* (December, 1986), p. 28.

40

Economic Systems and Economic Development

Comparative economics:
The study of the differences in economic systems; particularly, the differences between capitalist and socialist economic systems.

Past chapters have focused on the operation of a mixed capitalist economy, in which a private market sector plays the primary role in the production and distribution of goods and services. The study of **comparative economics** analyzes the differences between capitalist systems and other types of economic systems, particularly socialist economies. Under socialism, the state (the public sector) plays a primary economic role in the economy. The state controls most of the nonhuman productive resources in the economy and makes decisions about the allocation of these resources. The overall distribution and variety of goods and services available to final consumers are essentially determined by the state. Historically, socialism has taken many forms. In this chapter, we focus on what used to be called Soviet-style socialism—an extreme form of socialism that has fallen out of favor. Increasingly, existing socialist systems are mixed, with differing degrees of reliance on central planning and markets to determine production and allocation of goods and services. A number of historically socialist economies are experimenting with democracy and greater economic freedom. "Soviet-style" socialism no longer means what it once did. What role will economics and the implementation of market systems play as these countries search for economic efficiency and prosperity?

This chapter also introduces the study of economic development and the economic challenges facing the poorer economies of the world. For example, per capita income in 1990 in India and Burma was less than $300. Why are these countries so poor? How can they be made richer? What is the proper role of richer countries, such as the United States, in helping poor countries reach higher standards of living? While a complex array of cultural, political, and institutional factors affect economic development, economic systems and the incentives they create are key to understanding the varying levels of growth in these countries. When you complete Chapter 40 you should understand

- some of the underlying differences between socialist and market economic systems in generating economic efficiency.
- the historical role of central planning in the Soviet Union and other socialist nations.

- how the Soviet Union's and Eastern Europe's recent attempts to transform some of the basics of their economic systems from planning to market orientations have fared.
- some of the economic aspects of development and growth in developing countries.

COMPARATIVE ECONOMIC SYSTEMS

What do we mean by an economic system? The economic system of a given country is based on institutions of ownership, incentives, and decision making, which underlie all economic activity.

Recall the device we used in Chapter 3 to compare economic systems—the spectrum that ranges from pure capitalism to pure communism. Again, a society organized along the lines of **pure capitalism** is one in which most resources are privately owned and in which government economic control is minimal. In such a society, government's role is limited to protecting and enforcing private property rights and to providing pure public goods such as national defense. An economic system characterized by common ownership of productive resources, both human and nonhuman is **pure communism.** In between is **socialism,** in which the state owns some nonhuman productive resources and makes production decisions by planning the economy's output. The real world is complex, however; there simply are no pure economic systems (although there are some that come close).

Although there are many complex differences between any two economies, we can focus on two basic types of systems. To a varying degree, the economies of the United States, the United Kingdom, and France, for example, share the characteristics of **mixed capitalism.** In such a system, the state is an important participant in the economy, but by and large the bulk of productive activity is undertaken by private firms and individuals.

In a decreasing number of countries the dominant economic institutions are fundamentally different from those in capitalist societies. For many years, China and the Soviet Union headed lists of such countries—communist countries. As we will see, even these two models have attempted, to varying degrees, to mix market or capitalist elements and socialist planning in recent years. Under extreme socialism (that which is termed *communism* in the real world but which falls short of the pure communism on our spectrum), resource allocation is determined by central planning rather than by market forces. At least in theory, resources are allocated and utilized according to a centrally determined and administered overall economic plan. The quantity and composition of output, the relative proportions of consumption and investment, the use of resources in production, and the allocation of final output are all decided by the central authorities. The central plan is also likely to include detailed decisions on quantities of raw materials and inputs, techniques of production, prices, wages, location of plants and industries, and the pattern of employment of the labor force. The objectives of the central plan reflect the goals and preferences of the central planners. Consumers themselves have no direct input into the planning process; central planning effectively replaces the consumer sovereignty of capitalism.

Pure capitalism:
An economic system in which most resources are owned, and most relevant decisions are made, by private individuals.

Pure communism:
An economic system in which most productive resources, both human and nonhuman, are publicly owned.

Socialism:
An economic system in which most nonhuman productive resources are owned by the state.

Mixed capitalism:
An economic system in which most economic decisions are made by the private sector but in which government also plays a substantial economic and regulatory role.

Under Mikhail Gorbachev's stewardship as leader of the Soviet Union, numerous economic reforms have been proposed. Included in these reforms are attempts to streamline the bureaucracy of central planning, to build more economic incentives into production decisions, and to liberalize the Soviet economy's international trading relations.

In part heeding Gorbachev's example, in part reading into it a more tolerant mood in Moscow, most of Eastern Europe—namely, Poland, Romania, East Germany, Czechoslovakia, Hungary, and Bulgaria—minimized or eliminated the influence of socialist planning in their own economies. In 1989 and 1990, all of these nations, along with the Soviet Union, restructured, in varying degrees, their political systems to permit freer elections and "democratization." In other words, there has been a great deal of movement away from the pure communism end of our pure capitalism–pure communism spectrum. However, in the belief that it is impossible to understand where these countries are today without knowing where they have been, we present in this chapter a somewhat stylized comparison of capitalist and socialist systems.

THE GENERALITY OF ECONOMIC ANALYSIS

The basic economic problem of scarcity confronts all economic systems. Scarcity means that choices have to be made. To have more of one thing means having less of another. If a socialist economy wants to have a larger army, the resources for the army must come from alternative uses in the economy, such as agricultural labor. The fact that an economy is socialist does not make such trade-offs go away. Scarcity pervades economic organization; it is not something that confronts capitalism but not socialism.

Scarcity is not the only economic concept that applies generally to all economies. We consider the relevance of the following economic principles to the study of comparative economic systems: the law of demand, opportunity cost, diminishing marginal returns, and self-interest.

The Law of Demand

The law of demand is a general proposition about human behavior, not simply an economic law that applies to capitalism and private markets. The law of demand says that, other things being equal, price and quantity demanded will vary inversely. That is, the lower the price, given quality, the greater the quantity demanded, and vice versa. If socialist planners want to encourage the use of public transit and discourage the purchase of private cars, they will set relatively low prices on transit tickets and relatively high prices on cars. Consumers will respond according to the law of demand. If meat is scarce, its price will be set high to reflect its relative scarcity, and consumers will reduce their purchases of meat in state stores. If the socialist planners set zero prices on basic services such as medical care, quantity demanded will be so great that queues will develop and forms of nonprice rationing will emerge to determine who receives medical care.

Opportunity Cost

There is no such thing as a free lunch—in any economic system. It may well be that a socialist republic offers "free" medical care at zero price to recipients. But in no sense are the resources allocated to medical care free. They do not come out of thin air; they are directed away from alternative uses in the economy. The best alternative uses of these resources are a measure of their opportunity cost. If a socialist government wishes to increase its spending on space research, the resources must be reallocated from some other sector of the economy. The opportunity cost of a larger space program might be resources otherwise available for producing consumer goods.

Diminishing Marginal Returns

The law of diminishing marginal returns states that the increased application of a resource will ultimately lead to smaller and smaller increments of output, other things being equal. This phenomenon can be found in all economic systems. Worldwide, agriculture exhibits the law of diminishing returns. Generally, the stock of land in an economy is fixed, and the increased application of capital, such as tractors or fertilizer, to the fixed stock of land will lead to diminishing marginal returns. Soviet agriculture as well as American agriculture is subject to diminishing marginal returns. The only way that societies overcome the law of diminishing marginal returns over time is by investing in capital goods production and technological change. That is, as societies expand their resource base and technical capabilities, they are able to produce more output.

Self-Interest

Economic analysis is based on the idea that individuals weigh the costs and benefits of economic choices and normally respond according to their individual self-interest. Self-interest does not mean that individuals are totally

Drawing by Koren; © 1984 The New Yorker Magazine, Inc.

selfish. Individuals can demand or want anything, including a better life for others. Economics simply says that the amount of things individuals actually choose is determined by the costs and benefits of having those things.

Some socialist scholars have argued that self-interested behavior will disappear under socialism and that individuals will come to work for the common good instead. This is perhaps an appealing thought, but it does not seem to be true. The structure of personal incentives helps determine the actions of individuals in both capitalist and socialist economies. For example, in the Soviet Union managers of oil prospecting teams were once rewarded in a piece-rate fashion according to the number of meters they drilled. But drilling goes harder and slower as one drills deeper, with a greater chance that the pipe and drill bits will crack or break. With meters drilled rather than oil discovered as the indicator of success, drillers quickly concluded that they should drill only shallow holes, and lots of them, significantly retarding the discovery of new oil reserves. As this one example indicates, even socialist producers and consumers weigh costs and benefits in terms of self-interest. Ignoring such tendencies often results in poor economic performance.

THE EXPERIENCE OF CENTRAL PLANNING

With the understanding that the economic realities of the law of demand, opportunity cost, diminishing marginal returns, and self-interested behavior prevail in all economic systems, we turn now to an examination of how socialist states—in particular, the Soviet Union—have determined what gets produced, how, and for whom. One thing is certain, whatever economic systems the Soviet Union and its neighbors ultimately settle on: These new systems will be colored by decades of a much purer form of socialism.

In 1917, the Bolsheviks, a group of revolutionary socialists, came into political power in Russia and formed a new state, the Soviet Union. The Bolsheviks, influenced by the writings of Karl Marx and Friedrich Engels and the leadership of Vladimir Ilyich Lenin, sought to implement pure socialism— an economy in which all the means of production were owned and operated by the state and in which all economic activity would be centrally planned and controlled by the central government. Although Lenin, the revolutionary leader, did not live to see these goals accomplished, Joseph Stalin, his successor, was responsible for implementing them to a very great extent in the 1930s. In 1928, Stalin embarked on an ambitious mission to institute central planning in the Soviet economy, focusing his efforts on agriculture. The First Five-Year Plan emphasized heavy industry and established collective farms. Almost immediately, factory workers were needed—not farmers. Implementation of the plan, therefore, required the displacement of millions of peasants. The defiant were murdered; the rest had no choice but to move to the cities, where living conditions were dreadful.

Subsequent plans were less socially disruptive, and a sense of permanence—if not, eventually, correctness—settled over the notion of economic planning. The repeated failure of central planning to provide levels of real

Perestroika:
Economic reformation of the Soviet Union's command economy.

income even half those of Western (capitalist) nations led to reforms in the Soviet system in the 1980s, however. Mikhail Gorbachev's policy of **perestroika,** or restructuring, actually has meant a dismantling of many of the principles of planning. However, until markets guide most production, distribution, and consumption decisions in the Soviet Union as they do in capitalist nations, we will do better to approach the Soviet economy from the perspective of long-standing differences between their planned economy and the U.S. market economy. The Soviet economy entered the 1990s on the verge of collapse, yet resistance within the entrenched bureaucracy to drastic changes ensured the survival of certain elements of the command economy.

A Command Economy

Command economy:
An extreme form of socialist economy characterized by less private economic decision making than exists in a socialist economy.

The Soviet economy is sometimes loosely described as a **command economy.** Under authoritarian control, its economy is directed by a central planning system that oversees the production and distribution of most of its resources. The managers of individual state-owned enterprises follow orders imposed by the central plan that tell them what to produce, how to produce, and how to organize production. In effect, socialist managers are more like floor supervisors than the chief executive officers of capitalist firms; they have little independent authority.

The Soviet government basically owns and operates all industry, including the capital goods sector, transportation, communication, banking and financial institutions, and even the entire wholesale and retail network. In one sense, the Soviet economy is like a giant vertically and horizontally integrated firm. However, the analogy should not be taken too far. As we will see, the socialist state is not like a giant corporation, and its citizens are not its shareholders. Whereas corporate decisions are implemented by voluntary contractual agreements, the decisions of the central planning board are coercive.

In the case of the Soviet Union, the Communist party has historically played an important role in the management of the planned economy. This has been true of many other planned economies based on the Soviet model, such as those of Poland, East Germany, and China, although many of the economies of Eastern Europe as well as that of China have instituted market and democratic reforms in the 1980s. The Communist party is responsible for the selection of enterprise managers; it monitors the performance of both labor and management for the central planning board. This party monitoring is carried out through the various ministries of industry, which administer the central plan in individual enterprises.

Central Planning

Although the details of the actual operation of a large economy with millions of participants are extremely complex, the basic pattern of operations of a centrally planned economy is briefly summarized in Figure 1.

The state central planning agency (called Gosplan in the Soviet Union) drafts an economic plan for the entire economy. This plan includes a long-range five-year plan as well as an annual plan. These plans have the force of law. The basic economic plan is directed to the more than 200,000 different Soviet enterprises, setting production targets and allocating inputs to each

FIGURE 1

Basic Macroeconomic Sectors in an Idealized Command Economy

This is a highly simplified model of the command economy. Households supply labor inputs to enterprises in exchange for money. Labor inputs are assigned to firms by the planning process and not by a labor market. Money earned by labor is in turn exchanged for consumer goods and services produced by the enterprises. Exchange takes place in terms of money, although prices are fixed by the central planning board and remain fixed for long periods. In this simplified model, production takes place entirely within the state production establishment. Composition of output is determined not by consumers but by the central planning board.

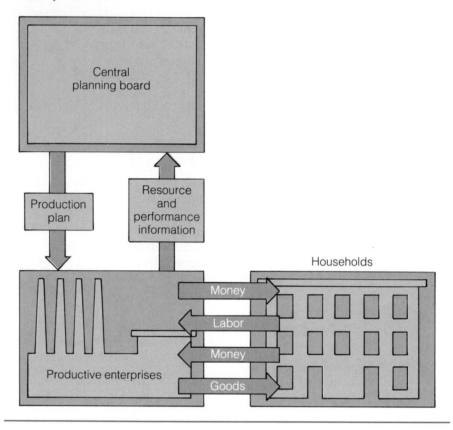

enterprise for all resources, including labor. Virtually all Soviet production is organized in the form of enterprises, which include everything from huge steel mills to small local baking plants. The manager of each enterprise is responsible for taking the resource inputs that have been allotted and using them to accomplish the goal assigned to the enterprise by the central plan. These targets are used to judge the performance of the firm over particular periods and to reward or penalize the responsible manager accordingly. For example, the plan might call for a steel mill to increase its production of rolled steel 5 percent over its previous year's output and reward the manager with a bonus for meeting the assigned quota (and a greater bonus for exceeding the quota).

Essentially, the central planning board attempts to ration raw materials throughout the entire economy without having to resort to the price system used in capitalist economies. It performs this task by the method of **materials balancing**—the maintaining of a balance sheet of all available supplies in the economy and of all sources of demand. In other words, the central planning board attempts to keep a comprehensive inventory of all raw materials and factor inputs—minerals, timber, labor, and so on—as well as a similar listing of the demand for these inputs by all the production units, given their assigned production goals. The method of materials balancing works out a consistent pattern of resource allocation throughout the economy that is compatible

Materials balancing:
A method of central planning entailing the monitoring of the quantity and availability of resources so as to allocate these resources among state enterprises to produce final output; a substitute for the price system method of allocating resources.

with the established planning priorities—that is, allocating necessary inputs perhaps first to military production, then to agricultural development, and so on.

In contrast to a capitalist economy, the socialist economy's central planners exercise essentially full control over production in the economy and can direct resources to whatever ends they choose. Production in the economic system is not directed by the final demand of consumers, who instead play a passive role. This is a fundamental difference in the two economies. In a capitalist economy the mix of goods provided reflects the demands of consumers. But in a centrally planned economy, the mix of goods provided reflects the decisions of the central planners. For example, if the Soviet government estimates that military spending should be 15 percent of GNP, it can reallocate resources accordingly to achieve this goal, without having to convince consumers or voters to rearrange their priorities.

The Problems of Central Planning

Central planning has never been without problems. Yet not until the 1980s did these problems become acute. The major problem of central planning is this: The central planning board must coordinate millions of different inputs and potential output—an enormous, perhaps impossible, task. Computer technology makes a coordinated overall plan feasible in principle, but the system must be constantly revised to accommodate unplanned circumstances; droughts and other climatic events may cause crop failures, for example, creating a need to revise agricultural plans. In recent years, the planning system in the Soviet Union has consistently failed to adjust to changed circumstances rapidly enough to prevent food shortages and reductions in overall GNP growth. Consumer unrest has been the result.

Other types of unforeseen events also can severely disrupt the central plan. In 1986, the nuclear reactor at Chernobyl underwent a disastrous meltdown. This reactor supplied electrical power to a large area of the Soviet Union's Ukraine region. Not only has power had to be diverted from other areas (thus creating shortages in those areas) in order to make up for lost power in the Chernobyl area, but a significant amount of both residential and farm land in the Soviet Union as well as in neighboring countries may have been contaminated and made unusable.

Planning, some arbitrary set of production goals and prices, robs the economy of flexibility. Planning eliminates the price system's ability to provide accurate information about relative scarcities and surpluses. Production bottlenecks arise when prices are inhibited from performing their rationing and information-signaling functions. When prices do not reflect actual resource scarcities, a supplier could unexpectedly fail to deliver a critical input. The customer, who may in turn be some other enterprise's supplier, is not free to place an order with some other supplier of the necessary input. Enterprises have assigned suppliers, and securing official permission for shifting suppliers can be difficult and extremely time-consuming. Enterprise managers may be confronted with the choice of cutting corners where they can—perhaps radically reducing the quality of the goods they produce—or missing an assigned quota (or even failing to produce any output at all). An alternative is to make unofficial and basically illegal private arrangements with other enterprise managers to overcome bottlenecks by switching suppliers. But such arrangements, however necessary, amount to cheating on the central planning process and to a partial introduction of the market process.

The Soviet planners must constantly monitor managerial performance to detect such cheating. To do so, the central planning board depends on information supplied by the managers themselves, whereas a capitalist economy would rely on a firm's success or failure in marketing its output. The incentives thus created can encourage managers to fabricate reports of available resources to avoid blame or to satisfy output quotas. Soviet planners have long been aware of these and many other problems with planning and—with great fanfare—have periodically undertaken programs to overcome them. While Gorbachev's *perestroika* is the latest attempt at "reforming" the economic system, previous attempts have not succeeded.

The Legal and Extralegal Private Sectors in the Soviet Economy

Although it seems inconsistent with the rhetoric of social planning, a legal private sector has always existed in the Soviet Union and in most other centrally planned economies. *Glasnost,* a new openness, and *perestroika* have provided the atmosphere for an expanded private sector. Private economic activity, while not entirely prohibited by Soviet law, is restricted in two major respects. First, a private individual cannot act as a middleman; second, no employee can be hired for the purpose of making a profit. These two restrictions obviously greatly limit the extent to which legally sanctioned private enterprise may operate. Effectively, the only areas in which private enterprise is permitted are personal services and farming. Professionals such as doctors and teachers and craft laborers like carpenters and shoemakers are free to sell their services to consumers. And peasants working on state-owned farms are permitted to grow crops on small assigned plots and are free to sell whatever they produce. In both cases, production of personal services or of goods for private sale can legally take place only after the completion of the day's labor in the individual's state-sector job. In effect, only moonlighting is legally permissible in the private sector.

Despite these restrictions, activities in the legal private sector realize a considerably higher rate of productivity than do comparable activities in the state sector. The primary evidence for this productivity differential is the output record of the privately cultivated agricultural plots. These private plots, which constitute only slightly more that 1 percent of land under cultivation in the Soviet Union, account for approximately 25 percent of the nation's total agricultural output, in spite of the fact that the private plots are typically far below the optimum size for efficient production of the crops grown on them.

The productivity of private plots is strong evidence for the crucial role of incentives in determining rates of output. The private plot owners gain the full value of any increase in the efficiency of resource use on their own plots. In marked contrast, the collectivized state agricultural sector is plagued by poor efficiency and poor productivity. It is true that relatively more land-intensive agricultural products—such as cotton and wheat—are grown on collective farms, partially accounting for the disparity in productivity because the value per acre of these crops tends to be relatively low. But this fact only explains a small portion of the difference. Incentives clearly play a large role in the productivity of private Soviet agriculture.

Although evidence concerning the relative performance of the privately provided personal services industry is scarce, the productivity advantages there are similar. Quality seems higher, too. Although in theory medical treatment is provided free to all Soviet citizens, the quality of such care often tends to be low. Some surgeons are able to command private fees of over 1000 rubles (about $1350) for major operations from individual patients concerned with the quality of their care.

In addition to the legally sanctioned private sector in the Soviet Union, there has been a booming underground or extralegal private economy, somewhat like the underground economy in the United States. The private sector continues to be much larger than that permitted by Soviet law. An underground sector characterized by black market activity will likely continue to flourish as long as the Soviet economy continues as an essentially planned economy.

Some underground activity involves theft of state-owned resources, but a large part of it involves what might be termed "capitalist acts between consenting adults." John Lennon records, blue jeans, and moonshine have been objects of trade, but the underground economy does not function solely to shift consumer goods to the highest bidder. The extralegal private sector helps ease shortages and reduce inefficiency in the planned sectors of the economy, as well. Managers of collective farms admit that often the only way to meet production targets is to buy supplies on the black market. In the Soviet economy and in other planned economies as well, production has always depended on extensive bribery to function; Russian enterprise managers have employed professional expeditors, who bribe suppliers to provide necessary inputs.

In general, bribery (both actual payments and favors) has performed a vital role in greasing the wheels of the planned economy. The underground private sector provides coordinating services that increase the efficiency of the planned sector.

Comparative Performance

Despite the problems of centrally planned socialist economies, their performance relative to capitalist economies is worth noting. See Table 1 for a comparison of U.S. and Soviet production. In general, the Soviets have concentrated, through the force of central planning, on capital goods infrastructure—especially that related to defense—rather than on consumer goods and services.

The total output of the U.S. economy is roughly twice that of the Soviet Union, although the Soviet Union has both a larger land area and a larger population. More food per person is produced in the United States by fewer agricultural workers; the United States also produces many more automobiles. However, the Soviet Union produces more oil and steel than the United States.

The Soviet Union has emphasized investment over consumption to a much greater extent than the United States. The Soviet growth rate in investment lagged to 3.2 percent between 1980 and 1985 but rose to an average of 5 percent during the Twelfth Five-Year Plan, 1986–1990. Centralized planning

TABLE 1

A Comparison of U.S. and Soviet Production Characteristics, 1985–1986

Production patterns in the United States and the Soviet Union for 1985–1986 reflect basic differences in the two economies and the natural resources abundant in each country.

	United States	Soviet Union
Total output (trillions of dollars per year)	4.0	2.2
Per capita GNP (dollars per year)	16,492	7,736
Steel (million metric tons)	80.1	154.7
Oil (million metric tons)	428.2	615.0
Electricity (billions of kwh)	2,583	1,598.9
Coal (million metric tons)	738.9	512.9
Wheat (million metric tons)	50.8	92.3
Corn (million metric tons)	209.6	12.5
Meat (million metric tons)	17.9	14.0
Population (millions)	244	284
Land area (million square miles)	3.6	8.6

Source: U.S. Bureau of the Census, *Statistical Abstract of the United States,* 1989 (Washington, D.C.: U.S. Government Printing Office, 1989).

allows planners to stress industrial development and capital accumulation. In the United States, both investment and capital accumulation are dependent on the savings and investment decisions of individuals and, in the long run, on the decisions of consumers.

While the investment rate in the Soviet Union has been relatively high, the efficiency of investment has remained generally low. Productivity of both labor and capital lags appreciably behind that of Western economies. For example, while Soviet investment in agriculture has increased fivefold since World War II, the growth in Soviet agricultural output has been low, and negative per capita growth rates in annual grain production are common. (Other problems have arisen in the Soviet economy; see Focus, "Soviets Plagued by Budget Deficits and Inflation.")

In the early 1970s, the growth rate of the Soviet economy appeared to be relatively high. Table 2 presents data on the growth of real gross national product during the period 1984–1989 for a variety of countries, including the United States and the Soviet Union. Over the entire period, the Soviet growth rate was 1.9 percent. The U.S. growth rate was higher, 4.0 percent. China's unusually high growth rate over the period in large part reflects the market-oriented economic reforms that have been underway there since the late 1970s.

At times, Soviet GNP growth has been quite high, however. The rate of economic growth in 1961–1965 averaged 5 percent. This figure encompassed a high of 7.6 percent in 1964 and a low of 2.2 percent in 1963—which suggests something important about Soviet growth rates: They have tended to be erratic (see Figure 2). Analysts suggest that Soviet GNP growth is gradually declining because of the increasing cost of raw materials as more accessible sources dry up. The Soviet Union is extraordinarily rich in raw materials, holding a large proportion of the world reserves of most economically important minerals, as well as oil and natural gas. But reserves of these resources

FOCUS   Soviets Plagued by Budget Deficits and Inflation

Budget deficits and inflation are apparently not limited to market economies such as the United States. In late 1988, in the wake of Gorbachev's economic reforms, the Supreme Soviet adopted a 1989 budget of $795 billion, with a projected budget deficit of over $55 billion at the official exchange rate. The projected Soviet deficit for 1989 was about 4 percent of domestic production; the corresponding figure for the United States was 3 percent. Deficits may be as severe in the Soviet Union as they have been in recent U.S. experience, but probably for different reasons.[a]

In the Soviet Union, a bureaucracy has for years set prices and production quotas in state-run enterprises without regard to supply and demand and virtually without any system of accounting to show profit and loss. When prices are determined by a planning bureau without reference to opportunity costs, accounting values cannot accurately reflect the real cost of producing goods and services. For many decades, the Soviets have geared production to provide low-priced necessities, resulting in incredible prices for items that are deemed luxuries. When prices are robbed of their signaling power, shortages, surpluses and noneconomic, inefficient production develops. Consumers either do not get what they want or do not get goods and services in the quantities they desire. The absence of market-determined interest rates has also meant that capital investment is used inefficiently; modern capital equipment sits unused and unfinished construction projects dot the urban landscape. Soviet finance authorities acknowledge that huge numbers of bankrupt businesses and budget deficits have resulted from their attempts to sidestep the price system, since revenues from goods production have not covered actual costs.

These same finance authorities, keen to introduce the reforms suggested by Gorbachev, are introducing a West-ern-style accounting system into Soviet production. Soviet legislators are attempting to increase production of consumer goods, so several hundred factories are being retooled. This move will tend to reduce the deficit if additional revenues are produced. (Critical to the success of these programs to introduce more consumer goods, however, is allowing supply and demand to decide what goods will be produced and sold.) For the present, massive production misallocations are occurring under price controls, and these are contributing to inflation.

Inflation—often thought to be a major curse of capitalism—is an actual and much-feared problem in the Soviet Union. While Soviet economists officially estimated inflation at 1.5 percent in 1988, some concede that the rate was actually over 7 percent, which is closer to the calculations of Western observers. In addition to massive dislocations in production, inflation also results from the overuse of the Soviet printing press. Wage pressures are also building up the threat of a Western-style wage-price spiral (fueled and validated by printing more money). If, as promised, Gorbachev lifts price and wage controls in the consumer goods system and decontrols the prices factories pay for fuel, tools, and raw materials in 1990, some experts predict a short-term rise in the inflation rate of from 10 to 20 percent.

Deficits and inflation, well known in capitalist societies, are certainly not new to the Soviet Union. The secrecy of central planning and the lack of any accurate accounting system merely kept them hidden for many decades.

[a]For an interesting account of Soviet deficit and inflation problems, see Bill Keller, "Deficits in Soviet Budgets Are Disclosed by Kremlin: Wasteful Subsidies Blamed," *New York Times* (October 28, 1988), pp. A1, A11.

---

are increasingly located in more remote areas, making exploitation more costly.

Finally, comparisons of Soviet and Western GNP do not take into account the qualitative aspects of the goods produced. The quality of Soviet consumer goods is generally recognized to be quite poor relative to similar Western goods. As the planned economy does not function on the basis of consumer sovereignty, a considerable proportion of production represents low-quality goods—indeed, goods that consumers do not want at all.

Income Distribution in a Command Economy

One of the stated goals of socialist economies is to reduce income inequality among members of society. What can be said about the performance of socialist economies in this regard?

TABLE 2

Average Annual Rate of Growth in Real GNP for Various Economies, 1984–1989

Real GNP growth rates differed significantly over the period 1984–1989 across various national economies. Japan led Western-style democracies in terms of percentage growth, while China led less-developed nations.

Country	Rate of Growth, GNP
United States	4.0%
Canada	4.4
West Germany	2.9
United Kingdom	3.4
USSR	1.9
China	9.3
Eastern Europe	1.5
Japan	4.6

Source: Council of Economic Advisers, *Economic Report of the President* (Washington, D.C.: U.S. Government Printing Office, 1990), p. 419.

Data issued by the Soviet government are fragmentary, but they allow a rough comparison of income distribution in the Soviet Union with that in Western countries. One such comparison, involving the Soviet Union, the United States, and Sweden (a socialist democracy), is presented in Table 3. Interestingly, differences in the degree of inequality in the respective income distributions appear to be comparatively minor. The percentage of low-income individuals is about the same in the three economies, as is the percentage of individuals earning the highest incomes.

But this comparison may understate the degree of inequality in the Soviet economy. As we saw in Chapter 18, real transfer payments such as health care or subsidized food would indicate a greater degree of equality in Soviet (and Swedish) income distributions. Conversely, special privileges are available to an enormous extent to Communist party members and bureaucrats, especially at the upper levels. For example, automobiles can usually be quickly purchased by members of the elite. An ordinary citizen, however, may have to place an order and wait for a year or more or attempt to purchase a used car on the black market at an inflated price. Soviet party officials and specially favored

TABLE 3

Estimated Shares of Personal Income, by Quintile

Estimates of income quintiles in the United States, Sweden, and the Soviet Union show surprisingly small differences in income distribution.

Income Quintile	Share of Income (percent)		
	United States	Sweden	Soviet Union
Lowest	6.9	7.7	7.5
Second through fourth	52.5	56.5	55.0
Highest	40.6	35.9	37.5
Top 5 percent	15.9	12.9	14.0

Source: Lowell Gallaway, "The Folklore of Unemployment and Poverty," in S. Pejovich, *Governmental Controls and the Free Market* (College Station: Texas A&M University Press, 1976), pp. 41–72.

FIGURE 2

Soviet economic growth was erratic between 1975 and 1989 and has generally declined over time.

Sources: Hearings Before the Joint Economic Committee of the Congress of the United States, *Allocation of Resources in the Soviet Union and China, 1982,* 97th Cong., 2nd sess. (Washington, D.C.: U.S. Government Printing Office, 1981), p. 4; Council of Economic Advisers, *Economic Report of the President* (Washington, D.C.: U.S. Government Printing Office, 1990), p. 419.

Growth of Soviet GNP

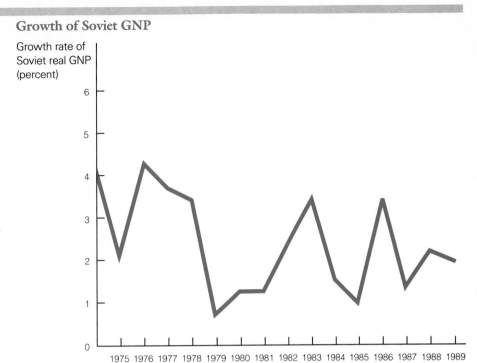

Growth rate of Soviet real GNP (percent)

groups are permitted to shop in special stores stocked with foreign goods unavailable to ordinary citizens. Thus, the elite are often protected from the problems of shortages, waiting in long lines, and poor-quality goods that plague ordinary citizens. These special privileges mean that the effective degree of inequality in Soviet society is much higher than published figures suggest. Focus, "Soviet Economists on Living Standards and Wealth Distribution in the USSR," suggests that when wealth rather than income is considered, the Soviet Union has a very small middle class.

The Gorbachev Reform Proposals

The lackluster performance of the Soviet economy under central planning has led, under the leadership of Communist party chairman and General Secretary Mikhail Gorbachev, to a policy of *glasnost,* or "openness." The policy brings a new openness into Soviet society, especially in the realm of human rights and greater social freedom, as well as in the functioning of the Soviet economy. As you know, *perestroika* seeks to reform central planning to include a greater role for the price system in allocating and distributing resources, and the devotion of more resources to consumer goods production. Gorbachev has tacitly admitted that planning schemes of the past did not motivate people to produce at high-efficiency levels, and he has proposed new profit incentives for the purpose of achieving greater economic growth.

Perestroika is an admission that technology and investment cannot be fully imposed from above. In the past, the growth potential inherent in new investment or new technology was completely determined by the uses to which it was put by bureaucratic industry and firm managers. With little or no

FOCUS Soviet Economists on Living Standards and Wealth Distribution in the USSR

As the "liberalization" of the Soviet economic system proceeds under *glasnost* and *perestroika,* Soviet economists have taken a hard look at their system. For example, Table 3 in this chapter shows a very similar income distribution between the Soviet Union and the United States (unadjusted for factors such as medical care and other welfare transfers). According to recent research by two Russian economists, such figures wildly overstate the well-being of the average Soviet citizen.[a] The true measure of equality, according to Soviet economists Andrei Kuteinikov and Alexander Zaichenko, is not *income* but *wealth* in the Soviet Union. Zaichenko utilizes consumer goods as a proxy for wealth (since Soviet citizens may own no liquid private property such as stocks or bonds) and finds a radical disparity between rich and poor. According to his estimates, originally published in the Soviet weekly *Argumenti i Fakti*, the "super-rich elite" comprise 2.3 percent of the population, while the poor make up the vast majority—86.5 percent. Within this social pyramid, the middle class, those who own an apartment or home, a car, and (perhaps) a summer house, comprise only 11.2 percent of the population. In Western countries the middle class represents 50 to 70 percent of the population. Even in Hungary, East Germany, and Czechoslovakia, 40 to 50 percent of the population would be considered middle class, using wealth as a standard.

According to Kuteinikov, official Soviet statistics bear out Zaichenko's estimates. Welfare expenditures account for only about 20 percent of Soviet GNP, compared to 28.5 percent in the United States. Kuteinikov also argues that disproportionate welfare benefits (such as health care, recreation facilities, and education) go to the Soviet elite. Old-age pensions are likewise disproportionately channeled to "personal pensioners"—retired members of the elite—who receive 500 rubles per month rather than the 84 rubles per month received by everyone else. (At black market rates, 84 rubles equals $12.50.)

Who are the elite? According to Zaichenko, the elite (estimated at about 400,000 individuals) come from the spheres of politics, science, sports, art, and diplomacy. Also included are cooperative managers, black marketeers, and service sector workers (who have access to desirable goods and who can facilitate black market sales). All of this points up potential problems for reform in the Soviet Union. A weak middle class means less stability in society. Furthermore, cooperation for system reforms from those in control of wealth will be difficult to obtain. Although economic reform was initiated by the Soviet leadership, Soviet citizens eventually began pressuring their leaders for more rapid implementation of new policies. The system seems to be responding. In March of 1990, the Soviet Union passed a law permitting private citizens and companies to buy land, buildings, and factories—for the first time in seventy years.[b] Further, foreign investment and joint ventures with outside investors are being encouraged by the government. Gains in output and welfare will be costly, but an ultimately more equitable distribution of wealth may well be the result.

[a]Andrei Kuteinikov, "Soviet Society—Much More Unequal Than U.S.," *Wall Street Journal* (January 26, 1989), p. A14.

[b]Kevin Maney, "U.S.S.R. Permits Private Ownership," *USA Today* (March 7, 1990), p. 1B.

incentive to manage resources and technology efficiently, managers were complacent and inefficient. (This outcome was predicted by Ludwig von Mises; see Economics in Action, "The Socialist Calculation Debate and the Transition from Planning to Markets.")

Gorbachev initially proposed that productive energies at all levels be guided by the partial use of profits and prices, (partially) replacing poor production incentives that have become institutionalized within the Soviet economic system. But the inadequacy of any half measure to fix the Soviet economy soon became evident. Faced with political pressure from new Russian Republic president Boris Yeltsin and rising discontent with a still-deteriorating economy, Gorbachev unveiled a more radical reform plan in autumn 1990. This plan would put up to 70 percent of the Soviet Union's factories, stores, and service enterprises up for sale—effectively ending government subsidies and necessitating sharp cutbacks in the central planning system. Some skeptics wonder whether Gorbachev will be able to push truly dramatic reforms past party conservatives and entrenched bureaucrats—or whether, if implemented, even these changes are enough.

Soviet leader Mikhail Gorbachev

Eastern Europe in the Early 1990s: No Gain Without Pain?

The opening of the Berlin Wall in 1989 (followed by the monetary and political union of East and West Germany in 1990), the election of democratic-minded leaders in Poland and Czechoslovakia, and outright declarations of independence from the Soviet Union by the Baltic states—Estonia, Lithuania, and Latvia—are all manifestations of political change left in the wake of *glasnost*. By 1990, most of the East European nations had withdrawn from exclusive international trade within the Soviet bloc, opening the way for bilateral trade negotiations with countries throughout the world. Table 4 provides data on population, per capita GNP, and hard currency debt—debt measured in dollars—for six Eastern European countries.

TABLE 4

GNP, Population, and Debt in Six Eastern European Countries

Comparative statistics show that East Germany had the highest per capita (adjusted) gross domestic product in Eastern Europe for the year shown, while Romania had the lowest. As these countries struggle to raise growth rates and economic performance, they will be faced with hard currency debt to other countries.

Country	Population (1989, in millions)	Adjusted GDP per capita (1986, in U.S. dollars)	Hard currency debt (1988, in billions of dollars)
Poland	38.2	$3250	$38.5
Romania	23.2	2770	2.2
East Germany	16.6	5660	19.5
Czechoslovakia	15.6	4910	6.1
Hungary	10.6	3890	18.0
Bulgaria	9.0	3540	7.1

Sources: New York Times (January 7, 1990), p. E3; Central Intelligence Agency; Population Reference Bureau; Jan S. Hogendorn, *Economic Development* (New York: Harper & Row, 1987).

While events in Eastern Europe were greeted with amazement and encouragement in the West, difficult periods of adjustment clearly await these economies. The transitions from central planning (of one form or another) to markets will be painful. Poland was the first country to plunge into market reforms in the face of a deteriorating economy.[1] As such, it is a model for the formerly planned nations of Eastern Europe and elsewhere.

In the late 1980s, the Polish economy experienced an inflation rate of several thousand percent annually, along with nearly bare shelves, thriving black markets, and consumer-goods smuggling. With the financial backing of the United States, West Germany, and other industrialized democracies, Poland launched an effort to stabilize its currency in 1990. (Both Poland and Czechoslovakia sharply devalued their currencies against the U.S. dollar in 1990.) The government—headed by officials of the formerly outlawed Solidarity union—began by reducing subsidies on housing, food, and fuel, and, as expected, the artificially low prices on these items rose. Almost immediately, bread prices rose 38 percent; coal prices rose 600 percent. As gasoline and automobile insurance prices soared out of reach, thousands of Poles turned in their license plates. These very painful steps were necessary to create a market mechanism in which supply, demand, prices, and the value of money are rationally interrelated. The choice between artificially low prices for low-quality goods in short supply and higher-priced, higher-quality goods of more dependable supply is a very real one for citizens of Eastern Europe and the Soviet Union.

The link between politics and economics is evident as these countries struggle for reforms that lead to prosperity and political freedom. In the context of economic systems, moreover, it is unclear whether these "democratic" changes will translate into economic reforms for freer markets. Entrenched interests can be expected to fight reforms, unless they can be convinced that change would create new benefits for them. For instance, workers long guaranteed a job might be reluctant to test their fortunes on free and open markets. The same goes for bureaucratic managers, planning directors, and other vested interests who enjoyed privileges in these economies for years. While private property was introduced in a limited way in both Poland and Czechoslovakia, the Czechs have been reluctant to privatize manufacturing in order to modernize technology. Politicians who want to be reelected do not want reputations for lowering living standards, although this is necessary as a short-run measure to achieve long-term prosperity. High levels of international debt also plague the economies of Eastern Europe (see Table 4). A great deal of international cooperation is needed to help Eastern Europe handle its external debt problem.

The ultimate outcome of the transition of Eastern European nations from centrally planned to wholly or partially democratic societies fueled by market systems is unpredictable. The mix of planning and market functioning that will result in a particular country cannot now be predicted, especially given the differing cultures and institutions. Most economists believe that expanded international trade holds great promise, but many wonder how far the price and profit system could be allowed to go without a fundamental restructuring of the goals of socialism. Capitalism, even modified capitalism,

---

[1]See Craig R. Whitney, "East Europe Joins the Market and Gets a Preview of the Pain," *New York Times* (January 7, 1990), p. E3, from which some of this section is derived.

may be incompatible with the goals of a socialist society. Whatever else is accomplished in the stirrings of the Soviet Union and the Eastern bloc toward democracy and market orientation, economists now have an unparalleled opportunity to compare the results of central planning and markets.

THE PROBLEM OF ECONOMIC DEVELOPMENT

We turn now from comparisons of socialist and capitalist economic systems to a consideration of the disturbing differences between developed and developing countries.

Economic development:
The process through which an economy achieves long-run economic growth; involves capital formation, the development of markets, productivity growth, and the improvement of entrepreneurial ability and labor skills.

In economic terms, development is not quite the same as growth. Economic growth usually refers to the increase in per capita GNP in an economy; **economic development** is the process of capital formation, entrepreneurial and labor skills improvement, and the growth in economic productivity that causes rates of economic growth to rise. The history of the U.S. economy provides a model of successful economic development, leading to high and sustained rates of economic growth combined with a growing population. The U.S. economy in 1776 was in many respects an underdeveloped economy. The transition from a low to a high state of development occurred rapidly during the nineteenth century.

In the modern world, the developed nations are the relatively rich economies, and the developing nations are the relatively poor economies. Many, though not all, developing countries are relatively stagnant economically. While population in these countries is often growing rapidly, per capita income grows slowly, if at all. As we will see, the form of economic institutions plays an important role in determining the extent to which economies develop.

The Characteristics of Less-Developed Countries

Less-developed countries:
Countries with relatively low levels of per capita real GNP; generally characterized by a large subsistence agriculture sector, low saving rates, and high population growth.

Most countries of the world, including the most populous, China, are defined as developing, or **less-developed, countries;** three-quarters of the world's population lives in less-developed countries. But there is an amazing amount of diversity among these countries; the only thing they have in common is their less-developed status. Economically, what characteristics are associated with the low development rates of less-developed countries?

In describing less-developed countries, there is general agreement that four features stand out: low per capita income, a dominant agricultural-household sector, relatively low saving rates, and rapid population growth.

A less-developed country is a poor country in the sense that its per capita GNP is low. Compared with poverty in developed countries, poverty in less-developed countries is more severe. In many of the countries, the plight of the lowest income group has not changed dramatically in hundreds of years. The second defining characteristic of less-developed countries is a dominant agricultural-household sector. In a way, this is merely another way of saying that less-developed countries are poor—a large proportion of their population is engaged in subsistence agriculture. Nearly two-thirds of the labor force of the low-income countries of Asia, Africa, and South America are employed in agriculture. In contrast, only 2 percent of the U.S. labor force is employed in agriculture. The size of the household (or nonmarket) sector in less-developed countries is generally much larger than in developed nations. Most households in less-developed countries are engaged in subsistence production in the sense that they raise their own food, make their own clothes, and construct their own homes. The degree of specialization in production in these economies is limited, compared to the more-developed economies. With the degree of specialization limited and a large amount of time devoted to subsistence production, the opportunities for welfare-enhancing exchange and trade with others in the society becomes relatively limited also. (Greater household production in less-developed countries does mean that real income levels in these countries are not as low, by comparison with developed countries, as suggested by measured income levels.)

The other two characteristic features found in most less-developed countries (although there are exceptions) are low saving rates and high rates of population growth. Many poor economies have low saving rates because saving is very difficult (or even impossible) when income is at or near the subsistence level. Low saving rates mean that very little income is set aside each year for investment in capital goods for increased production. This inability to save, in turn, contributes to continuing low rates of development. The term sometimes used for this problem is the **vicious circle of poverty.**

Vicious circle of poverty: An attempt to explain why some countries remain less developed that centers on low savings and investment causing low real incomes, which in turn lead to low saving and investment rates.

Rapid population growth is another condition commonly associated with less-developed countries. The population of the poor countries of Asia, Africa, and South America has been expanding at an average rate of about 2.5 percent per year. At this rate, the populations of these nations double every twenty-five or thirty years. In contrast, the populations of developed nations grow less than 1 percent per year on average. The difference is often taken to mean that rapid population growth is a major contributor to low rates of development because such growth imposes an increasing burden on the limited resources of less-developed countries. The more people, the greater the need to provide education, health care, and other basic services—which require resources that would otherwise be available for capital investment. To the extent that rapid population growth represents more mouths to feed, per capita income will decline as population grows, other things being equal.

THE ECONOMIC GAP BETWEEN DEVELOPED AND LESS-DEVELOPED COUNTRIES

Like wealth and poverty, development and underdevelopment are relative concepts. In 1750, England was probably the richest and most-developed country in the world, but by modern standards mid-eighteenth-century England was relatively poor and undeveloped. Moreover, we cannot judge reliably whether any given country should be counted as a developed or less-developed economy on the basis of secondary characteristics—such things as the rate of population growth, degree of literacy, or degree of industrialization. There are, for example, some developed countries that have high rates of population growth and a lesser degree of industrialization than do some less-developed countries. A more reliable way to distinguish quantitatively between the developed and less-developed countries is by per capita income—that is, the level of a country's GNP divided by its population.

Comparing per capita income across countries is problematic, however. Per capita income measures the availability of goods and services to individuals, but we cannot draw meaningful comparisons between incomes in Mexico, China, and Australia when GNP in each case is calculated in terms of a different national currency—pesos, yuan, and pounds, respectively. The simplest means of overcoming this problem is to use the exchange rate between national currencies to convert the GNP of each nation into a common currency. Most international income comparisons follow this technique, with U.S. dollars usually constituting the common currency. The term for this technique is the **exchange rate conversion method.**

Exchange rate conversion method:
The comparison of real GNP across countries by converting all nations' GNPs to a common currency denomination through the use of exchange rates.

Unfortunately, even international income comparisons based on the exchange rate conversion method can be misleading. When international comparisons are made, the intention is to measure the differences in standards of living between different countries. Exchange rate conversion may reflect these differences poorly. While the exchange rate generally reflects differences in the purchasing power of currencies for goods that are traded across international markets, it may be a poor indicator of differences in the purchasing power of currencies with respect to goods and services that are not exchanged across international markets. For example, if 1 U.S. dollar will purchase 1½ Chinese yuan in the foreign exchange market, this exchange rate does not mean that the dollar will purchase exactly 1½ yuan of housing, dental care, or education in the United States (as 1½ yuan would in China). Differences in climate, culture, and tastes must be taken into account.

A technique for greatly improving international income comparisons involves expressing the conversion ratio between currencies in terms of their ability to purchase a typical bundle of goods and services in the countries where they are issued.[2] For example, the bundle of goods for the United Kingdom might include relatively expensive housing, heating, and food products, and the bundle for Thailand relatively cheap housing, heating, and food products. The United Nations International Comparison Project, a study begun in 1968 by the U.N. Statistical Office, has devised a workable purchasing power index for several currencies. In this **purchasing power parity method,** each category in the bundle of typical goods and services is weighted according to its contribution to GNP. The dollar cost of purchasing the typical bundle is then compared to the dollar cost of purchasing a similar bundle in the United States. After the purchasing power of the nation's currency is determined in terms of the typical bundle, this information is used to convert the GNP of the country in question to a common currency unit, the U.S. dollar.

Purchasing power parity method:
The comparison of real GNP across countries by converting GNPs to a common currency through use of the comparative cost of purchasing a typical assortment of goods and services in each country.

The size of the gap in per capita income between the developed and the less-developed countries has been calculated by the World Bank using both methods. The results are shown in Table 5. Using the exchange rate conversion method, per capita income in the industrial market economies in 1987 was estimated to be $14,324, while that in less-developed countries was estimated to be $1160. By this method of comparison, the industrial market economies appeared to have a per capita income twelve times greater than that of the less-developed countries. However, the relative figures calculated in terms of the

---

[2]Dan Usher, *The Price Mechanism and the Meaning of National Income Statistics* (Oxford: Clarendon Press, 1968).

TABLE 5

Measuring the Economic Gap Between Developed and Less-Developed Countries: Per Capita GNP, 1987

Per capita GNP in industrial market economies was more than twelve and one-half times that in less-developed countries in 1987. Per capita purchasing power (in U.S. dollars) in the developed world was more than five times greater than that of developing nations.

Country Group	Exchange Rate Conversion Method (dollars)	Purchasing Power Parity Method (dollars)
Less-developed countries	1,160	2,454
Industrial market economies	14,324	12,047

Source: World Bank, *World Bank Development Report 1981* (New York: Oxford University Press, 1981), p. 17, and authors' calculations.

purchasing power parity method indicate that the more-developed countries' per capita GNP is only five times greater than that of the less-developed countries.

Purchasing power parity estimates of per capita income are a more accurate indicator of relative international performance. The problem is that they are more difficult to construct. However, even in purchasing power parity terms, there is still a very significant gap between the incomes of developed nations and less-developed nations.

UNDERDEVELOPMENT: CAUSES AND CURES

Looking at the economic policies of underdeveloped countries that have succeeded in achieving substantial rates of economic growth and at the policies of countries that have failed to develop, it becomes clear that there is no single secret to economic development. Policies that appear to work in one country often fail when applied elsewhere. Nonetheless, we can talk confidently about certain keys to achieving economic growth: (1) an economic system that relies on a price system to efficiently allocate resources; (2) growth in the foreign sector based on the principle of comparative advantage; (3) acquisition of human capital; (4) increased savings and investment to acquire technology; and (5) efficient agricultural techniques. This is not to suggest that a country that takes these five steps will necessarily be a success or that economic development is impossible in countries that fail to pursue these five objectives.

Even if the government of an underdeveloped country implements a market system and pursues free-trade policies, the goal of economic development often proves to be elusive; success may be thwarted by an unmotivated or unconvinced populace. The acquisition of human capital requires that some family members undertake training or schooling when, instead, they could be earning income in the work force or producing goods at home. This is a luxury families on the verge of starvation cannot afford. Similarly, when the vast majority of families are poverty-stricken, encouraging saving and investment may be futile. A high percentage of output goes for consumption in many poor countries; very little is left for saving and investment. Because attaining agricultural efficiency hinges on use of capital equipment, it may be that many poor countries can do nothing but fail—they are trapped in the vicious circle of poverty.

Population Growth and Economic Development

One of the characteristics shared by most developing countries is rapid population growth. The population of poor countries in Africa, Asia, and South America has been expanding in recent years at an annual rate of about 2.5 percent. By contrast, the population of the developed countries of Europe, Japan, and North America has been growing at a rate of about 1 percent per year. A cause-and-effect relation between rapid population growth and retarded economic growth of less-developed countries has often been claimed. Surely, the argument goes, rapid population growth must impose substantial costs on less-developed countries, insofar as education and health care—as well as elemental necessities like food and clothing—must be provided from limited available resources. While this line of reasoning is plausible on the surface, there are reasons to believe that blaming underdevelopment on rapid population growth is an oversimplification; in economic terms, both costs and benefits may be associated with population growth.

First, the high rate of population growth in less-developed countries is fostered not by increasing birth rates but by stable birth rates combined with a sharp decline in mortality, or death, rates. Mortality rates in the less-developed world have fallen by 50 percent in the last thirty years because of advances in disease control. Although infant mortality remains relatively high, life expectancy at birth in the less-developed world increased from about thirty-five years in 1950 to about fifty-eight years in 1990. Life expectancy at birth is an important measure of economic development. Hence, the population explosion in less-developed countries evidences, paradoxically, economic advance.

High rates of fertility in less-developed countries—that is, a high demand for children—are also cited as a cause of underdevelopment. Both modern and traditional methods of birth control are generally available in less-developed countries, but this has not slackened demand for large families. High rates of fertility, other things being equal, do imply reduced per capita income. But the costs of having children that families in less-developed countries must face are lower than the costs faced by families in Western countries. In less-developed countries, children frequently represent valuable capital assets. It is common for quite young children—four or five years of age—to enter the labor force, especially in the agricultural sector. Only very young children are usually dependent in the sense that the marginal product of their labor does not substantially offset the cost to their families of clothing and feeding them. This usefulness of the young is reflected in the high labor force participation rates for many less-developed countries compared with developed countries. In short, children in less-developed countries apparently make a more substantial contribution to aggregate output than children in developed countries.

International Wealth Distribution and Economic Development

Is economic exploitation by richer countries a cause of underdevelopment? If so, will financial help from more-developed countries solve the problem? In 1974, the U.N. General Assembly adopted a Declaration on the Establishment of a New International Economic Order (NIEO), in which it asserted that only large-scale redistribution of wealth from rich to poor countries can accelerate the latter's agonizingly slow development process.

Two ideas lie behind the NIEO: the vicious circle of poverty and the responsibility of developed countries for the underdevelopment of poor countries. In the minds of NIEO advocates, presently developed countries are colonial powers who developed their own economies largely through a redistribution of resources taken from less-developed countries. Today, the less-developed countries' circle of poverty is unbreakable unless the redistribution of wealth is reversed through trade preferences for less-developed countries, commodity agreements (in effect, long-run contracts for various agricultural and other goods), and, most important, cancellation of some of the enormous foreign debts owed by less-developed countries to foreign banks. An important clause of the declaration states that discrimination (that is, any restrictions on the use of funds) should not be involved in grants of aid to governments of less-developed countries. What those governments choose to do with the aid should be entirely left to them.

The claims of the advocates of the NIEO are understandable. Many presently developed nations long colonized many of the presently less-developed nations. International trade has continued among developed and less-developed countries on a large scale, yet the less-developed countries have not yet been brought to high stages of development. Finally, common sense would seem to suggest that additional aid could only help matters.

The NIEO proposal, however, has many opponents, who refute the claim that past and present commercial contact between the developed countries and the less-developed countries is a source of the less-developed countries' persistent poverty. Opponents point out that the list of the least-developed countries consists almost entirely of those that have had little or no involvement with international trade, such as Burundi, Chad, Rwanda, and Bhutan. Those with a record of the most extensive contacts with developed countries, including Mexico, Singapore, and Brazil, are among the most advanced poorer countries.

Opponents of NIEO also challenge the notion that trade between the developed nations and the less-developed nations has been a one-way street. They stress that there were and are gains to the less-developed countries from this trade. Opponents also disagree with NIEO's proposal to abolish economic discrimination against the less-developed countries, which would effectively allow them to follow any sort of economic policy. Opponents cite economic policies of the less-developed countries that have severely retarded their own economic development, including persecution and expulsion of productive minority groups (Asians in East Africa, Chinese in Southeast Asia, and many others), enforced collectivization of farming, the establishment of state export monopolies, and the confiscation of the property of productive groups for political purposes.

Thus, the economic policies pursued by governments in less-developed countries seem to play a crucial role in their own economic development.

Many government policies seem to inhibit economic growth and reduce the performance of the economy. In this context, critics question unrestricted aid to less-developed countries. The same governments that promulgate policies detrimental to economic development are unlikely to invest foreign aid in an economically efficient manner. To opponents of the NIEO proposals, the theory of exploitation from without underestimates the importance of internal institutions and economic policies in the development process. These critics argue that development is not determined by the greed or generosity of already developed nations but, to a large degree, by economic policies in the less-developed countries themselves.

Property Rights Arrangements and Economic Development

Can differences in economic institutions be pinpointed as a major cause of underdevelopment? It is often argued that economists are not able to bring societies into the laboratory and use the experimental method to test their theories. While this is certainly true, economists are able to make careful observations of how different economic institutions affect economic performance. There are contemporary examples of different economic systems that have a common basic cultural setting, a similar climate, and a common ethnic-religious origin but that have taken radically different routes to economic development (recall Economics in Action, "Contrasts in Economic Institutions: The Two Koreas," in Chapter 3). Comparison of such countries helps shed some light on the causes of underdevelopment.

Mainland China, Hong Kong, and Taiwan. The People's Republic of (Mainland) China is the world's most populous economy, with an estimated population in 1988 of over a billion (1,088,169,000). Unlike some other communist countries, until recently China apparently did not have a legally sanctioned private sector in its economy; economic activity was even more tightly controlled by the state than in the Soviet Union. Unlike the case of the Soviet economy, there has been little evidence in China of an underground economy, which in the Soviet Union restores some degree of flexibility to the centrally planned system.

Since 1959, China has not issued economic statistics, so evaluation of the country's economic performance is based on outside estimates. But there is general agreement that despite promising reserves of oil, gas, coal, iron ore and other natural resources, China is still one of the world's poorest countries. In 1985, the (estimated) GNP per capita was $318. However, even this low figure tends to overstate the standard of living in China, where quality consumer goods remain in scarce supply. Relative to average wages, goods tend in general to be more expensive than similar goods in the West. A worker can reasonably hope to save enough to buy a bicycle, but definitely not a car. In the past decade, the Chinese leadership has begun relaxing the reliance on central planning by encouraging greater initiative on the part of enterprise management and encouraging private economic ventures to a limited extent.

In 1978, China introduced a contract responsibility system for some of its 800 million peasant farmers. The system allowed these farmers to sell their crops on the open market after they had turned over a certain percentage of their yield to the government. The response of China's farmers to these economic reforms, which basically vested farmers with partial property rights over their production, was phenomenal. Between 1981 and 1985, wheat production in China rose by 43 percent, the production of cotton increased by 40 percent, and meat production rose by 39 percent. It is unlikely that such dramatic production increases were due solely to technological advancement or to favorable climatic conditions. In 1984, China extended this free-market experiment to urban workers. In the past, urban workers had little incentive to produce; each job was guaranteed for a worker's lifetime, and both industrious and laggard workers were equally rewarded. Now, state-run plants are able to keep whatever profits they earn in excess of state taxes and distribute these profits to workers in the form of wage incentives. Managers are able to hire and fire workers and to set different wages for different jobs.

The most significant change in China's economy has been its adoption of a modified price system. The government has slowly relaxed its controls over prices, and the costs of many basic consumer items now fluctuate in response to supply and demand.

Although many Chinese are enjoying greater prosperity because of these changes, the overall success of China's attempt to bring market principles into a command economy will depend on many factors, including the stability of the country's leadership. Eventually, the world's most populous nation may become a powerful economic force in international trade.

Although the people of Taiwan and Hong Kong are ethnically identical to the Chinese people, Taiwan and Hong Kong are market economies, with relatively small public sectors. In fact, in both countries government regulation of the economy is considerably more limited than it is in the United States. Of the two, Taiwan has the greater endowment of natural resources. Hong Kong is very poor in natural resources; it has little level land for agriculture and must import both food and water from the mainland. Yet each of these economies has enjoyed successful economic development. Estimated 1985 GNP per capita for Taiwan was $3109; for Hong Kong, $6330. The standard of living in each economy is high and visibly improving. Largely unrestricted by government, individual entrepreneurship thrives. Whether Hong Kong's rapid economic growth will continue after it is returned to mainland China in 1999 is uncertain. The Chinese have assured Hong Kong businesspeople of some freedom of action after the switch in regimes.

CONCLUSION: EXPLAINING ECONOMIC DEVELOPMENT

Why have economies developed at different rates? More specifically, why do less-developed countries seem to have such difficulty matching the levels of development typical of Europe, Japan, and North America? This question is the object of much controversy; we have already discussed some of the major issues in the debate, such as the vicious circle of poverty. It appears that neither the vicious circle of poverty nor large populations have prevented development of economies such as Hong Kong, Taiwan, and South Korea, which have developed rapidly by attracting foreign investment, rather than relying primarily on foreign aid.

Likewise, the level of technology in most less-developed countries tends to be low. But this is an effect, not a cause, of low levels of development. Poor countries are unable to afford equipment and techniques common in rich countries. The technology itself—inventions, new processes and techniques—is widely available to less-developed countries. The knowledge necessary to improve productivity is not lacking, but the economic development making that technical knowledge worthwhile is. Less-developed countries often have untapped reserves of entrepreneurial ability, a problem that countries such as China are only beginning to address.

In terms of economic growth, economists are generally satisfied that economic incentives matter. Property rights arrangements and institutions that reward economic efficiency and permit consumers to choose freely the kinds and amounts of goods and services produced tend to promote development. Consider Japan. Despite its dense population and sparse resource base, Japan has risen rapidly from a poor agricultural country to a model for what a capitalist-style market structure and incentives to savings and investment can accomplish.

SUMMARY

1. The study of comparative economic systems focuses on the alternative institutional arrangements of different economies—such as who owns productive resources and who makes economic decisions—and the impact of these arrangements on economic performance.

2. Capitalism is an economic system in which a large proportion of economic activity is conducted by private individuals and firms. The private ownership of resources and the freedom to employ resources as the owner sees fit are a hallmark of capitalist economic systems. By contrast, socialism is an economic system in which the state owns most nonhuman productive resources. Resource allocation under socialism is determined in the main by central planning rather than by private initiative.

3. The basic economic concepts introduced in the earlier chapters of this book have general applicability to all economic systems. The law of demand, opportunity cost, diminishing marginal returns, and self-interest, for example, apply equally to capitalist and socialist economies.

4. Historically, the Soviet economy has been a command economy, in which virtually all economic decisions were made through a detailed system of central planning. The recent introduction of *perestroika,* or economic restructuring, is a move toward less central planning and a somewhat greater reliance on markets to provide goods and services.

5. There is a growing legal private sector in the Soviet Union in agriculture and personal services. Until recently, private agricultural plots have occupied a small percentage of cultivated land but have been quite productive. There is also an extensive extralegal private sector in the Soviet Union that eases the bottlenecks caused by central planning.

6. Comparisons of the performance of the Soviet economy and other economies are tricky, especially since the Soviet economy is in transition. Data seem to indicate that the Soviet Union has achieved high but erratic growth rates over recent years. Moreover, when comparisons involving the quality of output are involved, Soviet performance in the consumer goods sector is generally poor.

7. Though an aim of Soviet policy is avowed to be greater equality in income distribution, the available evidence indicates that the effective distribution of income in the Soviet Union is similar to that in the capitalist U.S. economy and the democratic socialist economy of Sweden.

8. Economic development is the study of how countries grow economically.

9. The less-developed countries of the world are characterized by low per capita income, large and growing populations, and low saving and investment rates.

10. Comparisons of per capita income between the industrial countries and the less-developed countries can be made by the exchange rate conversion method or the purchasing power parity method. However the computation is handled, the economic gap between the developed and the less-developed countries is large.

11. The vicious circle of poverty refers to the fact that there is little saving in a poor economy and, therefore, little chance for future development. Economies are thus said to be poor tomorrow because they are poor today. This idea has some merit in explaining underdevelopment, but it must be applied carefully.

12. Population growth is a serious obstacle to economic development. However, much of the recent popula-

tion growth in less-developed countries is due to a declining death rate and to the need for young children to augment the labor supply in the agricultural sector, so the phenomenon of population growth in the less-developed countries must be interpreted cautiously.

13. There have been various responses to the New International Economic Order (NIEO) adopted by the United Nations in 1974. Under the NIEO, the rich countries of the world would transfer wealth to the poor countries. This and similar proposals are pred-

icated on the idea that the poverty of the poor countries is due to the policies of the rich countries and not to policies and institutions that prevail in the poor countries.

14. Comparative economic development suggests that property rights, incentives, personal freedom, and other similar institutions are important in sparking economic growth. The examples of Hong Kong, Taiwan, and Japan support the validity of this approach to development.

KEY TERMS

comparative economics
pure capitalism
pure communism
socialism
mixed capitalism

command economy
materials balancing
perestroika
economic development
less-developed countries

vicious circle of poverty
exchange rate conversion method
purchasing power parity method

QUESTIONS FOR REVIEW AND DISCUSSION

1. Would you expect the illegal private sector to be larger in the United States or in the Soviet Union? Why?

2. A socialist economy does not recognize private property rights. The state "owns" all resources. Name three consequences of this lack of private property rights.

3. Is income distribution in the Soviet Union fundamentally different from that in Western economies? Why or why not?

4. Give three examples not discussed in the text of how basic economic principles apply to a command economy.

5. What are the primary characteristics of a less-developed economy?

6. The vicious circle of poverty asserts that the less-developed countries are poor today because they were poor yesterday. Do you agree? Explain.

7. Evaluate this statement: "To achieve economic growth, an economy requires lots of resources, including land, and a low rate of population growth."

8. Explain why you agree or disagree with the following statement: "A major difference between a planned economy and a market economy is that the supply of any particular good in a planned economy is perfectly inelastic while in a free market it is elastic."

ECONOMICS IN ACTION
The Socialist Calculation Debate and the Transition from Planning to Markets

The astonishing turn of events in the Soviet Union in the 1980s gave way to events in Eastern Europe that were characterized as "unthinkable." While the news media and others may have been caught by surprise, economists were somewhat better prepared—having for years debated

whether socialism could exist as envisioned by Marx and Lenin, and then whether socialism could survive.

The debate originated with Austrian economist Ludwig von Mises (1881–1973) and a paper he published in 1922 entitled "Economic Calculation in the Socialist Commonwealth." Mises attacked the position taken by contemporary socialist theorists that after a socialist state abolished money, the price system, and markets, it would be able to plan and direct all production. He argued that money prices determined across markets were necessary for rational economic calculation. The price system allowed resources to flow to their most highly valued uses in society. For example, although it would be technically feasible to build subway rails out of platinum, this would be an economically inefficient allocation if less expensive substitutes were available for the rails. But only the price system, representing the competing bids of all potential users of platinum, allows for such judgments to be made. Without it, Mises argued, resources could not be allocated efficiently, and the economy could function only at a primitive level at best. A modern, technologically advanced, and complex economy would be impossible to achieve under socialism.

Socialists took Mises's challenge very seriously, and some prominent writers (Oskar Lange and Abba Lerner, in particular) acknowledged that Mises had identified a very important weakness in the socialist position. Lange even half-seriously proposed that in the future socialist commonwealth, a statue be erected in Mises's honor so that no one would forget that prices and markets would be essential under socialism, too. In effect, the socialist counterattack partially retreated from the original socialist position. Lange claimed that socialism might still work if central planning were abandoned in favor of a system wherein the state would set prices for goods and factors of production. Managers of state-owned firms would then produce until the marginal cost of their output equaled the assigned price of the good. These managers would simply requisition the inputs necessary to produce according to this rule: The state would adjust the prices it assigned in response to any shortages or surpluses of the factors of production.

While this plan seemed clever, Mises and his student, Friedrich von Hayek, countered that these "market socialist" schemes failed to solve the real problem of socialism. Although the socialist state could establish an arbitrary set of prices, it would not perform the function of a market price system unless these "prices" were able to convey an equal amount of information regarding the true opportunity costs associated with resource use. For the socialist state's prices to serve this purpose, they would have to reflect an enormous amount of information regarding the availability of resources, updated continually. If this task were possible at all, it would require high transaction costs. Furthermore, for such a system to approximate the efficiency of a market

economy, incentives would have to be structured to ensure that individuals within the system would use information and resources efficiently. But this could be possible only where factors of production were privately owned, while the market socialists insisted that all resources be owned by the state.

The seven-decade-long record of central planning bears out many points Mises made. As predicted, centrally planned economies, including those in Eastern Europe, failed to achieve the early goals of Marx and Lenin due to an inability to use prices as information. These early socialist theorists and later practitioners also underestimated the drag placed on the system by the inevitable bureaucracies.[a]

When Mises first voiced doubts about the practicality of socialism, socialism and central planning were just theories. We now know that a socialist system founded on central planning can exist; planning was the hallmark of Soviet bloc countries for many years, and growth did occur. Mises's primary point, however, was that no economy could approach high levels of efficiency and development without a price system and free markets to guide resources into their most highly valued uses. On this point, there is substantial empirical evidence that planning does not maximize the welfare of consumers or economic efficiency in society.

The socialist calculation debate, even with the recent shifts from planning to greater reliance on markets, cannot tell us what the future of formerly planned economies will be. Some people believe there is a third way, a middle ground between communism and capitalism where the excesses of the two systems can be reconciled in some form of social democracy or mixed economy. Mises and Hayek argued that all forms of social democracy are inherently unstable and will—owing to costs and inefficiencies generated by planning of any form—evolve into freedom and market capitalism or into socialist planning and totalitarianism. Where the recent steps taken by the countries of the Soviet bloc will lead only time will tell.

Question

Does Mises's indictment of central planning mean that planning is impossible or, rather, that, due to some ever-present characteristics of human nature and institutions, planning can seldom if ever guarantee that the goals of planners are reached? Explain. Does Mises's insight have any contemporary relevance for Western societies?

[a]Ludwig von Mises, *Bureaucracy* (New Haven, Conn.: Yale University Press, 1944).

P. T. Bauer

Gunnar Myrdal

P. T. Bauer and Gunnar Myrdal: Third World Development and Trade

PETER TAMAS BAUER (b. 1915) is the most distinguished critic of development theory. Bauer's studies of the rubber industry and the West African trade paved the way for his works on development—*Dissent on Development* (1972) and *Reality and Rhetoric: Studies in the Economics of Development* (1984). Bauer struck his central theme concerning economic development in earlier works: Economic growth, Bauer argued, is the product of voluntary responses and efficient domestic and international markets—not of state intervention or central planning by governments.

Born in Hungary in 1915, Bauer was a fellow of Gonville and Caius College at Cambridge (England) between 1946 and 1960 and again from 1968 and 1984. He was also professor of economics in the University of London at the London School of Economics from 1960 until his retirement in 1983. While in these academic posts, Bauer launched attacks on the conventional wisdom regarding economic development, including theories relating to the widening gap of income differences within and between countries, the vicious circle of poverty, the operation of marketing boards and commodity agreements in developing countries, and the operation of foreign aid. Principally, Bauer targeted the economic development theories of Gunnar Myrdal.

GUNNAR MYRDAL (1898–1987), sociologist and economist, was a joint recipient of the Nobel Memorial Prize in economics with Friedrich A. von Hayek in 1974. Myrdal is best known for his work on racial discrimination and social problems. His most famous work, *An American Dilemma:*

The Negro Problem and Modern Democracy, began as a study commissioned by the Carnegie Corporation in 1938 and had an enormous impact on American attitudes toward integration. His later works explored trade and economic development: *The Political Element in the Development of Economic Theory* (1935) focused on the philosophical foundations of classical free-trade doctrine, and *Rich Lands and Poor: The Road to World Prosperity* (1957) discussed the application of the free-trade doctrine to the problems of economic development.

Myrdal was born in the Gustaf parish of Sweden. He studied law as an undergraduate at the University of Stockholm and received his PhD in law from the university in 1927. In 1924, he married Alva Reimer, with whom he researched and wrote a study of Sweden's decreasing population, which was published in 1934. After graduation, Myrdal taught economics, traveled abroad, and served the government of Sweden both as a representative of the Social Democratic party and as cabinet minister. In 1947, he was appointed executive secretary of the United Nations Economic Commission for Europe, a position he retained for the next ten years. In 1960, he became a professor of international economics at the University of Stockholm.

WHAT IS THE PROBLEM?

Both Bauer and Myrdal pursued answers to timeless questions regarding the economic development of Third World nations. Does free trade promote or impede economic development in poor nations? Which is more conducive to economic growth and progress in developing nations—central planning or free markets? What is the nature and what are the effects of economic aid from industrialized nations to poor and developing nations of the world?

Bauer and Myrdal occupy opposite ends of the philosophical spectrum; they could not agree on what the problem of economic development is, much less any solution. Myrdal, for example, would center the investigation around the causes of poverty, while Bauer would have economists investigate the causes of prosperity and development. In other words, the burden of any theory of development is either to explain how certain nations and people got rich (Bauer) or why certain nations remained poor (Myrdal).

Not only are Myrdal and Bauer worlds apart on the definition of the problem of development, they stand apart on the philosophical nature of equality and power. Of great importance here is the concept of "equality," which both economists support, but in vastly different forms. As an important modern commentator on their views has remarked, "Whether Myrdal or Bauer is more in favor of equality depends entirely on whether equality is conceived as equality of economic results or equality of political process. Myrdal clearly believes more in equality of economic results—and Bauer equally clearly prefers equality of social processes."[a] In other words, the goal of economic development, in Myrdal's view, is to promote economic equality—similar levels of development and equitable income distributions—between rich and poor nations. Economic power exemplified by concentrations of monopoly power, Myrdal believed, is the root cause of inequalities. Bauer, on the other hand, believes that economic development requires that social processes and *access* to economic activity be open to all and be free and unfettered. In Bauer's view, power restricts the choices of others, most often exemplified by government planning and regulation. The rich, according to Bauer, most often get that way by expanding the choices and opportunities of others.

TRADE, CENTRAL PLANNING, AND ECONOMIC AID

Not surprisingly, the philosophical differences between Bauer and Myrdal show very different views of key elements in economic development. Here we consider only three of these key elements.

TRADE

In Myrdal's view, the principle of comparative advantage and free trade works in favor of rich nations and keeps poor nations locked within a vicious cycle of poverty. The low saving rates of poor countries mean low investment, which means low economic growth, which means low savings, and so on. To Myrdal, trade with other countries does not unlock this vicious cycle. In *Rich Lands and Poor: The Road to World Prosperity,* he writes, "The forces in the market tend to increase, rather than to decrease, the inequalities between regions." Myrdal points to the so-called banana republics, underdeveloped nations that specialize in one product. In Myrdal's view, such overspecialization leaves a country vulnerable to changes in demand and its economy in continuous peril. He suggests that tariffs and subsidies would provide the impetus for developing nations to diversify production and to reduce dependence on one or a few exports.

In Bauer's analysis of trade, these views are wrongheaded and counterproductive. In the first place, Bauer denies that there is a vicious cycle of poverty in underdeveloped countries. Saving and investment take place even where people are poor and illiterate. In his classic study of the rubber industry, Bauer showed that very rapid growth was possible as a consequence of voluntary responses by peasants to expanded opportunities and contacts of developed countries in the West.[b] Further, Bauer argued that trade restrictions and attempts to substitute domestic production for goods that can be obtained more cheaply abroad were a certain path to welfare reductions and to lower growth and development. Development could be maximized only with free interaction between *all* trading nations.

CENTRAL PLANNING AND AID

Myrdal urged central planning as an extension of his belief that unequal distribution of power and property was the principal obstacle to equitable economic growth. Institutional planning, production goals, and price planning are all parts of the system that Myrdal urged on developing nations as prerequisites to growth and changing attitudes. He had faith that, with enough information and competent managers, planning would be superior to any other method of achieving growth and human development. Further, he believed the role of industrialized countries was to provide aid to poor nations.

Sentiments expressed by Bauer twenty years ago have a very contemporary feel. Bauer pointed out then that planning, if it works at all, does not maximize an economy's opportunities. All investment undertaken for political motives is wasted. Bauer likewise criticized foreign aid as intergovernmental grants of taxpayers' money. While such aid augments resources in recipient countries, Bauer believes there is no reason to expect that, in the hands of politicians, bureaucrats, and administrators, it will be put to productive uses. With few exceptions, foreign aid promotes centralized and closely controlled economies (factors that choke growth), and it sometimes generates resentment and suspicion toward the donor.[c] Of far greater effect is aid provided on a commercial basis, direct foreign investment in developing nations, and—of ultimate importance in Bauer's view—free and open trade between rich nations and poor.

[a]Thomas Sowell, *A Conflict of Visions* (New York: William Morrow and Company, 1987), p. 159.

[b]A. A. Walters, "Peter Tamas Bauer," in *The New Palgrave: A Dictionary of Economics,* edited by John Eatwell, Murray Milgate, and Peter Newman (London: The Macmillan Press Limited, 1987), vol. I, p. 207. For further information on Myrdal, see Paul Streeten, "Gunnar Myrdal," *The New Palgrave,* vol. III, pp. 581–83.

[c]For more on economic aid, see P. T. Bauer, *Dissent on Development: Studies and Debates in Development Economics* (Cambridge: Harvard University Press, 1972), p. 114–35.

GLOSSARY

Numbers in parentheses indicate pages on which key terms are discussed.

Ability-to-pay principle: The notion that tax bills should vary directly with income levels or the capacity of individuals to pay taxes; a method of determining individuals' tax burdens on the basis of those most capable of paying taxes. (536, 725)

Absolute advantage: The ability of an economic entity to specialize and produce a greater amount of some good than another entity can. (51)

Accommodation of cost-push inflation: Increases in the money supply designed to offset a decrease in aggregate supply caused by monopoly or union action or by an aggregate supply shock; increased aggregate demand results, preventing decreases in real output. (826)

Accounting costs: Actual money expenditures associated with any activity; payments a firm actually makes to resource suppliers; out-of-pocket costs or explicit costs. (9, 193)

Accounting profit: The amount by which total revenues exceed total accounting, or explicit, costs; total revenues minus total explicit payments for inputs or out-of-pocket costs. (195, 438)

Adaptive expectations theory: A proposition suggesting that consumers and businesses form expectations of future inflation on the basis of actual inflation from the recent past. (817)

Adjusted income: An individual's income after all taxes and all government transfer payments are accounted for. (458)

Administrative lag: The amount of time between recognition of a destabilizing economic event and the implementation of a policy designed to correct for it. (848)

Advertising: Any communication or information that firms offer consumers to increase demand for a product. (287)

Age-distributed income: The distribution of income broken down by age ranges in the population, usually by ten-year intervals. (464)

Aggregate concentration: A measure of the percentage of the total productive assets in an economy owned by the largest one hundred or two hundred firms in the economy. (323)

Aggregate demand: The total spending that occurs in an economy at various price levels during a specified period of time. (588)

Aggregate demand curve: Graphical relation showing the different levels of national income that exist at different price levels. (689)

Aggregate supply: The total output that will be produced by an economy at various price levels during a specified period of time. (588)

Aggregate supply curve: A graph showing the different levels of aggregate output produced at different price levels. (694)

Aggregate supply of land: The total amount of land available for use by the entire economy. (425)

Allocative efficiency: A situation in which the socially optimal amount of a good or service is produced in an industry; the socially optimal amount depends on the tastes and preferences of society and on the opportunity cost of the resources used to produce the good or service. (238)

Antitrust policy: Regulations established by laws and government agencies that attempt to preserve business competition. (478)

Appreciation: An increase in the equilibrium exchange market value of a country's currency in a flexible-rate system; a decrease in the number of units of a country's money required to purchase one unit of a foreign country's money. (944)

Arc elasticity: A measure of the average elasticity between two points on the demand curve. (125)

Artificial barriers to trade: Restrictions created by the government that inhibit or prevent trade; includes import quotas and tariffs. (53)

Asset: Anything of value owned by a firm that adds to the firm's net worth. (187)

Asset income: Earnings from interest on savings, from capital investments, and from land; all result from forgone consumption in the past. (450)

Automatic stabilizers: Taxes and government expenditures whose levels do not depend on decisions by policy-makers for change but instead change countercyclically in response to changes in the level of economic activity. (718)

Autonomous consumption: Consumption expenditures that are independent of the level of income. (642)

Autonomous consumption multiplier: The multiple by which equilibrium income will change given a change in autonomous consumption expenditure: $1/MPS$. (665)

Autonomous government expenditures: Government expenditures that are independent of the level of income. (671)

Autonomous investment: Investment expenditures that are independent of the level of income. (649)

Average cost pricing: A regulatory policy that causes a firm to charge a price equal to average cost, inducing the firm to produce an output such that economic profits are zero. (490)

Average fixed cost: Total fixed costs divided by the level of output. (197)

Average product: Total output divided by the number of units of the variable input used to produce the total output; output produced per unit of variable input used. (200)

Average propensity to consume (*APC*): The percent of a particular level of income that is spent on consumption; total consumption divided by total income. (641)

Average propensity to save (*APS*): The percent of total income that is saved; total saving during any given period divided by total income in the same period. (641)

Average tax rate: The percentage of income paid in taxes; total tax liability divided by total income. (538)

Average total cost: Total costs divided by the level of output. (197)

Average variable cost: Total variable costs divided by the level of ouput. (197)

Backward induction: The incentive each player has to cheat in the last period of the game; exists because there are no future periods left to play in which possible consequences from cheating could occur. (305)

Balance of payments: An official accounting record of all the foreign transactions of a nation's residents, businesses, and governments. (954)

Balance of trade deficit: Occurs when the value of a nation's exports is less than the value of a nation's imports; also called a trade deficit. (950)

Balance of trade surplus: Occurs when the value of a nation's exports exceeds the value of a nation's imports; also called a trade surplus. (950)

Balance sheet: An accounting representation of the assets, liabilities, and net worth of a firm. (187)

Barter: Direct exchange of one good or service for another without the use of money. (14, 63)

Barter economy: An economy in which money is not used to facilitate exchange between individuals and firms; goods trade directly for other goods. (742)

Benefit principle: The notion that people who receive the benefits of publicly provided goods or services should pay for their production; a method of determining individuals' tax burdens on the basis of the beneficiaries of the expenditures that are financed by taxes; an example is a gasoline tax. (535, 725)

Bilateral monopoly: A market in which there is only one buyer and only one seller of a resource or product. (393)

Binding arbitration: An agreement between the buyers and sellers of labor to allow a third party to determine the conditions of a work contract. (395)

Bonds: Financial instruments that create future obligations on the part of the issuers to make principal repayments and, in most cases, interest payments. (724)

Bretton Woods system: The fixed exchange rate system established among Western countries after World War II. (960)

Budget constraint: A line that shows all possible combinations of two goods that a consumer is able to purchase given some money income and the prices of the goods. (165)

Budget deficit: The amount by which government's expenditures exceed government's tax revenues in a year. (719)

Budget surplus: The amount by which government's tax revenues exceed government's expenditures in a year. (719)

Bureaus: The arms of government that serve to implement and enforce legislation and to administer programs created by legislation. (565)

Business cycles: Recurrent, systematic fluctuations in the level of business activity; usually measured by changes in the level, or rate of growth, of real GNP over time; or the variation through time of the level of real GNP around its long-term trend. (586, 862)

Capital consumption: A decrease in the capital stock; occurs when the rate of depreciation is greater than the rate of capital formation. (407)

Capital deepening: Increases in the total stock of capital in conjunction with increases in the ratio of the capital stock to the labor force; occurs when the capital stock grows at a faster rate than the labor force. (888)

Capital formation: An increase in the stock of capital due to roundabout production; the process whereby the stock of capital in an economy increases. (406, 898)

Capital stock: The amount of nonhuman resources available in the economy, including tools, land, machinery, equipment, and so on; the total amount of capital goods that exist in an economy at any point in time. (39, 406)

Capitalized monopoly profits: What the sum of all future monopoly profits is worth today. (266)

Capture, or interest group, theory of regulation: Argues that regulations are constructed so as to further the interests of the existing firms within a particular industry. (487)

Cartel: An alliance of firms that act collusively to reduce output and increase price in an industry in order to increase profits. (300)

Cartel enforcement: Attempts by members of a cartel to prevent other members from cheating and thus destroying economic profit potential. (314)

Cash reserves: Commercial banks' and other depository institutions' holdings of vault cash or deposits at the Federal Reserve district banks. (765)

Ceteris paribus: The Latin phrase for "all other things held constant." (88)

Change in demand: A shift of the entire demand curve to the right or left. (89)

Change in the demand for labor: A shift of the entire labor demand curve; caused by a change in the marginal product of labor, by a change in the demand for the product produced by the type of labor in question, or by a change in the price of some other factor of production. (360)

Change in quantity demanded: A change in the amount of a good a consumer is willing and able to purchase that is caused by a change in the price of the good or service. (89)

Change in quantity supplied: A change in the amount of a good a producer is willing and able to produce and sell that is caused by a change in the price of the good or service. (96)

Change in supply: A shift of the entire supply curve to the right or left. (96)

Cheating: The act of violating a collusive agreement; may result in an increase in short-run economic profits to the firm that cheats, followed by zero economic profits in the long run. (305)

Checkable deposits: Demand deposits plus other types of transaction accounts that pay interest but that may carry some restrictions on use, including minimum balance and limits on the number of checks that can be written per month. (748)

Choices at the margin: Decisions based on the additional benefits and costs of small changes in a particular activity. (35)

Circular flow of income: The movement of real goods and services, payments, and receipts between households and business firms. (63)

Classical long-run equilibrium: The hypothetical adjustment of an economy to full employment given an actual supply of resources, population, technology, and degree of specialization. (620)

Classical macroeconomic theory: A view of the macroeconomy as being self-adjusting and capable of generating full employment and maximum output in the long run without government intervention; dominant from the late eighteenth through the early twentieth century. (618)

Classical process of economic growth: A process based on the division of labor but also involving increases in saving, investment, capital accumulation, and, ultimately, growth in real GNP. (618)

Classical range: A vertical segment of the aggregate supply curve; indicates that attempts to increase aggregate output will result only in a higher price level since resources are fully employed. (695)

Classical self-adjustment mechanism: The theory that, through Say's law, full employment will be reached given interest rate flexibility and price-wage flexibility. (629)

Coase theorem: States that the amount of an externality-generating activity will be the same regardless of the assignment of property rights if bargaining costs are small. (512)

Collective bargaining: The process of buyers and sellers negotiating, rather than competing individually, in order to determine a wage rate. (394)

Collusion: An explicit or implicit agreement among firms in an industry not to engage in competitive behavior. (333)

Command economy: An extreme form of socialist economy characterized by less private economic decision making than exists in a socialist economy. (975)

Commercial bank: Chartered financial institution that accepts deposits of various types, especially demand deposits, and that makes commercial and consumer loans. (753)

Commodity money: An item that serves as a medium of exchange and that is also a good itself. (743)

Common ownership: An arrangement whereby the property rights to a resource are nonexistent or poorly defined; by default, anyone may use or consume the resource. (504)

Comparable worth: A proposal that advocates government regulations requiring employers to pay employees in different but comparable occupations equally. Comparability between occupations is based on the amount of training and education required for each job and on working conditions. (376)

Comparative advantage: An economic entity's (an individual's or a nation's) ability to produce a good at a lower marginal opportunity production cost than some other entity. (45, 914)

Comparative economics: The study of the differences in economic systems; particularly, the differences between capitalist and socialist economic systems. (970)

Competition: A market situation satisfying two conditions—a large number of buyers and sellers and freedom to enter and exit the market—and resulting in prices equal to the costs of production plus a normal profit for sellers. (67)

Competitive labor market: A labor market in which the wage rate is determined by the interactions of a large number of sellers (suppliers) of labor and a large number of demanders (buyers) of labor. Neither group acts in a collusive manner. (354)

Complementary inputs: Inputs with a relation such that increased usage of one input due to a fall in its price results in increased employment of the other(s). (361)

Complements: Products that are related such that an increase in the price of one will decrease the demand for the other or a decrease in the price of one will increase the demand for the other; two goods whose cross elasticity of demand is negative: $\epsilon_c < 0$. (91, 134)

Constant-cost industry: An industry in which the minimum *LRATC* of production does not change as the number of firms in the industry changes; expansion (contraction) of the number of firms does not bid up (down) input prices; long-run industry supply is horizontal. (235)

Constant returns to scale: As plant size either increases or decreases, long-run average total cost does not change. (209)

Constitutional decision making: The process of choosing which set of rules (voting rules, for example) society will adapt for its use. (554)

Consumer equilibrium: A situation in which a consumer chooses quantities of goods that maximize total utility given a budget constraint; equilibrium implies that the per-dollar marginal utility obtained from the last unit of each good consumed is equal for all goods. (150)

Consumer-initiated discrimination: Wage discrimination arising from consumers' preferences for goods or services produced by individuals of a certain sex, race, religion, or national origin. Consumers must pay a premium in the form of higher prices or lower quality to exercise such discrimination. (466)

Consumer price index (CPI): A price index that uses the prices of goods and services consumers generally buy to calculate the price level and the rate of inflation. (610)

Consumers' surplus: The difference between the amount of money that consumers would be willing to pay for a certain quantity of a good and what they actually pay; the area above the price line and below the demand curve. (272)

Consumption function: The positive relationship between levels of consumption expenditures and levels of income, holding all other relevant factors that determine consumption constant. (642)

Consumption possibilities curve: All the possible combinations of two goods that could be consumed by first specializing according to comparative advantage and then trading at the terms of trade. (917)

Contestability: Characteristic of a market in which the entry of competitors is possible. (492)

Contestable markets theory: A theory of industrial organization that suggests that where entry and exit are costless, a single supplier in an industry will produce the same price and output result as a competitive firm. (336)

Contractionary gap: The amount by which total planned expenditures at the level of full-employment income fall short of the level required to generate full-employment income; also called a recessionary gap. (668)

Contrived scarcity: A situation in which a monopoly produces an output below what a competitive industry would produce; the contrived scarcity results in price and profits above competitive levels. (273)

Corporation: A firm owned by one or more individuals who own shares of stock that define ownership and rights to profits. Liability is limited to the value of corporation assets. (181)

Costs: An implication of scarcity; the necessary sacrifices associated with making any choice. (4)

Cost-benefit analysis: A procedure used to estimate the difference in costs and benefits, or the net benefits, of a project. (521)

Cost-price spiral: The process whereby increased production costs lead to increased final goods prices, which lead to further increases in resource prices and production costs; for the spiral to continue, the money supply must continually increase or real output must continually fall. (827)

Cost-push inflation: Increases in the price level caused by monopoly and/or union power or by shocks to the economy that reduce aggregate supply. (825)

Countercyclical fiscal policy: Changes in government expenditures or taxes that are designed to reverse changes in private expenditures or savings that produce unemployment or inflation. (676)

Cournot-Nash solution: The likely outcome of a one-shot game or a game with a known end point; in this case, both firms cheat, thus bringing profits below the joint profit-maximizing level. (304)

Craft union: Workers with a common skill who organize to restrict the supply of labor in their trade and obtain some market power; also called a trade union. (384)

Creative destruction theory: A business cycle theory that emphasizes the role of the entrepreneur as an innovator supplying new products and services, thereby creating new profit opportunities and destroying old ones; competitors follow the innovator's lead, which creates business cycles. (877)

Credit controls: The method or tools that the Federal Reserve System uses in efforts to control the monetary base and the money supply, including reserve requirements, open market operations, the discount rate, and other selective credit controls. (787)

Cross elasticity of demand: Measures buyers' relative responsiveness to a change in the price of one good in terms of the change in the quantity demanded of another good. The percentage change in the quantity demanded of one good divided by the percentage change in the price of another good. (133)

Crowding out: The competitive pressure exerted on private investment by government expenditures. (730)

Currency-deposit ratio: The percentage of total deposits held that people also wish to hold in the form of currency; currency holdings expressed as a decimal fraction of checkable deposit holdings. (777)

Curve: Any curved or straight line showing the relation between two variables on a graph. (26)

Cyclically balanced budget: A long-term view of the budget, in which surpluses generated during expansions match deficits created during recessions over a period of years. (719)

Decreasing-cost industry: An industry in which the long-run industry supply is downward-sloping; expansion (contraction) of the number of firms bids down (up) input prices; minimum *LRATC* of production falls as the number of firms in the industry increases. (237)

Deflation: Sustained decreases in the average level of prices. (582)

Demand curve: A graphic representation of the quantities of a product that people are willing and able to purchase at all possible prices. (87)

Demand deficiency unemployment: A short-run situation in which the level of employment is less than if the full-employment level of output were produced; arises when aggregate demand is insufficient to purchase the full-employment output given the price level. (704)

Demand deposit: A type of transaction account with virtually no restrictions as to the size, timing, or number of checks that can be written on the account. (748)

Demand elasticity coefficient: The numerical representation of the price elasticity of demand: $\epsilon_d = (\Delta Q/Q) \div (\Delta P/P)$. (119)

Demand for loanable funds: A curve or schedule that shows the various amounts individuals are willing and able to borrow at different interest rates. (408)

Demand-pull inflation: Increases in the price level caused by increases in aggregate demand. (825)

Demand-side policy: Fiscal or monetary policy intended to alter the overall level of spending, or aggregate demand. (591)

Deposit expansion: The total amount of additional money or checkable deposits created by some given amount of excess reserves. (772)

Depreciation: The wearing out of capital goods that occurs with usage over time; a decrease in the equilibrium exchange market value of a country's currency in a flexible-rate system; an increase in the number of units of a country's money that are required to purchase one unit of a foreign country's money. (407, 944)

Depression: A severe, persistent recession that may last several years. (863)

Deregulation: The removal of some or all government regulations from a previously regulated industry in an effort to improve the allocation of resources. (497)

Derived demand: The demand for factors of production that exists because of the demand for the products that the factors produce. (353)

Devaluation: An official change in a country's exchange rate in a fixed-rate system; the number of units of a country's money that purchases one unit of another country's currency is *increased* by the government. (951)

Differentiated product: A product with features that make it distinct, in consumers' eyes, from close substitutes. (285)

Direct government purchases: Real goods and services, such as equipment, buildings, and consulting services purchased by all levels of government. (74)

Discount rate: The interest rate a firm uses to determine the present value of an investment in a capital good; the interest rate charged by the Federal Reserve to depository institutions on loans of reserves from the Federal Reserve. (419, 791)

Diseconomies of scale: A situation in which, beyond a point, the long-run average total cost of producing output increases as plant size increases. (209)

Discretionary fiscal policies: Government policy actions that attempt to influence aggregate demand. (693)

Discretionary policy: A policy or change in policy that is determined by choices or decisions of policymakers. (590)

Disposable personal income: Personal income minus taxes; income available to spend. (607)

Dissaving: Occurs when consumption is greater than income; the use of previous years' savings or borrowing to finance consumption expenditures that are greater than income. (642)

Divestiture: The breaking up of a single firm into two or more smaller, independent firms as the result of a legal decree. (485)

Division of labor: An economic principle whereby individuals specialize in the production of a single good, service, or task, thereby increasing overall productivity and economic efficiency; the result of specialization. (43, 172)

Dominant solution: A situation in game theory in which each player has the same best choice no matter what course of action other players may choose. (303)

Double coincidence of wants: A situation in trading in which each party to the trade has what the other wants and wants what the other has. (743)

Dumping: The selling of goods in foreign markets at prices lower than those charged in domestic markets. (930)

Dynamic efficiency: A condition summarized in the idea that monopolies may, over time, be more innovative and efficient than competitive forms at developing new products and new production techniques. (277)

Econometrics: The combined use of both economic theory and formal statistical techniques to analyze, explain, and predict economic phenomena. (864)

Economic development: The process through which an economy achieves long-run economic growth; involves capital formation, the development of markets, productivity growth, and the improvement of entrepreneurial ability and labor skills. (987)

Economic efficiency: The correct allocation of resources, from the firm's perspective, so that maximum benefit is achieved at minimum cost. (296)

Economic goods and services: Goods and services that are scarce. (4)

Economic growth: A sustained or permanent increase in the productive capacity of an economy over time; increases in real GNP or per capita GNP over time. (40, 584, 887)

Economic indicators: Important data, or statistics, such as the money supply, investment spending, unemployment, and inventories that are used to help forecast economic activity and business cycles; these indicators are classified as leading, lagging, and coincident indicators. (865)

Economic mobility: The movement of individuals among income ranges. (462)

Economic profit: The amount by which total revenues exceed total opportunity cost; total revenue minus total opportunity costs of production. (194, 438)

Economic stabilization: The goal of governments' attempts to prevent adverse swings of inflation rates, interest rates, unemployment rates, and economic growth rates over time in the economy; a situation in which the price level and the unemployment rate vary from desired levels only temporarily and by small amounts. (72, 586)

Economic system: The part of the social system determining what, how, and for whom goods and services are produced. (59)

Economic wage discrimination: A situation in which individuals in the same occupation who have the same productive abilities are paid different wage rates by a given employer. The wage-rate differences are based on race, sex, religion, or national origin rather than on productive differences. (466)

Economic welfare: The value society places on goods and services consumed. (296)

Economies of scale: A situation in which long-run unit costs ($LRATC$) decline as plant output increases. (208)

Elastic demand: A situation in which buyers are relatively responsive to price changes; the percentage change in quantity demanded is greater than the percentage change in price: $\epsilon_d < 1$. (119)

Elasticity: A measure of the relative responsiveness of one variable to a change in another variable; the percentage change in a dependent variable divided by the percentage change in the independent variable. (117)

Elasticity of demand for labor: Measures the relative responsiveness of employment of a type of labor to changes in the wage rate; percent change in amount of labor hired divided by percent change in wage rate. (363)

Elasticity of supply: A measure of producers' or workers' relative responsiveness to price or wage changes; the percentage change in quantity supplied divided by the percentage change in price or wage rate. (134)

Entrepreneur: An individual who perceives profit opportunities, organizes resources into productive ventures, and bears the uncertain status of residual claimant of the resulting risky economic outcome. (438)

Equation of exchange: An identity used to derive the quantity theory of money; $MV \equiv PQ$. (807)

Equilibrium level of national income: In the income-expenditures model, the level of income at which total private expenditures equal total output. (652)

Equilibrium price: The price at which quantity demanded is equal to quantity supplied; other things being equal, there is no tendency for this price to change. (101)

Escalator clause: Provision of a labor contract that ties changes in nominal wages to changes in some price index. (823)

Ex ante distribution: The distribution of income before government transfer payments and taxes are accounted for. (450)

Excess capacity: A situation in which industry output in not produced at minimum average total cost. The output actually produced is less than the output that would minimize average total cost. (296)

Excess reserves: Total reserves minus required reserves. (765)

Exchange costs: The opportunity costs of the resources used in making trades; includes transaction costs, transportation costs, and artificial barriers to trade. (52)

Exchange rate: The (relative) price of one national currency in terms of another national currency. (939)

Exchange rate conversion method: The comparison of real GNP across countries by converting all nations' GNPs to a common currency denomination through the use of exchange rates. (989)

Excise tax: A tax that is based on the quantity of a good sold; a per unit tax. (528)

Exclusive territories: Given geographic areas in which one retailer or wholesaler has the exclusive, manufacturer-granted right to sell or distribute the manufacturer's product. (338)

Expansionary gap: The amount by which total planned expenditures at the level of full-employment income exceed the level required to generate full employment without inflation; also called an inflationary gap. (668)

Expected inflation rate: The rate of inflation that consumers and businesses expect to exist over a relevant future period, such as the coming year. (817)

Explicit costs: Accounting costs. (9)

Exploitation of labor: A situation in which the wage rate paid to an input is less than the input's marginal revenue product. (392)

Exports (X): Total spending by foreigners on domestically produced goods and services. (603, 675)

Ex post distribution: The distribution of income after government transfer payments and taxes are accounted for. (450)

External costs: The opportunity costs of production that are not borne, or paid, by producers. (195)

Externality: Benefits or costs of an individual's activity that the individual does not receive or bear. (507)

Externally held debt: The amount of a country's total federal debt that is owned by foreign governments, businesses, and individuals. (732)

Factor market: A market in which the prices of productive resources (factors of production, or inputs) are determined by the interaction of firms acting as buyers with households and firms acting as suppliers of resources. (352)

Factors affecting demand: Anything other than price, such as consumer income and preferences, that determines the amount of a product or service that consumers are willing and able to purchase. (88)

Factors affecting supply: Anything other than price, such as technology or input costs, that determines the amount of a product or service that sellers are willing and able to produce and offer for sale. (97)

Fallacy of composition: Incorrectly generalizing that what is true for a part is also true for the whole. (18)

Family income: The total of all incomes from all sources except transfers received by members of a household. (451)

Federal debt: The total value of federal government bonds outstanding; arises from both current and past budget deficits. (719)

Federal funds rate: A market-determined interest rate on loans and borrowings of bank reserves among commercial banks and other depository institutions. (788)

Federal Open Market Committee (FOMC): A committee of the Federal Reserve System made up of the seven members of the Board of Governors of the Federal Reserve System and five presidents of Federal Reserve district banks; directs open market operations (buying and selling of securities) for the system. (758)

Federal Reserve System: The central bank of the United States; regulates financial institutions and establishes and conducts monetary policy. (754)

Fiat money: Money, usually paper, that is made acceptable in exchange by law; usually not backed by any commodity such as gold. (744)

Final goods: Goods sold to the final consumers of the goods. (597)

Firm: An economic institution that purchases, organizes, and assembles resources to produce goods and services. (172)

Firm coordination: The process that directs the flow of resources into the production of a particular good or service through the forces of management organization within the firm. (173)

Firm's long-run demand for labor: The relationship between all possible wage rates and quantities demanded of labor at those wage rates, given that the firm has enough time to vary the usage of all inputs. (360)

Fiscal policy: The use of government spending and taxation to effect changes in aggregate economic variables. (590)

Fixed costs: The costs of inputs that cannot be varied in the short run. (196)

Fixed exchange rate system: An international monetary arrangement in which exchange rates are set by the government, which then must intervene in the foreign exchange market in order to maintain the pegged exchange rate. (940)

Fixed input: A factor of production whose level of usage cannot be changed in the short run. (196)

Fixed plant: A given amount of equipment and size of production facilities with which the firm can use variable inputs in the short run. (198)

Flexible, or floating, exchange rate system: An international monetary arrangement in which exchange rates are determined by private suppliers and demanders without government intervention. (940)

Flow of earnings: Total income received by resource suppliers during any given time period. (599)

Flow of expenditures: Total spending of consumers, businesses, and government on final goods and services during any given time period. (599)

Foreign exchange: The monies of countries that are used to facilitate international trade in goods, services, and financial assets. (939)

Foreign exchange market intervention: Purchases or sales of foreign exchange by government, usually a central bank, with the goal of maintaining a fixed exchange rate or influencing the exchange rate in a flexible-rate system. (949)

Foreign exchange markets: The interaction of the suppliers and demanders of foreign exchange through which exchange rates are determined in a flexible exchange rate system. (939)

Foreign exchange reserves: The stock of foreign exchange held by a central bank that is available for use in exchange market intervention. (949)

Fractional reserve banking system: A banking system in which banks hold only some percentage of deposits as reserves. (753)

Franchise bidding: The privatization of traditionally governmental responsibilities via a bidding process. (494)

Franchising: A form of vertical relationship in which, for a fee, a franchisee is granted the right to sell a good or service in a format designed and controlled by the franchiser. (340)

Free enterprise: Economic freedom to produce and sell or purchase and consume goods without government intervention. (66)

Free goods and services: Things that are available in sufficient amounts and provide all that people want at zero cost. (6)

Free rider: An individual who receives the benefit of consuming a public good or service without paying for it. (518)

Free trade: The exchange of goods between countries without the presence of artificial trade barriers such as tariffs and quotas. (920)

Full employment: A situation in which unemployment exists only because of normal market adjustments to changing demand or supply or to outmoded skills of workers; also a numerical federal government goal for the unemployment rate; to the classical economist, a situation in which all workers willing and able to work at the current market real wage rate are employed. (578, 709)

Full price: The total opportunity cost to an individual of obtaining a good; includes money price and all other costs such as transportation costs or waiting time costs. (112)

Game theory: A theory involving decision making in an atmosphere of mutual interdependence and imperfect information. (301)

Gini coefficient: A number between 0 and 1 calculated to estimate the degree of inequality in the distribution of income; the larger the number, the less the degree of equality. (453)

Gold standard: An international monetary system in which currencies are redeemable in gold at fixed rates or prices. (953)

Goods: All tangible things that satisfy people's wants and desires. (2)

Government license: A legal right granted by state, local, or federal governments to enter an occupation or industry. (254)

Government purchases (G): Total spending by federal, state, and local governments on final goods and services. (603)

Government transfer payments: Money transferred by government through taxes from one group to another, either directly or indirectly; also called income security transfers. (74)

Greenmail: Stock purchase made by incumbent management of a corporation to prevent corporate takeover by a hostile stockholder or group of stockholders. (184)

Gross domestic product (GDP): A measure of the final goods and services produced by a country with resources located within that country. (79)

Gross national product (GNP): The dollar value measured at market prices of all final goods and services produced in an economy over a given period of time, usually a year. (79, 584, 594)

Gross private domestic investment (I): Total spending by private businesses on final goods, including capital goods and inventories. (602)

Growth absorption: Increases in total spending sufficient to purchase additional output generated by increases in productive capacity. (894)

Historical costs: Costs measured by the cost of a resource at the time the resource was purchased. (194)

Homogeneous product: A good or service for which the consumer is indifferent as to which firm produces it; each firm's product is a perfect substitute for other firms' products in the eyes of the consumer. (218)

Horizontal equity: A tax structure under which people with equal incomes pay equal amounts of taxes. (536)

Human capital: Any quality, characteristic, or skill an individual has that enhances the individual's productivity, such as education and job experience. (370)

Human resources: All forms of labor and skill used to produce goods and services. (6)

Ideology: A set of beliefs or preferences that are held by the legislator independently of his or her constituents' self-interest. (563)

Imperfect competition: Market models, such as oligopoly, cartels, monopoly, and monopolistic competition, in which individual sellers' actions influence price. (284)

Implicit costs: Nonpecuniary costs associated with the cost of a good or service; the opportunity cost of resources used in production, for which no explicit payments are made. (9, 193)

Implicit price deflator: A price index that uses the most comprehensive set of prices to calculate the level of prices and the rate of inflation facing households, businesses, and government; also called the GNP deflator. (610)

Imports (*M*): Total spending by domestic residents on foreign-produced goods and services. (603, 675)

Income effect: The change in the quantity demanded of a good that results from a change in real income. (157)

Income statement: A summary of a firm's revenues and expenses over a month, a quarter, a year, or some other time period; facilitates assessments of a firm's well-being. (187)

Income elasticity of demand: A measure of consumers' relative responsiveness to income changes; the percentage change in quantity demanded divided by the percentage change in income, holding price constant. (132)

Income-expenditures model: A theory suggesting that private expenditures are basically determined by the level of national income and that these expenditures in turn determine the levels of output and employment in the economy. (638)

Income velocity: The average number of times that a unit of money (a dollar) is used, or changes hands, in purchasing nominal GNP. (807)

Increasing-cost industry: An industry in which the expansion (contraction) of the number of firms bids up (down) input process; minimum *LRATC* of production changes as the number of firms in the industry changes; long-run industry supply is upward-sloping to the right. (236)

Increasing returns to scale: As plant size increases, long-run average total cost decreases. (210)

Indifference curve: A curve that shows graphically all the combinations of two goods that yield the same level of utility to a consumer. (163)

Indifference map: A graph that shows two or more indifference curves for a consumer. (164)

Indifference set: A group of combinations of two goods that yield the same total level of utility to a consumer. (162)

Individual income: The earnings individuals receive from their labor, from their assets, and from government transfer payments, minus their tax payments. (448)

Industrial union: Workers in a given industry organized independently of their skills in an effort to obtain market power. (385)

Industry concentration ratios: A measure of the degree to which the largest firms in an industry account for total industry assets, sales, or some other factor. (323)

Industry regulation: Government rules to control the behavior of firms, particularly regarding prices and production techniques. (71)

Inefficient tax: A tax that decreases the overall productive capacity of the economy; a tax that decreases the supply of resources or decreases the efficiency of resource use. (543)

Inelastic demand: A situation in which buyers are relatively unresponsive to price changes; the percentage change in quantity demanded is less than the percentage change in price: $\epsilon_d<1$. (120)

Infant industry: A new or developing domestic industry whose unit production costs are higher than those of established firms in the same industry in other countries. (928)

Inferior good: A good that a consumer chooses to purchase in smaller quantities as income rises, or in larger amounts as income falls. (90)

Inflation: A sustained increase in the general level of prices; inflation reduces the purchasing power of money. (14, 142)

Inflation rate: The percent by which the average level of prices in an economy rises; usually expressed as a percent per year. (413)

Information: A scarce and important element in the process of economic exchange and growth. (7)

Inframarginal rent: That portion of a payment to a factor of production whose supply is upward-sloping in excess of the factor's opportunity cost. (424)

In-kind transfer payments: Transfer payments that take the form of goods and services such as public housing, veterans' hospitals, or a mass transit system. (458)

Institutions: The sum total of the traditions, mores, laws, and governmental structures of an economy. (8)

Interest: The compensation to savers for the act of saving (forgoing present consumption) or the payment made by borrowers; when measured as a percent of the amount borrowed or lent, it is referred to as an interest rate. (407)

Interest groups: Collections of individuals with one or more common characteristics, such as occupation, who seek collectively to affect legislation or government policy so as to benefit members of the group. (561)

Interest rate effect: The effect on investment spending that results from a change in the interest rate produced by a change in the price level. (689)

Intermediate goods: Goods used as inputs in the production of final goods. (597)

Intermediate range: A positively sloped segment of the aggregate supply curve; indicates that aggregate output and the price level will both change in the same direction. (695)

Internally held debt: The amount of a country's total federal debt that is owned by the country's various governments, businesses, and individuals. (732)

International Monetary Fund: An international organization, established along with the Bretton Woods system, designed to assist in the efficient functioning of the Bretton Woods fixed exchange rate system. (960)

Investment function: In the income-expenditures model, all investment is autonomous or independent of the level of income. The investment function is horizontal when plotted against income. (649)

Investment multiplier: The multiple by which equilibrium income will change given a change in autonomous investment expenditure: $1/MPS$. (663)

Investment spending: Expenditures made by businesses on capital goods plus any change (positive or negative) in business inventories. (648)

Investment tax credit: A percentage or amount of new investment expenditure that is directly subtracted from the investor's tax bill in calculating total taxes. (727)

Joint unlimited liability: The unlimited liability of a partnership, which is shared by all partners. (180)

Keynesian range: A horizontal segment of the aggregate supply curve; shows that output can increase with no change in the price level because of some unemployment of resources. (695)

Kinked demand: A demand curve in which the marginal revenue curve has a discontinuous segment; the result of qualitatively different price reactions by competitors to increases and decreases in the firm's price. (306)

Labor income: The payments an individual receives from supplying work time; equal to the wage rate times the number of hours supplied. (448)

Labor-managed firm: A firm that is owned and managed by the employees of the firm, who are also the residual claimants to firm profits. (185)

Labor union: A group of individual workers organized to act collectively in an attempt to affect labor market conditions. (383)

Laffer curve: A curve that shows the relation between the tax rate and tax revenues; it demonstrates graphically how as the tax rate rises, tax revenues rise, reach a maximum, and then fall. (534)

Laissez-faire: A public policy of not regulating to any degree or interfering with market activities (from the French, meaning, roughly, "allow to do"). (496)

Laissez-faire economy: A market economy that is allowed to operate according to competitive forces with minimal government intervention. (67)

Law of demand: The price of a product or service and the amount purchased are inversely related. If price rises, then quantity demanded falls; if price falls, quantity demanded increases, all other things held constant. (86)

Law of diminishing marginal returns: A situation in which adding more and more of a variable input to a fixed plant results in smaller and smaller amounts of additional output produced. (198)

Law of increasing costs: As more scarce resources are used to produce additional units of one good, production of the other good falls by larger and larger amounts. (38)

Law of one price: In perfect markets, the market forces of supply and demand produce a single, equilibrium price for a good or service. (99)

Law of supply: The price of a product or service and the amount that producers are willing and able to offer for sale are positively related. If price rises, then quantity supplied rises; if price decreases, quantity supplied decreases. (95)

Legal barriers to entry: Government actions that prohibit other firms or individuals from producing particular products or entering particular occupations or industries; such barriers take the form of legal franchises, licenses, and patents. (253)

Less-developed countries: Countries with relatively low levels of per capita real GNP; generally characterized by a large subsistence agriculture sector, low saving rates, and high population growth. (987)

Liability: Anything owed as a debt by a firm, reducing net worth. (187)

Limit-entry pricing: A pricing strategy of a firm that discourages entry by setting price below the short-run profit-maximizing price. (497)

Limit pricing: A pricing policy consisting of temporarily setting a price lower than the short-run profit-maximizing price in order to deter entry and maximize profits in the long-run. (310)

Limited liability: A legal principle implying that the owner(s) of a corporation are not personally responsible for the firm's debts, except up to the value of their shares. (182)

Linear relation: One variable changes by a constant rate, and the other variable also changes by a constant rate. (27)

Liquidity: The ease with which any asset or commodity can be converted into money with little or no risk of loss to the holder. (748)

Liquidity preference theory: A theory stating that the interest rate is determined by the interaction of real money demand and supply, and that interest rate changes due to real money demand or supply changes produce changes in real economic activity. (805)

Logrolling: The exchange of votes by legislators, usually in order to gain support for particular legislation. (559)

Long run: An amount of time sufficiently long that all input usage levels can be varied. (196)

Long-run average total cost: The lowest per-unit cost of producing any level of output when the usage of all inputs can be varied. (207)

Long-run competitive equilibrium: A market situation in which economic profits are zero for all firms; each firm produces output at minimum average total cost. (231)

Long-run industry supply: The quantities of a product that all firms in an industry are willing and able to offer for sale at various prices when the number of firms and the scale of operations of each firm are allowed to adjust. (234)

Long-run marginal cost: The additional cost of producing an additional unit of output when all inputs, including plant size, can be varied. (207)

Long-run Phillips curve: A vertical line at the natural rate of unemployment; indicates that if there is enough time for workers' expectations to adjust to the actual rate of inflation, then changes in the inflation rate produce no change in the rate of unemployment. (874)

Lorenz curve: A curve plotting the actual cumulative distribution of income in percentages; usually compared to a curve showing a perfectly even distribution of income. (880)

Lump-sum tax: A fixed level of total taxes; total taxes do not change as the level of income changes. (673)

M-1 money multiplier: The multiple by which the money supply will change given a change in the monetary base. (797)

Macroeconomics: Analysis of the behavior of an economy as a whole. (19)

Malthusian population principle: The notion that the population has the capability to grow geometrically while the food supply can only grow arithmetically; leads to the concept of the subsistence wage. (894)

Managed flexible-rate system: Primarily a flexible exchange rate system, but with occasional government purchases or sales of foreign exchange intended to influence the exchange rate. (941)

Manager: An individual or group of individuals that organizes and monitors resources within a firm to produce a good or service. (173)

Margin: The difference between the costs and benefits in an existing situation and after a proposed change. (12)

Marginal analysis: Looking at changes in the costs and benefits of a change from the status quo to a proposed new situation. These marginal changes in costs and benefits are the basis for rational economic choice. (12)

Marginal cost: The additional cost of producing one more unit of output; the change in total costs divided by the change in output. (197)

Marginal cost pricing: A regulatory policy that forces a firm to charge a price equal to marginal cost, resulting in a socially optimal allocation of resources. (490)

Marginal factor cost of labor (MFC_L): The change in total costs associated with employing one additional unit of labor. (357)

Marginal opportunity cost: The extra cost associated with the production of an additional unit of a product; this cost consists of the unproduced amounts of some alternative product. (94)

Marginal opportunity production cost: The number of units of one good that do not get produced when one additional unit of another good is produced. (45)

Marginal private cost: The change in total cost that only the firm bears when output changes by one unit. (513)

Marginal product: The additional output produced by employing one additional unit of a variable output. (199)

Marginal product of labor (MP_L): The additional output produced that results from hiring an additional unit of labor; change in total output divided by change in quantity of labor input used. (355)

Marginal propensity to consume (MPC): The percent of an additional dollar of income that is spent on consumption; change in consumption divided by change in income. (640)

Marginal propensity to save (MPS): The percent of an additional dollar of income that is saved; change in saving divided by change in income. (641)

Marginal rate of substitution: The amount of one good a consumer is willing to give up to get one more unit of another good such that the consumer's total utility remains constant. (164)

Marginal revenue: The change in total revenue resulting from the sale of one additional unit of output; the change in total revenue divided by the change in output. (223, 258)

Marginal revenue product of labor (MRP_L): The additional revenue that results from selling the additional output produced by hiring an additional unit of labor; marginal revenue times marginal product of input. (356)

Marginal social cost: The change in total cost borne by the economy as a whole (the firm plus all others, or society) that results from a one-unit change in the firm's output. (513)

Marginal tax rate: The percentage of an increase in income that must be paid in taxes; the change in tax liability divided by the change in taxable income. (538, 719)

Marginal utility: The amount by which total utility changes when consumption of a good or service changes by one unit; calculated by dividing the change in total utility by the change in quantity consumed. (147)

Market: A collection of buyers and sellers exchanging resources, goods, or services. Prices tend toward equality through the continuous exchange between suppliers and demanders. (13, 99, 218)

Market coordination: The process that directs the flow of resources into the production of goods and services through the price signaling mechanism. (173)

Market demand: The total amount consumers are willing and able to purchase of a product at all possible prices, obtained by summing the quantities demanded at each price over all buyers. (92)

Market demand curve for a public good: Obtained by summing vertically, instead of horizontally, all individuals' demands for the public good. Vertical summation is used because consumption is noncompeting. (519)

Market demand for labor: The total quantity of labor demanded at various wage rates, other things constant. The sum of all individual firms' demands for a type of labor. The firms may or may not all be in the same industry. (354)

Market failure: A situation in which the socially optimal amount of a good or service does not get produced by the private market; usually stems from unclear property rights assignments. (503)

Market for legislation: The interaction between interest groups acting as demanders of legislation beneficial to the group and legislators acting as suppliers of the legislation; legislation generally entails some type of wealth transfer. (562)

Market, or nominal, interest rate: The interest rate computed from the money values of a borrowing or lending arrangement, such as a savings account; the interest rate unadjusted for expected inflation. (816)

Market power: A situation in which an established firm has influence over price and profit levels due to barriers impeding the entry of rival firms. (306)

Market society: An economic system in which individuals acting in their own self-interest determine what, how, and for whom goods and services are produced, with little government intervention. (61)

Market supply: The total amount producers are willing and able to offer for sale of a product at all possible prices; obtained by summing the quantities supplied at each price over all producers. (98)

Market supply of labor: The sum of all individuals' supplies of a type of labor. The total quantity of labor people will offer to the market at various wage rates, other things being equal. (354)

Materials balancing: A method of central planning entailing the monitoring of the quantity and availability of resources so as to allocate these resources among state enterprises to produce final output; a substitute for the price system method of allocating resources. (976)

Mean income: A measure of average income; can be computed as per capita, per family, or per earner of income. (463)

Measure of economic welfare (MEW): A concept of social and economic well-being that accounts for the production of all goods and services, not just those transacted for in markets. (597)

Medium of exchange: An item that is generally acceptable as payment for goods and services. (743)

Merger: The combining of the ownership of two firms' assets, which results in a single firm. (333)

Microeconomics: Analysis of the behavior of individual decision-making units, including individuals, households, and business firms. (19)

Mixed capitalism: An economic system in which most economic decisions are made by the private sector but in which government also plays a substantial economic and regulatory role. (60, 971)

Model: A simplified abstraction of the real world that approximates reality and makes problems easier to analyze; also called a theory. (17)

Monetarism: A theory that centers on money supply growth, real money demand, nominal and real interest rates, and inflationary expectations in explaining the process of inflation or deflation. (815)

Monetary base: The sum of depository institutions' reserves plus currency held by the public. (787)

Monetary policy: The use of money supply changes to effect changes in aggregate economic variables. (590)

Monetary rule: A monetary policy consisting of a fixed rate of growth of the money supply. (849)

Money: A generally accepted medium of exchange. (14, 748)

Money expansion: The increase in the money supply created by some given amount of excess reserves. (773)

Money price: The dollar price that sellers receive from buyers; a price expressed in terms of money, not in terms of an amount of another good. (112)

Monitor: An individual in management who coordinates team production, measures the performance of team members, and discourages shirking. (176)

Monopolistic competition: A market model with freedom of entry and exit and firms producing similar but differentiated products. (285)

Monopoly rent: The payment to owners of fixed capital in a monopolized industry that exceeds the opportunity cost of capital; also called monopoly profit. (424)

Monopsony: A single buyer of a resource or product; sometimes found in labor markets as the single buyer of labor. (391)

Moral suasion: The use of advice and suggestion, rather than concrete policy actions, by the Federal Reserve to induce depository institutions to follow a certain course of action. (796)

Mutual interdependence: A relation among firms in which the decisions and actions of one firm have significant impact on the decisions, actions, and profits of other firms. (300)

National income (NI): Total earnings of resource suppliers during a given period of time. (604)

National income accounting: The process of statistically measuring the nation's aggregate economic performance. (594)

Natural monopoly: A combination of market demand and cost conditions that results in only one firm in an industry being able to produce output profitably; occurs when decreasing long-run average costs exist up to the level of total industry demand. (255, 327, 478)

Natural rate of unemployment: A theoretical concept; the unemployment rate that coexists with macroeconomic stability or labor-market equilibrium in the long run; the rate of unemployment due to frictional unemployment plus structural unemployment that will exist when expectations of inflation reflect actual inflationary conditions and all short-run macroeconomic adjustments have been made. (578, 709)

Negative externality: A cost of producing or consuming a good that is not paid entirely by the sellers or buyers but is imposed on a larger segment of society, such as pollution; a situation that arises when an individual or other economic entity imposes costs on others without first compensating them. (69, 507)

Negative income tax: An income tax system that pays a subsidy, or a negative tax, to individuals with incomes below a certain level. Below this level, as income increases, the subsidy decreases—but by less than the amount income increases. (469)

Negative, or inverse, relation: The variables change in opposite directions. A negative relation is graphed as a downward-sloping curve. (26)

Neo-Austrian political business cycle: A business cycle that results from political action to influence specific markets and industries rather than broad macroeconomic variables; microeconomic manipulation distorts industry-specific investment decisions and leads to a business cycle. (881)

Net exports (X − M): Total spending by foreigners on domestically produced goods and services minus total spending by domestic residents on foreign-produced goods and services. (603)

Net national product (NNP): GNP minus capital consumption allowances (depreciation); the value of total output less the value of the capital used up in producing output. (606)

Net worth: The owners' net value of a firm, determined by subtracting liabilities from assets; also called equity. (187)

Neutrality of money: A proposition stating that in the long-run the relative prices of goods and services are not affected by changes in the money supply. (809)

Neutral tax: A tax that has no effects on the production or consumption of goods. (527)

Nominal GNP: The economy's total production of final goods and services measured in dollars unadjusted for changes in the price level. (585)

Nominal income: Income measured in terms of money, not in terms of what the money can buy. (582)

Nominal rate of interest: The market-determined rate of interest; usually expressed as a percentage per year of the dollar or nominal amount of the loan. (413)

Nonhuman resources: All resources other than human resources, such as machines and land. (6)

Nonlinear relation: One variable changes by a constant rate, and the other variable changes by a rate that is not constant. (27)

Nonmarket activities: Anything an individual does that directly or indirectly yields utility while not working. (366)

Nonprice competition: Any means other than pricing decisions that firms use to sell output. (285)

Nonprofit firm: A firm that has no residual claimant(s) or shareholders. Such a firm may have a charitable or research objective for which it raises and expends funds. (186)

Nonproprietary: Relating to nonprivate ownership; entails motivations other than strictly profit motivations; individuals do not always fully bear the consequences of their decisions. (550)

Nontariff trade barriers: Alternative (to tariffs and quotas) means of restricting trade; examples include domestic content legislation and health and safety regulation. (926)

Normal good: A good that a consumer chooses to purchase in smaller (larger) amounts as income falls (rises). (90)

Normative economics: Value judgments based on moral principles or preferences about how economic life should be. (18)

Normative public choice: Economic analysis that determines shortcomings and failures of the political process and suggests improvements. (549)

Oligopoly: Market models characterized by a few firms producing either homogeneous or differentiated products, with entry of new firms very difficult or prevented. (300)

Open market operations: The purchase or sale of securities by the Federal Reserve System in order to affect the monetary base and the money supply; the major tool of monetary policy. (788)

Opportunity costs: The highest-valued alternative forgone in making any choice. (9, 33)

Opportunity cost of capital: The return that could be received from the next-best alternative investment. (193)

Opportunity costs of production: The opportunity cost of resources used to produce goods and services. (192)

Overvalued: A term describing the foreign exchange market value of a country's money; occurs when the number of units of a country's money that purchases one unit of a foreign currency is *less* than the equilibrium exchange rate. (949)

Ownership claims: The legal titles that identify owners of the assets of a firm. (187)

Partnership: A firm with two or more owners-residual claimants with unlimited liability. (180)

Patent: A monopoly right granted by government to an inventor for a product or process; valid for seventeen years in the United States. (254)

Per capita income: Average income per person; the total income of a population divided by the number of people in the population. (463)

Perestroika: Economic reformation of the Soviet Union's command economy. (945)

Perfect information: A situation that arises when information about prices and products is costless to obtain; complete knowledge about the market. (220)

Perfect market: A market in which there are enough buyers and sellers that no single buyer or seller can influence price. (99)

Personal consumption expenditures (C): Total spending by households on final goods and services. (602)

Personal income (PI): Total earnings resource suppliers actually receive during a given period of time plus transfer payments. (606)

Personal saving: Disposable personal income less personal consumption expenditures. (607)

Phillips curve: A graph showing the relation between the rate of inflation and the unemployment rate. (870)

Policy trade-off: A situation in which a policy that promotes the attainment of one macroeconomic goal necessarily implies that the attainment of another macroeconomic objective becomes more difficult. (590)

Political business cycle: A business cycle that results from the manipulation of policy tools by incumbent politicians hoping to stimulate the economy prior to an election and thereby improve their reelection chances. (879)

Positive economics: Observations, explanations, or predictions about economic life; scientific economics. (18)

Positive externality: A benefit of producing or consuming a good that does not accrue to the sellers or buyers but can be realized by a larger segment of society, such as vaccinations; a situation that arises when an individual or other economic entity creates benefits for others without receiving any compensation in return. (69, 508)

Positive public choice: Economic analysis of political decision making and other political behavior that aims to understand, explain, and predict such behavior. (550)

Positive, or direct, relation: Both variables change in the same direction. A positive relation is graphed as an upward-sloping curve. (26)

Post hoc **fallacy:** The incorrect linking of unrelated events as a cause-and-effect relationship simply because one event happens after the other. (18)

Poverty: A substandard level of income. (464)

Precautionary demand: Money demand that arises from the desire of businesses and consumers to hold money in order to facilitate unexpected purchases. (805)

Predatory pricing: The temporary pricing of goods or services below cost in order to reduce or eliminate competition. (479)

Present value: The value today of a payment to be made or received in the future; a future sum discounted by the current rate of interest. (416)

Price ceiling: A form of regulation in which a maximum legal price is established by government above which exchange between buyers and sellers is illegal. (107)

Price control: The setting, by government, of a price in a market different from the equilibrium price. (107)

Price discrimination: The practice of charging one buyer or group of buyers a different price than that charged to others. The price difference is not due to differences in the cost of supplying the two groups. (267)

Price elasticity of demand: A measure of buyers' relative responsiveness to a price change; the percentage change in quantity demanded divided by the percentage change in price. (119)

Price floor: A form of regulation in which a minimum legal price is established by govern-

ment below which exchange between buyers and sellers is illegal. (108)

Price index: A statistic used to calculate the price level and the rate of inflation. (608)

Price leadership: A market where a single firm sets industry price, with the remaining firms charging what the price leader charges. Industry price changes are initiated by the leader. (308)

Price level: The average of the prices of all goods and services in the economy; used for calculating the inflation rate and for converting nominal into real values. (608)

Price searcher: A firm that is able to choose a profit-maximizing price from a range of prices rather than have price imposed by market conditions and competition; such a firm faces a downward-sloping demand curve. (255)

Price-specie flow mechanism: The channels by which gold inflows would cause price level increases or decreases in a country on the gold standard, thereby eliminating trade surpluses and deficits. (953)

Price stability: A situation of no inflation or deflation in the economy; no change in the overall level of prices of goods, services, and resources. (578)

Price taker: An individual seller who faces a single market price and is able to sell as much as desired at that price. (220)

Prices: The market-established opportunity costs of goods and services obtained through exchange. (13)

Price-wage flexibility: An economic principle whereby prices and wages can fluctuate with changing economic conditions; thus the economy will be self-adjusting toward full employment even in response to shocks in supply and demand. (626)

Principle of diminishing marginal utility: The more of a good or service being consumed, the smaller the marginal utility obtained from consuming one additional unit of the good or service, all other factors equal. (147)

Prisoner's dilemma: A scenario that illustrates the mutual interdependence of decision making; the basis for game theory. (302)

Private costs: The opportunity costs of production by producers. (195)

Private good: A good over which a consumer can establish property rights. (289)

Private sector: All parts of the economy and activities that are not part of the government. (72)

Private-sector equilibrium: A situation of equality between total private expenditures and output. In this equilibrium, there is no unplanned investment and no tendency for the level of output to change. (651)

Producer price index (PPI): A price index that calculates the general level of prices and the rate of inflation of goods businesses purchase. (610)

Product market: The forces created by buyers and sellers that establish the prices and quantities exchanged of goods and services. (84)

Production possibilities frontier: The curve that graphs all the possible combinations of two goods that an economic entity can produce given the available technology, the amount of productive resources available, and the fact that these resources are fully utilized. (37)

Productive efficiency: A condition in which total industry output is produced at the lowest possible opportunity cost of resources. (238)

Productivity of labor: Output per worker over any given period of time. (888)

Profit-maximizing price: The price associated with the quantity sold at which the difference between total revenue and total cost is greatest; the price associated with the quantity sold at which marginal revenue equals marginal cost. (261)

Profits: The amount by which total revenue exceeds total opportunity cost of production. (222)

Progressive income tax: A tax based on a percentage of income that varies directly with the level of income. (536, 726)

Property rights: Any legal and/or enforceable rights to the use of resources of any kind. (8)

Proportional income tax: A tax based on a fixed percentage of income for all levels of income. (536, 726)

Proprietary: Relating to private ownership and profit motivation; individuals directly bear consequences of their decisions. (550)

Proprietorship: A firm with a single owner-residual claimant who has unlimited liability for the firm's debts. (179)

Public assistance programs: Efforts by government to provide a more equitable distribution of income. (70)

Public choice: The economic analysis of political decision making, politics, and the democratic process. (549)

Public employees' union: Workers employed by either federal, state, or local governments who organize in an effort to obtain market power. (385)

Public finance: The study of how governments at the federal, state, and local levels tax and spend. (525, 720)

Public franchise: A firm or industry's exclusive, government-granted right to produce and sell a good or service. (253)

Public good: A good such that, once produced, one individual's consumption of the good does not reduce and exclude the ability of other individuals to consume the good. (516)

Public goods: Goods that no one individual can be excluded from consuming once they have been provided to another, such as national defense. (69)

Public interest theory of regulation: Maintains that regulations are contrived so as to promote the public interest by correcting market failures and improving economic efficiency. (487)

Publicly owned firm: A firm owned and operated by government. (186)

Purchasing power parity method: The comparison of real GNP across countries by converting GNPs to a common currency through use of comparative cost of purchasing a typical assortment of goods and services in each country. (989)

Purchasing power parity (PPP) theory: A theory that predicts that the equilibrium exchange rate will adjust so as to equate the purchasing power of a unit of each country's money. (954)

Pure capitalism: An economic system in which most resources are owned, and most relevant decisions are made, by private individuals. (60, 971)

Pure communism: An economic system in which most productive resources, both human and nonhuman, are publicly owned. (60, 971)

Pure economic rent: The total payment to a factor of production whose supply curve is perfectly inelastic. (424)

Pure inflation tax: The reduction in purchasing power of an individual's nominal money holdings due to inflation. (823)

Pure interest: The interest associated with a risk-free loan. The interest rate that produces pure interest is called the risk-free rate. (415)

Pure monopoly: An industry in which a single firm produces a product that has no close substitutes and in which entry of new firms cannot occur. (252)

Pure socialism: An economic system in which most nonhuman productive resources are owned by the state. (60)

Purely competitive market: The interaction of a large number of buyers and sellers under the condition that entry and exit are not restricted. (218)

Quantity demanded: The amount of any good or service consumers are willing and able to purchase at various prices. (86)

Quantity supplied: The amount of any good or service that producers are willing and able to produce and sell at some specific price. (95)

Quantity theory of money: A theory stating that in the long run with output and velocity fixed, changes in the money supply cause proportional changes in the price level. (627, 805)

Quasi-rent: The payment to owners of fixed capital in a competitive industry in the short-run situation that exceeds the opportunity cost of their capital; also called economic profit. (424)

Quota: A restriction or limit on the quantity of an imported good. (919)

Rate of inflation: The percentage change in the average level of prices over a period of time; the speed at which prices in general are rising. (580)

Rate of monetary expansion: The annual percent by which the nominal money supply is changing. (818)

Rate of return on investment capital: Profits earned during a period of time divided by the value of invested capital; usually measured as a percent per year. (437)

Rate of return regulation: A cap imposed by a regulatory commission on the allowable percentage that a utility can earn on its investments in capital and other resources. (490)

Rate of time preference: The percent increase in future consumption over present consumption that is necessary to just induce an individual to be indifferent between present and future consumption. (407)

Rational expectations theory: A theory of behavior that assumes people make efficient use of all past and present relevant information in forming expectations; implies that people's reactions to policy may neutralize the intended effects of the policy. (851)

Rational self-interest: The view of human behavior espoused by economists. Given circumstances and preferences, people weigh the costs and benefits of choices in order to do the best they can for themselves. (10)

Rationing: The allocation of goods among consumers with the use of prices. The equilibrium price rations the limited amount of a good produced by the most willing and able suppliers, or sellers, to the most willing and able demanders, or buyers. (101)

Real balance effect: The effect on investment and consumption spending of a change in the price level that alters the real value of pecuniary assets. (686)

Real GNP: The total production of final goods and services measured in dollars that have been adjusted for changes in the price level. (585)

Real income: The buying power of a consumer's budget; determined by the consumer's money income and the prices of goods and services; the quantity of goods and services that money income can buy. (157, 582)

Real interest rate: The nominal interest rate minus the expected rate of inflation. (816)

Real money demand: Demand on the part of individuals and businesses to hold purchasing power in the form of cash and checkable deposits. (804)

Real per capita GNP: Real GNP divided by the population size; real output per person in the economy. (887)

Real rate of interest: The nominal interest rate minus the rate of inflation; the interest measured in terms of real buying power; measures the true incentives and costs that savers and investors face. (413, 624)

Recession: A contraction in overall economic activity, usually defined as a decrease in real GNP over a period of at least six months. (863)

Recognition lag: The amount of time it takes policymakers to realize that a destabilizing economic event has occurred. (848)

Regressive income tax: A tax based on a percentage of income that varies inversely with the level of income. (537, 726)

Regulatory policies: Administrative or legal attempts to influence the behavior of firms or industries when competitive goals cannot be realized or when positive goals are to be pursued. (478)

Relative price: The price ratio or "trade-off" in consumption between one product (or service) and another product (or service) or between one good and other goods taken as a whole. (86)

Rent: A payment to a factor of production in excess of the factor's opportunity cost. (424)

Rent seeking: The behavior associated with the use of scarce resources in the pursuit of monopoly profits created by government action; the process of using scarce resources in an effort to obtain rents or a transfer of wealth. (275, 436)

Required reserves: Reserves against checkable deposits that banks and other depository institutions are required by the Federal Reserve to keep in the form of cash reserves; equal to the required reserve ratio times checkable deposits; also called legal reserves. (765)

Resale price maintenance: A stipulated minimum price for a product imposed on a retailer by a manufacturer. (338)

Reserve bank credit: The total value of loans and securities owned or held by the Federal Reserve System. Changes in Reserve bank credit affect member institutions' reserves. (784)

Reserve ratio: The percentage of checkable deposits that banks and other depository institutions hold as reserves. (765)

Residual claimant: The individual or group of individuals that shares in the profit of the firm. (177)

Resource market: The forces created by buyers and sellers that establish the prices and quantities exchanged of resources such as land, labor services, and capital. (84)

Resource specialization: A situation in which resources are relatively more adept at one or a few tasks rather than a variety of uses; the result of a comparative advantage. (429)

Resources: Those things used to produce goods and services. These include land, machines, energy, and human labor and ingenuity. Resources are also called factors of production. (3)

Revaluation: An official change in a country's exchange rate in a fixed-rate system; the number of units of a country's money that purchases one unit of another country's currency is decreased by the government. (951)

Revealed preference: A consumer's ordering of combinations of goods demonstrated through observations of the consumer's actions. (162)

Right-to-work law: A law that prevents unions from requiring that individual workers join the union as a condition of employment by a particular firm. (397)

Risk: The chance that a borrower will default or fail to repay a loan. (412)

Roundabout production: The current production of capital goods so that greater amounts of consumption goods can be produced in the future. (406)

Sales tax: A tax that is based on the total expenditures on a particular product. (527)

Saving: The act of forgoing present consumption in order to increase future consumption. (406)

Saving function: The positive relationship between levels of current saving and levels of income, holding constant all other relevant factors that determine saving. (644)

Say's law: A proposition of the classical economists that the production of goods and services will generate incomes sufficiently large that those goods and services will be purchased. (622)

Scale of production: The relative size of a physical plant, which can be measured by the amount or value of the firm's capital. (179)

Scarcity: The condition whereby the resources, goods, and services available to individuals and society are limited relative to the wants and desires for them. (4)

Service industries: Those industries whose major, or sole, output is a consumer service, such as banking, entertainment, and health care. (903)

Services: All forms of intangible but useful activities that are valued by people. (2)

Shares: The equal portions into which ownership of a corporation is divided. (181)

Share transferability: The ability of an economic entity to sell ownership shares in a corporation without the approval of other shareholders. (181)

Shirking: A sometimes rational type of behavior of team members in which the individual exerts a less than expected or normal productive effort. (176)

Shortage: The amount by which a quantity demanded exceeds quantity supplied at a price below the equilibrium price. (100)

Short run: An amount of time insufficient to allow the usage of all inputs to vary. (196)

Short-run firm supply curve: That portion of a firm's marginal cost curve above the minimum point on the average variable cost curve. (230)

Short-run industry supply curve: The horizontal sum of all existing firms' short-run supply curves. (230)

Short-run Phillips curve: A downward-sloping curve indicating an inverse relation between the rate of inflation and the unemployment rate, holding constant the inflation expectations of workers. (872)

Shutdown: A loss-minimizing procedure in which the firm stops production to eliminate all variable costs, although it must still pay fixed costs. (228)

Simple money multiplier: The reciprocal of the reserve ratio. (772)

Slope: The ratio of the change in (Δ) the y value to the change in (Δ) the x value; Δy divided by Δx. (30)

Social costs: The opportunity cost of all resources used in the production of goods and services; the sum of private plus external costs. (195)

Socialism: An economic system in which most nonhuman productive resources are owned by the state. (971)

Socialization: Government ownership and operation of a firm or industry. (493)

Specialization: An economic entity's (an individual's or a nation's) producing only one good or service, or the performance of a single task in a production process by an individual. (41, 911)

Speculation: The buying and selling of currencies on the foreign exchange market with the intent of profiting from possible devaluation or revaluation in a fixed-rate system or from possible future movements in the exchange rate in a flexible-rate system. (961)

Speculative motive or demand: Money demand arising from uncertainty of future interest rates and the fact that people can substitute between holding money and holding bonds. (805)

Standard of deferred payment: A standard measure for expressing contractual values over time, such as the future payments associated with loans and debts; a function of money. (747)

Standard of living: The real value of the quantity of goods and services consumed by the average member of the economy. (886)

Static inefficiency: A condition associated with the welfare loss due to the presence of a monopoly. The loss can be summarized as the production of too little output sold at too high a price. (277)

Stock margin requirement: The percentage of the price of a stock purchase that must be paid in cash rather than borrowed. (795)

Store of value: The ability to own wealth in the form of some item, such as money: a function of money. (747)

Strike: A collective refusal to work at the current wage or under current working conditions. (395)

Structure-conduct-performance: A theory of industrial organization that emphasizes the importance of structural elements such as the number of firms in determining the competitive conduct and performance of the industry. (334)

Subsistence wage: A real wage rate that is only high enough to allow for a zero rate of population growth. (894)

Substitute inputs: Inputs with a relation such that increased employment of one input due to a fall in its price results in decreased usage of the other(s). (362)

Substitutes: Products that are related such that an increase in the price of one will increase the demand for the other or a decrease in the price of one will decrease the demand for the other; two goods whose cross elasticity of demand is positive: $\epsilon_c > 0$. (91, 133)

Substitution effect: The change in the quantity demanded of a good that results only from a change in the relative price of the good. (156)

Sunk costs: Previously incurred, irretrievable costs of a currently owned resource. (194)

Supply curve: A graphic representation of the quantities of a product or service that producers are willing and able to sell at all possible prices. (95)

Supply of loanable funds: A curve or schedule that shows the various amounts individuals are willing and able to lend or save at different interest rates. (408)

Supply shock inflation: Price level increases stemming from a decrease in aggregate supply; decreased aggregate supply usually occurs because of sudden increased scarcity of essential resources. (827)

Supply-side economics: Policy designed to stimulate production by altering incentives of producers; policy that has the purpose of shifting the aggregate supply curve to the right. (711)

Supply-side policy: Fiscal or monetary policy intended to directly alter the incentives to produce output; policies designed to shift aggregate supply. (591)

Surplus: The amount by which quantity supplied exceeds quantity demanded at a price above the equilibrium price. (99)

Sustainable monopoly: A monopoly that can forestall the entry of competitors in the absence of regulation. (492)

Tacit collusive solution: A possible outcome in game theory when, given an indefinite time horizon and no formal communication, rivals recognize that it is in their best interest to act so that joint profits are maximized. (304)

Takeover bid strategy: The attempt by one or more entrepreneurs to gain voting control over a corporation by buying vast quantities of the corporation's stock. (183)

Tangency solution: A long-run equilibrium situation in which the firm's downward-sloping demand curve is just tangent to its *LRATC* curve; zero economic profits are earned. (292)

Tariff: A tax or levy on imported goods. (919)

Tax avoidance: Legal means—tax shelters and loopholes—by which individuals can reduce tax liabilities. (539)

Tax base: The item or action—such as the amount of a good produced, the sales of a good, the income of a business or household, or the wealth of an individual—upon which a tax rate is applied in order to determine total tax liability. (527)

Tax incidence: The burden, or final resting place, of a tax or loss of welfare due to a tax. (534)

Taxable income: The amount of income that is subject to income taxes; total income minus deductions and exemptions. (537)

Tax indexation: Periodic adjustment of the tax brackets of a progressive income tax so as to base taxes on real, not nominal, income; eliminates bracket creep and increased income taxes due solely to inflation. (583, 825)

Team production: An economic activity in which workers cooperate as team members in order to accomplish an objective. (175)

Technology: Knowledge of production methods associated with producing a particular good. (7)

Terms of trade: The number of units of one good that exchange in the market for one unit of some other good; a relative price. Although not expressed in terms of money, it is a price nonetheless. (49, 917)

Terms of trade argument: Defending the use of artificial trade barriers combined with monopoly or monopsony power in international markets in order to produce an improvement in a country's terms of trade. (930)

Total cost of production: The total opportunity cost of all resources used in production; the sum of all explicit and implicit production costs. (193)

Total costs: All the costs of a firm's operations; total variable costs plus total fixed costs. (196)

Total expenditure: The total amount spent by consumers on a good or service; calculated as equilibrium price times equilibrium quantity. (126)

Total product: The total amount of output produced. (199)

Total revenue: Total receipts of businesses; always equal to total expenditures by consumers; calculated as market price multiplied by the amount of output sold; the dollar value of sales. (126, 224)

Total utility: The total amount of satisfaction derived from consuming any given quantity of a good or service. (148)

Total wage bill: The total cost of labor to firms; equal to wage rate times quantity of labor employed. (387)

Transaction costs: The opportunity costs of the resources directly associated with trade; includes time costs, brokers' fees, and so on. (52)

Transactions accounts: Demand deposits or other checkable accounts that allow the transfer of funds by writing a check. (748)

Transactions demand: Money demand that arises from the desire of businesses and consumers to facilitate exchange with the use of money. (804)

Transfer payment: A resource received by an individual from government that is not directly or explicitly paid for by that individual; it may be in the form of money or goods and services such as education or health care. (451)

Transitivity of preferences: A rational characteristic of consumers that suggests that if *A* is preferred to *B* and *B* is preferred to *C*, then *A* is preferred to *C*. (164)

Transportation costs: The value of resources used in the transportation of goods that finalize any trade. (53)

Trust: An institution that organizes firms in the same industry in an effort to increase profits by decreasing competition. (332)

Undervalued: A term describing the foreign exchange market value of a country's money; occurs when the number of units of a country's money that purchases one unit of a foreign currency is *greater* than the equilibrium exchange rate. (948)

Unemployed: A labor-force status characterized by an individual who is actively seeking employment but is not working. (576)

Unemployment rate: The percentage of the labor force without jobs. (576)

Unemployment of resources: A situation in which some human and/or nonhuman resources that can be used in production are not used. (38)

Unit elasticity of demand: A condition where the percentage change in quantity demanded is equal to the percentage change in price: $\epsilon_d = 1$. (120)

Unit of account: A standard measure, such as the dollar, that is used to express the values of goods and services; a function of money. (747)

Unlimited liability: A legal principle implying that the owner(s) of or partners in a firm are personally responsible for the debts of the firm up to the total value of their wealth. (179)

Utility: A measure of the satisfaction that the consumption of goods or services yields an individual. (146)

Value added: The increase in value or market worth of a good associated with each stage of production. (598)

Variable costs: The costs of inputs whose usage levels can be changed in the short run. Variable costs change as output changes. (196)

Variable input: A factor of production whose level of usage may be changed in the short run. (195)

Velocity: The average number of times a unit of money changes hands per year in financing the purchase of GNP. (628)

Vertical equity: A tax structure under which people with unequal incomes pay unequal taxes; people with higher incomes pay more taxes than people with lower incomes. (536)

Vertical restraints: Agreements between manufacturers and retailers that restrict the marketing options of one or both parties. (338)

Vicious circle of poverty: An attempt to explain why some countries remain less-developed that centers on low savings and investment causing low real incomes, which in turn lead to low saving and investment rates. (988)

Wage-price spiral: The process whereby increased prices of final goods cause increased wage rates and other resource prices, which in turn result in still-higher prices of final goods; for the spiral to continue, the money supply must continually increase or real output must continually fall. (826)

Wealth: The total value of monetary plus nonmonetary assets in existence at a point in time; a stock variable. (685)

Welfare loss due to monopoly: The consumers' surplus lost by consumers and not gained by the monopolist that results from a monopoly producing a less-than-competitive amount of output and charging a greater-than-competitive price; also called *dead-weight cost*. (274, 331)

Welfare loss to society: The *net* loss to an economy resulting from the imposition of an artificial trade barrier; government revenues plus producer gains minus consumer losses. (925)

x-axis, y-axis: Perpendicular lines on a coordinate grid system for measuring variables in a two-dimensional graph. The x-axis is the horizontal line; the y-axis is the vertical line. The intersection of the x-axis and the y-axis is the origin. (26)

X-inefficiency: The increase in costs of a monopoly resulting from the lack of competitive pressure to reduce costs to a minimum possible level. (276)

Zero economic profits: A condition in which total revenue equals total opportunity cost of production. Firms earn a normal rate of return and $P = MR = LRMC = LRATC$. (231)

ACKNOWLEDGMENTS

Photo

Unless otherwise acknowledged, all photos are the property of HarperCollins. Page abbreviations are as follows: (T) top, (C) center, (B) bottom, (L) left, (R) right.

p. 5: Robert E. Murowchick/Photo Researchers; p. 11: Copyrighted, Chicago Tribune Company, all rights reserved; p. 20: © Sam C. Rawls 1984; p. 112: Photo supplied by authors; p. 142L: The Granger Collection, New York; p. 142R: The Granger Collection, New York; p. 161: Gamma-Liaison; p. 220: Eli Reed/Magnum Photos; p. 282: Courtesy U.S. Postal Service; p. 349L: Historical Pictures Service, Chicago; p. 349R: Peter Lofts Photography, Cambridge, England; p. 381: UPI/Bettmann Newsphotos; p. 398: Randy G. Taylor/Gamma-Liaison; p. 441: UPI/Bettmann Newsphotos; p. 475L: The Granger Collection, New York; p. 475R: Courtesy of Gary Becker; p. 570L: Photo by V. H. Mottram/National Portrait Gallery, London; p. 570R: Courtesy of Ronald Coase; p. 581: S. Logure/Gamma-Liaison; p. 613: UPI/Bettmann Newsphotos; p. 699: SHOEMAKER'S SHOP, Greek 520–510 B.C., B/F amphora. H: .361 m, H. L. Pierce Fund 01.8035, Courtesy, Museum of Fine Arts, Boston; p. 738L: The Bettmann Archive; p. 738R: The Bettmann Archive; p. 745: The University Museum, University of Pennsylvania, Neg. S4-139881; p. 761: Neg. No. A53972, Courtesy The American Red Cross; p. 802: Reprinted with special permission of King Features Syndicate, Inc.; p. 828: NYT Pictures; p. 835L: Courtesy of Milton Friedman; p. 835R: T. Charles Erickson, Yale University Office of Public Information; p. 858: Reprinted by permission, Los Angeles Times Syndicate; p. 907L: Courtesy of Paul Samuelson; p. 907R: Courtesy of Robert Lucas; p. 985: UPI/Bettmann Newsphotos; p. 998L: John Cole/Impact Photos; p. 998R: The Bettmann Archive.

Text

p. 76: Figure 6 data from *Facts and Figures on Government Finance* (Washington, D.C.: Tax Foundation, Inc., 1983); p. 178: Table 1 from *Business Week,* May 7, 1990. Copyright © 1990 by McGraw-Hill, Inc. Reprinted by permission; p. 214: Text from *Case Studies in American Industry,* Second Edition, by Leonard W. Weiss, p. 38. Copyright © 1971 by John Wiley & Sons, Inc. Reprinted by permission of John Wiley & Sons, Inc.; p. 215: Figure 8 from *Case Studies in American Industry,* Second Edition, by Leonard W. Weiss, p. 76. Copyright © 1971 by John Wiley & Sons, Inc. Reprinted by permission of John Wiley & Sons, Inc.; p. 245: Table 2 from *Case Studies in American Industry,* Second Edition, by Leonard W. Weiss, p. 38. Copyright © 1971 by John Wiley & Sons, Inc. Reprinted by permission of John Wiley & Sons, Inc.; p. 271: Table 2 excerpted from *USA Today* (November 10, 1986), p. 11A. Copyright 1986, USA Today. Excerpted with permission; p. 290: Table 1 data adapted from Lee Benham, "The Effect of Advertising on the Price of Eyeglasses," *Journal of Law and Economics* 15 (October 1972), p. 342; pp. 298–99: Text adaptation from "Demand Uncertainty and Sales: A Study of Fashion and Markdown Pricing" by B. Peter Pashigian in *The American Economic Review,* vol. 78, no. 5, Dec. 1988. pp. 936–51. Copyright © 1988 the American Economic Association; p. 299: Figure 6 adapted from "Demand Uncertainty and Sales: A Study of Fashion and Markdown Pricing" by B. Peter Pashigian in *The American Economic Review,* vol. 78, no. 5, Dec. 1988. p. 941. Copyright © 1988 the American Economic Association; Table 2 adapted from "Demand Uncertainty and Sales: A Study of Fashion and Markdown Pricing" by B. Peter Pashigian in *The American Economic Review,* vol. 78, no. 5, Dec. 1988. p. 947. Copyright © 1988 the American Economic Association; p. 301: Text adapted from Richard O. Beil, Jr., *Collusion in Experimental Oligopoly Markets* (Unpublished doctoral dissertation, Texas A&M University, 1988). Used by permission of the author; p. 380: Figure 12 from "Flow of Third World Immigrants Alters Weave of U.S. Society," *The New York Times,* June 30, 1986. Copyright © 1986 by the New York Times Company. Reprinted by permission; p. 410: List of stocks from *The Wall Street Journal,* April 30, 1985. Reprinted by permission of *The Wall Street Journal,* © 1985 Dow Jones & Company, Inc., All Rights Reserved Worldwide; p. 459: Table 4 from Edgar K. Browning, "The Trend Toward Equality in the Distribution of Net Income," *Southern Economic Journal* 43 (July 1976): 914. Copyright

INDEX

Boldface numbers indicate pages on which definitions of key terms appear.

SELECTED U.S. MACROECONOMIC DATA, 1929–1989

Year	Gross National Product	Personal Consumption Expenditure	Gross Private Domestic Investment	Government Purchases	Net Exports	Gross National Product	Personal Consumption Expenditure	Gross Private Domestic Investment	Government Purchases	Net Exports	Real GNP per capital
	(in billions of dollars)					(in billions of 1982 dollars)					(in 1982 dollars)
1929	103.9	77.3	16.7	8.9	1.1	709.6	471.4	139.2	94.2	4.7	5822
1933	56.0	45.8	1.6	8.3	.4	498.5	378.7	22.7	98.5	−1.4	3966
1939	91.3	67.0	9.5	13.6	1.2	716.6	480.5	86.0	144.1	6.1	5469
1945	213.4	119.6	11.3	83.0	−.5	1354.8	592.7	76.5	704.5	−18.9	9682
1950	288.3	192.1	55.1	38.8	2.2	1203.7	733.2	234.9	230.8	4.7	7935
1955	405.9	257.9	69.7	75.3	3.0	1494.9	873.8	259.8	361.3	0	9045
1956	428.2	270.6	72.7	79.7	5.3	1525.6	899.8	257.8	363.7	4.3	9069
1957	451.0	285.3	71.1	87.3	7.3	1551.1	919.7	243.4	381.8	7.0	9056
1958	456.8	294.6	63.6	95.4	3.3	1539.2	932.9	221.4	395.3	−10.3	8839
1959	495.8	316.3	80.2	97.9	1.5	1629.1	979.4	270.3	397.7	−18.2	9200
1960	515.3	330.7	78.2	100.6	5.9	1665.3	1005.1	260.5	403.7	−4.0	9213
1961	533.8	341.1	77.1	108.4	7.2	1708.7	1025.2	259.1	427.1	−2.7	9299
1962	574.6	361.9	87.6	118.2	6.9	1799.4	1069.0	288.6	449.4	−7.5	9644
1963	606.9	381.7	93.1	123.8	8.2	1873.3	1108.4	307.1	459.8	−1.9	9896
1964	649.8	409.3	99.6	130.0	10.9	1973.3	1170.6	325.9	470.8	5.9	10281
1965	705.1	440.7	116.2	138.6	9.7	2087.6	1236.4	367.0	487.0	−2.7	10741
1966	772.0	477.3	128.6	158.6	7.5	2208.3	1298.9	390.5	532.6	−13.7	11233
1967	816.4	503.6	125.7	179.7	7.4	2271.4	1337.7	374.4	576.2	−16.9	11428
1968	892.7	552.5	137.0	197.7	5.5	2365.6	1405.9	391.8	597.6	−29.7	11784
1969	963.9	597.9	153.2	207.3	5.6	2423.3	1456.7	410.3	591.2	−34.9	11953
1970	1015.5	640.0	148.8	218.2	8.5	2416.2	1492.0	381.5	572.6	−30.0	11781
1971	1102.7	691.6	172.5	232.4	6.3	2484.8	1538.8	419.3	566.5	−39.8	11964
1972	1212.8	757.6	202.0	250.0	3.2	2608.5	1621.9	465.4	570.7	−49.4	12426
1973	1359.3	837.2	238.8	266.5	16.8	2744.1	1689.6	520.8	565.3	−31.5	12948
1974	1472.8	916.5	240.8	299.1	16.3	2729.3	1674.0	481.3	573.2	.8	12760
1975	1598.4	1012.8	219.6	335.0	31.1	2695.0	1711.9	383.3	580.9	18.9	12478
1976	1782.8	1129.3	277.7	356.9	18.8	2826.7	1803.9	453.5	580.3	−11.0	12961
1977	1990.5	1257.2	344.1	387.3	1.9	2958.6	1883.8	521.3	589.1	−35.5	13431
1978	2249.7	1403.5	416.8	425.2	4.1	3115.2	1961.0	576.9	604.1	−26.8	13993
1979	2508.2	1566.8	454.8	467.8	18.8	3192.4	2004.4	575.2	609.1	3.6	14182
1980	2732.0	1732.6	437.0	530.3	32.1	3187.1	2000.4	509.3	620.5	57.0	13994
1981	3052.6	1915.1	515.5	588.1	33.9	3248.8	2024.2	545.5	629.7	49.4	14114
1982	3166.0	2050.7	447.3	641.7	26.3	3166.0	2050.7	447.3	641.7	26.3	13614
1983	3405.7	2234.5	502.3	675.0	−6.1	3279.1	2146.0	504.1	649.0	−19.9	13964
1984	3772.2	2430.5	664.8	735.9	−58.9	3501.4	2249.3	658.4	677.7	−84.0	14771
1985	4014.9	2629.0	643.1	820.8	−78.0	3618.7	2354.8	637.0	731.2	−104.3	15122
1986	4231.6	2797.4	659.4	872.2	−97.4	3717.9	2446.4	639.6	761.6	−129.7	15389
1987	4524.3	3010.8	699.9	926.1	−112.6	3853.7	2513.7	674.0	781.8	−115.7	15800
1988	4880.6	3235.1	750.3	968.9	−73.7	4024.4	2598.4	715.8	785.1	−74.9	16339
1989	5233.2	3470.3	777.1	1036.7	−50.9	4142.6	2668.5	724.5	805.8	−56.3	16650

Sources: U.S. Department of Commerce, Bureau of Labor Statistics, Federal Reserve System, Council of Economic Advisers.